C.N.—A

THE COMMON LAW LIBRARY

NUMBER 6

NEGLIGENCE

AUSTRALIA
The Law Book Company Ltd.
Sydney : Melbourne : Brisbane

CANADA AND U.S.A.
The Carswell Company Ltd.
Agincourt, Ontario

INDIA
N. M. Tripathi Private Ltd.
Bombay

ISRAEL
Steimatzky's Agency Ltd.
Jerusalem : Tel Aviv : Haifa

MALAYSIA : SINGAPORE : BRUNEI
Malayan Law Journal (Pte.) Ltd.
Singapore

NEW ZEALAND
Sweet and Maxwell (N.Z.) Ltd.
Wellington

PAKISTAN
Pakistan Law House
Karachi

THE COMMON LAW LIBRARY

NUMBER 6

CHARLESWORTH
ON
NEGLIGENCE

FIFTH EDITION

BY

R. A. Percy, M.A.

Barrister-at-Law of the Middle Temple and North-Eastern Circuit

A Deputy Chairman of Quarter Sessions for the County of Durham

LONDON

SWEET & MAXWELL LIMITED

1971

First Edition	(1938)	By J. Charlesworth
Second Edition	(1947)	,, ,,
Third Edition	(1956)	,, ,,
Second Impression	(1959)	,, ,,
Fourth Edition	(1962)	By R. A. Percy
Fifth Edition	(1971)	,, ,,

SBN 421 14260 X

Published in 1971 by
Sweet & Maxwell Limited of
11 New Fetter Lane, London,
and printed in Great Britain
by The Eastern Press Limited
of London and Reading

PREFACE

In 1960, when I commenced to make plans for the preparation of the Fourth Edition of *Charlesworth on Negligence*, I did not think that it was either apposite or essential, especially so soon after the learned author's death, to bring about any fundamental changes to his book. I therefore proceeded upon that assumption which, upon reflection and even after using hindsight, I think was the right decision in the circumstances that prevailed at that time.

However, some nine years later when I was further entrusted with the similar task of preparing for the production of this, the Fifth Edition, all the considerations seemed to be completely different. Indeed, during the annual preparations of the cumulative supplements, it had become apparent that whatever the regrets may be for the passing of the old, I had to think in terms of making profound changes. The problems to be faced, which seemed to be immense, were, first, how to absorb into the book all the details of the prolific development in the law of negligence since March 1, 1962, both at common law and by statute, and, secondly, where to begin if these were to be solved by having to adapt the existing structure of the text. It was clearly going to be an intriguing challenge and, in my view, by no means an easy task but it called for a bold initial decision to be made, if *Charlesworth on Negligence* were to be brought forward successfully into the nineteen seventies. I hope that I have managed to achieve this aim and that this edition advances with vigour but with great respect the original concept that was laid down by Dr. John Charlesworth in 1938.

Accordingly I set about my work by starting with the reframing of the Chapters and their headings, then by putting these into a more acceptable form of congruity, thereby reducing their number from thirty to nineteen. I hasten to explain that this reduction was never intended as an illusion to mask the reality of an inevitable increase that would have to be made to the length of the text itself. In fact the increase is nearly 140 pages, despite the drastic pruning out of much of the old and out-of-date law contained in the earlier editions.

Chapters 3, 13 and 17 are entirely new and other chapters such as Chapters 4, 7, 8, 12, 14 and 16 have required substantial reorganisation and rewriting. Perhaps Chapter 2 has been so extensively rewritten that it too, probably, qualifies for the description of being virtually new; assuredly it was the most difficult to formulate and to attain in its final form and yet, in many ways, it was all the more rewarding for that. As a general study of the duty of care situation, it gave the greater scope for individual expression of opinion however controversial that always tends to be. Chapter 10 on Animals, without doubt, was the most frustrating because I had made a start on it before the original Animals Bill had got under way in Parliament. The chequered career of the Bill, with its re-introduction in the following Parliament and amendments throughout, necessitated continual revision of the chapter. Likewise the Law Reform (Miscellaneous Provisions) Act 1971 has caused a certain amount of cliff-hanging and suspense since it only received the Royal Assent on July 1, 1971, which meant my having to make at the late proof-reading stages last-minute adjustments to the law stated in those chapters dealing with the Limitation Acts and the Fatal Accidents Acts. On the advantage side the net result of these two particular matters as well as other Acts passed in 1971, *inter alia*, is that I have effectively been able to fix today's date as that at which the law is stated; some Acts have yet to come into force, such as the Animals Act on October 1, 1971. As regards Chapter 18, in view of its slightly different role, I have omitted all discussions of the regulations made under the provisions of the successive Factories Acts. To have included any references to them at all, I felt, would have needed a full analysis of their provisions in order to serve any useful purpose, which in turn would probably have added another hundred pages at least to its already increased size.

So far as the common law is concerned after the rapid strides of advance brought about by the decision in *Hedley Byrne & Co. Ltd.* v. *Heller & Partners Ltd.* [1964] A.C. 465 it remains to be seen what will be the true extent of the nullifying effect of the majority opinion of the Privy Council in *Mutual Life & Citizens' Assurance Co. Ltd.* v. *Evatt* [1971] 2 W.L.R. 23. This sort of " Stop: Go " approach adds much to the confusion of the law and the difficulty in understanding it and, regrettably, it is not altogether unknown to emanate from their Lordships' House. On occasions their Lordships seem to be called upon to state the most obvious, *e.g.* *Barnes* v. *Hampshire C.C.* [1969] 1 W.L.R. 1563 (how *was* it ever doubted that the school authorities were liable in negligence?), yet at other times they miss golden opportunities of restoring common sense and reason, *e.g.* *Naylor* v. *Yorkshire Electricity Board* [1968] A.C. 529. One of an editor's major tribulations is the constant change and development in the law, and the law of negligence is particularly subject to this. It seems inevitable that major decisions will be reported during the final preparation of a manuscript and its passage through the publishers' and printers' hands. This edition of *Charlesworth* is no exception and the 1970 volume of Appeal Cases produced, *inter alia*, *Parry* v. *Cleaver* (page 1); *Mallett* v. *McMonagle* (page 166); *Henderson* v. *Henry E. Jenkins & Sons* (page 282); *Baker* v. *Willoughby* (page 407) and *Dorset Yacht Co. Ltd.* v. *Home Office* (page 1004). Their Lordships thereafter continued to make further contributions and up to July 31, 1971, the following were accommodated in the text with varying degrees of success, *viz.*: *Boys* v. *Chaplin* [1971] A.C. 356; *Distillers Co. (Biochemicals)* v. *Thompson* [1971] A.C. 458; *Mulholland* v. *Mitchell* [1971] 2 W.L.R. 93; *Todd* v. *Davison* [1971] 2 W.L.R. 898 and *Albert* v. *Motor Insurers' Bureau* [1971] 3 W.L.R. 291. I am afraid that it has proved to be quite impossible to include either in Chapter 2 or Chapter 3 anything more than a reference in the footnotes to *Dorset Yacht Co. Ltd.* v. *Home Office*, *ante*, a case deserving much fuller treatment. However, I have sought to remedy this omission as best I can by a fuller, factual, reference to it in the text of Chapter 13.

It is with pleasure that I now express my most sincere thanks to my various colleagues at the Bar and all those behind the scenes who have given me so much assistance and encouragement over the past two years of industry, working on this edition. In particular, to my secretaries Mrs. June Brown and her sister Mrs. Nancy Henderson I extend my most grateful appreciation for their efficiency and combined efforts in transcribing my manuscripts, usually after normal working hours in Chambers, and typing out the whole of the pages for presentation to the Publishers in order to meet their scheduled deadline date; to the Publishers for their expert guidance and for resolving most of my editorial worries; and to D. C. H. Percy for his assistance in carrying out the tedious time-consuming tasks of proof-reading, locating printing errors, making corrections and carrying out the necessary cross-referencing.

Last but not least, I apologise to my wife for my negligence in failing to keep her society during the thousand hours and more when somehow I had to find the time instead to do this work. I thank her for her cheerfulness, patience and restraint. Now that it is over, I feel almost at peace with the world and it is very pleasant to relax and watch it go by in its accustomed and negligent way!

Newcastle-upon-Tyne, 1.
August 1, 1971.

R. A. PERCY

TABLE OF CONTENTS

TABLE OF STATUTES

[*Repealed Statutes are printed in italics.*]

TABLE OF STATUTORY REGULATIONS

TABLE OF CASES

TABLE OF CASES

PARA.

Barnes U.D.C. *v.* London General Omnibus Co. (1908) 100 L.T. 115; 7 L.G.R. 349; 73 J.P. 68 .... 787, 840, 965, 986
Barnett *v.* Chelsea and Kensington Hospital Management Committee [1969] 1 Q.B. 428; [1968] 2 W.L.R. 422; 111 S.J. 912; [1968] 1 All E.R. 1068 .. 80, 287
—— *v.* Cohen [1921] 2 K.B. 461; 90 L.J.K.B. 1307; 125 L.T. 733; 37 T.L.R. 629; 19 L.G.R. 623 .... 1285, 1287, 1294
—— *v.* Packer [1940] 3 All E.R. 575 .... 26, 629
Barraclough *v.* Brown [1897] A.C. 615; 66 L.J.Q.B. 672 1188
Barrington *v.* Kent Rivers Catchment Board (1947) 64 T.L.R. 35; 112 J.P. 85; 92 S.J. 27; [1947] 2 All E.R. 782 1253
Barry *v.* Cleveland Bridge Engineering Co. Ltd. [1963] 1 All E.R. 192 .. 1223, 1250
—— *v.* McDonald (1966) 110 S.J. 56 855
Bartlett *v.* Tottenham [1932] 1 Ch. 114; 101 L.J.Ch. 160; 145 L.T. 686 .... 417, 451
Bartonshill Coal Co. *v.* McGuire (1858) 3 Macq. 300; 4 Jur.(N.S.) 772; 6 W.R. 697; 111 R.R. 906 216
—— *v.* Reid (1858) 3 Macq. 266; 4 Jur.(N.S.) 767; 6 W.R. 664; 111 R.R. 896 216, 224
Barwick *v.* English Joint Stock Bank (1867) L.R. 2 Ex. 259; 36 L.J.Ex. 147; 16 L.T. 461; 15 W.R. 877 923
Bass *v.* Hendon U.D.C. (1912) 28 T.L.R. 317; 76 J.P. 13 940
Basted *v.* Cozens & Sutcliffe, Ltd. [1954] 1 W.L.R. 1069; 98 S.J. 525; [1954] 2 All E.R. 735n. 900
Bateman *v.* Poplar Board of Works (1887) 37 Ch.D. 272; 57 L.J.Ch. 579; 58 L.T. 720; 36 W.R. 501 1213
Bates *v.* Batey & Co. [1913] 3 K.B. 351; 82 L.J.K.B. 963; 108 L.T. 1036; 29 T.L.R. 616 633
—— *v.* Parker [1953] 2 Q.B. 231; 97 S.J. 226; [1953] 1 All E.R. 768 .. 207, 208, 357, 359
—— *v.* Stone Parish Council [1954] 1 W.L.R. 1249; [1954] 3 All E.R. 38 352
Bath *v.* British Transport Commission [1954] 1 W.L.R. 1013; 98 S.J. 472; [1954] 2 All E.R. 542; [1954] 1 Lloyd's Rep. 463 .... 131, 204, 1253
Bathurst (Borough of) *v.* Macpherson (1879) 4 App.Cas. 256; 48 L.J.P.C. 61 689
—— *v.* McDonald (1966) 110 S.J. 56 855
Bativala *v.* West [1970] 1 Q.B. 716; [1970] 2 W.L.R. 8; 113 S.J. 856; [1970] 1 All E.R. 332 .... 596, 598, 851
Batt *v.* Metropolitan Water Board [1911] 2 K.B. 965; 80 L.J.K.B. 1354 685
Batten *v.* Wedgwood Coal & Iron Co. (1886) 31 Ch.D. 346; 55 L.J.Ch. 396; 54 L.T. 245; 34 W.R. 228 311
Battersby *v.* Anglo-American Oil Co. Ltd. [1945] K.B. 23; 114 L.J.K.B. 49; 171 L.T. 300; 61 T.L.R. 13; 88 S.J. 423; [1944] 2 All E.R. 387 1141
Batting *v.* London Passenger Transport Board [1941] 1 All E.R. 228 1136
Batts Combe Quarry Co. *v.* Barclays Bank, Ltd. (1931) 48 T.L.R. 4 .... 243, 264
Baugh *v.* Delta Water Fittings, *The Times*, May 13, 1971 1287
Baxter *v.* Gapp & Co. [1939] 2 K.B. 271; 108 L.J.K.B. 522; 160 L.T. 533; 55 T.L.R. 739; [1939] 2 All E.R. 752 .... 238, 327
—— *v.* Stockton-on-Tees Corpn. [1959] 1 Q.B. 441; [1958] 3 W.L.R. 275: 122 J.P. 443; 102 S.J. 562; [1958] 2 All E.R. 675; 56 L.G.R. 349 ...... 693, 701, 704
Bayley *v.* Wolverhampton Waterworks (1860) 6 H. & N. 241; 30 L.J.Ex. 57; 123 R.R. 487 685
Beadon *v.* Capital Syndicate (1912) 28 T.L.R. 427 893
Beadsley *v.* United Steel Companies, Ltd. [1951] 1 K.B. 408; 66 T.L.R. (Pt. 2) 902; 114 J.P. 565; 94 S.J. 704; [1950] 2 All E.R. 872 .... 1243, 1250
Beal *v.* E. Gomme, Ltd. [1949] W.N. 235; 65 T.L.R. 543; 93 S.J. 423; 47 L.G.R. 601 1226
Beals *v.* Hayward [1960] N.Z.L.R. 131 1083
Beaman *v.* A.R.T.S. Ltd. [1949] 1 K.B. 550; 65 T.L.R. 389; 93 S.J. 236; [1949] 1 All E.R. 465 1145
Bean *v.* Wade (1885) 2 T.L.R. 157 .... 310, 319, 1142
Beard *v.* London General Omnibus Co. [1900] 2 Q.B. 530; 69 L.J.Q.B. 895; 83 L.T. 362; 48 W.R. 658 931
Bearn, The [1906] P. 48; 75 L.J.P. 9; 94 L.T. 265; 22 T.L.R. 165; 10 Asp.M.C. 208 .... 330, 341
Beatty *v.* Cullingworth, Brit.Med.J., Nov. 21, 1896 274
Beauchamp *v.* Turrell [1952] 2 Q.B. 207; [1952] 1 All E.R. 719; [1952] 1 T.L.R. 695; [1952] 1 Lloyd's Rep. 266 137
Beaulieu *v.* Fingham (1401) Y.B. 2 Hen. 4, 18, pl. 6 490
Beaumont *v.* Surrey County Council (1968) 112 S.J. 704; 66 L.G.R. 580 .... 297, 299
Beaumont-Thomas *v.* Blue Star Line, Ltd. (1939) 55 T.L.R. 852; [1939] 3 All E.R. 127 .... 370, 800, 1108, 1113

Table of Cases

PARA.

Shoreditch Corpn. *v.* Bull (1904) 90 L.T. 210; 19 T.L.R. 64; 20 T.L.R. 254 .. 678, 701, 704
Short *v.* McCarthy (1820) 3 B. & Ald. 626; 22 R.R. 503 1156
Shrimpton *v.* Hertfordshire C.C. (1911) 104 L.T. 145; 27 T.L.R. 251; 75 J.P. 201; 55 S.J. 270; 9 L.G.R. 397; 48 Sc.L.R. 737 307
Sidor *v.* National Coal Board (1956) 106 L.J. 218 224
Sigurdson *v.* British Columbia Electric Ry. [1953] A.C. 291 .... 77, 90, 1023, 1027
Sill *v.* Thomas (1839) 8 C. & P. 762 315
Silverton *v.* Marriott (1888) 69 L.T. 69; 52 J.P. 677 728
Simkin *v.* L. & N.W. Ry. (1888) 21 Q.B.D. 453; 59 L.T. 797; 53 J.P. 85 784
Simmonds *v.* Newport, etc., Co. [1921] 1 K.B. 616; 90 L.J.K.B. 609; 124 L.T. 557; 37 T.L.R. 165; 85 J.P. 109; 65 S.J. 114 .... 1196, 1203, 1206
Simmons *v.* Bovis, Ltd. [1956] 1 W.L.R. 381; 100 S.J. 283; [1956] 1 All E.R. 736 .... 224, 1199
—— *v.* Heath Laundry Co. [1910] 1 K.B. 543; 79 L.J.K.B. 395; 102 L.T. 210; 26 T.L.R. 326; 54 S.J. 392 .... 906, 907, 909
—— *v.* Pennington & Son [1955] 1 W.L.R. 183; 99 S.J. 146; [1955] 1 All E.R. 240 .... 192, 320
Simms *v.* Leigh Rugby Football Club [1969] 2 All E.R. 923 .... 364, 1065
Simon *v.* Islington B.C. [1943] K.B. 188; 112 L.J.K.B. 337; 168 L.T. 65; 59 T.L.R. 87; [1943] 1 All E.R. 41 .... 690, 698, 704
—— *v.* London General Omnibus Co. (1907) 23 T.L.R. 463 787
Simpson, *In the Estate of*; Gunning, *In the Estate of* [1936] P. 40; 105 L.J.P. 7; 154 L.T. 136; 52 T.L.R. 117; 79 S.J. 861 1150
—— *v.* Metropolitan Water Board (1917) 15 L.G.R. 629 .... 119, 687
Sims *v.* Foster Wheeler Ltd. [1966] 1 W.L.R. 769; 110 S.J. 189; [1966] 2 All E.R. 313; 1 K.I.R. 1 .... 949, 954
—— *v.* Howard (William) & Son Ltd. [1964] 2 Q.B. 409; [1964] 2 W.L.R. 794; 108 S.J. 174; [1964] 1 All E.R. 918 148
Simson *v.* London General Omnibus Co. (1873) L.R. 8 C.P. 390; 42 L.J.C.P. 112; 28 L.T.(N.S.) 560 .... 845, 987
Sincock *v.* Bangs (Reading) [1952] C.P.L. 562; 160 E.G. 134 255
Siner *v.* G.W. Ry. (1869) L.R. 4 Ex. 117; 38 L.J.Ex. 67; 20 L.T.(N.S.) 114; 17 W.R. 417 760
Singleton *v.* E.C. Ry. (1859) 7 C.B.(N.S.) 287; 121 R.R. 496; 29 L.J.C.P. 13; 6 Jur.(N.S.) 228; 2 L.T.(N.S.) 95; 8 W.R. 88 1036
—— *v.* Williamson (1861) 7 H. & N. 410; 31 L.J.Ex. 17; 8 Jur.(N.S.) 60; 5 L.T. (N.S.) 644; 10 W.R. 174; 126 R.R. 678 611
"Singleton Abbey," S.S. *v.* S.S. "Paludina" [1927] A.C. 16; 95 L.J.P. 135; 135 L.T. 707; 17 Asp.M.C. 177; 25 Ll.L.R. 281 .... 117, 120, 1013
Skelton *v.* L. & N.W. Ry. (1867) L.R. 2 C.P. 631; 36 L.J.C.P. 249; 16 L.T.(N.S.) 563; 25 W.R. 925 781
Skilton *v.* Epsom U.D.C. [1937] 1 K.B. 112; 106 L.J.K.B. 41; 154 L.T. 700; 52 T.L.R. 494; 100 J.P. 231; 34 L.G.R. 389; 80 S.J. 345; [1936] 2 All E.R. 50 690
Skinner *v.* L.B. & S.C. Ry. (1850) 5 Ex. 787; 19 L.J.Ex. 162; 82 R.R. 881; 15 Jur. 299 .... 742, 753, 984
Skrine *v.* Gould (1912) 29 T.L.R. 19 1102
Slade *v.* Battersea & Putney Hospital Management Committee [1955] 1 W.L.R. 207; 119 J.P. 212; 99 S.J. 169; [1955] 1 All E.R. 429 288
Slater *v.* Baker (1767) 2 Wils. C.P. 359 274
—— *v.* Clay Cross Co. [1956] 2 Q.B. 264; [1956] 3 W.L.R. 232; 100 S.J. 450; [1956] 2 All E.R. 625 .... 362, 364, 396, 1061, 1078
—— *v.* Worthington's Cash Stores, Ltd. [1941] 1 K.B. 488; 57 T.L.R. 468; [1941] 3 All E.R. 28 .... 430, 711
Slatter *v.* British Railways Board, 110 S.J. 688; 1 K.I.R. 336; [1966] 2 Lloyd's Rep. 395 .... 33, 785
Sleafer *v.* Lambeth Metropolitan Borough Council [1960] 1 Q.B. 43; [1959] 3 W.L.R. 485; 103 S.J. 599; [1959] 3 All E.R. 378; 57 L.G.R. 212 377
Smeaton *v.* Ilford Corpn. [1954] Ch. 450; 118 J.P. 200; 98 S.J. 251; [1954] 1 All E.R. 923; 52 L.G.R. 253 .... 413, 414, 419, 480, 481, 515
Smerkinich *v.* Newport Corpn. (1912) 76 J.P. 454; 10 L.G.R. 959 ...... 308, 1035
Smith *v.* Auckland Hospital Board [1965] N.Z.L.R. 191 245
—— *v.* Austin Lifts, Ltd. [1959] 1 W.L.R. 100; 103 S.J. 73; [1959] 1 All E.R. 81; [1958] 2 Lloyd's Rep. 583 .... 207, 208, 220, 357, 1061
—— *v.* Baker [1891] A.C. 325; 60 L.J.Q.B. 683; 65 L.T. 467; 55 J.P. 660 .. 200, 211, 216, 222, 224, 1002, 1057, 1058, 1060, 1061, 1068, 1080

PARA.

Thornton *v.* Fisher & Ludlow Ltd. [1968] 1 W.L.R. 655; 112 S.J. 214; [1968] 2 All E.R. 241; 4 K.I.R. 107 .... 1232, 1251
—— *v.* Shoe Lane Parking Ltd. [1971] 2 W.L.R. 585; [1971] 1 All E.R. 686; [1971] R.T.R. 79 1103
Thorp *v.* King Bros. (Dorking), *The Times*, February 23, 1957 850
Thrussell *v.* Handyside (1888) 20 Q.B.D. 359; 57 L.J.Q.B. 347; 58 L.T. 344; 52 J.P. 279 .... 398, 1059
Thurman *v.* Wild (1840) 11 A. & E. 453; 3 Per. & Dav. 289 893
Thurogood *v.* Van den Berghs & Jurgens, Ltd. [1951] 2 K.B. 537; [1951] 1 T.L.R. 557; 115 J.P. 237; 95 S.J. 317; [1951] 1 All E.R. 682 .. 58, 70, 214, 224, 1050, 1240
Thwaites *v.* Mackerson (1828) 3 C. & P. 341; M. & M. 199 315
Tidy *v.* Battman [1934] 1 K.B. 319; 103 L.J.K.B. 158; 150 L.T. 90 .... 855, 985
Tillett *v.* Ward (1882) 10 Q.B.D. 17; 52 L.J.Q.B. 61; 47 L.T. 546; 31 W.R. 197; 47 J.P. 438 .... 614, 849, 1082
Tilley *v.* Stevenson [1939] 4 All E.R. 207 .... 438, 486, 520
Tilling *v.* Dick Kerr & Co. [1905] 1 K.B. 562; 74 L.J.K.B. 359; 92 L.T. 731; 21 T.L.R. 281; 53 W.R. 380; 69 J.P. 172; 3 L.G.R. 369 676
Tingle Jacobs & Co. *v.* Kennedy [1964] 1 W.L.R. 638n.; 108 S.J. 196; [1964] 1 All E.R. 888n. 814
Tinline *v.* White Cross Insurance Association, Ltd. [1921] 3 K.B. 327; 90 L.J.K.B. 1118; 125 L.T. 632; 37 T.L.R. 733 .... 903, 1098, 1099
Tinsley *v.* Dudley [1951] 2 K.B. 18; [1951] 1 T.L.R. 315; 95 S.J. 106; [1951] 1 All E.R. 252 .... 334, 335
Tinto *v.* Stewarts & Lloyds Ltd., 1962 S.L.T. 314 1258
Tisbury *v.* Ship Carbon Co. of Great Britain Ltd. (1965) 109 S.J. 352 1258
Toal *v.* N.B. Ry. [1908] A.C. 352; 77 L.J.P.C. 119; 1908 S.C.(H.L.) 29 .. 396, 758, 771, 984
Tobin *v.* R. (1864) 16 C.B.(N.S.) 310; 33 L.J.C.P. 199; 139 R.R. 504; 10 Jur.(N.S.) 1029; 10 L.T.(N.S.) 762; 12 W.R. 838 860
Todd *v.* Davison [1971] 2 W.L.R. 898; [1971] 1 All E.R. 994; H.L.; affirming [1971] 1 W.L.R. 267 1148
—— *v.* Flight (1860) 9 C.B.(N.S.) 377; 30 L.J.C.P. 21; 127 R.R. 684; 7 Jur.(N.S.) 291; 3 L.T.(N.S.) 325; 9 W.R. 145 721
Tolhausen *v.* Davies (1888) 58 L.J.Q.B. 98; 59 L.T. 436; 52 J.P. 804; affirming 57 L.J.Q.B. 392 987
Tolhurst *v.* Webster (1936) 53 T.L.R. 174; 80 S.J. 1015; [1936] 3 All E.R. 1020 .. 830
Tomlinson *v.* Broadsmith [1896] 1 Q.B. 386; 65 L.J.Q.B. 308; 74 L.T. 265; 44 W.R. 471 320
—— *v.* Railway Executive [1953] 1 All E.R. 1 766
Toogood *v.* Wright [1940] 2 All E.R. 306 595
Toohey *v.* Hollier (1955) A.L.R. 302 163
Toole *v.* Sherbourne Pouffes Ltd., *The Times*, July 29, 1971 304
Toomey *v.* L.B. & S.C. Ry. (1857) 3 C.B.(N.S.) 146; 27 L.J.C.P. 39; 111 R.R. 585; 6 W.R. 44 .... 765, 993
Torrance *v.* Ilford U.D.C. (1909) 25 T.L.R. 355; 73 J.P. 255; 7 L.G.R. 554; 53 S.J. 301 1070
Tournier *v.* National Provincial & Union Bank [1924] 1 K.B. 461; 93 L.J.K.B. 449; 130 L.T. 682; 40 T.L.R. 214; 68 S.J. 441; 29 Com.Cas. 129 370
Townley *v.* Jones (1860) 8 C.B.(N.S.) 289; 29 L.J.C.P. 299; 6 Jur.(N.S.) 1159; 125 R.R. 667 316
Townsend *v.* Bishop, 160 L.T. 296; 55 T.L.R. 433; [1939] 1 All E.R. 805 177
—— *v.* Wathen (1808) 9 East 277; 9 R.R. 553 .... 356, 562
Tozeland *v.* West Ham Union [1907] 1 K.B. 920; 76 L.J.K.B. 514; 22 T.L.R. 306; 94 L.T. 486; 54 W.R. 531; 70 J.P. 134; 4 L.G.R. 411 920
Transwell *v.* Nelson, *The Times*, February 11, 1959 271
Travers *v.* Gloucester Corpn. [1947] K.B. 71; 115 L.J.K.B. 517; 175 L.T. 360; 62 T.L.R. 723; 110 J.P. 364; 90 S.J. 556; [1946] 2 All E.R. 506 .... 402, 526
Travers (Joseph) & Sons, Ltd. *v.* Cooper [1915] 1 K.B. 73; 83 L.J.K.B. 1787; 111 L.T. 1088; 30 T.L.R. 703 1110
Tredegar (Lord) *v.* Roberts [1914] 1 K.B. 283; 83 L.J.K.B. 159; 109 L.T. 731; 58 S.J. 118 1280
Treloar *v.* Henderson [1968] N.Z.L.R. 1085 319
Tremain *v.* Pike [1969] 1 W.L.R. 1556; 113 S.J. 812; [1969] 3 All E.R. 1303; 7 K.I.R. 318 225
Trent, *Re* (1868) L.R. 4 Ch. 112 157
Trevett *v.* Lee [1955] 1 W.L.R. 113; 99 S.J. 110; [1955] 1 All E.R. 406 676
Trinder *v.* G.W. Ry. (1919) 35 T.L.R. 291 787

CHAPTER 1

MEANING OF NEGLIGENCE

1 **Three meanings of negligence.** In current forensic speech negligence has three meanings. They are: (1) a state of mind, in which it is opposed to intention; (2) careless conduct, and (3) the breach of a duty to take care imposed by common or statute law. All three meanings are applicable in different circumstances but any one of them does not necessarily exclude the other meanings.

2 **(1)—Negligence as a state of mind.** Negligence as a state of mind is the opposite of intention. An act is intentional when it is purposeful and done with the desire or the object of producing a particular result.[1] An act is negligent when it is done, not with the desire of producing a particular result, but actually producing that result by carelessness or indifference. There may be negligence as to the act, as where a man thoughtlessly leaves open the gate of a field so that cattle escape onto the highway, or negligence as to the consequences of the act, as where a man intentionally throws a stone over a wall, careless as to the chances of anyone on the other side of the wall being hit by the stone, but without intending to hit anyone. A negligent state of mind is consistent with an intention to exercise at any rate some care, as where a motorist, in a hurry, drives quickly down a crowded street and collides with a pedestrian; here, he does not intend to have a collision and exercises as much care as he can, consistently with his desire to drive quickly. His negligence consists in his carelessness or indifference in exposing pedestrians to the risk of a collision, because he is not prepared to subordinate his desire for speed to his desire to drive carefully.

In this sense negligence is subjective and often means the same as inadvertence but this is not so always. A man may advert to the consequences of his act and yet decide to do it. If the consequence adverted to in fact happens, it cannot be said to be intended; it was not intended, it was risked, on grounds which the event has proved to have been insufficient. Eve J. described such state of mind as " an attitude of mental indifference to obvious risks." [2] An illustration of this mental indifference is afforded by *Vaughan* v. *Menlove*,[3] where the defendant stacked his hay in such a way as to give rise to the probability of fire. He was warned of the danger, was advised to take the rick down but he said that he would chance it.

[1] *Gollins* v. *Gollins* [1964] A.C. 644, *per* Lord Reid at pp. 663, 664. In *Imperial Chemical Industries Ltd.* v. *Shatwell* [1965] A.C. 656 see Lord Reid's reference at p. 672 to the " inaccurate habit of using the word ' negligence ' to denote a deliberate act done with full knowledge of the risk."

[2] *Hudston* v. *Viney* [1921] 1 Ch. 98, 104.

[3] (1837) 3 Bing.N.C. 468.

As a result the rick caught fire, which was due to his negligence and not to the defendant's intention at all that it should occur.

3 The use of the word negligence to describe a state of mind is to be found in the judgment of Lord Denman C.J. in *Filliter* v. *Phippard*,[4] dealing with the way in which a fire may be started, when he said: "In strictness the word 'accidental' may be employed in contradistinction to 'wilful,' and so the same fire might begin both accidentally and be the result of negligence. But it may equally mean a fire produced by mere chance or incapable of being traced to any cause." Fry J. used it in the same sense where he said: "Fraud imports design and purpose; negligence imports that you are acting carelessly and without that design." [5] Illustrations from the Statute Book are to be found in the Civil Aviation Act 1949, section 40 (2) of which provides that damages shall be recoverable from the owner of an aircraft "without proof of negligence or intention," and the Bills of Exchange Act 1882, section 90 of which provides: "A thing is deemed to be done in good faith, within the meaning of this Act, where it is in fact done honestly, whether it is done negligently or not."

4 **(2)—Negligence as careless conduct.** Negligence is often used in the sense of careless conduct without reference to any duty to take care. The use of the term in this sense has introduced some confusion into the subject, and has tended to obscure the true meaning of negligence. When there is a duty to take care, the standard of care frequently is that of the reasonable man, although this is not always so, and consequently, failure to take reasonable care and negligence are sometimes used as synonymous terms regardless of whether or not there is any duty. This is the sense in which negligence was used in the well-known definition of Alderson B.: "Negligence is the omission to do something which a reasonable man, guided upon those considerations which ordinarily regulate the conduct of human affairs, would do, or doing something which a prudent and reasonable man would not do." [6] This definition does not recognise the necessity for any duty to take care, and therefore naturally does not go on to consider what degree of care is imposed by the duty in any given case. In so far as the definition assumes a duty of care, it also assumes that the degree of care is exactly the same in each case, namely, a degree measured by the standard of a reasonable man, and this, as appears from the following pages, is by no means a complete or an accurate statement. It is clear, however, that the definition was not given with reference to any duty but was defining negligence in the abstract as meaning careless conduct.

5 Further illustrations of the use of the word negligence in this sense, of careless conduct, are as follows: "Although it may be true, that if a

[4] (1847) 11 Q.B. 347, 357.
[5] *Kettlewell* v. *Watson* (1882) 21 Ch.D. 685, 706.
[6] *Blyth* v. *Birmingham Waterworks Co.* (1856) 11 Ex. 781, 784.

person keeps an animal of known dangerous propensities, or a dangerous instrument, he will be responsible to those who are thereby injured, independently of any negligence in the mode of dealing with the animal or using the instrument; yet when the legislature has sanctioned or authorised the use of a particular thing, and it is used for the purpose for which it is authorised, and every precaution has been observed to prevent injury, the sanction of the legislature carries with it this consequence, that if damage results from the use of such thing independently of negligence, the party using it is not responsible.[7] " Here the plaintiffs must be taken to have consented to this collection of the water, which was for their own benefit, and the defendant can only be liable if he was guilty of negligence." [8] " It is now thoroughly well established that no action will lie for doing that which the legislature has authorised, if it be done without negligence, although it does occasion damage to anyone; but an action does lie for doing that which the legislature has authorised, if it be done negligently." [9] " The way in which the case was tried was that it was put to the jury as a case of negligence, and the learned judge told the jury that unless the plaintiff proved that the defendants had been guilty of negligence, he was out of court. That mode of putting the case was far too favourable to the defendants." [10] " The foundation of the action was a claim based upon the familiar doctrine established by the case of *Fletcher* v. *Rylands*,[11] which depends upon this—that even apart from negligence the use of land by one person in an exceptional manner that causes damage to another, and not necessarily an adjacent owner, is actionable." [12] " A man is entitled to be as negligent as he pleases towards the whole world if he owes no duty to them." [13] " It is common knowledge among lawyers that mere negligence in itself is not a cause of action. To give a cause of action there must be negligence which amounts to a breach of duty towards the person claiming. There are many cases where there has been clear negligence, in the absence of which damage would not have happened, and yet there is no liability under English law." [14] " I treat it, therefore, as established that a public authority, whether doing an act which it is its duty to do, or doing an act which it is merely empowered to do, must in doing the act do it without negligence, or, as it is put in some of the cases, must not do it carelessly or improperly." [15]

6 Another illustration emerges sometimes from cases concerning the doctrine of estoppel by negligence. Lord Denman C.J. in *Pickard* v.

[7] Cockburn C.J. in *Vaughan* v. *Taff Vale Ry.* (1860) 5 H. & N. 679, 685.
[8] Bramwell B. in *Carstairs* v. *Taylor* (1871) L.R. 6 Ex. 217, 222.
[9] Lord Blackburn in *Geddis* v. *Proprietors of Bann Reservoir* (1878) 3 App.Cas. 430, 455, 456.
[10] Swinfen Eady M.R. in *Miles* v. *Forest Rock Graine Co.* (1918) 34 T.L.R. 500, 501.
[11] (1865) L.R. 1 Ex. 265; (1868) L.R. 3 H.L. 330.
[12] Lord Buckmaster in *Rainham Chemical Works* v. *Belvedere Fish Guano Co.* [1921] 2 A.C. 465, 471.
[13] Lord Esher M.R. in *Le Lievre* v. *Gould* [1893] 1 Q.B. 491, 497 (the ratio of this decision was, however, considered by the H.L. to be wrong in *Hedley Byrne & Co. Ltd.* v. *Heller & Partners Ltd.* [1964] A.C. 465).
[14] Greer L.J. in *Farr* v. *Butters Bros. & Co.* [1932] 2 K.B. 606, 618.
[15] Lord Atkin in *E. Suffolk Rivers Catchment Board* v. *Kent* [1941] A.C. 74, 90.

Sears [16] stated the proposition that the rule of law is clear where one by his words or conduct, wilfully causes another to believe the existence of a certain state of things and induces him to act on that belief so as to alter his own previous position, the former is concluded from averring against the latter a different state of things as existing at the same time. Later, in *Gregg* v. *Wells* [17] Lord Denman stated the principle more broadly by saying that a party, who negligently or culpably stands by and allows another to contract on the faith and understanding of a fact that he can contradict cannot afterwards dispute that fact in an action against the person whom he has himself assisted in deceiving. Blackburn J. in *Swan* v. *North British Australasian Co.*[18] said "It is pointed out by Parke B.[19] . . . that in the majority of cases in which an estoppel exists, 'the party must have induced the other so to alter his position that the former would be responsible to him in an action for it'; and he had before pointed out that 'negligence,' to have the effect of estopping the party, must be 'neglect of some duty cast upon the person who is guilty of it.' And this, I apprehend, is a true and sound principle. A person who does not lock up his goods, which are consequently stolen, may be said to be negligent as regards himself, but inasmuch as he neglects no duty which the law casts upon him, he is not in consequence estopped from denying the title of those who may have, however innocently, purchased those goods from the thief, unless it be in market overt."

7 An illustration from the Statute Book was given by the Bills of Exchange Act 1882, section 82 of which afforded protection to a banker who "in good faith and without negligence receives payment for a customer" of a crossed cheque. In this connection "without negligence" meant "without want of reasonable care in reference to the interests of the true owner." [20] As Scrutton L.J. put it: "A question at once arises, as there is no 'negligence' without a legal duty, what was the exact duty imposed on the bank, and to whom? . . . In my view, section 82 lessened the duty of the bank by limiting it to an obligation only to use reasonable care in dealing with the cheque, or by providing that if the bank proved that it had used reasonable care in discharging its obligation to the true owner not to convert his property, it was discharged from liability though it had converted that property." [21] Section 82 has now been repealed by the Cheques Act 1957, but section 4 of the 1957 Act in effect re-enacts section 82 and its subsequent amendments [22] and extends the protection to uncrossed cheques.

8 The Sale of Goods Act 1893 serves as a further example by section 21,

16 (1837) 6 A. & E. 469, 474.
17 (1839) 10 A. & E. 90, 98.
18 (1863) 2 H. & C. 175, 181.
19 In *Freeman* v. *Cooke* (1848) 2 Ex. 654.
20 Kennedy J. in *Hannan's Lake View Central* v. *Armstrong & Co.* (1900) 5 Com.Cas. 188, 191.
21 *Savory & Co.* v. *Lloyds Bank Ltd.* [1932] 2 K.B. 122, 130.
22 Revenue Act 1883, s. 17, the Bills of Exchange (Crossed Cheques) Act 1906 and the Bills of Exchange Act (1882) Amendment Act 1932.

which deals with the transfer of title and the provision that the buyer acquires no better title to goods than the seller had unless the owner of the goods is " by his conduct precluded from denying the seller's authority to sell." This section was considered in *Mercantile Credit Co.* v. *Hamblin* [23] where the defendant knew P. for an apparently respectable motor-car dealer, whom she approached in order to raise a substantial loan of money on her Jaguar motor-car. P. gave the defendant his blank cheque stating that she could fill in the amount, when he had arranged the loan and had told her the amount he had been able to raise for her. At P.'s suggestion the defendant signed in blank certain hire-purchase forms, which she did not read in the belief that they were mortgage documents. P. then completed the forms and arranged the transaction on the basis that the motor-car was his and was being sold by him to the plaintiffs and thus by the plaintiffs on hire-purchase terms to the defendant. The defendant in due course refused to honour those terms and was sued by the plaintiffs in detinue and conversion. It was held that since title by estoppel does not arise under section 21 (1) of the Sale of Goods Act in a case of negligence unless (a) the owner owes a duty of care to the buyer, (b) there is a breach of duty, and (c) the negligence was the proximate or real cause of the buyer's loss, the plaintiff's claim failed because the defendant was not in fact negligent, although she did owe them a duty of care in the circumstances, which duty she had discharged.

9 Perhaps the best illustration of the use of " negligence " in the sense of careless conduct is to be found in the phrase " contributory negligence." Here, the word negligence does not mean breach of a duty to take care, but simply means careless conduct on the part of the person in question in not preventing or avoiding the consequences of the other person's breach of duty to take care.[24] A person who in broad daylight falls into an unfenced hole in the highway through not looking where he is going may be unable to succeed fully in an action because of the degree of his contributory negligence, but this is not on account of any duty which he owes to the person who dug the hole and left it unfenced—it is on account of his failure to take reasonable care for his own safety.

Negligence in the performance of a contract is yet another typical example of this second meaning under discussion.

With this meaning, negligence is the opposite of diligence.

0 **Degrees of negligence.** Used in the sense of meaning careless conduct it is true to say that there are degrees of negligence. As used in the expressions " gross negligence," " ordinary negligence " and " slight negligence," it is clear that the term negligence means carelessness and that these expressions mean gross carelessness, ordinary carelessness and slight carelessness respectively. When Rolfe B. said that he " could see no difference between negligence and gross negligence, that it was the

[23] [1965] 2 Q.B. 242.
[24] See Chap. 16.

same thing with the addition of a vituperative epithet," [25] he was using "negligence" in the sense of a breach of duty to take care and his criticism was justified. That is not to say, however, that the expression "gross negligence" has always the same meaning as "negligence." It is an expression in regular use among lawyers, and to deny it a meaning would be pedantic. It is intended to denote a high degree of careless conduct such as where a defendant did not intend a particular consequence to happen but nevertheless he must have been able to foresee its occurrence and in this sense it is of considerable practical utility.

Used in the sense of meaning a breach of the duty to take care, there are no degrees of negligence. "Epithets applied to negligence, so far as the common law is concerned, are really meaningless. Negligence is well known and well defined. A man is either guilty of negligence or he is not guilty of negligence. Gross negligence is not known to the English common law so far as civil proceedings are concerned." [26]

11 **Criminal negligence.** Degrees of negligence are recognised in criminal law. In *R.* v. *Bateman* [27] Lord Hewart C.J. said: "If A has caused the death of B by alleged negligence, then, in order to establish civil liability, the plaintiff must prove (in addition to pecuniary loss caused by the death) that A owed a duty to B to take care, that that duty was not discharged, and that such default caused the death of B. To convict A of manslaughter, the prosecution must prove the three things above mentioned and must satisfy the jury, in addition, that A's negligence amounted to a crime. In the civil action, if it is proved that A fell short of the standard of reasonable care required by law, it matters not how far he fell short of that standard. The extent of his liability depends, not on the degree of negligence, but on the amount of damage done. In the criminal court, on the contrary, the amount and degree of negligence are the determining question." In this passage "negligence" is sometimes used in the sense of a breach of the duty to take care and sometimes as meaning careless conduct. In the first two places in which it occurs it is used in the former meaning, in the second two in the latter meaning. The expression "the amount and degree of negligence" is unintelligible if negligence never means anything but the breach of a duty to take care, but is easily understood if it is taken to mean carelessness or careless conduct.

12 A use of the word negligence similar to the above occurred in Lord Atkin's speech in *Andrews* v. *Director of Public Prosecutions*.[28] He said: "It is only necessary to consider manslaughter from the point of view of an unintentional killing caused by negligence, that is, the omission of a duty to take care." [29] He there defined negligence in accordance with the

[25] *Wilson* v. *Brett* (1843) 11 M. & W. 113. Approved by Willes J. in *Grill* v. *Iron Screw Collier Co.* (1866) L.R. 1 C.P. 600, 612.
[26] *Pentecost* v. *London District Auditor* [1951] 2 K.B. 759, *per* Lynskey J. at p. 764.
[27] (1925) 94 L.J.K.B. 791.
[28] [1937] A.C. 576.
[29] *Ibid.* p. 581.

third meaning given above. Further on in his judgment he said: " The principle to be observed is that cases of manslaughter in driving motor-cars are but instances of a general rule applicable to all charges of homicide by negligence. Simple lack of care such as will constitute civil liability is not enough: for purposes of the criminal law there are degrees of negligence: and a very high degree of negligence is required to be proved before the felony is established." [30] Here, " simple lack of care " and " very high degree of negligence " must be contrasted terms. The " degrees of negligence " referred to are degrees of carelessness or careless conduct, and it is clear that in the second passage the word " negligence " is used in this sense. The same meaning was given to the word by Lord Porter, when he said: " A higher degree of negligence has always been demanded in order to establish a criminal offence than is sufficient to create civil liability. An obvious illustration is the difference between the degree of negligence in accident cases required to prove the crime of manslaughter and that sufficient to create civil liability." [31]

3 **(3)—Negligence as the breach of a duty to take care.** The third meaning of negligence is used in an objective sense and refers to a breach of a duty to take care, imposed by common or statute law. " The ideas of negligence and duty are strictly correlative, and there is no such thing as negligence in the abstract; negligence is simply neglect of some care which we are bound by law to exercise towards somebody." [32] Willes J. said that: " It is really the absence of such care as it was the duty of the defendant to use." [33] Lord Macmillan said: " The law takes no cognisance of carelessness in the abstract. It concerns itself with carelessness only where there is a duty to take care and where failure in that duty has caused damage. In such circumstances carelessness assumes the legal quality of negligence and entails the consequences in law of negligence. . . . The cardinal principle of liability is that the party complained of should owe to the party complaining a duty to take care, and that the party complaining should be able to prove that he has suffered damage in consequence of a breach of that duty." [34] Talbot J. speaks of actionable negligence as " depending on breach of duty owed by defendant to plaintiff." [35] Lord Wright says: " In strict legal analysis, negligence means more than heedless or careless conduct, whether in omission or commission: it properly connotes the complex concept of duty, breach, and damage thereby suffered by the person to whom the duty was owing." [36] " Negligence is the failure to use the requisite amount of care required by the law in the case where a duty to use care exists." [37] Accordingly when one comes to consider whether there is a breach of some duty owed to another, it is

[30] *Ibid.* at p. 583.
[31] *Riddell* v. *Reid* [1943] A.C. 1, 31.
[32] Bowen L.J. in *Thomas* v. *Quartermaine* (1887) 18 Q.B.D. 685, 694.
[33] *Grill* v. *General Iron Screw Collier Co.* (1866) L.R. 1 C.P. 600, 612.
[34] *Donoghue* v. *Stevenson* [1932] A.C. 562, 618, 619.
[35] *Cunard* v. *Antifyre Ltd.* [1933] 1 K.B. 551, 558.
[36] *Lochgelly Iron and Coal Co.* v. *M'Mullan* [1934] A.C. 1, 25.
[37] Lord Porter in *Riddell* v. *Reid* [1943] A.C. 1, 31.

legally irrelevant to inquire into a person's actual state of mind, since it is his conduct which need be judged.

Negligence, meaning a breach of duty, is " a specific tort in itself and not simply . . . an element in some more complex relationship or in some specialised breach of duty." [38] It is this specific tort of negligence which is to be dealt with in this book. Negligence as a tort in itself is a comparatively recent legal conception dating only from about 1824.[39] It has, however, developed very rapidly from about the middle of the last century, and during its progress it has swallowed large portions of the law of nuisance and of trespass, particularly trespass to the person.

As an example, it was held in *Letang* v. *Cooper* [40] that where a motor-car driver ran over the plaintiff's legs, whilst she was sunbathing on the grass in the private grounds of a hotel, having failed to notice her lying there, her action lay in negligence only and not in trespass to the person.

It therefore becomes necessary to analyse it so as to find out the elements of this tort of negligence.

14 **Breach of contractual duty to take care.** As appears from the quotations given above, negligence is the breach of a duty to take care. A duty to take care can be imposed by law or can be created by contract or trust. The breach of the contractual duty to take care, however, is not negligence in the sense in which the word is now being used. It is not uncommon to speak of the negligent performance of a contract, but in that case " negligent " is used in the second meaning explained above, *i.e.* in the sense of careless. In *Brown* v. *Boorman*,[41] indeed, the court actually treated breach of contract as negligence, when Lord Campbell said: " Whenever there is a contract, and something to be done in the course of the employment which is the subject of that contract, if there is a breach of a duty in the course of that employment, the plaintiff may either recover in tort or in contract." This, however, was only because " the introduction of assumpsit as a special kind of action on the case did not affect the earlier form of action in any way, or prevent it from being used in a proper case, even where assumpsit was a possible alternative." [42] It is now well recognised that breach of a contractual duty must be dealt with according to the law of contract, and cannot be regarded as the tort of negligence,[43] although the same facts may in some cases amount to a breach of contract and also the tort of negligence. This may be illustrated in a case of the relationship of master and servant where the Court of Appeal decided that the common law placed an employer under a duty to take all reasonable care for the safety of his servants in the course of their work and that the servant, having sustained personal injury owing to the employer's alleged breach of such duty, was entitled to claim damages, following his

38 *Grant* v. *Australian Knitting Mills* [1936] A.C. 85, *per* Lord Wright at p. 103.
39 Winfield, 42 L.Q.R. 184.
40 [1964] 2 Q.B. 53.
41 (1844) 11 Cl. & F. 1.
42 Sir F. Pollock, preface to 61 R.R.
43 See *Courtenay* v. *Earle* (1850) 10 C.B. 73.

election to sue either in tort or for breach of this implied term of the contract.[44] A further illustration would be in the case of a surgeon negligently performing an operation, the two rights of action are quite separate and the person entitled to sue in contract may be different from the person entitled to sue in tort. However, Diplock L.J. in *Bagot* v. *Stevens Scanlan & Co. Ltd.*[45] considered that this principle did not apply to those distinctive professional relationships of the kind where someone undertook to exercise by contract his professional skill in relation to the matter, *e.g.* an architect to supervise the building work.

Breach of trust being dealt with in courts of equity was never in danger of being regarded as a tort.

15 **Breach of statutory duty to take care.** Is breach of a duty, created by statute, negligence? The Trustee Act 1925, for example, imposes various duties upon trustees, and there is an increasing tendency to embody rules of law in a statutory form. Does a breach of duty become negligence when the duty is embodied in a statute if, before the statute was passed, the same breach of duty was not negligence? It seems clear that it does not. The trustee who has committed a breach of the duty imposed upon him by the Trustee Act 1925 is liable for breach of trust but has not committed the tort of negligence. The conclusion which may be arrived at, accordingly, is that the material source of the rule of law imposing the duty is irrelevant. Breach of statutory duty however may be negligence,[46] such as was described by Fletcher Moulton L.J.: " The effect . . . is that breaches of its provisions become statutorily equivalent to negligence " [47] but whether or not it is so is independent of the fact that it is embodied in statutory form. Nevertheless this use of the term " negligence " appears to be against the trend of modern decisions.[48] In order to exclude breaches of duty created by contract or trust and embodied in statutory form, we may include, in our definition, the statement that negligence is a tort. See further Chapter 18, *post*.

16 **Actual damage necessary.** Negligence is only actionable if actual damage is proved. There is no right of action for nominal damages.[49] Lord Reading C.J. in a passage approved by Lord Simon,[50] said: " Negligence alone does not give a cause of action; damage alone does not give a cause of action; the two must co-exist." [51]

17 **Wilful negligence.** Negligence may in this context consist in a wilful

44 *Matthews* v. *Kuwait Bechtel Corporation* [1959] 2 Q.B. 57. See also note in 75 L.Q.R. 300.
45 [1966] 1 Q.B. 197.
46 *Lochgelly Iron and Coal Co.* v. *M'Mullan* [1934] A.C. 1, *per* Lord Wright at pp. 23, 27. "As a rule the statutory duty involves the notion of taking care not to injure and in such cases actions for breach of statutory duty come within the category of negligence." Lord Atkin in *E. Suffolk Rivers Catchment Board* v. *Kent* [1941] A.C. 74, 88.
47 *David* v. *Britannic Merthyr Coal Co.* [1909] 2 K.B. 146, 164.
48 *L.P.T.B.* v. *Upson* [1949] A.C. 155, *per* Lord Wright at p. 168; *Riddell* v. *Reid* [1943] A.C. 1. 24–25.
49 See Chap. 4. § 126, *post*.
50 *E. Suffolk Rivers Catchment Board* v. *Kent* [1941] A.C. 74, 86.
51 *Munday* v. *L.C.C.* [1916] 2 K.B. 331, 334.

or an intentional act.[52] This is because negligence as the breach of a duty to take care is concerned with conduct and not with intention. It is no defence to prove that the defendant intentionally inflicted the damage in question and did not cause it by mere carelessness. If the driver of a heavy lorry deliberately runs into a bicycle and destroys it he can be sued for negligence, just as if he had destroyed it by careless driving. If a trench is made in the highway with a red lamp to give warning of its presence and A seeing X approaching and intending to cause him to fall into the trench, removes the red lamp and X does fall into the trench, A is liable in negligence, his intention instead of being a defence being a matter which facilitates proof of negligence.

18 Actionable negligence can be a wilful act and the expression " wilful negligence " is one which is well established. In *Emblen* v. *Myers*,[53] the defendant had asked the plaintiff, who was the owner of a stable next to the defendant's house, to sell the stable to him, but the plaintiff refused. The defendant thereupon, being required to pull down his house, pulled it down in such a reckless manner that the roof of the stable was damaged and, on the plaintiff's remonstrating, told his workmen to " work anyhow," and further damage to the plaintiff's property was done. The plaintiff sued for negligence and succeeded. Bramwell B. said: " It is said that the act of the defendant was wilful, and therefore the plaintiff cannot recover on this declaration; but the act was negligent as well as wilful. In my opinion, the plaintiff is entitled to recover the whole amount which he has chosen to claim." Channell B. said that the declaration must be read " as charging the defendant with wilful negligence," and added, " if in actions of trespass the plaintiff may recover damages beyond the amount of the actual injury, I see no reason why the same rule should not extend to wilful negligence."

In *Re City Equitable Fire Insurance Co.*,[54] a case of negligence on the part of directors of a company, Romer J. in a passage approved on appeal by Warrington and Sargant L.JJ., said: " An act, or an omission to do an act, is wilful where the person of whom we are speaking knows what he is doing and intends to do what he is doing. But if that act or omission amounts to a breach of his duty, and therefore to negligence, is the person guilty of wilful negligence? In my opinion, that question must be answered in the negative unless he knows that he is committing, and intends to commit, a breach of his duty, or is recklessly careless in the sense of not caring whether his act or omission is or is not a breach of duty." Later, he defines wilful negligence by saying: " A wilful act, which act amounts to negligence, is not wilful negligence unless there is a will to be negligent." [55]

[52] Some confusion arises from earlier decisions where " wilful " is used not as a term of art but too often is used as meaning no more than a high degree of carelessness or recklessness: *Caswell* v. *Powell Duffryn Associated Collieries Ltd.* [1940] A.C. 152, 176–177.
[53] (1860) 6 H. & N. 54.
[54] [1925] Ch. 407, 434.
[55] *Ibid.* at p. 436.

However the courts have sought to draw a difference, in order to distinguish their use of this term, in the case of personal injuries. Lord Denning M.R. in *Letang* v. *Cooper*: " If he does not inflict injury intentionally, but only unintentionally, the plaintiff has no cause of action today in trespass. His only cause of action is in negligence, and then only on proof of want of reasonable care. . . . If intentional, it is the tort of assault and battery. If negligent and causing damage, it is the tort of negligence." [56]

In *Imperial Chemical Industries Ltd.* v. *Shatwell*, Lord Reid criticised the inaccurate habit of using the word " negligence " to denote a deliberate act done with full knowledge of the risk, although this was said in connection with the matter under consideration, namely contributory negligence.[57]

19 **Definition.** The following definition may therefore be suggested: Negligence is a tort, which is the breach of a duty to take care imposed by common or statute law, resulting in damage to the complainant.[58]

20 **Essentials of actionable negligence.** Accordingly the essential ingredients of actionable negligence are:

1. the existence of a duty to take care owing to the complainant by the defendant;
2. failure to attain that standard of care prescribed by the law;
3. damage suffered by the complainant, which is causally connected with the breach of duty to take care.

These essentials are to be considered in the following chapter in greater detail, but it must be appreciated that there is still no major measure of agreement on the limits of these three elements, which becomes apparent from a study of the many and varied judicial opinions.[59]

Nevertheless, once these requirements are satisfied, the defendant in law will be held liable in negligence, whereupon it is then necessary to proceed to decide the extent of that damage, which is traceable to the defendant's negligence, and finally its value must be converted into a monetary estimation.

[56] [1965] 1 Q.B. 232, 239–240.
[57] [1965] A.C. 656, 672.
[58] In *Lochgelly Iron and Coal Co.* v. *M'Mullan* [1934] A.C. 1, Lord Wright at p. 25 opined: " In strict legal analysis, negligence means more than heedless or careless conduct, whether in omission or commission: it properly connotes the complex concept of duty, breach, and damage thereby suffered by the person to whom the duty is owing." See also *The Wagon Mound* (*No.* 1) [1961] A.C. 388, 425.
[59] For an example, see *Roe* v. *Minister of Health* [1954] 2 Q.B. 66 where Denning L.J. said at p. 85: " In all these cases you will find that the three questions, duty, causation and remoteness, ran continually into one another. It seems to me that they are simply three different ways of looking at one and the same problem. Starting with the proposition that a negligent person should be liable, within reason, for the consequences of his conduct, the extent of his liability is to be found by asking the one question: ' Is the consequence fairly to be regarded as within the risk created by the negligence? ' If so, the negligent person is liable for it: but otherwise not."

Chapter 2

THE DUTY TO TAKE CARE

1. General Aspects of the Duty of Care

21 **The need for a duty of care to exist.** There can be no doubt, as has been stated above in paragraph 16, *ante*, that damage must be suffered before the courts will recognise as actionable the tort of negligence and, likewise, actions in negligence must fail unless a duty to take care has been established. Perhaps, the clearest illustration of this need for a duty of care to exist is to be found in the words of Lord Wright in *Grant* v. *Australian Knitting Mills Ltd.*[1] where he said: " All that is necessary as a step to establish the tort of actionable negligence is to define the precise relationship from which the duty to take care is to be deduced. It is, however, essential in English law that the duty should be established: the mere fact that a man is injured by another's act gives in itself no cause of action: if the act is deliberate, the party injured will have no claim in law even though the injury is intentional, so long as the other party is merely exercising a legal right: if the act involves lack of due care, again no case of actionable negligence will arise unless the duty to be careful exists." Put in a compendious form, a man is entitled to be as negligent as he pleases towards the whole world, provided that he does not owe them a duty to take care.[2]

22 The circumstances under which a duty to take care arises have been gradually evolved by the courts, but it has not been easy to arrive at some general principle forming the basis of those circumstances. Lord Atkin said in *Donoghue* v. *Stevenson* [3] " It is remarkable how difficult it is to find in the English authorities statements of general application defining the relations between parties that give rise to the duty. The courts are concerned with the particular relations which come before them in actual litigation and it is sufficient to say whether the duty exists in those circumstances." Lord Atkin continued by saying: " At present I content myself with pointing out that in English law there must be, and is, some general conception of relations giving rise to a duty of care, of which the particular cases found in the books are but instances." [4] Judges, however, have been cautious in framing this general conception because " they find themselves in a difficulty if they state too wide propositions and find that

[1] [1936] A.C. 85, 103.

See Lord Esher M.R. at p. 497 in *Le Lievre* v. *Gould* [1893] 1 Q.B. 491. This decision was not followed but was explained by the H.L. in *Hedley Byrne & Co. Ltd.* v. *Heller & Partners* [1964] A.C. 465, " English law does not recognise a duty in the air, so to speak; that is, a duty to undertake that no one shall suffer from one's carelessness ": *Bottomley* v. *Bannister* [1932] 1 K.B. 458, *per* Greer J. at p. 476.

1932] A.C. 562, 579.

Donoghue v. *Stevenson*, *supra*, at p. 580.

they do not suit the actual facts." [5] Lord Atkin said also: " In the branch of the law which deals with civil wrongs dependent in England, at any rate, entirely upon the application by judges of general principles also formulated by judges, it is of particular importance to guard against the danger of stating propositions of law in wider terms than is necessary, lest essential factors be omitted in the wider survey and the inherent adaptability of English law be unduly restricted." [6] Asquith L.J. has also added his comments where he said in *Candler* v. *Crane, Christmas & Co.*[7] that the law governing the duty owed seems to have been built up in disconnected slabs exhibiting no organic unity or structure. General principles, however, must be formulated if the law is to be a coherent body of material rather than an isolated number of decisions, and a textbook writer must attempt to do what judges refrain from doing, his position of greater freedom and less responsibility preventing his statement of his conclusions from restricting the inherent adaptability of the law.

23 **Duty only exists when special relationship.** One view is that a duty to take care only exists when certain special relationships have been established between the parties, and that those relationships have been exhaustively defined by decided cases and now cannot be extended.[8] This view was argued in *Haseldine* v. *Daw & Sons Ltd.*,[9] but rejected on the ground that it was contrary to *Donoghue* v. *Stevenson.*[10] It was also argued in *Jackson* v. *Mayfair Window Cleaning Co., Ltd.*[11] and rejected. This view is an unduly narrow one which involves defining accurately the special relationships in question, a task which the following pages will show is an almost impossible one to perform and one which, if it were performed, would tend to cause injustice when new or unforeseen situations arose. Whether a duty exists or not is a matter of law and not of fact [12] so that there are many different classes of situations where the courts have held that a duty of care was imposed by reason of such relationships. An important illustration of this occurred recently in *Hedley Byrne & Co. Ltd.* v. *Heller & Partners Ltd.*[13] where the House of Lords expressed the opinion that the law will imply a duty of care, when a party seeking information from another, possessed of a special skill, trusts him to exercise all due care and that party knew or ought to have known that reliance was being placed on his skill and judgment. Some further examples may be considered:

[5] Scrutton L.J. in *Farr* v. *Butters Bros. & Co.* [1932] 2 K.B. 606, 612.

[6] *Donoghue* v. *Stevenson*, [1932] A.C. 562, 583.

[7] [1951] 2 K.B. 164, 188. The decision itself, however, was overruled by the H.L. in *Hedley Byrne & Co. Ltd.* v. *Heller & Partners* [1964] A.C. 465.

[8] Forcibly expressed by P. A. Landon in *Pollock on Torts*, 15th ed., pp. 326, 327, and 57 L.Q.R. 179.

[9] [1941] 2 K.B. 343, 358. See the judgment of Scott L.J.

[10] *Supra.*

[11] [1952] 1 All E.R. 215 (cleaners when cleaning the defendant's room caused a chandelier to fall from the ceiling—held liable for negligence in causing it to fall).

[12] *Per* Lord Kinnear in *Black* v. *Fife Coal Co. Ltd.* [1912] A.C. 149, 159; *per* du Parcq L.J. in *Deyong* v. *Shenburn* [1946] K.B. 227, 233; and *per* Lord Denning M.R. in *Letang* v. *Cooper* [1965] 1 Q.B. 232, 241.

[13] *Supra.*

24 In *Rootes* v. *Shelton* [14] it was held that where a participant in a game or pastime is injured by the act or omission of another participant, the existence and extent of a duty of care are to be determined in the light of all the circumstances, including the risks, which may reasonably be inferred to have been accepted by the fact of participation.

A railway passenger does owe a duty to any other person who is likely to be injured by his negligent act, such as a porter who was, in fact, standing on a station platform and was struck by a carriage door that had been opened by the railway passenger.[15] Other examples of such categories are between: an occupier of premises and his lawful visitors; a schoolmaster and his pupil; a professional man and his client; a person in a skilled occupation and his customer; a manufacturer and the ultimate consumer; the repairer of a chattel and its user; a local authority exercising its statutory powers to the injury of a member of the public.[15a]

25 **Duty as expressed in Heaven v. Pender.** In *Heaven* v. *Pender*,[16] Brett M.R. enunciated the following principle: " Whenever one person is by circumstances placed in such a position with regard to another that everyone of ordinary sense who did think would at once recognise that if he did not use ordinary care and skill in his own conduct with regard to those circumstances he would cause danger of injury to the person or property of the other, a duty arises to use ordinary care and skill to avoid such danger." However this principle was clearly stated too widely,[17] and accordingly later, when he had become Lord Esher, he qualified it by saying: " If one man is near to another or is near to the property of another, a duty lies upon him not to do that which may cause a personal injury to that other, or may injure his property." [18] The principle, thus qualified, was taken by Lords Atkin, Thankerton and Macmillan in *Donoghue* v. *Stevenson* as a " sound guide," Lord Atkin [19] quoting from A. L. Smith L.J.[20]: " The decision of *Heaven* v. *Pender* was founded upon the principle that a duty to take due care did arise when the person or property of one was in such proximity to the person or property of another that, if due care was not taken, damage might be done by one to the other," and adding: " I think that this sufficiently states the truth if proximity be not confined to mere physical proximity, but be used as I think it was intended, to extend to such close and direct relations that the act complained of directly affects a person whom the person alleged to be bound to take care would know would be directly affected by his

[14] (1947) 41 A.L.J.R. 172. The rules of the game are a relevant but not a determining factor.

[15] *Booker* v. *Wenborn* [1962] 1 W.L.R. 162.

[15a] *Dutton* v. *Bognor Regis U.D.C.* [1971] 2 All E.R. 1003.

[16] (1883) 11 Q.B.D. 503, 509. The principle was not approved by Cotton and Bowen L.JJ. (p. 516) and was frequently criticised until it was approved by the H.L. in *Donoghue* v. *Stevenson.*

[17] By Cotton and Bowen L.JJ. in giving their judgments in *Heaven* v. *Pender* at pp. 516–517. Also by Greer and MacKinnon L.JJ. in *Barnes* v. *Irwell Valley Water Board* [1939] 1 K.B. 21, 33, 46. See, too, Lord Atkin in *Donoghue* v. *Stevenson, supra*, at p. 580.

[18] *Le Lievre* v. *Gould* [1893] 1 Q.B. 491, 497 and by Bowen and Smith L.JJ. at pp. 502 and 509.

[19] *Donoghue* v. *Stevenson* [1932] A.C. 562, 581.

[20] In *Le Lievre* v. *Gould, supra*, p. 504.

careless act." Proximity in this connection is explained by Lord Wright as meaning that " the want of care and the injury are in essence directly and intimately connected . . . ' proximity ' can only properly be used to exclude any element of remoteness, or of some interfering complication between the want of care and the injury." [21]

26 **Duty as further expressed and developed in Donoghue v. Stevenson.** This duty has been expressed in terms as the " neighbour " principle. In *Donoghue* v. *Stevenson* [22] the defendants were manufacturers of ginger beer. They bottled some of their ginger beer in a bottle which was alleged to have contained the decomposed remains of a snail, with the result that the consumer of the ginger beer, who had no contract with the manufacturers, became ill. The manufacturers were held to owe a duty to the consumer to take care in the manufacture and bottling of their ginger beer. Lord Atkin, after approving, as set out above, the judgment of Brett M.R. in *Heaven* v. *Pender*,[23] stated the principle in this way [24]: " The rule that you are to love your neighbour becomes in law, you must not injure your neighbour; and the lawyer's question, Who is my neighbour? receives a restricted reply. You must take reasonable care to avoid acts or omissions which you can reasonably foresee would be likely to injure your neighbour. Who, then, in law is my neighbour? The answer seems to be—persons who are so closely and directly affected by my act that I ought reasonably to have them in contemplation as being so affected when I am directing my mind to the acts or omissions which are called in question." This statement of the law by Lord Atkin, as explained in *Grant* v. *Australian Knitting Mills Ltd.*,[25] has been generally accepted as correct, and establishes the " general concept of reasonable foresight as the criterion of negligence." [26]

Besides establishing clearly the principle that a manufacturer did owe a duty to the consumer, the real importance of the decision in *Donoghue* v. *Stevenson* lies in the fact that all doubts were thereby removed whether or not the tort of negligence was firmly bound down by existing precedents. It followed that it was not so bound, thus the tort was open to further expansion,[27] as indeed, it has expanded since

21 *Grant* v. *Australian Knitting Mills* [1936] A.C. 85, 104.
22 [1932] A.C. 562.
23 (1883) 11 Q.B.D. 503.
24 *Donoghue* v. *Stevenson, supra,* at p. 580.
25 [1936] A.C. 85, *per* Lord Wright at p. 104.
26 *Bourhill* v. *Young* [1943] A.C. 92, 107, *per* Lord Wright. Lord Atkin's proposition, too, has been rejected as being too wide notably by Scrutton L.J. in *Farr* v. *Butters Bros. & Co.* [1932] 2 K.B. 606, 613–614; by Roche L.J. in *Haynes* v. *Harwood* [1935] 1 K.B. 146, 167–168; by Singleton J. in *Barnett* v. *H. & J. Packer Co. Ltd.* [1940] 3 All E.R. 575, 577 and by Lord Thankerton in *Bourhill* v. *Young* [1943] A.C. 92, 98.
27 An example of such expansion occurs in the judgment of Marshall J. who cited the neighbour principle as his authority for imposing a new duty on a carrier in *Lee Cooper Ltd.* v. *Jeakins & Sons Ltd.* [1967] 2 Q.B. 1. The defendants, who were transport contractors, as bailees for reward of the plaintiffs' goods, albeit their contractual duty was owed to some others as bailors, owed to the plaintiffs a duty of care, since they knew that the plaintiffs and not the bailors were the owners of such goods. During the defendants' transport of the plaintiffs' goods their driver left their lorry unlocked and unattended at a roadside cafe and, upon his return a few minutes later, he discovered the lorry and its

then.[28] It follows that the word "duty" connotes the relationship between one party and another, imposing on the one an obligation for the benefit of that other to take reasonable care in all the circumstances.

27 **More than one duty can exist at a time.** Nevertheless some particular duty can displace that based generally upon proximity as emerged from *Commissioner for Railways* v. *Quinlan* [29] where it was held, *inter alia*, that no general principle is to be deducted from *Donoghue* v. *Stevenson*, which throws any particular light on the legal rights and duties that arise, when a trespasser is injured on a railway level crossing. More particularly it is not correct in principle to suppose that the mere fact that there was a likelihood, apparent to the occupier, of a trespasser being present on the crossing at some time or another is sufficient to impose on the occupier any general duty of care towards such a trespasser. On the other hand in *Commissioner for Railways* v. *McDermott* [30] it has become more clear that in a given situation two duties of care, the general duty and the special or limited duty, can exist simultaneously, neither displacing the other. Many situations arise where duties exist other than just to one class of persons at a time. In *Chadwick* v. *British Transport Commission* [31] Waller J. held, following a serious railway accident at Lewisham caused by the defendants' negligence, that the defendants owed a duty in respect of nervous shock to the passengers, since such injury was foreseeable, and that because these passengers had been put in such peril it could reasonably have been foreseen that someone would attempt to rescue them and would, in the process, suffer shock too. Accordingly, the defendants were held to owe the plaintiff, a rescuer, the like duty of care and were liable since he had become a psychoneurotic, as a result of this experience.

28 Situations also exist where more than one person owes a duty to a plaintiff at the same time. For example in *Griffiths* v. *Arch Engineering Co. (Newport) Ltd.*[32] where the plaintiff's employers hired a pneumatic portable grinding machine, which in fact was defective, as an essential item of equipment to be used in connection with their welding work it was held that both the employers and the hirers were equally liable for the plaintiff's injuries sustained whilst using it. The employers had failed to warn the plaintiff of the dangers involved in using it since they were in

load to have been stolen. It was held that the defendants were in breach of their duty in tort to the owners of the goods and were thus liable in damages to the plaintiffs for the value of their goods stolen.

28 *Per* Lord Macmillan, *supra*, at p. 619 where he said: "The criterion of judgment must adjust and adapt itself to the changing circumstances of life. The categories of negligence are never closed." See also *Candler* v. *Crane, Christmas & Co.* [1951] 2 K.B. 164, *per* Asquith L.J. at p. 192, although the decision itself was overruled in *Hedley Byrne & Co. Ltd.* v. *Heller & Partners Ltd.* [1964] A.C. 465; see to the same effect *per* Lord Devlin at p. 531; *Weller & Co.* v. *Foot and Mouth Disease Research Institute* [1966] 1 Q.B. 569; *The World Harmony* [1967] P. 341; *Electrochrome Ltd.* v. *Welsh Plastics Ltd.* [1968] 2 All E.R. 205.

29 [1964] A.C. 1054, 1070.

30 [1967] A.C. 169, 187.

31 [1967] 1 W.L.R. 912. See criticism of this decision by Professor Street, *The Law of Torts*, 4th ed., p. 142.

32 [1968] 3 All E.R. 217.

control of it and ought to have known about its defects. Also the hirers should have foreseen that the machine would be used by the employees of other contractors and would be likely to be used without some independent examination of it, in which event it was incumbent on them to take reasonable precautions against risk of injury to a person, using the machine in the manner it was foreseen it would be used.

2. FORESEEABILITY OF DAMAGE

29 **Duty based on reasonable foreseeability of damage.** Lord Atkin's statement was not intended to be complete or exhaustive.[33] It requires to be limited and explained as is stated below.[34] Subject to this, it agrees with the succinct statement of Scrutton L.J.[35]: " To determine whether an act is negligent, it is relevant to determine whether any reasonable person would foresee that the act would cause damage." Foreseeability is a question of fact, since it is only by a reference to the circumstances of each case under consideration that it can be determined.

30 **Reasonable foreseeability of damage is not the only criterion.** There were undoubtedly exceptions, firmly established in the law before *Donoghue* v. *Stevenson* in 1932, to the foresight of the reasonable man principle [36] where the defendant had avoided all liability in negligence, although it was perfectly apparent that he must have foreseen the likelihood of harm to the plaintiff. Examples are the immunity from liability of an occupier towards a trespasser,[37] of a vendor to his purchaser,[38] of lessor to his lessee or any other persons entering the premises during the currency of the lease [39] and the absence of any duty upon the owner of a domestic animal, not known to be dangerous, to prevent such an animal straying.[40] Not only have some of these earlier decisions been re-affirmed upon the ground that the principle of *Donoghue* v. *Stevenson* could not have applied to them but other exceptions have since been made; notably it has been held that an employer owes no duty to take care to protect his servant's property from the felonious act of a third party [41] and, perhaps with many academic sighs of relief, that a university owes no duty, through its

[33] *Herschtal* v. *Stewart & Ardern Ltd.* [1940] 1 K.B. 155, 160, *per* Tucker J. and *Haseldine* v. *Daw & Son Ltd.* [1941] 2 K.B. 343, 362, where Scott L.J. said: " It is because the critics have fallen into the error as in the case of Lord Esher, of assuming that Lord Atkin was intending to formulate a *complete* criterion almost like a definition in the prolegomena to a new theory of philosophy."

[34] *Post*, § 59.

[35] *Re Polemis & Furness, Withy & Co.* [1921] 3 K.B. 560, 577 (although the decision was disapproved in *The Wagon Mound* (*No.* 1) [1961] A.C. 388).

[36] See *per* Lord Macmillan at p. 620: " It is sometimes said that liability can only arise where a reasonable man would have foreseen and could have avoided the consequences of his act or omission."

[37] Chap. 8, § 387 *et seq.*

[38] Chap. 8, § 401 *et seq.*

[39] Chap. 8, § 401 *et seq.*

[40] Chap. 10, § 596 *et seq.*

[41] *Deyong* v. *Shenburn* [1946] K.B. 227 (actor's property stolen from theatre in which he was rehearsing; *Edwards* v. *West Herts. Group Hospital Management Committee* [1957] 1 W.L.R. 415 (a resident house physician had his belongings stolen from the hostel which adjoined the hospital). *Cf.*, however, a servant's duty to protect his master's property: *Stansbie* v. *Troman* [1948] 2 K.B. 48.

examiners, to its students should they negligently judge its undergraduates during the university examinations.[42] Foresight, further, can have no relevance when considering strict liability.[43]

"Where then do we get the obligation?" posed du Parcq L.J. in *Deyong* v. *Shenburn* [44] then he proceeded to answer his rhetorical question thus: "There are well known words of Lord Atkin in *Donoghue* v. *Stevenson* as to the duty towards one's neighbour and the method of ascertaining who is one's neighbour. It has been pointed out (and this only shows the difficulty of stating a general proposition which is not too wide) that unless one somewhat narrows the term of the proposition as it has been stated, one would be including in it something which the law does not support. It is not true to say that wherever a man finds himself in such a position that unless he does a certain act another person may suffer, or that if he does something another person will suffer, then it is his duty in the one case to be careful to do the act and in the other case to be careful not to do the act. Any such proposition is much too wide. There has to be a breach of a duty, which the law recognises, and to ascertain what the law recognises regard must be had to the decisions of the courts." [45]

These exceptions to the "neighbour" principle must originate from the fact that the situation, whence an obligation or duty will be inferred, only arises where the law will recognise: (1) the kind of harm, (2) the carelessness, causing such harm, and (3) the kind of persons both on whom and by whom this harm is inflicted. These will now be considered.

(a) *The Kind of Harm*

31 As a general rule, at common law, in cases where personal injury of a physical nature has been sustained or where actual damage to or loss of a person's property has been suffered, the courts have not been slow to impose liability and to provide a remedy, where a duty to take care exists. Where, however, the personal injury sustained is not physical in character but consists of an emotional distress and nervous shock or where the loss is purely financial in nature then the law has been extremely reluctant and devious in its recognition of such damage, which is a very real one in human affairs.

Ultimately having accepted that in certain circumstances pecuniary losses may be recoverable if they had resulted from careless acts, where they had been occasioned by careless statements instead had raised great

42 *Thorne* v. *University of London* [1966] 2 Q.B. 237; *Sammy* v. *Birkbeck College*, *The Times*, May 20 1965.

43 Chap. 9.

44 [1946] K.B. 227, 233.

45 *Cf. per* Lord Somervell in *Qualcast* (*Wolverhampton*) *Ltd.* v. *Haynes* [1959] A.C. 743, 757, 758: "Now that negligence cases are mostly tried without juries, the distinction between the functions of judge and jury is blurred. A judge naturally gives reasons for the conclusion formerly arrived at by a jury without reasons. It may sometimes be difficult to draw the line, but if the reasons given by a judge for arriving at the conclusion previously reached by a jury are to be treated as "law" and citable, the precedent system will die from a surfeit of authorities."

resistance until 1963, when a unanimous House of Lords in *Hedley Byrne & Co. Ltd.* v. *Heller & Partners Ltd.*[46] held that in principle there was no difference at all in law between physical loss and financial loss. Professor Heuston in *Salmond on Torts* [47] described the *Hedley Byrne* decision as the most striking decision in the field of negligence, perhaps in torts in general, since *Donoghue* v. *Stevenson*,[48] and in this he must be correct.

The kind of harm, therefore, is best considered under (a) physical damage; (b) nervous shock; (c) pecuniary and economic loss resulting from careless acts; and (d) pecuniary and economic loss resulting from careless statements.

32 **Physical damage to persons and property.** The name of litigation in personal injuries claims is Legion and the glut of cases, being reported in these modern times is so much on the increase year by year, that law library shelves fill up with alarming alacrity. For the textbook writer the tasks of selection and preparation become progressively harder to avoid an inundation from this amorphous mass, so that beyond the introduction above not much more need be said.

Therefore typically, as an example, if a motorist is injured and his motor car is crushed and damaged by the negligent driving of another road user, then the motorist victim can recover compensation not only in respect of his physical injuries sustained but also for the damage suffered to his motor car and to his other property, such as his torn or blood-stained clothing, his broken spectacles, watch and the like losses.

Further a person can suffer damage by losing his property such as by having it stolen, which is actionable, where a breach of duty can be established. In *Petrovitch* v. *Callinghams* [49] where the defendants, a firm of decorators, were carrying out internal painting work to the plaintiff's house but had left the street door open and unguarded, as a result of which omission a thief had entered and stolen the plaintiff's jewellery, it was held that the defendants were under a duty not to behave in such a way as to expose the occupier of a house to the risk of such reasonably foreseeable injury from loss. On the other hand in *Langbrook Properties Ltd.* v. *Surrey C.C.*[50] Plowman J. held on the trial of a preliminary issue as to whether the plaintiffs had any cause of action against any of the defendants that no action lay in negligence or nuisance in respect of subsidence of neighbouring land caused by a landowner abstracting water percolating under his own land.

33 **Nervous shock and emotional distress.** It is intended here to consider only that situation where the plaintiff suffers adversely in physical health as a result of the nervous shock experienced by any given occurrence. This must be distinguished from those cases where the plaintiff is merely

46 [1964] A.C. 465.
47 15th ed., pp. 269, 270.
48 [1932] A.C. 562.
49 (1969) 210 E.G. 1299.
50 [1970] 1 W.L.R. 161.

startled or frightened and so is " shocked " momentarily, whereby he does something and personal injury results. An example of this latter type of case is *Slatter* v. *British Railways Board*[51] where a shunter knew that the plaintiff was examining a line of wagons in the shunting yard but he failed to prevent some wagons from crashing into one end of that line with such an exceptional and unnecessarily violent bang, causing the plaintiff to be startled out of his wits so that he jumped, stumbled and fell injuring himself, the shunter's employers were held to be liable in negligence. A further example is *Brook* v. *Cook*[52] where a West African grass monkey suddenly appeared on the plaintiff's garden wall, frightening her so that she turned away, fell accidentally and injured her wrist.

For the former situation, where the plaintiff's health suffers as a result of nervous shock, a convenient introduction can be found in the case of *Victorian Railways Commissioners* v. *Coultas*[53] where the female plaintiff was a passenger in a buggy, being driven across a level-crossing by her husband, when a train approached them, going at a rapid speed. The engine passed by very close to the back of the buggy but did not actually touch it. The experience proved to be so frightening that the plaintiff fainted as a result of receiving a severe nervous shock and she suffered ill health, which persisted for a substantial time thereafter. The Privy Council, finding for the defendants, expressed the opinion that damages for a nervous shock or mental injury caused by fear of an impending collision were too remote.

This case is illustrative of the reluctance of the courts to award damages for shock. One can only presume that this resistance stemmed from the fact that the courts feared a spate of litigation based upon an allegation of this kind of injury, with its attendant risks of fictitious claims being made and of their avoiding detection due to the lack of precise medical and scientific knowledge then. Nevertheless by 1901 recognition did come in *Dulieu* v. *White & Sons*[54] where the plaintiff was held to be within the area of foreseeable impact, as a result of a pair of horses being negligently driven into the public-house, where she was serving behind the bar, it was held that she could recover damages for nervous shock that had induced her to give birth prematurely to a child which had been rendered an idiot thereby. By 1915 it was now " fully established by authority—recent and strong authority—that physical impact or lesion is not a necessary element in the case of recovery of damage in ordinary cases of tort."[55]

34 In *Bourhill* v. *Young*[56] Lord Macmillan said: " It is no longer necessary to consider whether the infliction of what is called mental shock may

[51] (1966) 1 K.I.R. 336.
[52] (1961) 105 S.J. 684 (this injury was not foreseeable as it did not result from an attack of any sort by the monkey, assuming it to be *ferae naturae*).
[53] (1888) 13 App.Cas. 222.
[54] [1901] 2 K.B. 669.
[55] *Brown* v. *John Watson Ltd.* [1915] A.C. 1, 14, *per* Lord Shaw.
[56] [1943] A.C. 92, 103.

constitute an actionable wrong. The crude view that the law should take cognisance only of physical injury resulting from actual impact has been discarded, and it is now well recognised that an action will lie for injury by shock sustained through the medium of the eye, or the ear without direct contact. The distinction between mental shock and bodily injury was never a scientific one, for mental shock is presumably in all cases the result of, or at least accompanied by, some physical disturbance in the sufferer's system. And a mental shock may have consequences more serious than those resulting from physical impact. But in the case of mental shock there are elements of greater subtlety than in the case of an ordinary physical injury and these elements may give rise to debate as to the precise scope of legal liability." It followed from *Dulieu* v. *White & Sons* [57] that when the negligence of the defendant gives rise to an apprehension on the part of the plaintiff of danger limited to himself, and that apprehension of danger results in nervous shock, the plaintiff can recover damages. Again where the pursuer, whilst walking on the footpath, saw a tramcar approaching down an incline at an excessive speed and out of control, and she knew that between her and the tram there was a dangerous turn where an accident had occurred before, and as the speed increased she was thrown into a state of terror lest the tram should leave the rails and run her down, with the result that she sustained a nervous shock and had a miscarriage, it was held that a relevant case was stated.[58] When the plaintiff, a midget working in the funfair of a circus, sustained a " shock " owing to an elephant, which had got out of control, coming over the top of a booth where the midget was going to perform, £25 was awarded for the extent to which the shock resulted in physical and mental harm to the midget.[59] If a nervous shock is caused by fear of injury not to the plaintiff himself but to some other person, then whether damages are recoverable is not in all cases free from doubt.

35 The further question whether a person can recover for nervous shock sustained from witnessing an accident or from fear of seeing a third person killed or injured is also unsettled. The authorities on the point are as follows:

In *Wilkinson* v. *Downton* [60] Wright J. referred to the unreported case of *Smith* v. *Johnson & Co.*, and said: " Bruce J. and I held that where a man was killed in the sight of the plaintiff by the defendant's negligence, and the plaintiff became ill, not from the shock from fear of harm to himself but from the shock of seeing another person killed, this harm was too remote a consequence of the negligence." In *Dulieu* v. *White* [61] Kennedy J. said: " It is not, however, to be taken that in my view every nervous shock occasioned by negligence and producing physical injury to the sufferer gives a cause of action. There is, I am inclined to think,

[57] [1901] 2 K.B. 669.
[58] *Brown* v. *Glasgow Corporation*, 1922 S.C. 527.
[59] *Behrens* v. *Bertram Mills Circus Ltd.* [1957] 2 Q.B. 1.
[60] [1897] 2 Q.B. 57, 61.
[61] [1901] 2 K.B. 669, 675.

at least one limitation. The shock, where it operates through the mind, must be a shock which arises from a reasonable fear of immediate personal injury to oneself. A has, I conceive, no legal duty not to shock B's nerves by the exhibition of negligence towards C, or towards the property of B or C." Phillimore J., in the same case, is silent on this point.

36 In *Hambrook* v. *Stokes Bros.*[62] the defendants negligently left a motor-lorry, with its engine running, at the top of a steep bank unattended. The lorry started and ran down the incline, and the plaintiff's wife, from fear for her own safety and also for the safety of her children, who had just left her but were out of sight around the bend in the road and must have met the lorry in its course, had a severe nervous shock from the effects of which she died. The trial judge, following the dictum of Kennedy J. quoted above, directed the jury that the plaintiff was only entitled to recover if the shock was caused by fear of harm to herself and not to the children. This was held to be a misdirection. Bankes L.J. said that " the dictum of Kennedy J. laid down in quite general terms . . . cannot be accepted as good law applicable in every case," [63] but he also said: " It may well be that the duty of a person to take care does not extend to a person in the position of the plaintiff in *Smith* v. *Johnson & Co.* or to the person indicated as B in Kennedy J.'s illustration, and yet may extend to a person in the position of the plaintiff's wife." [64] Atkin L.J., however, said: " I can find no principle to support the self-imposed restriction stated in the judgment of Kennedy J. in *Dulieu* v. *White* that the *shock* must be a shock which arises from a reasonable fear of immediate personal injury to oneself. . . . Personally, I see no reason for excluding the bystander in the highway who receives injury in the same way from apprehension of or the actual sight of injury to a third party. There may well be cases where the sight of suffering will directly and immediately physically shock the most indurate heart; and if the suffering of another be the result of an act wrongful to the spectator, I do not see why the wrongdoer should escape." [65] Nevertheless it is submitted that it is very doubtful whether a duty was owed to this plaintiff's wife at all, in the circumstances, despite Atkin L.J. saying that the duty of a driver of a vehicle on the highway was " owed to all wayfarers, whether they are injured or not; though damage by reason of the breach of duty is essential before any wayfarer can sue." [66] Seemingly the defendants by admitting negligence conceded inevitably that they owed a duty to her and were in breach of that duty but this admission may have been a fundamental error of the defence in the case.

37 In Scotland Lord Hunter in *Brown* v. *Glasgow Corporation*,[67] basing

[62] [1925] 1 K.B. 141. In *Bourhill* v. *Young* [1943] A.C. 92 this case was discussed without disapproval by the House of Lords. Lord Wright said (at p. 111) that it " now lays down the law." In *King* v. *Phillips* [1953] 1 Q.B. 429 the Court of Appeal treated it as good law, Singleton and Denning L.JJ. both expressly approving the decision.

[63] *Ibid.* at p. 151.

[64] *Ibid.* at p. 150.

[65] *Ibid.* at p. 157. See now *Hinz* v. *Berry* [1970] 2 Q.B. 40 and § 147, *post*.

[66] *Ibid.* at p. 156.

[67] 1922 S.C. 527. For the facts, see *ante*, § 34.

himself on Kennedy J.'s dictum, said: " The sight of an occurrence like that may perfectly well unnerve a person in the delicate condition in which the pursuer was. At the same time, a shock occasioned by a sight of that sort, where there is no real fear of injury to the pursuer herself, would not, in my opinion, be a good ground of action against the defenders." Later, however, in *Currie* v. *Wardrop*,[68] after considering *Hambrook* v. *Stokes Bros.*, he preferred to reserve his opinion. In *Currie* v. *Wardrop* a young man and a young woman were walking arm in arm along the highway when a motor omnibus collided with them. The man was struck and received considerable physical injury. The woman was not struck, but she suffered severely from shock from fear for her personal safety aggravated by anxiety for the safety of the man, and she was awarded damages on that basis. It was held, on appeal, that the jury ought not to have been asked to discriminate between these two heads of damage, and a contention that the jury should have been directed to disregard shock occasioned by anxiety for the safety of the man was rejected. In a dissenting judgment, Lord Alness, with whom three other members of the court were inclined to agree on this point, expressed his agreement with the dissenting judgment of Sargant L.J. in *Hambrook* v. *Stokes Bros.*, on the ground that no duty was owed to the plaintiff so far as fear of danger to persons other than herself was concerned.

38 In *Owens* v. *Liverpool Corporation* [69] a tramcar was so negligently driven that it collided with a hearse in a funeral procession and overturned the coffin. The mourners, who were relatives of the deceased, suffered a severe mental shock from witnessing the collision and were held entitled to recover. In *Bourhill* v. *Young* [70] a motor-cyclist passed a tramcar on its near side and negligently collided with a motor-car. A fishwife was getting her creel on her back on the offside of the tramcar some forty-five feet away, and the noise of the collision gave her a nervous shock, as a result of which she gave birth to a stillborn child, prematurely born a month afterwards. Her claim failed on the ground that, as she was not within his line of vision, she " was not so placed that there was any reasonable likelihood of her being affected by the cyclist's careless driving," [71] so that the cyclist, " was under no duty to the pursuer to

[68] 1927 S.C. 538.

[69] [1939] 1 K.B. 394. This decision was adversely criticised by Lords Porter and Wright in the H.L. in *Bourhill* v. *Young* [1934] A.C. 92, but in *King* v. *Phillips* [1953] 1 Q.B. 429 Singleton and Denning L.JJ. apparently approved of it. In *Behrens* v. *Bertram Mills Circus Ltd.* [1957] 2 Q.B. 1, Devlin J. said that *Owens* went " as far as any court can go " but did not treat it as overruled.

[70] [1943] A.C. 92. This case is discussed by Prof. Goodhart in 8 C.L.J. 265, and criticised by the author in 59 L.Q.R. 150. In " Shock Cases and Area of Risk," 16 M.L.R. 14, Prof. Goodhart effectively disposes of the fallacy that there can be found an " area of physical risk " within the limits of which alone can the actor be made legally responsible for his negligent acts.

[71] *Ibid.* at p. 105, *per* Lord Macmillan. In 8 C.L.J. 265, Professor Goodhart points out the unsatisfactory nature of the " area of physical impact " test. In 16 M.L.R. 14 he expresses the opinion that " there may be dicta which give rise to trouble in future cases."

foresee that his negligence in driving at an excessive speed and consequently colliding with a motor-car might result in injury to the pursuer, for such a result could not reasonably and probably be anticipated." Lord Porter said: "The duty is not to the world at large." Great stress was laid upon the fact that the cyclist could not see the fishwife because she was behind the tram, but it is well settled that knowledge of the presence of the injured party is not a condition precedent to liability in a highway collision.[72] As she had "suffered substantial damage and suffered it owing to the conduct of the cyclist" [73] there would seem to be some defect in the law, which does not provide her with a remedy against him, the wrongdoer. The plaintiff, however, could still recover damages if the injury by nervous shock should reasonably have been contemplated, even although she was outside the area of foreseeable danger from an impact. The case was distinguished in *Farrugia* v. *G.W.R.*[74] where a lorry, loaded with a large container, was driven under a bridge which was so low that the container was thrown off. In falling off it injured the plaintiff who was, unknown to the driver, running behind the lorry, on which he had just before been riding as a trespasser, but it was held that the defendants were liable. Lord Greene M.R. explained the defendants' duty [75]: "the duty was a duty to take care *vis-à-vis* anyone—not this plaintiff as such, but anyone—the general class of persons who, at the moment when the danger materialised, might happen to be in the near neighbourhood."

39 In *King* v. *Phillips* [76] a taxi cab backed into a small boy on a tricycle, causing slight damage to them, but giving the child's mother a nervous shock, when, upon hearing the boy screaming seventy yards away, she looked out of a window of her home. The Court of Appeal dismissed her suit in negligence on the ground that in the circumstances no duty was owed her. Denning L.J. said [77]: "There can be no doubt since *Bourhill* v. *Young* that the test of liability for shock is foreseeability of injury by shock," which view of the law was endorsed in *Overseas Tankship (U.K.) Ltd.* v. *Morts Dock and Engineering Co. Ltd.*[78] By contrast, in *Boardman* v. *Sanderson* [79] the defendant, in reversing his car out of the garage, negligently injured an eight-year-old boy by running over his foot. The child's father, who to the defendant's knowledge was within earshot, did indeed hear the screaming of his son; he ran to his assistance but suffered a shock in the process. The Court of Appeal, in holding the

[72] See, *e.g. Haynes* v. *Harwood* [1935] 1 K.B. 146 (where the plaintiff was inside the police station when the defendant's horses were left unattended); *Dulieu* v. *White* [1901] 2 K.B. 669 (where the injured plaintiff was behind the bar in a public-house); *Carmarthenshire C.C.* v. *Lewis* [1955] A.C. 549.
[73] *Ibid., per* Lord Wright at p. 106.
[74] [1947] 2 All E.R. 565.
[75] *Ibid.* at p. 567.
[76] [1953] 1 Q.B. 429. See article "Emotional Shock and the Unimaginative Taxi Driver" (Goodhart) 69 L.Q.R. 347.
[77] *Ibid.* at p. 441.
[78] [1961] A.C. 388, 426.
[79] [1964] 1 W.L.R. 1317.

defendant liable, did so upon the decisive factor that here he actually knew of the child's father's presence, after the Court had rejected the argument advanced that only eye-witnesses to an accident could recover damages for injury by nervous shock.

A more anxious field for development of the law concerns liability for those persons who suffer shock where they are not themselves put in any danger and the emotional involvement with the supposed victim is not so close as that considered already, *e.g.* parent and child. It has been held that a nervous shock caused by seeing a fellow workman injured during his employment is an accident within the meaning of the Workmen's Compensation Acts. Thus where a miner, hearing a cry for help, went and saw a man at the next working place knocked down by a fall of coal and bleeding all over his head and from his ears and eyes, injuries from which he died within fifteen minutes, it was held that the resulting shock which he sustained was an accident.[80] Where a tramdriver was involved in a road accident and suffered no physical injury but sustained a shock so that he was unfit to drive because of his nervous condition, he was held entitled to damages.[81] *Dooley* v. *Cammell Laird & Co. Ltd.*[82] provides a further illustration of this point, where a sling broke and its load dropped into the hold of a ship, watched helplessly by the plaintiff, who was operating the crane concerned. He suffered severe shock for the safety of his fellow workmen, whom he could not see but whom he knew to be below deck and directly in the line of the danger. It was held that he was entitled to recover damages but it is not easy to see how it was contended that the employers ought reasonably to have anticipated suffering by nervous shock as a result of their negligence, where the workman was outside the danger area, if that is the test to be applied. If it is because the defendants must have anticipated that their crane driver would be watching intently the slings being lowered by him and hence would be likely to be shocked at seeing the slings break, then why should they not anticipate likewise the presence of others of their workmen in the vicinity, observing the frightening incident, since the employers could expect them, too, to be in a position of danger, even if, as a fact, they were not. Where then is or must the line be drawn? The answer of McNair J. in *King* v. *Phillips*[83] it is submitted, is the correct one where he stated: " I should humbly reply in the language of Lord Wright, used admittedly in a slightly different context, that it should be drawn ' where in the particular case the good sense of the jury or judge decides.' " This is not an altogether unknown escape hatch used in our legal system in order to explain what is

80 *Yates* v. *South Kirby, etc., Collieries* [1910] 2 K.B. 538.

81 *Durward* v. *Dunoon Motor Services Ltd.*, 1952 S.L.T. (Notes) 2.

82 [1951] 1 Lloyd's Rep. 271.

83 Quoted by Singleton L.J. [1953] 1 Q.B. 429, 451. See also *per* Lord Denning M.R. in *S.C.M. (United Kingdom)* v. *W. J. Whittall & Son* [1971] 1 Q.B. 337, " Where is the line to be drawn? Lawyers are continually asking that question. But the judges are never defeated by it. We may not be able to draw the line with precision, but we can always say on which side of it any particular case falls," which seems to be as good a way of answering it as any other.

otherwise difficult to explain, but it must suffice that each case has to be decided on its facts and upon its merits.[83]

40 It is difficult to see, in principle, why nervous shock caused by fear of injury, or seeing the results of injury, to a third person owing to the negligence of the defendant is not actionable. The grounds for saying that it is not actionable are (1) remoteness, and (2) no breach of duty. As to remoteness, if the shock is actually due to what has been seen or feared as a result of the defendant's negligence, it is the direct result and can hardly be too remote,[84] although this is the ground on which Denning L.J. decided for the defendant in *King* v. *Phillips*.[85] As to there being no breach of duty, this involves a consideration of what the duty is. In the words of Atkin L.J.: " The duty of the owner of a motor-car in a highway is not a duty to refrain from inflicting a particular kind of injury upon those who are in the highway. If so, he would be an insurer. It is a duty to use reasonable care to avoid injuring those using the highway. It is thus a duty owed to all wayfarers, whether they are injured or not; though damage by reason of the breach of duty is essential before any wayfarer can sue. Further, the breach of duty does not take place necessarily when the vehicle strikes or injures the wayfarer. The negligent act or omission may precede the act of injury." [86] The contrary opinion is based on the view that, " as the defendant did not do anything which could reasonably or naturally be expected to cause the harm in question to the plaintiff, there was no evidence of any breach of duty towards him for which the defendant could be rendered liable." [87] The decision of the House of Lords in *Bourhill* v. *Young* [88] favours the latter opinion. Nervous shock is only a particular form of damage, no different in principle from a broken limb, so that if there is a breach of the duty to take care and nervous shock is caused by the breach, damages should be awarded as a matter of course. In the words of Atkin L.J., " The cause of action . . . appears to be created by breach of the ordinary duty to take reasonable care to avoid inflicting personal injuries, followed by damage, even though the type of damage may be unexpected—namely, shock." [89]

41 **Nervous shock: summary.** The following conclusions may be drawn:

1. When there is a breach of the duty to take care, the damage may take the form of a shock without a direct physical impact.[90]

2. Reasonable fear of immediate physical injury to the plaintiff himself resulting in a shock is actionable.[91]

3. Reasonable fear of immediate physical injury to the plaintiff's

[84] See *Hambrook* v. *Stokes Bros.* [1925] 1 K.B. 141, *per* Sargant L.J. at p. 162.
[85] [1953] 1 Q.B. 429, 442. See Goodhart's criticism of this reason in 69 L.Q.R. at p. 352.
[86] [1925] 1 K.B. 141, 156.
[87] *Ibid.*, *per* Sargant L.J. at p. 163.
[88] [1943] A.C. 92.
[89] *Hambrook* v. *Stokes Bros.* [1925] 1 K.B. 141, 158.
[90] *Bourhill* v. *Young* [1943] A.C. 92, *per* Lord Macmillan at p. 103; *per* Lord Wright at p. 106.
[91] *Dulieu* v. *White* [1901] 2 K.B. 669.

family,[92] or to his friends,[93] or, doubtfully, to third parties,[94] resulting in a shock is actionable.

4. The sight of an accident causing physical injury to the plaintiff's family, or to his friends,[95] or, doubtfully, to third parties,[96] resulting in a shock is actionable.

5. Hearing the noise of an accident causing physical injury to human beings resulting in a shock is by itself not actionable.[97]

6. The sight of physical injury caused otherwise than to a human being, *e.g.* to a corpse, to an animal or to property, resulting in a shock is not actionable.[98]

7. A report by a third party that physical injury to a member of the plaintiff's family has been caused by the defendant's negligence, resulting in a shock, is not actionable,[99] unless such intervening act by the third party was reasonable in the circumstances or to be expected.[1]

42 **Pecuniary and economic loss resulting from careless acts.**[2] Whilst the duty to take care to avoid causing physical injury to persons or property has been widely recognised as the general rule at common law, it has always been extremely reluctant to extend its recognition to non-physical or purely pecuniary loss however easily foreseeable.[3] An early example of this is to be found in *Cattle* v. *Stockton Waterworks Co.*[4] where the defendants had laid a water main, which in fact was defective, under a turnpike road. The resulting leakage of water seriously hampered the contractor's work of tunnelling underneath the road causing him to suffer a loss of profit on his contract with the road owners. The court, holding that he had no cause of action, regretted having to make that decision because said Blackburn J.: " If we did so, we should establish an authority for saying that, in such a case as that of *Fletcher* v. *Rylands* the defendant would be liable, not only to an action by the owner of the drowned mine,

92 *Hambrook* v. *Stokes Bros.* [1925] 1 K.B. 141; In *Hinz* v. *Berry* [1970] 2 Q.B. 40, the deceased's widow was awarded £4,000 damages in respect of the shock and subsequent ill health she suffered as a result of witnessing the accident, in which her husband was killed, and seeing her children being injured when the defendant collided with their Dormobile van, parked in a lay-by.

93 *Bourhill* v. *Young* [1943] A.C. 92, 117, *per* Lord Porter.

94 *Hambrook* v. *Stokes Bros.* [1925] 1 K.B. 141, 157, *per* Atkin L.J.

95 This is covered by the authorities quoted in notes 92 and 93. In *Turbyfield* v. *G.W. Ry.* (1938) 54 T.L.R. 221 £25 was awarded to a girl as damages for shock in seeing her sister killed through a motorist's negligence. No reasons were given.

96 Note 94, but the contrary view is expressed by Lord Porter in *Bourhill* v. *Young*, at p. 117. However, see *Carlin* v. *Helical Bar* (1970) 9 K.I.R. 154, where Rees J. awarded damages for nervous shock suffered by a cranedriver who had witnessed a fatal accident caused by negligence during the use of his crane.

97 *Bourhill* v. *Young* [1943] A.C. 92.

98 This seems to follow from the adverse criticism of *Owens* v. *Liverpool Corporation* [1939] 1 K.B. 394 in *Bourhill* v. *Young* [1943] A.C. 92.

99 *Hambrook* v. *Stokes Bros.* [1925] 1 K.B. 141 where shock suffered by the plaintiff's wife from what she was told by bystanders—that a child answering to the description of her own child had been injured—was held not actionable.

1 *Schneider* v. *Eisovitch* [1960] 2 Q.B. 430 where the plaintiff, herself injured in an accident, was told of her husband's death in the same crash, so that she suffered further shock, she was entitled to recover damages for such additional injury. See also *novus actus interveniens*, *post*, § 113 *et seq.*

2 See " Negligence and Economic Loss " (Lewis) 120 New L.J. 851.

3 " The reluctance to grant a remedy for the careless invasion of financial or pecuniary interests is longstanding, deep-rooted and not unreasonable," Professor Heuston, *Salmond on Torts*, p. 262.

4 (1875) L.R. 10 Q.B. 453.

and by such of his workmen as had their tools or clothes destroyed but also to an action by every workman and person employed in the mine, who in consequence of its stoppage made less wages than he would otherwise have done. And many similar cases to which this would apply might be suggested. It may be said that it is just that all such persons should have compensation for such a loss, and that, if the law does not give them redress, it is imperfect. Perhaps it may be so." [5] In 1956 a similar conclusion was reached in *Brandon Electrical Engineering Co. (Leeds) Ltd.* v. *William Press & Son Ltd.*[6] where the defendants negligently damaged a water main causing it to burst and the escaping water to damage an electrical cable, whereby the power at the plaintiffs' factory was cut off and work was brought to a standstill for some hours, resulting in wasted wages and loss of production. The defendants were held not liable on the ground that they owed no duty to the plaintiffs.

43 An important decision undoubtedly occurred in *Weller & Co.* v. *Foot and Mouth Disease Research Institute.*[7] The defendants occupied premises, where they carried out experimental work in connection with foot and mouth disease, but, when cattle in the vicinity of these premises became infected with the disease, the Ministry of Agriculture, Fisheries and Food made an order closing two local marts. During this enforced closure, the plaintiffs, auctioneers, were unable to auction cattle at these marts and brought actions against the defendants for damages for loss of business alleging that they owed the plaintiffs a duty to take reasonable care of which they were in breach by negligently allowing an escape of the virus. Widgery J. upheld the defendants' contention, raised by a preliminary issue, that even if they were to admit the escape and/or the negligence, as well as foreseeability of the loss to the plaintiffs, none of these constituted harm of the sort, which the law should grant a remedy.

Then again in *Electrochrome Ltd.* v. *Welsh Plastics Ltd.*[8] where B's servant negligently damaged a fire-hydrant belonging to C, as a result of which the water supply to A's factory was interrupted, causing A to suspend work, thereby to suffer considerable financial loss, it was held by Geoffrey Lane J. that B's duty of care was owed only to C, the owner of the fire-hydrant, and not to A, who could not recover damages. On the other hand, where strips of metal foil blew across from one factory on a trading estate and short circuited the bus-bars of the electricity sub-station,

[5] *Ibid.* at p. 457.

[6] (1956) 106 L.J. 332. But damage, consisting of loss of profits due to electrically driven machinery being put out of action as a result of the defendant demolition contractors interfering negligently with the power supply cable, was held to be recoverable in tort: *J. W. Moore (North Shields) Ltd.* v. *Sharp* (1964) 108 S.J. 453 there being a distinction from the decision in *Perera* v. *Vandiyar* [1953] 1 W.L.R. 672 where a landlord deliberately turned off his tenant's gas and electricity supplies in order to drive him out of the premises where in the circumstances there was a breach. See now *S.C.M. (United Kingdom) Ltd.* v. *W. J. Whittall & Son Ltd.* [1971] 1 Q.B. 337, affirming [1970] 1 W.L.R. 1017, Thesiger J. See article: " Negligence and Economic Loss " (Hewitt) 115 S.J. 255.

[7] [1966] 1 Q.B. 569.

[8] [1968] 2 All E.R. 205. See article: " Damnum Sine Injuria " (Powell Smith) (1968) 118 New L.J. 739.

thus bringing another factory's production to a grinding halt, as a result of the ensuing power failure, Lawton J. in *British Celanese* v. *A. H. Hunt (Capacitors) Ltd.*[9] held that the defendants did, indeed, owe the plaintiffs a duty to take reasonable care to prevent the foil from escaping from their factory premises in such a way as to foul the exposed conductors of their electricity supply. This decision of Lawton J. was held by the Court of Appeal to have been decided correctly in *S.C.M. (United Kingdom) Ltd.* v. *W. J. Whittall & Son Ltd.*[10] where the defendant contractors were preparing to build a boundary wall when they negligently pierced and damaged an 11,000 volt cable running alongside the road and thereby cut off the electric power to the plaintiffs' factory as well as to many other factories. The plaintiffs had suffered particularly severely from the power failure, which lasted over seven hours, because they had molten metals in their machines which solidified owing to lack of heat. It was held that the contractors were liable for the material damage done to the plaintiffs and the loss of profit truly consequent on it but not for any other economic loss, which was too remote and therefore was irrecoverable.

44 **Pecuniary and economic loss resulting from careless statements.** This aversion of the courts from holding that a duty exists in tort to avoid inflicting pecuniary loss, similarly falls to be considered in relation to careless statements, as opposed to careless acts, where that type of damage has resulted. It ought to be emphasised that the courts in the past have consistently recognised, where the making of careless statements has resulted in harm to the person or personal injuries, that a duty of care to avoid such kind of harm did arise and that liability ensued,[11] so that we are not concerned with those situations here. Historically it is significant that Lord Esher [12] spoke of " injury to the person or property of the other " whilst Lord Atkin [13] referred only to personal injury in this connection, so that, for example, no action arose in respect of pecuniary damage from negligent misrepresentation. Since fraud is an essential element in the action of deceit, without fraud, statements made even with " gross negligence " gave rise to no cause of action.[14] Again, an expression of opinion given without due care or skill by one person to another knowing that it was likely to be acted upon by a third party, gave no right of action to the third party if he acted upon it to his detriment. Where a

[9] [1969] 1 W.L.R. 959.

[10] [1971] 1 Q.B. 337. See article: " Negligence and Economic Loss " (Hewitt) 115 S.J. 255.

[11] *e.g. De Freville* v. *Dill* (1927) 96 L.J.K.B. 1056 (where doctor negligently certified plaintiff to be of unsound mind, which led to his detention in a mental home); *Clayton* v. *Woodman & Son (Builders) Ltd.* [1962] 2 Q.B. 533 reversing the decision on other grounds (where it was held that an architect was liable to a bricklayer for careless statements about how to carry out the work on the building, which resulted in the bricklayer, relying on such instruction, getting hurt when a gable end collapsed upon him). See articles founded on this case 24 M.L.R. 797; 111 L.J. 831; 78 L.Q.R. 107.

[12] *Heaven* v. *Pender* (1883) 11 Q.B.D. 503, 509; *Le Lievre* v. *Gould* [1893] 1 Q.B. 491, 497.

[13] *Donoghue* v. *Stevenson* [1932] A.C. 562, 580. See also *Old Gate Estates Ltd.* v. *Toplis* [1939] 3 All E.R. 209, 216 and *Heskell* v. *Continental Express Ltd.* [1950] 1 All E.R. 1033, 1042.

[14] *Derry* v. *Peek* (1889) 14 App.Cas. 337, but Parliament subsequently intervened to nullify its effect. See now Companies Act 1948, s. 43 (1).

surveyor negligently, *i.e.* carelessly, issued progress certificates to a builder on the strength of which a mortgagee advanced money to the builder and thereby suffered loss, it was held that the surveyor was not liable to the mortgagee.[15] Bowen L.J., referring to "the suggestion that a man is responsible for what he states in a certificate to any person to whom he may have reason to suppose that the certificate may be shown," adds that "the law of England does not go to that extent: it does not consider that what a man writes on paper is like a gun or other dangerous instrument, and, unless he intended to deceive, the law does not, in the absence of contract, hold him responsible for drawing his certificate carelessly." [16]

45 In *Australian Steam Shipping Co.* v. *Devitt* [17] the management committee of Lloyd's Register approved the plans of a ship, saw that the ship was built in accordance with those plans, and then issued a certificate that the ship was of the 100 A 1 class. On the ship's first voyage the foundations of some of the hold pillars gave way, because they were not strong enough to support the weight put upon them, and the ship was damaged. The committee were held not liable for negligence, on the ground that they owed no duty to the plaintiffs, the owners of the ship. In his judgment, Sankey J. said: "Mr. Roche (counsel for the plaintiffs) had said the defendants were doing work to the plaintiffs' property. That was an entire fallacy. The only persons doing work on the plaintiffs' property were the builders; the defendants were only asked to approve of the plans of the vessel and then to see whether the vessel had been built in accordance with those plans." If the defendants had been doing work to the ship a duty to take care would have arisen, and the distinction is between doing or omitting to do an act likely to cause physical damage to person, or property, and the expression of an opinion or the giving of advice.

46 A Lloyd's surveyor, who negligently passed as sound a mast which was unfit for use, was held to be under no obligation to the owner of the yacht for the expense he incurred in abandoning his cruise. Rowlatt J., in deciding that the surveyor was under no duty of care to the yacht owner, said: "No doubt where one person's body or property may be endangered by want of care and skill of another there are many classes of circumstances in which a duty of care or skill does arise independently of contract on the part of the latter towards the former. For breach of such a duty resulting in damage an action in tort will lie, damages being the gist of the matter. But it is not in every set of circumstances where the interests of one person depend really upon the care of another that this duty arises." [18] When a surveyor negligently made a valuation of some property, being instructed to value it by the promoters of a company, and in reliance on the valuation the company bought the property

[15] *Le Lievre* v. *Gould* [1893] 1 Q.B. 491.
[16] *Ibid.* at p. 502.
[17] (1917) 33 T.L.R. 178.
[18] *Humphery* v. *Bowers* (1929) 45 T.L.R. 297.

at an overvalue and suffered loss, the surveyor was held not liable. *Le Lievre* v. *Gould*[19] was followed, and it was held that the principle of *Donoghue* v. *Stevenson*[20] was " confined to negligence which results in danger to life, danger to limb or danger to health." [21] The words " or to property " should be added.[22]

7 Where a bill of lading was issued carelessly stating that goods were shipped, whereas they were not shipped, it was held that, on the authority of *Le Lievre* v. *Gould*,[23] it could not give rise to an action for breach of duty to the public, *i.e.* for negligence.[24] Again, when accountants were instructed by a company to prepare the company's accounts and they did so negligently, knowing that the accounts were to be shown to the plaintiff, who was contemplating making an investment in the company, and the accounts prepared gave a false view of the company's financial position, it was held that the accountants were not liable to the plaintiff who relied on the accounts and lost money. The ground of the decision was that the principle laid down by *Derry* v. *Peek*[25] and *Le Lievre* v. *Gould*[23] had in no way been qualified by the decision in *Donoghue* v. *Stevenson*.[26]

8 The first hint of a query concerning these earlier authorities came from Salmon J. in *Clayton* v. *Woodman & Son* (*Builders*) *Ltd.*[27] where he said: " May it be that the latter cases (*Derry* v. *Peek*; *Le Lievre* v. *Gould*; *Candler* v. *Crane, Christmas & Co.*) can be read as authorities for excluding from the ambit of *Donoghue* v. *Stevenson* only careless misstatements resulting in financial loss, but not those causing physical damage? . . . It may be difficult to think of a logical reason why there should in some circumstances be a duty to take care in making a statement causing physical damage but never such a duty in making a statement causing only financial loss. Logic and common sense, however, are uncertain guides in this breach of the law and the distinction between the two classes of careless misstatement may have its roots in the historical development of the law of torts."

9 In 1963, there was delivered a most important decision, which has had far reaching effects, in that the House of Lords unanimously decided in *Hedley Byrne & Co. Ltd.* v. *Heller & Partners Ltd.*[28] that in principle there

[19] [1893] 1 Q.B. 491.
[20] [1932] A.C. 562.
[21] *Old Gate Estates Ltd.* v. *Toplis & Harding & Russell* [1939] 3 All E.R. 209, 217.
[22] *Candler* v. *Crane, Christmas & Co.* [1951] 2 K.B. 164 at p. 189, *per* Asquith L.J.; at p. 198, *per* Cohen L.J. (overruled by *Hedley Byrne & Co. Ltd.* v. *Heller & Partners Ltd.* [1964] A.C. 465).
[23] [1893] 1 Q.B. 491 (disapproved by *Hedley Byrne*), *supra*.
[24] *Heskell* v. *Continental Express Ltd.* [1950] 1 All E.R. 1033.
[25] (1889) 14 App.Cas. 337.
[26] *Candler* v. *Crane, Christmas & Co.* [1951] 2 K.B. 164. There is considerable literature about this case, based on the view that the law ought to be different. See, *e.g.* Morison, 67 L.Q.R. 212; Seavey, 67 L.Q.R. 466; Wilson, 15 M.L.R. 160.
[27] [1961] 3 All E.R. 249, 256. So far as the architect is concerned his appeal was allowed in [1962] 2 Q.B. 533.
[28] [1964] A.C. 465.

was no difference at all between financial loss and physical loss and that, whenever there was a special relationship in existence, there was a duty to take care in making statements, which would found liability for a breach, unless there was a disclaimer of responsibility.

The material facts are that a bank made inquiries both by telephone and letter to the respondents, who were merchant bankers, concerning the financial position of one of their customers, stating that they wanted to know this information in confidence and without responsibility on the part of the respondents. The respondents' replies, subject to their disclaimer of responsibility, were to the effect that the customer was a respectably constituted company and was considered to be good for its normal business engagements, and this information was duly passed on by the bank to one of its customers, namely, the appellants, who were advertising agents. However, relying on this information, the appellants entered into a business transaction with the respondents' customer, Easipower Ltd., who shortly afterwards went into liquidation, and the appellants lost over £17,000 on the advertising contracts. The appellants sued the respondents for the amount of such loss, alleging that the respondents' replies to the bank's inquiries were given negligently in the sense of misjudgment by making a statement which gave a false impression as to the credit of Easipower Ltd. In fact, negligence was proved at the trial, but the respondents' disclaimer of responsibility for their replies on the occasion of the first inquiry was sufficient to exclude the assumption by them of a legal duty of care, and accordingly the appellants' action failed.

The further importance of this decision in *Hedley Byrne & Co. Ltd.* v. *Heller & Partners Ltd.* where the distinction from all other actions in negligence is that the only subject-matter of complaint was negligence in word, which caused financial loss, and not negligence in deed resulting in physical injury to person or property, is the disapproval of the long-standing decision of the Court of Appeal in *Le Lievre* v. *Gould* [29] and the emergence of the law prior to it (*e.g.* as stated by Chitty J. in *Cann* v. *Willson*).[30]

The House of Lords has thus expressed the opinion that if in the ordinary course of business including professional affairs a person seeks advice or information from another who is not under any contractual or fiduciary obligation to give it, in circumstances in which a reasonable man so asked would know that he was being trusted or that his skill or judgment was being relied on, and such person then chooses to give the requested advice or information without clearly disclaiming any responsibility for it, then he accepts a legal duty to exercise such care as the circumstances require in making his reply; for a failure to exercise that care, an action for negligence will lie if damage or loss results.

50 In considering the nature of this proximity of relationship between the parties Lord Devlin [31] stated his opinion: " I shall therefore content

[29] [1893] 1 Q.B. 491.
[30] (1888) 39 Ch.D. 39.
[31] [1964] A.C. 465, 530.

myself with the proposition that wherever there is a relationship equivalent to contract, there is a duty of care. Such a relationship may be either general or particular. Examples of a general relationship are those of solicitor and client and of banker and customer. For the former *Nocton* v. *Lord Ashburton* [32] has long stood as the authority and for the latter there is the decision of Salmon J. in *Woods* v. *Martins Bank Ltd.*,[33] which I respectfully approve. There may well be others yet to be established. Where there is a general relationship of this sort, it is unnecessary to do more than prove its existence and the duty follows. Whereas in the present case what is relied on is a particular relationship created *ad hoc*, it will be necessary to examine the particular facts to see whether there is an express or implied undertaking of responsibility.

I regard this proposition as an application of the general conception of proximity. Cases may arise in the future in which a new and wider proposition quite independent of any notion of contract will be needed."

In *Nocton* v. *Lord Ashburton* [32] Viscount Haldane L.C. said: " Although liability for negligence in word has in material respects been dealt with in our law differently from liability for negligence in act, it is nonetheless true that a man may come under a special duty to exercise care in giving information or advice. I should accordingly be sorry to be thought to lend countenance to the idea that recent decisions have been intended to stereotype the cases in which people can be held to have assumed such a special duty. Whether such a duty has been assumed must depend upon the relationship of the parties and it is at least certain that there are a good many cases in which that relationship may be properly treated as giving rise to a special duty of care in statement." [34]

Lord Devlin, in considering *Nocton's* case, said: " In my judgment the effect of this case is as follows. The House clearly considered the view of *Derry* v. *Peek* [35] exemplified in *Le Lievre* v. *Gould* [36] too narrow. It considered that outside contract (for contract was not pleaded in the case), there should be a special relationship between parties which imposed a duty to give careful advice and accurate information. The majority of their Lordships did not extend the application of this principle beyond the breach of a fiduciary obligation but none of them said anything at all to show that it was limited to fiduciary obligation. Your Lordships can therefore proceed upon the footing that there is such a general principle and that it is for you to say to what cases, beyond those of fiduciary obligation, it can properly be extended." [37]

51 Lord Morris stated that it followed from the guidance which Lord Haldane gave in *Nocton's* case, which was repeated by him in *Robinson* v. *National Bank of Scotland*,[38] that " it should now be regarded as settled

[32] [1914] A.C. 932.
[33] [1959] 1 Q.B. 55.
[34] *Supra*, at p. 948.
[35] (1889) 14 App.Cas. 337.
[36] [1893] 1 Q.B. 491.
[37] [1964] A.C. 465, 523.
[38] 1916 S.C.(H.L.) 154.

that if someone possessed of a special skill undertakes, quite irrespective of contract, to apply that skill for the assistance of another person who relies upon such skill, a duty of care will arise. The fact that the service is to be given by means of or by the instrumentality of words can make no difference. Furthermore, if in a sphere in which a person is so placed that others could reasonably rely upon his judgment or his skill or upon his ability to make careful inquiry a person takes it upon himself to give information or advice to, or allows his information or advice to be passed on to, another person who, as he knows or should know, will place reliance upon it, then a duty of care will arise." [39] However, as a result of this decision in *Hedley Byrne & Co. Ltd.* v. *Heller & Partners Ltd.*, it must not be assumed that, upon every occasion when economic loss is a foreseeable consequence of a careless statement, an action will lie even in the absence of a duty recognised at law. On the contrary the overriding principle is that the existence of such a duty, independently of any question of carelessness and foreseeability, must still be established; indeed, it will be an essential fact to be proved in any given case that the defendant had assumed responsibility for giving his opinion, advice or even information. A pertinent example of this is given by Professor Street in his 4th edition of the *Law of Torts* [40]: " the commuter, who sees his fellow-passenger reading the *Financial Times* and asks him what shares he should buy has no remedy, if he receives careless advice and acts on it to his loss." Then in *Jones* v. *Still* [41] an honest misrepresentation, even if negligent, was held to give no cause of action, since no duty to take care in making the statement arose because there was no contract, fiduciary relationship or reliance by the representee upon the special skill, knowledge or training possessed by the representor. The duty of care in giving gratuitous advice arises only where the advisor carries on the business or profession of giving advice of the kind sought, for otherwise there is no accepted standard of skill and care which the advisee can legitimately expect to be observed. Accordingly the Judicial Committee of the Privy Council held that a policy holder who had received incorrect advice from an insurance company, without its disclaiming liability, about the financial stability of one of its subsidiaries, upon which he intended to act after making an inquiry about it from the insurance company, did not have a cause of action. [42]

52 In *W. B. Anderson & Sons Ltd.* v. *Rhodes* (*Liverpool*) *Ltd.* [43] certain inquiries were made of the defendants, who were in the potato marketing business, about the credit-worthiness of a potential customer of the plaintiffs. The defendants very well knew of the purpose of such inquiries and that upon the strength of their recommendations the plaintiffs would probably rely and act. Negligently they informed the plaintiffs that the

[39] *Supra*, at pp. 502, 503.
[40] pp. 204–205.
[41] [1965] N.Z.L.R. 1071.
[42] *Mutual Life & Citizens' Assurance Co.* v. *Evatt* [1971] 2 W.L.R. 23, Lords Reid and Morris of Borth-y-Gest dissenting. " Negligent Statements—the Wilderness Revisited " (Harvey) 120 New L.J. 1155.
[43] [1967] 2 All E.R. 850.

potential buyer was credit-worthy but he was not in fact so worthy and the plaintiffs lost money through giving credit, based upon the defendants' said advice. The defendants were held liable. In *F. H. Wright* (*Constructions*) v. *Frodoor* [44] it was held on the facts that an accountant was not under a duty to consider the enforceability in law of debts but there can be little doubt that if *Candler* v. *Crane, Christmas & Co.*[45] fell to be decided again in the light of the *Hedley Byrne* case the accountants would be held liable. They had carelessly prepared a company balance sheet, which they knew would be shown to a prospective investor in the company. The latter, being duly impressed by the financial state of the company as disclosed on the inaccurate balance sheet and relying upon it, invested a considerable sum of money. Within a year the company was wound up and the plaintiff lost the whole of his £2,000 investment.

Accordingly the future trend has been set whereby these principles will extend beyond professional advice given by accountants, bankers, valuers and others, to businessmen generally and those engaged in commerce. How far the courts will go in providing a remedy for economic losses, which could be vast in the circumstances, as referred to above, remains to be seen. In principle they are recoverable but it will have to be foreseeable damage, which, in practice, may not be so easy to prove.[46]

(b) *The Carelessness Causing the Harm*

53 Coleridge J. in *Lumley* v. *Gye* [47] pointed out that courts of justice should not " allow themselves, in the pursuit of perfectly complete remedies for all wrongful acts, to transgress the bounds, which our law, in a wise consciousness as I conceive of its limited powers, has imposed on itself, of redressing only the proximate and direct consequences of wrongful acts." Typically, therefore, English law in its early stages of development only recognised the direct infliction of harm, the remedy for which lay in trespass, whilst the remedy for indirect or consequential harm lay in actions on the case, but after the abolition of the forms of action this distinction ceased to be relevant. Nevertheless there falls to be considered now the division of carelessness into (a) acts of commission, (b) acts of omission and (c) its causing harm, the further division of carelessness into careless acts and careless statements having already been discussed, although as Scott L.J. said in *Read* v. *J. Lyons & Co.*[48]: " It is the act of the defendant which entails liability on him for the harm happening to another, whether the act be one of commission or omission."

54 **Acts of commission.** There is no liability in law unless the wrong

[44] [1967] 1 W.L.R. 506.
[45] [1951] 2 K.B. 164 (which was overruled by the *Hedley Byrne* case).
[46] The Misrepresentation Act 1967 gives an action for damages in certain cases where a person has been induced to enter into a contract, as a result of which he has suffered loss or damage, by the innocent although negligent misrepresentation of the other party to the contract.
[47] (1853) 2 E. & B. 216, 252.
[48] [1945] K.B. 216, 228.

complained of can be attributed to the conduct of the defendant, where a duty to take care is owed. Where the particular head of liability requires an act of the defendant, as distinct from where liability arises from an omission, the requirement of an act involves a bodily movement resulting from an operation of the will.[49] From a study of the facts of many of the cases set out in these texts examples of acts of commission are readily discernible. However it may be helpful only to draw a distinction where the defendant may well be under a duty of care to the plaintiff, who is injured, but the injury may not be due to his act or of some person for whom he is responsible such as where a railway company was held not liable for the conduct of a crowd on the station platform.[50] Further examples are provided where an occupier, without negligence, was held not liable for the escape of a dangerous thing, under the rule in *Rylands* v. *Fletcher*, where the escape is caused by the act of a stranger [51] or where the occupier did not consent to the presence of the dangerous thing on his land [52] and in cases of contributory negligence where it was the plaintiff's fault which actually caused his injury.[53]

55 **Acts of omission.** At the outset it is necessary to draw an important distinction between two different situations: (1) where a failure in the course of doing something is, in fact, nothing more than performing negligently a duty to take care and is therefore indistinguishable in its legal effect from an act of commission, and (2) the total failure to do anything at all.

An illustration of the first situation is easily recognisable from the everyday example of the motorist, who fails to sound his horn at a blind crossing and/or to stop at a " Halt " sign, as a result of which some accident occurs. Such motorist would be liable for having performed a negligent but active operation in driving his vehicle so that this situation need not be examined further. It is only an omission in the second sense, which needs to be studied in more detail.

As a general rule, a mere omission to act, when there is no duty to act gives rise to no cause of action, even when damage is caused. Willmer L.J. expressed the law in this manner in *Zoernsch* v. *Waldock* [54]: " An omission on the part of one or other of the defendants would not furnish the plaintiff with any cause of action in the absence of some duty to act owed by the defendants to the plaintiff. No such duty is alleged, nor in my judgment could it be."

A person who undertakes a task which he is not obliged to perform owes no duty to take care in its performance so long as he does not

49 Holmes, *The Common Law*, p. 54.
50 *McCallum* v. *North British Railway*, 1908 S.C. 415.
51 *Rickards* v. *Lothian* [1913] A.C. 263.
52 *Whitmores Ltd.* v. *Stanford* [1909] 1 Ch. 427.
53 *Grand Trunk Railway* v. *McAlpine* [1913] A.C. 838.
54 [1964] 1 W.L.R. 675, 685. See also du Parcq L.J. in *Deyong* v. *Shenburn* [1946] K.B. 227, 233, where he said: " It is not true to say that whenever a man finds himself in such a position that, unless he does a certain act, another person may suffer, or that if he does something another person will suffer, then it is his duty in the one case to be careful to do the act and in the other not to do the act. Any such proposition is much too wide."

thereby add to the damage which would have been caused had he done nothing.[55] Thus, where a catchment board, which had a statutory power but no duty to repair a wall built to prevent a river from flooding the adjacent marshland, negligently repaired a breach in the wall so that work which should have taken fourteen days actually took 164 days, and the plaintiff's fields remained flooded longer than they should have been, the board were held not liable.[56] " Where a statutory authority is entrusted with a mere power, it cannot be made liable for any damage sustained by a member of the public by reason of a failure to exercise that power. If in the exercise of their discretion they embark upon an execution of the power, the only duty they owe to any member of the public is not thereby to add to the damages that he would have suffered had they done nothing.[57]

Again, an approved society, with power under its rules to institute proceedings on behalf of its members, owes no duty to a member for whom it contemplates bringing proceedings against a local authority for damages for personal injuries to take care that it starts the proceedings before the action is barred by the Public Authorities Protection Act 1893.

No duty is owed by a person who sees the person or property of another in danger, not caused by him, to take care to protect him from or minimise that danger. When a barge was moored by a wharfinger in a safe position at a wharf and removed by a third party to an unsafe berth, it was held that the wharfinger, on learning of the barge's danger, owed no duty to the owner to move the barge before she grounded and was damaged.[58]

56 Perhaps typical cases of this class, which ought to be mentioned here, are the " rescue cases " although these will be dealt with in greater detail at paragraph 67, *post*. It is sufficient to use only one, albeit an intriguing one, as an illustration at this juncture. In *Matthews* v. *McLaren, Jones and The Ogopogo* [59] M and H were invited guests on board D's pleasure cruiser but M fell overboard and was lost; after D's abortive attempts to save M had been made, H dived in but he also died. The Ontario Supreme Court held that, on the claim by M's dependants, D's failure to ensure that his visitors wore life belts was not actionable negligence since the relationship required a legal duty in D to aid and to rescue. However once he had taken positive steps in a rescue bid he was by law regarded as assuming a duty to act and thus would thereafter be liable for negligence, if it caused M's death by preventing his life being saved. On the other

[55] This is well illustrated by the facts in *Grange Motors* (*Cwmbran*) v. *Spencer* [1969] 1 W.L.R. 53. If a driver, standing beside his parked motor vehicle, elects to give a signal to another motorist, upon which he can anticipate that such motorist will intend to rely even though there is no obligation to give any signal at all, as a result of which the latter then proceeds to overtake the stationary vehicle, he owes a duty to him to give him an accurate signal which will not precipitate him into danger such as by driving forward into a head-on collision with another vehicle approaching from the opposite direction, coming around the bend. See also *White* v. *Broadbent*, *The Times*, November 29, 1957.

[56] *E. Suffolk Rivers Catchment Board* v. *Kent* [1941] A.C. 74.

[57] *Ibid.*, *per* Lord Romer at p. 102.

[58] *Butler* v. *Alcock* [1941] 3 All E.R. 411. The Public Authorities Protection Act 1893 is repealed by the Law Reform (Limitation of Actions) Act 1954, s. 1.

[59] [1969] 1 Lloyd's Rep. 374.

hand, on the claim by H's dependants, D's negligence in effecting M's rescue induced H to come to the rescue and the court held that such negligence was the cause of H's death. In allowing an appeal against this latter finding of the court below it was held [60] *inter alia* that (a) it was immaterial whether D was under a duty to rescue M since he voluntarily had undertaken a rescue operation; (b) D was not primarily negligent and hence responsible for M's plight in the first instance; (c) D would be under no liability to M if he had abandoned rescue operations once undertaken, if discontinuance of such had not left M in a worse condition than when D had taken charge and his efforts had not left M in a worse condition; (d) even if D were negligent, H's intervention was not reasonably foreseeable and (e) there was no authority that a defendant was liable to a rescuer where his negligence had not imperilled the person whose rescue the rescuer had attempted.

57 Up to August 3, 1964, local authorities were only liable for misfeasance, which was the bad performance of some active operation, and not for non-feasance, which was the non-performance of an operation. Now the Highways (Miscellaneous Provisions) Act 1961 [61] has imposed liability for non-feasance from the aforesaid date, subject to the statutory defence additionally available to the local authority to prove that they had taken such care as in all the circumstances was reasonably required to secure that the part of the highway to which the action relates was not dangerous.

58 **Remoteness.** The concept of reasonable foresight is relevant not only in testing the existence of a duty but also in considering the question of remoteness of damage, once the liability for negligence has been established. It is only intended to deal with the first aspect here, since the intricacies of causation must necessarily be reserved to the next chapter dealing with Damage.[62] In *Bourhill* v. *Young* [63] Lord Russell of Killowen expressed the view that: " In considering whether a person owes to another a duty, a breach of which will render him liable to that other in damages for negligence, it is material to consider what the defendant ought to have contemplated as a reasonable man. This consideration may play a double role. It is relevant in cases of admitted negligence (where the duty and breach are admitted) to the question of remoteness of damage, *i.e.* to the question of compensation or to culpability, but it is also relevant in testing the existence of a duty as the foundation of the alleged negligence, *i.e.* to the question of culpability not to compensation."

Regrettably this dual function has led in the past to very considerable confusion, especially when the test of duty was reasonable foresight, whilst the test of remoteness of damage was the directness of the damage resulting

[60] [1970] 1 Lloyd's Rep. 257.
[61] See also Chap. 12.
[62] Chap. 3, § 1.
[63] [1943] A.C. 92, 101.

from the breach, even though they were not foreseeable.[64] A good illustration of this is to be found in *Woods* v. *Duncan* [65] where the submarine *Thetis* was sunk with the loss of life of all of her crew except four men, because the rear door of a torpedo tube was ordered to be opened by Lieutenant Woods at a time when the bow-cap at the seaward end was also open. In the door was a test-cock, consisting of a small hole, from which water should have been trickling had the bow-cap been open, but this hole was blocked by paint. Because of this and other matters, it was held that Woods was not negligent. The painters were negligent in blocking the hole with paint and the builders also were negligent in not detecting the blockage, but an action against them by the dependants of the drowned seamen failed because the damage was too remote, in that a whole series of unlikely events had to happen before the blocking of the hole by paint could lead to the sinking of the submarine.

59 The reasonable man can only foresee the natural and probable consequences of his act, and in estimating these he is entitled to assume that the conditions governing those consequences will be normal unless he has actual notice to the contrary. " One who suffers from the terrible tendency to bleed on slight contact, which is denoted by the term 'a bleeder' cannot complain if he mixes with the crowd and suffers severely, perhaps fatally, from being merely brushed against. There is no wrong done there. A blind or deaf man who crosses the traffic on a busy street cannot complain if he is run over by a careful driver who does not know of and could not be expected to observe and guard against the man's infirmity. These questions go to 'culpability, not compensation.' " [66]

The reasonable man is only bound to foresee the probable consequences of his act and not also the possible consequences, because in the simplest and what appear to be the least harmful acts there are always possibilities of damage, improbable though that damage may be. It is always possible that a man may come in slight contact with a " bleeder " and cause him serious injury, while a normal man would not be injured at all, but experience shows that this is so unlikely that a reasonable man may quite properly fail to foresee it. As is pointed out by Lord Maugham [67] the " mere possibility of accident is not enough to establish liability." A similar view is expressed by Denning L.J.[68]: " Is the consequence fairly to be regarded as within the risk created by the negligence? If so, the negligent person is liable for it: but not otherwise."

It is a question of fact what consequences are reasonably foreseeable.[69]

60 As a result of the Privy Council's judgment in *The Wagon Mound*

[64] *Re Polemis & Furness Withy & Co. Ltd.* [1921] 3 K.B. 560; *Thurogood* v. *Van Den Berghs & Jurgens Ltd.* [1951] 2 K.B. 537; *Aldham* v. *United Dairies Ltd.* [1940] 1 K.B. 507.
[65] [1946] A.C. 401.
[66] *Bourhill* v. *Young* [1943] A.C. 92, *per* Lord Wright at p. 109.
[67] *Searle* v. *Wallbank* [1947] A.C. 341, 351. See also the American case of *Palsgraf* v. *Long Island Railroad Co.*, 248 N.Y. 339 (1928).
[68] *Roe* v. *Minister of Health* [1954] 2 Q.B. 66, 85.
[69] *Ante*, § 29.

(*No.* 1) [70] and *The Wagon Mound* (*No.* 2) [71] it must now be accepted that foresight is the test to be applied both when considering remoteness as regards the duty to take care and remoteness as regards damage where it does not matter that the precise chain of events leading up to that damage was not foreseeable.[72]

Having said that, in practice difficulties will still continue to be experienced in deciding whether the facts of the particular case under consideration are different in kind or only in degree from those which ought reasonably to have been foreseen and which, consequently, ought to have been guarded against in the circumstances. An obvious example of this difficulty is to contrast the cases of *Hughes* v. *Lord Advocate* [73] and *Doughty* v. *Turner Manufacturing Co. Ltd.*[74] each of which was dealing with an " explosion " in somewhat different circumstances, resulting from different causes.

61 In *Hughes* v. *Lord Advocate* a manhole in a street of Edinburgh was opened for the purpose of maintaining underground telephone equipment, pursuant to statutory powers. The hole was covered with a tent and, in the evening, it was left by the workmen unguarded but surrounded by red warning paraffin lamps. An eight-year-old boy went into the tent, knocked over or lowered one of the lamps down the hole, as a result of which an explosion occurred causing severe personal injury to him. It was held by the House of Lords that although under the law of negligence the duty to take reasonable care was confined to those dangers, which were reasonably to be foreseen, the fact that the danger actually materialising was not identical with the danger reasonably foreseeable does not necessarily result in liability being avoided. Thus the workmen were in breach of a duty of care to safeguard the boy against this type of occurrence which had arisen out of a known source of danger, which was reasonably foreseeable, namely the lamp with an inflammable liquid in it, despite that particular source of danger having acted in an unpredictable way.

Lord Pearce stated that the accident to the child in question " was but a variant of the foreseeable." [75]

[70] *Overseas Tankship* (*U.K.*) *Ltd.* v. *Morts Dock & Engineering Co. Ltd.* [1961] A.C. 388.
[71] *Overseas Tankship* (*U.K.*) *Ltd.* v. *The Miller Steamship Co. Pty.* [1967] 1 A.C. 617.
[72] [1961] A.C. 388; at p. 424 Viscount Simonds said: " After the event even a fool is wise. But it is not the hindsight of a fool; it is the foresight of the reasonable man which alone can determine responsibility." As regards remoteness of damage in *Smith* v. *Leech Brain & Co. Ltd.* [1962] 2 Q.B. 405, Parker C.J. thought that the decision in *The Wagon Mound* (*No.* 1) had not made inroads into the doctrine that you must take your victim as you find him in that they were not saying that a man was liable only for the extent of damage, which could be anticipated, if the type of damage done was anticipated. *Smith* v. *Leech Brain & Co. Ltd.* was followed by Paull J. in *Warren* v. *Scruttons* [1962] 1 Lloyd's Rep. 497 (the plaintiff injured a finger on a frayed rope, which was a foreseeable injury, as a result of the negligence of the employers in supplying such a rope for use, and in consequence suffered an aggravation of an existing eye complaint). Also see articles " Negligent Tortfeasor Still Takes His Victim As He Finds Him," 25 L.Q.R. 393; " Foreseeability in Negligence to Children," 107 S.J. 994; and " Risk and Remoteness," 27 M.L.R. 344; " Down with foreseeability! Of thin skulls and rescuers " (Linden) 47 Can.B.R. 545.
[73] [1963] A.C. 837. Followed in *Malcolm* v. *Broadhurst* [1970] 3 All E.R. 508.
[74] [1964] 1 Q.B. 518.
[75] [1963] A.C. 837, 858.

62 In *Doughty* v. *Turner Manufacturing Co. Ltd.* the defendants had two cauldrons in their factory's heat treatment room into which they subjected metal parts to heat by immersing them in a hot molten solution. They provided suitable covers for the cauldrons, in order to conserve the heat, which had been made by reputable manufacturers from asbestos cement and nobody had supposed that if one of these covers were immersed into the cauldron there would result any serious consequences. In fact a cover was accidentally knocked into the cauldron so that it slid beneath the molten liquid, although it never occurred to anybody to withdraw from the vicinity merely because of that. Suddenly the liquid erupted violently and the plaintiff sustained severe personal injuries as a result of being splashed. It was held by the Court of Appeal, that even if the inadvertent immersion of the cover was negligent, the defendants were not liable for the damage resulting from the explosion, because it was not damage of such a kind as could reasonably have been foreseen. Further, although risk by splashing was foreseeable, as would be caused by displacement from bodies falling on to its surface, this was an accident of an entirely different kind, its cause being the intrusion of a new and unexpected factor, *viz.* the chemical change of the asbestos compound due to the extreme heat.

Then in *Stewart* v. *West African Terminals* [76] Lord Denning M.R. emphasised that the proposition that a person is not liable for the consequences of his negligence except so far as they are reasonably foreseeable must be taken subject to this, namely it was not necessary for the precise concatenation of circumstances to be envisaged, if the consequence is one which is within the general sphere of contemplation and not of an entirely different kind, which no one can anticipate. In this case the plaintiff, a boiler maker, had been working repairing a broken winch before luncheon and afterwards had returned to pick up his tools. Whilst proceeding along the deck, a preventer wire, which formed part of the rigging of a derrick being operated by stevedores, was sagging and obstructing his path so that he lifted it with one hand and by an involuntary act placed his other hand on another wire of the derrick as a means of support. This latter wire suddenly began to run and the plaintiff's fingers were trapped in the block.

(c) *The Kind of Person*

63 Lord Macmillan in *Donoghue* v. *Stevenson* [77] raised the next question to be considered in this manner: "Does he owe a duty to take care and to whom does he owe that duty?" In order to discover who owes a duty and, then, to whom that duty is owed, it is first essential to discover the categories of person, who are capable of being recognised by law as: (a) a defendant and (b) as a plaintiff, so that the situation, where a duty to take care is imposed, can be completed. Next, the foresight principle is applied in order to determine whether or not liability can be fixed in the given circumstances of a particular case: *i.e.* (c) the foreseeable plaintiff.

[76] (1964) 108 S.J. 838.
[77] [1932] A.C. 562, 619–620.

64 **A defendant.** The Sovereign is exempt from liability and, prior to the Crown Proceedings Act 1947 the Crown was also exempt. As regards foreign diplomats, diplomatic privilege does not impart immunity from legal liability but only exemption from local jurisdiction. The privilege is the privilege of the Sovereign, by whom the diplomatic agent is accredited and it may be waived with the sanction of the Sovereign or of the official superior of the agent.[78] Before 1962 [79] neither husband nor wife could sue the other in tort, except where a wife could sue for a remedy in respect of her own property only, but the Law Reform (Husband and Wife) Act 1962 has rightly removed that particular injustice so that, for example, a wife, who is a passenger in a car being driven by her husband, can now sue him in the ordinary way if she sustains damage, due to his negligent driving.

Other exemptions or limits thereof, such as of occupiers, of lessors or vendors of dangerous premises and of professional persons, for example, barristers, will all be considered in later chapters. Unless there be some exemption any person [80] can be sued as a defendant, who has caused the plaintiff damage, which is recoverable, where there has been a breach of duty owed.

65 **A plaintiff.** With regard to damage to property, only the owner or the person in possession when the tort was committed will be recognised by law.[81]

The House of Lords in *Donoghue* v. *Stevenson* [82] by establishing the principle that the duty in tort is completely independent of any contract, which may exist, as has been emphasised already in the earlier parts of this chapter, has given very considerable extension to the classes of persons entitled to a remedy in law.

However at common law nobody could sue for the death of another so that statute law has had to make available the action and the remedy in the form of the Fatal Accidents Act 1846.[83] Since then further Acts were passed up to the Fatal Accidents Act 1959 [84] which widened the scope of specified dependants of a deceased person who were given a right of action where they had suffered pecuniary loss from the death of that person. Further, the personal representatives of a deceased person can now bring an action for the benefit of a deceased's estate or can continue an action, commenced by a deceased before his death, by virtue of the Law Reform (Miscellaneous Provisions) Act 1934.

78 *Taylor* v. *Best* (1854) 14 C.B. 487; *Re Suarez* [1918] 1 Ch. 176; *Dickinson* v. *Del Solar* [1930] 1 K.B. 376.
79 *Broom* v. *Morgan* [1953] 1 Q.B. 597.
80 *e.g.* the Home Office, as in *Dorset Yacht Co.* v. *Home Office* [1970] A.C. (negligently allowing borstal inmates to escape), and the Ministry of Transport as in *Levine* v. *Morris* [1970] 1 W.L.R. 71 (the negligent siting of road signs).
81 *Margarine Union G.m.b.H.* v. *Cambay Prince Steamship Co. Ltd.* [1969] 1 Q.B. 219.
82 [1932] A.C. 562.
83 ss. 2, 5. See also Law Reform (Miscellaneous Provisions) Act 1934, s. 2 (1), although it has now been repealed and replaced by the Fatal Accidents Act 1959, s. 3 (3).
84 s. 1.

Generally, in cases of a breach of statutory provisions, where a duty is imposed and a remedy is available to a member of the class of persons for whose benefit the protection is intended, it is essential for the plaintiff to establish that he belongs to that class.[85]

A husband is recognised as being entitled to sue for the loss of his wife's consortium caused by the negligence of another but a wife does not have any similar remedy in respect of being deprived of her husband's consortium.[86]

Certain classes of persons are not recognised as regard certain methods of inflicting harm or in respect of certain kinds of harm, such as occupiers towards trespassers, who, as a class, do not have any remedy for injuries inflicted on them by negligence, as opposed to their being inflicted wilfully or recklessly, *e.g.* by the laying of a spring gun to trap or to injure a trespasser.

66 **The foreseeable and/or the unforeseeable plaintiff.** As a duty to take care arises whenever a reasonable man would foresee that if he did not take care he would cause danger of injury to the person or property of another, the question arises whether he must foresee that if he did not take care there was a likelihood that he would injure the plaintiff, or whether it is enough that he would foresee that some person was likely to be injured. This is the question asked by Lord Atkin, "Who is my neighbour?", to which he gave the reply that they were the persons whom he ought to have in contemplation as likely to be affected by his acts. This reply must be taken in conjunction with the other passage in his speech in which he points out that there must be "proximity"[87] between the actor and the injured party. In view of the fact that "'proximity' can only properly be used to exclude an element of remoteness or of some interfering complication between the want of care and the injury,"[88] it seems that the duty is owed generally to everyone within the class of those who are likely to be injured if care is not taken.

Lord Esher M.R. in *Le Lievre* v. *Gould*[89] illustrated the question of proximity in a more dramatic manner: "If a man is driving on Salisbury Plain, and no other person is near him, he is at liberty to drive as fast and as recklessly as he pleases. But if he sees another carriage coming near him, immediately a duty arises not to drive in such a way as is likely to cause an injury."

Greer L.J. pointed out in *Haynes* v. *Harwood*[90] that: "it is not necessary to show that this particular accident and this particular damage were probable; it is sufficient if the accident is of a class that might well be

[85] *e.g. Hartley* v. *Mayoh & Co.* [1954] 1 Q.B. 383.
[86] *Best* v. *Samuel Fox & Co. Ltd.* [1952] A.C. 716.
[87] In *Hanson* v. *Wearmouth Coal Co.* [1939] 2 All E.R. 47, 54, Goddard L.J. said: "The legal conception of duty to 'proximity' has been authoritatively laid down by the H.L. in *Donoghue* v. *Stevenson*, and the modern tendency is to enlarge and not to restrict the ambit of that duty."
[88] *Grant* v. *Australian Knitting Mills Ltd.* [1936] A.C. 85, *per* Lord Wright at p. 104.
[89] [1893] 1 Q.B. 491, 497.
[90] [1935] 1 K.B. 146, 156.

anticipated as one of the reasonable and probable results of the wrongful act." To which Barry J. added in *Baker* v. *T. E. Hopkins & Sons Ltd.*,[91] " The essence of the *Haynes* v. *Harwood* [90] doctrine, as I understand it, is that among the persons who fall within that class are those who might attempt to rescue the man or woman placed in acute peril by the negligent act complained of. Whether that act of negligence arises out of the relationship between master and servant or any other relationship which involves a duty of care, seems to me to be quite immaterial."

67 Special mention can conveniently be made here about the position of rescuers and how they have been treated by the courts. If a person by his negligence creates a dangerous situation whereby other people [92] or their property [93] are likely to suffer damage or if he puts himself in peril [94] he owes a duty of care to those altruistically brave people, whom he ought reasonably to foresee may hasten to the rescue. [94a]

In *Haynes* v. *Harwood* [95] the defendants' two-horse cab was left unattended in a London Street, where mischievous children were likely to be, and the horses bolted. A policeman, inside the police station, saw the horses and van coming and, knowing that children might be knocked down, rushed out and stopped the horses, being injured himself in doing so. He was held entitled to recover damages on the ground that when horses were left unattended in such circumstances it should be contemplated that they might bolt and that " if horses run away it must quite obviously be contemplated that people are likely to be knocked down. It must also, I think, be contemplated that persons will attempt to stop the horses and try to prevent injury to life or limb." [96] The duty owed to a rescuer is quite independent of any duty which is owed to the person who has been endangered.[97]

In *Videan* v. *British Transport Commission* [97] the Court of Appeal held that a trolley-driver, driving along the railway lines, should have foreseen that his negligent driving might cause the occurrence of an emergency, in that someone might be put in peril, if the trolley approached too fast and without a proper lookout being kept. In this case the driver mowed down the station-master, who had leapt from the platform on to the line in a vain attempt to rescue his infant son, who had trespassed on to the permanent way in order to play. However, the presence of the station-master, who was an employee of the defendants, on the track was something that was foreseeable by the driver, and, as he was not a trespasser, a duty was owed to him. Lord Denning M.R. expressed the

[91] [1958] 1 W.L.R. 993, 1003. In this case a doctor went down a well shaft to the rescue of two workmen who had been overcome by fumes from a petrol-driven pump, but in doing so he became unconscious himself from poisoning by carbon monoxide, and died later on the way to hospital. This decision was affirmed by the Court of Appeal [1959] 1 W.L.R. 966. See also note in 75 L.Q.R. 19.

[92] *Ward* v. *T. E. Hopkins Ltd.* [1958] 1 W.L.R. 966.

[93] *Hyett* v. *G.W. Railway* [1948] 1 K.B. 345.

[94] *Baker* v. *T. E. Hopkins & Sons* [1958] 1 W.L.R. 993.

[94a] " Rescuers and good Samaritans " (Linden) 34 M.L.R. 241.

[95] [1935] 1 K.B. 146.

[96] *Per* Findlay J. which was quoted with approval by Maugham L.J. at p. 163.

[97] See *Videan* v. *B.T.C.* [1963] 2 Q.B. 650, 669, 675–676 and 682–683.

view in this manner: "Foreseeability is necessary but not foreseeability of the particular emergency that arose."

In *Chadwick* v. *British Railways Board* [98] where a serious railway accident had occurred at Lewisham in December 1957 causing the deaths of ninety people and the plaintiff's late husband had gone immediately to the scene of the crash to take part in the rescue operations, as a result of which experiences he had become psychoneurotic, Waller J. held that the defendants, having by their negligence put their passengers in peril, could reasonably have foreseen that someone would attempt to rescue those passengers and would suffer injury in the process. Accordingly they owed a duty to such rescuer and the fact that the risk run by the rescuer was not of the same kind as that run by the persons being rescued did not deprive the rescuer of his remedy.

68 Leaving aside the question of rescuers, the situation often arises where a person is in breach of his duty to another, yet a third person suffers damage. In *Smith* v. *London & South Western Railway Co.*[99] the defendants could have foreseen that sparks from their engine would set fire to the dried grass and hedge trimmings lying in an adjoining field. The court held the defendants liable to the owner of a cottage about 200 yards away across a road when the fire, which was fanned by a strong wind in summer, crept up to and destroyed the cottage, although they could not have foreseen this harm to the cottage's owner. A contrary view was taken in the American case of *Palsgraf* v. *Long Island Railroad Co.*[1] where two servants of the defendants, whilst assisting a passenger at their railway station, somehow managed to knock a parcel out of the passenger's hands. The parcel probably contained fireworks, although that fact was unknown at the time, but the resulting explosion caused a weighing machine some twenty-five feet away to topple and fall upon the plaintiff, hurting her. The majority of the New York Court of Appeals held that her action failed, Cardozo C.J. saying that the conduct of the defendants' guard if a wrong in its relation to the holder of the package, was not a wrong in its relation to the plaintiff, standing far away.

69 In *Glasgow Corporation* v. *Muir* [2] a picnic party of children were allowed by the manageress of a public tea room to have their tea in the tea room, access to which was gained through the small front shop. Whilst a tea urn was being carried through the shop one of the persons carrying it somehow slipped and the urn fell scalding six children when the boiling hot tea escaped. The House of Lords held that as a reasonable person would not have foreseen such a danger the occupiers were not liable.

In *Woods* v. *Duncan* [3] the facts of which have sufficiently been considered above in relation to remoteness, the action by the widows of the

[98] [1967] 1 W.L.R. 912.
[99] (1870) L.R. 6 C.P. 14.
[1] 248 N.Y. 339 (1928).
[2] [1943] A.C. 448.
[3] [1946] A.C. 401. *Ante*, § 58.

drowned seamen against the builders and the contractors, who carried out the painting, was dismissed by the House of Lords on the ground that the disaster to the submarine *Thetis* which resulted in their deaths could not reasonably have been foreseen as the result of the blocking by paint of the test-cock in the torpedo tube's door.

70 So far as employees are concerned an example can be found in *Thurogood* v. *Van Den Berghs & Jurgens Ltd.*[4] an electric fan was being tested in the defendants' maintenance shop, by being set in motion at a high speed on the floor of the shop without a guard, when the plaintiff, an electrician employed in making the test, had his hand caught in the rotating blades in some unexplained manner. It was held that the defendants should have contemplated that the act of operating the fan, on the floor, without a guard might result in some damage, for example, through a necktie or clothing being caught in the blades. The damage in fact did not result in any such way, it was caused by an unexplained act of inadvertence, but the defendants were held liable on the ground that, " although reasonable foresight of possible injury is the true criterion where negligence *vel non* is the issue, an employer who has created or permitted a dangerous condition to arise is reasonably expected to foresee and provide against the possibility of injury arising therefrom even though it so results through the intervention of an act of inadvertence by the employee and even though that act of inadvertence be of a character which cannot be precisely forecast and remains in the event ' unexplained.' It is enough if he ought reasonably to anticipate that injury or damage of some sort to a workman was likely to result." [5]

An illustration of a different situation arises in *Carmarthenshire C.C.* v. *Lewis.*[6] There a boy of four who attended the defendant's nursery school, was left unattended and in some way got out of the school onto the highway, there a lorry driver, in attempting to avoid him, collided with a telegraph post and was killed. It was argued that no duty was owed to the lorry driver by the defendants as school authority, but it was held that they owed a duty, which they had neglected to perform, to take reasonable care to prevent the child from getting onto the highway and, once he was on the highway, it was reasonably foreseeable that damage of some sort would result either to the child himself or to other road users. The widow's action succeeded.

71 **An unborn child.** Whether any care need be taken in respect of an unborn child is a question which has never arisen in England. In *Walker*

[4] [1951] 2 K.B. 537.
[5] *Ibid.* at p. 554, *per* Asquith L.J.
[6] [1955] A.C. 549. *Bourhill* v. *Young* [1943] A.C. 92 was distinguished; *per* Lord Reid (at p. 566), " if I am right in the view which I have already expressed that injury to other road users was reasonably foreseeable if the child was allowed to escape on to the street, then the reasoning in *Bourhill* v. *Young* is very much against the appellants." *Per* Lord Keith (at p. 571), " The case is clearly distinguishable from *Bourhill* v. *Young*, where the circumstances were such as to put the pursuer outside the field of persons to whom the motor cyclist in that case owed a duty." He did not say why no duty was owed to the pursuer in *Bourhill* v. *Young* while a duty was owed to the deceased in *Lewis.*

v. *G.N. Ry. of Ireland*[7] the plaintiff's mother was injured in a railway collision caused by the defendants' negligence, and as a result the plaintiff then unborn was born deformed. The action failed on the ground that the defendants owed no duty to the plaintiff, as they were not aware of her existence or presence on the train. On the other hand, in Canada[8] where the plaintiff's mother was injured in a tram accident and the plaintiff, then unborn, was born with club feet as a result, it was held that the plaintiff succeeded on the ground that unborn children, if subsequently born alive, have all the rights they would have had if born at the material time. It is undoubted that in English law a child *en ventre sa mere*, if subsequently born alive, is deemed to be born when it is necessary for the benefit of the child, not only in respect of real property but also in respect of personal property.[9] If the action of such a child fails it must be on the ground that there is no duty to take care owing to it. From the point of view of duty, it would seem that although it is possible that a woman, to whom a duty of care is owing, may be carrying a child, it is not probable that she is doing so; so that any duty, which otherwise might have been owing to the unborn child, is excluded by remoteness, and that the Irish case is correctly decided. On the other hand, if it be known that a woman, to whom the duty is owed, is actually carrying a child, which is subsequently born alive but is deformed as a result of the breach of duty, on the principles stated above, such child would be able to recover damages for negligence.[10]

In *Pinchin* v. *Santam Insurance Co.*[11] it was held by the Supreme Court of South Africa (Witwatersrand Local Division) that a child has an action to recover damages for pre-natal injuries sustained.

Nevertheless Hinchcliffe J. was faced with the anxious problem of assessing damages in two representative actions concerning those ill-fated children who had been born grossly deformed after their mothers had taken the drug " thalidomide," marketed by the defendants. The drug had been intended by the defendants to be used as a tranquilliser, *inter alia*, by pregnant mothers. However the issue of liability has not been decided, since the court approved a compromise whereby the defendants undertook to pay 40 per cent. of the damages agreed or assessed by the court upon the plaintiffs withdrawing all their allegations of negligence.[12]

7 (1890) 28 L.R.Ir. 69.
8 *Montreal Tramways* v. *Leveille* [1933] S.C.R. 456; 4 D.L.R. 337. See Winfield, " The Unborn Child," 8 C.L.J. 76.
9 *Villar* v. *Gilbey* [1907] A.C. 139; *Williams* v. *Ocean Coal Co. Ltd.* [1907] 2 K.B. 422.
10 The significance of knowledge is well illustrated in *Boardman* v. *Sanderson* [1964] 1 W.L.R. 1317.
11 1963 (2) S.A. 254.
12 *S.* v. *Distillers Co.* (*Biochemicals*) [1970] 1 W.L.R. 114.

CHAPTER 3

CAUSATION AND REMOTENESS OF DAMAGE

1. CAUSATION

72 **Damage suffered which is causally connected.** As has been emphasised in Chapter 1, once a duty of care and a breach of that duty have been established it must be proved, as the next essential ingredient, that damage has been suffered. This must have been caused by such breach of duty, in order to give a good cause of action in negligence.[1]

73 **Causation and remoteness of damage.** Thousands of hours of judicial time must have been spent over the many years in attempting to resolve the most difficult of all questions: *viz.* that concerning remoteness of damage. The question involves consideration of what items the law will give recognition to and to what extent. This must be answered before the court can turn to the next question, namely what is the measure of damages.

In order to keep matters in chronological order the discussion of the measure of damages will be postponed to Chapter 4, where the subject is dealt with fully.

The undoubted complexity of the question of remoteness is probably due to the fact that it is frequently raised in three different aspects in the law. The first has already been introduced in Chapter 2 at paragraph 58, namely that remoteness is an involved consideration of the duty of care as well as one of causation. Denning L.J. in *Roe* v. *Minister of Health*[2] commented pertinently: " In all these cases you will find that the three questions, duty, causation, and remoteness, run continually into one another." Thus if damage is not of the kind that was foreseeable the law will not provide any remedy. In *Overseas Tankship* (*U.K.*) *Ltd.* v. *Morts Docks & Engineering Co. Ltd. The Wagon Mound* (*No.* 1)[3] it was held that, although the spillage of ships' furnace oil onto the harbour water could do foreseeable damage by fouling shore installations, since fire damage to such premises had been found as a fact at the trial not to be foreseeable, damage by fire was too remote in such circumstances.

74 Secondly a plaintiff may only be able to prove that he has suffered

[1] See *Accidents, Compensation and the Law* (Atiyah), p. 217 *et seq.* exposing the defects in the present tort system for damages in personal injury cases. See comments upon such views in the article " Fault as Basis of Compensation " (Samuels), 120 New L.J. 798. Seemingly the abolition of the fault principle alone, according to expert opinion in the insurance industry, would cost between £70 m. and £100 m. annually, involving an increase of 125 per cent. to 150 per cent. in payments and a 25 per cent. to 40 per cent. increase in premiums, all at a time of raging inflation with spiralling prices. For jurisdiction generally of the court to hear the plaintiff's cause of action, see Chap. 17.

[2] [1954] 2 Q.B. 66, 85.

[3] [1961] A.C. 388.

damage which the law does not recognise. An example is to be found in *Cattle* v. *Stockton Waterworks Co.*[4] where the defendants had laid a water main, which in fact was defective, under a turnpike road. The resulting leakage of water seriously hampered the contractor's work of tunnelling underneath the road causing him to suffer a loss of profit on his contract with the road owners. Blackburn J. in holding that the contractor had no cause of action said: "Courts of justice should not 'allow themselves, in the pursuit of perfectly complete remedies for all wrongful acts, to transgress the bounds, which our law, in a wise consciousness as I conceive of its limited powers, has imposed on itself, of redressing only the proximate and direct consequences of wrongful acts.'"[5] These latter words connote remoteness but they lead up to the difficulties highlighted by the decision in *The Wagon Mound* (*No.* 1).[6]

75 Thirdly, a difficulty arises when one has to try to draw a line between those items of damage for which a defendant is answerable and those for which he is not. As Lord Wright said in *Liesbosch Dredger* (*Owners*) v. *S.S. Edison* (*Owners*)[7]: "the law cannot take account of everything that follows a wrongful act; it regards some subsequent matters as outside the scope of its selection, because 'it were infinite for the law to judge the cause of causes' or consequences of consequences." It is not easy always to draw such a line because, as Blackburn J. commented in *Hobbs* v. *London and South Western Railway Co.*[8]: "It is something like having to draw a line between night and day; there is a great duration of twilight when it is neither night nor day; but . . . though you cannot draw the precise line, you can say on which side of the line the case is." Thus, whilst a person is not answerable for each and every consequence that follows on from his conduct indefinitely, he may not necessarily be able to avoid consequences of which he complains that he has had no notice. Somewhat graphically this point was illustrated by Scrutton L.J. in *The Arpad*[9] in these words: "Damages are constantly given for consequences of which the defendant had no notice. You negligently run down a shabby-looking man in the street, and he turns out to be a millionaire engaged in a very profitable business which the accident disables him from carrying on; or you negligently and ignorantly injure the favourite for the Derby whereby he cannot run. You have to pay damages resulting from the circumstances of which you have no notice. You have to pay the actual loss to the man or his goods at the time of the tort, which is fixed by the circumstances at the time of the demand."

76 **Evidence of causation must be given on behalf of plaintiff.** Before a case can be considered, evidence must be called on behalf of the plaintiff,

[4] (1875) L.R. 10 Q.B. 453.
[5] Blackburn J. at p. 456 adopted with approval the words of Coleridge J. in *Lumley* v. *Gye* (1853) 2 E. & B. 216, 252.
[6] [1961] A.C. 388.
[7] [1933] A.C. 449, 460.
[8] (1875) L.R. 10 Q.B. 111, 121.
[9] [1934] P. 189, 202, 203.

whether it be direct or circumstantial evidence, which tends to show how the accident happened and how he sustained his personal injuries or suffered his damage from the negligence of the defendant. If he fails to establish that the defendant caused the harm, or some part of it, of which he complains, then his action will fail, whether this happens to be stated for reasons of remoteness or in terms of causation.

It is a question of law whether such evidence adduced allows a reasonable finding of causation [10] but it is a question of fact whether any particular head of damage is so caused by a defendant's negligence.[11]

In *Wakelin* v. *London and South Western Railway Co.*[12] the dead body of the plaintiff's husband was found on the defendant's railway line near a level crossing at night, the deceased having been killed by a train, although no evidence was given of the circumstances under which he had got on to the line. It was held by the House of Lords, even assuming (but without deciding) that there was evidence of negligence, there was still nothing to connect the happening of the accident with any such negligence.

77 **What is the cause of an accident?** Lord Wright, in considering what is the *cause* of an accident said: " Causation is to be understood as the man in the street, and not as either the scientist or the metaphysician, would understand it. Cause here means what a . . . man would take to be the cause without too microscopic analysis but on a broad view." [13] Lord Reid added: " One may find that as a matter of history several people have been at fault and that if any one of them had acted properly the accident would not have happened, but that does not mean that the accident must be regarded as having been caused by the faults of all of them. One must discriminate between those faults which must be discarded as being too remote and those which must not. Sometimes it is proper to discard all but one and to regard that one as the sole cause, but in other cases it is proper to regard two or more as having jointly caused the accident. I doubt whether any test can be applied generally." [14] What the causes of an accident were is a question of fact and, as the passage just cited shows, no test has yet been formulated to enable this question to be decided.

Accordingly the whole approach to the concept of causation is unfettered and permits infinite variation with freedom to choose one or more causes out of a selection of factors which contributed towards the actual happening of the event.[15] Frequently one hears

[10] In *Re Pickles* v. *N.C.B.* (*Intended Action*) [1968] 1 W.L.R. 997, 1000, Lord Denning M.R. said: " In the ordinary way attributability or causation is regarded as a point of law."

[11] *Per* McNair J. in *Mehmet Dogan Bey* v. *G. G. Abdeni & Co. Ltd.* [1951] 2 K.B. 405, 411.

[12] (1886) 12 App.Cas. 41.

[13] *Yorkshire Dale S.S. Co.* v. *Minister of War Transport* [1942] A.C. 691, 706. See also *Sigurdson* v. *British Columbia Electric Railway* [1953] A.C. 291, 299: " Causation and Responsibility in English law " (Lord Wright) [1955] C.L.J. 163.

[14] *Stapley* v. *Gypsum Mines Ltd.* [1953] A.C. 663, 681. In *Imperial Chemical Industries Ltd.* v. *Shatwell* [1965] A.C. 656, 670, Lord Reid agreed that *Stapley's* case " gives authoritative guidance on the question of causation." See Hart and Honore in 72 L.Q.R. 260 and 398, also " Causation in the law " (Glanville Williams) [1961] C.L.J. 62.

[15] *Norris* v. *W. Moss & Sons Ltd.* [1954] 1 W.L.R. 346. See *per* Vaisey J. at p. 351 upon this point.

trial judges applying what they care to believe to be the "common-sense" approach and yet it is remarkable just how often the appellate courts come to a conclusion quite different from that of the judge of first instance, still purporting to be deciding it upon the same principle. In *Stapley* v. *Gypsum Mines Ltd.*[16] two men were ordered to take down an unsafe roof in a mine. After attempting it for a time they gave up trying and Stapley returned to work under the unsafe roof, which then fell and killed him. In the House of Lords two members thought that the sole cause of the accident was the act of Stapley in returning to work under a roof, which he knew to be unsafe, but three members held that it was only partly the cause, the other part being the act of his fellow workman in leaving the roof in such a state.

78 In the absence of any formulated test, the courts must choose, after considering all the relevant factors, that cause or that combination of causes which was most probably responsible for the happening of the accident.

This is illustrated in the following cases. In *Quinn* v. *Burch Brothers (Builders) Ltd.*[17] it was held that the defendants, as the main contractors, were in breach of contract in failing to supply a step-ladder to the plaintiff, an independent sub-contractor. However, when the plaintiff borrowed a trestle, which he failed to have footed, and fell, it was held that even if the defendants could have foreseen that their failure to supply the plaintiff with the step-ladder might have resulted in the accident, yet their breach of contract did not cause the accident. Their breach merely gave the plaintiff the opportunity to injure himself by the negligent use of unsuitable equipment, which he had selected, and his action failed. In *McKew* v. *Holland & Hannen & Cubitts (Scotland)*[18] a servant suffered an accident for which his master was liable and then suffered a second accident, allegedly as a result of a weakness in the leg from the first accident, by falling and hurting himself after jumping down some steep stairs. It was held that as there had been an intervening act, which had broken the chain of causation, the second accident had not been caused by the initial negligence, so that the resulting injuries were not the natural and probable or the natural and direct result of the negligence; thus the claim in respect of this subsequent accident failed. However, by way of contrast, in *Wieland* v. *Cyril Lord Carpets*[19] the plaintiff had suffered a neck injury due to the defendants' negligence and, because her neck was constricted by a fitted medical collar that she was obliged to wear, she was unable to use her bifocal spectacles with her accustomed usual skill so that she tripped and fell while going downstairs thereby sustaining further personal injuries. It was held that this subsequent fall was attributable to the defendants' original negligence.

16 *Supra*; followed, *Williams* v. *Sykes & Harrison Ltd.* [1955] 1 W.L.R. 1180; *Hodkinson* v. *Henry Wallwork & Co.* [1955] 1 W.L.R. 1195.
17 [1966] 2 Q.B. 370.
18 [1969] 3 All E.R. 1621, H.L.
19 [1969] 3 All E.R. 1006.

79 In *Kelly* v. *W.R.N. Contracting Ltd. and Another* (*Third party*) [20] the third party had parked his car on a bend, without negligence, but in contravention of certain traffic sign regulations. The defendants' lorry, in which the plaintiff was travelling as a passenger, was being driven at such an excessive speed that, when the driver applied the brakes to avoid the car and negotiate the bend, the lorry skidded, crashed through a wall, ran down an embankment and overturned, pinning the plaintiff underneath, whereby he sustained severe personal injuries. It was held that since the third party had contravened the regulations it had had a causative effect on the accident. Hence a civil cause of action lay against him for breach of statutory duty, which made him liable to make contribution to the extent of 10 per cent. towards the damages payable to the plaintiff.

In *Matthews* v. *McLaren, Jones and The Ogopogo* [21] M. and H. were invited guests on board the defendants' pleasure cruiser but M. fell overboard and was lost; upon the failure of the defendants in their rescue bid, H. then dived into the water in order to save his friend but he died from shock. On the claim by H.'s dependants the Ontario Supreme Court held that the defendants were liable in that their negligence in effecting M.'s rescue so induced the deceased to act in the way he did that it caused his death. This decision, however, was reversed on appeal.[21a]

80 In *Barnett* v. *Chelsea and Kensington Hospital Management Committee* [22] three fellow night-watchmen presented themselves complaining to a nurse on duty that they had been vomiting for three hours after drinking tea. The doctor on casualty duty failed to examine them and, instead, referred them to their own doctors. Some five hours later, one of them died from arsenical poisoning, which substance had somehow been introduced into the tea that they had drunk in such a large quantity that he probably would have died in any event. The widow's claim failed because, despite the casualty officer's negligence in failing to examine or admit the deceased, he would have died irrespective of any treatment, if given him, thus causation could not be established.

In *Smith* v. *Leech Brain & Co. Ltd.*[23] the employers negligently failed to provide the plaintiff with adequate protection against the risk of receiving burns whilst working at a tank containing molten metal during galvanising operations. A droplet of molten metal splashed on to his lower lip causing a burn but this, acting as the promoting agent, further caused cancer to develop at the site of the burn so that some three years later he died from the disease. The employers were rightly held liable for causing the deceased's death so that his widow's claim for damages succeeded.

81 Cases undoubtedly do occur where causation cannot be apportioned,

[20] [1968] 1 W.L.R. 921.
[21] [1969] 1 Lloyd's Rep. 374.
[21a] [1970] 1 Lloyd's Rep. 257. See *ante*, § 56.
[22] [1969] 1 Q.B. 428.
[23] [1962] 2 Q.B. 405.

for example, where one cause is the responsibility of the defendant but the other is the responsibility of the plaintiff and each are equally probable causes. Where such a situation arises the courts inevitably will find that the plaintiff has failed to discharge the onus not only to establish the breach of duty, but also the causal connection between the breach and the injury.

In *McWilliams* v. *Sir William Arrol & Co. Ltd.*[24] an experienced steel erector, working on the erection of a steel lattice tower, fell some 70 feet from his place of work and was killed. His widow claimed damages in respect of his death against his employers on the ground that his death was caused by their negligence in failing to provide him with a safety belt, but it was held, by irresistible inference, that he would not have worn it even if one had been provided. Thus her action failed, there being no obligation on the deceased's employers to exhort him to wear one.

In *Vinnyey* v. *Star Paper Mills Ltd.*[25] where the defendants' factory floor had become slippery, following the spillage of some viscous fluid on it due to the negligence of their workmen in making a proper connection in a pipe, the plaintiff was instructed by the foreman to mop up the mess using squeegees. In order to carry out this work satisfactorily the plaintiff had first to remove a number of pallets, using a fork lift truck, but he chose to move even more pallets so to expose a wider area of the floor. When he slipped and fell whilst standing on a slippery patch it was held by Cumming-Bruce J. that there was no reasonably foreseeable risk that the plaintiff, charged expressly to perform such a simple task, would injure himself in carrying it out. Since there was no causal connection between the earlier negligence which caused the spillage, and the subsequent fall of the plaintiff, his claim for damages failed.

32 **Where there are concurrent causes.** Where separate and independent acts of negligence on the part of two or more persons together result in damage, any one of which probably would have caused the like damage, then the tortfeasor of each negligent act will be liable for the full damage suffered. This is because each negligent act is a substantive cause in producing the end-result.[26]

In *Burrows* v. *March Gas and Coke Co.*[27], where the gas company had fitted a defective service pipe to convey gas into the plaintiff's shop so that gas had leaked and an explosion had occurred when a servant of the gas fitters had approached the leak carrying a lighted candle, it was held that the gas company could be held liable for the whole amount of the damage.

In *Hale* v. *Hants & Dorset Motor Services Ltd.*[28] a local authority,

[24] [1962] 1 W.L.R. 295.
[25] [1965] 1 All E.R. 175.
[26] See *e.g. per* Lord du Parcq in *Grant* v. *Sun Shipping Co. Ltd.* [1948] A.C. 549, 563.
[27] (1872) L.R. 7 Ex. 96.
[28] [1947] 2 All E.R. 628.

which planted trees near the highway, negligently allowed the branches to overhang the road's surface. The plaintiff was a passenger in the defendants' bus, which was negligently driven so close to the trees that a low branch struck the bus window as a result of which the plaintiff was blinded by flying broken glass. The court held that the corporation as well as the bus company were each liable for the damage to the plaintiff although the apportionments made were different between the two defendants, since each was negligent in failing to foresee the harm which was likely to happen in combination with others' negligence. A similar decision was reached in *Hartley* v. *Mayoh & Co.*,[29] where the electricity board carried out some electrical wiring in a factory but negligently transposed two wires, so that the current remained on even after the switch had been turned off. The plaintiff, a fireman called to fight a fire, was electrocuted despite the switching off of what was believed by the occupiers to be the main switch. It was held that they, as well as the electricity board, were liable because they ought to have known which was their main switch, and the accident would not have happened had it not also been for the breach of their duty.

83 A distinction needs to be drawn between those cases where the damage suffered by the plaintiff was caused separately by the negligence of the concurrent, independent wrongdoers and where it was caused by the overlapping as well as consecutive damage caused by successive wrongdoers.

In *Performance Cars Ltd.* v. *Abraham* [30] the defendant negligently caused his motor car to collide with the plaintiff's Rolls Royce motor car damaging its front wing and thereby necessitating a paint re-spray to the whole of the lower part of the bodywork. However, the same Rolls Royce car had suffered an earlier accident due to the negligence of another driver, which damage also necessitated a similar re-spray, but this repair had not been carried out before the accident with the defendant. Further, the plaintiffs had been unable to recover that cost from the other car driver, because the judgment obtained was unsatisfied. Accordingly, the plaintiffs sought to recover this damage from the defendant who had caused the second collision. The Court of Appeal held that as the defendant had damaged a motor car which was, at the time of the accident, in need of re-spraying, this re-spraying did not flow from the defendant's wrongdoing so that he was not liable for that cost incurred, the plaintiffs having suffered no extra burden.

84 In *Baker* v. *Willoughby* [31] the plaintiff's leg had been broken in an accident, for which he claimed damages for personal injuries, which

[29] [1954] 1 Q.B. 383.
[30] [1962] 1 Q.B. 33.
[31] [1970] A.C. 467. See articles " Causation and Supervening Injury " (Casson) 119 New L.J. 1108; " Scope and application of the ' but for ' causal test " (Strachan) 33 M.L.R. 386; " Variations on an enigma: successive causes of personal injury " (McGregor) 33 M.L.R. 378.

included possible degenerative changes taking place. Before trial, however, the same leg had to be amputated as a result of its sustaining further injury, through a subsequent gunshot wound, caused when the plaintiff was a victim in an armed robbery, and this removed entirely the severe consequences of the first injury. The Court of Appeal held that the plaintiff's damages were limited to compensation for loss suffered up to the date of the shooting only, on the basis that no court must ever speculate when it knows the facts. Hence the second wrongdoer takes his victim as he finds him, *i.e.* not as a man with an already injured leg, only, but as one who also has the right to be compensated for the first accident. It is to be observed that no authority was cited for this somewhat novel proposition: *Performance Cars Ltd.* v. *Abraham*,[32] appears to be inconsistent with that principle, which was not cited in any of the judgments. The House of Lords reversed the Court of Appeal and restored the judgment of Donaldson J., who held [33] that a distinction had to be made between a supervening event which prevented an anticipated loss from occurring and a supervening event which caused a greater loss, whether or not of the same kind, in which the anticipated loss was merged or submerged. In the latter case the original loss was in no way reduced so that the plaintiff's actual and prospective loss flowing from the defendant's negligence had not been reduced by the subsequent loss of the leg at all.

Lord Reid added [34]: "If the later injury suffered before the date of the trial either reduces the disabilities from the injury for which the defendant is liable, or shortens the period during which they will be suffered by the plaintiff, then the defendant will have to pay less damages. But if the later injuries merely become a concurrent cause of the disabilities caused by the injury inflicted by the defendant, then in my view they cannot diminish the damages."

There can be little doubt that *Baker* v. *Willoughby* should be regarded as the most important and instructive decision on causation delivered for many years. It has clarified one of the most difficult aspects of the principle and removed a very substantial limitation on the extent of the wrongdoer's liability.

35 A situation can arise where two persons may be engaged in a joint venture but only one, to the exclusion of the other, could have inflicted the damage to the plaintiff. If it cannot be determined who actually caused the injury because of equal possibility, liability will attach to both since a prima facie case will be raised by the plaintiff against each defendant. In *Oliver* v. *Mills* [35] two men on a shooting expedition negligently fired their shotguns simultaneously causing a pellet to strike the plaintiff. It was impossible to decide from which gun the pellet

[32] *Supra.*
[33] [1969] 1 Q.B. 38.
[34] [1970] A.C. 467, 494.
[35] 144 Missouri 852 (1926).

in fact came but it could only have come from one of them. Accordingly both parties were held liable to the plaintiff for his damage.

86 **Participation in a joint enterprise which ends in disaster.** In *Imperial Chemical Industries Ltd.* v. *Shatwell* [36] two brothers, A and B, who were experienced shot firers, decided to test in the open the continuity of the electrical circuit, which was connected to a number of detonators, without waiting for the proper equipment to be brought up to them and in plain breach of the statutory regulations. Both men were seriously injured in the resulting explosion, whereupon A sued the employers upon the basis of their vicarious liability for the part taken by B. Since the defence of *volenti non fit injuria* succeeded, that was sufficient in the circumstances, but the alternative defence, that B's conduct had no causal connection with the accident, was specifically rejected. Where he was considering the effect of *Stapley's* case [37] Lord Donovan expressed the view: " Causation must, primarily, be a question of fact; but nevertheless a question of law was in my opinion also decided by the case, namely, whether a workman, who is injured in consequence of a breach of statutory duty, and of negligence of which both he and a fellow workman are together guilty, is precluded from contending that his fellow workman's breach and negligence was a cause of the ensuing injury. It was held that he was not so precluded." [38]

87 **The negligence of the plaintiff contributing to the cause.** Lord Atkin said in *Caswell* v. *Powell Duffryn Associated Collieries Ltd.*[39]: " I find it impossible to divorce any theory of contributory negligence from the concept of causation. It is negligence which ' contributes to cause ' the injury." Thus if a plaintiff be negligent, unless such negligence can be regarded as one of the causes or is not so venial that it cannot safely be disregarded, he cannot be held guilty of contributory negligence.[40] Any question of contributory negligence has to be considered broadly and upon a common-sense basis.[41] A fuller discussion of contributory negligence is reserved to Chapter 16, *post*.

88 **The suggested test of " last opportunity."** It was thought at one time that there existed a rule known as the rule of " the last opportunity " which could be applied to determine whose fault caused the accident.[42] The rule was, " When an accident happens through the combined negligence of two persons he alone is liable to the other who had the last opportunity of avoiding the accident by reasonable care." [43]

36 [1965] A.C. 656.
37 [1953] A.C. 663.
38 [1965] A.C. 656, 690, 691.
39 [1940] A.C. 152, 165: " contributes to cause," a phrase taken by Lord Atkin from the opinion of Lord Penzance in *Radley* v. *London and North Western Railway Co.* (1876) 1 App.Cas. 754.
40 See *e.g. per* Lord Asquith in *Stapley* v. *Gypsum Mines Ltd.* [1953] A.C. 663, 687.
41 See *The Volute* [1922] 1 A.C. 129, *per* Lord Birkenhead at p. 144; *Stapley* v. *Gypsum Mines Ltd., supra, per* Lord Reid at p. 681.
42 See, for an account of this, Williams, *Joint Torts and Contributory Negligence*, pp. 223–280.
43 *Service* v. *Sundell* (1929) 99 L.J.K.B. 55, *per* Scrutton L.J. quoting *Salmond on Torts*, 6th ed., p. 59.

In *Davies* v. *Mann* [44] the plaintiff hobbled an ass and turned it loose on the highway, where it was run into by the defendant's wagon, driven " at a smartish pace," and was killed. Lord Abinger stated the law to be: " As the defendant might, by proper care, have avoided injuring the animal, and did not, he is liable for the consequences of his negligence, though the animal may have been improperly there." Parke B. adding: " Were this not so, a man might justify the driving over goods left on a public highway, or even over a man lying asleep there, or the purposely running against a carriage going on the wrong side of the road." Again in *Radley* v. *L. & N.W. Ry.*[45] the defendants, the railway company, were in the habit of taking full trucks from the siding of the plaintiffs and returning empty trucks there. Over the siding was a bridge, and the plaintiffs left for return to the siding a truck containing another truck, the combined height of which exceeded the height of the bridge. The defendants pushed this truck towards the bridge and, on feeling resistance, continued to push and so brought down the bridge. The trial judge directed the jury that unless the accident was caused solely by the defendants' negligence and without any contributory negligence on the part of the plaintiffs, they must find for the defendants. The jury found contributory negligence on the part of the plaintiffs and judgment was accordingly entered for the defendants, but on appeal a new trial was ordered on the ground of misdirection, Lord Penzance saying: " Though the plaintiff may have been guilty of negligence, and although that negligence may, in fact, have contributed to the accident, yet if the defendant could in the result, by the exercise of ordinary care and diligence have avoided the mischief which happened, the plaintiff's negligence will not excuse him."

89 In *British Columbia Electric Ry.* v. *Loach* [46] a horse-drawn wagon was driven onto a level crossing, but the driver, who was not keeping a proper lookout, failed to notice an approaching train and the train, owing to defective brakes, could not stop, and a collision occurred. The railway authority was held liable. Here, the wagon would appear to have had the last opportunity of avoiding the accident, but, to fit into the rule of the last opportunity, the case was explained by saying that a person who by his negligence has deprived himself of the last opportunity of avoiding the accident (in this case the railway authority, because of defective brakes) is to be deemed in law to have had the last opportunity. It is unnecessary to go further into this rule, the weakness of which was that it meant finding out who had the last opportunity for avoiding the accident rather than whose negligence caused it. It was not followed in *Swadling* v. *Cooper* [47] and was rejected in *The Volute*.[48] There, Lord

44 (1842) 10 M. & W. 546.
45 (1876) 1 App.Cas. 754.
46 [1916] 1 A.C. 719.
47 [1931] A.C. 1.
48 [1922] A.C. 129. See also *Anglo-Newfoundland Development Co.* v. *Pacific Navigation Co.* [1924] A.C. 406.

Birkenhead said: " the question of contributory negligence must be dealt with somewhat broadly and upon common-sense principles as a jury would probably deal with it. And while no doubt, where a clear line can be drawn, the subsequent negligence is the only one to look to, there are cases in which the two acts come so closely together, and the second act of negligence is so much mixed up with the state of things brought about by the first act, that the party secondly negligent, while not held free from blame under the *Bywell Castle* rule, might, on the other hand, invoke the prior negligence as being part of the cause of the collision so as to make it a case of contribution." [49] An illustration of the application of this is the Admiralty case of *The Eurymedon* [50] where the *Corstar* sued the *Eurymedon* for damages for collision. The *Corstar* was lying at anchor athwart the fairway, and a collision occurred between her and the *Eurymedon* from the failure of the *Eurymedon* to keep a proper lookout. It was held that both vessels were equally to blame.

Finally, in the *Boy Andrew* [51] Lord Simon said: "The suggested test of ' last opportunity ' seems to me inaptly phrased and likely in some cases to lead to error, as the Law Revision Committee said in their report (Cmd. 6032 of 1939, p. 16): ' In truth, there is no such rule—the question, as in all questions of liability for a tortious act, is, not who had the last opportunity of avoiding the mischief, but whose act caused the wrong.' " In that case the *S.R.* was attempting to overtake the *B.A.* and was passing too close, when the *B.A.* changed her course in front of the *S.R.* and a collision occurred. The *B.A.* was held two thirds to blame and the *S.R.* one third.

90 Although as a principle of law the rule of the last opportunity (if it ever existed) is now dead, it may sometimes be a useful test to apply in deciding, as a matter of fact, whether an accident was caused by the fault of one or both of the parties. The chronological order of events is important and may well be decisive, as in *Davies* v. *Mann* [52] and *British Columbia Electric Ry.* v. *Loach* [53] and the 1945 Act does not, as a matter of law, compel the tribunal of fact to find that when both parties are negligent there must of necessity be an apportionment of the damages. It is still necessary to find out whose act caused the wrong, whether it is a combination of the acts of both parties or the sole act of one of them. " I am persuaded that it is still part of the law of this country that two causes may both be necessary preconditions of a particular result—damage to X—yet the one may, if the facts justify that conclusion, be treated as the real, substantial, direct or effective cause and the other

[49] [1922] 1 A.C. at p. 144.
[50] [1938] P. 41.
[51] [1948] A.C. 140, 149. See also, to the same effect, *Grant* v. *Sun Shipping Co.* [1948] A.C. 549, 563, *per* Lord du Parcq; *Davies* v. *Swan Motor Co. Ltd.* [1949] 2 K.B. 291 and *Harvey* v. *Road Haulage Executive* [1952] 1 K.B. 120, 126, where Denning L.J. said that the last opportunity rule " cannot survive the effect of the Law Reform (Contributory Negligence) Act." See also " Contributory Negligence " (Lord Wright) 13 M.L.R. 1.
[52] (1842) 10 M. & W. 546.
[53] [1916] 1 A.C. 719.

dismissed as at best a *causa sine qua non* and ignored for the purpose of legal liability. This is a doctrine affirmed by your Lordships' House and not, in my view, displaced by the Law Reform (Contributory Negligence) Act 1945." [54] An illustration of this is *Sigurdson* v. *British Columbia Electric Ry.*[55] where S., wanting to drive from one side of the street to the other, after beginning to turn, stopped on a street-car track in the centre of the road. The driver of an approaching street-car had an unobstructed view, but did not see S. until he was seventy-five feet away, so that there was a collision. The jury found, that the street-car driver was negligent in not keeping a proper lookout, but that S. was not negligent. The decision, after being reversed on appeal, was upheld by the Judicial Committee. They disapproved the proposition that "where one party (A) actually knows of the dangerous situation created by the negligence of another (B) and fails by the exercise of reasonable care thereafter to avoid the danger A is, generally speaking, liable, but that if A by reason of his own negligence did not actually know of the danger or by his own negligence or deliberate act has disabled himself from becoming aware of the danger he can only be held liable for a proportion of the resulting damage." On the question of fact the Judicial Committee might have come to a different conclusion but they held that the jury were not prevented in law from arriving at that conclusion if they thought fit. Again, if the only effective cause of the accident is the plaintiff's own negligence, he is not entitled to recover any damages.[56] So, where a scaffold was erected which was in breach of the Building Regulations in that one of the uprights was not vertical but the plaintiff, a scaffolder, tried to remedy the defect in a manner described as " fantastically wrong " which caused the scaffold to collapse, whereby he was injured, it was held there was no causal connection between the breach of statutory duty and the plaintiff's injury, and the plaintiff failed to recover.[57] Further, where a workman put his hand deliberately into the moving parts of a crushing machine in order to clean the grooves out, although the employers were in breach of their statutory duty to fence, under section 14 (1) of the Factories Act 1937, they were held not to be liable in damages because the cause of the accident in the sense of the operative act and effective cause, was the workman's own negligence.[58]

91 Nevertheless in considering whose fault it was, what must be ascertained is the fault causing the damage, since this may not necessarily be the same as the fault causing the accident, which in turn caused the damage. An example of this can be found in *Davies* v. *Swan Motor (Swansea) Ltd.*[59] where a collision took place between an omnibus and a dust-cart, owing to the negligence of the drivers of both vehicles, and the plaintiff's

54 Lord Asquith in *Stapley* v. *Gypsum Mines* [1953] A.C. 663, 687.
55 [1953] A.C. 291. See the interesting note on this case by C. J. Hamson in [1954] C.L.J. 42.
56 *C. P. Ry.* v. *Frechette* [1915] A.C. 871.
57 *Norris* v. *W. Moss & Sons Ltd.* [1954] 1 W.L.R. 346.
58 *Rushton* v. *Turner Brothers Asbestos Co. Ltd.* [1960] 1 W.L.R. 96.
59 [1949] 2 K.B. 291.

husband was killed. He had been standing on the steps of the dust-cart, where he was forbidden to be, and was crushed in the collision, which was in no way caused or contributed to by his presence there. It was nevertheless held that his death was contributed to by his negligence in riding in a forbidden position and the damages payable to his widow were reduced by one-fifth. Similarly, in *Jones* v. *Livox Quarries Ltd.*[60] the plaintiff, employed by the defendants, was, contrary to orders, riding on the back of a traxcavator, which was run into from behind by a dumper negligently driven by another employee of the defendants. The plaintiff was found guilty of contributory negligence, on the ground that he had unreasonably and improperly exposed himself to this particular risk, even though his conduct was not a cause operating to produce this particular accident. A further illustration is *Cork* v. *Kirby Maclean Ltd.*[61] where an epileptic, who had been warned by his doctor not to work at heights, and had not told his employers of this, was working on a platform some twenty feet above the ground when he had a fit, fell to the ground and was killed. The employers were in breach of their statutory duty in not providing toe boards and hand rails, and it was held that the epileptic's conduct and the employer's breach of duty were equally causes of the accident, so that the responsibility for the accident should be equally shared between them.

92 In *Cakebread* v. *Hopping Brothers*[62] a skilled workman so disliked working a circular saw with a guard brought down low to comply with the Woodworking Regulations that, after the foreman had protested to him about the dangerous height to which he had adjusted it, he agreed to a compromise position of the guard. However, it was not capable of adjustment properly to comply with the employers' statutory duty, and the plaintiff accidentally injured his hand by striking it against the revolving blade, which could not have occurred if the guard had been adjusted to its lowest possible position. The Court of Appeal apportioned liability equally between the plaintiff and the defendant.

2. REMOTENESS OF DAMAGE

93 **The remoteness of the damage caused.** The principle that a causal connection between the negligence and the damage must be established before the wrongdoer can be held responsible for the damage (subject to the rule concerning remoteness), has been considered in the preceding paragraphs. As Denning L.J. said in *Roe* v. *Minister of Health*[63]: " It is only when those two preliminary questions—duty and causation—are answered in favour of the plaintiff that the third question, remoteness of damage, comes into play." It is now necessary to consider remoteness, because where damage is too remote a consequence of the negligence

[60] [1952] 2 Q.B. 608.
[61] [1952] 2 All E.R. 402. Also *Laszczyk* v. *N.C.B.* [1954] 1 W.L.R. 1426.
[62] [1947] K.B. 641.
[63] [1954] 2 Q.B. 66, 85.

complained of, damages cannot be recovered. Whether or not damage is too remote can be ascertained by the application of the principles set out below. It is a question of law to be determined by the judge whether a particular item of damage is too remote or not.[64]

4 **Intended consequence not too remote.** A consequence which is intended cannot be too remote.[65] So where the defendant in pulling down his building intentionally caused materials to fall on the stable of the plaintiff, he was liable for the damage suffered.[66] Where a person acts, regardless of the consequences, such recklessness implies intention and so for all practical purposes the terms are synonymous. In *Scott* v. *Shepherd*[67] a person for a joke threw a lighted squib amongst a crowd of people in a covered market place. The first person nearest to whom it had fallen, saw it and he reacted in self-defence by throwing it away towards another, who, in turn, picked it up and threw it away. Whereupon it exploded and put out the plaintiff's eye. It was held that the mischievous person, who had originated the incident by lighting and throwing the squib was liable to the plaintiff because he must have intended that the firework should explode somewhere in the crowd. Further, the risk of injury to somebody, as a result of his action, was at least foreseeable. It follows that a defendant will also be liable for the damage, which was intended, despite the fact that it actually resulted from the action of a third party.[68] A further illustration occurs in *Cutler* v. *McPhail*.[69] The defendant wrote a letter containing matter which defamed the plaintiff to a local councillor in circumstances in which Salmon J. considered it to be privileged but, as the defendant also had intended that the same letter should be republished to others in a local newspaper, it was unprivileged in that regard and the defendant was held liable.

5 **Natural and probable consequences or reasonable foreseeability.** Where the consequences that result are unintended, then consideration must be given to the proposition that the wrongdoer is liable only for that damage which was the natural and probable consequence of his wrongful act. In this context, a consequence is natural and probable when it is one which is so likely to result from the act that the wrongdoer, acting as a reasonable man, would have foreseen it, because of his state of knowledge or his means of knowledge, and thus would have avoided doing the act. Approached in this manner, remoteness of damage is treated on exactly the same basis as the test for the existence of a duty of care and its neglect which has already been considered.[70]

64 *The Argentino* (1889) 14 App.Cas. 519; *Hobbs* v. *L. & S.W. Ry.* (1875) L.R. 10 Q.B. 111, 122; *Cork* v. *Kirby McLean Ltd.* [1952] 2 All E.R. 402, 407, *per* Denning L.J.
65 *Per* Lord Lindley in *Quinn* v. *Leathem* [1901] A.C. 495, 537; "The intention to injure the plaintiff disposes of any question of remoteness."
66 *Emblen* v. *Myers* (1860) 6 H. & N. 54.
67 (1773) W.Bl. 892.
68 See further "*Novus actus interveniens*" § 113, *post.*
69 [1962] 2 Q.B. 292.
70 Chap. 2, *ante.* § 58.

However, this test of foreseeability of damage was rejected by the Court of Appeal in *Re an Arbitration between Polemis and Another and Furness, Withy & Co. Ltd.*,[71] more conveniently referred to hereinafter as *Re Polemis.* Then the test was equally as forcefully accepted by the Judicial Committee in *Overseas Tankship (U.K.) Ltd.* v. *Morts Dock and Engineering Co. Ltd.*,[72] more conveniently referred to hereinafter as *The Wagon Mound No.* 1, some forty years later.

In view of this apparent conflict it will be necessary to discuss each of these two authorities in detail.

96 **Re Polemis [73]: Direct physical consequences not too remote.** The facts were that by a charterparty Messrs. Polemis and Boyazides, the owners of the Greek steamship *Thrasyvoulos* chartered their said steamship to Furness, Withy & Co. Ltd. for the period of the duration of the war in 1917. She proceeded to various ports and in Lisbon was loaded with further cargo, part of which consisted of cases of benzine which was destined for Casablanca and other ports on the Moroccan coast. Upon arrival at Casablanca the cargo was prepared to be discharged by Arab workmen and for this purpose they had placed heavy planks across the forward end of the hatchway in the 'tween decks. These planks were used as a platform in the process of transferring the cases of benzine from the lower hold to the 'tween decks but a considerable quantity of these cases had suffered damage, either through handling or by rough weather on the voyage, so that some leakage had occurred into the hold. In the course of heaving a sling of the benzine cases from the hold the rope came into contact with the planks, causing one of them to fall into the lower hold. The fall caused a spark which was instantaneously followed by a rush of flames from the lower hold, and this resulted eventually in the total destruction of the ship by fire.

The shipowners accordingly claimed the value of the ship from the charterers, who relied on the " excepted perils " clause in the charterparty, by way of their defence, and also that the damage was too remote. Hence questions in both contract and tort had to be decided and the experienced arbitrators, from whom the appeal was brought, found, *inter alia*, the following *important fact*:—" The causing of the spark could not reasonably have been anticipated from the falling of the plank, although some slight damage, which was not specified, might reasonably have been expected to occur to the ship as a result of the fall." The Court of Appeal unanimously decided that the charterers were liable to the owners on the ground that the " exception clause " did not protect the charterers in the circumstances and that as the fall of the plank was due to the negligence of the stevedores, their servants, the charterers were liable for all the direct consequences of the negligent act, even although those consequences could not reasonably have been anticipated. The charterers

[71] [1921] 3 K.B. 560.
[72] [1961] A.C. 388.
[73] *Supra.*

were therefore liable for the loss of the ship by fire, damages for which were assessed at £196,165 1s.11d. Bankes L.J. said: " It is immaterial that the causing of the spark by the falling of the plank could not have been reasonably anticipated. . . . Given the breach of duty which constitutes the negligence, and given the damage as a direct result of that negligence, the anticipations of the person whose negligent act has produced the damage appear to me to be irrelevant." [74] In his judgment Scrutton L.J. said: " To determine whether an act is negligent, it is relevant to determine whether any reasonable person would foresee that the act would cause damage: if he would not, the act is not negligent. But if the act would or might probably cause damage, the fact that the damage it in fact causes is not the exact kind of damage one would expect is immaterial, so long as the damage is in fact directly traceable to the negligent act, and not due to the operation of independent causes having no connection with the negligent act, except that they could not avoid its results. Once the act is negligent, the fact that its exact operation was not foreseen is immaterial." Then he continued: " In the present case it was negligent in discharging cargo to knock down the planks of the temporary staging, for they might easily cause some damage either to workmen, or cargo, or the ship. The fact that they did directly produce an unexpected result, a spark in an atmosphere of petrol vapour which caused a fire, does not relieve the person who was negligent from the damage which his negligent act directly caused." [75]

7 There can be little doubt that in *Re Polemis* two different interpretations are capable of being discerned. The first is that if the defendant has been negligent as regards somebody, whether or not that person had been in any foreseeable danger from the negligent act, then he will be held liable for all the direct consequences which flow from that negligence. The second is that the defendant will be liable to the plaintiff for the damage he has suffered to its fullest extent, even if this extent was unforeseeable, provided that the damage was the direct result of the original negligence and so long as it was reasonably foreseeable that the plaintiff would sustain some damage thereby, whether or not it would be only slight damage to person or property.[76]

As has been discussed [77] the first interpretation is wholly objectionable, since it is contrary to the basic requirement that in the tort of negligence there must always be a breach of duty towards the particular plaintiff and not towards the world at large. Additionally it would be in complete conflict with leading decisions of the House of Lords such as *Bourhill* v. *Young* [78] and others [79] in which it had been held, vitally to the result,

[74] *Ibid.* at pp. 571–572.
[75] *Ibid.* at p. 577.
[76] *Cf.* Lord Reid's view of the law, *post*, in *Czarnikow Ltd.* v. *Koufos* (*The Heron II*) [1969] 1 A.C. 350, 385, 386.
[77] Chap. 2, *ante*, § 65 *et seq.*
[78] [1943] A.C. 92.
[79] *e.g.*, *Glasgow Corporation* v. *Muir* [1943] A.C. 448; *Woods* v. *Duncan* [1946] A.C. 401.

that there was no damage foreseeable to the plaintiff at the time of the negligence.

It follows that the second interpretation of the case must be the correct one, since it is not inconsistent with these House of Lords cases, and it is justified upon the arbitrator's said finding of fact that some damage to the ship *might* reasonably have been anticipated from the mere falling of the plank.

98 In this respect the opinion of Lord Reid expressed in *Czarnikow Ltd.* v. *Koufos* (*The Heron II*)[80] is of considerable significance although the House of Lords were there considering remoteness of damage arising out of contract. His Lordship stated: " For over a century everyone has agreed that remoteness of damage in contract must be determined by applying the rule (or rules) laid down by a court including Lord Wensleydale (then Parke B.), Martin B. and Alderson B. in *Hadley* v. *Baxendale.*[81] But many different interpretations of that rule have been adopted by judges at different times." [82] He continued after reciting the relevant facts of the decision: " In cases like *Hadley* v. *Baxendale* or the present case it is not enough that in fact the plaintiff's loss was directly caused by the defendants' breach of contract. It clearly was so caused in both. The crucial question is whether, on the information available to the defendant when the contract was made, he should, or the reasonable man in his position would, have realised that such loss was sufficiently likely to result from the breach of contract to make it proper to hold that the loss flowed naturally from the breach or that loss of that kind should have been within his contemplation. The modern rule of tort is quite different and it imposes a much wider liability. The defendant will be liable for any type of damage which is reasonably foreseeable as liable to happen even in the most unusual case, unless the risk is so small that a reasonable man would in the whole circumstances feel justified in neglecting it. And there is good reason for the difference. In contract, if one party wishes to protect himself against a risk which to the other party would appear unusual, he can direct the other party's attention to it before the contract is made, and I need not stop to consider in what circumstances the other party will then be held to have accepted responsibility in that event. But in tort there is no opportunity for the injured party to protect himself in that way, and the tortfeasor cannot reasonably complain if he has to pay for some very unusual but nevertheless foreseeable damage which results from his wrongdoing. I have no doubt that today a tortfeasor would be held liable for a type of damage as unlikely as was the stoppage of Hadley's Mill for lack of a crankshaft: to anyone with the knowledge the carrier had that may have seemed unlikely but the chance of it happening would have been seen to be far from

[80] [1969] 1 A.C. 350, applying *Victoria Laundry (Windsor) Ltd.* v. *Newman Industries Ltd.* [1949] 2 K.B. 528.
[81] (1854) 9 Exch. 341.
[82] *Supra* at p. 383.

negligible. But it does not at all follow that *Hadley* v. *Baxendale* would today be differently decided." [83]

9 Nevertheless a curious conflict of judicial opinion did result from the decision in *Re Polemis* and that concerned the precise effect it had on the existing state of the law. In *Morrison Steamship Co. Ltd.* v. *Greystoke Castle* (*Cargo Owners*) [84] Lord Porter said: " One method of ascertaining the damages in an action of tort is to ask what loss would a reasonable man anticipate as a result of the wrongful act. To this the *Polemis* case added a further liability, *viz.* damage consisting of the direct physical consequences of the tortious act whether they would reasonably be anticipated or not. It has not narrowed the liability which was previously held to exist." Atkin L.J. on the other hand remarked in *Hambrook* v. *Stokes Bros.*[85]: " The full effect of the decision in *Re Polemis and Furness, Withy & Co.* has not yet, I think, been fully realised, even though that case laid down no new law."

Atkin L.J. further went on to say, with reference to the damage suffered by the plaintiff: " No doubt the particular injury was not contemplated by the defendants, but it is plain from *Re Polemis and Furness, Withy & Co.* that this is immaterial." In *Roe* v. *Minister of Health* [86] Denning L.J. considered that the decision in *Re Polemis* was of very limited application, since there were two preliminary questions to be answered before it could be brought into play: (a) whether there was a duty of care owed to the plaintiff, which depended upon foreseeability; and (b) whether the neglect of duty was a cause of the injury sustained in the proper sense of that term.

00 **What are " direct consequences "?** It would seem that the most helpful approach to an understanding of the problem raised by *Re Polemis* is to discover what was the real meaning to be attached to the term " direct consequences," since as Scrutton L.J. observed in *The San Onofre* [87] " the question whether damage is sufficiently direct consequence of negligence to be recoverable, or is too remote, is rather a question of first impression." It is submitted that a direct physical connection means that there is no independent cause intervening between the negligence and the damage. This view is expressed by Lord Wright in *Liesbosch Dredger* (*Owners*) v. *Edison* (*Owners*) [88] who said that *Re Polemis* " was concerned with the immediate physical consequences of the negligent act, and not with the co-operation of an extraneous matter such as the plaintiff's want of means." In that case the dredger *Liesbosch* was lying moored alongside a breakwater in a harbour when the steamship *Edison* fouled the dredger's moorings and carried her out to sea where she sank

83 *Ibid.* at pp. 385, 386.
84 [1947] A.C. 265, 295, 296.
85 [1925] 1 K.B. 141, 156.
86 [1954] 2 Q.B. 66, 84–85.
87 [1922] P. 243, 253.
88 [1933] A.C. 499, 461.

and was lost. The owners of the dredger required it for the performance of their contract with the Harbour Commissioners, delay in the completion of which work involved payment of heavy penalties. Due to lack of funds a substitute dredger could not be bought so that they were obliged to hire one at a more expensive rate but it was held that their increased loss suffered by their impecuniosity could not be recovered since this lack of money was a separate and concurrent cause which was not traceable to the defendants' negligence.[89]

In *Domine* v. *Grimsdall* [90] to the like effect Atkinson J. said: " Damage is recoverable if, without intervening causes having no connection with the negligent act, it is directly traceable to the negligent act." Lord Wright in *Bourhill* v. *Young* [91] stated the proposition that: " It must be understood to be limited, however, to ' direct ' consequences to the particular interest of the plaintiff which is affected. *Liesbosch* (*Owners*) v. *Edison* (*Owners*) illustrates this limitation." Whilst it is apparent that other aspects of the law, where the courts have evaluated the particular interests of the plaintiff invaded, such as in rescue cases,[92] may be cited in support of such a proposition, it is not easy to understand why such a distinction should be drawn between consequences which are " immediate physical " and other consequences, or to know, indeed, where the line is to be drawn.[93]

101 **The Wagon Mound (No. 1)** [94]**: reasonable foreseeability.** The facts were that the respondents owned and used a wharf, where they carried on business in the port of Sydney, Australia, repairing ships, for which purpose they used tools and equipment stored on the wharf, including both electric and oxy-acetylene welding equipment. The appellants, who were the charterers of the *S.S. Wagon Mound*, by their servants, carelessly discharged bunkering oil from the ship on October 30, 1951, whilst it was moored about 200 yards away from the respondents' premises. Some six hours later the ship set sail and left its moorings for the high seas but the oil, left behind on the surface of the water, was carried along by wind and tide beneath the respondents' wharf and around a vessel which was moored there and was undergoing a refit. After the appellants had received advice that it was safe for them to recommence their welding work despite the continued presence of the floating oil, and some two-and-a-half days after the *Wagon Mound's* departure, molten metal fell down from the welding operations and set fire to some cotton waste, which was floating on the surface beneath the wharf. This waste material, acting

[89] *Cf. Muhammed Issa El Sheikh Ahmed* v. *Ali* [1947] A.C. 414 where the plaintiff recovered the increased loss due to his lack of funds. It is to be noted that neither counsel in argument nor the Judicial Committee referred to the *Liesbosch* case at all. See *Monarch Steamship Co. Ltd.* v. *Karlshamns Oljefabriker* (*A/B*) [1949] A.C. 196, *per* Lord Wright at p. 224.

[90] (1937) 106 L.J.K.B. 386, 390.

[91] [1943] A.C. 92, 110.

[92] See Chap. 2, *ante*, § 67.

[93] See *The Wagon Mound* (*No.* 1) [1961] A.C. 388, 424.

[94] [1961] A.C. 388.

like a wick, set fire to the oil, as a result of which the flames engulfed the respondents' wharf causing considerable damage both to it and their equipment stored there. The respondents sued the appellants in negligence and nuisance, although the case proceeded upon the basis of negligence. It is to be emphasised as an essential feature that the trial judge made an important finding of fact that the respondents had suffered some damage, unquestionably a direct and reasonably foreseeable result of the escape of the oil, which consisted of the fouling up of the slipways due to the presence of the congealed oil adhering to them. However the trial judge further found that fire was *unforeseeable*, because expert opinion at the time of the happening indicated that it was unlikely to be set afire, when spread thinly on water.[95]

102 On these findings the Judicial Committee reversed the decision of the Full Court of the Supreme Court of New South Wales, declared *Re Polemis* to have been wrongly decided and remitted the case for a decision on the issue of nuisance which had been pleaded in the alternative as a ground for a finding of liability. More of the case itself has not reached our law reports but repercussions from the decision reverberated for a long time thereafter. Judging by the drawn out discussions in the mass of literature,[96] produced as a foreseeable result of this head-on collision between *Re Polemis* and *The Wagon Mound* (*No.* 1), these, irresistibly, must have been the outcome of the persistent burning of much midnight oil in an entertaining, if fruitless, academic exercise of seeking to explain the inexplicable or in attempting to reconcile the irreconcilable.[97] Even prior to *The Wagon Mound* (*No.* 1) reaching the Judicial Committee for decision, *Re Polemis* had been subjected to devastating and destructive crossfire in argument. Manning J. in giving the judgment of the Full Court of the Supreme Court of New South Wales considered that it would be a gross understatement to say that he was able to apply that decision with any degree of confidence and expressed the hope that the House of Lords or the Judicial Committee of the Privy Council would pronounce on it in the near future. Then, when before the Judicial Committee itself the mood was set at the outset by counsel for the appellants seeking to show that *Re Polemis* was wrong in law. Clearly the Judicial Commissioners were so persuaded because in the judgment of their Lordships, delivered by Viscount Simonds, there was said[98]: " Enough has been said to show that the authority of *Polemis* has been severely shaken though lip service has from time to time been paid to it. In their Lordships' opinion it should no longer be regarded as good law. It is not probable that many cases will for that reason have a different result, though it is hoped that the law will be thereby simplified and that in some cases, at

[95] But *cf.* " Oil of this character with a flash point of 170° F. is extremely difficult to ignite in the open. But we now know that it is not impossible ": as a finding of fact in *The Wagon Mound* (*No.* 2) [1967] A.C. 617, 633.
[96] See list of such literature [1962] C.L.J. 178, n. 2, and [1967] C.L.J. 63, n. 4.
[97] For a courageous attempt see Professor Street's *The Law of Torts*, 4th ed., Chap. 8, Sect. 3 *et seq.*
[98] *Ibid.* at pp. 422–423.

least, palpable injustice will be avoided. For it does not seem consonant with current ideas of justice or morality that for an act of negligence, however slight or venial, which results in some trivial foreseeable damage the actor should be liable for all consequences however unforeseeable and however grave, so long as they can be said to be 'direct.' It is a principle of civil liability, subject only to qualifications which have no present relevance, that a man must be considered to be responsible for the probable consequences of his act. To demand more of him is too harsh a rule, to demand less is to ignore that civilised order requires the observance of a minimum standard of behaviour."

103 In order to complete the history of events, two ships the *Corrimal* and the *Audrey D* which were undergoing refit at Sheerlegs Wharf, Morts Bay, Sydney Harbour, also suffered damage in the conflagration of November 1, 1951. Accordingly the owners brought fresh separate actions against the defendants alleging nuisance and negligence which also reached the Privy Council for opinion by the Judicial Committee in *Overseas Tankship* (*U.K.*) *Ltd.* v. *The Miller Steamship Co. Pty. The Wagon Mound* (*No.* 2).[99] At the trial Walsh J. held that these actions failed where based upon negligence, following *The Wagon Mound* (*No.* 1) since the damage by fire was not *reasonably* foreseeable although there was a remote risk, which was foreseeable but which he felt entitled to ignore. However, the actions succeeded where based upon nuisance. The Judicial Committee reversed this decision holding that, as the plaintiffs had proved by evidence *some* foreseeability of fire, whatever that degree of remote possibility may happen to be, since fire was a foreseeable kind of damage the defendants were liable in negligence for the escape of the bunkering oil. Whilst this may seem a surprising result in that the Judicial Committee were reversing in effect their previous decision in *The Wagon Mound* (*No.* 1) it is plain that there was no alternative upon that very significant and different finding of fact. It is to be noted with interest that despite counsel's dangling the carrot of "*The Polemis* heresy," any reference to its ghost was avoided entirely in the judgment of their Lordships, delivered by Lord Reid.

104 **Re Polemis and The Wagon Mound [1] in retrospect.** Whilst there may be good reasons for the controversy that has raged, particularly as regards why the Judicial Committee thought that the facts in the cases each raised precisely the same issue as a justification for holding that *Re Polemis* is no longer good law, in practice there can be no significant difference, if the approach of *The Wagon Mound* (*No.* 2) is correct. Can there be any real distinction between damage, which is a direct or an immediate physical consequence, as in *Re Polemis*, and damage which a defendant can reasonably foresee " however unlikely it may be, unless

[99] [1967] 1 A.C. 617.

[1] *Cf. The Wagon Mound,* where it was the molten metal, which fell as a result of the *plaintiff's* work that started the fire, and *Re Polemis* where it was the falling plank caused by the *defendants'* negligence that resulted in the outbreak of the fire.

it can be brushed aside as far fetched "?[2] It almost defies one being drawn. Nevertheless *The Wagon Mound* (*No.* 1), being a decision of the Judicial Committee, is not binding on the English courts, following strict precedent, although it may be of persuasive authority. However, this situation has produced its own complication in that the Court of Appeal has considered itself free to follow *The Wagon Mound* since it ought to be treated as the law whether it " is or is not binding on this Court."[3] Even the House of Lords in *Hughes* v. *Lord Advocate*[4] treated it as correctly stating the law, although it proceeded to distinguish it on the facts.

Without doubt the greatest benefit flowing from *The Wagon Mound* (*No.* 1) decision is the simplification which results in that the same test of foreseeability must now be applied to all three essentials of negligence as a tort namely (a) duty, (b) breach and (c) damage, even though the foresight principle has produced its own uncertainties as the sole criterion of liability (see Chap. 2). In doing so *The Wagon Mound* has displaced the proposition that unforeseeability is irrelevant if damage is said to be " direct " and has established the test of foresight *viz.*: whether the damage is of such a kind as the reasonable man should have foreseen, thereby bringing it into line with the general effect of *Donoghue* v. *Stevenson.*[5] In reasserting this principle the Judicial Committee conceived that they did not depart from but followed and developed the law of negligence as laid down by Baron Alderson in *Blyth* v. *Birmingham Waterworks Co.*[6]

05 **Where The Wagon Mound principle has no application.** Reasonable foreseeability as a test of remoteness has no application in the following instances:

(*a*) *Unforeseeable extent of damage.* As has been stated above, once the type or kind of damage, be it physical injury to person or property, could have been foreseen in a general way,[7] the defendant is liable for the full extent of the harm even though that extent was unforeseeable.

In *Smith* v. *Leech Brain & Co. Ltd.*[8] a workman suffered a burn of his lip, which was a foreseeable happening, as a result of the defendant's negligence but, because the workman had a predisposition to cancer, a carcinoma developed on the site of the burn, which was not a foreseeable happening, and in due course the workman died from the disease. Lord Parker C.J. in explaining certain dicta in *The Wagon Mound* (*No.* 1)[9] doctrine said: " Lord Simonds is clearly there drawing a distinction between the question whether a man could reasonably anticipate a type of injury, and the question whether a man could reasonably anticipate the

2 *C. Czarnikow Ltd.* v. *Koufos* (*The Heron II*) [1969] 1 A.C. 350, *per* Lord Upjohn at p. 422.
3 *Per* Harman L.J. in *Doughty* v. *Turner Manufacturing Co. Ltd.* [1964] 1 Q.B. 518, 528. See also *per* Diplock L.J. at p. 532.
4 [1963] A.C. 837.
5 [1932] A.C. 562. See p. 580, *per* Lord Atkin.
6 (1856) 11 Exch. 781, 784.
7 *Hughes* v. *Lord Advocate* [1963] A.C. 837.
8 [1962] 2 Q.B. 405. For fuller summary of the facts see § 80, *ante.*
9 [1961] A.C. 388, 416.

extent of injury of the type which could be foreseen. The Judicial Committee were, I think disagreeing with the decision in the *Polemis* case that a man is no longer liable for the type of damage which he could not reasonably anticipate. The Judicial Committee were not, I think, saying that a man is only liable for the extent of damage which he could anticipate, always assuming the type of injury could have been anticipated." [10]

In an earlier passage of his judgment [11] Lord Parker C.J. had said: " For my part, I am quite satisfied that the Judicial Committee in *The Wagon Mound* case did not have what I may call, loosely, the thin skull [12] cases in mind. It has always been the law of this country that a tortfeasor takes his victim as he finds him." [13]

Or as Mackinnon L.J. said in *Owens* v. *Liverpool Corporation*: " But one who is guilty of negligence to another must put up with idiosyncrasies of his victim that increase the likelihood or extent of damage to him: it is no answer to a claim for a fractured skull that its owner had an unusually fragile one." [14] The following are examples:

106 In *Love* v. *Port of London Authority* [15] the defendants, through their negligence, caused the plaintiff workman to sustain a head injury and from such injury he developed a neurosis although this was aggravated by a pre-existing heart condition. Edmund Davies J. stated [16]: " One has to remember, of course, that the defendants must take the plaintiff as they find him, that is to say, with his already vulnerable personality . . . if what we may call the 70 per cent. heart neurosis would not have prevented the plaintiff from working, but the addition of the 30 per cent. accident neurosis produced total incapacity, the defendants have to recompense the plaintiff for all special damages arising from the 100 per cent. neurosis which developed from these two causes."

In *Warren* v. *Scruttons* [17] where the plaintiff injured a finger on a frayed rope, which was a foreseeable injury, as a result of the negligence of the employers in supplying such a worn rope for use, and in consequence suffered an aggravation of an existing eye injury, Paull J. held the defendants liable also for the eye injury.

107 In *Sayers* v. *Perrin* [18] where a plaintiff, due to his employer's negligence,

[10] *Ibid.* at pp. 414, 415.

[11] *Ibid.* at p. 414.

[12] Under this category of a hypersensitive victim would come the sufferer from haemophilia referred to by Lord Wright as " a bleeder " in his giving examples in *Bourhill* v. *Young* [1943] A.C. 92, 109.

[13] See *Bourhill* v. *Young* [1943] A.C. 92, *per* Lord Wright at pp. 109–110. See also article " Negligent Tortfeasor Still Takes His Victim As He Finds Him " 25 M.L.R. 393, and *Malcolm* v. *Broadhurst* [1970] 3 All E.R. 508 (the exacerbation of a plaintiff's nervous condition was held to be a foreseeable consequence of injuring her; since the defendant must take a plaintiff as he finds her, there is no difference in principle between an egg-shell thin skull and an egg-shell thin personality).

[14] [1939] 1 K.B. 394, 400–401.

[15] [1959] 2 Lloyd's Rep. 541.

[16] *Ibid.* at p. 545.

[17] [1962] 1 Lloyd's Rep. 497.

[18] [1966] Q.L.R. 89.

suffered an electric shock which damaged nerve cells, thereby allowing poliomyelitis virus to attack these injured cells in his body and bring about paralysis, it was held that as the liability of the employers depended not upon the reasonable foreseeability of the actual result which ensued, but upon whether they could reasonably foresee an injury of such type which might directly result in the condition giving rise to the action, the plaintiff was entitled to succeed.

In *Oman* v. *McIntyre*[19] the Court of Session, Outer House, followed *Smith* v. *Leech Brain & Co. Ltd.* and held the defendants liable in full where the deceased had sustained a leg injury while working for the defendant, which led to fat embolism, broncho-pneumonia and then to his eventual death.

In *Bradford* v. *Robinson Rentals Ltd.*[20] a plaintiff radio engineer was required to drive for a long period of time in freezing conditions in his employers' van, which was not equipped with a car heater, and suffered frostbite as a result. The court held that even if the plaintiff was abnormally susceptible to frostbite as distinct from other more usual consequences of prolonged exposure to below-freezing conditions, it would be no defence, since a defendant must still take his victim as he finds him.

108 There is no reason to suppose that a defendant would not be held similarly liable for the unforeseeable extent of damage to a person's property. Willes J. interjected, during the expansion of counsel's arguments in *Mullett* v. *Mason*,[21] that there had been a case in the Exchequer tried by him at Newcastle Spring Assizes 1859, in which a chemist who sold ointment to rub sheep with was held liable to pay to their owner the whole of their value (£2,000 and upwards) its having killed them, " although it was hard that a man who could only make a profit of a few pence should be made responsible for so heavy a loss."

109 (*b*) *The kind of damage in cases of strict liability at common law.* The Judicial Committee expressly stated that in *The Wagon Mound* (*No.* 1) nothing that their Lordships had said was intended to reflect on the so-called rule of " strict liability " exemplified in *Rylands* v. *Fletcher*.[22] Liability is " strict " in such cases since a defendant is liable without fault on his part if the harmful event occurs, even though its happening was not to be foreseen. However, once he is liable, because the harmful event or the escape of the dangerous thing has taken place, he is only liable to compensate the plaintiff for the kind of damage, which foreseeably would be expected to follow the event. In the result the test for remoteness must be directness and not foresight.

110 (*c*) *The kind of damage in cases of strict liability imposed by statute.* The

19 1962 S.L.T. 168.
20 [1967] 1 W.L.R. 337.
21 (1866) L.R. 1 C.P. 559, 561.
22 (1868) L.R. 3 H.L. 330. Presumably this must include cattle-trespass and liability for dangerous animals.

same principle applies where there is the breach of statutory provision which has imposed an absolute duty on the defendant.

Examples are typified by cases under section 12, 13 and 14 of the Factories Act 1961 which relate to obligations to fence dangerous moving parts of sources of power, transmission and other machinery.

In *Galashiels Gas Co. Ltd.* v. *Millar* [23] the defendant's electrically operated lift failed, when the deceased stoker was using it to raise a full bogey of coke which was being removed from a retort after its discharge. By the appropriate section under the Factories Act 1937 an absolute and continuing obligation was imposed so that proof of any failure in the mechanism of a hoist or lift established a breach of the statutory duty, even though it was impossible to anticipate that failure before the event or to explain it afterwards and even though all reasonable steps had been taken to provide a suitable hoist or lift and to maintain it properly. Since the death of the deceased was a foreseeable kind of damage resulting, the defendants were liable.

111 (*d*) *Under the Fatal Accidents Acts claim.* Since the right of action is given to certain specified dependants of a deceased person for the pecuniary loss they have suffered from the death of that person caused by the wrongful act, neglect or default of the defendant, once that causal nexus has been established then the extent of their actual and prospective losses, even if unforeseeable, are recoverable. This is because such losses are the kind of harm for which the statutory law gives compensation.

The same principle would apply to an action by a husband suing for the loss of consortium of his wife, since he has been deprived of her services, so that the test of remoteness is once more directness and not foresight.

112 (*e*) *Where the damage is not of the kind against which it was the defendant's duty to guard.* When a statute creates a duty with the object of preventing a mischief of a particular kind, a person who, by reason of another's neglect of the statutory duty, suffers a loss of a different kind is not entitled to maintain an action in respect of such loss.

An illustration of this is to be found in *Gorris* v. *Scott* [24] where the defendant ship owner undertook to carry the plaintiff's sheep from Hamburg to Newcastle upon Tyne. On the voyage across some of the sheep were washed overboard by reason of the defendant's neglect to take a precaution enjoined by an order of Privy Council, made under the authority of the Contagious Diseases (Animals) Act 1869, s. 75, requiring the place on board the ship occupied by the sheep to be divided into pens by substantial divisions. The Court of Exchequer held that the plaintiff's claim failed, since the object of the statutory provisions was to prevent the spread of contagious disease amongst the animals and not to provide protection for them against perils of the sea.

[23] [1949] A.C. 275.
[24] (1874) L.R. 9 Ex. 125.

113 **Novus actus interveniens.** It is necessary at this stage to consider those situations where damage has resulted from the act of a third party, who is independent of the defendant himself, since it can often become a very difficult matter to discover any causal connection between the defendant's wrongful act and the damage suffered by the plaintiff. In *Weld-Blundell* v. *Stephens* [25] Lord Sumner said: " In general (apart from special contracts and relations and the maxim *respondeat superior*), even although A is in fault, he is not responsible for injury to C, which B, a stranger to him, deliberately chooses to do. Though A may have given the occasion for B's mischievous activity, B then becomes a new and independent cause." [26] So, too, said Lord Wright: " To break the chain of causation it must be shown that there is something which I will call ultroneous, something unwarrantable, a new cause which disturbs the sequences of events, something which can be described as either unreasonable or extraneous or extrinsic." [27]

It is not at all easy to find out from the authorities what tests have to be applied in order to find the solution to the problem in hand. It is revealing that Lord Wright found it very difficult to formulate any precise and all-embracing rule and said: " Certain well-known formulae are invoked, such as that the chain of causation was broken and that there was a *novus actus interveniens.* These phrases, sanctified as they are by standing authority, only mean that there was not such a direct relationship between the act of negligence and the injury that the one can be treated as flowing directly from the other. Cases have been cited which show great difference of opinion on the true answer in the various circumstances to the question whether the damage was direct or too remote. . . . It may be said that in dealing with the law of negligence it is possible to state general propositions, but when you come to apply those principles to determine whether there has been actionable negligence in any particular case, you must deal with the case on its facts." [28]

114 **Reasonableness as a test as well as foreseeability.** If the act of another is done reasonably as a result of the defendant's negligence the consequences of that fresh act are not too remote. Lord Herschell [29] considered that damages which flowed directly and naturally or " in the ordinary course of things " from the wrongful act could not be regarded as too remote. To which Lindley L.J. added in *The City of Lincoln*: " We have then to consider what is the meaning of ' the ordinary course of things.' Sir Walter Phillimore has asked us to exclude from it all human conduct. I can do nothing of the kind. I take it that reasonable human conduct is part of the ordinary course of things. So far as I can see my way to

25 [1920] A.C. 956.
26 *Ibid.* at p. 986. As was pointed out in *Stansbie* v. *Troman* [1948] 2 K.B. 48, this dictum was not intended to apply to cases where the act of negligence itself consisted in the failure to take reasonable care to guard against the very thing that did in fact happen.
27 *The Oropesa* [1943] P. 32, 39. See also the discussion of *novus actus interveniens* in *Minister of Pensions* v. *Chennell* [1947] K.B. 250.
28 *Ibid.* at p. 36.
29 *The Argentino* (1889) 14 App.Cas. 519, 523.

any definite proposition I should say that the ordinary course of things does not exclude all human conduct, but includes at least the reasonable conduct of those who have sustained the damage, and who are seeking to save further loss." [30]

115 It follows that the intervening conduct must be regarded in the light of whether it was done reasonably or not as a result of the defendant's negligence by balancing it against the latter's wrongful act. It is only where the unreasonableness of the intervening act so overwhelms the latter's wrongdoing that it can be said to be a *novus actus interveniens* otherwise the defendant as the original wrongdoer, cannot avoid responsibility. It is a matter of opinion based upon the facts of each case whether the intervening act is reasonable and arises in " the ordinary course of things." The question of foreseeability too was dealt with by Hamilton L.J. who said: " No doubt each intervener is a *causa sine qua non*, but unless the intervention is a fresh, independent cause, the person guilty of the original negligence will be the effective cause, if he ought reasonably to have anticipated such interventions and to have foreseen that if they occurred the result would be that his negligence would lead to mischief." [31]

116 Nevertheless foreseeability must not be regarded as the only or even the decisive test of *novus actus interveniens*.[32] On this point Salmon L.J. said: " Although the foreseeability test is a handmaiden of the law, it is by no means a maid-of-all-work. To my mind, it cannot serve as the true criterion when the question is, how was the damage caused? It may be a useful guide, but it is by no means the true criterion. For example, in *Bolton* v. *Stone* [33] the celebrated case of the cricket ball being hit for a six out of the ground and injuring the plaintiff, it was held that the defendant was not negligent because it could not reasonably be foreseen that a cricket ball hit out of the ground was likely to injure a passer-by. So the damage that occurred in that case was not reasonably foreseeable. Yet quite obviously that damage was caused by the cricket ball being hit out of the ground." [34] It seems therefore that both reasonableness and foreseeability, as tests, play two distinct roles, which may well be concurrent or may even overlap in any given case. Hence consequences due to a fresh, independent act, which is not one that ought

[30] (1890) 15 P.D. 15, 18.

[31] *Latham* v. *R. Johnson & Nephew Ltd.* [1913] 1 K.B. 398, 413. See also *Iron and Steel Holdings and Realisation Agency* v. *Compensation Appeal Tribunal* [1966] 1 W.L.R. 480, *per* Winn L.J. at p. 492: " In my opinion, wherever any intervening factor was itself foreseeable or reasonably foreseeable by the actor, the person responsible for the act which initiated the chain of causes leading to the final result, that intervening cause is not itself, in the legal sense, a *novus actus interveniens* breaking the chain of causation and isolating the initial act from the final result."

[32] Whilst foreseeability according to *The Wagon Mound* (*No.* 1) [1961] A.C. 388 should be considered to be the test in every case, yet, as pointed out in the text, this cannot be the only criterion.

[33] [1951] A.C. 850.

[34] *Quinn* v. *Burch Bros.* (*Builders*) *Ltd.* [1966] 2 Q.B. 370, 394.

reasonably to have been foreseen as likely to follow the negligent wrongdoing are too remote.

117 Accordingly, when the defendants' railway engine negligently entered the plaintiff's garden and damage was caused, not only by the engine itself and by those engaged in removing it, but also by a crowd of persons who entered the garden to gratify their curiosity, it was held that damage due to the crowd could not be recovered.[35] Again, where a railway company negligently permitted a carriage to be overcrowded, and the plaintiff was hustled and robbed in the overcrowded carriage, it was held that the plaintiff could not recover because, among other grounds, the overcrowding did not conduce in any way, directly or indirectly, to the robbery.[36] Also, when three ships, the *Paludina*, the *Singleton Abbey* and the *Sara* were moored by their sterns to the quay, the *Paludina*, as a result of negligence, dragged her anchors and fell down upon the *Singleton Abbey*. In their struggles to get free, the *Singleton Abbey* parted from her moorings and fell down upon the *Sara* and cast her adrift, with the result that some twenty minutes later there was a collision between the *Singleton Abbey* and the *Sara* in which the *Sara* was sunk. It was held, in an action to decide the liability for the final collision between the *Singleton Abbey* and the *Sara*, that the final collision was not caused by the negligence of the *Paludina*, the action of the *Sara* constituting a *novus actus interveniens.*[37]

118 Where the plaintiff's employers provided him with a chisel, the steel for which had been provided but had been negligently hardened by the manufacturers' suppliers (the third party), and the plaintiff was injured whilst using it, it was held that the employers alone were liable, since they had not withdrawn the implement from use after an accident had occurred some four weeks previously, when the chisel had thrown off a splinter whilst in use. The manufacturers of the chisel were held by Baker J. not to be vicariously liable for their suppliers' negligence because, *inter alia*, the keeping of the chisel in use by the plaintiff's employers with the knowledge that it was dangerous broke the chain of causation.[38]

119 On the other hand in *The Oropesa* [39] a collision occurred at sea between the *Oropesa* and the *Manchester Regiment*, causing it severe damage, which was due to the negligent navigation of the former vessel. The captain of the *Manchester Regiment* put out in a lifeboat in order to consult with the captain of the *Oropesa* with a view to saving the damaged ship but the lifeboat capsized during the voyage in heavy seas with loss of life. In the ensuing action against the *Oropesa* it was contended that the

[35] *Scholes* v. *North London Ry.* (1870) 21 L.T. 835. *Cf. Scott's Trustees* v. *Moss* (1889) 17 R. 32 (crowd gathered to watch an advertised parachute descent).
[36] *Cobb* v. *G.W. Ry.* [1894] A.C. 419.
[37] *Singleton Abbey* (*SS.*) v. *Paludina* (*SS.*) [1927] A.C. 16.
[38] *Taylor* v. *Rover Co.* [1966] 1 W.L.R. 1491.
[39] [1943] P. 32. But *cf. The Empire Squire* (1943) 169 L.T. 252 where it was held that the master's action was unreasonable.

death of the seamen was the result of the decision of the captain of the *Manchester Regiment* in putting to sea in the lifeboat and not of the negligence of the *Oropesa* in causing the collision. The Court of Appeal held that as the captain's decision was a reasonable one in the circumstances, it did not constitute a *novus actus interveniens*. Similarly in *The Guildford* [40] the captain of the damaged ship refused an offer of immediate towage by the other ship, which was heavily laden, on the ground that it was impracticable to be towed by it in such circumstances. Later, whilst being towed by a tug, she sank within a short distance of a suitable place where she could have been beached. It was held that the refusal of the immediate towage was reasonable and so did not constitute a *novus actus interveniens*. When a water board maintained in the street a metal cover for a valve box and some third person unknown pulled it open so that the plaintiff, while crossing the road with reasonable care, tripped over it and fell, it was held that the water board were liable, because they ought to have anticipated some such conduct on the part of mischievous boys.[41] The suicide of a man injured by the defendants' negligence, which is directly traceable to his injury, is not a *novus actus interveniens* so as to break the chain of causation between the injury and the death despite " the deceased's irrational and, no doubt, felonious act in taking his own life." [42] In *Schneider* v. *Eisovitch* [43] a motor accident happened in which the plaintiff was seriously injured and her husband was killed, due to the negligence of the defendant driver. When she recovered consciousness she had to be told of her husband's death whereupon she suffered an additional shock which produced further illness. It was held that the defendant was liable for this additional injury, since the fact of her being told of the death in the circumstances was the direct result of his negligence and also, because the fact of telling her was a reasonable thing to be expected to be done, so that it had not broken the chain of causation. A deliberate unlawful act such as housebreaking will not necessarily exempt the defendant from his liability for his antecedent negligence, where such an act could be reasonably foreseen and ought to have been guarded against at the time. Thus when a painter decorator, working in a house under contract with the occupier, knowing that he was alone in the home left the door unlocked whilst he went away for two hours to fetch more

40 [1956] P. 364.

41 *Wells* v. *Metropolitan Water Board* [1937] 4 All E.R. 639. But *cf. Simpson* v. *Metropolitan Water Board* (1917) 15 L.G.R. 629. Further, in *McCarthy* v. *Wellington City* [1966] N.Z.L.R. 481, where the occupiers of premises, containing stored explosives, failed to guard against the foreseeable mischievous acts of children, they were held liable. In a similar case, however, whilst it was held that the railways board were under a duty to use reasonable care to keep their detonators, which were dangerous things, safely, they could not have foreseen in the circumstances the theft of such detonators by trespassing boys: *Kingzett* v. *British Railways Board, The Times*, July 10, 1968. See also *Haynes* v. *Harwood* [1935] 1 K.B. 146 (where a mischievous child frightened an unattended horse in the street).

42 *Pigney* v. *Pointers Transport Services Ltd.* [1957] 1 W.L.R. 1121, *per* Pilcher J. at p. 1126, following *Cavanagh* v. *London Transport Executive, The Times*, October 23, 1956; but *cf. Freeman* v. *Minister of Pensions and National Insurance* [1966] 1 W.L.R. 456; *Farmer* v. *Rash* [1969] 1 W.L.R. 160

43 [1960] 2 Q.B. 430.

wallpaper and, during that time, a thief entered the house and stole valuables, the decorator was held liable in damages.[44]

20 Where the plaintiff was thrown down whilst climbing on to a tramcar, because some unknown person had rung the starting bell whilst the conductor, in breach of his duty, was still upstairs and was not on the platform, it was held that the defendants were liable on the basis that an unauthorised or wrongful act of a third person does not break the chain of causation, if it might be reasonably foreseen.[45] When a barge was properly tied up at a wharf on the Thames at a place where it was known that children and youths were wont to interfere with barges, and some unknown persons loosened the barge so that it collided with an eight-oared skiff rowed by a ladies' rowing eight crew, the barge owners were held liable for not fastening the barge more securely; it was not enough for them to prove that the cause of the damage was wrongful interference.[46]

The illustrations given in the preceding paragraph show that it is immaterial whether the act of the third party is a wilful act, a negligent act or even a lawful act, the sole question being whether it ought reasonably to have been foreseen as likely to follow upon the defendant's negligence.[47]

21 **The fresh independent act of the plaintiff.** The fresh independent act may be that of the plaintiff himself or of his servants or agents. This is illustrated by the *San Onofre*.[48] There, the vessels of the plaintiffs and the defendants came into collision owing to the defendants' negligence. The defendants' vessel was seriously damaged but the plaintiffs' vessel was only slightly damaged, whereupon the plaintiffs' vessel endeavoured to save the defendants' vessel by lashing her alongside and towing her inshore. During this towage the plaintiffs' vessel grounded in a fog and was further damaged, and it was held that this further damage was too remote a consequence of the original negligence. In his judgment Scrutton L.J. said: " The question whether damage is sufficiently direct consequence of negligence to be recoverable, or is too remote, is rather a question of first impression. I am clear that if a negligent driver on the road injures himself in a collision with another vehicle, whose driver and a stranger thereupon take the injured man to hospital and meet with an accident in so doing, neither of them can recover damages for the accident from the negligent driver as consequences of his original negligence. The present case seems to be exactly similar." [49]

[44] *Stansbie* v. *Troman* [1948] 2 K.B. 48. See also *Dorset Yacht Co. Ltd.* v. *Home Office* [1970] A.C. 1004.
[45] *Davies* v. *Liverpool Corporation* [1949] 2 All E.R. 175.
[46] *Newby* v. *General Lighterage Co. Ltd.*, [1955] 1 Lloyd's Rep. 273.
[47] *S.S. Singleton Abbey* v. *S.S. Paludina* [1937] A.C. 16, *per* Lord Sumner at p. 28: " Cause and consequence in such a matter do not depend on the question, whether the first action, which intervenes, is excusable or not, but on the question whether it is new and independent or not."
[48] [1922] P. 243.
[49] *Ibid.* at p. 253.

122 In *Quinn* v. *Burch Brothers* (*Builders*) *Ltd.*[50] it was held that the defendants, as the main contractors, were in breach of contract in failing to supply a step-ladder to the plaintiff, an independent sub-contractor. However, when the plaintiff borrowed a trestle, which he failed to have footed, and fell it was held that even if the defendants could have foreseen that their failure to supply the plaintiff with the step-ladder might have resulted in the accident, yet their breach of contract did not cause the accident. Their breach merely gave the plaintiff the opportunity to injure himself by the negligent use of unsuitable equipment, which he had selected, so that his action failed.

In *Alston* v. *Marine & Trade Insurance Co. Ltd.*[51] the plaintiff was involved in a motor accident, for which the defendants had accepted liability in negligence, as a result of which he sustained a brain injury that was held to be properly treated by the use of a drug called parstellin. Unfortunately, he ate cheese, which was not an unreasonable thing to do in the light of medical knowledge then, but in the event he suffered a stroke because the consumption of cheese when combined with the taking of the drug produced dangerous side-effects. The court held that the defendants were not liable in respect of the stroke, since the eating of the cheese constituted a *novus actus interveniens*. This case, perhaps, provides an unusual illustration not only of the fact that the fresh independent act was that of the plaintiff himself but that the test applied in the case could not have been the one of reasonableness, since the plaintiff's conduct in eating cheese was a perfectly reasonable one.

123 On the other hand, the following are examples of where the defendants have not succeeded in avoiding liability although the intervening conduct was the deliberate act of the plaintiff.[52] Where the defendants by mistake delivered five cases of scrap film to the plaintiffs' premises, instead of to another address along the same street, and the plaintiffs' typist touched a piece of the scrap with a lighted cigarette end, with the intention of making " a small innocuous fire," a serious explosion resulted, whereby the plaintiffs' premises were damaged by fire. The court held that the typist's act was not *novus actus interveniens*, relieving the defendants of liability for their original negligence, since although she knew that the scrap would burn, she had no idea that it was so violently inflammable.[53] Where the plaintiff knew that there was danger in cleaning the window of her home, because one sash had already broken, her conduct in opening and cleaning the window which fell and crushed her hand, was lawful, reasonable and free from blame and was in the ordinary

[50] [1966] 2 Q.B. 370. See also *Vacwell Engineering Co. Ltd.* v. *B.D.H. Chemicals Ltd.* [1971] 1 Q.B. 88; *McKew* v. *Holland & Hannen & Cubitts* (*Scotland*) [1969] 3 All E.R. 1621, H.L. But *cf.* the decision of Eveleigh J. in *Wieland* v. *Cyril Lord Carpets* [1969] 3 All E.R. 1006.

[51] 1964 (4) S.A. 112.

[52] In *Weld-Blundell* v. *Stephens* [1920] A.C. 956 Lord Sumner at pp. 984–985 set out a series of situation categories, where this could happen.

[53] *Philco Radio and Television Corporation of Great Britain Ltd.* v. *J. Spurling Ltd.* [1949] 2 All E.R. 882.

course of things so that the defendants could not avoid liability.[54] Where the plaintiff's husband had suffered a shock by falling glass from a skylight in the roof of a shop, due to the defendant's negligence in carrying out repairs, the plaintiff, reasonably believing her husband to be in danger, instinctively clutched his arm and tried to pull him clear. In so doing she strained herself and suffered injury for which the defendants were held liable.[55] Where a plaintiff, finding herself locked in a cubicle of the defendants' public lavatory, fell and was injured whilst returning to floor level after making an unsuccessful attempt to climb out over the top, it was held that the defendants were liable. It was the duty of the court to balance the risk taken by the plaintiff against the consequences of the defendants' breach of duty and, since the inconvenience caused to her was appreciable, she had not taken any risk which was so disproportionate to the necessities of her situation.[56] Also under these considerations, generally, come the " rescue cases " since it may be foreseeable that attempts at rescue would be made and in so far as such an attempt or act of rescue is reasonable in the circumstances of the case it does not eclipse the wrong created by the negligence of the defendants in the first instance.[57]

124 **Acts done to minimise the plaintiffs' damage.** Since it is the duty of the plaintiff to minimise his damage, no act which he does reasonably towards that end will break the chain of causation.[58] Lord Wrenbury said: " It is undoubted law that a plaintiff who sues for damages owes the duty of taking all reasonable steps to mitigate the loss consequent upon the breach and cannot claim as damages any sum which is due to his own neglect." [59] Thus, " if a man suffering from a sprained leg wishes to win a prize in a high-jump competition and proceeds to endeavour to win it and thereby makes his leg so much worse that it takes an additional six months to recover he is only entitled to damages for such part of his suffering as was not due to such heedless conduct. Upon the other hand it could scarcely be suggested that the fact of a man who is suffering from an injury to his eye glancing at a newspaper occasionally before his eye has quite regained its usual strength, would be wanton, heedless, or careless action on his part." [60]

Further a plaintiff may not increase the damages claimed by his own

[54] [1943] A.C. 283. *Cf. Leach* v. *Standard Telephones & Cables Ltd.* [1966] 1 W.L.R. 1392.
[55] *Brandon* v. *Osborne, Garrett & Co. Ltd.* [1924] 1 K.B. 548.
[56] *Sayers* v. *Harlow U.D.C.* [1958] 1 W.L.R. 623.
[57] See *Cutler* v. *United Dairies* (*London*) *Ltd.* [1933] 2 K.B. 297; *Haynes* v. *Harwood* [1935] 1 K.B. 146; *The Gusty* [1940] P. 159; *Morgan* v. *Aylen* [1942] 1 All E.R. 489; *Hyett* v. *Great Western Railway* [1948] 1 K.B. 345; *Baker* v. *T. E. Hopkins & Sons Ltd.* [1959] 1 W.L.R. 966; *Videan* v. *B.T.C.* [1963] 2 Q.B. 650; *Chadwick* v. *B.R.B.* [1967] 1 W.L.R. 912. See also § 67, *ante*.
[58] *Dee Conservancy Board* v. *McConnell* [1928] 2 K.B. 159.
[59] *Jamal* v. *Moolla Dawood Sons & Co.* [1916] A.C. 175, 179.
[60] *Jones* v. *Watney, Combe, Reid & Co. Ltd.* (1912) 28 T.L.R. 399, *per* Lush J. at pp. 399–400. Failure to wear a crash helmet reduced a moped rider's damages by 15 per cent., *O'Connell* v. *Jackson, The Times*, July 8, 1971.

unnecessary act. In *Admiralty Commissioners* v. *S.S. Amerika*,[61] where a submarine was sunk by the defendants' negligence and the crew were drowned, the Commissioners claimed as an item of damage the capitalised amount of the pensions payable by them to the crew's relatives. Since the pensions were voluntary payments in the nature of compassionate allowances, the court held that this could not be recovered: although the defendants' negligence had provided the occasion, it was not the cause of the damage. In *Attorney-General* v. *Valle-Jones* [62] it was held that the Crown was entitled to maintain a claim against the defendant for loss of service of the men by his negligence and to recover any damage which it had thereby suffered. The measure of that damage was the amount of the wages and rations of the men during their incapacity and the expenses of their hospital treatment, the amount of which payments, allowances and expenses, if they had not been borne by the Crown, could have been recovered by the men from the defendant as damages. Where a plaintiff refuses to accept medical advice or treatment, such refusal may in all the circumstances be unreasonable; thus damages should be assessed as if the plaintiff had undergone the treatment and it had been as successful as opined.[63] On the other hand, the defendant will be held liable in full if the original injury still subsists, but in an aggravated form, despite his undergoing an operation, prudently advised, which had been properly carried out.[64] If a damaged chattel was unique in character its owner may be entitled to the cost of repairing it at a cost considerably exceeding its market value [65] but not otherwise since he has not taken reasonable steps to mitigate his loss.[66] The question what is reasonable for a plaintiff to do in mitigation of his damages is not a question of law but one of fact in each case, the burden of proof being upon the defendant.[67]

125 **Failure of an expected intervening act to occur.** Finally, the situation must be considered where the defendant anticipates that a third party will do some intervening act and, if he is reasonably entitled to rely upon that other doing so, he may be relieved of liability. Thus in actions against the manufacturers, retailers, repairers and transferors of goods the damage is not too remote if no examination of the goods is anticipated.[68] On the other hand if such manufacturer, retailer, repairer or transferor of goods could reasonably expect an intermediate examination or some important instruction to be carried out he can avoid liability for the damage arising from the defect, which would have been disclosed by such

61 [1917] A.C. 38.
62 [1935] 2 K.B. 209.
63 *McAuley* v. *London Transport Executive* [1957] 2 Lloyd's Rep. 500.
64 *Hogan* v. *Bentinck West Hartley Collieries (Owners) Ltd.* [1949] 1 All E.R. 588.
65 *O'Grady* v. *Westminster Scaffolding Ltd.* [1962] 2 Lloyd's Rep. 238. (The car had been a 1938 M.G. but had been converted into a unique article " like a mechanised replica of the Lord Mayor's coach " and was proudly called " Hortensia " but she was somewhat unkindly referred to as a " freak " by Pennycuick J. [1963] 1 W.L.R. 1079.) See § 158, *post*.
66 *Darbishire* v. *Warran* [1963] 1 W.L.R. 1067.
67 *Roper* v. *Johnson* (1873) L.R. 8 C.P. 167, 181, *per* Brett J.
68 *Donoghue* v. *Stevenson* [1932] A.C. 562; *Brown* v. *Cotterill* (1934) 51 T.L.R. 21.

examination, or for the damage arising from the failure to carry out the instructions properly.[69] For example, if a noxious hair dye is manufactured and supplied without any instruction for a skin test to be made before use, the resulting damage is not too remote [70] but if such instructions are given but are disregarded by the plaintiff, then the damage is too remote and the defendant can avoid liability.[71] A building contractor was not liable for damage which resulted from making the passage of an air-raid shelter dark, because it had been passed by inspection of the local authority as being in accordance with the contract.[72] A sub-contractor equally avoided liability, where a stop-cock had been carelessly painted over, but it was reasonably anticipated that the work would have to be inspected and passed under contract.[73] Where a building contractor's labourer was injured when a dangerous wall which had been left purposely standing by the demolition contractors, who were acting under the advice of an architect, collapsed, although no one had carried out a proper inspection of it beforehand it was held that the architect, the demolition contractors and the workman's employers were all jointly liable. The architect and the demolition contractors could not escape liability, unless they could show that such examination by the building contractors was reasonably to be expected as a probability.[74]

69 *Haseldine* v. *Daw & Son* [1941] 2 K.B. 343, approving *Herschtal* v. *Stewart & Ardern* [1940] 1 K.B. 155.
70 *Parker* v. *Oxolo Ltd.* [1937] 3 All E.R. 524.
71 *Holmes* v. *Ashford* [1950] 2 All E.R. 76.
72 *Buckner* v. *Ashby* [1941] 1 K.B. 321.
73 *Duncan* v. *Cammell Laird* [1943] 2 All E.R. 621 (reversed on other grounds *sub nom. Woods* v. *Duncan* [1946] A.C. 401).
74 *Clay* v. *A. J. Crump & Sons Ltd.* [1964] 1 Q.B. 533; followed in *Driver* v. *W. Willett (Contractors) Ltd.* [1969] 1 All E.R. 665.

CHAPTER 4

DAMAGES

1. INTRODUCTION

126 **General Principles.** The principle on which damages for negligence are assessed is that they are to be regarded as compensation for an injury sustained and not punishment for a wrong inflicted. Since damage is essential to an action for negligence, no such action lies for nominal damages.[1] The measure of damages is that the injured party is to be placed as far as money can do it in the same position as he would have been in but for the negligence of the defendant, subject to the rules of law as to remoteness of damage, with the addition, in cases of personal injuries, of a reasonable sum for the pain and suffering sustained.[2]

127 **General and special damages.** Damages are divided into general and special damages. General damages are those which the law presumes to flow from the negligence complained of. These damages must be proved, but it is not necessary to allege them in detail in the statement of claim, and particulars will not be ordered.[3] Special damages in this connection means some specific item of loss which the plaintiff alleges is the result of the defendant's negligence in the particular case, although it is not presumed by the law to flow from the negligence as a matter of course. Full particulars of all special damage must be given and, if not given, will be ordered.[4] Loss of profits is special damage and must be specifically pleaded, it being insufficient merely to claim "damages."[5] Further, there should also be pleaded any special circumstances, which probably will lead the injured plaintiff to suffer financial losses in the future that may not in the ordinary way reasonably be expected to flow from the accident.[6]

[1] *Munday Ltd.* v. *L.C.C.* [1916] 2 K.B. 331 (in an action for negligence payment into court admitting negligence but denying damage is a denial of liability, as damage is the gist of the Action); *Hambrook* v. *Stokes Bros.* [1925] 1 K.B. 141, 156, *per* Atkin L.J.; *The Amerika* [1917] A.C. 38, 60, *per* Lord Sumner.

[2] *Livingstone* v. *Haywards Coal Co.* (1880) 5 App.Cas. 25, *per* Lord Blackburn at p. 39; *Phillips* v. *L. & S.W. Ry.* (1879) 5 Q.B.D. 78, 87, *per* James L.J.; *The Mediana* [1900] A.C. 113, 119; *The Liesbosch* v. *The Edison* [1933] A.C. 449, *per* Lord Wright, "the dominant rule of law is the principle of *restitutio in integrum*"; *Admiralty Commrs.* v. *SS. Susquehanna* [1926] A.C. 655, 661. In *Rushton* v. *N.C.B.* [1953] 1 Q.B. 495, *per* Romer L.J. at p. 502: "The principle has been adopted (and it is the only possible principle which can be adopted) of trying to compensate a man in the plight in which this plaintiff finds himself by awarding what may fairly be described as notional or theoretical compensation to take the place of that which is not possible, namely, actual compensation." For a slight injury, see *Parry* v. *English Electric Co. Ltd.* [1971] 2 All E.R. 1094.

[3] *London and Northern Bank* v. *George Newnes Ltd.* (1900) 16 T.L.R. 433.

[4] *Watson* v. *North Metropolitan Tramways Co.* (1886) 3 T.L.R. 273.

[5] *Perestrello E. Companhia Ltd.* v. *United Paint Co.* [1969] 1 W.L.R. 570.

[6] *Domsalla* v. *Barr* [1969] 1 W.L.R. 630.

Exemplary damages. Exemplary damages can be given in actions of negligence, although they are virtually unknown. They are only given in cases of "wilful negligence," that is where the negligence is accompanied with a contempt of the plaintiff's rights and convenience. Where the defendant was required by the police to pull down a dilapidated building adjoining the stable of the plaintiff, and did so in such a reckless manner that a large piece of timber fell on the plaintiff's stable, knocked in the roof and damaged the plaintiff's horse and cart, and, on the plaintiff's remonstrating with him, he told the workmen to "work anyhow," whereby great quantities of bricks were thrown upon the stable, it was held that the defendant was liable to pay exemplary damages.[7] During the argument, Pollock C.B. said: "It is very improbable that the question of motive should arise in an action for negligence; but if it does, the judge is warranted in telling the jury that if the defendant did not intend any wrong, they should limit their verdict to the damage really sustained; but if the injury was committed in an insolent way, they might take into consideration the motive and give exemplary damages," [8] and Wilde B. said; "Suppose a servant, while driving, was in the act of pulling up to prevent running against some person, and his master said: 'Never mind drive on,' might not the jury take that into consideration?" [9]

9 **Minimising the damages.** Damages can be diminished by showing that the loss, or part of it, was the result of unreasonable conduct [9a] on the part of the plaintiff subsequent to the defendant's negligence. "No person aggrieved by an injury is by common law entitled to increase his claim for damage by any voluntary act; on the contrary, it is his duty, if he reasonably can, to abstain from any act by which the damage could be in any way increased." [10] So, it was held that pensions paid voluntarily by the Admiralty to the dependants of sailors in the Navy who were drowned as the result of the defendant's negligence were not recoverable from the defendants. The same principle was stated by MacKinnon J. thus: "A person is entitled to recover only those damages which he has incurred while acting reasonably, and, if acting reasonably he could have minimised or reduced the damage that he has sustained to a smaller amount, it is only that smaller amount that he can recover." [11] The standard of reasonableness depends on the circumstances, and it is not unreasonable for an employer to refrain from dismissing a servant injured by the defendant's negligence, although he could legally do so, with the sole object of minimising the damages recoverable from the

[7] *Emblen* v. *Myers* (1860) 6 H. & N. 54. Followed, *Bell* v. *Midland Ry.* (1861) 10 C.B.(N.S.) 287; *Thompson* v. *Hill* (1870) L.R. 5 C.P. 564.

[8] *Ibid.*, at pp. 57, 58.

[9] *Ibid.* at p. 58.

[9a] *Eley* v. *Bedford, The Times*, May 5, 1971 (failure to claim disablement benefit was held not to be unreasonable conduct). Further see *post*, § 150.

[10] *Per* Lord Parker in *Admiralty Commrs.* v. *SS. Amerika* [1917] A.C. 38, 42, *e.g.* the plaintiff did not act reasonably or mitigate his loss when he had his damaged car repaired at a cost exceeding its market value: *Darbishire* v. *Warran* [1963] 1 W.L.R. 1067.

[11] *Att.-Gen.* v. *Valle-Jones* [1935] 2 K.B. 209, 219. This decision, however, was not approved in *Att.-Gen. for New South Wales* v. *Perpetual Trustee Co. Ltd.* [1955] A.C. 457.

defendant.[12] In an action for damages for personal injuries, Lush J. put to the jury " Has the plaintiff by any wanton, careless or needless conduct retarded her own recovery? " and on their answering it in the negative, intimated to them that had their answer been in the affirmative they would have had to deduct from the damages such portion as was attributable to her own conduct.[13] In *James* v. *Woodhall Duckham Construction Co.*[14] the Court of Appeal held that where the plaintiff was informed that his pain would disappear when his claim was settled, it was his duty to proceed expeditiously, hence he could not obtain damages for wages lost during a period of delay, which was due to his own fault and inaction. Similarly, a person who unreasonably refuses to undergo an operation or training cannot recover damages for incapacity which the operation [15] or the training [16] would have removed.

130 **Interference by appellate courts with awards of damages.** Prior to 1965 it was always stressed how, in considering an appeal on an award of damages assessed by a jury the approach of the court was different from its approach in cases tried by a judge alone.[17] Thus it was said, in the absence of any misdirection [18] or improper conduct at the trial, when damages had been assessed by a jury, the court would not set aside the assessment unless the amount was so small or so large that twelve sensible jurors could not reasonably have given the verdict, or such as to lead the court to the conclusion that the jury must have taken into consideration matter which they ought not to have considered, or that they have omitted to pay regard to matter which they ought to have considered. As an example, in *Morey* v. *Woodfield* [19] an infant plaintiff aged eleven who had become a quadriplegic as a result of the defendant's negligence was awarded £50,000 by a jury. The Court of Appeal refused to upset the jury's award, stating that the sum awarded was not such as no twelve reasonable men could have awarded, and that it was not out of all proportion.

131 While on a trial by judge alone, an appeal was a re-hearing of the case and accordingly the Court of Appeal could vary the amount of damages awarded to what they consider was the proper amount.[20] Then in 1965 an important landmark was reached when the full Court of Appeal in

12 *Att.-Gen.* v. *Valle-Jones, supra.*
13 *Jones* v. *Watney Combe & Co. Ltd.* (1912) 28 T.L.R. 399.
14 [1969] 1 W.L.R. 903.
15 *Tutton* v. *Majestic* [1909] 2 K.B. 54; *Warncken* v. *Moreland* [1909] 1 K.B. 184.
16 *McGowan* v. *Coltness Iron Co.*, 1945 S.L.T. 325.
17 *Johnston* v. *G.W. Ry.* [1904] 2 K.B. 250; *Smith* v. *Schilling* [1928] 1 K.B. 429; *Phillips* v. *L. & S.W. Ry.* (1879) 5 Q.B.D. 78. *Scott* v. *Musial* [1959] 2 Q.B. 429 at p. 438; *Wise* v. *Kaye* [1962] 1 Q.B. 638.
18 *Warren* v. *King* [1964] 1 W.L.R. 1; the jury's award of £50,000 was set aside by the Court of Appeal on the grounds that there had been such a misdirection that there had been a miscarriage of justice within the words of R.S.C., Ord. 58, r. 10 (2), and a new trial was ordered accordingly. A compromise of £35,000 was approved by the Court. See [1964] 1 W.L.R. 122n.
19 (No. 2) [1964] 1 Q.B. 1.
20 *Reaney* v. *C.W.S. Ltd.* [1932] W.N. 78.

Ward v. *James* [21] met to consider the whole problem anew and it confirmed the strict view that it should only be in exceptional cases of actions for personal injuries that a jury trial should be ordered in the future. Where, however, juries were so used the Court of Appeal no longer felt the same restraint in disturbing their awards as it had done in the past, Lord Denning M.R. saying: " We cannot change the principle on which [previous] cases were decided but we can, I think, alter the emphasis. In future this court will not feel the same hesitation as it formerly did in upsetting an award of damages by a jury. If it is ' out of all proportion to the circumstances of the case ' (that is, if it is far too high or far too low) this court will set it aside. On setting it aside this court has power, I think, to order the fresh assessment to be made by a judge alone." [22] As regards a trial by a judge alone the court has, however, said: " Unless we come to the conclusion that the learned judge took an erroneous view of the evidence as to the damage suffered by the plaintiff, or made some mistake in giving weight to evidence that ought not to have affected his mind, or in leaving out of consideration something that ought to have affected his mind, we ought not to interfere." [23] The appellate court will not interfere, merely because its members would themselves have decided upon a different figure, unless the judge has made " a wholly erroneous estimate of the damage suffered." [24] Although the Court of Appeal is slow to interfere with the award of a judge, it will do so more readily than in the case of the award of a jury, and in particular it will interfere if the sum awarded is out of line with the run of awards made in comparable cases in recent years.[25] It would seem therefore unlikely in practice that there will be any real difference in approach by the Court of Appeal when deciding whether or not to interfere with an award of damages, be it by a jury or a judge alone, on appeal against quantum. The tendency is towards a standardisation of damages, although it is recognised that exact standardisation is impossible and that the limits of variation are wide.

An award of damages to a plaintiff, whose injuries cannot be determined finally for a few years and thus may or may not become worse, will not be reduced on appeal unless wholly erroneous. In such a case

21 [1966] 1 Q.B. 273.

22 *Ibid.* at p. 301.

23 *Owen* v. *Sykes* [1936] 1 K.B. 192, 198, *per* Greer L.J. See also *Flint* v. *Lovell* [1935] 1 K.B. 354.

24 *Davies* v. *Powell Duffryn Associated Collieries* [1942] A.C. 601, 617, *per* Lord Wright. Damages were increased in *Roach* v. *Yates* [1938] 1 K.B. 256 (£2,750 to £6,542), *Davies* v. *Powell Duffryn Collieries Ltd.* [1942] A.C. 601 (£250 to £750), *Wormald* v. *Cole* [1954] 1 Q.B. 614 (£500 to £1,500) and *Nolan* v. *C. & C. Marshall Ltd.* [1954] 2 Q.B. 42 (£500 to £1,200), reduced in *Johnson* v. *Hill* [1945] 2 All E.R. 272 (£4,750 to £2,750), *Greenham* v. *Tecalemit Ltd.* [1948] W.N. 452 (£750 to £350), *Billingham* v. *Hughes* [1949] 1 K.B. 643 (£24,000 to £14,000) and *Bath* v. *British Transport Commission* [1954] 1 W.L.R. 1013 (£4,600 to £3,600), undisturbed, though thought to be very high in *Owen* v. *Sykes* [1936] 1 K.B. 192 (£10,000) and *Heaps* v. *Perrite Ltd.* [1937] 2 All E.R. 60 (£10,000).

25 *Bird* v. *Cocking & Sons Ltd.* [1951] 2 T.L.R. 1260 (£10,000 reduced to £7,000); *Rushton* v. *N.C.B.* [1953] 1 Q.B. 495 (£10,000 reduced to £7,000); *Mulready* v. *J. H. & W. Bell Ltd.* [1953] 2 Q.B. 117 (£7,600 reduced to £5,600); *Phillips* v. *Price*, *The Times*, October 29, 1957 (£1,750 reduced to £1,000); *Feistner* v. *Wills*, *The Times*, June 12, 1956 (£900 increased to £1,800); *Wilson* v. *Pilley* [1957] 1 W.L.R. 1138 (£75 increased to £200); *Clarke* v. *E .R. Wright & Son* [1957] 1 W.L.R. 1191 (£100 increased to £250).

the defendant should apply for a postponement of the issue of damages under R.S.C., Order 35, r. 3, or for an order for their assessment by a master or, preferably, a judge in court under Order 33, r. 5.[26]

As a general rule the Court of Appeal will only examine a party's physical condition at the hearing, in a case where the impression to be gained was purely objective, *e.g.* in cases of scarring or shortening of a limb, which could be seen but not where it depended in any way on the co-operation of the party being examined.[27]

Since, under R.S.C., Order 59, rr. 3 (1) and 10 (2), an appeal is by way of rehearing as at the date of such rehearing, the Court has a discretionary power to admit or refuse to admit new evidence and will generally admit it where the whole basis for the assessment of damages has altered in the meanwhile between the dates of the trial, and the hearing of the appeal.[28]

See Chapter 15, *post*, as regards other considerations where the appeal is from a county court.

132 **Survival of deceased's right of action.** The Law Reform (Miscellaneous Provisions) Act 1934, made an alteration in the law by providing that causes of action vested in a person at his death shall survive for the benefit of his estate. This Act was no doubt passed partly to provide a remedy against the estate of a person who was killed by his own negligence in an accident in which another was injured, and partly to deal with the state of affairs in such cases as *Pulling* v. *G.E. Ry.*,[29] where it was held that the administratrix of a person who was killed by the negligence of a railway company could not recover the loss of wages sustained and the expenses of medical attention and nursing which had been incurred between the date of the accident and the death. The Act provides:

" 1.—(1) Subject to the provisions of this section, on the death of any person after the commencement of this Act all causes of action subsisting against [30] or vested in him shall survive against, or, as the case may be for the benefit, of his estate. . . .

" (2) Where a cause of action survives as aforesaid for the benefit of the estate of a deceased person, the damages recoverable for the benefit of the estate of that person—

(*a*) shall not include any exemplary damages; . . .

(*c*) where the death of that person has been caused by the act or

[26] *Hawkins* v. *New Mendip Engineering* [1966] 1 W.L.R. 1341.

[27] *Stevens* v. *William Nash* [1966] 3 All E.R. 156.

[28] *Curwen* v. *James* [1963] 1 W.L.R. 748; in *Murphy* v. *Stone Wallwork* (*Charlton*) [1969] 1 W.L.R. 1023, the H.L. further increased an award of damages made by the C.A. which had assessed damages upon the basis that the employers would continue to employ the injured workman, when in fact they had dismissed him some fortnight after the successful hearing of his appeal.

[29] (1882) 9 Q.B.D. 110.

[30] If representation is not taken out, the court may appoint a person to defend the action under Ord. 16, r. 46, or a grant may be made to the Official Solicitor: *In the Goods of Knight* [1939] 3 All E.R. 928.

omission which gives rise to the cause of action, shall be calculated without reference to any loss or gain to his estate consequent on his death, except that a sum in respect of funeral expenses may be included.

"(3) No proceedings shall be maintainable in respect of a cause of action in tort [31] which by virtue of this section has survived against the estate of a deceased person, unless either—

(*a*) proceedings against him in respect of that cause of action were pending at the date of his death; or

(*b*) proceedings are taken in respect thereof not later than six months after his personal representative took out representation.[32]

"(4) Where damage has been suffered by reason of any act or omission in respect of which a cause of action would have subsisted against any person if that person had not died before or at the same time as the damage was suffered, there shall be deemed, for the purposes of this Act, to have been subsisting against him before his death such cause of action in respect of that act or omission as would have subsisted if he had died after the damage was suffered.

"(5) The rights conferred by this Act for the benefit of the estates of deceased persons shall be in addition to and not in derogation of any rights conferred on the dependants of deceased persons by the Fatal Accidents Acts 1846 to 1908,[33] and so much of this Act as relates to causes of action against the estates of deceased persons shall apply in relation to causes of action under the said Acts as it applies in relation to other causes of action not expressly excepted from the operation of subsection (1) of this section.

"(6) In the event of the insolvency of an estate against which proceedings are maintainable by virtue of this section, any liability in respect of the cause of action in respect of which the proceedings are maintainable shall be deemed to be a debt provable in the administration of the estate, notwithstanding that it is a demand in the nature of unliquidated damages arising otherwise than by a contract, promise or breach of trust."

3 The object of section 1 "is to put a person, who has by his negligence caused damage to someone who has subsequently died, in the same position as regards liability (subject to certain qualifications . . .) as he would have been in, if the injured person had sued and recovered

[31] Proceedings for contribution under s. 6 (1) (*c*) (*post*, § 895) of the Law Reform (Married Women and Tortfeasors) Act 1935 were not "proceedings . . . in respect of a cause of action in tort": *Harvey* v. *R. G. O'Dell Ltd., and Galway* [1958] 2 Q.B. 78 where it was held further that although the cause of action for contribution under the Act of 1935 did not arise until the time of judgment in the action by virtue of s. 1 (4) of the Act of 1934 it was to be deemed to have been a cause of action subsisting against the third party before his death, thus the defendant's claim under the Act of 1935 was not barred by s. 1 (3) of the Act of 1934.

[32] As amended by the Law Reform (Limitation of Actions, etc.) Act 1954, c. 36, s. 4.

[33] See now the Fatal Accidents Acts 1846–1959 and the Carriage by Air Act 1961.

judgment while still alive." [34] Accordingly, there can be recovered for the benefit of the estate of the deceased not only any expense to which the estate has been put, as was the case in *Pulling* v. *G.E. Ry.*,[35] but also damages for the pain and suffering experienced by the deceased and for his loss of expectation of life.[36] When the death results almost immediately from the injury or when the deceased is rendered unconscious by the accident and never recovers consciousness before death, or he exists in a cabbage-like state [37] or he remains in an unnatural state of euphoria,[38] until then no damages are recoverable for pain and suffering because none have been sustained.[39]

The damages include the costs of obtaining a grant of administration, if the grant was obtained solely to enable an action to be brought, but not the additional costs incurred by the personal representatives in consequence of the action, such as the cost of filing a corrective affidavit.[40]

Damages awarded under the Act for the benefit of the estate of the deceased must be taken into account so far as they increase the share coming to any individual dependant under the Fatal Accidents Acts and they will be deducted pound for pound.[41] Situations can arise where all the damages will be apportioned under the Act and none under the Fatal Accidents Acts at all.[42]

134 **Actions against the deceased's estate.** The aforesaid provisions of subsection (2) (*c*), that damages are to be calculated without reference to any loss or gain to the deceased's estate consequent on the death, prevent any account being taken of sums payable to his estate under policies of life or accident insurance, and also prevent account being taken of any loss his estate may have sustained through the loss of the deceased's earning capacity or of any other source of income, such as an annuity, which is terminable on his death.

The provisions of subsection (4) are presumably intended to deal with cases in which damage is essential to the cause of action. For example, a negligent manufacturer might manufacture noxious ginger beer which is not consumed for some months. If the consumer suffered damage from drinking it after the death of the manufacturer, he would have a right of action against the manufacturer's estate as if the manufacturer had died immediately after the consumer suffered damage, and

[34] *Rose* v. *Ford* [1937] A.C. 826, 838, *per* Lord Russell of Killowen.
[35] (1882) 9 Q.B.D. 110.
[36] *Rose* v. *Ford* [1937] A.C. 826. In this case " no issue arose " before the H.L. " on the question of amount ": *Benham* v. *Gambling* [1941] A.C. 157, 162.
[37] *McGrath Trailer Equipment Pty. Ltd.* v. *Smith* [1956] V.L.R. 738, and as in *West* (*H.*) *& Son Ltd.* v. *Shephard* [1964] A.C. 326.
[38] *Hayman* v. *Pike* [1958] S.A.S.R. 72.
[39] *Benham* v. *Gambling* [1941] A.C. 157, 162.
[40] *Thomas* v. *Cunard White Star* [1951] P. 153.
[41] *Rose* v. *Ford, supra*; *Davies* v. *Powell Duffryn Associated Collieries Ltd.* [1942] A.C. 601; *Bishop* v. *Cunard White Star Ltd.* [1950] P. 240.
[42] *Farmer* v. *Rash* [1969] 1 W.L.R. 160 (the plaintiff had been living separate and apart from her husband, who committed suicide a year after sustaining severe personal injuries in a motor accident).

his right of action would not be barred by the manufacturer's subsequent death. The effect of the subsection is, therefore, that in cases of negligence on the part of the deceased resulting in damage after his death, the right of the injured party to obtain damages from his estate is preserved, irrespective of the fact that the six months' period may have expired after his personal representative had taken out representation. For example, a claim for contribution under the Law Reform (Married Women and Tortfeasors) Act 1935, s. 6, can be brought by virtue of this subsection against the personal representatives of a deceased wrongdoer, regardless of the fact that the claimant's cause of action for contribution did not begin to exist until the injured party had proved liability against him and hence did not subsist against the deceased at the time of his death.[43]

5 The provisions of subsection (5) of section 1 of the Act of 1934 make the remedy against the estate of the deceased additional to remedies under the Fatal Accidents Acts and the Carriage by Air Act 1932.[44-45] The effect of this upon claims under the Fatal Accidents Acts is that if the damages awarded under the Law Reform (Miscellaneous Provisions) Act 1934 go, either on an intestacy or under the terms of the deceased's will, to any person who is a dependant under the Fatal Accidents Acts, they will *pro tanto* reduce the amount payable to that dependant under the latter Acts.[46] This is because in estimating pecuniary loss regard must be had to any benefits, other than certain benefits which have been or will be paid as a result of the death, *i.e.* any insurance money including a return of premiums, any National Insurance benefit or payment by a friendly society or trade union, paid for the relief or maintenance of a member's dependants, or any pension including a return of contributions or any lump sum payment in respect of a person's employment.[47]

6 If the damages recovered under the Law Reform Act 1934 are reduced under section 1 of the Law Reform (Contributory Negligence) Act 1945, any damages recovered under the Fatal Accidents Acts 1846 to 1959 must be reduced to a proportionate extent.[48] An action may be brought for the benefit of the estate under the Law Reform Act 1934, although a previous action has been brought and damages recovered under the Fatal Accidents Acts in respect of the same accident.[49] When the personal representative brings an action both under the Law Reform Act 1934 and the Fatal Accidents Acts, any payment into court must be made in respect of each claim separately, as the beneficiaries are not necessarily the same in each case.[50]

37 **Limitation of damages under Merchant Shipping Act 1894.**[51] Under

43 *Harvey* v. *R. G. O'Dell Ltd.* [1958] 2 Q.B. 78.
44-45 Repealed and re-enacted by the 1961 Act.
46 *Rose* v. *Ford, supra*; *Davies* v. *Powell Duffryn Associated Collieries Ltd.* [1942] A.C. 601.
47 *Pym* v. *G.N. Ry.* (1863) 4 B. & S. 396, and *post*, § 1282 and the Fatal Accidents Act 1959.
48 Law Reform (Contributory Negligence) Act 1945, s. 1 (4).
49 *May* v. *Sir Robert McAlpine & Sons Ltd.* [1938] 3 All E.R. 85.
50 *Gears* v. *Braley* [1940] 2 K.B. 442.
51 As amended by the Merchant Shipping (Liability of Shipowners and Others) Act 1958, s. 2 (1).

section 503 of this Act a shipowner can limit his liability to pay damages for the deaths of or personal injuries caused to members of the crew of the ship by his breach of statutory duty [52] or by the breach by his servants of his common law duty to take reasonable care for the safety of the crew.[53]

See Chapter 19, *post*, regarding the assessment of damages under the Fatal Accidents Acts.

2. HEADS OF DAMAGE AND ASSESSMENT

138 **Personal injuries.** In actions for damages for personal injuries, the matters to be taken into account in ascertaining the damages are: the pain and suffering endured, past, present and future, the inconvenience and loss of enjoyment of life sustained, past, present and future, injury to health, any shortening of the expectation of life, and the present and future financial loss. These were expressed by Cockburn C.J. as follows: " We think that a jury cannot be said to take a reasonable view of the case unless they consider and take into account all the heads of damage in respect of which a plaintiff complaining of a personal injury is entitled to compensation. These are the bodily injury sustained; the pain undergone; the effect on the health of the sufferer, according to its degree and its probable duration as likely to be temporary or permanent; the expenses incidental to attempts to effect a cure, or to lessen the amount of injury; the pecuniary loss sustained through inability to attend to a profession or business as to which, again, the injury may be of a temporary character, or may be such as to incapacitate the party for the remainder of his life." [54] The judge is under no duty to itemise his award of general damages for pain, loss of future earnings and the like, although he may do so, if he desires.[55] However, the Court of Appeal has given a warning that in assessing total general damages, particularly in a case where the plaintiff's life had been transformed by the severity of his injuries, there is considerable danger of overlapping if the total be arrived at merely by adding up sums calculated under separate heads.[56]

139 **Pain and suffering.** Damages for pain and suffering are clearly incapable of exact estimation and their assessment must necessarily be a matter of degree. They must be assessed on the basis of giving reasonable compensation for the actual and prospective suffering entailed, including that derived from the plaintiff's medical care, operations and treatment. Bramwell L.J. said that the proper direction for a jury was: " You must give the plaintiff a compensation for his pecuniary loss, you must give him compensation for his pain and bodily suffering; of course it is almost impossible for you to give to an injured man what can be strictly called a compensation; but you must take a reasonable view of the

[52] *The Truculent* [1952] P. 1.
[53] *Beauchamp* v. *Turrell* [1952] 2 Q.B. 207.
[54] *Phillips* v. *L. & S.W. Ry.* (1879) 4 Q.B.D. 406, affd. 5 Q.B.D. 78.
[55] *Watson* v. *Powles* [1968] 1 Q.B. 596. However, in view of the compulsory award of interest on personal injury claims after January 1, 1970, when the Administration of Justice Act 1969 came into force, itemisation in practice may become essential. See further " Interest " § 171, *post*.
[56] *Fletcher* v. *Autocar and Transporters* [1968] 2 Q.B. 322. But see § 171, *post*.

case, and must consider, under all the circumstances, what is a fair amount to be awarded to him." [57] It has been said that an attempt ought not to be made to give a perfect compensation.[58] This, however, can only mean that the assessment of damages must not be based on an attempt to fix the price which the injured party would have accepted for undergoing the injuries he has received.[59] It does not mean that a smaller sum must be awarded than is considered to be adequate compensation for the injuries sustained. The fact that the plaintiff is and will remain completely unconscious eliminates those heads of damage, which exist by being felt, thought or experienced irrespective of the serious nature of his injuries,[60] but a plaintiff who realises his condition of being seriously injured must be awarded compensation for the mental suffering involved thereby on a comparable basis to actual physical pain.[61]

Loss of enjoyment of life. As a result of the decision of the House of Lords in *H. West & Son Ltd.* v. *Shephard* [62] it is now authoritatively settled that damages will be awarded for the loss of amenities of life on an objective basis. Lord Morris said: "The fact of unconsciousness is therefore relevant in respect of and will eliminate those heads or elements of damage which can only exist by being felt or thought or experienced. The fact of unconsciousness does not, however, eliminate the actuality of the deprivation of the ordinary experiences and amenities of life which may be the inevitable result of some physical injury." [63] Hence loss of enjoyment of life and the hampering effect of the injuries in the carrying on of the normal social and personal routine of life, with the probable effect on the health and spirits of the injured party, are proper to be taken into account. Among the loss of the amenities of life are to be considered the injured person's inability to engage in indoor or outdoor games,[64] his dependence, to a greater or less extent, on the help of others in his

57 *Phillips* v. *L. & S.W. Ry.* (1879) 5 C.P.D. 280.

58 *Armsworth* v. *S.E. Ry.* (1847) 11 Jur. 758, *per* Parke B. In *Fowler* v. *Grace*, *The Times*, February 20, 1970, Edmund Davies L.J. confessed that he had felt troubled for years by Baron Parke's words that a jury must not attempt to give damages to the full amount of a perfect compensation, since these words were sometimes invoked as justifying an award of an amount less than perfect whereas it was the manifest duty of the tribunal (whether judge alone or jury) to give as perfect a sum as was within its power. Perhaps the key to the true meaning of those words lay in the words that followed in the judgment of Parke B., namely, that the jury was : "to take a reasonable view of the case and give what you consider a fair compensation." (The Court of Appeal proceeded to dismiss the defendants' appeal and to uphold the jury's award of £46,650 damages to the quadriplegic plaintiff, a housewife, who had sustained her disastrous injuries in a motor accident.) *Rowley* v. *L. & N.W. Ry.* (1873) L.R. 8 Ex. 221; *Phillips* v. *L. & S.W. Ry.*, *supra*, *per* Brett L.J.

59 See *Owen* v. *Sykes* [1936] 1 K.B. 192, *per* Greer L.J.

60 *Wise* v. *Kaye* [1962] 1 Q.B. 638; *Andrews* v. *Freeborough* [1967] 1 Q.B. 1.

61 *H. West & Son Ltd.* v. *Shephard* [1964] A.C. 326; *Cutts* v. *Chumley* [1967] 1 W.L.R. 742.

62 *H. West & Son Ltd.* v. *Shephard* [1964] A.C. 326.

63 *Supra*; see *per* Lord Devlin at p. 355. Since this decision substantial damages for loss of amenities have been awarded, *e.g. Hindmarsh* v. *H. & L. Slater Ltd.* (1966) 110 S.J. 429; *Andrews* v. *Freeborough* [1967] 1 Q.B. 1; *Cutts* v. *Chumley* [1967] 1 W.L.R. 742.

64 *Rushton* v. *National Coal Board* [1953] 1 Q.B. 495, 501, *per* Birkett L.J. See also *Owen* v. *Sykes* [1936] 1 K.B. 192, where a doctor, aged 39, an athlete, in large practice who was so injured that he would have to employ an assistant for the rest of his life was awarded £10,000.

daily life [65] and his inability to lead the life he wants to lead and was able to lead before his injuries.[66] In this connection the age of the injured person must be taken into account, as an elderly man will not suffer the same loss in this respect as a young man.[67] If the injury has resulted in disfigurement, this must be taken into account among the matters mentioned above.[68]

141 In assessing damages for physical injuries it is an irrelevant consideration that a victim may be unable to enjoy personally any award of damages and may be ignorant of the loss he has suffered except that such ignorance will be an element in the assessment of damages for pain and suffering.[69] So that where a sixteen-year-old athletic, intelligent public school boy sustained appalling injuries in a road accident, which turned him into a spastic, whereby he remained paralysed, mute and in a state of coma, it being unlikely that he would ever become aware of his plight, he was awarded substantial damages for loss of amenities. But Edmund Davies J. held that there should be no award of damages for loss of future earnings or the cost of providing private medical care.[70] In *S.* v. *Distillers Co.* (*Biochemicals*) [71] Hinchcliffe J. was required to assess damages in two representative actions arising out of that all too large number of children who were born pitifully deformed after their mothers had taken the drug thalidomide as a tranquilliser during their pregnancies. Whilst there could never have been cases in which there were so many imponderables, nevertheless the court had to determine what was fair and reasonable both to the plaintiffs as well as to the defendants upon the broadest view.

In assessing damages the court is not concerned to consider to what use the money will be put.[72]

142 **Shortening of expectation of life.** Injury to health resulting in a shortening of the injured person's expectation of life—the loss of " the prospect of an enjoyable, vigorous and happy old age " [73]—is a matter to be taken into account. This is because " a man has a legal right in

[65] *Heaps* v. *Perrite Ltd.* [1937] 2 All E.R. 60, where a young labourer lost both his hands and would always require daily assistance was awarded £10,000. See also *Rushton* v. *N.C.B., supra.*

[66] *Heaps* v. *Perrite Ltd.* [1937] 2 All E.R. 60. See also *Keating* v. *Elvan Reinforced Concrete Co. Ltd.* [1967] 3 All E.R. 611.

[67] *Bird* v. *Cocking & Sons Ltd.* [1951] 2 T.L.R. 1260, where a man aged 61 had one hand amputated and the other rendered useless was awarded £10,000 which was reduced by the C.A. to £7,000.

[68] See *Lampert* v. *Eastern National Omnibus Co.* [1954] 1 W.L.R. 1047; *McLaurin* v. *N.B. Ry.* (1892) 19 R. 346.

[69] *Wise* v. *Kaye* [1962] 1 Q.B. 638 which was approved by the Lords in *H. West & Son* v. *Shephard* [1964] A.C. 326, where it was pointed out that the guidance in *Benham* v. *Gambling* [1941] A.C. 157 concerning the award of moderate damages in fatal accident cases was intended to apply only to damages for loss of expectation of life and not to loss of amenities of life.

[70] *Maxwell* v. *Maxwell Scientific International* (*Distribution Services*), *The Times*, June 28, 1963.

[71] (1969) 113 S.J. 672.

[72] *H. West & Son* v. *Shephard, supra*; *Andrews* v. *Freeborough* [1967] 1 Q.B. 1.

[73] *Flint* v. *Lovell* [1935] 1 K.B. 354, *per* Acton J. Possibly, this was the first instance of this head of damage being admitted by the court.

his own life." [74] Lord Wright explained it thus: "I think he has a legal interest entitling him to complain if the integrity of his life is impaired by tortious acts not only in regard to pain, suffering and disability, but in regard to the continuance of life for its normal expectancy. A man has a legal right that his life should not be shortened by the tortious act of another. His normal expectancy of life is a thing of temporal value, so that its impairment is something for which damages should be given." [75] In assessing damages under this head, regard must be had to the injured party's normal expectation of life and not to his expectation of life in his injured condition, or to the fact that his injuries are such that he does not want his life to be prolonged or does not know it has been shortened.[76] Loss of the wages he would have earned during the years by which his life has been reduced are to be disregarded. "The only relevance of earnings which would have been earned after death is that they are an item of damages for loss of expectation of life, in the sense that they are one of the minor elements which indicate that a person earning a reasonable livelihood is more likely to have an enjoyable life." [77] Nothing can be awarded for loss of the prospects of making provision for dependants.[77a] Where a plaintiff who had become a paraplegic as a result of the serious injuries he had sustained when he was a boy of sixteen, during the course of the trial became aware of the shortening of his expectation of life, Marshall J. held that the boy's knowledge of his condition and its consequences should be taken into account in assessing damages, but that it should not be the subject of a separate award.[78]

3 **Loss of expectation of life.** In *Flint* v. *Lovell*,[79] where a sixty-nine-year-old plaintiff sustained serious personal injuries as a result of which his expectation of life was considerably diminished, it was held that he was entitled to damages for this loss. Further, damages for loss of expectation of life may be awarded, notwithstanding that the deceased himself, from the suddenness of his death or the fact of his unconsciousness until

[74] *Armsworth* v. *South Eastern Ry.* (1847) 11 Jur. 758.
[75] *Rose* v. *Ford* [1937] A.C. 826, 847, 848. See *ante*, § 133.
[76] *Roach* v. *Yates* [1938] 1 K.B. 256.
[77] *Harris* v. *Brights Asphalt Contractors Ltd.* [1953] 1 W.L.R. 341, 351 *per* Slade J. (man of 35 with an A1 life reduced to two years' expectation, £500 awarded; £5,000 awarded for past and future physical and mental pain and suffering—plaintiff paralysed below waist), differing from dicta to the contrary in *Roach* v. *Yates*, *supra*. A contrary view was expressed in *Pope* v. *D. Murphy & Son Ltd.* [1961] 1 Q.B. 222, Streatfeild J. holding that where injuries have reduced both the plaintiff's earning power and his expectation of life, the proper approach to the question of loss of earning capacity was one which compensated him for what he had in fact lost, namely, the prospective earnings for the remainder of his normal expectation of working life and not for the reduced period of such life, which resulted from the injuries. However, this decision was disapproved by the Court of Appeal in *Oliver* v. *Ashman* [1961] 1 Q.B. 337 where it was stated that lost wages during the "lost years" were only an ingredient of loss of expectation of life and were not to be valued as an item on their own. Also see *Wise* v. *Kaye* [1962] 1 Q.B. 638, and article by Jolowicz [1960] C.L.J. 160.
[77a] *Richards* v. *Highway Ironfounders Ltd.* [1955] 1 W.L.R. 1049.
[78] *Forrest* v. *Sharp* (1963) 107 S.J. 536.
[79] [1935] 1 K.B. 354. See also *Phillips* v. *L.S.W.Ry.* (1879) 5 Q.B.D. 78, 80.

death, did not know that his life was shortened.[80] The amount of the damages is to be based on the fact that continuance of life is a thing worth having, and therefore its loss is a thing for which compensation is to be awarded in the same way as pain and suffering is to be the subject of compensation.[81] It is not to be looked upon from the point of view of "what price the man would have put upon his life." [82] Loss of expectation of life is, like pain and suffering, something which is independent of the financial position or the station in life of the person who suffers it and is accordingly assessed without regard to such circumstances. "The damages are in respect of loss of life, not of loss of future pecuniary prospects." [83]

An action can be brought under the Law Reform (Miscellaneous Provisions) Act 1934, s. 1, although the deceased is killed instantaneously.[83a]

144 In assessing damages under this head, it must be borne in mind that "damages which would be proper for a disabling injury may well be much greater than for deprivation of life." [84] The sum arrived at must be "by way of damages for the loss of a measure of prospective happiness," [85] with the knowledge that the damages will not be received by the person who suffered the damage.[86] The damages "should not be calculated solely, or even mainly, on the basis of the length of life that is lost." [87] In the case of a very young child, damages should be less than in the case of an adult with settled prospects, because of the uncertainty of the child's future.[88] Acting on these principles, in 1940 the House of Lords reduced an award of £1,200 to £200 for damages for loss of expectation of life in the case of a child of two and a half, and said that even this would be excessive were it not that the infant's circumstances were most favourable.[89] Viscount Simon L.C. pointed out that "the thing to be valued is not the prospect of length of days, but the prospect of a predominantly happy life," hence the right conclusion is not to be reached by applying statistical or actuarial tests.[90] In addition the wealth and position of the victim is irrelevant since happiness does not depend on them. It follows that the decision in *Benham* v. *Gambling* has been accepted as the authoritative guidance to the courts to award only very moderate damages. Since then,

[80] *Rose* v. *Ford* [1937] A.C. 826.
[81] *Ante*, § 139.
[82] Lord Sands in *Reid* v. *Lanarkshire Traction Co.*, 1934 S.C. 79, quoted with approval by Lord Roche, in *Rose* v. *Ford*, *supra*, at p. 860.
[83] *Benham* v. *Gambling* [1941] A.C. 157, 167.
[83a] *Morgan* v. *Scoulding* [1938] 1 K.B. 786.
[84] *Ibid.* p. 168.
[85] *Ibid.* p. 166. Lower damages than normal were awarded when there was evidence that the life of the deceased was not a happy one: *Jordan* v. *Mullis*, *The Times*, December 2, 1952.
[86] *Ibid.* p. 168.
[87] *Ibid.* p. 166.
[88] *Ibid.* p. 167.
[89] *Benham* v. *Gambling* [1941] A.C. 157. The favourable circumstances were that the child was healthy, lived in a village off the main road, and his father was in regular employment.
[90] *Ibid.* at p. 166.

however, the change in the value of money has been taken into account,[91] so that damages in most favourable cases are now usually about £500.[92]

Naylor v. *Yorkshire Electricity Board: a disappointing decision.* The first determined attempt by the Court of Appeal to increase this conventional assessment to a more realistic figure occurred in *Naylor* v. *Yorkshire Electricity Board*[93-94] when an award of £500 was raised to £1,000. The decision reflected not only the changed value of money since 1940 but also the fact that the deceased was a healthy vigorous male aged twenty years who was established in life with some real prospects of a successful and happy future, compared with that situation found in *Benham* v. *Gambling* where the prospects of such a small child were necessarily uncertain. This laudable attempt regrettably was doomed to frustration by a short-sighted decision on appeal by the House of Lords[95] whereby the figure of £500 was reinstated, on the basis that because the trial judge, Ashworth J., fixed upon that figure as a result of his great experience in these matters, it could not be said that it was erroneous, still less wholly erroneous. This seems to be a classic example of judicial "begging the question." Had Ashworth J. felt *free* to award a figure in the region of £1,000 one wonders if the likelihood is that he probably would have taken that opportunity but his undoubted great experience dictated that he had to conform without option.

Nevertheless the House of Lords have still not committed themselves to any precise figures and it is submitted it would be wrong to limit the maximum award in every case to one of £500 which seems to be the popular belief and trend since this decision.[96] It is to be noted that Viscount Dilhorne[97] said: "I doubt if anyone would think even in these days that a sum much in excess of £500 could be regarded as a very moderate sum, it is not for this House to lay down what sum should be awarded in all cases for this loss or what should be the minimum and the maximum award."

Lord Devlin, taking a broad view, considered that it would be: "a great improvement if this head of damage was abolished and replaced by a short Act of Parliament fixing a suitable sum which a wrongdoer whose act has caused death should pay into the estate of the deceased. While the law remains as it is, I think it is less likely to fall into disrespect if judges treat *Benham* v. *Gambling*[98] as an injunction to stick to a fixed

[91] *Hart* v. *Griffiths-Jones* [1948] 2 All E.R. 729.

[92] See *Garcia* v. *Harland & Wolff Ltd.* [1943] 2 All E.R. 477, 486, where £500 was awarded. (The report in [1943] K.B. 731 does not deal with this point.) If that figure be correct now, then the law is indeed an ass.

[93-94] [1967] 1 Q.B. 244.

[95] *Sub nom. Yorkshire Electricity Board* v. *Naylor* [1968] A.C. 529. See article "The Value of Life," 101 L.T. 71.

[96] See *Cutts* v. *Chumley* [1967] 1 W.L.R. 742 (£1,000 awarded by Willis J. was reduced to £500 by a compromise); *Andrews* v. *Freeborough* [1967] 1 Q.B. 1; *Cain* v. *Wilcock* [1968] 1 W.L.R. 1961 (the child was aged two-and-a-half years and properly received £500 in the circumstances, yet can there really be any comparison with the deceased in *Yorkshire Electricity Board* v. *Naylor, supra*?)

[97] *Ibid.* at p. 541.

[98] [1941] A.C. 157.

standard than if they start revaluing happiness, each according to his own ideas."

146 **Nervous shock.** Damages may be recovered for nervous shock occasioned to the plaintiff through the negligence of the defendant.[1] It was at one time held [2] that it was necessary to prove physical contact before damages could be recovered but it is now " fully established by authority—recent and strong authority—that physical impact or lesion is not a necessary element in the case of recovery of damages in ordinary cases of tort." [3] " It is now well recognised that an action will lie for injury by shock sustained through the medium of the eye or the ear without direct contact." [4] Nervous shock in this connection does not mean fright or agony or distress of mind, but means a visible and provable illness, or physical damage, caused by the negligence of the defendant, although there was no actual impact upon the body of the plaintiff.[5] The circumstances under which nervous shock gives rise to a claim for damages have been considered in Chapter 2, *ante*, § 33 *et seq.*

147 In *Hinz* v. *Berry* [6] the plaintiff was picking bluebells near to a lay-by, where her husband, the deceased, had parked their Dormobile van. The defendant was driving his Jaguar motor-car when a tyre burst and the car crashed violently into the van. The plaintiff, on hearing the sounds of the collision, turned around in time to see the last of the catastrophe, which resulted in her husband's death and some of her children being injured. In consequence she received a very severe nervous shock, which caused her to suffer from a state of morbid depression that lasted for five years up to the trial. O'Connor J. awarded her £4,000 as damages for her extreme mental anguish and the illness that followed from it as a result of being present at the scene of the disaster. The Court of Appeal did not interfere with this assessment of damages although Lord Pearson did consider it to be a high figure. The former category of nervous shock namely, " distress of mind," if it is unaccompanied by physical injury, will not attract an award of damages [7] but where damages are awarded in personal injury cases, the figure for general damages not unusually includes something by way of compensation for such mental suffering, whether it consisted of a fright or distress of mind.[8]

1 See article: " Price of nervous shock " (Bradbury) 120 New L.J. 365; " Compensation for neurosis " (Cretney) 114 S.J. 307.

2 *Victorian Ry. Commrs.* v. *Coultas* (1888) 13 App.Cas. 222.

3 *Brown* v. *John Watson Ltd.* [1915] A.C. 1, 14, *per* Lord Shaw.

4 Lord Macmillan in *Bourhill* v. *Young* [1943] A.C. 92, 103.

5 See *Wilkinson* v. *Downton* [1897] 2 Q.B. 57 (defendant, as a joke, falsely told plaintiff that her husband was seriously injured in an accident); *Janvier* v. *Sweeney* [1919] 2 K.B. 316 (private detective to induce plaintiff to show him some letters falsely threatened her with a prosecution for espionage).

6 [1970] 2 Q.B. 40. Followed in *Carlin* v. *Helical Bar* (1970) 9 K.I.R. 154.

7 *Per* Kennedy J. in *Dulieu* v. *White* [1901] 2 K.B. 669, 673; *Schneider* v. *Eisovitch* [1960] 2 Q.B. 430, 441.

8 *Per* Coleridge J. in *Blake* v. *Midland Railway* (1852) 18 Q.B. 93, 111; *Schneider* v. *Eisovitch*, *supra*, at p. 442.

Assessment of damages.[9] It is impossible to frame any formula by which damages for pain and suffering, loss of the amenities of life, injury to health and loss of expectation of life can be measured. Some injuries are so severe that no money can be an adequate compensation, yet money must be awarded because it is the only remedy which it is in the power of the law to give. The only general principles which can be applied are that the damages must be fair and reasonable, that a just proportion must be observed between the damages awarded for the less serious and those awarded for the more serious injuries, and that although " it is impossible to standardise damages "[10] an attempt should be made to award a sum which accords " with the general run of assessments made over the years in comparable cases."[11] In the interests of justice it is of some importance that attempts should be made to obtain a measure of consistency in the assessment and the award of damages. This may require the judge to consider awards in comparable cases if he decides in his discretion to do so, but he is under no obligation to do so and his discretion should be exercised sparingly.[12] It is equally important, however, that comparable, and, especially, " conventional " awards of damages are realistic at the date of judgment.[13] One method of checking that judges' awards do keep and continue to keep abreast of these times of spiralling prices rising with devaluation of monetary values obviously is to employ more jury trials. However, the Court of Appeal has ruled that only in exceptional cases should a jury be used for the assessment of damages.[14]

Deductions for industrial injury and disablement benefits. In actions for damages for personal injuries, there must be taken into account against any loss of earnings or profits " one half of the value of any rights which have accrued or probably will accrue to [the injured person] therefrom in respect of industrial injury benefit, industrial disablement benefit or sickness benefit for the five years beginning with the time when the cause of action accrued,"[15] any increase of an industrial disablement

9 See article: " Assessment of damages—the Law Commission's proposals " (Deas), 67 L.S.Gaz. 553.

10 *Rushton* v. *National Coal Board* [1953] 1 Q.B. 495, 500, *per* Singleton L.J. (man of 36 who lost his right arm with no possibility of having an artificial arm fixed, awarded by C.A. £7,000 for loss of the amenities of life).

11 *Bird* v. *Cocking & Sons Ltd., supra, per* Birkett L.J. p. 1263. Awards of damages are collected in Kemp and Kemp, *Quantum of Damages.* In Scotland, see Walker, *Law of Damages in Scotland,* p. 796.

12 *Waldon* v. *War Office* [1956] 1 W.L.R. 51 (man of 28 earning £9 15s. a week with bright prospects—£12,875 increased to £17,000).

13 The conventional sum for the loss of an eye was usually between £2,000 and £3,000, which in 1965 ought to be nearer the £3,000 mark: *Quinn* v. *J. W. Green (Painters) Ltd.* [1966] 1 Q.B. 509, 521; or £3,500 in 1971: *Watson* v. *Heslop* (1971) 115 S.J. 308, *per* Salmon L.J.

14 *Ward* v. *James* [1966] 1 Q.B. 273; *Sims* v. *William Howard & Son Ltd.* [1964] 2 Q.B. 409. See *Hodges* v. *Harland & Wolff Ltd.* [1965] 1 W.L.R. 523 for an example of such an exceptional case.

15 Law Reform (Personal Injuries) Act 1948, s. 2 (1). Edmund Davies J. in *Perez* v. *C.A.V. Ltd.* [1959] 1 W.L.R. 724 held that the proper deduction to be made under this section was such sum as would bear the same proportion to half the gratuity as that part of the five years from the accident, which remained unexpired when the gratuity was paid, bore to the plaintiff's expectation of life. This was approved by the Court of Appeal in *Hultquist*

pension in respect of the need of constant attention being disregarded.[16] It has been decided that all the sums which were in fact paid or likely to be payable in accordance with the statute in respect of the injuries which put the statute into operation are to be taken into account and not merely the payments made during the period of incapacity as found by the court[17]; and that the court is bound to deduct from the loss of earnings claimed one-half of the payments already made and the estimated value of future payments and has not merely a discretion as to the amount of deduction to be made, the expression " taken into account " being used in a book-keeping sense.[18]

It is not necessary for a court to find separately the gross amount of the damage before taking these rights into account and the net amount after taking them into account. When the damages are reduced on account of contributory negligence or are limited by any Act or by contract, the reduction is from the gross amount and the limitation refers to that amount.[19]

150 **Matters not to be taken into account in assessing damages.** In awarding damages for personal injuries, account should not be taken of the fact that the injured party has a private income,[20] that he will receive compensation under a contract of insurance,[21] that he has received money from a fund voluntarily subscribed from charitable motives by third parties after the damage has been caused [22] or that he is awarded a disablement pension on being invalided out of the Royal Navy in consequence of the accident.[23]

151 In *Parry* v. *Cleaver* [24] the plaintiff, a police officer, aged thirty-five

v. *Universal Pattern and Precision Engineering Co. Ltd.* [1960] 2 Q.B. 467, overruling *Roberts* v. *Naylor Bros. Ltd.* [1959] 1 W.L.R. 718, where Paull J. had held that one-half of the disablement gratuity paid in a lump sum should be deducted from the plaintiff's loss of earnings because the gratuity had accrued and had been paid within five years of the accrual of the cause of action.

16 *Ibid.* s. 2 (2).

17 *Stott* v. *Sir William Arrol & Co. Ltd.* [1953] 2 Q.B. 92 (injured plaintiff off work five weeks lost £47 15s. 6d. in wages and was paid £12 17s. 6d. industrial injury benefit during that time. On returning to work he was paid a further £126 13s. for disablement benefit. It was held that half of both these sums was to be taken into account and not merely half of £12 17s. 6d.).

18 *Flowers* v. *George Wimpey & Co.* [1956] 1 Q.B. 73. (Workman sustained bruising and shock and a tumour developed later. He was paid industrial injury benefit and industrial disablement benefit during the whole time he was off work—over a year. The court found the tumour was not the result of the accident and that the accident only disabled the workman for three or four weeks—held, one-half of the total sum of benefits received should be deducted from the loss of the three or four weeks' earnings, so that general damages only were awarded.)

19 Law Reform (Personal Injuries) Act 1948, s. 2 (3).

20 *Phillips* v. *L. & S.W. Ry.* (1879) 5 Q.B.D. 78.

21 *Bradburn* v. *G.W. Ry.* (1874) L.R. 10 Ex. 1, which was applied by the H.L. in *Parry* v. *Cleaver* [1970] A.C. 1. *Eley* v. *Bedford, The Times*, May 5, 1971.

22 *Redpath* v. *Belfast & County Down Ry.* [1947] N.I. 167.

23 *Payne* v. *Railway Executive* [1952] 1 K.B. 26. The ratio decidendi of Sellers J. at the trial and of Cohen L.J. on appeal were approved by the House of Lords in *Parry* v. *Cleaver*, *supra*.

24 [1970] A.C. 1, approving and following *Bradburn* v. *G.W. Ry.*, *supra*, but distinguishing and, in effect, overruling *Browning* v. *War Office* [1963] 1 Q.B. 750. See article: " Deduction for benefits received " (Samuels) (1969) 119 New L.J. 288.

years, who had served for twelve years in the police force, was severely injured whilst directing traffic, due to the defendant's negligent driving. He had made compulsory contributions to a police pension fund out of his pay, which entitled him as of right to a pension on being discharged from the police force for disablement, so that when he was discharged for that reason he received thereafter a police pension for the rest of his life. The House of Lords held that in computing damages for loss of his earning capacity, this ill-health award was not deductible in assessing damages in respect of the head of claim for his loss of earnings as a policeman up to the date of retirement, but it would have to be brought into account as a relevant factor in respect of the loss in amount of his retirement pension. Lord Reid, by considering that the products of the sums paid into the pension fund were in fact delayed remuneration for current work, hence why pensions are regarded as earned income, said: " The true situation is that wages are a reward for contemporaneous work, but that a pension is the fruit, through insurance, of all the money which was set aside in the past in respect of his past work." [25] Thus by treating a pension, however it was contributed to, as equivalent to payment under some insurance policy, it followed that, because such payments should not be taken into account,[26] pensions too must be treated upon an equal footing. Further, Lord Reid emphasised one other matter which he regarded as of great importance: " It appears to me that public policy must enter largely into our decision and that therefore it is very relevant to see what policy Parliament has followed in dealing with a closely related subject. . . . If public policy, as now interpreted by Parliament,[27] requires all pensions to be disregarded in actions under the Fatal Accidents Acts, I find it impossible to see how it can be proper to bring pensions into account in common law actions." [28]

Where a plaintiff becomes entitled to receive a pension, not by reason of the accident, but by reason of the contributions he had made during his service with his employers, a wrongdoer should not be allowed to appropriate the benefit of such, and therefore the pension should be disregarded in assessing damages, whether the contributions to the superannuation fund were compulsory or not.[29] The defendant's means are also irrelevant.

52 *Parry* v. *Cleaver* [30] has no application to a case where an injured plaintiff continues to receive his wages from his employers, whilst

[25] *Ibid.* at p. 16.
[26] *Bradburn* v. *G.W. Ry.*, *supra.*
[27] Fatal Accidents Act 1959, which by s. 2 changed the law in this respect.
[28] *Ibid.* at pp. 19, 20.
[29] *Judd* v. *Hammersmith, West London and St. Mark's Hospitals Board of Governors* [1960] 1 W.L.R. 328.
[30] *Supra. Parry* v. *Cleaver* was applied by Park J. in *Hewson* v. *Downs* [1970] 1 Q.B. 73, when he held that the damages were not to be reduced because a plaintiff received a state retirement pension, where the personal injuries sustained had caused him to retire, and by the Court of Appeal in *Turner* v. *Minister of Defence* (1969) 113 S.J. 585 where the plaintiff's special damages consisted of his wages less the " sick pay " paid to him by the defendants, his employers, whilst he was off work.

incapacitated, since the payment of wages is intrinsically different from the receiving of a pension.[31] If such wages had to be paid, since the employers were under a legal obligation to do so, the plaintiff cannot recover for their loss as a part of his damages, whether or not he intended to reimburse them.[32] On the other hand if the plaintiff receives nothing from his employers by way of wages whilst he is off work due to the defendant's negligence, or if the plaintiff receives some such wages as voluntary payments, then his claim is not reduced thereby and he is entitled to sue the defendant for the full amount of his loss suffered. Normally the plaintiff, having received voluntary payments from his employers during the period of his inability to work, will undertake to reimburse them, but there is some authority, albeit doubtful, that he can be ordered to repay an equivalent sum to them out of the award of damages he recovers from the defendant.[33]

1 53 **Financial loss.** The injured party is also entitled to damages for his financial loss, actual and prospective. Actual financial loss may consist of loss of earnings, medical and nursing expenses,[34] additional cost of buying invalid diet, damage to clothing, the employment of extra household or other assistance, and all other loss which is the direct consequence of the injury,[35] including the cost of convalescence after the injury, necessitating a change of air in some place away from the injured party's home.[36] The fact that payment has not actually been made in respect of liabilities incurred under any of these heads of damage is immaterial, as long as the liability is a genuine liability actually incurred. Where, therefore, a husband incurred liability to a hospital for attendance upon his wife, it was held that he could claim the amount of the liability from the negligent defendant although he had not paid the amount and it was

31 *Ibid. per* Lord Reid at p. 16.

32 *Metropolitan Police District Receiver* v. *Croydon C.C.* [1957] 2 Q.B. 154 and it will only be in the exceptional case that the employers themselves could bring an action against the tortfeasor by the limited scope of the action *per quod servitum amisit*.

33 *Dennis* v. *L.P.T.B.* [1948] 1 All E.R. 779, by virtue of the reasoning in *Parry* v. *Cleaver supra, per* Lord Reid and *per* Lord Pearce.

34 Medical expenses include the expenses of treatment incurred upon the advice of experts, even though the experts' diagnosis was mistaken and the treatment unnecessary: *Reubens* v. *Walker*, 1946 S.C. 215. Nursing expenses may include loss sustained through a daughter in wage-earning employment leaving that employment to look after her injured parent, and so being unable to pay her usual contribution towards the household expenses: *Hawkes* v. *Torquay Corpn.* [1938] 4 All E.R. 16. Similarly the plaintiff's wife and sister-in-law gave up their work to nurse him: *Roach* v. *Yates* [1938] 1 K.B. 256. The possibility of avoiding these expenses by taking advantage of the National Health Service Act 1946, c. 81, is to be disregarded: Law Reform (Personal Injuries) Act 1948, c. 41, s. 2 (4); but if advantage is taken of this free service, a plaintiff is not entitled to recover the sum of money he would have had to pay had the expense been incurred privately: *Harris* v. *Brights Asphalt Contractors Ltd.* [1953] 1 Q.B. 617, 635 *per* Slade J.

35 See *Liffen* v. *Watson* [1940] 1 K.B. 556 (domestic servant whose injuries prevented her from following her employment entitled to damages for loss of board and lodging, in addition to loss of wages, although she was living with her father who provided her with free board and lodging); *Pitt* v. *Jackson* [1939] 1 All E.R. 129 (injured schoolmistress not allowed expenses for taxi fares in going to school).

36 *Phillips* v. *L. & S.W. Ry.* (1879) 5 Q.B.D. 78, 80. A deduction may be made for board and lodging when the cost of staying at a nursing home is claimed; *Shearman* v. *Folland* [1950] 2 K.B. 43; *Oliver* v. *Ashman* [1962] 2 Q.B. 210; *Cutts* v. *Chumley* [1967] 1 W.L.R. 742.

unlikely, or perhaps impossible owing to its being statute-barred, that the hospital would enforce payment from the husband.[37] On the other hand the court is entitled to advert to future probabilities when considering financial loss already sustained by the plaintiff at the date of trial. Thus in *Cutler* v. *Vauxhall Motors*,[38] where the plaintiff suffered an injury at work, which necessitated an operation, as a result of which he lost net wages of £173, he claimed as special damages this sum in his action against his employers. However, since it was proved that the plaintiff suffered from a pre-existing condition which would in all probability have made the same operation essential in four to five years' time, the only effect of the injury was to accelerate the operation so that he was only entitled to receive £10 general damages and his claim for special damages was disallowed.

Future financial loss is an estimate formed of the financial loss likely to be sustained by the injured party after the date of the trial. A director, a shareholder in a private company, who was incapacitated from doing work for the company as a result of which the profits of the company had declined and the amount distributed to him by way of dividends had been reduced accordingly, could recover the loss.[39]

4 **Loss of earnings.** In assessing loss of earnings, the plaintiff's tax liability must be considered and the net amount of the earnings only can be awarded. The assessment can be made on broad lines and it is not necessary to do it with mathematical accuracy.[40] Lord Goddard suggested this direction to a jury: " You know what the plaintiff was earning before the accident and what he had left to support himself and his family after tax was paid. You know his age. It is for you to consider for how long he would be likely to earn at the present rate. If he is a member of a partnership, take into consideration his position in the firm at the time of the accident. If a junior partner you may well think that his earnings would have increased as time went on, while if a senior partner they might well decrease as he ceases to give the same amount of time to the business of the firm. Remember that whatever he earned would be subject to tax and that you will already have in mind when assessing his pre-accident income. No one can foresee whether tax will go up or down, and I advise you not to speculate on the subject but to deal with it as

[37] *Allen* v. *Waters & Co.* [1935] 1 K.B. 200. The majority of the C.A. thought that the debt was not statute-barred. Goddard J. thought that it was but that, nevertheless, it was recoverable. See § 165, *post*, generally for the recovery as special damage of losses suffered by a third party, husband or parent of an injured person.

[38] [1970] 2 W.L.R 961.

[39] *Lee* v. *Sheard* [1956] 1 Q.B. 192.

[40] *B.T.C.* v. *Gourley* [1956] A.C. 185 overruling *Billingham* v. *Hughes* [1949] 1 K.B. 643; *Jordan* v. *The Limmer and Trinidad Lake Asphalt Co. Ltd.* [1946] K.B. 356. Where loss of remuneration is pleaded as special damage by the plaintiff, the defendants are entitled to further particulars of the assessments to income tax and surtax since the plaintiff's real claim for special damage is the amount of his net loss and the particulars are necessary in order to enable this special damage to be calculated: *Phipps* v. *Orthodox Unit Trusts Ltd.* [1958] 1 Q.B. 314. See articles on *B.T.C.* v. *Gourley* at 19 M.L.R. (Baxter); 73 L.Q.R. (Hall); [1959] C.L.J. (Jolowicz); [1959] C.L.J. 185 (Tucker); [1966] Canadian Bar Rev. 66.

matters are at present. You cannot tell what his health would have been had he not been injured nor what fortune, good or bad, he might have met with. You know he had, when he was injured, a spendable income of so much (adding if the plaintiff was in partnership ' you have heard the provisions of his partnership deed providing for an alteration in the shares and you may consider whether his injury may affect the earnings of the partnership '). Taking all these matters into consideration you will consider what is fair that a man of this age should receive in respect of the amount of disability which you find this accident has imposed upon him, remembering also that what you give is given once and for all." [41] In addition to deductions in respect of tax liability Lawton J. considered that national insurance contributions also should be taken into account: " It seems to me that the object of damages is to compensate the plaintiff for what he has lost, and what he has lost is what would have been in his pay packet when he took it home. . . and it seems to me that when special damages are being calculated there should be deducted the amount of any national insurance contributions the plaintiff would have had to make if he had remained in work." [42]

155 Wages lost can be recovered even though they have been paid by the employer, if the plaintiff is under a moral obligation to repay them in the event of his recovering them from the defendant.[43] Loss of earning capacity may include loss of ability to earn a higher income in the future. A man twenty-eight years old who had been trained for the position of a superintending marine engineer, which by reason of his injuries he was incapable of obtaining, was held entitled to be awarded compensation for the prospective loss he had sustained.[44] An American club professional golfer was held to be entitled to substantial damages for the loss of opportunity of competing in five tournaments, the ensuing loss of experience and prestige, and the loss of the chance of winning prize money, following some relatively minor injuries to his left hand.[45] In assessing damages for loss of earnings, sums which the plaintiff would have earned during the normal span of life had it not been shortened by injury should not be taken into account.[46] The future financial loss is an estimate formed on the financial loss likely to be sustained by the injured party after the date of the trial, but the possibility of future depreciation in the value of money is not a factor to be taken into consideration when assessing damages for personal injuries as either relevant to compensation for loss of future earnings or to the necessity of future expenditure.[47]

41 [1956] 1 Q.B. 192, 209.
42 *Cooper* v. *Firth Brown Ltd.* [1963] 1 W.L.R. 418 at p. 420.
43 *Dennis* v. *L.P.T.B.* [1948] 1 All E.R. 779 (plaintiff received equivalent of wages partly from the Ministry of Pensions and partly from sick pay from his employers—a direction was made by the court that the amounts so received should be repaid out of the damages recovered). But see reimbursement of a third party's losses, § 165, *post*.
44 *Johnston* v. *G.W. Ry.* [1904] 2 K.B. 250.
45 *Mulvaine* v. *Joseph* (1968) 112 S.J. 927.
46 *Wise* v. *Kaye* [1962] 1 Q.B. 638.
47 *O'Brien* v. *Mckean* (1968) 42 A.L.J.R. 223; *Gollan* v. *Duncan* [1961] N.Z.L.R. 60. See

There is no rule that actuarial tables or an actuary should be consulted for guidance about future loss of earnings.[48] However, actuarial computation may assist at times.[49]

6 **Damage to chattels.** In the case of damage to chattels the general rule is that the measure of damages is the difference between the value of the chattel before the damage and its value as damaged. This will usually be, in the case of a partial loss, the cost of repairing the chattel and any depreciation in value, being the difference between the value of the chattel when repaired and the value before the damage, less any increase in value due to the substitution of new for old material. In addition, consequential loss may be recovered, such as the cost of hiring another chattel during the time taken to repair the damaged chattel,[50] loss of profits during the time taken by the repairs, and damages for loss of the use of the chattel. In *Macrae* v. *Swindells* [51] the plaintiff's Standard car was damaged through the defendant's negligence and the defendant, a garage proprietor, lent the plaintiff a Morris car while the plaintiff's car was being repaired. The Morris car was damaged in a collision caused by the negligence of the plaintiff, who hired a third car until his Standard car was repaired. It was held that the plaintiff was entitled to recover from the defendant the cost of hire because he was compelled to hire this car as a result of the defendant's negligence and not as a result of his own negligence in driving the Morris car; he mitigated his loss by using the Morris car as long as it was available and the reason for its ceasing to be available was irrelevant. If no other chattel is hired during repairs but the owner brings into use a similar chattel which he has in hand to provide against some such emergency, he is entitled to be paid for providing such chattel, because he is nonetheless entitled to damages when, instead of hiring a chattel, he invests his money in purchasing one.[52] The cost of taking the chattel to the repairers may also be recovered. However, where a motor-car was damaged by separate tortfeasors by successive torts, although each tort, if occurring alone, would have rendered necessary the same work of repair, namely, a paint respray, it was held that the plaintiffs were not entitled to recover this cost from the subsequent tortfeasor, because the damage did not flow from his wrongful act.[53]

7 If a chattel is hired to replace the damaged chattel during the repairs,

also *Mallett* v. *McMonagle* [1970] A.C. 176 *per* Lord Diplock to the same effect under the Fatal Accidents Acts. *Cf. Miller* v. *B.R.S.* [1967] 1 W.L.R. 443 and *Woods and Hartley* v. *Wood* (1967) 117 New L.J. 654 where constant inflation was considered to be a relevant factor to be borne in mind.

48 *Watson* v. *Powles* [1968] 1 Q.B. 596; *Mitchell* v. *Mulholland* (No. 2) [1971] 2 W.L.R. 1271, C.A.

49 *Hodges* v. *Harland & Wolff Ltd.* [1965] 1 W.L.R. 523.

50 *The Greta Holme* [1897] A.C. 596; *Hughes* v. *Quentin* (1838) 8 C. & P. 703 (damage to horse)—so far as this case decides that the plaintiff was not entitled to the cost of hiring another horse while his own was recovering from its injuries, it must be taken to be erroneous—see *Davis* v. *Oswell* (1837) 7 C. & P. 804; *The Mediana* [1900] A.C. 113.

51 [1954] 1 W.L.R. 597.

52 *The Greta Holme*, *supra*, *per* Lord Herschell.

53 *Performance Cars Ltd.* v. *Abraham* [1962] 1 Q.B. 33.

there will, as a rule, be no ground for claiming loss of profits, but if a profit-earning chattel is damaged and not replaced, the profits lost during the time of the repairs can be recovered.[54] If there is no loss because the chattel is incapable of earning profit from other causes while it is being repaired, no damages for loss of use can be recovered.[55] "It is a sufficiently familiar head of damages between individuals that, if one person injures the property of another, damages may be recovered, not only for the amount which it may be necessary to spend in repairs, but also for the loss of the use of the article injured during the period that the repairing may occupy." [56] Even if there has been no loss of profits and no expense in temporarily replacing the chattel, damages may be recovered for loss of use. "I take it to be clear law that in general a person who has been deprived of the use of a chattel through the wrongful act of another is entitled to recover damages in respect thereof, even though he cannot prove what has been called 'tangible pecuniary loss,' by which I understand is meant that he is a definite sum of money out of pocket owing to the wrong he has sustained." [57] Damages for loss of use will normally be a total sum made up of depreciation of the chattel, interest on the capital value, cost of maintenance and expenditure on wages thrown away.[58] In *Lord Citrine* (*Owners*) v. *Hebridean Coast* (*Owners*) [59] a collision occurred between a collier and another ship, causing damage to the former, but the plaintiffs had failed to show that they had chartered tonnage to replace the ship. Lord Reid said: "With a non-profit-earning ship there is no direct financial loss and one must ask what harm was done to the owner by his being deprived of the use of his ship. Then comes what may be a very difficult task, to put a value in money on the harm which the owner has suffered. But you must first prove the harm. If no harm is proved beyond the mere fact that the owner is deprived of the services of his ship during the period of repairs, the opinion of Lord Herschell in *Steam Sand Pump Dredger No. 7* (*Owners*) v. *Greta Holme* (*Owners*) [60] appears to have given rise to the practice of awarding damages based on interest on the value of the ship." [61]

158 Where the chattel is completely destroyed or so damaged as not to be worth repairing, the measure of damages is the market value of the chattel or the cost of its replacement together with any consequential

[54] *The Argentino* (1889) 14 App.Cas. 519; *Re Trent* (1868) L.R. 4 Ch. 112, 117; *cf. The Soya* [1955] 1 W.L.R. 1246. In *Dixons* (*Scholar Green*) v. *J. L. Cooper* (1970) 114 S.J. 319 the C.A. held that where a valuable profit-earning articulated lorry, which had been in constant demand, had been put out of use for eleven weeks due to the defendant's negligence, the court had a duty to award substantial damages and not merely £2 nominal damages, hence an award of £450.

[55] *Carslogie SS. Co.* v. *Royal Norwegian Government* [1952] A.C. 292.

[56] *The Greta Holme, supra, per* Lord Halsbury at p. 601; see also *The Argentino* (1889) 14 App.Cas. 519.

[57] *The Greta Holme, supra, per* Lord Herschell at p. 604; see also *Admiralty Commissioners* v. *SS. Chekiang* [1926] A.C. 637.

[58] *Sunley & Co. Ltd.* v. *Cunard White Star Ltd.* [1940] 1 K.B. 740.

[59] [1961] A.C. 545.

[60] *Supra.*

[61] *Ibid.* at pp. 577, 578.

loss following on the destruction of the chattel [61a] If the chattel is profit earning, its value will take into account the profits which it was likely to earn in the future, and so no additional damages can be recovered for loss of future profits, except such profits as were being earned when the chattel was destroyed.[62] Consequential loss may include such items as the expense of procuring a substitute (not the cost of the substitute), and damage to interruption of business owing to the chattel not being available, but not extra damage due to the financial position of the injured party whereby the lost chattel could not be replaced within a reasonable time. In *Liesbosch (Owners)* v. *Edison (Owners)* [63] the plaintiffs' dredger, while engaged in connection with constructive works at Patras harbour, was sunk by the negligence of the defendants. As a result the works were held up and the plaintiffs became liable for penalties. Owing to their financial position the plaintiffs experienced considerable delay in replacing the dredger and suffered a greater financial loss than would ordinarily have been suffered. It was held that they were not entitled to this extra loss, and that the measure of damages was the value of the dredger to the plaintiffs as a profit-earning dredger at the time and place of her loss, including (1) a capital sum made up of (a) the market price on the date of the loss of a comparable dredger; (b) the cost of adapting a new dredger and transporting and insuring her to Patras; and (c) compensation for disturbance and loss in the carrying out of the works from the date of the loss until the date on which the substituted dredger could reasonably have been available for use at Patras, including overhead charges and expenses of staff and equipment and the like thrown away; and (2) interest on that sum from the date of loss. When a motor-car was so damaged as to be a constructive total loss, it was held that the measure of damages was the market value of the car at the date of the loss and the cost of hiring a substitute until a new car could be procured and made fit for use, less the scrap value of the damaged car.[64] Where a motor-car owner had his damaged vehicle repaired at a cost exceeding its market value, instead of trying to purchase a comparable motor-car at the market price, he cannot recover the cost of such repairs since it is his duty to mitigate his loss.[65] But where the motor-car involved was unique in character, *e.g.* a mechanised version of the Lord Mayor's carriage, and quite irreplaceable, the owner was held to be entitled to the cost of repairing it at a cost considerably in excess of its market value as a motor-vehicle.[66]

Damage to land and buildings. The measure of damages when land is damaged is the same as in the case of chattels. If a building is damaged, the plaintiff can recover (1) the cost of repairs; (2) any

[61a] *e.g. Moore* v. *D.E.R.*, *The Times*, June 19, 1971 (ordered a replacement Rover 2000 and hired one, too.)
[62] *The Llanover* [1947] P. 80.
[63] [1933] A.C. 449.
[64] *Pomphrey* v. *James A. Cuthbertson Ltd.*, 1951 S.C. 147.
[65] *Darbishire* v. *Warran* [1963] 1 W.L.R. 1067 distinguishing *O'Grady* v. *Westminster Scaffolding* [1962] 2 Lloyd's Rep. 238. See also § 124, *ante*.
[66] *O'Grady* v. *Westminster Scaffolding, supra*.

depreciation in value, namely, the difference in market value between the building as repaired and the building before the damage; and (3) the expense of obtaining equivalent accommodation while the repairs are being carried out. Consequential loss such as loss of business or loss of production in a factory can also be recovered.[67] In the case of total destruction of a building the measure of damages is the value of the building destroyed and not the cost of replacement.[68] Where a surveyor had negligently surveyed a house, the question of quantum in a seller's market was based by Paull J. on the cost of remedying the defects, and added to that sum must be the expense to which the plaintiff was put having to move out of the premises while the work was being carried out.[69]

160 In the case of land without buildings, the measure of damages is the diminished value of the land. This usually means the cost of restoring the land to its original condition, but there are cases in which this is not so, for example, when a ditch was widened and, in doing so a strip of a field was cut and carried away, it was held that the cost of restoration was not the true measure of damages.[70] In *Rust* v. *Victoria Graving Dock Co.*[71] the plaintiff's building estate was flooded owing to the negligence of the defendants. It was held that he could recover as damages (1) the cost of repairing the damaged houses and the rent lost during the period of repairs; (2) in respect of houses in course of erection on which the plaintiff was bound by contract to make and had made advances to builders by way of security, the amount by which the houses were a less sufficient security for the plaintiff's advances than they were before; and (3) loss of estimated rent through delay in letting the unbuilt-on land, owing to the flooding; but not (4) loss arising from the prejudice against the neighbourhood caused by the flood; or (5) loss arising from the depreciation in the selling value of the ground rents arising from leasing the houses to the builders, when it was found that there would be no damage due to the flood which would last to the end of the leases.

67 *e.g. S.C.M.* (*United Kingdom*) *Ltd.* v. *W. J. Whittall & Son Ltd.* [1971] 1 Q.B. 337 See, however, *per* Lord Denning M.R. and Winn L.J. that economic loss without damage to person or property which arises from a negligent act is not recoverable as damages, except where such loss is the immediate consequence of the negligence, since such damage is otherwise too remote. *British Celanese Ltd.* v. *A. H. Hunt* (*Capacitors*) *Ltd.* [1969] 1 W.L.R. 959. See further Chap. 2, § 42, *ante*, " Pecuniary and economic loss resulting from careless acts."

68 *Moss* v. *Christchurch R.D.C.* [1925] 2 K.B. 750. In *Hutchison* v. *Davidson*, 1945 S.C. 395, the cost of replacement was allowed.

69 *Hood* v. *Shaw* (1960) 176 E.G. 1291. Paull J. also held the measure of damages, where the plaintiff had to move out of his house and resell at a loss, to be (a) the difference between the market value at the time of purchase and the lower market value at resale; (b) the solicitors' costs incurred of the resale, the agents' costs and the costs of levelling a floor prior to resale. The plaintiff was not, however, entitled to solicitors' costs on the purchase: *Hardy* v. *Wamsley-Lewis* (1967) 203 E.G. 1039. However, where straying cattle derailed a train the cost of restoration of the permanent way, *inter alia*, was held to be the measure of damages: *Cooper* v. *Railway Executive* [1953] 1 W.L.R. 223.

70 *Jones* v. *Gooday* (1841) 8 M. & W. 146.

71 (1886) 36 Ch.D. 113. See also *Nitro-Phosphate and Odam's Chemical Manure Co.* v. *London and St. Katharine Docks* (1878) 9 Ch.D. 503, 520; *Workman* v. *G.N. Ry.* (1863) 32 L.J.Q.B. 279.

1 **Master's right to damages for injury to servant.** A master can recover for the reasonable expense to which he has been put in consequence of his servant being injured by the defendant's negligence. This is the action *per quod servitium amisit* and is of ancient origin. It appears to be a survival from the time when service was a status [72] and rests " at bottom on the idea that the master had a quasi-proprietary interest in his servant's services; and that idea is connected with ideas as to the status of a servant, which originated in the rules of law applicable to villein status." [73] It is well established that loss of services caused by the negligence of the defendant gives the master a right to recover damages,[74] but this right of the master only exists where the servant is a menial servant, in the sense that he is *intra moenia* as part of the household or family. It would include anyone living in the house or its curtilage, such as a domestic servant, a gardener, a chauffeur living in the house or in a cottage or lodge in the grounds, a nurse for children, a governess, and a private secretary living in the house and employed by someone living in the house, but not by a company.[75] " It is well settled that when by the tort of a third party a master has lost the services of his servant he can recover damages in respect of that loss of service. . . . If he has got a substitute to do the work of the servant, his damages may be the extra cost to which he has been put, over and above the payment he makes to the servant who is incapacitated. If he has put an end temporarily to the contract of service of the injured servant and pays him nothing, his damages would be the amount, if any, that he has to pay to the substitute. The payment, if any, that he makes to the substitute may of course be equal to, more or less than the wage of the injured servant . . . where he does not employ a substitute, if he continues to pay the wages to the injured servant, he clearly loses any benefit arising from that payment, because he is getting nothing in return for it. In that case, therefore, his damages are, prima facie, the amount of the wages that he has thus paid for nothing." [76] The action only lies when the relationship of master and servant exists and damage has been suffered by the master, but it does not lie at the instance of governments, limited companies, corporations or other employers who keep no household.[77] A constable is not a servant but the holder of an office,[78] and so

[72] *Admiralty Commissioners* v. *SS. Amerika* [1917] A.C. 38, 60, *per* Lord Sumner. Blackstone (Vol. 3, p. 142) says " it is the property which the master has by his contract acquired in the labour of the servant."

[73] Holdsworth, *H.E.L.*, Vol. 8, p. 429.

[74] *Martinez* v. *Gerber* (1841) 3 M. & G. 88; *Berringer* v. *G.E. Ry.* (1879) 4 C.P.D. 163.

[75] *I.R.C.* v. *Hambrook* [1956] 2 Q.B. 641; Parker L.J. adding that action would not lie if the servant were a mere clerk or typist who was not resident in the household.

[76] *Per* MacKinnon J. in *Att.-Gen.* v. *Valle-Jones* [1935] 2 K.B. 209, 216 (liability was admitted). But this case must be taken to be wrongly decided: *I.R.C.* v. *Hambrook* [1956] 2 Q.B. 641. When the action does lie, the amount paid to the servant as sick pay may be claimed, not as such, but as evidence of the amount of the loss suffered by the master. No deduction can be made from the damages payable to the master because of the servant's negligence. See note on this case, 74 L.Q.R. 53.

[77] *I.R.C.* v. *Hambrook* [1956] 2 Q.B. 641.

[78] *Att.-Gen. for New South Wales* v. *Perpetual Trustee Co.* [1955] A.C. 457; *Receiver for the Metropolitan Police District* v. *Croydon Corpn.* [1957] 2 Q.B. 154.

is a member of the armed forces [79] and an established civil servant,[80] so that no action lies by the Crown or any other person for damage caused by the loss of their services. A company cannot sue for loss of the services of a director.[81] When the servant assisted the master in a music hall turn and the servant was injured owing to a defect in the stage, the master recovered the loss he sustained through being unable to perform the turn during the servant's incapacity,[82] but this must be of doubtful authority now.

Proposals for the reform of the law and the abolition of this action have now been made.[83]

162 **Servant's right to damages for injury to master.** A servant who suffers damage because his master is injured through the defendant's negligence has no right of action against the defendant, since there is no principle or authority in English law on which such an action could be founded.[84]

163 **Damages for loss of consortium.**[83] If a wife is injured by the negligence of the defendant, the husband has an action against the defendant for loss of his wife's consortium. Blackstone says if " the husband is deprived at any time of the company and assistance of his wife, the law then gives him a separate remedy by an action upon the case . . . *per quod consortium amisit*, in which he shall recover a satisfaction in damages." [85] Whether the loss of consortium must be total or may be partial was undecided,[86] but in *Adams* v. *Railway Executive* [87] it was decided that it must be total. As has been said,[88] " little, if any, attention is paid to a loss of consortium which involves other considerations beyond " the expenses to which a husband is put for loss of his wife's services, and, save in exceptional cases, the damages likely to be awarded will be small.[89] A wife has no right of action for loss of her husband's

[79] *Att.-Gen. and Minister for Defence* v. *Ryan's Car Hire* (1964) 101 I.L.T.R. 57 (a sergeant in the defence force).

[80] *I.R.C.* v. *Hambrook* [1956] 2 Q.B. 641.

[81] *Lee* v. *Sheard* [1956] 1 Q.B. 192.

[82] *Mankin* v. *Scala Theodrome Co. Ltd.* [1947] K.B. 257.

[83] See Law Reform Committee's 11th Report (Cmnd. 2017 of 1963) and the Law Commission's Working Paper No. 19 (interim proposals circulated on June 14, 1968).

[84] *Best* v. *Samuel Fox & Co. Ltd.* [1952] A.C. 716; *Kirkham* v. *Boughey* [1958] 2 Q.B. 338.

[85] Vol. 3, p. 140. See also Holdsworth, *H.E.L.*, Vol. 8, p. 430 and *Brockbank* v. *Whitehaven Ry.* (1862) 7 H. & N. 834.

[86] In *Best* v. *Samuel Fox & Co. Ltd.* [1952] A.C. 716. In the C.A. all three judges thought it must be total, in the H.L. Lord Goddard and Lord Porter (tentatively) agreed with this view, but Lord Reid and Lord Oaksey differed. See on this, Todd, 15 M.L.R. 246, 16 M.L.R. 92 and Ross Parsons, 18 M.L.R. 514 dealing with the Australian case *Toohey* v. *Hollier* (1955) Argus L.R. 302. The present writer finds it difficult to resist the reasoning of Lord Reid.

[87] (1952) 96 S.J. 361. In *Spaight* v. *Dundon* (1960) 96 I.L.T.R. 69, the Supreme Court in Eire held that a husband whose wife had been injured by the negligence of a third party cannot successfully maintain an action for the impairment as opposed to the total loss of her consortium arising from the injury. But in *Lawrence* v. *Biddle* [1966] 1 All E.R. 575 Brabin J. held that, notwithstanding the fact that the loss of consortium had at no time been total, the husband was entitled to damages for the impairment of it and the damages need not be nominal; indeed such damages awarded may, in appropriate cases, be substantial. See, for example, *Cutts* v. *Chumley* [1967] 1 W.L.R. 742 where the plaintiff's husband was awarded £5,000 for total loss of services and £200 for loss of society.

[88] *Best* v. *Samuel Fox & Co. Ltd.*, *supra*, *per* Lord Porter.

[89] In *Sellars* v. *Best* [1954] 2 All E.R. 389, £100 was awarded for loss of consortium in an action for breach of contract. In *Hare* v. *B.T.C.* [1956] 1 All E.R. 578, £20 was awarded —wife 12 weeks in hospital but *cf. Cutts* v. *Chumley*, *supra.* For the recovery of special

consortium. The husband's right is regarded as an historical anomaly which should not be extended to a wife. So, where a husband, through the negligence and breach of statutory duty of the defendants, suffered an accident which deprived him of sexual capacity, it was held that the wife had no right of action in respect thereof.[90] If, however, the wife were injured by the defendant's negligence and suffered such disfigurement as to cause her husband to leave her, it may well be that she could recover damages for this as part of the consequential damage from the defendant's negligence.[91]

164 **No damages for death of a human being.** When the injured party has died as a result of the injuries inflicted by the negligence of the defendant, no action at all can be brought by a person, whether husband or master, who has sustained special damage thereby. This was decided in *Baker* v. *Bolton*,[92] where the plaintiff and his wife were injured by the negligence of the proprietors of a stage coach, and the wife died of the injuries. It was held that the husband could only recover damages for his own injuries and not for the loss of his wife's help in his business or for his grief and distress of mind, Lord Ellenborough saying: "In a civil court, the death of a human being could not be complained of as an injury." This was followed in *Osborn* v. *Gillett*,[93] where it was held that a father was not entitled to damages for injuries caused to his "daughter and servant" by the negligence of the defendant, resulting in his daughter's death, either in respect of the loss of her services or of the expense to which he had been put in burying her. On the same principle, it was held that the Admiralty Commissioners could not recover the amount of the pensions payable by them to the relatives of an officer and seamen, the crew of a submarine, who were drowned as a result of a collision caused by the negligence of the defendants.[94] The law, as stated above, is not affected by the provisions of the Law Reform (Miscellaneous Provisions) Act 1934,[95] so that the result is that special damage sustained by a third party in respect of the death of another caused by the negligence—as opposed to the breach of contract [96] —of the defendant is irrecoverable.

165 **Reimbursement of a third party's losses.** At one time there was considerable support for the view that a person could sue if he had necessarily incurred expense as a result of the defendant's negligence. So, a parent could sue for expense he had incurred through injuries caused to his

damages as an alternative to damages for loss of consortium, see *McNeill* v. *Johnstone* [1958] 1 W.L.R. 888, *post*, § 168.

90 *Best* v. *Samuel Fox & Co. Ltd.* [1952] A.C. 716.

91 *Lampert* v. *Eastern National Omnibus Co.* [1954] 1 W.L.R. 1047.

92 (1808) 1 Camp. 493.

93 (1873) L.R. 8 Ex. 88, followed and approved by the C.A. in *Clark* v. *L.G.O.* [1906] 2 K.B. 648.

94 *The Amerika* [1917] A.C. 38.

95 *Rose* v. *Ford* [1937] A.C. 826; *per* Lord Russell of Killowen at p. 839, *per* Lord Roche at p. 854.

96 *Jackson* v. *Watson & Sons* [1909] 2 K.B. 193.

child by the defendant's negligence.[97] Also, the Receiver for the Metropolitan Police District who had paid, under statutory powers, the pay and allowances of a member of the metropolitan police force injured by the defendant's negligence, could recover from the defendant the sums he so paid,[98] and the Crown could sue for wages paid to an airman injured by the defendant's negligence.[1] However, in *Receiver for the Metropolitan Police District* v. *Croydon Corporation* [2] a police constable was injured while on duty by the defendants' negligence as a result of which he was incapacitated from performing his duties for several months. During that period the police authority, acting under statutory regulations, had to pay the constable his full wages and allowances, and in due course he successfully sued for damages but made no claim for any loss of wages. Basing their claim on unjust benefit, the police authority then sued the defendants for the amount of wages and allowances so paid to the constable. The Court of Appeal held, since the police authority had not been called upon to pay anything which they would not otherwise have had to pay, there was no obligation on the defendants to repay the police authority what they had paid the constable. The defendants had paid to the constable by way of damages all that they were in law liable to pay, which did not include any loss of wages since none had been incurred in the circumstances. Following this decision now, the earlier view must be considered to be erroneous and those cases in support of it wrongly decided.

166 A child who gives up paid work to look after a parent injured by the defendant's negligence has no right of action against the defendant because the defendant has not committed a breach of duty towards the child.[3] This, however, is not a case of the child incurring expense on behalf of the parent, it is the case of the child itself suffering a loss. If, on the other hand, the parent paid the child for its services those payments would be recoverable by the parent as part of the parent's damage, provided they were reasonably and properly incurred.

167 Normally therefore such third party will have no remedy directly against the wrongdoer,[4] since no duty is owed by the defendant to him. Thus it becomes necessary to consider if any indirect method can be employed to achieve the desired result. Accordingly in an action for damages

97 See *Barnes* v. *Pooley* (1935) 51 T.L.R. 391 (stepchild. This was decided on an admission of liability, there being no contention to the contrary). In *Cook* v. *Wright* [1967] N.Z.L.R. 1034 where parents claimed for the expense of visiting their 15-year-old son in hospital, following an accident to him, it was held that the remedy is separate and distinct from that of the infant in respect of the original negligence and that the judgment on the infant's claim was not binding on either party, if the parents should later make a claim.

98 *Receiver for Metropolitan Police* v. *Tatum* [1948] 2 K.B. 68.

1 *Att.-Gen.* v. *Valle-Jones* [1935] 2 K.B. 209.

2 [1957] 2 Q.B. 154; *Att.-Gen. for New South Wales* v. *Perpetual Trustee Co. Ltd.* [1955] A.C. 457.

3 See *Best* v. *Samuel Fox & Co. Ltd.* [1952] A.C. 716, 734, *per* Lord Morton.

4 The exceptions are dealt with *ante*, § 161 and § 163 being the ancient actions of *per quod servitum amisit* and *per quod consortium amisit* which will not be extended in their scope since they are both anachronistic: *Att.-Gen. for New South Wales* v. *Perpetual Trustee Co. Ltd.* [1955] A.C. 457.

for personal injuries the question often arises whether the injured person can include in his claim for special damage that sum of money needed to reimburse in full a third party, who had incurred expense or even financial losses by coming to his assistance reasonably required as a result of the defendant's negligence. For example, a relative or friend may have given up gainful employment temporarily or even permanently in order to provide the injured plaintiff with nursing services that he needs as a result of the defendant's negligence. Where there is no legal obligation to reimburse the third party, even though the plaintiff feels under a moral obligation to do so, difficulties are met in enabling him to recover these sums of money due to the reluctance of the courts to award such damages.[5] On the other hand, where the plaintiff is under a legal obligation to reimburse his benefactor, such losses of wages or expenses raise no problems, since these are ordinary and reasonable expenses properly incurred by the plaintiff as a result of the defendant's negligence and are recoverable as special damage.[6] In *Roach* v. *Yates* [7] the plaintiff sustained by reason of the defendant's negligence a severe brain injury, which made it necessary that he should have day and night services of some nurse or friend to look after him for the rest of his life. This service was provided by his wife and his sister-in-law, both of whom willingly gave up their employment in order to nurse him, resulting in the loss of their weekly wages. Whilst there was no legal obligation placed upon either to do so, Greer L.J. considered that the plaintiff " would naturally feel that he ought to compensate them for what they have lost by giving up the work at which they were earning the sum of £3 a week." Accordingly the Court of Appeal awarded him damages under this head. In *Schneider* v. *Eisovitch* [8]

[5] *e.g. Kirkham* v. *Boughey* [1958] 2 Q.B. 338; *McDonnell* v. *Stevens, The Times*, April 8, 1967; *Fabiszewski* v. *Hutchings* (1969) 4 D.L.R. (3d) 187.

[6] *e.g. Inland Revenue Commissioners* v. *Hambrook* [1956] 2 Q.B. 641, 656–657, where Lord Goddard C.J. said: " Often it happens that a considerate employer, relative, or some kindly disposed friend gives an injured man a sum equivalent to his wages during incapacity on the terms that if he recovers his loss of wages as part of his special damage in an action he should repay what is advanced to him. Sometimes, too, I have known a loan to enable an injured man to go away for convalescence or to receive some special treatment which he could not afford from his own resources. I have never known these items when claimed as special damage to be disallowed, provided they were reasonable."

[7] [1938] 1 K.B. 256; where a wife lost her wages by taking time off to nurse the plaintiff, her disabled husband, it was held that this loss was recoverable and it was irrelevant that the plaintiff was not legally bound to repay his wife the loss of her wages: *Wattson* v. *Port of London Authority* [1969] 1 Lloyd's Rep. 95. See however *McDonnell* v. *Stephens, The Times*, April 8, 1967, where the husband stayed off work to nurse his wife, there being no principle which entitled him to recover in the absence of a contractual obligation. *per* Swanwick J. It is submitted that this case must be wrongly decided in the light of the Court of Appeal in *Roach* v. *Yates, supra*, and *Hawkes* v. *Torquay Corporation* [1938] 4 All E.R. 16 (daughter's nursing services). However where his children gave up their jobs to work at the plaintiff's farm, during his recuperation following an accident, it was held that because the father was not legally bound to pay his children for their services he could not recover damages for their lost earnings, despite the fact that he had undertaken to pay over such amounts to them: *Fabiszewski* v. *Hutchings, supra*.

[8] [1960] 2 Q.B. 430, 440, where a plaintiff sought to recover the expenses incurred by her brother-in-law and his wife when they flew out to France to assist her back home to England and, at the same time, to assist her in making the necessary arrangements for her husband's body to be brought back for burial. This decision was followed by Megaw J. in *Wattson* v. *Port of London Authority, supra*. However, it appears to be contrary to the *ratio decidendi* of the Court of Appeal in *Allen* v. *Waters & Co., supra* (see 76 L.Q.R. 187).

Paull J. held that whilst a moral obligation only to reimburse was insufficient for a third party's out-of-pocket expenses incurred to be recovered they could be recovered if the plaintiff could show: " first that the services rendered were reasonably necessary as a consequence of the tortfeasor's tort; secondly that the out-of-pocket services are reasonable bearing in mind all the circumstances including whether expenses would have been incurred had the friend or friends not assisted; and, thirdly, that the plaintiff undertakes to pay the sum awarded to the friend or friends." Thus if the special damage can be regarded as the damage of the injured person it can be included in the injured person's claim and it has been directed to be paid to the person who actually incurred it [9] although this order would seem to be of doubtful authority.

168 A husband can sue for medical and other expenses to which he has been put as a result of personal injuries inflicted on his wife if he is liable to pay them, even though he has not actually paid them at the date of the trial.[10] " The judge is entitled to give damages which have been suffered by a husband and wife arising out of the wife's accident. It not infrequently occurs that a husband has become liable to a doctor for fees which have not been paid at the time when the action is brought, and it sometimes happens that they could not have been paid; nevertheless, there was the liability to pay and, whether the fees have been paid or not, a claim in respect of them is in practice allowed as good and added to the sum which is recoverable as damages." [11] The husband, in such a case, can also claim any expense to which he has been put in the way of engaging a housekeeper to manage his household during his wife's illness, and the additional expense to which he is put owing to his household costing him more when managed by a housekeeper than when managed by his wife.[12] But where the wife sustains personal injuries as a result of the defendant's negligence and the husband thereupon sustains a loss of earnings owing to his taking less remunerative work to enable him to look after the children and to visit his wife in hospital, that loss is not recoverable.[13] In this instance it was held that the husband's damages were limited to damages for loss of consortium and the expense to which he was put in respect of medical treatment and convalescence. " Visits by a spouse may well be a factor in the recovery of a patient and a visit

Meanwhile in *Gage* v. *King* [1961] 1 Q.B. 188 where a husband and wife were injured in a car collision with the defendant's car, for which the husband was held two-thirds to blame and the defendant one-third, and the wife incurred medical expenses which the husband paid from a joint banking account, Diplock J. considered the fact of payment out of the joint account to be irrelevant, and the real question depended on which of them incurred the legal liability to pay the expense. It was held that the sole liability was incurred by the husband and thus was recoverable as special damage caused to him and not to the wife.

9 *Dennis* v. *L.P.T.B.* [1948] 1 All E.R. 779; see also *Allen* v. *Waters & Co.* [1935] 1 K.B. 200.

10 *Allen* v. *Waters & Co.* [1935] 1 K.B. 200.

11 *Ibid., per* Lord Hanworth M.R. at p. 206.

12 *Berry* v. *Humm & Co.* [1915] 1 K.B. 627; *Feay* v. *Barnwell* [1938] 1 All E.R. 31.

13 *Kirkham* v. *Boughey* [1958] 2 Q.B. 338. Likewise the loss of her earnings because she had had to give up her work in order to look after her husband, rendered a permanent invalid by the defendant's negligence, was irrecoverable in law: *Janney* v. *Gentry* (1966) 110 S.J. 408.

to a wife in hospital may thus be a proper step in mitigating the damage sustained by loss of consortium by reducing the period during which the consortium is lost. But if the sole justification for the visit is the comfort or pleasure which it gives to the wife, then I think it is not recoverable." [14]

169 The husband's right to claim medical expenses in respect of his wife is based on his legal obligation to maintain her and provide her when necessary with proper medical and surgical aid, but his right to recover the domestic expenses is based on his ancient right to sue for damages for loss of her services.[15] For the husband's right to recover damages for loss of his wife's consortium as an alternative to special damages, see *ante*, § 163. If the damage to the wife was caused partly through her own negligence, so that her own claims against the defendant had been reduced under the Law Reform (Contributory Negligence) Act 1945, the husband can still recover the full amount of the expenses to which he has been put as a result of his wife's injuries, because his right of action is not derived from his wife but is a separate action resulting from marriage.[16]

170 **Interest.** By the Law Reform (Miscellaneous Provisions) Act 1934,[17] interest on the damages from the date of the wrongful act may be awarded in cases where it would be reasonable for a court to do so, but it ought to be calculated only upon the balance of the award after bringing into account other compensation received by the plaintiffs. Where the plaintiffs' factory was burnt down due to the defendants' negligence, the plaintiffs were awarded £146,000 by way of damages. In addition they were awarded £26,835 by way of interest, but the trial judge had failed to take into consideration the fact that the plaintiffs had received substantial sums from their insurance company soon after the disastrous fire, namely, £50,000 within eight weeks, £40,000 within a few months and yet further sums of money. The Court of Appeal held that, whilst acknowledging that an award of interest was discretionary, normally the basis of such an award was that the defendant had kept the plaintiff out of his money, had had the use of it himself and ought to compensate the plaintiff as a result. However that reasoning did not apply when the plaintiff had not

14 *Per* Diplock J. at p. 343. Also see note on this case, 74 L.Q.R. 6. However a different view was expressed in *Behrens* v. *Bertram Mills Circus Ltd.* [1957] 2 Q.B. 1, where a husband and wife, both midgets, were injured. They earned their living by performing together, but the husband was the more important wage-earner of the two. The husband recovered first, but did not perform again until his wife was fit to perform again. It was held that, in the peculiar circumstances, the husband had acted reasonably and could be awarded damages for what he lost when he was not performing. In *McNeill* v. *Johnstone* [1958] 1 W.L.R. 888 where a husband took a month's unpaid leave from the United States Air Force to be with his wife, lying some distance away in hospital, following a motor accident, it was held that he, having given up his earnings to preserve his consortium, was entitled to recover his loss of earnings as an alternative to damages for loss of consortium.

15 *Best* v. *Samuel Fox & Co. Ltd.* [1952] A.C. 716, *per* Lord Goddard.

16 *Mallett* v. *Dunn* [1949] 2 K.B. 180. In *Curran* v. *Young* (1965) 112 C.L.R. 99 the High Court of Australia affirmed the principle that contributory negligence of a wife acting otherwise than as the servant or agent of her husband affords no defence to an action brought by the husband for his loss in respect of the injuries caused to her by the defendant's negligence.

17 s. 3.

been kept out of his money, *e.g.* where he had been indemnified by his insurers. Thus sums received from the insurance company should go in relief of the defendants, hence an award of interest should be made only upon the outstanding balance.[18] Until January 1, 1970, the power of the courts to award interest in all cases was discretionary, but in cases now where the claim consists of or involves personal injuries the power must be exercised compulsorily as a result of the Administration of Justice Act 1969.[19] As only was to be expected where the matter had been left to the courts to decide the principles on which interest should be awarded, scores of cases came before the judges, each of whom applied a different answer. Out of the confusion therefore the Court of Appeal, in *Jefford* v. *Gee*, [20] felt that it was duty bound to set out the guide-lines, even though in some respects Lord Denning thought that their observations might be *obiter dicta*. Accordingly, by gathering together the best of the reasoning from older authorities [21] the principles to be applied in awarding interest are: interest should not be awarded as compensation for the damage done; it should only be awarded to a plaintiff *for being kept out* of money which ought to have been paid to him.

171 It seems necessary that in order to carry out this compulsory provision of the 1969 Act the court would have to itemise the damages in most personal injury cases. In general, interest should be awarded on the following lines: interest on special damage should be allowed from the date of the accident to the date of trial at half the appropriate rate; no interest should be allowed on loss of future earnings; interest should be awarded on the damages given for pain and suffering and loss of amenities at the appropriate rate from the date of service of the writ [21a] to the date of trial; the same principle should apply to interest on Fatal Accidents Acts awards; and the appropriate rate should be the rate allowed by the court on the short-term investment account, taken as an average over the period for which interest was awarded. In most cases coming up for decision in 1970–71 the average could be taken to be 6 per cent. The judgment should state the rate of interest and the period for which it was awarded and should state it as a gross sum without deducting tax. Payment into court should be made without regard to interest.[22] The court has no power to award interest on damages where the payment in has been taken out of the court by the plaintiff in settlement of his claim.[23] In exceptional

[18] *Harbutt's " Plasticine " Ltd.* v. *Wayne Tank & Pump Co. Ltd.* [1970] 1 Q.B. 447. See article: " Fundamental Breach and Exemption Clauses, Damages and Interest " (Legh Jones and Pickering), 86 L.Q.R. 513.

[19] s. 22.

[20] [1970] 2 Q.B. 130. See articles: 120 New L.J. 237 and 308; " Interest on damages ": 114 S.J. 612.

[21] *e.g. London Chatham and Dover Railway Co.* v. *S.E. Railway Co.* [1893] A.C. 429, 437, *per* Lord Herschell. In *May* v. *A. G. Basset & Sons* (1970) 114 S.J. 269 the plaintiff duly succeeded in a fatal accident claim but only after the action had been adjourned at the plaintiff's request. It was held that notwithstanding the fact that the adjournment was through no fault of the defendants, they still had had use of the money throughout the time so that under s. 22 of the Act they should be ordered to pay interest up to the date of the trial.

[21a] In *Slater* v. *Hughes* (1971) 115 S.J. 428, it was held that a third party, who was eventually made a defendant, should pay interest only from the date of issue of the third party notice and not from the date of writ.

cases, such as when one party had been guilty of gross delay, the court might depart from the above suggestions by diminishing or increasing the award of interest or altering the periods for which it was allowed.[23a]

Where the Court of Appeal has increased the award of damages on appeal, in awarding interest on that increase of damages, credit should be given to the interest automatically allowable under the Judgments Act 1838.[24]

172 **Right to recover damages from insurer.** When death or bodily injury to any person is caused by or arises out of the use of a motor-vehicle on a road, then, subject to the qualifications stated below, the damages may be obtained from the insurers of the defendant by whose negligence the death or bodily injury was caused. It is compulsory for every person who drives a motor-vehicle to be insured against his liability for the death of or bodily injury to any person due to the use of his vehicle on the road except (1) in respect of accidents arising out of and in the course of his employment to a servant employed by the person insured; and (2) in the case of a lorry or other vehicle in which passengers are not carried for reward, in respect of accidents to persons carried in or upon or entering or getting onto or alighting from the vehicle at the time of the accident.[25] When such insurance is effected and a certificate of insurance has been delivered under the Road Traffic Act 1960, s. 205 (1) (3), judgment in respect of a liability covered by the policy—which will not be less than is required by the statute as stated above—obtained against a person insured by the policy may be enforced against the insurer for the full amount of the judgment including costs and interest, notwithstanding that the insurer may be entitled to avoid or cancel the

[22] It is not convincing that this would bring about a fair result where, for example, the payment in is close to the apparent value of the claim. Consider a typical case of a payment into court of £2,000: if the plaintiff decides to accept it he must waive his rights to the interest it would otherwise attract; whilst if he proceeds to judgment and is awarded precisely £2,000 (a not-unknown coincidence) he would then be awarded the compulsory interest on that sum, thereby increasing his financial compensation. But, because he had failed to beat the *payment* in and since interest for this purpose must be ignored, he would lose substantially on the costs. Accordingly the additional dilemma facing the plaintiff in such circumstances is that if he be minded to accept the payment in he cannot obtain the extra sum to which he should be entitled by way of interest except against the penalty of paying the costs. This seems hardly conducive to achieving settlements, which the courts admittedly have to rely upon in order to shorten their lists, especially at Assizes when a civil action can be listed, but miss two sittings before being heard at the third Assizes some nine months or more later, by which time even more valuable interest is at stake!

[23] *Newall* v. *Tunstall* [1971] 1 W.L.R. 105. See also *Waite* v. *Redpath Dorman Long Ltd.* [1971] 1 Q.B. 294, where it was held that an order under R.S.C., Ord. 22, r. 5, being neither a judgment for a sum of money nor a judgment given in proceedings tried in court, was not a judgment falling within s. 3 of the Law Reform (Miscellaneous Provisions) Act 1934, so that the plaintiff was entitled only to the money paid into court and not to any interest thereon. In *Blundell* v. *Rimmer* [1971] 1 W.L.R. 123 it was held that interest cannot be obtained by a plaintiff signing interlocutory judgment with an order for the damages to be assessed by a judge after money has been paid into court.

[23a] *e.g. Chadwick* v. *Parsons*, *The Times*, January 23, 1971.

[24] *Cook* v. *J. L. Kier & Co.* [1970] 1 W.L.R. 774.

[25] Road Traffic Act 1960, s. 203. A workman who is carried on a lorry or other non-passenger vehicle in pursuance of some contract of employment with another employer, not the owner of the vehicle, can recover under this section from the insurer if he is injured in a collision. *Izzard* v. *Universal Insurance Co. Ltd.* [1937] A.C. 773.

policy.[26] The judgment cannot be enforced against the insurer unless, before or within seven days of the commencement of the proceedings against the person insured, notice of the proceedings was given to the insurer.[27] The insurer is also freed from liability if, before the accident, the policy was cancelled and the certificate of insurance was surrendered to the insurer within fourteen days from the taking effect of the cancellation of the policy, or the insurer within the fourteen days took proceedings in respect of the failure to surrender the certificate.[28] Also the insurer is not liable if, in an action commenced within three months of the commencement of proceedings by the injured person or the dependants or the personal representatives of the deceased, he has obtained a declaration that, apart from any provision in the policy, he is entitled to avoid it on the ground that it was obtained by the non-disclosure of a material fact [29] or by a representation of fact which was false in some material particular, and, within seven days of the commencement of his action for a declaration, he has given notice to the injured person or other plaintiff of the non-disclosure or false representation on which he proposes to rely.[30] If the insurer denies liability under the policy, he can be joined as a third party by the defendant who is sued by the person injured.[31]

173 The provisions set out in the preceding paragraph only apply to damages for death or personal injury. When a person who is insured against liabilities to third parties of any kind becomes bankrupt or makes a composition or arrangement with his creditors or, being a company, goes into liquidation or has a receiver appointed, his rights against the insurer are transferred to and vest in the third party to whom the liability is incurred.[32] This gives the third party who has suffered damage arising from a risk covered by the policy the right to enforce the policy to the same extent, but no further, that the insured person could have done.[33]

174 **Effect of the Road Traffic Act 1960 on drivers of motor-vehicles.** Owing to the compulsory nature of the insurance required by the Road Traffic Act 1960 [34] it is usual, and indeed almost essential for business purposes, for the owner of a motor-vehicle to insure against third party risks not only when he is driving the vehicle himself, but also when the vehicle is being driven by any person on his order or with his permission. When this is so, the insurer is liable to indemnify such person

[26] *Ibid.*, s. 207. [27] *Ibid.*, s. 207 (2) (*a*). [28] *Ibid.*, s. 207 (2) (*c*).

[29] " Material " means of such a nature as to influence the judgment of a prudent insurer in determining whether he will take the risk, and, if so, at what premium and on what conditions: s. 207 (5).

[30] Road Traffic Act 1960, s. 207 (3). [31] *Harman* v. *Crilly* [1943] K.B. 168.

[32] Third Parties (Rights against Insurers) Act 1930. The rights transferred by this Act are (subject to the provisions of s. 207 of the Road Traffic Act 1960) subject to the rights of the insurer against the assured. For the application of this Act to road traffic cases, see s. 208 of the Act of 1960; *Smith* v. *Pearl Assurance Co.* [1939] 1 All E.R. 95.

[33] *Vandepitte* v. *Preferred Accident Insurance Corpn. of New York* [1933] A.C. 70; *Hindmarch* v. *Carterthorne Colliery Ltd.* (1928) 21 B.W.C.C. 44.

[34] Which repealed and re-enacted the earlier Road Traffic Acts.

against any liability which the policy purports to cover in respect of that person,[35] and the indemnity can be enforced by that person in an action against the insurer, although he is not a party to the contract of insurance.[36] The owner of a motor-vehicle who permits his vehicle to be used by a person who is not insured against third-party risks is liable in damages to a third party who is injured by the negligent driving of the uninsured person.[37]

The result of the Road Traffic Act is that in most cases in which death or bodily injury is caused through the driving of a motor-vehicle on the road, the insurers will be liable to the injured party. But, apart from the cases contemplated by section 207, there are cases in which the insurers are under no liability. For example, they are not liable when a motor-vehicle insured for one kind of use, such as "for social, domestic and pleasure purposes" is used for another kind of use, such as business purposes.[38] They are also not liable if the owner of the vehicle has sold it and handed the insurance policy to the buyer, but the buyer has not taken out a policy of his own, because the policy lapses when the insured ceases to be the owner of the vehicle insured.[39]

175 **Right of hospitals and medical practitioners against negligent driver.** A registered medical practitioner who gives emergency treatment to a person injured by a motor-vehicle on a road, can recover the fees laid down in sections 212–214 from the person using the vehicle at the time, and that person can recover in respect of his liability from the person whose wrongful act caused the injury.[40] A hospital rendering emergency treatment is in the same position for this purpose as a medical practitioner. Payment made by an insurer in respect of the death of or injury to a person arising out of the use of a motor-vehicle on a road must include the reasonable expenses, not exceeding £50, of any treatment that person has received in hospital.[41]

176 **Motor Insurers' Bureau.** By an agreement of February 1, 1971, [41a] the Motor Insurers' Bureau agreed to satisfy a judgment not satisfied within seven days in respect of any liability which is required to be covered by insurance by Part VI of the Road Traffic Act 1960 (which deals with third-party claims). The Bureau must be given notice of the proceedings within twenty-one days of their being brought. The Bureau is not liable under the agreement in respect of the death of or injury to a servant of the owner of a motor-vehicle which arises out of or in the course of the

[35] Road Traffic Act 1960, s. 206 (3).
[36] *Tattersall* v. *Drysdale* [1935] 2 K.B. 174; *Austin* v. *Zurich Insce. Co.* [1945] K.B. 250.
[37] *Monk* v. *Warbey* [1935] 1 K.B. 75; *Houston* v. *Buchanan*, 1940 S.C.(H.L.) 17.
[38] *Jones* v. *Welsh Insurance Corpn. Ltd.* [1937] 4 All E.R. 149.
[39] *Peters* v. *General Accident and Life Assurance Corpn.* [1938] 2 All E.R. 267.
[40] Road Traffic Act 1960, s. 213.
[41] *Ibid.*, ss. 212 (1), (2), 214 (1) and 216 (1). See *Royal Victoria Hospital* v. *London Guarantee and Accident Corpn.* [1937] N.I. 64.
[41a] Which replaces the 1946 agreement. An earlier agreement, dated April 21, 1969, widened the scope of the 1946 agreement by covering "untraceable drivers." Nevertheless the M.I.B. still cannot both maintain as well as defend an action: *White* v. *London Transport Executive* [1971] 3 W.L.R. 169.

servant's employment[42]; on the other hand it is liable to satisfy the judgment, where at the time of the accident the injured person was being carried " for hire or reward." These words, which are contained in the proviso to section 203 of the Road Traffic Act 1960, must be construed, particularly in the context of a penal statute, as applying only to a *vehicle* in which passengers were systematically carried for hire or reward, " which went beyond the bounds of mere social kindness." [43] The agreement does not prevent a plaintiff from recovering damages under the principle of *Monk* v. *Warbey* [44] from an owner who has allowed an uninsured driver to drive his car.[45] The fact that an unsuccessful legally aided defendant is supported by the Bureau is a circumstance which is relevant to the question whether the order for costs made against him should be a full order or not.[46] The Bureau is not liable when a collision occurs on a road which is not a " road " within the meaning of the Road Traffic Act 1960, s. 257 (1).[47] However where a person on private land was injured by a lorry, the greater part of which was on a public road, and suffered injuries arising out of the use of the vehicle on a road within the meaning of ss. 203 (3) (*a*) and 257 of the said Act it was held that he was entitled to recover from the Bureau.[48]

177 **One action only for one cause of action.** In an action for negligence damages must be assessed once for all at the trial. Even if it is found later that damage suffered was much greater than was originally supposed, no further action can be brought.[49] Again, " it is a well-settled rule of law that damages resulting from one and the same cause of action must be assessed and recovered once for all." [50] Two actions, therefore, will not lie by one plaintiff against the same defendant for personal injuries sustained in the same accident. When a child was killed by the negligence of the defendant and an action was brought under the Law Reform (Miscellaneous Provisions) Act 1934, for damages in respect of the death but not for loss of expectation of life (which, owing to the decision of the Court of Appeal in *Rose* v. *Ford*,[51] was thought not to be a head of damage),

42 *Lees* v. *Motor Insurers' Bureau* [1952] 2 All E.R. 511.
43 *Albert* v. *Motor Insurers' Bureau, The Times*, July 10, 1971, where the H.L. favoured the " business test " as the correct approach. Viscount Dilhorne considered *Connell* v. *Motor Insurers' Bureau* [1969] 2 Q.B. 494, wrongly decided (uninsured passenger in a private motor car who paid the vehicle owner 10s. and stood him a drink on occasions, which constituted a binding contract for reward, was held unable to recover from the Bureau). Similarly, *Coward* v. *Motor Insurers' Bureau* [1963] 1 Q.B. 259. However, see further § 795, *post*, for the effect of compulsory insurance for passengers proposed.
44 [1935] 1 K.B. 75.
45 *Corfield* v. *Groves* [1950] 1 All E.R. 488.
46 *Godfrey* v. *Smith* [1955] 1 W.L.R. 692.
47 *Buchanan* v. *Motor Insurers' Bureau* [1955] 1 All E.R. 607 (road in dock).
48 *Randall* v. *Motor Insurers' Bureau* [1968] 1 W.L.R. 1900.
49 See *Conquer* v. *Boot* [1928] 2 K.B. 336; unless time for appeal has not expired so that leave can be obtained to adduce further evidence at the hearing of the appeal.
50 *Brunsden* v. *Humphrey* (1884) 14 Q.B.D. 141, 147, *per* Bowen L.J. See also *The Oropesa* [1943] P. 32, (collision between the M.R. and the O., in which the O. is to blame. Action for loss of drowned seaman's personal effects does not bar subsequent action for damages for loss of expectation of life).
51 [1936] 1 K.B. 90.

it was held that the acceptance of the sum paid into court in satisfaction of the claim barred a second action for damages for loss of expectation of life brought after the decision of the Court of Appeal had been reversed.[52] But, negligence resulting in personal injuries and also in damage to property gives rise to two causes of action because two different rights are infringed, and so a cabman, who was involved in a highway collision owing to the negligence of the defendant, after having recovered in an action for damage done to his cab, was held entitled to bring another action for damages for personal injuries sustained in the same collision.[53] In *Marginson* v. *Blackburn Corpn.*,[54] a collision took place between the plaintiff's motor-car and the defendants' omnibus in which a third party suffered damage. The third party sued both the plaintiff and the defendants, who served third-party notices against each other and were held equally to blame. The plaintiff then sued the defendants for damages for personal injuries and also as administrator of his wife, who was killed in the same collision, for damages under the Law Reform Act 1934, and the Fatal Accidents Acts 1846 to 1908. It was held that the judgment in the original action estopped him in his claim for personal injuries but not in his claims as administrator of his wife, because they were made by him in a different capacity. Again, when a son, driving his father's motor-car, was involved in a collision with the defendant, it was held that an action by the father for damage to his car did not prevent the son from bringing an action against the same defendant for damages for personal injuries.[55]

178 A passenger in a motor-car who was injured in a collision between the car and a lorry in France caused, as the French court held, by the negligence of both drivers (three-fourths to the lorry and one-fourth to the car), after recovering damages in France against the lorry driver was held entitled to damages from the car driver. The amount of damages was not that fixed by the French court but had to be assessed by the English court. The plaintiff was willing to give credit for the damages recovered from the lorry driver, so that no decision was given whether he was bound to do so.[56]

179 **Knock-for-knock agreement.** Payment by the plaintiff's insurance company of the cost of repairs to the plaintiff's motor-car under the terms of a " knock-for-knock " agreement with the defendant's insurance company does not prevent the plaintiff, although requested not to do so by his insurance company, from suing the defendant for damages for negligence, including the cost of the repairs.[57] Such proportion of the damages recovered as were attributable to the cost of the repairs would be held by the plaintiff as trustee for his insurance company.

[52] *Derrick* v. *Williams* [1939] 2 All E.R. 559.

[53] *Brunsden* v. *Humphrey* (1884) 14 Q.B.D. 141.

[54] [1939] 2 K.B. 426. See " Estoppel and the Law of Negligence," by H. Street, 73 L.Q.R. 358, in which it is argued that *Marginson* v. *Blackburn Corporation* wrongly decided that there was an estoppel.

[55] *Townsend* v. *Bishop* [1939] 1 All E.R. 805.

[56] *Kohnke* v. *Karger* [1951] 2 K.B. 670.

[57] *Morley* v. *Moore* [1936] 2 K.B. 359.

CHAPTER 5

THE STANDARD OF CARE

180 **Standard of care a question of law.** Once it has been shown that a duty to take care arises, it becomes necessary to inquire how much care the law requires to be exercised.[1] The standard of care is a question of law. Whether that standard has been attained in any given case is a question of fact.[2] The standard is usually proportioned to the gravity and imminence of the risk, but this is not invariably the case, as the law occasionally lays down different standards to be applied when the risk is the same. For example, the standard of care required from a motorist is to drive with reasonable care, but if he approaches a pedestrian crossing he must take much more care than usual.[3]

181 **The reasonable man as the standard of care.** The standard of care usually adopted is that of a reasonable man—what is called reasonable care. In Alderson B.'s classic words,[4] " Negligence is the omission to do something which a reasonable man, guided upon those considerations which ordinarily regulate the conduct of human affairs, would do: or doing something which a prudent and reasonable man would not do." But, it is necessary to inquire somewhat more carefully into the standard of the reasonable man. The reasonable man knows the standard of care which the law exacts from him, and therefore complies with it, and, accordingly, it is a truism to say that the amount of care required by the law is to be measured by the conduct of a reasonable man. A reasonable man who drives a motor-car has the skill of a competent driver, has a complete knowledge of the Highway Code and the various statutory regulations dealing with the driving of motor-cars, and complies with them, but when this has been said it affords very little information as to the standard of care required by law from motorists. The fact is that in numerous operations of life, of which driving motor-cars may be taken as an example, the law has worked out definite rules which must be complied with, and these rules represent the legal standard of care in that case. These rules vary from time to time as social conditions and habits

1 As Lord Wilberforce said in *Goldman* v. *Hargrave* [1967] 1 A.C. 645, 663: " So far it has been possible to consider the existence of a duty, in general terms. But the matter cannot be left there without some definition of the scope of his duty. How far does it go? What is the standard of the effort required?"

2 The House of Lords has pointed out several times the undesirability of courts attempting to reduce to rules of law the question whether or not in any given case reasonable care has been taken: *e.g. Qualcast* (*Wolverhampton*) *Ltd.* v. *Haynes* [1959] A.C. 743, Lord Keith at p. 755 and Lord Somervell at pp. 757–758; *Cavanagh* v. *Ulster Weaving Co. Ltd.* [1960] A.C. 145, Lord Keith at pp. 163–164; *Brown* v. *Rolls-Royce Ltd.* [1960] 1 W.L.R. 210, Lord Keith at p. 214 and Lord Denning at p. 215.

3 *Bailey* v. *Geddes* [1938] 1 K.B. 156.

4 *Blyth* v. *Birmingham Waterworks* (1856) 11 Ex. 781, 784.

of life vary, but they regulate the standard of care at any given time. Just as it would be wrong for a tribunal of fact to apply to a motorist its own view of the conduct of a reasonable man under the circumstances, without regard to such things as the rule of the road and the other rules of conduct which are embodied in the Highway Code and the statutory regulations, so it is equally wrong to apply the abstract test of reasonableness to other cases in which definite rules have been laid down.

182 No doubt the standard of care required under various different sets of circumstances is one which is derived from a common source, namely, what was reasonable under those circumstances. But situations tend to repeat themselves, persons find that if they do what was found to be reasonable under similar circumstances in the past they will themselves be free from liability, and accordingly the general rule of reasonable conduct tends to be split up into a number of branches, each of which contains directions as to the way in which a reasonable man would behave under the circumstances in question. This result is both inevitable and beneficial. One of the objects of law is to prescribe rules of conduct so that the individual will know how to act in any given set of circumstances, and to direct him to act as a reasonable man without telling him in more detail how a reasonable man is found by experience to act under those circumstances is to give him very little guidance. When new sets of circumstances arise, it is necessary to fall back on the general test of reasonable conduct viewed in the light of such of the existing rules of conduct as seem most nearly appropriate to the case. For example, the advent of the motor-car gave rise to a new series of problems. These are being solved by adopting the old rules with regard to horse-drawn traffic and modifying them where it is reasonable to do so. They are not solved by discarding the old rules as to horse-drawn traffic and beginning afresh to apply the test of reasonable conduct to motor-cars.

183 The result is that to say that the standard of care is that of a reasonable man is to beg the question. A jury can only be directed to apply the standard of reasonable care if it is explained to them what amount of care the law regards as reasonable under the circumstances of the case they are trying. If reasonable care alone were the only test, the following pages would be superfluous.

This view just expressed is dealt with by Lord Atkin in connection with breach of statutory duty. He said: " The employer is alleged to have committed a breach of a duty owed by him to his servant to take a particular precaution (namely, support of the roof) for his servant's safety whereby the servant was injured. In my opinion that state of facts constitutes negligence of the employer; and I am unable to conceive of any accurate definition of negligence which could exclude it. All that is necessary to show is a duty to take care to avoid injuring; and if the particular care to be taken is prescribed by statute, and the duty to the injured person to take care is likewise imposed by statute, and the breach is proved, all the essentials of negligence are present. I cannot think that the true position is, as appears to be suggested, that in such cases negligence only exists where the tribunal of fact agrees with the legislature that the precaution is one that ought to be taken. The very object of the legislation is to put that particular precaution beyond controversy." [5] The same result follows where the particular care to be taken has been laid down by judicial decisions. Where no particular care has been laid down, the tribunal of fact can apply the broad test of reasonable care according to its own ideas of what is reasonable under the circumstances. It follows that it is in this flexibility where the true value of the principle of reasonableness can be found.

184 **Matters to be taken into account.** In *Morris* v. *West Hartlepool Steam Navigation Co. Ltd.*[6] Lord Reid said: " It is the duty [of an employer], in considering whether some precaution should be taken against a foreseeable risk, to weigh, on the one hand, the magnitude of the risk, the likelihood of an accident happening and the possible seriousness of the consequences if an accident does happen, and, on the other hand, the difficulty and expense and any other disadvantage of taking the precaution." It will be convenient to consider these matters in greater detail.

185 **(1)—Magnitude of the risk.** The degree of care to be taken depends on the magnitude of the risk, the greater the risk the more care should be taken. " The degree of care for the safety of others which the law requires human beings to observe in the conduct of their affairs varies according to the circumstances. There is no absolute standard, but it may be said generally that the degree of care required varies directly with the risk involved. Those who engage in operations inherently dangerous must take precautions which are not required of persons engaged in the ordinary routine of daily life." [7] When dangerous things, such as explosives, are handled " the law exacts a degree of diligence so stringent as to amount practically to a guarantee of safety." [8] At the other extreme, the degree of risk may be so small that no care need be taken. For example, in *Glasgow Corpn.* v. *Muir* [9] the manageress of a tea room, in which there were children buying sweets from a counter, gave permission to two men, members of a church picnic party, to carry a tea urn, full of hot tea, to the tea room through a narrow passage, on one side of which was the counter. While carrying the urn one of the men let go of the handle, so that the tea was spilled and scalded some of the children. The manageress owed a duty of care to the children and the question was whether she had

[5] *Lochgelly Iron and Coal Co.* v. *M'Mullan* [1934] A.C. 1, 9.
[6] [1956] A.C. 552, 524.
[7] *Glasgow Corporation* v. *Muir* [1943] A.C. 448, 456 *per* Lord Macmillan. See also *Read* v. *J. Lyons & Co. Ltd.* [1947] A.C. 156, 173.
[8] *Donoghue* v. *Stevenson* [1932] A.C. 562, 612, *per* Lord Macmillan.
[9] [1943] A.C. 448.

discharged it. It was held that in the simple operation of carrying a tea urn through the passage it was so unlikely that one of the men would let go the handle of the urn that the manageress was not bound to anticipate it. " It was a mere possibility, not a reasonable probability . . . the risk of negligence was a mere unlikely accident which no reasonable person in [the manageress's] position could naturally be expected to foresee." [10]

Again, in *Bolton* v. *Stone* [11] a cricket ball was driven out of a cricket ground and injured a person walking on the highway. The occupiers of the cricket ground clearly owed a duty to take care for the safety of persons on the adjacent highway, but on the facts of the case it was held that they were not liable for the improbable injury suffered by the plaintiff. The degree of care they were bound to exercise was to take care to prevent probable accidents, they were not bound to guard against improbable but possible accidents. " It is therefore not enough for the plaintiff to say that the occupiers of the cricket ground could have foreseen the possibility that a ball might be hit out of the ground by a batsman and might injure people on the road; she must go further and say that they ought, as reasonable men, to have foreseen the probability of such an occurrence." [12]

186 If a factory is damaged so that, to the knowledge of the employer, there is a risk of the roof falling or the risk of a wall collapsing on the workmen, the degree of care to be taken may well be to close down the factory until such time as the roof or the wall has been made safe,[13] but when part of the floor of a factory became slippery from floodwater and oil it was held that " the degree of risk was too small to justify, let alone require, closing down " [14] and the employer was not liable to a workman who was injured by slipping on the floor.

Generally, the principle is, " the degree of care . . . must be

[10] *Ibid. per* Lord Wright at p. 465.
[11] [1951] A.C. 850.
[12] *Ibid. per* Lord Normand at p. 861. So, too, where the defendant hooked his drive off the tee and the golf ball hit another player 200 yards away, the risk of such an accident happening was held to be either unforeseeable or was so slight that it could be ignored: *Brewer* v. *Delo* [1967] 1 Lloyd's Rep. 488. By way of contrast, where the occupiers allowed children to play football on a piece of open grassland from which, from time to time, balls were kicked out onto the road, so that on one such occasion a passing motor-cyclist was struck accidentally and died as a result of his being knocked off his machine, it was held that the occupiers had failed to take reasonable care in all the circumstances: *Hilder* v. *Associated Portland Cement Manufacturers Ltd.* [1961] 1 W.L.R. 1434. The proximity of the road, the amount of traffic, the age of the children, the nature of their amusements and the frequency with which the green was used were all matters which a reasonable man must have considered. The risk of damage to persons using the road as a result of the children's activities was not so small that it could be safely disregarded. In *Lamond* v. *Glasgow Corporation*, 1968 S.L.T. 291 the golf course owners were held liable to a pedestrian, who was injured by being hit on the head by a golf ball, whilst walking along a narrow public lane. About 6,000 shots a year were played over the fence onto this lane, so that, although there was no previous history of any accident, it was nevertheless a foreseeable happening.
[13] *Latimer* v. *A.E.C. Ltd.* [1952] 2 Q.B. 701, *per* Singleton L.J. in a judgment approved in the H.L.
[14] *Latimer* v. *A.E.C. Ltd.* [1953] A.C. 643, 662, *per* Lord Asquith.

proportioned to the degree of risk involved if the duty should not be fulfilled." [15]

187 (2)—**Likelihood of injury.** The likelihood of injury or damage being caused is a matter to be taken into account in determining what degree of care, if any, need be taken in any given circumstances when a duty to take care exists. If the chance of injury is small, little or no precautions need be taken against it, but if it is great, precautions should be taken to prevent or avoid it. A greater risk of injury is a relevant matter to take into consideration,[16] so whether a two-eyed workman should be provided with goggles by his employer depends on whether the risk of accident is appreciable.[17] In *Bolton* v. *Stone*,[18] Lord Porter held [19] that one element to be taken into account was whether injury was likely to follow if a cricket ball was driven out of the ground.

Each situation therefore requires its own assessment of the likelihood of injury. Thus where the defendant was felling a tree, watched by children as well he knew, it was not enough for him just to warn them to stand well clear before the tree fell and he should have taken active steps to make sure that they were out of harm's way, since young children could not be expected to appreciate the danger involved in watching such an attraction.[20]

The fact that under comparable circumstances for a reasonable number of years there have been no or only infrequent accidents is strong evidence that the existing standard of care is a proper one [21] though it is not conclusive.[22]

188 (3)—**Gravity of the consequences.** As Lord Wright said: "The degree of care which [a] duty involves must be proportioned to the degree of risk involved if the duty should not be fulfilled." [23] The graver the consequences of a failure to take due care, the greater the degree of care which must be taken. A one-eyed man, working with a hammer and chisel on metal, runs the risk of getting a chip of metal in his one eye and becoming totally blind, so that the degree of care owed to him by an employer who knows that he is one-eyed is greater than the care owed to a two-eyed man. He should be provided with goggles, although it may not

[15] *Northwestern Utilities Ltd.* v. *London Guarantee & Accident Co. Ltd.* [1936] A.C. 108, 126, *per* Lord Wright. See also *Glasgow Corpn.* v. *Muir* [1943] A.C. 448, 456; *Read* v. *J. Lyons & Co. Ltd.* [1947] A.C. 156, 173.

[16] In *Paris* v. *Stepney B.C.* [1950] 1 K.B. 320, 323 Asquith L.J. said, "A greater risk of injury is not the same thing as a risk of greater injury: the first alone is relevant to liability." The H.L. held [1951] A.C. 367 that both were relevant to the degree of care to be taken.

[17] *Paris* v. *Stepney B.C.* [1951] A.C. 367. The H.L. did not decide whether goggles should have been provided for two-eyed workmen in that case.

[18] [1951] A.C. 850.

[19] *Ibid.* p. 858.

[20] *Mourton* v. *Poulter* [1930] 2 K.B. 183; see also *Excelsior Wire Rope Co. Ltd.* v. *Callan* [1930] A.C. 404.

[21] See, *e.g. Wright* v. *Cheshire C.C.* [1952] 2 All E.R. 789.

[22] See, *e.g. Hurley* v. *J. Sanders & Co. Ltd.* [1955] 1 All E.R. 833.

[23] *Northwestern Utilities Ltd.* v. *London Guarantee & Accident Co. Ltd.* [1936] A.C. 108, 126.

be necessary to provide them for a two-eyed man.[24] Lord Simonds said: " I see no valid reason for excluding as irrelevant the gravity of the damage which the employee will suffer if an accident occurs." [25] If gas be brought onto a ship in containers during the course of construction the degree of care to be exercised by those who brought it on board must be measured by the danger, which is involved. [26]

189 (4)—**Cost and practicability of overcoming risk.** Few things can be done without some risk. Crossing the street in a town is a risk and yet the street must be crossed. Cleaning the windows of a high building is a risk and yet the windows must be cleaned. Going to sea is a risk and yet shipping must be carried on. Some of the risks both of everyday life and of many occupations can only be completely overcome by refraining to carry on the relevant activity, such as by not crossing the street, not having the windows cleaned or not going to sea. Such a course is clearly impracticable, and consequently the standard of care to be taken is laid down by the common law or by statute in view of the special circumstances of the case. There are some cases, however, in which the risk can be reduced or eliminated, though at great cost, and the question then arises, at what point can the cost be taken into account in considering the degree of care to be taken? In *Latimer* v. *A.E.C. Ltd.*,[27] where the question was whether the slippery condition of the floor of part of a factory made it necessary to close that part until the floor was dry, Denning L.J., who held it was not necessary to do so, said, " In every case of a foreseeable risk it is a matter of balancing the risk against the measures necessary to eliminate it." On the other hand, in *Bolton* v. *Stone*,[28] where a batsman hit a cricket ball out of the ground and struck a person on the highway, Lord Reid in considering the question whether " a reasonable man in the position of the appellants, considering the matter from the point of view of safety would have thought it right to refrain from taking steps to prevent the danger," said " I think that it would be right to take into account; not only how remote is the chance that a person might be struck; but also how serious the consequences are likely to be if a person is struck, but I do not think it would be right to take into account the difficulty of remedial measures." [29]

190 In considering the difficulty, or cost, of remedial measures it is necessary to take into account not only the risk but also the importance of the object to be attained by the activity which creates the risk. If the activity in question is of little or no national importance, it might be that cost should not be taken into account, but in other cases there must be

24 *Paris* v. *Stepney B.C.* [1951] A.C. 367; *Porteous* v. *N.C.B.*, 1967 S.L.T. 117.
25 [1951] A.C. 367, 375.
26 *Beckett* v. *Newalls Insulation Co.* [1953] 1 W.L.R. 8.
27 [1953] A.C. 643; [1952] 2 Q.B. 701; but *cf. Johnson* v. *Rea* [1961] 1 W.L.R. 1400, where soda ash seeped through the hessian sacks in which it was contained and spilled onto the floor of a shed making it dangerously slippery.
28 [1951] A.C. 850. See *ante*, § 185.
29 *Ibid.* at p. 67.

a point, as in practice there is, beyond which further remedial measures are prohibitive by reason of cost.[30] A slight risk may be run if the cost of remedying it is unreasonably high,[31] but the greater the risk the greater must be the cost of remedying it before remedial measures can be dispensed with. As regards the liability of public authorities it seems that account must be taken of the social functions which need to be discharged in deciding the relevance of cost. Lord Thankerton said: " It does appear to me that there are special circumstances in the case of statutory bodies, such as the appellants, which should lead to the application of a somewhat less exacting standard than ordinarily prevails. . . . The provision of staff, plant and material adequate to deal with sudden emergencies, let alone their somewhat cramped financial resources, present great difficulty, and, when you add the importance and the urgency of remedial measures, it does seem to me that much may be condoned as well-meant error of judgment, which under other circumstances might be considered as unjustifiably risky." [32] It is a question of degree in each case to be considered together with the importance of the end to be attained.

191 In *Daborn* v. *Bath Tramways Ltd.*[33] Asquith L.J. said: " In determining whether a party is negligent, the standard of reasonable care is that which is reasonably to be demanded in the circumstances. A relevant circumstance to take into account may be the importance of the end to be served by behaving in this way or in that. As has often been pointed out, if all the trains in this country were restricted to a speed of five miles an hour, there would be fewer accidents, but our national life would be intolerably slowed down. The purpose to be served, if sufficiently important, justifies the assumption of abnormal risk." This passage was quoted with approval in *Watt* v. *Hertfordshire C.C.*[34] where a fireman, going to a fire in an emergency in a lorry which contained a heavy jack which could not be lashed to anything, was injured when the driver applied the brakes suddenly and the jack moved forward and struck him. The fire authority were held not liable, although they were held to be under a duty to take reasonable care to avoid exposing the fireman to unnecessary risks, on the ground that in saving life they were justified in taking greater risks than if they had been concerned in a commercial enterprise. Denning L.J. said: " It is well settled that in measuring due care you must balance the risk against the measures

[30] See the decisions on what is " reasonably practicable," *post*, Chap. 18.
[31] See *Latimer* v. *A.E.C. Ltd.* [1953] A.C. 643.
[32] *East Suffolk Rivers Catchment Board* v. *Kent* [1941] A.C. 74, 95, 96 (where the Board took 164 days to repair a breach in the sea wall, work which could easily have been done in a fortnight). However in *Haley* v. *London Electricity Board* [1965] A.C. 778 the defendants were held liable for failing to take precautions against a blind man falling down an inadequately guarded hole. A proper form of fencing such as a light portable guard could have been provided at a reasonable cost. *Keating* v. *Elvan Reinforced Concrete Co. Ltd.* [1968] 1 W.L.R. 722.
[33] [1946] 2 All E.R. 333, 336 (driver of ambulance with left-hand drive not negligent when, in wartime, she turned to the right without giving a signal).
[34] [1954] 1 W.L.R. 835, 838.

necessary to eliminate the risk. To that proposition there ought to be added this: you must balance the risk against the end to be achieved." [35]

192 **Common practice as the standard of care.** Common practice by persons habitually engaged in a particular operation is strong evidence of what is reasonable care in the performance of that operation.[36] "A defendant charged with negligence can clear [himself] if he shows that he has acted in accordance with general and approved practice." [37] "A plaintiff who seeks to have condemned as unsafe a system of work which has been generally used for a long time in an important trade undertakes a heavy onus; if he is right it means that all, or practically all, the numerous employers in the trade have been habitually neglecting their duty to their men." [38] In *Cavanagh* v. *Ulster Weaving Co. Ltd.*[39] it was held that it does not necessarily follow that the evidence as to trade practice alone should be treated as conclusive in favour of an employer, although if the employer has adopted a widely used system concerning which there has been no complaint he can rely on it as at least a prima facie defence to an action for negligence. Since compliance with common practice is evidence that reasonable care has been used, but is not conclusive, it is open to the court to hold that common practice does not make proper provision for a known risk.[40] For example, when a local authority, who were the water undertakers for the district, took the usual precautions taken by similar undertakers to discover escapes of water from their pipes, it was held that the fact that the precautions taken were usual did not prevent them from being inadequate to comply with the legal standard of care.[41] Conversely, merely because a defendant has failed to conform to common practice that is not necessarily conclusive evidence of negligence. For example, where employers had failed to supply the pursuer, a machine oiler, with a barrier cream, which was commonly supplied by other employers to their workmen doing this same type of work, as a result of which work he contracted dermatitis, it was held that in the circumstances they had not failed in their duty. The efficacy of the barrier cream had not been proved as a precaution against the disease or that it would probably have prevented him from contracting

[35] *Ibid.* at p. 838.

[36] *Mahon* v. *Osborne* [1939] 2 K.B. 14, 43, *per* MacKinnon L.J.; *Whiteford* v. *Hunter* [1950] W.N. 553; *Wright* v. *Cheshire C.C.* [1952] 2 All E.R. 789. *Simmons* v. *Pennington & Son* [1955] 1 W.L.R. 183; *Morris* v. *West Hartlepool Steam Navigation Co. Ltd.* [1956] A.C. 552; *Stokes* v. *Guest, Keen and Nettlefold (Bolts and Nuts) Ltd.* [1968] 1 W.L.R. 1776, 1783; *Henderson* v. *H. E. Jenkins & Sons* [1969] 2 Q.B. 188.

[37] *Vancouver General Hospital* v. *McDaniel* (1934) 152 L.T. 56, 57, *per* Lord Alness.

[38] *General Cleaning Contractors Ltd.* v. *Christmas* [1953] A.C. 180, 192, *per* Lord Reid.

[39] [1960] A.C. 145.

[40] *Morris* v. *W. Hartlepool S.N. Co.* [1956] A.C. 552; *Bank of Montreal* v. *Dominion Guarantee Co.* [1930] A.C. 659; *Lloyds Bank Ltd.* v. *Savory & Co.* [1933] A.C. 201; *Blenkiron* v. *Great Central Gas Consumer Co.* (1860) 2 F. & F. 437; *Brown* v. *John Mills & Co. (Llanidloes)* (1970) 8 K.I.R. 702 (C.A.).

[41] *Manchester Corpn.* v. *Markland* [1936] A.C. 360. The point is brought out better in the C.A. [1934] 1 K.B. 566. See also *Shell-Mex Ltd.* v. *Belfast Corpn.* [1952] N.I. 72.

it, thus the employer's omission satisfied the test of " the conduct and judgment of a reasonable and prudent man." [42]

193 Again, in connection with an employer's duty to his servant, Lord Dunedin, in an often quoted passage, said [43]: " Where the negligence of the employer consists of what I may call a fault of omission, I think it is absolutely necessary that the proof of that fault of omission should be one of two kinds, either to show that the thing which he did not do was a thing which was commonly done by other persons in like circumstances, or to show that it was a thing which was so obviously wanted that it would be folly in anyone to neglect to provide it." Lord Dunedin's test must be read with Lord Normand's gloss in *Paris* v. *Stepney B.C.*[44]: " If there is proof that a precaution is usually observed by other persons, a reasonable and prudent man will follow the usual practice in the like circumstances. Failing such proof, the test is whether the precaution is one which the reasonable and prudent man would think so obvious that it was folly to omit it." In *Cavanagh* v. *Ulster Weaving Co.*[45] Lord Keith: " Lord Dunedin cannot, in my opinion, have intended to depart from or modify the fundamental principle that an employer is bound to take reasonable care for the safety of his workmen, and in every case the question is whether the circumstances are such as to entitle judge or jury to say that there has or has not been a failure to exercise such reasonable care. It is immaterial, in my opinion, whether the alleged failure in duty is in respect of an act of omission or an act of commission . . . Lord Dunedin was laying down, I think, no principle of law but stating the factual framework within which the law would fall to be applied." [46] This principle is not confined to employer-and-servant cases, although it is chiefly involved in such cases. It is of general application. If in any set of circumstances there is a known danger for which common practice makes no or no adequate provision, the proper standard of care is not attained unless it is proved that there are no further precautions which a reasonably prudent man would have taken to diminish the danger.[47]

[42] *Brown* v. *Rolls-Royce Ltd.* [1960] 1 W.L.R. 210; the fact that it is proved that the defendants had not followed the common practice of the trade did not necessarily raise a presumption of negligence, so that the onus did not shift to them to rebut it. The *legal* burden of proof, properly so called, which is imposed by the law itself, still falls on the pursuer to discharge, and it must be distinguished from the *provisional* burden which is raised by the state of the evidence (*per* Lord Denning, p. 215).

[43] *Morton* v. *William Dixon Ltd.*, 1909 S.C. 807, 809. " Folly " does not mean " ridiculous "; *Morris* v. *W. Hartlepool S.N. Co.* [1956] A.C. 552, 578; applied in *Graham* v. *Co-operative Wholesale Society Ltd.* [1957] 1 W.L.R. 511 (dust from West African mahogany of a type called sapele caused dermatitis to the plaintiff, which inherent danger had only very recently been discovered but the defendants had no knowledge of such danger at the time despite their efforts to keep up to date on the subject).

[44] [1951] A.C. 367, 382 and the decision of the H.L. in *Morris* v. *W. Hartlepool S.N. Co.* [1956] A.C. 552.

[45] [1960] A.C. 145 (the plaintiff, a labourer, fell from a crawling ladder which had no handrail whilst he was carrying up a bucket of cement on to a roof; expert evidence called at the trial was that this system of work was " perfectly in accord with good practice ").

[46] *Ibid.* at p. 166.

[47] *General Cleaning Contractors Ltd.* v. *Christmas* [1953] A.C. 180; *Drummond* v. *British Building Cleaners Ltd.* [1954] 1 W.L.R. 1434; *Hurley* v. *J. Sanders & Co. Ltd.* [1955] 1 All E.R. 833; *Barkway* v. *S.Wales Transport Co.* [1950] 1 All E.R. 392.

Accordingly, as a useful guidance for the purpose of determining the standard of care, the approved common practice may be a powerful indication but is not inflexible. Where there has been a failure to take into account some proved danger, it is negligent not to depart from the common practice. It follows therefore that if employers know that their employees are engaging in a dangerous method of work, albeit it has developed into a common practice, and condone that method then they are guilty of negligence.[48] It is no defence in such circumstances that many other employers permit the same method of work or that there have been no accidents over a considerable period of time.

Compliance with the statutory regulations applicable to a particular operation is evidence that the standard of care has been complied with, but it is not conclusive.[49]

194 **Acts requiring special skill.** Where something is to be done which may give rise to a danger to the person or property of another, and can only be safely performed by a person who has the necessary skill and ability, the reasonable man would not attempt it unless he was competent to do it. This clear distinction was drawn and illustrated by McNair J. in *Bolam* v. *Friern Hospital Management Committee* [50] where he said: " In the ordinary case which does not involve any special skill, negligence in law means a failure to do some act which a reasonable man in the circumstances would do, or the doing of some act which a reasonable man in the circumstances would not do; and if that failure or the doing of that act results in injury, then there is a cause of action. How do you test whether this act or failure is negligent? In an ordinary case it is generally said you judge it by the action of the man in the street. He is the ordinary man. In one case it has been said you judge it by the conduct of the man on the top of a Clapham omnibus. He is the ordinary man. But where you get a situation which involves the use of some special skill or competence, then the test as to whether there has been negligence or not is not the test of the man on the top of a Clapham omnibus, because he has not got this special skill. The test is the standard of the ordinary skilled man exercising and professing to have that special skill. A man need not possess the highest expert skill; it is well established law that it is sufficient if he exercises the ordinary skill of an ordinary competent man exercising that particular art." [51] The law, therefore, requires that a person who does such an act shall exercise the skill of a competent man in doing it. The standard of care is that he should do " all that any skilful person could

[48] *Brown* v. *John Mills & Co.* (*Llanidloes*) *Ltd.* (1970) 8 K.I.R. 702 (C.A.) (the plaintiff, a skilled turner, used the common practice of polishing the outside of a brass nut he was making by holding against it a piece of emery cloth, wrapped around his finger, as it revolved at high speed held in the chuck when he ought to have used a polishing stick but he had not been provided with one); applying *Blenkiron* v. *Great Central Gas Consumers Co.* (1860) 2 F. & F. 437.

[49] *Franklin* v. *Gramophone Co.* [1948] 1 K.B. 542.

[50] [1957] 1 W.L.R. 582.

[51] *Ibid.* at p. 586.

reasonably be expected to do in such a case." [52] A person driving a motor-car on the highway, for example, was bound to exercise the skill of a reasonably careful driver even before the introduction of driving tests, and, if he failed to do so, was not excused by the fact that he was using such care and skill as he possessed.

195 The principle stated above does not depend on the fact that a person holds himself out as having any special skill; it is based on the actual performance of an act which can only safely be done by a skilled person. A surgical operation, for example, must be performed in the manner in which a skilled surgeon, accustomed to perform that operation, would perform it and, with the possible exception of a sudden emergency, it would be no defence if damage was done through its being unskilfully performed, whether the unskilfulness arose from the operator's lack of a surgical qualification or from any other cause. In *Phillips* v. *Whiteley Ltd.*[53] the plaintiff had her ears pierced for earrings by a jeweller, with the result that her ears became inflamed. It was found that a surgeon would have sterilised his instruments, which the jeweller had not done, and that the operation was performed with the skill to be expected from a jeweller but not with the skill to be expected from a surgeon. It is submitted that, in tort, the degree of care to be expected from anyone who performs a particular operation is the same for all. In contract a different standard can be exacted from different persons, depending on the terms of the contract, but in the tort of negligence the same standard of care is exacted from all. It may be that in the operation of piercing ears for earrings the jeweller's standard of care is enough, but if that is so a surgeon who complied with it, though falling short of the standard which might be exacted from him in contract, would not be liable in tort. In *Wells* v. *Cooper*,[54] the Court of Appeal held that a man who had some experience as an amateur carpenter was justified in undertaking such a trifling domestic replacement as fitting a new door handle with three screws. Jenkins L.J. said: "We think the standard of care and skill to be demanded of the defendant in order to discharge his duty of care to the plaintiff in the fixing of a new handle . . . must be the degree of care and skill to be expected of a reasonably competent carpenter doing the work in question. This does not mean that the degree of care and skill required is to be measured by reference to the contractual obligations as to the quality of his work assumed by a professional carpenter working for reward, which would in our view set the standard too high." [55]

196 **Care towards disabled persons.** The standard of care in any given case is based on the conditions being normal. If, however, any of the persons involved in the occurrence are maimed, halt or blind, or from

52 *Jones* v. *Bird* (1822) 5 B. & Ald. 837, 845, *per* Bayley J.
53 [1938] 1 All E.R. 566.
54 [1958] 2 Q.B. 265. See note on this case, 74 L.Q.R. 474.
55 *Ibid.* at p. 271.

age or youth or from deafness or any other cause [56] are not within the description of normal persons, and that condition is known to the actor, a different standard of care is exacted from him. A measure of care appropriate to the inability or disability of those who are immature or feeble in mind or body is due from others who know of or ought to anticipate the presence of such persons within the scope and hazard of their own operations. Nothing can usefully be added except to point out that the reasonable man would take more care to avoid causing damage to such persons than to normal persons and that the additional amount of care he would take would be proportioned to the measure of disability known to him.[57] Thus it was held because the plaintiff had only one eye that fact placed on the defendants an obligation to take extra care so that he should not suffer damage to his remaining eye, which would result then in total blindness.[58] Further, in *Haley* v. *London Electricity Board* [59] the defendants excavated a trench along a pavement, which they guarded by placing a punner hammer across the path, but the plaintiff, a blind man, walking along failed to locate it with his stick, tripped up and fell. It was the duty of the defendants to take reasonable care not to act in a way likely to endanger other persons who might reasonably be expected to walk along the pavement. That duty however was owed to blind persons too if the defendants ought to have foreseen that such disabled people might walk along the path and was in no way different from the duty owed to persons with sight, though the standard of care, namely the carrying out of the duty, might involve extra precautions in the case of blind pedestrians.

197 Similar considerations apply where a person knows that he suffers from some infirmity or disability. If that person causes damage as a result of having, for example, a black-out whilst driving, well knowing that he was subject to such sudden attacks, he may be liable in negligence. This is not because he had experienced a black-out but because he failed to take adequate precautions against the occurrence and then driving in such circumstances.[60]

198 **Special circumstances.** The standard of care required by law under various different sets of circumstances is set out in the chapters to follow.

[56] *e.g. Hawkins* v. *Ian Cross* (*Castings*) [1970] 1 All E.R. 180 (an Indian labourer's imperfect knowledge of the English language did not enable him to respond to shouts).
[57] See *Paris* v. *Stepney B.C.* [1951] A.C. 367.
[58] *Paris* v. *Stepney B.C.*, *supra*.
[59] [1965] A.C. 778.
[60] See *e.g. Hill* v. *Baxter* [1958] 1 Q.B. 277; *R.* v. *Sibbles* [1959] Crim.L.R. 660.

CHAPTER 6

MASTER AND SERVANT AT COMMON LAW

1.—COMMON LAW DUTY OF MASTER

199 **General duty.**[1] A master owes a duty to his servant at common law and also under various statutes, such as the Factories Act. In this chapter only the common law duty is considered, the statutory duty being dealt with in Chapter 18.

At common law the duty of an employer to his servants is to take reasonable care for their safety, but he was not liable for damage caused to them through the negligence of a fellow servant in the course of his employment, when both the servant injured and the servant causing the injury were engaged in a common employment. The doctrine of common employment has been abolished in cases where the cause of action accrued after July 5, 1948,[2] so that it is no longer necessary to deal with it. A full account will be found in the second edition, Chapter 25. It is, however, necessary to bear the doctrine in mind when considering cases decided before the date of its abolition.

200 The general nature of the duty owed by a master to a servant was described by Lord Wright as follows [3]: "I think the whole course of authority consistently recognises a duty which rests on the employer and which is personal to the employer, to take reasonable care for the safety of his workmen, whether the employer be an individual, a firm, or a company, and whether or not the employer takes any share in the conduct of the operations. The obligation is threefold, as I have explained [*i.e.* 'the provision of a competent staff of men, adequate material, and a proper system and effective supervision ']." [4] Lord Wright describes the duty as threefold because the doctrine of common employment was still in existence. Now, however, it is unnecessary to put the duty under three heads. It is a single duty.[5] "The duty of an employer towards his servant is to take reasonable care for the servant's

[1] See article " Common law duties of employer towards employee." (Carby-Hall) 114 S.J. 694, 713.

[2] Law Reform (Personal Injuries) Act 1948.

[3] *Wilsons & Clyde Coal Co.* v. *English* [1938] A.C. 57, 84.

[4] *Ibid.* p. 78. There should be added: " a safe place of work."

[5] In *Wilson* v. *Tyneside Window Cleaning Co.* [1958] 2 Q.B. 110, 123–124 Parker L.J. said: " I think that this case is a very good example of the difficulties that one gets into in treating the duty owed at common law by a master to his servant as a number of separate duties . . . It is no doubt convenient, when one is dealing with any particular case, to divide that duty into a number of categories; but for myself I prefer to consider the master's duty as one applicable in all the circumstances, namely, to take reasonable care for the safety of his men, or . . . to take reasonable care so to carry out his operation as not to subject those employed by him to unnecessary risk."

safety in all the circumstances of the case." [6] It has also been described as "the duty of taking reasonable care . . . so to carry on his operations as not to subject those employed by him to unnecessary risk." [7]

An employer at sea is under the same liability as one on land and must have due regard in the prevailing circumstances to the reasonable safety of his men and the avoidance of anticipated perils. [8] The Employers' Liability (Compulsory Insurance) Act 1969 imposes on every employer carrying on business in Great Britain a duty to insure and maintain insurance under one or more approved policies with an authorised insurer against liability for bodily injury or disease sustained by employees and arising out of and in the course of their employment in Great Britain.[9]

201 **The contractual relationship.** The relationship itself of master and servant is necessarily based upon contract but it has been doubted whether the common law duties regarding the servant's safety are contractual duties or whether they lie in tort. In *Lister* v. *Romford Ice and Cold Storage Co. Ltd.*[10] Lord Radcliffe said: "It was much canvassed in argument before your Lordships whether, if there was some such duty on the appellant, it was anything more than the general duty he owed the world to avoid the tort of negligence. . . . The existence of the duty arising out of the relationship between employer and employed was recognised by the law without the institution of an analytical inquiry whether the duty was in essence contractual or tortious. What mattered was that the duty was there. A duty may exist by contract, express or implied. Since, in any event, the duty in question is one which exists by imputation or implication of law and not by virtue of any express negotiation between the parties, I should be inclined to say that there is no real distinction between the two possible sources of obligation. But it is certainly, I think, as much contractual as tortious. Since in modern times the relationship between master and servant, between employer and employed, is inherently one of contract, it seems to me entirely correct to attribute the duties which arise from that relationship to implied contract. It is a familiar position in our law that the same wrongful act may be made the subject of an action either in contract or in tort at the election of the claimant, and, although the course chosen may produce certain incidental consequences which would not have followed had the other course been adopted, it is a mistake to regard the two kinds of liability as themselves necessarily exclusive of

6 Lord Oaksey in *Paris* v. *Stepney B.C.* [1951] A.C. 367, 384; Lord Somervell in *Cavanagh* v. *Ulster Weaving Co. Ltd.* [1960] A.C. 145, 166, 167; *Savory* v. *Holland & Hannen & Cubitts* (*Southern*) *Ltd.* [1964] 1 W.L.R. 1158 *per* Diplock L.J. at p. 1164.

7 Lord Herschell in *Smith* v. *Baker* [1891] A.C. 325, 362. This alternative form of expressing the duty is the older way of stating the law, but was also used by Singleton L.J. at p. 406 in *Street* v. *British Electricity Authority* [1952] 2 Q.B. 399.

8 *Saul* v. *St. Andrews Steam Fishing Co.* (1965) 109 S.J. 392.

9 Commencement day January 1, 1972. See article on the Act (Blackshaw) 67 L.S. Gaz. 263.

10 [1957] A.C. 555, 587.

each other." Further in *Matthews* v. *Kuwait Bechtel Corporation* [11] where the servant was employed under a contract of service (which was expressed to be construed in accordance with English law) made between himself and his employer, resident abroad, and was injured in the course of his employment, it was held that he had the right to elect whether to sue in tort or in contract, there being an implied term of the contract to take reasonable care to prevent injury to him. Sellers L.J. said: "The argument of counsel for the defendants was that the common law had imposed certain duties upon employers in regard to the safety of the workman in the course of his work but the obligation so imposed, it was said, was entirely in tort. That the duties arose from the common law I think is established. . . . The question is whether those duties are contractual duties. The authorities to which I have referred show that they may be implied terms of the contract, attached to or incorporated in the contract, to apply Lord Tucker's view. It is at the election of the workman in circumstances such as these whether, relying on the recognised common law duties as established by Lord Cairns' speech in *Wilson* v. *Merry* [12] and following decisions, he will sue in contract or sue in tort. In this case, if it suits his purpose, he may sue in contract. It may be that that will have a somewhat limiting effect on his rights against the employer as compared with his more extensive rights at common law if he sues in tort, but I make no further comment on that." [13]

202 The duty of the master is not an absolute one. It can be performed by the exercise of due care and skill,[14] and while "a high standard of care is exacted" [15] it is "desirable in these days, when there are in existence so many statutes and statutory regulations imposing absolute obligations upon employers, that the courts should be vigilant to see that the common law duty owed by a master to his servants should not be gradually enlarged until it is barely distinguishable from his absolute statutory obligations." [16]

Moreover the duty is owed to each particular servant as an individual.[17]

[11] [1959] 2 Q.B. 57.

[12] (1868) L.R. 1 Sc. & Div. 326.

[13] At p. 67.

[14] Lord Wright in *Wilsons & Clyde Coal Co.* v. *English* [1938] A.C. 57, 78. See on this, Glanville Williams, "Liability for Independent Contractors" (1956) C.L.J. 190–192, who points out that the duty of an employer to provide proper staff, premises, plant and system of work cannot be delegated to a contractor, although as he says (p. 191), "it is not easy to see why the employer should be liable in tort where he has used every care to employ a responsible contractor." *Cf.* Occupiers' Liability Act 1957, s. 2 (4) (*b*), which does not, however, apply to master and servant cases.

[15] Lord Porter in *Winter* v. *Cardiff R.D.C.* [1950] 1 All E.R. 819, 822. "The law exacts from employers a high standard of care; ignorance and inexperience which result in the creation of unnecessary risk cannot, in law, provide an excuse for departure from that standard": *per* Barry J. in *Baker* v. *T. E. Hopkins & Sons Ltd.* [1958] 1 W.L.R. 993, 1001. Affirmed by the Court of Appeal [1959] 1 W.L.R. 966. See Morris L.J. at p. 993.

[16] Lord Tucker in *Latimer* v. *A.E.C. Ltd.* [1953] A.C. 643, 658; also *Chipchase* v. *British Titan Products* [1956] 1 Q.B. 545.

[17] The fact that a servant is, for example, employed as a maintenance fitter who may be called upon to put right defects that have occurred in the plant and apparatus on the employers' premises, does not alter the general duty owed him, although it might vary those precautions which the employers ought to take in the circumstances: *McPhee* v. *General Motors* (1970) 8 K.I.R. 885.

The master's " liability in tort arises from his failure to take reasonable care in regard to the particular employee and it is clear that, if so, all the circumstances relevant to that employee must be taken into consideration." [18] So, when a workman, known by his employers to be one-eyed, was employed in a garage, it was held that it was the duty of the employers to provide him with goggles when he was employed on work involving the risk of a chip of metal entering his remaining eye, although they might well be under no such duty towards a man with two eyes.[19] The duty may be considered under five heads [20]: (1) to provide a safe place of work, including a safe means of access; (2) to employ competent servants; (3) to provide and maintain adequate appliances, (4) to provide a safe system of work, and (5) other cases.

203 **(1) Safe place of work.** The duty of employers to provide the servant with a safe place of work was explained by Goddard L.J. to be " not merely to warn against unusual dangers known to them, . . . but also to make the place of employment . . . as safe as the exercise of reasonable skill and care would permit." [21] The duty thus described is a higher one than that in *Indermaur* v. *Dames*.[22] The language used suggests that it was intended to indicate the duty owed to persons entering premises under a contract.[23] In any case the employer is liable if the failure to exercise reasonable care and skill is that of an independent contractor, and is only excused from liability if the danger is due to a latent defect, not discoverable by reasonable care and skill on the part of anyone.

When a fitter's mate was working in a kiosk where transformers of electricity were housed and was electrocuted owing to the failure to

[18] Lord Simonds in *Paris* v. *Stepney B.C.* [1951] A.C. 367, 375. In *Withers* v. *Perry Chain Co.* [1961] 1 W.L.R. 1314 it was held that the duty on employers merely was to take all reasonable care, having regard to the fact that the plaintiff had had dermatitis.

[19] *Paris* v. *Stepney B.C.* [1951] A.C. 367.

[20] See *Winter* v. *Cardiff R.D.C.* [1950] 1 All E.R. 819, 823, *per* Lord MacDermott that they " are not absolute in nature. They lie within and exemplify, the broader duty of taking reasonable care for the safety of his workmen which rests on every employer."

[21] *Naismith* v. *London Film Productions Ltd.* [1939] 1 All E.R. 794, 798. *Ebbs* v. *James Whitson & Co. Ltd.* [1952] 2 Q.B. 877; *Graham* v. *Co-operative Wholesale Society Ltd.* [1957] 1 W.L.R. 511. Further, an employer is under a duty to his employees to take adequate precautions against risk from fire. Persons who were employed to work in the second and third floor of a building above a floor where a business was carried on by a third party, which business involved the storage of paper, and were injured when a fire broke out in the floor below, recovered from their employer because " the defendants' premises, being above two industrial premises and reached only by a wooden staircase, were a veritable trap in the event of fire occurring below," and it should have been practicable to have made arrangements for means of escape from fire (McNair J.): *Nicholls* v. *Reemer, Waugh & Reemer* (1957) 107 L.J. 378.

[22] (1866) L.R. 1 C.P. 274. The common law duties laid down in this case are, as from January 1, 1958, abolished as between occupiers of premises and their invitees and licensees. The common duty of care laid down by ss. 2 and 3 of the Occupiers' Liability Act 1957 is substituted. The Occupiers' Liability Act 1957 does not apply to the relationship of master and servant: see Law Reform Committee, Third Report (Cmd. 9305), para. 95 (5) (i).

[23] Chap. 8, *post*. " The duty of a master to his servant is higher than that of an invitor to an invitee," Lord Porter in *London Graving Dock* v. *Horton* [1951] A.C. 737; see also *per* Denning L.J. in *Christmas* v. *General Cleaning Contractors* [1952] 1 K.B. 141, 148. The duty owed to persons entering premises, when it is based on an implied term of the contract under which they enter, is now altered by s. 5 of the Occupiers' Liability Act 1957, but it does not affect the law stated in the text.

insulate the full length of the kiosk, it was held that his employers were liable for their failure "to provide a safe place for their workmen." [24] Goddard L.J. said: "This is a duty which cannot be avoided by delegation. [24a] It is no answer to say . . . 'We employed competent contractors to provide a safe place or plant.'"

204 It has been suggested that the employer's duty as to the condition of the premises is less than that in respect of the plant and appliances (*post*, § 211). This, however, is at variance with the authorities quoted above.[25] Moreover, the duty to provide a safe place of work is fulfilled by providing a place as safe as care and skill can do it, having regard to the nature of the place. If the workman is working on a scaffold or a roof it must be a safe scaffold or roof, but no complaint can be made that working there is not as safe as working on level ground. As long as the employer makes the working place as safe as it can reasonably be made, he has satisfied his obligation. Thus situations must frequently arise where there exist possible dangers, the risk of which a prudent employer can foresee and yet the particular danger cannot be removed easily, if at all. The employer's duty in such circumstances is to take reasonable precautions for his workmen's safety which, for example, could have required the provision of: an adequate fencing to meet the contingency of a servant falling off a narrow platform, whilst working with his back to a steep drop [26]; a handrail on a short but steep and irregular flight of steps [27]; a safety belt to save a ship's painter from falling whilst working from slippery steps in a dry dock [28]; a guard-rail round the open hatchway giving access to the 'tween deck of a ship out at sea [29]; a handhold on a crawling ladder used for carrying buckets of cement up on to a roof [30]; a line of demarcation on a roof, over which a ropeway was operated [31]; a different type of engine so that the driver was not obliged to lean out of the cab to observe a signal placed near a bridge with an unusually narrow clearance [32]; the re-siting of a vertical points lever which had a clearance of only eight inches between it and a passing locomotive's steps, on which shunters habitually stood to ride [33]; a fence to divide the British Transport Commission's railway lines from a private line along which workmen were accustomed to walk.[34]

The employer's duty at common law is not higher than that imposed

[24] *Paine* v. *Colne Valley Electricity Co.* [1938] 4 All E.R. 803, 807.

[24a] See especially *Riverstone Meat Co. Proprietary Ltd.* v. *Lancashire Shipping Co. Ltd.* [1961] A.C. 807; *Sumner* v. *William Henderson & Sons Ltd.* [1963] 1 W.L.R. 823.

[25] In *Davidson* v. *Handley Page Ltd.* [1945] 1 All E.R. 235, Lord Greene M.R. said at p. 237: "I very much doubt the correctness of that proposition."

[26] *Bath* v. *British Transport Commission* [1954] 1 W.L.R. 1013.

[27] *Kimpton* v. *Steel Co. of Wales Ltd.* [1960] 2 All E.R. 274.

[28] *Hurley* v. *J. Saunders & Co. Ltd.* [1955] 1 W.L.R. 470.

[29] *Morris* v. *West Hartlepool Steam Navigation Co. Ltd.* [1956] A.C. 552.

[30] *Cavanagh* v. *Ulster Weaving Co. Ltd.* [1960] A.C. 145.

[31] *Quintas* v. *National Smelting Co. Ltd.* [1961] 1 All E.R. 630.

[32] *McArthur* v. *British Railways Board* (1968) 6 K.I.R. 40 (alternatively the engine should have been re-routed).

[33] *Hicks* v. *British Transport Commission* [1958] 1 W.L.R. 493. See note on this case, 74 L.Q.R. 337.

[34] *Braithwaite* v. *South Durham Steel Co. Ltd.* [1958] 1 W.L.R. 986.

by sections 28 and 29 of the Factories Act 1961.[35] Indeed, Lord Tucker in *Latimer* v. *A.E.C. Ltd.*[36] warned " that the courts should be vigilant to see that the common law duty owed by a master to his servant should not be gradually enlarged until it is barely distinguishable from his absolute statutory obligations." To fulfil it, the place of work must have such protective devices as experience has shown to be desirable in other working places of the same or a similar kind, but even this may not be enough. In *Bath* v. *British Transport Commission* [37] the deceased was concreting the side of a dry dock, working from a ledge or " altar " some 2 ft. 6 ins. wide which was unfenced and immediately above the bottom of the dock forty feet below, when he fell and was killed. The employers were held liable, although the work had been going on for three years without mishap and without complaint, because the place was so dangerous that some protection, such as a fence, should have been provided.

205 Apart from its construction, a place of work may become unsafe owing to some temporary condition or some obstruction being created on it. In such a case the test to be applied is whether a reasonably prudent employer would have caused or permitted the existence of that state of affairs, which is complained of, so that what constitutes a breach of his duty in any given set of circumstances is a question of degree. However if a place has become unsafe due to some temporary or exceptional danger, *e.g.* an unexploded shell, and the only knowledge of the danger was that of fellow servants, who were neither foremen nor charge-hands, it has been held that the employers were not in breach of their duty to provide a safe place of work, because such knowledge ought not to be imputed to them.[38] When a workman slipped on a patch of oil or water or both which had accumulated, possibly in a depression, on the concrete floor of a passage in a factory, Somervell L.J. said that he felt it impossible to say that the mere existence of these conditions " indicates any failure to take reasonable care to protect those employed from unnecessary risk." [39] Again, when the entrance to a factory became slippery owing to a sudden fall of snow which froze as it fell a quarter of an hour or so before the factory opened, and a workman slipped in entering, the employers were held not liable, on the ground that there had been no failure to exercise reasonable care.[40] In *Latimer* v. *A.E.C. Ltd.*[41] after an

[35] Which came into force on April 1, 1962, and repealed the Factories Acts 1937–59. Under the 1937 Act the relevant sections were s. 25 and s. 26. See the earlier decision of *Thomas* v. *Bristol Aeroplane Co. Ltd.* [1954] 1 W.L.R. 694. This only dealt with s. 26 but the observations of Somervell L.J. at p. 697 applied equally to s. 25. For the duty imposed by these sections see chap. 18, *post*.

[36] [1953] A.C. 643, 658; *Trott* v. *Smith (Erectors) Ltd.* [1957] 1 W.L.R. 1154, 1158.

[37] [1954] 1 W.L.R. 1013.

[38] *O'Reilly* v. *National Rail and Tramway Appliances Ltd.* [1966] 1 All E.R. 499.

[39] *Davies* v. *De Havilland Aircraft Co.* [1951] 1 K.B. 50, 52.

[40] *Thomas* v. *Bristol Aeroplane Co.* [1954] 1 W.L.R. 694. No breach of the employers' common law duty was proved in *Powley* v. *Bristol Siddeley Engines* [1965] 3 All E.R. 612 but Megaw J. held that there had been a breach of s. 28 of the Factories Act 1961 in their failure to have the office steps cleared of ice, the statutory obligation being a higher duty than the common law duty in the circumstances.

[41] [1953] A.C. 643.

exceptionally heavy storm the floor of a factory became flooded. When the water drained away it left an oily film on the floor which was slippery. Sawdust was put down but, owing to the large area of the floor, there was not enough to cover all the floor and a workman slipped on a part of the floor which had no sawdust. Lord Tucker said that the only question was " Has it been proved that the floor was so slippery that, remedial steps not being possible, a reasonably prudent employer would have closed down the factory rather than allow his employees to run the risks involved in continuing work?" [42] As there was no evidence of any complaint or of any other person being in difficulty from the floor, the employers were held not liable, since they had taken all reasonable steps to deal with the conditions short of closing the factory or part of it, which would have been unreasonable in the circumstances. In *Vinnyey* v. *Star Paper Mills* [43] Cumming-Bruce J. held that there was no reasonably foreseeable risk that a workman brought to the scene where some slippery substance had been allowed negligently to escape on to the floor, and charged expressly with the duty of cleaning up the mess with a squeegee, would slip in the course of performing such a simple duty.

206 **Servant working on premises of another.** In *Mace* v. *R. and H. Green and Silley Weir Ltd.* Lord Parker C.J. said [44]: " At one time it was often thought that where a master sent his servant to work on somebody else's premises he owed no duty to the servant in regard to those premises. I think that that was a misunderstanding as to the true position and that, as has been indicated by the Court of Appeal in *Davie* v. *New Merton Board Mills Ltd.*[45] and in *Wilson* v. *Tyneside Window Cleaning Co.*[46] a duty to take reasonable care is always there but the performance of it will vary according to all the circumstances, including the question whether the premises are in the occupation and control of another person."

207 Thus the general duty of an employer to his servant to take reasonable care for his safety does not come to an end merely because the servant is sent to work at premises which are not in the occupation of the employer but it remains throughout the course of his employment.[47] Earlier Parker L.J. had said in *Wilson* v. *Tyneside Window Cleaning Co.*: "The duty is there, whether the premises on which the workman is employed are in the occupation of the master or of a third party . . . ; but what reasonable care demands in each case will no doubt vary." [48] To this Holroyd Pearce

[42] *Ibid.* at p. 659.
[43] [1965] 1 All E.R. 175.
[44] [1959] 2 Q.B. 14, 21 (the plaintiff, a boilermaker employed by ship repairers, while ascending a ladder, fell as a result of catching his foot in a rope wound around one of the rungs. The employers were exonerated from liability but the shipowners were held to be liable for the plaintiff's accident).
[45] [1958] 1 Q.B. 210 (affirmed in House of Lords [1959] A.C. 604).
[46] [1958] 2 Q.B. 110.
[47] *General Cleaning Contractors Ltd.* v. *Christmas* [1953] A.C. 180; *Thomson* v. *Cremin* [1953] 2 All E.R. 1185; *Smith* v. *Austin Lifts Ltd.* [1959] 1 W.L.R. 100.
[48] *Supra*, at p. 124. *Cf.* the facts of this case with the similar facts in *Baker* v. *White's Window & General Cleaning Co. Ltd.*, *The Times*, March 1, 1962, where the employers'

L.J. had added: "The master's own premises are under his control: if they are dangerously in need of repair he can and must rectify the fault at once if he is to escape the censure of negligence. But if a master sends his plumber to mend a leak in a respectable private house, no one could hold him negligent for not visiting the house himself to see if the carpet in the hall creates a trap. Between these extremes are countless possible examples in which the Court may have to decide the question of fact." [49] Since the performance of the duty to provide a safe place of work may become impracticable where it is in the occupation or under the control of another, before sending his men out to work on such premises the employer may have to go and inspect them to find out whether they are reasonably safe for the work to be done on them in order to fulfil his duty to provide a safe system of work (*post*, § 216). If such a visit be made and the inspection reveals a danger which is out of his hands to remedy it may be sufficient for the employer merely to warn the workmen of its existence [50] but there may be instances where the risks are too great or the giving of a warning is quite insufficient so that a prudent employer ought not to permit his servant to work there until the occupier has rendered the premises safe.[51] The workman will be, of course, a lawful visitor of the occupier and thus be entitled to the common duty of care under the Occupiers' Liability Act 1957 although if the occupier be sued he can plead that he is entitled to expect that a skilled workman will guard against the normal risks of his calling.[52] In other cases the employer may be compelled to take positive steps to protect his workman in order to discharge his duty of care [53] and if he fails to do so the fact that the servant knowingly incurs the risk only concerns the degree of his contributory negligence.[54] The view was taken by Lord Wright in *Thomson* v. *Cremin* [55] that: "To hold a master stevedore, in the absence of special circumstances of suspicion, subject to a general duty towards his men to inspect the structure of the vessel, whether

liability was established. The plaintiff, a window cleaner, had had a casual conversation with his working foreman, who had himself suffered an accident on the premises, about the unreliability of certain gun metal handles on the upper sash of a window 20 feet above ground level when the foreman told him: "Be careful, Harry, you know what happened to me!" The plaintiff nevertheless forgot, he relied on the handles which gave way and he fell injuring himself. The court held that no express order had been given him by the employers that he must not put any weight on these handles and that the casual conversation referred to could not be relied upon as a substitute for the performance by them of their duty to take reasonable care for the plaintiff's safety. The plaintiff was, however, held to be one third to blame.

49 *Ibid.* at pp. 121–122.

50 *Smith* v. *Austin Lifts Ltd.*, *supra.*

51 *Ibid.* at p. 117.

52 For example, a householder is entitled to expect that a self-employed window cleaner will take his own precautions against all those risks which he must know are incidental to his work such as loose plywood: *Bates* v. *Parker* [1953] 2 Q.B. 231; handles screwed into unsound woodwork; *Wilson* v. *Tyneside Window Cleaning Co.*, *supra.*

53 *Smith* v. *Austin Lifts Ltd.*, *supra*, at p. 117: "by requiring the occupiers to make the [place] safe."

54 *A. C. Billings & Sons Ltd.* v. *Riden* [1958] A.C. 240; *Bill* v. *Short Bros. & Harland*, *The Guardian*, May 22, 1962; *Baker* v. *White's Window & General Cleaning Co.*, *The Times*, March 1, 1962, where the plaintiff was held to be one third to blame for trusting his weight to a sash window handle which gave way under the strain.

55 [1953] 2 All E.R. 1185, 1192. Followed in *Szumczyk* v. *Associated Tunnelling Co.* [1956] 1 W.L.R. 98.

permanent or temporary, whether shifting-boards, stanchions or the like, would, I think, be contrary to practice and inconsistent with the exigencies of the case." In that case, a master stevedore was held not liable to his servant, who was injured by the fall of a " shore " while unloading cargo on a ship.

208 Where a carpenter, employed by building contractors, was sent to repair a house which had suffered bomb damage and was injured by the collapse of a floor, it was held that the employers were not liable.[56] Again, a welding firm doing work on a ship as sub-contractors for shipwrights who were repairing the ship in their shipbuilding yard were held not liable to one of their workmen who was injured owing to defects in the scaffolding erected by the shipwrights on the ground that " the work in question was to be done by them in premises over which they had no control whatsoever." [57] Where contractors were employed to paint a crane in their employers' factory and, before starting, asked whether the crane was safe and were told that it was, it was held they were not liable for the death of one of their workmen due to the crane being unsafe, because they had done all that could be expected of them in the circumstances by asking whether the crane was safe and getting the assurance that it was.[58] Where a plumber's mate, while working in a private dwelling-house, went up to the loft to investigate the overflow of the water tanks, but owing to a faulty electrical conduit he was electrocuted, the employer was held not liable, as it was not reasonable to expect him to look over the house before sending his men to work there.[59] Obviously if the employer knew of a danger in the house it would be his duty to warn the servant or take other appropriate steps to avoid subjecting him to unnecessary risks. Thus the employers of a workman were held to be liable when they failed to visit the premises occupied by another, to see that the place of work was safe, when they knew of the defective state of the doors of the lift's machine house since they had notified the occupiers of the urgent need for repairs on four previous occasions.[60]

If the employer intends to use part of the premises for his own work so as to put a greater strain upon that part than it usually bears, *e.g.* if a builder is going to use a chimney stack as a support for his staging while he repairs the roof [61] it would seem he is under a duty to take reasonable care to see that it is fit for that purpose before putting it to that use.[62]

[56] *Taylor* v. *Sims & Sims* [1942] 2 All E.R. 375. In *Garcia* v. *Harland & Wolff Ltd.* [1943] K.B. 731, a distinction was drawn between the safety of the premises and safety due to the nature of the work. The employer was held liable for danger of the latter kind.

[57] *Hodgson* v. *British Arc Welding Co.* [1946] K.B. 302.

[58] *Bott* v. *Prothero Steel Tube Co.* [1951] W.N. 595.

[59] *Cilia* v. *James & Sons* [1954] 1 W.L.R. 721.

[60] *Smith* v. *Austin Lifts Ltd.* [1959] 1 W.L.R. 100.

[61] See *per* Goddard L.J. in *Bates* v. *Parker* [1953] 2 Q.B. 231, 236.

[62] On the other hand, it was not suggested in *General Cleaning Contractors Ltd.* v. *Christmas* [1953] A.C. 180, that a window-cleaning company were under a duty to see if the windows were safe to hold on to. Their duty was said to be to tell their men to test the windows and to provide them with apparatus to prevent their closing unexpectedly. In *Wilson* v. *Tyneside Window Cleaning Co.* [1958] 2 Q.B. 110, a window-cleaning firm were held not liable to one of their workmen, who had had a life-long experience in the trade and who

209 **Safe means of access.** It is probable that an employer is under a duty to take reasonable care to provide a reasonably safe means of access from the highway to the place of work. When the place of work immediately adjoins the highway, his duty begins as soon as the workman leaves the highway and enters the place of work. When the place of work does not adjoin the highway but is reached by a way over land in the occupation of a third party, the employer is under a duty to take reasonable care to see that the way is reasonably safe for his workman. This was decided in *Ashdown* v. *Samuel Williams & Sons Ltd.*[63] where the access to the place of work was over land occupied by a third party, crossed by railway lines on which railway wagons were shunted from time to time. Havers J. held that there was a duty to warn of the danger and on failure to do so the employer was liable when an employee was injured by the shunting, but his decision was reversed on appeal[64] on the ground that the employer had provided a safe means of access and there was no duty to warn that there were rails to be crossed on which shunting took place from time to time, as the employee already knew this. The Court of Appeal rejected a submission on the part of the employer that he owed no duty to the employee until the employee arrived at the employer's premises, on the ground that it was too wide, and seemed to hold that the employer was under a duty to take reasonable care to provide a reasonably safe means of access, which duty he had discharged.

Where the defendants knew that the plaintiff, a ringmaster, because of his bulk and weight of some twenty-three stones would have difficulty in getting in and out of the caravan which was supplied by them as his dressing room annexed to the circus, they were held to be guilty of negligence in failing to provide steps or some other suitable substitute for use as a means of access, the absence of which had caused the plaintiff to fall and break his ankle.[65]

210 **(2) Competent servants and supervision.** The master is under a duty to take reasonable care to employ competent servants. This duty was of importance while the doctrine of common employment existed, on the ground that " The servant, when he engages to run the risks of his service, including those arising from the negligence of fellow servants, has a right to understand that the master has taken reasonable care to protect him from such risk by associating him only with persons of ordinary skill and

was injured when he fell as a result of a handle by which he was supporting himself, giving way. The workman had often cleaned that particular window before, and knew that the woodwork around the handle was unsound; and again in *Clements* v. *General Services (London), The Times*, March 10, 1961, the employers of a window cleaner were held not liable when a window frame fell out due to some latent defect, causing him to overbalance and fall onto some railings, just as he was about to climb back into a room from a balcony. But see *Baker* v. *Whites Window and General Cleaning Co., The Times*, March 1, 1962.

[63] [1956] 2 Q.B. 580, 593.

[64] [1957] 1 Q.B. 409.

[65] *Emney* v. *Chipperfields Circus & Zoo, The Times*, October 17, 1961.

care." [66] Now that the doctrine of common employment has been abolished this duty is no longer of much practical importance, except in such instances as where a workman had repeatedly made a nuisance of himself to his fellow workmen by " his almost incurable habit of tripping people up or otherwise engaging in horse-play and skylarking " and eventually had caused injury to the plaintiff by getting hold of him from behind and forcing him onto the ground whereby the plaintiff's wrist was broken, the employers were held liable for not taking proper steps to put an end to that workman's conduct.[67] See further Chapter 14, *post*, §§ 937–939.

A master is not liable to a servant for personal injuries sustained, which were caused by the negligence of a fellow servant, who is not acting in the course of his employment, when he perpetrates some isolated mischievous act, such as a practical joke, that could not reasonably have been foreseen.[68] However it does not necessarily follow that merely because the practical joke happens to have been an isolated incident that the employer can automatically avoid liability by arguing that the perpetrators of it were not acting in the course of their employment. Such an argument would not avail a master where he owed a duty of care to the plaintiff who was bound to obey the joker's instructions.[69] If a master has reason to anticipate misconduct by a servant which is likely to be dangerous to fellow employees, the master is under a duty to those other servants to take reasonable steps to avoid harm arising from it, *e.g.* by reprimanding him, so that if these reprimands are disregarded the duty ultimately involves the dismissal of such mischievous or vicious servant.[70] On the other hand where a master employs an unskilled foreign worker an added risk may well be incurred that would have to be accepted by him should some misunderstanding arise which causes an accident. This was illustrated in *Hawkins* v. *Ian Ross* (*Castings*) *Ltd.*[71] where the plaintiff and a seventeen-year-old Indian labourer were required to carry a hand shank full of molten metal for pouring into moulds at the defendants' foundry. Whilst pouring the metal the plaintiff received personal injuries by losing his balance because the Indian, whose knowledge of English was indifferent, did not respond to his shouts to stop pouring. Fisher J. held, *inter alia*, that a servant's imperfect knowledge of the English

[66] Alderson B. in *Hutchinson* v. *York, Newcastle and Berwick Ry.* (1850) 5 Ex. 343, 353.

[67] *Hudson* v. *Ridge Manufacturing Co.* [1957] 2 Q.B. 348.

[68] *Smith* v. *Crossley* (1951) 95 S.J. 655 (a practical joke by two young apprentices in the misuse of a compressed air pipe which they shoved up another boy's rectum); *Coddington* v. *International Harvester Co. of Great Britain Ltd.* (1969) 6 K.I.R. 146 (a tin containing " thinners " was set alight and another workman, passing by, as a joke flicked the tin with his foot in the direction of a fellow servant, who in the agony of the moment kicked the burning tin violently away so that it overturned and its highly inflammable contents spilled over the plaintiff, enveloping him in a sheet of flames); *Wood* v. *Duttons Brewery* (1971) 115 S.J. 186.

[69] *Chapman* v. *Oakleigh Animal Products* (1970) 8 K.I.R. 1063, C.A.

[70] *Smith* v. *Ocean S.S. Co. Ltd.* [1954] 2 Lloyd's Rep. 482 (a ship's officer was stabbed by a native labourer but his claim failed since the employers had no reason to expect any danger from employing native labour); *Walden* v. *Court Line* (1965) 109 S.J. 151 (a ship's cook was injured by a crew member, who had previously assaulted others, but the employers were held not to be liable in the circumstances since they were not negligent in keeping the man on in their employment).

[71] [1970] 1 All E.R. 180.

language imposed a higher standard of care on his employers in such circumstances.

In addition to the provision of competent servants the master undoubtedly owes a duty to give adequate supervision [72] and to give proper instruction in appropriate cases.[73] In many instances, particularly in the cases of the less skilled or of younger employees, it is quite insufficient merely to supply adequate plant or appliances, then to leave them to their own devices in order to use them.

211 **(3) Adequate plant and appliances.** The master's duty as to the appliances used by the servant has been stated by Lord Herschell to be [74]: " The contract between employer and employed involves on the part of the former the duty of taking reasonable care to provide proper appliances, and to maintain them in a proper condition." Lord Wright added: " The obligation to provide and maintain proper plant and appliances is a continuing obligation." [75]

The obligation is not absolute. It is to take reasonable care to provide and maintain adequate plant. Where, therefore, a steel rope, which had been holding some trucks on a haulage way in a mine, broke so that the trucks ran away and injured a miner, the Coal Board were not liable on proving that they had provided a safe rope and that their system of inspection was proper, reasonable and customary.[76] The obligation " is limited to reasonable exercise of care and skill to guard against danger which, as reasonable people, the employers ought to have anticipated." [77] So, where a circular saw, properly guarded in accordance with the Woodworking Machinery Regulations 1922, ejected a piece of wood which struck the operator—an accident " outside normal experience and such as could not reasonably have been anticipated "—the employers were not liable.[78] But statutory regulations defining an employer's duty concerning a particular machine do not *per se* relieve him from taking reasonable care to make the use of that machine safe.[79]

The fulfilment of this duty of the master may include the carrying out of regular inspections of and all necessary repairs to the plant and appliances provided by him as are reasonable in the circumstances. Thus the employer was held to be negligent when a screw on an electric drill loosened and, as a result, a part of the drill flew off and struck the workman, although the drill was only a year old and had recently been examined for

[72] *Smith* v. *Crossley Bros. Ltd.*, *supra.*
[73] *General Cleaning Contractors Ltd.* v. *Christmas* [1953] A.C. 180.
[74] *Smith* v. *Baker* [1891] A.C. 325, 362.
[75] *Wilsons & Clyde Coal Co.* v. *English* [1938] A.C. 57, 84.
[76] *Turner* v. *N.C.B.* (1949) 65 T.L.R. 580. See also to the same effect *Wilsons & Clyde Coal Co.* v. *English* [1938] A.C. 57, 78.
[77] *Nicholls* v. *F. Austin* (*Leyton*) *Ltd.* [1946] A.C. 493, 503, *per* Lord Wright.
[78] *Nicholls* v. *F. Austin* (*Leyton*) *Ltd.*, *supra.*
[79] *Quinn* v. *Horsfall & Bickham Ltd.* [1956] 1 W.L.R. 264. Although the decision in this case has been reversed in the Court of Appeal [1956] 1 W.L.R. 652, the statement in the text remains correct. Failure to fence a horizontal milling machine (assumed not to be required to be fenced by statute) was held to be a breach of the employers' common law duty " to take reasonable care so as not to subject their employees to unnecessary risks."

an electrical fault but the screw in question had never been checked for tightness.[80]

212 **Employers' liability for defective equipment.** Prior to the invasion of the common law by the Employer's Liability (Defective Equipment) Act 1969,[81] which came into force on October 25, 1969, the employer was only liable on proof of negligence, if equipment which he provided was in fact defective and injury was occasioned thereby to his employee. Thus the employer was held to be under no obligation to examine tools of a standard pattern bought from reputable manufacturers before these were issued for use to his workmen. Where, for example, a workman was using a drift to knock out a key by striking it with a hammer, the metal of the drift having been tempered dangerously too hard, and a chip of metal flew into the workman's eye, the employer was held not liable as the defect was not apparent.[82]

However, since October 25, 1969, where an employee is injured because of a defect in equipment provided by his employer for the purposes of his business and the defect is attributable to the fault of some third party, the injury nevertheless is to be deemed to be attributable also to the " fault " of the employer, who is thereby declared guilty of negligence, even though he is entirely blameless. The Act, accordingly, has had the profound effect not only of reversing the decision in *Davie* v. *New Merton Board Mills Ltd.*[83] but also the very principle of law on which all liability for personal injury is founded. Whilst the innocent employer's rights of contribution or indemnity are preserved, for what they may be worth, the practical result seems to be indistinguishable from the imposition of absolute liability, subject only to the law relating to contributory negligence.[84] Equipment is defined as including: " any plant and machinery, vehicle, aircraft and clothing." [85]

213 **Provision of protective device or clothing.** If the nature of the work is such that a reasonable employer would provide his workmen with some protective device or clothing while doing the work, there is a duty to provide it and to take reasonable care to see that it is used.[86] If a one-eyed man is employed to loosen a bolt with a hammer, goggles must be provided.[87] A man employed in a piano-fitting shop who used synthetic glue and contracted dermatitis was entitled to recover because he was not

[80] *Bell* v. *Arnott & Harrison* (1967) 2 K.I.R. 825.
[81] Articles (Ingman) 33 M.L.R. 70; (Maggs) 67 L.S.Gaz. 262; (J. A. K.) 114 S.J. 895.
[82] *Davie* v *New Merton Board Mills Ltd.* [1959] A.C. 604. See also article based on this case, 74 L.Q.R. 397: " A master's liability for defective tools " discussing the law as it stood then, and *Mason* v. *Williams & Williams Ltd.* [1955] 1 W.L.R. 549.
[83] [1959] A.C. 604.
[84] s. 1 (1).
[85] s. 1 (3).
[86] *James* v. *Hepworth & Grandage Ltd.* [1968] 1 Q.B. 94. (Employers were under no duty to ascertain whether or not their workmen were literate when they had no reason to believe otherwise, so that where they had made protective clothing available to the plaintiff and had advertised that fact by the display of notices to that effect, they had not been negligent.)
[87] *Paris* v. *Stepney B.C.* [1951] A.C. 367. The H.L. did not decide whether a two-eyed man should have had goggles.

required to use the protective cream which he ought to have used.[88] "When [an employer] asks his men to work with dangerous substances, he must provide proper appliances to safeguard them; he must set in force a proper system by which they use the appliances and take the necessary precautions; and he must do his best to see that they adhere to it." [89] If he supplies the necessary protective measure and instructs the workmen how to use it the employer is not liable.[90] Likewise, where an experienced moulder was burnt whilst handling a ladle of molten metal when it slipped, splashing the metal onto his foot, the House of Lords held that the employers were not liable for not having ordered or advised him to wear the protective spats provided by them as a precaution against that very type of injury.[91] If the process was not known to be dangerous, the employer is not liable [92] but failure to know what is common knowledge may result in damage being found to be foreseeable, *e.g.* decompression causing septic bone necrosis.[92a]

214 **Situations generally.** The master has been held liable, when a workman employed to hoist an iron cylinder was killed owing to the tackle provided being of insufficient strength, so that it broke and the cylinder fell on him [93]; when a servant, employed to lubricate dangerous machinery, was injured owing to the failure of the employer to maintain adequate fencing around the machinery [94]; where a servant was injured owing to the collapse of a rotten scaffold pole, which the master had failed to have inspected [95]; where a film actress had to cover her feet with some inflammable material which caught fire during the shooting of a film sequence [96]; where a workman was struck by the blades of a large fan, electrically driven, revolving at high speed, unguarded during testing on the factory floor [97]; where they failed to provide crawling boards for risky work on a roof but instead relied wholly on the plaintiff's skill as an experienced man [98]; where the servant, a stevedore, was injured owing to the breaking of a chain which had been in use for seven years without any examination or testing by the master [99]; where the servant was employed on an elevated tramway belonging to his employers, who provided no ladder or other safe means of ascending to or descending from the tramway, and in descending from the tramway his foot slipped and he was killed [1];

88 *Clifford* v. *Charles Challen & Sons Ltd.* [1951] 1 K.B. 495. See also *Crookall* v. *Vickers-Armstrong Ltd.* [1955] 2 All E.R. 12; *Snell* v. *J. Shelbourne & Co.* (1965) 109 S.J. 270; *Voller* v. *Schweppes* (*Home*) (1969) 7 K.I.R. 228.

89 *Clifford* v. *Charles Challen & Sons, supra, per* Denning L.J. at pp. 497, 498.

90 *Woods* v. *Durable Suites Ltd.* [1953] 1 W.L.R. 857.

91 *Qualcast* (*Wolverhampton*) *Ltd.* v. *Haynes* [1959] A.C. 743. See the words of caution by Lord Radcliffe regarding the "much vaguer obligation of encouraging, exhorting or instructing" workmen to make regular use of the protective measures provided (at p. 753).

92 *Ebbs* v. *James Whitson & Co.* [1952] 2 Q.B. 877; *Graham* v. *Co-operative Wholesale Society Ltd.* [1957] 1 W.L.R. 511.

92a *Ransom* v. *Sir Robert McAlpine and Sons* (1971) S.J. 326.

93 *Weems* v. *Mathieson* (1861) 4 Macq. 215.

94 *Clarke* v. *Holmes* (1862) 7 H. & N. 937.

95 *Webb* v. *Rennie* (1865) 4 F. & F. 608.

96 *Naismith* v. *London Film Productions Ltd.* [1939] 1 All E.R. 794.

97 *Thurogood* v. *Van den Berghs & Jurgens Ltd.* [1951] 2 K.B. 537.

98 *Jenner* v. *Allen West & Co. Ltd.* [1959] 1 W.L.R. 554.

99 *Murphy* v. *Phillips* (1876) 35 L.T. 477.

1 *Williams* v. *Birmingham Battery and Metal Co.* [1899] 2 Q.B. 338.

where a dock labourer was employed in loading a ship and injured in climbing an unsafe rope ladder provided by his employers instead of a fixed iron ladder [2]; where a commercial traveller was injured in trying to start a motor-car provided by his employers owing to the defective starting gear of the car [3]; where a boilermaker was injured by the collapse of an improvised staging, erected by himself owing to the employer's failure to supply him with proper materials [4]; where a cartman was injured through driving an unsafe horse [5]; where a ladder was provided which was not in an efficient state and in good repair [6]; where a highly skilled rigger faced with a matter of urgency had had to adopt a method of doing the job that was obviously less safe than the method he would have preferred to use if the appropriate appliances had been provided.[7]

215 The duty of an employer to provide safe appliances covers appliances not only directly connected with the work, but also appliances used for purposes normally and reasonably incidental to the work. When a woman, employed in a factory, fell on a slippery duckboard in going to wash a teacup for her own use, the employer was held liable.[8] Where a waitress touched an electric fire which had been provided in her bedroom in the hotel, and the fire was defective to the employer's knowledge so that she received burns it was held that they were liable since they should reasonably have foreseen what happened as a possible consequence of their breach of duty.[9]

On the other hand the master was held not to be liable where the workman failed to make proper use of the equipment provided [10] and where, as an act of folly on the workman's part, he chose the wrong tool to do the job [11]; where, in answering an emergency call, the fire service transported a heavy piece of lifting gear on a flat-platformed lorry instead of on a vehicle, especially designed to carry it, as a result of which the gear (a mobile jack) moved forward and crushed the plaintiff's foot when the lorry braked hard and stopped [12]; where a skilled man, who was allowed to repair his own tools, selected brittle materials from the stores.[13]

216 **(4) Safe system of work.** If the master has instituted a defective system of work, as a result of which a servant is injured, although there is no negligence in the actual working of the system, the master is liable. This was laid down in *Sword* v. *Cameron*,[14] where the servant was

[2] *Monaghan* v. *Rhodes & Co.* [1920] 1 K.B. 487.
[3] *Baker* v. *James* [1921] 2 K.B. 674, where McCardie J. refused to follow *Griffiths* v. *London and St. Katherine Docks* (1884) 13 Q.B.D. 259.
[4] *Lovell* v. *Blundells* [1944] K.B. 502.
[5] *Bowater* v. *Rowley Regis Corpn.* [1944] K.B. 476.
[6] *Jones* v. *Crosville Motor Services Ltd.* [1956] 1 W.L.R. 1425.
[7] *Machray* v. *Stewarts & Lloyds Ltd.* [1965] 1 W.L.R. 602.
[8] *Davidson* v. *Handley Page Ltd.* [1945] 1 All E.R. 235.
[9] *McBrien* v. *Arden & Cobden Hotels* (1963) 107 S.J. 791.
[10] *Parkinson* v. *Lyle Shipping Co.* [1964] 2 Lloyd's Rep. 79.
[11] *Leach* v. *British Oxygen Co.* (1965) 109 S.J. 157; *Johnson* v. *Croggan & Co. Ltd.* [1954] 1 All E.R. 121 (chose an unsuitable ladder for the job).
[12] *Watt* v. *Hertfordshire C.C.* [1954] 1 W.L.R. 835.
[13] *Bristol Aeroplane Co.* v. *Franklin* [1948] W.N. 341.
[14] (1839) 1 Dunlop 493.

employed at a stone quarry and was injured through blasting operations, owing to the warning signal not having been given in sufficient time to enable him to put himself in a position of safety. In *Bartonshill Coal Co.* v. *Reid*,[15] Lord Cranworth, referring to this case, said: " The injury was evidently the result of a defective system not adequately protecting the workmen at the time of the explosions." Also, in *Smith* v. *Baker*,[16] Lord Halsbury said: " I think the cases cited at your Lordships' Bar of *Sword* v. *Cameron* [14] and *Bartonshill Coal Co.* v. *McGuire* [17] established conclusively the point for which they were cited, that a negligent system or a negligent mode of using perfectly sound machinery may make the employer liable."

217 A system of work is the term used to describe the organisation of the work, the way in which it is intended the work shall be carried out, the sequence of events, the taking of precautions for the safety of the men and at what stages, the number of men required to do the job, the parts to be taken by the various men employed and the time at which they shall do their various parts. Further, " it includes . . . or may include according to circumstances, such matters as the physical layout of the job—the setting of the stage, so to speak—the sequence in which the work is to be carried out, the provision in proper cases of warnings and notices, and the issue of special instructions. A system may be adequate for the whole course of the job or it may have to be modified or improved to meet circumstances which arise. Such modifications or improvements appear to me equally to fall under the head of system." [18]

218 An employer is under a duty to prescribe a system of work even where the operation is a single one if it is necessary in the interests of safety.[19] " A system of working normally implies that the work consists of a series of similar or somewhat similar operations, and the conception of a system of working is not easily applied to a case where only a single act of a particular kind is to be performed. Recently, however, this obligation has been extended to cover certain cases where only a single operation is involved. I think that the justification for this is that, where the operation is of a complicated or unusual character, an employer, careful of the safety of his men, would organise it before it was begun and in that sense provide

15 (1858) 3 Macq. 266, 290.

16 [1891] A.C. 325, at p. 339. See also *C.P. Ry.* v. *Fréchette* [1915] A.C. 871.

17 (1858) 3 Macq. 300.

18 Lord Greene M.R. in *Speed* v. *Thomas Swift and Co.* [1943] K.B. 557, 563, 564. In *Colfar* v. *Coggins and Griffith* (*Liverpool*) *Ltd.* [1945] A.C. 197, 202, Lord Simon said that the judgments in this case " carry the analysis of ' system of working ' to the furthest point that can be reached."

19 *Vernon* v. *B.T.C.* (1963) 107 S.J. 113 (where it was held that an employer should have made allowances for the fact that workmen do stumble sometimes, the deceased having done so and having been crushed to death during the tipping of coal); *Field* v. *Jeavons & Co. Ltd.* [1965] 1 W.L.R. 996 (where the occupiers of a factory must watch out and be prepared for some degree of stupidity and forgetfulness on the part of those working in the factory, *e.g.* electric saw switched on accidentally by electrician testing the circuit); *McArthur* v. *B.R.B.* (1968) 6 K.I.R. 40 (engine driver was killed when he was obliged to lean out of the cab to observe a signal placed near a bridge with an unusually narrow clearance).

a safe system of working for it. Where such an organisation is called for, an employer must provide it . . . but cases in which such a duty has been found to exist are comparatively few, and it has never even been suggested that such an obligation arises in every case where a group of the employer's servants are doing some work which may involve danger if negligently performed." [20]

Accordingly a system of work must be provided when the work is of a regular and uniform kind, such as in a mine, a factory or on a railway and it is necessary in the interests of safety or when the danger is one which is constantly found so as to call for a system to meet it. In other cases it is only necessary to prescribe a system in the circumstances indicated by Lord Reid. So, when a heavy voltage regulator was carried on a lorry and no instructions were given to the chargehand to secure it so that it should not move about, it was held that there was no need to prescribe a system of work "as the job required the exercise of judgment on the spot." [21]

219 The duty to prescribe a safe system of work is not an absolute duty. Thus where, for example, some commercial necessity requires that an employer will expose a workman to some risks, he may avoid liability for his failure to guard against such dangers.[22] It is a duty "to take reasonable steps to provide a system which will be reasonably safe, having regard to the dangers necessarily inherent in the operation. In deciding what is reasonable, long established practice in the trade, although not necessarily conclusive, is generally regarded as strong evidence in support of reasonableness." [23] It is not, however, conclusive, because there may be a danger which is so obvious that, although there is a general practice to neglect it, it ought not to be neglected.[24] For example, if window cleaners are to clean windows high above the ground by standing on a sill, little over six inches wide, without any instructions to ensure that the windows should be tested before cleaning or any apparatus, such as wedges, to prevent them from closing,[25] or, being provided with safety belts, are not instructed to attach them to available transoms,[26] there is a failure to provide a safe system of work. This is well expressed in a

20 Lord Reid in *Winter* v. *Cardiff R.D.C.* [1950] 1 All E.R. 819, 835.

21 *Winter* v. *Cardiff R.D.C.*, *supra*. This case was decided before the doctrine of common employment was abolished. Today, the employer would be liable for the chargehand's negligence in not securing the regulator. *Campion* v. *Scruttons* [1968] 2 Lloyd's Rep. 469. But *cf. Roy* v. *Co-ordinated Traffic Services* (1969) 113 S.J. 162 where the decision of the man on the spot should not have been relied on in the circumstances.

22 *Vickers* v. *B.T.D.B.* [1964] 1 Lloyd's Rep. 275.

23 Lord Tucker in *General Cleaning Contractors Ltd.* v. *Christmas* [1953] A.C. 180, 195.

24 See generally Chap. 5, § 192, *ante*, "Common practice as standard of care." Where a dangerous method of work used by a plaintiff had become a common practice amongst his fellow workmen, a fact which was known to the chief shift engineers but not to the Works Manager, the employers could not thereby avoid liability: *Bell* v. *Greater London Council* (1969) 119 New L.J. 153.

25 *General Cleaning Contractors Ltd.* v. *Christmas*, *supra*. *Baker* v. *White's Window & General Cleaning Co.*, *The Times*, March 1, 1962.

26 *Drummond* v. *British Building Cleaners Ltd.* [1954] 1 W.L.R. 1434. A further case concerning the provision of safety belts is *Roberts* v. *Dorman Long & Co. Ltd.* [1953] 2 All E.R. 428, but see note 31 below.

judgment of Lord Dunedin, frequently quoted, where he said: " Where the negligence of the employer consists of what I may call a fault of omission, I think it is absolutely necessary that the proof of that fault of omission should be one of two kinds, either to show that the thing which he did not do was a thing which was commonly done by other persons in like circumstances, or to show that it was a thing which was so obviously wanted that it would be folly in anyone to neglect to provide it." [27] Where a danger is known to exist it may be insufficient for an employer, in order to avoid liability, merely to issue orders that something must not be done without doing more to see that such prohibition is observed.[28]

220 The operation may be one specifically dealt with by statute or statutory regulation, and in such a case compliance with the statutory requirements is evidence that the common law duty has been fulfilled.[29] This is illustrated where a plaintiff, employed by a tunnelling company to work in a coal mine, was injured by a fall of stone from the roof. The mine was owned and occupied by the National Coal Board, who were under a statutory duty to secure the roof, and the system of working, so far as it concerned support for the roof, was that advocated by the Board. It was held that the tunnelling company had used reasonable care in following the advice of the Board and were not in breach of their duty to the plaintiff.[30] It is not, however, conclusive evidence, and in exceptional circumstances, or where some special peril is to be met, the common law duty is not restricted by the statutory requirements.[31]

[27] *Morton* v. *William Dixon Ltd.*, 1909 S.C. 807, quoted in *Paris* v. *Stepney B.C.* [1951] A.C. 367, 382. See *ante*, § 193; *Cavanagh* v. *Ulster Weaving Co.* [1960] A.C. 145, *per* Lord Somervell of Harrow: " Lord Dunedin's observation was, in its context, clearly only intended to apply where the practice proved was clearly proved and where the circumstances covered by the practice were precisely similar to those in which the accident happened. There may be many cases in which, although the circumstances are not precisely similar, evidence of practice should be given some though less weight." In *Cavanagh's* case the plaintiff, a labourer employed by the defendants, was seriously injured when he fell from a crawling ladder whilst descending from the factory roof, at a time when he was carrying a bucket of cement in one hand and was wearing rubber boots, supplied by the defendants, which were too big and which they knew were bound to be wet and slippery. Further see *Graham* v. *Co-operative Wholesale Society Ltd.* [1957] 1 W.L.R. 511; *Riddick* v. *Weir Housing Corporation* [1970] S.L.T. 71.

[28] *Baker* v. *T. E. Hopkins & Son Ltd.* [1959] 1 W.L.R. 966.

[29] *Caulfield* v. *Pickup Ltd.* [1941] 2 All E.R. 510; *Franklin* v. *Gramophone Co.* [1948] 1 K.B. 542, 558; *England* v. *N.C.B.* [1953] 1 Q.B. 724, 731, *per* Somervell L.J. (the case was reversed on other grounds [1954] A.C. 403); *Chipchase* v. *British Titan Products Co. Ltd.* [1956] 1 Q.B. 545; *Smith* v. *Austin Lifts Ltd.* [1959] 1 W.L.R. 100.

[30] *Szumczyk* v. *Associated Tunnelling Co. Ltd.* (1956), unreported in the C.A., affirming [1956] 1 W.L.R. 98.

[31] *Roberts* v. *Dorman Long & Co. Ltd.* [1953] 2 All E.R. 428, 436. (See the observations of Lord Evershed M.R. at p. 231 and Parker L.J. at p. 233, when *Haynes* v. *Qualcast* (*Wolverhampton*) *Ltd.* [1958] 1 W.L.R. 225 was considered by the Court of Appeal, for their observations that this case and *Drummond* v. *British Building Cleaners Ltd.*, *ante*, note 26, have not been overruled by the House of Lords in *Bonnington Castings* v. *Wardlaw* [1956] 1 A.C. 613. Further, see Lord Denning at p. 762 when *Qualcast's* case was before the House of Lords: [1959] A.C. 743.) However, *Roberts* v. *Dorman Long & Co. Ltd.* was disapproved by the House of Lords in *McWilliams* v. *Sir William Arrol & Co.* [1962] 1 W.L.R. 295 in so far as it purported to lay down any contrary principle that a causal connection must be established between a breach by an employer either of his duty at common law or under a statute and the damage suffered by his employee. Further see *Harriman* v. *Martin* [1962] 1 W.L.R. 739 and *Jones* v. *N.C.B.* [1965] 1 W.L.R. 532 (where a breach of the common law duty was found but not a breach of statutory duty); *cf. Kelly* v. *John Dale Ltd.* [1965] 1 Q.B. 185 (vice versa).

221 Prescribing a safe system of work is not a discharge of the employer's duty unless it is also accompanied by taking reasonable care to see that it is followed, such as by supervision in appropriate cases. Thus a man ought not to be given a task to carry out, which is beyond his competence and initiative, without adequate supervision being given.[32] On the other hand an experienced man does not need any warnings or advice about risks with which he is thoroughly familiar,[33] even although he may require such, if he be made to do a task, with which he is thoroughly unfamiliar. The mere giving of written instructions, which set out and explain the system, then telling the workman to comply with them without more was held not to be enough.[34] Providing the necessary protective clothing such as goggles or masks or barrier cream may not be enough unless reasonable steps are taken by pointing out the risk of not using it and by explaining its benefit to encourage men to use it.[35] However in *James* v. *Hepworth and Grandage Ltd.*[36] it was held that in providing protective spats and exhibiting two prominent notices in the workshop stating that they were available free of charge and should be worn, the employers had fulfilled their common law duty, despite the fact that, unknown to them, the employee was illiterate and had no idea what the notices stated. Nevertheless in *Qualcast* (*Wolverhampton*) *Ltd.* v. *Haynes*,[37] Lord Radcliffe said: "though indeed there may be cases in which an employer does not discharge his duty of care towards his workmen merely by providing an article of safety equipment, the courts should be circumspect in filling out that duty with the much vaguer obligation of encouraging, exhorting or instructing workmen or a particular workman to make regular use of what is provided." It has been held to be an answer to a claim for failing to provide the necessary protective clothing to say that the workmen would probably not have used it.[38] In *Qualcast's* case Lord Denning said: "It is often said that a person who omits to do his duty 'cannot be heard to say' that it would have made no difference even if he had done it. . . . But this is an overstatement. The judge *may* infer the omission

32 *Byers* v. *Head Wrightson & Co. Ltd.* [1961] 1 W.L.R. 961.

33 *Qualcast* (*Wolverhampton*) *Ltd.* v. *Haynes* [1959] A.C. 743.

34 *Barcock* v. *Brighton Corpn.* [1949] 1 K.B. 339. But the House of Lords queried in *Boyle* v. *Kodak Ltd.* [1969] 1 W.L.R. 661 whether there is any duty at common law to instruct workmen when the statutory obligation is to do no more than a skilled man must know to be necessary.

35 *Crookall* v. *Vickers-Armstrong Ltd.* [1955] 2 All E.R. 12; *Clifford* v. *Challen & Sons Ltd.* [1951] 1 K.B. 495. *Cf. Woods* v. *Durable Suites Ltd.* [1953] 1 W.L.R. 857, where the duty was satisfied. In *Watson* v. *Ready Mixed Concrete*, *The Times*, January 18, 1961, Edmund Davies J. held that the value of barrier cream was, on the present state of scientific evidence, extremely questionable and that failure to provide such cream had not been proved to be a substantial causative factor by a plaintiff who had probably suffered from a constitutional skin disease.

36 [1968] 1 Q.B. 94. *Percival* v. *Leicester Corporation* [1962] 2 Lloyd's Rep. 43. Fireman drowned while practising aqua-lung swimming. He had received adequate instructions but he had disregarded orders to use a safety line.

37 [1959] A.C. 743, 753. Approved by Viscount Simonds L.C. in *McWilliams* v. *Sir William Arrol & Co. Ltd.* [1962] 1 W.L.R. 295.

38 *McWilliams* v. *Sir William Arrol & Co. Ltd.* [1962] 1 W.L.R. 295, which was applied in *Wigley* v. *British Vinegars Ltd.* [1964] A.C. 307; see also *Nolan* v. *Dental Manufacturing Co. Ltd.* [1958] 1 W.L.R. 936.

to be a cause, but he is not bound to do so. If at the end of the day he thinks that, whether the duty was omitted or fulfilled, the result would have been the same, he is at liberty to say so." [39] Conversely, if it be a probability that the workman would have used the safety equipment had they provided it, the employers will be liable once causation has been proved.[40]

When a plaintiff raises the issue that the system of work is unsafe, usually he must set out in his statement of claim what the proper system of work was and in what relevant respects it was not observed.[41] However in *Dixon* v. *Cementation Co. Ltd.*[42] the court held that it was not necessary in every case where an unsafe system of work was alleged for the plaintiff to undertake the burden of pleading and proving an alternative system of work which could have been adopted and which would have been safe. On this subject Devlin L.J. stated [43]: " There may be cases in which the plaintiff will not get very far with an allegation of unsafe system of work unless he can show some practicable alternative, but there are also cases—and I think this is one of them—in which a plaintiff can fairly say: ' If this is dangerous, then there must be some way of doing it that can be found by a prudent employer and it is not for me to devise that way or say what it is'."

222 It is a question of fact whether or not a system of work should be prescribed in any given circumstances, so that in deciding it regard ought to be had to the nature of the work, *i.e.* whether it properly requires careful organisation and supervision in the interests of safety of all those persons carrying it out or it can be left by a prudent employer to the care of the particular man on the spot to do it reasonably safely.[44] Thus in addition to the cases quoted in the preceding paragraphs by way of illustration it has been held to be an unsafe system: when stones, likely to fall, were slung over the heads of men working below without making provision for warning the men before the stones were slung [45]; when the haulage in a mine was continued during the time at which it was known that men would be travelling along the road at the end of their shift [46]; when an aeroplane at a flying school was started prematurely as a result of a misunderstanding due to the method of teaching [47]; when lighting of great intensity was used in making a film, and no warning was given to the actors or any precautions taken against injury to their eyes [48]; when a large quantity of highly combustible material was kept in

39 [1959] A.C. 743, 762.
40 *Machray* v. *Stewarts & Lloyds Ltd.* [1965] 1 W.L.R. 602.
41 Lord Simon in *Colfar* v. *Coggins & Griffith* (*Liverpool*) *Ltd.* [1945] A.C. 197, 203. See the comment on this in *General Cleaning Contractors Ltd.* v. *Christmas* [1953] A.C. 180, *per* Lord Oaksey at p. 190; *per* Lord Tucker at p. 195.
42 [1960] 1 W.L.R. 746.
43 *Ibid.* at p. 748.
44 See *Jenner* v. *Allen West & Co. Ltd.* [1959] 1 W.L.R. 554.
45 *Smith* v. *Baker & Sons* [1891] A.C. 325.
46 *Wilsons and Clyde Coal Co.* v. *English* [1938] A.C. 57.
47 *Olsen* v. *Corry* [1936] 3 All E.R. 241.
48 *Russell* v. *Criterion Film Productions Ltd.* (1936) 53 T.L.R. 117.

immediate proximity to a boiler so constructed that sparks were likely to be emitted from it on its being fired [49]; when, in unloading a ship, no adequate barricade was placed on the deck to prevent cargo, which frequently slipped from the slings, from rolling over the ship's side onto a barge below [50]; when, in loading a ship, a rail was not removed, with the result that a hook caught it, causing some timber to fall onto a barge below [51]; when a man was working in a ship on the 'tween deck under closed hatches in proximity to an open hatchway, and no adequate light or fencing to the hatch was provided [52]; where the upper deck hatches were battened down but the 'tween deck hatch covers were left off and no guard-rail was erected round the hatchway, the employers were held liable for sending a seaman down to the 'tween deck while the ship was at sea, as a result of which he fell into the hold and was injured [53]; when a man was required to wheel a heavy load onto a narrow ledge where it was likely to, and did, overbalance [54]; when a workshop contained a grinder which created dust and no exhaust appliance was provided [55]; when wartime supports of corrugated iron sheets on which a workman had to crawl were not examined before use [56]; when men were working on the permanent way of a railway at the exit of a tunnel with a lookout man so placed that he could not warn the men in time to enable them to get out of the way of approaching trains [57]; when a workman was repairing a ship in dry dock, not taking any steps to prevent him from falling into the hold [58]; not providing boards for men to stand on when they were working on a roof from which they were likely to fall [59]; where a workman died from scrotal cancer, which had been caused by his regular contact over many years with mineral oil in the course of his employment, the defendants' factory doctor was held to be negligent in failing to warn him about the dangers to which he was being exposed and the precautions he ought to have taken and in failing to institute six-monthly medical examinations in the circumstances [60]; where the employers failed to warn an experienced cement labourer of the danger of dermatitis, to encourage him to take precautions and to provide adequate washing facilities, his conditions of work with dry cement being exceptionally bad [61]; where a workman was required to handle detergents, which were likely to cause dermatitis, for use in cleaning work, but the employers supplied him with

49 *D'Urso* v. *Sanson* [1939] 4 All E.R. 26.
50 *Grantham* v. *New Zealand Shipping Co.* [1940] 4 All E.R. 258.
51 *Speed* v. *Thomas Swift & Co. Ltd.* [1943] K.B. 557.
52 *Garcia* v. *Harland & Wolff Ltd.* [1943] K.B. 731.
53 *Morris* v. *West Hartlepool Steam Navigation Co.* [1956] A.C. 552.
54 *Rees* v. *Cambrian Wagon Works* (1946) 62 T.L.R. 512 ("It was no answer to say that if the workman or the manager had looked about elsewhere proper materials could have been found").
55 *Franklin* v. *Gramophone Co.* [1948] 1 K.B. 542.
56 *Whitby* v. *Burt Boulton & Hayward Ltd.* [1947] K.B. 918.
57 *Dyer* v. *Southern Ry.* [1948] 1 K.B. 608.
58 *Donovan* v. *Cammell Laird & Co.* [1949] 2 All E.R. 82.
59 *Harris* v. *Brights Asphalt Contractors Co.* [1953] 1 Q.B. 617.
60 *Stokes* v. *Guest Keen & Nettlefold (Bolts & Nuts)* [1968] 1 W.L.R. 1776. Similarly see *Wright* v. *Dunlop Rubber Co.*, *The Times*, April 22, 1971.
61 *Snell* v. *J. Shelbourne & Co.* (1965) 109 S.J. 270. But *cf. Riddick* v. *Weir Housing Corpn.* [1970] S.L.T. 71.

gloves which only extended a few inches up his forearms instead of up to the elbows as a result of which his skin was contaminated and he developed the disease.[62]

223 It has been held that the system was not unsafe: when girls working mechanical mincers were first employed for a week on general work and then, if thought suitable, were instructed to work the mincer by an experienced worker [63]; when loading operations on a ship were temporarily suspended and the derrick arm was insecurely fastened, as a result of which, when work was resumed, the arm swung and caused some of the cargo which was being loaded to fall [64]; when a workman, insufficiently skilled for the purpose, was allowed to make a tool and was killed when using it, owing to the tool being inadequate [65]; when a workman contracted dermatitis owing to the hypersensitiveness of his skin [66]; when a coachmaker used Monsonia wood, which caused dermatitis in a workman, and in the then state of knowledge it was not possible to say that a reasonable employer ought to have anticipated that exposure to dust from the wood was likely to result in injury [67]; when employers provided an omnibus service to take their workmen from the working site and a workman was crushed in a disorganised rush by the waiting workmen to get into the bus [68]; when a workman in a shipyard lifted a cable which was across the track of a bogie to let the bogie pass and was injured by the bogie [69]; when a farm labourer, to clean out a loose box in which was kept a fierce bull, was instructed to secure the bull through a window and not to enter the loose box while the bull was not secured [70]; when scaffolding, not provided by the defendants but by other contractors working on the same building, had platform boards with spaces between them and no toe boards [71]; cutting barbed wire by placing it on the metal head of a sledge hammer and striking it with a smaller hammer [72]; where an experienced workman knowingly used a wrong tool for the job and alleged that his employers ought to have warned or reminded him to use the correct tool supplied [73];

224 **(5) Other cases.** In addition to the heads of liability considered above, the employer is liable to his servant for damage caused through the negligence of his fellow servant acting in the course of his employment.[74]

[62] *Voller* v. *Schweppes* (*Home*) (1969) 7 K.I.R. 228.
[63] *Wood* v. *L.C.C.* [1940] 4 All E.R. 149, reversed on another point [1941] 2 K.B. 232.
[64] *Colfar* v. *Coggins and Griffith* (*Liverpool*) *Ltd.* [1945] A.C. 197.
[65] *Franklin* v. *Bristol Aeroplane Co.* [1948] W.N. 341.
[66] *Clayton* v. *Caledonian Stevedoring Co. Ltd.* (1948) 81 Ll.L.R. 332.
[67] *Ebbs* v. *James Whitson & Co. Ltd.* [1952] 2 Q.B. 877; *Graham* v. *Co-operative Wholesale Society Ltd.* [1957] 1 W.L.R. 511, *cf. Stokes* v. *Guest Keen & Nettlefold* (*Bolts & Nuts*) [1968] 1 W.L.R. 1776.
[68] *Ramsay* v. *Wimpey & Co.*, 1952 S.L.T. 46.
[69] *Grace* v. *Stephen & Sons*, 1952 S.L.T. 61.
[70] *Rands* v. *McNeill* [1955] 1 Q.B. 253.
[71] *Hughes* v. *McGoff & Vickers Ltd.* [1955] 2 All E.R. 291.
[72] *Baker* v. *Harvey Farms* (*Thorpe*), *The Times*, October 26, 1961.
[73] *Leach* v. *British Oxygen Co.* (1965) 109 S.J. 157.
[74] *Staveley Iron & Chemical Co. Ltd.* v. *Jones* [1956] A.C. 627. See the comment on this case [1956] C.L.J. 158. See also *Simmons* v. *Bovis Ltd.* [1956] 1 W.L.R. 381.

Formerly, in most cases, the doctrine of common employment provided the employer with a complete defence, but this is so no longer. It is only when it is not possible to prove negligence on the part of a fellow servant that it is necessary to rely on one of the grounds already considered. These, however, are only a convenient method of grouping the most usual cases of the duty of the employer. His duty is to take reasonable care for the safety of his servant and failure to perform this renders him liable even though the facts do not show any failure to perform one of the duties set out above, or do not fit conveniently into any of the categories hitherto considered. This is sometimes expressed by saying that the employer's duty is "so to carry on his operations as not to subject those employed by him to unnecessary risk." [75] An unnecessary risk is "any risk that the employer can reasonably foresee and which he can guard against by any measures, the convenience and expense of which are not entirely disproportionate to the risk involved." [76] For example, when an electric fan was being tested in the maintenance shop of a factory by being operated at a high speed on the floor without any guard and an electrician, in some unexplained way, had his hand caught in the revolving blades, the employers were held liable on the broad ground that in the circumstances it was reasonably foreseeable that some damage might result.[77]

225 Similarly, if an employer knows that accidents to workpeople are caused from time to time by wire ejected from a machine, it is his duty to take reasonable care to protect his workpeople from injury by such accidents, even though there is no breach of section 14 (1) of the Factories Act 1937 (now the Factories Act 1961), in relation to such machine. Where it was known that wire was from time to time ejected from a machine revolving at 800 revolutions a minute in a wire rope factory and had caused a number of minor accidents without any steps being taken by the employers to prevent them, it was held that the employers were liable when an ejected piece of wire destroyed the sight of one of the operator's eyes.[78] Again, where a workman was employed in a factory in which were 500 machines, twelve of which were dangerous to lubricate during motion, and he was injured whilst so oiling one of the twelve, the employers were held liable at common law because "(i) they failed to issue proper instructions to the plaintiff to ensure that he did not oil

[75] *Smith* v. *Baker* [1891] A.C. 325, 362, *per* Lord Herschell. See also *Bartonshill Coal Co.* v. *Reid* (1858) 3 Macq. 266, *per* Lord Cranworth; *Hutchinson* v. *York, etc., Ry.* (1850) 5 Ex. 343, *per* Alderson B. As to discovery of previous accidents, see *Edmiston* v. *B.T.C.* [1956] 1 Q.B. 191. In *Houghton* v. *Hackney Corporation* (1961) 3 K.I.R. 615 it was held that there had been no breach of duty to see that a rent collector was not exposed to unnecessary risks when he, in the course of his employment, had been robbed with violence of the money he had collected, whereby he had sustained injuries. The test was whether the employers had taken reasonable precautions in all the circumstances, and it was found that they had so taken by employing a uniformed porter to be about when rent was being collected.

[76] *Harris* v. *Brights Asphalt Contractors Ltd.* [1953] 1 W.L.R. 341, 344.

[77] *Thurogood* v. *Van den Berghs & Jurgens Ltd.* [1951] 2 K.B. 537. See also *Sidor* v. *N.C.B.* (1956) 106 L.J. 218.

[78] *Kilgollan* v. *William Cooke & Co. Ltd.* [1956] 1 W.L.R. 527.

any of these twelve dangerous machines when in motion; and (ii) they took no effective step to ensure that instructions not to oil such machines when in motion were carried out." [79] Where a servant suffered frostbite as a result of a long journey travelling in an unheated motor-van during freezing weather conditions it was held that his employers were under a duty to take steps to protect him against reasonably foreseeable hazards. If as a result of failure to take such steps the servant suffered injury of a kind that was reasonably foreseeable, even though its precise nature was not foreseen, the master will be liable.[80]

226 On the other hand when a workman, using a swab to clean the "tucking blades" of a rotary press while the machine was stationary, the blades being sharpish but by no means of razor-blade sharpness, cut his hand on one of the blades, it was held that the employers were not liable as there was no breach of duty on their part [81]; and where a cabinet maker, employed in a factory, contracted dermatitis through wood dust settling on his skin and it was proved that the ventilation of the factory was adequate for ordinary purposes and that furniture manufacturers took no precautions to prevent dermatitis from West African hard wood dust, since it was not then thought likely to cause it, the defendants were held not liable.[82] An employer is not liable to a servant for the negligence of a fellow servant who is not acting in the course of his employment, as where personal injury was caused by the wilful misbehaviour of the fellow servants (in this case a practical joke) which the employer could not reasonably have foreseen.[83]

There is no legal duty on an employer to refuse to employ or to prevent an adult employee doing work he is willing to do merely because the employer thought it is not in the latter's best interests. In circumstances where a plaintiff had returned to work after an attack of dermatitis and commenced other work which she knew was likely to exacerbate this condition, the employers were exonerated from blame, since their duty was limited to the taking of all reasonable care, having regard to the fact that the plaintiff had had dermatitis.[84] Moreover there was no duty at common law requiring an employer to dismiss an employee rather than

79 *Lewis* v. *High Duty Alloys Ltd.* [1957] 1 W.L.R. 632 (the plaintiff was held one third to blame).

80 *Bradford* v. *Robinson Rentals* [1967] 1 W.L.R. 337 which was distinguished by Payne J. in *Tremain* v. *Pike* [1969] 1 W.L.R. 1556, since injury from extreme cold was foreseeable, even if the degree of injury was not, whilst the risk of the initial infection from the rare Weil's disease contracted through contact with rat's urine was not reasonably foreseeable and was entirely a different risk from, for example, the effect of a rat's bite or food poisoning by the consumption of food or drink contaminated by rats. See also the distinction drawn from *Smith* v. *Leech Brain & Co. Ltd.* [1962] 2 Q.B. 405.

81 *Buckingham* v. *Daily News Ltd.* [1956] 2 Q.B. 534. The plaintiff and his witnesses said that a long-handled brush should have been used; the defendants called no evidence; the judge, at the parties' request, had a view before giving his decision, and the Court of Appeal held he was entitled to follow his own impressions formed at the view.

82 *Graham* v. *Co-operative Wholesale Society Ltd.* [1957] 1 W.L.R. 511; *Ebbs* v. *James Whitson & Co. Ltd.* [1952] 2 Q.B. 877.

83 *Smith* v. *Crossley Bros.* (1951) 95 S.J. 655. See generally § 210, *ante* "(2)—Competent servants and supervision."

84 *Withers* v. *Perry Chain Co. Ltd.* [1961] 1 W.L.R. 1314.

to retain him in employment and allow him to earn his wages merely because there might be some risk since in such cases it was for the employee to weigh the risk against the desirability or necessity of the employment. Thus in *Jones* v. *Lionite Specialities* (*Cardiff*) the employers were not liable where they had failed to prevent a servant from exposing himself to danger when they allowed him to enter and remain in a tank, being degreased using trichloro-ethylene, to which the employers knew he was addicted, as a result of which the servant inhaled an overdose and died.[85] The employer's duty extends to taking reasonable steps to guard employees from criminal assaults or injury in carrying out their tasks [86] but he owes no duty to take care to protect his servant's property from the felonious act of a third party.[87]

227 **No liability for ordinary risks of service.** An employer is not liable to his servant for damage suffered by him from one of the ordinary risks of the service when there is no negligence on the part of himself or his servants. The death of a seaman drowned at sea, either in a shipwreck or other disaster, gives no cause of action if the ship was properly manned and equipped and there is no negligence on the part of the captain or the crew, because the risk of drowning is an ordinary risk of the service. This principle is expressed by Glyn-Jones J. in these words [88]: " A great deal of work which has to be done is dangerous, and if it is not reasonably practicable for the master to eliminate or diminish the danger, then the risk is a necessary incident of this employment and a risk which the servant is paid to take." Lord Tucker emphasised " Sailors are, of course, necessarily exposed to many risks by the very nature of their calling, and no one would suggest that the courts should be ready to interfere with the practice based upon past experience with regard to such occupational risks." [89] A workman who slipped on the ice at the entrance to the factory failed to recover because " the danger of finding surfaces icy is one of the incidents of winter in our country which everyone encounters." [90] A fireman who was injured by a jack while travelling on a lorry, not specially fitted for carrying the jack, in an emergency, failed to prove liability because the risk to which he was exposed was a risk incidental

[85] (1961) 105 S.J. 1082. See also below for " ordinary risks of service."

[86] *Houghton* v. *Hackney Corporation* (1961) 3 K.I.R. 615, followed in *Williams* v. *Grimshaw and Orse* (1967) 3 K.I.R. 610, where no breach of duty was proved by the stewardess of a cricket club, who was injured in an attempted robbery by a thief trying to grab the cash takings that she was taking home with her under escort.

[87] *Deyong* v. *Shenburn* [1946] K.B. 227 (actor's property stolen from theatre in which he was rehearsing—employer not liable), which was followed in *Edwards* v. *West Herts Group Hospital Management Committee* [1957] 1 W.L.R. 415 (a resident house physician, living in a staff hostel adjoining the hospital, cannot recover against the hospital if his personal effects are stolen from the hostel, as the hospital owes no duty to the physician to safeguard his property against theft by a third party who comes into the hostel). *Cf.* Factories Act 1961, s. 59; *McCarthy* v. *Daily Mirror Newspapers Ltd.* [1949] 1 All E.R. 801, and Offices, Shops and Railway Premises Act 1963, s. 12. Article " A master's duty of care for his servants property " (Foulkes) (1964) 114 L.J. 486.

[88] *Hurley* v. *J. Sanders & Co. Ltd.* [1955] 1 All E.R. 833, 836.

[89] *Morris* v. *West Hartlepool Steam Navigation Co. Ltd.* [1956] A.C. 552, 576.

[90] *Thomas* v. *Bristol Aeroplane Co.* [1954] 1 W.L.R. 694, 696, *per* Somervell L.J.

to the fire service.[91] A night-watchman injured when falling over a loose plank on a building site failed because " one would expect that on a building site there would be obstructions and obstacles such as the plank in question, and a night-watchman must take the risk of them." [92] Nevertheless where a boy of seventeen was left alone on the crew accommodation deck to clean out the scupper pipe on the port side and was never seen again, having fallen in shark-infested waters in the Indian Ocean, the shipowners were held liable for having failed to provide him with an assistant. Hodson L.J. said that the case had to be approached with the knowledge that sailors had by their calling to perform dangerous tasks at sea and it was not always practicable to take effective steps to eliminate risk, but the duty of employers to safeguard their men from unnecessary risk applied at sea as on land.[93] Where the defendant's skipper could not have foreseen the risk of a sea breaking over the side of the trawler which was fishing during bad weather and in heavy sea conditions so as to cause any real danger to the plaintiff deck hand, the plaintiff's claim in negligence failed.[94] Where a servant had placed a loaded gun on top of a harvester machine in disobedience to his master's instructions and the gun fired accidentally, injuring the driver, a fellow servant, it was held that as the " scope of employment " must be construed liberally the master was vicariously liable for his servant's act in adding a further danger to the risk of the work.[95]

228 **Which employer liable.** When a servant in the general employment of one employer is placed on loan and at the disposal of another employer on a temporary basis, a question arises which employer is liable for injury caused to the servant. In *O'Reilly* v. *Imperial Chemical Industries Ltd.*[96] Parker L.J. said: " If a duty of master to servant is to be found in any case it can only be where there is either a true relation of master and servant or a relationship of master and servant of a temporary character as that envisaged in the *Mersey Docks and Harbour Board* case.[97] Unless one or other of those features is proved I cannot see any possibility of maintaining a claim for a breach of the duty owed by a master to his servant." If the injury is caused by the negligence of a fellow servant, the employer of the fellow servant will be liable. On the other hand, if it is

91 *Watt* v. *Hertfordshire C.C.* [1954] 1 W.L.R. 835.

92 *Field* v. *Perrys (Ealing) Ltd.* [1950] W.N. 320, *per* Devlin J.

93 *Ellis* v. *Ocean Steamship Co. Ltd.* [1958] 2 Lloyd's Rep. 373.

94 *The Farnella* [1965] 2 Lloyd's Rep. 299.

95 *Spencer* v. *Curtis Bros.* (1962) 106 S.J. 390.

96 [1955] 1 W.L.R. 1155, 1162 (and *per* Jenkins L.J. at p. 1164). See 72 L.Q.R. 6. In *Savory* v. *Holland & Hannen & Cubitts (Southern) Ltd.* [1964] 1 W.L.R. 1158 the Court of Appeal commented that the decision in *O'Reilly's* case is of no authority today in view of the Occupiers' Liability Act 1957, which would now require the occupiers to use reasonable care towards the lorry driver concerned. Whilst this may be so as regards providing a safe place of work it cannot be correct as regards the other aspects of the employers' duty of care.

97 *i.e. Mersey Docks and Harbour Board* v. *Coggins & Griffith (Liverpool) Ltd.* [1947] A.C.1 where the House of Lords held that the harbour authority as the general permanent employer was liable since it had not discharged the heavy burden of proof placed on it so as to shift to the stevedores, the temporary employer, its prima facie responsibility for the negligence of the craneman.

caused by unsafe premises, defective plant or materials or an unsafe system of work, different considerations apply. It does not follow that the person who is regarded as the employer for the purpose of being held liable for the negligence of the servant [98] is the same person as the employer who is regarded as liable for injury to the servant.[99] If the injury is caused by unsafe premises, the employer in occupation and control of the premises is liable. If the injury is caused by defective plant or materials, the employer supplying them is liable. Where an electrician in the general employment of A was lent to B to work in his factory and, on his asking B's foreman for a trestle, was told to look round and find one, it was held that B was liable and not A, when the electrician was injured owing to the trestle's defects.[1] If the injury is caused by an unsafe system, the employer who prescribed and operated the system is liable.[2]

A distinction nevertheless must be drawn between the lending of a servant, thereby transferring the right of control to the temporary employer, and the making available merely the benefit of his services whereby the control essentially still remains with the permanent employer. Hence, since the burden of proof of transfer is a heavy one,[3] it can only be in the exceptional case that the right of control over a servant is transferred away from the general to the temporary master, particularly where the servant has been lent together with some valuable equipment. The inference that control has been transferred may be more readily drawn where an unskilled workman alone is lent.[4]

2.—LIABILITY BETWEEN FELLOW SERVANTS

229 **Duty of servants to each other.** Two or more servants working for the same employer owe a duty to each other to take reasonable care and are liable to each other for damage caused by failure to perform that duty. Where one servant injured another through his breach of statutory regulations, as a consequence of which the employer had to pay workmen's compensation to the injured servant, it was held that the employer was entitled to an indemnity from the servant causing the injury on the ground that the circumstances created a legal liability in that servant towards the injured servant.[5] Again, where an actress on the stage negligently let a club slip from her hand and injured a member of the orchestra, it was held that she was liable to the injured person.[6]

230 One servant owes a duty to take care to a fellow servant when they

98 See Chap. 14, § 910.

99 *Garrard* v. *Southey & Co.* [1952] 2 Q.B. 174, *per* Parker J. See also 20 M.L.R. 189.

1 *Garrard* v. *Southey & Co., supra.* The electrician was held to be, for the time being, in the employment of B.

2 See *Holt* v. *Rhodes & Son Ltd.* [1949] 1 All E.R. 478.

3 *Mersey Docks and Harbour Board* v. *Coggins & Griffith (Liverpool) Ltd., supra.*

4 *Denham* v. *Midland Employers' Mutual Assurance Ltd.* [1955] 2 Q.B. 437 (a brickfield labourer was lent to contractors drilling on the site and was placed under orders from their foreman).

5 *Lees* v. *Dunkerley Bros.* [1911] A.C. 5. Workmen's Compensation Act 1925, s. 30 (now repealed by the National Insurance (Industrial Injuries) Act 1946, s. 89, Sched. IX).

6 *Laubach* v. *Co-optimists' Entertainment Syndicate* (1926) 43 T.L.R. 30.

are working together in a joint operation. The plaintiff, one of a gang of six stevedores, was injured by the collapse of bags of sodium carbonate which the gang were unloading from a barge. The collapse was due to the unsafe method of unstowing adopted by the gang, including the plaintiff, contrary to the express instructions of the foreman. The employers were held liable for the negligence of the other members of the gang, but the damages were reduced by 50 per cent. because of the plaintiff's contributory negligence. " If a number of men engage in an occupation which is contrary to instructions, and which is also dangerous, there nevertheless is a duty owed by one to the other to use reasonable care, and that duty is not abrogated by joining together and carrying out a common operation. Even the assent to carrying out that operation might in certain circumstances amount to a breach of duty to a man who is also carrying it out; it is a breach of duty that one man owed to the other." [7]

3.—LIABILITY OF SERVANT TO MASTER

231 **Duty of servant to master.** In *Century Insurance Co. Ltd.* v. *Northern Ireland Transport Board* Lord Wright expressed the view that " the duty of the workman to his employer is so to conduct himself in doing his work as not negligently to cause damage either to the employer himself or his property or to third persons or their property and thus to impose the same liability on the employer as if he had been doing the work himself and committed the negligent act. This may seem too obvious as a matter of common sense to require either argument or authority." [8] Accordingly the servant owes a duty to take reasonable care as regards the employer but unlike the similar duty in tort owed between fellow servants to one another,[9] it is deemed to be an implied contractual obligation arising out of the servant's contract of service.[10] Should the servant be in breach of this duty then the master has a cause of action and may recover damages unless they are too remote. A negligent servant is liable therefore to indemnify his master against the damages which the master is liable to pay because of his vicarious liability for his servant's negligence as well as for any direct physical injury sustained.[11] In *Lister* v. *Romford Ice and Cold Storage Co. Ltd.*[12] the defendant, a lorry driver employed

[7] *Williams* v. *Port of Liverpool Stevedoring Co. Ltd.* [1956] 1 W.L.R. 551, *per* Lynskey J. at pp. 555, 556.

[8] [1942] A.C. 509, 519.

[9] *Supra*, §§ 229, 230.

[10] *Lister* v. *Romford Ice & Cold Storage Co. Ltd.* [1957] A.C. 555.

[11] *Digby* v. *General Accident Fire and Life Insurance Corporation Ltd.* [1943] A.C. 121 (the famous pre-war film actress Miss Merle Oberon sustained personal injuries, whilst travelling as a passenger in her Buick motor car, which was being driven by her chauffeur, and she recovered £5,000 general damages for these injuries caused by his negligent driving).

[12] *Supra.* (See note on this case 74 L.Q.R. 169 and 20 M.L.R. 437.) Distinguished in *Harvey* v. *R. G. O'Dell Ltd.* [1958] 2 Q.B. 78. (A workman used his own motor-cycle combination to transport himself and a fellow servant and drove negligently, injuring his fellow employee, riding as a passenger. However, as he was employed as a storekeeper and not as a driver there was no implied term in his contract of employment that he would indemnify the employers for failure on his part to drive with care whilst using his vehicle on their business.) See note on this case, 74 L.Q.R. 170.

by the plaintiffs, negligently ran into and injured his father, who also was employed by the plaintiffs as a driver's mate. The father obtained judgment against the plaintiffs on the ground of the defendant's negligence for which they were vicariously liable and the House of Lords by a bare majority held that the plaintiffs could recover from the defendant the amount of that judgment, on the ground that the defendant was in breach of an implied term in his contract of service that he would drive with reasonable care and skill. Lord Simons said, expressing what he believed to be the unanimous opinion: "The servant owes a contractual duty of care to his master and the breach of that duty founds an action for damages for breach of contract." [13]

232 In *Weld-Blundell* v. *Stephens* [14] Warrington L.J. said: "It may well be that if a servant by his negligent act inflicts an injury on a third person who recovers damages therefor from the master, the latter may recover the amount from the servant in an action against him for breach of his duty. But in such a case the right of action against the master and his legal liability themselves result from the servant's negligent act, and but for that act would not have existed."

233 In *Ryan* v. *Fildes* [15] a schoolboy received a box on the ear from the schoolmistress. This was held to be excessive correction and the boy recovered damages from the mistress and her employers, the school managers. The managers obtained contribution from the schoolmistress of 100 per cent., amounting to a complete indemnity, and the question was discussed whether, instead of applying for contribution, the managers could have recovered in an action for indemnity. The conclusion, though not expressed, seems to be that they could have done so.

234 Where a master and servant are joint tortfeasors it is now settled law that the master can claim contribution from such servant to the extent which the court considers to be just and equitable in all the circumstances under the Law Reform (Married Women and Tortfeasors) Act 1935,[16] which could amount in an appropriate case to an indemnity. It follows that if the employer himself is negligent or he is liable by reason of some negligence of another of his servants [17] he will not be entitled to an indemnity but only to a contribution. Thus in *Jones* v. *Manchester Corpn.*[18] the widow of a deceased patient at a hospital recovered damages against the hospital authority and a doctor employed by them for the death of her husband, caused by the doctor's negligence. The hospital authority claimed an indemnity or alternatively contribution from the doctor and

[13] *Ibid.* at p. 573.

[14] [1919] 1 K.B. 520, 536. See also *Gregory* v. *Ford* [1951] 1 All E.R. 121, 124, *per* Byrne J. "A servant is, of course, liable at the suit of his master for damage which is the result of the servant's negligence."

[15] [1938] 3 All E.R. 517, which was expressly approved by Lord Simonds in *Lister* v. *Romford Ice & Cold Storage Co. Ltd.* [1957] A.C. 555, 580.

[16] See articles "Vicarious Liability and Master's Indemnity" (Williams), 20 M.L.R. 220. "Right to Indemnity between Master and Servant" (Jolowicz), 22 M.L.R. 71, 189.

[17] *e.g. Harvey* v. *R. G. O'Dell Ltd. supra*, (which was in fact 100 per cent in this case.).

[18] [1952] 2 Q.B. 852.

it was held that there had been negligence on their part contributing to the loss so they were not entitled to an indemnity, although they were entitled to contribution amounting to one-fifth. Singleton L.J. after quoting without disapproval a passage from *Salmond on Torts* [19] to the effect that the employer had a right of indemnity from the servant, said that there was no such right when the employer had himself contributed to the loss. Denning L.J., after saying that the statement " if a master is made liable for the negligence of his servant he is entitled to indemnity from that servant " has often been assumed to be the law, pointed out that there was no reported decision to that effect, and expressed the opinion that the master and servant in such a case were joint tortfeasors, so that contribution only and not indemnity can be obtained. On the other hand, Hodson L.J. was of opinion that there was an implied term in the doctor's contract of employment to exercise reasonable skill, that the finding of negligence was proof of breach of that term and that the doctor was liable to indemnify the hospital authority.

235 In *Semtex Ltd.* v. *Gladstone* [20] one servant negligently drove a car taking some of his fellow servants to work, as a result of which there was an accident in which one was killed and several others injured. The employer, having paid the damages awarded against him, sued the driver for an indemnity. Finnemore J. expressed his preference for Hodson L.J.'s judgment in *Jones*' case and said that " the defendant is, in my view, quite plainly liable at common law to his masters " and also found the driver (the defendant) liable to make 100 per cent. contribution if he was to be regarded as a joint tortfeasor.

[19] 10th ed., p. 78; see 15th ed., p. 648.
[20] [1954] 2 All E.R. 206, which was expressly approved by Lord Simonds, but disapproved by Lord Somervell (dissenting)—*Lister* v. *Romford Ice & Cold Storage Co. Ltd. supra*, at pp. 570, 600.

Chapter 7

PERSONS PROFESSING SOME SPECIAL SKILL

1.—Actions Against Skilled Persons Generally

236 **Care and skill.** Where special skill is required for the work to be done, a reasonable man would not be expected to attempt it unless he is capable of performing it by possessing such special skill, in which event he is bound to exercise the skill and competence of an ordinarily competent practitioner in that profession. " Every person who enters into a learned profession undertakes to bring to the exercise of it a reasonable degree of care and skill. He does not undertake, if he is an attorney, that at all events you shall gain your case, nor does a surgeon undertake that he will perform a cure; nor does he undertake to use the highest possible degree of skill. There may be persons who have higher education and greater advantages than he has, but he undertakes to bring a fair, reasonable and competent degree of skill." [1]

The same rule applies to any man exercising a skilled trade or business. " If a smith prick my horse with a nail, etc., I shall have my action upon the case against him, without any warranty by the smith to do it well . . . for it is the duty of every artificer to exercise his art rightly and truly as he ought." [2]

In *Bolam* v. *Friern Hospital Management Committee*,[3] McNair J. said: " Where you get a situation which involves the use of some special skill or competence, then the test as to whether there has been negligence or not is not the test of the man on the top of a Clapham omnibus, because he has not got this special skill. The test is the standard of the ordinary skilled man exercising and professing to have that special skill. . . . A man need not possess the highest expert skill; it is well established law that it is sufficient if he exercises the ordinary skill of an ordinary competent man exercising that particular art."

It follows that an action for negligence will lie for damage caused by the failure to exercise due care and skill by proving either that the defendant did not possess the requisite skill or by showing that, although he possessed it, he did not exercise it in the particular case.

237 As the standard of care and skill is that possessed by a man of ordinary competence exercising the same calling, it follows that the opinions of persons exercising that calling as to the conduct of a reasonably skilful

[1] *Lanphier* v. *Phipos* (1838) 8 C. & P. 475, *per* Tindal C.J. See also *Harmer* v. *Cornelius* (1858) 5 C.B.(N.S.) 236; *Jones* v. *Bird* (1822) 5 B. & Ald. 837, 845, *per* Bayley J.; *Seare* v. *Prentice* (1807) 8 East 348.
[2] F.N.B. 94 D.
[3] [1957] 1 W.L.R. 582, at p. 586.

man under the particular circumstances are admissible in evidence. In an action against an insurance broker for negligently effecting an insurance, Tindal C.J. said: " The point, therefore, to be determined is, not whether the defendant arrived at a correct conclusion upon reading the letter, but whether, upon the occasion in question, he did or did not exercise a reasonable and proper care, skill and judgment. This is a question of fact, the decision of which appears to us to rest upon this further inquiry, *viz.*, whether other persons exercising the same profession or calling, and being men of experience and skill therein, would or would not have come to the same conclusion as the defendant. For the defendant did not contract that he would bring to the performance of his duty, on this occasion, an extraordinary degree of skill, but only a reasonable and ordinary proportion of it; and it appears to us, that it is not only an unobjectionable mode, but the most satisfactory mode of determining this question, to show by evidence whether a majority of skilful and experienced brokers would have come to the same conclusion as the defendant. If nine brokers of experience out of ten would have done the same as the defendant under the same circumstances, or even if as many out of a given number would have been of his opinion as against it, he who only stipulates to bring a reasonable degree of skill to the performance of his duty would be entitled to a verdict in his favour." [4]

238 Reasonable skill includes a practical working knowledge of the law relating to the calling in question.[5]

This duty to exercise reasonable care and skill is applicable to everyone practising a calling involving personal skill, such as: accountants and auditors,[6] agents,[7] architects, engineers and surveyors,[8] auctioneers,[9] barristers [10] (when engaged on non-litigious matters), dentists,[11] directors of companies,[12] divers,[13] nurses,[14] patent agents,[15] physicians and surgeons,[16] solicitors,[17] stockbrokers,[18] insurance brokers,[19] valuers [20] and veterinary practitioners.

4 *Chapman* v. *Walton* (1833) 10 Bing. 57.
5 *Jenkins* v. *Betham* (1855) 15 C.B. 168; *Lee* v. *Walker* (1872) L.R. 7 C.P. 121.
6 *Post*, § 246.
7 *Keppel* v. *Wheeler* [1927] 1 K.B. 577; *Price* v. *Metropolitan House Investment Agency* (1907) 23 T.L.R. 630; *Gokal* v. *Ram* (1938) 55 T.L.R. 15.
8 *Post*, § 255.
9 *Parker* v. *Farebrother* (1853) 1 C.L.R. 323; *Hibbert* v. *Bayley* (1860) 2 F. & F. 48; *Cyril Andrade Ltd.* v. *Sotheby & Co.* (1931) 47 T.L.R. 244.
10 *Post*, § 268.
11 *Post*, § 271.
12 *Re City Equitable Fire Insurance Co.* [1925] Ch. 407.
13 *Wilton* v. *Hampton*, *The Times*, November 10, 1959, where a professional diver, who allowed his former pupil, the day after the latter had qualified as a master diver, to dive in unfavourable diving conditions, was held not to be negligent in allowing him to dive.
14 *Post*, § 295.
15 *Lee* v. *Walker*, *supra*.
16 *Post*, § 272.
17 *Post*, § 310.
18 *Neilson* v. *James* (1882) 9 Q.B.D. 546.
19 *Chapman* v. *Walton* (1833) 10 Bing. 57; 2 L.J.C.P. 210; *Coolee Ltd.* v. *Wing Heath & Co.* (1930) 47 T.L.R. 78; *United Mills Agencies Ltd.* v. *R. E. Harvey Bray & Co.* [1952] 1 All E.R. 225n.
20 *Baxter* v. *Gapp & Co.* [1939] 2 K.B. 271; *post*, § 326.

239 **Is cause of action contract or tort?** In all these cases of action for negligence against professional and other skilled persons the cause of action is primarily breach of contract, but it can also be based on negligence on the ground that a reasonable man, owing a duty of care in such circumstances, would exercise the care of a skilled man in doing the work.[21] In some cases, therefore, it is also permissible to sue in tort.[22] The reason for this is largely due to historical causes. Under the old forms of action the action of trespass upon the case lay against a person who had undertaken to do something to the person or property of another and did it so as to cause damage. From this there developed the action of assumpsit, which was for damage suffered as a result of a failure to carry out an undertaking or of improperly performing a duty which had been undertaken—in other words, for damages for breach of contract.[23] As long as the old forms of action remained, an action for misfeasance in the performance of a duty could be brought either in case or in assumpsit. The position was thus stated by Tindal C.J.: " That there is a large class of cases in which the foundation of the action springs out of privity of contract between the parties, but in which, nevertheless, the remedy for the breach, or non-performance, is indifferently either assumpsit or case upon tort, is not disputed. Such are actions against attorneys, surgeons and other professional men, for want of competent skill or proper care in the service they undertake to render; actions against common carriers, against shipowners on bills of lading, against bailees of different descriptions; and numerous other instances occur in which the action is brought in tort or contract at the election of the plaintiff. . . . The principle in all these cases would seem to be that the contract creates a duty, and the neglect to perform that duty, or the nonfeasance, is a ground of action upon a tort." [24] This would seem to indicate that every breach of contract was also a tort, but even before the abolition of forms of action by the Common Law Procedure Act 1852 it was recognised that mere breach of contract, such as non-payment of a debt, was not a tort.[25]

240 Now that forms of action are abolished it is possible to look at the substance of the matter to ascertain whether the action is in contract or tort. The importance of this is that in order to determine the scope of the action, an action of contract only lies between the parties to the contract, while an action of tort has a much wider range, and the measure of damages may well be quite different.

[21] *Heaven* v. *Pender* (1883) 11 Q.B.D. 503, 507; *Grant* v. *Australian Knitting Mills Ltd.* [1936] A.C. 85, 103; *Gold* v. *Essex C.C.* [1942] 2 K.B. 293; *Cotton* v. *Wallis* [1955] 1 W.L.R. 1168; *Wells* v. *Cooper* [1958] 2 Q.B. 265.

[22] *Pippin* v. *Sheppard* (1822) 11 Price 400; *Gladwell* v. *Steggall* (1839) 5 Bing.N.C. 733 (surgeons); *Edwards* v. *Mallan* [1908] 1 K.B. 1002 (dentist); *Turner* v. *Stallibrass* [1898] 1 Q.B. 56 (bailee).

[23] See Sutton's *Personal Actions at Common Law*, pp. 63–65; Maitland, *Forms of Action at Common Law*, lecture 6.

[24] *Boorman* v. *Brown* (1841) 3 Q.B. 511, 525, affd. 11 Cl. & F. 1.

[25] *Courtenay* v. *Earle* (1850) 10 C.B. 73 (counts alleging non-payment of money are counts in assumpsit and cannot be joined with counts in case).

The distinction between contract and tort turns on the origin of the duty. In contract the duty arises from the agreement of the parties; in tort it is independent of agreement and is imposed upon the parties by the law.[26] The duty in tort may also be covered by a duty in contract, and the question then arises, is the duty in tort superseded by the duty in contract, or is there a choice of remedies open to the injured party? The answer is that there is a choice of remedies, but " where the defendant has protection under a contract, it is not permissible to disregard the contract and allege a wider liability in tort." [27] In *Jarvis* v. *Moy, Davies, Smith, Vandervell and Co.*,[28] Greer J. said: " The distinction in the modern view, for this purpose, between contract and tort may be put thus: where the breach of duty alleged arises out of a liability independently of the personal obligation undertaken by contract, it is tort, and it may be tort even though there may happen to be a contract between the parties, if the duty in fact arises independently of that contract. Breach of contract occurs where that which is complained of is a breach of duty arising out of the obligations undertaken by the contract." Diplock L.J. in *Bagot* v. *Stevens Scanlan and Co. Ltd.*[29] considered the above quotation to be an accurate statement of the law and continued by saying: " It can be properly said, as it was in such cases as *Lister* v. *Romford Ice and Cold Storage Co. Ltd.*[30] that, independently of contract, there existed from the mere status a relationship which gave rise to a duty of care not dependent upon the existence of a contract between the parties. But I do not think that that principle applies to professional relationships of the kind . . . where someone undertakes to exercise by contract his professional skill in relation to the matter."

241 Apart from the possible overlapping of contract and tort, it remains to be considered whether a skilled person does owe any duty in tort. Generally,[31] the duty to take care only arises when the foreseeable result of a failure or omission to take care will cause injury, loss or damage whether to person or property. From this it appears that a duty in tort will arise although the type of damage may well differ; *e.g.* in the case of persons such as doctors, dentists, barbers, plumbers and similar people the loss is more likely to be physical damage, whilst in the case of such others as solicitors, architects, accountants, surveyors, bankers and stockbrokers, the damage is more likely to be financial loss.

242 So, it has been held that an action against a banker for wrongfully

26 *Jarvis* v. *Moy, Davies & Co.* [1936] 1 K.B. 399, *per* Greer L.J. See also *Jackson* v. *Mayfair Window Cleaning Co.* [1952] 1 All E.R. 215 (damage to chandelier caused by persons who had contracted to overhaul and clean it is an action in tort. " If the defendants . . . interfere with [the plaintiff's] property whether with or without her permission and whether in pursuance of a contract or otherwise—they are under an obligation not to damage that property as a result of their negligence, or in other words, they are bound to take reasonable care to keep it safe "); Winfield, *Province of the Law of Tort*, pp. 40, 64.

27 *Hall* v. *Brooklands Auto-Racing Club* [1933] 1 K.B. 205, 213, *per* Scrutton L.J.

28 [1936] 1 K.B. 399, at p. 405.

29 [1966] 1 Q.B. 197, at p. 205.

30 [1957] A.C. 555.

31 *Ante*, Chap. 2.

dishonouring a cheque is an action founded on contract,[32] that an action against stockbrokers for negligently carrying out their instructions as to the purchase of shares is founded on contract,[33] and that an action against an architect for negligence in supervising the erection of a house is founded on contract.[34] In the latter case Phillimore J. said [35]: " There are certain cases of bailment in which the contract, from unexpected reasons, becomes impossible of fulfilment, while the bailee nevertheless remains in possession of the bailor's chattels and becomes subject to duties which arise out of the fact of possession. This occurs when perishable articles are entrusted to a carrier to deliver at a wrong address, or when, by reason of sea peril, the cargo becomes incapable of being carried to its destination. In these cases it may be quite sound to say that the claim arising from breach of duty is wholly a claim in tort.[36] But it seems to me scientifically incorrect to say that the other cases of claims for breach of duty arising out of bailment or of the employment of a professional man are claims in tort and not claims in contract." It is submitted that this is an accurate statement of the law. Even a solicitor, who was formerly liable to be sued in case as well as in assumpsit, cannot be said to be under any duty in tort to his client or to any other person.[37] His duty arises solely by virtue of his contract with his client, and therefore his liability for negligence arises solely out of contract and not in tort.[38]

Regarding the duty as a contractual one, the standard of care and skill which can be demanded will depend on the terms of the contract. In the absence of a special contract to the contrary the care and skill which can be demanded must not fall below that of a person of average competence in that calling. The contract, however, may be that a higher degree of skill is to be exercised.

243 **Special relationships.** In 1963 by a unanimous decision in *Hedley Byrne & Co. Ltd.* v. *Heller & Partners Ltd.*[39] the House of Lords held, *inter alia*, that a duty to take reasonable care in making statements existed,

32 *Marzetti* v. *Williams* (1830) 1 B. & Ad. 415.
33 *Jarvis* v. *Moy, Davies & Co.* [1936] 1 K.B. 399.
34 *Steljes* v. *Ingram* (1903) 19 T.L.R. 534.
35 *Ibid.* at p. 535.
36 As Prof. Winfield points out (*Province of the Law of Tort*, Chap. 5), breach of bailment is not a tort. For the purposes of the County Courts Act 1934 the liability of a bailee was founded on tort (*Turner* v. *Stallibrass* [1898] 1 Q.B. 56), but to ascertain the standard of care which was required from a bailee the nature of the bailment must be inquired into. This is part of the law of bailment and not of the law of torts. Under the County Courts Act 1959 the distinction whether an action is commenced in contract or in tort is immaterial.
37 *Robertson* v. *Fleming* (1861) 4 Macq. 167. See also *Carl-Zeiss Stiftung* v. *Herbert Smith & Co.* [1969] 2 Ch. 276 (*Quaere* if solicitors had had knowledge of a trust in such circumstances?). However, see now " Special relationships " in next paragraph.
38 See *Nocton* v. *Ashburton* [1914] A.C. 932, *per* Lord Haldane, at p. 956, and Lord Dunedin at p. 964; *Groom* v. *Crocker* [1939] 1 K.B. 194, 222; *Otter* v. *Church, Adams, Tatham & Co.* [1953] Ch. 280, *per* Upjohn J. at p. 285.
39 [1964] A.C. 465. See articles founded on this momentous decision: " Liability for Professional Negligence—the New Approach," 67 Accountants' Mag. 518; " Negligent Misstatements and 'Special Relationships,' " 107 S.J. 582; " Bankers' References," 234 L.T. 381; " Taking a Risk with Counsel," 107 S.J. 622; " Negligence and Liability

wherever a special relationship had been created and there had been no disclaimer of responsibility. The facts were that the appellants were advertising agents and they were anxious to discover information about the creditworthiness of Easipower Ltd., from whom they had obtained instructions to arrange substantial advertising contracts, since the terms were that they were personally liable for the cost of the orders. Accordingly they asked their bankers, the National Provincial to make inquiries into the company's financial stability whereupon the bankers on two separate occasions made approaches to the respondents, a firm of merchant bankers, who were financing the company, as well as their being the company's bankers. The respondents gave favourable references but stipulated that these were " without responsibility " and in due course this reference was passed on to Hedley Byrne & Co. Ltd., the appellants, who relied upon them and placed certain orders which resulted in a loss of £17,000 when Easipower Ltd. went into liquidation. The House of Lords, however, by holding that the disclaimers were sufficient to negative any duty of care which might have existed by assuming that a special relationship had been created between the parties in the circumstances, did not proceed further to consider whether or not Heller & Partners had been negligent. Nevertheless the decision affirms, as well as extends, the principle that a duty to take reasonable care may exist where a special relationship is created independently of any contractual relationship between the parties such as where in its widest sense there is a fiduciary relationship.[40] This duty is quite distinct from a duty to be honest.[41]

244 In *Candler* v. *Crane, Christmas & Co.*[42] Denning L.J. in his dissenting judgment [43] held that accountants, exercising a calling which requires knowledge and skill, owed a duty to use care in the work, which resulted in their accounts and reports as well as in the rendering of such. They owed that duty not only to their clients, with whom they had contracted, but also to any third person to whom they showed their accounts and reports or to whom they knew that their clients were going to show them, when they knew that that person would consider their accounts and reports with a view to the investment of money or taking other action to his gain

for Statements," 113 L.J. 779; " Judicial Creativity and Doctrinal Possibility " (Stevens), 27 M.L.R. 121; " Professional Negligence: a Postcript " [1964] J.B.L. 231; " Liability for Innocent but Negligent Misrepresentations " (Goodhart), 74 Yale L.J. 286; " Effect of *Hedley Byrne* " (Coote), 2 N.Z.U.L.R. 263; " Liability for Financial Loss; *Hedley Byrne* and After " (North), 116 New L.J. 407, and (Honore) 8 J.S.P.T.L. 284; " Negligence and Economic Loss " (Atiyah), 83 L.Q.R. 248 and 101 I.L.T. 333; " Careless Talk Costs Money " (Borrie), 118 New L.J. 788; " Further adventures of *Hedley Byrne* " (Whincup), 119 New L.J. 1073.

40 No exhaustive description of such possible relationships was given but see [1964] A.C. at pp. 465, 502, 514, 529, 539 for the formulae proffered by the Law Lords. In *Nocton* v. *Ashburton* [1914] A.C. 932 a fiduciary relationship was held to exist.

41 See *Parsons* v. *Barclay & Co. Ltd.* (1910) 26 T.L.R. 628; *Batts Combe Quarry Co.* v. *Barclays Bank Ltd.* (1931) 48 T.L.R. 4. Also see § 264, *post.*

42 [1951] 2 K.B. 164.

43 *Ibid.* commencing at p. 174, which judgment was approved by Lords Hodson, Devlin and Pearce in *Hedley Byrne & Co. Ltd.* v. *Heller & Partners Ltd.*, *supra*, at pp. 503, 530 and 539.

or detriment. However the duty only extended in respect of those transactions for which the accountants knew that their accounts were required and Denning L.J. considered that surveyors, valuers and analysts were under a similar duty.

245 The limits of the *Hedley Byrne* doctrine are not at all certain [43a]; it would scarcely seem to be desirable that liability should be imposed on a bystander who, when asked for directions, carelessly misdirected the inquirer on his way so that he missed some important appointment [44] or on a mere agent who misrepresented his authority.[45] The answer would seem to lie in limiting such liability to that category of defendants who have some special knowledge, *viz.*: those whose trade, business or profession requires them, in the normal course of events, to make statements or to give information [46] upon which they anticipate that reliance will be entrusted and some action will result. The following are examples: where a person gives another a reference as to the character, honesty and integrity of a prospective employee which is grossly misleading [47]; where a doctor gives a misleading answer to an inquiry from a patient concerning the seriousness of an operation, about which he needs to arrive at a decision [48]; where a business man carelessly misleads a person, inquiring into the creditworthiness of a third party.[49]

2.—ACCOUNTANTS AND AUDITORS [50]

246 **Nature of the duty.** Accountants and auditors are liable for failing to use that skill and diligence which a reasonably competent and careful accountant or auditor would exercise. Their duty arises out of contract or out of an obligation imposed on them under some statute, such as the Companies Act 1948.

247 **Duty depends on terms of employment.** Although the standard of care and skill which can be demanded of an accountant is constant, the exact scope of his duties depends on the terms of his contract. Where, therefore, accountants were employed to certify a return made by a branch office of an insurance company to the head office, but not to make an audit of the branch books, it was held that they were not liable for failing to detect the fraud of one of the employees at the branch office.[51] Where accountants were employed to investigate the accounts of a business before money was advanced by their client to the business, and the stock sheets which they examined in fact overvalued the stock by 3 per cent., but they failed to discover it, it was held that

43a Especially since *Mutual Life & Citizens' Assurance Co. Ltd.* v. *Evatt* [1971] 2 W.L.R. 23 which may even have nullified its effect altogether? See § 51, *ante*.

44 *Hedley Byrne & Co. Ltd.* v. *Heller & Partners Ltd.*, *supra*, at pp. 495, 502, 510, 539 but see Lord Devlin at p. 529, *contra*.

45 *Jones* v. *Still* [1965] N.Z.L.R. 1071.

46 For a distinction between " a statement " and " an instruction " see *Clayton* v. *Woodman & Sons (Builders) Ltd.* [1962] 2 Q.B. 533, 544.

47 *Technovision Ltd.* v. *Reed, The Times*, April 14, 1964.

48 *Smith* v. *Auckland Hospital Board* [1965] N.Z.L.R. 191.

49 *Anderson (W. B.) & Sons Ltd.* v. *Rhodes* [1967] 2 All E.R. 850.

50 Articles " Liability for Negligence," 163 Acct. 761; " Law of Negligence" (Francis) 22 Comm. Acc. 85.

51 *Maritime Insurance Co.* v. *Fortune & Son* (1931) 41 Ll.L.R. 16.

they were not negligent,[52] Lord Alverstone saying: "It was not the duty of an auditor to take stock, but the plaintiffs alleged that the stock sheets showed suspicious circumstances. It had been said that an auditor was not a detective, it was his duty to exercise what was reasonable care in the circumstances.[53] The most that could be said was that he must make a reasonable and proper investigation of accounts and stock sheets, and if a reasonably prudent man would have concluded on that investigation that there was something wrong it was his duty to call his employer's attention to the fact."

Where an accountant was employed to check books of account, but not to make a full audit, he was held to be negligent in drawing up a balance sheet without checking the cash by looking at the bank pass book or getting a certificate from the bank, but taking the figures of cash at bank and cash in hand from the cash book, in which wrong figures had been entered by a dishonest clerk.[54] Even where a plaintiff informally employed a partner in a firm of accountants to advise him upon the sale of two businesses it was held that a contractual relationship existed between the parties, which gave rise to liability for negligence in the accountant's failure to advise the plaintiff properly.[55]

The plaintiff, an ex-solicitor, who had been struck off the Roll, failed to recover damages, although the defendants had been negligent in failing to detect deficiencies in his accounts because the plaintiff's loss and damage were due solely to his own dishonesty.[56]

248 **Duty to keep client's affairs secret.** An accountant is under a duty to take reasonable care of any documents entrusted to him by his client and not to disclose confidential information communicated to him. For breach of this duty he is liable in damages.[57]

249 **Duties under the Companies Acts.** When auditors of companies are appointed under the Companies Acts, their duties are governed by those Acts and reference must be made to books on company law for a detailed statement of those duties. It has been held that the duty of an auditor is "not to confine himself merely to the task of verifying the arithmetical accuracy of the balance sheet, but to inquire into its substantial accuracy, and to ascertain that it contained the particulars specified in the articles of association (and consequently a proper income and expenditure account), and was properly drawn up, so as to contain a true and correct representation of the state of the company's affairs." [58] Accordingly, where the audited accounts showed that the company was entitled to "moneys lent" to the amount of £29,515 15s. when

52 *Henry Squire Cash Chemist Ltd.* v. *Ball, Baker & Co.* (1911) 27 T.L.R. 269, affd. on other grounds, 28 T.L.R. 81.
53 *Re Kingston Cotton Mill Co.* [1896] 2 Ch. 279, 284.
54 *Fox* v. *Morrish Grant & Co.* (1918) 35 T.L.R. 126.
55 *Bradford* v. *Wright Stevens and Lloyd*, *Guardian*, February 27, 1962.
56 *Luscombe* v. *Roberts and Pascho* (1962) 106 S.J. 373.
57 *Weld-Blundell* v. *Stephens* [1920] A.C. 956.
58 *Per* Stirling J. in *Leeds Estate Co.* v. *Shepherd* (1887) 36 Ch.D. 787, 802.

this was not the fact, as a result of which dividends were paid out of capital, the auditor was held liable for negligence.[59] The auditor's duty is to see that the accounts put before the shareholders accurately state the company's financial position; it is not enough for him merely to indicate the means of ascertaining that position.[60] He fulfils this duty by examining books of the company, but he must also see that the books themselves show the company's true financial position. "An auditor, however, is not bound to do more than exercise reasonable care and skill in making inquiries and investigations. He is not an insurer; he does not guarantee that the books do correctly show the true position of the company's affairs; he does not even guarantee that his balance sheet is accurate according to the books of the company." [61]

250 When frauds have been committed and money of a company has been misappropriated so that it appears that the company's audited accounts have been inaccurate, a question arises as to whether the auditors can be successfully sued for negligence. In such a case, everything depends on the manner in which the fraud has been committed. An auditor is not bound to be suspicious as opposed to his being reasonably careful.[62] The test to be applied, therefore, is whether a reasonably competent auditor on making a reasonable and proper investigation of the company's accounts would have discovered the frauds in question. Where the managing director of a large insurance company had fraudulently misappropriated a large part of the company's funds, and the books showed £250,000 owing by his firm to the company, to conceal which, he, for three successive years, bought Treasury Bills for £200,000 just before the audit, thus reducing his firm's indebtedness to £50,000, and sold the bills immediately after the audit, thus restoring the original indebtedness, it was held that although these transactions, when isolated, should have led the the auditors to entertain suspicions, yet as they formed only one item in a large audit there was no negligence on the auditors' part.[63] Where auditors, who had been put on inquiry by alteration of invoices, negligently failed to investigate the matter and accordingly gave a falsely favourable picture of the profits of a company, as a result of which the company declared dividends it would not otherwise have declared, it was held to be no defence that they had not been given enough time to do their job. As regards damages they should be ordered to repay the dividends, the costs of recovering the extra tax and any of the extra tax not recoverable.[64]

251 When the audited accounts are incorrect because of an overvaluation of the assets, the liability of the auditors depends on the circumstances. If they know that the assets are overvalued, they should so report to

59 *Ibid.*
60 *Re London and General Bank* [1895] 2 Ch. 673.
61 *Re London and General Bank*, *supra*, *per* Lindley L.J. at p. 683.
62 *Re Kingston Cotton Mill Co.* [1896] 2 Ch. 279, *per* Lindley L.J. at p. 284.
63 *Re City Equitable Fire Insurance Co.* [1925] Ch. 407.
64 *Re Thomas Gerrard & Son* [1968] Ch. 455. See "Auditors and stocktaking" (Pennington) Accountancy, 694.

the shareholders, and if they fail to do so they are negligent. So, where the auditors reported to the directors they that considered that the security for certain loans was insufficient, and that there would be difficulty in realisation, but only reported to the shareholders that the value of the assets was dependent on realisation, they were held liable for negligence.[65] On the other hand, the auditors are entitled to accept the certificate of the appropriate official of the company as to the value of the stock, unless there are circumstances which ought to have suggested to them, as reasonably competent auditors, that the certificate is incorrect. Where the manager certified the value of the stock and this was accepted by the auditors although, if they had compared the amount of the stock at the begining of the year with the purchases and sales during the year, they would have suspected that it was incorrect, it was held that the auditors were not negligent.[66] Auditors are entitled to call for explanations of items in a stock sheet, and failure to ask for an explanation of items apparently lumped together may be negligence.[67]

252 Auditors should satisfy themselves that the company's securities in fact exist and are in safe custody, that is, in the custody of the company itself, or of some person, such as a bank, who in the usual course of his business keeps securities for his customers. Where the auditors accepted the certificate of the company's stockbrokers, in which the company's managing director was the senior partner, that they held certain securities on behalf of the company and the securities were non-existent, it was held that the auditors were negligent.[68]

253 **Duty to client only.** Apart from his statutory duties, an accountant's duty is in contract only. He owes no duty to anyone but his client and those persons to whom he stands in a fiduciary relationship.[69]

254 **Liability for ignorance of law.** As in the case of other professional men, an auditor is bound to have a knowledge of the practical rules of law which affect him in the exercise of his profession. In auditing a company's accounts he is bound to know the provisions of the articles and the provisions of the Companies Acts affecting his duties.[70] If an item appears in the balance sheet as a payment, when it is not in accordance with the articles or the Companies Acts, the auditor will be liable in negligence as a general rule. Where, however, the auditor passed the payment of a commission, authorised by a board resolution but contrary to the articles, and the payment of profit costs to a solicitor director, who was not authorised by the articles to contract with the company, it was

65 *Re London and General Bank*, *supra*.
66 *Re Kingston Cotton Mill Co.*, *supra*.
67 *Mead* v. *Ball, Baker & Co.* (1911) 28 T.L.R. 81.
68 *Re City Equitable Fire Insurance Co.*, *supra*.
69 See " Special relationships " § 243, *ante*, and *Hedley Byrne & Co. Ltd.* v. *Heller & Partners Ltd.* [1964] A.C. 465.
70 *Re Republic of Bolivia Exploration Syndicate Ltd.* [1914] 1 Ch. 139; *Thomas* v. *Devonport Corpn.* [1900] 1 Q.B. 16.

held that in the special circumstances the auditor was not liable.[71] However, accountants, who were employed to value a company by determining the difference between the assets and liabilities were not bound to consider the enforceability in law of debts admitted by both parties; in particular they were not under a duty to consider whether the Moneylenders Act applied to the transactions, which they were taking into account.[72]

254A **Liquidators.** The liquidator of a company is liable for negligence in the discharge of his statutory duties. This renders him liable in damages to an injured creditor,[73] and to the creditors in general by means of a summons for misfeasance.[74]

3.—ARCHITECTS, SURVEYORS AND ENGINEERS

255 **Nature of the duty.** The duty of architects and engineers is to use the reasonable care and skill of an architect, surveyor or engineer of ordinary competence measured by the professional standard of the time. The duty is a contractual one and the standard is the same as that of other professional men.

An architect and engineer of a bridge has been held liable in negligence for not properly examining the foundations on which the bridge was to be built. " If a surveyor, who makes an estimate, sues those who employ him for the value of his services, and it appears that he was so negligent, that he did not inform himself, by boring or otherwise, of the nature of the soil of his foundation, and it turned out to be bad; this goes to his right of action; and if he went upon the information of others, which now turns out to be false or insufficient, he must take the consequences; for every person, employed as a surveyor, must use due diligence." [75] Again, an architect and surveyor instructed to inspect a farm and to give a general opinion and not to make a detailed survey was held to be negligent in not discovering dry rot, woodworm and settlement.[76]

256 Where an architect, employed to prepare plans of a building to be erected on a specified site, acted on information as to the size of the site, supplied by a person who was not authorised by the building owners to supply any such information, and did not himself measure or survey the site, as a result of which he prepared plans for a site much smaller than the actual site, he was held to be negligent.[77] Architects are also liable for not properly superintending actual construction of the building.[78] They are entitled to leave details to be superintended by the clerk of the

[71] *Re Republic of Bolivia Exploration Syndicate Ltd., supra.*
[72] *Frank H. Wright (Constructions)* v. *Frodoor* [1967] 1 W.L.R. 506.
[73] *Pulsford* v. *Devenish* [1903] 2 Ch. 625.
[74] *Re Windsor Coal Co.* [1929] 1 Ch. 151; *Re Home and Colonial Insurance Co.* [1930] 1 Ch. 102.
[75] *Moneypenny* v. *Hartland* (1824) 1 C. & P. 352, *per* Abbott C.J.
[76] *Sincock* v. *Bangs (Reading)* [1952] C.P.L. 562; *Philips* v. *Ward* [1956] 1 All E.R. 874.
[77] *Columbus Co.* v. *Clowes* [1903] 1 K.B. 244.
[78] *Armstrong* v. *Jones* (1869) 2 Hudson's B.C., 4th ed., 6; *Saunders and Collard* v. *Broadstairs L.B.* (1890) 2 Hudson's B.C., 4th ed., 164; *Rogers* v. *James* (1891) 8 T.L.R. 67; *Steljes* v. *Ingram* (1903) 19 T.L.R. 534; *Florida Hotels Pty.* v. *Mayo* (1965) 113 C.L.R. 588.

works, and are not liable for negligence in respect of those details properly so left to such clerk. But where, owing to the fraud of the clerk of the works, floors were laid contrary to the specification so that dry rot was set up in the floors, the architect was held liable for not seeing that the floors were properly laid.[79] In requiring a builder to remedy faults, an architect is entitled to take into account the fact that the building is being erected at a low cost.[80] An architect was held to be negligent in approving drawings of a defectively designed building where he had delegated specialised design tasks to qualified sub-contractors, he having no authority under the contract to employ such sub-contractors.[81]

257 An architect or a surveyor will be liable for negligence in measuring the work or otherwise ascertaining the amount due from his employer to the builder. If, however, the contract provides that the architect in granting his final certificate shall be in the position of an arbitrator, he is not liable for negligence, because his duty is owed to both parties to the contract and is to decide impartially what is due from one to the other.[82] In such a case he is only liable for fraud or collusion. Whether or not he is liable for negligence in issuing interim certificates is doubtful.[83] Where, however, an architect issued interim certificates which included the cost of certain prime cost items actually delivered on the site, but for which he knew that the building owners and not the contractors would have to pay, it was held, on the construction of the contract, that there was no negligence on the architect's part and that all necessary financial adjustments could be made when the final certificate was issued.[83]

A clause in the contract providing that the decision of the architect as to the state of the works or in any wise relating to the execution of the works should be final and binding, only relates to disputes between the building owner and the contractor, so that a final certificate given under such a clause is no estoppel in an action by the building owner against the architect for negligence.[84]

258 Architects, surveyors and engineers are expected to have a practical working knowledge of the law relating to their professions, sufficient to enable them to perform their duties adequately. So, where valuers of ecclesiastical property, employed to make a valuation as between an incoming and outgoing incumbent, valued on the basis applicable between an incoming and outgoing tenant because they did not know the difference between the two bases of valuation, they were held liable for negligence, Jervis C.J. saying: " We agree with my learned brother, that the defendants could not be expected to supply minute and accurate

[79] *Leicester Guardians* v. *Trollope* (1911) 75 J.P. 197.
[80] *Cotton* v. *Wallis* [1955] 1 W.L.R. 1168.
[81] *Moresk Cleaners* v. *Hicks* [1966] 2 Lloyd's Rep. 338.
[82] *Chambers* v. *Goldthorpe* [1901] 1 K.B. 624; *Stevenson* v. *Watson* (1879) 4 C.P.D. 148; *Tharsis Sulphur Co.* v. *Loftus* (1872) L.R. 8 C.P. 1; *Boynton* v. *Richardson* (1924) 69 S.J. 107.
[83] *Wisbech R.D.C.* v. *Ward* [1928] 2 K.B. 1.
[84] *Rogers* v. *James* (1891) 8 T.L.R. 67.

knowledge of the law; but we think, that, under the circumstances, they might properly be required to know the general rules applicable to the valuation of ecclesiastical property, and the broad distinction which exists between the cases of an incoming and an outgoing tenant, and an incoming and an outgoing incumbent." [85]

The amount of damages recoverable for negligence is the loss resulting from the negligence, arrived at in accordance with the ordinary law relating to damages. There is no rule restricting the damages to the professional charges of the negligent person.[86] Where a surveyor had negligently surveyed a house, Paull J. decided that in a sellers' market the quantum of damages was based on the cost of remedying the defects, and added to that sum must be the expense to which the plaintiff was put having to move out of the premises whilst the work was being carried out.[87]

259 **Evidence of negligence.** Failure of the works which he was employed to design and superintend may be evidence of negligence on the part of the architect or engineer concerned, throwing upon him the burden of proving that he was not negligent. If, however, he is employed to do something in the nature of an experiment, failure by itself will be no evidence of negligence. Where an architect was employed to design and superintend the erection of model lodging-houses, with instructions to put in a new patent concrete roofing which was much less costly than a lead or a slate roof, he was held not to be negligent when the roof proved a failure and let in water. In directing the jury, Erle J. said: " You should bear in mind that if the building is of an ordinary description in which, he [the defendant] had had abundance of experience, and it proved a failure, this is an evidence of want of skill or attention. But if out of ordinary course, and you employ him about a novel thing, about which he has had little experience, if it has not had the test of experience, failure may be consistent with skill. The history of all great improvements shows failure of those who embark in them." [88] In the absence of expert evidence that the omission of an architect to provide for downstairs toilets in the " £8,000 price range " houses, to be built in Mill Hill, N.W., was in breach of standard practice or of evidence that indicated incompetence, unless it was so glaring an omission as to require no such evidence (*i.e.* the provision of a staircase having been overlooked), an architect was held not to be negligent by the Court of Appeal.[89]

260 **Duty is contractual.** The duty owed by architects, surveyors and engineers to their clients is purely a contractual duty; they are not liable for negligence generally to a person to whom they are under no contractual

[85] *Jenkins* v. *Betham* (1855) 15 C.B. 168. See also to the same effect *Lee* v. *Walker* (1872) L.R. 7 C.P. 121 (negligence of patent agent in not knowing a recent legal decision).
[86] *Saunders and Collard* v. *Broadstairs L.B.* (1890) 2 Hudson's B.C., 4th ed., 164.
[87] *Hood* v. *Shaw* (1960) 176 E.G. 1291; *Hardy* v. *Wamsley-Lewis* (1967) 203 E.G. 1039.
[88] *Turner* v. *Garland* (1853) 2 Hudson's B.C., 4th ed., 1.
[89] *Worboys* v. *Acme Investments, The Times*, March 26, 1969.

obligation. In *Le Lievre* v. *Gould* [90] a surveyor negligently granted progress certificates to a builder, knowing that they would be shown by the builder to his mortgagees for the purpose of obtaining an advance of money from them, it was held that he was under no liability to the mortgagees. Bowen L.J. dealing with " the suggestion that a man is responsible for what he states in a certificate to any person to whom he may have reason to suppose that the certificate may be shewn " says: " The law of England does not go to that extent: it does not consider that what a man writes on paper is like a gun or other dangerous instrument, and, unless he intended to deceive, the law does not, in the absence of contract, hold him responsible for drawing his certificate carelessly." [91] But in the light of the authority of the House of Lords in *Hedley Byrne & Co. Ltd.* v. *Heller & Partners* [92] it is clear that a duty to be careful may exist in situations where a special relationship [93] is created between the parties of a wide fiduciary nature, which depends for its existence on the degree of proximity between them. In *Clayton* v. *Woodman & Son* (*Builders*) *Ltd.*[94] an architect instructed the plaintiff, a bricklayer employed by the building contractors, to cut a chase in the gable but omitted to give any instructions as to shoring or strutting of the wall, which was against the express wishes of the plaintiff, who had thought the gable was unsafe. However the chase was duly cut by the plaintiff but the whole gable suddenly toppled inwards and fell injuring the plaintiff. Salmon J. held the architect liable on the ground that, having regard to the close relationship between him and the plaintiff, he owed the latter a duty of care which included his giving him proper instructions how to do the job in safety since the architect knew that his orders would be obeyed by the plaintiff.

261 *Hedley Byrne & Co. Ltd.* v. *Heller & Partners Ltd.* was applied in *Clay* v. *Crump & Sons Ltd.*,[95] where the Court of Appeal held that an architect's duty was not confined to his contractual duty to the owners of a dangerous wall which had purposely been left standing after partial demolition and which had collapsed injuring a builder's workman, on the ground that the duty extended to all those persons who would be so closely and directly affected by his acts and omissions that he ought reasonably to have them in contemplation as being so affected. Applying that test, the architect ought reasonably to have foreseen that the builder's workman would be affected by his carelessness. He was held 42 per cent. to blame, the demolition contractors 38 per cent. and the workman's

90 [1893] 1 Q.B. 491 and see note 92 below; see also *Love* v. *Mack* (1905) 93 L.T. 352.
91 *Ibid.* p. 502.
92 [1964] A.C. 465. Lord Reid (at p. 488) considered that: " The actual decision in *Le Lievre* v. *Gould* may therefore be correct. But the decision was not put on that ground (*i.e.* the degree of proximity necessary to establish a relationship giving rise to a duty of care): if it had been, *Cann* v. *Willson* (1888) 39 Ch.D. 39 would not have been overruled."
93 See " Special relationships " § 243, *ante*.
94 [1962] 2 Q.B. 533. The Court of Appeal nevertheless allowed the architect's appeal (*ibid.* at p. 546) on the facts in that the architect had not taken on himself the responsibility of ordering the plaintiff to do dangerous work or to do it in an unsafe manner.
95 [1964] 1 Q.B. 533; see article, " Negligent Architects—Falling Walls and Perils of Polling," 27 M.L.R. 216.

employers 20 per cent. The High Court of Australia in *Voli* v. *Inglewood Shire Council and Lockwood*[96] came to a similar conclusion and held that an architect owes a duty of care quite apart from his contract of employment and may be liable to anyone lawfully entering a structure designed by him whom it could reasonably have been expected might be injured as a result of his negligent design.

Nevertheless as the duty of an architect to his client is based on contract, he is not liable for tortious negligence so that time begins to run for the purposes of the Limitation Act 1939, from the date of the act of alleged negligence and not from the time when damage is first suffered.[97]

262 A surveyor of thirty years' experience, although he had undergone no training, advised a prospective purchaser that damp in the basement of a building she was interested in was due to condensation and that so long as it was kept properly aired, it would be all right, whereupon she decided to buy the property. In fact the trouble was due to rising damp and wet and dry rot, which cost £550 to eradicate. It was held that the purchaser only could recover damages for breach of contract and that the management company to which the purchaser had conveyed the property had no status to sue, not being either a party to the contract or an assignee of the purchaser's right of action[98]; where the owner of a yacht employed Lloyd's Register to survey his yacht for classification, and one of the surveyors employed negligently certified the mast as sound when in fact it was rotten and unfit for use, it was held that the surveyor was under no liability to the yacht owner, as there was no contract between them.[99]

4.—AUCTIONEERS

263 An auctioneer, in common with others who profess to carry on a business which requires knowledge and skill, must exercise that due care and skill as is reasonably to be expected from a competent auctioneer. Their liability to their client, the vendor, arises out of contract only and it is their duty to sign a proper contract which is binding on the purchaser. Any omission to do so will make the auctioneers liable to the vendor for the damage suffered as a result of their neglect.[1] They are under a duty to account for all moneys received on the vendor's behalf and to pay over such moneys to him.[2] Auctioneers must follow the course of business that is ordinarily recognised by custom[3] as well as that prescribed by statute.[4] It has been held that were an auctioneer, exercising his judgment, did not insist upon payment of a deposit by a purchaser he had not acted

[96] (1963) 56 Q.L.R. 256.
[97] *Bagot* v. *Stevens Scanlan & Co.* [1966] 1 Q.B. 197 applying *Clark* v. *Kirby-Smith* [1964] Ch. 506. Where, however, the breach of contract has been concealed by fraud see *Applegate* v. *Moss* [1971] 1 Q.B. 406.
[98] *Freeman* v. *Marshall & Co.* (1966) 200 E.G. 777.
[99] *Humphery* v. *Bowers* (1929) 45 T.L.R. 297.
[1] *Peirce* v. *Corf* (1894) L.R. 9 Q.B. 210.
[2] *Re Cotton, ex p. Cooke* (1913) 108 L.T. 310, C.A.
[3] *Russell* v. *Hankey* (1794) 6 Term Rep. 12.
[4] *Coppen* v. *Moore* (No. 2) [1898] 2 Q.B. 306; *Christie, Manson and Woods* v. *Cooper* [1900] 2 Q.B. 522.

negligently.[5] Although the point was deliberately left undecided by Kennedy J. in *Rainbow* v. *Howkins*,[6] an action would lie in all probability against an auctioneer for failing to enter a memorandum of sale, binding his principal, in his books. Nevertheless this was doubted by Pennycuick J. in *Richards* v. *Phillips* [7] where he considered that it was not clear how an implied agency on behalf of the purchaser could make it part of the auctioneer's duty to the purchaser to sign the memorandum on behalf of the vendor. The auctioneer, being a bailee for reward, must exercise ordinary care and diligence in keeping the goods, which have been entrusted to him by the vendor.

There would appear to be no reason why a special relationship could not be created as in *Hedley Byrne & Co. Ltd.* v. *Heller & Partners Ltd.*[8] which would give rise to an action in negligence.

5.—BANKERS

264 A banker must exercise due care and skill in the business of banking, but it is no part of his ordinary business to advise as to investments. Where therefore a customer, on the advice of his bank manager, advanced money on mortgage to a company who were customers of the bank and suffered loss owing to the company's failure, it was held that the bank owed no duty to advise their customer carefully or at all and that they were not liable for his loss.[9] However, in *Woods* v. *Martins Bank Ltd.*[10] Salmon J. said: " In my judgment the limits of a banker's business cannot be laid down as a matter of law. The nature of such a business must in each case be a matter of fact . . . I have found that it is part of the defendant's business to advise customers and potential customers on financial matters of all kinds. . . . No doubt the defendant Johnson could have refused to advise the plaintiff, but, as he chose to advise him, the law in these circumstances imposes an obligation on him to advise with reasonable care and skill." [11]

When a bank is asked for information as to the financial position of one of their customers, they are under a duty to answer honestly on the information before them but under no duty to make inquiries elsewhere. If they are asked for their opinion as to whether their customer can be considered trustworthy in the way of business for a specified sum of money, and express their honest opinion, they are not liable even if on the facts before them other bankers might have expressed a different opinion.[12]

[5] *Andrade (Cyril) Ltd.* v. *Sotheby & Co.* (1931) 47 T.L.R. 244.
[6] [1904] 2 K.B. 322, at p. 326.
[7] [1967] 3 All E.R. 876, at p. 881. This decision was affirmed without reference to this aspect of the case [1968] 2 All E.R. 859.
[8] [1964] A.C. 465.
[9] *Banbury* v. *Bank of Montreal* [1918] A.C. 626.
[10] [1959] 1 Q.B. 55, at p. 70 (approved by H.L. in *Hedley Byrne & Co. Ltd.* v. *Heller & Partners Ltd.* [1964] A.C. 465).
[11] [1959] 1 Q.B. 55, at p. 72.
[12] *Parsons* v. *Barclay & Co. Ltd.* (1910) 26 T.L.R. 628; (contrast the facts and the situation with those in *Hedley Byrne & Co. Ltd.* v. *Heller & Partners Ltd.*); *Batts Combe Quarry Co.* v. *Barclays Bank Ltd.* (1931) 48 T.L.R. 4. In *Macken* v. *Munster and Leinster Bank*

Since the decision of the House of Lords in *Hedley Byrne & Co. Ltd.* v. *Heller & Partners Ltd.*[13] there is a clear distinction to be made from a duty to be honest and the duty to take reasonable care, which arises where a special relationship exists quite independently of any contractual relationship between the parties.[14]

265 The standard of care which the law requires of a bank with regard to the collection of a cheque is that shown in the ordinary practice of careful bankers. Where Nield J. found that the bank had not fallen short of such standard, the bank was protected by section 4 of the Cheques Act 1957. The Court of Appeal, in affirming this decision, added that it did not constitute any lack of reasonable care to refrain from making inquiries of a customer, which it was improbable would lead to detection of the potential customer's dishonest purpose, if he were dishonest, and which were calculated to offend him and maybe drive away his custom, if he were honest.[15]

Where there had been no failure to communicate information of sufficient importance to the plaintiffs concerning a customer, who had been refused a loan by the defendant bank, it was held that they were not liable to contribute towards the plaintiffs' ultimate loss resulting through the default in repayment by that customer, to whom the plaintiffs had advanced money.[16]

6.—BARBERS AND HAIRDRESSERS

266 **Barbers.** The duty of a barber to exercise due care and skill is not confined to the actual operation of shaving or haircutting, but includes a duty to keep his razors and other instruments in a clean condition. Where a person contracted an infectious disease through being shaved with a razor which had not been properly cleaned, it was held that evidence was admissible that two other persons had, shortly before, contracted the same disease after suffering abrasions of the skin when being shaved in the defendant's shop, on the ground that "evidence to show that a similar practice in other barbers' shops had led to the communication of disease, and was therefore dangerous, would be admissible. If so, evidence to show that the practice had led to the communication of disease in the defendant's own establishment would be equally admissible."[17]

267 **Hairdressers.** A hairdresser, like a barber, is under a duty to exercise reasonable care and skill. Where a hairdresser used a process of

(1960) 95 I.L.T.R. 17 Judge Deale held that a bank manager was negligent when he failed to take reasonable care when supplying information to the plaintiff concerning the financial position of a certain Dutchman, as a result of which the plaintiff signed a promissory note, on which the Dutchman defaulted.

13 [1964] A.C. 465. For the facts see § 243 *ante*.

14 See § 243 *ante*.

15 *Marfani & Co.* v. *Midland Bank Ltd.* [1968] 1 W.L.R. 956.

16 *Mutual Mortgage Corporation* v. *Bank of Montreal* (1965) 55 D.L.R. (2d) 164.

17 *Hales* v. *Kerr* [1908] 2 K.B. 601.

permanent waving in regard to which the manufacturers issued a warning that over-bleached hair should not be waved without a preliminary test being first made, it was held that the hairdresser was liable to a customer whose hair was bleached and brittle so that it fell off when the waving process was put into operation, because he failed to test the hair or to warn the customer of the risk.[18] Similarly, if a hair dye is used without a test, when the manufacturer has issued a warning that a test must be made before use.[19] If the customer passes the test but gets dermatitis, the hairdresser will probably be liable although the manufacturer of the dye may be also.[20]

7.—BARRISTERS

268 For over a century now it has been held that barristers cannot be sued for breach of duty which rule appears to be based on the ground that they are under no contractual obligation towards their clients. The fees received by a barrister are considered to be in the nature of an honorarium. In *Swinfen* v. *Lord Chelmsford* [21] Pollock C.B. said: " We are all of opinion that an advocate at the English Bar, accepting a brief in the usual way, undertakes a duty, but does not enter into any contract or promise, express or implied. Cases may, indeed, occur where, on an express promise (if he made one), he would be liable in assumpsit; but we think a barrister is to be considered not as making a contract with his client, but as taking upon himself an office or duty, in the proper discharge of which not merely the client, but the court in which the duty is to be performed, and the public at large, have an interest."

In *Fell* v. *Brown* [22] an action was brought against a barrister for unskilfully and negligently settling and signing a bill filed by the plaintiff in the Court of Chancery. Lord Kenyon held that the action could not be maintained, saying: " If this action could be supported, it would equally lie against a counsel for inserting a count in a declaration, or putting matter in a plea which ought not to be there, and which the court should think improper and impertinent." He added that he believed the action to be the first of the kind. In *Purves* v. *Landell* [23] Lord Campbell, in discussing the liability of a law agent in Scotland for negligence, said: " Against the barrister in England, and the advocate in Scotland, luckily, no action can be maintained."

[18] *Dobbin* v. *Waldorf Toilet Saloons Ltd.* [1937] 1 All E.R. 331. *Cf. Parker* v. *Oxolo Ltd.* [1937] 3 All E.R. 524 (application of hair dye causes dermatitis); *Watson* v. *Buckley* [1940] 1 All E.R. 174 (hair dye causes dermatitis—hairdresser liable in contract, distributor liable in tort). It is a defence in contract to prove that the customer had an abnormally sensitive skin: *Griffiths* v. *Peter Conway Ltd.* [1939] 1 All E.R. 685. In the case of a dangerous thing it is no defence if it is used without a test: *Ingham* v. *Emes* [1955] 2 Q.B. 366.

[19] See *Holmes* v. *Ashford* [1950] 2 All E.R. 76.

[20] See *Ingham* v. *Emes* [1955] 2 Q.B. 366, where the customer sued in contract but failed as she did not disclose to the hairdresser that she was, as she knew, allergic to that dye. See also Chap. 11, § 645, *post.*

[21] (1860) 5 H. & N. 890, 920.

[22] (1791) 1 Peake 131.

[23] (1845) 12 Cl. & F. 91, 103.

269 In *Swinfen* v. *Lord Chelmsford*[21] an action was brought against a barrister for compromising a cause contrary to his client's instructions. In this case it was held by the court that: " A counsel is not subject to an action for calling or not calling a particular witness, or for putting or omitting to put a particular question, or for honestly taking a view of the case which may turn out to be quite erroneous. If he were so liable, counsel would perform their duties under the peril of an action by every disappointed and angry client." Pollock C.B. also expressed his own opinion " that provided an advocate acts honestly, with a view to the interests of his client, he is not responsible at all in an action. It seems admitted on all hands that he is not responsible for ignorance of law, or any mistake in fact, or for being less eloquent or less astute than he was expected to be. According to my view of the law, a barrister, acting with perfect good faith and with a single view to the interests of his client, is not responsible for any mistake or indiscretion or error of judgment of any sort." [24]

270 Following the decision in *Hedley Byrne & Co. Ltd.* v. *Heller & Partners Ltd.*[25] inevitably the question arose whether this immunity could possibly survive it, since a special relationship undoubtedly was created between a barrister and his lay client. Nevertheless the problem remained unresolved by authority until the decision of the House of Lords in *Rondel* v. *Worsley*.[26] The facts were that the appellant was indicted and tried on a charge of having caused grievous bodily harm to a certain named person and was convicted. He had been represented by the respondent, a barrister, who had appeared on a " dock brief." Later the appellant issued a writ and statement of claim against the respondent claiming damages for professional negligence in the respondent's dealing with the evidence. The master ordered the statement of claim to be struck out as disclosing no reasonable cause of action, which order was upheld by Lawton J. and by the Court of Appeal. On further appeal the House of Lords held that a barrister was immune from an action for negligence in such a case at the suit of a client and preliminary work connected therewith such as the drawing of pleadings. That immunity was not based on the absence of contract between barrister and client but on public policy and long usage in that (a) the administration of justice required that a barrister

24 *Supra*, at p. 924.

25 [1964] A.C. 465.

26 [1969] 1 A.C. 191. In an article " Taking a Risk with Counsel " (107 S.J. 622) the author suggests that if counsel does have this new head of liability in tort then the further position arises of the possibility of both counsel and solicitors being joint tortfeasors. Further see articles: " Negligence and the Bar," 114 L.J. 202 and 144 L.J. 299; " Negligence and the Advocate," 116 New L.J. 367; " Negligence—the Advocate's Reprieve," 100 I.L.T. 125; " Carte Blanche for Counsel? " 1966 S.L.T. 209; " Professional Negligence—Immunity of Counsel," 63 L.S.Gaz. 498; " *Hedley Byrne* to *Rondel* v. *Worsley* " (North), 118 L.J. 137, 148; " *Rondel* v. *Worsley* " (Davis), 1968 S.L.T. 45; " *Rondel* v. *Worsley* and criminal proceedings " (North) [1968] Crim.L.R. 183; " Looking over the advocate's shoulder: an Australian view of *Rondel* v. *Worsley* (Heerey), 42 A.L.J. 3; " Liability of an advocate and solicitor for negligence in the course of his professional duties " (Hill) (1968) M.L.J. 16; " *Rondel* v. *Worsley*: immunity of the Bar " (Sir R. Roxburgh), 84 L.G.R. 513.

should be able to carry out his duty to the court fearlessly and independently; (b) actions for negligence against barristers would make the retrying of original actions inevitable and so prolong litigation, contrary to public interest; and (c) a barrister was obliged to accept any client, however difficult, who sought his services.

However, there was opinion expressed *obiter* that as public policy did not require that a barrister should be immune from action for negligence in relation to non-litigious matters, if he failed to exercise the ordinary care and skill that can reasonably be expected of him, he should be and was in no better position than any other professional man. It follows that since *Rondel* v. *Worsley* has laid down that there is a special relationship which gives rise to a duty of care between barrister and lay client, it seems clear that unless the former can now bring himself within this exceptional immunity, which is shared by all those taking part in the judicial process, he can be sued in negligence.

8.—DENTISTS

71 The duty of a dentist to exercise due care and skill in his treatment of his patients is the same as that of a surgeon and a physician.[27] If a tooth is extracted, and, after the extraction, the jaw is found to be fractured, that, of itself, is no evidence of negligence against the dentist, even if there is also part of the root of the tooth left in the jaw.[28] It has been held that a dentist was entitled to rely upon a doctor's opinion as to the general response of a patient to antibiotic treatment, unless that opinion was quite clearly inconsistent with the facts as observed by the dentist.[29] Likewise, if a jaw has been dislocated during an extraction of teeth, that is no evidence of negligence, but it was negligence not to notice the existence of such dislocation during his further examinations over the subsequent months of treatment.[30]

9.—DOCTORS, SURGEONS, PHYSICIANS AND PSYCHIATRISTS

72 **Nature of duty.** The civil liability of medical men towards their patients is compendiously stated in *R.* v. *Bateman* [31] as follows: " If a person holds himself out as possessing special skill and knowledge and he is consulted, as possessing such skill and knowledge, by or on behalf of a patient, he owes a duty to the patient to use due caution in undertaking the treatment. If he accepts the responsibility and undertakes the treatment and the patient submits to his direction and treatment

[27] *Edwards* v. *Mallan* [1908] 1 K.B. 1002.

[28] *Fish* v. *Kapur* [1948] 2 All E.R. 176. See also *O'Neill* v. *Kelly*, *The Times*, December 15, 1961 and Chap. 15, *post*, Res Ipsa Loquitur.

[29] *Transwell* v. *Nelson*, *The Times*, February 11, 1959, where a patient had had some teeth extracted by her dentist, who then referred her to a doctor, when her condition worsened. A doctor diagnosed an abscess and treated her with antibiotics, but later it was discovered that she was suffering from osteomyelitis. The patient could not succeed in an action against the dentist.

[30] *Lock* v. *Scantlebury*, *The Times*, July 25, 1963.

[31] (1925) 94 L.J.K.B. 791. See also *Akerele* v. *The King* [1943] A.C. 255.

accordingly, he owes a duty to the patient to use diligence, care, knowledge, skill and caution in administering the treatment. No contractual relation is necessary, nor is it necessary that the service be rendered for reward. . . . The law requires a fair and reasonable standard of care and competence. This standard must be reached in all the matters above mentioned. If the patient's death has been caused by the defendant's indolence or carelessness, it will not avail to show that he had sufficient knowledge; nor will it avail to prove that he was diligent in attendance, if the patient has been killed by his gross ignorance and unskillfulness. . . . As regards cases where incompetence is alleged, it is only necessary to say that the unqualified practitioner cannot claim to be measured by any lower standard than that which is applied to a qualified man. As regards cases of alleged recklessness, juries are likely to distinguish between the qualified and the unqualified man. There may be recklessness in undertaking the treatment and recklessness in the conduct of it. It is no doubt, conceivable that a qualified man may be held liable for recklessly undertaking a case which he knew, or should have known, to be beyond his powers, or for making his patient the subject of reckless experiment. Such cases are likely to be rare. In the case of a quack, where the treatment has been proved to be incompetent and to have caused the patient's death, juries are not likely to hesitate in finding liability on the ground that the defendant undertook, and continued to treat, a case involving the gravest risk to his patient, when he knew he was not competent to deal with it, or would have known if he had paid any proper regard to the life and safety of his patient."

273 The duty of a doctor was limited to the sphere of medicine so that unless he had received specific instructions to that effect he was not concerned in any way with the sphere of legal liability. In the absence of any special circumstances a doctor was not required to contemplate or foresee any question connected with a third party's liability. Thus in *Stevens* v. *Bermondsey and Southwark Group Hospital Management Committee*,[32] due to a negligent diagnosis by the hospital's casualty officer, the plaintiff was unaware as to the true nature of his disability, which he had sustained in an accident, so that he proceeded to settle his claim against the tortfeasor at a much lower figure than otherwise he would have done. Paull J. held that damages were not recoverable based on the difference between the damages he had settled for and the damages to which he would have been entitled if the full extent of his injuries had been known, as a result of the limited duty stated above.

274 **Liability in contract.** A distinction must be drawn between liability in contract and liability in tort. In contract, liability depends on the express or implied terms of the contract, and is based on what the medical man in question contracts to do. If he holds himself out as a person who undertakes the cure or treatment of human ailments " there is on his part

[32] (1963) 107 S.J. 478.

an implied warranty that he is of skill reasonably competent to the task he undertakes—*Spondes peritiam artis*. . . . The public profession of an art is a representation and undertaking to all the world that the professor possesses the requisite ability and skill." [33] The amount of skill which must be displayed depends on the extent of the profession of the person employed. A specialist, for example, is one from whom, in a case of contract, more skill can be demanded than from a general practitioner. If an unqualified man is employed, then, unless he professes to be equal or more than equal in skill to a qualified practitioner, he is only liable for not employing such skill as he professes to have.[34]

The duty in contract is only owed to the parties to the contract, but it would seem that there is in most cases a contract between patient and medical practitioner, even if the patient himself is not liable for payment of the services rendered, such payment being made by someone else. A medical man cannot examine, treat or operate upon a patient without the patient's consent except by committing a trespass or assault.[35] This consent, which may be implied, amounts to an agreement on the part of the patient to allow himself to be treated and is sufficient consideration for an implied promise to exercise proper care and skill.[36]

Nevertheless circumstances could arise whereby consent to general treatment is not enough and that a specific consent should be obtained. In *Male* v. *Hopmans*,[37] a patient with an injured knee gave his consent to general treatment for it. The doctor fearing serious infection or even fatal results, decided without first obtaining the patient's specific consent to use a drug with known possible side effects. He failed to carry out recommended tests, of which he was aware, to discover whether such side effects were happening and the patient in fact suffered immediately from them, It was held that the doctor, having obtained incipient consent to general treatment had used his discretion properly in deciding to use the drug without first obtaining the patient's specific consent but was negligent in failing to carry out the recommended known tests.

75 **Liability in tort.** In tort, no question of warranty, undertaking or profession of skill can arise. The duty arises from the fact that the practitioner does something to a human being which is likely to cause physical damage unless it is done with proper care and skill. It is well settled that under those circumstances the practitioner owes a duty in tort to the patient.[38] There seems to be no good reason for thinking that

[33] *Per* Willes J. in *Harmer* v. *Cornelius* (1858) 5 C.B.(N.S.) 236.

[34] See *Shiells & Thorne* v. *Blackburne* (1789) 1 H.Bl. 158, *per* Heath J. His opinion deals with the gratuitous rendering of services, but payment in these cases only goes to the amount and not to the existence of consideration.

[35] *Slater* v. *Baker* (1767) 2 Wils. 359; *Beatty* v. *Cullingworth*, Brit.Med.J., November 21, 1896, where a surgeon was alleged to have removed a woman's ovaries without her consent.

[36] *Gladwell* v. *Steggall* (1939) 5 Bing.N.C. 733; *Everett* v. *Griffiths* [1920] 3 K.B. 163, 193, *per* Scrutton L.J.

[37] (1967) 64 D.L.R. (2d) 105.

[38] *Pippin* v. *Sheppard* (1822) 11 Price 400; *Gladwell* v. *Steggall, supra*; *Edgar* v. *Lamont*, 1914 S.C. 277.

the duty is in any respect different if, in an emergency, an unqualified person renders medical or surgical aid to another. The officious aid of a well-meaning but unskilled person may cause as much damage as the original accident, and, accordingly, it is negligence if such a person gives more treatment than is reasonably necessary in the special circumstances.

276 **Standard of care.** The standard of care and skill to satisfy the duty in tort is that of the ordinary competent medical practitioner exercising the ordinary degree of professional skill.[39] " A defendant charged with negligence can clear himself if he shows that he acted in accordance with general and approved practice."[40] This means the practice approved at the date when he is said to have been negligent not the practice which has become approved at a later date. A surgeon was held to be not liable when he made an incorrect diagnosis through his failure to use an instrument which was very rare in England at the material date.[41] An anaesthetist was held not liable when he administered an anaesthetic which had been kept in a manner thought to be safe at the time, which later experience showed to be dangerous.[42] A medical man " is not guilty of negligence if he has acted in accordance with a practice accepted as proper by a responsible body of medical men skilled in that particular art . . . merely because there was a body of opinion who would take a contrary view." [43] It is not required in discharge of his duty of care that he should use the highest degrees of skill, since they may never be acquired. Deviation from normal professional practice is not necessarily evidence of negligence.[44] To be so, it must be proved, (1) there is a normal practice applicable to the case, (2) the defendant has not adopted it, and (3) the course he took

[39] *Rich* v. *Pierpont* (1862) 3 F. & F. 35; *Chin Keow* v. *Government of Malaysia* [1967] 1 W.L.R. 813.

[40] *Marshall* v. *Lindsey C.C.* [1935] 1 K.B. 516, 540, *per* Maugham L.J., approved by H.L. in *Whiteford* v. *Hunter* [1950] W.N. 553.

[41] *Whiteford* v. *Hunter, supra.* See also *Chapman* v. *Rix, The Times,* December 22, 1960; *McCormack* v. *Redpath Brown & Co., The Times,* March 24, 1961.

[42] *Roe* v. *Minister of Health* [1954] 2 Q.B. 66. For other cases concerning the use of anaesthetics, see: *Williams* v. *North Liverpool Hospital Management Committee, The Times,* January 17, 1959; and *Moore* v. *Lewisham Group Hospital Management Committee, The Times,* February 5, 1959; but *cf. O'Donovan* v. *Cork C.C.* [1967] I.R. 173.

[43] *Per* McNair J. in *Bolam* v. *Friern Hospital Management Committee* [1957] 1 W.L.R. 582, 587. In *Hucks* v. *Cole* (1968) 118 New L.J. 469, Lord Denning M.R. said: " A charge of professional negligence against a medical man was serious. It stood on a different footing to a charge of negligence against the driver of a motor car. The consequences were far more serious. It affected his professional status and reputation. The burden of proof was correspondingly greater. As the charge was so grave, so should the proof be clear. With the best will in the world, things sometimes went amiss in surgical operations or medical treatment. A doctor was not to be held negligent simply because something went wrong. He was not liable for mischance or misadventure; or for an error of judgment. He was not liable for taking one choice out of two or for favouring one school rather than another. He was only liable when he fell below the standard of a reasonably competent practitioner in his field so much so that his conduct might be deserving of censure or inexcusable."

[44] In *Holland* v. *Devitt and Moore Nautical College, The Times,* March 4, 1960, Streatfeild J. expressed the view that a doctor was entitled to use his common sense and experience and judgment in the treatment of each particular case, and a slight departure from the textbook would not of itself establish negligence.

is one which no professional man of ordinary skill would have taken had he been taking ordinary care.[45]

The competent practitioner will know when a case is beyond his skill, and thereupon it becomes his duty either to call in a more skilful person or to order the removal of the patient to a hospital where skilled treatment is available. When a consultant has thus taken over the responsibility for the treatment of a case, it is a defence to the competent practitioner that he acted on the specific instructions given to him by such consultant.[46] Failure to use due skill in diagnosis, so that wrong treatment is given, is negligence.[47]

.77 Negligence may consist in failing to obey an urgent summons from a person who has been accepted as a patient, in failing to warn of the dangers of certain treatment and in unskilful or careless treatment of a complaint properly diagnosed. When a patient in a mental hospital injured himself through being given electro-convulsive therapy and alleged there was negligence in not warning him of the dangers of this treatment there are two questions to be considered: " First, does good medical practice require that a warning should be given to a patient before he is submitted to E.C.T. treatment; and, secondly, if a warning had been given, what difference it would have made? Are you satisfied that the plaintiff would have said: ' You have told me what the risks are. I will not take those risks. I prefer not to have the treatment '?" [48] Whether leaving a wad of gauze in a patient's body after an operation is negligence depends on the nature of the operation and the circumstances generally. When the operation is a piece of team work it may be that the surgeon is entitled to leave part of the work, such as the counting of the swabs taken from the patient's body, to some other member of the team.[49] Where in giving treatment by injection a needle

[45] *Hunter* v. *Hanley*, 1955 S.C. 200; see also *Landau* v. *Werner* (1961) 105 S.J. 1008.

[46] *Junor* v. *McNichol*, *The Times*, March 26, 1959, where the House of Lords held that a house surgeon was not liable for the treatment of a child, who had to have an arm amputated because he was not given sufficient penicillin, since the prescribed treatment was being given under the instructions of a responsible consultant.

[47] See *Pudney* v. *Union-Castle Mail SS. Ltd.* [1953] 1 Lloyd's Rep. 73. In *Newton* v. *Newton's Model Laundry*, *The Times*, November 3, 1959, Salmon J. held that a doctor had been negligent in failing to diagnose a broken patella after the plaintiff had fallen 12 feet on to a concrete floor. But in *Crivon* v. *Barnet Group Hospital Management Committee*, *The Times*, November 18, 1958, the Court of Appeal held that a wrong diagnosis was not necessarily an unskilled or negligent diagnosis, where a pathologist had diagnosed cancer and the plaintiff had been treated accordingly until it was discovered that this diagnosis had been wrong.

[48] *Per* McNair J. in *Bolam* v. *Friern Hospital Management Committee* [1957] 1 W.L.R. 582, at p. 588.

[49] Negligence was found in *Dryden* v. *Surrey C.C.* and *Stewart* [1936] 2 All E.R. 535, *James* v. *Dunlop* (1931) C.A., unreported but referred to in *Mahon* v. *Osborne* [1939] 2 K.B. 14; *Hocking* v. *Bell* [1948] W.N. 21 (drainage tube left *in situ*), and *Urry* v. *Bierer*, *The Times*, July 15, 1955. In *Cooper* v. *Nevill*, *The Times*, March 24, 1961, the Judicial Committee held a surgeon liable for leaving an abdominal swab in a patient's body, there being no justification in the circumstances for any departure from the normal routine. Lord Denning expressed the view that if the swab were a mopping pack it was negligent to lose control of it, whilst if it were a restraining pack, then having regard to the small number used, their obvious position, the absence of movement and the lack of any particular need for haste at the end of the operation, it was negligence on the part of the surgeon not to remove it, since the responsibility for doing so was admittedly his. On

was broken, without negligence, and left in the patient's body, it was held to be negligence not to tell the patient of the presence of the broken needle.[50] Similarly, a doctor was held liable for negligently giving his patient a hypodermic injection for malaria, as a result of which he pierced the sciatic nerve and caused foot drop [51]; where he injected cocaine instead of procaine [52]; where pentothal was injected while the patient was already under an anaesthetic [53] and so caused the death of the patient; and where he had failed to administer penicillin for a condition of fulminating septicaemia of a finger, after the finish of a five day course of tetracycline.[54] Where a woman was admitted as a paying patient to hospital to be confined and was placed in the same ward with a woman suspected of and later found suffering from puerperal fever, as a result of which she caught puerperal fever herself, it was held she could recover damages from the doctor attending her for his negligence in not isolating her when the other case was suspected and taking steps to prevent her from becoming infected.[55]

278 A psychiatrist was held liable in negligence towards his patient by introducing social contacts with him into his treatment of her, particularly as in her then emotional state she was already in love with him, which fact he well knew. There was no body of professional opinion which would have considered it desirable for a doctor to have such social contact with his patient in these circumstances.[56]

Negligence may also consist in failing to make adequate arrangements for a patient [57]; failing to give proper instructions [58]; failing to communicate his findings to others responsible for continuing a patient's treatment [59]; and in failing to make proper inquiries to discover what treatment, if any, a patient had already received elsewhere [60]:

the other hand no negligence was found in *Mahon* v. *Osborne* [1939] 2 K.B. 14; *Chasney* v. *Anderson* [1950] 4 D.L.R. 223 and *White* v. *Westminster Hospital Board of Governors*, *The Times*, October 26, 1961.

50 *Gerber* v. *Pines* (1933) 79 S.J. 13. Not followed, *Daniels* v. *Heskin* [1954] I.R. 73.

51 *Caldeira* v. *Gray*, *The Times*, February 15, 1936.

52 *Collins* v. *Hertfordshire C.C.* [1947] K.B. 598.

53 *Jones* v. *Manchester Corpn.* [1952] 2 K.B. 852.

54 *Hucks* v. *Cole* (1968) 118 New L.J. 469.

55 *Heafield* v. *Crane*, *The Times*, July 31, 1937.

56 *Landau* v. *Werner* (1961) 105 S.J. 257; affirmed (1961) 105 S.J. 1008.

57 In *Corder* v. *Banks*, *The Times*, April 9, 1960, McNair J. held a plastic surgeon liable who allowed his patient to go home after an operation but failed to make proper arrangements for receiving telephone messages from that patient in the event of bleeding taking place during the first 48 hours after the operation.

58 In *Waters* v. *Park*, *The Times*, July 15, 1961, it was held that it did not fall short of the proper standards of the medical profession, where an operation for sterilisation had been carried out to protect a woman's health but the surgeon did not immediately tell her that there was a slight risk of her further pregnancy or advise her to use contraceptives.

59 *Chapman* v. *Rix*, *The Times*, November 10, 1958, where a hospital doctor was held by Barry J. to be negligent when he failed to communicate his findings, following his examination of a wound in the deceased's stomach, to the deceased's own doctor, since such failure inevitably meant a failure to keep the deceased's condition under observation after his discharge from hospital. However, on the facts, this finding was reversed by the Court of Appeal: (1959) 103 S.J. 940. See also *McCormack* v. *Redpath*, *The Times*, March 24, 1961, where a hospital's casualty officer allowed the plaintiff to leave after suffering an accident at work where he had been struck on the head by a falling spanner. In fact there was a depressed fracture of his skull.

60 *Coles* v. *Reading and District Hospital Management Committee* (1963) 107 S.J. 115.

Although it may be unusual for a doctor to prescribe drugs without first seeing a patient it is not necessarily negligent to do so in the circumstances; nor was it held to be negligent in failing to follow up a patient's change of address and to search for him in the absence of any suggestion or urgent treatment being required.[61]

279 A medical practitioner is liable for the negligence of an assistant or a *locum tenens* employed by him.[62] He is not, however, liable for the negligence of nurses at a hospital, when the nurses are not employed by him. Where, therefore, two surgeons ordered that the plaintiff, a patient in a hospital, should have a hot bath and, owing to the negligence of the nurses, the plaintiff was injured, it was held that the surgeons were not liable because the giving of a bath was a thing properly left to the nurses and it was no part of the surgeons' duty to superintend personally the bathing of the plaintiff.[63] Again, where a surgeon agreed to perform an operation upon the plaintiff and to give the case his personal attention, and some three months after the plaintiff's discharge from hospital a tube was found in the plaintiff's bladder, it was held that the surgeon was not liable on proof being made that the treatment after the operation demanded the frequent insertion and replacement of tubes in the plaintiff's body and that this treatment was done by the resident surgeons and nurses at the hospital.[64] Tucker J. said: "I think it is well established as a matter of law that the resident medical officers in a hospital of this kind, and the nursing staff, are not the agents of a specialist surgeon who comes and performs an operation of this kind, at any rate in so far as they are performing the ordinary routine duties which have to be carried out at a hospital of this kind."

280 The obligation to use proper care and skill is confined to cases where the patient is being treated or operated upon by the physician or surgeon concerned and does not arise, apart from contract, when there is no relation of doctor and patient between the parties. Accordingly, when a man, injured in a railway accident, was examined by a doctor sent by the railway company and told that his injuries were very slight, as a result of which he accepted a small sum in compensation, it was held that, assuming that the injuries were more serious than the doctor had reported, he had no right of action against the doctor for negligence because he had sustained no injury in consequence of neglect in examination.[65] Again, where a doctor, at the request of a relieving officer, negligently gave a certificate under the Lunacy Act 1890,[66] s. 20, as to the state of the plaintiff's mind, whereupon the plaintiff was taken to an infirmary, it was held that the doctor was not liable.[67] In this

[61] *Kavanagh* v. *Abrahamson* (1964) 108 S.J. 320.
[62] *Hancke* v. *Hooper* (1835) 7 C. & P. 81.
[63] *Perionowsky* v. *Freeman* (1866) 4 F. & F. 977.
[64] *Morris* v. *Winsbury-White* [1937] 4 All E.R. 494.
[65] *Pimm* v. *Roper* (1862) 2 F. & F. 783.
[66] Now repealed by the Mental Health Act 1959.
[67] *Thompson* v. *Schmidt* (1891) 8 T.L.R. 120. See also *Urquhart* v. *Grigor* (1864) 3 M. 283, 287.

case the doctor "was expressing an opinion to satisfy the relieving officer's mind, upon whom alone rested the responsibility for action. He was in no different position than if he had been a neighbour to whom the relieving officer had addressed an inquiry as to the man's sanity." [68]

281 **Mentally disordered patients.** A medical practitioner who gives a certificate under a statute which provides for the giving of a certificate to enable something to be done under the statute is bound to exercise proper care and skill in giving the certificate.

The Mental Health Act 1959, s. 26, provides that an application for the admission into hospital of a person suffering from a mental disorder, for observation or treatment, must be founded on the written recommendations of two medical practitioners. Section 141 (1) provides that no liability arises concerning acts done in pursuance of the Act unless done in "bad faith or without reasonable care." [69]

The medical practitioner, in giving such a recommendation, owes a duty to the patient to exercise proper care and skill, and if he fails to perform that duty he is liable in damages to him.[70] His duty "is not merely a duty to take reasonable care in making inquiries, that is, in ascertaining the necessary data, but includes a duty to exercise reasonable professional skill in forming a conclusion from such data." [71] In *Hall* v. *Semple*,[72] Crompton J. directed the jury that "if a person assumes the duty of a medical man under [this statute] and signs a certificate of insanity which is untrue, without making the proper examination or inquiries which the circumstances of the case would require from a medical man using proper care and skill in such a matter—if he states that which is untrue, and damage ensues to the party thereby, he is liable to an action." [72] This direction has been consistently upheld.[73]

282 Before an action can be brought against a medical practitioner for negligently recommending a mentally disordered patient for hospital treatment, leave must be obtained from the High Court and leave shall not be given unless the court is "satisfied that there is substantial ground for the contention that the person to be proceeded against has acted in bad faith or without reasonable care." [74]

The medical superintendent of a mental hospital may be made liable

[68] *Everett* v. *Griffiths* [1920] 3 K.B. 163, 216, *per* Atkin L.J.

[69] This is substantially the same as the Lunacy Act 1890, s. 330, as substituted by the Mental Treatment Act 1930, s. 16.

[70] *De Freville* v. *Dill* (1927) 96 L.J.K.B. 1056; decided under the Lunacy Act 1890, s. 16, which provided for the signing of a medical certificate before an order could be made for the detention of a lunatic in an institution.

[71] *Everett* v. *Griffiths* [1920] 3 K.B. 163, 216, *per* Atkin L.J.

[72] *Hall* v. *Semple* (1862) 3 F. & F. 337.

[73] *Everett* v. *Griffiths* [1920] 3 K.B. 163, *per* Bankes L.J. and Atkin L.J.; [1921] 1 A.C. 631, *per* Lord Finlay and Lord Cave; *Harnett* v. *Fisher* [1927] A.C. 573, *per* Lord Blanesburgh; *De Freville* v. *Dill*, *supra*.

[74] Mental Health Act 1959, s. 141 (2), which replaced the Mental Treatment Act 1930, s. 16 (2). For the construction of this and the Lunacy Act 1890, s. 330, see *Re Frost* [1936] 2 All E.R. 182; *Shackleton* v. *Swift* [1913] 2 K.B. 304; *Williams* v. *Beaumont* (1894) 10 T.L.R. 489, 543; *Re Shoesmith* [1938] 2 K.B. 637.

if he negligently allows a mental patient to be at large. If the patient has been convicted of a criminal offence and assaults a member of the public during his period of freedom,[75] he may be liable provided that he knew or should have known that the patient, if not kept under control, was likely to commit an act of violence.[76]

10.—HOSPITALS

283 It was long held that public hospitals were not liable for the negligence of physicians, surgeons and nurses at the hospital while acting in the discharge of their professional functions. As Lord Wright pointed out,[77] this was rather an anomalous position, because the professional staff is appointed by the hospital authorities, and the general rule is that " those who engage in an undertaking the actual conduct of which involves expert scientific or professional skill and knowledge which the principals do not possess, cannot escape liability to outsiders who are injured by the negligence of those who advise or act for the principals, on the ground that they, as principals, are laymen and must necessarily be guided by, or act through, experts." The principle, however, seemed to be firmly settled that, if reasonable care was taken to select competent physicians, surgeons and nurses, the hospital authorities were not responsible for their negligence in the course of their professional duties.[78] In the words of Kennedy L.J.: " I see no ground for holding it to be a right legal inference from the circumstances of the relation of hospital and patient that the hospital authority makes itself liable in damages, if members of its professional staff, of whose competence there is no question, act negligently towards the patient in some matter of professional care or skill, or neglect to use or use negligently, in his treatment the apparatus or appliances which are at their disposal." [79]

284 The hospital authority were held not liable for negligence in the following cases: Where the plaintiff's son was discharged from hospital by the order of the physician, while he was still in an infectious condition as a result of an attack of scarlet fever, with the consequence that the other children of the plaintiff contracted scarlet fever, causing the plaintiff to be put to expense [80]; where the plaintiff entered a hospital to be medically examined under an anaesthetic, and he was negligently placed on the operating table so that his arms were burnt and bruised and became paralysed [81]; where a patient at a hospital died as a result of the negligence of two nurses who administered a dose of six ounces of

[75] *Holgate* v. *Lancashire Mental Hospitals Board* [1937] 4 All E.R. 19.

[76] *Ellis* v. *Home Office* [1953] 2 All E.R. 149. [The report in [1953] 2 Q.B. 135 is only on the question of Crown privilege.]

[77] *Lindsey C.C.* v. *Marshall* [1937] A.C. 97, 122.

[78] *Lindsey C.C.* v. *Marshall*, *supra*, *per* Lord Hailsham at p. 108, *per* Lord Sankey at p. 113, *per* Lord Macmillan at p. 119, Lord Wright doubting; *Hillyer* v. *St. Bartholomew's Hospital* [1909] 2 K.B. 820; *Strangways-Lesmere* v. *Clayton* [1936] 2 K.B. 11.

[79] *Hillyer* v. *St. Bartholomew's Hospital*, *supra*, at p. 829.

[80] *Evans* v. *Liverpool Corpn.* [1906] 1 K.B. 160.

[81] *Hillyer* v. *St. Bartholomew's Hospital* [1909] 2 K.B. 820.

paraldehyde instead of six drachms as prescribed by the doctor [82]; where a patient, who had been operated upon in a hospital was discharged with a wad of surgical gauze in her body as a result of the negligence of the surgeon and nurses in the conduct of the operation.[83] All these cases, with the possible exception of the last, would now be decided differently. However, the hospital was held not liable when a mental patient receiving electro-convulsive therapy sustained, during treatment given in accordance with a considerable body of medical opinion, fractures of the pelvis on each side caused by the head of the femur being driven through the acetabulum.[84] Although a greater degree of care and supervision was required in the case of a patient of known or suspected suicidal tendencies, there was no negligence found where a woman succeeded in eluding the nursing staff and returned to her home, there to commit suicide whilst mentally ill but not insane.[85]

285 The hospital authority were liable for the negligence of physicians, surgeons and nurses appointed by them for all acts which were not done in the exercise of their professional duty. Such acts were described as ministerial or administrative. To quote Kennedy L.J.: " It may well be, and for my part I should, as at present advised, be prepared to hold, that the hospital authority is legally responsible to the patients for the due performance of their servants within the hospital of their purely ministerial or administrative duties, such as, for example, attendances of nurses in the wards, the summoning of medical aid in cases of emergency, the supply of proper food, and the like.[86]

286 **Hospital liable for negligence of staff.** The distinction drawn by Kennedy L.J. between professional duties and ministerial or administrative duties has been disapproved, and the law now is that hospitals are liable for the negligence of the members of the hospital staff whether they are nurses [87] or doctors.[88] Accordingly, when a patient in a hospital was injured by the negligence of the radiographer, a whole-time servant of the hospital, in failing to provide adequate screening material in using X-rays, the hospital were held liable.[89] The hospital has also been held liable, when the house surgeon, who was unqualified, negligently injected a patient with cocaine in mistake for procaine, a harmless drug [90]; when the medical staff were negligent in the post-operational treatment

82 *Strangways-Lesmere* v. *Clayton* [1936] 2 K.B. 11, overruled by *Gold* v. *Essex C.C.* [1942] 2 K.B. 293.
83 *Dryden* v. *Surrey C.C.* [1936] 2 All E.R. 535.
84 *Bolam* v. *Friern Hospital Management Committee* [1957] 1 W.L.R. 582.
85 *Thorne* v. *Northern Group Hospital Management Committee* (1964) 108 S.J. 484.
86 *Hillyer* v. *St. Bartholomew's Hospital*, *supra*, at p. 829. See also *per* Lord Sankey in *Lindsey C.C.* v. *Marshall* [1937] A.C. 97, 114.
87 *Wardell* v. *Kent C.C.* [1938] 2 K.B. 768. *Voller* v. *Portsmouth Corpn.* (1947) 203 L.T.J. 264 (nursing staff negligent in not properly disinfecting the apparatus for giving injections). *Fox* v. *Glasgow S.W. Hospitals Board*, 1955 S.L.T. 337.
88 *Cassidy* v. *Ministry of Health* [1951] 2 K.B. 343; *Macdonald* v. *Glasgow S.W. Hospitals Board*, 1954 S.C. 453.
89 *Gold* v. *Essex C.C.* [1942] 2 K.B. 293.
90 *Collins* v. *Hertfordshire C.C.* [1947] K.B. 598.

of a patient [91]; when an anaesthetic was negligently administered by a physician on the hospital staff [92]; and when the casualty officer failed to discover a depressed fracture of the skull and penetration of the bone into the brain tissue [93]; and where a nurse at a cottage hospital had failed to give an anti-tetanus injection to a man who had suffered a severe crush injury to a finger whilst shovelling coal or had failed to take steps to communicate to others to ensure that the plaintiff got the proper treatment elsewhere.[94]

287 A medical man employed part-time at a hospital is a member of the staff for whose negligence the hospital is responsible.[95] In a voluntary hospital the consulting physicians and surgeons are not employed by the hospital, which is therefore not liable for their negligence,[96] but in the case of a hospital under the National Health Service Act 1946, the consultants or specialists are employed under the terms of the Act so that the hospital is liable for their negligence.[97]

A hospital management committee is liable for negligence in the treatment of a patient at the hospital and is not protected by section 72 of the National Health Service Act 1946.[98]

A hospital authority, which provides a casualty department, owes a duty of care towards persons presenting themselves there, complaining of illness. Nevertheless, in *Barnett* v. *Chelsea and Kensington Hospital Management Committee* [99] the plaintiff widow's claim failed because, despite the casualty officer's negligence in failing to examine or admit the deceased, the latter had, unknowingly, consumed so much arsenic in some contaminated tea that he would have died in any event, irrespective of any treatment if it had been given.

288 **Duty as to hospital premises.** In *Lindsey C.C.* v. *Marshall* [1] the plaintiff was admitted to a nursing home to be confined. Shortly before her admission, a case of puerperal fever occurred at the home. The medical superintendent gave instructions, which were carried out, for disinfecting the home and the nursing staff, but no warning was given to the plaintiff, and in consequence she entered the home and caught the fever. The hospital authority were held liable because they knew or ought to have known that the hospital was dangerous and failed to warn

91 *Cassidy* v. *Ministry of Health* [1951] 2 K.B. 343.
92 *Jones* v. *Manchester Corpn.* [1952] 2 K.B. 852.
93 *McCormack* v. *Redpath Brown & Co., The Times*, March 24, 1961.
94 *Coles* v. *Reading and District Hospital Management Committee* (1963) 107 S.J. 115.
95 *Roe* v. *Minister of Health* [1954] 2 Q.B. 66.
96 *Gold* v. *Essex C.C., supra*; *Collins* v. *Hertfordshire C.C., supra*; *Cassidy* v. *Ministry of Health, supra*. Denning L.J.'s view, which he repeated in *Roe* v. *Minister of Health, supra*, was that the hospital was liable if it provided the specialist, but not if the patient obtained him.
97 See *Razzel* v. *Snowball* [1954] 3 All E.R. 429; *Higgins* v. *N.W. Metropolitan Hospital Board* [1954] 1 W.L.R. 411; *Hayward* v. *Board of Management, R.I. of Edinburgh*, 1954 S.L.T. 226.
98 *Bullard* v. *Croydon Hospital Group Management Committee* [1953] 1 Q.B. 511.
99 [1969] 1 Q.B. 428; hence causation could not be established. See article: " Doctors duty to see his patient " (Samuels) 112 S.J. 1017.
1 [1937] A.C. 97; *Heafield* v. *Crane, The Times*, July 31, 1937, is a similar case.

the plaintiff of the danger. This case may be compared with *Vancouver General Hospital* v. *McDaniel.*[2] There the plaintiff, who was in hospital for diphtheria, developed smallpox owing to being placed in a room on the same floor as patients suffering from smallpox and attended by nurses who also attended those patients. This system of dealing with patients was, according to the evidence, in accord then with the most approved medical practice and the best system known to medical science; the plaintiff, accordingly, failed. In the light of modern knowledge this case would probably be decided differently.

Where a boy, aged seven, was admitted to hospital suffering from scarlet fever and was placed on the ground floor in a bed near a window the lower part of which was open, it was held that the hospital were liable for negligence when, in the absence of a nurse, the boy somehow fell out of the window and was injured on the ground below.[3] Where a plaintiff suffering from a form of epilepsy characterised by a dangerous condition of post-epileptic automatism jumped from a high window of a hospital and was severely injured, it was held that in the absence of physical safeguards it was the duty of the hospital, who knew of the patient's condition, to ensure that the plaintiff was kept under the constant care of a competent servant of theirs at all times.[4] On the other hand, when a girl of nine, in the temporary absence of the orderly, injured herself by running into glass swing doors, the hospital was held not liable.[5] The hospital's duty, apart from the medical side, was said to be that of an ordinary prudent parent.

A hospital authority must " take by themselves or by their officers all proper steps to keep the premises safe for the admission of the public, or if they have not done so either to exclude the public altogether, or at least to warn them of the danger." [6] Their duty towards patients and persons coming to visit them, as far as the condition of the premises is concerned, is that of an occupier to a visitor, namely " common duty of care." [7]

289 **Hospital's duty to medical staff.** A hospital owes no duty to a resident house physician, living in a staff hostel adjoining the hospital, to

[2] [1934] W.N. 171.

[3] *Newnham* v. *Rochester and Chatham Joint Hospital Board, The Times*, February 28, 1936.

[4] *Lepine* v. *University Hospital Board* (1964) 50 D.L.R. (2d) 225, affirmed (1965) 54 D.L.R. (2d) 340. Likewise in *Selfe* v. *Ilford and District Hospital Management Committee* (1970) 114 S.J. 935 the hospital was guilty of negligence in failing to provide continuous supervision of the plaintiff, a psychiatric patient and a known suicide risk, who left his bed by a ground floor window, climbed to a roof and threw himself off thereby sustaining severe personal injuries.

[5] *Gravestock* v. *Lewisham Group Hospital Management Committee, The Times*, May 27, 1955.

[6] *Lindsey C.C.* v. *Marshall* [1937] A.C. 97, 119, *per* Lord Macmillan.

[7] The Occupiers' Liability Act 1957, ss. 1 (2) and 2 (1) which came into force on January 1, 1958. Prior to that date the duty was that of an invitor to an invitee; see the earlier decisions in *Lindsey C.C.* v. *Marshall, supra, per* Lord Wright at p. 125; *Weigall* v. *Westminster Hospital* (1936) 52 T.L.R. 301 (visitor to patient slips on a mat—hospital liable); and *Slade* v. *Battersea and Putney Hospital Management Committee* [1955] 1 W.L.R. 207 (wife of a patient fell on a slippery floor in process of being polished—hospital liable).

safeguard his personal effects against theft by a third party who comes into the hospital.[8]

290 **Private nursing home.** In the case of a private nursing home, there will usually be a contractual duty. As to the duty in tort, it is difficult to see any principle on which the duty in such a home can differ from that in a public hospital.[9]

291 **Nursing association.** A nursing association which takes reasonable care to provide competent nurses is not liable for the negligence of the nurses it provides.[10]

11.—INSURANCE AGENTS AND BROKERS

292 The liability of an insurance agent to his principal is determined by the principles of the law of agency, since the relationship is purely a contractual one. Accordingly if an insurance agent chooses to undertake to procure an insurance he is legally bound to use all due care and skill in performance of the duties. The question which is raised in each case is whether the act or omission complained of is inconsistent with that reasonable degree of care and skill which persons of ordinary prudence and competence ought to show in any given situation.[11] Further it is a question of construction of the terms of the contract of agency whether the agent has contracted merely to use due care and skill to procure an effective insurance or has given an absolute undertaking that he will procure an effective insurance.[12] He is assumed to have knowledge of the ordinary well settled rules relating to insurance law and other insurance matters, such as to know all the necessary details to make the policy a legally valid instrument.[13] Whether an insurance broker has exercised reasonable care and skill in all the circumstances is a question of fact.[14] Brokers were not negligent in failing to see that an assured read through an application for insurance before he signed it.[14a]

293 In *Osman* v. *J. Ralph Moss Ltd.*[15] the plaintiff took out a motor insurance policy on the recommendation of the defendants who were insurance brokers but the insurance company were unsound financially and were wound up. The defendants failed to tell the plaintiff of this and to advise him that he was no longer insured but the plaintiff only found out following an accident for which he was not only fined but had judgment entered against him in civil proceedings. The Court of Appeal held that the defendants were guilty of negligence for they had recommended the plaintiff to insure with a company which they ought to have known was in financial difficulties. On the issue of remoteness of damage it was

[8] *Edwards* v. *West Herts Group Hospital Management Committee* [1957] 1 W.L.R. 415. See also note, 73 L.Q.R. 313.

[9] See *Powell* v. *Streatham Manor Nursing Home* [1935] A.C. 243; *Gold* v. *Essex C.C.* [1942] 2 K.B. 293.

[10] *Hall* v. *Lees* [1904] 2 K.B. 602.

[11] *Chapman* v. *Walton* (1833) 10 Bing. 57, at p. 63, *per* Tindal C.J.

[12] *Hood* v. *West End Motor Car Packing Co.* [1917] 2 K.B. 38.

[13] *Turpin* v. *Bilton* (1843) 5 Man. & G. 455.

[14] *Hurrell* v. *Bullard* (1863) 3 F. & F. 445.

[14a] *O'Connor* v. *Kirby* [1971] 2 W.L.R. 1233.

[15] [1970] 1 Lloyds Rep. 313.

reasonably foreseeable that the plaintiff would continue to drive since he had no cause to believe that he was not entitled to do so and the fact that he might be involved in an accident was also reasonably foreseeable because that was the very risk against which he had sought to insure himself. Evidence is admissible of persons engaged in the same business in order to assert what would have been the conduct of a reasonably careful and skilful broker in the circumstances of the case under consideration.[16]

There can be no doubt that a special relationship can be created outside the contractual one so that the principle laid down in *Hedley Byrne & Co. Ltd.* v. *Heller & Partners Ltd.* would apply to impose liability in negligence.[17] It has been held, however, that a broker who effected an insurance with an underwriter was not his agent and was under no legal liability to him to use care or skill in effecting the insurance.[18]

12.—JEWELLERS

294 **Jewellers.** The same standard of care is exacted from a jeweller who undertakes to pierce his customer's ears for the reception of earrings. When a jeweller was sued for negligence in carrying out such an operation, Goddard J. said: "The defendants were bound to conform to the standard of skill and care which might be expected from a jeweller. Of course, if the operation was negligently performed by the use, for instance, of a wholly unsuitable instrument, that would render the defendants liable. Again, the degree of care in seeing that the instruments used were clean must be that which was to be expected of a jeweller. To say, however, that a jeweller undertook to use instruments which had the degree of surgical cleanliness which would be expected of a doctor in the case of a serious operation was putting the matter too high. If a person desired to secure such a standard of care he should go to a doctor. If he went to a jeweller he must expect the operation to be carried out in the way a jeweller might be expected to do it." [19]

13.—NURSES

295 Nurses, like other persons who are doing acts which are likely to cause physical damage, if done negligently, are under a duty to exercise due care and the professional skill of a reasonably competent nurse towards their patients. Accordingly, a nurse who administered six ounces of paraldehyde instead of six drachms as ordered by the doctor was held to be negligent.[20]

[16] See the principles laid down by Tindal C.J. in *Chapman* v. *Walton*, *supra*, but *cf.* *Campbell* v. *Rickards* (1833) 5 B. & Ad. 840 where such evidence was excluded as inadmissible.

[17] See *ante*, § 243.

[18] *Empress Assurance Corporation* v. *Bowring & Co.* (1905) 11 Com.Cas. 107; *Glasgow Assurance Corporation* v. *William Symondson & Co.* (1911) 104 L.T. 254.

[19] *Phillips* v. *William Whiteley Ltd.* (1938) 54 T.L.R. 379. See the criticism of this case, *ante*, § 195.

[20] *Strangways-Lesmere* v. *Clayton* [1936] 2 K.B. 11. *Cf.* *Dryden* v. *Surrey C.C.* [1936] 2 All E.R. 535 where the nurses were held not negligent. Also see generally § 284, *ante*.

14.—QUASI-ARBITRATORS

296 A quasi-arbitrator, such as one who is asked by a buyer and a seller of shares to fix the value of the shares according to the method prescribed by the contract between them, is under no duty to exercise due care or skill, his only duty being to act honestly.[21] "He is not liable to an action unless he is dishonest." [22]

15.—SCHOOLS AND SCHOOLTEACHERS

297 **Duty of schoolteacher.** The duty of a schoolteacher has been said to be to take such care of his pupils as a reasonably careful father would take of his own children of the family.[23] The standard of such care required was that of a parent, applying his mind to school life rather than to that at home,[24] but having as many children [25] and of the type of children as are in the class.[26] Whilst the standard of care required is high, it is no more than what would be reasonably expected in any given case; nevertheless it is higher than the common duty of care under the Occupiers' Liability Act 1957.[27]

It is no part of the duty of a schoolmaster to foresee every act of stupidity that might take place [28] but at the same time it is necessary to strike a proper balance between too strict a supervision of children at every waking moment of their school life and the desirable object of encouraging the sturdy independence of children whilst they grow up, which, after all, is an important facet of their education.[29] In *Camkin* v. *Bishop* [30] where a schoolboy aged fourteen received injuries when ragging about, as a result of being struck by a flying clod of earth thrown at him by another boy, Goddard L.J., in exonerating the defendant from blame, said: "If every master is to take precautions to see that there is never ragging or horseplay among his pupils, his school would indeed be too awful a place to contemplate." However where a schoolboy aged fifteen was injured in the course of ragging at school as a result of his hand breaking through a glass panelled door, Edmund Davies J. held, *inter alia*,

21 *Finnegan* v. *Allen* [1943] K.B. 425; *Boynton* v. *Richardson* [1924] W.N. 262.

22 *Dean* v. *Prince* [1954] Ch. 409, 427, *per* Lord Denning L.J. However for a "special relationship" see *Hedley Byrne & Co. Ltd.* v. *Heller and Partners Ltd.* [1964] A.C. 465.

23 *Per* Lord Esher M.R. in *Williams* v. *Eady* (1893) 10 T.L.R. 41; *Shepherd* v. *Essex C.C.* (1913) 29 T.L.R. 303, *per* Darling J.; *Rawsthorne* v. *Ottley* [1937] 3 All E.R. 902, *per* Hilbery J.; *Ricketts* v. *Erith C.B.* [1943] 2 All E.R. 629; *Prince* v. *Gregory* [1959] 1 W.L.R. 177. But see the criticism of this test without more, by Geoffrey Lane J. in *Beaumont* v. *Surrey C.C.* (1968) 112 S.J. 704. Article: "The Schoolteacher and the Law of Negligence" (Linehan), 31 Ir. Jur. 38. "Injuries at School" (Brown), 114 S.J. 216.

24 *i.e.* where there was more skylarking to be expected as in *Lyes* v. *Middlesex C.C.* (1962) 61 L.G.R. 443; applied in *Jacques* v. *Oxfordshire C.C.* (1967) 66 L.G.R. 440.

25 *Nicholson* v. *Westmorland* C.C., *The Times*, October 25, 1962, *viz.*: "a parent with a family of twenty children"; *Crouch* v. *Essex C.C.* (1966) 64 L.G.R. 240. "It is unrealistic, if not unhelpful, to say the standard of care owed by the headmaster of a school of 900 pupils is that of the reasonably careful and prudent father towards his own children," *per* Geoffrey Lane J. in *Beaumont* v. *Surrey C.C., supra.*

26 *e.g.* deaf and dumb children, *Ellis* v. *Sayers Confectioners* (1963) 61 L.G.R. 299.

27 See *Reffell* v. *Surrey C.C.* [1964] 1 W.L.R. 358.

28 *Perry* v. *King Alfred School Society, The Guardian*, October 28, 1961.

29 *Jeffery* v. *L.C.C.* (1954) 52 L.G.R. 521.

30 [1941] 2 All E.R. 713, at p. 716.

that the defendants were guilty of negligence in not preventing such skylarking in the circumstances.[31]

298 Applying this standard of care it has been held that the act of a teacher, in telling a girl of about fourteen to go into the teachers' common room to poke the fire and pull out the damper of a grate with which she was not familiar, in consequence of which the girl's apron caught fire and she sustained injuries, was negligent.[32] It has also been held to be negligent to fail to provide a guard for a gas stove in a cookery class which was attended by an eleven-year-old girl.[33] On the other hand, when a master told a boy of twelve to carry an oil can with a long spout from one classroom to another and, while the boy was carrying the oil can, another boy, coming suddenly round the corner in the passage, collided with the can and injured his eye, it was held that there was no negligence on the master's part.[34] Also there was held to be no negligence where a fourteen-year-old girl was scalded when carrying a large teapot full of hot tea down a school passageway and a boy, running along, collided with her, since the carrying of a pot of tea was an ordinary domestic duty.[35]

299 It is a schoolmaster's duty to take all reasonable and proper steps to prevent any of his pupils, bearing in mind their known propensities, from suffering injury from inanimate objects, from the actions of their fellow pupils [36] or from a combination of the two. Thus he should not leave about, in a place to which his pupils have access, anything which is likely to injure them or with which they are likely to interfere and to injure each other. Accordingly, when some phosphorus was left in a conservatory where the boys could get at it, a schoolmaster was held liable for injury caused to one of the boys by the phosphorus, Kay L.J. saying: "Was it not evidence of negligence to have left the bottle of phosphorus lying about in a place to which the boys had access knowing what boys are?" [37]

If things likely to injure the pupils are left lying about by a third party, the schoolmaster is liable if he knew or ought to have known that they were left where his pupils could get at them and injure themselves. Where a contractor, in order to carry out some repairs to a school, left a truck of "rough stuff," consisting of three parts sand and one part lime, in a corner of the playground, and the schoolmaster knew of it, and, thinking it would be dangerous to the boys, telephoned to the contractor to remove it, the schoolmaster was held liable for injury caused to one of the boys through being struck in the eye by a ball of "rough stuff" thrown by another boy. The contractor was also

31 *Lyes* v. *Middlesex C.C.* (1962) 61 L.G.R. 443.
32 *Smith* v. *Martin and Hull Corporation* [1911] 2 K.B. 775.
33 *Fryer* v. *Salford Corporation* [1937] 1 All E.R. 617.
34 *Wray* v. *Essex C.C.* [1936] 3 All E.R. 97. *Cf. Crouch* v. *Essex C.C.* (1966) 64 L.G.R. 240.
35 *Cooper* v. *Manchester Corporation, The Times*, February 13, 1959.
36 Thus a school may be liable for injuries caused to a boy by the "horse plav" of other pupils: *Beaumont* v. *Surrey C.C.* (1968) 112 S.J. 704.
37 *Williams* v. *Eady* (1893) 10 T.L.R. 41.

held liable for his failure to remove the rough stuff within a reasonable time after receiving the schoolmaster's message.[38] This case was distinguished in *Rich* v. *L.C.C.*[39] where the school authority was held not liable where there was an unfenced heap of coke in the school playground and a pupil threw a piece of coke at another, injuring him. It was found that there was proper supervision, and the trial judge's judgment in favour of the plaintiff was reversed on the ground that when the supervision was adequate there was no obligation to prevent the boys from having access to the coke by erecting some structure over which they could not climb.

300 What things are likely to injure pupils is a question of degree depending on the nature of the thing and the age of the pupils. "To leave a knife about where a child of four could get at it would amount to negligence, but it would not if boys of eighteen had access to it." [40] It would seem that the test it: Is the thing one of a class which children of that age are, in the ordinary course of things, not allowed to use without supervision? For example, where a child at a public elementary school, with the consent of the teacher, brought some toy soldiers to play with, and another child, aged five, was injured through the lance of one of the toy soldiers piercing his eye, it was held that there was no negligence on the part of the teacher in allowing the children to play with the soldiers, on the ground that they were playthings in ordinary use in every nursery.[41] On the other hand, to allow children of tender years to have fireworks without supervision on the part of the schoolmaster is negligence.[42]

301 **Duty to exercise supervision.** A schoolmaster is under a duty to exercise supervision over his pupils when they are on the school premises, either in the schoolroom or the playground. It extends to those simple tasks, reasonably left to be performed by the children, which will result in the continuing safety of the school premises.[43] The amount of supervision required depends on the age of the pupils and what they are doing at the material time. During hours of instruction a greater degree of supervision is required than during hours of recreation. Where a fifteen-year-old boy in a chemistry class of twenty-five children was struck in the face by a strong solution of caustic soda being squirted at him through a pipette by another pupil, it was held that neither the master in charge of the class nor the education authority was liable. The standard of discipline maintained was sufficient from the safety point of view even if it

[38] *Jackson* v. *L.C.C. and Chappell* (1912) 28 T.L.R. 359.

[39] [1953] 2 All E.R. 376. In a similar case Lord Parker C.J. held that there was no obligation on the school authorities to provide sufficient supervisors to watch all parts of the playground all the time: *Newton* v. *East Ham Corporation, The Guardian,* July 11, 1963.

[40] *Per* Cave J. in *Williams* v. *Eady* (1893) 9 T.L.R. 637. Further, see *Clark* v. *Monmouthshire C.C.* (1954) 118 J.P. 244.

[41] *Chilvers* v. *L.C.C.* (1916) 32 T.L.R. 363.

[42] *King* v. *Ford* (1816) 1 Stark.N.P. 421, *per* Lord Ellenborough.

[43] *Martin* v. *Middlesbrough Corporation* (1965) 109 S.J. 576 (the children failed to remove crates of empty milk bottles so that some broke and a child sustained lacerations).

did not succeed in putting down all impertinence and high spirits.[44] A teacher was held not to be under a duty to require all work to cease in class, whilst she had to give individual attention to a particular child, during which time the plaintiff, a child of nine to ten years of age, accidentally lost an eye as a result of her class-mate waving about in the air a pair of pointed scissors, when she was supposed to be cutting out some paper illustrations.[45]

A local authority which operates a school bus owes a duty to see that it is reasonably safe for the children using it for that purpose and this includes, where necessary, the provision of supervision. In *Jacques* v. *Oxfordshire C.C.*[46] the fourteen-year-old plaintiff, who was struck in the eye by a pellet, failed to prove liability, where, as was the normal practice, the discipline over the forty-two pupils using the bus was entrusted to two responsible prefects. When boys were doing farm work during a half-holiday and one boy injured another by throwing a clod of earth at him, it was held that the headmaster was not liable, as he was under no duty to provide supervision for the boys.[47] When normally healthy children of school age are in the playground, it is not necessary that they should be under continuous supervision,[48] even if some of the children are only six years old.[49] Where a boy sustained the loss of sight in an eye when he was struck by a rounders bat whilst playing in an unofficial game of rounders during the mid-day luncheon break in the school playground, it was held that there had been no failure of supervision.[50] Where a pupil, during instruction in a gymnasium, vaulted over a horse, fell and injured himself, it was held to be negligence on the master's part not to take reasonable care to prevent a fall, and the education authority was held liable on the ground that " the games master does not seem to have acted with that promptitude which the law requires." [51] On somewhat similar facts, a boy of twelve who was injured in vaulting over a " buck " failed to prove liability. There were four classes in the gymnasium and the instructor was supervising another class at the time, but it was proved that the supervision was in accordance with approved practice and had been followed with safety for many years, so that it was held there was no negligence.[52]

302 If the schoolmaster knows or ought to know that the pupils on the school premises are playing dangerous games or doing acts in such a manner or in such a place as are likely to cause injury to one another, and does not prevent it, he is liable in negligence. He is not liable

44 *Crouch* v. *Essex County Council* (1966) 64 L.G.R. 240.
45 *Butt* v. *Cambridgeshire and Isle of Ely C.C.* (1969) 119 New L.J. 1118.
46 (1967) 66 L.G.R. 440.
47 *Camkin* v. *Bishop* [1941] 2 All E.R. 713.
48 *Rawsthorne* v. *Ottley* [1937] 3 All E.R. 902. *Newton* v. *East Ham Corporation, The Guardian*, July 11, 1963.
49 *Ricketts* v. *Erith B.C.* [1943] 2 All E.R. 629 (school not liable when boy of ten injured girl of six during the break with a toy bow and arrow, in the teacher's absence).
50 *Price* v. *Caernarvonshire County Council, The Times*, February 11, 1960.
51 *Gibbs* v. *Barking Corpn.* [1936] 1 All E.R. 115.
52 *Wright* v. *Cheshire C.C.* [1952] 2 All E.R. 789.

for injury caused to a pupil through playing one of the ordinary school games, properly conducted. For example, when a pupil at an instruction centre of a county council was playing a compulsory game of "riders and horses," during the ordinary course of which some of the players were thrown to the ground, and he was injured in falling, it was held that there was no negligence on the part of the instructor in ordering the game to be played and no liability on the county council.[53] Again, when a boy of fourteen took part in a relay race at a play centre and injured himself by putting his arm through a glass partition at the other end of the room, Porter J. held that the master owed a duty of care, but that as the boys were told to touch the master and run back, and not told to touch the glass partition, the local authority who provided the play centre were not liable.[54]

303 If the schoolmaster knows or ought to know that a game is being played in a dangerous manner or in an unsuitable place likely to make it dangerous,[55] he is negligent if he does not take proper steps to prevent danger. So, where the plaintiff, while playing a game of "touch," was chased by another boy and unwittingly put his hand through a glass partition on one side of the hall where the game was played, the trial judge held that a reasonable and prudent father would have contemplated the possibility of such an accident and gave judgment for the plaintiff. The Court of Appeal held that the correct test had been applied and affirmed the decision.[56] When a boy in the school buildings was hit in the eye by a golf-ball struck by another boy from the playground, the schoolmaster was held not liable, because the injured boy said that he had never known a boy hit a golf-ball in the playground before.[57] But if in that case the plaintiff's allegations that the schoolmaster (1) failed to exercise proper supervision over his pupils; (2) knew or ought to have known that pupils were in the habit of hitting golf-balls in a manner likely to be dangerous to other pupils, had been proved, the schoolmaster would have been liable in negligence.[58] Even if there is a breach of the duty to exercise supervision, a schoolmaster is not liable for sudden acts which could not have been prevented by supervision, as where in a school for blind children one of the children during the temporary absence of the person in charge, jumped on the back of another and injured him,[59] or for accidents which could not be anticipated, such as an injury to a child at a swimming bath caused by one child suddenly letting go a spring-board to which she was clinging while the injured child was about to

[53] *Jones* v. *L.C.C.* (1932) 48 T.L.R. 368.
[54] *Cahill* v. *West Ham Corpn.* (1937) 81 S.J. 630.
[55] *Gillmore* v. *L.C.C.* [1938] 4 All E.R. 331 (county council liable for providing hall with a slippery floor in which physical training classes were held when an adult pupil slipped and injured himself).
[56] *Ralph* v. *L.C.C.* (1947) 63 T.L.R. 546.
[57] *Langham* v. *Governors of Wellingborough School* (1932) 101 L.J.K.B. 513.
[58] *Langham* v. *Governors of Wellingborough School*, *supra*, *per* Greer L.J. at p. 517.
[59] *Gow* v. *Glasgow Education Authority*, 1922 S.C. 260; *Langham* v. *Governors of Wellingborough School* (1932) 101 L.J.K.B. 513, *per* Scrutton L.J.

jump from it.[60] Where a gas company delivered a load of coke in a tip-up lorry to a school, and the lorry arrived while the boys were in the playground, but the headmaster did not know of its arrival, it was held that the schoolmaster was not liable for injury caused to one of the boys through a number of the boys jumping on to the lorry and causing it to tip up. The gas company were also held not liable, on the ground that their driver could not reasonably have anticipated such interference with his lorry.[61]

304 In the case of very young children it is the duty of the school to take reasonable care to prevent them from getting out of the school and onto the highway. When a boy of four at a nursery school was dressed up for a walk and, during the teacher's temporary absence, got onto the highway through a gate which was either open or possible for him to open, and a lorry driver in an attempt to avoid the child collided with a lamp-post and was killed, the school was held liable. The unexplained presence of the child on the highway was evidence of negligence on the part of the school, and no explanation consistent with the exercise of proper care had been given.[62]

There is no duty to supervise children after they leave the school following the breaking-up time when the day's work is done. When a child aged five years fell through the glass roof of the children's lavatory in the playground after school hours the school authority was held not liable. There the children under five years of age were kept under supervision, until they were collected by their mothers, but not those of five or over, thus, it was held that there was no negligence in failing to supervise the over-fives.[63] But where a five-year-old child was released from school about five minutes earlier than the normal breaking-up time and had set to walk home alone, since her mother had not yet arrived to fetch her in accordance with usual practice, the education authority were held liable when the child sustained severe personal injuries as a result of being knocked down, whilst crossing over the main road.[64]

305 **Duty as to school premises.** The local education authority are bound by statute to secure that the premises of every school maintained by them conform to the standards prescribed by the Minister of Education for schools of the description to which the school belongs.[65] Under earlier statutes they were bound to maintain and keep efficient all public elementary schools in their area which were necessary [66] and for breach of this duty they were liable in damages. When a boy, who was playing in the playground, caught his foot in the asphalt covering of the ground,

60 *Clarke* v. *Bethnal Green B.C.* (1939) 55 T.L.R. 519.
61 *Rawsthorne* v. *Ottley* [1937] 3 All E.R. 902.
62 *Carmarthenshire C.C.* v. *Lewis* [1955] A.C. 549. See further *Toole* v. *Sherbourne Pouffes Ltd., The Times*, July 29, 1971 (school authority liable for the negligence of their traffic warden's failure to prevent a young child darting across a pedestrian crossing).
63 *Jeffery* v. *L.C.C.* (1954) 52 L.G.R. 521.
64 *Barnes* v. *Hampshire C.C.* [1969] 1 W.L.R. 1563. See article: " Safety in School and the Danger Without " (1969) 119 New L.J. 939.
65 Education Act 1944, s. 10, which is included in the Education Acts 1944–1968.
66 Education Act 1921, s. 17.

he was held entitled to recover, Lord Halsbury saying: " Anyone charged with that duty [to keep the playground in proper condition] was bound to take care that the playground where the boys were expected to play . . . should be in such a condition that they should not be exposed to unnecessary danger while playing there." [67]

306 The local education authority must not only keep the school premises in good repair, but must construct them so that they are not dangerous to children of the age intended to use them. Where a girl of seven, being told by the teacher to leave the room, had to open a heavy swing door with a powerful spring and caught her hand in the door, it was held that the door was unsuitable for the school in question and dangerous to children of that age and the education authority were liable. The door had originally been put in the school by a school board, from which the school was transferred by the Education Act 1902 to the local education authority, but it was held to be a breach of their statutory duty for the authority to allow the door to remain after the school was transferred to them.[68] Where a fifteen-year-old schoolboy was injured in the course of ragging at school as a result of his hand breaking through a glass panelled door, Edmund Davies J. held the defendants liable in that they were in breach of regulation 5 of the Schools Grant Regulations 1951 [69] and section 10 (2) of the Education Act 1944, in that the glass panel was too thin and the door was therefore not " efficient." [70] Also, a girl aged twelve, whose hand was injured when it went through the glass panel of a door swinging back towards her, succeeded in her claim for damages for breach of statutory duty under regulation 51 of the Standards for School Premises Regulations 1959 [71] in that the " construction and properties of the materials," *viz.* the glass panel, were not such that the " safety of the occupants shall be reasonably assured." [72]

307 In *Ward* v. *Hertfordshire C.C.*[73] where an eight-year-old pupil fell in the playground and injured himself against the boundary wall, which had been built with sharp flint stones, Hinchcliffe J. did not consider that such a wall came within the ambit of regulation 51 of the Standards for School Premises Regulations 1959 [69] thus the local education authority was under no absolute duty [74] concerning it and the safety of the occupants of the school. However he held that the authority was liable in negligence for breach of the " common duty of care " under the Occupiers' Liability Act 1957 [75] for failing to cement-render the wall or to put up railings or netting, which would have protected the infant plaintiff against the injury

[67] *Ching* v. *Surrey C.C.* [1910] 1 K.B. 736.
[68] *Morris* v. *Carnarvon C.C.* [1910] 1 K.B. 840, which was decided under the Education Act 1902.
[69] 1951 S.I. No. 1743.
[70] *Lyes* v. *Middlesex C.C.* (1962) 61 L.G.R. 443.
[71] 1959 S.I. No. 890.
[72] *Reffell* v. *Surrey C.C.* [1964] 1 W.L.R. 358.
[73] [1969] 1 W.L.R. 790.
[74] *Reffell* v. *Surrey C.C.* [1964] 1 W.L.R. 358 decided that the statutory duty is absolute in its nature and that also a duty exists at common law independently of such statutory duty.
[75] ss. 1 and 2.

he sustained, although the Court of Appeal reversed the decision upon this finding.[76] Where a cleaner had brushed the loose snow from the step outside the church school but had failed to place ashes or grit on the icy surface beneath it, upon which the infant plaintiff later slipped and hurt himself due to its dangerous condition, the local authority were held liable.[77] Where an education authority had decided to provide transport facilities for taking children to and from school it must be a reasonably safe conveyance. Thus, where a pupil, a girl aged thirteen was injured by falling off the step at the rear of the vehicle, the authority was held liable on the ground that as it had provided a conveyance it was its duty to provide for the safety of children using it. The jury found that the accident was due to the negligence of the driver and the non-provision of a conductor to help children on and off the conveyance, and the House of Lords held that the education authority ought to have provided a conductor under the circumstances.[78]

When a child of eleven was injured in the school playground where she slipped and fell, cutting herself on a piece of broken glass of a milk bottle, it was held that the defendants were negligent in failing to insist upon a safe system for storing and carrying away empty bottles and in failing to provide any proper supervision for these tasks.[79]

308 In the case of chattels which the pupils are invited or directed to use, there is a duty to see that such chattels are reasonably fit for the intended use. Where a youth of nineteen who was a pupil at technical classes provided by the local education authority was injured in using a circular saw and the negligence alleged was the failure to provide a guard, it was held that the authority were liable if the suggested guard was the recognised method of guarding saws of the kind, but otherwise not.[80] Although section 14 of the Factories Act 1961 did not apply so as to impose a statutory duty on the school authority to fence a dangerous part of a machine, the school authority nonetheless owed a similar duty at common law to provide for the safety of pupils against such a danger.[81] Where a girl of eleven, attending a cookery school, was injured through her dress catching fire at a gas stove, it was held that the school authority were liable for not providing a guard for the stove.[82]

Apart from the liability in tort explained above, where pupils enter school premises under a contract, there is presumably the same implied warranty of safety as in the case of guests staying at an hotel.[83]

309 Towards schoolmasters and other persons employed by the school, the same liability for the defective state of the premises exists as in the

[76] [1970] 1 W.L.R. 356.
[77] *Woodward* v. *Mayor of Hastings* [1945] K.B. 174.
[78] *Shrimpton* v. *Hertfordshire C.C.* (1911) 104 L.T. 145; See also *Jacques* v. *Oxfordshire C.C.* (1967) 66 L.G.R. 440.
[79] *Martin* v. *Middlesbrough Corporation* (1965) 63 L.G.R. 385.
[80] *Smerkinich* v. *Newport Corporation* (1912) 76 J.P. 454.
[81] *Butt* v. *Inner London Education Authority* (1968) 66 L.G.R. 379.
[82] *Fryer* v. *Salford Corporation* [1937] 1 All E.R. 617.
[83] *Ante*, Chapter 8. *Maclenan* v. *Segar* [1917] 2 K.B. 325.

other case of master and servant.[84] Knowledge of the defective condition of the school will not prevent the schoolmaster or other servant from recovering, subject to any contributory negligence on his part. Accordingly an action for breach of statutory duty can be brought not only by pupils attending the school, but also by a schoolmaster who is injured by the breach, so that when a schoolmaster was injured by the bursting of a heating apparatus, known by the managers of a non-provided school to be defective, the managers were held liable for breach of their statutory duty under the Education Act 1902, s. 7, to provide a school house.[85]

Towards persons who are not pupils, liability depends on the character in which they enter the premises, whether as " visitors " or " trespassers " and the ordinary rules explained in Chapter 8 apply.

Liability for the defective state of the school premises is on the occupiers of the school premises, who are usually the governors or other the proprietors of the school. In county schools, the local education authority are the occupiers and in voluntary schools the managers or governors.[86]

16.—SOLICITORS

310 **Nature of duty.** Solicitors are bound to exercise a reasonable degree of care, skill and knowledge in all legal business they undertake. Their liability arises out of contract.[87] They were formerly also liable in tort [88] but this is so no longer.[89] The exact duty of a solicitor depends on what he is employed to do. A solicitor who was consulted to advise whether his client's workmen's compensation payments were in danger of being reduced was held not to be negligent in failing to advise on his client's prospects of success in a common law action.[90]

311 **Duty to client alone.** A solicitor owes no duty to a person who is not his client, and is not liable in negligence to anyone but his client, except

84 *Ante*, § 203.
85 *Abbott* v. *Isham* (1920) 90 L.J.K.B. 309.
86 Education Act 1944, s. 22 (3).
87 Damages for neglect of duty were recoverable in contract only; there is no alternative claim in tort for negligent misstatement: *Clark* v. *Kirby-Smith* [1964] Ch. 506, where Plowman J. at p. 241 said: " I do not accept the argument that the *Hedley Byrne* case is an authority for saying that the liability of a solicitor to his client for negligence is a liability in tort." See articles, " Professional Negligence of Solicitors and Attorneys," 107 S.J. 207 and 226; " Taking a Risk with Counsel," 107 S.J. 622; " Hazards of an Uncommon Calling—Negligence Claims against Solicitors " (Goodman), 108 S.J. 906, 929; " Liability by Negligence " (Glasgow), 49 *Secretaries Chronicle* 442; " Who is a Lawyer's Neighbour ? " (De Pinna) 118 New L.J. 89.
88 *Howell* v. *Young* (1826) 5 B. & C. 259; *Blyth* v. *Fladgate* [1891] 1 Ch. 337.
89 *Groom* v. *Crocker* [1939] 1 K.B. 194; *Davies* v. *Lock* (1844) 3 L.T. (o.s.) 125; *Bean* v. *Wade* (1885) 2 T.L.R. 157. However, a registrar of a local land charges registry owes a statutory duty to incumbrancers, under s. 17 of the Land Charges Act 1925 as applied by the Land Charges Rules 1934, to include in his certificate to a purchaser all the entries on the register and he is liable in damages if he fails so to do: *Ministry of Housing and Local Government* v. *Sharp* [1969] 3 W.L.R. 1020. If the clerk procures another officer of the local authority to carry out the search then that officer is liable in damages in the event of causal negligence and the local authority is accordingly vicariously liable. Articles: " Incorrect Land Charge Search Certificate: Liability in Negligence," 119 New L.J. 550; " Negligence—Counting the Cost " (Cretney), 119 New L.J. 544.
90 *Griffiths* v. *Evans* [1953] 1 W.L.R. 1424.

in cases where his is liable as an officer of the court.[91] On this point, Lord Campbell said: " I never had any doubt of the unsoundness of the doctrine . . . that A, employing B, a professional lawyer, to do any act for the benefit of C, A having to pay B, and there being no intercourse of any sort between B and C—if, through the gross negligence or ignorance of B in transacting the business, C loses the benefit intended for him by A, C may maintain an action against B, and recover damages for the loss sustained. If this were law, a disappointed legatee might sue the solicitor employed by a testator to make a will in favour of a stranger, whom the solicitor never saw or before heard of, if the will were void for not being properly signed and attested." [92] Where a law agent in Scotland was instructed by his client to prepare the necessary document to give a security over the client's property in favour of a third party and negligently omitted to complete it so that the third party suffered loss, it was held that the law agent was under no liability to the third party.[92]

An answer to a casual inquiry made by a person not a client will probably not impose any liability on the solicitor. So, where a portion of the wages of a workman was paid to a trustee to be held on certain trusts, and the workman asked the employer's attorney whether, on his leaving his employment, he was entitled to the trust money, it was held the mistake of the attorney in wrongly answering the question in the affirmative so that the workman gave notice and failed to get the trust money, imposed no liability on the attorney towards the workman.[93] But in view of the decision in *Hedley Byrne & Co. Ltd.* v. *Heller & Partners Ltd.*[94] a solicitor who gives upon request any advice or material information negligently, whether gratuitously or not, to a non-client then if he has reason to believe that such is going to be acted upon, in the absence of a clear disclaimer of responsibility, he may well be liable should loss or damage be suffered as a result by the non-client.

312 **Standard of care.** The standard of care and skill which can be demanded from a solicitor is that of a reasonably competent and diligent solicitor. Lord Ellenborough has said: " An attorney is only liable for *crassa negligentia.*" [95] Again, Lord Campbell in discussing the essential elements to sustain an action for negligence has said: " What is necessary to maintain such an action? Most undoubtedly that the professional adviser should be guilty of some misconduct, some fraudulent proceeding, or should be chargeable with gross negligence or with gross ignorance. It is only upon one or other of those grounds that the client can maintain an action against the professional adviser." [96] This, however, does not

[91] *Batten* v. *Wedgwood Coal and Iron Co.* (1886) 31 Ch.D. 346; *Re Dangar's Trusts* (1889) 41 Ch.D. 178.
[92] *Robertson* v. *Fleming* (1861) 4 Macq. 167.
[93] *Fish* v. *Kelly* (1864) 17 C.B.(N.S.) 194, approved by the H.L. in *Hedley Byrne & Co. Ltd.* v. *Heller & Partners Ltd.* [1964] A.C. 465.
[94] *Supra.*
[95] *Baikie* v. *Chandless* (1811) 3 Camp. 17, 20.
[96] *Purves* v. *Landell* (1845) 12 Cl. & F. 91, 102. Lords Brougham and Lyndhurst expressed similar opinions.

mean that the standard of care imposed upon a solicitor is below that imposed on other professional men; it only means that it is not enough to prove that the solicitor has made an error of judgment or shown ignorance of some particular part of the law, but that it must be shown that the error or ignorance was such that an ordinarily competent solicitor would not have made or shown it. " It would be extremely difficult to define the exact limit by which the skill and diligence which a solicitor undertakes to furnish in the conduct of a case is bounded, or to trace precisely the dividing line between that reasonable skill and diligence which appears to satisfy his undertaking, and that *crassa negligentia*, or *lata culpa* mentioned in some of the cases, for which he is undoubtedly responsible. It is a question of degree and there is a borderland within which it is difficult to say whether a breach of duty has or has not been committed." [97]

313 **Ignorance of law.** It may be negligence on the part of a solicitor to be ignorant of the law applicable to the case, but, in the words of Abbott C.J.: " No attorney is bound to know all the law; God forbid that it should be imagined that an attorney, or a counsel, or even a judge is bound to know all the law; or that an attorney is to lose his fair recompense on account of an error, being such an error as a cautious man might fall into." [98] His general duty in this respect is summed up by Tindal C.J.: " He is liable for the consequences of ignorance or non-observance of the rules of practice of this court; for the want of care in the preparation of the cause for trial; or of attendance thereon with his witnesses; and for the mismanagement of so much of the conduct of a cause as is usually and ordinarily allotted to his department of the profession. Whilst, on the other hand, he is not answerable for error in judgment upon points of new occurrence, or of nice or doubtful construction, or of such as are usually entrusted to men in the higher branch of the profession of the law." [99]

Although a solicitor is not bound to know the contents of every statute of the realm, there are some statutes which it is his duty to know. The test for deciding what he ought to know is to apply the standard of knowledge of a reasonably competent solicitor. He is bound to know the statutes of limitation, and if he finds that the time of limitation is so near its end as to be likely to bar his client's right of action, he must warn his client of the position. Where a solicitor, instructed by a client to bring an action for personal injuries against a local authority, omitted to do so within the time limited by the Public Authorities Protection Act 1893,[1] it was held that he was liable for negligence and bound to pay to his client the amount the client would have recovered from the local authority.[2]

[97] Scrutton L.J. in *Fletcher & Son* v. *Jubb Booth & Helliwell* [1920] 1 K.B. 275, 281, following Tindal C.J. in *Godefroy* v. *Dalton* (1830) 6 Bing. 460. See also *Parker* v. *Rolls* (1854) 14 C.B. 691.

[98] *Montriou* v. *Jefferys* (1825) 2 C. & P. 113.

[99] *Godefroy* v. *Dalton, supra.*

[1] Now repealed by the Law Reform (Limitation of Actions, etc.) Act 1954.

[2] *Fletcher & Son* v. *Jubb Booth & Helliwell* [1920] 1 K.B. 275; *cf. Yardley* v. *Coombes* (1963) 107 S.J. 575.

If a solicitor is in fact ignorant of the law on a point, he should take steps to inform himself of it.[3] If he considers the point to be difficult or doubtful he should inform his client of this and take his instructions on whether or not counsel's opinion should be taken. If the client refuses to take counsel's opinion, the solicitor is only liable " where the law would presume him to have the knowledge himself." [4] If he takes upon himself to advise on a difficult or doubtful point without warning the client of the difficulty and suggesting that counsel's opinion should be taken, he is negligent.[5]

314 **Effect of taking counsel's opinion.** If counsel's opinion is taken and acted upon by the solicitor, he is under no liability for negligence.[6] To obtain this protection, however, he must lay all relevant facts before counsel,[7] included among which are all private Acts of Parliament and statutory regulations known by the solicitor to be likely to be relevant.[8]

315 **Duty in contentious matters.** In contentious matters, it is the duty of a solicitor on taking his client's instructions to ascertain the relevant facts so as to enable him to form an opinion as to whether or not there is a right of action.[9] If he comes to the conclusion that there is no cause of action he should so advise his client,[10] but if, notwithstanding that advice, he is instructed to proceed with the action he is under no liability for negligence.[11] He must communicate to his client any offer of compromise made by the other party, and not reject it without first taking instructions.[12]

A solicitor has an implied authority to settle an action on behalf of his client. If, however, the compromise was made against the client's express instructions he will be liable to an action for damages for breach of duty, even though he compromised on the advice of counsel.[13] " It is within the scope of a solicitor's authority to compromise and if he uses all due diligence and acts bona fide and reasonably no action will lie against him; but if he has been expressly forbidden to compromise, and

[3] *Parker* v. *Rolls* (1854) 14 C.B. 691.

[4] *Per* Tindal C.J. in *Godefroy* v. *Dalton, supra.* Tindal C.J. suggests that in matters which the law presumes a solicitor to know, he cannot protect himself " by consulting another." If, however, he takes counsel's opinion even upon a point which he is presumed to know himself, he is protected if he acts on the opinion.

[5] *Richards* v. *Cox* [1943] K.B. 139 (advising on the construction of an insurance policy without counsel's opinion—liable for negligence).

[6] *Potts* v. *Sparrow* (1834) 6 C. & P. 749; *Kemp* v. *Burt* (1833) 4 B. & Ad. 424; *Andrews* v. *Hawley* (1857) 26 L.J.Ex. 323; *Re Clark* (1851) 1 De G.M. & G. 43, 49. See also *Francis* v. *Francis & Dickinson* [1956] P. 87, 96, *per* Sachs J.: " As a general rule a solicitor acting on the advice of properly instructed counsel can hardly be said to be acting unreasonably, save perhaps in a very exceptional set of circumstances."

[7] *Ireson* v. *Pearman* (1825) 3 B. & C. 799.

[8] *Glebe Sugar Refining Co.* v. *Greenock Harbour Trustees* (1921) 37 T.L.R. 436.

[9] *Gill* v. *Lougher* (1830) 1 Cr. & J. 170; *Long* v. *Orsi* (1856) 18 C.B. 610; *Thwaites* v. *Mackerson* (1828) 3 C. & P. 341; *Ottley* v. *Gilby* (1845) 8 Beav. 602; *Lawrence* v. *Potts* (1834) 6 C. & P. 428.

[10] *Jacks* v. *Bell* (1828) 3 C. & P. 316.

[11] *Re Clark* (1851) 1 De G.M. & G. 43.

[12] *Sill* v. *Thomas* (1839) 8 C. & P. 762.

[13] *Fray* v. *Voules* (1859) 1 E. & E. 839.

he does compromise, then, however beneficial that compromise may be, an action will lie against him for disregarding that express negative direction." [14] If a solicitor advises his client not to defend an action brought against him, his liability depends on the same principles.[15]

A solicitor is negligent if, in a collision case, he delivers a defence admitting negligent driving by his client without first obtaining his client's instructions or consent to the admission. Where an action for personal injuries sustained in a motor accident was brought against the client, who put his defence into the hands of his insurance company, who in turn instructed a solicitor, it was held that the solicitor must act in the interests of the client and not subordinate the client's interests to those of the insurance company, with the result that when the solicitor delivered a defence admitting negligent driving on the part of the client —which defence was delivered to give effect to a pooling arrangement among insurance companies and with the object of saving the insurance company money—the solicitor was held to be negligent because he had not first obtained his client's consent to the admission.[16]

316 A solicitor has been held liable in negligence for: proceeding under a wrong section of a statute [17]; deliberately allowing time to run out, without getting any instructions, so that an action for damages became statute-barred [18]; bringing an action in a court which has no jurisdiction [19]; bringing an action, which might have been taken in the county court, in a superior court without first warning his client of the possible consequences as to costs [20]; not informing his client, the assignee of an insolvent debtor, that he was personally liable for the costs of an action unless he obtained the consent of the creditors to bring the action [21]; not warning his client that unusual expense might have to be borne by the client himself whatever the result of the action [22]; being instructed to defend an action, allowing judgment to go by default of defence [23]; failing to watch the court list, so that his client was unrepresented at the hearing [24]; where counsel was necessary, failing to instruct counsel [25]; failing to see that the witnesses were at hand when they were required at the trial [26]; failing to take proofs of the witnesses before the

14 Farwell J. in *Re Newen* [1903] 1 Ch. 812.
15 *Hill* v. *Finney* (1865) 4 F. & F. 616.
16 *Groom* v. *Crocker* [1939] 1 K.B. 194.
17 *Hart* v. *Frame* (1839) 6 Cl. & F. 193.
18 *Kitchen* v. *Royal Air Force Association* [1958] 1 W.L.R. 563.
19 *Williams* v. *Gibbs* (1836) 5 A. & E. 208; *Cox* v. *Leech* (1857) 1 C.B.(N.S.) 617.
20 *Lee* v. *Dixon* (1863) 3 F. & F. 744. In *Barker* v. *Fleetwood Improvement Comrs.* (1890) 62 L.T. 833, there was held to be no negligence in bringing an action, which might have been brought in the county court, in the Lancaster Palatine Court.
21 *Allison* v. *Rayner* (1827) 7 B. & C. 441.
22 *Re Blyth and Fanshawe* (1882) 10 Q.B.D. 207; *Re Roney & Co.* [1914] 2 K.B. 529. In these cases the solicitor was disallowed the items on taxation as between solicitor and client.
23 *Godefroy* v. *Jay* (1831) 7 Bing. 413.
24 *Burgoine* v. *Taylor* (1878) 9 Ch.D. 1.
25 *R.* v. *Tew* (1752) Say. 50; *De Roufigny* v. *Peale* (1811) 3 Taunt. 484; *Hawkins* v. *Harwood* (1849) 4 Ex. 503; *Townley* v. *Jones* (1860) 8 C.B.(N.S.) 289.
26 *Reece* v. *Rigby* (1821) 4 B. & Ald. 202; *Price* v. *Bullen* (1825) 3 L.J.(O.S.) K.B. 39; *Hawkins* v. *Harwood, supra.*

trial [27]; where his personal attendance was necessary, failing to attend at the hearing [28]; when, acting for the purchaser of property, he has made no inquiry as to the standard rent [29]; mistake in the examination of a witness under the Old Chancery practice [30]; mistake in drawing up a decree [31]; failing to deliver a pleading [32]; failing to take steps to set aside an irregular order [33]; failing to take reasonable steps to ascertain the truth of a statement made to the court, whereby a wrong order was made [34]; neglecting to attend a summons whereby the master was unable to proceed with an order of reference [35]; failing to issue execution [36]; failing to register a *lis pendens* [37]; bringing an appeal for his own purposes and not in the interests of his client [38]; failing to make an application for review on behalf of an injured infant workman within six months of his attaining twenty-one [39]; when on being instructed to draft wills for two clients, man and woman, wishing to confer benefits on each other, and being told that they were likely to marry each other at some indefinite future time, he failed to warn them that marriage would revoke the wills [40]; allowing a client's action to be dismissed for want of prosecution due to the inexcusable delay in bringing the action to trial [41]; failing to ascertain his client's current address, so that she was not informed of the hearing of her husband's divorce petition, which she desired to defend [42]; allowing a client's husband's divorce suit to go undefended so that she lost her right to an award of maintenance for herself and maintenance for her child [43]; advising a client to enter into a collusive bargain in contemplation of divorce proceedings and failing to file an

27 *Manley* v. *Palache* (1895) 73 L.T. 98.

28 *Swannell* v. *Ellis* (1823) 1 Bing. 347; *Nash* v. *Swinburne* (1841) 3 M. & G. 630.

29 *Goody* v. *Baring* [1956] 1 W.L.R. 448. " It is still the duty of a purchaser's solicitor to make the appropriate requisitions and inquiries after the formal contract is signed, even if the preliminary inquiries have been so complete that it is only necessary to ask whether the answers thus received are still complete and accurate " (p. 456).

30 *Stokes* v. *Trumper* (1855) 2 K. & J. 232.

31 *Re Bolton* (1846) 9 Beav. 272.

32 *Re Massey and Carey* (1884) 26 Ch.D. 459.

33 *Frankland* v. *Cole* (1832) 2 Cr. & J. 590.

34 *Re Spencer* (1870) 39 L.J.Ch. 841.

35 *Ridley* v. *Tiplady* (1855) 20 Beav. 44.

36 *Harrington* v. *Binns* (1863) 3 F. & F. 942.

37 *Plant* v. *Pearman* (1872) 41 L.J.Q.B. 169.

38 *Harbin* v. *Masterman* [1896] 1 Ch. 351.

39 *Ashton* v. *Philip Conway Thomas & Co.* (1939) 32 B.W.C.C. 246.

40 *Hall* v. *Meyrick* [1957] 2 Q.B. 455. This case was reversed in the Court of Appeal (also reported [1957] 2 Q.B. 458 on the ground that an amendment of the statement of claim had been improperly allowed setting up a cause of action which was statute barred at the issue of the writ. On the merits, Hodson L.J. (with whom the other members of the court agreed) said (at p. 475): " I would not for one moment suppose that it was the duty of a solicitor in all cases to draw the attention of persons who come into his office to make wills to the effect of marriage on a will." Ormerod L.J. added (p. 482): " I have no doubt it would be the clear duty of a solicitor on being instructed to prepare a will, to advise his client of the effect of subsequent marriage on the will if, in fact, the client told him that he was intending to get married in the near future, or even, perhaps, if the client's intention came to the knowledge of the solicitor in a less direct way."

41 *Fitzpatrick* v. *Batger & Co. Ltd.* [1967] 1 W.L.R. 706; *Welburn* v. *Mayberry* (1971) 115 S.J. 468.

42 *D.* v. *D.* [1963] 1 W.L.R. 194.

43 *Cook* v. *Swinfen* [1967] 1 W.L.R. 457 (affirming Lawton J.'s decision on this point [1966] 1 W.L.R. 635).

Answer both of which resulted in financial loss to the client [44]; An agreement that a solicitor shall not be liable for negligence in respect of any contentious business is void.[45]

317 Where actions were dismissed for want of prosecution brought about by the laches of their solicitors, clients can claim damages against their solicitors for being deprived thereby of their causes of action.[46] An action may be dismissed for want of prosecution even although the plaintiff may not have a good claim in negligence against the Trade Union's solicitors, with whom he had no contractual relationship, who did as they were instructed. In such a case it is not the function of the court to attribute or apportion blame but simply to ask: " Was the delay inexcusable? " [47]

Where in proceedings costs are incurred improperly or without reasonable cause or are wasted by undue delay or by any other misconduct or default, the court may make an order under R.S.C., Ord. 62, r. 8 against any solicitor whom it considers to be responsible, requiring *inter alia* that the solicitor personally should indemnify such other parties against costs payable by them. Such an order was made in *Jakeman* v. *Jakeman and Turn* [48] where the co-respondent's solicitor negligently failed in his duties to represent his client, which caused a retrial to the issue of damages to be ordered, thus adding to the costs of the cause.

318 **Liability in acting as an advocate.** In *Rondel* v. *Worsley* [49] opinions were expressed by Lords Reid, Morris of Borth-y-Gest, Pearce and Upjohn that a solicitor ought to be given the same immunity in litigious work, which would have been done by a barrister had he been engaged, as the barrister would have had. See generally § 270, *ante*.

319 **Duty in non-contentious matters.** In non-contentious matters,[50] the duty of a solicitor depends on the nature of the transaction which he is carrying out on behalf of his client. The general standard of care and skill is as stated above, but for a more detailed statement of a solicitor's duty reference must be made to works dealing with vendor and purchaser, conveyancing or other the particular business for which the solicitor is engaged. A solicitor has been held negligent for: Not explaining to his client the documents which he is being asked to execute and the consequences to him of executing them [51]; when acting for a purchaser of property, not warning him that he was obtaining only a

[44] *Bryant* v. *Goodrich* (1966) 110 S.J. 108.
[45] Solicitors Act 1957, s. 60 (4).
[46] *Allen* v. *Sir Alfred McAlpine & Sons Ltd.* [1968] 2 Q.B. 229; *Reggentin* v. *Beecholme Bakeries Ltd.* [1968] 2 Q.B. 276.
[47] *Rowe* v. *Tregaskes* [1968] 1 W.L.R. 1475.
[48] [1964] P. 420.
[49] [1969] 1 A.C. 191 at pp. 232, 244, 267, 284.
[50] See Articles: " Leases—the duty of care " (Cretney), 119 New L.J. 454; " Negligence and covenants restrictive of user " (Stratton), 113 S.J. 807; " Solicitors duty to warn client," 113 S.J. 785. " Negligence: a Solicitor's Liability," 100 I.L.T. 441.
[51] *Stannard* v. *Ullithorne* (1834) 10 Bing. 491.

possessory title to the land [52]; not explaining the nature and terms of a composition deed to his client [53]; not making the usual searches [54]; not calling for the last receipt for rent when advising the purchaser of farming produce which was to be left on the ground [55]; failing to give notice of new trustees of a reversionary interest to the trustees of the settlement fund [56]; failing to give a notice so as to secure priority for his client [57]; failing to inform his clients that a club, which they had formed, had been refused registration by the magistrate's clerk [58]; failing to inform his client that a local search showed that plans of the building erected on land his client had agreed to buy had not been approved by the local authority [59]; advising his client that his interest in real estate was an absolute one, whereas in reality it was entailed, with the result that no disentailing assurance was executed and, on the client's death the property did not form part of his estate [60]; when acting for the purchaser of property, failing to discover that the vendor's title was defective because being one trustee of his father's will the vendor had bought from the trustees [61]; allowing his client, a prospective purchaser, to gain possession and spend money on repairs pending execution of the contract when the vendor thereafter changed his mind and decided not to proceed with the sale [62]; where he was acting for both parties, his failure to take proper instructions from one party [63]; failing to explain to his client, who was considering taking a lease, the meaning of any clause in the proposed lease, which he knew or ought to have realised his client did not fully understand,[64] failing in duty to inform clients that contracts had been exchanged.[64a]

When a solicitor is acting for a client who is lending money on security, it is his duty to see that the necessary legal steps are taken to make the security proper and sufficient in point of form; for example, that there is no prior incumbrance of which his client was not aware when he entered into the transaction [65]; but he is not liable for any inadequacy in the value of the security,[66] unless he is instructed to advise his client on the value of his security and does so advise him.[67] He is,

52 *Allen* v. *Clark* (1863) 7 L.T. 781.

53 *Watts* v. *Hyde* (1846) 2 Coll. 368.

54 *Cooper* v. *Stephenson* (1852) 21 L.J.Q.B. 292.

55 *Waine* v. *Kempster* (1859) 1 F. & F. 695.

56 *Bean* v. *Wade* (1885) 2 T.L.R. 157.

57 *Stevenson* v. *Rowand* (1830) 2 Dow & Cl. 104; *Donaldson* v. *Haldane* (1840) 7 Cl. & Fin. 762.

58 *Ashton* v. *Wainwright* [1936] 1 All E.R. 805.

59 *Lake* v. *Bushby* [1949] 2 All E.R. 964.

60 *Otter* v. *Church, Adams, Tatham & Co.* [1953] Ch. 280.

61 *Pilkington* v. *Wood* [1953] Ch. 770 (negligence was admitted).

62 *Attard* v. *Samson* (1966) 110 S.J. 249.

63 *Treloar* v. *Henderson* [1968] N.Z.L.R. 1085.

64 *Sykes* v. *Midland Bank Executor and Trustee Co. Ltd.* [1969] 2 Q.B. 518 (reversed on the question of damages [1971] 1 Q.B. 113).

64a *Stinchcombe & Cooper* v. *Addison, Cooper, Jesson & Co.* (1971) 115 S.J. 368.

65 *Whiteman* v. *Hawkins* (1878) 4 C.P.D. 13.

66 *Brinsden* v. *Williams* [1894] 3 Ch. 185; *Scholes* v. *Brook* (1891) 63 L.T. 837, affd. 64 L.T. 674; *Howell* v. *Young* (1826) 5 B. & C. 259; *Stewart* v. *M'Lean*, 1915 S.C. 13. A solicitor advising trustees should advise them as to the rule of the court about the margin of safety between the value of the property and any sum lent on mortgage. *Stokes* v. *Prance* [1898] 1 Ch. 212.

67 *Rae* v. *Meek* (1889) 14 App.Cas. 558; *Morgan* v. *Blyth* [1891] 1 Ch. 337.

however, liable if he advises his client about the value of the security without making full disclosure of all material facts known to him when he gives his advice. When a solicitor advised his client to release a security mortgaged to him, representing that his client's sub-mortgagee had agreed to release it but not pointing out the difference between the position of his client and that of the sub-mortgagee if the security were released, he was held to be negligent.[68] Where a solicitor failed to tell the plaintiff widow, his client, about the borrower's untrustworthiness relating to money matters, which was known to him and which made the plaintiff's loan unwise, it was held that the plaintiff had been negligent for it was his duty either to advise the plaintiff of the material facts or, if he felt this would be in breach of professional confidence, to advise her to consult another solicitor.[69] Where a solicitor allowed his client to sign the contract to purchase a house, when the application for a mortgage was still outstanding, after warning him of the risk that he might lose his deposit, he was held not to be liable since his duty was sufficiently discharged by giving his client the warning of the risk which he then incurred.[70]

320 It was held that there was no negligence: When a solicitor, employed by the managing partner of a business firm to defend an action against the firm, kept the partner by whom he was employed informed of the progress of the action but did not inform the other partners [71]; when his client, the wife of a licensed victualler, had lent money to her husband for the purpose of his business, and the solicitor did not advise the registration of a bill of sale or the necessity of the transfer of the licence to the wife [72]; when instructed by an intending mortgagee who had instructed valuers to value the proposed security, omitting to call his client's attention to the fact that the value assessed by the valuers was considerably more than the price last paid for the property, although the solicitor had called the valuer's attention to this [73]; when the owner of land, having contracted to sell the land to X, rescinded the contract, wrongfully as the court subsequently held, and sold to Y, advising Y that he could safely complete [74]; when acting for a vendor of land, answering a requisition made by the purchaser in accordance with general conveyancing practice, although as a result of the answer the purchaser was enabled to refuse to complete and recover his deposit.[75]

321 A solicitor is under a duty to take reasonable care of all documents entrusted to him by his client and not to disclose confidential information

68 *Nocton* v. *Ashburton* [1914] A.C. 932.
69 *Neushul* v. *Mellish and Harkavy* (1967) 111 S.J. 399.
70 *Buckland* v. *Mackesy* (1968) 112 S.J. 841.
71 *Tomlinson* v. *Broadsmith* [1896] 1 Q.B. 386.
72 *Faithfull* v. *Kesteven* (1910) 103 L.T. 56.
73 *Scholes* v. *Brook* (1891) 63 L.T. 837 (the appeal, 64 L.T. 674, only deals with the valuers' liability).
74 *Bell* v. *Strathern & Blair* (1954) 104 L.J. 618.
75 *Simmons* v. *Pennington & Son* [1955] 1 W.L.R. 183.

communicated to him. For breach of this duty he will be liable for any damage suffered by his client resulting from the breach.[76]

322 **No duty to advise on business matters.** A solicitor is under a duty to advise his client on law but not, unless he expressly undertakes to do so, on matters of business. He is under no duty to remind his client of the approach of the date for giving notice to determine a lease.[77]

323 **Measure of damages.** The duty being in contract, damages are limited to the pecuniary loss sustained and do not include general damages for injury to the client's general reputation and feelings.[78]

When the negligence consisted in advising a landowner that he had an absolute title when he had only an entailed interest, the measure of damages was the loss to the estate suffered by the passing of the property to the next tenant in tail.[79] When the negligence was failing to detect a flaw in the title of the vendor of land, the measure of damages was the difference between the market value of the land, at the date of the breach of contract, with a good title and its market value at that date with a defective title.[80] The client was held to be under no duty to mitigate the damages by suing the vendor on his covenant for title "in order to protect his solicitor from his own carelessness." Special damage in respect of the cost of the valuation of the property required by the client's bankers at the time of the purchase and interest on the overdraft which remained because the client could not sell the property were not allowed because they were not reasonably within the contemplation of the parties at the date of the breach. When the negligence consisted of not serving a notice to quit, so that the client was unable to get possession of his house, there were allowed as damages the cost to the client of storing his furniture, garage expenses and general damages for the inconvenience and discomfort he had suffered, but no damages in respect of the annoyance and mental distress he had suffered.[81]

324 Where a solicitor failed to prosecute in time his client's claim for damages for personal injuries alleging the employer's negligence, so that the claim became statute barred, Edmund Davies J. held that the client's claim would have had a reasonable chance of success, in which event he might have expected an award of £3,000. However, allowing for all contingencies, for the deprivation of the right of action against his employers, the court was only prepared to award £1,000.[82] In *Piper* v.

[76] *Weld-Blundell* v. *Stephens* [1920] A.C. 956 (action against an accountant for negligently communicating confidential instructions).

[77] *Yager* v. *Fishman & Co.* [1944] 1 All E.R. 552.

[78] *Groom* v. *Crocker* [1939] 1 K.B. 194 (solicitor, in breach of duty, admits negligence of client in a collision action, but the damages are paid by the client's insurers— judgment for £1,000 reduced to 40s.).

[79] *Otter* v. *Church, Adams, Tatham & Co.* [1953] Ch. 280.

[80] *Pilkington* v. *Wood* [1953] Ch. 770.

[81] *Bailey* v. *Bullock* [1950] 2 All E.R. 1167.

[82] *Yardley* v. *Coombes* (1963) 107 S.J. 575. See also a very similar decision by the Court of Session in *Yeoman's Executrix* v. *Ferries*, 1967 S.L.T. 332. In another case McNair J.

Daybell Court-Cooper & Co.[83] Nield J. held that, where a solicitor failed to inform his client, who was purchasing a house, that there was a right of way over the premises in favour of a neighbour, in addition to special damages the client was entitled to general damages under the two-fold principle laid down in *Hadley* v. *Baxendale*.[84] As well as the damages, which he would have recovered had his action been timeously tried, a plaintiff is entitled to compensation for his worsening nervous condition over the previous intervening years caused by the defendant solicitor's subsequent acts of negligence, since their obligation was a continuing one.[85] Where delay in failing to prosecute a client's claim for personal injuries caused the latter's condition to worsen it was held that the damages must be assessed without reference to such deterioration, the value of such deterioration being the solicitors' responsibility to discharge.[86] The measure of damages for negligently advising a client that land he buys is free from a restriction, to which it is subject, is the difference between the market value of the land and the price paid and is not the difference between its market values subject to and free from the restrictions.[87] Where no special damage has been proved a nominal amount of forty shillings would normally be awarded but since the parties had agreed that on such a finding the damages should be nil the court would not award any figure at all, hence the action had to fail. Where a solicitor, who represented a prisoner charged with the crime of robbery, failed to trace and to have available a witness to support an alibi, the accused, after his conviction, proved the solicitor to have been in technical breach of his duty to his client and was awarded £2 nominal damages.[88]

17.—STOCKBROKERS

325 **Liability of stockbrokers.** Stockbrokers are liable for failing to use that skill and diligence which a reasonably competent and careful stockbroker would exercise. Where a customer instructed his stockbroker to sell shares at a time when there was a market for them and the latter failed to do so, despite further instructions by the customer to sell at a time when he knew of the broker's failure, the broker was held liable. The Alberta Supreme Court held by a majority that the measure of damages was the named price of the shares less commission and taxes, the broker keeping the shares, which he had not been able to sell.[89]

There can be no room for doubt that, since the decision in *Hedley Byrne & Co. Ltd.* v. *Heller & Partners Ltd.*[90] if a stockbroker gratuitously

assessed the value of the loss of the right of action against the employers to be three quarters of the damages likely to be awarded, but added 12 per cent. interest for the delay which had resulted: *Gregory* v. *Tarlo* (1964) 108 S.J. 219.

[83] (1969) 210 E.G. 1047.

[84] (1854) 9 Ex. 341.

[85] *Malyon* v. *Lawrence Messer & Co.* (1968) 112 S.J. 623.

[86] *Wales* v. *Wales* (1967) 111 S.J. 946.

[87] *Ford* v. *White* [1964] 1 W.L.R. 885.

[88] *Scudder* v. *Prothero and Prothero* (1966) 110 S.J. 248. This decision was doubted by the House of Lords in *Rondel* v. *Worsley* [1969] 1 A.C. 191, *per* Lord Reid at p. 231. See also § 270, *ante*.

[89] *Pankhurst* v. *Gairdner & Co.* (1960) 25 D.L.R. (2d) 515.

[90] [1964] A.C. 465.

but negligently gives any advice or material information on request to a person then, if he has reason to believe that such is going to be acted upon, in the absence of a clear disclaimer of responsibility, he may well be liable should loss or damage be suffered as a result of such negligence.

18.—VALUERS AND ESTATE AGENTS

326 Valuers must exercise the standard of care and skill possessed by a competent valuer. Their duty, as in all cases, depends on the nature of their engagement. When valuers were instructed to advise whether a licensed hotel should be sold and whether brewery companies should be approached and, the hotel being the only free house in Melton Mowbray, they advised against an approach to brewery companies, so that it was sold privately and, within seven days, re-sold at a profit to a brewery company, the valuers were held to be negligent.[91]

327 Valuers are liable to their clients for negligence in making a valuation, but are not liable to third parties who rely on their valuation,[92] unless they knew or had reason to believe that such, if given negligently was going to be relied and acted upon by them. In that event in the absence of any clear disclaimer of responsibility they will be liable should any resulting loss or damage be suffered by third parties. Thus in *Cann* v. *Willson*[93] an intending mortgagor applied to a firm of valuers for a valuation of his property following a request from an intending mortgagee's solicitors; the solicitors upon receipt of the valuers' valuation particularly called the valuers' attention to the purpose for which the valuation was wanted and to the responsibility they were undertaking. The valuers affirmed their valuation, which was communicated to the intending mortgagee, who then advanced money to the owner on the security of a mortgage of his property. In due course the owner defaulted in payment and the property proved insufficient to answer the mortgage. Chitty J. held the valuers liable on the basis that they having sent a document called a valuation for the purpose of inducing the mortgagee to advance money and, having placed themselves in that special position, in point of law incurred a duty towards the mortgagee to use reasonable care in the preparation of such document. He likened the case to *George* v. *Skivington*,[94] and continued: " In this

[91] *Bell Hotels* (1935) *Ltd.* v. *Motion* [1952] C.P.L. 403.

[92] *Le Lievre* v. *Gould* [1893] 1 Q.B. 491; *Love* v. *Mack* (1905) 93 L.T. 352; *Old Gate Estates* v. *Toplis* [1939] 3 All E.R. 209. However the decision in *Le Lievre* v. *Gould* has been disapproved by the House of Lords in *Hedley Byrne & Co. Ltd.* v. *Heller & Partners Ltd.* [1964] A.C. 465. At p. 506 Lord Hodson said: " It was thought by Wrottesley J. in *Old Gate Estates Ltd.* v. *Toplis and Harding and Russell*, that he was precluded from awarding damages in tort for a negligent valuation made by a firm of valuers which knew it was to be used by the plaintiffs since the doctrine of *Donoghue* v. *Stevenson* was confined to negligence which results in danger to life, limb or health. I do not think that this is the true view of *Donoghue* v. *Stevenson* but the decision itself, although its effect has been extended to cases where there was no expectation as contrasted with opportunity of inspection (see *Grant* v. *Australian Knitting Mills Ltd.*) and to liability of repairers (see *Haseldine* v. *C. A. Daw & Son Ltd.*) has never been applied to cases where damages are claimed in tort for negligent statements producing damage."

[93] (1888) 39 Ch.D. 39, which had wrongly been overruled by the Court of Appeal in *Le Lievre* v. *Gould, supra*, has now been specifically approved by the House of Lords in *Hedley Byrne & Co. Ltd.* v. *Heller & Partners Ltd.* [1964] A.C. 465.

[94] (1869) L.R. 5 Ex. 1.

case the document supplied appears to me to stand upon a similar footing and not to be distinguished from that case as if it had been an actual article that had been handed over for the particular purpose of being so used. I think, therefore, that the Defendants stood with regard to the Plaintiff—quite apart from any question of there being a contract or not in the peculiar circumstances of this case—in the position of being under an obligation or duty towards him." [95] Valuers may be interrogated as to the basis of their valuation.[96] When making a valuation of property they must use competent care in ascertaining the date on which the valuation should be made, but are under no obligation to inquire into the financial position of the person to whom money will be advanced upon their valuation or into the title of the property.[97] They must have a knowledge of the general rules of law applicable to the subject of their valuation.[98] The measure of damages for negligently valuing property for a mortgagee has been held to be the total of (a) the difference between the sum advanced and the proceeds of sale; (b) the amount of interest which the mortgagor failed to pay; (c) cost of insurance and repair while the mortgagee was in possession; (d) expenses of abortive attempts to sell and the agent's commission when a sale was made, and (e) legal charges of possession and sale.[99] The measure of damages for negligently valuing a house and farm is the difference between the value of the house and farm in the condition described in the report and their value as they should have been described.[1]

19.—VETERINARY SURGEONS AND PRACTITIONERS

328 **Nature of duty.** The civil liability of veterinary surgeons towards the owners of animals is similar in all respects to that of medical men towards their patients, and they are liable for any damage caused by their negligence.[2] Additionally, a veterinary practitioner impliedly warrants any drugs or substances he uses as being reasonably fit for the purpose for which it is required, namely for administration to animals. Thus in *Dodd and Dodd* v. *Wilson and McWilliam* [3] the plaintiffs, who were farmers and cattle breeders consulted the defendant, a veterinary surgeon, for advice concerning the use of a serum called corynebacterium toxoid, a preparation which purported to be a preventative of summer mastitis among cattle. The defendant admitted that he had administered the toxoid to other herds and had obtained reasonably good results and, although he would not guarantee that the toxoid would prevent or cure the disease, it could do no harm. As a result, the defendant was asked

95 *Ibid.* p. 43.
96 *Turner* v. *Goulden* (1873) L.R. 9 C.P. 57.
97 *Beck* v. *Smirke* (1894) Hudson's B.C., 4th ed., Vol. 2, p. 259.
98 *Jenkins* v. *Betham* (1855) 15 C.B. 168.
99 *Baxter* v. *Gapp & Co.* [1939] 2 K.B. 271. When the property was not sold, the damages were based on what the mortgagees would have got had they realised their security: *Eagle Star Insce. Co.* v. *Gale & Power* (1955) 105 L.J. 458.
1 *Philips* v. *Ward* [1956] 1 All E.R. 874.
2 See § 272, *ante*.
3 [1946] 2 All E.R. 691.

to carry out the necessary inoculations of the plaintiffs' cattle, but many of the beasts became seriously sick because there was something defective with the serum used. It was held, *inter alia,* that there was an implied condition in the contract entered into between the plaintiffs and the defendant that the toxoid to be used for the inoculation would be reasonably fit for the purpose for which it was required but that condition had not been fulfilled. Nevertheless since there had been a breach of the implied condition of fitness under the Sale of Goods Act 1893, s. 14, the defendant might have recourse against the suppliers, the third party, and the third party against the manufacturers, the fourth party, for the damages awarded.

329 In *Chute Farms Ltd.* v. *Curtis* [4] the defendant, a veterinary surgeon, had been brought in by the plaintiffs to treat their thoroughbred yearling colt, valued at £5,000, which had become lame, although its treatment was placed in the hands of his assistant who merely applied a poultice to its injured leg and the colt died soon afterwards. It was held that the defendant was vicariously liable for his assistant's negligence in failing to use reasonable care and skill in the treatment prescribed. Elwes J. considered that there could be no doubt that a competent veterinary surgeon called in to a horse with an injured foot, through which tetanus corpuscles could enter, would without fail inject with anti-tetanus serum, since experience had shown that a prophylactic dose, administered in time, was successful in the vast majority of such cases.

[4] *The Times*, October 10, 1961.

CHAPTER 8

DANGEROUS PREMISES

1.—THE PREMISES

330 **Generally.** The premises to which the following principles apply, where a duty is owed, are not restricted to buildings, houses and other real property, but include objects upon the land as well, which the visitor to the premises has been invited or permitted to use. Illustrations are to be found in such things as grandstands,[1] electricity pylons,[2] and diving-boards at swimming pools.[3] Further, the duty is not confined, either, to fixed premises but extends to all movable structures and conveyances in or on which human beings are invited and permitted to entrust their safety. Accordingly, it includes any aircraft, railway carriages,[4] road carriages,[5] lorries,[6] trucks,[7] ships,[8] ladders,[9] lifts,[10] stagings [11] and scaffolds.[12] It also includes wharves and berths to which ships are invited for the purpose of loading or unloading.[13] The principles do not govern any negligence on the part of the driver or the person operating or in charge of such movable structures or conveyances, but they do apply in so far as the damage has arisen from the dangerous structural condition of the object in question.

331 **Liability for dangerous premises.** Liability for dangerous premises must be considered in connection with (1) persons who are injured whilst a visitor on the premises, and (2) persons who are injured when they are not on the premises but whose injuries are caused by the dangerous state of the premises (*post*, § 406).

332 **Common law duty to persons visiting premises.** When persons were injured on the premises, their rights depended on the circumstances under which they came to be on the premises. The different categories of duty at common law were described by Hamilton L.J. thus: " The duty of the

1 *Francis* v. *Cockrell* (1870) L.R. 5 Q.B. 501.
2 *Kenny* v. *Electricity Supply Board* [1932] I.R. 73.
3 *Perkowski* v. *Wellington Corporation* [1959] A.C. 53; *Periscinotti* v. *Brighton West Pier*, *The Times*, June 7, 1961.
4 *Foulkes* v. *Metropolitan Ry.* (1880) 5 C.P.D. 157 and see Chap. 7; *Readhead* v. *Midland Ry.* (1869) L.R. 4 Q.B. 379.
5 *Moffatt* v. *Bateman* (1869) L.R. 3 P.C. 115; *White* v. *Steadman* [1913] 3 K.B. 340.
6 *Lomas* v. *M. Jones & Son* [1944] K.B. 4.
7 *Elliott* v. *Hall* (1885) 15 Q.B.D. 315.
8 *Hillen* v. *I.C.I. (Alkali) Ltd.* [1936] A.C. 65; *London Graving Dock* v. *Horton* [1951] A.C. 737.
9 *Marney* v. *Scott* [1899] 1 Q.B. 986.
10 *Haseldine* v. *Daw & Sons* [1941] 2 K.B. 343; *Sandford* v. *Eugene* (1970) 115 S.J. 33.
11 *Heaven* v. *Pender* (1883) 11 Q.B.D. 503.
12 *Woodman* v. *Richardson* [1937] 3 All E.R. 866.
13 *The Moorcock* (1889) 14 P.D. 64; *The Calliope* [1891] A.C. 11; *The Bearn* [1906] P. 48; *The Humorist* [1944] P. 28.

owner or occupier to use care, if it exists at all, is graduated distinctly, though never very definitely measured. . . . Contractual obligations, of course, stand apart. The lowest is the duty towards a trespasser. More care, though not much, is owed to a licensee—more again to an invitee." [14] These three categories of invitee, licensee, and trespasser were rigid and there were no intermediate stages between them.[15] Accordingly, such expressions as " bare licensee," " licensee with an interest," " licensee for payment " were meaningless except in so far as they could be referred to one of the three classes set out above. As Atkin L.J. had pointed out [16]: " It is no doubt unfortunate that the law as to the obligation of owners of property towards those who come upon it compels distinctions to be drawn which are subtle and apt to be confused. On the other hand they correspond to real differences in the nature of the user of property and in the reasonable claims to protection of those who are permitted such use."

333 **The Occupiers' Liability Act 1957.** Since January 1, 1958, however, the common law rules of the duty owed to lawful visitors are replaced by the statutory provisions of the Occupiers' Liability Act 1957,[17] which provides [18] that the new rules enacted by sections 2 and 3 " shall have effect, in place of the rules of the common law, to regulate the duty which an occupier of premises owes to his visitors in respect of dangers due to the state of the premises or to things done or omitted to be done on them." In so far as the duties owed to them are concerned, the three categories [19] of invitee, licensee and trespasser have, accordingly, been merged into two, namely Visitors and Trespassers. Persons, who, up to that date, were treated as invitees or licensees are, since then, treated as visitors [20] and the duty owed to them is the " common duty of care," [21] but the Act does not alter in any way the common law relating to trespassers.[22] The duty as to movable structures is also the " common duty of care." It is specifically provided [23] that the rules laid down in sections 2 and 3 apply to regulate " the obligations of a person occupying or having control over any fixed or moveable structure, including any vessel, vehicle or aircraft." Whilst the " common duty of care " under the Occupiers'

[14] *Latham* v. *Johnson* [1913] 1 K.B. 398 at p. 410.

[15] *Robert Addie & Sons (Collieries) Ltd.* v. *Dumbreck* [1929] A.C. 358; *Liddle* v. *Yorkshire (North Riding) C.C.* [1934] 2 K.B. 101, 119, *per* Greer L.J.; *Sutton* v. *Bootle Corpn.* [1947] K.B. 359. For the old law, see Chap. 9, 3rd ed., *Charlesworth on Negligence*.

[16] In *Coleshill* v. *Manchester Corpn.* [1928] 1 K.B. 776, 791.

[17] Which followed the Law Reform Committee's Third Report (Cmd. 9305) in 1954.

[18] s. 1 (1).

[19] These three categories still exist at common law. It is only the distinction between the duty owed to invitees and that owed to licensees which has been abolished and replaced by statute.

[20] s. 1 (2).

[21] s. 2 (1). This duty is defined in s. 2 (2) and is: " A duty to take such care as in all the circumstances of the case is reasonable to see that the visitor will be reasonably safe in using the premises for the purposes for which he is invited or permitted by the occupier to be there." See further § 345, *post*.

[22] See § 387, *post*.

[23] s. 1 (3) (*a*).

Liability Act [24] is restricted to the occupier or the notional occupier of premises [25] (since the Act does not apply to non-occupiers), a duty to take care is owed also by other persons who are on the premises on the invitation or by the permission of the owner or occupier and even by trespassers.[26] But firstly the duty itself must be considered in connection with the state of the premises, and also in connection with wrongful or negligent acts done on the premises.

34 **Duty confined to physical state of premises.** At common law the duty to an invitee was confined to the physical condition of the premises. For negligent acts done on the premises the occupier was under his ordinary common law duty. Where a customer at a public-house left his motorcycle in a covered yard marked " garage," from which it was stolen, the occupier of the public-house was held not liable.[27] " There is no warrant . . . for holding that an invitor, where the invitation extends to the goods as well as the person of the invitee, whereby by implication of law assumes a liability to protect the invitee and his goods not merely from physical dangers arising from defects in the premises, but from the risk of the goods being stolen by some third party." [28]

The 1957 Act has not altered the common law on this point. It is provided by section 1 (1) that sections 2 and 3 (the common duty of care) " regulate the duty which an occupier of premises owes to his visitors in respect of dangers due to the state of the premises or to things done or omitted to be done on them."

These words " things done or omitted to be done on " the premises must also be read in conjunction with section 1 (2), which states that the rules enacted in sections 2 and 3 shall not alter the rules of the common law as to the persons to whom a duty is owed. This means that the occupier is liable to his visitor for his negligent acts or omissions done on the premises by himself and others for whose conduct he is under a common law liability.[29] The law laid down in *Tinsley* v. *Dudley*,[30] that the occupier was under no duty to guard his invitee's goods brought on to the premises against the risk of theft, remains unaltered. *Tinsley* v. *Dudley* was followed in *Edwards* v. *West Herts Group Hospital Management Committee*,[31] which was also decided before the passing of the Occupiers' Liability Act 1957, when it was held that a resident house physician, living in a staff hostel adjoining the hospital, cannot recover against the hospital if his personal effects are stolen from the hostel by a

[24] See s. 1 (2) and (3).
[25] s. 6 provides that the Act shall bind the Crown, but as regards the Crown's liability in tort shall not bind the Crown further than the Crown is made liable in tort by the Crown Proceedings Act 1947, and that Act and in particular section 2 of it shall apply in relation to duties under sections 2 to 4 of this Act as statutory duties.
[26] *Post*, § 403.
[27] *Tinsley* v. *Dudley* [1951] 2 K.B. 18. *Cf. Deyong* v. *Shenburn* [1946] K.B. 227.
[28] *Ibid.*, *per* Jenkins L.J. at p. 31.
[29] See also below, " Dangerous use of premises."
[30] *Supra.*
[31] [1957] 1 W.L.R. 415.

person unknown, as the hospital owes no duty to the physician to safeguard his property against theft by a third party who comes into the hostel.

335 **Damage to property.** As to property brought by a visitor on to the premises, section 1 (3) provides that the rules enacted by sections 2 and 3 apply to regulate " the obligations of a person occupying or having control over any premises or structure in respect of damage to property including the property of persons who are not themselves his visitors." [32] Having regard to section 1 (2) that the rules enacted in section 2 and 3 " shall not alter the rules of the common law as to the persons on whom a duty is so imposed or to whom it is owed," the reference in section 1 (3) (*b*) to the property of persons who are not themselves the occupier's visitors must mean property not belonging to a visitor but which, nevertheless, he is invited or permitted to bring on to the premises, such as articles in his possession under a hire-purchase agreement or otherwise or articles of which he is bailee. Damages are not limited by section 1 (3) (*b*) to damages in respect of physical damage but may include damages in respect of consequential financial loss.[33] Accordingly as an example posed by Mocatta J.,[34] where a visitor had brought on to the occupier's premises a car used by him for hiring out, upon its suffering damage due to the dangerous state of these premises, the visitor can recover not only the cost of repairs to the vehicle but also his loss of earnings for hiring whilst it is being repaired.

As has been pointed out in the previous paragraph, this section of the Act does not create any new liability (*e.g.* for the theft of goods) where none existed at common law.[35]

336 **Dangerous use of premises.** At common law the duty to take reasonable care to prevent damage from unusual danger applied not only to the structural condition of the premises but also " to the use which the occupier (or whoever has control so far as material) of the premises permits a third party to make of the premises." [36] The question then was whether a reasonable person would know or ought to know that the invitee would be exposed to unusual danger from the acts of the third party in using the premises in the permitted way. It had been held that to permit an urn full of hot tea to be carried by third parties through a shop where there were a number of children to a tea room did not expose the children to an unusual danger, so that the occupiers of the shop were not liable when the third parties negligently spilt the tea and injured the children.[37] The common law in this regard has not been altered by the 1957 Act. The

[32] At common law the invitor's duty was to prevent not only personal injury but also damage to an invitee's goods. s. 1 (3) (*b*) now affirms and extends the common law. Damage to property does not include the loss of property (see *Tinsley* v. *Dudley*, *supra*) but indicates that the occupier is under a duty to prevent physical damage to a visitor's chattels whilst they are on his premises.

[33] *A.M.F. International* v. *Magnet Bowling* [1968] 1 W.L.R. 1028.

[34] *Ibid.* p. 1050.

[35] Mocatta J. expressed this view also at p. 1050, *ibid.*

[36] Lord Wright in *Glasgow Corporation* v. *Muir* [1943] A.C. 448, 462.

[37] *Glasgow Corporation* v. *Muir*, *supra.*

occupier owes the "common duty of care" not only in respect of dangers due to the state of the premises but also in respect of dangers due to "things done or omitted to be done on them."[38] This includes things done or omitted to be done by persons permitted by the occupier to make use of the premises when reasonably using the premises for the purposes for which they are invited or permitted to be there.[39] Accordingly where a firework party was held at a riverside bungalow which was later set on fire as a result of a "jumping jack" accidentally finding its way into the lounge from the vicinity of the porch and there setting alight some other fireworks especially stored in a cubby-hole made for the occasion, it was held by Paull J. that there was no breach of duty under the Act since the occupiers had done all that could reasonably be expected of them to store the fireworks safely.[40]

In the absence of evidence that the defendant occupier knew that his camping site was being used for the giving of driving lessons by one of the campers it was held that the defendant was not negligent in failing to provide a suitably marked-out area for such driving activities or to make or to draw attention to regulations requiring that no vehicles should be driven in the vicinity of the tents erected on the site.[41]

2.—THE PERSON LIABLE FOR DANGEROUS PREMISES

337 **Liability of occupier.** Liability for dangerous or defective premises is primarily on the occupier, whether he is the owner or not, and is based on the fact that he has the immediate control and supervision and has given an invitation or licence to come on premises in his possession. The persons who are to be treated as occupiers under the Act[42] are the same as the persons who would at common law be treated as occupiers. Therefore an occupier is any person who is in actual occupation for the time being or having possession or physical control over the premises concerned or over the fixed or the movable structures including such things as vessels, vehicles or aircraft.[43] For example a contractor converting a vessel, lying in a dry dock, into a troopship, occupies the vessel[44]; a sideshow concessionaire on a show-ground occupies his premises[45] and, likewise, local authorities, which had requisitioned houses, occupy such premises.[46] However, to the contrary, it has been held that a road contractor does not occupy land adjacent to a part of the road where his workings are finished[47] and that an electricity company does not occupy land over which it has a wayleave agreement to erect poles or pylons and to pass cables across.[48]

38 s. 1 (1).

39 See also previous paragraph.

40 *Horsenail* v. *Kennedy, The Times*, April 30, 1964.

41 *Crickmar* v. *Cleavers, The Times*, October 8, 1964.

42 Occupiers' Liability Act 1957, s. 1 (2).

43 *Ibid.* s. 1 (3) (*a*).

44 *Hartwell* v. *Grayson Rollo and Clover Docks Ltd.* [1947] K.B. 901.

45 *Humphreys* v. *Dreamland (Margate) Ltd.* (1931) 100 L.J.K.B. 137.

46 *Greene* v. *Chelsea Borough Council* [1954] 2 Q.B. 127; *Hawkins* v. *Coulsdon and Purley U.D.C.* [1945] 1 Q.B. 319.

47 *Creed* v. *J. McGeoch & Sons Ltd.* [1955] 1 W.L.R. 1005.

48 *Buckland* v. *Guildford Gas Light and Coke Co.* [1949] 1 K.B. 410.

As regards requisitioning authorities, they are treated as occupiers since the residents are those persons licensed by the authority. Denning L.J. said in *Hawkins* v. *Coulsdon and Purley U.D.C.*[49]: "They cannot shift their responsibility on to the occupants of the house for the simple reason that they retained the possession and control and are responsible in law. They cannot get rid of their responsibility by the plea that they are only a requisitioning authority."

338 Nevertheless more than one person can be in occupation of the same premises and a clear illustration of this is found in *Wheat* v. *E. Lacon & Co. Ltd.*[50] The defendants, who were brewers, were the owners of a public-house the management of which they entrusted to a manager employed by them under a service agreement. The first floor was used by the manager and his wife exclusively as their private dwelling but the defendants allowed them, as a privilege, to take in paying guests for their own profit. The plaintiff and her husband were staying in the private part of the premises as paying guests of the manager's wife and at about 9 p.m. one evening the husband left the plaintiff on the first floor in order to go downstairs to buy some drinks from the bar. He was subsequently found at the foot of the back staircase with a fractured skull from which he later died. There was a handrail down the left-hand side of the staircase and there was an electric light at the top of the stairs, although there was no bulb in it at the material time. It was held that both the manager and the brewery company were the occupiers, so they each owed the common duty of care to their visitor. However, the widow plaintiff's claim failed because there was not sufficient evidence that the back staircase, although unlit, was dangerous to someone using it with proper care.

The mere fact that a local authority is liable to maintain a privately owned footpath does not make that authority an occupier of that road for the purposes of the Act.[51]

339 **Liability of owner.** An owner, who is not in occupation, and who has not contracted to keep the premises in question in repair, is under no liability to the occupiers' visitors.[52] So, where there was a forecourt between a shop and the highway and a customer to the shop was injured because the forecourt was in bad repair, the owner, who was not in occupation, was not liable.[53] On the other hand in *Jones* v. *City of Calgary*[54] where a municipality owned an electric transformer on the premises of a supermarket shopping centre which was not adequately kept locked

49 [1954] 1 Q.B. 319, 338.

50 [1966] A.C. 552. See also *Fisher* v. *C. H. T. Ltd.* [1966] 2 Q.B. 475, where it was held that the proprietors of a club as well as the managers of a restaurant on the club premises were the occupiers of the restaurant for the purpose of the Act. See article: "The Service Agreement and Occupiers' Liability" (Samuels) (1966) 110 S.J. 515.

51 *Whiting* v. *Hillingdon London Borough Council* (1970) 68 L.G.R. 437 (plaintiff tripped over a hidden tree stump, which protruded over the footpath, as she stepped to one side into the grass and foliage in order to pass some other pedestrians).

52 *Lane* v. *Cox* [1897] 1 Q.B. 415; *Bromley* v. *Mercer* [1922] 2 K.B. 126.

53 *Howard* v. *Walker* [1947] K.B. 860. The shopkeeper was held liable.

54 (1969) 3 D.L.R. (3d) 455.

or surrounded by a barrier, and a nine-year-old boy received an electric shock from it, it was held that as the municipality could not be said to be the occupiers of the land on which the transformer stood, the boy was not a trespasser. Nor could the municipality succeed on the basis that the boy was a trespasser to the transformer itself, because it was an allurement and its attraction to children was foreseeable. Further, the owners of the supermarket itself were not to be held liable as being under any duty, since the municipality had kept exclusive control of the transformer, thus only the latter was in breach of its common duty of care, by reason of the lack of fencing and warning.

340 **Liability for acts of occupier's visitors.** The occupier owes the "common duty of care," not only in respect of dangers due to the state of the premises but also in respect of dangers due to "things done or omitted to be done on them." [55] Otherwise, the occupier is not liable for damage caused by one of his invitees or licensees to another unless he could reasonably have foreseen that damage of that kind would be caused by that invitee or licensee acting within the limits of his invitation or licence. Accordingly, the occupier of a shop, with a tea room behind, was held not liable when tea-room customers, in carrying an urn of hot tea through the shop, negligently scalded customers in the shop.[56] The occupiers of a wharf at which the plaintiff's barges were moored were held not liable when a ship, arriving at night at the wharf, moved the barges to an unsafe berth further up the wharf.[57]

341 **Liability of invitor or licensor not in occupation of premises.** A person not in occupation [58] of premises may give an invitation or licence to others to enter on the premises. This may occur, for example, in the case of a dance hall, where the hall is retained in the possession and control of the occupiers, but an invitation or licence to enter is given by the promoters of the dance or other entertainment. In such a case at common law the guests would be the invitees [59] of the occupiers. But, in addition to the occupiers, the promoters of the dance or other entertainment may be liable as the persons who have given the invitation or licence. "When a person invites another to a place where they both have business, the invitation creates a duty on the part of the invitor to take reasonable care that the place does not contain or to give warning of hidden dangers, no matter whether the place belongs to the invitor or is in his exclusive occupation." [60] During the construction of a building the head contractor is the invitor of the sub-contractors and their workmen, but his duty as invitor ceases when he hands over exclusive control of any part of the

[55] Occupiers' Liability Act 1957, s. 1 (1).
[56] *Glasgow Corpn.* v. *Muir* [1943] A.C. 448.
[57] *The Majfrid* [1942] P. 145.
[58] The Occupiers' Liability Act 1957 does not apply to non-occupiers. See *post*, § 403.
[59] *Kelly* v. *Woolworth & Co.* [1922] 2 Ir.R. 5. After January 1, 1958, both invitees and licensees would be classed as "visitors" to the premises.
[60] Lord Oaksey L.J. in *Hartwell* v. *Grayson Rollo & Clover Docks Ltd.* [1947] K.B. 901, 913.

premises to a sub-contractor.[61] Where a ship, at the invitation of a railway company, who were occupiers of a wharf, went to a berth at a harbour under the control of harbour trustees and was damaged owing to the condition of the berth, both the railway company and the trustees were held liable—the railway company because as invitors they should have taken reasonable care to see that the berth was safe or to have given warning that they had not done so, and the trustees as occupiers because they should have taken reasonable care to keep the berth in a fit condition.[62] Accordingly, a tenant of a flat, who invited a visitor to see him on business, was presumably liable to his visitor for injury he sustained owing to an unusual danger in the staircase retained by the landlord in his own possession, if he knew or ought to have known of the danger, and gave no warning of it.[63] The tenant of the flat, in the circumstances would not be affected by the provisions of the Occupiers' Liability Act 1957, so that his liability would be as before the Act. The landlord, on the other hand, by reason of his occupation of the staircase would owe the visitor the common duty of care.[64]

342 **Liability of actual wrongdoer.** In addition to the occupier, the person who actually created the danger is also liable if he has reason to expect that persons will be lawfully on the premises during the existence of the danger which he has created. " If a person creates a dangerous condition of things (something in the nature of a concealed trap) whether in a public highway, or on his own premises, or on those of another, and he sees some other person who to his knowledge is unaware of the existence of the danger lawfully exposing himself or about to expose himself to the danger which he has created he is under a duty to give such a person a warning . . . the duty arises quite independently of the occupation of premises. It does not arise out of any invitation or licence." [65] Such person's liability is to take such care as is reasonable in all the circumstances [66] and even a trespasser may have a successful claim.[67] Where a licensee using a private road stumbled in the dark over a heap of slates left by a builder with the permission of the owner, it was held that the builder was liable.[68] So also was a mason who negligently erected a tombstone in a churchyard so that it fell

61 *Canter* v. *Gardner & Co.* [1940] 1 All E.R. 325 (an example where an invitee may recover against another invitee).

62 *The Bearn* [1906] P. 48. See also *The Grit* [1924] P. 246; *The Calliope* [1891] A.C. 11; *The Moorcock* (1889) 14 P.D. 64; *The Empress* [1923] P. 96; *The Kate* [1935] P. 100; *The Unique* [1939] W.N. 60.

63 *Fairman* v. *Perpetual Bdg. Socy.* [1923] A.C. 74, 85, 95; *Howard* v. *Walker, supra.*

64 Occupiers' Liability Act 1957, s. 4.

65 *Kimber* v. *Gas Light & Coke Co.* [1918] 1 K.B. 439 at 445, *per* Bankes L.J.

66 The broad principle of *Donoghue* v. *Stevenson* [1932] A.C. 562 normally regulates the duty of care of non-occupiers.

67 *Buckland* v. *Guildford Gas Light & Coke Co.* [1949] 1 K.B. 410 (schoolgirl of 13 who climbed an oak tree and was electrocuted upon touching the bare high-voltage wires, running concealed through the branches and foliage); *Miller* v. *South of Scotland Electricity Board*, 1958 S.L.T. 227 (child trespasser received shock from live cable left carelessly disconnected in a house about to be demolished).

68 *Corby* v. *Hill* (1958) 4 C.B.(N.S.) 556 (an example where a licensee may recover against another licensee).

upon the plaintiff and injured him.[69] Again, where the owner of a house employed builders to put it into repair, and the builders employed a gas company to do the necessary work in connection with the gas fittings, and a prospective tenant who was viewing the house fell into an unfenced hole made by the gas company's servants, it was held that the gas company were liable.[70] In this case the plaintiff was not invited or licensed by the gas company to be on the premises. Scrutton L.J. described their duty as follows: " It is A's [the gas company's] duty to carry on his work with due precautions for the safety of those whom he knows, or ought reasonably to know, may be lawfully in the vicinity of this work; and the most obvious precaution would be to warn B, [the plaintiff] who is going towards the hidden danger A has created." The same duty is owed by one sub-contractor working on premises to the workmen of another.[71] A workman on a ship who fell down a hatchway, left open by stevedores employed by the shipowner to unload the ship, was held entitled to recover against the stevedores on the ground that there is " a common law obligation upon one invitee working upon the premises to warn another invitee working there of any danger which he may have created, and for which he is responsible." [72] The defendant stevedores, knowing that they had created a slippery condition on the shop floor due to the presence of soda ash spillage on it, owed a duty to the plaintiff, who was also a licensee of the premises, not merely to warn him of the danger but to take such reasonable steps as could be taken to protect him from injury as a result of the very danger that they had created.[73] An Electricity Board which carried out wiring for electricity in a factory and negligently transposed two wires so that the current remained on after the switch, which apparently controlled the electricity supply to them, had been switched off were held liable for the death of a fireman called to the factory to extinguish a fire.[74] Where the Ministry of Fuel and Power, under statutory authority, entered a field, not in their occupation, to bore for coal and their contractors left a heap of timber which injured the occupier's horse grazing in the field, both the Ministry and their contractors were held liable.[75] A contractor who was employed to destroy the existing safe means of access to a building and construct a new one was held liable when, during the course of the work, he left the access unsafe so that a person coming to visit the caretaker of the building was injured.[76]

343 The person creating the danger may not be liable for damage resulting

[69] *Brown* v. *Cotterill* (1934) 51 T.L.R. 21.
[70] *Kimber* v. *Gas Light and Coke Co.* [1918] 1 K.B. 439.
[71] *Canter* v. *Gardner & Co.* [1940] 1 All E.R. 325, 332.
[72] *Hawkins* v. *Thames Stevedore Co.* [1936] 2 All E.R. 472.
[73] *Johnson* v. *Rea Ltd.* [1962] 1 Q.B. 373.
[74] *Hartley* v. *Mayoh & Co.* [1954] 1 Q.B. 383.
[75] *Darling* v. *Att.-Gen.* [1950] 2 All E.R. 793.
[76] *A. C. Billings & Sons Ltd.* v. *Riden* [1958] A.C. 240, a case described by H. Street as a " decision of the House of Lords " which " is a decisive stage in recent progress towards a general theory of negligence for non-occupiers ": see *The Law of Torts*, 4th ed., p. 194.

from it if he has reasonable grounds for believing that the danger will be removed or guarded against by someone else. For example, a contractor doing work in a dark passage may assume, in most cases, that the occupier will light the passage.[77] Where a plasterer, employed about a new building, for the convenience of his operations opened a passage or communication from the staircase of an adjoining house, and afterwards went away for a time before his work was finished, with the intention of returning to complete it, and both while he was there and during the time he was absent other workmen employed about the premises used the passage or communication, it was held that a man who, at night, fell into the passage owing to its not having been properly secured by the other workmen, when they left, could not recover against the plasterer.[78] Lord Redesdale said: " It appeared that Milne [the plasterer] had quitted the premises, and left others working there; it was their duty and not Milne's to close it up," and Lord Eldon said: " If, after the operation, Milne had left his work at night, without guarding against consequences, no doubt . . . Milne would have been liable." On the other hand, if the person creating the danger has no reasonable grounds for believing that someone else will remove it, he will be liable. In *Grant* v. *Sun Shipping Co.*[79] a stevedore working on a ship fell into the hold through the open hatch covers which were unlighted. The hatch covers were removed by some repairers, who should have replaced them but omitted to do so. The shipowners were held to be under a duty to the stevedore, an invitee, to take care to see that the hatch covers were replaced, but as between the repairers and the shipowners it was the repairers' duty to replace the covers. The repairers were held liable to the stevedore and were not excused by the subsequent negligence of the shipowners.[80]

If a sub-contractor, working on a building under construction, leaves his work in a safe condition he is not liable if another sub-contractor or some other person does something to make his work unsafe.[81] A builder is not liable if the building owner, during the carrying out of the work and while the building is unfinished, goes round the building unattended and injures himself by slipping on a loose plank.[82]

344 A person doing work on a building will not be liable for damage done by his work if his work has been examined and passed by competent examiners. When contractors roofed in a passage and left a sole plate near a pillar which tripped up the plaintiff as he was walking along the passage, it was held that the contractors were not liable because their contract was to do the work to the satisfaction of the employers, and the work had been inspected and passed by the employers' works

77 *Buckner* v. *Ashby & Horner Ltd.* [1941] 1 K.B. 321.
78 *Milne* v. *Smith* (1814) 2 Dow 390; 3 E.R. 905.
79 [1948] A.C. 549.
80 The shipowners were also liable, and damages apportioned 75 per cent. to the repairers, and 25 per cent. to the shipowners.
81 *Canter* v. *Gardner & Co.* [1940] 1 All E.R. 325.
82 *Nabarro* v. *Cope* [1938] 4 All E.R. 565.

supervisor.[83] But, " in the case of a danger concealed from the occupiers of premises and their licensees," for instance in the case of a balcony which a builder has been employed to repair, the fact that the work had been approved would not exonerate the contractor if it were badly done, the defect not being apparent.[84] This was the case in *Hartley* v. *Mayoh & Co.*[85] where the work of installing electricity in a factory was done by an Area Electricity Board which negligently transposed some wires. The work was accepted, but the occupiers did not know and were not negligent in failing to discover this, and it was held that the Board were not exonerated from liability when a fireman was killed as a result of their negligent work.

3.—THE DUTY OWED

345 **What is the duty owed?** The duty owed in respect of dangerous premises is a single duty and is the " common duty of care." Section 2 (1) of the Act provides:—

" An occupier of premises owes the same duty, the ' common duty of care,' to all his visitors, except in so far as he is free to and does extend, restrict, modify or exclude his duty to any visitor or visitors by agreement or otherwise." Then by section 2 (2), the Act proceeds to define the said duty of care: " The common duty of care is a duty to take such care as in all the circumstances of the case is reasonable to see that the visitor will be reasonably safe in using the premises for the purposes for which he is invited or permitted by the occupier to be there."

The Law Reform Committee had recommended: " that the law can and should be simplified by the abolition of the existing categories of invitees and licensees, and the substitution of one uniform duty of care owed by the occupier of premises to all persons coming upon them at his invitation or by his permission, express or implied." [86] This has clearly been implemented by the Act so that all those irksome distinctions [87] between unusual dangers and concealed traps, etc., disappear, and as Lord Pearce said: " Once the duty of care is imposed, the question whether a defendant failed in that duty becomes a question of fact in all the circumstances." [88]

Then section 2 (3) goes on to provide:

" The circumstances relevant for the present purposes include the degree of care, and of want of care, which would ordinarily be looked for in such a visitor . . ."

346 By way of illustrations, an occupier has been held not liable: where a stevedore alleged that he had injured himself slipping on an oily patch

[83] *Buckner* v. *Ashby and Horner Ltd.* [1941] 1 K.B. 321.
[84] *Ibid., per* Lord Goddard L.J. at p. 338. See also *Brown* v. *Cotterill* (1934) 51 T.L.R. 21.
[85] [1954] 1 Q.B. 383.
[86] Cmd. 9305, para. 78.
[87] " A jungle of technicalities and refinements " *per* Mocatta J. in *AMF International Ltd.* v. *Magnet Bowling Ltd.* [1968] 1 W.L.R. 1028, at p. 1043.
[88] *Wheat* v. *E. Lacon & Co. Ltd.* [1966] A.C. 552, at p. 587.

on the deck of a ship [89]; where a customer in a shop was injured by a fall of part of the ceiling which had been plastered recently by a firm of independent contractors [90]; where an elderly lady slipped on the stairs of a block of flats when the lighting over this access was turned off due to the faulty adjustment of the time switch controlling the electricity supply [91]; where a customer in a shop fell over some cartons stacked up in a gangway [92]; where a man, who was a paying guest, was found dying at the foot of a staircase and there was no landing light at the top of the stairs, since the electric bulb was missing, and the handrail was alleged to have been inadequate [93]; where a visitor to a club sat on a chair which had been repaired negligently by another member, a skilled craftsman, but which had collapsed under the visitor's weight [94]; where a visitor to a public-house tripped up over a dog in the bar, which had not been kept on a lead but was not making a nuisance of itself.[95]

On the other hand an occupier has been held liable: where a plasterer was redecorating a restaurant and came into contact with a live electric light wire which had been carelessly switched on by the occupier's maintenance electrician [96]; where a cleaner slipped on a highly polished floor which was dangerous in the circumstances [97]; where a visitor, a passenger on the railway, was walking along the platform and, finding himself hemmed in by goods trolleys and a fallen bag, had tried to step over it but had tripped and fallen [98]; where a visitor was electrocuted because the occupiers had failed to warn him of the existence of a high voltage cable some twenty-two feet above the exhibition site at an agricultural show which he accidentally had touched with a metal flag pole that he was in the process of erecting.[99]

347 **Extension, restriction, modification or exclusion of liability.** The aforesaid words contained in section 2 (1): " in so far as he is free to," would seem to be designed to ensure that an occupier's power to extend, restrict, modify or exclude his duty shall not be any greater than the position was at common law. As regards the words: " by agreement or otherwise," these enable the occupier to exclude liability to his visitors not only by agreement with them but also by, for example, the provisions of any by-laws, rules or regulations which he may have power to make or, of course, by the exhibition of a clear notice disclaiming liability for injury. In *Ashdown* v. *Samuel Williams & Sons Ltd.*[1] it was held that

[89] *Lowther* v. *H. Hogarth & Sons Ltd.* [1959] 1 Lloyd's Rep. 171.
[90] *O'Connor* v. *Swan & Edgar* (1963) 107 S.J. 215; but see the judgment of Nield J. in *Sharpe* v. *E. T. Sweeting & Son Ltd.* [1963] 1 W.L.R. 665 at p. 675.
[91] *Irving* v. *L.C.C.* (1965) 109 S.J. 157.
[92] *Doherty* v. *London Co-operative Society* (1966) 110 S.J. 74.
[93] *Wheat* v. *E. Lacon & Co. Ltd.* [1966] A.C. 552.
[94] *Carrol* v. *Hibbert* (1967) 117 New L.J. 353.
[95] *Carrol* v. *Garford* (1968) 112 S.J. 948.
[96] *Fisher* v. *C. H. T.* [1966] 2 Q.B. 475.
[97] *Adams* v. *S. J. Watson & Co.* (1967) 117 New L.J. 130.
[98] *Blackett* v. *B.R.B.*, *The Times*, December 19, 1967.
[99] *McDowell* v. *F.M.C. (Meat)* (1968) 5 K.I.R. 456.
[1] [1957] 1 Q.B. 409 applying *Parker* v. *South Eastern Rail Co.* (1877) 2 C.P.D. 416. See article: " Knowledge and Exemption in Occupiers' Liability " (Bradbury) 119 New L.J. 520.

an occupier was not liable to a licensee because: (a) the conditions, which excluded liability, on which she was permitted to be on the land had been sufficiently brought to her attention by the posting of a notice, and, having read enough of the notice to know that she was on the land at her own risk, she was bound by the terms of the notice, although she had not read all of it; and (b) the words of the notice were sufficient to exclude liability not only for dangers of the property in its static condition but also for activities carried on there negligently. It follows, therefore, that *Ashdown's* case, although decided before the passing of the Act, would be unaffected by it, since the terms of the licence, held to be binding on the licensee, excluded the occupier's liability to take reasonable care.

348 **Liability to children.** Section 2 (3) then continues, by providing that: "an occupier must be prepared for children to be less careful than adults." In this regard it is helpful, as a guide, to consider the decided cases at common law, since the principles relating to the duty owed to invitees, licensees and trespassers applied to children as well as to adults. Farwell L.J. said: "I am not aware of any case that imposes any greater liability on the owner towards children than towards adults: the exceptions apply to all alike, and the adult is as much entitled to protection as the child. If the child is too young to understand danger, the licence ought not to be held to extend to such a child unless accompanied by a competent guardian." [2] Nevertheless, although the principles of liability were the same in respect of children as of adults, their application to the facts of any particular case required separate consideration.

349 **Traps for children at common law.** In *Cooke* v. *Midland Great Western Ry. of Ireland* [3] a railway company kept an unlocked turntable on their land close to a public road. They knew that children were in the habit of playing with the turntable and that they obtained access to the land through a gap in the fence. A child of just over four was injured in playing with the turntable, and the railway company were held liable, Lord Macnaghten saying: "It does not seem unreasonable to hold that, if they allow their property to be open to all comers, infants as well as children of maturer age, and place upon it a machine attractive to children and dangerous as a plaything, they may be responsible in damages to those who resort to it with their tacit permission, and who are unable, in consequence of their tender age, to take care of themselves." [4] This case "rests upon the ground that there was evidence from which the jury were entitled to infer that the plaintiff was on the turntable with the leave and licence of the railway company, and that the turntable was in the nature of a trap." [5]

[2] *Latham* v. *Johnson* [1913] 1 K.B. 398, 407. See also *Glasgow Corporation* v. *Taylor* [1922] 1 A.C. 44, 67, *per* Lord Sumner.

[3] [1909] A.C. 229. The headnote in the *Law Reports* says that the child was a trespasser. This is inaccurate, as the speeches themselves and the cases referred to in note 5 below show, but it gave rise to an erroneous impression that this case had extended the duty to children.

[4] *Ibid.* at p. 236.

[5] *Per* Lord Hailsham in *Robert Addie & Sons (Collieries) Ltd.* v. *Dumbreck* [1929] A.C.

350 Liability to children who were upon premises as licensees or invitees accordingly depended on the same principles as liability to adults. The respects in which it differed were: (1) things which were not unusual dangers or traps to adults might well be such to children, and accordingly steps had to be taken by lighting, guarding or otherwise to prevent them from being dangerous to children; (2) a notice or warning of the danger which might be adequate in the case of adults might not be adequate in the case of children, and accordingly, if warning was relied upon as a defence it had to be one which was capable of being understood by the children; and (3) there was a duty to guard children, lawfully on the land, from things, dangerous to a child, with which the child might be tempted to meddle. If there was no unusual danger or trap upon the premises there was no liability to an infant licensee or invitee. So, where a child of between two and three years old, a licensee, hurt itself when playing on a heap of stones, the occupier was held not liable, Hamilton L.J. saying: " What objects which attract infants to their hurt are traps even to them? Not all objects with which children hurt themselves simpliciter. A child can get into mischief and hurt itself with anything if it is young enough. In some cases the answer may rest with the jury, but it must be matter of law to say whether a given object can be a trap in the double sense of being fascinating and fatal. No strict answer has been, or perhaps ever will be, given to the question, but I am convinced that a heap of paving stones in broad daylight in a private close cannot so combine the properties of temptation and retribution as to be properly called a trap." [6]

351 What was a concealed danger or trap had to depend to some extent on the age of the child. In *Phipps* v. *Rochester Corpn.*[7] Devlin J. distinguished between big children and little children—" children who know what they are about and children who do not," [8] adding " a licensor who tacitly permits the public to use his land without discriminating between its members must assume that the public may include little children. But as a general rule he will have discharged his duty towards them if the dangers which they may encounter are only those which are obvious to a guardian or of which he has given a warning comprehensible by a guardian," subject to the exception that the occupier " may have to take into account the social habits of the neighbourhood. No doubt there are places where little children go to play unaccompanied. If the licensor knows or ought to anticipate that, he may have to take steps accordingly." [9] Where, therefore, the public was in the habit of going over land in the process of being developed as a building estate and a boy of five, whilst out blackberrying with his sister of seven, fell into

358, 366. The decision in *Cooke's* case is subjected to a careful examination by Hamilton L.J. in *Latham* v. *Johnson* [1913] 1 K.B. 398, 417. See also *per* Lord Atkinson in *Glasgow Corpn.* v. *Taylor* [1922] 1 A.C. 44, 54, and *Liddle* v. *Yorkshire* (*North Riding*) *C.C.* [1934] 2 K.B. 101.

[6] *Latham* v. *Johnson* [1913] 1 K.B. 398, 416.

[7] [1955] 1 Q.B. 450, where the principal cases on this subject are well reviewed.

[8] *Ibid.* p. 458.

[9] *Ibid.* p. 472.

an unguarded trench dug for the purpose of laying a sewer, the estate developers were held not liable, on the ground that there was no evidence to show that they should have anticipated the presence of little children unaccompanied. Devlin J. further commented: " But the responsibility for the safety of little children must rest primarily upon the parents; it is their duty to see that such children are not allowed to wander about by themselves, or at least to satisfy themselves that the places to which they do allow their children to go unaccompanied are safe for them to go to. It would not be socially desirable if parents were, as a matter of course, able to shift the burden of looking after their children from their own shoulders to those of persons who happen to have accessible bits of land. Different considerations may well apply to public parks or to recognised playing grounds where parents allow their children to go unaccompanied in the reasonable belief that they are safe." [9]

The following have been held *not* to be allurements or traps to children so as to impose liability on the occupier: A pond,[10] a river,[11] a swing,[12] a chute,[13] an unhorsed van,[14] a tip-up lorry in the charge of a competent driver,[15] a stack of steel lattice work on a road,[16] a heap of soil at the foot of a wall adjoining the highway,[17] a scaffold with a rope coiled round a pulley thirty-five feet from the ground,[18] a trench on land in process of being developed,[19] a hole in the ground,[20] and a pile of mortar.[21]

352 The unusual danger or trap might take the form of some object with which the child was not invited or licensed to meddle. In such a case, if the child was licensed or invited to be on the land, the occupier would be liable for injury sustained by the child in meddling with the object if it was of such a nature that he ought to have anticipated that the child would meddle with it.[22] The object, though forbidden, might be an allurement [23] or temptation to a child. " The allurement may arise after he [the child] has entered with leave or as of right. Then the presence in a frequented place of some object of attraction, tempting him to meddle where he ought to abstain, may well constitute a trap, and in the case of a child too young to be capable of contributory negligence, it may impose full liability on the owner or occupier, if he ought, as a reasonable man, to have anticipated the presence of the child and the attractiveness and peril

10 *Hastie* v. *Edinburgh Magistrates*, 1907 S.C. 1102.
11 *Stevenson* v. *Glasgow Corpn.*, 1908 S.C. 1034.
12 *Purkis* v. *Walthamstow B.C.* (1934) 151 L.T. 30; *Sutton* v. *Bootle Corporation* [1947] K.B. 359.
13 *Dyer* v. *Ilfracombe U.D.C.* [1956] 1 W.L.R. 218.
14 *Donovan* v. *Union Cartage Co.* [1933] 2 K.B. 71.
15 *Rawsthorne* v. *Ottley* [1937] 3 All E.R. 902.
16 *Morley* v. *Staffordshire C.C.* [1939] 4 All E.R. 92.
17 *Liddle* v. *Yorkshire (North Riding) C.C.* [1934] 2 K.B. 101.
18 *Cutress* v. *Scaffolding (Great Britain) Ltd.* [1953] 2 All E.R. 1075, 1081.
19 *Phipps* v. *Rochester Corpn.* [1955] 1 Q.B. 450.
20 *Perry* v. *Thomas Wrigley Ltd.* [1955] 1 W.L.R. 1164.
21 *Prince* v. *Gregory* [1959] 1 W.L.R. 177.
22 *Gough* v. *N.C.B.* [1954] 1 Q.B. 191; *Holdman* v. *Hamlyn* [1943] K.B. 664, 668, *per* du Parcq L.J.
23 See *per* Asquith L.J. in *Sutton* v. *Bootle Corpn.* [1947] K.B. 359, 369.

of the object." [24] The following *have* been held to be allurements and traps to children: A horse and cart left unattended in the street,[25] a railway turntable,[26] a moving staircase at a railway station,[27] a poisonous berry of attractive and appetising appearance,[28] an insecure wall where bird's-nesting could be carried on,[29] a rope haulage system with a rope on which to swing,[30] a lorry laden with sugar,[31] the opening on a threshing machine through which sheaves of grain were put to be threshed,[32] a chute in a children's playground,[33] broken glass on waste land where children were allowed to play,[34] a paddling pool, provided by the local authority for the children to play in but which contained a broken piece of glass hidden in the sand [35]; a tree, close to a footpath, which could be easily climbed by children and above which there was stretched a live electricity cable [36]; slow-moving trams on an unguarded track which people, including children, had been permitted to cross,[37] a bomb-damaged house in course of demolition.[38]

353 If children were invited or permitted to come on premises, there was no duty to erect a fence or otherwise to prevent them from wandering from the land on which they were lawfully playing. So, where a railway company permitted children to play on a pile of sleepers adjoining a railway line, they were held to be under no liability to a child of two and a half years old who got onto the railway line and was injured by a train.[39] Again, where children were allowed to play in a sand pit and one of them, of less than two years old, wandered from the sand pit onto a level crossing and was injured by a train, the local authority, who occupied the sand pit, were held to be under no liability.[40] When a child of four got through a gap in the fence of a public recreation ground and went onto a railway line where it was injured by a live rail, the defendants, who provided the recreation ground, were held not liable.[41]

354 **Licence conditional on adult companion.** It might be that the invitation or licence was only given to young children when accompanied by

[24] *Per* Hamilton L.J. in *Latham* v. *Johnson* [1913] 1 K.B. 398, 416.
[25] *Lynch* v. *Nurdin* (1841) 1 Q.B. 29.
[26] *Cooke* v. *M.G.W. Ry. of Ireland* [1909] A.C. 229.
[27] *Hardy* v. *Central London Ry.* [1920] 3 K.B. 459. In this case the child was a trespasser but would have succeeded had he been a licensee—*per* Lord Dunedin in *Robert Addie & Sons (Collieries) Ltd.* v. *Dumbreck*, *supra*, at p. 376.
[28] *Glasgow Corpn.* v. *Taylor* [1922] 1 A.C. 44.
[29] *Boyd* v. *Glasgow Iron and Steel Co.*, 1923 S.C. 758.
[30] *Excelsior Wire Rope Co.* v. *Callan* [1930] A.C. 404.
[31] *Culkin* v. *McFie & Sons Ltd.* [1939] 3 All E.R. 613.
[32] *Holdman* v. *Hamlyn* [1943] K.B. 664.
[33] *Bates* v. *Stone Parish Council* [1954] 1 W.L.R. 1249; *Dyer* v. *Ilfracombe U.D.C.* [1956] 1 W.L.R. 218.
[34] *Williams* v. *Cardiff Corpn.* [1950] 1 K.B. 514.
[35] *Ellis* v. *Fulham Corporation* [1938] 1 K.B. 212.
[36] *Buckland* v. *Guildford Gas Light & Coke Co.* [1949] 1 K.B. 410.
[37] *Gough* v. *N.C.B.* [1954] 1 Q.B. 191.
[38] *Davis* v. *St. Mary's Demolition and Excavation Co.* [1954] 1 W.L.R. 592.
[39] *Jenkins* v. *G.W. Ry.* [1912] 1 K.B. 525.
[40] *Schofield* v. *Bolton Corpn.* (1910) 26 T.L.R. 230.
[41] *Bint* v. *Lewisham B.C.* [1946] W.N. 12. See article: "An Infant Trespasser on Railway Lines," 79 L.Q.R. 586. But see *Herrington* v. *B.R.B.* [1971] 2 W.L.R. 477 and article "Forgive Us Our Trespasses" (Lewis) 121 New L.J. 134.

an older person. If this were so, there was no liability to a young child not so accompanied. So, where a child of four in going up the steps leading to the defendant's front door, fell off the steps owing to a defective railing, it was held that the occupier was not liable, Lindley J. saying: "There was no invitation to the plaintiff if he was not guarded, and, if guarded, then there was no trap." [42]

The question of a conditional licence was carefully considered in *Phipps* v. *Rochester Corpn.*[43] by Devlin J., who came to the conclusion that it involved difficulties. When there was no express licence, the implication of a licence at all was often rather unreal and to attach conditions to a licence which had not been consciously given would be more unreal still. In *Phipps*' case,[44] however, as an alternative ground of his decision, he held there was a conditional licence, that the condition had not been fulfilled and the claim failed. It has been held that a child, just over three, accompanied by a boy of fourteen, was accompanied by a competent guardian,[45] but a boy of five accompanied by his sister of seven was not.[44]

Where a child's hand was injured in a potato riddling machine in a barn on a farm in 1952, the Court of Appeal considered that the proper inference on the facts was that the occupier took the child's mother on to work with an agreement by implication that when she came to work she would bring her children with her on the footing that the children were to be in her charge. On this basis the occupier was entitled to assume that the child would be kept reasonably safe from danger.[46]

355 **Trespassing children.**[47] When the child was a trespasser his position was exactly the same as an adult, and no higher duty was owed to him. "In cases of trespass there can be no difference in the case of children and adults, because if there is no duty to take care that cannot vary according to who is the trespasser. It is quite otherwise in the case of licensees, because there you are brought into contact with what is known as trap and allurement." [48] Again, "there can be no general duty on the part of the landowner to keep his land safe for children, or even free from hidden dangers, if he has not directly or by implication invited or licensed them to come there." [49] Accordingly, the occupier of the land was held

[42] *Burchell* v. *Hickisson* (1880) 50 L.J.Q.B. 101. The passage from Lindley J.'s judgment was quoted with approval by Hamilton L.J. in *Latham* v. *Johnson.* See also to the same effect, Farwell L.J. in *Latham* v. *Johnson,* at p. 407, and *Schofield* v. *Bolton Corpn., supra.*

[43] [1955] 1 Q.B. 450.

[44] *Ante,* § 351.

[45] *Coates* v. *Rawtenstall B.C.* [1937] 3 All E.R. 602.

[46] *McCullie* v. *Butler, The Times,* March 19, 1959.

[47] See further "Trespassers," *post,* § 387 *et seq.* The C.A. in *Herrington* v. *B.R.B.* [1971] 2 W.L.R. 477, when granting leave to appeal to the H.L. in a case involving a six-year-old child injured whilst trespassing on a railway line, said that the English law on the question was in a confused state and should be altered.

[48] *Per* Lord Dunedin in *Robert Addie & Sons (Collieries) Ltd.* v. *Dumbreck* [1929] A.C. 358, at p. 376.

[49] *Per* Holmes J. in *United Zinc and Chemical Co.* v. *Van Britt* (1922) 258 U.S. 268, 276, quoted with approval by Scrutton L.J. in *Liddle* v. *Yorkshire (North Riding) C.C.* [1934] 2 K.B. 101.

not liable under the following circumstances: Where a child of two and a half trespassed on a railway line and was run over by a train,[50] where a child of six trespassing in a house owing to its parents, the tenants, holding over, fell out of a window from which the sash had been removed,[51] where a child of five, playing on a moving staircase at a railway station, caught his hand in the band which worked it,[52] where a child was injured through going into a harmless-looking pond which contained water poisoned by a chemical works,[53] where a boy of four was killed by being crushed in the terminal wheel of a haulage system belonging to a colliery company,[54] where a boy of seven climbed on a high wall adjoining a highway and fell off,[55] where a child of nine went upon a piece of vacant land and fell down a deep hole,[56] where a boy of eleven went into a railway yard to watch some rubbish being burnt and was injured through the explosion of a detonator accidentally concealed in the rubbish,[57] where a boy of eleven played in an air-raid shelter and was electrocuted by interfering with an electric cable laid on the ground,[58] where boys went into a minefield on sand dunes to which the public had access in peace-time and were injured by a mine explosion,[59] where a boy aged ten years, who was a cub member of a scout group, visited a lion's cage, climbed between two fences, was mauled by the lion and died later [60]; where a boy of twelve got onto a railway bank, through the dilapidated fence separating it from the public footpath, then proceeded to climb through the barbed wire fence surrounding a 2,500 volt transformer, which he well knew was intended to keep him out, and was injured by an electric shock, it was held that he was not entitled to recover.[61]

On the other hand, if the child, although a trespasser, was known to be present, an act likely to injure him, such as felling a tree when the child was standing in the probable line of its fall, ought not to be done without first seeing that the child was out of danger.[62]

356 **Allurement.** In some of the cases dealing with trespassing children reference was made to "allurement." However, an object should not be

[50] *Jenkins* v. *G.W. Ry., supra*; *Videan* v. *B.T.C.* [1963] 2 Q.B. 650.
[51] *Coffee* v. *McEvoy* [1912] 2 Ir.R. 290.
[52] *Hardy* v. *Central London Ry.* [1920] 3 K.B. 459.
[53] *United Zinc and Chemical Co.* v. *Van Britt, supra.*
[54] *Robert Addie & Sons (Collieries) Ltd.* v. *Dumbreck, supra.*
[55] *Liddle* v. *Yorkshire (North Riding) C.C.* [1934] 2 K.B. 101.
[56] *Proctor* v. *British Northrop Loom Co.* (1937) 81 S.J. 611.
[57] *Breslin* v. *L. & N.E. Ry.*, 1936 S.C. 816.
[58] *Walder* v. *Hammersmith Corpn.* [1944] 1 All E.R. 490.
[59] *Adams* v. *Naylor* [1944] K.B. 750; affd. on other grounds by the H.L. [1946] A.C. 543.
[60] *Murphy* v. *Zoological Society of London, The Times*, November 14, 1962 (the deceased was held to have been a trespasser at that place and since no dangerous animal had "escaped" the defendants were not liable).
[61] *McGlone* v. *B.R.B.* (1966) S.C. (H.L.) 1. But *cf. Herrington* v. *B.R.B.* [1971] 2 W.L.R. 477 (a child of six years who was trespassing was injured when he stepped on to the live rail of an electrified railway, having got through the broken fence which the defendants had permitted to become dilapidated at a point which had clearly been used as a route for pedestrians to cross over the railway. Failure to fence securely imposed liability on the Board). See *ante*, note 47.
[62] *Mourton* v. *Poulter* [1930] 2 K.B. 183; *Excelsior Wire Rope Co.* v. *Callan* [1930] A.C. 404, §§ 395, 403, *post*.

considered an allurement unless the temptation which it presents is such that no normal child could be expected to restrain himself from intermeddling, even if he knows that to intermeddle is wrong. Therefore where a child who was stealing a ride on a low-loader passing through a town at walking pace was killed when attempting to jump off, it was held that that vehicle was not an allurement.[63] An allurement might either tempt children to come upon premises where they were not permitted to be, so that they were trespassers, or it might tempt children invited or licensed to be on the premises to meddle with the allurement. In the second case the occupier might be liable in the circumstances set out above.[64] In the first case he was under no liability and the presence of an allurement was irrelevant, except in so far as it might be evidence of licence. In the case of *Townsend* v. *Wathen*,[65] a landowner placed baited traps on his own land near to the plaintiff's premises with the intention of trapping dogs, and it was held that he was liable to the plaintiff whose dogs he had trapped. This case, however, had no application to children unless it could be shown that the landowner intentionally attracted children to his land. Hamilton L.J. said: " It is hard to see how infantile temptations can give rights, however much they may excuse peccadilloes. A child will be a trespasser still, if he goes on private ground without leave or right, however natural it may have been for him to do so." [66] The same view was expressed by Warrington L.J. where he said: " Much stress was laid in argument on the ' allurement ' afforded by the moving staircase. Such a fact may be a material element in considering whether under all the circumstances, leave and licence is to be inferred, but where, as I think is the case here, leave and licence is distinctly negatived, the fact ceases to be relevant." [67]

357 **Entry of visitors to work, etc.** Section 2 (3) further continues by providing that: " (*b*) an occupier may expect that a person, in the exercise of his calling, will appreciate and guard against any special risks ordinarily incident to it, so far as the occupier leaves him free to do so." This gives effect therefore to the recommendation of the Law Reform Committee that: " any redefinition of the occupier's duty should expressly provide that where a visitor enters premises for the purpose of carrying out any work of construction, maintenance, repair or other similar operation, the occupier should not merely in that capacity be held liable for damage arising to such visitor from any danger encountered in the course of such operation if the danger is not one which would have been encountered in the normal use of the premises. For example, if a window cleaner (not being a servant of the occupier) sustains injury through the insecurity of some part of the exterior of the premises which he uses as a foothold or handhold for the purpose of cleaning the outside of the

63 *O'Leary* v. *Wood* (1963) 99 I.L.T.R. 194.
64 *Ante*, § 352.
65 (1880) 9 East 277; 9 R.R. 553.
66 *Latham* v. *Johnson* [1913] 1 K.B. 398, 415.
67 *Hardy* v. *Central London Ry.* [1902] 3 K.B. 459, 470.

windows, the occupier merely as such should not be liable.[68] *Aliter*, if the window cleaner is injured through some defect in the staircase when going upstairs in the ordinary way to reach the windows on an upper floor." [69]

358 Thus in *Woollins* v. *British Celanese Ltd.*[70] it was held that the particular subsection under consideration deals with the special risks incident to the work being carried out on the occupiers' premises by the visitor, such as live wires to an electrician, and does not apply to the ordinary risks incident to the premises themselves, such as the unsafe fragile roofing upon which a Post Office engineer put his foot when attempting to remove a cable from the occupiers' factory. On the other hand an occupier was held not liable: where an experienced and skilled window cleaner fell while cleaning windows when some ornamental trellis-work up against which he had knocked broke away and resulted in him losing his balance [71]; where a clerk of works fell from a scaffold which was not in any way defective, there being no risk other than that ordinarily incident to the use of any scaffold.[72] In *Roles* v. *Nathan* [73] two chimney-sweeps were killed by carbon monoxide poisoning whilst they were engaged in sealing up a sweep-hole in a flue leading from the occupier's boiler room. Lord Denning said: " The occupier here was under no duty of care to these sweeps, at any rate in regard to the dangers which caused their deaths. If it had been a different danger, as for instance, if the stairs leading to the cellar gave way, the occupier might no doubt be responsible, but not for these dangers which were special risks ordinarily incidental to their calling." [74]

359 **General matters to be taken into consideration.** Clearly the court is free to take into consideration all those matters which under the old law in the past have proved to have been relevant in order to arrive at a decision whether the occupier has fulfilled the common duty of care. Accordingly it should have regard to such things as the purpose of the visit, the conduct of the visitor that is to be expected of him, the nature of the danger and whether it be obvious or not, what warnings, if any, should be given, what guarding, lighting and precautions should be taken, the state of knowledge of the occupier and the age of the visitor.

By way of illustration drawn from the old common law decisions dangers have been held to exist: where there was a loose end of a carpet

68 This subsection shows that *Christmas* v. *General Cleaning Contractors Ltd.* [1953] A.C. 180 is still good law under the Act.

69 Cmd. 9305, para. 77 (iii); *Bates* v. *Parker* [1953] 2 Q.B. 231. The Committee added that in their view the provision of proper safeguards for window cleaners in factories, shops, offices and private houses was a matter which might usefully receive further attention. See also *Smith* v. *Austin Lifts* [1959] 1 W.L.R. 100; *Heggie* v. *Edinburgh and Leith Window Cleaning, etc., Co.*, 1959 S.L.T. 30.

70 (1966) 1 K.I.R. 438. See articles: " The ' Occupier ' and his ' Visitors,' " 130 J.P.J. 38; " Knowledge and Exemption in Occupiers' Liability " (Bradbury), 119 New L.J. 520.

71 *Caddis* v. *Gettrup* (1967) 202 E.G. 517.

72 *Howitt* v. *A. Bagnall & Sons* [1967] 2 Lloyd's Rep. 370.

73 [1963] 1 W.L.R. 1117.

74 *Ibid.* at pp. 1123–1124.

laid at the entrance to a room [75]; a piece of vegetable matter on a shop floor upon which a customer slipped and fell [76]; where some steps leading from a clubhouse had been removed and re-erected in a different position but not lit so as to warn members of the alteration.[77] On the other hand no danger was held to exist: where a rug had been laid on top of a floor highly polished elsewhere but not under the rug [78]; where a window which was safe enough for ordinary purposes was not safe when held onto by a window cleaner.[79]

360 **Warning and knowledge of dangers.** It is implicit from the wording of section 2 (4) of the Act that all relevant general matters noted above can and should be taken into consideration by the court. It provides: "In determining whether the occupier of premises has discharged the common duty of care to a visitor, regard is to be had to all the circumstances, so that (for example)—

(*a*) where damage is caused to a visitor by a danger of which he had been warned by the occupier, the warning is not to be treated without more as absolving the occupier from liability, unless in all the circumstances it was enough to enable the visitor to be reasonably safe . . ."

The effect in *London Graving Dock* v. *Horton* [80] was that the House of Lords had held that notice to or knowledge by the visitor of the risk was quite sufficient to exonerate the occupier from liability, provided that it could be shown the visitor had recognised the full significance of the risk. Further if the required degree of knowledge was brought home to the visitor his claim would be equally defeated whether he freely and voluntarily undertook the risk or not. However this decision has now been overruled by section 2 (4) (*a*). Thus knowledge of the danger by the visitor is now just one of the circumstances of the case to be taken into consideration when deciding whether reasonable care has been taken to see that the visitor will be reasonably safe for the purposes for which he is invited or permitted to be there. A warning, accordingly, on the facts of the particular case may or may not be sufficient. Singleton L.J. in dealing with this aspect said: "Whether the notice (or knowledge) is sufficient to absolve the occupier must depend on a variety of circumstances, including the nature of the risk and the position of the injured party. If a veterinary surgeon is called to a farm at night time to attend to a sick animal and the farmer tells him: 'Be careful how you go down the yard or you may fall into a tank,' and, in spite of every care, the veterinary surgeon meets with an accident through an unusual danger, though of the kind envisaged, he may be entitled to recover notwithstanding the warning or notice. On the other hand, if a shopkeeper says to a customer

[75] *Kimber* v. *Wm. Willett Ltd.* [1947] K.B. 570.
[76] *Turner* v. *Arding & Hobbs Ltd.* [1949] 2 All E.R. 911.
[77] *Prole* v. *Allen* [1950] 1 All E.R. 476.
[78] *Jennings* v. *Cole* [1949] 2 All E.R. 191.
[79] *Christmas* v. *General Cleaning Contractors* [1952] 1 K.B. 141 (affirmed on other grounds [1953] A.C. 180). S. 2 (3) (*b*) shows that this case is still good law under the Act: *Bates* v. *Parker* [1953] 2 Q.B. 231.
[80] [1951] A.C. 737.

some such words as: 'Do not go to the far side of the shop; there is a hole there and it is dangerous,' and the customer disregards the warning and thereby meets with an accident, it is unlikely that he could recover even if he would be regarded as an invitee at that spot." [81] Lord MacDermott also proffered an example where in his opinion a warning would not be sufficient: "A, at the end of his day's work, repairs to the local railway station to go home. He goes to the ticket office by the usual and only means of approach. The roof overhead is in a dangerous state and bits of it are liable to fall at any moment. The railway company know of this and could readily avert the danger of those beneath by placing a temporary screen under the defective part. But all they do is to post a notice describing the danger in clear terms. A reads and understands this before he enters the perilous area, but hurries on in order to get his ticket and is hurt by a piece of falling glass. He was not *volens* or careless." [82] In *Roles* v. *Nathan* [83] two chimney-sweeps, in defiance of repeated warnings of the dangers involved given to them by the occupiers' agent, entered into the confined space of an alcove in order to obtain access to the sweep-hole with a view to sealing it up, and died from carbon monoxide gas as a result. The Court of Appeal held that in the circumstances the occupiers by their warnings had discharged under section 2 (4) (*a*) of the Occupiers' Liability Act 1957 the common duty of care that they owed to the chimney-sweeps.

361 In *Bunker* v. *Charles Brand & Son Ltd.*[84] the plaintiff, an employee of a constructional engineering firm, was engaged in work in a section of the Victoria Tube tunnel, which was being cut by a machine hired by the defendants, the main contractors, for constructing such tunnel. As the machine progressed in its cutting operation the normal way to reach the front of the machine was by walking along the line of free-running rollers supported on angle irons, which was what the plaintiff was doing when he missed his footing, slipped off onto the rollers, which moved, and fell, hurting himself. O'Connor J. held that although the plaintiff knew of the risk involved in walking over the rollers, knowledge of the danger did not absolve the occupier from liability unless in all the circumstances it was enough to enable the visitor to be reasonably safe, and he considered that on the facts something more ought to have been done by the defendants.

362 If the occupier has exempted himself from liability by "agreement or otherwise," [85] "in so far as he is free to and does" so, no duty of care is owed to the visitor.

[81] *Horton* v. *London Graving Dock Co.* [1950] 1 K.B. 421, at pp. 428–429.
[82] [1951] A.C. 737, at pp. 764–765.
[83] [1963] 1 W.L.R. 1117.
[84] [1969] 2 Q.B. 480. See articles: "Knowledge and Exemption in Occupiers' Liability" (Bradbury), 119 New L.J. 520; "Occupiers' Liability: '*Scienti*' or '*Volenti non fit injuria*,'" 7 Legal Executive 184.
[85] s. 2 (1). See also *ante*, § 347.

Thus it is seen from the above matters, at common law, when an invitee had full knowledge of the nature and extent of the danger, no duty of care was owed to him by the occupier.[86] The Act accordingly recognises the common law principle that a danger, if known to a visitor, may cease to be a danger to him, but, in each case, it is a question of fact whether such knowledge on the part of such visitor successfully relieves the occupier from liability. As Denning L.J. had said in *Slater* v. *Clay Cross Co. Ltd.*: " Even in cases which concern the condition of premises . . . knowledge of the danger is only a bar where the party is free to act on it, so that his injury can be said to be due solely to his own fault. . . . Where knowledge of the danger is not such as to render the accident solely the fault of the injured party, then it is not a bar to the action but only a ground for reducing the damages." [87]

Whilst it is clear from the wording of section 2 (5) that the defence of " *volenti non fit injuria* " is preserved,[88] its application will, probably, be rare, since a finding of contributory negligence will be the more likely.

363 **Contributory negligence.** Although the Law Reform Committee [89] specifically recommended that this defence should be available the Act is silent on this point. Contributory negligence is not in itself a bar to a plaintiff's claim, but is merely a ground for the reduction of damages, since the passing of the Law Reform (Contributory Negligence) Act 1945, which provides that the defendant's conduct must constitute: " negligence, breach of statutory duty or other act or omission which would give rise to a liability in tort." It would seem that the " common duty of care " owed by an occupier under the Occupiers' Liability Act 1957 must fall within this definition, so that it is submitted that the qualified defence of contributory negligence is open to an occupier under the Act in claims arising after January 1, 1958.[90]

364 **Volenti non fit injuria.** In *Letang* v. *Ottawa Electric Ry.*[91] it was stated: " If the defendants desire to succeed on the ground that the maxim ' *volenti non fit injuria* ' is applicable, they must obtain a finding of fact that the plaintiff freely and voluntarily, with full knowledge of the nature and extent of the risk he ran impliedly agreed to incur it." Thus a defendant has not broken any duty of care towards a plaintiff according to the ordinary principles of negligence when it is found as a fact that he has voluntarily assumed the risk. The same principles apply to the duty under

[86] *London Graving Dock* v. *Horton* [1951] A.C. 737.
[87] [1956] 2 Q.B. 264, 271. See further *A. C. Billings & Sons Ltd.* v. *Riden* [1958] A.C. 240, *per* Lord Somervell at p. 266.
[88] *Letang* v. *Ottawa Electric Ry.* [1926] A.C. 725, at p. 731, citing *Osborne* v. *London and North Western Ry.* (1888) 21 Q.B.D. 220.
[89] Cmd. 9305, para. 95.
[90] *Wheat* v. *E. Lacon & Co. Ltd.* [1966] A.C. 552, at p. 570. Then there have been findings of contributory negligence in, for example: *Woollins* v. *British Celanese Ltd.* (1966) 1 K.I.R. 438; *Blackett* v. *B.R.B., The Times*, December 19, 1967; *McDowell* v. *F.M.C. (Meat)* (1968) 5 K.I.R. 456.
[91] [1926] A.C. 725, at p. 731, citing *Osborne* v. *London & North Western Ry.* (1888) 21 Q.B.D. 220.

the 1957 Act which provides by section 2 (5): " The common duty of care does not impose on an occupier any obligation to a visitor in respect of risks willingly accepted as his by the visitor (the question whether a risk was so accepted to be decided on the same principles as in other cases in which one person owes a duty of care to another)." Thus where the plaintiff was injured through slipping on the polished floor of a hall in which physical training classes were conducted, it was held that he did not agree to take upon himself the risk of slipping upon a floor which was not reasonably fit for the purpose of physical training.[92] On the other hand a rugby footballer was held willingly to have accepted the risk of playing the game on the defendant's ground, which, although it complied with the by-laws of the Rugby Football League, had a concrete wall running at a distance of 7 ft. 3 in. away from and along the touchline.[93] Nevertheless since the Law Reform (Contributory Negligence) Act 1945 it is more common for the conduct of the visitor to be dealt with as contributory negligence rather than as a voluntary assumption of risk, since this defence amounts to a complete answer to his claim for damages, whilst under contributory negligence the court can apportion the blame.[94] For a more detailed discussion of this maxim, see Chapter 16, § 1053, *post*.

365 **Liability for independent contractors.** In order to understand the present law it is helpful to consider the position prior to January 1, 1958. It was then held that the occupier ought to have known of dangers created by himself and his servants or agents, but not necessarily those which were unknown to him, but were known to his sub-contractors. Accordingly it depended on the circumstances whether he ought to have known of these. However, there was considerable judicial doubt what the true position was at common law, because in *Haseldine* v. *Daw* [95] and *Woodward* v. *Hastings Corpn.*[96] the Court of Appeal laid down the principle as stated above, whilst in *Thomson* v. *Cremin* [97] the House of Lords appeared to say that the occupiers' duty was personal and not to be avoided by entrusting its performance to an independent contractor.[98] Nevertheless whatever was the precise effect of *Thomson* v. *Cremin* there seemed to be no question of *Haseldine* v. *Daw* being overruled. Further in *Green* v. *Fibreglass Ltd.*[99] an office cleaner was injured when cleaning

92 *Gillmore* v. *L.C.C.* [1938] 4 All E.R. 331. For the occupier's or promoter's duty in respect of sports premises and sporting activities, see *post*, § 372.
93 *Simms* v. *Leigh Rugby Football Club* [1969] 2 All E.R. 923.
94 *Slater* v. *Clay Cross Co.* [1956] 2 Q.B. 264.
95 [1941] 2 K.B. 343.
96 [1945] K.B. 174.
97 [1953] 2 All E.R. 1185; this case was first drawn to the attention of the legal profession by Heuston in *Salmond on Torts*, 11th ed., p. 563. See now 15th ed., p. 350.
98 For a full discussion of the differences and the case-law upon the subject by the author, see 3rd ed., pp. 198–201.
99 [1958] 2 Q.B. 245. Salmon J. considered this dictum of Lord Wright in *Thomson* v. *Cremin*, and said (at p. 253): " With great diffidence I doubt whether it is helpful to import into this branch of the law the conception of warranty. That seems to me to belong exclusively to the law of contract. The obligation of an invitor to an invitee has nothing to do with the law of contract or quasi-contract but is part of the law of tort. The invitee's cause of action lies in negligence and nothing else."

an electric fire which was " alive " due to faulty wiring leading from the mains to the switch, thence to the socket into which the fire had been plugged. It was held that the occupier was not liable since he had discharged his duty to the plaintiff, as invitor, by employing competent electrical contractors, who had completely rewired the offices some five years previously.

366 The Act now substantially reproduces, as a statutory example of the general proposition, that: " In determining whether the occupier of premises has discharged the common duty of care to a visitor, regard is to be had to all the circumstances,"[1] the Law Reform Committee's recommendations,[2] by means of section 2 (4) (*b*). This provides that the occupier is not liable for damage caused to a visitor owing to the faulty execution of any work of construction, maintenance or repair done by an independent contractor, if (1) he acted reasonably in entrusting the work to an independent contractor, and (2) he had taken such steps as he reasonably ought to satisfy himself that the contractor was competent and that the work had been properly done.

In *A.M.F. International Ltd.* v. *Magnet Bowling Ltd.*[3] Mocatta J. stated: " I approach the point of construction with a self-confessed reluctance to adopt too rigid and technical an interpretation of an Act passed to bring order into what had become, notwithstanding the clarity of the words of Willes J. in *Indermaur* v. *Dames*,[4] a jungle of technicalities and refinements. It seems to me that if a builder in the course of constructing a building fails to take adequate precautions against flooding and that causes damage to the property of a visitor, it would be altogether too technical to hold this not within the true construction of the words ' a danger due to the faulty execution of any work of construction, maintenance or repair.' "

367 It would seem therefore that the wording of section 2 (4) (*b*) effectively overrules *Thomson* v. *Cremin*[5] on this point and provides statutory confirmation of *Haseldine* v. *Daw & Sons Ltd.*[6] Presumably *Woodward* v. *Hastings Corporation* would still be decided in the same way. Also would be decided with the like result *Green* v. *Fibreglass Ltd.*[7] since the occupiers' common duty of care would be discharged by the employment of the competent electrical contractors to carry out rewiring of the premises in the circumstances. If an occupier undertakes to do work himself, which requires such a degree of highly specialised skill or knowledge that a normal occupier would reasonably be expected to and would employ competent experts to do it, he may well find himself in breach of duty, but

[1] s. 2 (4).
[2] Cmd. 9305, para. 78 (v).
[3] [1968] 1 W.L.R. 1028, at p. 1043.
[4] (1866) L.R. 1 C.P. 274.
[5] [1953] 2 All E.R. 1185.
[6] *supra*.
[7] *supra*. There could have been no answer to the claim had it been brought against the electrical contractors.

not if he undertakes some trifling domestic repair work. Accordingly, where a door handle came away in a visitor's hand, the Court of Appeal held in *Wells* v. *Cooper* [8] that a man who had some experience as an amateur carpenter was justified in undertaking such a trifling domestic replacement as fitting a new door handle with three screws. Jenkins L.J.[9] said: " We think the standard of care and skill to be demanded of the defendant in order to discharge his duty of care to the plaintiff in the fixing of a new handle . . . must be the degree of care and skill to be expected of a reasonably competent carpenter doing the work in question. This does not mean that the degree of care and skill required is to be measured by reference to the contractual obligations as to the quality of his work assumed by a professional carpenter working for reward, which would, in our view, set the standard too high." Towards the end of his judgment Jenkins L.J., after stressing the fact that the occupier's duty was no more than to take reasonable care and that the standard required of him was not raised to anything higher than that by the circumstances that he might choose to employ an independent contractor to do the work for him, said [10]: " It does not follow that because the degree of care and skill exercised by the independent contractor falls short of the standard required of him under his contract with the invitor it also falls short of the standard required of the invitor as between himself and his invitee. The two standards are by no means necessarily the same."

368 Where, however, the safety of the visitor depends on acts which the occupier could and ought to have done personally and which do not involve the performance of work requiring technical skill or special knowledge, he cannot avoid liability for his own neglect to do those acts merely by delegating it to an independent contractor, who had negligently performed the work. When the occupier has acted reasonably in entrusting the work to an independent contractor, and has satisfied himself that such contractor was competent, the taking of such further steps to satisfy himself that the work has been properly done may require the provision of expert supervision which is beyond his capabilities. Failure to employ the necessary specialised supervision by a properly qualified man, when such is called for on the facts, undoubtedly could result in the occupier being found guilty of negligence. As Mocatta J. said further [11]: " In the case of the construction of a substantial building or of a ship, I should have thought that the building owner, if he is to escape subsequent tortious liability for faulty construction should not only take care to contract with a competent contractor or shipbuilder, but also to cause that work to be supervised by a properly qualified professional man such as an architect or surveyor, or a naval architect or Lloyd's surveyor. Such cases are different in fact and in everyday practice from having a flat re-wired."

[8] [1958] 2 Q.B. 265.
[9] At p. 271.
[10] At p. 274.
[11] *AMF International Ltd.* v. *Magnet Bowling Ltd., supra*, at p. 1044.

369 **Effect of contract on occupiers' liability to third party.** At common law it was considered that the duty owed by the occupier to a third person in regard to the safety of the premises, was exactly the same as that which he owed to the person with whom he had contracted for the use of the premises on the basis that that person would be entitled to permit a third person to use them under the terms of such contract.[12] This was an unsatisfactory position which the Law Reform Committee recommended should be reformed and which the Act has attempted to do by the provisions of section 3.

Section 3 (1) provides: "Where an occupier of premises is bound by contract to permit persons who are strangers to the contract to enter or use the premises, the duty of care which he owes to them as his visitors cannot be restricted or excluded by that contract[13] but (subject to any provision of the contract to the contrary) shall include the duty to perform his obligations under the contract,[14] whether undertaken for their protection or not, in so far as those obligations go beyond the obligations otherwise involved in that duty." Section 3 (3) defines "stranger to the contract" as "a person not for the time being entitled to the benefit of the contract as a party to it or as the successor by assignment or otherwise of a party to it, and accordingly includes a party to the contract who has ceased to be so entitled." The duty now owed by the occupier to such strangers to the contract is the same common duty of care that he owes to all lawful visitors unless the contract has imposed more onerous terms on the occupier.[15] By way of illustration if the lessor of a block of offices has retained control of the common staircase he cannot exclude or limit in the terms of the lease his common duty of care to the tenants' lawful visitors when using this means of access. Indeed, the tenants' said visitors will be able to claim the benefit of any more onerous obligations undertaken in the lease, unless it contains terms contrary to the provision.[16]

Section 3 (4) next provides: "Where by the terms or conditions governing any tenancy (including a statutory tenancy which does not in law amount to a tenancy) either the landlord or the tenant is bound, though not by contract, to permit persons to enter or use premises of which he is the occupier, this section shall apply as if the tenancy were a contract between the landlord and the tenant." Then lastly by section 3 (5) it is explained and enacted that: "This section, in so far as it prevents the common duty of care from being restricted or excluded, applies to contracts entered into and tenancies created before the commencement of

12 Cmd. 9305, para. 55; see also *Fosbroke-Hobbes* v. *Airwork Ltd.* [1937] 1 All E.R. 108, 112.

13 Normally the common duty of care can be restricted or excluded altogether, so that such visitors in this instance are in a privileged position (see s. 2 (1)).

14 Provided an occupier has taken all reasonable care, he is not responsible for the default of an independent contractor unless the contract provides expressly that he should be (see s. 3 (2) of the Act).

15 The case of *Jacobs* v. *London County Council* [1950] A.C. 361, would now be decided differently because the appellant being a licensee on the landlord's forecourt would be in the position of being a lawful visitor, whilst approaching the tenant's shop premises, in which event she must be entitled to the benefit of the common duty of care provided by s. 2 of the Occupiers' Liability Act 1957.

16 Cmd. 9305, paras. 79 and 95 (1) (ii).

this Act, as well as to those entered into or created after its commencement; but, in so far as it enlarges the duty owed by an occupier beyond the common duty of care, it shall have effect only in relation to obligations which are undertaken after that commencement or which are renewed by agreement (whether express or implied) after that commencement."

370 **Contractual duty to persons entering the premises.** When payment is made for admission to premises, a contractual relation is established between the payer and the person receiving payment. The terms of the contract may be contained in some document, such as a ticket,[17] and in that case liability depends on the construction of the document. On the other hand, there may be no express terms, and then liability depends on the implied terms. Whether or not terms are to be implied is a question of law for the court.[18] Terms will only be implied to carry out the presumed intention of the parties and not merely because it would be reasonable to imply them. When there is a contract, express or implied, between the parties regulating their rights, it is not permissible to disregard the contract and allege a wider duty in tort.[19]

At common law when persons entered premises under a contract, the circumstances might be such that, unless there was an express or implied term to the contrary, there was an implied warranty that the premises were as safe as reasonable care and skill could make them. This was not an absolute warranty, and did not cover defects, such as latent defects, which could not have been discovered by the exercise of reasonable care and skill. However, as a result of the uncertainties which had developed around the terms to be implied,[20] all these distinctions were abolished by the Act, which has greatly simplified the law. Now, in lieu of the terms implied at common law, section 5, which applies to contracts entered into after January 1, 1958, enacts:

"(1) Where persons enter or use, or bring or send goods to, any premises in exercise of a right conferred by contract with a person occupying or having control of the premises, the duty he owes them in respect of dangers due to the state of the premises or to things done or omitted to be done on them, in so far as the duty depends on a term to be implied in the contract by reason of its conferring that right, shall be the common duty of care.

[17] See *Rogers* v. *L.M.S. Ry.* (1930) 46 T.L.R. 238: *Thompson* v. *L.M.S. Ry.* [1930] 1 K.B. 41; *Penton* v. *Southern Ry.* [1931] 2 K.B. 103; *Beaumont-Thomas* v. *Blue Star Line Ltd.* [1939] 3 All E.R. 127.

[18] *Comptoir Commercial Anversois* v. *Power Son & Co.* [1920] 1 K.B. 868; *Tournier* v. *National Provincial and Union Bank* [1924] 1 K.B. 461, 483–485; *Hall* v. *Brooklands Auto-Racing Club* [1933] 1 K.B. 205.

[19] *Hall* v. *Brooklands Auto-Racing Club, supra, per* Scrutton L.J. at p. 213.

[20] Broadly speaking in the case where a contract was one for the use of the premises (as distinct from a contract incidentally involving the use of premises) the occupier had to keep them as safe for the purposes contemplated as reasonable care and skill could make them: *Francis* v. *Cockrell* (1870) L.R. 5 Q.B. 501; *Maclenan* v. *Segar* [1917] 2 K.B. 325. On the other hand, where the use of the premises was merely incidental to the main purpose of the contract, the occupiers' duty would appear to have been limited to taking reasonable care to see that the premises were reasonably safe for the purpose for which they were to

(2) The foregoing subsection shall apply to fixed and moveable structures as it applies to premises.

(3) This section does not affect the obligations imposed on a person by or by virtue of any contract for the hire of, or for the carriage for reward of persons or goods in, any vehicle, vessel, aircraft or other means of transport, or by or by virtue of any contract of bailment."

371 In this connection it is necessary to consider the problems arising out of: (a) Spectacles and Entertainments, and (b) Landlord and Tenant. Although, as provided by section 5 (1) above, the duty is now the "common duty of care,"[21] the matters set out in the following text would probably be taken into account as forming part of the "circumstances of the case."

(a) *Spectacles and Entertainments*

372 **Duty as to structure.** At common law if the premises were to be used for the purpose of watching some sport, spectacle or theatrical entertainment, the warranty was that they were reasonably fit for that purpose having regard to the normal risks of the particular entertainment. The person receiving payment was not "under any obligation to provide safety under all circumstances, but only to provide against damage to spectators which any reasonable occupier in their position would have anticipated as likely to happen."[22] Accordingly, when a spectator at a motor race meeting at Brooklands was injured by a car which came through the railing dividing the track from the space appropriated to the spectators, and it was proved that no similar accident had happened since the track was opened over twenty years before, it was held that the spectator had no cause of action.[23] Similarly, when a polo pony at Ranelagh ran through a hedge and injured a spectator, it was held that the spectator could not recover.[24]

373 The normal risks of the particular sport, spectacle or entertainment might, however, require that some additional safety device should have been added to the structure and, if this was not done, there would be a breach of duty of care. "The performance may be of such a kind as to render the structure an unsafe place to be in whilst the performance is going on, or it may be of such a kind as to render the structure unsafe unless some obvious precaution is taken. As an illustration under the latter head I would instance a case where a tightrope dancer performs on a rope stretched over the heads of the audience. In such a case the

be used: *Gillmore* v. *L.C.C.* [1938] 4 All E.R. 331. The validity of this distinction was seriously cast into doubt by the decision in *Thomson* v. *Cremin* [1953] 2 All E.R. 1185.

21 s. 2 (2). 22 *Per* Greer L.J. in *Hall* v. *Brooklands Auto-Racing Club* [1933] 1 K.B. 205, 225.

23 *Hall* v. *Brooklands Auto-Racing Club, supra*; *Wilks* v. *Cheltenham Homeguard Motor Cycle and Light Car Club* [1971] 1 W.L.R. 668. *Cf. Australian Racing Drivers Club* v. *Metcalf* (1961) 106 C.L.R. 177. The respondent, a spectator, who had paid a charge for admission to a motor-car race meeting organised by the appellants, was injured by a racing car which left the track at a point where it was unfenced. The High Court of Australia held the appellants liable for the failure under their contractual duty to provide a safety fence.

24 *Pidington* v. *Hastings*, *The Times*, March 12, 1932.

provision of a net under the rope to protect the audience in case the performer fell seems so obvious a precaution to take that in the absence of it the premises could not be said to be reasonably safe." [25] So, where a performer on a tightrope negligently dropped a chair upon one of the audience, and no net was provided, the proprietors of the hall were held liable for breach of implied contract that the seats were reasonably safe.[26]

374 **Duty as to the performance.** Apart from the duty as to the structure, there was a duty as to the entertainment. It was said that there was a duty not to give an entertainment of an intrinsically dangerous nature.[27] This, however, could mean no more than that reasonable care must have been taken to make the premises safe having regard to the nature of the entertainment. A circus showing performing lions or bears was giving an entertainment which was intrinsically dangerous unless proper precautions were taken, but there was no duty not to give it.

375 If there was no breach of duty as to the structure, there was no liability on the person with whom the contract was made when damage was caused without any lack of care on the part of the performers. When a racing car at Brooklands got among the spectators without any negligence on the part of the driver, and the track was reasonably safe, it was held that the proprietors of Brooklands were not liable.[28] A visitor at a golf club who, while putting on a green, was struck by a ball driven by a player from an adjoining tee, was held to have no right of action against the club, because his injury was due to a risk of the game and not to any lack of care in the design or construction of the course.[29] Similarly, at a cricket or football match a spectator who was hit by a ball struck or kicked in the course of play had no right of action against the occupiers of the ground. A child of six, a spectator at an ice-hockey match, who was injured through the puck leaving the arena and coming among the spectators, failed to recover on its being proved that the rink was structurally safe and the risk was a risk of the game.[30] On the other hand, when there was negligence on the part of the performers, the occupier of the place of entertainment was liable if they were his servants.[31]

[25] *Per* Bankes L.J. in *Cox* v. *Coulson* [1916] 2 K.B. 177, 191–192; 85 L.J.K.B. 1081.

[26] *Welsh* v. *Canterbury and Paragon Ltd.* (1894) 10 T.L.R. 478. A plea that there was contributory negligence on the part of the plaintiff in sitting underneath the rope while the performance was going on was rejected by Mathew J. The provisions of s. 2 (4) (*b*) of the Occupiers' Liability Act 1957 would not apply, and the plaintiff would only succeed now if the court found that in the circumstances a net should have been provided to make the premises reasonably safe for use.

[27] *Cox* v. *Coulson, supra, per* Pickford L.J. at p. 187; *Sheehan* v. *Dreamland* (*Margate*) *Ltd.* (1923) 40 T.L.R. 155.

[28] *Hall* v. *Brooklands Auto-Racing Club, supra. Cf. Australian Racing Drivers Club* v. *Metcalf, supra.*

[29] *Potter* v. *Carlisle and Cliftonville Golf Club Ltd* [1939] N.I. 114. See also § 1063 *et seq.*

[30] *Murray* v. *Harringay Arena Ltd.* [1951] 2 K.B. 529. The implied term in the contract did not become wider because one of the parties was an infant.

[31] In *Wooldridge* v. *Sumner and British Horse Society, The Times*, December 6 and 7, 1961, a competitor was held not to be a servant of the occupiers, and the occupiers were dismissed from the case. This was not the subject of any appeal at [1963] 2 Q.B. 43. The duty of

If they were not his servants, he was not liable for their negligence unless he knew or ought to have known that in the course of the performance a dangerous thing [32] would be employed. So where the plaintiff paid for admission to the defendant's theatre, at which a travelling company, not the servants of the defendant, were performing, and the plaintiff was injured through the firing of a pistol by one of the actors in the course of the performance, it was held that the defendant was bound to take reasonable care to see that such incidents as the firing of pistols were performed without risk to the audience.[33] Pickford L.J. said: "In this case it is obvious that firearms would be used, and it is common knowledge that unless proper care is taken in loading them they are dangerous, and I think there was an obligation on his [the defendant's] part to take reasonable care that they were so loaded as not to be dangerous. I do not think that such an obligation necessarily imposes on him a liability for every unexpected act of negligence on the part of one of the actors." [34]

376 When a dangerous thing was not used and the person negligent was not a servant of the occupier of the premises, the occupier was not liable.[35] Accordingly, when the plaintiff entered a show-ground under a contract with the defendants and went into a sideshow where she was injured owing to the negligence of a person employed by the sideshow concessionaire, it was held that the defendants were not liable, as the sideshow was not intrinsically dangerous.[36] When a member of the audience at a theatre was struck in the face by the heel from one of the performers' shoes during a performance which was not intrinsically dangerous, the claim failed.[37]

(b) *Landlord and Tenant*

377 **Obligation of landlord.** It remains to consider whether a landlord is under any contractual duty to his tenant in respect of defective premises. The general rule is that, apart from contract, the landlord is under no duty to his tenant as to the state of the demised premises. "A landlord who lets a house in a dangerous state is not liable to the tenant's customers

care which a competitor or participant in a sport or game owes to a spectator depends on the standard of conduct which the sport or game permits or involves, and a spectator takes the risk of damage done to him by participants in the course of and for the purposes of that sport or game notwithstanding that such damage may be the result of an error of judgment by the competitor, provided that it is not reckless or deliberate. See further *Wilks* v. *Cheltenham Homeguard Motor Cycle and Light Car Club* [1971] 1 W.L.R. 668.

[32] See *post*, Chap. 9.

[33] *Cox* v. *Coulson* [1916] 2 K.B. 177. The duty was based rather on the relationship of invitor and invitee than on contract.

[34] *Ibid.* at p. 187.

[35] See *Payne* v. *Maple Leaf Gardens* [1949] 1 D.L.R. 369, where a spectator at an ice-hockey game was injured when one player attacked another to take away his stick. The occupier was held not liable but the player was held liable.

[36] *Sheehan* v. *Dreamland* (*Margate*) *Ltd.* (1923) 40 T.L.R. 155. Where no payment was made for entrance to the show-ground, but a sideshow was entered for payment made to a cashier employed by the show-ground but under a contract made with the concessionaire, it was held that there was no contractual relation between the show-ground proprietors and the person entering the sideshow and also no relation of invitor and invitee between them. *Humphreys* v. *Dreamland* (*Margate*) *Ltd.* (1931) 100 L.J.K.B. 137.

[37] *Fraser-Wallas* v. *Waters* [1939] 4 All E.R. 609 (the action was against the persons who engaged the artists at a variety entertainment and not against the occupiers of the theatre, but the liability of the occupiers could not be greater than that of the persons sued).

or guests for accidents happening during the term; for, fraud apart, there is no law against letting a tumbledown house; and the tenant's remedy is upon his contract, if any." [38] Unless the tenant has an express contract that the landlord will keep the demised premises in repair, he has no remedy against the landlord if he is injured through the non-repair of the premises, because it is well settled that in the case of the letting of unfurnished houses or flats there is no implied contract on the part of the landlord that the premises are fit for habitation at the commencement of the letting [39] or will be maintained in repair during the tenancy. Even if the landlord in fact does the repairs, he is under no implied obligation to his tenant to do so.[40] An exception to this rule has been introduced in the case of small houses by the Housing Act 1957.[41] It is provided by section 6 (2): " Subject to the provisions of this Act, in any contract to which this section applies [42] there shall, notwithstanding any stipulation to the contrary, be implied a condition that the house is at the commencement of the tenancy, and an undertaking that the house will be kept by the landlord during the tenancy, fit for human habitation." This does not apply to a letting for not less than three years without the option of determination during the term, on condition that the house shall be put by the lessee into a state reasonably fit for human habitation.[43] It does, however, apply to a house occupied by an agricultural worker as part of his

[38] *Per* Erle C.J. in *Robbins* v. *Jones* (1863) 15 C.B.(N.S.) 221. See also *Auto-Scooters (Newcastle) Ltd.* v. *Chambers* (1966) 197 E.G. 457. But see article "Coming shortly: The Defective Premises Bill" (Gillett) 103 Chart. Surv. 567.

[39] *Hart* v. *Windsor* (1844) 12 M. & W. 68; *Cruse* v. *Mount* [1933] Ch. 278; *Manchester Bonded Warehouse Co.* v. *Carr* (1880) 5 C.P.D. 507. But for furnished house see *Smith* v. *Marrable* (1843) 11 M. & W. 5; *Collins* v. *Hopkins* [1923] 2 K.B. 617.

[40] *Morgan* v. *Liverpool Corpn.* [1927] 2 K.B. 131; *Wilchick* v. *Marks* [1934] 2 K.B. 56; *Sleafer* v. *Lambeth Metropolitan Borough Council* [1960] 1 Q.B. 43. (Where the landlords, who in practice did carry out repairs, failed to repair the front door so as to ease its shutting and the tenant, in an endeavour to close it, pulled hard at the door handle, which came away in his hand, causing him to fall heavily, it was held that in the absence of a contractual obligation to repair there was no duty on the landlords to do such repairs to the demised premises.) See also *Turner* v. *Waterman* (1961) 105 S.J. 1011.

[41] Which repealed the Housing Act 1936 (Part 1).

[42] It applies to those set out in the Housing Act 1957, s. 6 (1) namely:

(*a*) to a contract made before July 31, 1923, for letting for human habitation a house at a rent not exceeding—

(i) in the case of a house situate in the administrative county of London, £40;

(ii) in the case of a house situate in a borough or urban district outside the administrative county of London, being a borough or district which at the date of the contract had according to the last published census a population of 50,000 or upwards, £26;

(iii) in the case of a house situate elsewhere, £16, and

(*b*) to a contract made on or after the said July 31 and before July 6, 1957, for letting for human habitation a house at a rent not exceeding—

(i) in the case of a house situate in the administrative county of London, £40;

(ii) in the case of a house situate elsewhere, £26, and

(*c*) to a contract made on or after the said July 6, 1957, for letting for human habitation a house at a rent not exceeding—

(i) in the case of a house situate in the administrative county of London, £80;

(ii) in the case of a house situate elsewhere, £52.

" Rent " means the actual rent agreed to be paid and not the rent after deduction of rates: *Rousou* v. *Photi* [1940] 2 K.B. 379.

[43] Housing Act 1957, s. 6 (2); for definition of standard of fitness, see ss. 4 and 5.

remuneration and not as a tenant.[44] Section 6 of the Housing Act 1957 is overlapped and supplemented by sections 32 and 33 of the Housing Act 1961, which provides that irrespective of the amount of the rent payable under the lease there shall be implied covenants by the lessor to keep in repair the structure and exterior of the dwelling-house, inclusive of drains, gutters and external pipes, and to keep in repair and in proper working order the various installations in the dwelling-house, *i.e.* for the supplies of water, gas, electricity, sanitation and heating. It has been held that there is no breach of the statutory condition if the house is from time to time invaded from without by rats in considerable numbers,[45] if a common staircase, not included in the letting, is in an unsafe condition,[46] or when the hot water system is out of order but the house has alternative means of heating water, such as a gas cooker, and gas and electricity are laid on.[47] A defective sash-cord is a breach of the condition,[48] and so is a defective step leading from the kitchen to the back kitchen.[49] The landlord must have notice of the defect before he can be made liable.[49]

378 As there is no obligation upon a landlord (apart from express contract or the statutory obligation under the Housing Act 1957) to keep the demised premises in repair, the question arises whether he is under any contractual obligation to repair the means of access to the demised premises, such as a common staircase, or the roof of a block of flats which he keeps under his own control. He owes a duty in tort in respect of those parts of the premises which he keeps under his own control,[50] but it is difficult to see how there can be implied in the contract of tenancy an obligation to repair, *e.g.* a common staircase, when there is no such obligation to repair the demised premises themselves. When the landlord is under an obligation to repair premises in his own possession, it is not necessary to give notice of want of repair before the landlord can be held liable.[51] In *Dunster* v. *Hollis* [52] Lush J. held that there was an implied undertaking on the part of a landlord to keep the means of access to the demised premises in a reasonably safe condition. This decision was based on *Miller* v. *Hancock*,[53] since

[44] *Ibid.* s. 7.

[45] *Stanton* v. *Southwick* [1920] 2 K.B. 642. Lord Wright in *Summers* v. *Salford Corpn.* [1943] A.C. 283, 295, disagreed with this decision.

[46] *Dunster* v. *Hollis* [1918] 2 K.B. 795. The meaning of the expression " unfit for human habitation " is discussed in *Hall* v. *Manchester Corpn.* (1915) 84 L.J.Ch. 732, and *Estate and Trust Agencies Ltd.* v. *Singapore Improvement Trust* [1937] A.C. 898.

[47] *Daly* v. *Elstree R.D.C.* [1948] 2 All E.R. 1.

[48] *Summers* v. *Salford Corpn.* [1943] A.C. 283.

[49] *McCarrick* v. *Liverpool Corpn.* [1947] A.C. 219.

[50] Thus where the four-year-old child of a tenant in a block, belonging to the local authority, fell through a gap in the balustrade on the staircase, it was held that having regard to the position and size of the gaps the staircase did not comply with the duty of care owed to a child of the age of the plaintiff: *Moloney* v. *Lambeth London B.C.* (1966) 110 S.J. 406.

[51] *Melles & Co.* v. *Holme* [1918] 2 K.B. 100; *Bishop* v. *Consolidated London Properties* (1933) 102 L.J.K.B. 257.

[52] [1918] 2 K.B. 795, which would probably still be decided the same way after January 1, 1958, as regards the duty under the Occupiers' Liability Act 1957.

[53] [1893] 2 Q.B. 177, overruled by *Fairman* v. *Perpetual Investment Bdg. Socy.* [1923] A.C. 74. In *Devine* v. *London Housing Society Ltd.* [1950] 2 All E.R. 1173, Croom-Johnson J. thought *Dunster* v. *Hollis* was not based on *Miller* v. *Hancock*.

overruled, and cannot be considered to be satisfactory in principle. In *Cockburn* v. *Smith*[54] where the landlord of a block of flats retained the roof under his own control and was held liable in tort to his tenant for damage caused through the roof being out of repair, Bankes L.J. said: " It cannot now be suggested that there was any agreement express or implied which can accurately be described as an agreement to repair the roof or the guttering," but Scrutton L.J. and Sargant L.J. expressly reserved their opinion on this point. It has been held that the landlord of a block of flats is under no implied obligation to light the common staircase.[55] It is submitted that a landlord does not impliedly contract to keep in repair the premises he retains under his own control, but at common law he was liable in tort to his invitees and licensees, and, since the coming into operation of the Occupiers' Liability Act 1957, namely, January 1, 1958, he, as the occupier of the means of access, owes the " common duty of care " to his visitors, including the tenant's wife, family and guests, even though he may have effectively contracted out of liability to his tenant. When, by the terms of the tenancy, either the landlord or the tenant is bound, though not by contract, to permit persons to enter or use premises of which he is the occupier, the duty owed by the occupier to such persons cannot be restricted or excluded by the tenancy.[56]

379 When a landlord *has* contracted to repair, he is no longer liable in contract only to his tenant, but he will not be liable under the Act, unless notice of the need for repair has been given to him, since such notice is necessary before his breach of covenant is actionable at the suit of his tenant.[57] Whether the tenancy was created before or after January 1, 1958, he owes " to all persons who or whose goods may from time to time be lawfully on the premises " the common duty of care.[58] Nevertheless, where a landlord has not contracted to repair, he is under no liability to a workman, employed by the tenant, who is injured owing to a defective staircase[59] or to one of the tenant's friends, who is injured by a defective wall,[60] or to the tenant's wife, who is injured due to the dangerous condition of the premises.

[54] [1924] 2 K.B. 119.
[55] *Devine* v. *London Housing Socy. Ltd., supra.* The proposition that there is a general duty on all landlords to light common staircases at all times of darkness is too wide: *Irving* v. *L.C.C.* (1965) 109 S.J. 157, *per* Paull J.
[56] Occupiers' Liability Act 1957, s. 3 (4).
[57] *e.g. Uniproducts (Manchester) Ltd.* v. *Rose Furnishers Ltd.* [1956] 1 W.L.R. 45.
[58] Occupiers' Liability Act 1957, s. 4. The effect of this is to overrule in the main *Cavalier* v. *Pope* [1906] A.C. 428; but *Cameron* v. *Young* [1908] A.C. 176 being a Scottish case is not affected by s. 4. Likewise *Ryall* v. *Kidwell & Son* [1914] 3 K.B. 135 and *Middleton* v. *Hall* (1912) 108 L.T. 804, are overruled. S. 4 (1) has not overruled that part of the *ratio decidendi* of *Cavalier* v. *Pope, supra,* which remains House of Lords authority for the proposition that a landlord does not owe any duty to his tenant's visitors when he has let a house knowing it to be in a defective state of repair, *unless* he has contracted with the tenant either expressly or impliedly or is subject to a statutory obligation to to let such house in a fit state of repair or maintenance.
[59] *Lane* v. *Cox* [1897] 1 Q.B. 415.
[60] *Bromley* v. *Mercer* [1922] 2 K.B. 126.

The effect of section 4 is that a visitor can sue not only the immediate landlord but also any superior landlord who has covenanted to repair, provided that the default amounts to a breach of covenant actionable by the immediate tenant of each landlord or superior landlord sued by the visitor; and provided, too, that there is an unbroken chain of such covenants from the superior landlord sued down through each sub-letting, to the occupying tenant.[61] However, the landlord is not liable to the visitor merely because there is a breach of his covenant to the tenant since, in addition, there must be a breach of the common duty of care that he owes to the visitor. For breach of the contract or the statutory obligation to repair, the tenant may recover any special damage he has suffered in consequence of injury to his wife or family living with him.[62]

4.—THE VISITOR

380 **Generally.** The persons who are to be treated as visitors are the same as those who would at common law have been treated as invitees or licensees [63] so that in this respect the common law rules as to the persons to whom the occupier owed a duty have not been affected by the Occupiers' Liability Act at all.

381 **Invitation or licence, express or implied.** Clearly the invitation or licence to a visitor to enter or use the occupier's premises can be either express or implied. Where, therefore, members of the public habitually visit the premises of the occupier which he well knows but takes no steps to prevent such user, a licence may be readily inferred according to the circumstances. By way of illustration implied permissions existed where a road had been constructed on a housing estate under construction but the road had not yet been dedicated to the public [64]; and where a field was habitually used by members of the public as a short cut, which fact was well known to the occupier.[65] On the other hand no licence was inferred where the occupier had warned off his premises persons frequently and whenever he had seen their presence there [66]; and where the occupier had fenced off his premises, which although broken from time to time he continuously put back and kept in repair.[67]

Problems do arise where an invitation or permission to enter one part of the occupier's premises cannot be interpreted as an invitation or licence to enter other parts of the same premises, hence the duty owed to such a visitor may be limited to some specified area. Accordingly the area of invitation of licence extends to those places only into which the visitor may reasonably be expected to be likely to go and which the visitor reasonably believes that he can do so within the purpose and scope of his

[61] s. 4 (2) and (4).
[62] *Allen* v. *Waters & Co.* [1935] 1 K.B. 200.
[63] s. 1 (2).
[64] *Coleshill* v. *Manchester Corporation* [1928] 1 K.B. 776.
[65] *Lowery* v. *Walker* [1911] A.C. 10.
[66] *Hardy* v. *Central London Ry.* [1920] 3 K.B. 459; *Robert Addie & Sons (Collieries) Ltd.* v. *Dumbreck* [1929] A.C. 358.
[67] *Edwards* v. *Railway Executive* [1952] A.C. 737.

visit.[68] Scrutton L.J. gave a graphic example of this where he said: "When you invite a person into your house to use the staircase, you do not invite him to slide down the banisters. You invite him to use the staircase in the ordinary way in which it is used." [69]

382 It has been held, that a guest, who wandered about a hotel during the darkness and somehow found himself in a service room, had entered that part of the premises to which he had not been invited [70]; a customer was not invited into a shop after the shutters had been placed in position but the door had not yet been locked [71]; the proprietor of an amusement park, who had invited the public to enter, did not invite these members to enter that part of the land which had been let to a concessionaire for his use as a side-show.[72] Nevertheless an involuntary encroachment outside the permitted or invited place which is caused by the occupier's neglect cannot convert a lawful visitor into a trespasser merely because of his presence in that forbidden area.[73] Thus, where a customer in a public-house is invited to use the lavatory he remains a lawful visitor even although he happens to stray whilst making a reasonable search for it.[74] Where a person enters premises in order to call upon the occupier, be it for canvassing business or begging or because he intends making a social call which he reasonably believes to be acceptable, he will remain a lawful visitor only so long as he confines himself to that part of the premises which provides the normal access to the premises.[75] If such person has been forbidden to enter under any circumstances at all either by express prohibition or by the exhibition of a clear and general notice, then he is not even a visitor to use the access up to the premises.[76] Where there is some frequent trespass taking place, of which the occupier is aware but has taken no steps to curb, the facts of the case may show that he has acquiesced in the use and hence has impliedly permitted the trespasser to be present.[77] However the court, it is urged, should be slow to hold that there is such implied permission. As the House of Lords held in *Edwards* v. *Railway Executive* [78] the burden was on the plaintiff to establish a licence, which onus was not discharged by showing that children had broken through a properly constructed fence, which had been repaired whenever it had been broken by trespassing children or others. Where the defendants knew that unauthorised persons habitually trespassed upon their property they must show that they resented intrusion and took

[68] *Mersey Docks and Harbour Board* v. *Procter* [1923] A.C. 253, *per* Lord Cave.
[69] *The Carlgarth*; *The Otarama* [1927] P. 93, at p. 110.
[70] *Lee* v. *Luper* [1936] 3 All E.R. 817.
[71] *Mason* v. *Langford* (1888) 4 T.L.R. 407; see also *Prole* v. *Allen* [1950] 1 All E.R. 476.
[72] *Humphreys* v. *Dreamland* (*Margate*) *Ltd.* (1931) 100 L.J.K.B. 137.
[73] *Braithwaite* v. *South Durham Steel Co.* [1958] 1 W.L.R. 986.
[74] *Gould* v. *McAuliffe* [1941] 2 All E.R. 527. See also *Pearson* v. *Coleman Bros.* [1948] 2 K.B. 359 (a similar situation at a circus).
[75] *Mersey Docks and Harbour Board* v. *Procter*, *supra*; *Hillen* v. *I.C.I.* (*Alkali*) *Ltd.* [1936] A.C. 65. *Cf. Braithwaite* v. *South Durham Steel Co.* [1958] 1 W.L.R. 986.
[76] *Dunster* v. *Abbott* [1954] 1 W.L.R. 58.
[77] *Lowery* v. *Walker* [1911] A.C. 10.
[78] [1952] A.C. 737.

steps to prevent it, but neither omission to take every possible step nor the knowledge that intrusion had occurred was in itself sufficient to support the inference of the grant of a tacit licence.

383 **Children.** Whilst the same considerations apply in the case of a child as in the case of an adult, the Law Reform Committee recognised the problem whether a child can claim to be a licensee when prima facie he is a trespasser.[79] It recorded: " The mere fact that the occupier has upon his premises a dangerous object alluring to children does not make him liable to a trespassing child who meddles with and is injured by it; but the presence of such an object in a place accessible to children may aid the inference of an implied licence." See *ante*, § 348, " Liability to Children " for a fuller discussion.

384 **Persons entering as of right.** A question which had often been raised at common law was whether there was a class of persons who came within the description of persons entering as of right since they came on property not because they were invited or permitted to do so but because the occupier had no power to prevent them from entering.[80] The problem is no longer of any great moment since section 2 (6) provides that: " For the purposes of this section, persons who enter premises for any purpose in the exercise of a right conferred by law are to be treated as permitted by the occupier to be there for that purpose, whether they in fact have his permission or not." Accordingly they are entitled to the benefit of the common duty of care which the occupier owes to all his lawful visitors (*i.e.* a duty to take reasonable care to see that the premises are reasonably safe for the purpose in hand). Such persons who enter as of right include employees of public utilities (*e.g.* gas and electricity boards), police with search warrants, and a numerous class of enforcement officers and inspectors who have statutory rights to enter premises,[81] as well as the members of the public who use premises provided for them such as public parks, playgrounds, libraries, shelters and conveniences.

385 The Act has made no changes in the common law rules of liability relating to those persons who exercise public rights of way. Therefore, since a highway is merely a public right of way over land which remains throughout in the occupation of the owner of the land in question, the grantor of a public right of way owes no duty of care with regard to the condition of the road or highway. Thus passengers on a highway are in a different class and it is only for acts of positive misfeasance which result in obstruction or danger on the highway that make an occupier liable, although he is also liable for maintaining his property adjoining a highway in such a dangerous state that it constitutes a nuisance. See also *post*, Chapter 12. As a result of the decision of the Court of Appeal in

[79] Cmd. 9305, para. 30. *Cooke* v. *Midland G.W. Ry. of Ireland* [1909] A.C. 229; *Gough* v. *N.C.B.* [1954] 1 Q.B. 191.
[80] More fully discussed in 3rd ed., *Charlesworth on Negligence*, Chap. 9, pp. 220, 221.
[81] Cmd. 9305, para. 38. *Hartley* v. *Mayoh & Co.* [1954] 1 Q.B. 383 (firemen).

Greenhalgh v. *British Railways Board* [82] it seems equally clear that in the case of a person who exercises a private right of way, he is in no different position to a person exercising a public right of way in that he is not now a visitor on the premises within the meaning of the Act. Lord Denning M.R. said of the appellant, who had tripped up over the pot-holed surface of an accommodation bridge over a railway, whilst walking over it and had injured herself: " It was said that she was a ' visitor.' But I do not think she was. Section 1 (2) shows that, in order to determine whether a person is a ' visitor,' we must go back to the common law. A person is a ' visitor ' if at common law he would be regarded as an invitee or licensee; or be treated as such, as for instance, a person lawfully using premises provided for the use of the public, *e.g.* a public park, or a person entering by lawful authority, *e.g.* a policeman with a search warrant. But a ' visitor ' does not include a person who crosses land in pursuance of a public or private right of way. Such person was never regarded as an invitee or licensee, or treated as such." [83] Then, after considering the words of section 2 (6) of the Act, he continued: " The important words to notice are the opening words: ' For the purpose of this section,' *i.e.* for the purpose of section 2, which defines only the *extent* of the occupier's duty to acknowledged visitors. It does not expand the range of persons who are to be treated as visitors."

386 It is expressly provided by section 1 (4) of the Act that: " A person entering any premises in exercise of rights conferred by virtue of an access agreement or order under the National Parks and Access to the Countryside Act 1949, is not, for the purposes of this Act, a visitor of the occupier of those premises." It is to be observed that where an access agreement or order is in force in respect of any land, a person who enters upon such land for the purpose of an open-air recreation, without breaking or damaging any wall, fence, hedge or gate or who is on such land for that purpose after having so entered thereon, shall not be treated as a trespasser on that land or incur any other liability by reason only of so entering or being on the land.[84]

5.—TRESPASSERS

387 A trespasser is one who wrongfully enters on land in the possession of another, and has neither right nor permission to be on the land. He is one " who goes on the land without invitation of any sort and whose presence is either unknown to the proprietor or, if known, is practically objected to." [85]

82 [1969] 2 Q.B. 286.
83 At pp. 292, 293.
84 The National Parks and Access to the Countryside Act 1949, s. 60 (1); but s. 66 (2) provides that the operation of s. 60 (1) in relation to any land shall not increase the liability, under any enactment not contained in the Act or under any rule of law, of a person interested in that land or adjoining land in respect of the state thereof or of things done or omitted thereon.
85 *Robert Addie & Sons (Collieries) Ltd.* v. *Dumbreck* [1929] A.C. 358, 371, *per* Lord Dunedin.

The Occupiers' Liability Act 1957 does not alter the common law affecting trespassers or entrants, other than lawful visitors, so that they are wholly outside the scope of the Act. By section 1 (4) the Act provides: "A person entering any premises in exercise of rights conferred by virtue of an access agreement or order under the National Parks and Access to the Countryside Act 1949 is not, for the purpose of this Act, a visitor of the occupier of those premises."

88 **Intention with regard to trespasser.** Neither the occupier nor any other person may intentionally inflict personal injury on a trespasser either by direct violence, or indirectly by doing on the land some act the effect of which he must know will be to injure the trespasser. So, where spring-guns were placed on land and a trespasser, not knowing of the spring-guns, was shot and injured, it was held that he could recover.[86] Such a case "is just to arrange to shoot him without personally firing the shot"[87]; and liability is imposed because there is an intention to injure. If, however, a landowner puts something on his land with the principal object of keeping trespassers off his land, he is not liable to a trespasser who sustains injury from it because the protective measures he has taken have caused, and were likely to cause, such injury. So, glass or spikes may be placed on the top of a wall[88] and a savage dog may be kept for the protection of premises[89] without rendering the occupier liable.

89 When a person is on the land of another, the burden of proof is on him to prove he is not a trespasser. It is for him to show that he was authorised by law to enter on another's land or that he did so by the leave and licence of the occupier. Acquiescence in trespass, known to the occupier, is some evidence of an implied licence, but "repeated trespass of itself confers no licence,"[90] and "to find a licence there must be evidence either of express permission or that the landowner has so conducted himself that he cannot be heard to say that he did not give it."[90] A court "is not justified in lightly inferring"[91] a licence. Whether acquiescence in trespass amounts to an implied licence is a question of fact.[92] As far as the condition of the premises is concerned, no duty at all is owed to a trespasser, but the occupier must not create

86 *Bird* v. *Holbrook* (1828) 4 Bing. 628; 6 L.J.(O.S.)C.P. 146. Spring-guns, except for protecting a dwelling-house, are illegal: Offences against the Person Act 1861, s. 31.

87 *Per* Lord Dunedin in *Robert Addie & Sons (Collieries) Ltd.* v. *Dumbreck*, *supra*, at p. 376.

88 *Deane* v. *Clayton* (1817) 7 Taunt. 489, 521, *per* Dallas J.; *The Carlgarth* [1927] P. 93, 109, *per* Scrutton L.J.

89 *Brock* v. *Copeland* (1794) 1 Esp. 203; *Sarch* v. *Blackburn* (1830) 4 C. & P. 297.

90 Lord Goddard in *Edwards* v. *Railway Executive* [1952] A.C. 737.

91 Lord Porter in *Edwards*' case, *supra*.

92 An implied licence was found in the following cases: *Cooke* v. *Midland Great Western Ry. of Ireland* [1909] A.C. 229; *Lowery* v. *Walker* [1911] A.C. 10; *Jenkins* v. *G.W. Ry.* [1912] 1 K.B. 525; *Latham* v. *Johnson & Nephew Ltd.* [1913] 1 K.B. 398. There was no implied licence in *Hardy* v. *Central London Ry.* [1920] 3 K.B. 459; *Walder* v. *Hammersmith Corpn.* [1944] 1 All E.R. 490; *Robert Addie & Sons (Collieries)* v. *Dumbreck* [1929] A.C. 358; *Adams* v. *Naylor* [1944] K.B. 750, affd. [1946] A.C. 543; *Edwards* v. *Railway Executive* [1952] A.C. 737.

a concealed danger or trap on the premises with the intention of injuring the trespasser. Lord Hailsham stated the position as follows: " Towards the trespasser the occupier has no duty to take reasonable care for his protection or even to protect him from concealed danger. The trespasser comes on to the premises at his own risk. An occupier is in such a case liable only where the injury is due to some wilful act involving something more than the absence of reasonable care. There must be some act done with the deliberate intention of doing harm to the trespasser, or at least some act done with reckless disregard of the presence of the trespasser." [93] In *Commissioner for Railways* v. *Quinlan* [94] the view was expressed that the contents and limits of the duty owed by an occupier to a trespasser were that the owner of the property is under a duty not to injure the trespasser wilfully; not to do a wilful act in reckless disregard of ordinary humanity towards him; but otherwise a man " trespasses at his own risk." Moreover no general principle is to be deduced from *Donoghue* v. *Stevenson* which throws any particular light on the legal rights and duties that arise when a trespasser is injured on land nor is it correct in principle to suppose that the mere fact that there was a likelihood, apparent to the occupier, of a trespasser being present on the land at some time or another is sufficient to impose on the occupier any general duty of care towards him.

390 The trespasser failed to recover in the following cases: Where his servant, driving his horses along a private road not dedicated to the public, drove into an unlighted trench dug for the purpose of laying drains, and the trespasser was injured [95]; where he got off the highway and, in wandering over the land of a railway company, fell into a reservoir in the dark [96]; where a child, when playing on a moving staircase at a railway station in spite of being warned off by the railway company's servants, was injured [97]; where a girl, aged nine, trespassed upon a piece of vacant land and fell down a deep hole [98]; where a police constable entered the defendant's premises in the dark with a view to discovering a suspected offence (held under the circumstances to be a trespasser), fell into an unfenced sawpit and was injured [99]; when a person crossing a field was injured by a savage horse [1]; when a person, without the owner's permission, got onto a cart which broke down [2]; where a boy climbed up the wall of a warehouse, leaned over into an aperture in

[93] *Robert Addie & Sons (Collieries) Ltd.* v. *Dumbreck*, *supra*, at p. 365.
[94] [1964] A.C. 1054. See articles: " Trespassers: an Out-of-date Approach " (Munkman), 114 L.J. 316; " No humanity for Trespassers " (Samuels), 27 M.L.R. 464; " An adult Trespasser on the Railway Lines " (Goodhart), 80 L.Q.R. 559.
[95] *Murley* v. *Grove* (1882) 46 J.P. 360.
[96] *Hardcastle* v. *South Yorkshire Ry.* (1859) 4 H. & N. 67.
[97] *Hardy* v. *Central London Ry.* [1920] 3 K.B. 459.
[98] *Proctor* v. *British Northrop Loom Co. Ltd.* (1937) 81 S.J. 611.
[99] *G.C. Ry.* v. *Bates* [1921] 3 K.B. 578.
[1] *Lowery* v. *Walker* [1910] 1 K.B. 173; reversed [1911] A.C. 10, on the ground that the plaintiff was not a trespasser, but otherwise not affecting the decision—see *per* Lord Halsbury at p. 13.
[2] *Lygo* v. *Newbold* (1854) 9 Ex. 302.

the wall and was injured by a descending lift [3]; where a ship entered an Admiralty harbour during prohibited hours and collided in the dark with an unlighted wreck [4]; where the trespasser was injured by an innocent-looking pond which contained poisonous matter [5]; where a tenant held over after the expiration of his tenancy, the landlord removed a window-sash, and the tenant's child fell through the window in consequence of there being no sash [6]; where stevedores, knowing it was a wrong thing to do, used the hatch cover of a barge in order to load cargo from it [7]; where a boy entered a railway yard to watch rubbish being burnt in the yard and was injured by the explosion of a detonator concealed in the rubbish [8]; where a boy played in an air raid shelter and was electrocuted by interfering with an electric cable laid on the ground [9]; where boys entered a minefield on sand dunes to which the public had access in peacetime and were injured by a mine explosion [10]; where a boy went onto a railway line adjacent to a recreation-ground and was run over [11]; where a girl, aged ten, went onto a bombed site which was used as a car park, threw a lighted match into the petrol tank of a lorry, and was injured by the resultant explosion [12]; where a stationmaster's child strayed onto the railway lines to play.[13]

On the same principle, if an animal trespasses on land and is injured, the occupier is not liable. Accordingly, where the plaintiff's horse stretched its head over the boundary of the defendant's land and ate the leaves of a yew tree on the defendant's land, with the result that it died, the defendant was held not liable.[14]

391 The distinction between doing an act with the intention of injuring a trespasser and doing an act with the intention of preventing trespassing on the premises is clearly explained by Gibbs C.J. in *Deane* v. *Clayton*.[15] In that case, the plaintiff's dog, trespassing on the defendant's land in chase of a hare, was killed by a dog spear on the land, and Gibbs C.J. said: " It has also been said that because I could not justify killing or maiming dogs, which were found wandering over my land without right, therefore I cannot justify the setting up a defence which is likely to produce the same effect. But the two cases are widely different. In the one, I make an immediate and direct attack on the animals, with no object in view but their destruction, which I have no right to effect, if they can be removed from my land by less violent means; in the other,

3 *Stiefsohn* v. *Brook* (1889) 53 J.P. 790.
4 *H.M.S. Glatton* [1923] P. 215.
5 *United Zinc and Chemical Co.* v. *Van Britt* (1922) 258 U.S. 268, quoted by Scrutton L.J. in *Mourton* v. *Poulter* [1930] 2 K.B. 183.
6 *Coffee* v. *McEvoy* [1912] 2 Ir.R. 290.
7 *Hillen* v. *I.C.I. (Alkali) Ltd.* [1936] A.C. 65.
8 *Breslin* v. *L. & N.E. Ry.*, 1936 S.C. 816.
9 *Walder* v. *Hammersmith Corpn.* [1944] 1 All E.R. 490.
10 *Adams* v. *Naylor* [1944] K.B. 750; affd. in H.L. on other grounds [1946] A.C. 543.
11 *Edwards* v. *Railway Executive* [1952] A.C. 737.
12 *Adcock* v. *Loveridge, The Times*, June 21, 1956.
13 *Videan* v. *British Transport Commission* [1963] 2 Q.B. 650.
14 *Ponting* v. *Noakes* [1894] 2 Q.B. 281. See also *Blyth* v. *Topham* (1607) Cro.Jac. 158.
15 (1817) 7 Taunt. 489.

I merely set up a guard against all wrongdoers generally; the primary object of this guard was protection to my own property, not mischief to theirs." [16] In *Deane* v. *Clayton* the court was evenly divided, but in *Jordin* v. *Crump* [17] the opinion of Gibbs C.J. was approved and it was held that the plaintiff, under such circumstances, had no right of action.

392 Even if something is put on the land with the intention of injuring a trespasser, a trespasser who was warned of the presence of the danger cannot recover if he is injured by it. So, in *Ilott* v. *Wilkes*,[18] before spring-guns were made illegal, a person trespassing in a wood with notice that spring-guns were set there, was held to be unable to recover when he was injured by a spring-gun.

In *Sycamore* v. *Ley* [19] the question was discussed but not decided whether the owner of a motor-car, left in the highway, was liable to a trespasser who was bitten by a savage dog kept confined in the car with the object of preventing pilfering from or interference with the car. In view of the authorities cited above, it would seem that the owner is under no liability to a trespasser in such circumstances.

393 **Liability to a trespasser for negligence.** In addition to a duty not intentionally to inflict injury on a trespasser, the occupier is under a duty not to do any act "with reckless disregard of the presence of the trespasser." [20] This duty, however, only arises when the trespasser is known to be present on the land; there is no duty to anticipate his presence. So, a landowner shooting over his own land and seeing a trespasser in the line of fire must exercise reasonable care for the trespasser's safety when he shoots, but if no trespassers are known to be present he is not bound to search for them before beginning to shoot. Lord Atkin states the law to be: "I know of no duty to a trespasser owed by the occupier of land other than, when the trespasser is known to be present, to abstain from doing an act which if done carelessly must reasonably be contemplated as likely to injure him, and, of course, to abstain from doing acts which are intended to injure him." [21]

394 Accordingly, a trespasser on a railway train who was injured in a railway collision caused by the negligence of the railway company's servants was held to be unable to recover.[22] Again, when a colliery company had on their premises an endless wire cable passing over an iron wheel which was not visible from the pithead from which the motor operating the cable was worked, and a boy was killed owing to the wheel being set in motion, it was held that as the boy was a trespasser the colliery company were under no liability.[23] Where a child had seated himself on

16 *Ibid.* at p. 534.
17 (1841) 8 M. & W. 782.
18 (1820) 3 B. & Ald. 304, quoted with approval in *Jordin* v. *Crump, supra.*
19 (1932) 147 L.T. 342.
20 *Per* Lord Hailsham in *Robert Addie & Sons (Collieries) Ltd.* v. *Dumbreck* [1929] A.C. 358.
21 *Hillen* v. *I.C.I. (Alkali) Ltd.* [1936] A.C. 65, 70.
22 *Grand Trunk Ry. of Canada* v. *Barnett* [1911] A.C. 361.
23 *Robert Addie & Sons (Collieries) Ltd.* v. *Dumbreck* [1929] A.C. 358.

the running-board of a van, unknown to the driver, and was thrown off when the van moved, it was held that the van owners were under no liability, as the driver was under no duty to look for trespassers before starting the van.[24] Where a person, in attempting to cross a railway line by means of a track, not a highway, crawled under a line of trucks and was killed owing to the trucks being moved without warning, the railway company were held to be under no duty to have a man stationed to warn trespassers likely to use the track that the line was being used for traffic.[25]

395 When the trespasser is known to be present or it is reasonably foreseeable that a trespasser will be on the premises,[25a] a duty to take care arises. In *Videan* v. *British Transport Commission*[26] Lord Denning M.R. considered it a duty to use reasonable care whilst Pearson L.J. expressed it as a duty substantially less than the duty of care which is owing to a lawful visitor, namely to treat the trespasser with common humanity and not a duty to make the land and operations thereon safe for him in his trespassing. A company operating haulage machinery in a field adjoining a children's playground, knowing that children were in the habit of playing with the machinery, which was only put in motion about three times a week, and that it was extremely likely that children would be playing with it, were held liable for putting the machinery in motion without first seeing that the children were clear, although the children were trespassers.[27] The difference between this case and *Addie's* case[23] would seem to be that in this case it was known that it was extremely likely that the children were playing with the machinery, while in *Addie's* case it was not so known.[28] When a nursery man was felling a tree with a number of children trespassing on the land and watching him at his work, he was held liable to a child injured through the fall of the tree because of his failure to warn the child of the direction the fall would take.[29] Where a man starts a wheel, fells a tree, or sets off a blast when he knows that people are standing near, "in each of these cases he owes a duty to these people, even though they are trespassers, to take care to give them warning." [30]

6.—LIABILITY FOR NEGLIGENT ACTS ON PREMISES

396 **Liability generally.** Closely connected with the question of liability for the condition of the premises is the question of liability for negligent acts on the premises. Neither the occupier nor any other person is

[24] *Howard* v. *Pickfords Ltd.* (1935) 79 S.J. 69.
[25] *French* v. *Hills Plymouth Co.* (1908) 24 T.L.R. 644.
[25a] See *Herrington* v. *B.R.B.* [1971] 2 W.L.R. 477, and article : " Forgive Us Our Trespasses," (Lewis) 121 New L.J. 134.
[26] [1963] 2 Q.B. 650. See articles: " Liability in Tort to Trespassers," 234 L.T. 631, 644, and " The Occupier's Duty to Trespassing Children," 107 S.J. 1031; also " Trespassers Will be Prosecuted," 27 M.L.R. 88.
[27] *Excelsior Wire Rope Co.* v. *Callan* [1930] A.C. 404.
[28] See Scrutton L.J.'s explanation of the distinction between these two cases in *Mourton* v. *Poulter* [1930] 2 K.B. 183, 190.
[29] *Mourton* v. *Poulter* [1930] 2 K.B. 183.
[30] *Per* Scrutton L.J. at p. 191.

entitled to act negligently towards persons whom he knows or ought reasonably to know will be lawfully on the premises. In this connection at common law there was no difference between liability to invitees and licensees. So, when a licensee was injured in using a private way by the negligence of the owner's servants in lowering goods from a warehouse, Coleridge C.J. said: "The grantee must use the permission as the thing exists. It is a different question, however, when negligence on the part of the person granting the permission is superadded. It cannot be that, having granted permission to use a way subject to existing dangers, he is to be allowed to do any further act to endanger the safety of the person using the way." It was held that the licensee could recover.[31] The defendant's liability was based not on the ground that he was the occupier of the premises but on the ground that he was doing an act which he knew or ought to have known would cause damage to persons whom he knew or ought to have known were lawfully on the premises. So, railway companies were liable for the negligence of their porters in wheeling luggage along the platforms so as to collide with persons lawfully on the platforms,[32] and for the negligence of their servants in leaving open the doors of railway carriages so as to strike persons lawfully on the platform.[33] Where a licensee, walking along a railway tunnel, was injured through the negligent driving of a train by a servant of the occupiers, she recovered damages on the ground that, as the driver knew that persons such as the plaintiff used the tunnel, he was under a duty to take reasonable precautions before entering the tunnel.[34] But a notice in adequate terms which has been brought sufficiently to the attention of the visitor will clearly exclude the occupiers' liability to take reasonable care.[35] A person driving his motor-car up a private avenue to his own house, knowing that tradesmen and others lawfully calling at the house were likely to be on it, was bound to drive as carefully as on the highway.[36] A person who was given a ride by a friend in his motor-car—when he was a licensee in the car—was entitled to be driven by the friend with the skill of a reasonably competent driver.[37] The principle was thus expressed by Denning L.J.[38]: "In regard to current operations, the duty of the occupier—or of the person conducting the operations—is simply to use reasonable care in all the circumstances. This duty is owed alike to all persons lawfully on the premises who may be affected by his activities; and it is the same whether the person injured is an invitee or a licensee, a volunteer or a guest."

[31] *Gallagher* v. *Humphrey* (1862) 6 L.T. 684. See also *Corby* v. *Hill* (1858) 4 C.B.(N.S.) 556.
[32] *Tebbutt* v. *Bristol and Exeter Ry.* (1870) L.R. 6 Q.B. 73, Chap. 12, *post*, § 771.
[33] *Thatcher* v. *G.W. Ry.* (1893) 10 T.L.R. 13; *Toal* v. *N.B. Ry.* [1908] A.C. 352; *Burns* v. *N.B. Ry.*, 1914 S.C. 754; *Hare* v. *B.T.C.* [1956] 1 W.L.R. 250.
[34] *Slater* v. *Clay Cross Co. Ltd.* [1956] 2 Q.B. 264.
[35] *Ashdown* v. *Samuel Williams* [1957] 1 Q.B. 409.
[36] *Bowie* v. *Shenkin*, 1934 S.C. 459.
[37] *Harris* v. *Perry & Co.* [1903] 2 K.B. 219; *Pratt* v. *Patrick* [1924] 1 K.B. 488.
[38] *Dunster* v. *Abbott* [1954] 1 W.L.R. 58, 63.

397 The duty of an occupier of premises to his visitors in respect of negligent acts done or omitted to be done on the premises is governed as from January 1, 1958, by the Occupiers' Liability Act 1957,[39] which does not apply to persons who are not occupiers. The duty owed is the "common duty of care."[40]

398 **Nature of liability.** The liability of any person doing negligent acts on the premises is the same as that of the occupier. A contractor doing work on premises is bound to warn other persons lawfully on the premises of dangers, even hidden ones, which he has created and is also under a duty "not actively and negligently to injure other persons on the premises, as by carelessly dropping hammers on their heads."[41] Where two sets of workmen, working for different employers, were working in the same building and one workman injured another by negligently dropping a piece of iron on his head, it was held that the injured workman could recover from the employer of the negligent workman.[42] Again, where workmen employed by the occupier and workmen employed by a contractor were working together in the same building and one of the occupier's workmen negligently erected a scaffold which collapsed and injured one of the contractor's workmen, the occupier was held liable, not as occupier, but as employer of the negligent workman.[43] Where a ship arrived at a wharf at night and, to get a safe berth, moved some barges further up the wharf to a berth which was unsafe, the ship was held liable for the damage to the barges.[44] A licensee, who was injured on private land by a shot fired by the defendant while shooting pigeons, recovered because the defendant, though the licensee was visible to him, did not first look to see whether anyone was in the line of fire.[45] A farmer taking delivery on his farm of a heifer from a cattle lorry, who was injured by the negligence of the driver in allowing the lorry door to fall on him, recovered.[46]

399 Failure to appreciate the principle stated at the beginning of the preceding paragraph led to the unsatisfactory case of *Malone* v. *Laskey*.[47] There, the landlord of premises, during the currency of a tenancy, negligently fixed an iron bracket to support a water tank. The bracket was left in a condition dangerous to persons on the premises and, three months after the work was done, the bracket fell on the wife of the sub-tenant of the premises and injured her. The defendant was held not liable on the grounds (1) that there was no contractual relation between the plaintiff and the defendant; (2) the doing of the work was a voluntary act on the part of the defendant and not an act done in

39 ss. 2 and 3. See *ante*, §§ 345 *et seq.* and §§ 369 *et seq.*
40 s. 2 (2), which defines this duty. See *ante*, §§ 333 and 345.
41 *Kimber* v. *Gas Light and Coke Co.* [1918] 1 K.B. 439, *per* Scrutton L.J.
42 *Thrussell* v. *Handyside* (1888) 20 Q.B.D. 359.
43 *Clelland* v. *Edward Lloyd Ltd.* [1938] 1 K.B. 272.
44 *The Majfrid* [1942] P. 145.
45 *Chettle* v. *Denton* (1951) 95 S.J. 802.
46 *Lomas* v. *M. Jones & Son* [1944] K.B. 4.
47 [1907] 2 K.B. 141, Kennedy L.J. doubting. "A person executing works on premises . . .

pursuance of a duty; and (3) the defendant was not in control of the premises and the plaintiff was not his invitee. As to ground (1), it is clear that the absence of a contractual duty is irrelevant in considering the duty in tort [48]; ground (2) is equally irrelevant in tort; while ground (3) confuses the duty of the defendant as landlord with his duty as a person doing work on the premises after the possession of the premises was in the sub-tenant. A landlord doing work on premises in the possession of his tenant owes the same duty of care to persons lawfully on the premises as a contractor. This case was distinguished by Talbot J.[49] on the ground that the facts were " somewhat peculiar," and it is submitted that it was wrongly decided on the question of negligence.

400 In *Ball* v. *L.C.C.*,[50] Tucker L.J. accepted, " there is no authority which establishes that once a landlord has let premises or has sold them, if thereafter he goes into these premises at the request of the tenant or the purchaser . . . the mere fact that he happens to be the landlord or the vendor absolves him from the duties which would otherwise attach to a contractor or builder or any other person who is called in to carry out operations on the premises," but it was held that a landlord who negligently installed a boiler after the commencement of the tenancy was not liable for the resultant damage to the tenant's daughter when the boiler exploded. The ground of the decision was that *Malone* v. *Laskey* had decided that in such circumstances there was no duty of care owed to members of the tenant's family. While no criticism can be directed against the result in *Ball's* case, because the boiler had been installed some seven years previously and the plaintiff, who had used it during that time, attempted to light it when the water system was frozen, nevertheless it is submitted that the landlord did owe a duty of care when he installed the boiler.[51]

7.—LIABILITY OF VENDOR OR LESSOR [51a]

401 **Liability of vendor or lessor.** Apart from contract or implied warranty, neither a vendor nor a lessor of property is under any tortious liability for its dangerous condition after he has parted with possession to the purchaser or lessee.[52] " The authorities show that if a landlord, or if a

is under a general duty to use reasonable care for the safety of those whom he knows or ought reasonably to know may be affected by or lawfully in the vicinity of his work ": Lord Somervell of Harrow in *A. C. Billings & Sons Ltd.* v. *Riden* [1958] A.C. 240. In *Billings*' case the House of Lords held that *Malone* v. *Laskey* was overruled so far as it dealt with negligence and that *Ball* v. *L.C.C.*, so far as it was based on *Malone* v. *Laskey*, could not be regarded as an authority.

48 *Donoghue* v. *Stevenson* [1932] A.C. 562.

49 *Cunard* v. *Antifyre Ltd.* [1933] 1 K.B. 551. Atkinson J., however, treated it as good law in *Otto* v. *Bolton* [1936] 2 K.B. 46. In *Blacker* v. *Lake and Elliott* (1912) 106 L.T. 533, Hamilton J. said that *George* v. *Skivington* (1869) L.R. 5 Ex. 1, (which was approved by the H.L. in *Donoghue* v. *Stevenson*), was inconsistent with *Malone* v. *Laskey*.

50 [1949] 2 K.B. 159. See the criticism of this case by P. S. James in 12 M.L.R. 500, and by A. L. Goodhart in 65 L.Q.R. 518. See also note 47 above.

51 See the cases quoted above, and, in addition, *Haseldine* v. *Daw* [1941] 2 K.B. 343, and *Bottomley* v. *Bannister* [1932] 1 K.B. 458, 478, *per* Greer L.J.

51a The Law Commission (Chairman : The Hon. Mr. Justice Scarman) has published Law Com. No. 40, " Civil liability of vendors and lessors for defective premises."

52 *Robbins* v. *Jones* (1863) 15 C.B.(N.S.) 221. See *ante*, § 377 for the qualifications of this in the case of lettings of small houses, under the Housing Acts 1957 and 1961.

vendor of property, sells or lets a house which is defective to such an extent as to be a danger to the tenant and his family, or the purchaser, and of course to other persons entering the house, he is absolved from liability; he is not under any duty in law resulting from the defective condition of the premises which he sells or lets. That position is so even if he is himself the person who has put the house into that condition and, of course, has knowledge of the dangerous condition in which it is. It follows that, if he is not under any such obligation to the lessee or purchaser, equally he is not under any obligation to a stranger who happens to be visiting the premises." [53]

402 In *Bottomley* v. *Bannister* [54] a firm of builders sold a house in which was installed a gas boiler without a flue, thereby rendering the installation dangerous to use. As a result of using the apparatus the purchaser of the house died. The builders were held not liable, and the question was discussed whether, as vendors, they owed any duty to the purchaser as to defects in the house, and it was held that they owed no such duty. Greer L.J. said: " The result is unsatisfactory, because in the present case, if the landlord instead of doing the work himself before he sold the house, had done it afterwards as a contractor to Mr. Bottomley [the purchaser] he would have been liable if there were sufficient evidence that it was negligence on his part to have installed the Halliday boiler without a flue." [55] This decision was given before *Donoghue* v. *Stevenson*,[56] which remedied the unsatisfactory result that was produced by the earlier cases dealing with manufacturers of chattels, and it might well have been thought that the principle of that case was not restricted to the negligent manufacture of chattels but included the negligent manufacture or building of houses, stands and other things attached to the land. The contrary, however, was held in *Otto* v. *Bolton*.[57] In that case, a builder negligently built the ceilings of a house which he afterwards sold. During the occupation of the house by the purchaser one of the ceilings fell and injured a person lawfully in the house. The builder was held to be not liable, on the ground that the principle of *Donoghue* v. *Stevenson* applied only to chattels.[56] A second ground of the decision was that the defects in the ceiling were not hidden or latent, but plainly to be seen so as to put anyone making a proper examination on his guard, and that an examination, although an inadequate one, was in fact made.[58]

53 Tucker L.J. in *Ball* v. *L.C.C.* [1949] 2 K.B. 159, 167. *Otto* v. *Bolton* [1936] 2 K.B. 46.
54 [1932] 1 K.B. 458.
55 [1932] 1 K.B. 458, 478.
56 [1932] A.C. 562. See in particular, *post*, § 405. In *Sharpe* v. *E. T. Sweeting & Son Ltd.* [1963] 1 W.L.R. 665, Nield J. at p. 675 said: " It was submitted on behalf of the defendants that the principles in *Donoghue* v. *Stevenson* [1932] A.C. 562 are only applicable in the case of chattels and their manufacture, repair or installation and do not apply in relation to realty. The observations of Scrutton L.J. to this effect in *Bottomley* v. *Bannister* are *obiter* and I am of the view with great respect that they should not be followed without reservation in these days."
57 [1936] 2 K.B. 46.
58 To what extent this can be regarded as a good defence is discussed *post*, § 644.

Similarly, in *Davis* v. *Foots*[59] a flat was let to a man and his wife and, before the tenancy commenced, the landlord disconnected a gas fire, which was not wanted by the tenants, from one of the bedrooms. In doing so, he negligently removed the tap so that the gas, when turned on at the meter, went into the room and asphyxiated the man and injured his wife. The landlord was held not liable on the ground that he owed no duty to the tenants as to defects in the house. In *Sharpe* v. *E. T. Sweeting & Son Ltd.*[60] it was conceded that Middlesbrough Corporation as owners of the realty and the landlords of the tenant whose wife was injured by the fall of a defective canopy outside the front door, enjoyed an immunity from liability for defects in the construction of the building. This immunity was considered by Nield J. who came to the conclusion that this rule was too deeply embedded in the common law to be capable of disturbance, and that whilst an owner, who was also the builder, did have such owner's immunity, when the builder is not the owner he does not enjoy any such immunity. In this case the defendants were held not to be the agents of the owners but were held to be independent contractors who, having erected the canopy in circumstances in which they did not and could not have reasonably anticipated that there would be any intermediate examination such as would be likely to reveal the defects which existed, owed a duty of care to the tenant's wife and accordingly were liable to her in damages. This decision followed that in *Gallagher* v. *McDowell*[61] where the Court of Appeal in Northern Ireland held that the landlords, who were also the builders, were under a duty to the tenant's wife as a lawful user of the house, which they had constructed, to take reasonable care in the repair of the hole in a defective floorboard, particularly where, in the circumstances, they could not reasonably have anticipated any examination, which would have revealed the defect in the floorboard, in which the plaintiff caught the heel of her shoe. It was further held that the principles in *Donoghue* v. *Stevenson* applied.

8.—LIABILITY OF NON-OCCUPIERS

403 **Liability of persons not in occupation.** The duty to take care when it is known that a person is present and is likely to be injured unless care is taken, does not depend upon the ownership or occupation of land. It is a duty which is owed by everybody about to do an act which will cause injury unless care is taken, whether the doer of the act is the owner, the occupier, an invitee, a licensee or even a trespasser. Nevertheless the law regarding this general liability for negligence in this particular sphere has developed very slowly, mainly because the courts seemed reluctant to subject non-occupiers to any such liability. In *Excelsior Wire Rope Co.* v. *Callan*[62] the rope company were neither

59 [1940] 1 K.B. 116. *Travers* v. *Gloucester Corpn.* [1947] K.B. 71 (defective installation by landlord of gas geyser causing lodger's death—landlord not liable) is a similar case.
60 *supra.*
61 [1961] N.I. 26.
62 [1930] A.C. 404.

the owners nor the occupiers of the land, but carried on their operations under a licence from the landowner. Their liability to trespassers, however, was the same as if they had been occupiers. In *Mourton* v. *Poulter* [63] the defendant was an independent contractor engaged by the landowner to fell the tree, but it was not suggested that his liability was in any way affected by this circumstance.

404 The duty of one who is neither the owner nor the occupier of land may in some cases be greater than that of the owner or occupier. If he is doing something on the land which he knows or ought to know will be a source of danger to persons on or likely to come on the land and meddle with the subject of his activity, he is under a duty to take precautions to prevent damage. Electricity undertakers, who placed high voltage wires across a field near to a tree which could be easily climbed and the foliage of which prevented the wires from being easily seen, were held liable for the death of a girl of thirteen who climbed the tree and came in contact with the wires. It was held that even if the girl was a trespasser on the tree, they should have contemplated that such an accident might occur and taken steps to prevent it.[64] Demolition contractors, who had demolished a house to the level of the first floor ceiling, were held liable to a boy of twelve who trespassed on the house and was injured by playing with a wall in an unsafe condition. The contractors knew that children were in the habit of playing on a cleared site behind the house and should have foreseen that children were likely to come to the building and interfere with the brickwork.[65] Contractors engaged in road making who left a trailer, attractive to children, on some waste land not in their occupation, near to their work were held liable to a child of five who was injured when playing with the trailer.[66] On the other hand contractors were not held to be liable for the injuries sustained by a child trespasser, who fell through the skylight of a building, which was waiting to be demolished.[67] Likewise a householder could not reasonably be expected to apprehend danger to children from lime mortar which had been left in a heap in the gutter outside his house prior to its use for repairs.[68]

405 In *Miller* v. *South of Scotland Electricity Board*,[69] where the House of Lords held the defenders liable for negligently disconnecting their electricity supply to premises about to be demolished so that a child trespasser received a serious electric shock, Lord Denning said: " We are concerned with the duty of care that is owed by a person doing work—or anything else—on land: and that duty is today best found by

[63] [1930] 2 K.B. 183.
[64] *Buckland* v. *Guildford Gas Light & Coke Co.* [1949] 1 K.B. 410. See also, *post*, § 533.
[65] *Davis* v. *St. Mary's Demolition Co. Ltd.* [1954] 1 All E.R. 578. See the discussion of this case by Montrose, 17 M.L.R. 368.
[66] *Creed* v. *McGeoch & Sons Ltd.* [1955] 1 W.L.R. 1005. See 19 M.L.R. 79.
[67] *Aldrich* v. *Henry Boyer Ltd.*, *The Times*, January 16, 1960.
[68] *Prince* v. *Gregory* [1959] 1 W.L.R. 177.
[69] 1958 S.C.(H.L.) 20.

resort to the general principle enunciated by Lord Atkin in *Donoghue* v. *Stevenson.*[70] Such a person—be he occupier, contractor, or anyone else—owes a duty to all persons who are so closely and directly affected by his work that he ought reasonably to have them in contemplation when he is directing his mind to the task." [71] Further, the recent House of Lords decision in *A. C. Billings & Sons Ltd.* v. *Riden,*[72] which is an important milestone in that *Malone* v. *Laskey* [73] and *Ball* v. *London County Council* [74] were overruled, held that a contractor working on premises owed a duty to take reasonable care to prevent damage to persons whom he may reasonably expect to be affected by his work when destroying the normal safe access to a building. Thus the road is now effectively cleared to extend the broad principle of *Donoghue* v. *Stevenson* to those cases where visitors and even trespassers are injured on premises as a result of the negligence of non-occupiers, so that the occupier is no longer the only person who can be held responsible. So far as the Occupiers' Liability Act [75] is concerned it has no application in the case of a non-occupier.

9.—LIABILITY TO PERSONS ON ADJOINING PREMISES

406 **Persons on adjoining premises.** There remains to be considered the question of liability to persons who are not on the premises or on the highway, but are nevertheless injured owing to the defective condition of the premises. If a person lawfully on the adjoining premises is injured because the premises have not been maintained in a reasonably safe condition, his legal position is the same as if he had been injured while lawfully passing along the highway.[76] This was laid down in *Cunard* v. *Antifyre Ltd.*[77] There, the defendants were lessees and occupiers of a building let out in flats, the main roof and guttering of which were vested in them as occupiers. The male plaintiff was a sub-tenant of a flat on the third floor, and while his wife was in the kitchen a heavy piece of the guttering fell from the main roof through the glass roof of the kitchen and injured his wife. The guttering fell because it had never been properly supported, and the want of proper support was obvious to anyone looking at it. The defendants were held liable, Talbot J. saying: " The plaintiffs' true cause of action (if they have one) is for negligence, for failure by an occupier of property to take reasonable care that his property does not get into such a state as to be dangerous

70 [1932] A.C. 562, 580.
71 1958 S.C.(H.L.) 20, 37.
72 [1958] A.C. 240.
73 [1907] 2 K.B. 141. See *ante*, § 399, note 47.
74 [1949] 2 K.B. 159. See *ante*, § 400, note 50.
75 s. 2 (1). The common duty of care, which extended by virtue of section 1 (3) of the1957 Act to persons occupying or having control of a structure, was not thereby imposed on the contractors whose sub-contractors were in occupation and control of a particular working platform and scaffolding being erected amongst the roof members and trusses: *Kearney* v. *Eric Waller* [1967] 1 Q.B. 29.
76 *Post*, Chap. 12.
77 [1933] 1 K.B. 551.

to adjoining property or persons lawfully thereon." [78] Again, he said: "There is no doubt that if this guttering had overhung the street in the condition proved in the case before us, and had fallen on someone passing below and injured him, that person would have had an action against the defendants on the principle of *Tarry* v. *Ashton*.[79] What is that principle? It is in our opinion that anyone in occupation and control of something hung over a place, in which people may be expected lawfully to be, is bound to take reasonable care that it does not fall and injure them. This seems to us to be both law and justice; and, as we have already said, it is in our opinion immaterial whether in such a case the plaintiff is in the place where he is injured as one of the King's subjects entitled to use the highway, or in the exercise of any other legal right. A closely similar principle applies to work done or chattels kept or moved in the like dangerous situations: see such cases as *Byrne* v. *Boadle* [80]; and it makes no difference whether the plaintiff was on the highway, as in that case, or in any other place where he had a right to be, and where people might be expected to be: *Scott* v. *London and St. Katherine Docks Co.*" [81] Again, where three rooms in a house were let by the owners, and the daughter of the tenant was injured by a brick falling from a chimney stack, the owners were held liable. "The landlord . . . who negligently allowed the brickwork to remain for a matter of five years in this dangerous state was equally liable at law whether the brick fell on his tenant, on his tenant's daughter or on a casual passer-by and whether the tenant or the daughter or the passer-by was in the yard or on the highway or on the property of an adjoining owner." [82] In this case there was no demise of the chimney stack. The general rule as between landlord and tenant is that the tenant must take the premises as he finds them, and has no right of action if yew trees on the landlord's land which were overhanging his land at the time of the demise subsequently poison his cattle,[83] or if rotten overhanging timber falls and injures him or his servant.[84]

407 If the owner of property causes work to be done on his property, either by way of repairs or rebuilding, he is under a duty to use reasonable care to see that the work does not cause damage to adjoining property. In *Hughes* v. *Percival* [85] there were three houses belonging to A, B and C respectively, B's house being separated from the houses of A and C by party walls. B's house was pulled down for the purpose of rebuilding, and the new building was tied into the party wall between A's house and B's house. The builder employed by B negligently cut

[78] *Ibid.* p. 557.
[79] (1876) 1 Q.B.D. 314. Also see *post*, § 705.
[80] (1863) 2 H. & C. 722.
[81] (1865) 3 H. & C. 596; *Cunard* v. *Antifyre Ltd., supra*, at p. 562.
[82] *Taylor* v. *Liverpool Corpn.* [1939] 3 All E.R. 329—Stable J. at p. 337.
[83] *Cheater* v. *Cater* [1918] 1 K.B. 247. See *Lemmon* v. *Webb* [1895] A.C. 1 for an abatement of such nuisance.
[84] *Shirvell* v. *Hackwood Estates* [1938] 2 K.B. 577.
[85] (1883) 8 App.Cas. 443.

into the party wall between B's house and C's house, as a result of which the new building, which was nearly finished, fell and dragged down A's house with it. B was held liable to A, because he owed to A a duty, as to which Lord Blackburn said: " I do not think that duty went so far as to require him absolutely to provide that no damage should come to the plaintiff's wall from the use he thus made of it, but I think that the duty went as far as to require him to see that reasonable skill and care were exercised in those operations which involved a use of the party wall, exposing it to this risk." Again, where a house was pulled down so negligently that damage was caused to a stable on the adjoining land and to a horse and cart in the stable, the person who ordered the house to be pulled down was held liable.[86]

An owner of property who pulls down a wall under statutory powers is not liable to the adjoining owner for damage he has sustained owing to his rooms being unprotected. The statute, in such a case, authorises the wall to be pulled down, but does not oblige the person pulling it down to do an independent act, such as putting up a hoarding.[87]

[86] *Emblen* v. *Myers* (1860) 6 M. & N. 54.
[87] *Thompson* v. *Hill* (1870) L.R. 5 C.P. 564.

CHAPTER 9

DANGEROUS THINGS: RYLANDS v. FLETCHER [1]

1.—PRINCIPLES OF LIABILITY

408 **Duty in respect of dangerous things.** The duty imposed on those who control or interfere with dangerous things goes beyond a mere duty to take care. Before considering the extent of the duty an attempt will be made to ascertain the things to which it applies, in other words, what is the legal meaning of the expression "dangerous things."

409 **Meaning of dangerous things.** Most things are sources of danger if they are used negligently, such as a stick, a loose slate on the roof of a building and an unlighted heap of stones in the highway. Such things, however, when used by any person impose upon him the ordinary liability for negligence. It is the circumstances under which the thing in question is used rather than the thing itself which gives rise to the danger. A motor-vehicle, for example, is not a dangerous thing although thousands of people are killed every year by motor accidents. The definition of "dangerous things" must therefore be such as to exclude such things as motor-vehicles, railway trains, mechanically propelled vehicles and machinery of all kinds. Liability for these depends on negligence.

On the other hand, things like fire, dynamite, gas and electricity are themselves dangerous, quite apart from any carelessness in handling them. A motor-car, when stationary, is safe, and when put in motion it becomes dangerous only because of the way in which it is driven. Even if it has defective brakes or is otherwise unfit to be put on the road, it is safe enough unless and until it is used by a person who negligently, *i.e.* in breach of the duty to take care imposed by law on those who drive motor-cars, uses it. There are things, however, which, like a savage animal, require to be chained up, otherwise they are a perpetual source of danger quite apart from any user by an individual. Gas and fire are good illustrations of this. Other things, again, are of such a nature that special precautions have to be taken to prevent people from coming in contact with them to prevent danger which is otherwise inevitable. Such things as electricity and poisons are illustrations of this. There are, in addition, things, of which explosives are the best illustration, which require great care in storage and handling, otherwise physical damage is liable to be caused far beyond the immediate neighbourhood of the person storing or handling them.

410 The things indicated above seem to differ from other things in two ways. In the first place, they are always dangerous in that they always

[1] See Law Commission report (Law Com. No. 32).

require the greatest care in being stored or handled, as opposed to things which are only dangerous in certain circumstances, such as machinery which is safe when at rest but may be dangerous when in motion.

Secondly, the things indicated above are dangerous in themselves or what may be described as inherently or essentially dangerous. They have been termed actively dangerous. The danger in such things as gas, electricity, fire, water, poison and explosives is derived from the quality of the thing itself and not from external circumstances. The conditions under which such things are used may be adequate to prevent them from doing harm, but the danger is only kept in check and not removed, so that if the conditions alter the danger will reassert itself.

The distinction between dangerous things and other things has been criticised,[1a] but it is well recognised. Lord Wright said[2]: " A distinction has been drawn in some cases between things intrinsically dangerous or dangerous *per se* and other things which are not dangerous in the absence of negligence. The correctness or value of that distinction has been doubted by eminent judges. I think, however, that there is a real and practical distinction between the two categories. Some things are obviously and necessarily dangerous unless the danger is removed by appropriate precautions. These things are dangerous *per se*. Other things are only dangerous if there is negligence."

411 There is no judicial interpretation of the expression " dangerous things." Judicial descriptions are: " anything likely to do mischief if it escapes "[3]; " an instrument in its nature dangerous . . . as a loaded gun "[4]; " the other class of things where the thing is actually dangerous in itself; that is to say, where there is what I may call active danger in it, such as the case of a loaded gun, poison, or fire. The decided case of a squib is a good instance of that "[5]; " articles dangerous in themselves, such as loaded firearms, poisons, explosives, and other things *ejusdem generis* "[6]; " an instrument noxious or dangerous in itself which might produce an accident from the mere handling of it "[7]; " implements or substances dangerous in themselves, such as flame-bearing instruments or explosives."[8] " The case of things dangerous in themselves, or, as they are sometimes called, inherently dangerous, is a case separate and distinct and holds a special place in the law of negligence. Where you are dealing

[1a] See *Hodge & Sons* v. *Anglo-American Oil Co.* (1922) 12 Ll.L.Rep. 183, 187, *per* Scrutton L.J.; *Donoghue* v. *Stevenson* [1932] A.C. 562, *per* Lord Atkin; see also *Salmond on Torts*, 15th ed., p. 389.

[2] *Glasgow Corpn.* v. *Muir* [1943] A.C. 448, 463, 464.

[3] *Fletcher* v. *Rylands* (1866) L.R. 1 Ex. 265, 279, *per* Blackburn J.

[4] *Longmeid* v. *Holliday* (1851) 6 Ex. 761, *per* Parke B.

[5] *Reilly* v. *Greenfield Coal and Brick Co.*, 1909 S.C. 1328, 1336, *per* Lord Dunedin.

[6] *Dominion Natural Gas Co.* v. *Collins* [1909] A.C. 640, 646, *per* Lord Dunedin. A similar description is given by Atkin L.J. in *Jefferson* v. *Derbyshire Farmers Ltd.* [1921] 2 K.B. 281, 289.

[7] *Caledonian Ry.* v. *Mulholland* [1898] A.C. 216, 232. For further judicial explanations of this phrase, see Stallybrass, 3 C.L.J. 376.

[8] *The Pass of Ballater* [1942] P. 112, 117. See also *Balfour* v. *Barty-King* [1956] 1 W.L.R. 779 at p. 787.

with a dangerous thing you are dealing with something which, if left, may at any moment and under modern circumstances cause damage. Such articles are things like a gun or a pistol. If a gun or a pistol is left about loaded, in a condition in which it may go off if handled in a certain way, if anyone handles an instrument of that sort the risk of danger is obvious. . . . It may not be possible precisely to say what article is inherently dangerous and what is not by any general definition, yet when you come to particular articles there is, I think, no difficulty in drawing the line you take as the standard in the one case. Things like a naked sword or a hatchet or a loaded gun or an explosive are clearly inherently dangerous—that is to say, they cannot be handled without a serious risk. On the other hand, you have things in ordinary use which are only what is called 'potentially dangerous': that is to say, if there is negligence or if there is some mischance or misadventure, then the thing may be a source of danger; but that source of danger is something which is not essential to their ordinary character; it merely depends on the concurrence of certain circumstances—in particular, generally, negligence on the part of someone." [9]

412 The passages quoted in the preceding paragraph emphasise the essentials that (a) the danger is always present; and (b) that the danger is caused by some characteristic of the thing itself and not by the accident of circumstances. It is submitted, however, that neither a naked sword nor a hatchet is a dangerous thing because they have no inherent or active danger in themselves. Neither of them has ever been held to be a dangerous thing, and their inclusion would mean that all sharp instruments such as a penknife, a saw and a sharp stone, were within the category, and this is certainly not the case.

Whether or not a thing is a "dangerous thing" is a question of law.[10] The fact that the thing was not known to be dangerous is immaterial if it is within the class of things dangerous in themselves.[11]

413 The following things have been held to be "dangerous things": Water artificially accumulated,[12] sewage,[13] fire,[14] gas,[15] electricity,[16] explosives,[17] poison,[18] dangerous animals,[19] petrol,[20] oil,[21] paraffin,[22]

[9] *Wray* v. *Essex C.C.* [1936] 3 All E.R. 97, *per* Lord Wright at pp. 101, 102.

[10] *Blacker* v. *Lake and Elliott Ltd.* (1912) 106 L.T. 533. In *Read* v. *J. Lyons & Co. Ltd.* [1947] A.C. 156, 176, Lord Porter said it was a question of fact, "subject to the ruling of a judge as to whether the particular object can be dangerous."

[11] *Rainham Chemical Works* v. *Belvedere Fish Guano Co.* [1921] 2 A.C. 465; *West* v. *Bristol Tramways* [1908] 2 K.B. 14.

[12] *Rylands* v. *Fletcher* (1866) L.R. 3 H.L. 330. *Charing Cross Electricity Supply Co.* v. *Hydraulic Power Co.* [1914] 3 K.B. 442.

[13] *Humphries* v. *Cousins* (1877) 2 C.P.D. 239; *Smeaton* v. *Ilford Corpn.* [1954] Ch. 450.

[14] *Jones* v. *Festiniog Ry.* (1868) L.R. 3 Q.B. 733. This includes fire from a flame-bearing instrument such as an ignited blowlamp: *Balfour* v. *Barty-King* [1956] 1 W.L.R. 779 (affirmed [1957] 1 Q.B. 496).

[15] *Northwestern Utilities* v. *London Guarantee and Accident Co.* [1936] A.C. 108.

[16] *National Telephone Co* v. *Baker* [1893] 2 Ch. 186.

[17] *Rainham Chemical Works* v. *Belvedere Fish Guano Co.*, *supra.*

[18] *West* v. *Bristol Tramways* [1908] 2 K.B. 14.

[19] *Filburn* v. *People's Palace and Aquarium Co.* (1890) 25 Q.B.D. 258.

[20] *Jefferson* v. *Derbyshire Farmers* [1921] 2 K.B. 281, 290, *per* Atkin L.J.; *Marshall* v. *Russian*

airborne oily smuts containing sulphur compounds,[23] a noxious hair dye,[24] a roundabout known as a chair-o-plane,[25] a cleaning fluid which generated an explosive gas on coming into contact with cast-iron,[26] an electric space heater,[27] colliery spoil which slid down the hill.[28] Other things which have been held to be dangerous things but, it is submitted, wrongly, are discussed in §§ 420–421, *post*.

The following have been held not to be dangerous things: A steam roller,[29] a person who had recovered from scarlet fever and was discharged from hospital while in an infectious condition,[30] an oil can,[31] a brazing lamp,[32] a tree with a branch, in a condition rendering it liable to fall, overhanging the highway,[33] a motor-car,[34] a stationary unhorsed van in a highway,[35] an aeroplane,[36] a domestic boiler without a safety valve,[37] an air rifle,[38] a cricket ball,[39] the operation of shooting " swarf " into barges.[40]

414 **Absolute liability for dangerous things.** Liability for damage caused by dangerous things is absolute,[41] that is to say, it is not necessary to prove any negligence or lack of care on the part of anyone, provided

Oil Products, 1938 S.C. 773, 796. Also a motor-vehicle with petrol in its tank, although the vehicle itself is not dangerous, *Musgrove* v. *Pandelis* [1919] 2 K.B. 43, and petrol fumes in an otherwise empty tank of a vehicle, *Perry* v. *Kendricks Transport Ltd.* [1956] 1 W.L.R. 85.

21 *Smith* v. *G.W. Ry.* (1926) 135 L.T. 112. See article "Oil Pollution—*Rylands* v. *Fletcher*." (Ingram) 121 New L.J. 183.

22 *Mulholland & Tedd Ltd.* v. *Baker* [1939] 3 All E.R. 253.

23 *Halsey* v. *Esso Petroleum Co. Ltd.* [1961] 1 W.L.R. 683.

24 *Watson* v. *Buckley* [1940] 1 All E.R. 174.

25 *Hale* v. *Jennings Bros.* [1938] 1 All E.R. 579. It is difficult to see why this is a dangerous thing when an aeroplane is not; see note 36 *infra*.

26 *Anglo-Celtic Shipping Co. Ltd.* v. *Elliott & Jeffrey* (1926) 42 T.L.R. 297.

27 *Robinson* v. *Technico Ltd.* (1953) unreported—a decision of the Supreme Court in Eire. See 70 L.Q.R. 170.

28 *Attorney-General* v. *Cory Bros.* [1921] 1 A.C. 521.

29 *Chichester Corpn.* v. *Foster* [1906] 1 K.B. 167.

30 *Evans* v. *Liverpool Corpn.* [1906] 1 K.B. 160.

31 *Wray* v. *Essex C.C.* [1936] 3 All E.R. 97.

32 *Blacker* v. *Lake and Elliott Ltd* (1912) 106 L.T. 533.

33 *Noble* v. *Harrison* [1926] 2 K.B. 332.

34 *Ruoff* v. *Long & Co.* [1916] 1 K.B. 148.

35 *Donovan* v. *Union Cartage Co. Ltd.* [1933] 2 K.B. 71.

36 *Fosbroke-Hobbes* v. *Airwork Ltd.* [1937] 1 All E.R. 108, 110.

37 *Ball* v. *L.C.C.* [1949] 2 K.B. 159 (overruled by *A. C. Billings* v. *Riden* [1958] A.C. 240 in so far as it was based on *Malone* v. *Laskey* [1907] 2 K.B. 141).

38 *Donaldson* v. *McNiven* [1952] 1 All E.R. 1213, affd. [1952] 2 All E.R. 691.

39 *Bolton* v. *Stone* [1951] A.C. 850.

40 *Burley* v. *Stepney Corpn.* [1947] 1 All E.R. 507.

41 The expression " absolute liability " in this connection is well established by judicial usage. In addition to its use by Blackburn J. in *Rylands* v. *Fletcher*, it is used by Lord Moulton in *Rickards* v. *Lothian* [1913] A.C. 263, 281, Scrutton L.J. in *Charing Cross Electricity Supply Co.* v. *Hydraulic Power Co.* [1913] 3 K.B. 442, 449, and *St. Anne's Well Brewery Co.* v. *Roberts* (1928) 44 T.L.R. 703, 705, Atkin L.J. in *Belvedere Fish Guano Co.* v. *Rainham Chemical Works* [1920] 2 K.B. 487, 504, 505, by Slesser L.J. in *Honeywill and Stein Ltd.* v. *Larkin Bros.* [1934] 1 K.B. 191, by Lord Wright in *Noble* v. *Harrison* [1926] 2 K.B. 332, 342, and *Knott* v. *L.C.C.* [1934] 1 K.B. 126, 139, by Lord Uthwatt in *Read* v. *J. Lyons & Co. Ltd.* [1947] A.C. 156, and by Upjohn J. in *Smeaton* v. *Ilford Corpn.* [1954] Ch. 450, 483, to quote only some of the cases. The term " strict liability " invented by Prof. Winfield (42 L.Q.R. 37; *Tort*, 6th ed., p. 590) has been suggested as an alternative. It is submitted that the expression " absolute liability " more accurately describes liability without negligence and that " strict liability " has no precise meaning. In *Read* v. *J. Lyons & Co. Ltd.*, *supra*, at p. 171, Lord Macmillan described the expression " strict liability " as ambiguous.

that (1) the dangerous thing escapes from a place in the occupation of the defendant or over which he has control to a place outside his occupation or control [42] and, possibly, (2) its presence on the land constituted a " non-natural " user of the land. The defendant can only be excused liability by bringing himself within one of the exceptions stated below. This rule of absolute liability was laid down in *Rylands* v. *Fletcher* [43] where the defendants, through an independent contractor, made a reservoir on their land and, when the reservoir was filled, the water escaped through the disused re-filled shaft of an old mine into the plaintiff's mine and flooded it. The defendants were held liable on the grounds stated by Blackburn J. and subsequently approved by the House of Lords. " The question of law therefore arises, what is the obligation which the law casts on a person who, like the defendants, lawfully brings on his land something which, though harmless whilst it remains there, will naturally do mischief if it escape out of his land. It is agreed on all hands that he must take care to keep in that which he has brought on the land and keeps there, in order that it may not escape and damage his neighbours, but the question arises whether the duty which the law casts upon him, under such circumstances, is an absolute duty to keep it in at his peril, or is, as the majority of the Court of Exchequer have thought, merely a duty to take all reasonable and prudent precautions, in order to keep it in, but no more. If the first be the law, the person who has brought on his land and kept there something dangerous, and failed to keep it in, is responsible for all the natural consequences of its escape. If the second be the limit of his duty, he would not be answerable except on proof of negligence, and consequently would not be answerable for escape arising from any latent defect which ordinary prudence and skill could not detect." [44] Then Blackburn J. proceeded to add the words so often quoted:

" We think that the true rule of law is, that the person who for his own purposes brings on his lands and collects and keeps there anything likely to do mischief if it escapes, must keep it in at his peril, and, if he does not do so, is prima facie answerable for all the damage which is the natural consequence of its escape. He can excuse himself by showing that the escape was owing to the plaintiff's default; or perhaps that the escape was the consequence of *vis major*, or the act of God." [45]

415 **Necessity for escape.** The judgment quoted in the preceding paragraph deals with the case of dangerous things escaping from land, but the principle of *Rylands* v. *Fletcher* is not confined to the rights of

[42] *Read* v. *J. Lyons & Co. Ltd.* [1947] A.C. 156. This does not apply in the case of an escape of wild animals (Lord Simonds, at p. 182).

[43] (1866) L.R. 1 Ex. 265; affirmed in H.L., L.R. 3 H.L. 330, although Lord Cairns introduced an element of flexibility to the rule by restricting it to circumstances where there had been " a non-natural use " of the land by the defendant (at pp. 338–340).

[44] *Ibid.* at p. 279.

[45] *Ibid.* at pp. 279, 280.

adjacent landowners among themselves. Lord Sumner said: "I am satisfied that *Rylands* v. *Fletcher* is not limited to the case of adjacent freeholders. I shall not attempt to show how far it extends. It extends as far as this case [which dealt with the position of an electric supply company and a hydraulic power company both laying their mains in the streets], and that is enough for the present purpose," adding that in *Rylands* v. *Fletcher*, "both courts show that they have no intention of confining the principle to the case of adjacent freeholders."[46] It covers cases where the dangerous thing is brought or carried along the highway,[47] but the principle was held not to be applicable where there was an escape from a ship.[48] If the dangerous thing is brought on to another person's land the owners of the dangerous thing are liable although they have "no tenancy or independent occupation of the land, but use it thus by permission of the tenants or occupiers,"[49] and *a fortiori*, if they have no such permission. *Rylands* v. *Fletcher*, therefore, applies to dangerous things generally, and lays down the measure of liability for those who allow them to "escape."[50] Lord Wright, dealing with gas, says: "That gas is a dangerous thing within the rules applicable to things dangerous in themselves is beyond question. Thus the appellants who are carrying in their mains the inflammable and explosive gas are prima facie within the principle of *Rylands* v. *Fletcher*, affirming *Fletcher* v. *Rylands*: that is to say, that though they are doing nothing wrongful in carrying the dangerous thing so long as they keep it in their pipes, they come prima facie within the rule of strict liability if the gas escapes: the gas constitutes an extraordinary danger created by the appellants for their own purposes, and the rule established by *Rylands* v. *Fletcher* requires that they act at their peril and must pay for damage caused by the gas if it escapes, even without any negligence on their part. The rule is not limited to cases where the defendant has been carrying or accumulating the dangerous thing on his own land: it applies equally in a case like the present where the appellants were carrying the gas in mains laid in the property of the city (that is, in the subsoil) in exercise of a franchise to do so."[51]

416 The escape of the dangerous thing must be not only from the control of the person who keeps it but must also be an escape to some other place

[46] *Charing Cross Electricity Supply Co.* v. *Hydraulic Power Co.* [1914] 3 K.B. 772, 779. See also *per* Atkinson J. in *Shiffman* v. *Order of St. John* [1936] 1 All E.R. 557, 561.

[47] *Jones* v. *Festiniog Ry.* (1868) L.R. 3 Q.B. 733; *Powell* v. *Fall* (1880) 5 Q.B.D. 597; *Hasley* v. *Esso Petroleum Co.* [1961] 1 W.L.R. 683 (where the dangerous thing escapes onto the public highway and damages a personal chattel such as a motor-car parked outside by the roadside).

[48] *Miller Steamship Co.* v. *Overseas Tank Ship (U.K.) Ltd. The Wagon Mound (No. 2)* [1963] 1 Lloyd's Rep. 402, which point did not fall to be considered by the Privy Council [1967] 1 A.C. 617.

[49] *Rainham Chemical Works* v. *Belvedere Fish Guano Co.* [1921] 2 A.C. 465, 479, *per* Lord Sumner.

[50] See *Jones* v. *Festiniog Ry.*, *supra*; *Filburn* v. *People's Palace and Aquarium Co.* (1890) 25 Q.B.D. 258. *Cf.* Stallybrass, 3 C.L.J. 376.

[51] *Northwestern Utilities* v. *London Guarantee and Accident Co.* [1936] A.C. 108, 118.

not subject to his control.[52] In *Read* v. *J. Lyons & Co. Ltd.*[53] the defendants in time of war carried on the business of making shells. The plaintiff was an inspector employed by the Minister of Supply who in the course of her duty was in the shell-filling shop of the defendants inspecting the filling of shell cases when an explosion occurred which killed one person and injured others, including the plaintiff. The plaintiff, in her action, did not allege negligence but claimed on the principle of *Rylands* v. *Fletcher*, and she failed on the ground that there had been no "escape" of the explosive or of the explosion from the defendant's premises. Likewise there had been no escape where a yew tree growing on the defendant's land and never having extended its branches beyond his boundary had had some of its leaves eaten by the plaintiff's horse, reaching out over the fence for them, as a result of which it died from being poisoned.[54]

417 **Things naturally on the land not dangerous things.** It follows from what has been stated above, that the rule in *Rylands* v. *Fletcher* has no application to things naturally on the land, because they are not dangerous things. Accordingly, where land, which had been cultivated, was neglected so that thistles sprang up and their seeds were blown onto the adjoining land causing damage, the landowner was held not liable for the natural growth of the soil.[55] Similarly, when the branch of a beech tree overhanging the highway broke in consequence of some latent defect and damaged a vehicle which was passing along the highway, the landowner was held not liable, because (1) the tree was not a dangerous thing, and (2) it was the natural growth of the soil.[56] If the branch was in such a condition "that anyone could see that it might fall at any moment, and probably would fall very soon," there would be liability on the ground of negligence but not under the rule in *Rylands* v. *Fletcher*.[57] Again, where some rocks overhanging a steep slope, owing to the action of the weather, broke away and fell down the slope crashing into the plaintiff's dwelling-house the defendant was held not liable, Eve J. saying: "It is not a case where the landowner has erected or brought upon his land something of an unusual nature which is essentially dangerous in itself. The rocks in question are . . . part of the natural formation." [58] In this case also, if the fall

[52] *Read* v. *J. Lyons & Co. Ltd.* [1947] A.C. 156, *per* Viscount Simon at p. 168.
[53] *Supra.* See the criticism of this case in *Pollock on Torts*, 15th ed., p. 372.
[54] *Ponting* v. *Noakes* [1894] 2 Q.B. 281.
[55] *Giles* v. *Walker* (1890) 24 Q.B.D. 656. In *Davey* v. *Harrow Corporation* [1958] 1 Q.B. 60 at p. 72 Lord Goddard C.J., delivering the judgment of the Court of Appeal, tentatively expressed the opinion that today this case "if founded on nuisance and not on negligence . . . might be decided differently." But it could now be an offence under the Weeds Act 1959.
[56] *Noble* v. *Harrison* [1926] 2 K.B. 332.
[57] *Mackie* v. *Dunbartonshire C.C.* [1927] W.N. 247. *Cf. Bruce* v. *Caulfield* (1918) 34 T.L.R. 204 (tree on defendant's land blown down on to plaintiff's stable—held, defendant not liable as no evidence that the tree was dangerous); *Shirvell* v. *Hackwood Estates* [1938] 2 K.B. 577; *Cunliffe* v. *Banks* [1945] 1 All E.R. 459 (in both of these cases damage was caused by the fall of a tree, but the defendant was held not liable because he was not negligent).
[58] *Pontardawe R.D.C.* v. *Moore-Gwyn* [1929] 1 Ch. 656.

of the rocks had been caused by the removal of their natural support so as to render their dangerous condition both patent and imminent, the owner would have been liable on the ground of negligence. When a quarry became filled with water by rain and percolation the quarry owner was held not liable for the erosion of the adjoining land by the water, on the ground that it was " impossible to say that the defendants . . . are responsible for water which they have not themselves brought on to the land, but which is there naturally." [59]

418 **Natural and non-natural user of land.** In *Rylands* v. *Fletcher* Blackburn J. had held that the rule only applied to a thing " which was not naturally there " but in the House of Lords Lord Cairns, in addition to approving the reasons for the decision given by Blackburn J., also founded his judgment on the ground that the defendants had made a non-natural use of their land, which he described as " introducing into the close that which, in its natural condition, was not in or upon it." [60] As has been pointed out,[61] a non-natural use of land is not quite the same thing as bringing on land what was not naturally there, and it is not easy to understand what is meant by non-natural user.

In *Barker* v. *Herbert* [62] the railings round an area had become broken by boys playing football in the street, and the plaintiff, a child, fell through the broken railings into the area and was injured. It was contended that the defendant was under an absolute duty to fence his area, but Fletcher Moulton L.J. said: " We are not dealing in this case with anything analogous to the subject-matter of the decision in *Rylands* v. *Fletcher*. This is not a case where a landowner has erected or brought upon his land something of an unusual nature, which is essentially dangerous in itself." [63] This case was followed in *Ilford U.D.C.* v. *Beal*,[64] where it was held that the movement of a retaining wall, which cracked a sewer underneath it, imposed no liability on the owner of the retaining wall in the absence of knowledge of the existence of the sewer. Again, in *St. Anne's Well Brewery Co.* v. *Roberts*,[65] part of the ancient city wall of Exeter forming the back wall of an inn collapsed and demolished the inn, and the owners of the wall were held not to be liable. Also, where a house built on the upper part of a slope caused a retaining wall to collapse and damage a house on the lower part of the same slope, the owner of the upper house was held not liable.[66] In all these four cases it was argued that the principle of *Rylands* v. *Fletcher* applied and in all of them it was rejected; in the last three cases it was on the ground that erecting walls and

[59] *Rouse* v. *Gravelworks Ltd.* [1940] 1 K.B. 489. The quotation is from Goddard L.J. at p. 505. See also to the same effect, Goddard L.C.J. in *Neath R.D.C.* v. *Williams* [1951] 1 K.B. 115, 123; Lawrence L.J. in *Bartlett* v. *Tottenham* [1932] 1 Ch. 114, 131.
[60] (1866) L.R. 3 H.L. 330, 339.
[61] *Read* v. *J. Lyons & Co. Ltd.* [1947] A.C. 156, 166 (Lord Simon).
[62] [1911] 2 K.B. 633.
[63] At p. 642.
[64] [1925] 1 K.B. 671.
[65] (1928) 140 L.T. 1.
[66] *Wilkins* v. *Leighton* [1932] 2 Ch. 106.

buildings was a normal use of land. The decisions are more satisfactorily explained, it is submitted, by saying that erecting walls and buildings is not bringing or creating a dangerous thing on the land. As illustrating the uncertainty implied in the phrase " natural use of land," it may be pointed out that in *Pound* v. *Plumstead Board of Works*[67] Blackburn J. said that making a road was using land " for an artificial purpose."

419 The point that abnormal use alone is not enough to involve liability under *Rylands* v. *Fletcher* is brought out by Lord Moulton in *Rickards* v. *Lothian*,[68] where he says: " It must be some special use bringing with it increased danger to others, and must not merely be the ordinary use of the land or such a use as is proper for the general benefit of the community." Similarly, Atkin L.J. says: " Where a person brings upon land of which he is in *de facto* possession for purposes of his business dangerous materials which would not naturally be upon the land, he is under an obligation to keep those materials under control, so as not to cause mischief to his neighbours."[69]

It is submitted that the distinction between natural and non-natural use of land is one which it is impossible to draw with any accuracy.[70] No test for distinguishing one from another has ever been laid down.[71] Once it is agreed that non-natural user does not mean bringing on the land something which was not naturally there, it is necessary to find some other test. If it is a natural use to make, " such a use as is proper for the general benefit of the community,"[71] the use for the purpose of a reservoir (*e.g.* as in *Rylands* v. *Fletcher*) would appear to be a natural use, although the contrary was held in that case. In *Read* v. *J. Lyons & Co. Ltd.*,[72] Lord Simon and Lord Macmillan tentatively expressed the opinion that the making of munitions in time of war was not a non-natural use of land, apparently on the ground that it was beneficial to the country. It is submitted that liability under *Rylands* v. *Fletcher* is based on the escape of the dangerous thing from land in the occupation of the defendant and that if the escape causes damage there is no necessity to satisfy the further condition that the presence of that thing on the land constituted a non-natural use of the land.[73]

420 *Rylands* v. *Fletcher* has been held to apply in some few cases in which dangerous things were not present, but these cases are of doubtful

[67] (1871) L.R. 7 Q.B. 183.

[68] [1913] A.C. 263, 280.

[69] *Belvedere Fish Guano Co.* v. *Rainham Chemical Works* [1920] 2 K.B. 487, 502; affirmed [1921] 2 A.C. 465.

[70] The distinction is strongly criticised by Sir J. Salmond, *Law of Torts* (6th ed., the last by Sir J. Salmond himself), p. 260. *Cf.* 15th ed., p. 410.

[71] The distinction " awaits authoritative determination ": Upjohn J. in *Smeaton* v. *Ilford Corpn.* [1954] Ch. 450, 471.

[72] [1947] A.C. 156. At p. 166 Lord Simon said the test was " difficult to apply." Likewise there was held to be no non-natural use by the defendants of the harbour or the ship: *Miller Steamship Co.* v. *Overseas Tank Ship* (*U.K.*) *Ltd.*, *The Wagon Mound* (*No.* 2) [1963] 1 Lloyd's Rep. 402. (There was no appeal against this finding: [1967] 1 A.C. 617.)

[73] *Cf. Street on Torts*, 4th ed., pp. 248–249.

authority. In *Hoare & Co.* v. *McAlpine* [74] it was held to apply to vibrations set up by pile driving which caused damage to an old building. If this is correct, then it equally applies to all cases of nuisance caused by noise or smells. Nuisance, however, is only actionable by the occupier, and in some cases the owner of land, while under *Rylands* v. *Fletcher* any injured person can sue. Damage caused by vibrations would seem to be actionable as a nuisance or, possibly, as negligence, but to have no relation to *Rylands* v. *Fletcher*. In *Att.-Gen.* v. *Corke* [75] the owner of land who allowed persons to dwell there in caravans was held responsible for the acts of the caravan dwellers in trespassing and committing a nuisance on the adjoining land. The decision was based on the ground that the defendant had put his land to an abnormal use. The case seems to be an undue extension of *Rylands* v. *Fletcher* and makes a landowner liable for trespass committed by his licensees as if they were cattle. It is difficult to see why his liability should be higher than if he had accommodated the caravan dwellers in a lodging house or a hostel, in which cases it could not be suggested that he was liable. In *Firth* v. *Bowling Iron Co.*[76] the owners of a wire fence, the strands of which decayed and fell onto the adjoining land, were held liable for the death of a cow caused by swallowing a piece of the rusted and decayed wire. It is doubtful whether the decision was based on negligence or on *Rylands* v. *Fletcher* (which is not mentioned in the judgment). It would seem to be a case of trespass or negligence. In *Shiffman* v. *Order of St. John* [77] the view was tentatively expressed that a flagpole erected near a casualty tent in Hyde Park on the day of a jubilee celebration came within the rule of *Rylands* v. *Fletcher*. Liability for flagpoles, however, would seem to rest on the same basis as liability for lamps or other erections suspended over the highway, for bridges and for chimneys and other buildings, and to depend on negligence rather than on the rule of absolute liability.

421 In *Att.-Gen.* v. *Cory Bros.*[78] the House of Lords held that a colliery company which had tipped a vast mass of spoil on the side of a hill,

[74] [1923] 1 Ch. 167. See Sir F. Pollock's comment on this case (*Torts*, 15th ed., p. 377), which he describes as a " fallacious extension " of the rule in *Rylands* v. *Fletcher*; see also 39 L.Q.R. 145.

[75] [1933] Ch. 89. See the criticism by Holdsworth in 49 L.Q.R. 158. In the county court case of *Greenwell* v. *Prison Commissioners* (1951) 101 L.J. 486 (see 68 L.Q.R. 18), boys from an " open " Borstal Institution escaped and stole the plaintiff's lorry. It was held that the Institution was not a non-natural use of land with *Att.-Gen.* v. *Corke*, because it was maintained under statutory authority. The defendants were held liable in negligence because they knew one of the boys had escaped four times before. The necessity of proving a breach of a duty of care was confirmed by the Court of Appeal in *Dorset Yacht Co. Ltd.* v. *Home Office* [1969] 2 Q.B. 412 where it was held that the Crown may be liable in law for damage done to property by its boys, if its officers negligently permit them to escape from Borstal, and the damage, which results, is foreseeable; affirmed by the House of Lords [1970] A.C. 1004. See articles: " Borstals and the public " (Henderson), 1969 S.L.T. 81; " Escaping Borstal boys and the immunity of office " (Hamson) 27 C.L.J. 273.

[76] (1878) 3 C.P.D. 254.

[77] [1936] 1 All E.R. 557.

[78] [1921] 1 A.C. 521.

with the result that a landslide occurred, were liable on the ground of negligence and also on the principle of *Rylands* v. *Fletcher*. Their decision on the latter point was based on the ground " of liability for not keeping under control an artificial structure in its character dangerous," [79] in other words, they held that the spoil, from its size and position, was a dangerous thing. Although this heap of spoil would seem to differ only in degree from a lamp suspended over the highway, so as to make it very doubtful whether it was properly classed as a dangerous thing, yet if the classification is accepted as correct it confirms the view expressed above that *Rylands* v. *Fletcher* only applies in the case of dangerous things.

422 **Liability of owner of the dangerous thing.** The person primarily liable for the dangerous thing is the actual wrongdoer, whether or not he is in occupation of the land on which the dangerous thing is brought. This is the person who either owns it, as in the case of a reservoir or a savage animal, or has caused it to be in the position from which it has done damage, such as a gas or an electricity supply company in the case of an escape of gas or electricity from mains. If the dangerous thing escapes from the highway, such as sparks from a traction engine, the person who sent it on the highway is liable.[80] In the case of an explosion, the person carrying on the operations resulting in an explosion is liable.[81] If permission is given to a colliery company to tip colliery spoil onto a hill side, the colliery company are liable.[82]

423 **Liability of occupier of land.** The occupier of the land is liable if the dangerous thing is brought on to the land with his knowledge and consent. Accordingly, when a company manufactured explosives on land occupied by F and P and an explosion occurred, F and P were held liable on the ground that they had knowingly permitted the company to carry on its dangerous operations.[83] Dealing with this point, Lord Sumner said that F and P " clearly assented to the introduction and storing of the dinitrophenol and . . . they alone would benefit pecuniarily by the manufacture of picric acid from it. . . . As occupiers they would be under a personal obligation to their neighbours not to let this non-natural user of the land, which they occupied, become a source of damage to them. This obligation it was for them to discharge and, whether they employed agents or independent contractors in connection with the matter, their own obligation persisted. Even if they actually employed nobody, but simply suffered others to manufacture upon the site which they nevertheless continued to occupy, I think they are still under liability to third parties, if what is thus allowed by them, upon the land which they occupy, causes damage." On similar principles, the occupier of land

[79] *Per* Lord Haldane, *ibid.* at p. 537.
[80] *Powell* v. *Fall* (1880) 5 Q.B.D. 597.
[81] *Rainham Chemical Works* v. *Belvedere Fish Guano Co.* [1921] 2 A.C. 465.
[82] *Att.-Gen.* v. *Cory Bros.* [1921] 1 A.C. 521.
[83] *Rainham Chemical Works* v. *Belvedere Fish Guano Co., supra.*

who gives a licence to the owner of a travelling menagerie to exhibit his wild animals on his land will be liable if any of the animals escape and do damage.[84] Where oil leaked from an oil tank belonging to an oil company standing on the siding of a railway company, it was held that the railway company were not liable, but only on the ground that the escape was due to the wrongful act of third parties, namely the owners of the oil tank, in sending the oil tank on the railway in a leaky condition.[85]

424 In *Rylands* v. *Fletcher* Blackburn J. speaks of a person who collects, "for his own purposes," anything likely to do mischief if it escapes. These words, however, although appropriate to the decision in which they were used, are not to be taken as limiting liability to cases in which the defendant is obtaining some financial or other advantage from collecting the dangerous thing. The purpose for which it is collected by him is immaterial.[86] A somewhat different view, however, was taken in *Whitmores Ltd.* v. *Stanford.*[87] In that case an artificial watercourse was constructed and water diverted into it by erecting a weir across a river and controlling the flow into the watercourse by sluice gates. The watercourse flowed past a tannery and then past a mill and was used by the proprietors of both. The mill owner, who was also the owner of the weir and sluice gates, cut off the water supply from the tanner and, in an action to restrain him from continuing to interfere with the flow of water down the watercourse, argued that if he was bound to collect the water for the purpose of the tanner he would be liable under *Rylands* v. *Fletcher*, although he derived benefit from it. Eve J., dealing with this argument, said: "The rule does not appear to me to extend to make the owner of land liable for consequences brought about by the collecting and impounding on his land, by another, of water, or any other dangerous element, not for the purposes of the owner of the land, but for the purposes of such other." It is submitted that this goes too far. If an owner and occupier is bound by contract or prescription to collect a dangerous thing on his land for the purposes of another, while he is relieved from liability to that other if the dangerous thing escapes and damages him, he is not thereby relieved from liability to third parties. The occupier is liable because the dangerous thing was on his land with his knowledge and consent.

425 **Liability of owner of land.** The owner of the land who is not in occupation and is not the owner of or exercising control over the dangerous thing is under no liability in respect of it. The owner of land who lets it to another for the purpose of building a reservoir,

[84] See *Att.-Gen.* v. *Corke* [1933] Ch. 89, where the occupier was held liable for the acts of his licensees. This case is criticised *supra*, § 420, but if wild animals instead of human beings had been kept on the land there would have been no ground for criticism.
[85] *Smith* v. *G.W. Ry.* (1926) 42 T.L.R. 391.
[86] "It scarcely seems accurate to hold that the nationalised gas industry collects and distributes gas for its 'own purposes'" within the rule in *Rylands* v. *Fletcher*: *per* Sellers L.J. in *Dunne* v. *North Western Gas Board* [1964] 2 Q.B. 806.
[87] [1909] 1 Ch. 427.

building a factory for manufacturing munitions or keeping a zoo, is under no liability if these operations cause damage. He is not in the position of a landowner who has let his land for the purpose of doing an act likely to cause a nuisance,[88] and accordingly he is only liable if he has let the land for a purpose from which damage is bound to result without negligence on the part of his tenant.[89]

Where the landowner is also the owner of the dangerous thing, such as a reservoir, the question arises whether he is liable for damage done when the land and the dangerous thing is let to a tenant. The occupier of the land cannot escape liability by employing an independent contractor to perform his obligation,[90] and it would seem that, on principle, an owner is in the same position. This view is expressed by Atkin L.J. when, after saying that the principle of *Pickard* v. *Smith* [91] and *Penny* v. *Wimbledon U.D.C.*[92] applies to persons who bring dangerous materials onto land, he adds: " Can the person who has acquired a tiger, so long as he remains its owner, relieve himself of responsibility by contracting with a third person for its custody? " [93]

426 **Any person injured may sue.** Liability under the rule in *Rylands* v. *Fletcher* is owed to all the world, the only limitation being the ordinary rule governing the remoteness of damage. As is pointed out above,[94] the rule does not deal only with liability of landowners to each other but makes the owner of the dangerous thing liable " 'for any mischief thereby occasioned,' that is to say, not mischief necessarily occasioned to the owner of the adjoining land, but any mischief thereby occasioned." [95] Accordingly, Blackburn J. expressed the opinion that in *Rylands* v. *Fletcher* itself the workmen in the drowned mine would be

[88] See *Harris* v. *James* (1876) 45 L.J.Ch. 545; *Jenkins* v. *Jackson* (1888) 40 Ch.D. 71.

[89] *Att.-Gen.* v. *Cory Bros.* (1918) 34 T.L.R. 621. This point was not dealt with on appeal. In *St. Anne's Well Brewery Co.* v. *Roberts* (1928) 140 L.T. 1, the C.A. expressed the opinion that a landowner not in occupation of the land was never liable under *Rylands* v. *Fletcher*. This requires the limitation that he is not also the owner of the dangerous thing on the land.

[90] *Rainham Chemical Works* v. *Belvedere Fish Guano Co.* [1921] 2 A.C. 465, *per* Lord Sumner.

[91] (1861) 10 C.B.(N.S.) 470.

[92] [1899] 2 Q.B. 72.

[93] *Belvedere Fish Guano Co.* v. *Rainham Chemical Works* [1920] 2 K.B. 487, 504. *Cf.* Lord Wright in *Brackenborough* v. *Spalding U.D.C.* [1942] A.C. 310, 324: " In the case of dangerous animals, a transfer of actual possession and control would not necessarily terminate his [the owner's] responsibility."

[94] *Ante*, § 415.

[95] *Charing Cross Electricity Supply Co.* v. *Hydraulic Power Co.* [1914] 3 K.B. 772, 785, *per* Bray J. This decision was followed in *Halsey* v. *Esso Petroleum Co. Ltd.* [1961] 1 W.L.R. 683 where a plaintiff's motor car, left out on the highway, and washing, hung out to dry on his premises, were damaged by sulphuric acid smuts or oily drops escaping from the defendant's factory chimneys at their oil distributing depot, it was held that he was entitled to recover damages. See article " Wild beasts in Fulham " (nuisance by noise, smuts and fumes), 105 S.J. 579. *Cf. Vaughn* v. *Halifax-Dartmouth Bridge Commission* (1961) 29 D.L.R. (2d) 523, where flecks of paint were blown on to and damaged the the plaintiff's car from a bridge which the defendants were in the process of painting. The Nova Scotia Supreme Court held that the plaintiff could succeed on the basis of negligence but not on the basis of the rule in *Rylands* v. *Fletcher*, because such rule only applies with respect to damage affecting the use and occupation of land and because the painting of the bridge was a natural user of land.

entitled to recover the value of the tools they had lost,[96] and in gas explosions [97] and escapes of water from mains [98] members of the public passing along the highway who have been injured have been entitled to recover. Owners of stacks and other inflammable property in fields adjoining the highway have recovered when their property was damaged by fire set up by sparks emitted from railway engines [99] and traction engines.[1]

427 The damage must be caused by the escape of the thing to a place outside the occupation or control of the person who brought the thing to the place where it was before it caused the damage. Accordingly, when an explosion occurred in a munitions factory and injured the plaintiff, who was employed by the Ministry of Supply to inspect the work done there, it was held that in the absence of proof of negligence the plaintiff could not recover, as there had been no " escape." [2]

428 **The kind of damage is irrelevant.** The view has been expressed [3] that damages for personal injuries cannot be recovered under the doctrine of *Rylands* v. *Fletcher*. Whether the action is to be regarded as based on nuisance or negligence or on some special rule, there is neither principle nor authority for holding that whilst there can be liability for one kind of damage, namely to property, yet there can be no liability for another kind, *viz.* personal injuries, caused by the same wrong.

However this particular problem needs to be considered in the light of whether the plaintiff has any interest in the land that has been interfered with or not. Even where he has no such interest the right to damages for personal injuries under the doctrine of *Rylands* v. *Fletcher* was recognised by the Judicial Committee of the Privy Council [4] and such damages have later been awarded by the Court of Appeal.[5] It would seem that no doubt about it had ever been expressed before, until the dicta of some of the law lords in *Read* v. *Lyons*. In *Perry* v. *Kendricks Transport Ltd.* Parker L.J. said: " Though the decision in *Musgrove* v. *Pandelis* [6] has been the subject of some criticism (see the speech of Lord Porter in *Read* v. *J. Lyons & Co. Ltd.*[7]) it is still binding upon this court. Accordingly, I feel bound to approach the matter upon the basis that the facts here bring the

96 *Cattle* v. *Stockton Waterworks Co.* (1875) L.R. 10 Q.B. 453.
97 *Price* v. *South Metropolitan Gas Co.* (1895) 65 L.J.Q.B. 126.
98 *Markland* v. *Manchester Corpn.* [1936] A.C. 360.
99 *Jones* v. *Festiniog Ry.* (1868) L.R. 3 Q.B. 733.
1 *Powell* v. *Fall* (1880) 5 Q.B.D. 597; *Gunter* v. *James* (1908) 24 T.L.R. 868; *Mansell* v. *Webb* (1918) 88 L.J.K.B. 323.
2 *Read* v. *J. Lyons & Co. Ltd.* [1947] A.C. 156. See also *Howard* v. *Furness Lines Ltd.* [1936] 2 All E.R. 781.
3 By Lord Macmillan in *Read* v. *J. Lyons & Co. Ltd., supra*, at p. 121. The other members of the House expressed no concluded opinion.
4 *E. & S. A. Telegraph Co.* v. *Cape Town Tramways* [1902] A.C. 381, 390, 392. Also by the C.A. in *Perry* v. *Kendricks Transport Ltd* [1956] 1 W.L.R. 85. See also Tylor, 10 M.L.R. 369, 399.
5 *Miles* v. *Forest Rock Granite Co.* (*Leicestershire*) *Ltd.* (1918) 34 T.L.R. 500 and by Atkinson J. in *Shiffman* v. *Order of St. John* [1936] 1 All E.R. 557.
6 [1919] 2 K.B. 43.
7 [1947] A.C. 156, 176.

case within the rule in *Rylands* v. *Fletcher*: nor do I think it is open to this court to hold that the rule only applies to damage to adjoining land or to a proprietary interest in land and not to personal injury. It is true that in *Read* v. *Lyons & Co. Ltd.* Lord Macmillan, Lord Porter and Lord Simonds all doubted whether the rule extended to cover personal injuries, but the final decision in the matter was expressly left over and, as the matter stands at present, I think we are bound to hold that the defendants are liable in this case, quite apart from negligence, unless they can bring themselves within one of the well-known exceptions to the rule." [8]

On the other hand where the plaintiff has such an interest there can be little doubt that as an occupier he can recover damages in respect of personal injuries sustained by him as well as damage to his chattels.[9] Thus in *Hale* v. *Jennings Brothers* [10] where the plaintiff, a tenant of a stall at a fair, was struck and seriously injured by a chair complete with its occupant which had become detached from a chair-o-plane roundabout belonging to the defendants, it was held by the Court of Appeal that she had a good cause of action founded on *Rylands* v. *Fletcher*. This decision must therefore remain a binding authority until such time as it is authoritatively overruled.

In *Weller & Co.* v. *Foot and Mouth Disease Research Institute* [11] the defendants occupied premises where they carried out experimental work in connection with foot and mouth disease. As a result of an outbreak of the disease in cattle in the vicinity of these premises the Ministry of Agriculture, Fisheries and Food made an order closing two markets in the area, which resulted in the plaintiffs, auctioneers, suffering the loss of lucrative business since they were unable to carry out the auctioning of cattle at those marts. Nevertheless on the assumption that the defendants had imported an African virus onto their premises which had escaped and had caused the outbreak of the disease, resulting in the compulsory closure order of the marts, it was held, *inter alia*, that the plaintiffs were not entitled to recover damages for loss of profits under the rule in *Rylands* v. *Fletcher* because they had no interest in any land to which the virus could have escaped. Further, as the plaintiffs had no proprietary interest in any of the cattle, they had no claim in negligence, even if they had a proprietary interest in the market, because the escape of the virus could not possibly injure those premises.

2.—DEFENCES

(a) *Act of God*

29 Where the damage is caused by an act of God there is no liability under

[8] [1956] 1 W.L.R. 85, at p. 92 (where a child of 10 years old was seriously injured by the explosion of petrol fumes from the tank of a disused coach parked on the defendants' parking ground whilst he was crossing over some waste land returning home from school after some other boys had unscrewed the tank's cap and had dropped in lighted matches).

[9] *e.g.* to car parked outside house on the road and clothes on washing line: *Halsey* v. *Esso Petroleum Co. Ltd.* [1961] 1 W.L.R. 683. See article "Wild beasts in Fulham" 105 S.J. 579.

[10] [1938] 1 All E.R. 579.

[11] [1966] 1 Q.B. 569.

Rylands v. *Fletcher*. " *Rylands* v. *Fletcher* saved the question whether the act of God might not have afforded a defence, and this question was answered in the affirmative in *Nichols* v. *Marsland*,[12] in which the act of God had been established by the finding of the jury, though I have some doubt whether that finding was correct." [13] It is not established by decisions in the House of Lords that the act of God is a defence,[14] although an occurrence which falls within the description of " act of God " in this connection is one which can only occur very seldom.

An act of God is equivalent to *damnum fatale* in Scottish law, which was defined by Lord Westbury in *Tennant* v. *Earl of Glasgow* [15] as " circumstances which no human foresight can provide against, and of which human prudence is not bound to recognise the possibility, and which when they do occur, therefore, are calamities that do not involve the obligation of paying for the consequences that may result from them." This definition was approved by the House of Lords in *Greenock Corpn.* v. *Caledonian Ry.*[16] To be an act of God the occurrence in question must be due to natural causes and not to human agency. In the words of Lord Mansfield: " Now what is the act of God? I consider it to mean something in opposition to the act of man." [17] To be an act of God an occurrence must be, accordingly, (a) due to natural causes exclusively; (b) of an extraordinary nature; and (c) such that it could not be anticipated or provided against.

Before *Greenock Corpn.* v. *Caledonian Ry.* there were two views about the meaning of " act of God," each of them supported by a respectable body of authority. One view, now adopted by the House of Lords, was that the occurrence could only be an act of God if it could not be anticipated or guarded against [18]; the other view was that it was sufficient to show that it could not reasonably be anticipated or guarded against.[19] These two views do not differ as much as might appear. A man must anticipate as likely to occur natural phenomena which have already occurred in Great Britain, and, in some cases, in neighbouring countries. The margin of safety is not to be based on the average but on the extreme, and when the extremes are ascertained it must still be contemplated that the extremes may be exceeded. Lord Dunedin has said [20]

12 (1876) 2 Ex.D. 1.
13 Lord Parker in *Greenock Corpn.* v. *Caledonian Ry.* [1917] A.C. 556, 581.
14 *Greenock Corpn.* v. *Caledonian Ry.*, *supra*; *Att.-Gen.* v. *Cory Bros.* [1921] 1 A.C. 521.
15 (1864) 2 M.(H.L.) 22.
16 [1917] A.C. 556.
17 *Forward* v. *Pittard* (1785) 1 T.R. 27.
18 *Nugent* v. *Smith* (1875) 1 C.P.D. 19, 34, *per* Brett J.; *Hamilton* v. *Pandorf* (1886) 17 Q.B.D. 670, 675, *per* Lord Esher; *R.* v. *Commrs. of Sewers for Essex* (1885) 14 Q.B.D. 561, 574, *per* Coleridge C.J. and Cave J. *Cf. G.W. Ry.* v. *Owners of SS. Mostyn* [1928] A.C. 57, 105, where Lord Blanesburgh refers to an act of God as something which had taken a ship out of control " by an irresistible and unsearchable providence nullifying all human effort."
19 *Nugent* v. *Smith* (1876) 1 C.P.D. 423, *per* Cockburn C.J. (at p. 426) and James L.J. (at p. 444); *Nichols* v. *Marsland, supra*; *Nitro-Phosphate and Odam's Manure Co.* v. *London and St. Katherine Docks* (1878) 9 Ch.D. 503, *per* Fry J.; *Baldwin's Ltd.* v. *Halifax Corpn.* (1916) 85 L.J.K.B. 1769, *per* Atkin J.
20 *Greenock Corpn.* v. *Caledonian Ry.* [1917] A.C. 556, 577.

that there is "no clear-cut choice in law" between the two views, "but that it always comes to a question of fact whether such and such an occurrence was a *damnum fatale*."

In *Ruck* v. *Williams* [21] Bramwell B. said, when referring to an exceptional storm: "We call it extraordinary, but in truth it is not an extraordinary storm which happens once in a century, or in fifty or twenty years; on the contrary, it would be extraordinary if it did not happen. There is a French saying that 'there is nothing so certain as that which is unexpected.' In like manner, there is nothing so certain as that something extraordinary will happen now and then." It would seem therefore that whether there is a duty or not to take precautions against extraordinary events must depend on the facts but the avoidance of liability by raising this defence in appropriate cases may not be so easy in the light of extreme weather conditions which can be reliably forecasted and publicised as a result of modern sophisticated technological and meteorological skills.

30 **Extraordinary rainfall.** A rainfall of extraordinary violence is not an act of God. In *Greenock Corpn.* v. *Caledonian Ry.*[22] the corporation had diverted the course of a natural stream and constructed a paddling pond. Owing to an extraordinary rainfall the stream burst from its diverted channel and returned to its natural channel, with the result that the accumulated water damaged the railway company's premises. The corporation were held liable, Lord Finlay saying: "It is true that the flood was of extraordinary violence, but floods of extraordinary violence must be anticipated as likely to take place from time to time." On this point Lord Dunedin said: "The appellants argue that . . . if they can show that this rainfall was much in excess of what had been previously observed in Greenock that is enough. I do not think that you can rightly confine your view to Greenock alone. No one can say that such rainfall was unprecedented in Scotland; and I think the appellants were bound to consider that some day Greenock might be subjected to the same rainfall as other places in Scotland had been subjected to." [23]

In the earlier case of *Nichols* v. *Marsland* [24] a stream was diverted and dammed so as to form three pools. Owing to an extraordinary rainfall the dam burst and the resulting flood carried away some bridges. The jury found that the rainfall was so severe as to amount to *vis major*, which is equivalent to the act of God, and the defendants were consequently held to be not liable. This finding was criticised in *Greenock Corpn.* v. *Caledonian Ry.*,[25] with the result that it may be said that an extraordinary rainfall is not an act of God.[26] A somewhat similar view was taken by the court when a railway embankment in Canada,

21 (1858) 3 H. & N. 308, at p. 318.
22 [1917] A.C. 556.
23 *Ibid.* p. 577.
24 (1876) 2 Ex.D. 1.
25 [1917] A.C. 556.
26 *Att.-Gen.* v. *Cory Bros.* [1921] 1 A.C. 521, 536, *per* Lord Haldane; 35 T.L.R. at p. 574, *per* Scrutton L.J. A heavy snowfall was held not an act of God in *Slater* v. *Worthington's Cash Stores* [1941] 1 K.B. 488.

constructed under statutory powers, was carried away in a storm. Lord Chelmsford said: "The railway company ought to have constructed their works in such a manner as to be capable of resisting all the violence of weather which, in the climate of Canada, might be expected, though perhaps rarely, to occur." [27]

431 **High wind.** The principle which applies to an extraordinary rainfall applies to a high wind. "Before wind can amount to an act of God . . . the wind must not merely be exceptionally strong, but must be of such exceptional strength that no one could be reasonably expected to anticipate or provide against it." [28]

432 **High tide.** An extraordinary high tide would seem to be no different in this respect than an extraordinary rainfall. The view of Coleridge C.J. that "as soon as it was shown by experience that a tide of the height of that recorded in March 1874 might occur, the danger of its recurrence was a danger that could be foreseen in the future, and might be guarded against, whether it could have been foreseen in the past or not, and consequently that the owners of the sea-walls were bound to foresee and provide against it," [29] seems more in accordance with authority than that of Fry J. who said that an event which has happened once, when there is nothing to lead to the inference that it is likely to recur, does not, if it happens a second time, cease to be an act of God.[30]

433 **Lightning.** Lightning is one of the usual illustrations of an act of God,[31] but there is no decided case in which it has been involved.

434 **Rat.** Where water was collected from the roof of property by means of gutters into a box, and a rat gnawed a hole in the box with the result that the water flowed into the ground floor of the building and damaged the plaintiff's goods, it was held that the occupier of the upper floor was not liable because the escape of the water was due to *vis major* "as much as if a thief had broken the hole in attempting to enter the house, or a flash of lightning or a hurricane had caused the rent."[32] The action of the rat, however, cannot be regarded as an act of God,[33] and the other illustrations given show that this point was not considered very carefully by the court. In any event the action of the rat could both be foreseen and guarded against.[34]

27 *G.W. Ry. of Canada* v. *Braid* (1863) 1 Moo.P.C.(N.S.) 101, 121. See also *City of Montreal* v. *Watt and Scott Ltd.* [1922] 2 A.C. 555.

28 *Cushing* v. *Peter Walker & Son* [1941] 2 All E.R. 693, 695, *per* Hallett J.

29 *R.* v. *Commrs. of Sewers for Essex* (1885) 14 Q.B.D. 561, 574, affirmed (1886) 11 App.Cas. 449. See also *Greenwood Tileries Ltd.* v. *Clapson* [1937] 1 All E.R. 765.

30 *Nitro-Phosphate and Odam's Chemical Manure Co.* v. *London and St. Katherine Docks* (1878) 9 Ch.D. 503.

31 See *Carstairs* v. *Taylor* (1871) L.R. 6 Ex. 217; *Nichols* v. *Marsland* (1875) L.R. 10 Ex. 255, 260, *per* Bramwell B.; *Anon.* (1538) Dyer 33, Case (10).

32 *Carstairs* v. *Taylor* (1871) L.R. 6 Ex. 217.

33 *Cf. Bishop* v. *Consolidated London Properties* (1933) 102 L.J.K.B. 257, where a pigeon blocked an open gutter and caused an overflow, and the landlord of the property was held liable; *Pandorf* v. *Hamilton* (1887) 12 App.Cas. 518, where rats gnawed a hole in a pipe and caused sea water to damage the cargo.

34 *Cf. Northwestern Utilities* v. *London Guarantee and Accident Co.* [1936] A.C. 108, dealing with the act of a stranger.

435 **Sudden death.** The sudden death from heart failure of the driver of a motor-vehicle while at the wheel is an act of God.[35] On the other hand, if a driver had any reason to suspect that he was suffering from heart disease then of course different considerations apply, since he should never have been driving in such circumstances.

(b) *Default of the Plaintiff*

436 **The default of the plaintiff.** In *Rylands* v. *Fletcher* Blackburn J. says that the defendant " can excuse himself by showing that the escape was due to the plaintiff's default." This means that if the sole cause of the damage is the act or default of the plaintiff himself he cannot recover.[36] Accordingly, where the Postmaster-General negligently laid some telegraph lines close to some electric cables of a local authority and so exposed his lines to danger to which they need not have been exposed and which it was the duty of the person laying them to avoid, it was held that he could not recover although by the Telegraph Act 1878, s. 8, the local authority were made absolutely liable for damage to the lines caused by their cables.[37] A person, of course, is entitled to assume that others will properly perform their legal duties and to regulate his actions accordingly, so that, as a rule, it is not negligence on his part to omit to take precautions against the consequences of another failing to perform his duty under *Rylands* v. *Fletcher*.[38]

Persons who meddle with dangerous animals cannot recover if they are injured.[39]

(c) *Consent of the Plaintiff*

437 **Consent of the plaintiff.** If the injured person has agreed to run the risk of damage from the dangerous thing, he cannot recover unless he can prove that the damage was caused by the omission to use reasonable care, *i.e.* negligence, on the part of the defendant. So, when the owners of land gave permission to their lessees to tip colliery spoil on the side of a hill, it was held that they could not recover for damage caused by the sliding of the spoil down the hill into the valley below except on proof of negligence on the part of their lessees.[40] " A plaintiff who is himself a consenting party to the accumulation cannot rely simply upon the escape of the accumulated material; he must further establish that the escape was due to want of reasonable care on the part of the

[35] *Ryan* v. *Youngs* [1938] 1 All E.R. 522. See *J. Constantine S.S. Line Ltd.* v. *Imperial Smelting Corpn. Ltd.* [1942] A.C. 154, at p. 202. *Cf. The Saint Angus* [1938] P. 225 (a case of illness).

[36] If the damage is only partly the result of the plaintiff's act or default, the damages will be apportioned under the Law Reform (Contributory Negligence) Act 1945, *post*, Chap. 16.

[37] *Postmaster-General* v. *Liverpool Corpn.* [1923] A.C. 587.

[38] See *Miles* v. *Forest Rock Granite Co. Ltd.* (1918) 34 T.L.R. 500, where the plaintiff, who was injured while passing along the highway owing to the failure of the defendants to keep the results of their blasting operations on their own land, was not prevented from recovering by the fact that he disregarded the warnings of men with red flags posted by the defendants on the highway; also *Daniel* v. *Metropolitan Ry.* (1871) L.R. 5 H.L. 45.

[39] See the cases quoted in Chap. 10.

[40] *Att.-Gen.* v. *Cory Bros.* [1921] 1 A.C. 521.

person who made the deposit." [41] Again, a person who enters into occupation of premises " takes the premises as they are, and, accordingly, consents to the presence there of the installed water system with all its advantages and disadvantages." [42]

Whether or not the plaintiff has agreed, expressly or by implication, to take upon himself the risk of injury from the dangerous thing is a question of fact, but the mere fact that he occupies premises near to a gasworks or a munitions factory does not mean that he agrees to bear the risk of an explosion unless he can prove negligence. It would be otherwise if he were the owner of the land and had let it to a tenant for that purpose.

438 **Common benefit.** If the dangerous thing has been brought upon premises for the common benefit of the plaintiff and the defendant, there is an implied agreement to run the risk of damage, unless negligence on the part of the defendant can be proved. The chief example of this is to be found in cases where water is collected from the spouts of a building, or a cistern is maintained for the common use of the occupiers of different floors in the same building. [43] These cases are considered in detail later. [44] There is no common benefit or common interest, for this purpose, between a statutory supplier of gas, water or electricity and the individual consumer. [45]

In addition to these cases, there is a tendency to hold that damage caused by the ordinary domestic installation of gas, water and electricity is never actionable except on proof of negligence. [46]

(d) *Independent Act of Third Party*

439 **Independent act of a third party.** The rule in *Rylands* v. *Fletcher* does not apply when the damage is due to the independent act of a third party, which could not reasonably have been foreseen and guarded against. The ground of this exception is that the defendant has fulfilled his duty of keeping the dangerous thing harmless and that the cause of the damage was not his breach of duty but " the conscious act of another volition." [47]

This exception was first recognised in *Box* v. *Jubb* [48] where the defendants owned a reservoir connected with a main drain at the upper end by sluices by which it was supplied, and at the lower end by sluices by which the surplus water was returned. By the combined effect of the

[41] *Per* Lord Finlay, *supra*, at p. 539.
[42] *Peters* v. *Prince of Wales Theatre* [1943] K.B. 73, 79, *per* Goddard L.C.J.
[43] *Carstairs* v. *Taylor* (1871) L.R. 6 Ex. 217; *Rickards* v. *Lothian* [1913] A.C. 263; *Anderson* v. *Oppenheimer* (1880) 5 Q.B.D. 602; *Blake* v. *Woolf* [1898] 2 Q.B. 426; *Kiddle* v. *City Business Properties Ltd.* [1942] 1 K.B. 269.
[44] *Post*, § 482 (water); § 538 (electricity).
[45] *Northwestern Utilities Ltd.* v. *London Guarantee and Accident Co.* [1936] A.C. 108, 120.
[46] *Collingwood* v. *Home and Colonial Stores* [1936] 3 All E.R. 200; *Tilley* v. *Stevenson* [1939] 4 All E.R. 207.
[47] *Per* Lord Dunedin in *Dominion Natural Gas Co.* v. *Collins* [1909] A.C. 640, 647. See also *Northwestern Utilities* v. *London Guarantee and Accident Co.* [1936] A.C. 108, 120.
[48] (1879) 4 Ex.D. 76.

emptying of a reservoir belonging to a third person above that of the defendants and an obstruction in the drain below, an overflow occurred. The defendants had no control over the main drain or the other reservoir, or knowledge of the circumstances causing the overflow, and were held not liable on the ground that " the matters complained of took place through no default or breach of duty of the defendants, but were caused by a stranger over whom and at a spot where they had no control." [49] Similarly, when damage was caused to the occupier of the lower floor of a building by an overflow of water from the lavatory basin in the upper floor, and it was proved that the overflow was caused by the malicious act of a third person in turning the tap fully on and plugging the wastepipe, the occupier of the upper floor was held not liable.[50] Further, where a motor-coach with an empty petrol tank was in a car park and some boys threw a lighted match into the petrol tank which caused the petrol fumes in the tank to explode and injure the plaintiff, a boy of ten, who was close to the car park, the owners of the coach were held not liable because the explosion was caused by the act of strangers which the owners could not reasonably have anticipated and guarded against.[51] Lord Moulton said that a defendant cannot " be properly said to have caused or allowed the water to escape if the malicious act of a third person was the real cause of its escaping without any fault on the part of the defendant." [52] Again, in *Nichols* v. *Marsland*,[53] Bramwell B., dealing with the escape of water from a reservoir, said: " Suppose a stranger let it loose, would the defendant be liable? If so, then if a mischievous boy bored a hole in a cistern in any London house, and the water did mischief to a neighbour, the occupier of the house would be liable. That cannot be." [54]

The exception itself being firmly established, it remains to consider who is a third party within the meaning of the exception, and the circumstances under which his acts exempt the owner of the dangerous thing from liability.

40 **Meaning of " third party."** There is no authority defining the meaning of " third party " or " stranger " in this connection. It is clear that the owner is liable for the acts of his servants and agents in the course of their employment. He is also liable for the acts of independent contractors and of any other persons whom he authorises to interfere with the dangerous thing.[55] Does " third party " or " stranger " include persons who do not come within any of these categories? Sir John Salmond says: " But what shall be said of persons lawfully upon the defendant's land with his permission, but without authority to bring upon it, or to

[49] *Per* Kelly C.B.
[50] *Rickards* v. *Lothian* [1913] A.C. 263.
[51] *Perry* v. *Kendricks Transport Ltd.* [1956] 1 W.L.R. 85.
[52] *Ibid*. p. 278.
[53] (1876) 6 Ex.D. 1; affirming L.R. 10 Ex. 255.
[54] L.R. 10 Ex., at p. 259.
[55] *Hardaker* v. *Idle D.C.* [1896] 1 Q.B. 335; *Black* v. *Christchurch Finance Co.* [1894] A.C. 48.

deal with, dangerous things—for example, the members of his family, his servants, his guests, or licensees permitted to use the land? It is submitted that for the acts of all such persons in bringing or keeping dangerous things on the premises, or in meddling with such things already on the premises, the occupier is vicariously liable under the rule in *Rylands* v. *Fletcher*." [56] This opinion has been adopted by his editors.[57] Professor Winfield, on the other hand, thinks this goes too far, and suggests that the test is: " Can it be inferred from the facts of the particular case that the occupier had such control over the licensee or over the circumstances which made his act possible that he ought to have prevented it? If so, the occupier is liable, otherwise not." [58]

441 It is to be observed that the two passages quoted in the preceding paragraph are not dealing with exactly the same point. Sir John Salmond is ascertaining the meaning of " stranger," while Professor Winfield, leaving on one side the meaning of " stranger " is trying to determine when the defendant is liable for the act of a person who is a licensee on the defendant's land. The two questions should be kept distinct, because the defendant is liable without proof of negligence if the damage has been caused by the act of a person who is not a " stranger "; on the other hand, if the act has been done by a person who is within the category of a " stranger " he is only liable on proof of negligence.

It is submitted that " third party " or " stranger " in this connection means anyone who is not a servant or agent or independent contractor of the defendant, or some other person whom he has authorised to interfere with the dangerous thing, but does not include members of the defendant's family or persons on his land by his invitation or licence.[59] There is nothing, either on principle or authority, which would justify a departure from the normal meaning of " third party." [60] A person is not liable for the acts of those whom he invites or licenses to use his land [59] and there is no reason to suppose that his liability is any different in this respect because he has a dangerous thing on the land. The person injured is adequately protected by the requirement that even when the damage has been caused by the act of a stranger, the defendant is liable on proof of negligence.

Some light is thrown on this by the decision in *Smith* v. *G.W. Ry.*[61] In that case, oil escaped from an oil truck while the truck was in a railway

[56] *Law of Torts*, 6th ed. (the last by Sir J. Salmond), p. 268.
[57] *Salmond on Torts*, 15th ed., p. 421.
[58] *Tort*, 5th ed., p. 600.
[59] See now *Perry* v. *Kendricks Transport Ltd.* [1956] 1 W.L.R. 85.
[60] In *Perry* v. *Kendricks Transport Ltd.*, *supra*, at p. 92, Parker L.J. said a stranger was one over whom the defendant had no control (applied in *Emanuel* v. *G.L.C.*, *The Times*, July 21, 1970). In *Balfour* v. *Barty-King* [1957] 1 Q.B. 496 it was held that an independent contractor is not a stranger for this purpose. The defendants had control over an independent contractor " in that they chose him, they invited him to their premises to do work and he could have been ordered to leave at any moment ": (at p. 505, *per* Lord Goddard C.J.). See the note on this case by T. Ellis Lewis in [1957] C.L.J. 132.
[61] (1926) 42 T.L.R. 391.

siding, with the result that water in an adjoining watercourse was rendered unfit to be drunk by cattle. The truck was the property of the oil company, and the railway company had no reason to suppose that it was defective. Here, the oil company were in the position of invitees or licensees of the railway company as regards the truck.[59] It was held that the railway company were not liable, because the oil company were " third parties " within the meaning of *Rickards* v. *Lothian* and *Box* v. *Jubb*.[62]

442 Yet a further example can be found in *Baker* v. *Snell*[63] where the defendant was the owner of a dog which he knew to be savage. The dog was in the charge of his servant, a potman, who brought it into the kitchen and incited it to attack a maid, the plaintiff in the action. The plaintiff failed in the county court but, on appeal, a new trial was ordered to decide whether the potman was acting in the course of his employment at the time of injury. This shows that, in the view of the Court of Appeal, the potman, though a servant of the defendant, would be a " third party " or " stranger " within the meaning of the exception now being considered if he was not acting in the course of his employment.[64] *A fortiori*, persons who are not servants or agents of the defendant, but are lawful visitors[65] on his land, must be third parties. In *Behrens* v. *Bertram Mills Circus Ltd.*,[66] Devlin J. held that in the case of a dangerous animal on land the act of a licensee on the land was the act of a stranger. There, a circus elephant, held to be in law a dangerous animal, irritated by the barking and snapping of a dog belonging to the manager of the plaintiffs, who had a booth in the funfair adjoining the circus, got out of control and injured the plaintiffs, and it was held that the action of the manager's (a stranger's) dog was no defence to the owners of the elephant.

443 **Test of negligence.** Even if the damage has been caused by the act of a third party, the owner of the dangerous thing is liable if there is negligence on his part. Negligence in this connection means that the act of a stranger is one which the owner ought reasonably to have foreseen and guarded against, but has failed to do so. For example, in *Box* v. *Jubb*[67] the act of a stranger which exempted the defendants from liability was described as one which " the defendants could not possibly have been expected to anticipate," and which they had no means of preventing.

62 The decision may also be supported on the ground that the railway company neither owned nor controlled the oil.

63 [1908] 2 K.B. 825.

64 This case has been much criticised, *e.g.* in *Pollock on Torts*, 15th ed., p. 385, but the criticism is directed to the view of the majority in the C.A. that the owner of the animal is liable even if a stranger let it loose. It does not affect the actual decision, which is as set out in the text. In *Behrens* v. *Bertram Mills Circus Ltd.* [1957] 2 Q.B. 1, Devlin J. decided that in *Baker* v. *Snell* " it was held by a majority that the intervening act of a third party was no defence."

65 Provided that the occupier of the land has no control over them: *Perry* v. *Kendricks Transport Ltd.* [1956] 1 W.L.R. 85.

66 [1957] 2 Q.B. 1.

67 (1879) 4 Ex.D. 76. The same test was applied in *Smith* v. *G.W. Ry.* (1926) 42 T.L.R. 391.

443 In *Rickards* v. *Lothian* [68] it was held that the omission to ask the jury the question whether the defendant ought reasonably to have anticipated the act of the third party, was fatal to any attempt to render him liable when the damage was in fact caused by the third party's act. In a later case,[69] Lord Wright said: " Though the act of a third party may be relied on by way of defence in cases of this type, the defendant may still be held liable in negligence if he failed in foreseeing and guarding against the consequences to his works of that third party's act." Accordingly, where a gas main was broken in consequence of the removal of support from underneath it by a local authority who were constructing a sewer, it was held that, although the cause of the fracture was the act of a third party, the local authority, the gas company were liable for the consequent explosion, owing to their negligence in failing to guard against the possible damage to their mains from the excavations of the local authority.[70]

The exception only applies when the act of the third party is a fresh, independent act. It must be " the conscious act of another volition." [71] In *Rickards* v. *Lothian* [72] the act of the third party was described as " malicious," which was later interpreted as meaning a deliberate or conscious act.[73]

444 In *Philco* v. *J. Spurling Ltd.*[74] carriers by mistake delivered highly inflammable film scrap to the wrong address. No proper warning of its dangerous character was given and when it was on the plaintiff's premises one of the plaintiff's typists set it on fire with her cigarette. An explosion occurred causing serious damage. The defendants were held liable because the evidence did not establish that the fire was caused by the deliberate act of the typist. Had it been, the majority of the court would have held the defendants not liable.

445 The burden of proving the defence of a third party's independent act is on the defendant. On proof by the plaintiff that a dangerous thing for which the defendant is responsible has done the damage in question the defendant is liable unless he can prove (a) that the damage was caused by the independent act of a third party; and (b) that the act could not reasonably have been anticipated and guarded against by him. These two elements combined form the defence, and accordingly it is not enough for the defendant to prove (a) and then to throw the

68 [1913] A.C. 263, 274.

69 *Northwestern Utilities* v. *London Guarantee and Accident Co.* [1936] A.C. 108, 125. See also to the same effect, *per* Atkinson J. in *Shiffman* v. *Order of St. John* [1936] 1 All E.R. 557.

70 *Northwestern Utilities Ltd.* v. *London Guarantee and Accident Co.*, *supra.* The failure to make proper inspections of a spillway so as to keep it clear of logs and boulders even although such obstructions were caused partly by the act of another in diverting a small stream amounted to negligence, since it ought to have been foreseen: *Lewis* v. *District of North Vancouver* (1963) 40 D.L.R. (2d) 182.

71 *Per* Lord Dunedin in *Dominion Natural Gas Co.* v. *Collins* [1909] A.C. 640, 646.

72 [1949] 2 All E.R. 882.

73 *Per* Lord Wright in *Northwestern Utilities Ltd.* v. *London Guarantee and Accident Co.* [1936] A.C. 108, 119.

74 [1949] 2 All E.R. 882. See also *Prosser & Son Ltd.* v. *Levy* [1955] 1 W.L.R. 1224.

burden of proving (b) on the plaintiff. This is implicit in the judgment of Blackburn J. in *Rylands* v. *Fletcher* where, after laying down the rule of absolute liability for dangerous things, he says: "He [the defendant] can excuse himself by showing that the escape was owing to the plaintiff's default; or perhaps that the escape was the consequence of *vis major*, or the act of God." Again, in discussing this exception, Lord Wright said [75]: "In *Dominion Natural Gas Co.* v. *Collins and Perkins*,[76] in a case for this purpose not dissimilar the question was put: 'Have the defendants been able to show affirmatively that the true cause of the accident was the conscious act of another volition, *i.e.* the tampering with the machines by the railway company's workmen?'" Finally, in *Hanson* v. *Wearmouth Coal Co.*,[77] Goddard L.J., in delivering the judgment of the court, said: "A person who brings a dangerous thing onto his land and allows it to escape, thereby causing damage to another, is liable to that other unless he can show that the escape was due to the conscious act of a third party, and without negligence on his own part. Obviously, the burden of showing that there was no negligence is on the defendants, and it is not for the plaintiff to prove negligence affirmatively."

446 In *Wilson* v. *Newberry* [78] the declaration alleged that the defendant was possessed of yew trees, the clippings of which he knew to be poisonous, that it was his duty to take care to prevent such clippings from being placed on other land and that, in breach of his duty, clippings were placed on adjoining land whereby the plaintiff's horses were poisoned. It was held on demurrer that the declaration was bad, because the facts alleged were insufficient. The court rejected the plaintiff's contention "that where a person has yew trees growing on his land which are clipped by some means he must prevent the clippings from escaping onto his neighbour's land, and from being placed there by a stranger," and held that "the case of *Rylands* v. *Fletcher* has no analogy to this case." In view of these findings the case cannot be considered as throwing any light on the question of the burden of proof in the circumstances under consideration.

(e) *Statutory Authority*

447 **Statutory authority.** If the dangerous thing is created or maintained under statutory authority, there is no liability under the rule in *Rylands* v. *Fletcher* unless negligence is proved. This is on the principle that, "It is now thoroughly well established that no action will lie for doing that which the legislature has authorised, if it be done without negligence, although it does occasion damage to anyone; but an action does lie for doing that which the legislature has authorised, if it be done

[75] *Northwestern Utilities Ltd.* v. *London Guarantee and Accident Co.*, *supra*, at p. 120.
[76] [1909] A.C. 640, 647.
[77] [1939] 3 All E.R. 47, 53.
[78] (1871) L.R. 7 Q.B. 31.

negligently." [79] Accordingly, in actions against gas, water and electricity undertakings which operate under statutory powers the rule in *Rylands* v. *Fletcher* is not applicable.[80] The statutory authorisation may, however, preserve the liability of the statutory undertaker for nuisance, and in such a case it is unnecessary to prove negligence.[81] To be a defence, the statute must authorise the creation or maintenance of the dangerous thing expressly or by necessary implication [82]; it is not enough merely to permit it to be used.[83] The exact legal position depends on the construction of the statute in question.

448 In considering whether the statutory authority has been exercised without negligence, the degree of care to be taken must be proportioned to the degree of risk involved.[84] In the case of all dangerous things a very high degree of care is required. The statutory undertakers must use all reasonable care in the erection and maintenance of their works. They are not bound " to ransack science in the hope of discovering some scientific specific against possible accident," but they are bound " to use well-known scientific means." [85] This may involve their consulting outside experts in addition to the technical and scientific members of their own staffs.[86] They must use reasonable care to maintain their works in a state of efficiency, but they are not liable because they have not " adopted the last inventions of ever-changing, ever-advancing scientific discovery." [87] At the same time, " the authority to erect and work the plant and the obligation in both respects to use reasonable care and precautions are correlative, and erection cannot be so severed from use and maintenance as to entitle the undertakers to go on permanently using a plant with all its original imperfections unremedied, merely on the ground that original faults in construction must be deemed to be irremediable in subsequent use. Reasonableness applies not merely to construction but to improvement." [88] What amounts to negligence depends on the circumstances of each particular case [89] and is considered further in the following sections.

449 The burden of proof is on the statutory undertaker to prove that

[79] *Geddis* v. *Proprietors of Bann Reservoir* (1878) 3 App.Cas. 430, 455, *per* Lord Blackburn. See also *Dunne* v. *North Western Gas Board* [1964] 2 Q.B. 806.
[80] *Green* v. *Chelsea Waterworks Co.* (1894) 70 L.T. 547; *Northwestern Utilities Ltd.* v. *London Guarantee and Accident Co.* [1936] A.C. 108.
[81] *Midwood* v. *Manchester Corpn.* [1905] 2 K.B. 597; *Charing Cross Electricity Supply Co.* v. *Hydraulic Power Co.* [1914] 3 K.B. 772.
[82] *West* v. *Bristol Tramways* [1908] 2 K.B. 14.
[83] *Jones* v. *Festiniog Ry.* (1868) L.R. 3 Q.B. 733.
[84] *Northwestern Utilities Ltd* v. *London Guarantee and Accident Co., supra, per* Lord Wright, at p. 126.
[85] *Snook* v. *Grand Junction Waterworks* (1886) 2 T.L.R. 308.
[86] *Manchester Corpn.* v. *Farnworth* [1930] A.C. 171.
[87] *National Telephone Co.* v. *Baker* [1893] 2 Ch. 186, 205.
[88] *Manchester Corpn.* v. *Farnworth, supra, per* Lord Sumner, at p. 202.
[89] In addition to the cases already quoted, the following may be referred to: *Midwood* v. *Manchester Corpn.* [1905] 2 K.B. 597, 608; *Quebec Ry.* v. *Vandry* [1920] A.C. 662; *Eastern and South African Telephone Co.* v. *Cape Town Tramways* [1902] A.C. 381.

he has statutory authority to create, maintain or use the dangerous thing, and that he is exercising his powers without negligence.[90]

3.—WATER

450 **Liability for accumulating water.** A person who accumulates water on land is bound to keep the water so accumulated from doing damage at his peril. It matters not what form the accumulation takes, whether it is a reservoir,[91] a tank,[92] or a mound of earth. So, where the defendants maintained a mound of earth against the wall of the adjoining house, they were held liable for damage caused by rainwater percolating through the wall, on the principle that: " If anyone by artificial erection on his own land causes water, even though arising from natural rainfall only, to pass into his neighbour's land and thus substantially to interfere with his enjoyment, he will be liable to an action at the suit of him who is so injured." [93] A similar case was where water from a broken soil pipe of the defendant's discharged into an artificial mound of earth made by the defendant against the plaintiff's wall, and the defendant was held liable.[94] Again, the defendant was held liable when water, escaping from his pipes, collected in his cellar and percolated into the plaintiff's cellar,[95] and when a drain became blocked with refuse through neglect and the water flooded the adjoining garden.[96]

Where factory premises on the second floor of a building were used for the purpose of washing cinematograph films, which necessitated the use of large quantities of circulating water in a closed apparatus, a boiler, a sink and a number of containers, it was held that the occupiers of the factory were liable for damage caused by the escape of the water onto the lower floors of the building, although there was no negligence on their part.[97]

451 On the other hand, if the water has accumulated on the land as the result of natural causes only, as for example, in a pond or a stream, there is no liability for damage caused by the overflow. This is so even if it has accumulated in a quarry which has been excavated.[98]

If a landowner causes more water to be discharged from his land onto his neighbour's land than would normally be the case, or collects the drainage of his land into one place and discharges it onto his neighbour's land, he will be liable.[99] But he is not liable if he merely does something on his own land which causes water naturally on the land to flow more quickly onto his neighbour's land, provided he does not

90 *Manchester Corpn.* v. *Farnworth, supra.*
91 *Rylands* v. *Fletcher* (1868) L.R. 3 H.L. 330.
92 *Western Engraving Co.* v. *Film Laboratories Ltd.* [1936] 1 All E.R. 106.
93 *Hurdman* v. *North Eastern Ry.* (1878) 3 C.P.D. 168. To the same effect is *Maberley* v. *Peabody & Co.* [1946] 2 All E.R. 192.
94 *Broder* v. *Saillard* (1876) 2 Ch.D. 692.
95 *Snow* v. *Whitehead* (1884) 27 Ch.D. 588.
96 *Sedleigh-Denfield* v. *O'Callaghan* [1940] A.C. 880.
97 *Western Engraving Co.* v. *Film Laboratories Ltd.* [1936] 1 All E.R. 106.
98 *Rouse* v. *Gravelworks Ltd.* [1940] 1 K.B. 489.
99 *Hurdman* v. *North Eastern Ry., supra*; *Whalley* v. *L. & Y. Ry.* (1884) 13 Q.B.D. 131.

collect it in any way. Where the defendant dug a trench in order to lay a pipe on his land and, in doing so, tapped an underground spring as a result of which some water was discharged onto the plaintiff's land but no substantial damage was done, Lawrence L.J. gave judgment for the defendant, saying: "In the present case, the defendant has neither diverted any defined watercourse nor altered the level of her land nor erected any structure upon it so as to cause rainwater which would ordinarily soak into her ground to pass onto the plaintiff's land." [1]

452 **Water on the highway.** A highway authority are not entitled to discharge water from the highway onto the lands of adjoining occupiers, or to construct roads so inadequately drained as to cause water to flow onto the adjoining land. Where a local authority built a road on the side of a hill, so that it acted as a catch-water for the rainwater from the upper slopes which would otherwise have flowed onto the lower slopes, and also caught loose shale brought down by the rain, with the result that in a heavy rain vast quantities of water and shale were caught and overflowed onto property in the valley below, they were held liable for not making sufficient provision for carrying off the water and the shale.[2] Again, where two streams of water flowed down a lane and then under the main road through two separate culverts and the highway authority put a ridge across the lane which had the effect of diverting both streams to one culvert, as a result of which a flood was caused on the plaintiff's land, the highway authority were held liable.[3] It was contended that the Highway Act 1835 s. 67, was a defence, but it was held that the section did not justify the defendants in diverting water from its natural course so as to send it onto private property.

Where a highway authority raised the level of a footpath so that a wooden fence adjoining the footpath became decayed through the percolation of dampness from the adjoining soil, the authority were held liable.[4] They were similarly held liable when they raised a footpath adjoining the plaintiff's premises, the effect of the raising being to prevent water which fell upon the space between the plaintiff's warehouse and the road from draining into the road.[5]

453 **Diverting natural stream.** A person who diverts the course of a natural stream is liable for any damage caused by the water escaping from the channel into which it has been diverted, although there was no negligence on his part. Apart from the defences set out above,[6] he can only escape liability by proving that the diversion has been

[1] *Bartlett* v. *Tottenham* [1932] 1 Ch. 114.
[2] *Baldwin's Ltd.* v. *Halifax Corpn.* (1916) 85 L.J.K.B. 1769.
[3] *Thomas* v. *Gower R.D.C.* [1922] 2 K.B. 76. *Cf. Ely Brewery Co.* v. *Pontypridd U.D.C.* (1903) 68 J.P. 3 (retaining wall built across street—no interference with ordinary flow of surface water—diverted unusual flow caused by wrongful act of third parties onto plaintiff's land—highway authority not liable).
[4] *Rochford* v. *Essex C.C.* (1915) 85 L.J.Ch. 281.
[5] *Milward* v. *Redditch L.B.* (1873) 21 W.R. 429.
[6] §§ 429, 430.

" fortified by prescription " in the sense that " the existence of a state of things for the period of the long prescription may serve to prevent any person alleging that another state of things was the true state of nature." [7]

In *Fletcher* v. *Smith* [8] the defendants diverted the course of a stream and, on the occasion of a heavy fall of rain, the water flowed over the artificial bank of the new channel and went down certain holes and fissures in the surface, whence it flooded the plaintiff's mine. The jury found that the new channel was not as efficient as the old, and judgment was given for the plaintiff. Lord Penzance, in discussing the liability of the defendants in diverting the stream, said: " But, in diverting it what were their obligations? Was it enough to make the new and artificial watercourse as efficient but no more so, than the old and natural one, so that whatever defects, incapacity, or otherwise, the old one had, might, without responsibility, be reproduced in the new one? Or, secondly, were they bound (as they, for their own convenience, were making a new and artificial watercourse) to construct it in such a manner that it would be capable of conveying off the water that might flow into it from all such floods and rainfalls as might reasonably be anticipated to happen in that locality? Or, thirdly, were they bound to make provisions for any such quantities of water as might possibly be discharged into it from any mere rainfall, however heavy, however unusual, and however contrary to all previous experience? . . . For my own part, I incline to think that the second proposition defines the true measure of the defendants' obligations, but I desire to express no positive opinion to that effect." Commenting on this, Lord Dunedin said that " there is no clear-cut choice in law between " Lord Penzance's second and third propositions,[9] and Lord Parker said that " Lord Penzance's alternatives are not very clearly stated." [10]

54 **Damming natural stream.** In *Kerr* v. *Earl of Orkney* [11] a dam built across a stream gave way in time of flood and damage was caused to the pursuer's mill. The defender was held liable, Lord Justice-Clerk Hope saying: " If a person chooses upon a stream to make a great operation for collecting and damming up the water for whatever purpose, he is bound, as the necessary condition of such an operation, to accomplish his object in such a way as to protect all persons lower down the stream from all danger: He must secure them against danger. It is not sufficient that he took all the pains which were thought at the time necessary and sufficient. They were exposed to no danger before the operation. He creates the danger, and he must secure them against danger, so as to make them as safe notwithstanding his dam as they

[7] *Per* Lord Dunedin in *Greenock Corpn.* v. *Caledonian Ry.* [1917] A.C. 556, 578.
[8] (1877) 2 App.Cas. 781.
[9] *Greenock Corpn.* v. *Caledonian Ry., supra,* at p. 577.
[10] *Ibid.* at p. 581.
[11] (1857) 20 D. 298, approved by the H.L. in *Greenock Corpn.* v. *Caledonian Ry., supra.*

were before. It is no defence in such a case to allege the dam would have stood against all ordinary rains—it gave way in an extraordinary and unprecedented fall of rain, which could not be expected. The dam must be made perfect against all extraordinary falls of rain—else the protection is not afforded against the operation which the party must accomplish."

455 In *Nichols* v. *Marsland* [12] the defendant dammed up a natural stream and made a series of artificial pools. Owing to an unusually heavy rainfall, the dams burst and the resultant flood carried away four county bridges. The court had no doubt that the obligation of the defendant was that laid down in *Rylands* v. *Fletcher*, but held that the heavy rainfall was an act of God [13] so that the defendant was not liable.

In *Greenock Corpn.* v. *Caledonian Ry.*[14] the corporation had diverted the course of a natural stream, made a paddling pond for children and constructed other works necessitating the enclosing of the stream in a culvert. During a heavy rainfall the stream overflowed and burst from its artificial banks, with the result that the railway company's property was damaged. The corporation were held liable, Lord Finlay saying: "It is the duty of anyone who interferes with the course of a stream to see that the works which he substitutes for the channel provided by nature are adequate to carry off the water brought down even by extraordinary rainfall, and if damage results from the deficiency of the substitute which he has provided for the natural channel he will be liable."

If a bridge is built over a stream in such a way as to become choked in time of flood, the person building it is liable for damage caused by flooding.[15]

456 **Culverting streams.** If a stream is enclosed in a culvert and, owing to the bad state of repair of the culvert, it breaks through the culvert in time of flood and damages the neighbouring property, the owner of the culvert is liable on the principle of *Rylands* v. *Fletcher*.[16] Where an artificial watercourse was culverted and became blocked, so that the adjoining land was flooded, the occupier of the watercourse was held liable in nuisance.[17]

457 **Summary.** The effect of the cases may be summarised in the words of Lord Maugham: "At common law . . . the duty of one who obstructs the natural flow of a river is to prevent damage, and, if damage results to any persons, he will be liable to them, irrespective of whether or not they are riparian owners." [18]

[12] (1876) 2 Ex.D 1.
[13] This finding of fact by the jury was thought to be wrong by the H.L. in *Greenock Corpn.* v. *Caledonian Ry., supra*. See *ante*, § 454.
[14] [1917] A.C. 556.
[15] *Ferrand* v. *Midland Ry.* (1901) 17 T.L.R. 427.
[16] *Booth* v. *Thomas* [1926] Ch. 109, *per* Russell J.; affirmed on other grounds [1926] Ch. 397. *Pemberton* v. *Bright and the Devon C.C.* [1960] 1 W.L.R. 436.
[17] *Sedleigh-Denfield* v. *O'Callaghan* [1940] A.C. 880.
[18] *R.* v. *Southern Canada Power Co. Ltd.* [1937] 3 All E.R. 923, 928.

458 **Watercourses.** A person who constructs a watercourse on his land is under the same liability, in the event of water escaping from his watercourse and doing damage, as the owner of the reservoir in *Rylands* v. *Fletcher*. Where a landowner, in order to bring water from a river to his mill, made a watercourse with a shuttle at the head of it to control the flow of the water from the river into the watercourse, his successors in title were held liable for damage caused to neighbouring owners owing to their failure to keep the shuttle in repair, as a result of which flood water from the river got into the watercourse and overflowed onto the adjoining land.[19] Vaughan Williams L.J. said that the defendants were " under an obligation to the owners of adjoining land . . . to take care that the water so conducted along their watercourse did not break loose and do damage to those owners." If the watercourse was originally constructed for the mutual benefit of the plaintiff and the defendant there would be no liability in the event of damage being caused by an overflow, unless there was negligence on the part of the defendant.[20]

459 **Natural stream silting up.** The owner of the bed of a stream is not liable if the stream becomes silted up owing to the natural growth of weeds, with the result that flooding occurs.[21] " The owner of the bed of a stream is not under any obligation at common law to remedy the natural and gradual silting up of the stream; and makes no difference, in my opinion, whether the silting up is caused in one way or in another. . . . An obstruction may be caused by a heavy growth of weeds in the bed of the stream; or by sand and earth being washed down. It may also be caused by boulders or rocks being washed down a mountain stream; and I think that the common law of England has never imposed liabilities upon landowners for anything which happens to their land in the natural course of affairs if the land is used naturally." [22] Where water was diverted from a brook to form a canal and the canal was subsequently filled up so that the brook resumed its natural course but, owing to disuse, the channel had become silted up and overflowed in time of flood, the defendants who had filled up the canal were held not liable.[23] Where, however, the owners of a reservoir had power to discharge surplus water into a river through a little stream and, owing to the channel of the stream being silted up, the water overflowed the banks of the stream and caused damage, the owners were held liable because of their negligence in discharging water into a stream the channel of which was silted up.[24]

460 **Discharging accumulated water onto land of another.** If water has

19 *R. H. Buckley & Sons Ltd.* v. *N. Buckley & Sons* [1898] 2 Q.B. 608.
20 *Whitmores Ltd.* v. *Stanford* [1909] 1 Ch. 427.
21 *Hodgson* v. *York Corpn.* (1873) 28 L.T. 836; *Cracknell* v. *Thetford Corpn.* (1869) L.R. 4 C.P. 629. See River Boards Act 1948, for the powers to compel cleansing.
22 *Neath R.D.C.* v. *Williams* [1951] 1 K.B. 115, 121, *per* Goddard L.J.
23 *Mason* v. *Shrewsbury and Hereford Ry.* (1871) L.R. 6 Q.B. 578.
24 *Geddis* v. *Proprietors of Bann Reservoir* (1878) 3 App.Cas. 430.

accumulated naturally on a person's land he must not discharge it onto his neighbour's land. If it goes onto his neighbour's land in the ordinary course of nature, without any assistance from him, he is not liable for the resultant damage,[25] but he is liable if he digs a drain or does any other act to cause it to go onto his neighbour's land. Where a quantity of rainwater accumulated against a railway embankment and, to prevent the embankment from giving way, the railway company made cuttings which caused the water to go on the neighbouring land, the railway company were held liable, Brett M.R. saying: " An extraordinary misfortune happened, it fell upon the defendants, and if they had allowed things to remain as they were, they would have been the sufferers; but in order to get rid of the misfortune which had happened to them, and which, *rebus sic stantibus*, would not have injured the plaintiff, they did something which brought an injury upon the plaintiff. Under those circumstances it seems to me the defendants are liable." [26] In the same case, Brett M.R. also said: " If he [the defendant] has not brought the danger there, and without any act of his it breaks through his land on to his neighbour's land, I take it he is not liable." This occurred in *Tennent* v. *Earl of Glasgow*.[27] There, the defender substituted a wall for a hedge along the side of a road. A stream ran parallel with the road and eventually passed underneath it by means of a conduit. Owing to a heavy rainfall, the stream burst its banks and accumulated against the wall which it eventually burst. The defender was held not liable for the resultant damage.

461 **Barriers against floods.** A landowner can erect a barrier to prevent flood water from coming onto his own land, although the natural consequence of his doing so is to cause more water to flow onto his neighbour's land. Where the owners of a canal put planks in the canal to keep off flood water from a neighbouring river and, in consequence, a flood was caused which damaged the plaintiff's land, the defendants were held not liable on the ground that they " had the right to protect themselves against it, and the plaintiffs cannot complain although what the defendants did in so protecting themselves augmented the damage to them." [28] Similarly, where a railway company, who owned land, which was liable to flooding, near their railway line, in order to prevent flooding built an embankment which had the effect of diverting the water from coming upon their land and caused it to go onto the plaintiff's land, it was held that they were not liable for the damage caused.[29]

462 A landowner is not obliged to erect a barrier to keep off floods on the boundary of his land, and if he erects it some distance within the

25 *Rouse* v. *Gravelworks Ltd.* [1940] 1 K.B. 489.
26 *Whalley* v. *L. & Y. Ry.* (1884) 13 Q.B.D. 131, at pp. 137, 138.
27 (1864) 2 M.(H.L.) 22.
28 *Nield* v. *L. & N.W. Ry.* (1874) L.R. 10 Ex. 4.
29 *Maxey Drainage Board* v. *G.N. Ry.* (1912) 106 L.T. 429.

boundary he is not responsible for so much of the flood water as comes on his land and is diverted by the barrier onto the adjoining land.[30] If, however, the river has a flood channel he must not block it up or interfere with it to the detriment of neighbouring land.[31] "Where, indeed, there is a natural outlet for natural water, no one has a right for his own purposes to diminish it, and if he does so he is, with some qualification perhaps, liable to anyone who is injured by his act, no matter where the water which does the mischief came into the watercourse. I say with some qualification, because it may be that, even in the case of a natural watercourse, the riparian owner is entitled to protect himself against extraordinary floods by keeping off extraordinary water." [32] Where a railway company built an embankment over the flood channel of a river and provided insufficient arches for flood water to come through, it was held that the plaintiff was entitled to recover the difference between the damage he would have suffered in the ordinary course of nature and the damage he actually suffered in consequence of the railway company's works.[33] There seems to be no doubt that, as long as there is no defined course which the flood water was accustomed to take, a riparian owner can keep off flood water by raising the height of the river banks.[34] A landowner is not obliged, apart from contract or statute, to maintain a barrier against floods for the benefit of neighbouring owners.[35] If, therefore, a riparian owner, who maintains a river wall for the protection of his own property, pulls down the wall as a result of which his neighbour's land is flooded, he is not liable for the damage.[36]

463 **Barriers against sea.** A landowner is not bound at common law to maintain on his own land a barrier against the sea for the benefit of inland owners.[37] On the other hand, he is entitled to protect his land from the incursions of the sea by building a groin or sea wall, even though the effect of his doing so is to cause the sea to flow with greater violence against the adjoining land.[38] But he cannot remove a natural barrier against the sea, even when it is on his own land, if the removal causes damage to the adjoining land [39]; and the result is the same if the removal will cause damage to a sea wall and drainage system maintained as protective works.[40]

30 *Gerrard* v. *Crowe* [1921] 1 A.C. 395.
31 *Menzies* v. *Breadalbane* (1828) 3 Bligh(N.S.) 414; *Orr-Ewing* v. *Colquhoun* (1877) 2 App.Cas. 839, 857; *R.* v. *Trafford* (1831) 1 B. & Ad. 874.
32 *Nield* v. *L. & N.W. Ry., supra, per* Bramwell B. at p. 7.
33 *Workman* v. *G.N. Ry.* (1863) 32 L.J.Q.B. 279.
34 *Gerrard* v. *Crowe, supra*; *Lagan Navigation Co.* v. *Lambeg Bleaching Co.* [1927] A.C. 226.
35 *Mason* v. *Shrewsbury and Hereford Ry.* (1871) L.R. 6 Q.B. 578; *Nield* v. *L. & N.W. Ry., supra.*
36 *Thomas & Evans Ltd.* v. *Mid-Rhondda Co-operative Society* [1941] 1 K.B. 381.
37 *Hudson* v. *Tabor* (1877) 2 Q.B.D. 290.
38 *R.* v. *Pagham Commrs.* (1828) 8 B. & C. 355.
39 *Crossman* v. *Bristol and South Wales Union Ry.* (1863) 11 W.R. 981; *Att.-Gen.* v. *Tomline* (1880) 14 Ch.D. 58.
40 *Canvey Island Commissioners* v. *Preedy* [1922] 1 Ch. 179.

464 **Interference with barriers against sea and floods.** If a wall is maintained by statutory authority to prevent flooding from the sea or a river, anyone who interferes with the wall is liable for flooding caused by his interference. Where a river wall was maintained along the side of the Thames, and a dock company, acting under statutory powers, constructed a dock which communicated with the river by an artificial channel, it was held that they were under a common law duty to maintain the sides of their dock at the same height as that of the wall and were liable for damage caused by an overflow from their dock owing to their failure to do so.[41] Again, where a river bank was maintained under statutory powers, and a landowner built a wall so as to replace a portion of the bank, and during a particularly high tide the water broke through the wall, but not through the bank alongside, and flooded the neighbouring land, the landowner was held liable.[42] Branson J. explained the defendants' position as follows: "As soon as the wall fails it seems to me that their position is the same as the position of one who has cut through the bank and left a gap through which the sea enters. It seems to me that their position is really analogous to the position of the defendant in *Rylands* v. *Fletcher*. They have created a danger which they must guard at all events."

465 **Mining.** If a man carries on mining operations on his own land and, while carrying them on in accordance with good mining practice and without negligence, water goes by natural gravitation into an adjoining mine, the owner of the adjoining mine has no remedy. Accordingly, when the plaintiff and the defendant were owners of adjoining mines and the defendant worked coal which had the effect of allowing water, previously held up by his coal, to pass into the plaintiff's mine, the defendant was held not liable.[43] "The water is a sort of common enemy . . . against which each man must defend himself. And this is in accordance with the civil law, by which it was considered that land on a lower level owed a natural servitude to that on a higher, in respect of receiving, without claim to compensation, the water naturally flowing down to it." [44] In such a case the plaintiff must protect himself by erecting a barrier in his own mine. "But the mine-owner will be liable if he conducts the water from his mine to the lower mine or mines by means of some opening made or other work executed with the express purpose of so conducting the water and not for the purpose of getting minerals." [45]

466 If an artificial channel is made by which water is conducted to a place in another mine which it would not otherwise have reached, liability

[41] *Nitro-Phosphate and Odam's Chemical Manure Co.* v. *London and St. Katherine Docks Co.* (1878) 9 Ch.D. 503.
[42] *Greenwood Tileries Ltd* v. *Clapson* [1937] 1 All E.R. 765, at pp. 770, 771.
[43] *Smith* v. *Kendrick* (1849) 7 C.B. 515.
[44] *Ibid. per* Cresswell J. at p. 566.
[45] *Westhoughton Coal and Cannel Co.* v. *Wigan Coal Corpn.* [1939] Ch. 393, 405, *per* Luxmoore L.J.

depends on the answer to the question: "Has the conducting of the water through the artificial channel increased the burden on the owner of the lower mine or not?" The material time for answering it is when the channel was made.[46]

A mine-owner must not pump water, naturally in his mine, into another man's mine. "The defendants, as occupiers of the higher mine, have no right to be active agents in sending water into the lower mine. The plaintiffs, as occupiers of the lower mine, are subject to no servitude of receiving water conducted by man from the higher mine. Each mine-owner has all rights of property in his mine, and, among them, the right to get all minerals therefrom, provided he works with skill and in the usual manner. And if, while the occupier of a higher mine exercises that right, nature causes water to flow to a lower mine, he is not responsible for this operation of nature."[47]

467 If the working of a mine causes a subsidence on the surface and surface water comes through the cracks so made into the mine and from there gravitates into the adjoining mine, the mine-owner is under no greater liability than if the water had been naturally in the mine all the time.[48] On the other hand, if the water which gravitates into the adjoining mine has come through holes in the surface owing to a natural stream being diverted, the mine-owner who has diverted the stream is liable.[49] Whether a mine-owner is liable if his workings cause a subsidence in the bed of a natural stream as a result of which water comes into his mine and gravitates into the adjoining mine depends on whether he is working his mine in an ordinary, reasonable and proper way. Where, therefore, it was alleged that the defendants' mine could not be worked without letting in a river and flooding the defendants' mine and, through that, the plaintiffs' mine, a demurrer was overruled on the ground that the defendants had not an absolute right to work their mine, but only a right to work it in an ordinary, reasonable and proper way, which was a matter of evidence.[50]

468 A mine-owner is not liable if he stops up an opening by which water had been accustomed to flow into the adjoining mine, as a result of which the water accumulates and overflows by another passage into the same mine,[51] but he is liable if he uses pipes to send the water into the adjoining mine.[51] He is also not liable if, by an altered system of working, he causes an increased amount of water to flow into the adjoining mine.[52] He is, however, liable if he conducts the water in his mine to a weak spot in his neighbour's boundary so that it can flow

46 *Westhoughton Coal and Cannel Co.* v. *Wigan Coal Corpn.*, *supra*, affd. on other grounds [1939] Ch. 800.
47 *Baird* v. *Williamson* (1863) 15 C.B.(N.S.) 376, *per* Erle C.J. at pp. 391, 392.
48 *Wilson* v. *Waddell* (1876) 2 App.Cas. 95.
49 *Fletcher* v. *Smith* (1877) 2 App.Cas. 781.
50 *Crompton* v. *Lea* (1874) L.R. 19 Eq. 115.
51 *Lomax* v. *Stott* (1870) 39 L.J.Ch. 834.
52 *Scots Mines Co.* v. *Leadhills Mines Co.* (1859) 34 L.T.(O.S.) 34.

through the weak spot and thereby be removed from his mine,[53] if he pumps up water from the lower part of his mine so that it flows into the adjoining mine,[54] or if he interferes with the natural flow of water in his own mine so as to cause more water than would naturally do so to flow into the adjoining mine.[55] An alteration of the flow of water within his own mine which does not increase the burden on the adjoining mine is not actionable.[55]

469 **Canals.** Canals are always constructed under statutory authority and accordingly canal companies are not liable for damage caused by an escape of water from their canals unless it can be proved that they have acted negligently in the exercise of their statutory powers. Accordingly, where a mine was worked and caused the surface of the land to crack as a result of which water from the defendants' canal went through the cracks into the plaintiff's mine, it was held that the defendants were not liable as there was no negligence on their part.[56] On the other hand, where the defendants were liable to maintain a cut for carrying off water, and the banks of the cut were insufficient for the water the cut could contain, it was held that they were liable for an overflow caused by the stoppage of the outlet owing to the neglect of third parties to clear the outlet.[57] In this case there was negligence in the maintenance of the banks of the cut and also in sending water through it after it was known that the outlet was blocked. Pollock C.B. said that if A has a drain through the lands of B and C, and C stops the inlet, but A, after knowing of the stoppage, continues to send water through and damages B, A is liable to B. In a somewhat similar case a company, under statutory powers, constructed a cut parallel with the canal to carry off overflows from the canal. The cut became blocked owing to the acts of third parties and an overflow occurred flooding the plaintiff's premises through a drain which he had made between his premises and the cut. The company were held not liable as there was no negligence on their part.[58]

470 Where a mill, built on the banks of a canal, was damaged by the leakage of water from the canal into the mill due to the working of a coal-mine by third parties, the owners of the canal were held liable for negligence, as they might have prevented the damage.[59] But where, on the occasion of an unprecedented rainfall, the sluices of a canal were opened, resulting in the flooding of the plaintiff's premises, but it was proved that it was necessary to open the sluices to prevent the canal banks from giving way, the canal company were held not liable as there was no negligence on their part.[60]

53 *Westminster Brymbo Coal and Coke Co.* v. *Clayton* (1867) 36 L.J.Ch. 476.
54 *Baird* v. *Williamson, supra,* at p. 391.
55 *West Cumberland Iron and Steel Co.* v. *Kenyon* (1879) 11 Ch.D. 782.
56 *Dunn* v. *Birmingham Canal Co.* (1872) L.R. 8 Q.B. 42.
57 *Harrison* v. *G.N. Ry.* (1864) 3 H. & C. 231.
58 *Boughton* v. *G.W. Ry. of Ireland* (1873) I.R. 7 C.L. 178.
59 *Evans* v. *Manchester, Sheffield and Lincolnshire Ry.* (1887) 36 Ch.D. 626.
60 *Thomas* v. *Birmingham Canal Co.* (1879) 49 L.J.Q.B. 851.

The owners of a canal are entitled to erect a barricade or to raise the banks of the canal to prevent the canal from being flooded, and they are not liable if the consequence of their doing so is to cause the flood water to do damage elsewhere.[61] If they raise the banks of their canal and so cause flood water to accumulate on the land of an adjoining owner, that owner is not entitled to cut through the banks of the canal so as to drain the flood water from his own land.[62]

471 **Water companies' liability for reservoirs.** Water companies operating under statutory authority are only liable on proof of negligence. In the case of reservoirs, having regard to the serious damage which is likely to result from a burst, the degree of care required is a very high one.[63] Indeed, in the case of reservoirs constructed after January 1, 1931, in pursuance of powers granted after August 1, 1930, the fact that the reservoir was constructed under statutory authority does not exonerate the undertakers from any action or other proceedings to which they would otherwise have been liable.[64] The effect of this is to impose on such undertakers the full liability of *Rylands* v. *Fletcher*, namely, that of an insurer.

The Waterworks Clauses Act 1847, s. 27,[65] provides that nothing in their special Act shall prevent undertakers from being as liable for damage done to mines by means or in consequence of waterworks as if they had not statutory authority. The effect of this is that water companies are liable, without negligence, for damage, actual or threatened, to mines due to their conduct of their undertaking.[66]

472 **Water companies' liability for escapes from pipes.** The liability of a water company for escapes from its pipes or mains depends on negligence. The standard of care is what is reasonable in the prevailing circumstances to prevent escapes caused by foreseeable eventualities. Where a water main, laid down by a company under statutory powers, burst and caused damage, and the jury found that there was no negligence on the part of the water company, it was held that the water company was not liable.[67] Where an escape of water was caused by the fracture of a pipe due to a sudden contraction of the pipe from the difference in temperature between the incoming water and the iron

[61] *Nield* v. *L. & N.W. Ry.* (1874) L.R. 10 Ex. 4; *Lagan Navigation Co.* v. *Lambeg Bleaching Co.* [1927] A.C. 226.

[62] *Lagan Navigation Co.* v. *Lambeg Bleaching Co., supra.*

[63] See *Northwestern Utilities* v. *London Guarantee and Accident Co.* [1936] A.C. 108 (a gas case).

[64] Reservoirs (Safety Provisions) Act 1930, s. 7.

[65] This Act is repealed by the Water Act 1945. By s. 32 of that Act the Minister of Health, in the circumstances therein stated, may by order apply to any water undertaking such of the provisions of Sched. III to the Act as he thinks appropriate. Para. 18 of Sched. III in effect repeats the provisions of the Waterworks Clauses Act 1847, s. 27; Water Act 1948, s. 8 (5); Water Resources Act 1963, s. 79. See also *Dunne* v. *North Western Gas Board* [1964] 2 Q.B. 806.

[66] *Graigola Merthyr Co.* v. *Swansea Corpn.* [1928] Ch. 31; affirmed on other grounds [1929] A.C. 344.

[67] *Green* v. *Chelsea Waterworks Co.* (1894) 70 L.T. 547, followed in *Dunne* v. *North Western Gas Board* [1964] 2 Q.B. 806.

of the pipe, and the pipes were made of the same metal as all other water companies used, it was held that there was no negligence on the part of the water company.[68] Again, where a pipe burst twenty-seven years after it had been properly laid, and the evidence was that the usual length of life of such a pipe was eighty years, it was held that the water company was not negligent.[69] Where water escaped from a stopcock in the highway and loosened some paving stones near-by and also some paving stones farther off, on which latter stones the plaintiff slipped and fell, the water board were held not liable when there was no evidence to show that they knew or ought to have known that those stones were loose.[70]

The escape of water from a water undertaker's pipes or mains is prima facie evidence of negligence.[71]

473 Water companies are bound to take precautions to prevent water from escaping owing to frost. Where, however, a fire plug was prevented from acting properly owing to an accumulation of ice, and water was forced into the plaintiff's house, the water company was held to be free from negligence because the frost was of unprecedented severity.[72] " The defendants had provided against such frosts as experience would have led men acting prudently to provide against; and they are not guilty of negligence because their precautions proved insufficient against the effects of the extreme severity of the frost of 1855, which penetrated to a greater depth than any which ordinarily occurs south of the Polar regions. Such a state of circumstances constitutes a contingency against which no reasonable man can provide." [73] But in a later case where, although the frost was extraordinary, there was evidence that it was known that frost might cause the plugs to start, and that some precaution might be taken to prevent the water from escaping, it was held that the water company was liable for damage so caused.[74]

474 **Water company's duty to discover and remedy bursts.** Although an escape of water may have occurred without any negligence on the part of the water company they " have a duty to take all reasonable precautions to secure that leaks in their system should be brought to their knowledge and be repaired with promptitude." [75] In *Manchester Corpn.* v. *Markland* [76] a burst occurred in a service pipe on a Thursday, and water escaped onto the highway where it formed a pool. On the following Saturday night there was a sudden and severe frost which

68 *Snook* v. *Grand Junction Waterworks* (1886) 2 T.L.R. 308.
69 *Manchester Corpn.* v. *Markland* [1936] A.C. 360. The facts are more fully set out in [1934] 1 K.B. 566.
70 *Longhurst* v. *Metropolitan Water Board* [1948] 2 All E.R. 834.
71 *Snook* v. *Grand Junction Waterworks, supra.*
72 *Blyth* v. *Birmingham Waterworks Co.* (1856) 11 Ex. 781.
73 *Blyth* v. *Birmingham Waterworks Co.* (1856) 11 Ex. 781, *per* Alderson B. at pp. 784, 785.
74 *Steggles* v. *New River Co.* (1865) 11 W.R. 234; 13 W.R. 413.
75 *Per* Lord Tomlin in *Manchester Corpn.* v. *Markland* [1936] A.C. 360.
76 *Supra.*

froze the pool and, on the ice so formed, a motorist skidded and killed a pedestrian on the footpath. It was found that there was no negligence on the part of the motorist. The corporation, who were the water authority, had no knowledge of the burst until after the accident. They caused their pipes to be examined so that every part was visited about once in nine days, but otherwise they relied " entirely on the chance that some policeman or road officer, or other servant of another authority, or some householder or other person may give them information." It was held that this amounted to negligence on their part. It was also held that the plaintiff was not obliged to show what steps the corporation ought to have taken to obtain early notice of bursts. A water company who agree to cut off the water from a house must do so effectively so as to prevent a third party from turning it on again. If they fail to do so and the house is flooded, they are liable.[77]

475 **Water company's liability for nuisance.** If a water company's statutory powers provide that they are to remain liable for a nuisance caused by them, it is not necessary to prove negligence. In such a case they are under the liability of *Rylands* v. *Fletcher*.[78] The escape of water is itself a nuisance and it is not necessary to show that it has continued for a long time. Where hydraulic mains were laid under a road and, owing to a subsidence of the soil and the vibration of traffic, one of the mains burst and damaged some electric cables laid under the same road, it was held that the water company were liable, although there was no negligence on their part, for a nuisance caused by them for which their statutory powers preserved their liability.[78]

Although a water company may be liable for damage due to the escape of water from its pipes, as explained above, damage sustained by a person who has contracted to make a tunnel under an embankment and finds his contract unprofitable owing to the extra expense to which he is put in dealing with conditions caused by the leakage of water from a water main, is too remote.[79]

If water escapes from a service pipe and causes a gas pipe to rust, as a result of which a gas explosion occurs, the water company is not liable if the obligation to repair the pipe is put by statute upon the consumer and not upon the water company.[80]

476 **Water company breaking up streets.** The Water Act 1945[81] empowers water companies to break up streets for laying and repairing their pipes. When they do break up a street they are required by section 7 of the Public Utilities Street Works Act 1950 to complete the work with all convenient speed and to fill in the ground and reinstate and make good the street so broken up. If a breach of this duty causes

77 *Watson* v. *Sutton Water Co.* [1940] 3 All E.R. 502.
78 *Charing Cross Electricity Supply Co.* v. *Hydraulic Power Co.* [1914] 3 K.B. 772.
79 *Cattle* v. *Stockton Waterworks Co.* (1875) L.R. 10 Q.B. 453.
80 *Stacey* v. *Metropolitan Water Board* (1910) 9 L.G.R. 174.
81 Sched. III, para. 22.

damage to a third party they are liable.[82] They are not only liable to persons passing along the highway but also to a gas company whose pipes they have caused to fracture owing to their failure to ram in the earth properly, thereby depriving them of proper support.[83] The Act requires them to reinstate and make good such portion of the road as they have taken up, but has no bearing on their liability to answer for any other damage to the street.[84]

477 **Quality of water supplied by water company.** Apart from liability for the escape of water, a water company must give notice to consumers of anything in the quality of the water which is likely to render it unfit for any ordinary use in the conditions likely to prevail in the consumer's premises. Where the water supplied was of such a nature that in passing through lead pipes it took up lead and so caused lead poisoning in the persons who drank it, it was held that the water company were liable for not warning the consumers when there was a high degree of probability that the consumer would use lead pipes.[85]

Water companies must take reasonable care to supply water fit for human consumption; so that when they supplied water, which through their negligence contained typhoid germs, they were held liable.[86]

478 **Sewers and drains.** Liability for sewage is the same as liability for water. Parker J. said: "I think it clear that the principle of *Fletcher* v. *Rylands* would apply to the owner of a sewer, whether he made his sewer or not. His duty at common law would be to see that the sewage in his sewer did not escape to the injury of others, and mere neglect of this duty would give any person injured a good cause of action." [87] Where a drain from the defendant's house, after receiving the drainage of several other houses, turned back under the defendant's house and, owing to the decayed condition of the return drain, sewage escaped and got into the plaintiff's cellar, the defendant was held liable although there was no negligence on his part and he was not aware of the existence of the return drain.[88]

479 Under various statutes commissioners are empowered to construct and maintain drainage works for the benefit of a particular district. When damage is caused in consequence of those works, liability depends on the terms of the particular statutory provisions. As a general rule they are

[82] *Post*, § 678.

[83] *Huyton and Roby Gas Co.* v. *Liverpool Corpn.* [1926] 1 K.B. 146.

[84] *Longhurst* v. *Metropolitan Water Board* [1948] 2 All E.R. 834, *per* Lord Porter. The street works code of the Public Utilities Street Works Act 1950 replaced Sched. III, para. 26, of the Water Act 1945 (see Sched. V to the 1950 Act).

[85] *Barnes* v. *Irwell Valley Water Board* [1938] 2 All E.R. 650.

[86] *Read* v. *Croydon Corpn.* [1938] 4 All E.R. 631. The obligation under the Waterworks Clauses Act 1847, s. 35 (now Water Act 1945, Sched. III, para. 31), to supply wholesome water for domestic use is owed to ratepayers only.

[87] *Jones* v. *Llanrwst U.D.C.* [1911] 1 Ch. 393, 405.

[88] *Humphries* v. *Cousins* (1877) 2 C.P.D. 239. He clearly must have known there was a drain, and so his knowledge of the precise course it took was immaterial. If he had had no reason to suppose there was a drain he would not have been liable. *Ilford U.D.C.* v. *Beal* [1925] 1 K.B. 671, *per* Branson J.

only liable on proof of negligence,[89] but the statute may impose an absolute obligation upon them.[90] If flooding is caused through the opening of water gates in a time of heavy rainfall, the defendants, although prima facie liable for the damage on the principle of *Rylands* v. *Fletcher*, are protected by their statutory powers, the water gates being constructed expressly to be opened in times of flood.[91]

If a sewer is constructed so as to cause a subsidence of the adjoining land, the person constructing it is liable for the damage caused.[92]

Where an action was brought against a sanitary authority in respect of the death of one of their workmen from sewer gas, it was held that the authority were only liable for negligence and that, as no sewerage authority was shown to have reason to apprehend deaths from such a cause, there was no negligence in not taking precautions against it.[93]

480 **Overflows from sewers.** Public sewers and sewage disposal works are vested in local authorities by the Public Health Act 1936. By sections 14–30 of that Act and sections 12–19 of the Public Health Act 1961, they have a duty to provide for the sewerage of their district and given various powers for that purpose. Accordingly, if they carry out their statutory duty without negligence and damage is caused they are not liable under the principle of *Rylands* v. *Fletcher* [94]; they can only be held liable if negligence is proved. In *Pride of Derby* v. *British Celanese Ltd.*,[95] Denning L.J. doubted whether the doctrine of *Rylands* v. *Fletcher* [94] applied " in all its strictness to cases where a local authority, acting under statutory authority, builds sewers which afterwards overflow or sewage disposal works which later pour out a polluting element." [96] No such doubt had ever been expressed before, and it would be odd if a public utility service carried out by a local authority should be under any different liability for damage than a similar service carried out by another. Evershed M.R. did not share his doubt, but said: " It was suggested that local authorities have a special immunity from the so-called rule in *Rylands* v. *Fletcher*.[94] I am not, as at present advised, satisfied that that is certainly so." [97] In *Smeaton* v. *Ilford Corpn.*[98] Upjohn J. expressly dissented from Denning L.J.'s observations saying that the authorities did not establish his propositions,[99] adding " an

[89] *Collins* v. *Middle Level Commrs.* (1869) L.R. 4 C.P. 279; *Harrison* v. *G.N. Ry.* (1864) 3 H. & C. 231; *Boynton* v. *Ancholme Drainage and Navigation Commrs.* [1921] 2 K.B. 213; *Coe* v. *Wise* (1866) L.R. 1 Q.B. 711; *Sephton* v. *Lancashire River Board* [1962] 1 All E.R. 183.

[90] *R.* v. *Marshland Smeeth and Fen District Commrs.* [1920] 1 K.B. 155.

[91] *Dixon* v. *Metropolitan Board of Works* (1881) 7 Q.B.D. 418.

[92] *London General Omnibus Co.* v. *Tilbury Contracting Co.* (1907) 71 J.P. 534.

[93] *Digby* v. *East Ham U.D.C.* (1896) 13 T.L.R. 11.

[94] (1868) L.R. 3 H.L. 330.

[95] [1953] Ch. 149. Such doubts obtained support from the Court of Appeal in *Dunne* v. *North Western Gas Board* [1964] 2 Q.B. 806 where the view was stated that " it scarcely seems accurate to hold that a nationalised industry collects and distributes gas for ' its own purposes ' within the rule of *Rylands* v. *Fletcher*."

[96] [1953] Ch. 149 at p. 189. See the criticism on this in 16 M.L.R. 243.

[97] *Ibid.* p. 176.

[98] [1954] Ch. 450.

[99] *Ibid.* p. 470.

individual has an absolute responsibility for an escape of filth from his land, and I can see no justification for applying a different law to a local authority merely because it is a local authority, or that it is carrying out something beneficial to the community, or even that it is doing so pursuant to a statutory duty. However, if in imposing a statutory duty upon a local authority the legislature thinks fit to relieve that authority, by express provision or necessary implication, from the liability to which it would be otherwise subject, that is quite a different matter." [1]

481 If a sewer overflows or there is an escape of sewage, the sewer authority will be liable when there is negligence on their part, but otherwise not.[2] The negligence may consist in the original construction or maintenance of the sewer,[3] or diverting sewage from one sewer into another already overcharged with sewage.[4] Failure to enlarge the sewer to meet the growing requirements of the district is not negligence for this purpose.[5] It has been said that this is because a local authority, though liable for misfeasance in the performance of their public duties, are not liable for nonfeasance,[5] but this reason has been criticised. In the *Pride of Derby* case,[6] Denning L.J. roundly said: "the distinction between misfeasance and nonfeasance is valid only in the case of highways repairable by the public at large. It does not apply to any other branch of the law," [7] and Evershed M.R. seemed to be of the same opinion.[8]

The Public Health Act 1936, s. 31, provides: "A local authority shall so discharge their functions under sections 14 to 30 as not to create a nuisance." Local authorities create a nuisance if they discharge or cause to flow sewage on to another's land,[9] but if they "take over or construct a sewage and drainage system which is adequate at the time to dispose of the sewage and surface water for their district, but which subsequently becomes inadequate owing to increased building which they cannot control, and for which they have no responsibility, they are not guilty of the ensuing nuisance. They obviously do not create it, nor do they continue it merely by doing nothing to enlarge or improve the system. The only remedy of the injured party is to complain to the Minister." [10]

482 **Liability for water collected in buildings.** The question of the liability for the escape of water collected in a building occupied by two or more persons demands separate consideration. It has been said that there is

[1] *Ibid.* p. 478.
[2] *Hammond* v. *St. Pancras Vestry* (1874) L.R. 9 C.P. 316.
[3] *Fleming* v. *Manchester Corpn.* (1881) 44 L.T. 517; *Brown* v. *Sargent* (1858) 1 F. & F. 112.
[4] *Dent* v. *Bournemouth Corpn.* (1897) 66 L.J.Q.B. 395.
[5] *Hesketh* v. *Birmingham Corpn.* [1924] 1 K.B. 260; *Stretton's Derby Brewery Co.* v. *Derby Corpn.* [1894] 1 Ch. 431; *Robinson* v. *Workington Corpn.* [1897] 1 Q.B. 619.
[6] [1953] Ch. 149.
[7] *Ibid.* at p. 188; see also the note by A.T.D. in 55 L.Q.R. 343.
[8] *Ibid.* at p. 176.
[9] *Glossop* v. *Heston & Isleworth L.B.* (1879) 12 Ch.D. 102; *Att.-Gen.* v. *Dorking Union* (1882) 20 Ch.D. 595.
[10] Denning L.J. in [1953] Ch. 149 at p. 190. See also *Smeaton* v. *Ilford Corpn.* [1954] Ch. 450, 463.

no liability, except on proof of negligence where the water is kept for the common benefit of the parties.[11] There are many cases, however, in which it has been held that proof of negligence is essential to liability even when there has been no common benefit, and it now appears that common benefit is only evidence of consent. The principle is that when a person enters into occupation of premises he " takes the premises as they are, and, accordingly, consents to the presence there of the installed water system with all its advantages and disadvantages." [12] This is so whether the premises are used for business or residential purposes.

483 When the plaintiff and the defendant were occupiers under the same landlord of the ground and second floors respectively of the same building and water from the defendant's water closet, without any negligence on his part, percolated to the plaintiff's premises and damaged his stock-in-trade, it was held that the defendant was not liable.[13] The ground of the decision is that the plaintiff, in taking the ground floor, must be deemed to have accepted the risk of such damage. In a later case [14] the defendant, the landlord of the premises, let the second floor to the plaintiff. Some unknown person plugged the waste pipe of a lavatory basin on the top floor and turned the tap on, with the result that the overflow of water went to the plaintiff's part of the building and damaged his goods. The defendant was held not liable. " The provision of a proper supply of water to the various parts of a house is not only reasonable but has become, in accordance with modern sanitary views, an almost necessary feature of town life. It is recognised as being so desirable in the interests of the community that in some form or other it is usually made obligatory in civilised countries. Such a supply cannot be installed without causing some concurrent danger of leakage or overflow. It would be unreasonable for the law to regard those who instal or maintain such a system of supply as doing so at their own peril, with an absolute liability for any damage resulting from its presence even when there has been no negligence." [15] Similarly, when the plaintiffs occupied a shop, immediately above which was the defendant's flat and, owing to a burst in the rising main in the defendant's flat, water went into the shop and damaged the ceiling decorations, it was held that the defendant was not liable. The main was entirely embedded in plaster and it was held that the defendant was under no duty to have it inspected from time to time, in the absence of anything to lead her to think there was anything wrong with it. As soon as she discovered the burst the defendant turned off the main stopcock but it was held she was under no duty to warn the plaintiffs in the absence of anything to indicate there was a risk of water causing damage below.[16]

11 *Carstairs* v. *Taylor* (1871) L.R. 6 Ex. 217.
12 *Peters* v. *Prince of Wales Theatre* (*Birmingham*) *Ltd.* [1943] K.B. 73, 79, *per* Goddard L.J.
13 *Ross* v. *Fedden* (1872) L.R. 7 Q.B. 661.
14 *Rickards* v. *Lothian* [1913] A.C. 263.
15 *Per* Lord Moulton at p. 281.
16 *Irish Linen Manufacturing Co.* v. *Lowe* (1956) 106 L.J. 828.

484 Where a building was let, as to the ground floor to the plaintiffs, as to the first, second and third floors to the second defendants, the landlords, the first defendants, keeping the staircases and passages under their own control, and the tap on the second floor landing, only three and a half inches from the ground, was turned on by some unknown person, it was held the landlords were liable unless they could prove that the tap had been turned on by the deliberate and mischievous act of a third party. The negligent act of a third party was no defence. The second defendants were not liable as they were not in possession or control of the tap.[17]

485 Where the landlord of a house let it out in floors to separate tenants and supplied the different floors with water from a cistern at the top of the house, the water being distributed by a main pipe connected with the cistern, each floor having a separate branch inserted in the main pipe, and the branch pipe supplying the first floor burst, with the result that the plaintiffs' goods on the ground floor were damaged, the landlord was held not liable.[18] Brett and Cotton L.JJ. decided the case on the ground that the water supply was maintained for the common benefit of the plaintiffs and the other tenants of the house, but Thesiger L.J. put his judgment on the ground that the plaintiffs had taken their lease on the basis of there being the water supply on the premises and that " they took the benefit and must take the burden." Again, where the plaintiff occupied the ground floor of a building and the defendants were the owners of the house above and there was an overflow of water from the defendants' cistern, which was not used to supply the plaintiff's premises, the defendants were held not liable.[19] Stephen J. said: " Here it was the ordinary domestic apparatus which is in every house. The facts brought the case near *Ross* v. *Fedden*.[20] When they had to do with anything so artificial as a house in London, tenants must take it subject to the ordinary risks." The tenant of a shop, part of a building containing a theatre, was held to have no cause of action when the contents of his shop were damaged by water from burst sprinklers, designed to discharge large quantities of water in case of fire, caused by a severe frost and not by any negligence on the part of the occupiers of the theatre, on the ground that he had impliedly consented to the presence of the sprinklers.[21] The landlords of a building with several storeys, each let to separate tenants, kept the central heating system under their own control. The windows of the top storey were damaged by enemy action and had not been replaced Near to one of these windows was a radiator which burst, through frost, and the plaintiffs, who occupied the storey below, suffered damage from flooding. The landlords were held liable for not keeping

17 *Prosser & Son Ltd.* v. *Levy* [1955] 1 W.L.R. 1224.
18 *Anderson* v. *Oppenheimer* (1880) 5 Q.B.D. 602.
19 *Blake* v. *Land and House Property Corpn.* (1887) 3 T.L.R. 667.
20 (1872) L.R. 7 Q.B. 661.
21 *Peters* v. *Prince of Wales Theatre (Birmingham) Ltd.* [1943] K.B. 73.

the boiler fires lit or, if they could not keep them lit, for not warning the plaintiffs.[22]

486 When the damage is due to negligence, the person having the control of the domestic water supply, usually the occupier of the house, will be liable. His duty is to take the precautions taken by a prudent householder to see that his water supply does not give rise to an escape of water. Where the defendant's servant, in going to wash his hands, turned on the tap but, as no water flowed, forgot to turn it off again with the result that water subsequently flowing from the tap damaged the plaintiff's premises on the floor below, the defendant was held liable.[23] In a similar case the defendant was held liable for the negligence of his servant in blocking the waste pipe by emptying tea leaves into the sink.[24] Where, however, the defendant's clerk went into his employers' private lavatory into which he was forbidden to go, and forgot to turn off the tap, as a result of which the plaintiff's premises on the floor below were damaged, the defendant was held not liable, as the act of the clerk was outside the scope of his employment.[25] The defendant is not liable for the negligence of his independent contractor. Where, therefore, the owner of premises, on a leakage from his cistern being reported to him, employed a plumber to mend it and, in consequence of the plumber's negligence, an overflow occurred which damaged the goods of the plaintiff on the ground floor, the owner was held not liable.[26] The tenant of a flat, who did not go into occupation for some days, was held to be not liable to the tenant of the flat below when the water pipe burst during a frost before his occupation began, unless it could be proved that he knew or ought to have known that the water was turned on.[27]

487 In all the cases cited in the preceding paragraphs the parties were the occupiers of different parts of the same building. If the parties occupied different buildings the defence of consent would not apply. In *Anderson* v. *Oppenheimer*[28] Thesiger L.J. said: "If the apparatus for storing and distributing the water had been entirely unconnected with the plaintiff's premises, the matter might have worn a different aspect," and in *Humphries* v. *Cousins*,[29] a case of the escape of domestic sewage, Denman J. said: "It was contended that the present case was governed by *Ross* v. *Fedden*[30]; but that was a case in which the plaintiff and the defendant occupied separate storeys in the same house; and it was expressly distinguished from a case like the present, which depends

22 *George Frensham Ltd.* v. *Shorn & Sons Ltd.* [1950] W.N. 406.
23 *Ruddiman* v. *Smith* (1889) 60 L.T. 708.
24 *Abelson* v. *Brockman* (1890) 54 J.P. 119.
25 *Stevens* v. *Woodward* (1881) 6 Q.B.D. 318.
26 *Blake* v. *Woolf* [1898] 2 Q.B. 426.
27 *Tilley* v. *Stevenson* [1939] 4 All E.R. 207.
28 (1880) 5 Q.B.D. 602, 609, *ante*, § 485.
29 (1877) 2 C.P.D. 239, at p. 246.
30 (1872) L.R. 7 Q.B. 661, *ante*, § 485.

simply on those principles of law which regulate the rights and duties of occupiers of adjacent pieces of land." On the other hand, the principle laid down in *Rickards* v. *Lothian* [31] by Lord Moulton would cover damage done to adjoining premises by the escape of water from the domestic water supply, and in *Collingwood* v. *Home and Colonial Stores* [32] the Court of Appeal said that the doctrine of *Rylands* v. *Fletcher* did not apply to the use of water, gas or electricity for ordinary domestic purposes as distinguished from the handling of them in bulk in mains or reservoirs. Accordingly, it may be said that water stored in one building for use in connection with the provision of meals, baths, wash basins and water closets in that building, which escapes to another building does not give rise to an action except on proof of negligence. Water stored in a building for manufacturing purposes, as opposed to domestic purposes, which escapes to another building gives rise to the liability in *Rylands* v. *Fletcher* whether or not there is negligence.[33]

Whether the mere escape of water from the defendant's premises is evidence of negligence has not been decided. It would seem, however, to be within the principle of *res ipsa loquitur* [34] and to be more consistent with negligence on the part of the defendant than with any other cause.

488 **Escape of water collected on roofs.** When water is collected from the roof of a building to be conducted by gutters and pipes into the drains, an escape of the water so collected into the adjoining building is within the principle of *Rylands* v. *Fletcher*.[35] If, however, the plaintiff is one of the persons for whose benefit the water is so collected and conducted to the drains, for example, if he occupies premises under that roof, the defendant is only liable on proof of negligence. Where the plaintiff and the defendant occupied the ground and upper floors respectively of a building, and water from the roof was collected by gutters into a box from which it was discharged by a pipe into the drains, it was held that the escape of water from the box, by the action of a rat in gnawing a hole in it, imposed no liability on the defendant, the owner of the building, in the absence of negligence. As the defendant had used reasonable care in examining and seeing to the security of the gutters and the box it was held that he was not liable.[36] Again, where water from the roofs of both the plaintiff's and the defendant's buildings was discharged on to a flat roof belonging to the defendant, whence it escaped through a gulley and down a pipe into the drains, it was held that the defendant was not liable, without negligence, for a leakage of water into the plaintiff's building owing to a stoppage in the gulley.[37] In this case

[31] [1913] A.C. 263, *ante*, § 483.
[32] [1936] 3 All E.R. 200. See also to the same effect, *Miller* v. *Robert Addie & Sons (Collieries) Ltd.*, 1934 S.C. 150 (gas).
[33] *Western Engraving Co.* v. *Film Laboratories Ltd.* [1936] 1 All E.R. 106; *Peters* v. *Prince of Wales Theatre (Birmingham) Ltd.* [1943] K.B. 73, 79.
[34] Chap. 15, § 978, *post*.
[35] See *Cockburn* v. *Smith* [1924] 2 K.B. 119, 132, *per* Scrutton L.J.
[36] *Carstairs* v. *Taylor* (1871) L.R. 6 Ex. 217.
[37] *Gill* v. *Edouin* (1895) 71 L.T. 762; 72 L.T. 579.

the drainage system was maintained for the common benefit of both parties. The evidence was that the defendant never examined or cleaned the gutter but, as he had had no previous trouble from it and no notice of the stoppage, it was held that he was not negligent. The tenant of a shop whose goods were damaged by an overflow of rainwater from a blocked gutter under the control of his landlords was held not entitled to recover, in the absence of negligence, on the ground that he had " taken part of the defendant's premises with a sloping roof outside down which rain must run to the gutter provided to carry it off, and it therefore follows that if the flooding from the gutter occurred without negligence on the part of the landlords, the latter are not liable." [38]

489 A landlord of premises let to tenants who keeps the roof and gutters under his own control is liable for damage caused to his tenants by water from the roof escaping owing to a stoppage of the gutter, if he omits within a reasonable time to clear it after notice.[39] Even if there is no notice of the stoppage the landlord may still be liable. Where water was conducted from a building by means of open gutters through a box room in which pigeons were in the habit of nesting, and one of the gutters was blocked by the body of a dead pigeon, it was held that, in the circumstances, the landlord was negligent in not taking steps to protect and clean the gutters although he had no notice of the stoppage.[40]

Where a firm of builders, in pulling down a chimney stack on the instructions of the owner, negligently allowed rubbish to fall on to the roof, whence it was carried down the drain pipe into the gulley below, and so caused a flood in the basement, it was held that they were not liable in negligence to a tenant in occupation at the time of the flood but not in occupation at the date of the negligence.[41]

4.—FIRE

490 **Common law liability.** Liability for fire is based on the rule of *Rylands* v. *Fletcher* [42] and accordingly, except in cases in which the Fires Prevention (Metropolis) Act 1774 applies,[43] it is not necessary to prove negligence in an action for damage by fire.

The common law is stated in Rolle's Abridgment: " If fire (I know nothing of it) suddenly break out in my house and burn my goods, and also the house of my neighbour, my neighbour shall have an action on the case against me." [44] Again, in *Beaulieu* v. *Fingham* [45] Markham J.

38 *Kiddle* v. *City Business Properties Ltd.* [1942] 1 K.B. 269, at p. 274.
39 *Hargroves & Co.* v. *Hartopp* [1905] 1 K.B. 472; *Cockburn* v. *Smith, supra.*
40 *Bishop* v. *Consolidated London Properties* (1933) 102 L.J.K.B. 257.
41 *Konskier* v. *B. Goodman Ltd.* [1928] 1 K.B. 421. They were held liable in trespass. Probably *Donoghue* v. *Stevenson* [1932] A.C. 562, has overruled this decision on the point of negligence.
42 *Jones* v. *Festiniog Ry.* (1868) L.R. 3 Q.B. 733; *Powell* v. *Fall* (1880) 5 Q.B.D. 597; *Gunter* v. *James* (1908) 24 T.L.R. 868. See articles: " Vagaries in liability for the escape of fire " (Ogus), 27 C.L.J. 104; " Liability for fire before 1880 " (Foote), 20 N.I.L.Q. 141.
43 *Post*, § 493.
44 Action sur case (B) pur fewe, 2.
45 (1401) Y.B. 2 Hen. 4, 18, pl. 6. See also *Crogate* v. *Morris* (1617) 1 Brownl. 197; *Anon.* (1582) Cro.Eliz. 10; Winfield, 42 L.Q.R. 46, where the early authorities are discussed.

said: " A man is bound to answer for the act of his servant or of his guest in such a case, for if my servant or my guest puts a candle in a window and the candle sets light to the thatch and burns my house down and the house of my neighbour also, in this case I shall answer to my neighbour for the damage he sustained. . . . I shall answer to my neighbour for him who enters my house by my leave or knowledge, where he is guest to me or my servant, if he acts, or either of them acts, in such a way with the candle or other things that my neighbour's house is burned. But if a man outside my household against my will sets fire to the thatch of my house or does otherwise *per quod* my house is burned and also the houses of my neighbours, I shall not be held to answer to them, because this cannot be said to be ill on my part, but against my will."

491 The cases mentioned in the preceding paragraph refer to fires in buildings, but the law is the same if fire is made in a field or on land without buildings. In *Turberville* v. *Stampe* [46] the plaintiff made a fire to burn weeds in his field and the fire spread to the plaintiff's field and did damage. In giving judgment for the plaintiff, Holt C.J. said: " Every man must so use his own as not to injure another. The law is general; the fire which a man makes in his fields is as much his fire as his fire in his house; it is made on his ground, with his materials, and by his order; and he must at his peril take care that it does not, through his neglect, injure his neighbour; if he kindle it at a proper time and place, and the violence of the wind carry it into his neighbour's ground and prejudice him, this is fit to be given in evidence."

The same result follows if the fire comes from any other place. Where sparks from the defendants' railway engine set fire to the plaintiff's haystack, the defendants were held liable, Blackburn J. saying: " The general rule of common law is correctly given in *Fletcher* v. *Rylands*,[47] that when a man brings or uses a thing of a dangerous nature on his own land, he must keep it in at his own peril; and is liable for the consequences if it escapes and does injury to his neighbour. Here the defendants were using a locomotive engine with no express parliamentary powers making lawful that use, and they are therefore at common law bound to keep the engines from doing injury, and if the sparks escape and cause damage, the defendants are liable for the consequences though no actual negligence be shewn on their part." [48]

492 The law, apart from the Fires Prevention (Metropolis) Act 1774, is summed up by Lord Wright: " Before that Act if a fire spread from a man's premises and did damage to adjoining premises, he was liable in damage on the broad ground that it was his duty at his own peril to keep any fire that originated on his premises from spreading to and

[46] (1697) 1 Ld.Raym. 264. See also *Canterbury* v. *Att.-Gen.* (1842) 1 Phillips 306; *Vaughan* v. *Menlove* (1837) 3 Bing.N.C. 468; *H. & N. Emanuel Ltd.* v. *G.L.C.* [1971] 2 All E.R. 835.
[47] (1866) L.R. 1 Ex. 265.
[48] *Jones* v. *Festiniog Ry.* (1868) L.R. 3 Q.B. 733 at p. 736.

damaging his neighbour's premises." [49] He was not liable if the case came within any of the exceptions to the rule in *Rylands* v. *Fletcher*.[50] "If a stranger set fire to my house, and it burns my neighbour's, no action will lie against me." [51] A guest in the house is not a stranger for this purpose. "If my friend come and lie in my house and set my neighbour's house on fire, the action lieth against me." [52] Similarly, the occupier was held not liable for a fire caused by the act of his servant in cleaning the chimney, an act which was outside the scope of his employment.[53] On the other hand, he was liable for the act of his independent contractor.[54] The owners of land, who instructed an independent contractor to burn brushwood on their land, were held liable when the fire was carried by the wind to the adjoining land, where it did damage, on the ground that the lighting of a fire on open bushland was an operation attended with great danger and imposed a duty on the person ordering the operation to be carried out to see that all proper precautions were taken.[55]

493 **Fires Prevention (Metropolis) Act 1774.** The common law liability has been modified in respect of fires spreading from the defendant's land by the Fires Prevention (Metropolis) Act 1774, s. 86.[56] This enacts: "No action, suit or process whatever, shall be had, maintained or prosecuted against any person in whose house, chamber, stable, barn or other building, or on whose estate any fire shall . . . accidentally begin." The operation of this enactment is not confined to the metropolis but extends to the whole of England.[57] Its effect is to protect the occupier of land from being liable for damage caused by accidentally ("a term which has been construed to mean 'without negligence'" [58]) beginning on his land, the terms of the Act being comprehensive and the word "estate" applying "to land not built upon." [59]

The statute affords no protection in the case of fires caused or continued by negligence, or caused by a nuisance.[60] It applies to fires "produced by mere chance or incapable of being traced to any cause," [61] and even to fires which can be traced to a cause, if there was no

[49] *Collingwood* v. *Home and Colonial Stores* [1936] 3 All E.R. 200, 203.
[50] *Ante*, §§ 429–449.
[51] *Turberville* v. *Stampe* (1697) 1 Ld.Raym. 264, *per* Holt C.J.
[52] *Crogate* v. *Morris* (1617) 1 Brownl. 197. See *Allen* v. *Stephenson* (1700) 1 Lut. 90, to the contrary.
[53] *M'Kenzie* v. *M'Leod* (1834) 10 Bing. 385.
[54] *Balfour* v. *Barty-King* [1957] 1 Q.B. 496 (independent contractor invited into house to thaw frozen pipes, did so negligently, and set the house on fire). See note on this case by T. Ellis Lewis in [1957] C.L.J. 132.
[55] *Black* v. *Christchurch Finance Co.* [1894] A.C. 48.
[56] Re-enacting Apprehension of Housebreakers Act 1707, s. 6, which only applied to a "house or chamber." For the effect of this, see Blackstone, *Commentaries* 1, 431.
[57] *Filliter* v. *Phippard* (1847) 11 Q.B. 347; *Richards* v. *Easto* (1846) 15 M. & W. 244, *per* Parke B. Not to Scotland: *Westminster Fire Officer* v. *Glasgow Provident Society* (1888) 13 App.Cas. 699.
[58] *Per* Asquith J. in *Mulholland & Tedd Ltd* v. *Baker* [1939] 3 All E.R. 253, 255.
[59] *Per* Denman C.J. in *Filliter* v. *Phippard*, *supra*, p. 355.
[60] *Spicer* v. *Smee* [1946] 1 All E.R. 489 (defective electric wiring caused fire, owner liable).
[61] *Filliter* v. *Phippard*, *supra*, *per* Denman C.J.

negligence.[62] It has been held to be negligence in this connection when hay was stacked in a damp condition so that it burst into flames and the fire spread to the adjoining property of the plaintiff[63]; when an hotel caught fire through the ignition of a beam of wood owing to a defective scheme for conveying the smoke and burning soot from the kitchen chimney[64]; when some paper was lit in a yard to smoke out a rat in a drainpipe, and the fire spread to a packing case and exploded a drum of paraffin[65]; where packing cases, greasy machinery, tarpaulins, petrol, acetylene and paints, which were all highly combustible articles, had been stored in the defendants' yard in such conditions that if they caught fire the fire would be likely to spread, and they had so caught fire, spreading to the plaintiff's garden, causing damage[66]; and when a fire was caused by the use of a blowlamp in attempting to thaw a frozen pipe in a roof.[67] On the other hand, it has been held that the fire was accidental and there was no negligence when a fire broke out in the basement of a grocery store owing to some unknown defect in the electrical wiring,[68] a short circuit of the electric wires behind the panelling near the ventilator of the half landing of a building, where a stack of packing and wrapping material was stored, caused a fire,[69] and when a fire broke out in a tip[70] and in a garage[71] from some unknown cause.

494 A fire which originally started accidentally may be continued by negligence so as to prevent the defendant from obtaining the protection of the Fires Prevention (Metropolis) Act 1774. In *Musgrove* v. *Pandelis*[72] the defendant was the occupier of a garage, the rooms above which were occupied by the plaintiff. From some unexplained cause, and without any negligence on the part of the defendant's chauffeur, the petrol in the carburettor of the defendant's motor caught fire. The chauffeur could have prevented the fire from spreading by turning off the tap from the petrol tank, but he omitted to do so with the result that the fire spread and the plaintiff's rooms were burnt. The court held that the defendant was liable because there were two fires, the original fire and the fire caused by the omission to turn off the tap, and as the second fire was caused by the negligence of the defendant's servant the statute was no defence. In a later case, Scrutton L.J. said[73]: " I

62 For an example of this, see *Solomons* v. *R. Gertzenstein Ltd.* [1954] 1 Q.B. 565, reversed on other grounds [1954] 2 Q.B. 243.
63 *Vaughan* v. *Menlove* (1837) 3 Bing.N.C. 468.
64 *Maclenan* v. *Segar* [1917] 2 K.B. 325.
65 *Mulholland & Tedd Ltd.* v. *Baker* [1939] 3 All E.R. 253.
66 *Mason* v. *Levy Auto Parts of England* [1967] 2 Q.B. 530.
67 *Balfour* v. *Barty-King* [1957] 1 Q.B. 496.
68 *Collingwood* v. *Home and Colonial Stores* [1936] 3 All E.R. 200.
69 *Solomons* v. *R. Gertzenstein Ltd.* [1954] 1 Q.B. 565, reversed on other grounds [1954] 2 Q.B. 243.
70 *Job Edwards Ltd.* v. *Birmingham Navigations* [1924] 1 K.B. 341.
71 *Williams* v. *Owen* [1955] 1 W.L.R. 1293.
72 [1919] 2 K.B. 43.
73 *Job Edwards Ltd* v. *Birmingham Navigations, supra*, p. 361. Scrutton L.J. dissented, but his judgment was preferred by the H.L. in *Sedleigh-Denfield* v. *O'Callaghan* [1940] A.C. 880. The effect of the statute was not discussed by the other members of the court.

should respectively have thought that it was safer to say that the fire was continued by negligence, and that the cause of action was not for a fire accidentally begun, but for negligence in increasing such a fire." Scrutton L.J. also puts the case [74]: "Suppose the fire is caused by a trespasser, as if he throws down a match; and suppose the owner comes by immediately afterwards, sees the small fire, and could with no trouble extinguish it by stamping on it, but does not do so, so that the fire spreads and damages his neighbour, is he freed by the statute? He is then aware of a dangerous thing on his land which may damage his neighbour, and which by reasonable care he can prevent from damaging his neighbour, and he does nothing. I agree he is not an absolute insurer of that dangerous thing, for he did not himself create it, but I think on principle he is bound to take reasonable care of a dangerous thing which he knows to exist." This opinion is submitted as an accurate statement of the law. Accordingly where a fire broke out in a redgum tree, after it had been struck by lightning, on the defendant's land but the fire, in due course, spread to the plaintiff's properties, causing damage, because the defendant had failed to extinguish it properly after felling the tree, he was held liable in negligence. He owed a duty of care, which he had failed to discharge notwithstanding that the hazard initially had arisen accidentally, because the fire had revived through his neglect and had spread; thus it had not accidentally begun within the defence afforded by section 86 of the Act of 1774.[75]

495 An alternative ground for the decision in *Musgrove* v. *Pandelis* [76] was that the Act of 1774 was no defence when the fire originated from a dangerous thing. "If this motor-car with the petrol in its tank was potentially dangerous, such as a man's own fire, then it was the defendant's duty to see that the potential danger did not become an actual danger causing damage to his neighbour. The Act [of 1774] is no protection against that liability." [77] This ground of decision has been criticised,[78] but it was adopted and followed in *Mulholland & Tedd Ltd.* v. *Baker*.[79] As, however, it is the fire which is the dangerous thing, whether it is caused by petrol, paraffin or anything else, and the object of the statute is to give protection against accidental fires, it is difficult to understand why the statute should not protect as much in one case as in the other. The presence of inflammable matter on premises is important when the question of negligence is being considered (*post*, § 502), but if there is no negligence and it is found that the fire is accidental it is submitted that the statute is a defence to the occupier of the land on which it begins whatever may be the origin of the fire.

74 *Ibid.* p. 361. See also *per* Lush J. in *Musgrove* v. *Pandelis* [1919] 1 K.B. 314, 318.
75 *Goldman* v. *Hargrave* [1967] A.C. 645.
76 [1919] 2 K.B. 43.
77 *Ibid.* p. 49, *per* Warrington L.J. The other members of the court expressed themselves to the same effect.
78 *Collingwood* v. *Home and Colonial Stores* [1936] 3 All E.R. 200, 209.
79 [1939] 3 All E.R. 253.

496 If the fire has been started intentionally or by negligence of the occupier the statute affords him no protection. Accordingly in *Filliter* v. *Phippard* [80] where the defendant lit a fire on his land for the purpose of burning weeds, and the fire spread and consumed the hedges and fences on the adjoining land of the plaintiff, the statute was held to be no protection because of the words of the Act; also because there was negligence on the part of the defendant, *viz*: " suppose the fire to begin accidentally on the estate of him from whose estate it spreads. Now this fire did not begin accidentally, but was knowingly lighted by the defendant himself." [81] In *Sturge* v. *Hackett* [82] the defendant occupier of a flat lit a paraffin-soaked rag and negligently applied it to a sparrow's nest, built between a cornice and some wire netting which had been placed in position to keep out house-martins, as a result of which the nest caught fire but set alight to the roof so that the whole house was burned down. It was held that he was liable for damage caused by the escape of fire from the premises, quite apart from his being liable in negligence as the person whose negligent act had originated the fire. The result is that the rule in *Rylands* v. *Fletcher* applies to fires intentionally kindled.[83]

497 There is an exception to this where the fire is lit in a grate, when there must be negligence on the part of the person who causes the fire to be lit. When a lodger lit a fire in his room, where there was no fireguard and no fender, and left the room for a few hours, during which a spark from the fire set up a fire in the room which spread to the adjoining rooms, it was held that his landlady had no remedy in the absence of any evidence that he built up an excessive fire.[84] If the grate is defective so that the fire spreads beyond its intended confines, or if it is so constructed that burning fuel is likely to fall off and set up a fire outside the grate, the person liable for the condition of the grate or for creating the fire will be liable on the ground of negligence.

The statute was held to be no defence in a case where the plaintiff entrusted some books to a bookbinder to be bound and the bookbinder failed to deliver them to the plaintiff within a reasonable time, after the expiration of which the books were destroyed by an accidental fire on the bookbinder's premises, because " the breach of contract had been

80 (1847) 11 Q.B. 347.

81 *Filliter* v. *Phippard, supra*, p. 358, *per* Lord Denman C.J.

82 [1962] 1 W.L.R. 1257.

83 *Black* v. *Christchurch Finance Co.* [1894] A.C. 48; *Emanuel* v. *G.L.C., The Times*, July 21, 1970 (prefabricated bungalows were removed from council land by a contractor, employed by the Ministry of Public Building and Works, who lit a bonfire of the scrap wood and negligently allowed sparks to spread to the plaintiff's land where buildings and chattels were damaged).

84 *Sochacki* v. *Sas* [1947] 1 All E.R. 344. See also *Doltis* v. *Braithwaite & Sons* [1957] 1 Lloyd's Rep. 522, where setting fire to newspaper was held to be a natural user of a fireplace. The newspaper had been lit by the defendants' servant in order to test whether the chimney was clear. It was not known either to the plaintiffs or to the defendant contractors, who were installing a new boiler, that the chimney inter-communicated with another unused chimney on a different floor of the premises. Sparks came down this unused chimney causing extensive damage as a result of setting fire to the materials stored in that part of the premises.

committed before the fire occurred." [85] The Act of 1774 only affords protection to the occupier of the land on which the fire accidentally begins. A third party starting the fire will be under the liability of *Rylands* v. *Fletcher*, and the statute will be no protection to him, although the occupier will be protected on the ground that, as far as he is concerned, the fire is an accidental fire.

498 **Burden of proof.** The burden of proving that the origin of the fire was due to the negligence of the occupier, or his servants, agents or independent contractors, for whose acts or omissions he would also be liable, rests firmly on the plaintiff. It is not for the defendant to prove that the fire was either accidental in its origin [86] or, in invoking the protection of the Act, to disprove negligence.[87] However this does not apply where there is a bailment. In *Hyman (Sales) Ltd.* v. *Benedyke & Co. Ltd.*[88] it was held that at common law the onus of proof lay on the defendants, as bailees, to prove the absence of negligence on their part and that in those circumstances even where they had pleaded the provisions of this Act, it was still for them to prove the defence which they had set up, *i.e.* that the fire was accidental, which they had failed to do. It is to be observed that the Act provides expressly another exception, namely, the case of landlord and tenant.

499 **Provisions of other statutes.** The Factories Act 1961,[89] ss. 40–47, requires factories to be provided with means of escape in case of fire and also to have certain safety provisions in case of fire. Failure to comply with these provisions resulting in injury to any person employed in the factory will render the owner liable in damages for breach of statutory duty, even though the fire be accidental in its origin.[90] A similar result follows if there is a breach of the provisions of the London Building Acts dealing with the provision of fire escapes.[91] The by-laws of local authorities usually require the provision of a fire escape for a building exceeding a certain height used as an hotel, restaurant, hospital, boarding-house, common lodging-house, or school, and in shops of the same height where sleeping accommodation is provided for the persons employed, and failure to comply with the by-laws may be evidence of negligence in an action by an invitee or a person employed in the building against the occupier of the building.[92]

85 *Shaw & Co.* v. *Symmons & Sons* [1917] 1 K.B. 799.

86 See *Becquet* v. *MacCarthy* (1831) 2 B. & Ad. 951, 958, *per* Tenterden C.J.; *Musgrove* v. *Pandelis* [1919] 1 K.B. 314, 317, *per* Lush J.; *Collingwood* v. *Home and Colonial Stores* [1936] 3 All E.R. 200; *Williams* v. *Owen* [1955] 1 W.L.R. 1293.

87 *Mason* v. *Levy Auto Parts of England Ltd.* [1967] 2 Q.B. 530, 539, MacKenna J.

88 [1957] 2 Lloyd's Rep. 601; *Smith* v. *Taylor* [1966] 2 Lloyd's Rep. 231, where Blain J. held that although the plaintiff had not shown the probable cause of the fire, the onus was on the defendant, as a bailee, to prove that he was not negligent.

89 Which came into force on April 1, 1962, and repealed the Factories Acts 1937–1959.

90 *Groves* v. *Wimborne* [1898] 2 Q.B. 402; *Solomons* v. *R. Gertzenstein Ltd.* [1954] 2 Q.B. 243.

91 *Solomons* v. *R. Gertzenstein Ltd., supra.*

92 In *Maclenan* v. *Segar* [1917] 2 K.B. 325 the jury found no negligence on the part of the hotel proprietor in omitting to provide a fire escape. It does not appear from the report whether the omission was a breach of the by-laws.

500 **Sparks from highway.** A person who takes fire onto the highway is liable if it escapes from his control and damages persons or property on or adjoining the highway. The owner of a traction-engine was held liable for damage to a haystack which was set on fire by sparks from the engine, although the engine was being driven along the highway at a proper pace and there was no negligence on the part of his servants in its management.[93] Liability in such a case is based on *Rylands* v. *Fletcher*. The owner is equally liable even if he has fitted his engine with a special apparatus intended to prevent the escape of sparks.[94]

501 **Sparks from railway.** With the advent of the diesel engine being used throughout the country and with the passing of the steam engine only a very brief summary of the law now need be given.[95]

No liability is imposed upon railway authorities for fire caused by sparks emitted from a locomotive where the railway is operated under statutory authority [96] unless there has been negligence [97] and the burden of proving negligence is on the plaintiff and is not on the railway authorities.[98] However, the Railway Fires Acts 1905 and 1923 modified the law to a limited extent by providing that statutory authority is no defence when damage is caused to crops of agricultural land [99] from fire which arises from sparks or cinders emitted from a railway engine, when the claim does not exceed £200. If the damage exceeds £200, then, in order to recover that excess amount, negligence would have to be proved whereupon the claim for compensation under the Acts can be properly joined with the ordinary common law action in negligence.[1]

Where there is no statutory authority for the running of the railway then the absolute liability which is imposed by the common law remains.[2]

502 **Doing acts likely to result in damage by fire.** Persons doing acts likely to cause a fire or to result in damage by fire, as by handling objects which are likely to burn persons or property, by placing combustible material where it is likely to catch fire or by maintaining fires in stoves or braziers, are bound to take a high degree of care to prevent damage. In this connection they are liable for the negligence not only of their servants or agents but also of their independent contractors.[3]

Where ship repairers were doing work on a ship and, in doing so,

93 *Powell* v. *Fall* (1880) 5 Q.B.D. 597; *Gunter* v. *James* (1908) 24 T.L.R. 868.
94 *Mansell* v. *Webb* (1918) 88 L.J.K.B. 323.
95 For a fuller discussion see 4th edition, *Charlesworth on Negligence*, §§ 610–613.
96 The railways were nationalised by the Transport Act 1947 as amended by the Transport Act 1962. The property and functions of the railway companies were thereby vested in the Transport Commission who operate through regions.
97 *Vaughan* v. *Taff Vale Ry.* (1860) 5 H. & N. 679.
98 *Parker* v. *L.N.E. Ry.* [1946] W.N. 63.
99 The wide extents of which are defined in section 4 of the 1905 Act.
1 *Att.-Gen.* v. *G.W. Ry.* [1924] 2 K.B. 1. See also the point raised in *Langlands* (*Swanley*) *Ltd.* v. *B.T.C.* [1956] 1 W.L.R. 890.
2 *Jones* v. *Festiniog Ry.* (1868) L.R. 3 Q.B. 733.
3 *Honeywill & Stein Ltd.* v. *Larkin Bros. Ltd.* [1934] 1 K.B. 191; *Black* v. *Christchurch Finance Co.* [1894] A.C. 48; *Brooke* v. *Bool* [1928] 2 K.B. 578.

were carrying red-hot rivets close to an open hatchway which exposed a cargo of jute in the hold below, it was held that they were liable when one of their workmen slipped and let a rivet fall down the hold, where it set fire to the cargo.[4] Atkin L.J. held that they were liable because " anyone using such a dangerous element as fire is under an obligation to take special care, lest he injure his neighbour or his neighbour's property," [5] and, in expressly approving this judgment, Lord Birkenhead assented particularly to the illustration of Atkin L.J. that the ship repairers had " brought upon the respondents' ship that which was in fact dangerous." [6] Again, where the defendants were employed on board a ship to cut away a ventilator leading to a hold containing inflammable cargo and they used an acetylene flare without plugging the ventilator, as a result of which the cargo was set on fire by the sparks, which went down the ventilator, it was held that they were liable.[7]

503 A person who examines gas pipes with a naked light is liable for any explosion which occurs, because he is doing a highly dangerous act and accordingly his duty is " to take care that the dangerous operation which he had undertaken was done safely." [8] Where the defendants, in connection with their business as dealers, stored in their yard large quantities of combustible materials, which were kept in such condition that if they ignited the fire would be likely to spread to the plaintiff's land adjoining, they were held to be negligent when these materials had so caught fire which spread to the plaintiff's garden, causing damage.[9]

In *Mulholland & Tedd Ltd.* v. *Baker*,[10] the defendant, trying to destroy a rat which was believed to be in a drainpipe, lit some paper and put it in the pipe. Some of the burning paper set fire to some material in the yard and this, in turn, caused a drum containing twenty gallons of paraffin to ignite and explode. The defendant was held liable, Asquith J. saying: " the standard of care incumbent on a person lighting something within three feet of an intensely combustible object such as this packing case is high." Again, it is negligence to place highly combustible material near a boiler, so that when the boiler is fired, sparks from it may set the material on fire.[11]

504 Where carriers, by mistake, delivered highly inflammable celluloid scrap to the plaintiff's premises without giving proper warning of its

[4] *Ellerman Lines Ltd.* v. *H. & G. Grayson Ltd.* [1920] A.C. 466.
[5] [1919] 2 K.B. 514, 534.
[6] [1920] A.C. at p. 475.
[7] *Nautilus SS. Co.* v. *Henderson*, 1919 S.C. 605.
[8] *Brooke* v. *Bool* [1928] 2 K.B. 578, *per* Talbot J.
[9] *Mason* v. *Levy Auto Parts of England* [1966] 2 Q.B. 530.
[10] [1939] 3 All E.R. 253. See also *Balfour* v. *Barty-King* [1957] 1 Q.B. 496, where an independent contractor was employed to thaw frozen pipes in the second defendant's loft, which contained a large quantity of combustible material and the application of a blowlamp to the felt-lagged pipes caused a fire which spread rapidly throughout the whole loft and thus to the plaintiff's house, contiguous to the second defendant's.
[11] *D'Urso* v. *Sanson* [1939] 4 All E.R. 26.

dangerous character and, as a result, one of the employees of the plaintiff's carelessly set it on fire and burnt the premises, the carriers were held liable.[12]

A photographer who takes a flashlight photograph by a method which involves the creation of fire and explosion must take adequate precautions to prevent the fire so created from damaging persons or property near to his operations. The Court of Appeal was inclined to think that he was under an absolute obligation to prevent damage in such a case, but whether that is so or not, he is under an obligation to take special care.[13]

Where a gas company, in carrying out repairs to a gas main, placed a fire pail in the highway, and a boy accidentally knocked over the pail with the result that a child, playing near to it, was injured, the gas company were held liable.[14] Their duty in such a case was said to be to take " proper precautions to guard the public from injury."

505 Schoolmasters must take special care to prevent children under their charge from coming in contact with fire. The teacher and the education authority were held liable when a girl of fourteen was burnt in poking the fire in the teacher's room at the request of the teacher.[15] Also, the education authority were held liable when a girl of eleven, attending a cookery class, was injured in consequence of her apron catching fire from a gas-cooker which was not provided with a guard.[16]

Even persons who are not schoolmasters should not place fire or highly combustible material into the charge of a child too young to understand its dangerous nature. Where petrol was sold to a boy of nine, who used it to make a torch which caused him severe burns when he lit it, the seller was held liable on the ground that " to put a highly inflammable substance into the hands of a small boy is to subject him to temptation and the risk of injury, and this is no less true if the boy has resorted to deceit in order to overcome the suppliers' scruples." [17]

506 **Handling petrol.** The handling of petrol or benzol is an act which requires special precautions to guard against fire. The occupier of a garage was held liable for a fire caused through one of his servants lighting a cigarette and throwing the match on the garage floor while drawing benzol from a drum into a tin.[18] Atkin L.J. explained his duty as follows: " The servant must exercise reasonable care and skill in the circumstances in which he is called upon to act, and this duty is more imperious when the servant is handling articles dangerous in themselves, such as loaded

[12] *Philco Radio Ltd.* v. *J. Spurling Ltd.* [1949] 2 All E.R. 882.

[13] *Honeywill & Stein Ltd* v. *Larkin Bros. Ltd.* [1934] 1 K.B. 191 (where the method used was the then usual method of igniting magnesium powder in a tray).

[14] *Crane* v. *South Suburban Gas Co.* [1916] 1 K.B. 33.

[15] *Smith* v. *Martin and Hull Corpn.* [1911] 2 K.B. 775.

[16] *Fryer* v. *Salford Corpn.* [1937] 1 All E.R. 617.

[17] *Yachuk* v. *Oliver Blais Co. Ltd.* [1949] A.C. 386.

[18] *Jefferson* v. *Derbyshire Farmers Ltd.* [1921] 2 K.B. 281. See also *Ayoub* v. *Beaupre* (1964) 45 D.L.R. (2d) 411, where both the mechanic and his employers were found liable.

firearms, poisons, explosives, or the like: *Dominion Natural Gas Co.* v. *Collins.*[19] It could not be disputed that benzol is an article of that kind. In dealing with these and the like substances there is a special duty to take precautions that no damage shall accrue either to bystanders or to adjoining property by reason of explosion, fire, or other injury." [20] In a somewhat similar case, petrol was being delivered from a lorry to a tank at a garage. While the petrol was flowing from the lorry to the tank, the lorry driver lit a cigarette and threw the lighted match away, as a result of which a fire was caused, resulting in an explosion. The driver's employers were held liable.[21] When petrol is being delivered through a pipe or other container there is a duty to watch and control the flow of the petrol, and failure to do this resulting in a fire or an explosion renders the person in charge of the operation liable in damages.[22] When petrol is delivered in bulk in barrels or other containers, there is a duty to deliver it in containers which are fit to withstand the ordinary risks incident to delivery, so that where petrol was delivered in a barrel which burst on being rolled down a skid on the buyer's yard, the sellers were held liable.[23]

The keeping and transport of petrol is governed by the Petroleum (Consolidation) Act 1928 and the regulations made thereunder.[24]

07 **Firemen.** Where a fireman is called to attend a fire and is injured in the performance of his duty of fire fighting he does not become entitled *ipso facto* to recover damages from the person whose negligence caused the fire. Nevertheless, the fireman will become so entitled to succeed in his claim for damages if the occupiers of premises at which the fire takes place knew or ought to have known that they were creating or maintaining serious risks of fire and explosion on their premises which were likely to expose him to some grave and exceptional risk of injury from an explosion, which he would not otherwise be anticipating when he was called to extinguish the fire. Accordingly the occupiers of a factory, who allowed thick deposits of dust containing aluminium and carbon particles in combustible proportions to accumulate without taking any steps either to prevent or remove them, when they knew or ought to have known that they were creating and maintaining exceptional risks of fire and explosion were held liable when a fireman, called with the fire brigade to put out a fire in the factory, was injured by a fire and explosion caused by that dust.[25] A fireman, who was seriously injured while fighting a fire in a factory, was held to be outside the ambit of the provisions of section 29

[19] [1909] A.C. 640.
[20] *Jefferson* v. *Derbyshire Farms Ltd., supra,* at p. 289.
[21] *Century Insurance Co.* v. *Northern Ireland Road Transport Board* [1942] A.C. 509.
[22] *Kennedy* v. *Nascar* [1941] 3 D.L.R. 755.
[23] *Marshall* v. *Russian Oil Products Ltd.* 1938 S.C. 773.
[24] Although the plaintiff's employers were found guilty of negligence in *Heffer* v. *Rover Car Co., The Times,* November 26, 1964 in permitting petrol to be kept in an open tin, the plaintiff was found equally to blame since he had accidentally caused the lighting of the petrol during the lunch time by " larking " about at his place of employment. See article: " Petrol Delivery and Explosion Risks " by E. R. Hardy Ivamy, 105 L.J. 163.
[25] *Merrington* v. *Iron Bridge Metal Works Ltd.* [1952] 2 All E.R. 1101.

(1) of the Factories Act 1961 [26] in his claim for damages made against the occupiers.[27]

Where a volunteer intervenes in an attempt to rescue life or property he may be owed an ordinary duty of care, which has already been considered, under the principle of " rescue " cases.[28]

5.—GAS

508 **General rule of liability for gas at common law.** Gas is a dangerous thing and accordingly those who make, supply or use it are subject to the liability of the rule in *Rylands* v. *Fletcher*. Lord Wright explains it as follows: " That gas is a dangerous thing within the rules applicable to things dangerous in themselves is beyond question. Thus the appellants who are carrying in their mains the inflammable and explosive gas are prima facie within the principle of *Rylands* v. *Fletcher*,[29] affirming *Fletcher* v. *Rylands* [30]; that is to say, that though they are doing nothing wrongful in carrying the dangerous thing so long as they keep it in their pipes, they come prima facie within the rule of strict liability if the gas escapes: the gas constitutes an extraordinary danger created by the appellants for their own purposes, and the rule established by *Rylands* v. *Fletcher* requires that they act at their peril and must pay for damage caused by the gas if it escapes, even without any negligence on their part." [31]

509 **Public supply of gas.** The public supply of gas is carried out by Area Boards under the provisions of the Gas Act 1948, and so " the rule of strict liability has been modified by admitting as a defence that what was being done was properly done in pursuance of statutory powers, and the mischief that has happened has not been brought about by any negligence on the part of the undertakers." [32] The burden of proving that there was no negligence in the exercise of the statutory powers is on the Area Boards, and there is no obligation on the party suffering damage to prove negligence on their part.[33] Area Boards are accordingly liable in negligence for the escape of gas from their pipes; they are also liable for nuisance, as explained below.[34]

510 **Liability in negligence of Area Boards for gas escapes.** As Area Boards keep gas under pressure in mains and pipes a very high degree

[26] See generally Chap. 18, § 1254.
[27] *Flannigan* v. *British Dyewood Co.*, 1969 S.L.T. (O.H.) 223.
[28] *Ante*, Chap. 2, § 56; § 67.
[29] (1868) L.R. 3 H.L. 330.
[30] (1866) L.R. 1 Ex. 265.
[31] *Northwestern Utilities Ltd.* v. *London Guarantee and Accident Co.* [1936] A.C. 108, 118.
[32] [1936] A.C. at p. 119. In *Price* v. *South Metropolitan Gas Co.* [1895) 65 L.J.Q.B. 126, Russell C.J. said: " Where a gas company such as this, having statutory powers to lay pipes does so in the exercise of its statutory powers, the ' wild beast ' theory referred to in the well-known case of *Rylands* v. *Fletcher* is inapplicable." *Dunne* v. *North Western Gas Board* [1964] 2 Q.B. 806. However see the doubts expressed about this decision by Rees J. in *Pearson* v. *North Western Gas Board* [1968] 2 All E.R. 669, at p. 672.
[33] *Northwestern Utilities Ltd.* v. *London Guarantee & Accident Co.*, *supra*; *Manchester Corpn.* v. *Farnworth* [1930] A.C. 171; *Lloyde* v. *West Midlands Gas Board* [1971] 1 W.L.R. 749.
[34] *Post*, § 515.

of care is exacted of them. In *Northwestern Utilities Ltd.* v. *London Guarantee and Accident Co.*[35] an hotel was damaged by fire owing to an escape of gas from the mains of gas undertakers operating under statutory authority. The gas escaped because of a break in one of the joints of the main caused by the underground operations of a local authority in constructing a storm sewer. Lord Wright said that the gas undertakers owed " a duty to the respondents' [hotel] even though the case falls outside the rule of strict or absolute liability to exercise all care and skill that these [hotel] owners shall not be damaged. The degree of care which that duty involves must be proportioned to the degree of risk involved if that duty should not be fulfilled." It was held that the gas undertakers should have been vigilant to see that the operations of the local authority did not affect their mains and on their failure to do so they were held liable. It was not enough for them to assume that the local authority would properly fulfil its duty to support the gas main. In a somewhat similar case, where a gas pipe was laid ten and a half inches below the surface, and a sewer authority had recently excavated the ground but failed to leave proper support for the pipe, as a result of which it became cracked by the weight of traffic above, Russell C.J. said that the gas company " should be vigilant in seeing that when any other body had reason to excavate near their pipes the pipes were left in a safe condition," and that they were negligent because they ought " to have known that the ground under the pipe had been disturbed and had not been properly replaced." [36]

511 Again, when a gas main, laid in a public highway, was broken as a result of colliery subsidence and the escaping gas caused an explosion in a neighbouring dwelling-house, the gas undertakers were held liable in negligence because, though they knew of the likelihood of colliery subsidence and that they had no right of support for their mains, they took no precautions to guard their mains against the risk of subsidence.[37] On the other hand, when a gas pipe and a water pipe were laid close together and the gas pipe became rusted in consequence of water leaking from the water pipe, so that gas escaped and an explosion occurred, the gas company was held not liable.[38] Where a gas company allowed the escape of gas from its mains into a house where lights were burning, and an explosion occurred, the company was held liable.[39] Cockburn C.J., in directing the jury, said: " To allow a quantity of gas to escape into premises where lights are burning was necessarily attended with

[35] [1936] A.C. 108.

[36] *Price* v. *South Metropolitan Gas Co.* (1895) 65 L.J.Q.B. 126. A similar case is *Shell-Mex Ltd.* v. *Belfast Corpn.* [1952] N.I. 72.

[37] *Hanson* v. *Wearmouth Coal Co.* [1939] 3 All E.R. 47.

[38] *Stacey* v. *Metropolitan Water Board* (1910) 9 L.G.R. 174.

[39] *Blenkiron* v. *Great Central Gas Consumer's Co.* (1861) 2 F. & F. 437. In *Jackson* v. *Carshalton Gas Co.* (1888) 5 T.L.R. 69, the gas company was held not to have been negligent, but the report is too brief to be of any assistance.

danger of ignition, and must have been known to be so; and those who carry on operations dangerous to the public are bound to use all reasonable precautions—all the precautions which ordinary reason and experience might suggest to prevent the danger. It is not enough that they do what is usual if the course ordinarily pursued is imprudent and careless; for no one can claim to be excused for want of care because others are as careless as himself; on the other hand, in considering what is reasonable, it is important to consider what is usually done by persons acting in a similar business."

512 The unexplained escape of gas from a gas undertaker's mains or pipes is prima facie evidence of negligence on the part of the gas undertaker. If the escape was through a crack in the pipe, it is for the undertaker to prove that the crack was caused without any negligence on his part. If there is no crack, but the pipe leaks in some way, it is again for him to prove that the leak is not due to his negligence. "A person who brings a dangerous thing on his land [40] and allows it to escape, thereby causing damage to another, is liable to that other unless he can show that the escape was due to the conscious act of a third party, and without negligence on his own part. Obviously the burden of proving that there was no negligence is on the defendants, and it is not for the plaintiff to prove negligence affirmatively." [41] But the law offers no remedy to a person who suffers loss as a result of a gas explosion, which occurs without negligence either by that person or by the gas undertakers. In *Pearson* v. *North Western Gas Board* [42] where the explosion which killed the plaintiff's husband and destroyed their home was the result of the ignition of gas which had seeped into the house from a fractured gas main under a public footpath, such fracture having been caused suddenly by an exceptionally severe frost, negligence was not proved and the action failed.

513 Area Boards are bound to take all reasonable precautions to detect escapes of gas within their systems and to deal with escapes with reasonable promptitude. Where gas was escaping for three days and on the third day the gas company, on being informed, sent a man to investigate, who found there was an escape from the mains and went back to obtain the means to remedy it when an explosion occurred, it was held that the gas company was liable.[43] Pollock C.B., in directing the jury, said: "It was clear that there ought to be some system of supervision, and that men should always be in readiness to repair any leakage that might

[40] "The rule is not limited to cases where the defendant has been carrying or accumulating the dangerous thing on his own land. It applies equally . . . where the appellants were carrying gas in mains laid in the property of the city (that is, in the subsoil) in the exercise of a franchise to do so": Lord Wright in *Northwestern Utilities Ltd.* v. *London Guarantee & Accident Co.* [1936] A.C. 108.

[41] *Hanson* v. *Wearmouth Coal Co.* [1939] 3 All E.R. 47, 53, *per* Goddard L.J.

[42] [1968] 2 All E.R. 669.

[43] *Mose* v. *Hastings and St. Leonards Gas Co.* (1864) 4 F. & F. 324. See also *Manchester Corpn.* v. *Markland* [1936] A.C. 360, dealing with the detection of escapes from water mains, and *ante*, § 472, dealing with water companies.

be discovered; and that anything short of those precautions against accidents, which were thus liable, amounted to neglect, for which they would be liable." Again, where a pipe was cracked owing to the combined effect of the removal of support from underneath it and the weight of traffic above, and there was an escape and accumulation of gas for two or three days, of which the gas company was unaware, it was held that the gas company was negligent and liable for the damage caused by the resultant explosion.[44]

By paragraph 33 of the Third Schedule to the Gas Act 1948, an Area Board is liable to be fined if, after receiving notice in writing of a gas escape from any of its pipes, it does not prevent any further escape within twenty-four hours.

514 An Area Board is under no duty to inspect service pipes, which are not its property, unless it receives warning of some defect or should have been aware of it. Where a person on premises occupied by the first defendant was injured by a gas explosion caused by an escape of gas from a defective supply pipe and there had been a strong smell of gas, never present before, for about eight hours without any report being made to the Area Board, it was held that the Area Board was not liable but that the occupier was liable.[45] On the other hand in *Smith* v. *South Eastern Gas Board*[46] an explosion occurred, damaging three houses, as a result of a deliberate escape of gas made when one of the occupants had committed suicide. A strong smell of gas had been noticed and reported to the gas board, which matter was investigated by one of their representatives but he could not detect any fault, whereupon he left the vicinity and took no action at all. The gas board was held liable, their servant being negligent in leaving the situation as it was and in failing to appreciate that he must have been leaving a situation of great danger.

There is no liability if the escape of gas is due to the act of the plaintiff himself without any negligence on the part of the Area Board. Where the plaintiff was the owner of a house to which gas was supplied, and the only means of cutting off the gas was by a stopcock inside the house, it was held that the gas company was not liable for an explosion which occurred while the house was empty, owing to an omission to turn off the stopcock because " the plaintiff was himself wanting in the ordinary care of seeing that the stopcock in the inside was closed, which would have effectively prevented the gas from escaping." [47]

515 **Liability of Area Boards for nuisance.** By paragraph 42 of the Third Schedule to the Gas Act 1948, it is provided: " Nothing in this Act shall exonerate an Area Board from any indictment, action or other proceeding for any nuisance caused by them." This reproduces in almost identical

[44] *Price* v. *South Metropolitan Gas Co.* (1895) 65 L.J.Q.B. 126; *Shell-Mex Ltd.* v. *Belfast Corpn.* [1952] N.I. 72.
[45] *Glennister* v. *Condon & Eastern Gas Board* [1951] 2 Lloyd's Rep. 115.
[46] (1964) 108 S.J. 337.
[47] *Holden* v. *Liverpool New Gas & Coke Co.* (1846) 3 C.B. 1.

terms the provisions of the Gasworks Clauses Act 1871, s. 9. The escape of gas is itself a nuisance but if it is caused by the Area Board it is not actionable without proof of negligence.[48] If the escape is not caused by the Area Board, in that the pipe has been fractured or the escape otherwise caused by any other person, the Area Board is only liable if it negligently allows the gas to escape when, by taking prompt action it could have prevented the escape [49] or its continuance.[50]

To be a nuisance it is not necessary that the escape of gas should have been going on for any prolonged period of time.[51]

516 **Breaking up streets.** The Gas Act 1948, Third Schedule, paras. 1–7, as amended by the Fifth Schedule to the Public Utilities Street Works Act 1950, contains provisions empowering Area Boards to break up streets for the purpose of laying and repairing pipes, and imposes an obligation upon them of reinstating the streets so broken up with all convenient speed. For breach of this obligation they are liable in damages to any person injured.[52] When exercising these powers they must take reasonable care for the protection of persons passing along the highway. Accordingly, a gas company was held liable when its workmen, in laying gas pipes, so negligently conducted themselves that a piece of metal was projected against the plaintiff as he was walking along the highway and injured him.[53] Again, when a gas company, in repairing a gas main, placed a fire pail with a ladle containing molten lead on unenclosed land adjoining the highway, and a young child playing near the fire was injured owing to a passer-by accidentally knocking over the fire pail and spilling the molten lead upon her, it was held that the gas company was liable in negligence in leaving the fire unattended and unguarded, and in nuisance in putting a dangerous thing on land adjoining the highway without taking any steps to protect highway users.[54]

517 **Gas meters.** By the Gas Act 1948, Third Schedule, para. 13, Area Boards are obliged to supply any meters which they require consumers to use, and this paragraph impliedly imposes on them the obligation of fixing the meters. For negligence in doing so they are liable to any person

48 The C.A. has held that the gas board cannot be liable either on a basis of strict liability under the *Rylands* v. *Fletcher* rule or in nuisance, if the board had done what the statute had imposed upon it, without negligence, since it had been recognised that gas might escape as an incident of its statutory operations: *Dunne* v. *North Western Gas Board* [1964] 2 Q.B. 806, distinguishing *Midwood* v. *Manchester Corpn.* [1905] 2 K.B. 597 and *Charing Cross Electricity Supply Co.* v. *Hydraulic Power Co.* [1914] 3 K.B. 772; *Manchester Corpn.* v. *Farnworth* [1930] A.C. 171.

49 *Hanson* v. *Wearmouth Coal Co.* [1939] 3 All E.R. 47, 55; *Smeaton* v. *Ilford Corpn.* [1954] Ch. 450, 462; approved in *Dunne* v. *Northwestern Gas Board, supra.* See article " Damage Caused by Dangerous Things," 114 L.J. 152.

50 *Dunne* v. *Northwestern Gas Board, supra.*

51 *Midwood* v. *Manchester Corpn., supra*; *cf.* Salmond, 13th ed., p. 184.

52 *Goodson* v. *Sunbury Gas Co.* (1896) 75 L.T. 251; *Brame* v. *Commercial Gas Co.* [1914] 3 K.B. 1181.

53 *Scott* v. *Manchester Corpn.* (1857) 2 H. & N. 204.

54 *Crane* v. *South Suburban Gas Co.* [1916] 1 K.B. 33.

injured.[55] But where an inspector was sent to examine a meter which was out of order and, failing to remedy the defect with his penknife, went to bring other tools leaving his open penknife in the house where the plaintiff, a child of four, saw it and played with it, thereby causing injury to his eye, it was held that the gas company was not liable. The jury found that the inspector ought not to have anticipated reasonably that, if he left the knife where he did, some such accident as happened might result from it.[56]

518 **Installing or disconnecting gas.** In installing or disconnecting a supply of gas, an Area Board is only liable on proof of negligence.[56a] The degree of care and skill required, however, is a very high one because of the great danger resulting from an escape of gas and of the skill and experience which the statutory undertakers may be presumed to have in matters relating to the supply of gas. In one case, a gas company cut off the supply of gas to a meter but left a long piece of pipe projecting into the cellar where the meter was kept. This pipe, although stopped up, was connected with the mains, and some third parties, in attempting to carry away the meter, broke the pipe with the result that gas entered the cellar and an explosion occurred. The gas company was held liable, Lord Esher M.R. saying: " There was a precaution—in cutting off the supply at a perfectly safe point—which would have been both easy and effective. . . . Gas was so dangerous a thing that it required the greatest precaution, whether the supply was intended to be cut off permanently or even only temporarily. The jury had properly looked upon the fact of the defendants not having cut off the supply of gas to Ormerod's meter either at the main or at the place where it entered the cellar of the inn as showing negligence." [57] Again, when a gas company contracted to supply the plaintiff with a service pipe to convey gas from the main to the meter inside the house, and it supplied a defective pipe from which gas escaped, it was held that the company was liable for an explosion which occurred when a gasfitter's servant carried a lighted candle in order to find out the cause of the escape.[58] The company was held liable on the ground of breach of contract and also on the ground of negligence. " They ought to have taken care, before laying gas on, that the apparatus of which this pipe is a part was safe and sufficient. They have thus been guilty of a double default—first, in supplying a defective pipe; and secondly, in sending gas through it in quantities calculated to produce the catastrophe which occurred." [59] Where, however, the gas company did not supply the pipe but was asked to supply gas to a service pipe already laid by the

55 *Clayton* v. *Pontypridd U.D.C.* [1918] 1 K.B. 219.

56 *Forsyth* v. *Manchester Corpn.* (1912) 29 T.L.R. 15. Another ground given for the decision was that the inspector was acting outside the scope of his employment in repairing the meter, but this was unnecessary in view of the jury's finding.

56a But the plaintiff may be able to claim *res ipsa loquitur*, *e.g.* as in *Lloyde* v. *West Midlands Gas Board* [1971] 1 W.L.R. 749. Further see Chap. 15.

57 *Paterson* v. *Blackburn Corpn.* (1892) 9 T.L.R. 55.

58 *Burrows* v. *March Gas and Coke Co.* (1870) L.R. 5 Ex. 67.

59 *Per* Cockburn C.J. in L.R. 7 Ex. at p. 97.

owner of a flat, it was held that it was under no duty to test the service pipe or to wait and see after the gas was turned on whether it leaked or not.[60]

519 In *Dominion Natural Gas Co.* v. *Collins*[61] the gas company installed an apparatus for the supply of natural gas to a railway company. The gas was supplied at a very high pressure, and to make it fit for use a regulator, fitted with a safety valve, was provided. Owing to the negligence of the gas company, the safety valve was fixed so as to discharge indoors instead of out-of-doors, with the result that an explosion occurred killing one and injuring another of the railway company's servants. The gas company was held liable, Lord Dunedin saying: "In the case of articles dangerous in themselves, such as loaded firearms, poisons, explosives, and other things *ejusdem generis*, there is a peculiar duty to take precaution imposed upon those who send forth or instal such articles when it is necessarily the case that other parties will come within their proximity."

520 **Liability of persons other than Area Boards.** The liability of persons, other than Area Boards or others operating under statutory authority, in respect of gas owned or controlled by them is that laid down in *Rylands* v. *Fletcher*. If, however, gas escapes from an ordinary domestic supply, the owner is not liable except on proof of negligence.[62] Where, therefore, gas escaped from an outside service pipe belonging to the owner of several houses and caused an explosion in the house of one of his tenants, it was held that there was no liability to the persons injured, in the absence of negligence on the part of the owner in the maintenance of the service pipe.[63]

521 The liability of persons who instal or disconnect gas fittings is the same as that of gas companies—they are liable for negligence, but, as is pointed out above,[64] the degree of care required from those who are dealing with gas is a high one because of the dangerous nature of gas. Where a gasfitter was employed by the plaintiff's employer to repair a gas meter and, in doing so, he removed the meter and made a temporary connection by means of a flexible tube, it was held that he was liable to the plaintiff for the injuries he sustained through an explosion caused by an escape of gas owing to the insufficiency of his connection.[65] In giving judgment, Lopes J. said: "I think the plaintiff's right of action is founded on a duty which I believe attaches in every case where a person

60 *Henderson* v. *Newcastle and Gateshead Gas Co.* (1893) 37 S.J. 403; see also *Glennister* v. *Condon & Eastern Gas Board* [1951] 2 Lloyd's Rep. 115, *ante*, § 514.
61 [1909] A.C. 640. See also *Parry* v. *Smith* (1879) 4 C.P.D. 325.
62 *Bleach* v. *Blue Gate Products, The Times*, January 26, 1960 (defective tap on a gas cooker). See *ante*, § 482, dealing with the escape of water.
63 *Miller* v. *Robert Addie & Sons (Collieries)*, 1934 S.C. 150. *Quaere* whether this case does not go too far? *Cf. Peters* v. *Prince of Wales Theatre (Birmingham) Ltd.* [1943] K.B. 73; *Tilley* v. *Stevenson* [1939] 4 All E.R. 207; *Western Engraving Co.* v. *Film Laboratories Ltd.* [1936] 1 All E.R. 106 (water cases).
64 *Ante*, § 518.
65 *Parry* v. *Smith* (1879) 4 C.P.D. 325.

is using or is dealing with a highly dangerous thing, which, unless managed with the greatest care, is calculated to cause injury to bystanders. To support such a right of action, there need be no privity between the party injured and him by whose breach of duty the injury is caused, nor any fraud, misrepresentation, or concealment; nor need what is done by the defendant amount to a public nuisance. It is a misfeasance independent of contract."

522 A person doing an act likely to cause an escape of gas or a gas explosion is under a duty to take a very high degree of care to prevent any damage from being caused. When gas pipes are cracked owing to proper support not being left by persons working near to the pipes, the persons responsible for removing the support are liable.[66] Where a local authority employed an independent contractor to construct a sewer in a street and in doing so the contractor left a gas main unsupported, in consequence of which the main broke and an explosion occurred in an adjoining house, both the contractor and the local authority were held liable.[67] Again, where a gas main had been properly laid and had been in position for forty years without damage, but was cracked because of the carrying out of some road repairs, involving excavation under the main and the use of a heavy steam roller, the road authority were held liable for injury caused by the resulting explosion to a person passing along the highway.[68] Channell J. said that, assuming it was the duty of the gas company to ascertain and replace any subsidence under the mains, it was negligence on the part of the highway authority to use a heavy roller on roads under which there were gas mains which had not been touched for forty years.

A gas undertaker whose pipes, properly laid, are cracked by the use of heavy steam rollers by the highway authority is entitled to damages from the highway authority.[69] It is also entitled to recover for damage to its pipes caused by the action of water, sewer and other authorities, who have removed the support for its pipes in the course of carrying out their statutory or other duties.[70]

523 Where the owner of a lock-up shop let to a tenant, suspecting an escape of gas in the shop after the tenant had left for the night, went into the shop with a friend, and the friend with his approval examined the gas pipe with a naked light, thereby causing an explosion which damaged the goods in the shop, the owner was held liable to the tenant.[71] In giving judgment, Talbot J. said: " It is obvious that to examine a

[66] If the gas company has no right of support for its pipes, the person removing support will not be liable for any escape of gas: *Hanson* v. *Wearmouth Coal Co.* [1939] 3 All E.R. 47.

[67] *Hardaker* v. *Idle District Council* [1896] 1 Q.B. 335.

[68] *Driscoll* v. *Poplar Board of Works* (1897) 14 T.L.R. 99.

[69] *Gas Light & Coke Co.* v. *St. Mary Abbott's, Kensington* (1885) 15 Q.B.D. 1.

[70] *Ilford Gas Co.* v. *Ilford U.D.C.* (1903) 67 J.P. 365; *Huyton & Roby Gas Co.* v. *Liverpool Corpn.* [1926] 1 K.B. 146.

[71] *Brooke* v. *Bool* [1928] 2 K.B. 578.

place in which an escape of gas is suspected is highly dangerous, unless proper care is taken; and that one of the necessary precautions against disaster is to avoid the use of a naked light. In my opinion the defendant, having undertaken this examination, was under a duty to take reasonable care to avoid danger resulting from it to the shop and its contents, and, if so, he cannot escape liability for the consequences of failure to discharge this duty by getting, as he did, someone to make the examination, or part of it, for him, whether that person is an agent, or a servant, or a contractor, or a mere voluntary helper." [72]

524 In *Beckett* v. *Newalls Insulation Co.*[73] a refrigeration company and an insulation company were working on a ship under construction. The refrigerators were using Calor gas in a cylinder and left it in an outer chamber of the ship on a Friday, knowing that they would not be using it until the following Tuesday but that other men would be working on the ship during the intervening days. On the Sunday, a man employed by the insulators, without any negligence, moved the gas cylinder from the outer to the inner chamber. On the Tuesday, the plaintiff, employed by the insulators, entered the inner chamber, struck a match and caused an explosion which injured him. The refrigerators were held liable, because they had not taken the high degree of care imposed on them as the persons who had brought a dangerous thing on board the ship.

525 **Negligence of independent contractors.** A person dealing with a dangerous thing such as gas is liable not only for his own negligence but also for the negligence of any independent contractor whom he may employ to deal with the dangerous thing.[74] In *Rapson* v. *Cubitt*,[75] however, a builder employed to make alterations at a club-house, including the preparation and fixing of gas fittings, was held not liable for damage to the plaintiff caused by the negligence of his sub-contractor, a gasfitter, who forgot to turn off the gas. This case was decided in 1842 before the modern rule of liability for the acts of independent contractors was fully developed,[76] and must be considered to be superseded by later decisions to the contrary.[74]

526 **Liability of landlord or vendor of real property.** There is no liability on the part of a landlord to a tenant or of a vendor to a purchaser for negligence in the installation of gas or any other dangerous thing in the premises before the commencement of the tenancy or the completion of the purchase. In *Bottomley* v. *Bannister* [77] a firm of builders sold a house which they had built and in which they had installed a gas-boiler

72 *Ibid.* at p. 587.
73 [1953] 1 W.L.R. 8. (It was not proved how the gas escaped.)
74 *Hardaker* v. *Idle District Council* [1896] 1 Q.B. 335; *Honeywill & Stein Ltd.* v. *Larkin Bros. Ltd.* [1934] 1 K.B. 191; *Black* v. *Christchurch Finance Co.* [1894] A.C. 48; *Brooke* v. *Bool* [1928] 2 K.B. 578, 587, *per* Talbot J.
75 (1842) 9 M. & W. 710.
76 § 946 *et seq., post.*
77 [1932] 1 K.B. 458.

without a flue. The apparatus was safe if the burner was properly regulated but dangerous if it was not, and the gas company's representative properly regulated the burner. Shortly after going into possession the purchaser and his wife were found dead, poisoned by gas from the apparatus. At the time of the deaths the burner was regulated in such a way as to be dangerous, and, as it had been properly regulated by the gas company, the inference was that the purchaser himself had altered the burner and this, in itself, is sufficient to show that the builders were not liable for the death. The court, however, laid it down that a landlord was not liable to his tenant, or a vendor of real estate to a purchaser, for defects in the house rendering it dangerous even if the defects were due to his construction or were within his knowledge. This case was decided before *Donoghue* v. *Stevenson*,[78] but it has since been held that that case has no application to the sale or letting of a house.[79] In *Davis* v. *Foots* [80] a house was let to a man and his wife, and before the commencement of the tenancy a gas fire, not required by the tenants, was removed from a bedroom by the landlord. Owing to his negligence, no tap was left on the end of the gas pipe, so that when the gas was turned on at the meter it went into the room, where it asphyxiated the man and made his wife seriously ill. The landlord was held not liable, as he owed no duty to the tenant as to the condition of the house. Again, in *Travers* v. *Gloucester Corpn.*,[81] the negligent installation by the landlord of a gas geyser in a bathroom, as a result of which a lodger in the house was killed, was held not to be a breach of duty on the part of the landlord.

But different considerations apply if gas escapes from that part of the premises retained by the landlord into the tenant's part. In *Federic* v. *Perpetual Investments*,[82] where a landlord in operating a garage on his own premises, directly below a tenant's apartment, allowed gas to escape and penetrate the tenant's premises so that the tenant suffered chronic carbon monoxide poisoning, it was held that the landlord was strictly liable under *Rylands* v. *Fletcher*.

527 **Using light to detect gas escape.** When a person would be otherwise liable for an escape of gas, it is no defence for him to show that the immediate cause of the explosion was the act of a third person in using a naked light in an attempt to detect the place of the escape. Accordingly, where a gas company was negligent in supplying a defective service pipe and supplying gas through it, and a gasfitter's servant—found by a jury to be negligent—caused an explosion through using a naked light, it was held that the gas company was liable for the damage caused and that the negligence of the gasfitter's servant was no defence.[83] The

78 [1932] A.C. 562.
79 *Otto* v. *Bolton* [1936] 2 K.B. 46.
80 [1940] 1 K.B. 116.
81 [1947] K.B. 71.
82 (1968) 2 D.L.R. (3d) 50.
83 *Burrows* v. *March Gas and Coke Co.* (1872) L.R. 7 Ex. 96.

gasfitter would also have been liable for the negligence of his servant.[84] Whether the plaintiff was negligent in using the light depends on the circumstances prevailing at the time when he used it.

6.—ELECTRICITY

528 **General rule of liability for electricity.** Electricity is a dangerous thing and consequently the duty of those who own or control it is that laid down in *Rylands* v. *Fletcher*.[85] The liability for electricity is precisely the same as for gas.

529 **Public supply of electricity.** The public supply of electricity is carried out by the British Electricity Authority and Area Electricity Boards under the provisions of the Electricity Act 1947.[86] By section 57 (2) of that Act, the Schedule to the Electric Lighting (Clauses) Act 1899 is incorporated therewith subject to the adaptations and modifications in Part III of the Fourth Schedule.

By the Electric Lighting (Clauses) Act 1899, Sched., s. 77, as adapted and modified by the Electricity Act 1947, it is provided: "The Area Electricity Board shall be answerable for all accidents, damages, and injuries happening through the act or default of the Area Electricity Board, or of any person in their employment, by reason of or in consequence of any of the Area Electricity Board's works, and shall save harmless all authorities, bodies, and persons by whom any street is repairable, and all other authorities, companies and bodies collectively and individually, and their officers and servants, from all damages and costs in respect of those accidents, damages, and injuries." Probably this provision only renders the Area Electricity Boards liable when there is negligence on their part. It has been held a similar provision in the Tramways Act 1870, s. 55, does not render the tramway company liable in the absence of negligence,[87] but with regard to electricity Mathew L.J. has said [88]: "In the case of a tramway it may be enough to provide that the business shall be carried on with all reasonable care, because the incidents of that business are well known and obvious; but the difficulties and risks incidental to the business here in question are not well known and obvious, and so the legislature may reasonably provide by clause 67 [corresponding to section 77] as well as clause 70 [corresponding to section 81, below] that they shall be borne by the body who are authorised to carry it on, and not by innocent members of the public who may be damaged by reason of the concession made

84 *Brooke* v. *Bool* [1928] 2 K.B. 578.
85 *National Telephone Co.* v. *Baker* [1893] 2 Ch. 186; *Eastern and South African Telephone Co.* v. *Cape Town Tramways* [1902] A.C. 381; *Hiller* v. *Air Ministry, The Times*, December 8, 1962.
86 Which nationalised the electricity undertakings. The organisation of the industry, however, is now regulated by the Electricity Act 1957.
87 *Brocklehurst* v. *Manchester, etc., Tramways Co.* (1886) 17 Q.B.D. 118.
88 *Midwood* v. *Manchester Corpn.* [1905] 2 K.B. 597, 610.

to the defendants." The other members of the court decided the case on clause 70 (the nuisance clause) and expressed no opinion on this point, which is not supported by any other authority.

Apart altogether from this provision, Area Electricity Boards are liable for negligence in the exercise of their statutory powers, and, in addition, they are liable in nuisance.[89]

530 **Liability of Area Electricity Boards for negligence.** The Central Electricity Authority (originally named the British Electricity Authority) and Area Electricity Boards are not liable for damage caused by the exercise of statutory powers if they act without negligence.[90] The burden of proving that there was no negligence is on the Central Electricity Authority or the Area Board concerned and there is no obligation on the person who has suffered damage to prove negligence on their part.[91] The standard of care required is a high one owing to the dangerous nature of electricity.[92]

531 Where a tramway company, with statutory authority to use electric power, worked their trams on the single trolley system, under which each end of the wire passed into the earth which acted as a return conductor, and disturbed the wires of a telephone company, it was held that there was no negligence and that the tramway company were not liable.[93] Kekewich J., in giving judgment, said: "The defendants' system is, on the whole, the best which practical science has yet discovered; but there is no occasion really to go as far as this. It is enough to say, and about this I entertain no doubt that it is at least as good as any other, and has been proved by experience ... to be as likely as any other to meet the requirements of traffic and the convenience of all concerned in the protection of the site of tramways for the use of legitimate purposes other than those of the tramway undertaking." [94] Again, where electric tramways were worked under statutory authority and the tramway rails were used for the return current, as a result of which the cables of a telegraph company were interfered with, the tramway company were held not liable, because there was no negligence on their part. The statute provided that the tramway company were to be liable for "any electric leak," but it was held that this meant "some defect in apparatus not contemplated as a condition of the working of the system," and as there was no such defect, but the escape of electricity was a necessary result of the act authorised, the action failed.[95]

89 *Post*, § 536.
90 *Geddis* v. *Proprietors of Bann Reservoir* (1878) 3 App.Cas. 430, 455, and cases cited in note 85, above.
91 *Manchester Corpn.* v. *Farnworth* [1930] A.C. 171.
92 See *Northwestern Utilities* v. *London Guarantee and Accident Co.* [1936] A.C. 108 (gas).
93 *National Telephone Co.* v. *Baker* [1893] 2 Ch. 186.
94 *Ibid.* p. 204.
95 *Eastern and South African Telephone Co.* v. *Cape Town Tramways* [1902] A.C. 381.

532 Where an electric supply company had erected two overhead cables carrying high-tension current, and a violent wind tore a branch from a tree, drove it against the cables and broke them down, as a result of which high-tension current found its way along a low-tension cable, which supplied electricity to the plaintiff's house, and caused a fire, it was held that the company were liable for negligence. The negligence consisted in omitting to ground the wires of the transformers so that the electricity could pass harmlessly to earth instead of entering the neighbouring houses.[96] Dealing with the defence of statutory powers, Lord Sumner said: "Such powers are not in themselves charters to commit torts and to damage third persons at large, but that which is necessarily incidental to the exercise of the statutory authority is held to have been authorised by implication, and therefore it is not the foundation of a cause of action in favour of strangers, since otherwise the application of the general law would defeat the purpose of the enactment."[97] Again, where a company had statutory power to erect wires either overhead or underground, it was held that they were not negligent in putting them overhead. Accordingly, when a workman was operating a derrick in the street to raise a stone, and the derrick came in contact with the overhead wire as a result of which electricity was conducted down the cable of the derrick, rendered the workman unconscious, and killed two men who came to his assistance, it was held that the company were not liable. The jury found no negligence on the part of the workman's employers, but that the company were negligent, and the court held that there was no evidence of negligence on the company's part to go to the jury.[98]

533 When electricity is carried overhead by wires or cables great care must be taken in addition to any precautions required by statute, to see that it is not likely to become a source of danger. In *Buckland* v. *Guildford Gas Light & Coke Co.*[99] high voltage electric wires were taken across a field immediately over the top of a tree, part of which had been cut down to permit the passages of the wires. A girl of thirteen climbed the tree when it was in full leaf, came in contact with the wires and was killed. The electricity undertakers, were held liable on the ground that they should have foreseen that someone might climb the tree and, being unable to see the wires owing to the dense foliage, accidentally come in contact with them.[1] A different result was arrived at in the somewhat similar case of *McLaughlin* v. *Antrim Electricity Supply Co.*[2] There

[96] *Quebec Railway Light, Heat and Power Co.* v. *Vandry* [1920] A.C. 662.
[97] *Ibid.* p. 679.
[98] *Dumphy* v. *Montreal Light, Heat and Power Co.* [1907] A.C. 454.
[99] [1949] 1 K.B. 410.
[1] The girl was found not to be a trespasser on the tree, but as the defendants did not own the tree or the field in which it was growing, this is irrelevant except possibly on the question of foreseeability.
[2] [1941] N.I. 23. See also *Moyle* v. *Southern Electricity Board* [1962] 1 Lloyd's Rep. 607 (where a kite being flown from a steel wire touched an overhead cable the accident could not have been foreseen).

a boy aged twelve climbed a pylon, one leg of which was on public land and the other in a field used by children as a playground, came in contact with the wire and was injured. He failed to recover on the ground that he was a trespasser on the pylon and climbed at his own risk. It would seem, however, that the real question is not whether the boy was a trespasser but whether the electricity undertakers had fulfilled their duty to take care having regard to the situation and position of the wire and to the known circumstances generally.

534 Normally, the Area Boards' liability ends at the point where they deliver the electricity to the consumer. Where an electrical contractor installed at the plaintiff's house an electric boiler together with a new circuit, but failed to earth the new circuit properly, so that the plaintiff's wife got an electric shock from which she died, it was held that the Board were not liable.[3] They were under no duty to carry out any inspection or test of the new installation before supplying electricity. " They are responsible, of course, for bringing the electricity along their own lines and for making and continuing to have, it may be, a proper connection at the terminal supply points. Then if they have installed and they still have control of some electrical equipment on what is called the consumer's side by virtue of that installation and continuing control, they would be responsible for that also. It seems to me too much to say that the Board are responsible for what the occupier by himself and his contractors and agents may have done or omitted to do to his own chattels on his own premises." [4]

535 **Explosions.** Where an explosion occurred in the electric mains of a statutory undertaker, owing to the leakage of gas from a gas main being exploded by a spark from the electric main, and there was evidence that a ventilator would have prevented the explosion from occurring, it was held that there was negligence on the part of the electricity undertakers.[5] But, where there was a similar explosion, and it was found that the chamber in which it occurred was constructed properly, the electricity undertakers were held not liable.[6] In such a case both the gas and the electricity companies should have been made defendants, and the plaintiff, who in each case was a person passing along the highway, would have been able to recover against one or other on the grounds of negligence or nuisance.[7]

An explosion set up by an escape of electricity from the mains or wires of the Area Electricity Board is prima facie evidence of negligence on the part of the Board. Where the plaintiff, in walking along the highway, passed close to an electric lamp-post, beside which was a

[3] *Sellars* v. *Best* [1954] 2 All E.R. 389.
[4] *Ibid.*, *per* Pearson J. at p. 394.
[5] *Solomons* v. *Stepney Borough Council* (1905) 69 J.P. 360.
[6] *Goodbody* v. *Poplar Borough Council* (1915) 84 L.J.K.B. 1230.
[7] See *per* Sankey J. in *Goodbody* v. *Poplar Borough Council*, *supra*.

chamber sunk into the street, and an explosion occurred causing a metal plate to open and a flash to emanate, injuring the plaintiff, it was held that there was negligence on the part of the local authority who were the electricity undertakers.[8]

536 **Liability of Area Electricity Boards for nuisance.** By the Electric Lighting (Clauses) Act 1899, Sched., s. 81, as adapted and modified by the Electricity Act 1947, it is provided: " Nothing in this schedule or any local enactment shall exonerate any electricity board from any indictment, action or other proceedings for nuisance in the event of any nuisance being caused or permitted by them." If the nuisance is caused or permitted by the Area Board it is still necessary to prove negligence if it is to be actionable.[9] The mere escape of electricity causing damage, whether by means of an explosion or otherwise is a nuisance. Where a local authority, empowered by statute to supply electricity to their district, but with their liability for nuisance preserved, laid down mains in the street, and one of the mains fused, causing the bitumen in which it was laid to become volatilised into an inflammable gas which accumulated for three hours and then exploded, resulting in damage to the plaintiff's goods, the local authority were held liable for nuisance.[10] Collins M.R. said: " It cannot, I think, seriously be contended that, where the premises of an adjoining owner are blown up by an explosion brought about through the agency of the defendant's system of electric lighting, there is not a nuisance. Whether the defendants are liable in respect of it is, of course, another matter. There was a gradual accumulation of explosive gas brought about by the fusion of the bitumen by the operation of the overheated electric wires, which process went on for some three hours, and ultimately resulted in an explosion. If that was not a nuisance I do not know what would be one." [11] In the same case, Mathew L.J. said: " The provisions of the order [preserving liability for nuisance] seems to me to come to this. A concession is granted to the undertakers, giving them the right to carry on a dangerous business, to which latent risks may be incidental that cannot be prevented by any degree of care; and, that being so, it was thought reasonable that those who are empowered to carry on that business for their profit should have to bear the inevitable loss arising from such risks." [12]

537 **Breaking up streets.** The Electric Lighting (Clauses) Act 1899, Schedule, appendix, incorporates sections 6–12 of the Gasworks Clauses Act 1847, relating to the breaking up of streets, and is applied by the

[8] *Farrell* v. *Limerick Corpn.* (1911) 45 I.L.T. 169, *per* Palles C.B.; see also *Solomons* v. *Stepney Borough Council* (1905) 69 J.P. 360, *per* Alverstone C.J.

[9] *Dunne* v. *Northwestern Gas Board* [1964] 2 Q.B. 806, see *ante*, § 515, distinguishing *Midwood* v. *Manchester Corpn.* [1905] 2 K.B. 597 and *Charing Cross Electricity Supply Co.* v. *Hydraulic Power Co.* [1914] 3 K.B. 772.

[10] *Midwood* v. *Manchester Corpn.*, *supra*. (There was also an important finding of negligence.)

[11] *Ibid.* p. 604.

[12] *Ibid.* p. 610.

Electricity Act 1947, to electricity boards, so that electricity boards are under the same obligation as gas boards to take care in replacing the streets broken up.[13] These provisions are now affected by the Public Utilities Street Works Act 1950, which repealed sections 8 to 12 of the Gasworks Clauses Act 1847. The present law as to the breaking up of streets and their reinstatement is to be found in the Street Works Code in the 1950 Act.

538 **Liability of persons other than electricity boards.** The liability of persons who own or control electricity without any statutory authority is that laid down in *Rylands* v. *Fletcher*.[14] An exception, however, occurs in the case of " electric wiring which everybody or most people nowadays have in the house which they occupy whether for domestic use or for the purposes of trade," [15] when negligence must be proved to establish liability. Where there was some unknown defect in the electrical wiring in the basement of the defendant's grocery stores causing a fire to break out, and the adjoining shop of the plaintiff was damaged by the water used in extinguishing the fire, it was held that, as there was no evidence of negligence, the defendant was not liable.[15] Lord Wright said that the rule in *Rylands* v. *Fletcher* did not apply " to the ordinary domestic installation of electric wiring for the ordinary comfort and convenience of life." Again, when a fire was caused by a short circuit set up by the electric wires behind the panelling near a ventilator on the half landing of a building where a stack of packing and wrapping material was stored, it was held there was no liability.[16] On somewhat similar facts, however, the defendant was held liable in nuisance. In *Spicer* v. *Smee* [17] the plaintiff's house was destroyed by fire caused by a defect in the electric wiring of the adjoining house owned by the defendant. The condition of the wiring was found to be a nuisance created by the defendant or those for whom he was responsible, and as this nuisance caused the fire the defendant was held liable, quite apart from negligence. There was negligence on the part of an independent contractor employed by the defendant to instal the wiring but this was held to be no defence to the defendant. *Collingwood* v. *Home & Colonial Stores* was distinguished on the ground that there was no

13 *Ante*, § 516.

14 *National Telephone Co.* v. *Baker* [1893] 2 Ch. 186; *Eastern and South African Telephone Co.* v. *Cape Town Tramways* [1902] A.C. 381; *Hiller* v. *Air Ministry, The Times*, December 8th, 1962. The defendants had laid a high voltage cable under the plaintiff farmer's field in 1941, pursuant to powers conferred by Regulation 50 of the Defence (General) Regulations of 1939, but in 1959, whilst grazing in it, nineteen cows collapsed simultaneously as a result of being electrocuted following an escape of electricity from the cable. The defendants were liable since clearly the Regulations had not authorised such an escape and had in any event ceased to have effect in 1958 as a result of the Land Powers (Defence) Act 1958. Further the Regulations did not give the defendants a perpetual right to maintain and use the cable.

15 *Collingwood* v. *Home and Colonial Stores* [1936] 3 All E.R. 200.

16 *Solomons* v. *R. Gertzenstein Ltd.* [1954] 1 Q.B. 565, reversed on other grounds [1954] 2 Q.B. 243.

17 [1946] 1 All E.R. 489.

finding of fact that there was a nuisance or any negligence in installation or maintenance.

539 It is unsatisfactory, if it be the law, that liability for damage caused by the domestic installation of electric wiring should depend on whether the plaintiff sues in negligence or in nuisance. Possibly the two cases may be reconciled on the ground that a person who instals electricity on his premises owes a duty to take care to instal and to maintain the installation in a safe condition and, if he fails to do this, either by himself, his servants or agents or his independent contractors, he is liable for the resultant damage.

540 **Installing electrical equipment.** Persons installing or disconnecting electrical equipment are only liable for negligence, but a high degree of care is required. Their liability is the same as that of persons who instal or disconnect gas.[18] When a workman employed by an electricity supply company was electrocuted when working at a kiosk negligently made by the second defendants, the claim against those defendants failed because, before the death, the electricity supply company had had an opportunity of inspection, but it was said, " If the second defendants had been employed to supply and fix the kiosk and turn on the current, I think that it may well be that they would be considered to be in a relationship sufficiently proximate to a workman who might have to enter the kiosk after the current was turned on to put them under a duty towards him." [19] This occurred in *Hartley* v. *Mayoh*,[20] where an electricity board installed a new meter on premises and did not test the circuits after finishing the work. They had negligently crossed the leads, as a result of which a fireman, called to a fire on the premises, was killed. They were held liable on the ground that they should have contemplated that their omission to make a test might cause damage to persons lawfully on the premises who had occasion to come into contact with any part of the wiring system.

Again, an electrical contractor who installed at the plaintiff's house an electric boiler together with a new circuit but failed to provide a fully efficient earthing system for the circuit was held liable to the plaintiff for the death of his wife, who was electrocuted owing to there being no proper earthing system.[21] Wires carrying electric current must be kept properly insulated, and neglect of this duty causing damage is actionable. Where two persons were killed by an electric shock, when

18 *Ante*, § 519.

19 *Paine* v. *Colne Valley Electricity Supply Co.* [1938] 4 All E.R. 803, 808, *per* Goddard L.J. A somewhat similar case is *Eccles* v. *Cross and M'Ilwham*, 1938 S.C. 697 (builders' workman killed by electric shock while altering a building. The wire causing the shock was part of a temporary electric lighting system installed two months before by electricians under contract with owners. Electricians not liable as owners had opportunity of inspection. Owners liable).

20 [1953] 2 All E.R. 525. An appeal on another aspect of the case was made and dismissed [1954] 1 Q.B. 383. *Cf. Green* v. *Fibreglass Ltd.* [1958] 2 Q.B. 245.

21 *Sellars* v. *Best* [1954] 2 All E.R. 389. See 70 L.Q.R. 170.

using public baths, owing to the neglect of the local authority to earth the metal tubes employed in connection with the electric light system, the local authority were held liable.[22]

7.—EXPLOSIVES

541 **Explosives Act 1875.** The manufacture, keeping, sale, importation and conveyance of explosives are regulated by the Explosives Act 1875, as amended by the Explosives Act 1923. For breach of the provisions of these statutes and the orders made thereunder, the action, when it lies at all, is for breach of statutory duty.[23] It is provided by section 102 that " This Act shall not, save as is herein expressly provided, exempt any person from any action or suit in respect of any nuisance, tort, or otherwise, which might, but for the provisions of this Act, have been brought against him." It is a public nuisance to keep a powder magazine in such a place that it is a danger to life and property.[24]

542 **Liability for explosives.** Persons who manufacture or store explosives are liable under the rule in *Rylands* v. *Fletcher* [25] if damage is caused by their explosives, whether or not there is any negligence on their part. In *Rainham Chemical Works* v. *Belvedere Fish Guano Co.*[26] two men, F. and P., contracted with the Minister of Munitions to manufacture picric acid, and for that purpose formed a company. During the process of the work, a large quantity of dinitrophenol, which was stored at the works for the purpose of manufacturing picric acid, exploded and damaged the plaintiff's property. Both the company and F. and P. were held liable on the principle of *Rylands* v. *Fletcher*, Lord Sumner saying: " The explosive, to which in this case the rule in *Rylands* v. *Fletcher* has to be applied, is not a combination of dinitrophenol with old boxes or bags, which had contained nitrate of soda. These are only one of the conditions of explosion. What is material is the explosive itself. The dinitrophenol was lawfully brought on to the Range site and stored there by the company. They cannot escape any liability which otherwise attaches to them on storing it there merely because they have no tenancy or independent occupation of the land but use it thus by permission of the tenants or occupiers." The duty being to prevent an explosion, it is immaterial that the substance in question was not known to be an explosive. Lord Buckmaster said: " It may be accepted that it was not known to either of the defendants that this danger existed, but that in itself affords no excuse." [27] Where a twenty-gallon drum of paraffin

22 See *Re Fulham Borough Council and National Electric Construction Co.* (1905) 70 J.P. 55. (The local authority, however, failed to obtain an indemnity for breach of contract from the electrical contractors.)
23 *Post*, Chap. 18.
24 *R.* v. *Chilworth Gunpowder Co.* (1888) 4 T.L.R. 557.
25 *Ante*, § 414.
26 [1921] 2 A.C. 465, 479.
27 *Ibid.* p. 471.

exploded in a yard, the defendants were held liable under *Rylands* v. *Fletcher*.[28] When an explosion occurs in a factory where explosives are made or handled, there is no liability to persons who are injured in the factory itself, unless negligence is proved.[29]

An injunction may be granted to prevent a person from carrying on the business of manufacturing explosives so as to be a danger to the adjoining property, and where an explosion had occurred and there was a reasonable probability of another occurring so as to be an imminent danger to the plaintiff's property an injunction was granted.[30]

543 **Intentionally causing an explosion.** A person who intentionally causes an explosion, for example by blasting, does so at his peril and is liable for the resulting damage irrespective of negligence. Where a quarry near a highway was being worked, and men with red flags were posted on the highway to warn the public of the danger when blasting was in progress, it was held that a man who was injured on the highway as a result of the blasting was entitled to recover, although he had disregarded the warning. In giving judgment, Swinfen Eady M.R. said: "The way in which the case was tried was that it was put to the jury as a case of negligence, and the learned judge told the jury that, unless the plaintiff proved that the defendants had been guilty of negligence, he was out of court. That mode of putting the case was far too favourable to the defendants. This was a case in which the defendants had brought on their premises a quantity of explosives for their business, and fired considerable charges. . . . The duty of the defendants on bringing this foreign and dangerous material on the ground and exploding it there was to keep all the results of the explosion on their own lands, and it escaped from their own lands at their peril. The doctrine of *Rylands* v. *Fletcher* applied to the present case." [31]

544 **Doing acts likely to cause an explosion.** When an act is done which is likely to cause an explosion, there is a duty to take care that an explosion is not caused. The degree of care required is a high one, so much so that liability cannot be avoided by employing an independent contractor to do the act.[32] A telephone company, engaged in laying telephone wires in a street, employed a plumber, an independent contractor. The plumber, in the course of soldering some tubes, dipped a lamp into a cauldron of melted solder. This was the proper method of doing the work but, owing to the safety valve of the lamp being out of order as the plumber ought to have known, the lamp exploded and injured the plaintiff who was walking in the street. The telephone

28 *Mulholland & Tedd Ltd.* v. *Baker* [1939] 3 All E.R. 253.

29 *Read* v. *J. Lyons & Co. Ltd.* [1947] A.C. 156. See the criticism of this case by P. A. Landon in *Pollock on Torts*, 15th ed., p. 372, with which the author agrees.

30 *M'Murray* v. *Cadwell* (1889) 6 T.L.R. 76.

31 *Miles* v. *Forest Rock Granite Co.* (1918) 34 T.L.R. 500. Blasting which caused vixens in a silver fox farm to abort was held actionable in *Western Silver Fox Ranch* v. *Ross & Cromarty C.C.*, 1940 S.C. 601.

32 See *ante*, § 502, note 3; *The Pass of Ballater* [1942] P. 112.

company were held liable on the ground that " works were being executed in proximity to a highway, in which in the ordinary course of things an explosion might take place," and that they were " under an obligation to the public to take care that persons passing along the highway were not injured by the negligent performance of the work." [33] The principle of this decision is not confined to work done in or near to the highway. It " does not depend merely on the fact that the defendants were doing work on the highway, but primarily on its dangerous character, which imposes on the ultimate employers an obligation to take special precautions, and they cannot delegate this obligation by having the work carried out by independent contractors. This is equally true when the work being done by the independent contractor for the ultimate employer is being done on another person's premises." [34]

545 On the principle that there is a duty to take care not to cause an explosion when an act is being done which is likely to cause one, persons employing a firm of photographers, who were independent contractors, to take a flashlight photograph of the interior of a cinematograph theatre, were held liable for the negligence of the photographers. The negligence consisted in burning magnesium powder in a tray near to a curtain and so causing a fire.[35] In delivering the judgment of the court, Slesser L.J. said: " To take the photograph in the cinema with a flashlight was, on the evidence stated above, a dangerous operation in its intrinsic nature, involving the creation of fire and explosion on another person's premises, that is, in the cinema, the property of the cinema company. The appellants, in procuring this work to be performed by their contractors, the respondents, assumed an obligation to the cinema company which was, as we think, absolute,[36] but which was at least an obligation to use reasonable precautions to see that no damage resulted to the cinema company from these dangerous operations: that obligation they could not delegate by employing the respondents as independent contractors, but they were liable in this regard for the respondents' acts." [37] Similarly, the owner of a lock-up shop who went into the shop with a friend to try to locate an escape of gas was held liable to the tenant of the shop for damage caused to his goods by an explosion caused by the act of the friend in using a naked light to discover the source of the escape.[38] Again, where a firm of ship repairers, before using an oxyacetylene burner, employed a consulting engineer to make a report and on his reporting " gas free " used the burner, when an

[33] *Holliday* v. *National Telephone Co.* [1899] 2 Q.B. 392. The quotations are from the judgment of Lord Halsbury.
[34] *Honeywill & Stein Ltd.* v. *Larkin Bros. Ltd.* [1934] 1 K.B. 191, 199.
[35] *Honeywill & Stein Ltd.* v. *Larkin Bros. Ltd., supra.* This method of taking flashlight photographs has been superseded by the use of magnesium foil contained inside a glass bulb and by other safer devices, the most modern of which is the electronic flash.
[36] In this case the explosion was caused intentionally, so that the principle of *Miles* v. *Forest Rock Granite Co., ante*, § 543, would apply.
[37] *Honeywill & Stein Ltd.* v. *Larkin Bros. Ltd., supra*, at p. 200.
[38] *Brooke* v. *Bool* [1928] 2 K.B. 578.

explosion occurred, the ship repairers were held liable for the negligence of the engineer in not making a proper inspection before giving his certificate. Their duty, when dangerous things were to be used, was not merely to take care but to see that care was taken.[39]

546 The generating of steam in a boiler is an act which is likely to cause an explosion unless proper precautions are taken, and would appear to be within the principle stated in the preceding paragraphs. Where a ship's boiler exploded and injured a workman working on the ship, it was held that the shipowners were not liable in the absence of negligence, because there was no escape of steam from the ship.[40] The explosion was due to a faulty valve which had been fitted by a competent firm of marine engineers, and this defect was unknown to the shipowners and could not have been discovered by the exercise of reasonable care, so that they were held not liable to the workman as invitee.[41] It has since been held that an invitor may be liable for a danger created by an independent contractor,[42] so that the decision, in so far as it was based on the ground that the shipowners were not liable for the negligence of the marine engineers, must be regarded as of doubtful authority. But, for the law after 1957, see now *ante*, § 333 *et seq.*

In *Muir* v. *Stewart* [43] a customer in a chemist's shop produced a bottle and asked for nitric acid. The chemist asked what the bottle had contained and, on being told nitric acid, filled it. An explosion occurred, injuring another person in the shop. The chemist was held not liable as he had taken some care, and there was no evidence to show what was the practice of chemists in filling bottles.

547 **Evidence of negligence.** The fact that something, the property of the defendant, explodes, or that an explosion occurs out of and in the course of some operation carried out by or under the control of the defendant, is prima facie evidence of negligence on the part of the defendant.[44] Where an explosion occurred at a cartridge factory from an unknown cause, and the jury found that the owners of the factory were negligent in not supplying suitable machinery and in not taking sufficient precautions to prevent an explosion, it was held that exact proof of negligence was not necessary where the accident was the work of a moment, and its origin and cause were incapable of being detected.[45]

[39] *The Pass of Ballater* [1942] P. 112.
[40] *Howard* v. *Furness Houlder Argentine Lines Ltd.* [1936] 2 All E.R. 781. An additional ground was that the owners were not making an unnatural use of their steamship. This case was approved by the H.L. in *Read* v. *J. Lyons & Co. Ltd.* [1947] A.C. 156, 168.
[41] *Howard* v. *Furness Houlder Argentine Lines Ltd.*, *supra*, at p. 788.
[42] *Thomson* v. *Cremin* [1953] 2 All E.R. 1185. For the pre-1957 law, see *ante*, § 332.
[43] 1938 S.C. 590.
[44] See *Solomons* v. *Stepney Borough Council* (1905) 69 J.P. 360; *Farrell* v. *Limerick Corpn.* (1911) 45 I.L.T. 169.
[45] *McArthur* v. *Dominion Cartridge Co.* [1905] A.C. 72.

In *Read* v. *J. Lyons & Co. Ltd.*[46] where an explosion occurred in a munitions factory and injured a government inspector in the factory, negligence was not alleged.

It is not evidence of negligence merely to prove that an explosion occurred on a person's land without proving circumstances leading to an inference that some act or neglect of his was responsible for the explosion. Where a passenger in a railway train brought a parcel of bombs into the compartment and the bombs exploded, injuring the passengers in the compartment, it was held that the railway company was not liable in the absence of evidence that the parcels brought into the compartment were of such a size or nature as to suggest danger.[47]

548 **Setting off fireworks.** A person setting off fireworks is bound to take great care to prevent them from causing damage to others. In *Whitby* v. *Brock & Co.*[48] where the plaintiff went to the Crystal Palace to see a firework display carried out by the defendants and was struck on the leg by a firework, it was held that the defendants were liable. Lord Esher, in giving judgment, said that the defendants knew that fireworks were dangerous articles. Therefore, " there was a duty to manage with care their dealings with the fireworks. . . . The mere fact that the fireworks struck the plaintiff was sufficient prima facie evidence of negligence, because fireworks did not ordinarily strike the spectators and bystanders." When the defendant threw a lighted squib into a crowded building and the person near whom it came threw it away to another man who in turn threw it away so that it exploded and injured the plaintiff, the defendant was held liable because he had given the mischievous faculty to the squib and was responsible for its introduction into the building.[49] But where a firework party was held at a riverside bungalow which was later set on fire as a result of a " jumping jack " accidentally finding its way into the lounge from the vicinity of the porch and there setting alight some other fireworks especially stored in a cubby-hole made for the occasion, it was held by Paull J. that there had been no negligence, since the occupiers had done all that could reasonably be expected of them to store the fireworks safely.[50] When a schoolboy was injured at a firework display at the school on November 5, Lord Ellenborough stated his opinion " that if the master of a school, knowing that fireworks would be used, were to be guilty of negligence in not preventing the use of them, he would be amenable for the consequences." [51] Where a boy, aged eight, bought from the defendant's shop a firework which he later set off in such a manner that the explosion blinded him in one eye, Stable J. held that the

[46] [1947] A.C. 156, *ante*, § 542.
[47] *East Indian Ry.* v. *Kalidas Mukerjee* [1901] A.C. 396.
[48] (1888) 4 T.L.R. 241. Further, Lopes L.J. said that he adhered to what he had said in *Parry* v. *Smith* (1879) 4 C.P.D. 325, that under such circumstances the defendants were bound to use care and the fact that the plaintiff was struck was evidence of negligence.
[49] *Scott* v. *Shepherd* (1773) 2 W.Bl. 892.
[50] *Horsenail* v. *Kennedy*, *The Times*, April 30, 1964.
[51] *King* v. *Ford* (1816) 1 Starkie 421.

shopkeeper had been negligent in allowing a firework to be sold to so young a child.[52]

549 **Firing guns.** Loaded firearms must be used with the greatest caution. " The law of England, in its care for human life, requires consummate caution in the person who deals with dangerous weapons." [53]

Before firing a gun, care should be taken to see that anyone whose presence is known or might reasonably be anticipated is not within the line of fire. On this point, Blackburn J. said [54]: " If a man fires a gun across a road where he may reasonably anticipate that persons will be passing, and hits some one, he is guilty of negligence and liable for the injury he has caused; but if he fires in his own wood, where he cannot reasonably anticipate that any one will be, he is not liable to any one whom he shoots, which shows that what a person may reasonably anticipate is important in considering whether he has been negligent." Even a man who fires in his own wood will be liable if he shoots a person who is visible to him, without first looking to see whether that person is in the line of fire.[55]

In *Stanley* v. *Powell* [56] the defendant was a member of a shooting party and the plaintiff was employed to carry cartridges and birds. The defendant fired at a pheasant and a shot from his gun struck the bough of a tree, glanced off and struck the plaintiff. The distance between the plaintiff and the defendant was about thirty yards. The jury found no negligence on the defendant's part and judgment was given for the defendant. The case was not considered on the basis of the degree of care required from the defendant in using a dangerous weapon, such as a gun, and on the point of negligence the case can only be considered as a somewhat peculiar finding of fact by a jury.

550 Even if the gun is only intended to be loaded with blank cartridge, there is an obligation to take great care to see that blank alone is loaded before it is fired. When a member of the audience at a theatre was injured by a bullet fired from a pistol by one of the actors—the pistol being only intended to be loaded with blank cartridge, but in fact having a spent cartridge put in above the blank—it was held that the proprietor of the theatre would be liable, although the actor was employed by a theatrical company and not by the proprietor himself, if he failed to see that reasonable care was taken in the loading of the pistol. Pickford L.J. put his duty as follows: " In this case it is obvious that firearms would be used, and it is common knowledge that unless proper care is taken in loading them they are dangerous, and I think there was an obligation

52 *Beaver* v. *Cohen, The Times*, May 14, 1960.

53 *Per* Erle C.J. in *Potter* v. *Faulkner* (1861) 1 B. & S. 800, 805. See further the provisions of the Air Guns and Shot Guns, etc., Act 1962.

54 *Smith* v. *L. & S.W. Ry.* (1870) L.R. 6 C.P. 14, 22.

55 *Chettle* v. *Denton* (1951) 95 S.J. 802.

56 [1891] 1 Q.B. 86. In *Fowler* v. *Lanning* [1959] 1 Q.B. 426 at p. 438 Diplock J. expressed the view that the decision in *Stanley* v. *Powell* is still good law. (See also 75 L.Q.R. 161.)

on his part to take reasonable care that they were so loaded as not to be dangerous." [57]

If a person shot intentionally at another the cause of action was in trespass to the person but if the injury sustained by the plaintiff was caused unintentionally then negligence was a necessary ingredient to be proved, were he to succeed in an action for damages. In *Fowler* v. *Lanning* [58] Diplock J. held that the onus of proving negligence, where the trespass is not intentional, lies upon the plaintiff, whether the action be framed in trespass or in negligence.

551 **Entrusting firearms to incompetent persons.** There is a duty on the owner of a loaded gun not to entrust it to a person who by reason of his youth, his ignorance or his lack of intelligence is not competent to handle it. It is a question of fact whether he is competent or not. In *Dixon* v. *Bell* [59] the defendant sent his servant, a girl of about thirteen or fourteen, to a friend's house to fetch his gun, giving her a note asking the friend to remove the priming. The friend did so, as he thought, and the servant on her way home pointed the gun, as a joke, at a child and fired. The gun went off and the child was injured. The defendant was held liable, Lord Ellenborough saying: " It was incumbent on him, who, by charging the gun, had made it capable of doing mischief, to render it safe and innoxious. This might have been done by the discharge or drawing of the contents; and though it was the defendant's intention to prevent all mischief, and he expected that this would be effectuated by taking out the priming, the event has unfortunately proved that the order to Leman was not sufficient; consequently, as by this want of care, the instrument was left in a state capable of doing mischief, the law will hold the defendant responsible."

In the case of a competent person, the only duty is to give warning that the gun is loaded.[60]

There is a similar duty not to entrust a firearm, together with ammunition for it, to a person who is not competent to use it. A mere warning of the danger is not enough. In *Burfitt* v. *A. & E. Kille* [61] the defendants sold to a boy aged twelve what was called a " safety pistol "

57 *Cox* v. *Coulson* [1916] 2 K.B. 177, 187. The cause of action was breach of contract, but it was held that the duty owed by the defendant to the plaintiff was that of invitor to invitee.

58 *Supra.* Lord Denning M.R. in *Letang* v. *Cooper* [1965] 1 Q.B. 232, at p. 240 approved of the law as expounded by Diplock J. therein but added: " I would go this one step further: when the injury is not inflicted intentionally, but negligently, I would say that the only cause of action is negligence and not trespass. If it were trespass, it would be actionable without proof of damage; and that is not the law today."

59 (1816) 5 M. & S. 198.

60 See *per* Scrutton L.J. in *Hodge & Sons* v. *Anglo-American Oil Co.* (1922) 12 Ll.L.R. 183, 187.

61 [1939] 2 K.B. 743. Contrast *Ricketts* v. *Erith B.C.* [1943] 2 All E.R. 629, where the seller of a toy bow and arrow to a boy of ten was held not liable because the toy was not " a thing dangerous in itself in the hands of the particular purchaser " (Tucker J.). But compare the similar position where a seller was held liable in negligence for allowing a firework to be sold to a boy aged eight: *Beaver* v. *Cohen*, *The Times*, May 14, 1960; and petrol to a boy aged nine: *Yachuk* v. *Oliver Blais Co. Ltd.* [1949] A.C. 386.

and 100 blank cartridges. The pistol, although it could not be used with ball ammunition, was held to be highly dangerous by reason of its construction and the liability of the barrel to become blocked with fouling. The boy fired the pistol near to the plaintiff, another boy of about the same age, and a small piece of the rim of the cartridge entered the plaintiff's eye. The defendants were held liable for selling a dangerous thing to a small boy.

552 **Not keeping loaded guns in safe place.** In addition to the duty not to entrust firearms to incompetent persons, there is a further duty to keep loaded firearms in a safe place so that they cannot be used by anyone who is likely to use them carelessly. "You must not put anything dangerous in itself where the public may possibly have access to it, and the best known instance of that is the case of a loaded gun." [62] To the same effect is the illustration given by Lord Denman C.J.: "If, for example, a gamekeeper, returning from his daily exercise, should rear his loaded gun against a wall in the playground of schoolboys whom he knew to be in the habit of pointing toys in the shape of guns at one another, and one of these should playfully fire it off at a school-fellow and maim him, I think it will not be doubted that the gamekeeper must answer in damages to the wounded party." [63] This was followed in *Sullivan* v. *Creed* [64] where the defendant left a gun loaded and at full cock inside a fence on his land close to a path. His son, aged between fifteen and sixteen, pointed the gun in play at the plaintiff, fired, and injured him. The defendant was held liable, Fitzgibbon L.J. saying: "In the case of a gun loaded at full cock the measure of care is at its maximum. The scope of duty is the scope of danger, and it extends to every person into whose hands a prudent man might reasonably expect the gun to come, having regard to the place where he left it. The ground of liability here is not that the boy was the defendant's son, but the fact that the gun was left without warning, in a dangerous condition, within reach of persons using the pathway, and the boy was one of the very class of persons whom the defendant knew to be not only likely but certain to pass by, *viz.*, his own household."

553 In the cases cited in the previous paragraph the gun was fired by a child, but if it had been negligently, as opposed to intentionally, fired by an adult the result would have been the same. This is pointed out in *Sullivan* v. *Creed* by Holmes L.J.: "I do not attach much importance to the age of the defendant's son. He was old enough to know that it was dangerous to handle the gun on full cock. . . . Quite irrespective of the age of the persons who might use the path, I think that there was evidence from which the jury were at liberty to find that the defendant, when placing the gun against the fence, ought to have contemplated that it might fall into negligent hands. . . . I hold that in a case of this kind

62 *Per* Lord Dunedin in *Fardon* v. *Harcourt-Rivington* (1932) 48 T.L.R. 215.
63 *Lynch* v. *Nurdin* (1841) 1 Q.B. 29, 35.
64 [1904] 2 Ir.R. 317.

there is a marked distinction between a negligent act and a wilful act. A man who negligently lays aside a loaded gun ought to contemplate that it may be taken up by a person who will handle or use it negligently. But I think that it would not be within reasonable contemplation that the finder of it would wilfully discharge it at another."

554 **Airgun.** An airgun is not a thing dangerous in itself,[65] but it is capable of causing injury to others if it is negligently used. It should not therefore, be entrusted to a child who is too young [66] to be likely to use it safely, and if it is so entrusted and damage is caused, the parent or other person who gave the airgun to the child or allowed the child to use it will be liable. If the child is old enough to use it safely, provided that he is told of the danger and proper precautions, such as a reasonable and prudent parent would take, are taken, then the parent on giving the warning and taking the precautions is not liable. Thus an accident caused by an airgun pellet ricochetting, when fired by a boy of twelve, who had been properly instructed in its use and had not been pointing the gun at another boy, aged thirteen, was held to have been purely accidental by Thesiger J. and not to have been caused by any negligence.[67] Where a father allowed his son aged thirteen to have an airgun on condition that it was only used in the cellar of the house and not outside, but the boy, in breach of his promise to his father, used the airgun in the open and injured a child of five, the father was held not liable.[68] Similarly in *Gorely* v. *Codd* [69] the defendant, aged fourteen years, was found to be guilty of negligence which caused the accident to the plaintiff, aged sixteen years, when he was struck by an airgun pellet, whilst they were "larking about" together. The defendant's father was held not to be negligent, since he had given his son proper and sufficient instruction in the use of the rifle and the defendant was found by the court to be a responsible boy normally. The prohibition in section 1 (3) of the Air Guns and Shot Guns Act 1962 against persons under seventeen years of age possessing an air weapon only extended to a public place and, as the shooting had taken place in a private place, it was of no application in the case. On the other hand, if experience shows that the child cannot safely be allowed to have the airgun, the parent will be liable. So, where a father gave his son, aged fifteen, an airgun and the son, in March, broke a window in firing it, and in June shot another boy in the eye, it was held that the father was liable because "in leaving the air gun in his

[65] *Donaldson* v. *McNiven* [1952] 1 All E.R. 1213, 1216, *per* Pearson J.

[66] By section 1 (1) of the Air Guns and Shot Guns, etc., Act 1962 it is enacted that: "No person under the age of fourteen shall accept as a gift any air weapon or ammunition for an air weapon, and no person shall give any air weapon or ammunition for an air weapon to any person under that age." Contravention is a criminal offence and is punishable by virtue of section 3. See also the limited exceptions to the prohibition of possession of such an air weapon contained in section 1.

[67] *Rogers* v. *Wilkinson, The Times*, January 19, 1963.

[68] *Donaldson* v. *McNiven* [1952] 2 All E.R. 691. (It was conceded that the father was not negligent in allowing his son to have the airgun.)

[69] [1967] 1 W.L.R. 19.

boy's hands the defendant had not exercised such reasonable care as a prudent person ought to exercise." [70]

If in breach of section 19 (1) of the Firearms Act 1937, which forbids the sale of firearms and ammunition by a vendor, when he knows or has reasonable grounds for believing that the buyer was under the age of seventeen years, a person sells an air pistol to someone in fact under that age, then prima facie such person had been negligent. Accordingly in *Hinds* v. *Direct Supply Co.* (*Clapham Junction*) *Ltd.*[71] the sellers of an air pistol to an under-aged boy were held to be liable in damages for the personal injuries sustained by the victim of the shooting by that boy.

555 **Petrol.** When a motor-vehicle is parked in a parking ground occupied by the owner of the motor-vehicle and the tank contains petrol fumes, the owner is not liable to a person injured by an explosion caused by a lighted match thrown into the petrol tank whether by strangers [72] or by the injured person [73] because such an act could not reasonably have been foreseen. For explosions caused by handling petrol, see *ante*, § 506.

556 **Explosive substances.** The duty in the case of explosive materials is similar to that already explained in connection with firearms. If they are delivered to a person competent to understand and profit by a warning, a warning should be given. For example, when, by mistake, a carrier delivered celluloid scrap to a factory where it was not expected without giving warning of its dangerous character, and an employee in the factory, in ignorance of the explosive nature of the scrap, set it alight with a cigarette, thereby causing an explosion, the carrier was held liable.[74]

If the person to whom they are delivered is not competent to understand a warning, the substances should not be delivered to them at all. In *Yachuk* v. *Oliver Blais Co. Ltd.*[75] a boy of nine obtained petrol from a filling station by falsely saying that it was wanted for his mother's car which " was stuck down the street." He then used it to make a torch for a game he was playing with his younger brother and on lighting the petrol it exploded and he was injured. The owners of the filling station were held liable.

Similarly, explosive substances should be kept in a safe place where they are not likely to be interfered with. Where a schoolmaster left a bottle containing a stick of phosphorus in a conservatory to which the the boys had access, and the plaintiff, one of the boys, took the bottle and played with it so that it burst and he was injured, the schoolmaster was held liable. The Court of Appeal approved of the direction of

70 *Bebee* v. *Sales* (1916) 32 T.L.R. 413.
71 *The Times*, January 29, 1966.
72 *Perry* v. *Kendricks Transport Ltd.* [1956] 1 W.L.R. 85.
73 *Adcock* v. *Loveridge*, *The Times*, June 21, 1956.
74 *Philco Radio Ltd.* v. *Spurling Ltd.* [1949] 2 All E.R. 882.
75 [1949] A.C. 386. It was held that the act of the plaintiff was one which he might be reasonably expected to do, so that there was no contributory negligence or new intervening act.

Cave J. that if a man kept dangerous things he must keep them safely and must take such precautions as a prudent man would take, and to leave such things about in the way of boys would not be reasonable care.[76]

8.—POISON

557 **Liability for poisons.** Poison when in liquid or gaseous form imposes the same liability upon those who own or control it as does water or gas, and reference should be made to the previous sections dealing with those subjects.

558 **Poisonous fumes.** When a tramway company had statutory authority to lay wood paving between their tram lines and used creosoted wood blocks, the fumes from which damaged the crops of a market gardener, it was held that they were liable to the gardener.[77] "Creosote is like the wild animals in the old cases, the water in *Rylands* v. *Fletcher*, and the electric fluid in *National Telephone Co.* v. *Baker*."[78] In this case the statute authorised wood paving but not creosoted wood paving, and it was held that the defence of statutory authority could not be established without showing that creosoted wood blocks were authorised either expressly or by necessary implication. Further, it was held to be no defence that the authority had no knowledge of the poisonous nature of the substance. Again, when the defendants shipped ferro-silicon on board a keel belonging to the plaintiff's husband, and the ferro-silicon gave off poisonous fumes which killed her husband and injured the plaintiff herself, it was held that the defendants were liable to the plaintiff although they were ignorant of the danger arising from ferro-silicon.[79]

559 **Liquid poisons.** A highway authority who sprayed one of their roads with tar were held liable to the plaintiff whose watercress beds were damaged by tar acid from the road.[80] The defendants had statutory authority to spray their roads with tar, but it was held that this did not necessarily involve draining the water from the roads through the plaintiff's watercress beds. Where an oil company sent oil by rail in a defective tank from which the oil leaked and got into a watercourse, making the water unfit to be drunk by cattle, it was held that the company were liable for the resulting damage on the ground that they had consigned the tank in a condition in which oil was likely to escape from it.[81]

560 **Poisons left in an easily accessible position.** Poisons, like explosives, must not be left in a place easily accessible to third parties who may

76 *Williams* v. *Eady* (1893) 10 T.L.R. 41. *Cf. Shepherd* v. *Essex C.C.* (1913) 29 T.L.R. 303, where a jury found no negligence on the facts.
77 *West* v. *Bristol Tramways Co.* [1908] 2 K.B. 14.
78 [1893] 2 Ch. 186. *Per* Phillimore J. [1908] 2 K.B. 14 at p. 16, approved by the C.A.
79 *Bamfield* v. *Goole and Sheffield Transport Co.* [1910] 2 K.B. 94.
80 *Dell* v. *Chesham U.D.C.* [1921] 3 K.B. 427.
81 *Smith* v. *G.W. Ry.* (1926) 42 T.L.R. 391.

carelessly use them and so damage themselves or others.[82] A boat owner, who employed a joiner to repair his boats, was held liable for the act of the joiner in leaving scrapings of paint from the boats in a field where they poisoned a cow.[83] In giving judgment Lord Dundas said: "The job in question was quite a simple one. . . . It involved a risk that poisonous matter in the shape of chips or flakes might be left about on the surrounding grass. I think that risk imposed a duty on the defender to avoid dangerous consequences to the pursuer and to the public, and I do not think he could free himself by delegation." Again, a local authority who planted in a public park shrubs with poisonous berries of attractive appearance were held liable for the death of a boy of seven who ate some of the berries, on the ground that "there was fault in having such a shrub where it was without definite warning of its danger and definite protection against the danger being incurred."[84] When the poison is in a place to which the public has access, a mere warning of the danger is not enough; there must be some further precaution taken, either by removing the poisonous nature of the thing in question, if such a course is possible, or by putting it in such a position that it is not accessible. When the poison is not in a place to which the public has access, the duty is the same as that in respect of loaded guns and explosive substances.

561 **Yew trees.** The owner of yew trees, the leaves of which are poisonous to cattle, must prevent the leaves from projecting over the boundary of his neighbour's land. If he fails to do this, and his neighbour's cattle are poisoned through eating the leaves, he is liable for the damage on the principle of *Rylands* v. *Fletcher*.[85] On the other hand, if he fulfils his duty, but his neighbour's cattle are poisoned by putting their heads over the boundary fence or otherwise trespassing on his land, he is not liable.[86] But if the trespass is caused because he has failed to maintain a fence, which by contract, prescription or otherwise he is bound to maintain, between his land and that of his neighbour, and his neighbour's cattle are poisoned on his land, he is liable.[87] Nevertheless, if a landlord lets land to a tenant and, at the time of the letting, there are yew trees upon other land belonging to the landlord which overhang the tenant's land, so that the tenant's cattle are poisoned from eating the yew trees, the landlord is not liable.[88]

562 **Animals poisoned on defendant's land.** A person who puts poisoned food on his own land with the object of poisoning animals attracted

[82] *Ante*, §§ 552, 556.
[83] *Stewart* v. *Adams*, 1920 S.C. 129.
[84] *Glasgow Corpn.* v. *Taylor* [1922] 1 A.C. 44, 63. For liability in respect of public parks, see *ante*, § 384.
[85] *Crowhurst* v. *Amersham Burial Board* (1878) 4 Ex.D. 5; *Wilson* v. *Newberry* (1871) L.R. 7 Q.B. 31.
[86] *Ponting* v. *Noakes* [1894] 2 Q.B. 281.
[87] *Lawrence* v. *Jenkins* (1873) L.R. 8 Q.B. 274.
[88] *Cheater* v. *Cater* [1918] 1 K.B. 247; *Erskine* v. *Adeane* (1873) L.R. 8 Ch. 756.

by the food on to his land is liable to the owner of the animal.[89] But if the poison is put down for another purpose, the person putting it down is not liable unless he should have foreseen that it was likely to poison animals brought legitimately to his premises. A confectioner, who put some poisoned bread and cheese behind the counter of his shop with the object of poisoning rats and mice, was held not liable to the owner of a dog which was poisoned by going behind the counter and eating the poisoned food.[90]

When the land of the plaintiff was separated from that of the defendant by a wire fence which the defendant was bound by contract to maintain, and the wire decayed so that a piece broke off and fell on the plaintiff's land where it was swallowed by one of his cows which in consequence died, it was held that the defendant was liable.[91]

63 **Sale of poisons.** The sale of poisons is regulated by the Pharmacy and Poisons Act 1933, as amended by the Pharmacy and Medicines Act 1941 and the Pharmacy Act 1954.

9.—NUCLEAR INSTALLATIONS [92]

64 **Generally.** As a result of the first uses made of the release of atomic energy for military purposes, the harnessing of such enormous sources of power for peaceful purposes has become essential. Nevertheless, with the potential risks involved of widespread damage being caused, maybe costing many millions of pounds following any accidental release of a single emission of ionising radiations, the setting up of nuclear installations created entirely new problems which had not before been experienced. Not the least of these was that of legal liability generally for such a disastrous " escape," should it occur, since the common law was wholly inadequate to provide an acceptable solution in the circumstances, whether by action in negligence, nuisance or based on the rule of absolute liability under *Rylands* v. *Fletcher*. The solution, which has been reached, equally has had to be an innovation.

65 **Nuclear Installations Act 1965.** By virtue of the provisions of the Nuclear Installations Act 1965[93] no person other than the United Kingdom Atomic Energy Authority shall use any site for the operation of nuclear plant, unless a licence to do so has been granted by the Minister of Power in respect of it. Such licences for nuclear sites are granted only to cor-

[89] *Townsend* v. *Wathen* (1808) 9 East 277.
[90] *Stansfeld* v. *Bolling* (1870) 22 L.T. 799.
[91] *Firth* v. *Bowling Iron Co.* (1878) 3 C.P.D. 254.
[92] The leading work on this subject is the *Law Relating to Nuclear Energy* (1966) Street and Frame.
[93] Which consolidates with an exception (s. 29 (1)) the Nuclear Installations Acts 1959 and 1965 *i.e.* the Nuclear Installation (Licensing and Insurance) Act 1959 and the Nuclear Installation (Amendment) Act 1965. The Nuclear Installations Act 1965 (Commencement No. 1) Order 1965 (S.I. 1965 No. 1880) brought the Act into force on December 1, 1965, except for section 17 (5) which bars enforcement in the United Kingdom of certain foreign judgments.

porate bodies and are not transferable.[94] Liability can only arise in connection with any licensed nuclear site and it arises when a nuclear incident occurs at or in connection with certain nuclear installations, or in the course of carriage of nuclear matter. The Act applies to occurrences outside the United Kingdom.[95]

566 **Who is liable?** The principle of the Act has restricted all liability to licensees only, which has also simplified the necessary insurance arrangements, since there is no need to extend the cover to such additional persons such as the manufacturers, suppliers and contractors. Thus the Act confers on certain victims of exposure to the emission of radiation a statutory right to compensation against the licensee deemed responsible for the occurrence.[96] The United Kingdom Atomic Energy Authority and other Government Departments are likewise liable for emissions from their sites, by virtue of section 8.

Further, section 12 (1) provides that: " where any injury or damage has been caused in breach of a duty imposed " by the Act, then, subject to certain exceptions, " no other liability shall be incurred by any person in respect of that injury or damage." This effectively prevents the licensee from obtaining either an indemnity arising out of any contract [97] or contribution from any negligent third party [98] so that he alone still remains liable. Nevertheless in order to meet a situation where two or more licensees are responsible in respect of the same injury incurred, section 17 (3) expressly provides that both or all of those persons shall be treated as jointly and severally liable in respect of that injury or damage.

567 **The duty of the licensee.** It is enacted by section 7 (1): " It shall be the duty of the licensee to secure that—

(*a*) no such occurrence involving nuclear matter as is mentioned in subsection (2) of this section causes injury to any person or damage to any property of any person other than the licensee, being injury or damage arising out of, or resulting from the radioactive properties, or a combination of those and any toxic explosive or other hazardous properties, of that nuclear matter; and

(*b*) no ionising radiations emitted during the period of the licensee's responsibility—

(i) from anything caused or suffered by the licensee to be on the site which is not nuclear matter; or

[94] s. 3 (1).

[95] s. 12 (1).

[96] It is not actually necessary that the dangerous matter should " escape " as such from the site, where it is kept, on to other land, since by the very nature of radioactivity dangerous emissions occur constantly as do, for example, all the harmful rays of the sun.

[97] It should also prevent licensees from invoking the principle in *Lister* v. *Romford Ice Co. Ltd.* [1957] A.C. 555 as a means of claiming an indemnity from the employee whose negligence caused the nuclear occurrence.

[98] Contribution is only obtainable as between joint tortfeasors and for the purposes of the Act there can be only one tortfeasor, *viz.*: the licensee.

(ii) from any waste discharged (in whatever form) on or from the site,

cause injury to any person or damage to any property of any person other than the licensee."

The duty is one of absolute liability and it is unnecessary to prove negligence on the part of anyone. There is one exception only, which is contained in section 13 (4), to the absolute nature of this liability, *viz.* that it is a defence that the breach of statutory duty is attributable to hostile action in the course of any armed conflict, including any armed conflict within the United Kingdom. It is not, however, a defence which would be available otherwise under the rule in *Rylands* v. *Fletcher*, that the breach is attributable to a natural disaster, notwithstanding that the disaster is of such an exceptional character that it could not reasonably have been foreseen.[99] By virtue of section 13 (6) damages may be reduced by reason of the fault of the plaintiff if, but only if, and to the extent that, the causing of that injury or damage is attributable to any act of the plaintiff committed with the intention of causing harm to any person or property or with reckless disregard for the consequences of his act. This seems to be distinguishable from the provisions of the Law Reform (Contributory Negligence) Act 1945, where both the degree of blameworthiness and the causative potency of the plaintiff's act have to be taken into consideration in reducing damages. It would seem therefore that if a trespasser on the site is hurt by a nuclear incident, provided that he is not guilty of any such intentional or reckless conduct, he is not precluded from recovering damages in full.

568 **The damage suffered.** " Injury " for the purposes of the statutory obligation imposed by the Act means " personal injury and includes loss of life "[1] whilst " damage to any property " must be physical damage to the fabric or its contents. Losses which normally follow from such damage, namely loss of earnings, loss of profits, reduction of value and loss of use, etc., must also be recoverable but only in so far as they are consequential upon such injury or damage.[2] In the absence of any physical harm no remedy can lie.

569 **Special periods of limitation.** Section 15 (1) enacts that: " notwithstanding anything in any other enactment " a claim under the Act shall not be entertained " if made at any time after the expiration of thirty years from the relevant date," which date is that of the occurrence that gave rise to the claim and not of the infliction of damage. Where that occurrence was a continuing one or was one of a succession, all of which were attributable to a particular happening on a particular relevant site,

[99] s. 13 (4) (*b*).

[1] s. 26 (1).

[2] See generally " Economic loss," Chap. 2, § 42, *ante*. *S.C.M.* (*United Kingdom*) v. *W. J. Whittall & Son Ltd.* [1971] 1 Q.B. 337, affirming Thesiger J. [1970] 1 W.L.R. 1017. See also § 159 *ante*, note 67.

or to the carrying out from time to time on a particular relevant site of a particular operation, the limitation period begins to run from the date of the last of those events.

Where a claim arises in respect of injury or damage caused by an occurrence involving nuclear matter stolen from, or lost, jettisoned or abandoned by the person whose breach of statutory duty under the Act gave rise to the claim it is provided by section 15 (2) that the limitation period in such circumstances is the period of twenty years. This period is to be calculated " beginning with the day when the nuclear matter in question was so stolen, lost, jettisoned or abandoned."

570 **Arrangements for insurance.** The Act acknowledges the impossibility of meeting compensation without insurance, so that the licensees are required to take out an insurance cover against their statutory liability.[3] Since the insurance companies had refused to provide such cover for either unlimited damages or for an intended period, as a result of the carefully worked out arrangement between them and the Government, the ceiling figure of five million pounds sterling was agreed upon and the cover extends only in respect of the first ten years.

Where claims in excess of this five million pounds or other [4] limit are made or they are made more than ten years after the cause of action arose, the licensee is not required to pay in satisfaction of these uninsured losses unless Parliament has appropriated the necessary funds to meet them. In these circumstances the claim must be directed to the appropriate Minister.[5] The terms of section 12 (1) are wide enough to bar any claim against the licensee beyond the statutory limits of this new cause of action given by the Act; thus the above restrictions cannot ordinarily be evaded; by pursuing some alternative claim against the licensee based upon negligence, nuisance or, even, *Rylands* v. *Fletcher*.

[3] s. 19.

[4] But in respect of cover for compensation for course of carriage, s. 21 limited the aggregate amount to one and three quarter million pounds.

[5] s. 16 (3), *i.e.* if against the Authority (s. 8), it is the Minister of Technology; if against government departments to the Minister in charge of that department; in any other case, to the Minister of Power.

CHAPTER 10

ANIMALS

571 **Generally.** Although there are similarities between the tort relating to dangerous animals and the tort considered in the previous chapter, based on the rule in *Rylands* v. *Fletcher*,[1] in that they are both examples of strict liability in form, they are nevertheless still distinct and separate torts. One obvious difference between them is that no escape from the defendant's land is an essential ingredient of the tort, assuming that the animal had ever been on the defendant's land in the first place. Another distinction is that natural use of the land is not a defence in the case of a dangerous animal.[2]

572 **Principles of liability.** Prior to October 1, 1971, the law dealing with damage caused by animals was somewhat complicated.[3] From early days the owner had been liable for damage caused by his animals when trespassing on the land of another. Apart from trespass there was no liability at all for damage done by domestic animals. In time, however, the owner became liable for some damage done by domestic animals, but this was only for such damage as he knew the particular animal had a propensity to commit—liability was based on what was termed *scienter*.[4] For damage done by wild animals the owner was absolutely liable. Very much later it was recognised that the ordinary duty to take care to prevent damage applied to animals as well as to other things but this was a modern development which had to be fitted on to the earlier law, with the result of creating not only some complexity but also some uncertainty in the law. For example, it was not settled whether, in actions for trespass and negligence, the damages included injury to human beings in the absence of proof of *scienter*.[5]

Sensible and rational changes in the law took a long time in coming. In 1953 a report was produced on the law [6] but it was not until 1967 that the Law Commission resumed consideration of reform and reported

[1] (1868) L.R. 3 H.L. 330.

[2] *Rands* v. *McNeil* [1955] 1 Q.B. 253. See observations of Denning L.J. at p. 258; *Behrens* v. *Bertram Mills Circus Ltd.* [1957] 2 Q.B. 1, at pp. 21, 22.

[3] See Glanville Williams, "*Liability for Animals*" (Cambridge 1939) for a full account of the common law on this subject; Holdsworth 55 L.Q.R. 588–591.

[4] See § 578, *post*.

[5] For a fuller discussion of the state of the law prior to the passing of the Animals Act 1971, see *Charlesworth on Negligence*, Fourth Edition, Chap. 17. See also *post*, § 601, "Liability for Trespass."

[6] Report of the Committee on the Law of Civil Liability for Damage done by Animals (1953) Cmd. 8746.

to Parliament [7] submitting a draft Bill [8] to give effect to their recommendations. Finally the Animals Act 1971 has emerged, coming into operation on October 1, 1971.[9]

Liability for damage caused by animals must be considered under the heads: (1) Strict liability for damage done by animals; (2) Liability for negligence; and (3) Liability for trespass.

1.—STRICT LIABILITY FOR DAMAGE DONE BY ANIMALS

573 **Dangerous and non-dangerous species of animals.** At common law, under this heading, animals are divided into two classes. Bankes L.J. explained that " the first includes animals *ferae naturae*, for example a tiger or a gorilla, which are obviously of a dangerous nature, although individuals may be more or less tamed. A person who keeps an animal of this class keeps it at his peril. If he loses control of it and it does damage he is responsible. The second class includes dogs, cows, and horses, which are not naturally dangerous to mankind. Of this class individuals may develop dangerous propensities, but unless and until they do so they are not treated as belonging to the class of animals which the owner keeps at his peril; and, leaving trespass aside for the present, the owner is not responsible for damage which these animals may do when not trespassing. An individual of this class, however, may cease to be one for whose damage its owner is not responsible, if it has given him indications of a vicious or dangerous disposition. When the animal has been found by its owner to possess such a nature it passes into the class of animals which the owner keeps at his peril." [10] The test for deciding whether animals were *ferae naturae* for the purpose of liability was not whether they are *ferae naturae* as far as rights of property are concerned,[11] but whether they were dangerous to mankind.[12] In *McQuaker* v. *Goddard* [13] the test applied was whether the animal, in that case a camel, was wild or domesticated. It did not appear, however, that the court

[7] Law Commission Paper No. 13.

[8] The Bill, which was first introduced in the House of Lords, failed to reach the Statute Books before Parliament was dissolved in June 1970. It was therefore reintroduced in July 1970 giving effect with some modifications to the recommendations.

[9] By s. 13 (3). The Act received the Royal Assent on May 12, 1971. See article 112 New L.J. 584.

[10] *Buckle* v. *Holmes* [1926] 2 K.B. 125, at p. 128. See also *R.* v. *Huggins* (1730) 2 Ld.Raym. 1574; and 1 Hale P.C. 430 to the same effect.

[11] *Filburn* v. *People's Palace and Aquarium Co.* (1890) 25 Q.B.D. 258, 260, *per* Lord Esher M.R.

[12] *Buckle* v. *Holmes, supra, per* Bankes L.J. at p. 129; *Clinton* v. *Lyons & Co. Ltd.* [1912] 3 K.B. 198, *per* Ridley J. " The reason for imposing a specially stringent degree of liability upon the keeper of a savage animal is that such an animal has a propensity to attack mankind and, if left unrestrained, would be likely to do so ": *per* Devlin J. in *Behrens* v. *Bertram Mills Circus Ltd.* [1957] 2 Q.B. 1. Dr. Williams suggested (*Liability for Animals*, pp. 296–298) that the dangerous class includes animals not only dangerous to mankind but also animals " likely, if not controlled, to work substantial damage to property." Certainly the Animals Act 1971 in using the word " damage " which is defined in s. 11 does not *exclude* such damage to property.

[13] [1940] 1 K.B. 687, 695. See the criticism of this case by Dr. Williams in 56 L.Q.R. 354.

was attempting to introduce a new test which differed from previous authorities. " Wild animals," said Scott L.J. " are assumed to be dangerous to human beings because they have not been domesticated." The court found that camels were among the oldest domesticated animals in the world and were never found in a wild state so that they could not be dangerous to mankind. It is a question of law whether any particular kind of animal falls into one class or another.[14] Under the Animals Act 1971 [15] a dangerous species is a species [16]

" (*a*) which is not commonly domesticated in the British Islands; and
(*b*) whose fully grown animals normally have such characteristics that they are likely, unless restrained, to cause severe damage or that any damage they may cause is likely to be severe."

574 Where the defendant kept a monkey which bit the plaintiff, Lord Denman C.J. in giving judgment for the plaintiff, said: " Whoever keeps an animal accustomed to attack and bite mankind, with knowledge that it is so accustomed, is prima facie liable in an action on the case at the suit of any person attacked and injured by the animal, without any averment of negligence or default in the securing or taking care of it. The gist of the action is the keeping the animal after knowledge of its mischievous propensities," adding: " a person keeping a mischievous animal with knowledge of its propensities is bound to keep it secure at his peril, and . . ., if it does mischief, negligence is presumed, without express averment." [17] There is nothing unlawful about keeping a dangerous animal. " It is not unlawful or wrongful to keep such an animal; the wrong is in allowing it to escape from the keeper's control with the result that it does damage." [18]

575 If an animal is of a dangerous species, it is immaterial that the owner did not know it to be dangerous or believed that the individual animal

[14] *Filburn* v. *People's Palace and Aquarium Co., supra*; *Mason* v. *Keeling* (1699) 12 Mod. 332, 355; *Besozzi* v. *Harris* (1858) 1 F. & F. 92. Evidence was called in *McQuaker* v. *Goddard, supra*, that a camel was not a wild animal or dangerous to mankind. This was not evidence to prove a question of fact but was to assist the court, which had to take judicial notice of the ordinary course of nature, to ascertain the nature of a camel (Clauson L.J.). The Law Commission, in summarising its recommendations in para. 25 (ii), added: " The question whether an animal belongs to a dangerous species should depend, as is at present the position with the category of animals *ferae naturae*, upon a test prescribed by law; and in determining this question a court should regard as the decisive consideration the risks to persons or property in the circumstances of this country. A species of animals which is generally domesticated in the British Isles should not be regarded in law as dangerous, but with regard to other species their domesticated or non-domesticated character abroad should be taken into account only to the extent that this factor may be relevant to the degree of risk which such species present in the circumstances of this country."

[15] s. 6 (2).

[16] s. 11: " species " includes sub-species and variety.

[17] *May* v. *Burdett* (1846) 9 Q.B. 101. But where there has been no attack by the animal see *Brook* v. *Cook* (1961) 105 S.J. 684.

[18] *Knott* v. *L.C.C.* [1934] 1 K.B. 134, 138, *per* Lord Wright. See also *Jackson* v. *Smithson* (1846) 15 M. & W. 563, *per* Platt B. *Contra*, *Baker* v. *Snell* [1908] 2 K.B. 825, 833, *per* Farwell L.J.

was tame. Where a bear, "tame and docile in its habits," seized a woman as she was passing where it was chained, Crowder J., in directing the jury, said: "The statement in the declaration, that the defendant knew the bear to be of a fierce nature, must be taken to be proved, as every one must know that such animals as lions and bears are of a savage nature." [19] Again, where the plaintiff, in going to feed a bear in a cage, had his arm mauled by the bear, Huddleston B. said that "it mattered not whether the defendants knew or did not know that this bear was savage—they were equally liable and responsible in either case." [20] Where an elephant exhibited by the defendants attacked the plaintiff, and the jury found (1) that the elephant was not an animal dangerous to man; and (2) that the defendants did not know that the elephant was dangerous, the Court of Appeal upheld a judgment for the plaintiff on the ground that elephants as a class were dangerous animals and that it was immaterial whether the particular elephant was a dangerous one, or whether the defendants had any knowledge that it was so.[21] "People must not be wiser than the experience of mankind. If, from the experience of mankind, a particular class of animal is dangerous, though individuals may be tamed, a person who keeps one of the class takes the risk of any damage it may do." [22]

Nor is it a defence that damage resulted because the animal suddenly had been frightened and not from any vicious propensity in its character. Thus in *Behrens* v. *Bertram Mills Circus Ltd.*[23] the defendants were held liable where one of their obedient well behaved Burmese elephants, on the way to perform in the ring, was frightened by a small dog so that it knocked over a booth in which two midgets were on show. Devlin J. pointed out an important distinction when he said: "It does not follow . . . that if an elephant slips or stumbles, its keeper is responsible for the consequences. There must be a failure of control. But here there was such a failure, albeit a very temporary one." [24]

In addition to the animals mentioned above, it has been held that zebras [25] and leopards [26] are dangerous animals, and so is (by a county

19 *Besozzi* v. *Harris*, *supra*.
20 *Wyatt* v. *Rosherville Gardens Co.* (1886) 2 T.L.R. 282.
21 *Filburn* v. *People's Palace and Aquarium Co.* (1890) 25 Q.B.D. 258. *Behrens* v. *Bertram Mills Circus Ltd.* [1957] 2 Q.B. 1, is a similar case.
22 *Ibid.*, *per* Bowen L.J. at p. 261.
23 [1957] 2 Q.B. 1.
24 *Ibid.* at p. 19. *Cf.* the Law Commission's explanation set out in para. 19: "The strict liability which we recommend should be imposed for animals of a dangerous species and for other animals possessing known dangerous characteristics should not in our view depend on the 'escape from control' of the animal. In the circumstances suggested by Devlin J. in *Behrens* v. *Bertram Mills Circus Ltd.* if an elephant 'slips or stumbles' we think the keeper should be liable for any injury or damage which it thereby causes. We would favour the approach adopted by the Court of Appeal of British Columbia in *McNeill* v. *Frankenfield* (1963) 44 D.L.R. (2d) 132 where the Court, in dealing with the requirement of 'escape' in respect of a tethered dog, said that for a dog to 'escape' in this sense it was not necessary that it should get at large or loose, but merely that the control or restraint that one assumes a keeper will put on a vicious dog proved in fact insufficient to prevent the dog doing injury."
25 *Marlor* v. *Ball* (1900) 16 T.L.R. 239.
26 *Sylvester* v. *Chapman Ltd.* (1935) 79 S.J. 777.

court decision) a serval cat.[27] A camel is not since it is a domestic and not a wild animal in England or, indeed, anywhere else in the world.[28] Bees are probably not dangerous animals.[29]

576 **Liability for damage done by dangerous animals.** At common law the obligation of the owner [30] of an animal of the dangerous class was to keep it secure at his peril. It was not necessary to show that it had escaped from his land or from his control. A dangerous animal kept in a cage imposed liability on the owner if it caused damage by putting its paw or its teeth through the cage.[31] The animal had to be "so confined as to be incapable of doing damage." [32] The owner was liable for any damage it may do while it was out of control.[33] But where a boy aged ten years climbed in between the safety barriers in order to get up closer to a lion's cage and was mauled to death by the animal, the defendant owners were held not liable since the boy was a trespasser at that place where he had been seized and no lion had either escaped or had got out of control.[34]

The damage for which the owner was liable was not restricted to damage to human beings. It extended to all damage caused by the act of the animal. For example the owner of a mischievous dog, known to have a tendency to chase animals, has been held liable at common law for damage to sheep [35] and to game.[36] Liability was not confined to damage which was caused by viciousness, but even accidental damage was included so that considerations of malevolence or *mens rea* were quite irrelevant.[37]

577 From October 1, 1971, the common law rules imposing a strict liability in tort for damage done by an animal on the ground that the

27 *The Times*, November 13, 1923 (Judge Tobin, K.C.).

28 *McQuaker* v. *Goddard* [1940] 1 K.B. 687.

29 The responsibilities of an owner of contained (hived) bees is not entirely free from doubt. The Irish case of *O'Gorman* v. *O'Gorman* [1903] 2 Ir.R. 573, where a man was injured as the result of angered bees stinging his horse, was decided on a finding of negligence and is some authority for the proposition that bees are not *per se* "dangerous animals"; but in a later comparable Canadian case *Lucas* v. *Pettit* (1906) 12 O.L.R. 448 where the beekeeper was also held liable it was decided that the doctrine of *scienter* had no application. See also *Robins* v. *Kennedy* (1931) N.Z.L.R. 1134.

30 "Owner" in this connection includes the person having possession or control.

31 *Wyatt* v. *Rosherville Gardens* (1886) 2 T.L.R. 282; *Pearson* v. *Coleman* [1948] 2 K.B. 359; *Besozzi* v. *Harris* (1858) 1 F. & F. 92, where a bear was chained. In *Filburn's* case, *supra*, the elephant was performing when it attacked the plaintiff, a spectator, but it did not escape. See also, *per* Lord Simonds in *Read* v. *J. Lyons & Co. Ltd.* [1947] A.C. 156. In *Rands* v. *McNeil* [1955] 1 Q.B. 253, where a dangerous bull untethered in a loose box had injured a farm hand who had entered the box, the farmer was held not liable on the ground (*inter alia*) that the bull had not escaped. There were other and better grounds for the decision. It is submitted that this cannot be an authority for the proposition that the animal must escape before the owner is liable. *Cf.* the position of a trespasser, however, in *Murphy* v. *Zoological Society of London*, *The Times*, November 14, 1962.

32 *Pearson* v. *Coleman*, *supra*, *per* Evershed L.J.

33 *Behrens* v. *Bertram Mills Circus Ltd.* [1957] 2 Q.B. 1. See also 73 L.Q.R. 149.

34 *Murphy* v. *Zoological Society of London*, *supra*.

35 *Card* v. *Case* (1848) 5 C.B. 622. See "Dogs" *post*, § 592.

36 *Read* v. *Edwards* (1864) 17 C.B.(N.S.) 245.

37 *Behrens* v. *Bertram Mills Circus Ltd.*, *supra*, at p. 17 Devlin J. observed: "If a person wakes up in the middle of the night and finds an escaping tiger on top of his bed and suffers a heart attack, it would be nothing to the point that the intentions of the tiger were quite amiable."

animal was regarded as *ferae naturae* have been replaced by the new form of strict liability provided by the Animals Act 1971. By section 2 (1) it is enacted that where any damage [38] is caused by an animal which belongs to a dangerous species,[39] any person who is a keeper [40] of the animal is liable for the damage, except as otherwise provided by provisions of section 5.[41] A dangerous species [39] is a species [42] (a) which is not commonly domesticated in the British Islands; and (b) whose fully grown animals normally have such characteristics that they are likely, unless restrained, to cause severe damage or that any damage they may cause is likely to be severe.

578 On the other hand in the case of animals which were not dangerous to mankind, it was necessary to prove that the owner knew that the individual animal had a propensity [43] to do the kind of damage in question. This was termed proof of *scienter*. When *scienter* was proved, the owner was liable without proof of negligence. For example, where a ram, known to the owner to be accustomed to attack mankind, attacked and injured a woman the owner was held liable, Alderson B. saying: " There is no distinction between the case of an animal which breaks through the tameness of its nature, and is fierce, and known by the owner to be so, and one which is *ferae naturae*." [44] Also, where a bull, known to be accustomed to run at anything red, attacked a man who was wearing a red tie, in the street, the owner was held liable.[45] Again on *scienter* being proved, the owner was held liable for a dog killing sheep [46] and game [47] and biting human beings.[48] A propensity, known to the owner, of a horse to wander on to the highway did not, however, make the owner liable for the resulting damage, because an owner was under no duty to prevent his animals from straying on to the highway [49] but a propensity to leap over hedges on to passers-by on the highway would make him liable if he knew of it.[50] Therefore unless *scienter* could be proved, it was necessary to prove negligence or trespass if the plaintiff were to succeed. Accordingly, the plaintiff failed, in the absence of proof of *scienter*,

[38] Defined in s. 11 as including " the death of, or injury to, any person (including any disease and any impairment of physical or mental condition)."
[39] Defined in s. 6 (2).
[40] Defined in s. 6 (3).
[41] For these exceptions from liability see also § 587, *post*.
[42] Species is defined by s. 11 as including " sub-species and variety."
[43] *I.e.* " a propensity which is really likely to be dangerous," *per* Willmer L.J. and " a propensity to attack people," *per* Danckwerts L.J. in *Fitzgerald* v. *E.D. & A.D. Cooke Bourne* (*Farms*) *Ltd.* [1964] 1 Q.B. 249.
[44] *Jackson* v. *Smithson* (1846) 15 M. & W. 563. See also to the same effect, *per* Willes J. in *Cox* v. *Burbridge* (1863) 13 C.B.(N.S.) 430, *per* Atkin L.J. in *Manton* v. *Brocklebank* [1923] 2 K.B. 212, *per* Bankes L.J. in *Buckle* v. *Holmes* [1926] 2 K.B. 125.
[45] *Hudson* v. *Roberts* (1851) L.R. 6 Ex. 697.
[46] *Card* v. *Case, supra.*
[47] *Read* v. *Edwards, supra.*
[48] *Gould* v. *McAuliffe* [1941] 2 All E.R. 527.
[49] *Searle* v. *Wallbank* [1947] A.C. 341. But see now the provisions of s. 8 of the Animals Act 1971 and Chap. 12, " Highways," § 848 *et seq.*
[50] *Brock* v. *Richards* [1951] 1 K.B. 529.

when a horse on the highway kicked a child,[51] bit a man,[52] a mare in a field kicked a horse,[53] a cat with kittens attacked a woman,[54] a dog bit a man,[55] a cat killed some pigeons,[56] a bullock attacked a cyclist in the street,[57] a horse jumped over a hedge into a motor-cyclist on the highway,[58] a dog killed rabbits kept in a hutch for commercial purposes.[59]

579 However, the Court of Appeal in *Fitzgerald* v. *E.D. & A.D. Cooke Bourne* (*Farms*) *Ltd.*[60] affirmed emphatically that the propensity to be proved needed to be an unnatural one for the kind of animal in question, namely one that was really likely to be dangerous arising out of viciousness and hostility and not out of some mischievous playfulness. So where the plaintiff, while walking along a public footpath through a field, fell and was injured as a result of a young unbroken thoroughbred filly coming up to her at a gallop, prancing around then bumping into her with its shoulder, it was held that as the filly was merely indulging in a natural propensity to be playful in its joie de vivre only, there being no hostile attack, the plaintiff's claim for damages based on *scienter* failed.

580 From October 1, 1971, the common law rules imposing a strict liability in tort for damage done by an animal on the ground that its vicious or mischievous propensities were known or presumed to be known have been superseded by the new provisions of the Animals Act 1971. If therefore damage is done by an animal not belonging to a dangerous species, its keeper is liable only if the animal has abnormal characteristics making it likely that it will cause such damage and those characteristics are known to the keeper. By section 2 (2), except as otherwise provided by section 5 [61] a keeper of such an animal is liable for the damage: " if (*a*) the damage is of a kind which the animal, unless restrained, was likely to cause or which, if caused by the animal, was likely to be severe; and (*b*) the likelihood of the damage or of its being severe was due to characteristics of the animal which are not normally found in animals of the same species or are not normally so found except at particular times or in particular circumstances; and (*c*) those characteristics were known to that keeper or were at any time known to a person who at that time had charge of the animal as that keeper's servant or, where that keeper is the head of a household, were known to another keeper of the animal who is a member of that household and under the age of sixteen."

51 *Cox* v. *Burbridge* (1863) 13 C.B.(N.S.) 430.
52 *Glanville* v. *Sutton* [1928] 1 K.B. 571.
53 *Manton* v. *Brocklebank* [1923] 2 K.B. 212.
54 *Clinton* v. *Lyons & Co. Ltd.* [1912] 3 K.B. 198.
55 *Mason* v. *Keeling* (1699) 12 Mod. 332.
56 *Buckle* v. *Holmes* [1926] 2 K.B. 125.
57 *Lathall* v. *Joyce* [1939] 3 All E.R. 854.
58 *Brock* v. *Richards, supra.*
59 *Tallents* v. *Bell & Goddard* [1944] 2 All E.R. 474.
60 [1964] 1 Q.B. 249. See the comment upon this case by Professor Heuston (*Salmond on Torts* 15th ed. p. 435) but amusing as it may be in its inference, the decision of the Court of Appeal was clearly correct in the circumstances of the case.
61 See *post*, § 588.

581 **Who is liable?** Under the Animals Act 1971 the liability for damage done by a dangerous animal, whether it belongs to a dangerous species or otherwise because of the provisions of section 2 (2), falls upon the keeper of the animal. By virtue of section 6 (3) a person is a keeper of an animal if (subject to subsection (4) of the section):

"(*a*) he owns the animal or has it in his possession [62]; or

(*b*) he is the head of a household of which a member under the age of sixteen owns the animal or has it in his possession."

At common law an owner who was in possession of the animal could not escape liability by abandoning ownership either before or after the damage was done.[63] Until he had transferred the ownership to another he was liable for not keeping it under control. His liability being based on strict liability similar to the rule in *Rylands* v. *Fletcher* [64] he could not relieve himself from responsibility by delegating the performance of his duty to an independent contractor. In the words of Atkin L.J.: "Can the person who has acquired a tiger, so long as he remains its owner, relieve himself of responsibility by contracting with a third person for its custody?" [65] So, too, as Lord Wright observed: "In the case of dangerous animals, a transfer of actual possession and control would not necessarily terminate his [the owner's] responsibility." [66] Section 6 (3) preserves and embodies the common law on this point by adding that: "if at any time an animal ceases to be owned by or to be in the possession of a person, any person who immediately before that time was a keeper thereof by virtue of the preceding provisions of this subsection continues to be a keeper of the animal until another person becomes a keeper thereof by virtue of those provisions."

582 In view of the definition of "a keeper" more than one person can be held liable for the same animal namely the owner and, in addition, the person having its possession and control. So, where a dog, the property of a former servant of the defendant, was allowed to live at his premises by the defendant, it was held that the latter was liable for damage done by it on the ground that he was harbouring the dog.[67] But where the defendant's daughter aged seventeen, who lived with the defendant, was the owner and had the control of a savage dog, it was held that the fact that the dog lived on his premises did not make him liable.[68] For the same reason, a local authority, owners and occupiers of a school, were held not vicariously liable for damage done by a dangerous dog

[62] Lord Wright in *Knott* v. *L.C.C.* [1934] 1 K.B. 126, 134, 141, stated the common law position: "The true test of liability, namely that of ownership or possession and control."

[63] *Brady* v. *Warren* [1900] 2 Ir.R. 632; *Dee Conservancy Board* v. *McConnell* [1928] 2 K.B. 159, 163, *per* Scrutton L.J.

[64] *Filburn* v. *People's Palace and Aquarium Co.* (1890) 25 Q.B.D. 258; *Knott* v. *L.C.C.*, *supra* at p. 139, *per* Lord Wright; recognised in numerous cases.

[65] *Belvedere Fish Guano Co.* v. *Rainham Chemical Works* [1920] 2 K.B. 487, 504; commented on by Lords Buckmaster and Parmoor [1921] 2 A.C. 465 at pp. 477, 491.

[66] *Brackenborough* v. *Spalding U.D.C.* [1942] A.C. 310, 324.

[67] *M'Kone* v. *Wood* (1831) 5 C. & P. 1.

[68] *North* v. *Wood* [1914] 1 K.B. 629.

owned by a schoolkeeper, employed by them, although the dog was kept at the school with their consent.[69] The mere fact of the animal being on the defendant's premises when it does damage imposes no liability on the defendant, so that where a dog made a sudden incursion at a railway station, bit the plaintiff and disappeared just as suddenly as it had appeared, the railway company was held not to be liable.[70]

A person with the care and custody of the animal under contract with the owner is under the same liability as the owner, since both are keepers under the Act. A trainer who, under contract with the owner, had a horse which he knew was accustomed to bite in his custody was held liable when the horse, while being taken from the stables to a railway station, bit the plaintiff.[71]

The Act specifically provides that a person shall not be a keeper of an animal by virtue only of the fact of possession where he has taken it into and kept it in possession " for the purpose of preventing it from causing damage or of restoring it to its owner." [72]

583 **Abnormal characteristics known to keeper.** Considerable guidance can still be gained from the common law principles relating to proof of *scienter*.[73] Such proof is made by showing that the animal has a propensity to do the particular kind of damage in question and that the owner knows of it. The best evidence is that the animal has, to the owner's knowledge, done that kind of damage before but it is not essential to go as far as that. Proof of knowledge of unsuccessful attempts is enough.[74] In the case of a bull, evidence by one witness that the owner had said that the bull would run at anything red, and by another witness that he had said that a bull would run at anything red, was held sufficient evidence of *scienter* on the ground that " either expression was some evidence to go to the jury that the defendant knew that this animal was a dangerous one." [75] In an action for damages for being bitten by a dog, where there was no evidence that the dog had ever bitten any person, but it was proved that, to the defendant's knowledge, the dog rushed out of his kennel when any stranger passed and barked and attempted to bite, it was held that *scienter* was established.[76] But if the dog " merely

[69] *Knott* v. *L.C.C.*, *supra*.
[70] *Smith* v. *Great Eastern Ry.* (1866) L.R. 2 C.P. 4.
[71] *Walker* v. *Hall* (1876) 40 J.P. 456.
[72] s. 6 (4).
[73] The Law Commission in para. 18 reported: " The law at present achieves this imposition of strict liability by the *scienter* rule, but we think that this rule requires considerable modification and simplification. We would therefore abolish it in its common law form and substitute a new rule retaining what we conceive to be the essential rationale of the old law. . . ."
[74] See *Barnes* v. *Lucille Ltd.* (1907) 96 L.T. 680. See para. 18 (2) of the Law Commission's report.
[75] *Hudson* v. *Roberts* (1851) 6 Ex. 697.
[76] *Worth* v. *Gilling* (1866) L.R. 2 C.P. 1. See also to the same effect *Osborne* v. *Chocqueel* [1896] 2 K.B. 109. The decision to the contrary of Lord Ellenborough in *Beck* v. *Dyson* (1815) 4 Camp. 198, must be taken to be overruled. Thus the common suggestion that every dog is entitled to its first bite is scarcely accurate law.

had a habit of bounding upon people in play, even although in so doing he might frighten timid persons or cause some little annoyance, that would not sustain the action." [77] The fact that a dog is usually kept tied up is no evidence of *scienter*,[78] but a warning by the owner not to go near the dog is evidence of *scienter*,[79] and so is an offer of compromise, although the latter should carry little or no weight.[80]

584 Proof of *scienter* is established by evidence of one bite by a dog; it is not necessary that the dog should be generally prone to bite.[81] When the defendant went with his dog into a public-house and his dog bit the potman, and half an hour afterwards, in the street, it again bit the potman, it was held, reversing the court below, that the defendant was liable, because "the action was not for the first bite, but for the second. Half an hour had intervened between them, and during that time it was the duty of the defendant, who knew his dog had just bitten a man, to secure him in some way so as to prevent him from biting again." [82] Interrogatories are not admissible to ascertain the names of the persons alleged by the plaintiff to have been previously bitten by the dog.[83]

585 It is not necessary to prove that the defendant's animal is always ferocious, as long as it is proved that, to his knowledge, it is fierce at certain times. So, when it was proved that a bitch which had bitten the plaintiff was, to the defendant's knowledge, fierce when she had pups although harmless at other times, it was held that *scienter* was established, Darling J. asserting: "I do not think, further, that in order to make the owner of the dog liable the dog must be always and invariably ferocious. If the owner knows that at certain periods the dog is ferocious, then he has knowledge that at those times the dog is of such a character that he ought to take care of it." [84]

To prove *scienter* it must be proved that the owner had knowledge of the particular propensity which caused the damage. A disposition to attack men is not proved by showing a disposition to attack sheep.[85] In an action by a man for being bitten by a dog it is not enough to prove that the dog has previously bitten a goat,[86] and a defendant's knowledge that his horse has a propensity to bite horses is not evidence of knowledge of a propensity to bite mankind.[87]

77 *Line* v. *Taylor* (1862) 3 F. & F. 731, *per* Erle C.J.
78 *Beck* v. *Dyson*, *supra*; *Hogan* v. *Sharpe* (1837) 7 Car. & P. 755.
79 *Judge* v. *Cox* (1816) 1 Stark. 285. A "Beware of Dog" sign on the front gate did not imply knowledge that the dog was vicious: *Dolan* v. *Bright*, *The Times*, November 17, 1962.
80 *Thomas* v. *Morgan* (1835) 2 C.M. & R. 496. *Cf. Sanders* v. *Teape and Swan* (1884) 51 L.T. 263.
81 *Charlwood* v. *Greig* (1851) 3 Car. & Kir. 46; *Pacy* v. *Field* (1937) 81 S.J. 160.
82 *Parsons* v. *King* (1891) 8 T.L.R. 114.
83 *Knapp* v. *Harvey* [1911] 2 K.B. 725.
84 *Barnes* v. *Lucille Ltd.* (1907) 96 L.T. 680. *Cf. Howard* v. *Bergin O'Connor & Co.* [1925] 2 Ir.R. 110 (bullock savage when being unloaded from railway).
85 *Hartley* v. *Harriman* (1818) 1 B. & Ald. 620, *per* Ellenborough C.J.
86 *Osborne* v. *Chocqueel* [1896] 2 Q.B. 109.
87 *Glanville* v. *Sutton* [1928] 1 K.B. 571.

586 **Knowledge of keeper's servant.** Section 2 (2) (*c*) of the Animals Act has preserved and widened the scope of the position at common law as regards knowledge to be implied to a keeper by the words " those characteristics . . . were at any time known to a person who at that time had charge of the animal as that keeper's servant or, where that keeper is the head of a household, were known to another keeper of the animal who is a member of that household and under the age of sixteen." Accordingly the knowledge of the mischievous propensity of the animal need not be the personal knowledge of the owner himself, provided that such knowledge is possessed by his servant, who had the care and control of the animal, or by the manager or agent of the owner's business in connection with which the animal is kept. So, the knowledge of a coachman who kept the dog in the stable that the dog was savage was held to be the knowledge of the owner,[88] and complaints made to barmen, servants of the owner of a dog, that the dog had attacked customers in the bar were held to be notice to the owner that his dog was savage, although there was no evidence that the complaints were ever communicated to the owner.[89] A complaint to the owner's wife, who is living with him, is evidence of her husband's knowledge,[90] but a complaint to the owner's husband has been held not to be evidence against the owner in an action brought after her husband's death.[91] Knowledge of the owner's son, aged eleven, that a dog which he was taking out was savage has been held to be evidence of *scienter* on the part of the owner.[92] On the other hand, where the plaintiff was going to a steamship company's premises when he was bitten by their dog, and it was proved that some of the company's servants knew that the dog had previously bitten people, but not that those servants had control of the dog, or the management of the premises, the company were held not liable.[93] Similarly, where a schoolkeeper was allowed by the education authority to keep a dog for his own pleasure, the dog not being used or required for the guarding of the school, the knowledge of the schoolkeeper was held not to be the knowledge of his employers, because it was acquired by him not as servant of the education authority but as owner of the dog.[94] Complaints of a dog's ferocity, made to a domestic servant who did not have charge and which were not communicated to the defendant or his wife, were held not to be evidence of *scienter* on the part of the defendant.[95]

The knowledge required to impose liability is the actual knowledge of the keeper or his servant or agent. It is not enough to prove that he ought to have known of the propensity.[96]

[88] *Baldwin* v. *Casella* (1872) L.R. 7 Ex. 325.
[89] *Applebee* v. *Percy* (1874) L.R. 9 C.P. 647.
[90] *Gladman* v. *Johnson* (1867) 36 L.J.C.P. 153.
[91] *Miller* v. *Kimbray* (1867) 16 L.T. 360.
[92] *Elliott* v. *Longden* (1901) 17 T.L.R. 648.
[93] *Stiles* v. *Cardiff Steam Navigation Co.* (1864) 33 L.J.Q.B. 310.
[94] *Knott* v. *L.C.C.* [1934] 1 K.B. 126, 134.
[95] *Colget* v. *Norrish* (1886) 2 T.L.R. 471.
[96] *Mason* v. *Keeling* (1699) 12 Mod. 332.

587 **Exceptions from liability.** Since liability for dangerous animals and for non-dangerous animals known to have a propensity to cause a particular danger at common law had a similar basis as the rule in *Rylands* v. *Fletcher*, most of the exceptions to liability for damage under that rule also applied although there was considerable doubt whether the act of God was a defence.[97] Equally there was some doubt whether the independent act of a third party was a defence.[98]

On the other hand it was always a defence to prove that the injured person had brought the damage upon himself by meddling with the animal, or that he deliberately or rashly went too near the dangerous animal's cage [99] well knowing that it was dangerous.[1] Accordingly, the owner of some zebras was held not liable when he kept his animals secure in a stable but the plaintiff entered the stable and, in stroking one of the animals, was kicked into the next stall where another zebra bit him.[2] Also, where, seeing a smouldering cigarette on some straw, a servant of the defendants, who was not employed to look after the animals, climbed over the barrier separating the leopard's cage from the part to which the public were admitted and was mauled by the animal, it was held that the defendants were not liable.[3] A child who interfered with a dog of known mischievous propensity by attempting to play with it, was held to have no right of action when he was bitten.[4]

588 Section 2 of the Animals Act clearly imposes liability " except as otherwise provided " and these statutory exceptions from liability are contained in section 5 the first of which is that " a person is not liable . . . for any damage which is due wholly to the fault [5] of the person suffering it." [6] At common law it was also a good defence that the plaintiff was a trespasser [7] upon the defendant's premises when he was injured by the

97 By Bramwell B. in *Nichols* v. *Marsland* (1875) L.R. 10 Ex. 255, at p. 260. For the position after October 1, 1971, see *post*, § 614.

98 See *Charlesworth on Negligence*, 4th ed., § 744. The majority of the C.A. in *Baker* v. *Snell* [1908] 2 K.B. 825 and Devlin J. in *Behrens* v. *Bertram Mills Circus Ltd.* [1957] 2 Q.B. 1 were of the opinion that there was no such defence. *Aliter* the H.L. in the Scottish appeal of *Fleeming* v. *Orr* (1855) 2 Macq. 14 in which Lord Cranworth L.C. thought it was a defence and that the law of England and Scotland were in this respect the same.

99 *Murphy* v. *Zoological Society of London*, *The Times*, November 14, 1962 (a boy aged ten years who was a cub member of a scout group, visited a lion's cage, climbed between two fences, was mauled by the lion and died later). The deceased was held to be a trespasser at that place and as no animal had " escaped " the Zoological Society were not in breach of any duty owed him.

1 In *Behrens* v. *Bertram Mills Circus Ltd.* [1957] 2 Q.B. 1, at p. 19, Devlin J. said of the defence (of the plaintiff's own fault): " I see no reason why the same sort of defence should not prevail where the fault of the plaintiff does not amount to recklessness . . . but is failure of due diligence to look after his own safety."

2 *Marlor* v. *Ball* (1900) 16 T.L.R. 239.

3 *Sylvester* v. *Chapman Ltd.* (1935) 79 S.J. 777.

4 *Lee* v. *Walkers* (1940) 162 L.T. 89; see also *Sycamore* v. *Ley* (1932) 147 L.T. 342.

5 " Fault " is defined in s. 11 as having the same meaning as in the Law Reform (Contributory Negligence) Act 1945. See Chap. 16, *post*, §§ 1019—1022.

6 s. 5 (1).

7 *Lowery* v. *Walker* [1910] 1 K.B. 173; [1911] A.C. 10. Thus a farmer is entitled to keep a dangerous bull in his fields without being liable to a trespasser who enters his land and is attacked.

dangerous animal kept there but this was not necessarily so if the plaintiff was trespassing upon some third party's land. However, if the dangerous animal was kept there for the purpose deliberately of attacking a trespasser there were undoubtedly circumstances in which the defendant could have been held liable.[8] The common law in this respect is reflected in the statutory exception from liability contained in section 5 (3): " A person is not liable under section 2 of this Act for any damage caused by an animal kept on any premises or structure to a person trespassing there, if it is proved either—

(*a*) that the animal was not kept there for the protection of persons or property; or

(*b*) (if the animal was kept there for the protection of persons or property) that keeping it there for that purpose was not unreasonable."

589 Further, there was no valid reason for excluding the maxim of *volenti non fit injuria* from being a complete defence at common law just as it was one to other dangerous things where the plaintiff had agreed to run the risk.[9] Accordingly if a person intervenes to separate his dog involved in a dog-fight he could well expect to have this defence raised against him.[10] Section 5 (2) especially preserves the defence: " A person is not liable under section 2 of this Act for any damage suffered by a person who has voluntarily accepted the risk thereof." Where a farm hand was injured while cleaning out a stall in which a bull, known to be dangerous, was kept untethered without first seeing that the bull was secured (a precaution always taken when the mucking out took place) it was held that the injury was caused by his own fault so that he could not recover damages.[11] However, section 6 (5) provides for such a situation: " Where a person employed as a servant by a keeper of an animal incurs a risk incidental to his employment he shall not be treated as accepting it voluntarily."

590 **Contributory negligence.** Although the Animals Act is silent on the matter there is no reason to suppose that the partial defence that the plaintiff had contributed by his negligence to the injury or damage should be excluded in any way.[12]

[8] *Sarch* v. *Blackburn* (1830) 4 C. & P. 297. *Cf.* the keeping of a savage dog in order to deter a burglar.

[9] *Behrens* v. *Bertram Mills Circus Ltd.* [1957] 2 Q.B. 1.

[10] *Smith* v. *Shields* (1964) 108 S.J. 501.

[11] *Rands* v. *McNeil* [1955] 1 Q.B. 253, at p. 266 Jenkins L.J. said, " I do not think that this doctrine of absolute liability can reasonably be applied as between a farmer and the persons employed by him on his farm in relation to the handling by those persons of an animal such as a bull kept by the farmer." See, *per* Denning L.J. at p. 257 for a statement upon the duty of care at common law in a case such as this.

[12] Certainly the Law Commission recommended its retention in para. 21 and added in a footnote: " In view of the emphasis which we have placed on the possibility of insurance . . . it could be argued that the negligence of the plaintiff should be neither a complete nor a partial defence to any claim against the keeper of a dangerous animal, but we doubt whether public opinion would accept so great a departure from the traditional basis of tort liability."

591 **Doctrine of scienter: no application to breach of contract.** The doctrine of *scienter* never had any application to breach of contract. So where the plaintiff's horse was agisted with the defendant and was gored by a bull, not known by the defendant to be savage, which had got into the defendant's field owing to defective fences, it was held that the defendant was liable.[13] Blackburn J. said: " It is a question of fact whether he [the defendant] took sufficient care or not, and the doctrine of *scienter*, which, as I have said, depends mainly upon authority, ought not to be extended to a contract to take reasonable care." [14]

592 **Dogs.** With regard to dogs, the doctrine of *scienter* had been modified by statute firstly by the Dogs Act 1906 as amended by the Dogs (Amendment) Act 1928 and again by the Animals Act 1971,[15] section 3 of which provides: " Where a dog causes damage by killing or injuring livestock,[16] any person who is a keeper of the dog is liable for the damage, except as otherwise provided by this Act." These exceptions to liability are contained in section 5, subsection (1) of which exonerates a dog-keeper " for any damage which is due wholly to the fault of the person suffering it " and subsection (4) further exonerates a dog-keeper " if the livestock was killed or injured on land on to which it had strayed and either the dog belonged to the occupier or its presence on the land was authorised by the occupier." See § 607, *post*, regarding liability in the case of a dog that trespasses.

593 **Cats.** The owner of a cat was only liable for damage done by it, without negligence on the owner's part, on proof of *scienter*. Where a cat with kittens was kept on the premises of a teashop and, to the knowledge of the manageress, had a disposition to attack a dog in her neighbourhood, it was held that the owners of the cat were not liable for damage done by the cat to a person entering the teashop with a dog in her arms, on the ground that " the facts appear . . . to show that the cat was not dangerous to human beings but to dogs." It was also held, however, that they were not liable for the injury inflicted by the cat on the dog, having regard to the jury's finding that the owners knew that the cat, when with kittens, was dangerous to dogs it is difficult to accept this as a considered statement of the law.[17]

2.—Liability for Negligence

594 **Principles of liability.** Liability for animals which belong to a dangerous

13 *Smith* v. *Cook* (1876) 1 Q.B.D. 79.

14 *Ibid.* at p. 83.

15 s. 13 (2) of which repealed subs. (1) to (3) of s. 1 of the Dogs Act 1906 and the words " in both places where that word occurs " contained in s. 1 (1) of the Dogs (Amendment) Act 1928.

16 Defined in s. 11 as meaning: " cattle, horses, asses, mules, hinnies, sheep, pigs, goats and poultry, and also deer not in the wild state and, in s. 3 . . . also, while in captivity, pheasants, partridges and grouse."

17 *Clinton* v. *Lyons & Co. Ltd.* [1912] 3 K.B. 198. See Sir John Salmond's criticism on this point, *Law of Torts* (6th ed., the last by Sir J. Salmond), p. 473 (omitted in 13th ed.), which, it is submitted, is well founded. For trespass by cats, see *post*, § 608.

species or which are known to be dangerous is independent of negligence, but liability for animals not known to be dangerous depends on negligence.[18] There is a duty to take reasonable care to prevent damage from animals, what is reasonable care depending on the nature and habits of the kind of animal concerned, the circumstances of the case and the usual practice of mankind in dealing with that kind of animal. The rule is thus stated by Lord Atkin: " Quite apart from the liability imposed upon the owner of animals or the person having control of them by reason of knowledge of their propensities, there is the ordinary duty of a person to take care either that his animal or his chattel is not put to such a use as is likely to injure his neighbour—the ordinary duty to take care in the cases put upon negligence." [19] In a case where a plaintiff was injured by a playful filly whilst crossing a field over which there was a right of way Diplock L.J. said: " The owner of domestic animals which are not known to him to be vicious in the sense which I have explained, which are grazing upon land on which he has a right to depasture them, owes no duty to a person exercising his right of using a highway which passes across or adjoins that land to take any steps to prevent their causing damage in the course of following the natural propensities of their kind. The solution which the common law imposes in this conflict of rights is that this is a risk which users of country footpaths must themselves assume." [20]

595 **Cases of no negligence.** As a general rule there is no liability " where tame animals with no special individual mischievous propensity are lawfully let loose in the course of the ordinary use of them, and the only danger to be apprehended is from contact with other animals in places where they may all lawfully be." [21] The rule is the same as regards danger to human beings.[22] But the circumstances may be such as to show that damage is likely to result if the animal is allowed liberty, and the owner will then be liable if it does result. " The root of this liability is negligence, and what is negligence depends on the facts with which you have to deal. . . . If the possibility of danger emerging is only a mere possibility which would never occur to the mind of a reasonable man, then there is no negligence in not having taken extraordinary precautions." [23] Accordingly, where a dog was shut up in a motor-car, left in the highway, and the plaintiff was struck in the eye by a splinter of glass caused by the dog bounding about inside the car and breaking a window, the owner was held not liable because the occurrence was such that " according to no reasonable standard could it be said that it ought to have been foreseen by the most careful owner of a motor with a dog

[18] In their report the Law Commission recommended that the general principles of the existing law of negligence whereby the keeper of an animal is under a duty to prevent that animal causing injury or damage should not be disturbed. See paras. 26–28, which recommendation the Act has observed.

[19] *Fardon* v. *Harcourt-Rivington* (1932) 48 T.L.R. 215.

[20] *Fitzgerald* v. *E.D. & A.D. Cooke Bourne (Farms) Ltd.* [1964] 1 Q.B. 249, 272.

[21] *Manton* v. *Brocklebank* [1923] 2 K.B. 212, 232, *per* Atkin L.J.

[22] *Cox* v. *Burbidge* (1863) 13 C.B.(N.S.) 430.

[23] *Fardon* v. *Harcourt-Rivington, supra, per* Lord Dunedin.

in it on a highway."[24] Again, where a dog was kept in a motor-car confined by a leash which prevented it from projecting its nose more than three inches over the rim of the door, and a child of five when leaning over the motor-car was bitten, it was held that in the absence of *scienter* the owner of the dog was not liable.[25] Where a large Newfoundland dog, loose in a small garden, jumped over the garden wall and landed on the plaintiff's back while he was digging a hole and injured him, it was held that the owner was not liable.[26] Also the defendant was held not liable when his dog came out of the open gate of his property, dashed across the road, and being frightened by an oncoming motor-car, turned back and struck the plaintiff's bicycle, knocking the plaintiff down[27]; when his racing greyhound, in the charge of two small boys, while chasing a cat bit a woman who tried to rescue the cat[28]; and, where he had brought a dog into a public-house, there being no duty to keep a constant watch upon it, unless there was reason to believe that it was making a nuisance of itself.[29]

596 It was held not to be negligent to put cattle into a field with defective hedges, adjoining a highway, whence they strayed on to the roadway because there is no duty on a landowner to fence off his land from the highway. In *Searle* v. *Wallbank*[30] the House of Lords affirmed this clearly established rule, which according to Evershed M.R.[31] "is founded upon our ancient social conditions and is in no way related to, or liable to be qualified by, such matters as the relative levels of fields and highway, the nature of the highway, or the amount of traffic upon it." Also, if a horse comes through an open gate from the stable yard into the highway and collides with a motor-car, the owner is not liable.[32] The owner of a market franchise is under no duty to prevent beasts brought to market from getting on to the highway and injuring members of the public.[33]

597 **Cases of negligence.** When a large dog owned by the tenant of an upper flat came down the stairs unaccompanied and knocked against a woman who was coming up the stairs and injured her, it was held that the owner of the dog was not liable because there was no evidence to show how the dog got out of the flat. Scrutton L.J., however, said: "I reserve my opinion as to whether in other cases, where the owner of a dog is responsible for taking him into such a situation where the uncontrolled movements of the dog may cause damage, there may not

24 *Ibid., per* Lord Macmillan.
25 *Sycamore* v. *Ley* (1932) 147 L.T. 342.
26 *Sanders* v. *Teape & Swan* (1884) 51 L.T. 263.
27 *Gibb* v. *Comerford* [1942] Ir.R. 295, but *cf.* with the facts in *Gomberg* v. *Smith* [1963] 1 Q.B. 25, where the owner was held to be negligent.
28 *Toogood* v. *Wright* [1940] 2 All E.R. 306.
29 *Carroll* v. *Garford* (1968) 112 S.J. 948.
30 [1947] A.C. 341; *Jones* v. *Lee* (1911) 106 L.T. 123; *Ellis* v. *Banyard* (1911) 106 L.T. 51; *Heath's Garage Ltd.* v. *Hodges* [1916] 2 K.B. 370. But see the distinction drawn in *Bativala* v. *West* [1970] 1 Q.B. 716.
31 *Brock* v. *Richards* [1951] 1 K.B. 529, at p. 534.
32 *Hughes* v. *Williams* [1943] K.B. 574.
33 *Brackenborough* v. *Spalding U.D.C.* [1942] A.C. 310.

be a liability on the owner of the dog." [34] Such a case occurred when a dog, taken out into the street on a long lead, was so loosely held that it broke away from control to chase a cat, and in doing so the lead became entangled with the legs of the plaintiff, a woman of seventy-three, so that she was thrown to the ground and injured, and it was held that the defendant was liable for negligence.[35] An owner has also been held liable for exercising two greyhounds coupled together in the highway near to a town in the dusk so that the plaintiff was knocked down and injured [36]; when he allowed his dog to run at large in the vicinity of a mink farm during the whelping season, when he knew that there was a hostile reaction between mink and strange dogs [37]; for negligently driving a cow and calf on the highway, so that the cow tossed a woman on the pavement [38]; for insecurely tethering a pony in a stable so that it got loose, went into the streets of a town and caused the plaintiff to fall in the street and injure herself [39]; for negligently unloading bullocks, excited by a train journey, from a train so that they escaped through an open gate into the streets of a town and did damage [40]; also for keeping bees in unreasonable numbers, at an unreasonable place, smoking them out for an unreasonable time, so that they stung the plaintiff's horse which threw the plaintiff [41]; for supplying an unsuitable horse which bolted, throwing the plaintiff whom the riding stable's employee knew to be an inexperienced rider [42]; and for driving cattle four times a day along a road, bounded by the plaintiff's hedge, accompanied only by a boy incapable of controlling them, so that the cattle damaged the hedge and made it unsightly by pulling at it.[43]

598 Where a pony in a gymkhana ran out of the ring and onto a road, as a result of its suffering a fright when its rider had fallen off and its saddle had slipped underneath its belly and thus caused a motor collision, it was held that the rule in *Searle* v. *Wallbank* [44] had no application since the animal was under direct human control and its straying was a foreseeable reaction by the animal in the circumstances. Hence the organisers were negligent.[45] Highway collisions involving animals are more fully dealt with, *post*, in Chapter 12, § 846 *et seq.*

In cases where liability is based on negligence, the owner is not liable

34 *Hines* v. *Tousley* (1926) 95 L.J.K.B. 773.
35 *Pitcher* v. *Martin* [1937] 3 All E.R. 918.
36 *Jones* v. *Owen* (1871) 24 L.T. 587.
37 *Caine Fur Farms* v. *Kokolsky* (1963) 39 D.L.R. (2d) 134.
38 *Pinn* v. *Rew* (1916) 32 T.L.R. 451. Before meeting the plaintiff, the cow had met a dog, which she tossed. There was evidence that a cow with a calf might become dangerous on meeting a dog.
39 *Deen* v. *Davies* [1935] 2 K.B. 282.
40 *Howard* v. *Bergin, O'Connor & Co.* [1925] 2 Ir.R. 110.
41 *O'Gorman* v. *O'Gorman* [1903] 2 Ir.R. 573.
42 *Collins* v. *Richmond Rodeo Riding and Amundson* (1966) 56 D.L.R. (2d) 428.
43 *Allford* v. *Maton* (1936) 3 L.J.C.C.R. 167.
44 *Supra.* The Law Commission in para. 55 recommended that the rule in *Searle* v. *Wallbank* which excludes or restricts the duty of care which might otherwise be owed in respect of animals straying on to the highway should be abolished subject to certain qualifications.
45 *Bativala* v. *West* [1970] 1 Q.B. 716.

for the negligence of one who is not his servant or agent. So, where the defendant employed an auctioneer to hold a sale of horses in his yard and the plaintiff, attending the sale, was kicked by a horse which was being run up and down (it was alleged) in too narrow a space, it was held that the defendant was not liable for the negligence of the auctioneer, as he was not the defendant's servant.[46]

599 **Damages may be independent of scienter.** Assuming negligence to be proved, a question arises whether the defendant is liable for damage caused by a mischievous propensity in his animal, not known to the defendant—in other words, whether *scienter* must be proved. On this point, Lord Sterndale said: " When a cause of action, whether in trespass or negligence, has once been established, the defendant may well be liable for any damage produced by acts not alien to the nature of the animal and cannot say such damage is too remote." [47] But even if such damage is alien to the animal's nature, the owner may be liable. Greer L.J. said: " I agree that there may be cases in which a defendant may be liable for the bite of a dog even if the dog does not belong to the class of ferocious animals, if it be proved that the dog is put in such a position that a reasonable man would know that it was likely to cause danger and therefore he ought to regard himself as under an obligation to do something by way of precaution." [48] So, where a mare, known to be of an excitable and nervous disposition, was left unattended on a towpath where it kicked a man leading a quiet horse pulling a barge, the owner was held liable.[49] Again, where a pony attached to a milk cart was left unattended for half an hour and became restive, put its feet on the footpath and attacked the plaintiff as she was walking along the footpath, it was held that the owners were liable, in spite of a finding by the jury that the owners had no knowledge of any propensity on the part of the pony to attack human beings.[50] Where a bull attacked a cow in an auction yard, it was held that it was necessary for the plaintiff to prove that there was negligence on the part of the defendant in not having anticipated the probable danger, and that, if negligence were proved, it would be no answer for the defendant to set up absence of *scienter*.[51]

600 Absence of *scienter* may affect the damages on the ground of remoteness. Where a horse belonging to the defendants and not known to be vicious was negligently left unattended in the plaintiffs' yard, with the result that one of the plaintiffs' workmen in passing behind the horse was kicked so that he died, it was held that the defendants were not liable, as the accident was not the natural result of the negligence.[52]

46 *Walker* v. *Crabb* (1916) 33 T.L.R. 119.
47 *Manton* v. *Brocklebank* [1923] 2 K.B. 212, 223.
48 *Sycamore* v. *Ley* (1932) 147 L.T. 342, 345. See also *Fardon* v. *Harcourt-Rivington* (1932) 48 T.L.R. 215.
49 *Rose* v. *George Henry Collier Ltd.* [1939] W.N. 19.
50 *Aldham* v. *United Dairies (London), Ltd.* [1940] 1 K.B. 507.
51 *Hinckes* v. *Harris* (1921) 65 S.J. 781.
52 *Bradley* v. *Wallaces Ltd.* [1913] 3 K.B. 629.

If the defendants had done something to disturb the horse as the workman was passing behind it, no doubt they would have been held liable.[53] When a bullock which was being unloaded at a butcher's premises was negligently allowed to escape and, during its freedom, deliberately attacked a cyclist it was held that the defendant was not liable, in the absence of proof of a mischievous propensity on the part of the bullock, on the ground that the damage did not naturally flow from the negligence.[54] It has been held that an owner is not liable for disease communicated by his sheep to other sheep as a result of his negligence, unless he knows that his sheep are suffering from disease.[55]

3.—LIABILITY FOR TRESPASS

601 **Principles of liability.** Apart from negligence, an owner [56] is liable for damage caused by the trespass of his livestock.[57] This is confined to trespass to land, as there is no liability for trespass to person or goods by an animal in the absence of intention or negligence.[58] The common law was thus stated by Williams J.: " If I am the owner of an animal in which by law the right of property can exist, I am bound to take care that it does not stray into the land of my neighbour; and I am liable for any trespass it may commit, and for the ordinary consequences of that trespass. Whether or not the escape of the animal is due to my negligence is altogether immaterial. I am clearly liable for the trespass, and for all the ordinary consequences of the trespass, subject to a distinction which is taken very early in the books, that the animal is such that the owner of it may have a property in it which is recognisable by law. For instance, if a man's cattle, or sheep, or poultry, stray into his neighbour's land or garden, and do such damage as might ordinarily be expected to be done by things of that sort, the owner is liable to his neighbour for the consequences." [59] Accordingly, when the defendant's mare strayed into the plaintiff's field and kicked a horse, it was held that the defendant was liable and that the damage was not too remote.[60] Again, when the defendant's horse bit and kicked the plaintiff's mare through a wire fence, it was held that the protrusion of any part of the horse over the boundary line was enough to enable the plaintiff to succeed.[61] Where calves were penned on one side of a railway line and their

[53] See *Abbott* v. *Freeman* (1876) 35 L.T. 783, where the facts negatived negligence.
[54] *Lathall* v. *Joyce & Son* [1939] 3 All E.R. 854.
[55] *Cooke* v. *Waring* (1863) 2 H. & C. 332. Otherwise where the sheep were trespassing. *Post*, § 603.
[56] For meaning of " owner " in this connection see *post*, § 606.
[57] This is an ancient cause of action dating from the 14th century: *Wormald* v. *Cole* [1954] 1 Q.B. 614, 620; Williams' *Liability for Animals*, pp. 127, 135; Holdsworth, H.E.L., Vol. 8, pp. 470–471. See also Blackstone, Comm., III, 211.
[58] *Manton* v. *Brocklebank* [1923] 2 K.B. 212.
[59] *Cox* v. *Burbidge* (1863) 13 C.B.(N.S.) 430.
[60] *Lee* v. *Riley* (1865) 18 C.B.(N.S.) 722; *Holgate* v. *Bleazard* [1917] 1 K.B. 443.
[61] *Ellis* v. *Loftus Iron Co.* (1874) L.R. 10 C.P. 10. Otherwise where the horse was not trespassing: *Manton* v. *Brocklebank* [1923] 2 K.B. 212.

dams on the other, the fences between being erected and maintained by the railway authorities, and the dams by using exceptional force broke through the fence and got on to the line where some of them were killed in a collision with a train, their owner was held liable for the damage caused by the derailment on its being proved that the fence was properly maintained in accordance with the Railways Clauses Consolidation Act 1845, s. 68.[62] Also, when the defendants' cow got into the plaintiff's field where there was a bull which broke its leg in chasing and attempting to mount the cow, the plaintiff recovered on the ground that the damage to his bull was the natural consequence of the trespass.[63]

602 The common law rules imposing liability for cattle trespass have been superseded by the provisions of the Animals Act 1971.[64] Section 4 provides: " (1) Where livestock [65] belonging to any person strays on to land in the ownership or occupation of another and—

(*a*) damage is done by the livestock to the land or to any property on it which is in the ownership or possession of the other person; or

(*b*) any expenses are reasonably incurred by that other person in keeping the livestock while it cannot be restored to the person to whom it belongs or while it is detained in pursuance of section 7 of this Act, or in ascertaining to whom it belongs;

the person to whom the livestock belongs [66] is liable for the damage or expenses, except as otherwise provided by this Act."

From the above it is clearly intended that the straying of livestock should only be actionable upon proof of actual damage which should cover those reasonable expenses incurred in detaining the animals where there is a right to do so or in finding the person to whom they belong but which is otherwise limited to damage to land and chattels.

603 **Damages for livestock trespass.** When a trespass is committed by livestock, its owner is liable for the natural consequences of the trespass. At common law there was considerable uncertainty whether this included damages due to an abnormal propensity in the absence of *scienter*. In *Theyer* v. *Purnell* [67] where sheep suffering from disease trespassed upon

[62] *Cooper* v. *Railway Executive* [1953] 1 W.L.R. 223.

[63] *Eustace* v. *Ayre* (1947) 14 L.J.N.C.C.R. 106.

[64] See s. 1 (1) (*c*), which follows the recommendations of the Law Commission (Law Com. 13) contained in paras. 60–68 that the old common law rules of strict liability for cattle trespass should be abolished and a new form of strict liability for straying livestock should be provided in lieu.

[65] Livestock is defined in s. 11 as meaning any " cattle, horses, asses, mules, hinnies, sheep, pigs, goats and poultry and also deer not in the wild state." Poultry is, in turn, defined as meaning " the domestic varieties of the following, that is to say, fowls, turkeys, geese, ducks, guinea-fowls, pigeons, peacocks and quails." Cats and dogs are not " cattle," *Buckle* v. *Holmes* [1926] 2 K.B. 125 nor does " livestock " include wild animals which are not normally the object of ownership *e.g.* rabbits, foxes nor such imported wild animals such as lions and tigers, whether captive or free.

[66] s. 4 (2) provides that " for the purposes of this section any livestock belongs to the person in whose possession it is."

[67] [1918] 2 K.B. 333 distinguishing *Cooke* v. *Waring* (1863) 2 H. & C. 332, where the action was for negligence.

the plaintiff's land and infected his sheep, it was held that the defendant was liable for that damage, whether or not he was aware of the condition of his sheep at the date of the trespass, on the ground that the doctrine of *scienter* had no application to an action founded on trespass. There can be little doubt that after October 1, 1971, the same decision would be reached on the same facts but on the ground that the damage suffered was that covered by section 4 (1) (*a*) of the Animals Act 1971. On the other hand there were several opinions, but not decisions, expressing the contrary view. In *Fletcher* v. *Rylands*,[68] dealing with animals, Blackburn J. said: "The law as to them seems to be perfectly settled from early times; the owner must keep them in at his peril, or he will be answerable for the natural consequences of their escape; that is with regard to tame beasts, for the grass they eat and trample upon, though not for any injury to the person of others, for our ancestors have settled that it is not the general nature of horses to kick, or bulls to gore; but if the owner knows that the beast has a vicious propensity to attack man, he will be answerable for that too." The same view was later expressed by Atkin L.J.: "Where the owner is liable for the animal's trespasses it may be material to consider whether the damage it does is the result of a normal propensity. For this damage the owner is liable; but for damage resulting from an abnormal propensity not known to him he is not in my opinion liable, though he would of course be liable for the ordinary consequences of the trespass." [69]

It has been held that if a horse is trespassing it is not a natural consequence of the trespass that it should kick a human being, in the absence of *scienter*,[70] but in the cases which decided this the injured party was not the occupier of the land or otherwise authorised to sue in trespass.[70]

604 In *Wormald* v. *Cole* [71] the defendant's cattle strayed onto the defendant's land and the plaintiff, a woman of eighty, in trying to drive them away, was knocked down and trampled on, not as a result of an attack upon her but because they came up against her. The defendant was held liable on the ground that the accident was a natural consequence of the trespass. It was conceded on behalf of the plaintiff that had there been an attack by the cattle the plaintiff could not have recovered in the absence of *scienter*, but Goddard L.C.J. doubted whether this concession should have been made,[72] adding: "I leave open the question whether it follows that if a trespassing animal attacks the occupier he can recover, though I incline to the opinion that he can." [73] The other members of the court

[68] (1866) L.R. 1 Ex. 265, 280.
[69] *Buckle* v. *Holmes* [1926] 2 K.B. 125, 130. See to the same effect, Lord Sterndale M.R. in *Manton* v. *Brocklebank* [1923] 2 K.B. 212, 223.
[70] *Cox* v. *Burbidge* (1863) 13 C.B.(N.S.) 430 (the horse was trespassing on the highway, but not on land occupied by the plaintiff); *Bradley* v. *Wallaces Ltd.* [1913] 3 K.B. 629 (the injured man was a workman employed by the occupiers of the yard where the horse was trespassing).
[71] [1954] 1 Q.B. 614.
[72] *Ibid.* p. 620.
[73] *Ibid.* p. 625.

expressed no opinion on this point. Before this case the general opinion was that expressed by counsel for the plaintiff, that damage due to an abnormal propensity could not be recovered in the absence of *scienter*,[74] and the decision itself is no authority to the contrary, but it has the effect of unsettling the law. It seems, however, an unnecessary distinction to hold that, in the absence of *scienter*, the owner of a trespassing horse is liable if the horse kicks the occupier of the land but not liable if it kicks any other person on the land, or elsewhere.

605 Whilst section 11 of the Animals Act defines " damage " as including " the death of, or injury to, any person (including any disease and any impairment of physical or mental condition)," it is apparent that in section 4 the only relevant damage is limited to that done by trespassing livestock " to the land or to any property on it which is in the ownership or possession of the other person," and to any special damage, namely those expenses incurred in keeping the livestock until restoration is effected to the owner.

Section 7 has abolished the ancient right to seize and detain any animal by way of distress damage feasant but has replaced it with a more elaborate procedure for the detention and sale of trespassing livestock by way of remedy for the occupier of the injured land.

606 **By and against whom the action is brought.** The action for trespass can be brought by anyone who has possession of the land or any part of it, and so the purchaser of a crop of growing turnips can sue for turnips eaten by trespassing sheep.[75] Anyone who can bring trespass for the land can sue, such as one who has the exclusive right of pasture upon it.

At common law the owner of the animal was liable for its trespass. If, however, the animal was in possession of another under the contract of agistment when the trespass was committed, the owner was not liable, but the agister was.[76] This was on the principle that the person in possession and control of an animal was liable for the damage it caused, when there was any liability at all.[77]

Section 4 of the Animals Act has not changed the common law in this regard.

607 **Trespass by dog.** There is no liability for trespass to land committed by a straying dog.[78] This is, apparently, " on account—first of the difficulty

[74] The Report of the Committee on the Law of Civil Liability for Damage done by Animals (1953) Cmd. 8746 says (para. 3): " The result of the modern cases on this subject is that a person can recover for damage done to his land and crops by trespassing cattle irrespective of negligence on the part of their owner, but in the absence of *scienter* cannot recover for damage to the person whether caused to himself or his servants." For a full discussion of this, see Williams, *Liability for Animals*, pp. 157–173.

[75] *Wellaway* v. *Courtier* [1918] 1 K.B. 200.

[76] *Hammond* v. *Mallinson* (1939) 6 L.J.C.C.R. 357.

[77] See now §§ 581—582, *ante*, for the effect of the Animals Act 1971.

[78] *Brown* v. *Giles* (1823) 1 C. & P. 118; *Sanders* v. *Teape & Swan* (1884) 51 L.T. 263; *Beckwith* v. *Shordike* (1767) 4 Burr. 2092; *Mitten* v. *Faudrye* (1626) Poph. 161. A dog is not included in the definition, contained in s. 11 of the Animals Act 1971, of " livestock," for the trespassing of which the person to whom the livestock belongs is liable.

or impossibility of keeping the latter [dogs and cats] under restraint—secondly, the slightness of the damage which their wandering ordinarily causes—thirdly, the common usage of mankind to allow them a wider liberty—and lastly, their not being considered in law so absolutely the chattels of the owner, as to be the subject of larceny." [79] Accordingly, an owner was not liable for his trespassing dog which killed rabbits, kept for commercial purposes, in the absence of evidence of *scienter*.[80] If however, the dog has a known propensity to hunt for and to destroy game, the owner will be liable for the damage done as being the owner of a mischievous dog, and the fact that the dog was trespassing when the damage was done will not affect his liability.[81] Again, an owner who incites his dog to enter the land of another will be liable for the intentional trespass so committed.[82]

Although the owner of a dog is not liable for the damage it does when trespassing, he runs the risk of having his dog shot. A trespassing dog which attacks animals or livestock belonging to the occupier of the land may be killed if, at the time, it is attacking the animals or there is a danger that it will renew an attack already made if left alone, and it is reasonable for the protection of the animals to kill it.[83] If the animals chased are *ferae naturae*, in which the landowner has no property, such as pheasants, which are not in captivity, there is no right to shoot the trespassing dog.[84]

Section 9 of the Animals Act now has laid down and clarified the precise circumstances in which a defendant may justifiably kill or injure dogs worrying livestock.

608 **Trespass by cat.** A cat is in the same category as a dog when the liability of the owner for its trespasses is in question. Accordingly, when a cat went onto the plaintiff's land and killed some of his pigeons and fowls, it was held that the owner was not liable.[85] Presumably if the same cat repeated its performance on a later date the owner would be liable, not for trespass but for damage done by a cat with a known mischievous propensity.

609 **Trespass by deer.** The owner of deer has been held liable for trespass committed by them upon the neighbouring land. In this case the deer had escaped from his park some six years before, but they were in the habit of returning. The defendant's keeper fed the deer in the park in the winter time, and a jury found that the deer were tame and kept by the defendant and under his control.[86]

[79] *Read* v. *Edwards* (1864) 17 C.B.(N.S.) 245, *per* Willes J.
[80] *Tallents* v. *Bell and Goddard* [1944] 2 All E.R. 474.
[81] *Read* v. *Edwards, supra.*
[82] *R.* v. *Pratt* (1855) 4 E. & B. 860.
[83] *Cresswell* v. *Sirl* [1948] 1 K.B. 241; *Goodway* v. *Becher* [1951] 2 All E.R. 349. See also Dogs (Protection of Livestock) Act 1953.
[84] *Gott* v. *Measures* [1948] 1 K.B. 234.
[85] *Buckle* v. *Holmes* [1926] 2 K.B. 125.
[86] *Brady* v. *Warren* [1900] 2 Ir.R. 632.

610 **Wild animals.** There is no liability for wild animals, breeding or living on the land of one owner, which do damage on the land of another owner. "If a man makes coney-burrows in his own land, which increase in so great a number that they destroy his neighbour's land next adjoining, his neighbours cannot have an action on the case against him who makes the said coney-burrows." [87] Again, where rabbits bred on the defendant's land and were trapped by the defendant for profit, it was held that he was not liable for damage done by them in trespassing on the neighbouring land, although his predecessor had brought new rabbits onto the land to improve the breed.[86] If, however, a landowner brings game or other wild animals onto his land to an unreasonable amount, or causes them to increase to an unreasonable extent, he will be liable to his neighbours for any damage they sustain.[88] But the presence of a large number of pheasants on a man's land caused by natural increase and not by any unreasonable action on his part does not render him liable for damage done by the pheasants to crops on adjoining land.[89] "The birds were *ferae naturae* and I am unable to see that the fact that the plaintiff had no right to shoot them imposed any duty in law upon the defendant to shoot them himself." [90]

A bone manure manufacturer whose business was carried on near to the fields of a farmer was held not liable for damage done to the farmer's corn by rats which were attracted to his land by a heap of bones, it not being proved that the bones kept were excessive or unusual in quantity.[91] If, however, a nuisance be committed, the person committing it will be liable. Where the defendant had a heap of manure which was excessive in quantity and from its smell and the number of flies it attracted and bred amounted to a nuisance, it was held that an injunction should be granted to restrain the defendant from keeping it.[92] As regards bees, see § 575, *ante*, note 29.

611 **Only two exceptions from liability for trespass.** Firstly, at common law it was always a defence to an action for trespass by a person's livestock to show that the trespass was caused by breach of an obligation on the part of the plaintiff to fence. Whilst it is the duty of the person to whom the animal belongs to prevent it from trespassing, if by agreement or prescription that duty is imposed upon the plaintiff, then the latter cannot recover damages.[93]

[87] *Boulston's Case* (1597) 15 Rep. 104b; *sub nom. Bowlston* v. *Hardy*, Cro.Eliz. 547. It is suggested in Salmond, 15th ed., p. 451, that this case is no longer law, but the authorities do not support this view.

[88] *Farrer* v. *Nelson* (1885) 15 Q.B.D. 258.

[89] *Seligman* v. *Docker* [1949] Ch. 53.

[90] *Ibid., per* Romer J. at p. 66.

[91] *Stearn* v. *Prentice Bros.* [1919] 1 K.B. 394.

[92] *Bland* v. *Yates* (1914) 58 S.J. 612.

[93] *Star* v. *Rookesby* (1711) 1 Salk. 335 (prescription); *Singleton* v. *Williamson* (1861) 7 H. & M. 410 (enclosure award); *Lawrence* v. *Jenkins* (1873) L.R. 8 Q.B. 274. In *Wiseman* v. *Booker* (1878) 3 C.P.D. 184, the liability to fence was imposed by statute on a railway company for the benefit of the defendant, and when the defendant's horses put their heads over the fence and ate the crops of the plaintiff, who was the tenant of the railway

Section 5 (1) of the Animals Act 1971 preserves the defence that a person is not liable for the trespass of his livestock causing damage which is due wholly to the fault of the person suffering it. However this defence needs to be considered in the light of subsection (6) which provides that: "In determining whether any liability for damage under section 4 of this Act is excluded by subsection (1) of this section the damage shall not be treated as due to the fault of the person suffering it by reason only that he could have prevented it by fencing; but a person is not liable under that section where it is proved that the straying of the livestock on to the land would not have occurred but for a breach by any other person, being a person having an interest in the land, of a duty to fence."

612 To be a defence at common law the obligation to fence must have been enforceable by the defendant against the plaintiff. So, where a railway company was obliged by statute to fence its railway from the lands of the adjoining occupiers, and the plaintiff's sheep escaped from his land, owing to his own fences being out of repair, got onto the land of a third party adjoining the railway, and from there, owing to the railway company's defective fence, onto the railway where they were killed, it was held that the railway company was not liable.[94] Again, where the plaintiff and the defendant occupied adjoining fields and were both tenants of the same landlord under agreements whereby they undertook to keep the fences on their holdings in repair, it was held that the defendant could not rely on the breach by the plaintiff of his agreement with his landlord as a defence when his horses trespassed upon the plaintiff's field and injured a colt.[95] When a farm adjoined several allotments, the holders of which were under contract with their landlord, who was also the farmer's landlord, to maintain a fence and the farmer's cattle damaged the crops in one allotment owing to the fence having been broken by the acts of the allotment holders, the farmer was held liable.[96] A defence of leave and licence was rejected on the ground that there was no evidence that the cattle entered through any particular gap. If the plaintiff had broken down the fence and so let in the cattle, the defence would have succeeded. Again, when the defendant's sheep strayed from a moor, owing to the breach by a third party of their duty to fence, got on to the highway and from there on to the plaintiff's land, the defendant was held liable. Although the third party's failure to fence was a wrongful act, it did not excuse the defendant, as he was aware of the failure and could have guarded against it.[97]

company, the defendant was held not liable on the grounds, (1) the plaintiff could not be in a better position than the railway company, (2) the damage was caused by the company's breach of the statutory duty owed to the defendant.

94 *Ricketts* v. *East and West India Docks, etc., Ry.* (1852) 12 C.B. 160. See also *Child* v. *Hearn* (1874) L.R. 9 Ex. 176 (railway company bound to maintain fence—pigs got through and upset a railwayman riding a trolley—owner of pigs not liable).

95 *Holgate* v. *Bleazard* [1917] 1 K.B. 443.

96 *Park* v. *Jobson & Son* [1945] 1 All E.R. 222.

97 *Sutcliffe* v. *Holmes* [1947] 1 K.B. 147.

613 If the defendant was under an obligation to fence, he was liable for damage caused to his neighbour's cattle through breach of this obligation. Where the plaintiff, the bailee of a horse, turned it into a field, and from the bad state of the fence, which it was the defendant's duty to maintain, it fell into the defendant's field and was killed, it was held that the defendant was liable.[98] Again, when the plaintiff's cows got through a gap in the fence, which the defendant was by prescription obliged to maintain, caused by a tree which was negligently felled by a third party to whom the defendant had sold the right to cut timber, and ate yew leaves on the defendant's land so that they died, the defendant was held liable although he had no notice that the fence was broken before the escape of the cows.[99]

The obligation had also to be to fence against the kind of animal found trespassing. An occupier of land who was bound to fence against moorland cattle, including sheep, was held not bound to fence against sheep of a peculiarly wandering and active disposition which had jumped over his fence.[1]

614 Secondly at common law the occupier of premises which adjoin a highway was presumed to have accepted the risks that flowed from the passage of traffic along that highway. Accordingly where the defendant's ox, whilst being driven through the streets of a country town entered the plaintiff's ironmonger's shop which adjoined the street, through the open doorway and damaged his goods it was held that the plaintiff was unable to recover damages since the escape of the beast was not due to any negligence of the defendant.[2]

Section 5 (5) replaces the common law in this regard by providing that: " A person is not liable under section 4 of this Act where the livestock strayed from a highway and its presence there was a lawful use of the highway."

In view of the wording of section 4 (1) that the person to whom the trespassing livestock belongs is liable for the damage or expenses incurred except as otherwise provided by the Act [3] the uncertainty of the common law is thereby removed whether or not (a) the unlawful act of a third party and (b) an act of God were further exceptions to liability.[4]

[98] *Rooth* v. *Wilson* (1817) 1 B. & Ald. 59.

[99] *Lawrence* v. *Jenkins* (1873) L.R. 8 Q.B. 274.

[1] *Coaker* v. *Willcocks* [1911] 1 K.B. 649.

[2] *Tillett* v. *Ward* (1882) 10 Q.B.D. 17.

[3] *viz.*: only those two defences, which are set out above, contained in s. 5.

[4] See Law Commission's recommendation in para. 24: " We would abolish the defence of Act of God, which appears to be of little practical importance in this field and only to add an unnecessary complication to the law. We would also resolve any doubts which may remain in spite of the majority view in *Baker* v. *Snell* [1908] 2 K.B. 825 as to the availability of the defence of the act of a third party, by a clear rule that this defence is not available. In view of the rationale of strict liability for special risks [see para. 20] it is our view that the act of a third party is one of the circumstances against which the person creating the risk should take precautions."

CHAPTER 11

DANGEROUS CHATTELS: DONOGHUE v. STEVENSON

1.—GENERAL PRINCIPLES OF LIABILITY

615 **Duty of care.** The owner [1] of a dangerous chattel is under a duty to take care in respect of it. The owner of a chattel which is not dangerous may be under a duty of care in respect of it, for example, the owner of a motor-car owes a duty of care if he drives the motor-car along the highway, but that duty arises out of his use of the car and not out of his mere ownership. In the present chapter, the duty arising out of the ownership of the chattel as distinguished from the use to which it is being put is considered. When the owner of a chattel parts with possession of it or allows others to come in contact with it he is under no duty in tort in respect of it as a general rule. If the chattel is a dangerous chattel he does owe a duty of care and the nature and extent of that duty forms the subject of this chapter.

616 A dangerous chattel is a chattel containing one of the dangerous things explained in Chapter 9 or, if it does not, one which is likely to cause damage to person or property when used by a person taking reasonable care but ignorant of the dangerous nature of the chattel.[2] A distinction is drawn between chattels dangerous in themselves and chattels not dangerous as a class but dangerous in individual cases when defective. Chattels dangerous in themselves are dangerous things as explained in Chapter 9 contained in chattel form, such as a bottle containing poison. Chattels not dangerous as a class may become dangerous in individual cases, for example, ginger beer is not a dangerous drink but it may be harmful to drink if it contains the decomposed remains of a snail. This distinction though it has been criticised,[3] is still made. Dealing with it in *Donoghue* v. *Stevenson*,[4] Lord Atkin said: " I do not find it necessary to discuss at length the cases, dealing with duties where the thing is dangerous, or, in the narrower category, belongs to a class of things which are dangerous in themselves. I regard the distinction as an unnatural one so far as it is used to serve as a logical differentiation by which to distinguish the existence or non-existence of a legal right. In this respect I agree with what was said by Scrutton L.J. in *Hodge &*

[1] The word " owner " is used in this connection as including the person in possession of the chattel for the time being, the person who puts it into circulation and the person who instals it to enable it to be used, and " ownership " is used accordingly.

[2] " The product would I think, be dangerous if it might affect normal people adversely ": *per* Denning L.J. in *Board* v. *Thomas Hedley & Co. Ltd.* [1951] 2 All E.R. 431, 432.

[3] See *Salmond on Torts*, 15th ed., p. 389 or for a complete list see 14th edition pp. 428–430.

[4] [1932] A.C. 562, 595, 596. See article " Donoghue v. Stevenson in Retrospect," (Heuston) (1957) 20 M.L.R. 1.

Sons v. *Anglo-American Oil Co.*,[5] a case which was ultimately decided on a question of fact. ' Personally, I do not understand the difference between a thing dangerous in itself, as poison, and a thing not dangerous as a class, but by negligent construction dangerous as a particular thing. The latter, if anything, seems the more dangerous of the two; it is a wolf in sheep's clothing instead of an obvious wolf.'[6] The nature of the thing may very well call for different degrees of care, and the person dealing with it may well contemplate persons as being within the sphere of his duty to take care who would not be sufficiently proximate with less dangerous goods; so that not only the degree of care, but the range of persons to whom a duty is owed may be extended." He then quoted from Lord Dunedin: " It has, however, again and again been held that in the case of articles dangerous in themselves, such as loaded firearms, poisons, explosives, and other things *ejusdem generis*, there is a peculiar duty to take precaution imposed upon those who send forth or install such articles when it is necessarily the case that other parties will come within their proximity,"[7] and added: " This, with respect, exactly sums up the position. The duty may exist independently of contract. Whether it exists or not depends upon the subject-matter involved; but clearly in the class of things enumerated there is a special duty to take precautions. This is the very opposite of creating a special category in which alone the duty exists."

617 In the same case Lord Macmillan said: " The exceptional case of things dangerous in themselves, or known to be in a dangerous condition, has been regarded as constituting a peculiar category outside the ordinary law both of contract and of tort. . . . I rather regard this type of case as a special instance of negligence where the law exacts a degree of diligence so stringent as to amount practically to a guarantee of safety."[8] The exceptional position of dangerous things is also recognised by Lord Wright when he said: " The case of things dangerous in themselves, or, as they are sometimes called, inherently dangerous, is a case separate and distinct and holds a special place in the law of negligence."[9] Lord Wright approved the distinction. " A distinction has been drawn in some cases between things intrinsically dangerous or dangerous *per se* and other things which are not dangerous in the absence of negligence. The correctness or value of that distinction has been doubted by eminent judges. I think, however, that there is a real and practical distinction between the two categories. Some things are obviously and necessarily dangerous unless the danger is removed by appropriate precautions. These are things dangerous *per se*. Other things are only dangerous if

5 (1922) 12 Ll.L.R. 183, 187.

6 Commenting on this passage in *Burfitt* v. *Kille* [1939] 2 K.B. 743, 749, Atkinson J. said: " The distinction rests not on the measure of the danger but on the circumstances of the duty."

7 *Dominion Natural Gas Co.* v. *Collins* [1909] A.C. 640, 646.

8 *Donoghue* v. *Stevenson* [1932] A.C. 562, at p. 611.

9 *Wray* v. *Essex C.C.* [1936] 3 All E.R. 97, 101.

there is negligence. It is only in that contingency that they can cause danger." [10]

This passage points out the importance of the distinction. In the case of chattels dangerous in themselves the owner is always under a duty of care. In the case of chattels dangerous because they are defective, it must first be proved that circumstances exist which make the particular chattel dangerous, although chattels of the class to which it belongs are not dangerous, before the duty to take care arises.

It is a question of law whether any given chattel falls within the category of a chattel dangerous in itself but a question of fact whether it is dangerous having regard to all the circumstances in each case.[11]

618 **Duty in respect of chattels dangerous in themselves.** The duty in respect of chattels dangerous in themselves has been already explained in connection with petrol (§ 506), gas containers (§ 518), loaded guns (§ 549), explosives (§ 556), and poison (§ 558). It may be shortly stated as a duty to take reasonable care to prevent them from causing damage to persons likely to come in contact with them.[12] The standard of care in such a case is a very high one—" a peculiar duty to take precaution," [13] " a special instance of negligence where the law exacts a degree of diligence so stringent as to amount practically to a guarantee of safety," [14] " it is intended that the standard of care, where dangerous substances are concerned, should be maintained at the highest possible level." [15] It is not so high as the duty of an insurer. " There must always be found somewhere the element of negligence on his part to make the owner of a chattel liable for . . . injury. Take the extreme instance of a loaded gun. This is so obviously dangerous when it gets into unknown hands that the law holds it to be negligence on the part of the owner to let the gun leave his possession in that state and be put in inexperienced hands." [16]

619 When possession of a chattel dangerous in itself is transferred, there is a duty only to transfer it to a competent person who is given adequate warning of the danger,[17] unless he knows of it already. If such a person does not know of the danger and is not warned of it, the owner of the chattel is liable for the resulting damage.[18] The limits of the duty are

[10] *Glasgow Corpn.* v. *Muir* [1943] A.C. 448, 463, 464. See also, *per* Devlin J. in *Behrens* v. *Bertram Mills Circus Ltd.* [1957] 2 Q.B. 1, 18: " In the case of dangerous chattels . . . the law has recognised, though it is not now perhaps of much importance, the distinction between chattels that are dangerous in themselves and chattels that are dangerous when used for certain purposes."

[11] *Blacker* v. *Lake and Elliott* (1912) 106 L.T. 533.

[12] *Hodge & Sons* v. *Anglo-American Oil Co.* (1922) 12 Ll.L.R. 183, 188, *per* Scrutton L.J.

[13] *Donoghue* v. *Stevenson* [1932] A.C. 562, 596 (Lord Atkin); *Dominion Natural Gas Co.* v. *Collins* [1909] A.C. 640, 646 (Lord Dunedin).

[14] [1932] A.C. 562, at p. 612 (Lord Macmillan).

[15] *The Pass of Ballater* [1942] P. 112, 119 (Langton J.).

[16] *Oliver* v. *Saddler & Co.* [1929] A.C. 584, 599 (Lord Dunedin).

[17] *Hodge & Sons* v. *Anglo-American Oil Co.* (1922) 12 Ll.L.R. 183; *Robinson* v. *Technico* (1953) (unreported, Supreme Court in Eire) 70 L.Q.R. 170.

[18] *Farrant* v. *Barnes* (1862) 11 C.B.(N.S.) 553; *Anglo-Celtic Shipping Co. Ltd.* v. *Elliott* (1926) 42 T.L.R. 297; *Holmes* v. *Ashford* [1950] 2 All E.R. 76.

explained by Lord Dunedin. "The duty being to take precaution, it is no excuse to say that the accident would not have happened unless some other agency than that of the defendant had intermeddled with the matter. A loaded gun will not go off unless someone pulls the trigger, a poison is innocuous unless someone takes it, gas will not explode unless it is mixed with air and then a light is set to it. Yet the cases of *Dixon* v. *Bell*,[19] *Thomas* v. *Winchester*,[20] and *Parry* v. *Smith*[21] are all illustrations of liability enforced. On the other hand, if the proximate cause of the accident is not the negligence of the defendant, but the conscious act of another volition, then he will not be liable. For against such conscious act of volition no precaution can really avail."[22]

620 The transfer of a chattel dangerous in itself to a person who because of his age or infirmity cannot appreciate the nature of the danger renders the owner of the chattel liable for the damage caused by it. It is not enough for the owner, in such a case, to give a warning to a person who is not competent to profit by the warning, he must not transfer it at all to such a person, unless he is first able to make it safe. "A warning is not a sufficient discharge of duty if the person to whom the chattel is delivered is not a competent person."[23] A shopkeeper who sold a toy pistol and blank ammunition to a boy aged twelve was held liable when the pistol was defective, so that on being fired a piece of metal was discharged and hit another boy in the eye.[24] Where petrol was sold to a boy of nine who injured himself by lighting it, the seller was held to be negligent and liable to the boy.[25]

621 Failure to discharge the duty stated above renders the owner liable to all likely to be endangered by its breach, and not only to the immediate transferee. "If A places in the hands of B a chattel which belongs to a class of things dangerous in themselves in the hands of such a person as B, as distinguished from a chattel which is dangerous only because of some defect peculiar to the particular chattel handed over, a duty of care rests on A not only towards the recipient but also towards all such persons as may reasonably be contemplated as likely to be endangered."[26]

19 (1816) 5 M. & S. 198.
20 (1852) 6 N.Y.R. 397.
21 (1879) 4 C.P.D. 325.
22 *Dominion Natural Gas Co.* v. *Collins* [1909] A.C. 640, 646. Lord Atkin in *Donoghue* v. *Stevenson* (*supra*) at p. 596 said of this statement: "This, with respect, exactly sums up the position." In *Hodge* v. *Anglo-American Oil Co.*, *supra*, Scrutton L.J. expressed the opinion, which he repeated in *Bottomley* v. *Bannister* [1932] 1 K.B. 458, that it was difficult to see the distinction between the other agency, which is no excuse, and the conscious act of volition, which is an excuse. The distinction, however, is well recognised, although it may be difficult to draw in any given set of facts. See *Philco Radio Ltd* v. *J. Spurling Ltd.* [1949] 2 All E.R. 882, where the defendants, by mistake, delivered celluloid scrap to the plaintiff's premises where it was set on fire by a cigarette of one of the plaintiff's typists. The defendants were held liable on their failure to prove that the typist deliberately set the scrap alight.
23 *Burfitt* v. *Kille* [1939] 2 K.B. 743, *per* Atkinson J.
24 *Burfitt* v. *Kille*, *supra*.
25 *Yachuk* v. *Oliver Blais Co. Ltd.* [1949] A.C. 386.
26 *Burfitt* v. *Kille*, *supra*, at p. 746, *per* Atkinson J. No such duty exists in the case of things not dangerous in themselves. *Ricketts* v. *Erith B.C.* [1943] 2 All E.R. 629 (vendor of toy bow and arrow to boy of ten not liable to child injured by the shooting of the arrow).

This means that if A fails to give warning to B, or if B is not a competent person, A is liable to C.[24] If, however, adequate warning is given to a competent person who fails to pass it on to his transferee, the original transferor is not liable. A manufacturer of a hair dye, who supplied it in bottles to a hairdresser, together with a brochure containing a warning that a test should be made before use, was held not liable to a customer of the hairdresser who was injured through the failure of the hairdresser to warn the customer and to make the test.[27]

622 When a chattel is dangerous in itself the owner is liable for damage caused by it although he did not know it to be dangerous and was not negligent in failing to discover that it was dangerous. " The duty has never been stated to rest on knowledge. If A chooses to sell things of a class dangerous in themselves he cannot be heard to say he did not know of or appreciate the danger." [28] Where ferro-silicon was sent by a keel and its fumes poisoned the owner of the keel and his wife who was with him, it was held that the consignor was liable in respect of the death of the owner and the injury to his wife although he did not know, and the trial judge did not find that negligence could be imputed to him for not knowing that ferro-silicon was dangerous.[29] Again, the owners of a large quantity of dinitrophenol which exploded and caused damage were held liable, although at the time of the explosion it was not known by anyone that it was likely to explode.[30]

623 The owner of chattels dangerous in themselves is under a duty not to put the chattels " in a situation easily accessible to a third person who sustains damage " [31] from them. " You must not put anything dangerous in itself where the public may possibly have access to it, and the best known instance of that is the case of a loaded gun." [32] In addition to loaded guns,[33] illustrations of this rule are to be found in connection with phosphorus,[34] jars containing sulphuric acid,[35] poisonous berries in a public park,[36] and poisonous paint left in a field.[37]

The distinction between the duty owed in respect of things dangerous in themselves and other things is illustrated by *Ball* v. *L.C.C.*[38] In that case the landlords of a house installed in the house a boiler which was not

27 *Holmes* v. *Ashford* [1950] 2 All E.R. 76; see also *Kubach* v. *Hollands* [1937] 3 All E.R. 907 (*post*, § 636), to the same effect.
28 *Burfitt* v. *Kille* [1939] 2 K.B. 743, 749, *per* Atkinson J.
29 *Bamfield* v. *Goole and Sheffield Transport Co.* [1910] 2 K.B. 94.
30 *Rainham Chemical Works* v. *Belvedere Fish Guano Co.* [1921] 2 A.C. 465. See also *West* v. *Bristol Tramways Co.* [1908] 2 K.B. 14.
31 *Per* Parke B. in *Longmeid* v. *Holliday* (1851) 6 Ex. 761.
32 *Per* Lord Dunedin in *Fardon* v. *Harcourt-Rivington* (1932) 48 T.L.R. 215.
33 *Dixon* v. *Bell* (1816) 5 M. & S. 198; *Sullivan* v. *Creed* [1904] 2 Ir.R. 317.
34 *Williams* v. *Eady* (1893) 10 T.L.R. 41.
35 *Adelaide Chemical Co. Ltd.* v. *Carlyle* (1940) 64 C.L.R. 514.
36 *Glasgow Corpn.* v. *Taylor* [1922] 1 A.C. 44.
37 *Stewart* v. *Adams*, 1920 S.C. 129.
38 [1949] 2 K.B. 159. The House of Lords in *A. C. Billings & Sons Ltd.* v. *Riden* [1958] A.C. 240 overruled this decision of the Court of Appeal that there was no liability in negligence for installations connected with houses unless the installation itself was in fact a dangerous thing.

fitted with a safety valve. The water in the pipe connected with the boiler became frozen so that when the tenant's daughter lit the fire an explosion occurred in which she was injured. The boiler had been in use in the house for seven years before the explosion and it was held that it was not a thing dangerous in itself, with the result that the action failed. But, it was said: " if this boiler as constructed is a dangerous or noxious thing . . . then the defendants would be liable to strangers who might be contemplated as likely to visit the house." [39]

624 **Donoghue v. Stevenson.**[40] In this appeal the House of Lords were required to consider whether the averments made by the appellant, the pursuer, disclosed a good cause of action if the facts alleged in her condescendence were true. The action was brought in the Court of Session by the appellant, who was a shop assistant, seeking to recover damages from the respondent, who was a manufacturer of aerated waters. The damage that she alleged that she had suffered was as a result of consuming part of the contents of a bottle of ginger-beer which had been manufactured by the respondent and had contained the decomposed remains of a snail. In her pleadings she averred that the bottle of ginger-beer was purchased for her by a friend, whilst visiting the cafe occupied by one Minchella at Paisley; the bottle was made of dark opaque glass and she had no reason to suspect that it contained any foreign matter but pure ginger-beer; the said Minchella poured out some of the drink into a tumbler and she drank some of the contents; the friend was then proceeding to pour the rest of the bottle's contents into the tumbler when a snail, in a state of decomposition, floated out of the bottle; and as a result of the nauseating sight of the snail in such circumstances and the consequential impurities in the drink, which she had already partially consumed, she suffered from shock and severe gastro-enteritis. Upon these matters the House of Lords decided by a majority (Lord Atkin, Thankerton and Macmillan with Lords Buckmaster and Tomlin dissenting) that the appellant would have a good cause of action if she could prove these facts that she had averred.[41]

625 Firstly Lord Atkin dealt with the difficulties in finding some general principle of negligence and then proceeded to set out the doctrine of duty to one's neighbour which is the " broad rule " of this important decision already discussed fully in Chapter 2. He finally went on to state the " narrow rule " in his judgment in these terms: " My Lords, if your Lordships accept the view that this pleading discloses a relevant cause of action you will be affirming the proposition that by Scots and English

[39] [1949] 2 K.B. 159, *per* Tucker L.J. at p. 172.
[40] [1932] A.C. 562.
[41] Article by Professor Heuston (1957) 20 M.L.R. 1, 2, n. 5. The truth is that the issue of fact was never decided since the defender died before proof and the pursuer in consequence compromised the action and received £100 in settlement of her claim. The assertion by Jenkins L.J. in *Alder* v. *Dickson* [1954] 1 W.L.R. 1482, at p. 1483 is therefore incorrect that when the trial was finally heard there was no snail in the bottle at all! See further 71 L.Q.R. 472 and 220 L.T. 291.

law alike a manufacturer of products, which he sells in such a form as to show that he intends them to reach the ultimate consumer in the form in which they left him, with no reasonable possibility of intermediate examination, and with the knowledge that the absence of reasonable care in the preparation or putting up of the products will result in an injury to the consumer's life or property, owes a duty to the consumer to take that reasonable care.

It is a proposition which I venture to say no one in Scotland or England who is not a lawyer would for one moment doubt. It will be an advantage to make it clear that the law in this matter, as in most others, is in accordance with sound common sense." [42]

626 **Duty in respect of dangerous chattels.** The duty explained above applies to all dangerous chattels, both chattels dangerous in themselves and chattels not dangerous as a class but dangerous in individual cases.

The duty of an owner of a dangerous chattel who keeps it in his own possession and control and invites or permits others to use it is the same as that of the occupier of dangerous premises and has already been considered (Chapter 7).

The duty of an owner of a dangerous chattel who does not retain it in his own possession and control will be considered so far as it affects the manufacturer (*post*, § 628), the retailer (*post*, § 646), the repairer (*post*, § 655), the transferor (*post*, § 662), including the owner, the consignor for carriage and the carrier, and the installer (*post*, § 674).

2.—DUTY OF MANUFACTURER OF GOODS

627 **Duty in contract.** A manufacturer of goods is under a contractual duty to the buyer by section 14 of the Sale of Goods Act 1893. Unless the goods are sold under a patent or trade name, there is an implied condition that they are reasonably fit for the purpose for which they are sold.[43] There is also an implied condition that they are of merchantable quality,[44] which means that " the article sold, if only meant for one particular use in ordinary course, is fit for that use; . . . it is not merchantable in that event if it has defects unfitting it for its only proper use but not apparent on ordinary examination." [45]

Frequently there will not be any contractual relationship between the manufacturer and the consumer or user. For breach of any of the implied conditions under the Sale of Goods Act 1893, the actual seller

[42] *Ibid.* p. 599. This exposition of the obligation of a manufacturer which is owed in respect of chattels has never been questioned but has been adopted, applied and even expanded in over a hundred reported cases throughout the common law world since 1932. See 36 *English & Empire Digest* (1954) p. 85, para. 458.

[43] s. 14 (1).

[44] *Ibid.* s. 14 (2). This condition is implied even when the goods are sold under a patent or trade name. *Bristol Tramways Ltd.* v. *Fiat Motors Ltd.* [1910] 2 K.B. 831.

[45] *Grant* v. *Australian Knitting Mills Ltd.* [1936] A.C. 85, 100, *per* Lord Wright.

will be liable to the buyer and will, in turn, have a claim against the manufacturer for the damages he has had to pay to the buyer and any costs he had incurred in reasonably defending the action by the buyer.[46] In this way, liability for damage caused to the buyer is thrown upon the manufacturer; but unless the buyer is also the person who suffers damage from the goods, there is no contractual liability to the consumer or user.[47] In tort, however, the manufacturer may be liable to the consumer or user.

628 **Duty in tort.** A person who manufactures goods which he intends to be used or consumed by others is under a duty to take reasonable care in their manufacture so that they can be used or consumed in the manner intended, without causing physical damage to person or property. This was laid down in *Donoghue* v. *Stevenson*,[48] set out fully above (§§ 624–625, *ante*).

However this statement of duty must be modified in one respect. It is not essential that there should be no reasonable possibility [49] of intermediate examination, as long as the article is intended by the manufacturer to reach the ultimate consumer or user in the state in which it left him. " The decision in *Donoghue's* case did not depend on the bottle being stoppered and sealed: the essential point in this regard was that the article should reach the consumer or user subject to the same defect as it had when it left the manufacturer." This was laid down in *Grant* v. *Australian Knitting Mills*.[50] There the plaintiff bought from a retail shop a pair of underpants which had been manufactured by the defendants. The pants contained a chemical irritant which caused the plaintiff to contract dermatitis, and for this the defendants were held liable, on the ground of negligence in manufacture. In this case possibility of intermediate examination was present, because the pants were handled by the retailer before sale and there was the possibility that they might have been tampered with after they left the manufacturer, but, as there had been no such tampering in fact, this was held to be no defence. Again, the pants might have been washed by the user before use, and this would have removed the irritant. This, also, was held to be no defence, because " it was not contemplated that they should be first washed." [51] To the

46 *Kasler and Cohen* v. *Slavouski* [1928] 1 K.B. 78.

47 *Preist* v. *Last* [1903] 2 K.B. 148; *Frost* v. *Aylesbury Dairy Co.* [1905] 1 K.B. 608; *Jackson* v. *Watson & Sons Ltd.* [1909] 2 K.B. 193.

48 *Supra.* See article: " Manufacturers' Liability to Third Parties." (Johnson) 117 New L.J. 411 and 426.

49 Goddard L.J. suggested the substitution of " probability " for " possibility " in *Paine* v. *Colne Valley Electricity Supply Co.* [1938] 4 All E.R. 803, and in *Haseldine* v. *Daw & Son* [1941] 2 K.B. 343, 376.

50 [1936] A.C. 85, *per* Lord Wright at pp. 106, 107. When dermatitis is caused by defective clothing, it is a defence to prove that the plaintiff has an abnormally sensitive skin: *Griffiths* v. *Peter Conway Ltd.* [1939] 1 All E.R. 685. When dermatitis is contracted after wearing a suit cleaned by the defendants the burden is on the defendants to prove no negligence: *Mayne* v. *Silvermere Cleaners, Ltd.* [1939] 1 All E.R. 693.

51 *Ibid.* p. 105.

same effect is the earlier case of *George* v. *Skivington*,[52] which after undergoing much criticism has been expressly approved in *Donoghue* v. *Stevenson*.[53] There a chemist sold a hairwash, made by himself, to the plaintiff's husband knowing that it was to be used by the plaintiff. The hairwash was negligently compounded and was unfit for use, thereby injuring the plaintiff. The chemist was held liable on the ground that he knew that the plaintiff was to use his hairwash. Although the point was not made, it was obvious that the chemist contemplated that the hairwash would be used in the state in which he sold it without further examination.

629 A manufacturer of a sidecar, who negligently fitted it to a motor cycle, was held liable to a passenger in the sidecar who was injured when the cycle parted from the sidecar in climbing a hill. The ground of the decision was that the manufacturer must have contemplated that the sidecar was to be used by third parties without new tests.[54] Again, when a reconditioned motor-car was sold, the sellers knowing it was to be used immediately without any examination, although there was an opportunity of examining it, the sellers were held liable when, through their negligence, a wheel came off the first morning the car was used and the driver was injured.[55] Similarly, a monumental mason who erected a tombstone was held liable to a person on whom it fell owing to his negligence at the time of the erection, on the ground that he must have contemplated that his work would be accepted without any tests.[56]

A manufacturer of sweets who sold them to a wholesaler from whom they were bought by a retailer was held liable to the retailer when, on putting the sweets in his shop window, his hand was injured by a piece of wire in one of the sweets, although he had an opportunity of examining them when he took them out of the box.[57]

630 In *Dransfield* v. *British Insulated Cables Ltd.*,[58] it was held that the manufacturer owes no duty to the consumer or user if his product is in such a condition that there is a reasonable possibility of intermediate examination. In that case the manufacturers of a metal bull-ring supplied it for use to a local authority. The bull-ring was used in the local

[52] (1869) L.R. 5 Ex. 1; " After a long and rough crossing has limped into port," *per* Asquith L.J. in *Candler* v. *Crane, Christmas & Co.* [1951] 2 K.B. 164, 190. (The decision itself in *Candler* v. *Crane, Christmas & Co.*, however, was disapproved by the House of Lords in *Hedley Byrne & Co. Ltd.* v. *Heller & Partners Ltd.* [1964] A.C. 465.) *Blacker* v. *Lake and Elliott* (1912) 106 L.T. 533 (purchaser of brazing lamp which exploded owing to negligent manufacture, held not entitled to recover from manufacturer), in which *George* v. *Skivington* was not followed, must be considered to be overruled by *Donoghue* v. *Stevenson* (Lord Atkin, p. 594, Lord Macmillan, p. 616) on the ground that it did not give " sufficient attention to the general principle which governs the whole law of negligence in the duty owed to those who will be immediately injured by lack of care."

[53] [1932] A.C. 562.

[54] *Malfroot* v. *Noxal Ltd.* (1935) 51 T.L.R. 551.

[55] *Herschtal* v. *Stewart & Ardern Ltd.* [1940] 1 K.B. 155.

[56] *Brown* v. *Cotterill* (1934) 51 T.L.R. 21.

[57] *Barnett* v. *Packer Ltd.* [1940] 3 All E.R. 575.

[58] [1937] 4 All E.R. 382.

authority's overhead system of wires. Owing to negligence in manufacture, the bull-ring broke and killed a workman. It had not deteriorated since it left the manufacturers, and the local authority did not test it before use, but relied on the manufacturers. It was held that, as there was an opportunity for testing the bull-ring before use and such a test could have been easily made, the manufacturers were not liable for the death. This decision must be considered erroneous,[59] the test being not whether there was a possibility of examination before use but whether it was contemplated that the article would not be used until after an examination was made. So, where a cold chisel was supplied by the manufacturers to employers and was used by a workman who sustained an injury through a splinter of metal entering his eye because the head of the chisel, which he was properly using, was dangerously hard, the manufacturers were liable to the workman. The employers were held to be under no duty to examine the chisel before issuing it to the workman or to institute frequent inspections after use in the absence of anything to suggest that the chisel was defective.[60]

631 The duty of the manufacturer may be said to be to take reasonable care in the manufacture of his product, and failure to take such care will render him liable to any consumer or user whose person or property is injured by his product, provided (1) the product causing the injury has the same defect as it had when it left the manufacturer; and (2) the manufacturer should have contemplated that the product would be consumed or used in the same condition as it was in when it left him.

632 **Component parts.** A manufacturer's duty is not limited to those parts of his product which he makes himself. It extends to component parts, supplied by his sub-manufacturers or others, which he uses in the manufacture of his own products. He must take reasonable care, by inspection or otherwise, to see that those parts can properly be used to put his product in a condition in which it can be safely used or consumed in the contemplated manner by the ultimate user or consumer.[61]

633 **Container of goods.** The manufacturer's duty extends not only to his product, but also to any container in which he packs his product for

[59] It was not followed by Tucker J. in *Herschtal* v. *Stewart & Ardern Ltd.* [1940] 1 K.B. 155, and was said by Goddard L.J. in *Haseldine* v. *Daw & Son Ltd.* [1941] 2 K.B. 343, 376, to be wrongly decided. See also Goodhart in 54 L.Q.R. 59.

[60] *Mason* v. *Williams & Williams Ltd.* [1955] 1 All E.R. 808, which was referred to with approval by the House of Lords in *Davie* v. *New Merton Board Mills Ltd.* [1959] A.C. 604, where a fitter had his eye injured because a tool, supplied by a reputable supplier, was negligently made in that it was excessively hard. The trial judge, Ashworth J., said ([1957] 2 Q.B. 368, at p. 379): " Use of an article for a purpose materially different from that for which the maker designed it or which he might reasonably be taken to have contemplated, might afford him an answer to a claim founded on the article's dangerous or defective condition . . ." but ". . . I do not agree with the contention that use for a different, albeit similar, purpose *ipso facto* frees the makers from liability." See note on this case, 74 L.Q.R. 397.

[61] See *Macpherson* v. *Buick Motor Co.*, 217 N.Y. 282, referred to with approval by Lords Atkin and Macmillan in *Donoghue* v. *Stevenson.*

the purpose of sale. If he does not manufacture the container, he must exercise reasonable care to see whether it is fit for its purpose before he delivers it to his buyer. In *Bates* v. *Batey & Co.*,[62] manufacturers of ginger beer, who did not make their bottles, were sued by the purchaser of a bottle of their ginger beer who was injured owing to the bursting of the bottle. The jury found that the manufacturers did not know the bottle was defective but were negligent in not discovering whether it was defective or not, and on these findings the manufacturers were held not liable. This case must be taken to be overruled by *Donoghue* v. *Stevenson* on the ground stated by Lord Atkin[63]: " As the manufacturers must have contemplated the bottle being handled immediately by the consumer, they owed a duty to him to take care that he should not be injured externally by explosion, just as I think they owed a duty to him to take care that he should not be injured internally by poison or other noxious thing." In *Elliott* v. *Hall*[64] a colliery company who supplied coal in a defective truck, which they hired from a wagon company, were held liable to a servant of the buyers of the coal for damage caused to him through the defective condition of the truck, on the ground that, as they supplied their coal in a truck, they were under a duty to use reasonable care to see that the truck was safe for the purpose. In *Marshall* v. *Russian Oil Products*[65] petrol was delivered in a barrel which burst when it was being rolled down a skid. The suppliers were held liable for not taking reasonable care to see that the container was fit to withstand the ordinary risks of delivery. If, however, the defect in the container were a latent one, which could not be detected by reasonable care and skill on the part of the manufacturer, the manufacturer would not be liable.[66] In such a case, the maker of the container would be liable if the latent defect were due to negligence in the making.

634 **Duty to label goods.** The manufacturer owes a duty to take care in the labelling of his product, when failure to label it properly is likely to cause danger to person or property. If, by negligent labelling, he causes damage to the ultimate consumer or user he will be liable. " If

[62] [1913] 3 K.B. 351. This decision followed *Blacker* v. *Lake and Elliott, supra*, and did not follow *George* v. *Skivington*, and must therefore be taken to be overruled by *Donoghue* v. *Stevenson*. It is expressly disapproved by Lord Atkin (p. 595) with whose criticism of the cases Lord Thankerton concurred, and disapproved by implication by Lord Macmillan (p. 616). Horridge J., however, in *Pattendon* v. *Beney* (1933) 50 T.L.R. 10, expressed the opinion that it was not overruled. Nevertheless where a bottler used bottles for carbonated beverages repeatedly without having an adequate method of inspection in order to discover whether or not the bottles had become weakened by previous rough handling, he was held liable when a bottle suddenly exploded due to weakness whilst it was standing on the floor of a retail store and injured the plaintiff: *Hart* v. *Dominion Stores* (1968) 67 D.L.R. (2d) 675.

[63] *Donoghue* v. *Stevenson, supra*, p. 595.

[64] (1885) 15 Q.B.D. 315. As Lord Atkin points out in *Donoghue* v. *Stevenson*, at p. 585, this case was not decided on the ground that the truck was in the defendant's possession and that the plaintiff was an invitee.

[65] 1938 S.C. 773.

[66] *Elliott* v. *Hall, supra, per* Grove J.

a person, for example, manufactures two different articles, one being a deadly poison and the other safe, and through a careless blunder labels as safe an article which he ought to have known was of the other category and sells it under that description, I should be slow to say that in such a case he would not be responsible to persons who he knew would use the article."[67] In *Vacwell Engineering Co. Ltd.* v. *B.D.H. Chemicals Ltd.*[68] the defendants supplied the plaintiffs with boron tribromide in order technically to faciliate the plaintiffs' manufacture of transistor devices. This chemical was manufactured and distributed by the defendants in glass ampoules with a label affixed to each bearing the warning words " harmful vapour," since it was known that the chemical reacted on contact with water by emitting toxic vapour but neither of the parties knew that it reacted violently and exploded on such contact. Whilst two of the plaintiffs' physicists were engaged on washing the labels off the ampoules in two adjacent sinks of water the glass of one was broken and a violent explosion occurred killing one of these men and causing extensive damage to the plaintiff's premises. It was held, *inter alia*, by Rees J. that the defendants were negligent in that it was their duty to take reasonable care to ascertain major industrial hazards of chemicals marketed by them and to give proper warning of such hazards to their customers, which they had failed to do by using these misleading labels. In *Devilez* v. *Boots Pure Drug Co.*[69] it was held that the defendants had a duty to give some warning on the bottle of the corn solvent's dangerous characteristics and also to secure the bottle in some better way than with a cork to avoid accidental contamination should the bottle spill its contents as a result of the stopper accidentally falling out.

635 **Duty to give proper instructions for use.** Goods may be dangerous when used for a particular purpose unless certain precautions are taken. A drug, for example, may be perfectly safe if properly diluted, but dangerous if taken undiluted. In such a case it is the duty of the manufacturer to deliver adequate instructions for use with his product. Accordingly, manufacturers of a cattle dip, who negligently labelled the dip, so that when the labelled instructions were carried out the dip was insufficiently diluted and cattle were killed, were held liable in negligence to the buyers.[70] Again, manufacturers of a cleaning fluid, who sold some of their fluid to a firm of ship repairers, were held liable to the owners of a ship which was damaged by an explosion caused by their fluid because of their issuing inadequate instructions for its use to the

[67] Lush J. in *Blacker* v. *Lake and Elliott* (1912) 106 L.T. 533, 541.
[68] [1971] 1 Q.B. 88. (In the C.A. after seven days of argument the parties came to terms with the court's approval that judgment be entered for the plaintiffs on the issue of liability in negligence limited to 80 per cent. of the damages, and the issue of damages would be referred for assessment by an official Referee on the basis that that part of the judgment of Rees J. which dealt with remoteness of damage in negligence would not be challenged.
[69] (1962) 106 S.J. 552.
[70] *British Chartered Co. of S. Africa* v. *Lennon* (1915) 31 T.L.R. 585. In this case the buyers bought direct from the manufacturers, but this does not affect the principle.

ship repairers.[71] Also, when manufacturers of a hair dye knew that their dye was dangerous if used on a person without a skin test and sold it to a hairdresser without warning him of the necessity of a test before use, it was held that they were liable to one of the hairdresser's customers who developed dermatitis as a result of the application of the dye.[72] Although a warning was given concerning the use of a certain weedkiller, it was held to be an insufficient one by the Ontario High Court and thus the manufacturers were held liable for the damage to plants caused by the invisible mist produced when the weedkiller was being properly used.[73]

636 On the other hand, in *Kubach* v. *Hollands*,[74] manufacturers of chemicals sold what purported to be manganese dioxide to retailers who in turn sold it to a girls' school. The manganese dioxide was in fact mixed with antimony sulphide, as a result of which one of the pupils of the school, in making an experiment, was injured by an explosion and lost an eye. Manganese dioxide can be used " for a variety of purposes or in innocuous compounds or mixtures. The use of it for school experiments was only one of the many possible uses " and therefore it is not dangerous in itself. Moreover, the manufacturers had invoiced it to the retailers with a warning that it " must be examined and tested by user before use." The retailers neither examined and tested it themselves nor passed on the warning to the school, and the manufacturers were held not liable because they had discharged their duty by giving a proper warning. The retailers, on the other hand, were held liable because they contemplated that the school would use the chemicals without first testing them.

Similarly when a manufacturer of a hair dye supplied the dye to a hairdresser in labelled bottles together with a brochure of instructions, both of which contained a warning that a test should be made before use, and no test was made, the manufacturer was held not liable to one of the hairdresser's customers who contracted dermatitis. Warning to the hairdresser was enough.[75] " I think it would be unreasonable and impossible to expect that they [the manufacturers] should give warning in such a form that it must come to the knowledge of the particular customer who is to be treated." [76]

If a test is made and the plaintiff passes it but nevertheless gets dermatitis owing to her being allergic to the form of dye used, it is possible that the manufacturer might be liable to the plaintiff for making a dangerous dye, but this is not certain.[77]

[71] *Anglo-Celtic Shipping Co.* v. *Elliott* (1926) 42 T.L.R. 297.

[72] *Parker* v. *Oxolo Ltd.* [1937] 3 All E.R. 524.

[73] *Ruegger* v. *Shell Oil of Canada* (1963) 41 D.L.R. (2d) 183.

[74] [1937] 3 All E.R. 907.

[75] *Holmes* v. *Ashford* [1950] 2 All E.R. 76 (the hairdresser was held liable).

[76] *Ibid.*, *per* Tucker L.J. at p. 80.

[77] See *Ingham* v. *Emes* [1955] 2 Q.B. 366, where the plaintiff, who was tested for the dye and passed the test but got dermatitis, sued in contract on an implied warranty that the dye was fit to be used upon her. She knew she was allergic to that form of dye but did not tell the hairdresser. It was held that the warranty was only that the dye was fit to be used upon normal persons.

637 **Proof of negligence.** Negligence on the part of the manufacturer must be proved before liability is established, and the method of proof is the same as in any other case of negligence.[78] In *Donoghue* v. *Stevenson* Lord Macmillan said[79]: "There is no presumption of negligence in such a case as the present, nor is there any justification for applying the maxim *res ipsa loquitur*. Negligence must be both averred and proved." This, however, seems to go too far. While it is true that there is no presumption of negligence, the maxim *res ipsa loquitur* applies to negligence in manufacture, when the circumstances are such as to call for its application, equally with negligence in other cases. The mere presence of a snail in a stoppered and sealed bottle of ginger beer would appear to be within the maxim because, owing to retention of effective control by the manufacturer until the ginger beer reached the consumer, there is a greater probability of negligence on the part of the manufacturer than on the part of any other person. In *Grant* v. *Australian Knitting Mills*[80] the court apparently proceeded on the view that the presence of the chemical irritant in the garments was evidence of negligence. "If excess sulphites were left in the garment, that could only be because someone was at fault. The appellant is not required to lay his finger on the exact person in all the chain who was responsible, or to specify what he did wrong. Negligence is found as a matter of inference from the existence of the defects taken in connection with all the known circumstances."[81] Similarly, in the earlier case of *Chapronière* v. *Mason*[82] the presence of a stone in a bath bun manufactured by the defendant was held to be within the maxim *res ipsa loquitur* and to be evidence of negligence against the manufacturer. When dermatitis was contracted on wearing a suit just cleaned by the defendants it was held that the burden was on the defendants to prove no negligence.[83]

638 It is not necessary to specify any particular act of negligence. When a workman used a chisel, defective through excessive hardness, and was injured because of the defect it was held that on proving that the chisel came from the manufacturers and that the hardness had not been caused at his employer's factory he had discharged the burden of proof.[84]

When the issue is whether the product is dangerous or not, discovery

[78] Chap. 15, *post*.

[79] [1932] A.C. 562, 622. This dictum was applied in *Daniels* v. *White & Sons* [1938] 4 All E.R. 258 (manufacturers held to have proved that the presence of carbolic acid in their lemonade was not due to their negligence). However, the decision in *Daniels* v. *White & Sons* cannot be reconciled with either *Chapronière* v. *Mason* or *Grant* v. *Australian Knitting Mills*, which latter case appears not to have been cited. See Salmond, 15th ed., p. 400 and Winfield, 6th ed., p. 666. Meanwhile, in Street's *Law of Torts* 4th ed., pp. 174–175, the author advances a suggestion how these conflicting decisions may be so reconciled.

[80] [1936] A.C. 85 (Lord Macmillan was a member of this Judicial Committee, holding a contrary view to the dictum he expressed in *Donoghue's* case).

[81] Lord Wright at p. 101.

[82] (1905) 21 T.L.R. 633.

[83] *Mayne* v. *Silvermere Cleaners Ltd.* [1939] 1 All E.R. 693.

[84] *Mason* v. *Williams & Williams Ltd.* [1955] 1 All E.R. 808. See also *Davie* v. *New Merton Board Mills Ltd.* [1959] A.C. 604 (affirming the decision of the Court of Appeal [1958] 1 Q.B. 210). In the American case of *Escola* v. *Coca Cola Bottling Co. of Fresno* (1944)

may be obtained of complaints of personal injuries from users not only before but also after the date of the supply of the product.[85]

Defences

639 **User's knowledge of defect.** The manufacturer may not be liable when the consumer or user knows of the defect. "The principle of *Donoghue's* case can only be applied where the defect is hidden and unknown to the consumer, otherwise the directness of cause and effect is absent: the man who consumes or uses a thing which he knows to be noxious cannot complain in respect of whatever mischief follows, because it follows from his own conscious volition in choosing to incur the risk or certainty of mischance." [86] So, where the manufacturers of a crane sent it out in parts to be assembled by the buyers, and the buyers' foreman, in assembling it, noticed that it was defective but nevertheless assembled and worked the crane before the defects were remedied, with the result that he was killed, the manufacturers were held not liable in respect of the death on the ground that the chain of causation was broken.[87]

640 In spite of Lord Wright's dictum, quoted above, knowledge of the defect does not as a matter of law prevent the consumer or user from recovering. The manufacturer by negligently causing the defect has been guilty of a breach of duty. Whether any particular damage is causally connected with that breach or whether the chain of causation between the breach and the damage has been broken is a question of fact, depending on the circumstances, and not a question of law. The circumstances may show that, even with knowledge of the defect, the consumer or user is justified in incurring the danger which it suggests. The test whether he is so justified is the old test laid down in *Clayards* v. *Dethick*,[88] "whether the plaintiff acted as a man of ordinary prudence would have done, or rashly and in defiance of warning." In other words, it is whether in the circumstances he has acted reasonably. This is illustrated by *Denny* v. *Supplies & Transport Co. Ltd.*,[89] where a barge was loaded by the defendants with timber so badly as to make it dangerous to unload it. The plaintiff, who was employed to unload it, saw it was unsafe, but proceeded to unload it and was injured in doing so. It was held that he was entitled to recover on the ground that it was reasonable for him to unload, because the only alternative was to leave the barge loaded.

150 Pac. (2d) 436, the plaintiff was injured by a bottle of Coca Cola, bought by her employer and bottled and sold by the defendant, exploding in her hand. It was held that *res ipsa loquitur* applied and she was entitled to recover, although there was no evidence of specific acts of negligence and the defendant proved he used approved methods of inspection.

85 *Board* v. *Thomas Hedley & Co. Ltd.* [1951] 2 All E.R. 431.

86 Lord Wright in *Grant* v. *Australian Knitting Mills Ltd.* [1936] A.C. 85, 105.

87 *Farr* v. *Butters Bros. & Co.* [1932] 2 K.B. 606. See the criticism of this decision in Williams, *Joint Torts and Contributory Negligence*, p. 324.

88 (1848) 12 Q.B. 439.

89 [1950] 2 K.B. 374.

641 In *London Graving Dock* v. *Horton*,[90] Lord Porter expressed the view that knowledge of the true position would be " a complete answer to the claim " against the manufacturer, but *Horton's* case was a decision on the principle of *Indermaur* v. *Dames* (Chapter 8) and it was held that *Donoghue* v. *Stevenson* [91] could not have any application to the facts of that case. It is to be noted that *Denny's* case is not mentioned in any of the judgments. Nevertheless in *Gledhill* v. *Liverpool Abattoir Ltd.*,[92] Lord Porter's view was followed and approved by the Court of Appeal. The facts, however, in *Gledhill's* case do not seem to come within the point raised in this paragraph. In that case, the plaintiff's employers, by arrangement with the Liverpool Corporation, used the Corporation's abattoir in which to slaughter pigs. The pigs, after being stunned, were fixed to an elevator by chains supplied by the Corporation. When the chains became worn the Corporation supplied new chains at the employers' request. The new chains were strong and properly made but were unsuitable because they were of a heavier type than was necessary, so that one of the pigs on being lifted slipped and fell on the plaintiff, injuring him. These new chains had been in use for about a year without complaint to the Corporation although the plaintiff and his employers both knew of their unsuitability for the work. The plaintiff's action against the Corporation failed and Morris L.J.[93] said: " The Corporation were entitled to assume that if the chains did not prove suitable or convenient they would not be used. They cannot be held responsible for their user by those who had full knowledge that some difficulties were in some cases and on some occasions presented."

In this case there seems to have been no breach of duty on the part of the Corporation. The chains they supplied were not defective in any way and if they were not suitable for the purpose for which the plaintiff's employers required them that would not give rise to any liability in tort unless they were required for immediate use without any possibility of examination.[94]

642 **Contributory negligence.** Whether or not the manufacturer is liable if the consumer or user, although he does not know of the defect, could have discovered the defect by the exercise of reasonable care has not been decided. The consumer or user is presumably entitled to assume that the manufacturer has properly fulfilled his duty and is not bound to make an examination for defects.[95] On the other hand, if the defect

[90] [1951] A.C. 737, 750.
[91] *Ibid.* See the similar views expressed by Lord Normand and Lord MacDermott.
[92] [1957] 1 W.L.R. 1028.
[93] [1957] 1 W.L.R. 1028, at p. 1037.
[94] See note on this case, 74 L.Q.R. 7.
[95] See *Mason* v. *Williams & Williams* [1955] 1 All E.R. 808 where it was held that factory owners were not bound to examine tools supplied by reputable manufacturers for defects before issuing them to their workmen to use. In *Davie* v. *New Merton Board Mills Ltd.* [1959] A.C. 604 at p. 630, *per* Lord Reid: " The trial judge, Ashworth J., said: ' I also hold that no intermediate examination of the drift between the time of the manufacture and the time of its actual use was reasonably to be expected. It seems to me wholly unreasonable to expect an employer to test a drift for hardness before issuing it to his

would have become apparent to anyone consuming or using the article with reasonable care, the consumer or user may be prevented from recovering in full on the ground of his contributory negligence.

643 **Defect caused since the manufacturer parted with the goods.** The manufacturer is not liable when the defect is not due to his negligence but was caused by something which has happened after he has parted with the goods. As Lord Macmillan said: " I can readily conceive that where a manufacturer has parted with his product and it has passed into other hands it may well be exposed to vicissitudes which may render it defective or noxious, for which the manufacturer could not in any view be held to blame." [96] In considering whether the defect was due to the manufacturer's negligence, the lapse of time since the manufacturer parted with the article, the probability of damage from other causes, the speed with which articles of that kind deteriorate, and the necessity or otherwise of repair, are all matters to be taken into consideration.[97] So, where a windscreen fitted to a motor-car broke after about a year's use, for no apparent cause, the manufacturers were held not liable because, after the lapse of time and the many opportunities for damage the windscreen must have had, including that of being negligently fitted into its frame, it could not be said that the cause of the damage was negligence in manufacture.[98] Again, in the case put in *Grant* v. *Australian Knitting Mills* [99] of a foundry which had cast a rudder to be fitted to a ship and after some years of use the rudder broke, owing to negligent casting, causing great loss of life and damage to property, the makers would not be held liable, because " so many contingencies must have intervened between the lack of care on the part of the makers and the casualty."

If the article manufactured is only intended for temporary use, the lapse of the time for which it was contemplated it would be used will relieve the manufacturer from liability.[1]

644 **Inspection contemplated before use.** In *Donoghue* v. *Stevenson* the article manufactured was delivered in such a form as to preclude the possibility of intermediate examination, but, as is pointed out above (§ 628), the manufacturer is liable for defects caused by his negligence if he contemplates that his product will be used immediately without

employee, and no other examination would have revealed the danger existing in this particular drift.' This finding is not challenged by the appellant [plaintiff]. Accordingly, there was no negligence on the part of the respondents or any of their servants, including the appellant." *Taylor* v. *Rover Co.* [1966] 1 W.L.R. 1491.

96 *Donoghue* v. *Stevenson* [1932] A.C. 562 at p. 622.

97 As an example see *Gillespie* v. *Grahame* (1936) 106 L.J. 458, where a joiner had erected a henhouse on land and, in a wind, the roof of the henhouse was blown onto the adjoining land, causing damage, the joiner was held not liable. Lord Hill Watson held that the joiner's liability depended on whether there was or was not a reasonable opportunity for inspection by an ordinary prudent owner who was doing his duty.

98 *Evans* v. *Triplex Safety Glass Co.* [1936] 1 All E.R. 283.

99 [1936] A.C. 85.

1 *Eccles* v. *Cross & M'Ilwham*, 1938 S.C. 697 (electricians who installed a temporary electric lighting system not liable to builders' workman killed two months after).

any previous examination or test, even though he has not precluded the possibility of examination.

If the manufacturer contemplates that, in the ordinary course of things, his product will not be used until after an examination or test is first made, he is not liable for defects which the examination or test ought to have revealed. On this principle, when contractors did work subject to the approval of the local authority, and their work was passed by the local authority's works supervisor, it was held that they were not liable to a person who tripped over a soleplate which they had placed in a passage.[2] If an examination or test is made, whether contemplated or not, the manufacturer may not be liable for defects which that examination or test ought to have revealed. His liability depends on whether, in the circumstances of the case, the chain of causation is broken (see § 639). So, the builder of a house who negligently erected a defective ceiling which fell and injured a person lawfully in the house was held not liable when it was proved that the ceiling was obviously defective and that the defects should have been discovered by the person who was engaged by the purchaser to make an examination.[3] It has also been held that when a substantial period of time has elapsed between the delivery of the goods and the damage, during which an examination might have been made, the manufacturer is not liable.[4] It is submitted, however, that lapse of time between delivery and damage is only relevant to the question whether the goods were in the same condition as when they left the manufacturer. If they were, then the manufacturer is liable notwithstanding that there was an opportunity, which was not taken, of examining the goods [5] unless he contemplated that his goods would not be used without first being examined.

645 If the manufacturer sends out his goods accompanied by a warning that they are to be tested before use, he is under no liability for damage caused by his goods through failure to observe the warning. In *Kubach* v. *Hollands* [6] manufacturing chemists sold to retailers a quantity of manganese dioxide. The invoice stated: " The above goods are accurate as described on leaving our works but they must be examined and tested by user before use." The chemicals supplied in fact contained a mixture of another chemical, with the result that a schoolgirl, in performing an experiment at a school to which the chemicals were supplied by the retailers, was injured. The retailers were held to be liable to

[2] *Buckner* v. *Ashby & Horner Ltd.* [1941] 1 K.B. 321. See also *London Graving Dock* v. *Horton* [1951] A.C. 737, 750, *per* Lord Porter, " an examination by the retail vendor, if rightly expected, could be relied on by the manufacturer and would have been a complete answer to the claim."

[3] *Otto* v. *Bolton* [1936] 2 K.B. 46. This was not the case of the manufacturer of a chattel, but on the point under discussion it was decided on the same principle. See also *Davis* v. *Foots* [1940] 1 K.B. 116. See also *Gillespie* v. *Grahame* (1956) 106 L.J. 458.

[4] *Paine* v. *Colne Valley Electricity Supply Co.* [1938] 4 All E.R. 803 (interval of two years between delivery of machinery and installation by buyers—manufacturers not liable).

[5] See *Mason* v. *Williams & Williams Ltd.* [1955] 1 All E.R. 808. This decision was approved by the House of Lords in *Davie* v. *New Merton Board Mills Ltd.* [1959] A.C. 604.

[6] [1937] 3 All E.R. 907.

the schoolgirl, but the manufacturers were held to be not liable to indemnify the retailers, on the ground that the retailers " had ample and repeated opportunity of intermediate examination, and, if they had taken the simple precaution which the invoice warned them to take, no mischief would have followed." On the same ground, Lord Hewart C.J. expressed the opinion that the schoolgirl could not have sued the manufacturers.[7] Again, when a manufacturer supplied a hairdresser with a hair dye in labelled bottles accompanied by a brochure of instructions containing a warning that a skin test should be made before the dye was used, it was held that he was not liable to one of the hairdresser's customers, who contracted dermatitis, when the hairdresser used the dye on her without making a test.[8]

3.—DUTY OF RETAILER OF GOODS

646 **Contractual duty.** A retailer of goods is in contractual relationship with the buyer and accordingly may be liable for breach of contract if he sells defective goods. The extent of his liability is set out in the Sale of Goods Act 1893, s. 14. For breach of contract the retailer is only liable in damages to the buyer, but those damages may include expense to which the buyer has been put or pecuniary loss which he has sustained through injury to members of his family, living with him, caused by the breach of contract.[9] If there has been a breach of contract it is immaterial whether or not the seller has been negligent; he is equally liable for latent defects in the articles he sells as for defects discoverable on reasonable examination.[10]

647 **Fraud.** A retailer is liable if he makes any fraudulent misrepresentation in selling his goods; his liability extends to any person who ought to have been in his contemplation as likely to be injured as a result of his fraud. Accordingly, the seller of a gun, who warranted the gun to be safe when in fact he knew it was unsafe, was held liable to the buyer's son who was injured owing to the bursting of the gun.[11]

648 **Duty to warn of known defects.** Apart from any question of contract or fraud, a retailer owes a duty to the person to whom he supplies goods to warn him of any danger in the goods of which he knows and of which he could not reasonably expect the recipient to know. Similarly, he must warn him of any defect in the goods which renders them unfit for the purpose for which he contemplates they will be used, provided

7 [1937] 3 All E.R. 907 at p. 911; *cf. Ingham* v. *Emes* [1955] 2 Q.B. 366.

8 *Holmes* v. *Ashford* [1950] 2 All E.R. 76.

9 *Preist* v. *Last* [1903] 2 K.B. 148 (hot water bottle bursts and injures buyer's wife); *Frost* v. *Aylesbury Dairy Co.* [1905] 1 K.B. 608 (milk contains germs of typhoid fever, whereby buyer's wife dies); *Jackson* v. *Watson & Sons* [1909] 2 K.B. 193 (tinned salmon poisons buyer's wife). The contractual duty applies also to the container. *Geddling* v. *Marsh* [1920] 1 K.B. 688 (ginger beer).

10 *Randall* v. *Newson* (1877) 2 Q.B.D. 102 (carriage-pole); *Myers* v. *Brent Cross Service Co.* [1934] 1 K.B. 46 (connecting rod); *Grant* v. *Australian Knitting Mills* [1936] A.C. 85 (men's pants).

11 *Langridge* v. *Levy* (1837) 2 M. & W. 519; affd. 4 M. & W. 338.

that he knows of the defect. Failure to disclose the danger or defect will render him liable to the ultimate consumer or user of the goods who suffers damage directly attributable to the danger or defect. When the plaintiff was supplied by the sellers with a tin of disinfectant powder which, owing to previous complaints they had received, the sellers knew would be likely to cause injury unless the tins were opened with special care, and no warning was given of the danger, the plaintiff was held entitled to recover.[12] Similarly, it would appear that a retailer, who has negligently delivered goods, known by him to be dangerous, in mistake for harmless goods ordered by the buyer, is liable to the consumer or user of the goods delivered who has suffered damage through believing that the retailer had delivered the goods ordered.[13]

649 The retailer must also pass on to the buyer any instructions for use or warnings which he has received from the manufacturer. Where manganese dioxide was bought from a manufacturer with a warning that it must be " examined and tested by user before use," and the retailer failed to hand on the warning to his customer, with the result that no examination was made and an explosion occurred owing to the substance supplied being manganese dioxide mixed with antimony sulphide, the retailer was held liable.[14] The retailer, who has sold goods, which are dangerous by reason of a latent defect in them, may be able to escape liability for negligence to a person who uses them and suffers injury thereby, if it can be shown that he himself purchased them from well-known and reputable suppliers. Accordingly in *Fisher* v. *Harrods* [15] the retailers were held to be negligent in failing to make inquiries of the manufacturer of a jewellery cleaning liquid, which had exploded and injured a buyer, or to have it analysed and in marketing the product without giving a warning. If the retailers had made any inquiry they would have found that the manufacturer was a man of insufficient qualification for, or experience in, the manufacture of such a cleaning product.

650 **Duty not to render goods defective.** When the retailer does not know that the goods are defective or dangerous, and he sells goods which have been so packed or made up, in a bottle, tin or other container, that it is not reasonably possible for him to examine the goods without destroying the condition in which the manufacturer intended them to reach the buyer and in which the buyer expected to receive them, he is under no liability in tort to a consumer or user who receives the goods with the same defects as they had when they left the manufacturer. In *Gordon* v. *M'Hardy* [16] a retail grocer was sued for damages caused

[12] *Clarke* v. *Army and Navy Co-operative Society* [1903] 1 K.B. 155.
[13] *Cf. Macdonald* v. *Macbrayne Ltd.*, 1915 S.C. 716; *British Chartered Co. of S. Africa* v. *Lennon* (1915) 31 T.L.R. 585; *Philco Radio* v. *Spurling* [1949] 2 All E.R. 882.
[14] *Kubach* v. *Hollands* [1937] 3 All E.R. 907. The trial of the issue between the plaintiff and the retailer is reported in *The Times*, June 17, 1937.
[15] (1966) 110 S.J. 133.
[16] (1903) 6 F. 210. Apparently approved in *Donoghue* v. *Stevenson*, see p. 604 (Lord Thankerton), and at p. 622 (Lord Macmillan).

by the death of a person who had eaten tinned salmon sold by him, and it was held that, as the tin was only to be opened immediately before use, it was not reasonable to expect the grocer to examine the goods, and he was not liable.

651 Even in this case, however, it would appear that there may be some liability on the part of the retailer. If the damage to the consumer or user is caused, not by some defect which the goods had when they left the manufacturer but by some other defect, the retailer will be liable if that defect has been caused by his negligence. If the retailer is exempted from liability as the innocent distributor of the manufacturer's goods, he should at least use care to see that the goods are in the same condition as when they left the manufacturer, and that externally they are free from defects. If a tin containing the goods has been burst open, or any other container has been damaged while the goods are in the retailer's possession, so that the contents of the tin or other container have become defective, the retailer who knew or should have known of the defect, would be liable to the consumer or user who was injured.[17] Again, if complaints have been received from consumers or users of a particular consignment of goods, the retailer would be liable if he continued to sell the goods without taking precautions in the light of the complaints he received—either by discontinuing the sale of that consignment or, in so far as the complaint was capable of remedy, remedying the defect complained of.[18]

652 If the form in which the manufacturer makes his goods does not preclude the retailer from making an examination of them before sale, the question then arises, what is the liability of the retailer for damage caused by the goods he has sold when he does not know, although by the exercise of reasonable care he could have known, that the goods are defective?

653 It would appear that the retailer is liable for damage due to defects in his goods caused by his own negligence. If, for example, he stores his goods in such a position or in such a manner that they are contaminated from external sources, such as rats, damp or dirt, the principle of *Donoghue* v. *Stevenson* would render him liable to the ultimate consumer or user for his negligence just as the manufacturer is liable for negligence in manufacture. The same result would follow if he kept the goods in stock so long that they became defective.

654 A retailer is under no duty to examine goods for defects before resale, in the absence of circumstances suggesting that they might be defective,

[17] See *Gordon* v. *M'Hardy* (1903) 6 F. 210, where the Lord Justice-Clerk said that an averment that the tin was dented so as to cut through the metal and cause injury to the contents which the defender should have noticed, might have been ground for an action against him.

[18] See *Clarke* v. *Army and Navy Co-operative Society* [1903] 1 K.B. 155, where the retailers knew of the dangerous condition of the goods because of complaints they had received, and were liable for not giving warning, after knowledge of the danger.

when he obtains them from a manufacturer of repute.[19] If he obtains them from another source, he may be under a duty to examine them, depending on the nature of the goods and the probability or otherwise of danger to be expected from defects to which the goods are subject. Such a duty was held to exist in *Andrews* v. *Hopkinson* [20] where a secondhand motor-car, selected by the plaintiff and sold by the defendant (a dealer in secondhand cars) to a finance company who let it to the plaintiff on hire-purchase terms, had a defect in the steering. The defect could have been discovered by a competent mechanic, though probably not by an ordinary owner-driver, and the defendant had no reason to suppose that the car would be examined before use. The defendant was held liable, McNair J. stating [21]: "Having regard to the extreme peril involved in allowing an old car with a defective steering mechanism to be used on the road, I have no hesitation in holding that the defendant in the circumstances was guilty of negligence in failing to make the necessary examination, or at least in failing to warn the plaintiff that no such examination had been carried out." Similarly, in *Watson* v. *Buckley* [22] a hair dye was distributed by a firm, who were not the manufacturers, to a hairdresser who used it on the plaintiff, as a result of which the plaintiff contracted dermatitis. The reason was that the dye should have contained a 4 per cent. solution of acid but in fact contained a 10 per cent. solution. The distributors obtained the dye from "a gentleman who had emerged quite unexpectedly from Spain," advertised it as safe and fit for use without any preliminary test and gave directions for use but made no examination of the dye before distributing it. They were held to be negligent and liable to the plaintiff.

The duty of a retailer as stated above applies to all sellers of goods who are not manufacturers, whether they sell by retail or wholesale, because a wholesaler who distributes defective goods appears to be in the same position as the retailer.[23]

4.—DUTY OF REPAIRER OF GOODS

655 **Liability in contract and tort.** The case now being considered is that of a person who undertakes to repair a chattel or other property and so negligently performs his work that physical damage is caused to the person or property of a third party in consequence of his negligence. As far as his own work and its consequences are concerned, his duty is the same as that of a manufacturer.

[19] *Mason* v. *Williams & Williams Ltd.* [1955] 1 All E.R. 808, which was approved by the House of Lords in *Davie* v. *New Merton Board Mills Ltd.* [1959] A.C. 604. See *Gordon* v. *M'Hardy* (1903) 6 F. 210, *per* Lord Macdonald: "A grocer who gets a quantity of tins of preserved food and sells them to the public as he got them, cannot be liable for the condition of the contents of the tins if he buys from a dealer of repute."

[20] [1957] 1 Q.B. 229. See note on this case, 73 L.Q.R. 147.

[21] [1957] 1 Q.B. 229, at p. 237.

[22] [1940] 1 All E.R. 174.

[23] In *Goodchild* v. *Vaclight, The Times*, May 22, 1965, it was held that as the defendants, the distributors in England of vacuum cleaners made in Germany, both serviced and guaranteed them in this country they owed the same duty of care as the manufacturers.

It is quite clear that: "The fact that there is a contractual relationship between the parties which may give rise to an action for breach of contract, does not exclude the co-existence of a right of action founded on negligence as between the same parties, independently of the contract, though arising out of the relationship in fact brought about by the contract. Of this the best illustration is the right of the injured railway passenger to sue the railway company either for breach of the contract of safe carriage or for negligence in carrying him. And there is no reason why the same set of facts should not give one person a right of action in contract and another person a right of action in tort."[24] Some of the earlier cases are based on the view that facts which constitute a contract cannot have any other legal effect, but, as the passage just quoted shows, this view is erroneous. Equally erroneous is the view that if one person commits a breach of contract with another, a third party who is injured in consequence of the breach must, by reason of the breach, have a right of action in tort against the first party. In all cases the person suing in tort must show a breach of duty towards himself and cannot rely on a breach of duty towards any other person.

56 In *Winterbottom* v. *Wright*[25] the defendant had contracted with the Postmaster-General to provide a mail-coach, and the plaintiff's employer had contracted to convey the mail-coach along the road, the plaintiff himself being a coachman employed to drive the coach. The coach was defective and broke down injuring the plaintiff. The claim was based on the breach by the defendant of his contract to provide a safe coach, and the reliance by the plaintiff on the defendant's due performance of his contract. It was held that the claim failed, the chief ground of the decision being that the defendant's breach of contract gave no right of action to a person who was not a party to the contract. "Unless we confine the operation of such contracts as this to the parties who entered into them, the most absurd and outrageous consequences, to which I can see no limit, would ensue," was the opinion of Lord Abinger, who also regarded it as "an action of the first impression." In *Donoghue* v. *Stevenson*,[26] Lord Atkin's comment on this case was: "The actual decision appears to have been manifestly right; no duty to the plaintiff arose out of the contract; and the duty of the defendant under the contract with the Postmaster-General to put the coach in good repair could not have involved such direct relations with the servant of the persons whom the Postmaster-General employed to drive the coach as would give rise to a duty of care owed to such servant." Apparently, so far as the decision was based on tort, the damage was considered to be too remote.[27]

24 Lord Macmillan in *Donoghue* v. *Stevenson* [1932] A.C. 562, at p. 610.

25 (1842) 10 M. & W. 109. See § 658, *post*.

26 At p. 589. Lord Macmillan (p. 610) accepts the view of this case put forward in *Pollock on Torts*, 13th ed., p. 570, that the plaintiff did not have a cause of action. "Not in contract, for there was no contract between these parties; not in tort, for no bad faith or negligence on the defendant's part was shown."

27 See, *per* Brett M.R. in *Heaven* v. *Pender* (1883) 11 Q.B.D. 503.

657 In *Earl* v. *Lubbock* [28] the defendant contracted to keep in repair a number of vans owned by the plaintiff's employer. The plaintiff was a driver who was injured while driving one of the vans, owing to the wheel coming off. The van in question had been attended to by the defendant's workmen shortly before and also on the day of the accident. The plaintiff's case was put forward on the basis of the defendant's breach of contract, Mathew L.J. in his judgment saying: " The argument of counsel for the plaintiff was that the defendant's servants had been negligent in the performance of the contract with the owners of the van, and that it followed as a matter of law that anyone in their employment, or, indeed, anyone else who sustained an injury traceable to that negligence, had a cause of action against the defendant. It is impossible to accept such a wide proposition, and, indeed, it is difficult to see how, if it were the law, trade could be carried on." [29] It is clear that the proposition, as stated, is too wide, but it is not equally clear that if the proposition had been: " when a defendant has been negligent in the execution of his work, anyone who sustains physical injury as a direct consequence of that negligence has a cause of action against the defendants," it also would have been too wide, and the latter proposition is the one now being considered. Lord Atkin [30] said of *Earl* v. *Lubbock* that he agreed with the judgment of Mathew L.J. and added: " I have no doubt that in that case the plaintiff failed to show that the repairer owed any duty to him." Lord Macmillan's comment was [31]: " The case turns upon the rule that a stranger to a contract cannot found an action of tort on a breach of that contract. It was pointed out that there was no evidence that the plaintiff had been invited by the defendant to use the van, and the van owner was not complaining of the way in which the van had been repaired. The negligence, if negligence there was, was too remote, and the practical consequences of affirming liability in such a case were considered to be such as would render it difficult to carry on a trade at all."

658 The decisions of *Winterbottom* v. *Wright* and *Earl* v. *Lubbock* considered in the two preceding paragraphs cannot now be relied on. As decisions on the question of law raised in both cases, there can be no doubt that they are right, but they are not now authorities for the proposition that a repairer who negligently repairs an article entrusted to him, so that it is unsafe and causes damage to a person of a class who ought to have been in his contemplation as likely to be injured through its defect, is not liable to that person. In the words of Goddard L.J., " If properly pleaded that case [*Earl* v. *Lubbock*] would today be differently decided." [32] There are several decisions supporting this view.

[28] [1905] 1 K.B. 253. See § 658, *post*.
[29] *Ibid.* at p. 259.
[30] *Donoghue* v. *Stevenson* [1932] A.C. 562, at p. 592.
[31] *Ibid.* at p. 615.
[32] *Haseldine* v. *Daw & Son* [1941] 2 K.B. 343, 379. See also to the same effect, *Old Gate Estates* v. *Toplis* [1939] 3 All E.R. 209, *per* Wrottesley J.; *Buckner* v. *Ashby & Horner* [1941] 1 K.B. 321, 331, *per* Atkinson J.

In *Malfroot* v. *Noxal Ltd.*,[33] the defendants negligently fitted a sidecar to a motor-cycle, and as a result of their negligence, while the combination was climbing a gradient, the sidecar parted from the motor-cycle and the plaintiff, a passenger in the sidecar, was injured. Lewis J. applied the principle of *Donoghue* v. *Stevenson* and held that as the defendants were negligent and the sidecar was, to their knowledge, likely to be used without new tests by third parties, the defendants were liable in tort to the plaintiff. In *Brown* v. *Cotterill* [34] the defendant, a monumental mason, negligently erected a tombstone in a churchyard, with the result that it fell upon the plaintiff, who was lawfully in the churchyard, and injured her. Lawrence J., applying *Donoghue* v. *Stevenson,* held that the defendant would be liable unless the terms of his contract for the erection of the tombstone were such that an ordinarily prudent man would consider that his liability was at an end after the approval of the other party to the contract; he further held that the defendant could not have expected the person who ordered the tombstone to examine and approve of the method of erection, and he was therefore liable to the plaintiff. In *Howard* v. *Furness Houlder Ltd.*[35] the plaintiff was injured by the negligent reassembling of a valve in a steamship. He was held entitled to recover, on the ground that the defendants by their negligence had converted an article not dangerous in itself into a dangerous article.

659 In *Stennett* v. *Hancock* [36] a motor repairer negligently replaced the wheel of a lorry so that it came off and injured a pedestrian in the highway, and the repairer was held liable. In *Herschtal* v. *Stewart & Ardern Ltd.*[37] the suppliers of a reconditioned motor-car for the plaintiff's use were held liable to the plaintiff when a wheel came off and he was injured, on the ground that " the decision in *Donoghue* v. *Stevenson* is not intended to be limited only to manufacturers of goods but . . . it applies in a proper case to the repairer of an article." Finally, in *Haseldine* v. *Daw & Son Ltd.*[38] a firm of lift repairers were held liable to a passenger in the lift who was injured in consequence of their negligent work. " Where the facts show that no intermediate inspection is practicable or is contemplated, a repairer of a chattel stands in no different position from that of a manufacturer, and does owe a duty to a person who, in the ordinary course, may be expected to make use of the thing repaired." [39]

5.—DUTY OF TRANSFEROR OF GOODS

660 **Liability of transferors.** The duty of manufacturers, retailers and repairers of goods has already been considered. It now remains to

[33] (1935) 51 T.L.R. 551.
[34] (1934) 51 T.L.R. 21. The test applied by Lawrence J. in this case was applied by the C.A. in *Buckner* v. *Ashby & Horner* [1941] 1 K.B. 321.
[35] [1936] 2 All E.R. 781.
[36] [1939] 2 All E.R. 578. *Earl* v. *Lubbock* was not followed. The owner of the lorry was held not liable, as he had entrusted the repair to a competent repairer.
[37] [1940] 1 K.B. 155. An opportunity for intermediate examination which it was not reasonably anticipated would be exercised was held to be no defence.
[38] [1941] 2 K.B. 343.
[39] *Ibid., per* Goddard L.J. at p. 379.

consider the liability of other persons who transfer goods as a result of which damage is caused to the consumer or user of the goods. The other persons who transfer goods may be classified as (1) the owner, including a bailee with the right to use the goods, who transfers goods by way of loan or gift; (2) the owner or bailee who lets the goods on hire; (3) the owner or bailee who delivers the goods to a carrier for carriage; and (4) the carrier of goods who delivers them to a consignee. The liability of such a transferor may arise either out of contract or tort.

661 **Contractual duty.** Contractual liability will be only shortly considered. In the case of a gratuitous loan, the lender is bound to communicate defects in the goods lent with reference to the use to which they are to be put, if he knows of the defects. If he does not know of them, although he might have discovered them by the exercise of reasonable care, he is not liable for damage caused by the defects.[40] As to gifts, Willes J. said [41]: " The principle of law as to gifts is, that the giver is not responsible for damage resulting from the insecurity of the thing, unless he knew its evil character at the time, and omitted to caution the donee. There must be something like fraud on the part of the giver before he can be made answerable."

In the case of hiring, it is an implied term of the contract that the article let on hire is as fit for the purpose as reasonable care and skill can make it.[42] There is some doubt whether this implied term covers latent defects.[43]

In the case of carriage, there is an implied warranty on the part of the consignor that the goods are fit to be carried, and there is no exception in the case of latent defects.[44] The carrier's duty, in the absence of any contract to the contrary, depends on whether or not he is a common carrier, and need not be considered here.

662 **Duty in tort.** In tort, the duty of the owner of goods who delivers them by way of gift, loan or hire is much the same as that of a retailer. In all these cases the liability of the transferor does not depend on any contract he has entered into and " no question of consideration between the parties is relevant." [45] Therefore, the fact that the retailer of goods

[40] *Coughlin* v. *Gillison* [1899] 1 Q.B. 145 (defendants lend donkey-engine to plaintiff and others. Engine defective and burst, but defendants not liable in the absence of knowledge of the defect); *Blakemore* v. *Bristol and Exeter Ry.* (1858) 8 E. & B. 1035.

[41] *Gautret* v. *Egerton* (1867) L.R. 2 C.P. 371, 375.

[42] *Mowbray* v. *Merryweather* [1895] 2 Q.B. 640 which was distinguished in *Hadley* v. *Droitwich Construction Co.* [1968] 1 W.L.R. 37 where it was held that the implied warranty as to fitness of the crane when handed over was qualified by the hirer's undertakings to put a competent man in charge of it and to see that it was properly serviced but that this implied warranty could not survive the hirer's breach of those undertakings. *Vogan & Co.* v. *Oulton* (1889) 81 L.T. 435; *Hyman* v. *Nye* (1881) 6 Q.B.D. 685.

[43] In *Hyman* v. *Nye, supra*, Lindley J. said that a latent defect was a defence, but Mathew J. expressly reserved his opinion. In *Geddling* v. *Marsh* [1920] 1 K.B. 668, a Divisional Court thought that *Hyman* v. *Nye* decided that a contract of hiring differed from a contract of sale of goods in this respect, *sed quaere*?

[44] *Brass* v. *Maitland* (1856) 6 E. & B. 470; *G.N. Ry.* v. *L.E.P. Transport Co.* [1922] 2 K.B. 742; *Bamfield* v. *Goole and Sheffield Transport Co.* [1910] 2 K.B. 94.

[45] Lord Wright in *Grant* v. *Australian Knitting Mills Co.* [1936] A.C. 85, 103.

sells them does not make his liability in tort any higher than if he gives them as a present or lends them, with or without consideration being paid for their use. If the owner-transferor is also the manufacturer his liability is that of a manufacturer. Hence, in the case put by Denning L.J. in *Hawkins* v. *Coulsdon & Purley U.D.C.*,[46] suppose that the manufacturer of a special soap sent out samples by way of gift to members of the public, and owing to negligence in manufacturing a user of the soap suffers from dermatitis, the manufacturer would be liable, his manner of putting the soap in circulation whether by gift or by sale being irrelevant.

Accordingly, an owner who transfers goods, whether by gift, loan or hire, to another is under a duty to warn the transferee of defects, actually known to him, which render the goods unfit for the purpose for which he contemplates they will be used.[47] If he warns the transferee he is under no further liability; if he omits to warn the transferee he is liable to the consumer or user of the goods who suffers damage directly attributable to the defect.

663 When the owner does not know that the goods are defective, the general rule is that he is under no liability. So, if factory owners give a general permission to contractors to use their plant they do not contemplate that any particular piece of plant will be used for any particular work and are not liable to a workman employed by the contractors who is injured through using one of their ladders which is defective.[48] The owner's position as regards defects of which he ought to have known is rather different from that of a retailer. A retailer of new (as opposed to second-hand) goods has not used the goods, and delivers them in the same condition as they were in when he received them, subject only to such deterioration as they may have suffered in carriage (for which he should make some examination according to the nature of the goods) or as they have developed while in his custody (against which he ought to take reasonable steps to safeguard them). An owner, on the other hand, may have used the goods, so that they have become worn or defective or in need of repair, or he may not have used them, so that they have deteriorated by disuse and as a reasonable man he ought to know that they are unfit for the contemplated purpose. In such a case, an objective test will be applied and his knowledge of the facts rendering the goods defective will be considered knowledge of the defect.[49] Further, if he delivers the goods for immediate use, there is some authority for the view that he must take reasonable care to examine them to see that they are fit for the contemplated use.[50]

46 [1954] 1 Q.B. 319, 333.

47 *Clarke* v. *Army and Navy Co-operative Society* [1903] 1 K.B. 155; *White* v. *Steadman* [1913] 3 K.B. 340.

48 *Marshall* v. *Cellactite & British Uralite Ltd.* (1947) 63 T.L.R. 456; *Johnson* v. *Croggan & Co. Ltd.* [1954] 1 All E.R. 121.

49 See *Hawkins* v. *Coulsdon & Purley U.D.C.* [1954] 1 Q.B. 319.

50 See *Heaven* v. *Pender* (1883) 11 Q.B.D. 503, 511, *per* Brett M.R.; approved by Lord Atkin in *Donoghue* v. *Stevenson* [1932] A.C. 562, 581. In " The Liability of the Gratuitous

664 In *Heaven* v. *Pender*[51] a dock owner, as incident to the use of his dock, provided a shipowner with a staging to be used by workmen engaged in repairing the ship. The plaintiff was a painter, whose employer was under contract with the shipowner to paint the ship. The ropes of the staging had been scorched and were unfit for use and were supplied without a reasonably careful attention to their condition, so that they broke, as a result of which the plaintiff fell into the dock and was injured. The dock owner was held liable to the plaintiff on the ground that, although he did not retain control of the staging, he had a duty to use " reasonable care as to the state of the articles when delivered by him to the ship under repair for immediate use in relation to the repairers. For any neglect of those having control of the ship and the appliances he would not be liable, and to establish his liability it must be proved that the defect which caused the accident existed at the time when the article was supplied by the dock owner."[52]

665 In *Elliott* v. *Hall*[53] sellers of coal delivered the coal in a truck which they had hired from a wagon company. The truck was defective, in that the trap-door in the bottom was secured by a pin which was worn, and in getting into the truck to unload the coal a servant of the buyers fell through the trap-door and was injured. The truck had been examined by a servant of the sellers and no defect was found, but the jury found that the sellers were negligent in not discovering the defect. The sellers were held liable to the buyer's servant, as they must have contemplated that someone in his position would get into the truck to unload the wagon. In *Hawkins* v. *Smith*[54] the plaintiff was a dock labourer employed by a dock company to unload grain from a ship. The grain was loaded into sacks, which had been hired by the consignees from the defendant. One of the sacks was defective and broke when it was hoisted up, causing injury to the plaintiff. The defendant was held liable on the ground that he knew the purpose for which the sack was required, and had delivered a sack which was unfit for that purpose. In *White* v. *Steadman*[55] the plaintiff's husband hired from the defendant, who was a livery-stable keeper, a landau with a horse and driver for the purpose of taking a drive. The plaintiff went with him in the carriage. The horse shied, became unmanageable, and upset the carriage, injuring the plaintiff. The jury found that the defendant ought to have known that the horse was unsafe to send out with the landau, and the defendant was held liable to the

Transferor " (1950) 66 L.Q.R. 39, Marsh argues that there is no difference between the liability in tort of the gratuitous transferor and a transferor for reward—a view which is clearly right. He then argues that a gratuitous transferor " must . . . use reasonable care if he chooses to put the chattel into circulation." If this means he must use reasonable care to discover defects it is too wide.

51 (1883) 11 Q.B.D. 503.

52 (1883) 11 Q.B.D. 503, *per* Cotton L.J. at p. 515.

53 (1885) 15 Q.B.D. 315. Mentioned with approval by Lord Atkin in *Donoghue* v. *Stevenson*, at p. 585.

54 (1896) 12 T.L.R. 532. Mentioned with approval by Lord Atkin in *Donoghue* v. *Stevenson*, at p. 585.

55 [1913] 3 K.B. 340.

plaintiff on the ground that he owed a duty " not only to the person who contracts to hire it, but to all those persons for whose use it is supplied." As to his duty to discover defects, Lush J. said: " I think that a person who has the means of knowledge and only does not know that the animal or chattel which he supplies is dangerous because he does not take ordinary care to avail himself of his opportunity of knowledge is in precisely the same position as the person who knows. A person who keeps for hire horses, some of which he knows may be dangerous, cannot shelter himself behind his own want of knowledge, if that arises from his indifference or carelessness. If he has the means of knowledge and shuts his eyes to them, he does not thereby diminish or alter his duty towards those to whom he supplies a horse which is dangerous in fact."

66 In *Oliver* v. *Saddler & Co.*,[56] stevedores, in conjunction with porters, were unloading a ship. The cargo was hoisted in rope slings provided by the stevedores, who gratuitously permitted the porters to use the slings for transporting the cargo from the point where the stevedores' duty ended to the dock. While a sling was being used by the porters it broke killing one of the porters. The House of Lords held that the stevedores owed a duty to the porters to use reasonable care to see that the sling was fit to take the weight loaded upon it, and that they were liable to the dependants of the deceased man.

67 The duty upon the lender in the cases set out in the preceding paragraphs is only to use reasonable care to see that the goods lent for immediate use are reasonably fit for the intended purpose. Where a lorry driver was engaged in loading his lorry by means of wire slings belonging to the owners of a quay and was injured by a frayed sling, it was held that, on proof that reasonable care was taken to keep the slings in good condition and that the sling in question was in good condition when taken out of the store, the quay owners were not liable.[57]

The mere fact that the article lent breaks while being used by the borrower is in itself no evidence of negligence against the lender [58]; if the article lent is a sling, it may have been overloaded,[59] and in any case some affirmative evidence of negligence must be given.

68 In the cases last quoted the chattels were intended to be used at once, so that there was no reasonable opportunity of examination by or on behalf of the users before use. On the other hand, if there is such reasonable opportunity of examination the transferor is not liable, because the

[56] [1929] A.C. 584. *Cf. Gledhill* v. *Liverpool Abattoir Ltd.* [1957] 1 W.L.R. 1028, where the distinction was made that the stevedores knew that the porters relied on them to take care that the slings were safe, since the porters had no prior opportunity of examination, but where ample opportunity for independent examination of the chains being used by slaughtermen existed before the accident, the suppliers of the chains were held not to be liable.

[57] *Harwood* v. *Antwerp Quay* (1935) 51 Ll.L.R. 336.

[58] *Edwards* v. *Newton* (1934) 48 Ll.L.R. 155 (workman discharging cargo into lorry by means of ship's tackle—none of crew assisting—tackle breaks and workman is injured, no case of *res ipsa loquitur*).

[59] *McKinstry* v. *Johannes (Owners)* (1935) 52 Ll.L.R. 339.

transferee can see for himself whether the chattels are suitable for his purpose. In *Caledonian Ry.* v. *Warwick* [60] a wagon belonging to the Caledonian Railway Company was filled with coal and delivered to the system of the Glasgow and South Western Railway Company, in whose employment the deceased man was, to undergo a further journey to the premises of the consignees of the coal. The brake on the wagon was defective, so that it failed to act when the wagon was on a descent, with the result that the deceased was crushed between two wagons. The Caledonian Company was held not liable for the death, on the ground that they were not bound to examine the wagon to see that it was fit for a new journey. In *Oliver* v. *Saddler & Co.* this case was distinguished on the ground that " examination of the wagons was equally open to both persons by whom they were used," [61] and in *Donoghue* v. *Stevenson* Lord Atkin said: " There was ample opportunity for inspection by the second railway company. The relations were not proximate." [62]

669 The two earlier cases of *Blakemore* v. *Bristol and Exeter Ry.*[63] and *MacCarthy* v. *Young*,[64] so far as they were decided on tort and not on contract, must be regarded as wrongly decided,[65] unless they are illustrations of the principle that the transferor of a defective chattel is not liable when the transferee has a reasonable opportunity of inspecting it before use. In *Blakemore* v. *Bristol and Exeter Ry.*—" that melancholy case " [66]—the defendants lent a crane, which they knew to be unsafe, to consignees of goods to enable them to unload the goods from their railway. The crane broke and killed a servant of the consignees who was engaged in the work of unloading, and the defendants were held not liable. In *MacCarthy* v. *Young* [64] the defendant had allowed the plaintiff's employer to use a scaffold which the defendant himself had erected. The scaffold was defective, although the defendant was not aware of it, and gave way, injuring the plaintiff who was working on it. Following *Blakemore* v. *Bristol and Exeter Ry.*, the defendant was held not liable.

670 **Delivery to carrier.** An owner or bailee of goods who delivers them to a carrier for the purpose of carriage is under a duty to take reasonable care to see that they can be carried without causing physical damage to the person or property of others with whom the goods are likely to come in contact during the carriage. This would seem to follow from the statement of general principle above,[67] but the only cases on

[60] [1898] A.C. 216.
[61] Lord Buckmaster at p. 591. See also Lord Atkin (with whom Lord Shaw concurred) at p. 597.
[62] [1932] A.C. 562, 597.
[63] (1858) 8 E. & B. 1035.
[64] (1861) 6 H. & N. 329.
[65] " There can be little doubt that the cases of *Blakemore* v. *Bristol & Exeter Ry.* and *MacCarthy* v. *Young* . . . would be decided differently today ": Denning L.J. in *Hawkins* v. *Coulsdon & Purley U.D.C.* [1954] 1 Q.B. 319, 333.
[66] *Per* Erle C.J. in *Mears* v. *L. & S.W. Ry.* (1862) 11 C.B.(N.S.) 850.
[67] *Ante*, § 662.

the subject are those dealing with dangerous goods. In *Farrant* v. *Barnes*[68] the defendant sent a carboy of nitric acid to a carrier for carriage, without giving any warning of its dangerous character. Whilst the plaintiff, a servant of the carrier, was carrying the carboy it burst from some unexplained cause and injured him. The defendant was held liable on " the general principle that, wherever a person employs another to carry an article which from its dangerous character requires more than ordinary care, he must give him reasonable notice of the nature of the article, and that, if he fails to do so, he is responsible for the probable consequences of his neglect."[69] From Willes J.'s reference to goods " which in the absence of extraordinary care are likely by escaping to damage other parts of the cargo " it seems clear that the damage for which the consignor is liable includes damage to other goods carried as well as to individuals.[70] It would also seem to follow that for this purpose dangerous goods means goods, which, by reason of defects or otherwise, are unfit to be carried in the manner contemplated.

When a customer went to a chemist with a bottle, asked for nitric acid, and on the chemist's asking what the bottle had contained, said nitric acid, the chemist was held not liable for the results of an explosion which occurred when he filled the bottle with nitric acid, on the ground that he had, in the circumstances, taken enough care.[71]

671 **Delivery by carrier.** A carrier who delivers goods in the same condition as they were in when he received them for carriage is not liable to the consumer or user for damage caused to them through the goods being defective. This is because he is a mere agent for the transmission of the goods, and is not in any way responsible for their condition.

If, however, he delivers goods which are not in the same condition as they were in when he received them for carriage, and the change in condition is either due to his negligence or as a reasonable man he ought to have known of it, and the change is such as to render the goods unfit for the contemplated use, in the absence of his giving warning he will be liable to the consumer or user for damage caused through the goods being used for any purpose for which he ought to have contemplated they would be used.

672 In *Cramb* v. *Caledonian Ry.*[72] sugar was delivered to the railway company for carriage and was packed near some weedkiller. The weedkiller was poisonous and contaminated the sugar, with the result that some purchasers of the sugar from the consignee died, and others became ill. The railway company were held not liable to the injured

[68] (1862) 11 C.B.(N.S.) 553. When the goods are dangerous, the consignor is liable even if he did not know they were dangerous and was not negligent in failing to discover that they were dangerous. *Bamfield* v. *Goole and Sheffield Transport Co.* [1910] 2 K.B. 94.
[69] (1862) 11 C.B.(N.S.) 553, *per* Willes J. at p. 564.
[70] See *G.N. Ry.* v. *L.E.P. Transport Co.* [1922] 2 K.B. 742.
[71] *Muir* v. *Stewart*, 1938 S.C. 590.
[72] (1892) 19 R. 1054.

persons, in the absence of knowledge or means of knowledge of the poisonous character of the weedkiller. In *Macdonald* v. *Macbrayne Ltd.*,[73] the consignee had ordered two barrels of paraffin from the consignor, and the carrier delivered two barrels of paraffin and one of naphtha. The consignee's servants, without ascertaining the amount of paraffin ordered, received the consignment in the belief that all the barrels contained paraffin, and one of them, in that belief, drew off part of the contents of the barrel of naphtha by the light of a candle; an explosion ensued and the consignee's premises were burnt. The carrier was held liable to the consignee, Lord Salvesen saying: " Prima facie, it is not unreasonable to suppose than an ordinary and natural consequence of the delivery of naphtha to a person who does not know that it is highly inflammable, and is at the same time informed that it is paraffin, might well give rise to a fire in the premises of the receiver, as in fact happened." In *Taylor & Sons* v. *Union Castle Steamship Co.*[74] the defendants, who were shipowners, delivered to the plaintiffs some maize mixed with castor seed. The castor seed was poisonous and poisoned some horses belonging to a person who had bought the maize from the plaintiffs. The plaintiffs sued to recover from the defendants the amount they had paid to their buyer as damages. The defendants were held not liable, MacKinnon J. saying: " The question in each case must be whether the person delivering the article knew, or as a reasonable man ought to have known, that it was dangerous. Here the defendants were not dealers in grain and experts in that particular trade, but were shipowners carrying goods of every possible description." Where carriers by mistake delivered to the wrong consignees highly inflammable material, without giving warning of its nature, which caught fire owing to the negligence of one of the servants of the person to whom it had been delivered, they were held liable, as they should have contemplated what in fact happened.[75]

673 The carrier is not necessarily liable for all the consequences of his misdelivery. It might well be that as a reasonable man the carrier ought to have contemplated that the goods were unfit for use, and yet ought not to have contemplated that the person to whom he delivered them would fail to have made such an examination before using the goods, as would have discovered the defect.[76] So, in *Cunnington* v. *Great Northern Ry.*,[77] the carriers, a railway company, knew that the consignors were in the habit of sending empty casks to the consignees, who filled them with ketchup and returned them, and they negligently delivered casks which were not the casks of the consignors and were unfit for filling with ketchup because they had been used for the storage of

[73] 1915 S.C. 716.
[74] (1932) 48 T.L.R. 249.
[75] *Philco Radio* v. *Spurling* [1949] 2 All E.R. 882.
[76] In *Taylor & Sons* v. *Union Castle Steamship Co.*, *supra*, other buyers of the maize had discovered the presence of the castor seed, before delivery to the ultimate consumer, but it was unnecessary to decide whether the plaintiff's failure to discover the castor seed was negligence.
[77] (1883) 49 L.T. 392. *Cf. Muir* v. *Stewart*, 1938 S.C. 590, *ante*, § 670.

turpentine. The consignees filled the casks with ketchup, which was spoilt, and they consequently suffered damage. The carriers were held to be under no liability to the consignees, on the ground that it was not reasonable to suppose that, " in the ordinary course of any business, casks which are to be sent empty for the purpose of being filled with something, would not be examined at all so as to discover whether there was in those casks such a thing as the dregs of turpentine." [78]

6.—DUTY OF INSTALLER OF GOODS

674 **Duty of installer.** One who instals chattels on premises is under a duty to take care to instal them so that they are not a source of danger to those who might be injured if they were not properly installed. This has already been considered in connection with water (§ 485), gas (§ 518), electricity (§ 540) and premises (§ 399). Reference may also be made to *Brown* v. *Cotterill* (§ 629), *Howard* v. *Furness Houlder Ltd.* (§ 658) and *Buckner* v. *Ashby & Horner Ltd.* (§ 644).

[78] *Per* Brett M.R.

CHAPTER 12

HIGHWAYS

1.—DANGERS ON OR ADJOINING THE HIGHWAY

675 **Duties in respect of a highway.** It is a public nuisance to do any act on a highway which hinders or obstructs the free passage of the public along the highway, and for any damage sustained by an individual in consequence of such act, over and above the damage sustained by the public at large, an action will lie.[1] The circumstances which give rise to such an action by an individual member of the public may conveniently be considered as part of the law of negligence, because of the breach of duty which takes place whenever an obstruction or danger in the highway is created. It is proposed to deal with dangers (a) on the highway, (b) adjoining the highway, and (c) miscellaneous.

(a) *Dangers on the Highway*

676 **Obstructions on highway.** If a highway is obstructed, as for example, by placing a pole across it, a person who is injured without negligence on his part as a result of the obstruction, can recover damages.[2] Where a post was put in the middle of a footpath to prevent cattle from straying, it was held that a person who, in the dark, collided with the post could recover from the local authority who erected it.[3] If a heap of rubbish is lawfully left in the highway, for example during road repairs, but negligently left unguarded and unlit, a person injured by it can recover damages.[4] Digging a hole or a trench in the highway and leaving it unguarded is negligence.[5] So, too, if a ridge is left in the highway during road repairs so as to cause the driver of a vehicle to collide with

[1] *Benjamin* v. *Storr* (1874) L.R. 9 C.P. 400; *Fritz* v. *Hobson* (1880) 14 Ch.D. 542; *Vanderpant* v. *Mayfair Hotel Co.* [1930] 1 Ch. 138.

[2] *Butterfield* v. *Forrester* (1809) 11 East 60. *Harper* v. *Haden & Sons* [1933] Ch. 298 (the scaffolding and wooden hoarding were held not to be a nuisance by the Court of Appeal in the circumstances). Other examples of obstruction are to be found in: collecting a large crowd of people in the highway outside the doors of a theatre: *Barber* v. *Penley* [1893] 2 Ch. 447 (" Charley's Aunt " being performed at the Globe Theatre, Strand) but *cf. Dwyer* v. *Mansfield* [1946] K.B. 437 (queue for potatoes during wartime food shortages); leaving horses and carts standing for an unreasonable length of time or in an excessive number: *Fritz* v. *Hobson* (1880) 14 Ch.D. 542 (together with building materials in a narrow passageway called Fleur de Lis Court, Fetter Lane, London) or motor vehicles *Chesterfield Corpn.* v. *A. Robinson (Transport) Ltd.* (1955) 106 L.J. 61 (plaintiffs had to divert their bus route as a result of the town's main road being blocked for three days due to the defendants' negligence in conveying an outsize load of 83 tons on a large transporter lorry); *Stevens* v. *Kelland* [1970] R.T.R. 445 (two vehicles parked opposite each other).

[3] *Lamley* v. *E. Retford Corpn.* (1891) 55 J.P. 133.

[4] *Penny* v. *Wimbledon U.D.C.* [1899] 2 Q.B. 72.

[5] *Gray* v. *Pullen* (1864) 5 B. & S. 970: *Ellis* v. *Sheffield Gas Consumers Co.* (1853) 2 E. & B. 767.

a bridge, there is negligence.[6] The same result follows if a temporary set of tramlines, raised above the level of the highway, is laid down whilst the ordinary lines are being repaired.[7] It is negligence to cause a stream of water to spout up in the highway without taking any step to warn approaching traffic of its existence, and so if a horse takes fright, and as a result sustains injury, the persons responsible for the water are liable.[8] If a heap of stones is lawfully left in the roadway, but some of the stones are negligently tipped on to the footpath, a pedestrian who falls over them and is injured will be able to recover damages in full if he has not been guilty of contributory negligence.[9] The pedestrian may recover even when the material is not on the footpath if it is so near it as to be a nuisance, so that when a man tripped over a pile of slates in the highway near the kerb (held to be a nuisance) he recovered, and it was held that he was not negligent " if he does not constantly look down to his feet."[10] A similar result follows if a carpet is put on the footpath; " if a person puts anything across the pavement and a person stumbles over it, the owner is liable for the consequences. The passer-by is not bound to look for mats on the highway."[11]

On the other hand, when, during a drought, a small hosepipe was laid across the highway to enable water to be brought from a tank to the defendant's house and the plaintiff, while delivering milk, although she saw the pipe, tripped over it and fell, it was held that the plaintiff could not recover. The presence of the hosepipe on the highway was held not to be a nuisance, because in the circumstances it was reasonable for the defendant to put it there.[12]

677 **Trees.** The occupier of land is not liable if a tree, which he did not know, and had no reasonable grounds for knowing, to be unsafe, falls on to the highway and injures a person passing along the highway.[13] His duty is to act as a prudent landowner to prevent his trees which adjoin the highway from being a danger to persons passing along the highway, but he is not bound to call in an expert to examine his trees unless he has reason to believe that they may be unsafe. When a tree fell owing to disease of the roots not visible on an external examination and caused damage, the owner was held not liable.[14] When an elm tree, 130 years old, which had never been lopped, topped or pollarded, fell on a motor-car on the highway, owing to a long standing disease of the roots not detectable on external examination and it was not proved that expert

6 *Hill* v. *Tottenham U.D.C.* (1898) 79 L.T. 495.
7 *Tilling* v. *Dick Kerr & Co.* [1905] 1 K.B. 562.
8 *Hill* v. *New River Co.* (1868) 9 B. & S. 303.
9 *Gould* v. *Birkenhead Corpn.* (1910) 74 J.P. 105 (no contributory negligence was found).
10 *Almeroth* v. *Chivers Ltd.* [1948] 1 All E.R. 53.
11 *De Teyron* v. *Waring* (1885) 1 T.L.R. 414, *per* Coleridge C.J.; *Watson* v. *Ellis* (1885) 1 T.L.R. 317.
12 *Trevett* v. *Lee* [1955] 1 W.L.R. 113.
13 *Noble* v. *Harrison* [1926] 2 K.B. 332; *Cunliffe* v. *Banks* [1945] 1 All E.R. 459; *cf. Shirvell* v. *Hackwood Estates Ltd.* [1938] 2 K.B. 577.
14 *Cunliffe* v. *Banks* [1945] 1 All E.R. 459.

examination would have discovered it, the owner was held not liable.[15] But when a tree, which had been dying for some years and should have been known to be dangerous by an ordinary landowner, fell and caused damage, the owner was held liable.[16]

A local authority which plants trees near the highway is under a duty to cut them back when they grow over the highway so as to interfere with traffic, and was held liable on failure to do this when an overhanging branch broke a window in a bus and caused damage to a passenger.[17]

If a tree falls on to the highway without any negligence, the occupier of the land is not bound to light it or give warning of it, so that if a motorist collides with it the occupier is under no liability to him.[18] But if a local authority in the course of road widening operations leave a tree adjoining the highway in such danger of falling that the danger is both "patent and imminent," it is liable for damage caused by the fall to persons and vehicles on the highway.[19]

678 **Trench improperly filled in.** If a trench is lawfully dug in the highway, for example to lay gas or water pipes, it must be filled in so as not to be dangerous to traffic, either by leaving a hollow[20] or by creating a raised mound in the highway.[21] When a water company negligently filled in a trench in the highway, Phillimore J. declared their duty to be "to reinstate and to leave its reinstatement in such a condition that no further reinstatement will be required, and that the inequalities will only be produced by the natural consequences of wear and tear."[22] If a dangerous inequality in the highway is created, so as to cause a vehicle driven along the highway to be upset, the person creating the danger is liable.[23] Where a sewer authority dug a trench to lay a sewer and negligently filled in the trench so that a cab-driver, finding that the trench was soft, swerved to avoid it and ran into a heap of stones negligently left in the highway by a third party, the sewer authority were held liable.[24] If a pavement is taken up and the paving stones are so laid as to give a false appearance of safety to persons passing along the footpath, the persons taking up the pavement will be liable to anyone who is injured.[25] Again, when a telegraph pole was moved so as to allow the highway to be widened, and the hole was negligently filled in so that a wagon was damaged owing to one of its

15 *Caminer* v. *Northern & London Investment Trust* [1951] A.C. 88. The test as stated by Lord Normand therein was applied in *Quinn* v. *Scott* [1965] 1 W.L.R. 1004. (The owner of a tree on a highway who has means of knowing that it is diseased and may fall is liable in negligence if it falls and causes an accident.)

16 *Brown* v. *Harrison* [1947] W.N. 191.

17 *Hale* v. *Hants & Dorset Motor Services Ltd.* [1947] 2 All E.R. 628.

18 *Hudson* v. *Bray* [1917] 1 K.B. 520.

19 *Mackie* v. *Dunbartonshire C.C.* [1927] W.N. 247.

20 *Hartley* v. *Rochdale Corpn.* [1908] 2 K.B. 594.

21 *Peachey* v. *Rowland* (1853) 13 C.B. 182. The decision that the employer was not liable for the negligence of his independent contractor in creating such a danger in the highway must be considered to be overruled by *Penny* v. *Wimbledon U.D.C.* [1899] 2 Q.B. 72.

22 *Hartley* v. *Rochdale Corpn., supra* at p. 599.

23 *Goodson* v. *Sunbury Gas Co.* (1896) 75 L.T. 251.

24 *Shoreditch Corpn.* v. *Bull* (1904) 90 L.T. 210.

25 *Drew* v. *New River Co.* (1834) 6 C. & P. 754.

wheels sinking into the hole, it was held that the Post Office was liable for negligently filling in the hole, and the highway authority were also liable for throwing the road open for public use without first seeing that it was safe.[26] Where a local authority, who were both the highway and the sewer authority, employed a contractor to dig a trench, and the trench was afterwards improperly filled in so that the plaintiff's horse, in consequence of the surface giving way, was injured, it was held that the authority were liable.[27] The local authority are not liable, however, if the owner of houses in pursuance of a notice from them, digs a trench to connect his drains with the main sewer and improperly fills it in, because he is not their agent for doing the work.[28] When the local authority, in the course of laying a new sewer, came across an old service pipe, which they knew was likely to become leaky, but nevertheless neither laid down a new pipe nor took adequate steps to prevent the old one from leaking, it was held that when, a few months afterwards, the pipe leaked so that the earth subsided and caused a van to overturn, the local authority were liable.[29]

679 **Trench properly filled in but natural subsidence occurs later.** If a trench has been dug in the highway and properly filled in, but a natural and inevitable subsidence occurs later owing to the shrinkage of the materials, the person responsible for digging the trench is liable for damage caused by the subsidence. In *Hyams* v. *Webster* [30] a contractor employed by the Metropolitan Board of Works dug a trench in the highway in connection with the laying of sewers, and properly filled it in. This was finished in August, and in February a hole appeared, due, as the jury found, to natural subsidence. In going along the highway the plaintiff's horse put its foot in the hole and caused damage to the plaintiff. The Exchequer Chamber, affirming the Court of Queen's Bench,[31] held that the defendant was not liable on the ground that he was under no obligation, after the trench had been properly filled in and the road reinstated, to make good a subsequent subsidence. On the other hand, in *Newsome* v. *Darton U.D.C.*,[32] a local authority made a trench in the highway for the purpose of executing drainage work. The trench was filled in and the surface reinstated and the jury found that this was done without negligence. The work was finished in August, 1935, but in August, 1936, a subsidence occurred with the result that the plaintiff, a cyclist, was thrown from his bicycle. It was held that the local authority, having interfered with the surface of the road, were under a duty to restore it to its original condition and could only fulfil that duty by making good the inevitable subsidences as and when they

26 *Thompson* v. *Bradford Corpn. and Tinsley* [1915] 3 K.B. 13.
27 *Smith* v. *West Derby Local Board* (1878) 3 C.P.D. 423.
28 *Steel* v. *Dartford L.B.* (1891) 60 L.J.Q.B. 256.
29 *Cox* v. *Paddington* (*Vestry*) (1891) 64 L.T. 566.
30 (1868) L.R. 4 Q.B. 138.
31 L.R. 2 Q.B. 264.
32 [1938] 3 All E.R. 93. *Hyams* v. *Webster* was not referred to.

occurred. It was also held that they were negligent in not discovering and remedying the danger.

680 **Laying stopcocks, etc., in highway.** When the highway is broken up to lay sewers, gas or water pipes or other works which can lawfully be laid in the highway, there is a duty to make good the highway so that the reinstatement will, in normal circumstances, be serviceable for a reasonable time. When a local authority, who were also the water authority, laid a stopcock in the footpath of an unmade highway at the level to which the footpath would eventually have been made up but which, at the time, projected above the surrounding pathway and, to level it off, rammed in earth which was constantly being removed by the ordinary incidence of the weather, it was held that they were liable to a person who tripped over the projecting stopcock.[33] But where a stopcock in the highway leaked and loosened some paving stones immediately around it and also other paving stones some distance away, over one of which latter stones the plaintiff tripped and fell, the Water Board, which placed the stopcock in the highway, was held not liable on the ground that the leak was not due to any negligence on the board's part and there was no evidence that the board knew or ought to have known that the stone over which the plaintiff tripped was loose.[34]

681 **Gratings, coal plates, etc.** A person who puts in the footpath, or on any other part of the highway, a grating, skylight, coal plate or other structure, is bound to maintain it so as not to be a source of danger to users of the highway. So, when a man walked over a cellar cover set into the pavement and the cover collapsed, he was held entitled to recover.[35] Such structures are usually part of a building, and, when that is so, liability is on the occupier although it may be on the owner.[36] If the structure in question is not part of a building, but is part of the highway, the highway authority and not the occupier is responsible for its maintenance.[37] If it is neither part of a building nor part of the highway, then the person who put it on the highway is liable unless he can show that he had statutory authority for his action or in some other way was entitled to put it on the highway.

682 **Structure in existence before dedication of highway.** If the structure was in existence before the highway was dedicated to the public, there is no obligation to repair it. Accordingly, when a cellar flap projected above the street so that a passer-by, at night, stumbled over it and was injured, the occupier of the premises was held not liable when it was proved that the flap was in existence before the highway.[38] Blackburn J. said: " The law is clear that, if after a highway exists anything be newly

33 *Withington* v. *Bolton Borough Council* [1937] 3 All E.R. 108; see also *Rider* v. *Metropolitan Water Board* [1949] 2 K.B. 378.
34 *Longhurst* v. *Metropolitan Water Board* [1948] 2 All E.R. 834.
35 *Heap* v. *Ind Coope & Allsopp Ltd.* [1940] 2 K.B. 476.
36 See *post*, §§ 720, 721.
37 *Robbins* v. *Jones* (1863) 15 C.B.(N.S.) 221.
38 *Fisher* v. *Prowse* (1862) 2 B. & S. 770.

made so near it as to be dangerous to those using the highway—such, for instance, as an excavation: *Barnes* v. *Ward*[39]—this will be unlawful and a nuisance; as it also is if an ancient erection, as a house, is suffered to become ruinous, so as to be dangerous: *R.* v. *Watts*[40]; and those who make or maintain the nuisance in either case are liable for any damage sustained thereby, just as much as if the nuisance arose from an obstruction in the highway itself; but the question still remains, whether an erection or excavation already existing, and not otherwise unlawful, becomes unlawful when the land on which it exists, or to which it is immediately contiguous, is dedicated to the public as a way, if the erection prevents the way from being so convenient and safe as it otherwise would be; or whether, on the contrary, the dedication must not be taken to be made to the public, and accepted by them, subject to the inconvenience or risk arising from the existing state of things. We think the latter is the correct view of the law."

If the structure has been in existence as long as living memory, the inference ought to be drawn that it was in existence at the time of the dedication, in the absence of anything to suggest contrary inference.[41] The mere fact that it has been pulled down and rebuilt—as where stone steps leading from the street to the door of a house were removed and replaced by new steps on the level of the street being altered[42]—does not prevent the inference from arising.

683 A grating,[43] coal plate[44] or other structure which is the property of the owner of the building to which it is appurtenant, must be maintained in such a condition as not to be dangerous to the public. " The person who is in possession of the premises and who allows the coal plate to be in a dangerous condition is the person responsible to the public for any injury resulting from its being out of repair."[45] Although described as nuisance, the obligation is really based on negligence. There is no absolute duty to make the structure safe, and therefore if, for example, a grating breaks because of some latent defect, or for any other reason not due to negligence on the part of anyone, the occupier of the premises will not be liable.[46] He is, however, liable for the negligence of his independent contractors,[47] and for failing to keep the structure in a proper state of repair, even if he did not know that it was out of repair.[48]

684 When the structure does not form part of the adjoining premises the occupier or owner of those premises is not liable. Accordingly, when

39 (1850) 9 C.B. 392.
40 (1703) 1 Salk. 357.
41 *Fisher* v. *Prowse*, *supra*.
42 *Cooper* v. *Walker* (1862) 2 B. & S. 770.
43 *Gwinnell* v. *Eamer* (1875) L.R. 10 C.P. 658.
44 *Pretty* v. *Bickmore* (1873) L.R. 8 C.P. 401.
45 *Per* Bovill C.J. in *Pretty* v. *Bickmore*, *supra*.
46 See *Barker* v. *Herbert* [1911] 2 K.B. 633; *Tarry* v. *Ashton* (1876) 1 Q.B.D. 314; *Lambert* v. *Lowestoft Corpn.* [1901] 1 K.B. 590.
47 *Tarry* v. *Ashton*, *supra*.
48 *Wringe* v. *Cohen* [1940] 1 K.B. 229; *Heap* v. *Ind Coope & Allsopp Ltd.* [1940] 2 K.B. 476.

the highway authority made a gutter in the highway, covering the gutter with removable iron carriage plates, and were paid the cost of these works by the frontagers, it was held that a frontager was not liable to a person who was injured by catching her foot between two carriage plates, even though he was in the habit from time to time of removing the plates opposite his house for the purpose of cleaning the gutters.[49] Again, when there was a coal shoot to the defendant's house and, owing to the level of the pavement being raised, the local authority had left a hole to give access to the coal shoot, it was held that the defendant was not liable to a person who tripped in the hole so left, on the ground that there was no duty on a frontager to keep in repair a highway which had been taken over by the local authority.[50] Also, when a local authority raised a pavement and reset in it a metal slab covering a cellar hole, which slab before being reset was in good condition but after it had been reset projected above the pavement, and the plaintiff tripped over the projection, it was held that the frontager was not liable under the Public Health Acts Amendment Act 1890, s. 35 (1),[51] as he had not created a nuisance and had no power or duty to abate a nuisance created by the local authority.[52] But the frontager was held liable under this section where the purpose of the defective grating in the highway was to admit light to the cellar of the defendant's premises and the defendant knew of the condition of the grating.[53] However the Highways Act 1959, s. 154 (5), which imposes an obligation on the owner or occupier of premises to keep the covers of cellars in good condition, does not impose an absolute duty. If a plaintiff is injured by a breach of the section he must still prove either negligence or nuisance in order to recover damages; hence if a cover be broken without the knowledge or fault of the owner or occupier and very shortly afterwards an accident occurs as a result of this breakage liability may not be established.[54]

685 **Structures laid in highway under statutory powers.** Many structures are put upon the highway in connection with the supply of gas, water and electricity, and the provision of drains and sewers to the adjoining property. Such structures are made under statutory authority, and accordingly reference should always be made to the appropriate statute to see to what extent, if at all, the common law liability is affected. Apart from any special statutory provisions, the duty is to take reasonable care to instal and to maintain the structures so that they are not dangerous to persons using the highway with reasonable care.[55] So, where a water company laid in the street a stopcock, which was protected by a guardbox,

49 *Jones* v. *Rew* (1910) 79 L.J.K.B. 1030.
50 *Horridge* v. *Makinson* (1915) 84 L.J.K.B. 1294.
51 s. 35 was repealed by the Highways Act 1959 and replaced by s. 154 of that Act.
52 *Penney* v. *Berry* [1955] 1 W.L.R. 1021.
53 *Macfarlane* v. *Gwalter* [1959] 2 Q.B. 332, distinguishing *Penney* v. *Berry*, *supra*.
54 *Scott* v. *Green & Sons* [1969] 1 W.L.R. 301, distinguishing *Macfarlane* v. *Gwalter*, *supra*.
55 *Stockings* v. *Lambeth Waterworks Co.* (1891) 7 T.L.R. 460; *Hendra* v. *Chelsea Waterworks Co.* (1891) 8 T.L.R. 101; *Styles* v. *East London Waterworks Co.* (1887) 4 T.L.R. 190; *Strube* v. *Southwark and Vauxhall Water Co.* (1889) 5 T.L.R. 638.

it was held that a person who tripped over the lid of the guardbox, which was out of repair, could recover from the water company, who alone had power to break up the street for the purpose of effecting repairs.[56] Where a water company was bound by statute to fix fire plugs into its mains and to keep them in proper order, it was held liable when one of the caps to the plugs was broken and a horse put its foot in the plughole and was injured.[57] Again, when a stopcock box was placed in the pavement, and to make it level with the pavement it was the practice of the water company to put in a wad to fill the hole caused by the box, it was held that a person who caught her foot in the box because no wad or an insufficient wad was put in, could recover from the company.[58] In these cases, liability depends on the statutory duty to maintain. So, where the appropriate statute imposes the obligation to repair the box upon the owner or occupier of the house and not upon the water company, the company are not liable.[59]

686 If the work in question is properly maintained, but becomes dangerous owing to the wearing away of the surrounding highway, the person whose duty it is to maintain the work is not liable[60]; neither was the highway authority if the danger was only due to nonfeasance on their part.[61] On the other hand, if the highway has subsided owing to the negligent way in which the work was originally done, the person doing the work negligently is liable.[62] When a grating and framework were laid so as to cause a considerable depression in the road, but the work was done with due care and skill according to the usual method at the time, it was held that a cyclist, who was injured in consequence of the depression, had no remedy on the finding of a jury that neither the road authority nor the sewer authority knew, or could have known by the exercise of reasonable care, of the existence of the defect.[63]

687 **Lids raised by act of third party.** If the lid of a valve-box or other cover which ought to be maintained level with the surface of the road is pulled up by the act of a third party, the liability of the persons responsible for the maintenance of the lid or cover to persons falling over it depends on whether the nature of the lid or cover is such that the act of the third

56 *Chapman* v. *Fylde Waterworks Co.* [1894] 2 Q.B. 599.
57 *Bayley* v. *Wolverhampton Waterworks* (1860) 6 H. & N. 241.
58 *Osborn* v. *Metropolitan Water Board* (1910) 102 L.T. 217; *Rosenbaum* v. *Metropolitan Water Board* (1910) 103 L.T. 284, 739.
59 *Batt* v. *Metropolitan Water Board* [1911] 2 K.B. 965; *Mist* v. *Metropolitan Water Board* (1915) 84 L.J.K.B. 2041.
60 *Moore* v. *Lambeth Waterworks Co.* (1886) 17 Q.B.D. 462. *Cf. Withington* v. *Bolton B.C.* [1937] 3 All E.R. 108.
61 *Thompson* v. *Brighton Corpn.* [1894] 1 Q.B. 332. A similar case is *Chappell* v. *Dagenham Corpn.* [1948] W.N. 274 (metal street box, installed by electricity company in highway, protrudes owing to wearing away of the surrounding highway, and the plaintiff trips over it—highway authority not liable). See now the provisions of the Highway (Miscellaneous Provisions) Act 1961, *post*, § 698.
62 *Hartley* v. *Rochdale Corpn.* [1908] 2 K.B. 594.
63 *Papworth* v. *Battersea Corpn.* [1916] 1 K.B. 583.

party is one which ought reasonably to have been anticipated. Accordingly, in the case of a large cover which was pulled up and caused a dangerous obstruction in the street as a result of "the malicious act of a third person against which precautions would have been inoperative," the water board, which maintained the cover, were held not liable.[64] But where the lid was a small one which might easily be opened by a child, and the water board knew that children were apt to tamper with such lids, a person who tripped over an open lid in the roadway was held entitled to recover from the water board.[65]

688 **Liability of local authorities.** If a grid, covering the entrance to a sewer, is defective so as to injure persons passing along the highway, the sanitary authority are liable although, as highway authority, they were under no liability for nonfeasance.[66] Similarly, if a local authority, to enable them to water the streets, place a box covered with an iron flap in the footway, so that a person walking along the streets slips because the flap has become worn smooth, the authority is liable.[67] The same result follows with regard to a manhole.[68]

689 **Barrel drain.** Where a local authority built a barrel drain under the highway, and the drain got into disrepair as a result of which a hole was formed in the road, it was held that they were liable to a person who was injured through driving into the hole, which was left open and unfenced. Sir Barnes Peacock in giving judgment said: "The duty was cast upon them [the local authority] of keeping the artificial work which they had created in such a state as to prevent its causing a danger to passengers on the highway, which, but for such artificial construction, would not have existed, or, at the least, of protecting the public against the danger, when it arose, either by filling up the hole or fencing it." [69] There is no liability, however, if reasonable care has been taken to erect or maintain the work. Where, therefore, a sewer was constructed with due care and of proper materials and, owing to the mortar in one of the joints having been worked away by rats, a cavity was formed below the surface of the road, but the existence of the cavity was not known to and could not by the exercise of reasonable care have been discovered by the sewer authority, it was held that the plaintiff, whose horse while passing along the road fell through the road into the cavity, could not recover from the sewer authority.[70]

690 **Things put on highway.** Even before the Highways (Miscellaneous Provisions) Act 1961 came into force on August 3, 1964 the old common law

64 *Simpson* v. *Metropolitan Water Board* (1917) 15 L.G.R. 629.
65 *Wells* v. *Metropolitan Water Board* (1937) 54 T.L.R. 104.
66 *White* v. *Hindley Local Board* (1875) L.R. 10 Q.B. 219.
67 *Blackmore* v. *Vestry of Mile End Old Town* (1882) 9 Q.B.D. 451.
68 *Winslowe* v. *Bushey U.D.C.* (1908) 72 J.P. 259.
69 *Borough of Bathurst* v. *Macpherson* (1879) 4 App.Cas. 256, 265, explained in *Municipal Council of Sydney* v. *Bourke* [1895] A.C. 433.
70 *Lambert* v. *Lowestoft Corpn.* [1901] 1 K.B. 590.

rule that a highway authority was liable for misfeasance but not for non-feasance applied only to disrepair of the road *qua* road and did not extend to things on the road, such as gratings[71] or things created on the surface, such as ridges following the obliteration of the central white lines.[72] Accordingly a highway authority who place and maintain traffic studs on a highway must use reasonable care to maintain them in a safe condition. So, where such a stud had become loose and dangerous and remained so for three weeks, with the result that when a motorist drove over it, it shot across the road and knocked down a cyclist, the local authority were held liable.[73] Dealing with the question of whether the studs had been placed on the highway by the local authority in their capacity as highway authority, Slesser L.J. said that the test was not " whether the body which is sought to be made liable for non-reparation is or is not the same body as that which is responsible for the maintenance of the road, but whether the particular alleged nuisance or injury which they have permitted is one which they have done in their capacity as repairers of the road or in carrying out their obligations or powers under some different statute." [74] On this principle it has been held that a highway authority who have become owners of a tram track because of its abandonment by the undertakers are liable to a cyclist who was injured owing to the dangerous condition of the track, due to their failure to remove it and make good the surface of the road.[75]

691 Things temporarily placed in the highway while necessary work on the highway is being carried out by the highway authority give rise to no liability if they are clearly visible. So, where a highway authority painted a white line in the highway and marked it with red flags set in cans to show that it was newly painted, they were not liable when, in the daylight, a collision was caused owing to the failure of a driver of a vehicle to see them.[76]

If a drinking-fountain or similar structure is maintained in the highway, reasonable care must be taken to make it safe. Where, therefore, a stone on a drinking-fountain was loose so that, during a procession, it was dislodged by a person who climbed on the fountain to view the procession and struck the plaintiff, the local authority were held to be liable.[77]

692 If a local authority maintain a guard with spikes to protect something they have erected in the highway, they must put them in such a position that they are not likely to be dangerous to persons using the highway with reasonable care. Accordingly, where trees planted in the highway

[71] *Connolly* v. *Ministry of Transport* (1965) 63 L.G.R. 372 (C.A.).
[72] *Bright* v. *Ministry of Transport* (1971) 115 S.J. 226.
[73] *Skilton* v. *Epsom U.D.C.* [1937] 1 K.B. 112.
[74] *Ibid.* at p. 123.
[75] *Simon* v. *Islington B.C.* [1943] K.B. 188.
[76] *Hughes* v. *Sheppard* (1940) 163 L.T. 177. But where a lamp-post became stranded near to the centre of a busy road due to road widening operations, see *Davies* v. *Carmarthenshire C.C.* [1971] R.T.R. 112.
[77] *McLoughlin* v. *Warrington Corpn.* (1910) 75 J.P. 57. *Cf. O'Keefe* v. *Edinburgh Corpn.*, 1911 S.C. 18.

were guarded with iron spikes and the plaintiff, during the lighting restrictions in the war, collided with the spikes in the dark and injured his eye, a finding by a jury that reasonable care had not been taken to prevent the guard from being dangerous to the public was upheld. The duty was held to be not merely to make the guards reasonably safe at the date of their erection, but to continue to keep them reasonably safe.[78] Similarly, when a market was held in the public street near to a statue which was surrounded by a spiked railing, on which the plaintiff's cow spiked itself, it was held that the question was whether the place was reasonably safe for the standing of cattle, and a finding by the jury that it was not safe was upheld.[79]

693 **Lights on dangerous objects.** Where a local authority in pursuance of statutory powers put some structure in the highway which is dangerous if unlighted, or where they construct a road in such a position or manner that it is dangerous if unlighted,[80] they are under a duty to take reasonable steps to prevent their works from being a danger to the public. Jenkins L.J. said: "It appears to us that the real answer to Mr. Waller's submission is that failure to light or give some other form of warning of an obstruction on the highway by a highway authority who themselves created the obstruction is taken out of the category of mere nonfeasance and brought within the category of misfeasance by their positive act of creating the obstruction giving rise to the need for lighting or other means of warning."[81] An obvious means of discharging that duty during darkness is to light the works.[82] So, where a post was put in the middle of a footpath to prevent cattle from straying, a person who, in the dark, collided with the post owing to the absence of a light was entitled to recover from the local authority.[83] Again, when a local authority made a road ending in an unfenced ravine, so that it was dangerous to traffic unless sufficient lighting was maintained, it was held that a motorist who drove into the ravine in the dark could recover.[80] Also, where, under statutory authority, a wall was built across a road in a place where there had formerly been a level-crossing and a cyclist collided with the wall at night, both the railway authority and the local authority were held liable for not lighting the wall.[84]

694 The local authority were held liable when they erected a tram refuge in the middle of the street with a bollard, illuminated at night, at one end and the light failed with the result that a motorist collided with the

[78] *Morrison* v. *Sheffield Corpn.* [1917] 2 K.B. 866.
[79] *Lax* v. *Darlington Corpn.* (1879) 5 Ex.D. 28.
[80] *McClelland* v. *Manchester Corpn.* [1912] 1 K.B. 118.
[81] *Baxter* v. *Stockton-on-Tees Corpn.* [1959] 1 Q.B. 441, at p. 461, where a motor-cyclist, whilst riding along the highway at night, struck an unlit traffic island, which had been so constructed that it projected into the highway, and died as a result of his injuries. It was held that the defendant corporation were not liable because their fault consisted exclusively of nonfeasance since they had merely kept the island as they had found it when they took over the road from the county council.
[82] *Fisher* v. *Ruislip-Northwood U.D.C.* [1945] K.B. 584, 593, *per* Lord Greene M.R.
[83] *Lamley* v. *Retford Corpn.* (1891) 55 J.P. 133.
[84] *Law* v. *Railway Executive* [1949] W.N. 172.

bollard in the dark.[85] When a red lamp, which was usually lit on an air raid shelter, was out, so that a cyclist collided with the shelter in the dark, the local authority were held liable, although the ordinary street lighting was on, on the ground that the existence of normal street lighting did not absolve them from their duty to take reasonable care to give warning to the public of the presence of the shelter, by lighting or otherwise.[86]

If lighting is relied on, the duty is only to take reasonable care to maintain a light, but if the light is out at the material time the burden of proof is on them to show that they were not negligent in having failed to maintain the light.[85] Failure to provide enough night-watchmen to guard roads under repair in order to prevent people extinguishing or stealing the warning lights marking out the roadworks' danger area, where hooliganism is rife in the locality, may amount to negligence[87]; but where there has been no such vandalism previously it was held[88] that the defendants were under no duty to inspect periodically during the night their excavation, which they had left properly lighted and secured with barriers.

695 If normal lighting is prohibited, whether by reason of war restrictions or otherwise, the duty to take reasonable care to prevent the works from being a danger still exists, although different means of discharging that duty will have to be adopted. When spikes were placed round a tree, planted in the highway, to protect it and, owing to war restrictions, no lights were maintained, so that a person walking in the highway was injured by the spikes, the local authority were held liable on the ground that they had failed to take reasonable care to see that there was no danger in the altered circumstances.[89] Again, when a taxicab ran into an unlighted street refuge in wartime, the local authority were held liable for negligence in omitting to maintain a danger lamp on the refuge.[90] Also, where the lighting on a barrier across the highway near a bomb crater was not maintained,[91] and where there was no light on an air raid shelter which was usually lit,[92] in each case, the local authority were held liable in negligence. When a motorist in wartime collided with an unlighted air raid shelter erected in the highway, the local authority were held liable on the ground that it was their duty to take such steps as were reasonably possible, such as providing special danger lights, to safeguard the public.[93] On similar facts, the motorist failed, when it was

85 *Polkinghorn* v. *Lambeth Borough Council* [1938] 1 All E.R. 339. *Cf. Brown* v. *Lambeth Borough Council* (1915) 32 T.L.R. 61, where on somewhat similar facts a finding of no negligence on the part of the defendants was upheld on appeal.

86 *Whiting* v. *Middlesex C.C.* [1948] 1 K.B. 162.

87 *Murray* v. *Southwark London Borough Council* (1966) 65 L.G.R. 145.

88 *Lilley* v. *British Insulated Callenders Construction Co.* (1968) 67 L.G.R. 224.

89 *Morrison* v. *Sheffield Corpn.* [1917] 2 K.B. 866 (negligence was found by a jury and the C.A., while not agreeing with the finding, declined to disturb it).

90 *Baldock* v. *Westminster City Council* (1918) 88 L.J.K.B. 502 (negligence was found by a jury).

91 *Foster* v. *Gillingham Corpn.* [1942] 1 All E.R. 304.

92 *Knight* v. *Sheffield Corpn.* [1942] 2 All E.R. 411.

93 *Fisher* v. *Ruislip-Northwood U.D.C.* [1945] K.B. 584. This case is important because of the full discussion of the authorities by Lord Greene M.R. *Wodehouse* v. *Levy* [1940]

found that the local authority took reasonable care to keep the lights illuminated.[94]

The statutory authority under which the works are maintained may provide for absolute immunity, even though no care is taken. When a railway company maintained gate posts at the entrance to one of their stations under statutory powers which were construed as not imposing any duty to light them or otherwise to obviate the danger they caused, and a taxicab collided with them when they were unlighted in wartime, it was held that the railway company were not liable.[95]

696 **Statutory obligation to light.** If the local authority have not themselves created the danger, by " putting posts in the highway without warning," by " placing traps and dangers in the streets and not lighting them at night," or by making a road " with a sudden drop into the adjoining land below," [96] their liability depends on their statutory obligation to light. If they are under a duty to light, such as is imposed by section 130 of the Metropolis Management Act 1855, they are bound to see that every street is well and sufficiently lighted. Therefore, where the entrance to an archway was lighted by a light seventy feet away which, owing to war restrictions then in force, was dimmed and the driver of a van attempted to pass beneath the arch but was crushed between his van and the arch, it was held that the entrance was inadequately lighted so that a breach of statutory duty was committed.[97] On the other hand, where there is only a power and no obligation to light, as is the case under section 161 of the Public Health Act 1875, there is no obligation on the local authority to light any dangers except those created by themselves. So, where a highway was bounded by land at a higher level supported by a retaining wall, and the plaintiff, after the light on the retaining wall had been extinguished for the night at 9 p.m., missed his way, got on to the adjoining land, and fell over the retaining wall into the street, it was held that the local authority were not liable.[98]

697 **Non-repair of highway by local authority.** At common law, if a highway repairable by the inhabitants at large was allowed to get into a state of disrepair, as a result of which damage was caused to a person passing along the highway, no action lay. This immunity from liability is due to historical causes.[99] Originally, liability to repair public highways was upon the inhabitants of the various parishes through which the highway passed, each parish being responsible for that portion of the highway which was within its own boundaries. As the inhabitants were not

2 K.B. 561, *Lyus* v. *Stepney Corpn.* [1941] 1 K.B. 134, and *Fox* v. *Newcastle-upon-Tyne Corpn.* [1941] 2 K.B. 120, were not followed.

94 *Greenwood* v. *Central Service Co. Ltd.* [1940] 2 K.B. 447.

95 *Great Central Ry.* v. *Hewlett* [1916] 2 A.C. 511.

96 Scrutton L.J. in *Sheppard* v. *Glossop Corpn.* [1921] 3 K.B. 132 at p. 149.

97 *Carpenter* v. *Finsbury Borough Council* [1920] 2 K.B. 195.

98 *Sheppard* v. *Glossop Corpn.* [1921] 3 K.B. 132.

99 See Holdsworth, *History of English Law*, Vol. 10, pp. 314–319. Article: "Non-feasance relating to Highways," 113 S.J. 615.

incorporated there was no corporate fund from which damages could be recovered and it was considered to be impossible for an action to be brought against each individual for his proportion of the damages.[1] The only remedy for non-repair was by indictment.[2] The Highway Act 1835 transferred the duty of repairing highways to the surveyor of highways, and it was held that the surveyor was entitled to the same immunity as the inhabitants of the parish.[3] By the various Public Health Acts and Local Government Acts the duties of the surveyor of highways were transferred to local authorities, and they succeeded to the surveyor's immunity from liability for non-repair of highways.[4] The immunity only attached to authorities who had succeeded to the surveyor's position, however[5]; it never did apply to dock, railway and canal companies who maintained roads or bridges in connection with their statutory undertakings.[6]

698 **Highways (Miscellaneous Provisions) Act 1961.** This intractable position at common law was scarcely consistent with the modern requirements of this age in which we live so that, following pressures exerted favouring a change in the law,[7] Lord Molson introduced a Bill to amend the law in this respect. He said, *inter alia*: " My Lords, I never thought when, at Oxford many years ago, I first learned about the non-feasance rule, that it would fall to my lot nearly a generation later to move a Bill which would have the effect of bringing to an end what I think has generally been regarded as an anomaly which has resulted in injustice to many people." As a result the law is now affected by the Highways (Miscellaneous Provisions) Act 1961,[8] section 1 of which came into force three years after the passing of the Act but does not apply to damage resulting from an event which occurred before the expiration of that period,[9] *viz.* before August 3, 1964.

Section 1 of the Act provides that the rule of law exempting the inhabitants at large and any other persons as their successors from

1 *Russell* v. *Men of Devon* (1788) 2 T.R. 667.

2 This procedure was abolished (though it had long fallen into disuse) by the Highways Act 1959. The procedure is now by way of service of a notice on the highway authority: see ss. 59, 282 of the 1959 Act.

3 *Young* v. *Davis* (1862) 7 H. & N. 760; affd. 2 H. & C. 197; *M'Kinnon* v. *Penson* (1854) 9 Ex. 609.

4 *Cowley* v. *Newmarket L.B.* [1892] A.C. 345; *Thompson* v. *Brighton Corpn.* [1894] 1 Q.B. 332; *Maguire* v. *Liverpool Corpn.* [1905] 1 K.B. 767; *Municipality of Pictou* v. *Geldert* [1893] A C. 524; *Municipal Council of Sydney* v. *Bourke* [1895] A.C. 433.

5 *Swain* v. *Southern Ry.* [1939] 2 K.B. 560 at p. 574; *Att.-Gen.* v. *St. Ives R.D.C.* [1961] 1 Q.B. 366 (C.A.).

6 *Mersey Docks Trustees* v. *Gibbs* (1866) L.R. 1 H.L. 93; *Blundy, Clark & Co.* v. *London and North Eastern Ry.* [1931] 2 K.B. 334; *Parnaby* v. *Lancaster Canal Co.* (1839) 11 A. & E. 223; *Guilfoyle* v. *Port of London Authority* [1932] 1 K.B. 336; *Swain* v. *Southern Ry.* [1939] 2 K.B. 560 (railway company, responsible for repairing a bridge and its approaches, liable to a cyclist thrown off his machine by a dangerous rut—their duty is to maintain the surface so as to be fit for the traffic of the period at which their obligation arose).

7 Notably from the General Council of the Bar in 1960.

8 The Act was passed on August 3, 1961. The Act must be read with the Highways Act 1959. See articles on this Act 128 L.P.J. 40 and 120 New L.J. 389.

9 Highways (Miscellaneous Provisions) Act 1961, s. 1 (8).

liability for non-repair of highways [10] is abrogated.[11] However, in an action against a highway authority [12] in respect of damage [13] resulting from their failure to maintain a highway maintainable at the public expense, it shall be a defence to prove that the authority had taken such care as, in all the circumstances, was reasonably required to secure that the part of the highway to which the action relates was not dangerous for traffic.[14] This is without prejudice to any other defence or the law relating to contributory negligence.[15]

In relation to a defence under section 1 (2) the court shall have regard to the following matters [16]: (a) the character of the highway, and the traffic reasonably to be expected to use it; (b) the standard of maintenance appropriate to such a highway; (c) the state of repair in which a reasonable person would have expected to find the highway; (d) whether the highway authority knew, or could reasonably have been expected to know, that the condition of the part of the highway was likely to cause damage to the users of the highway; (e) where the highway authority could not have been expected to repair the highway before the cause of action arose, what warning notices of its condition had been displayed. It is no defence for the local authority to prove that it had arranged for a competent person to carry out the maintenance of the highway unless it is also proved that they had given him proper instructions concerning the maintenance and he had carried them out.[17] The section binds the Crown.[18] The Act applies whether the plaintiff sues in negligence, breach of statutory duty or in nuisance.[19]

699 **Nature of the statutory duty.** The precise nature of the duty imposed by the Act has already resulted in a sharp difference of opinion by the Court of Appeal. In *Griffiths* v. *Liverpool Corporation* [20] the elderly female plaintiff, whilst walking along the pavement of a busy highway, tripped up over a flagstone which had been left unrepaired and hurt herself. As a result of the highway authority's inability to establish the statutory

[10] Any reference to a highway in s. 1 includes a reference to a bridge: s. 1 (4).
[11] *Ibid.* s. 1 (1).
[12] *Ibid.* s. 1 (4) provides that in the application of this section to highways in London repairable by the inhabitants at large, references to the highway authority are references to the council responsible for the maintenance of the highway.
[13] This section does not apply to damage resulting from breaking, or opening or tunnelling or boring under a street by way of code-regulated works which occurred: (a) before the completion of the reinstatement or making good of the relevant part of the street (under the Public Utilities Street Works Act 1950, s. 7 (2)); or (b) where the relevant part of the street is the subject of an election (Public Utilities Street Works Act 1950, Sched. III): see subs. (7).
[14] *Ibid.* s. 1 (2).
[15] *Ibid.* " A person is guilty of contributory negligence if he ought reasonably to have foreseen that, if he did not act as a reasonable, prudent man, he might be hurt himself; and in his reckonings he must take into account the possibility of others being careless ": *Jones* v. *Livox Quarries Ltd.* [1952] 2 K.B. 608, *per* Denning L.J. at p. 615. See *post*, Chap. 15.
[16] *Ibid.* s. 1 (3).
[17] *Ibid.* s. 1 (3), which statutory provision confirms *Hardaker* v. *Idle District Council* [1896] 1 Q.B. 335.
[18] *Ibid.* s. 1 (5).
[19] For a choice of action see *Simon* v. *Islington Borough Council* [1943] K.B. 188.
[20] [1967] 1 Q.B. 374.

defence, since the flagstone was held to have been dangerous, her action for damages succeeded. Sellers L.J. took the view that the provisions of the Act " make negligence the essential and ultimate basis of a claim against a highway authority, as it has always been and still is in respect of misfeasance." [21] On the other hand the majority view of the court concluded that it was an absolute duty to which the defence, if proved, provided by section 1 (2) excused non-performance. Diplock L.J. said " The duty at common law to maintain, which includes a duty to repair a highway, was not based in negligence but in nuisance. It was an absolute duty to maintain, not merely a duty to take reasonable care to maintain, and the statutory duty which replaced it was also absolute. At common law the duty, being a duty to the public, was enforceable by indictment but its rigour was reduced by another rule of common law that a private individual who suffered damage as a result of a highway's being out of repair could not recover damages in a civil action against the inhabitants at large if the lack of repair was due to mere failure to repair (that is, non-feasance) and not to acts of repair or other acts in relation to the highway improperly performed (that is, mis-feasance). When the common law duty of the inhabitants at large was converted into a statutory duty of the highway authority the rule excluding liability for non-feasance was, by judicial construction, treated as applicable to the statutory duty as well. And so matters remained until August 3, 1964: the duty to maintain the highways in their area was an absolute duty of the highway authority but subject to an exemption from liability in a civil action by a private individual for damages sustained by him as a consequence of mere non-repair." [22] Salmon L.J. took the same view in saying " since the flagstone was dangerous, the defendants were liable to the plaintiff—absolutely and irrespective of any negligence on their part." [23] Although the point is open to the House of Lords this view upon the statutory construction must prevail and is binding on the courts.[24]

It was further held in *Griffiths*' case that although section 1 (1) provides that it should only be a defence for non-repair of a highway, if the responsible authority took such care as was reasonably required within section 1 (2), it is nevertheless a defence within the latter subsection that through no fault of its own the highway authority was unable to take the steps needed to keep the highway in repair because of the shortage of skilled labour.

700 Since this decision however, the courts have tended to adopt a more liberal view in their findings of fact in favour of the highway authorities.[25] Thus in *Meggs* v. *Liverpool Corporation* [26] the Court of Appeal held that

[21] *Ibid.* at p. 386.
[22] *Ibid.* at pp. 389, 390.
[23] *Ibid.* at p. 394.
[24] See comments in (1967) 83 L.Q.R. 4 and (1967) Camb. L.J. 21. Winn L.J. in *Meggs* v. *Liverpool Corpn.* [1968] 1 W.L.R. 689, at p. 692 felt he had not yet understood fully the scope of this section and that further argument may be necessary in the future.
[25] In effect following the exception to the finding of fact that the pavement was dangerous in *Griffiths* v. *Liverpool Corporation, supra,* as expressed by Sellers L.J. at p. 381.
[26] [1968] 1 W.L.R. 689.

although the highway authority were under the duty to keep the highway in repair under section 44 (1) of the Highways Act 1959, a plaintiff, in order to make a prima facie case against such authority, had to show that the highway was not reasonably safe *i.e.* that it was dangerous to the relevant traffic. Lord Denning M.R. stated: " It seems to me, using ordinary knowledge of pavements, that everyone must take account of the fact that there may be unevenness here and there. There may be a ridge of half an inch or three quarters of an inch occasionally, but that is not the sort of thing which makes it dangerous or not reasonably safe." [27] This approach was accepted and followed by Cumming-Bruce J. in *Littler* v. *Liverpool Corporation* [28] wherein he observed: " Uneven surfaces and differences in level between flagstones of about an inch may cause a pedestrian, temporarily off balance, to trip and stumble but such characteristics have to be accepted. A highway is not to be criticised by the standards of a bowling green." [29]

But in *Pridham* v. *Hemel Hempstead Corporation* [30] Mocatta J. considered that the local authority had not proved that it had done all that was reasonably practicable for it to do to secure that the particular piece of the footpath was not dangerous, or that it had taken such care as in all the circumstances it reasonably could to the same end. The plaintiff's shoe had become wedged so tightly in a three inch deep hole in the pavement that she was unable to release her foot until a passer-by came to her rescue and freed it from her shoe. Where a large pool of surface water accumulated during a torrential rainstorm in a roadway, the trial judge found that the highway authority had instituted a good system of maintenance but that their workmen had negligently failed to carry it out properly.[31]

701 **Distinction between nonfeasance and misfeasance.** At common law the distinction between nonfeasance and misfeasance was highly relevant since, as explained above, in the case of nonfeasance [32] immunity from liability existed whilst a highway authority has always been liable for misfeasance, that is, for doing work on the highway without taking reasonable care for the safety of users of the highway. The distinction between nonfeasance and misfeasance can be illustrated thus: if nothing at all is done, it is nonfeasance; but if the highway is interfered with, there immediately arises a duty to take reasonable care, and an omission, such as a failure to fence or light a heap of stones or a hole, is misfeasance as much as a positive act, such as causing inequalities in the road in the

[27] *Ibid.* at p. 692. For an example of the comparable situation where the local authority *creates* ridges on a highway, see generally misfeasance *post*, § 704 and *Bright* v. *Ministry of Transport* (1971) 115 S.J. 226, white lines obliterated on road surface in such a manner that longitudinal ridges were left into which the plaintiff's motor-cycle wheels got caught.
[28] [1968] 2 All E.R. 343.
[29] *Ibid.* at p. 345.
[30] *The Times*, December 19, 1969.
[31] *Burnside* v. *Emerson* [1968] 1 W.L.R. 1490 (the C.A. held that the deceased driver of the other vehicle, who negligently drove into the water at speed injuring the plaintiffs, was two-thirds to blame for the accident).
[32] See " Non-Feasance Revisited," by G. Sawer, 18 M.L.R. 541.

course of repairs. Lush J. explains the distinction as follows: "If a highway authority, therefore, leaves a road alone and it gets out of repair, there is, of course, no doubt that no action can be brought, although damage ensues. But this doctrine has no application to a case where the road authority have done something, made up or altered or diverted a highway, and have omitted some precaution, which, if taken, would have made the work done safe instead of dangerous. You cannot sever what was omitted or left undone from what was committed or actually done, and say that because the accident was caused by the omission therefore it was nonfeasance. Once establish that the local authority did something to the road, and the case is removed from the category of nonfeasance. If the work was imperfect and incomplete it becomes a case of misfeasance and not nonfeasance, although damage was caused by an omission to do something that ought to have been done. The omission to take precautions to do something that ought to have been done to finish the work is precisely the same thing in its legal consequence as the commission of something that ought not to have been done, and there is no similarity in point of law between such a case and a case where the local authority have chosen to do nothing at all." [33]

702 An immediate problem that is raised is whether or not this distinction between nonfeasance and misfeasance is still relevant. Certainly the introductory words of Lord Molson [34] when moving the Bill before Parliament indicated that what alone was intended to be removed was this anomaly, an unjustifiable and unsatisfactory exemption from liability for non-repair, which the court had declined to extend.[35] It is to be noted that the words used in the marginal note of section 1 read "Civil liability for non-repair of certain highways and bridges" and subsection 1 tersely provides that the rule of law exempting the inhabitants at large and any other persons as their successors from liability for non-repair of highways "is hereby abrogated." This would appear to exclude misfeasance and likewise the words in subsection 2 "failure to maintain a highway" must relate to nonfeasance only. It is submitted that this is the correct view and the law relating to misfeasance remains unaffected.

Despite the misgivings of some writers [36] that the old common law distinction should still be preserved, there is no good reason why the two should not stand together with their respective causes of action, *viz.*: nonfeasance where there has been a breach of the absolute duty to maintain the highway, subject to the statutory defence, excusing non-performance and, in the alternative, misfeasance where work has been carried out on the highway without taking reasonable care for the safety of users of it.

703 **Burden of proof.** In misfeasance cases the burden of proving negligence

[33] *McClelland* v. *Manchester Corpn.* [1912] 1 K.B. 118. See also *per* Lord Halsbury in *Shoreditch Corpn.* v. *Bull* (1904) 90 L.T. 210; and *Baxter* v. *Stockton-on-Tees Corporation* [1959] 1 Q.B. 441.

[34] See *ante*, § 698.

[35] *e.g.* by Salmon J. in *Att.-Gen.* v. *St. Ives R.D.C.* [1960] 1 Q.B. 312, 323.

[36] Professor H. Street, *The Law of Torts* 4th edition p. 470.

remains on the plaintiff. The fact that an independent contractor is employed and that he has committed the misfeasance is no defence to the highway authority, since the responsibility cannot be shifted by delegating the performance of that duty imposed on it to another.[37] In nonfeasance cases [38] the action involves three things: (a) the plaintiff must show that the road was in such a condition as to be dangerous for traffic, of which foreseeability is an essential element; (b) the plaintiff must prove that the dangerous condition was due to a failure to maintain, which includes a failure to repair the highway; and (c) if there is a failure to maintain, the highway authority is liable prima facie for any damage resulting therefrom. It can only escape liability if it proves that it took such care as in all the circumstances was reasonable.[39]

704 **Examples of misfeasance.** The following have been held to be misfeasance on the part of the highway authority and are still relevant authorities: partially filling up a hole in the roadway with soft, wet ballast [40]; repairing the road so as to leave a ridge in the carriageway [41]; obliterating the white lines on the road surface so as to leave longitudinal ridges [42]; leaving a heap of soil unlighted and unguarded in the highway in the course of doing road repairs [43]; digging a trench in the highway, filling it in so that it became soft within a few days, and allowing traffic to go over it [44]; making up a street, at the end of which was an unfenced ravine, and throwing it open to the public without taking steps by lighting, guarding or otherwise to warn the public of the existence of the ravine [45]; widening an existing road and throwing it open to the public without first seeing that a hole, caused by the removal of a telegraph pole to enable the road to be widened, was properly filled in [46]; constructing a road on the side of a steep hill without making proper provision for carrying off water and shale caught by the road [47]; in the course of road repairs, leaving the road, unlighted and unfenced, divided into two parts at different levels, one part consisting of loose stones rolled in by a steam roller and the other part being the undisturbed road [48]; removing a fence which was formerly erected to protect the public using the highway from going into

[37] *Hardaker* v. *Idle District Council* [1896] 1 Q.B. 335; *Penny* v. *Wimbledon U.D.C.* [1899] 2 Q.B. 72.
[38] For examples of " nonfeasance " see *Charlesworth on Negligence* 4th edition, § 353.
[39] *Burnside* v. *Emerson* [1968] 1 W.L.R. 1490 (the claim against the highway authority was founded separately in misfeasance, nonfeasance and negligence. However Lord Denning M.R. commenced his judgment: " This is an action for non-feasance against a highway authority. It has only been available since the Highways (Miscellaneous Provisions) Act 1961." *Whiting* v. *Hillingdon London Borough Council* (1970) 68 L.G.R. 437 (plaintiff tripped over a hidden tree stump protruding over a privately owned footpath which the local authority was liable to maintain. *Held* by James J. not to be in breach of their duty under the Highways Act 1959 and the defence under the Act of 1961 had been established).
[40] *Meeling* v. *Vestry of St. Mary, Newington* (1893) 10 T.L.R. 54.
[41] *Hill* v. *Tottenham U.D.C.* (1898) 79 L.T. 495.
[42] *Bright* v. *Ministry of Transport* (1970) 114 S.J. 475.
[43] *Penny* v. *Wimbledon U.D.C.* [1899] 2 Q.B. 72.
[44] *Shoreditch Corpn.* v. *Bull* (1904) 90 L.T. 210.
[45] *McClelland* v. *Manchester Corpn.* [1912] 1 K.B. 118.
[46] *Thompson* v. *Bradford Corpn.* [1915] 3 K.B. 13.
[47] *Baldwins Ltd.* v. *Halifax Corpn.* (1916) 85 L.J.K.B. 1769.
[48] *Parkinson* v. *West Riding C.C.* (1922) 66 S.J. 488.

a ditch at the side of the highway, so that, during a flood, a person driving along the highway drove into the ditch and was drowned [49]; raising the level of the highway above that of the neighbouring land so as to leave a dangerous drop of five or six inches without providing a fence or other protection [50]; omitting to make good a subsidence in the road caused by a trench which they had dug and filled up [51]; allowing tram lines, which had become vested in them, to get out of repair and become dangerous to users of the highway [52]; removing railings adjoining the highway when they were damaged in a collision and omitting to replace them [53]; in repairing the highway, reducing the headroom of a bridge so as to create an undue risk.[54] However, where a highway superintendent, noticing a subsidence in the road which had been caused by rat runs, sealed off one run, blocked the manhole to which it led and filled in the hole in the road, but failed to use broken glass as an ingredient in the filling material, it was held that there was no liability to a plaintiff who was injured when his foot sank into the surface due to the rats dislodging this new filling. Despite the great experience of the superintendent it was held that he had no reason to suppose that the events which occurred would happen.[55]

In the absence of express provision to the contrary, one local authority is not liable for the misfeasance of an authority to which it has succeeded.[56]

(b) *Dangers adjoining the Highway*

705 **Liability for dangerous buildings adjoining highway.** Buildings adjoining the highway must be maintained in such a condition as not to be dangerous to users of the highway. Such buildings constitute a public nuisance and liability is based on nuisance rather than on negligence, but as the element of negligence is not altogether absent the subject is dealt with here.

The occupier, and sometimes the owner,[57] of property is liable (1) for creating the nuisance, and (2) for continuing the nuisance after knowledge or presumed knowledge of its existence.[58] A nuisance is created if there is negligence in maintaining buildings adjoining the highway so that they get into a dangerous state of disrepair. The mere fact that their disrepair causes damage to a person in the highway, as by a slate coming off a roof or the collapse of a wall, is itself evidence of negligence throwing the burden of disproving it on the occupier or the owner. But if that burden is discharged, and it is proved that there is no negligence in maintaining a building, the question arises whether the owner or the occupier can be said to have created the nuisance. On this point the

[49] *Whyler* v. *Bingham R.D.C.* [1901] 1 K.B. 45.
[50] *Nicholson* v. *Southern Ry. and Sutton and Cheam U.D.C.* [1935] 1 K.B. 558.
[51] *Newsome* v. *Darton U.D.C.* [1938] 3 All E.R. 93.
[52] *Simon* v. *Islington B.C.* [1943] K.B. 188.
[53] *Drake* v. *Bedfordshire C.C.* [1944] K.B. 620.
[54] *Lewys* v. *Burnett and Dunbar* [1945] 2 All E.R. 555.
[55] *Birmingham* v. *East Ham Corpn., The Times*, October 20, 1961.
[56] *Nash* v. *Rochford R.D.C.* [1917] 1 K.B. 384. See also *Baxter* v. *Stockton-on-Tees Corpn.* [1959] 1 Q.B. 441.
[57] *Post*, § § 720, 721.
[58] *Sedleigh-Denfield* v. *O'Callaghan* [1940] A.C. 880.

authorities are conflicting. It is settled, however, that it is no defence to employ an independent contractor to keep the building in repair, the employer being liable for the negligence of the independent contractor.[59]

706 In *Kearney* v. *London and Brighton Ry.*[60] the plaintiff, as he was walking along the highway under a railway bridge, was struck by a brick which fell from one of the piers of the bridge. A train had passed over the bridge before he was struck. The railway company were held liable, Kelly C.B. saying: " There can be no doubt that it was the duty of the defendants, who had built this bridge over the highway, to take such care that, where danger can be reasonably avoided, the safety of the public using the highway should be provided for. . . . The bridge had been built for two or three years, and it was the duty of the defendants from time to time to inspect the bridge, and ascertain that the brickwork was in good order and all the bricks well secured." In this case the only material evidence was the fall of the brick, and there was no evidence that the railway company knew of the defective condition of the brickwork.

707 In *Tarry* v. *Ashton*[61] a lamp was fixed to the side of a house and suspended over the highway. As the plaintiff was walking along the highway the lamp fell and injured her. The jury found that the lamp was out of repair through general decay, but not to the knowledge of the defendant. They also found that there was no negligence on the part of the defendant, although there was negligence on the part of a contractor whom he had employed to examine his lamps and put them in thorough repair. The defendant was held liable, Blackburn J. saying[62]: " The occupier would be bound to know that things like this lamp will ultimately get out of order, and, as occupier, there would be a duty cast upon him from time to time to investigate the state of the lamp. If he did investigate, and there was a latent defect which he could not discover, I doubt whether he would be liable; but if he discovers the defect and does not cure it, or if he did not discover what he ought on investigation to have discovered, then I think he would clearly be answerable for the consequences." From this passage it is clear that the duty to take reasonable care involves a duty to inspect from time to time in order to discover defects due to wear and tear.

708 The burden of proof was discharged and the defendant was held not liable in *Palmer* v. *Bateman*.[63] In that case the plaintiff was injured in the highway by a piece of the gutter falling from the defendant's house, but,

59 *Tarry* v. *Ashton* (1876) 1 Q.B.D. 314.
60 (1871) L.R. 6 Q.B. 759.
61 (1876) 1 Q.B.D. 314.
62 The headnote in the Law Reports implies that Lush and Quain JJ. differed from the reasons given by Blackburn J. This, however, does not seem to be the case. Blackburn J. gave judgment first and went into the question more thoroughly than the other judges, who confined themselves to the question that the employment of an independent contractor was no defence. See the same opinion expressed by Sir F. Pollock, *Torts*, 13th ed., p. 541; 15th ed., p. 403, and Landon, 56 L.Q.R. 140.
63 [1908] 2 Ir.R. 393. In *Wringe* v. *Cohen* [1940] 1 K.B. 229, 242, the C.A. expressed the opinion that this case was wrongly decided.

on his proving that the house was periodically examined and repaired, the jury found that there was no negligence. O'Brien C.J. said: "I don't think it can be said that the owner of a house warrants to each member of the public that it is in an absolutely safe condition of repair; but if there be negligence in the keeping of the house in repair, and such negligence results in an injury to a member of the public, that is a wholly different thing. Indeed, I think the case of *Kearney* v. *London and Brighton Ry.*[64] concludes this case."

709 On the other hand, where the roof and three walls of a building were pulled down, leaving the fourth wall, which abutted upon the highway, still standing, the Irish Court of Appeal[65] held that when the fourth wall fell down and injured a person upon the highway the owner was liable, although the jury found that he neither knew nor ought to have known that the wall was dangerous.

In *Wringe* v. *Cohen*[66] the wall of a building collapsed, causing damage, and the owner was held liable though he neither knew nor ought to have known of the danger. It was expressly held that when the danger is caused by want of repair, proof of negligence is unnecessary. The reasoning of this case has not escaped criticism,[67] but it was followed in *Heap* v. *Ind Coope & Allsopp Ltd.*,[68] where a cellar flap in the highway collapsed owing to lack of repair. In a later case Atkinson J., who had delivered the judgment of the Court of Appeal in *Wringe* v. *Cohen*, explained: "A duty to prevent his house from becoming dangerous from want of repair connotes a duty to inspect and examine, and if a landlord fails to do either, it is right that he should not be allowed to rely upon his want of knowledge. There is nothing latent in the premises becoming in such disrepair as to be in danger of collapse. That was the point in *Wringe* v. *Cohen*."[69]

710 There is no liability if the danger is due to a latent defect, not discoverable by the exercise of reasonable care and skill on the part of anyone, or by "a secret and unobservable operation of nature, such as a subsidence under or near the foundations of the premises."[70] Again, it is a defence to show that the danger was caused by a trespasser and was not continued after knowledge or means of knowledge.[71] Where blast from an enemy bomb loosened a slate, which fell from the roof of

64 (1871) L.R. 6 Q.B. 759.

65 *Mullan* v. *Forrester* [1921] 2 Ir.R. 412. In *Noble* v. *Harrison* [1926] 2 K.B. 332, 343, Wright J. said that he preferred the dissenting judgment of Moore J. that the liability of the occupier depended on knowledge.

66 [1940] 1 K.B. 229. The wall fell on adjoining property and not on the highway, but it was held that there was no difference in the legal result. See Winfield, *Tort*, 6th ed., p. 570. The judgment in this case was not referred to at all by the H.L. in *Sedleigh-Denfield* v. *O'Callaghan* [1940] A.C. 880, possibly because at the time notice of appeal had been given in the former and so was *sub judice*.

67 Pollock, *Torts*, 15th ed., p. 324; Salmond, *Torts*, 15th ed., p. 87; Winfield, *Tort*, 8th ed. p. 376; 56 L.Q.R. 1; Landon, 56 L.Q.R. 140.

68 [1940] 2 K.B. 476 (negligence was found as a fact by the county court judge).

69 *Spicer* v. *Smee* [1946] 1 All E.R. 489, at p. 494.

70 *Wringe* v. *Cohen* [1940] 1 K.B. 229, 233; *Lambert* v. *Lowestoft Corpn.* [1901] 1 Q.B. 590.

71 *Wringe* v. *Cohen, supra*; *Barker* v. *Herbert* [1911] 2 K.B. 633.

a building in a high wind eighteen days later and injured a person in the highway, the occupier was held not liable on its being found that reasonable inspection of the roof did not disclose that the slate had been loosened by the blast.[72]

711 Liability is imposed for continuing a nuisance after it was or ought to have been known. When there was an accumulation of snow on the roof of a building and for four days the occupiers did not remove it, so that it fell on the plaintiff as she was walking on the footpath, the occupiers were held liable.[73] The occupier was also liable when an air raid on a Friday night broke the windows of an empty house and the damage remained unrepaired by the following Tuesday, when the plaintiff in the highway was injured by a fall of glass.[74]

712 **Dangerous fences and boundary walls.** The obligation to maintain premises adjoining the highway so that they are not dangerous to persons using the highway extends to fences and boundary walls adjoining the highway. If a person, in the ordinary and reasonable use of the highway, leans upon or otherwise comes in contact with the fence or wall so that it gives way and he is injured, he can recover from the occupier of the premises. So, where the defendants occupied a cellar in which scene-painting was going on and, to protect the area, a bar was put up against which the plaintiff, a child, was leaning, it was held that the plaintiff was entitled to recover for injuries sustained through falling into the area owing to the giving way of the bar.[75] Again, where a fence was maintained abutting on the highway and a child of four, in order to play with some children on the other side of the fence put his foot on the fence, when it fell on him and injured him, it was held that the child could recover.[76] A. L. Smith L.J. said: " A rotten fence close to a highway is an obvious nuisance. If I were on the highway and wanted to tie up my boot, or got tired and leaned against the fence, should I not have been lawfully using the highway? The present case is a stronger one." A boy of eight who climbed a wall in a ruinous and dangerous condition adjoining a public footpath and was injured by the wall collapsing on him, was held entitled to recover.[77] There is no liability, however, if the danger has been created by a trespasser and there is no negligence in failing to remove it. Accordingly, when the defendant was the owner of a vacant house, the area railings of which had been broken by boys playing football in the street, and the plaintiff, a boy between three and four, while clambering along the railings, fell into the area and was injured, it was held that the defendant was not liable on a finding of fact that the defendant had used reasonable care to prevent the premises becoming

[72] *Cushing* v. *Peter Walker & Sons Ltd.* [1941] 2 All E.R. 693.
[73] *Slater* v. *Worthington's Cash Stores Ltd.* [1941] 1 K.B. 488. See article, " Damage from Frost and Snow," 113 L.J. 179.
[74] *Leanse* v. *Egerton* [1943] K.B. 323.
[75] *Jewson* v. *Gatti* (1886) 2 T.L.R. 441.
[76] *Harrold* v. *Watney* [1898] 2 Q.B. 320, 322.
[77] *Robertson's Tutor* v. *Glasgow Corpn.*, 1950 S.C. 502.

dangerous to persons using the highway, and that he neither knew nor would have known by the exercise of reasonable care of the break in the railings.[78]

713 A fence or a wall does not become dangerous because persons on the highway may climb up it and fall off. So, where a wall, which was perfectly safe, adjoined the highway, it was held that the presence of a heap of soil at the side of the highway so placed as to enable a boy of seven to climb on top of the wall, imposed no liability on the owners and occupiers of the wall when the boy fell off and sustained injuries.[79]

714 **Dangerous siting of road signs.** In *Levine* v. *Morris and Ministry of Transport*,[80] it was held that the Ministry of Transport owed a duty of care to motorists in the siting of their road signs. Where motorists may inadvertently leave the road and collide with such signs, the duty is to select the site which is equally good as regards visibility but which involves the lesser hazard to the motorist. However, in practice, this need for special siting will arise only where the configuration of the road makes it foreseeable that there is an above average risk of a vehicle leaving the road's surface.

715 **Dangerous premises.** If premises by the side of the highway are so constructed as to be dangerous to users of the highway, they are a nuisance. In such a case the state of repair is immaterial, because the existence of the works constitutes the danger. So, where a barbed wire fence was maintained to fence off the defendant's premises from the highway, the plaintiff, who tore his coat upon it, was held entitled to recover.[81] Where in front of a shop window there was a wall, eighteen inches high, on the top of which was a row of spikes four and a half inches high, and the plaintiff, a girl aged five, was found injured under circumstances consistent with her having fallen upon the spikes, it was held that the spikes were a nuisance and the owners of the shop were liable.[82] But where the defendant had for seven years maintained a spiked fence, four and a half feet high, adjoining the highway, and one of the plaintiff's horses, drawing a cart along the highway up an incline, slipped and fell against the fence, thereby sustaining injuries, it was held that the defendant was not liable.[83] Lopes L.J. said that " the law no doubt was that if a person erected on his own land anything calculated to interfere with the use of a highway, what he so did was a nuisance." But he could not agree with the suggestion that " the erection of this iron fence, not with spikes jutting out into the road, but with perpendicular spikes, amounted to a nuisance."

78 *Barker* v. *Herbert* [1911] 2 K.B. 633. It was also held that even if the defendant was responsible for the nuisance, the injury was not the direct result of the nuisance.
79 *Liddle* v. *Yorkshire* (*North Riding*) *C.C.* [1934] 2 K.B. 101.
80 [1970] 1 W.L.R. 71.
81 *Stewart* v. *Wright* (1893) 9 T.L.R. 480. See Barbed Wire Act 1893.
82 *Fenna* v. *Clare & Co.* [1895] 1 Q.B. 199.
83 *Gibson* v. *Plumstead Burial Board* (1897) 13 T.L.R. 273. See also *Morton* v. *Wheeler*, *The Times*, February 1, 1956.

716 **Excavations adjoining highway.** The occupier of land is liable if he makes or continues an excavation on his own land which is a danger to persons using the highway. Where an area before a house was not fenced in so that the plaintiff, while walking along the street, fell in and was injured, the occupier was held liable although the premises were in the same condition as they were in when he became possessed of them.[84] Again, where land adjoining a highway was excavated for the erection of a building and the excavation was left unfenced so that the plaintiff, passing along the highway in the dark, was injured, it was held that the plaintiff could recover.[85] Maule J. said: " The defendant, in having made that excavation, was guilty of a public nuisance, even though the danger consisted in the risk of accidentally deviating from the road." Where the plaintiff, walking along the highway without negligence, fell into an unfenced hoist-hole fourteen inches from the highway, the occupiers were held liable, on the ground that they " would be liable for a nuisance to the highway, if the excavation was so near to it that a person lawfully using the way, and using ordinary caution, accidentally slipping might fall into it." [86] It was held to be no defence that the builder who made the hole might also be liable.

717 Liability is only imposed when the excavation is so near to the highway that a person going along the highway might fall into it. There is no liability if the person injured is a trespasser when he suffers the injury. " We think that the proper and true test of legal liability is, whether the excavation be substantially adjoining the way, and it would be very dangerous if it were otherwise—if in every case it was to be left as a fact to the jury, whether the excavation were sufficiently near to the highway to be dangerous." [87] Accordingly, the occupier has been held to be under no liability: where cattle strayed from the highway and fell into a pit thirty-six feet from the highway [88]; where a man wandered from the highway and fell into a reservoir some little distance from the highway [89]; where a man got off the towpath adjoining a canal, went across a strip of land twenty-four feet wide, and fell into the canal, which was unfenced [90]; where a boy climbed up three and a half feet to an unfenced aperture in a wall and put his head through the aperture, when he was injured by the descent of a lift, which was two feet from the edge [91]; when a man at night and in a fog got off the highway and fell into an unfenced dock forty-seven feet away [92]; when a man at night in the dark got into a private road from which he fell and was killed.[93]

84 *Coupland* v. *Hardingham* (1813) 3 Camp. 398.
85 *Barnes* v. *Ward* (1850) 9 C.B. 392.
86 *Hadley* v. *Taylor* (1865) L.R. 1 C.P. 53, *per* Erle C.J. at p. 55.
87 *Hardcastle* v. *South Yorkshire Ry.* (1859) 4 H. & N. 67, *per* Pollock C.B.
88 *Blyth* v. *Topham* (1607) Cro.Jac. 158.
89 *Hardcastle* v. *South Yorkshire Ry.*, *supra*.
90 *Binks* v. *South Yorkshire Ry.* (1862) 3 B. & S. 244.
91 *Stiefsohn* v. *Brook* (1889) 53 J.P. 790.
92 *Casely* v. *Bristol Corpn.* [1944] 1 All E.R. 14.
93 *Melville* v. *Renfrewshire C.C.*, 1920 S.C. 61.

718 Apart from cases within the principle stated above, there is no liability on the ground of nuisance if a person sustains damage after leaving the highway. Lord Simonds says[94]: " The House was referred to no case and my researches have led me to none where a plaintiff has deliberately left the highway to go elsewhere, and, having left it and having suffered injury on the adjoining land, has then been held entitled to recover on a claim of public nuisance in respect of which he has suffered special damage. Far as the law of nuisance has travelled beyond its original limits, this further extension appears to me to be justified neither by reason nor by authority." Accordingly, when shops owned by the defendants were separated from the highway by a forecourt in which was a stopcock about two feet from the highway projecting above the surface and the plaintiff going to one of the shops, which was let to a tenant, tripped over the stopcock, it was held that the defendants were not liable as the obstruction was not on the highway, so that it could not be a nuisance.[95] The plaintiff's remedy in such a case was to have sued the tenant of the shop as an invitor.[96] This was the position in *Howard* v. *Walker*,[97] where a customer at a shop fell owing to the defective paving of the forecourt between the shop and the highway. She was held entitled to recover from the shop tenant, who was an invitor, but not against the landlord who was not in occupation of the forecourt. Further see *ante*, Chapter 8, § 337.

If the highway is raised above the level of the surrounding land so as to leave a dangerous drop, the occupier of the land is under no obligation to erect a fence to prevent persons travelling along the highway from falling down the drop.[98] The highway authority are liable for building the highway without making any protection against such accidents.[98] The occupier of land is under no duty to fence a natural danger, such as a stream, from the highway.[99]

719 **Dangers due to diversion of highway.** When a highway is diverted, protection must be provided at the point of diversion so as to prevent persons going along the highway with reasonable care from going astray at the point of diversion. Where a railway company, in constructing their railway, diverted a footpath into a road but put nothing to indicate the point of the diversion, so that a person going along the footpath got on to the railway line and was injured, it was held that the railway company were liable.[1] Where a tunnel under an archway was substituted for a level crossing, so that a lad driving a van, was crushed under the archway, the local authority who had built the tunnel were held liable.[2]

94 In *Jacobs* v. *L.C.C.* [1950] A.C. 361, 377.
95 *Jacobs* v. *L.C.C., supra*, overruling *Owens* v. *Scott* [1939] 3 All E.R. 663.
96 See Chap. 8.
97 [1947] K.B. 860, expressly approved by the H.L. in *Jacobs* v. *L.C.C., supra.*
98 *Nicholson* v. *Southern Ry.* [1935] 1 K.B. 558.
99 *Morrison* v. *L.M.S. Ry.*, 1929 S.C. 1.
1 *Hurst* v. *Taylor* (1885) 14 Q.B.D. 918. See also *Evans* v. *Rhymney Local Board* (1887) 4 T.L.R. 72.
2 *Bedman* v. *Tottenham Local Board* (1887) 4 T.L.R. 22. See also *Law* v. *Railway Executive* [1949] W.N. 172, *ante*, § 693.

720 **Liability of occupier.** Liability for defective buildings adjoining the highway, defective coal plates, gratings and other structures in the highway, and defective fences and other erections adjoining the highway, has hitherto been treated as if it were on the occupier.

The rule is that the occupier is always liable,[3] apart from cases where the defect has been caused by the wilful act of a third person and there has been no negligence on the part of the occupier in remedying the defect.[4] He is liable even if the defect existed before he became occupier, because he has continued the nuisance and it was his "fault to contract for an interest in land on which there was a nuisance."[5]

721 **Liability of owner.** The owner of the premises is liable if he has contracted with the occupier to do the repairs. This was decided in *Payne* v. *Rogers*[6] where the plaintiff was injured by his leg slipping through a hole in the pavement into a vault or cellar, owing to some plates or bars, which went under the pavement, being out of repair. The owner is liable whether he has actual knowledge of the state of disrepair or not.[7]

The owner is also liable if he has let the premises knowing them to be in a ruinous or dangerous condition without taking any steps to remedy their condition. Where, therefore, houses were demised with chimneys in a dangerous condition so that they fell upon the neighbouring building and damaged it, the lessor was held liable.[8] If, however, the lessor takes a covenant from the lessee that the lessee shall do the repairs, the lessor is not liable even if he knew that the premises were out of repair at the date of the lease, because by taking the covenant he takes steps to put an end to the disrepair.[9] Accordingly, where an iron flap covering a coal cellar was out of repair before the date of the demise and the premises were let to a tenant who covenanted to keep them in repair, the landlord covenanting to put them in repair, a pedestrian on the highway who was injured through the flap giving way was held to have no action against the landlord when the accident happened after the tenant had entered into possession but the landlord's workmen were still executing the repairs which he had agreed to do.[10]

722 The owner is also liable if the premises get out of repair during the demise, where there is no covenant on the part of the occupier to do

[3] *Wilchick* v. *Marks and Silverstone* [1934] 2 K.B. 56, 68.
[4] *Barker* v. *Herbert* [1911] 2 K.B. 633.
[5] *Roswell* v. *Prior* (1701) 12 Mod. 635.
[6] (1794) 2 H.Bl. 350. This case was approved in *R.* v. *Pedly* (1834) 1 A. & E. 822; *Todd* v. *Flight* (1860) 9 C.B.(N.S.) 377; *Nelson* v. *Liverpool Brewery Co.* (1877) 2 C.P.D. 311.
[7] *Wringe* v. *Cohen* [1940] 1 K.B. 229, disapproving the opinion of Goddard J. in *Wilchick* v. *Marks and Silverstone* [1934] 2 K.B. 56, 66; *Heap* v. *Ind Coope & Allsopp Ltd.* [1940] 2 K.B. 476. See *ante*, § 709 for references to criticisms of this case.
[8] *Todd* v. *Flight*, *supra*. There is no reletting each week or month in a weekly or other periodic tenancy, and consequently a landlord is not liable, under this principle, for any damage through disrepair existing at the beginning of any week or month of the tenancy after the beginning of the letting. *Gandy* v. *Jubber* (1864) 5 B. & S. 78; *Bowen* v. *Anderson* [1894] 1 Q.B. 164.
[9] *Pretty* v. *Bickmore* (1873) L.R. 8 C.P. 401; *Gwinnell* v. *Eamer* (1875) L.R. 10 C.P. 658.
[10] *Pretty* v. *Bickmore*, *supra*.

the repairs and where the owner, although not contracting to repair, reserves the right to enter and do repairs.[11] So where the plaintiff, while passing along the highway, was injured through the fall of a shutter while it was being closed by the tenant's son, and there was no agreement between landlord and tenant as to repairs, it was held that both landlord and tenant were liable, the landlord on the ground that he had power to repair and, knowing of the disrepair, did not exercise it, and the tenant because he was under a duty to see that no injury befell members of the public who passed his house.[12] The position is the same when the owner, although he has not expressly reserved the right to enter and do repairs in practice does the repairs because in such a case there is an implied permission for him to enter to do the repairs.[13]

723 **Interferences with structures in or adjoining highway.** The owner of premises is not liable merely because there are cellar flaps, plates or doors so close to the highway that if they are opened suddenly and without due care persons passing along the highway will be injured.[14] Where premises had a door which opened outwards flush with the highway the owner was held not liable to a person who was injured by the door being opened suddenly when there was no evidence that it was opened by him or by anyone for whose acts he was responsible.[15] " The utmost that can be urged here is that the respondents own premises which if carelessly used by the occupant might be a cause of injury to an innocent passer-by. That is insufficient in my opinion to establish any liability against them for the accident that arose." [16] The occupier would have been prima facie liable in such a case.

724 In the event of cellar flaps or other structures in the highway being interfered with so as to render them dangerous, liability is primarily upon the person who interfered with the structures although the occupier is liable in certain circumstances. If cellar flaps are opened so as to leave a hole in the highway or an obstruction over which a person walking with reasonable care trips and falls the person who opened the flaps or caused them to be opened is liable. If he employs an independent contractor to do work which necessarily involves the creation of such a danger he is liable as where the lessee of refreshment rooms at a railway station employed an independent contractor to deliver coals through a hole into the coal cellar and was held liable for damage caused to a passenger who without any fault of his own, fell into the cellar

11 *Wringe* v. *Cohen* [1940] 1 K.B. 229.
12 *Wilchick* v. *Marks and Silverstone* [1934] 2 K.B. 56.
13 *Heap* v. *Ind Coope & Allsopp Ltd.* [1940] 2 K.B. 476. This case was followed in *Mint* v. *Good* [1951] 1 K.B. 517, where a boy on the highway was injured by the fall of a wall separating the forecourt of a house, let on a weekly tenancy, from the highway. There was no right to enter to do repairs reserved to the landlord, who in fact did the repairs, but the landlord was held liable. *Pretty* v. *Bickmore* was doubted by Denning L.J., but see 67 L.Q.R. 148 and 14 M.L.R. 348.
14 *De Boos* v. *Collard* (1892) 8 T.L.R. 338.
15 *Evans* v. *Edinburgh Corpn.* [1916] 2 A.C. 45.
16 *Ibid. per* Lord Buckmaster at p. 49.

owing to its being left insufficiently guarded.[17] The independent contractor is also liable in such a case.[18] When a coal merchant delivering coke to his customer's house through a cellar flap in the pavement left the flap open and unguarded for a short time so that a person passing along the highway fell in and was injured, both the coal merchant and the customer were held liable.[19] But if the work does not necessarily involve an interference with the highway, the employer is not liable. Accordingly, where a brewery company employed a contractor to deliver beer to a public house, and the occupier opened the cellar flaps, which were on the highway, it was held that the occupier but not the brewery company was liable for damage suffered by a boy in tripping over the flaps.[20] The ground of the decision was that the contractor was not employed to interfere with the highway. "Here the contractor was not employed in any sense to open the flap of this cellar. It was quite consistent with the contract of the contractor with the brewery company that the occupier of the house should himself have pushed back the flap, and if he did so and left it open, it was clearly his duty to see that it was not dangerous to the public using the highway."[21] This decision seems inconsistent with *Pickard* v. *Smith*[22] and *Whiteley* v. *Pepper*[23]; liability on the part of the occupier does not prevent the employer of the independent contractor from also being liable.

725 A canal company, with statutory authority to build a swivel bridge over a canal, are liable to persons who are injured through falling into the canal when the bridge is open if they provide no fence or warning. In such a case they create a danger in the highway by leaving an unfenced gulf in the highway whenever the bridge is opened for traffic.[24]

726 If the structure is interfered with by a third party, without the knowledge or consent of the occupier, the occupier is not liable if he has made the structure reasonably secure so that it will be safe unless intentionally, as opposed to accidentally, interfered with. Even if it is intentionally interfered with, the occupier will be liable if it is the sort of interference he should have anticipated would be likely to occur. Where a hogshead of wine was being lowered into a cellar, the flap of which was placed in a slanting position resting on a ledge about a foot above the pavement, when it fell on the plaintiff and injured him, Tindal C.J., directing the jury, said: "The defendants were bound, in placing the flap, to use such

17 *Pickard* v. *Smith* (1861) 10 C.B.(N.S.) 470. Although the accident happened in a railway station, "no sound distinction in this respect can be drawn between the case of a public highway and a road which may be and to the knowledge of the wrongdoer probably will in fact be used by persons lawfully entitled so to do."

18 *Whiteley* v. *Pepper* (1876) 2 Q.B.D. 276.

19 *Daniel* v. *Rickett Cockerell & Co.* [1938] 2 K.B. 322 (damages were apportioned as to nine-tenths to the coal merchant and one-tenth to the customer).

20 *Wilson* v. *Hodgson's Kingston Brewery Co.* (1915) 85 L.J.K.B. 270.

21 *Per* Avory J. at p. 272.

22 (1861) 10 C.B.(N.S.) 470.

23 (1876) 2 Q.B.D. 276.

24 *Manley* v. *St. Helens Canal Co.* (1858) 2 H. & N. 840.

precaution as would preserve it, under all ordinary circumstances, from falling down; but if it was so secured, and a third person, over whom they had no control, came and removed it, then I think the defendants will not be liable."[25] Again, where the facts were somewhat similar, but the plaintiff, a child, was injured through another child jumping from the flap and pulling it over, Pollock C.B. said: "It may be admitted that if a person, in passing along the street, had, without carelessness (as, for example, by his dress being blown against it), pulled the flap over, and been hurt thereby, he might have maintained an action against the defendants for the negligence or wrong in placing the flap so that, without any negligence in the plaintiff, it was likely to do, and had done, damage to him." It was held that the plaintiff could recover unless he was a joint actor with the child who jumped from the flap.[26] A cellar plate, which is left so insecure that any boy, poking about with a stick, can disturb it and make it loose, is a danger which imposes liability on the occupier if anyone in the highway is injured.[27]

727 A sun blind, which is securely fixed in front of a shop, does not give rise to liability on the occupier if it is pulled down by persons who jump up at it while they are passing along the highway. The occupier is not bound to fasten it so securely as to bear the weight of two men jumping up at it.[28] "The liability in a case of this kind is not a liability of insurance or warranty that the blind will never come down. The utmost which can be put against the shopkeeper is that he, as occupant, is bound to take such reasonable precautions as a reasonable man would exercise to avoid the result of an accident which might be reasonably foreseen."[29] On the same principle, a water board has been held to be not liable for damage caused through the act of a third person in raising the lid of a water-box in the highway, in the absence of a finding that the occurrence could or ought to have been foreseen and provided against.[30]

728 **Occupier continuing danger created by third party.** Although a third party may have interfered with a structure in the highway and so created a danger, the occupier will be liable if he allows the danger to continue. If, for example, a stranger opens cellar flaps, the occupier will not be liable for the opening of the flaps but he will be liable if he allows them to remain open after he knew or ought to have known that they were open. His duty is to shut or guard them within a reasonable time after knowledge which he actually has or ought to have under the circumstances. "The gravamen is the continuance of the nuisance and not the original causing

25 *Daniels* v. *Potter* (1830) 4 C. & P. 262.
26 *Hughes* v. *Macfie*, *Abbott* v. *Macfie* (1863) 2 H. & C. 744.
27 *Braithwaite* v. *Watson* (1889) 5 T.L.R. 331. To the same effect is *Findlay* v. *Angus* (1887) 14 R. 312 (shutter fastened by bolt fell when meddled with by children, occupier liable); also *Wells* v. *Metropolitan Water Board* [1937] 4 All E.R. 639, *ante*, § 687.
28 *Wheeler* v. *Morris* (1915) 84 L.J.K.B. 1435.
29 *Per* Cozens-Hardy M.R. at p. 1437.
30 *Mileham* v. *Marylebone Corpn.* (1903) 67 J.P. 110; *cf. Wells* v. *Metropolitan Water Board*, *supra.*

of it." [31] So, where a wall on the defendant's land was knocked down by trespassers so that the bricks were, to his knowledge, spread over the highway, the defendant was held liable for injury caused to a horse by the bricks, Field J. saying: "If an owner of land becomes aware of something on his premises, though through the act of a stranger, which is a source of risk and danger, a duty arises on him to guard against that risk and danger. There is a duty on him to keep and maintain his premises in such a condition that they shall not be injurious to the public at large using them." [32]

(c) *Miscellaneous Dangers*

729 **Dangerous machines left in highway.** Liability in respect of vehicles, horsed or unhorsed, left unattended in the highway is discussed elsewhere.[33] As to other objects, if a dangerous machine is left in the highway there will be liability to children, but in the case of adults liability will depend on the ordinary rule relating to obstructions in the highway.[34] "A man who leaves in a public place, along which persons, and amongst them children, have to pass, a dangerous machine which may be fatal to anyone who touches it, without any precaution against mischief, is not only guilty of negligence, but of negligence of a very reprehensible character, and not the less so because the imprudent and unauthorised act of another may be necessary to realise the mischief to which the unlawful act or negligence of the defendant has given occasion." [35] The duty to children in connection with dangerous machines in the highway is the same as the duty to children who are lawful visitors and is discussed *ante*.[36] In *Mangan* v. *Atterton* [37] a cutting machine was left unattended in a market place without being fastened or rendered harmless in any way, when boys returning from school played with it, one turning the handle, with the result that another boy's fingers were crushed, and it was held that the owner was not negligent. Bramwell B. said: "Suppose he had painted it with some poisonous paint, and the child had sucked it, would he have been liable?" The answer to this is clearly, yes.[38] This case is contrary to the trend of modern cases dealing with children, and must no longer be considered an authority.

730 **Vehicles on premises adjoining highway.** With regard to vehicles and machines which are left on premises adjoining the highway, they must be left in such a position and in such a manner as not to be dangerous to persons using the highway. If they are safe unless interfered with, the general rule is that the owner is under no liability when the acts of third persons make them unsafe and cause danger. So, where some railway

[31] Fletcher Moulton L.J. in *Barker* v. *Herbert* [1911] 2 K.B. 633, 642.
[32] *Silverton* v. *Marriott* (1888) 52 J.P. 677.
[33] *Post*, § 844.
[34] *Ante*, § 676 *et seq.*
[35] *Per* Cockburn C.J. in *Clark* v. *Chambers* (1878) 3 Q.B.D. 327, 339.
[36] Chap. 8, § 348 *et seq.*
[37] (1866) 4 H. & C. 388; 35 L.J.Ex. 161, disapproved in *Clark* v. *Chambers*, *supra.*
[38] *Glasgow Corpn.* v. *Taylor* [1922] 1 A.C. 44.

trucks were safely braked on a siding, which was on an incline running down to the highway, and some boys trespassed on to the railway line and released the brakes so that the plaintiff, while passing along the highway, was injured by the trucks, the railway company were held not liable.[39] The owner of the vehicle will, however, be liable if he knows that there is a real, as opposed to merely a possible, risk of his vehicle being interfered with in the position in which he has left it, unless he takes reasonable care to overcome that risk.[40]

731 **Duty to take care to avoid doing anything likely to injure persons on highway.** The duty to take care to avoid doing anything likely to injure persons on the highway is only part of the wider duty to take reasonable care in doing on or adjoining the highway anything which is likely to cause danger to persons passing along the highway. Where a telephone company were laying telephone wires in the street and employed a contractor to help them, it was held that they were liable when a lamp, used by one of the contractor's servants, exploded owing to the safety valve being out of order.[41] Lord Halsbury said: "The telephone company, by whose authority alone these works were done, were, whether the works were done by the company's servants or by a contractor, under an obligation to the public to take care that persons passing along the highway were not injured by the negligent performance of the work." [42] Similarly, where the defendants, who were working a quarry near the highway, injured a person passing along the highway by their blasting operations, it was held that they were liable because it was their duty to keep the results of their blasting operations on their own land.[43] Also, where the plaintiff slipped on the pavement on a piece of fat which had come from a butcher's shop, either from some chopping done by the butcher or by being carried on a customer's shoe, the butcher was held liable, both in nuisance and in negligence, because he should have foreseen the likelihood of fat from the shop getting on to the pavement.[44] When clouds of smoke were emitted so as to obscure the highway and no warning was given to approaching traffic, it was held that the person responsible for the smoke was liable for a highway collision caused by poor visibility.[45]

32 **Causing ice on highway.** When a van was washed in the street and the water flowed down the gutter but did not go down the grating, owing to its being frozen over, with the result that a sheet of ice was formed on which the plaintiff's horse, while being led past the spot, slipped and broke its leg, it was held that, although the defendant's act

39 *McDowall* v. *G.W. Ry.* [1903] 2 K.B. 331.
40 See *per* Vaughan Williams L.J. at p. 337.
41 *Holliday* v. *National Telephone Co.* [1899] 2 Q.B. 392.
42 *Ibid.* at p. 399.
43 *Miles* v. *Forest Rock Granite Co.* (1918) 34 T.L.R. 500.
44 *Dollman* v. *Hillman Ltd.* [1941] 1 All E.R. 355.
45 *Holling* v. *Yorkshire Traction Co.* [1948] 2 All E.R. 662. See also *Funnell* v. *C.P.R. & Bowden* (1964) 45 D.L.R. (2d) 481, where dense clouds of sand and dust blew across the highway as a result of the construction activities taking place on the adjoining land so that liability was established.

in washing the van in the highway was wrongful, the damage was too remote.[46] This decision, which could not stand after *Re Polemis*[47] was restored with approval by the Judicial Committee of the Privy Council in *The Wagon Mound* (No. 1).[48]

However in a somewhat similar case, when a pedestrian slipped on some ice on the pavement outside a garage yard, formed as a result of the washing of motor-vehicles in the garage on a November night, the garage proprietors were held liable, although it was not freezing when the vehicles were being washed, on the ground that they should have anticipated the possibility of the onset of a sudden frost and taken precautions to prevent the formation of ice on the pavement.[49] Again where water from a burst service pipe caused a pool of water to collect in the roadway, which lay unheeded for three days, and then a frost occurred forming ice upon which a motor car skidded, knocked down and killed a man, the water authority was held liable in negligence in not having taken prompt steps to attend to the leak and so to prevent the road from being dangerous to traffic.[50]

733 **Acid on highway.** When a carboy of sulphuric acid, fell off a lorry which was being driven along the highway and was cracked, thereby causing a pool of acid to be formed in the road, and a motor-cyclist, thinking it was water, attempted to ride through it, skidded and was burnt by the acid, it was held that the driver was liable for allowing the acid to remain on the road for half an hour after he knew that it was there without giving warning.[51]

734 **Sports grounds near highway.** A golf course adjoining the highway where a hole is so placed that players habitually drive into the highway is a nuisance, rendering the club liable to a person in the highway who is injured.[52] The player who struck the ball will also be liable, if he failed to take reasonable care, to keep his ball from going on to the highway.[53] The playing of cricket on a ground from which cricket balls are hit out of the ground on rare occasions only is not a nuisance, and the club is not liable to a person in the highway who is injured by a ball.[54]

46 *Sharp* v. *Powell* (1872) L.R. 7 C.P. 253.
47 [1921] 3 K.B. 560.
48 [1961] A.C. 388, at p. 418. "The judgment of Bovill C.J. is particularly valuable and interesting."
49 *Lambie* v. *Western S.M.T. Co. Ltd.*, 1944 S.C. 415. See article, "Damage from Frost and Snow," 113 L.J. 179.
50 *Manchester Corpn.* v. *Markland* [1936] A.C. 360. See also *Shepherd* v. *Midland Rail. Co.* (1872) 25 L.T. 879 (water trickled from a waste pipe at a railway station onto the platform and froze. The plaintiff, a passenger, stepped upon the ice, fell and was injured. The court held the defendant Railway Co. liable for negligence in not removing the ice); *Osborne* v. *London and North Western Rail. Co.* (1888) 12 Q.B.D. 220 (the plaintiff was injured by falling on steps leading to the defendant's railway station. The steps were worn and hollowed, and a light layer of snow which had been trodden down and formed ice had made them slippery).
51 *Pope* v. *Fraser* (1939) 55 T.L.R. 324.
52 *Castle* v. *St. Augustine's Links* (1922) 38 T.L.R. 615.
53 See *Cleghorn* v. *Oldham* (1927) 43 T.L.R. 465. Compare *Potter* v. *Carlisle and Cliftonville Golf Club Ltd.* [1939] N.I. 114.
54 *Bolton* v. *Stone* [1951] A.C. 850. But see *Hilder* v. *Associated Portland Cement Manufacturers Ltd.* [1961] 1 W.L.R. 1434 (footballs regularly kicked out of field).

735 **Vehicles calculated to frighten horses.** If a vehicle is brought on the highway which is likely to be a source of danger to persons or animals properly on the highway it is a nuisance, and the owner is liable for any damage caused. So, when a traction engine, by emitting sparks and smoke, frightened the plaintiff's horse upon the road, Erle C.J. directed the jury that: " The plaintiff is entitled to your verdict, if the engine was calculated by its noise and appearance to frighten horses, so as to make the highway dangerous to persons riding, or driving horses." [55] This was followed and approved by the Court of Appeal in *Galer* v. *Rawson*,[56] where Lord Esher M.R. said: " If an engine of this sort fulfilled all the requirements of the statute, and yet was calculated to frighten horses of ordinary nerve and courage on a highway, the engine was a nuisance, and there was nothing in the statutes to absolve the owner from liability to pay damages to those whose person or property was injured in consequence thereof." In the case of an engine of this sort, it is not necessary to prove that there was any negligence on the part of the driver.[57] The only engines which come within this principle are apparently traction engines and steam rollers.[58] It does not apply to tramcars.[59]

736 An attempt was made to establish that motor-vehicles, because they have a tendency to skid and get out of control on greasy roads, are a nuisance, but the attempt failed and liability for motor-vehicles depends exclusively on negligence.[60] It would seem that there is no real ground for imposing a higher liability upon the driver of a traction engine than upon the driver of a motor-car. The law of negligence adequately protects other highway users by providing that a vehicle must be driven with such care as is proportionate to the risk. The driver of a traction engine, which is known to be a vehicle likely to frighten horses in certain circumstances, must take special care when approaching horses,[61] but if he does take such care and an accident happens there seems no ground for holding him liable. It is submitted that a traction engine, the existence of which is recognised by statute, cannot be described as a public nuisance, and that the decisions basing liability on nuisance and not on negligence are erroneous.

A person who leaves on the highway, or on land adjoining the highway, anything calculated to frighten horses passing along the highway, is liable for damage caused as the result of a horse taking fright. So, where in one case a steam plough [62] and in another case an agricultural roller [63] was left on the roadside, the person leaving it was held liable for damage

55 *Watkins* v. *Reddin* (1861) 2 F. & F. 629.
56 (1889) 6 T.L.R. 17, reversing Stephen J.
57 *Galer* v. *Rawson, supra*; *Bantwick* v. *Rogers* (1891) 7 T.L.R. 542.
58 *Jeffery* v. *St. Pancras Vestry* (1894) 63 L.J.Q.B. 618.
59 *Brocklehurst* v. *Manchester etc., Tramways Co.* (1886) 17 Q.B.D. 118.
60 *Wing* v. *London General Omnibus Co.* [1909] 2 K.B. 652; *Parker* v. *London General Omnibus Co.* (1909) 101 L.T. 623.
61 See Highway Code, para. 64.
62 *Harris* v. *Mobbs* (1878) 3 Ex.D. 268.
63 *Wilkins* v. *Day* (1883) 12 Q.B.D. 110.

resulting from horses taking fright. Again, where a heap of rubbish was left on the defendants' land adjoining the highway and caused horses to shy, the defendants were held liable.[64] Evidence was held to be admissible that other horses had shied at the heap.

737 **Vehicles damaging the highway.** The use of a steamroller [65] or traction engine [66] of such a weight as to break gas or water pipes laid properly and at sufficient depth in the highway is actionable, on the ground that " an action lies for an injury to property, unless such injury is expressly authorised by statute, or is, physically speaking, the necessary consequence of what is so authorised." [67]

When a vehicle on the highway dislodged a paving stone on the footpath so that a pedestrian tripped over it, the driver of the vehicle was held liable.[68]

2.—DUTY OF CARRIERS

738 **Nature of duty.** A person who undertakes, either for reward or gratuitously, to carry another person in a vehicle is liable to that other if he causes him damage by negligence. His duty may be considered in connection with (a) the carriage of the passenger, and (b) the provision of the vehicle.

739 (a) **Duty as to carriage.** The duty as to carriage is to use reasonable care and skill. The carrier is not an insurer of the safety of the passenger. The law on this point, with special reference to the duty of stage-coach proprietors, is thus stated by Best C.J.: " The action cannot be maintained unless negligence be proved. . . . The coachman must have competent skill, and must use that skill with diligence; he must be well acquainted with the road he undertakes to drive; he must be provided with steady horses; a coach and harness of sufficient strength, and properly made; and also with lights by night. If there be the least failure in any one of these things, the duty of the coach proprietors is not fulfilled, and they are answerable for any injury or damage that happens. But with all these things, and when everything has been done that human prudence can suggest for the security of the passengers, an accident may happen. The lights may, in a dark night, be obscured by fog; the horses frightened, or, as it happened in the present case, the coachman may be deceived by a sudden alteration in objects near the road, by which he had used to be directed on former journeys. It is not his fault if, having exerted proper care and skill, he from accident gets off the road; and the proprietors are not answerable for what happens from his doing so." [69]

64 *Brown* v. *Eastern & Midlands Ry.* (1889) 22 Q.B.D. 391. On the subject of horses shying, see the observations of Scrutton L.J. in *Cutler* v. *United Dairies Ltd.* [1933] 2 K.B. 297, 303.

65 *Gas Light and Coke Co.* v. *St. Mary Abbott's, Kensington* (1885) 15 Q.B.D. 1; *Driscoll* v. *Poplar Board of Works* (1897) 14 T.L.R. 99.

66 *Chichester Corpn.* v. *Foster* [1906] 1 K.B. 167.

67 *Gas Light and Coke Co.* v. *St. Mary Abbott's, Kensington* (1885) 15 Q.B.D.1, *per* Lindley L.J. at p. 5.

68 *Conelly* v. *West Ham Corpn.* (1947) 62 T.L.R. 739.

69 *Crofts* v. *Waterhouse* (1825) 3 Bing. 319.

The duty is the same whether the carriage is undertaken for reward or gratuitously. " A person who undertakes to provide for the conveyance of another, although he does so gratuitously, is bound to exercise due and reasonable care." [70] His liability is not limited to responsibility for gross negligence only.[71] In *O'Connor* v. *British Transport Commission*,[72] the defendants were held not liable for the death of a young child, who fell out of a corridor-type guard's van, after he had opened the door with its handle specially provided on the inside for the guard's use, the plaintiff having failed to prove that there was any failure on the part of the defendants to take all due care to carry their passenger safely. The Court of Appeal held that the defendants were entitled to assume that children of tender years would be accompanied by persons who would take due care in looking after them.

40 (b) **Duty as to the safety of the vehicle.** The duty as to the safety of the vehicle imposed by any contract for the hire of, or for the carriage for reward of persons or goods in, any vehicle, vessel, aircraft or other means of transport, or by or by virtue of any contract of bailment, is governed by the common law. It is specifically provided by the Occupiers' Liability Act 1957 [73] that the common law duty in this respect is not affected in any way by the statute. The duty is similarly one to take reasonable care to provide a safe vehicle. Carriers are not under an absolute obligation to provide a safe vehicle. They must take " a high degree of care " and are under " the duty of exercising all vigilance to see that whatever is required for the safe conveyance of their passengers is in fit and proper order "; but they are not liable for " a disaster arising from a latent defect in the machinery which they are obliged to use, which no human skill or care could either have prevented or detected." [74] Accordingly, where a railway carriage ran off the line owing to the breaking of the tyre of one of the wheels, arising from a latent defect not attributable to any fault of the manufacturer and not detectable before the breakdown, the railway company were held not liable.[75] To rely on the defence of latent defect there must be proved (1) the nature of the defect, and (2) that it could not have been detected with reasonable care and skill.[76]

[70] *Lygo* v. *Newbold* (1854) 9 Ex. 302, 305, *per* Parke B. See also *Lewys* v. *Burnett and Dunbar* [1945] 2 All E.R. 555; *Hyman* v. *Nye* (1881) 6 Q.B.D. 685, 687.
[71] *Karavias* v. *Callinicos* [1917] W.N. 323; *Harris* v. *Perry & Co.* [1903] 2 K.B. 219; *Austin* v. *G.W. Ry.* (1867) L.R. 2 Q.B. 442.
[72] [1958] 1 W.L.R. 346.
[73] s. 5 (3).
[74] *Readhead* v. *Midland Ry.* (1869) L.R. 4 Q.B. 379, *per* Montague Smith J., at p. 393.
[75] *Readhead* v. *Midland Ry., supra.*
[76] *Ritchie* v. *Western Scottish M.T. Co.*, 1935 S.L.T. 13 (bus overturned owing to deflated tyre due to defect in metal of the flange under the tyre—company liable). When a road accident is solely due to a latent defect in a vehicle its owner may discharge the onus of showing that he has properly maintained it by proving that he has followed the common practice, where such practice has not been shown to be faulty or by taking reasonable care he would not have rendered patent the defect so that a better system could have been initiated: *Henderson* v. *Henry E. Jenkins & Sons* [1969] 2 Q.B. 188 (defendants discharged the onus). *Cf. Pearce* v. *Round Oak Steel Works* [1969] 1 W.L.R. 595 (defendants failed to discharge the onus).

741 The duty to exercise reasonable care involves the making of a reasonable examination of the vehicle from time to time in accordance with the practice of reasonably careful carriers.[77] The breakdown of the vehicle is evidence of negligence on the part of the carrier, throwing upon him the burden of showing that he exercised reasonable care and skill in detecting and remedying defects.[78]

The duty at common law set out above is a contractual duty and the duty in tort was once precisely the same, at any rate when the carrier provided the vehicle in the course of his business.[79] However the duty in tort is now modified by the Occupiers' Liability Act 1957,[80] section 1 (1) of which provides that the rules enacted by sections 2 and 3 " shall have effect, in place of the common law " to regulate the duty, which is owed to all " visitors." [81] The " common duty of care," as set out in these two sections, regulates also, " the obligations of a person occupying or having control over any fixed or moveable structure, including any vessel, vehicle or aircraft." [82] It is defined as the duty to take such care as in all the circumstances of the case is reasonable to see that the visitor will be reasonably safe in using the " premises " (*i.e.* the " vehicle ") for the purposes for which he is invited or permitted by the occupier to be there.[83] Such duty is owed to all visitors of the occupier, except in so far as he is free to and does extend, restrict, modify or exclude his duty to any of them by agreement or otherwise.[84] So far as the duty to warn a visitor of defects or dangers is concerned it is expressly provided that a warning by the " occupier " (*i.e.* the carrier) of the existence of the danger or defect does not, in itself, absolve him from liability unless in all the circumstances it was enough to enable the visitor to be reasonably safe.[85] Nevertheless, the defence of *volenti non fit injuria* is preserved, but only so far as it would have been available at common law.[86]

742 **Duty is owed to passengers.** The common duty of care set out above is owed to a passenger who is a lawful visitor but difficulty sometimes arises in determining who is such a passenger. To be one, it is not necessary that the person in question should have a contract with the carrier. Where a train had been hired for an excursion from a railway company by a benefit society, from whom the plaintiff had bought a ticket, and there was a railway accident caused by the negligence of the railway

77 *Bremner* v. *Williams* (1824) 1 C. & P. 414.
78 *Christie* v. *Griggs* (1809) 2 Camp. 79.
79 *Austin* v. *G.W. Ry.* (1867) L.R. 2 Q.B. 442; *Foulkes* v. *Metropolitan Ry.* (1880) 5 C.P.D. 157. See also *Elliott* v. *Hall* (1885) 15 Q.B.D. 315 and *White* v. *Steadman* [1913] 3 K.B. 340.
80 Which came into force on January 1, 1958 (s. 8 (3)).
81 The old distinction between the duties owed to invitees and licensees, made by the common law prior to January 1, 1958, has been abolished and the single duty now defined is owed to those persons who would have been invitees or licensees under the old law since they are now combined in one class called " visitors ": s. 1 (2). See *ante*, Chap. 8, for examples of people included in this new class of visitors.
82 s. 1 (3) (*a*).
83 s. 2 (2).
84 s. 2 (1).
85 s. 2 (4) (*a*).
86 s. 2 (5).

company, it was held that there was evidence on which a jury could find that the plaintiff was a passenger of the railway company.[87] Where a valet was travelling on a railway under a contract made between his employer and the railway company, and his portmanteau was lost owing to the company's negligence, it was held that he could recover "not by reason of any contract between him and the company, but by reason of a duty implied by law to carry him safely," which duty covered his luggage as well as himself.[88] Where newspaper reporters were supplied with free tickets on a railway and the plaintiff, a reporter, used a ticket bearing the name of another reporter of the same newspaper, the question arose whether he could recover on being injured by the railway company's negligence. It appeared that he showed his ticket to a porter, whose business it was to examine tickets, and was shown into a carriage. The jury found that he was lawfully in the carriage. The court held that "the point is whether or not the plaintiff was in the carriage under such circumstances as that he must be considered a trespasser," that this was a question of fact and affirmed a judgment for the plaintiff.[89] A passenger in an aeroplane who was present as the guest of the hirer of the aeroplane, was held entitled to recover from the owners of the aeroplane for the negligence of their pilot, on the ground that "the duty to him arose because he was carried in the aeroplane."[90]

3 **Passenger may be accepted as such without contract.** In the cases cited in the preceding paragraph the plaintiff has been in the vehicle under a contract, although not a contract to which he was a party. It is not necessary, however, that there should be a contract, provided that the plaintiff is accepted as a passenger. Where the plaintiff, "a gentleman considerably advanced in years," signalled to the driver of an omnibus to stop, and the driver did so but, just as the plaintiff was putting his foot on the step, the driver drove on and the plaintiff fell down and was injured, it was held that the plaintiff could recover because there was evidence that he had been accepted as a passenger.[91] Where a child, just over three years old, was taken into a railway train by his mother without any ticket having been taken for him and was injured by the railway company's negligence, it was held that he was entitled to recover, Blackburn J. saying: "I think that what was said in the case of *Marshall* v. *Newcastle and Berwick Ry.*[92] was quite correct. It was there laid down that the right which a passenger by railway has to be

[87] *Skinner* v. *L.B. & S.C. Ry.* (1850) 5 Ex. 787.

[88] *Marshall* v. *York, Newcastle and Berwick Ry.* (1851) 11 C.B. 655. The quotation is from the judgment of Jervis C.J. *Meux* v. *G.E. Ry.* [1895] 2 Q.B. 387 (servant contracted with railway company and lost his portmanteau, containing livery the property of his mistress, mistress entitled to recover) is a similar case. See also *Martin* v. *G.I.P. Ry.* (1867) L.R. 3 Ex. 9 (officer in India travelling on railway under contract between the Indian Government and the railway, loses luggage—recovers).

[89] *Great Northern Ry.* v. *Harrison* (1854) 10 Ex. 376.

[90] *Fosbroke-Hobbes* v. *Airwork Ltd.* [1937] 1 All E.R. 108.

[91] *Brien* v. *Bennett* (1839) 8 C. & P. 724. *Wilkie* v. *L.P.T.B.* [1947] 1 All E.R. 258, is a similar case.

[92] (1851) 11 C.B. 655.

carried safely, does not depend on his having made a contract, but that the fact of his being a passenger casts a duty on the company to carry him safely."[93]

744 **Position of passenger who has not paid the fare.** If the passenger has got on to the vehicle fraudulently intending not to pay his fare, or to pay only part of his fare or to pay only a lower class fare while travelling first class, he has still been accepted as a passenger and is entitled to sue for injuries caused by negligence. "A third-class passenger is not an outlaw when he travels in a first-class carriage. When he does so the railway company are still under a duty to him personally."[94] If such a passenger was travelling on an excursion train, on which passengers with tickets had, in consideration of a cheap fare, agreed to relieve the railway company from liability for negligence, the question would arise whether he was to be in a better position from not having made a contract than he would have been had he contracted. A similar question arises if such a passenger travels on an ordinary train on which are travelling passengers with ordinary tickets and also passengers with cheap day tickets limiting the railway company's liability.[95] It would seem that he cannot be in a better position than if he had taken the excursion or cheap day ticket or other the cheapest ticket available to the ordinary public on that particular train, because the railway company must be taken to have accepted him as a passenger only on those terms if he has not contracted for better terms.

745 **Position of passenger, who is in fact a trespasser.** A trespasser has been defined by Lord Dunedin as one: "who goes on the land without invitation of any sort and whose presence is either unknown to the proprietor or, if known, is practically objected to."[96]

The Occupiers' Liability Act 1957 does not in any way concern itself with trespassers since the statute applies only to those visitors who are lawfully present. Most probably the reason for this is that the owner of a vehicle is under no duty to those persons, the likelihood of whose presence on his vehicle he cannot reasonably foresee.[97] Accordingly, the carrier's obligation to any trespasser is still very limited and continues to be governed by the common law.[98] Thus there is a difference between the position of a passenger who gets himself accepted as a passenger, even by fraud, by boarding the vehicle in the usual way and travelling on the vehicle with the knowledge or acquiescence of the carrier and his servants, and one who is not so accepted.

93 *Austin* v. *G.W. Ry.* (1867) L.R. 2 Q.B. 442, 445, 446.
94 *Per* Atkin L.J. in *Vosper* v. *G.W. Ry.* [1928] 1 K.B. 340, 349 (passenger with third-class ticket travels in a first-class carriage and loses his luggage, held able to recover from the railway company).
95 See *Penton* v. *Southern Ry.* [1931] 2 K.B. 103.
96 *Robert Addie & Sons (Collieries) Ltd.* v. *Dumbreck* [1929] A.C. 358, at p. 371.
97 *Twine* v. *Bean's Express Ltd.* [1946] 2 All E.R. 202; *Conway* v. *Geo. Wimpey & Co. Ltd.* [1951] 2 K.B. 266; *Jones* v. *Livox Quarries Ltd.* [1952] 2 Q.B. 608.
98 See *ante*, Chap. 8, § 387 *et seq.*

746 **Stowaway.** A stowaway on a vehicle is one to whom no duty can be owed, because he is not known to be on it as well as the fact that he is a trespasser. Where a person, in breach of a by-law and without the permission of the railway company, travelled on a train which to his knowledge was not then in use as a passenger train, and was injured in a collision caused by the negligence of the railway company's servants, it was held that he was a trespasser and unable to recover.[99]

47 **Passenger on vehicle with consent of servant acting outside the scope of his employment.** If a servant, without his master's authority and acting outside the scope of his employment, allows a person to become a passenger in the vehicle, the master is under no liability to him because that person is a trespasser.[1] Where the defendant contracted to carry the plaintiff's goods in a cart and sent his servant with the cart, and the plaintiff, with the servant's permission but without the authority of the master, rode in the cart, which broke down, it was held that the plaintiff could not recover.[2]

48 **By whom the duty is owed.** There are three sets of circumstances to be considered in dealing with the question of the person who owes the duty.[3] They are (1) where the carrier contracts to carry the passenger partly on his own vehicle and partly on vehicles supplied by others, (2) where there is no contract but the carrier accepts the passenger who is carried partly on the carrier's vehicle and partly on vehicles supplied by others and, (3) where there is no contract for carriage between the carrier and passenger or any person contracting directly for his carriage. Dealing with these seriatim:

49 (1) Where the carrier contracts with the passenger for a journey to be performed partly on his own vehicle and partly on vehicles supplied by others. Here, unless there is anything in the contract to the contrary, the contracting party is liable not only for the negligence of himself and his servants but also for the negligence of those responsible for the other vehicles.[4] This is purely a contractual duty.

0 (2) Where there is no contract between the passenger and the carrier, but the carrier accepts the passenger as a passenger and the journey is performed partly on the carrier's own vehicles and partly on vehicles supplied by others. In this case each carrier is responsible for his own negligence and that of his servants. The original carrier is liable on the grounds stated above.[5] The subsequent carriers are also liable, because of their acceptance of the passenger as a passenger. Where, therefore, the

[99] *Grand Trunk Ry. of Canada* v. *Barnett* [1911] A.C. 361.

[1] *Twine* v. *Bean's Express Ltd.* [1946] 1 All E.R. 202, affd. 175 L.T. 131. The servant is liable. *Conway* v. *George Wimpey & Co. Ltd.* [1951] 2 K.B. 266 is a similar case. See on these cases, § 932, note 37.

[2] *Lygo* v. *Newbold* (1854) 9 Ex. 302. See also *Houghton* v. *Pilkington* [1912] 3 K.B. 308; *per* Blackburn J. in *Austin* v. *G.W. Ry.* (1867) L.R. 2 Q.B. 442.

[3] *Per* Thesiger L.J. in *Foulkes* v. *Metropolitan Ry.* (1880) 5 C.P.D. 157.

[4] *G.W. Ry.* v. *Blake* (1862) 7 H. & N. 987; *Thomas* v. *Rhymney Ry.* (1871) L.R. 6 Q.B. 266.

[5] *Ante*, §§ 742, 744.

plaintiff took a return ticket with railway company A and, by arrangement between the two railway companies, performed the return journey in the train of railway company B, and was injured owing to the height of the carriage and the platform being unsuitable to each other, it was held that company B was liable to him.[6] Again, where the plaintiff contracted with one company for a journey over the lines of that company and the defendant company, and his luggage was lost during the journey over the defendant company's lines owing to their negligence, it was held that he could recover from the defendant company because, having accepted the plaintiff as a passenger in one of their trains, it was their duty to take reasonable care of his luggage.[7] It would seem that, in the circumstances of the last cases, the company with which the contract was made would not be responsible in tort for the defective carriages or the negligence of the other company.[8] If, however, the railway company invite the passenger to entrust himself to carriages provided by someone else, such as a Pullman Car company, they will be under the same liability for defects in those carriages as if they were provided by themselves.

751 (3) Where there is no contract for carriage between the carrier and the passenger or any person contracting directly for his carriage. In this case the carrier owes a duty to take reasonable care not to injure the passenger if the circumstances are such that he should contemplate that the passenger will be injured through his failure to take reasonable care. In *Dalyell* v. *Tyrer*[9] the lessee of a ferry hired a ferry from the defendants to assist him in carrying his passengers. The defendants provided their own tackle and crew. The plaintiff, who had contracted with the lessee to be carried across the ferry, was injured on board the defendant's ferry by the breaking of some tackle owing to the negligence of the crew. He was held entitled to recover, because " if the negligence in question had injured a mere stranger, not on board, but standing, for instance, on the pier at the time, they would have been liable."[10] Again, where a passenger had taken a ticket with railway company A and was injured in a collision caused by the negligence of the signalman of railway company B, it was held that he could recover from company B " for a pure tort, such as would be committed if a vehicle in the highway were wrongfully driven against or across the path of another vehicle."[11]

What is negligence in this connection depends on the nature of the carriage and the circumstances of the case, and is considered below with reference to the more usual modes of carriage, namely: (a) Railways, (b) Road Carriage, (c) Ships, (d) Aircraft, and (e) Hovercraft.

[6] *Foulkes* v. *Metropolitan Ry.* (1880) 5 C.P.D. 157.
[7] *Hooper* v. *L. & N.W. Ry.* (1880) 50 L.J.Q.B. 103.
[8] See *Wright* v. *Midland Ry.* (1873) L.R. 8 Ex. 137 (plaintiff contracts with M. company—collision caused by negligence of L. company in disregarding M. company's signals—M. company not liable to plaintiff).
[9] (1858) E.B. & E. 899.
[10] *Per* Erle J. at p. 905.
[11] *Berringer* v. *G.E. Ry.* (1879) 4 C.P.D. 163.

(a) *Railways*

752 **Duty generally of railway undertakers.** The railway authority is under a duty to use reasonable care and skill in the provision and maintenance of its carriages, the provision and maintenance of its railway track, and the provision of a proper system of signalling so as to prevent accidents. It is also liable for the negligence of the signalmen and others operating the system and of the drivers and others in the driving and management of its trains. Bramwell B. expressed the duty as to see " that all persons connected with the carrying and with the means and appliances of the carrying, with the carriages, the road, the signalling, and otherwise, shall use care and diligence, so that no accident shall happen."[12] As a result of the provisions of the Transport Act 1947[13] the undertakings of the principal railway companies vested in the British Transport Commission on January 1, 1948. Now, by virtue of the Transport Act 1962[14] which provided for the reorganisation of the nationalised transport undertakings, the British Transport Commission is replaced by four public authorities and by a holding company among which the functions and the property of the Commission are divided as from September 1, 1962. The relevant authority is therefore the British Railways Board and the same principles of law apply to it as they did to the railway companies. The standard of care is that of a reasonably careful and skilful body of persons carrying on the work of such a transport undertaking.

53 **Collisions.** When a collision between two trains occurs[15] or a train runs off the lines[16] or a train drives into the buffers so as to cause a jolt[17] a prima facie case of negligence is established. This prima facie case, however, may be rebutted by proving a latent defect in the rolling stock[18] or by showing that the collision was caused by the wrongful act of a third person.[19] It is negligence to run a train over lines known to be defective and fractured.[20]

54 **Overcrowding.** Railway undertakers are bound to provide reasonable accommodation for their passengers and, if too many people are put into the same carriage, they are liable for the damage resulting therefrom.[21] They are also bound to take reasonable steps to prevent people from getting into carriages already full.[22] It has been held that it is not the natural result of overcrowding that a passenger should have his hand

12 *Wright* v. *Midland Ry.* (1873) L.R. 8 Ex. 137, 140.
13 Part II.
14 Which gave effect to proposals in the White Paper on this subject (Cmnd. 1248) which was presented to Parliament in December 1960.
15 *Skinner* v. *L.B. & S.C. Ry.* (1850) L.R. 5 Ex.787.
16 *Carpue* v. *London & Brighton Ry.* (1844) 5 Q.B. 747; *Dawson* v. *M.S. & L. Ry.* (1862) 5 L.T. 682.
17 *Burke* v. *M.S. & L. Ry.* (1870) 22 L.T. 442.
18 *Readhead* v. *Midland Ry.* (1869) L.R. 4 Q.B. 379.
19 *Latch* v. *Rumner Ry.* (1858) 27 L.J. Ex. 155.
20 *Pym* v. *G.N. Ry.* (1861) 2 F. & F. 619.
21 *Metropolitan Ry.* v. *Jackson* (1877) 3 App.Cas. 193, 209, *per* Lord Blackburn.
22 *Metropolitan Ry.* v. *Jackson* (1877) 3 App.Cas. 193, at p. 210.

trapped when the carriage door was shut,[23] or that he should be assaulted [24] or robbed [25] by other passengers. When a boy, aged thirteen, returning from his work, was travelling in a colliers' train and, owing to the crowd, was in the guard's van with some thirty other men and boys, it was held that there was no evidence of negligence against the railway company. The boy was injured because the men, as they usually did, made a rush to get out of the train before it stopped and the boy was caught in the rush and injured, but it was held that, even if the railway company were negligent in permitting overcrowding, the accident was not the result of the negligence.[26]

Further, there is a duty to prevent platforms from becoming overcrowded so that a passenger is pushed off the edge on to the line and injured.[27]

755 **Injury caused to one passenger by another.** Railway undertakers are not liable if one passenger negligently or wilfully injures another. Where, therefore, a passenger in a railway train brought into the carriage a parcel which appeared to be harmless, but in fact contained bombs, which exploded and injured a fellow-passenger, it was held that the railway authorities were not liable, because they were not bound to search every parcel taken into the carriage in the absence of anything to suggest danger.[28] If, however, the railway undertakers, through their servants, know that a person, by reason of disease, drunkenness or avowed intention, is likely to be a danger to other passengers, they are under a duty to prevent him from entering the train.[29] They are also under a duty to take all reasonable steps to remove disorderly persons from, and to preserve order in, their trains.

756 In *Pounder* v. *N.E. Ry.*[30] the plaintiff, after he had taken his ticket, was threatened with personal violence by a number of pitmen on the platform and, to avoid them, he got into the guard's van. The railway company's servants removed him from there and put him into a compartment. A number of pitmen, unrestrained by the railway company's servants, entered the compartment and assaulted him until the next station, when they got out and others got in and also assaulted him. This occurred at each station, but in spite of the plaintiff's complaints at each station no effort was made to afford him protection. The plaintiff sued the railway company and succeeded in the county court, but lost in the Divisonal Court. As the railway company knew that the plaintiff

23 *Ibid.*
24 *Pounder* v. *N.E. Ry.* [1892] 1 Q.B. 385.
25 *Cobb* v. *G.W. Ry.* [1894] A.C. 419.
26 *Machen* v. *L. & Y. Ry.* (1918) 88 L.J.K.B. 371.
27 *Hogan* v. *S.E. Ry.* (1873) 28 L.T. 271 but *cf. M'Callum* v. *N.B. Ry.*, 1908 S.C. 415. See further § 770, *post.*
28 *East Indian Ry.* v. *Kalidas Mukerjee* [1901] A.C. 396.
29 See *per* A. L. Smith J. in *Pounder* v. *N.E. Ry.* [1892] 1 Q.B. 385; *Murgatroyd* v. *Blackburn Tramways* (1887) 3 T.L.R. 451.
30 [1892] 1 Q.B. 385.

was first threatened and then the victim of violence in one of their compartments, from which he had no means of escaping from his assailants, and took no steps to prevent it, it is submitted that the decision of the Divisional Court was erroneous.[31]

When a passenger in a train was robbed by a gang of men who entered his compartment and at the next station he asked the stationmaster to detain the train so that the men could be given into custody and searched, it was held that a refusal to detain the train was not negligence on the part of the railway company, because they were not responsible for the robbery and under no duty to delay the train to enable the plaintiff to recover his property.[32]

757 **Shutting carriage doors.** Railway undertakers are under a duty to take reasonable care to see that the carriage doors are properly closed before the train leaves the station.[33] Where the plaintiff, while the train was in motion, got up and leant against the window, when the door opened and he fell out, it was held that the railway company were liable, Kelly C.B. saying: " Any passenger in a railway carriage, who rises for the purpose either of looking out of the window, or of dealing with, and touching, and bringing his body in contact with the door for any lawful purpose whatsoever, has a right to assume, and is justified in assuming, that the door is properly fastened; and if by reason of its not being properly fastened his lawful act causes the door to fly open, the accident is caused by the defendants' negligence." [34] In a train with corridor coaches the mere fact that a door comes open is no evidence of negligence against the railway company.[35] Where a child of four years falls out of a train, having opened the guard's van door by an internal handle, it was held that the carriers could not reasonably foresee that a mother, aware that such a door could be opened from the inside, would have let her child wander alone about the carriage, and therefore were not liable for the child's death.[36]

The actual shutting of the door must be done with reasonable care. When a passenger is in the act of getting into or out of a carriage, a warning should be given before the door is shut.[37] Failure to give warning in those circumstances is evidence of negligence.[38] When no warning is given, the question arises, what would the person whose duty it is to shut the doors reasonably have supposed the position of the plaintiff

[31] This decision was doubted by Lord Selborne in *Cobb* v. *G.W. Ry.* [1894] A.C. 419, at p. 423, *contra* Lord O'Hagan at p. 426. See the criticism of this case in *Beven on Negligence*, 4th ed., pp. 1198–1201.

[32] *Cobb* v. *G.W. Ry.*, *supra.*

[33] *Brookes* v. *L.P.T.B.* [1947] 1 All E.R. 506.

[34] *Gee* v. *Metropolitan Ry.* (1873) L.R. 8 Q.B. 161, 171. See also *Warburton* v. *Midland Ry.* (1870) 21 L.T. 835; *Richards* v. *G.E. Ry.* (1873) 28 L.T. 711; *Dudman* v. *N.L. Ry.* (1886) 2 T.L.R. 365; *Hamer* v. *Cambrian Ry.* (1886) 2 T.L.R. 508; *Inglis* v. *L.M.S. Ry.*, 1941 S.C. 551.

[35] *Easson* v. *L.N.E. Ry.* [1944] K.B. 421.

[36] *O'Connor* v. *British Transport Commission* [1958] 1 W.L.R. 346.

[37] *Richardson* v. *Metropolitan Ry.* (1868) L.R. 3 C.P. 374n.

[38] *Fordham* v. *L.B. & S.C. Ry.* (1869) L.R. 4 C.P. 619; *Atkins* v. *S.E. Ry.* (1885) 2 T.L.R. 94.

to be? [39] There is no negligence in shutting a door without warning if the passenger is seated in the carriage and is not in the act of getting out or in,[40] but slamming the door without warning or first giving the passenger reasonable opportunity to alight and without taking reasonable care to see that it is safe to shut the door is negligence.[41]

758 Where a passenger entered an electric train and before he had taken his seat the train started suddenly, causing him to lose his balance, so that he put out his hand which was caught by the sliding door closing through the motion of the train, it was held that there was evidence on which a jury could find negligence on the part of the railway company in starting the train with a jerk.[42]

Where a passenger was in a carriage, the door of which kept coming open, and, on trying to close it for the fourth time, the passenger fell out and was injured, it was held that he could not recover, because he was doing something obviously dangerous when he might have been sitting in the carriage in safety.[43]

If a carriage door is not shut and the train starts so that a passenger who has alighted from the train is struck by the door, there is evidence of negligence against the railway company [44] and where a passenger dashed onto and boarded a moving train and negligently left the door of the carriage open so that it struck a porter employed at the station, he was held liable in damages.[45]

The mere fall of a carriage window into its socket is no evidence of negligence against the railway company.[46]

759 **Invitation to join or alight.** Railway undertakers are bound to provide reasonable means for passengers to alight at the stations at which the trains stop.[47] Accordingly, if the platform provided is too low, having regard to the height of the carriage, it is evidence of negligence on the part of the railway company in not providing reasonable facilities for alighting.[48] In an action based on such negligence, evidence of the height of other platforms in the district is admissible.[49] If the train is too long for the platform and a passenger is asked by a porter to alight beyond the end of the platform and does so with reasonable care but is injured, the railway undertakers will be liable if " the place and the

[39] *Cohen* v. *Metropolitan Ry.* (1890) 6 T.L.R. 146.
[40] *Drury* v. *N.E. Ry.* [1901] 2 K.B. 322; *Benson* v. *Furness Ry.* (1903) 88 L.T. 268; see also *Metropolitan Ry.* v. *Jackson* (1877) 3 App.Cas. 193.
[41] *Bird* v. *Railway Executive* [1949] W.N. 196.
[42] *Metropolitan Ry.* v. *Delaney* (1921) 90 L.J.K.B. 721.
[43] *Adams* v. *L. & Y. Ry.* (1869) L.R. 4 C.P. 739. In *Gee* v. *Metropolitan Ry.* (1873) L.R. 8 Q.B. 161, Brett J. who was a party to the decision, said that the right principle had been wrongly applied to the facts. See now the Law Reform (Contributory Negligence) Act 1945.
[44] *Toal* v. *N.B. Ry.* [1908] A.C. 352.
[45] *Booker* v. *Wenborn* [1962] 1 W.L.R. 162.
[46] *Murray* v. *Metropolitan Ry.* (1873) 27 L.T. 762.
[47] *Robson* v. *N.E. Ry.* (1876) 2 Q.B.D. 85, *per* Mellish L.J. at p. 88.
[48] *Foulkes* v. *Metropolitan Ry.* (1880) 5 C.P.D. 157; *Wharton* v. *L. & Y. Ry.* (1888) 5 T.L.R. 142.
[49] *Manning* v. *L. & N.W. Ry.* (1907) 23 T.L.R. 222.

means of descent provided were not reasonably convenient." [50] Railway undertakers owe no special duty to passengers suffering from physical disability. Therefore, when a passenger of abnormal weight was injured in alighting from a carriage onto a platform which was safe for normal persons, it was held he could not recover damages.[51]

760 The mere fact of a carriage overshooting [52] or failing to reach [53] the platform is no evidence of negligence against the railway authority. If, therefore, the passenger in such circumstances chooses to alight and in doing so is injured, he has no claim.[54] On the other hand, if the passenger be invited to alight, either expressly or by implication, and he does so without negligence and is injured, owing to his carriage not being opposite the platform, he will be able to recover. Calling out the name of the station as the train is drawing up is not an invitation to alight immediately the train stops.[55] But if the name of the station has been called out, the train stopped, no warning given to the passengers not to alight, and a sufficient interval of time allowed to elapse so as to lead the passenger to suppose that the train, when it moves, will go on to the next station, there is evidence of an invitation to alight.[56] Accordingly, where the carriage in which the plaintiff was travelling was drawn up opposite a curved part of the platform, so that there was a gap between the footboard and the platform, and the train had been brought to a final standstill until it started for the next station, it was held that the plaintiff, who alighted in the dark and fell into the gap, could recover against the railway company because, under the circumstances, he might " reasonably infer that it is intended that he should get out if he purposes to alight at the particular station." [57] But where an intending passenger fell into the gap between an underground train and the curved edge of the platform, which was marked with a white line and was illuminated adequately, it was held that the defendants had not been negligent.[58] Again, where a train drew up at a platform with the rear carriages in a tunnel, the name of the station was called out and a passenger alighted in the tunnel, fell on some irregular ground and received injuries from which he died, it was held that the railway company were liable, Lord Hatherley saying: " When the name of a station has been called out, accompanied by a stoppage, and a

[50] *Foy* v. *L.B. & S.C. Ry.* (1865) 18 C.B.(N.S.) 225.
[51] *Henderson* v. *L.M.S. Ry.*, 1935 S.C. 734.
[52] *Lewis* v. *L.C. & D. Ry.* (1873) L.R. 9 Q.B. 66; *Weller* v. *L.B. & S.C. Ry.* (1874) L.R. 9 C.P. 126.
[53] *Bridges* v. *North London Ry.* (1874) L.R. 7 H.L. 213. However in *Struthers* v. *British Railways Board* (1969) 113 S.J. 268 the defendants were held to be negligent in stopping their train short of the platform at a station, without any compelling reason and in siting the illuminated station sign where it was, which had prompted the plaintiff passenger to alight opposite it (the plaintiff was held to be one-third to blame for failing to look where he was stepping).
[54] *Siner* v. *G.W. Ry.* (1869) L.R. 4 Ex. 117; *Harrold* v. *G.W. Ry.* (1866) 14 L.T. 440; *Owen* v. *G.W. Ry.* (1877) 46 L.J.Q.B. 486; *Abbott* v. *N.B. Ry.*, 1916 S.C. 306.
[55] *Lewis* v. *L.C. & D. Ry.* (1873) L.R. 9 Q.B. 66; *Plant* v. *Midland Ry.* (1870) 21 L.T. 836.
[56] *Weller* v. *L.B. & S.C. Ry.* (1874) L.R. 9 C.P. 126.
[57] *Cockle* v. *L. & S.E. Ry.* (1872) L.R. 7 C.P. 321.
[58] *Stracstone* v. *London Transport Board, The Times*, January 21, 1966.

considerable interval has elapsed . . . there is a certain amount of evidence to go to the jury to authorise the finding of a verdict for the plaintiff, unless some explanation could be given of the facts by the defendants, instead of their merely submitting that the plaintiff had not produced sufficient evidence to call upon them for a defence." [59]

761 When a train overshot the platform and stopped, and the plaintiff, after looking about for a railway servant, and waiting for some time, fearing that she would be carried beyond her destination, got out and was injured, it was held that there was evidence of negligence against the railways.[60] Similarly, when the train overshot the platform and porters called out to the passengers to keep their seats, but the plaintiff, being in the front, did not hear and got out, after waiting some little time, and was injured, it was held that there was evidence of negligence against the railways.[61]

Opening the door of the carriage is an invitation to alight.[62]

762 Even where there is an invitation to alight, a passenger must take reasonable care for his own safety. But, where a train in the daylight overshot the platform and the plaintiff, thinking she would alight on the platform in the usual way and without looking where she was going, stepped down and was injured, it was held that there was evidence on which a jury were justified in finding in favour of the plaintiff.[63] On the other hand, where the plaintiff was asleep and failed to hear the porters calling out to passengers to keep their seats, and, on waking up, got out in a hurry without looking to see what he was stepping on, and was injured, owing to his carriage being short of the platform, it was held that his own evidence proved such negligence on his own part as to prevent him from recovering.[64]

There is no invitation to alight if passengers are warned not to leave their seats, and therefore if a passenger disregards the warning or alights immediately the train stops and before the railway undertakers have had time to give warning, he has no cause of action.[65]

763 **Stopping and starting trains.** Trains must be started and stopped with reasonable care. If, therefore, a train is started with a sudden jerk as a result of which a passenger is injured, for example, by a sliding door being closed on his hand,[66] there is evidence of negligence against the railways. A violent and unusual stopping or starting of the train, causing injury to a passenger, is prima facie evidence of negligence. In the event of a sudden and violent stop the railways have " to show

59 *Bridges* v. *North London Ry.* (1874) L.R. 7 H.L. 213, 241.
60 *Robson* v. *N.E. Ry.* (1876) 2 Q.B.D. 85.
61 *Rose* v. *N.E. Ry.* (1876) 2 Ex.D. 248.
62 *Praeger* v. *Bristol and Exeter Ry.* (1871) 24 L.T. 105.
63 *London, Tilbury and Southend Ry.* v. *Glasscock* (1902) 19 T.L.R. 305.
64 *Sharpe* v. *Southern Ry.* [1925] 2 K.B. 311, distinguishing the case last quoted on the ground that the facts were insufficiently stated in the report.
65 *Anthony* v. *Midland Ry.* (1908) 100 L.T. 117.
66 *Metropolitan Ry.* v. *Delaney* (1921) 90 L.J.K.B. 721.

both that they acted reasonably and properly in suddenly stopping the train, and also that the cause which led to the necessity of stopping the train was not brought about by any negligence upon their part." [67] Accordingly, where the brakes of a train were suddenly applied, with the result that the plaintiff was thrown off his seat and injured, and it was proved that the train was stopped to avoid running over a passenger who was crossing the line, it was held that the railway undertakers were liable, because they had failed to show that the presence of the passenger on their line was not due to their negligence.[68]

If a train stops for a sufficient time to appear to be finally stopped and then gives a jerk by suddenly moving on, it is evidence of negligence against the railways.[69]

There is evidence of negligence on the part of a passenger if he stands in the carriage by an open door while the train is in motion,[70] or if he attempts to board [71] or leave [72] a train in motion.

764 **Duty to persons resorting to railway premises.** Persons resorting to railway premises, whether as passengers, intending passengers, or as the senders or consignees of goods, are in the position of invitees [73] and are "visitors" under the Occupiers' Liability Act 1957.[74] The railways are therefore under a duty to take care that their premises are reasonably safe for persons using them in the ordinary and customary manner and with reasonable care.

A person seeing a friend off at a railway station or meeting a passenger arriving by train is a visitor.[75] Where the plaintiff, after seeing his friends into the train, stood on the platform talking to another person and was knocked onto the railway line by the door of the guard's van when the train began to move, it was held that the railway authorities were liable.[76] They may, however, contract out of this liability by issuing a platform ticket with a condition that they shall be absolved from all liability. When such a ticket is issued it will protect the railways from liability for accidents happening, not only on that part of the platform from which the public without tickets are excluded, but also from accidents happening in going from the ticket machine or office to the restricted part of the platform.[77]

[67] Lord Loreburn L.C. in *Angus* v. *L.T. & S. Ry.* (1906) 22 T.L.R. 222.
[68] *Angus* v. *L.T. & S. Ry., supra.*
[69] *Langton* v. *L. & Y. Ry.* (1886) 3 T.L.R. 18; *L. & N.W. Ry.* v. *Hellawell* (1872) 26 L.T. 557; *Stockdale* v. *L. & Y. Ry.* (1863) 8 L.T. 289; *Goldberg* v. *G. & S.W. Ry.*, 1907 S.C. 1035, where the railway company succeeded.
[70] *Langton* v. *L. & Y. Ry., supra*; *Folkes* v. *North London Ry.* (1892) 8 T.L.R. 269. Such evidence is not conclusive: *Hall* v. *London Tramways Co.* (1896) 12 T.L.R. 611.
[71] *Avis* v. *G.E. Ry.* (1892) 8 T.L.R. 693; *Booker* v. *Wenborn* [1962] 1 W.L.R. 162.
[72] *Metropolitan Ry.* v. *Wright* (1886) 11 App.Cas. 152.
[73] *Norman* v. *G.W. Ry.* [1915] 1 K.B. 584. For duty to visitors, see Chap. 8, and *ante*, §§ 741, 742.
[74] s. 1 (2).
[75] *Watkins* v. *G.W. Ry.* (1877) 37 L.T. 193, *per* Denman J.; *Stowell* v. *Railway Executive* [1949] 2 K.B. 519 (father at station to meet his daughter arriving by train slips on patch of oil on platform—succeeds).
[76] *Thatcher* v. *G.W. Ry.* (1893) 10 T.L.R. 13; *Hare* v. *B.T.C.* [1956] 1 W.L.R. 250.
[77] *Rogers* v. *L.M.S. Ry.* (1930) 46 T.L.R. 238.

765 **Platforms.** The existence of an erection projecting above the level of the platform, so that persons taking reasonable care may stumble over it, is evidence of negligence. So, where a passenger going over a platform with a crowd of other passengers tripped over a box containing signal levers projecting two inches above the platform, the railway undertakers were held liable.[78] On the other hand, where there was on the platform a portable weighing machine, the foot of which projected six inches above the platform and the machine had been in the same position for five years without causing any accident, the railway undertakers were held not liable to a passenger who fell over it.[79] If the platform is reasonably safe for persons using it in a reasonable way, the railway undertakers are under no liability to persons who are using it in an unreasonable way. So, where two passengers ran arm-in-arm along a platform, safe for one person but too narrow for two abreast, used as a footpath from the station to a steamboat pier, and one of them fell on the line and was injured, the railway undertakers were held not liable.[80] Again, where on the platform there were two doors close together one marked " gentlemen " leading to the urinal, and the other marked " lamp room," and the plaintiff, intending to go to the urinal, by mistake went through the door marked " lamp room " and fell down some steps, it was held that the railway undertakers were not liable, as there was no negligence on their part.[81]

766 Apart from the duty in tort, a contractual duty is owed to a ticket-holding passenger to use reasonable care to make the platforms safe for use by the passenger in the usual way. So, where a contract ticket holder tripped in a crack between a paving stone and the coping stone at the edge of the platform and was injured, he was entitled to damages [82]; but where after a snowstorm, the porter at a station began to put sand on the snow but had to attend to other work before he had finished sanding and, during his temporary absence, a passenger alighting from a train slipped on the snow and was injured, it was held that there had been no failure of reasonable care and the claim failed.[83] Similarly, where the defendants' foreman saw a patch of oil at Paddington Station and sent for sawdust after calling out to stop passengers from going where this oil was, but the plaintiff, a passenger, did not hear his warnings, her action failed when she slipped on the oil and hurt herself.[84]

767 The opinion of a witness that a platform is dangerous is not evidence. The witness can give factual evidence about the state of the platform

[78] *Sturges* v. *G.W. Ry.* (1892) 8 T.L.R. 231.
[79] *Cornman* v. *E.C. Ry.* (1859) 4 H. & N. 781. See also to the same effect, ***Blackman*** v. *L.B. & S.C. Ry.* (1869) 17 W.R. 769.
[80] *Rigg* v. *M.S. & L. Ry.* (1866) 14 W.R. 834.
[81] *Toomey* v. *L.B. & S.C. Ry.* (1857) 3 C.B.(N.S.) 146.
[82] *Protheroe* v. *Railway Executive* [1951] 1 K.B. 376.
[83] *Tomlinson* v. *Railway Executive* [1953] 1 All E.R. 1.
[84] *Blackman* v. *Railway Executive* [1953] 1 W.L.R. 2, affd. [1954] 1 W.L.R. 220.

then the court will decide whether a platform in that condition is dangerous or not.[85]

If such things as ice, orange peel or banana skins are allowed to remain on the platform after they are known or ought to be known to be there, and a passenger slips and is injured, there is evidence of negligence against the railway undertakers.[86] In such cases, if the danger is obvious, it is always a question of fact whether there has been contributory negligence on the part of the passenger [87] which may apportion liability. See *post*, Chap. 14.

768 **Platforms when there is fog.** In foggy weather conditions the railway undertakers are under a duty to take all reasonable precautions to protect passengers from the dangers incidental to movement upon the platform. Where, therefore, the plaintiff, during a fog, fell off the platform, and several other passengers had also fallen during the same night, it was held that there was evidence of negligence against the railway company in not taking precautions to prevent such occurrences.[88] Again, where entrance to a platform was gained by a staircase, which came on to the platform at right-angles, the foot of the staircase being three yards from the edge of the platform, and the plaintiff, walking carefully in the fog, went over the edge on to the line and was injured, the railway undertakers were held liable because the lighting at the foot of the staircase was inadequate in the circumstances as well as there being no indication of the direction of the platform in relation to the staircase.[89]

769 **Lighting on platforms.** It is not only in foggy weather that a railway company are under a duty to light their platforms. They must use reasonable care to light them so as to make them safe for persons ordinarily using the platforms. As Maule J. said: "Railway companies are to light their railway not for their own servants alone, but for persons who have never been there before, and who may be in a great hurry to reach the train." So, where a passenger, in crossing in a hurry from one platform to another, tripped over a switch handle which he did not see owing to the bad light, it was held that there was evidence of negligence on the part of the railway undertakers.[90]

770 **Overcrowding on platforms.** Railway undertakers are under a duty to see that their platforms are not overcrowded, and to take reasonable care to control the crowd so as to prevent accidents. Where, therefore, a railway company ran an excursion train and allowed more persons on the platform than it could properly hold, as a result of which there was

85 *Rigg* v. *M.S. & L. Ry.* (1866) 14 W.R. 834.
86 *Shepherd* v. *Midland Ry.* (1872) 25 L.T. 879.
87 *Osborne* v. *L. & N.W. Ry.* (1888) 21 Q.B.D. 220; *Brackley* v. *Midland Ry.* (1916) 85 L.J.K.B. 1596; *Letang* v. *Ottawa Electric Ry.* [1926] A.C. 725.
88 *L.T. & S. Ry.* v. *Paterson* (1913) 29 T.L.R. 413. This decision is criticised in *Beven on Negligence*, 4th ed., p. 1187, on the ground that there were no further precautions which the railway company could have taken.
89 *Schlarb* v. *L.N.E. Ry.* [1936] 1 All E.R. 71.
90 *Martin* v. *G.N. Ry.* (1855) 16 C.B. 179.

a rush for the train when it arrived and the plaintiff was carried on to the line and injured, it was held that there was evidence of negligence against the railways.[91] On the other hand, if they employ an adequate station staff to look after the safety of passengers, they are not liable for an injury to a passenger by the rush of a crowd of people for the train.[92]

771 **Acts of misfeasance on platforms.** If a carriage door is left open so that it strikes a person standing on the platform, it is evidence of negligence against the railways.[93] Railway undertakers are liable for the negligence of their porters, so where the plaintiff was on the platform when he was injured through the negligence of a porter in pushing a truck of luggage so that a portmanteau fell and injured him, the railway undertakers were held liable.[94] They are not, however, liable for damage unless it is caused by their negligence or that of their servants. Accordingly, they are not liable for the negligence of their independent contractors,[95] or for the act of a stray dog in biting a passenger on the platform, in the absence of negligence in allowing it on the platform.[96] When a drunken man alighted from a train and was left by a porter lying on the platform, from which he got by some unexplained means on to the railway line where he was run over and killed, the railway authorities were held not liable.[97]

772 **Approaches.** If there is a footbridge or a staircase leading to a station, or between one platform and another, the railway undertakers' duty with regard to it is the same as to the platform itself. They must take reasonable care not to allow it to be or to remain in a dangerous condition. Where, therefore, a passenger slipped on a worn flight of steps and was injured, and it was found that "the steps had not been properly and efficiently swept and cleaned from the caked snow, which, added to the worn condition of the steps, caused the plaintiff to fall," it was held that the railway undertakers were liable.[98] On the other hand, under somewhat similar circumstances, it was held that, as the danger of slipping on the caked snow was open and obvious, the passenger must be deemed to have taken the risk upon himself.[99] This, however, seems to be

[91] *Hogan* v. *S.E. Ry.* (1873) 28 L.T. 271; *McGregor* v. *Glasgow District Subway Co.* (1901) 3 F. 1131; *Fraser* v. *Caledonian Ry.* (1902) 5 F. 41.

[92] *M'Callum* v. *N.B. Ry.*, 1908 S.C. 415. See also *Cannon* v. *M.G.W. Ry.* (1876) 6 L.R.Ir. 199 (railway company not liable when passenger pushed on to line from platform by sudden rush of people on to platform without permission).

[93] *Thatcher* v. *G.W. Ry.* (1893) 10 T.L.R. 13; *Toal* v. *N.B. Ry.* [1908] A.C. 352; *Burns* v. *N.B. Ry.*, 1914 S.C. 754; *Hare* v. *B.T.C.* [1956] 1 W.L.R. 250. However, no attempt was made to make the British Transport Commission liable to one of its servants who was injured by a passenger who had dashed to board a moving train and had negligently left the door of the carriage open, so that it had struck the plaintiff, who was a porter employed at the station: *Booker* v. *Wenborn* [1962] 1 W.L.R. 162.

[94] *Tebbutt* v. *Bristol and Exeter Ry.* (1870) L.R. 6 Q.B. 73.

[95] See Chap. 14 for liability for acts of independent contractors.

[96] *Smith* v. *G.E. Ry.* (1866) L.R. 2 C.P. 4.

[97] *M'Cormick* v. *Caledonian Ry.* (1903) 5 F. 362.

[98] *Osborne* v. *L. & N.W. Ry.* (1888) 21 Q.B.D. 220, recited at p. 221.

[99] *Brackley* v. *Midland Ry.* (1916) 85 L.J.K.B. 1596. The bridge in this case was held to have been dedicated to the public as a highway, but this does not affect the point under discussion.

unsatisfactory. If the railway undertakers maintain an approach on their premises and it is dangerous by reason of its worn condition or of the neglect to remove snow or ice from it, the sole question would appear to be whether the injury was only caused by the dangerous condition of the approach or contributed to by the negligence of the passenger in not taking reasonable care having regard to the apparent risk. In *Letang* v. *Ottawa Electric Ry.*[1] a passenger climbed up some steps coated with snow to a railway station, slipped on the steps and was injured; it was held that the railway undertakers were liable but no question of contributory negligence arose.

When there is more than one approach, it is no defence for the railway undertakers to show that the other route was the safer, because the passenger is entitled to avail himself of any approach provided by the railways.[2]

773 The railway undertakers are not bound to keep everything in such a condition that nobody could by any possibility hurt himself. So, where a woman tripped on an escalator by catching her heel in the space between the bottom of the escalator and the platform, it was held that, as the space did not exceed half an inch, there was no evidence of negligence on the part of the railway undertakers.[3] On the other hand, a passenger who tripped over a projecting nut and bolt, part of a weighing machine erected on a path leading from the platform to the street, has been held entitled to recover damages.[4]

The mere fact that a passenger slips on some steps is no evidence of negligence against the railway undertakers. Where a passenger slipped on some steps which were used with safety by hundreds of people every day, and it was proved that the nosing of the steps, being made of brass, had become worn and slippery, which would not have happened had lead been used, it was held that there was no evidence of negligence.[5] Again, where a consignee of goods sent a horse and cart to the defendants' goods yard to take delivery of the goods and on one side of the yard there was an unfenced grass slope, down which the horse and cart fell while the carter was signing for the goods, it was held that the bank being unfenced was not evidence of negligence.[6]

774 **Crossings between platforms.** Railway undertakers must take reasonable care in providing crossings to enable passengers to enter or leave the station or to go from one platform to another. The crossing may take the form either of a bridge over the line or a level crossing. If both are provided, but there is a notice prohibiting passengers to pass by the level crossing and directing them to use the bridge, the railway undertakers cannot set up the existence of the notice as a defence in an action

1 [1926] A.C. 725.
2 *Longmore* v. *G.W. Ry.* (1865) 19 C.B.(N.S.) 183; *Letang* v. *Ottawa Electric Ry., supra.*
3 *Alexander* v. *City and South London Ry.* (1928) 44 T.L.R. 450.
4 *Bloomstein* v. *Railway Executive* [1952] 2 All E.R. 418.
5 *Crafter* v. *Metropolitan Ry.* (1866) L.R. 1 C.P. 300.
6 *Norman* v. *G.W. Ry.* [1915] 1 K.B. 584.

if they have habitually acquiesced in passengers using the level crossing.[7] A passenger using a level crossing, however, must take reasonable care for his own safety, and therefore where, in the daylight, a passenger stepped on to a crossing and was immediately knocked down by a train which she could have seen if she had looked, the railway undertakers were not liable.[8] On the other hand, if a passenger is unable to see an approaching train owing to darkness or to a curve in the line and receives no warning either by way of a whistle from the engine or from a porter or other official that a train is expected, there is evidence of negligence against the railways.[9]

If a crossing place is provided, a passenger who is injured through jumping on the rails in order to cross from one platform to another has no claim against the railways.[10]

Where a passenger alighted from a train, which blocked up the ordinary level crossing, and proceeded, in accordance with the usual practice at that station, to cross the line behind the train when he stumbled over some hampers, put out of the train, which he was unable to see in the dark, it was held that there was evidence of negligence.[11] Again, when a passenger, arriving just in time to catch his train, was admitted on to the platform and ran along the line, where he ought not to have gone, tripped over a switch handle and was injured, it was held that there was evidence of negligence against the railways.[12] It was also held to be evidence of negligence when a passenger, in leaving the station by the usual route, was injured by a spark from the engine entering his eye, and there was nothing to screen the path from the railway.[13]

775 **Embankments and bridges.** Embankments and bridges must be maintained in a reasonably safe condition, and it is no defence to say that competent engineers have been employed to make or maintain them. If, however, there is no negligence on the part of anyone in construction or maintenance, but competent people have been employed, the best materials used and the best method adopted, the railway undertakers are not liable.[14] The mere collapse of an embankment or a bridge is evidence of negligence against the railway authority owning it, and it is no defence to say that the collapse was due to exceptional weather conditions, because "the railway company ought to have constructed their works in such a manner as to be capable of resisting all the violence of weather which in the climate . . . might be expected, though perhaps rarely, to occur."[15]

[7] *Dublin, Wicklow and Wexford Ry.* v. *Slattery* (1878) 3 App.Cas. 1155; *Rogers* v. *Rhymney Ry.* (1872) 26 L.T. 879.
[8] *Walker* v. *Midland Ry.* (1866) 14 L.T. 796; *Davey* v. *L. & S.W. Ry.* (1883) 12 Q.B.D. 70.
[9] *Dublin, Wicklow and Wexford Ry.* v. *Slattery*, *supra*; *Brown* v. *G.W. Ry.* (1885) 1 T.L.R. 614; *Wright* v. *Midland Ry.* (1885) 1 T.L.R. 406; *Crowther* v. *L. & Y. Ry.* (1889) 6 T.L.R. 18; *Dallas* v. *G.W. Ry.* (1893) 9 T.L.R. 344.
[10] *Wilby* v. *Midland Ry.* (1876) 35 L.T. 244.
[11] *Nicholson* v. *L. & Y. Ry.* (1865) 3 H. & C. 534.
[12] *Martin* v. *G.N. Ry.* (1855) 16 C.B. 179.
[13] *Atherton* v. *L. & N.W. Ry.* (1905) 21 T.L.R. 671.
[14] *Grote* v. *Chester and Holyhead Ry.* (1848) 2 Ex. 251.
[15] *G.W. Ry. of Canada* v. *Braid* (1863) 1 Moo.P.C.(N.S.) 101, not following *Withers* v. *North Kent Ry.* (1858) 27 L.J.Ex. 417, where an embankment which had stood for five years was washed away in an extraordinary storm and the railway company were held not liable.

When the highway is carried over the railway by a bridge, the railway undertakers are under a statutory duty to maintain the bridge and its approaches.[16] When the road over such a bridge was in bad repair, with several potholes and a large rut, and a cyclist was injured owing to the bad state of the road, the railway authority was held liable.[17]

776 **Level crossings over highways.** When a railway line crosses the highway by a level crossing, the railway undertakers are under a duty to keep the crossing in a proper state for the passage of traffic across the rails. They must take reasonable care to reduce the danger created by their line to a minimum, the nature of the measures to be taken depending on the circumstances.[18] Where the rails were placed too high above the surface of the road, as a result of which the plaintiff's carriage was caught by the rails and torn in two, the authorities were held liable.[19] The railway undertakers are liable to keep the crossing in proper repair, and their liability at common law extends to any inclined approaches which it may have been necessary to construct.[20] They are not bound, however, to reconstruct such approaches from time to time to meet modern traffic requirements.[21] In respect of the crossing, the railway undertakers, unlike the position of a surveyor of highways at common law, are liable for nonfeasance as well as misfeasance in keeping the crossing in repair.[22]

777 The Railways Clauses Consolidation Act 1845, s. 47,[23] provides that if a railway crosses a public carriage road on the level, the company must erect and maintain good and sufficient gates across the road, and must employ proper persons to open and shut them. The same Act, section 61, provides that if a railway crosses a highway other than a public carriageway on the level the company must, if the highway is a bridleway, erect and maintain good and sufficient gates, and, if it is a footway, good and sufficient gates or stiles at each side of the railway where the highway communicates with it. For neglect to perform their

16 Railways Clauses Consolidation Act 1845, s. 46.

17 *Swain* v. *Southern Ry.* [1939] 2 K.B. 560.

18 *Smith* v. *L.M.S. Ry.*, 1948 S.C. 125. *Commissioner for Railways* v. *Quinlan* [1964] A.C. 1054; In *Commissioner for Railways* v. *McDermott* [1967] A.C. 169 it was held that in running trains through a level crossing there was imposed on the railway authority a general duty of care towards persons lawfully on the crossing, which extended not merely to positive operations but included keeping the crossing itself in a reasonably safe condition. See articles: " Occupiers' Liability towards Trespassers," (Hall) 115 L.J. 87 (founded on this case); " Negligence at Level Crossings," 236 L.T. 101.

19 *Oliver* v. *N.E. Ry.* (1874) L.R. 9 Q.B. 409.

20 *Hertfordshire C.C.* v. *G.E. Ry.* [1909] 2 K.B. 403. The wide principle enunciated by Fletcher Moulton L.J. was said to be " too broadly expressed " in *Sharpness New Docks, etc., Co.* v. *Att.-Gen.* [1915] A.C. 654. The obligation under the Railways Clauses Consolidation Act 1845, s. 16, does not extend to repairing the approaches: *West Lancashire R.D.C.* v. *L. & Y. Ry.* [1903] 2 K.B. 394.

21 *Att.-Gen.* v. *G.N. Ry.* [1916] 2 A.C. 356.

22 *Guilfoyle* v. *Port of London Authority* [1932] 1 K.B. 336; *Swain* v. *Southern Ry.* [1939] 2 K.B. 560.

23 The Railways Clauses Act 1863, s. 6, requires the company to erect a lodge at the point where the railway crosses a public carriage road. The Road and Rail Traffic Act 1933, s. 42, and the Transport Act 1968, ss. 123, 124, contain other provisions relating to level crossings, not affecting the text.

statutory duty the railway company are liable. Where, therefore, a railway line crossed a footpath on the level and the company, in breach of their duty under section 61, had not erected a gate or stile, with the result that a child four-and-a-half-years old, having been sent on an errand, got onto the crossing and was injured by a train, the authority were held liable.[24]

In the absence of a gatekeeper as required by section 47, a member of the public should not attempt to open the gate, and if he does so and is injured, the railway undertakers are not liable.[25] Apart from section 47, the railway undertakers are under no obligation (except under a special Act) to employ a gatekeeper or a watchman at a level crossing.[26] The duty of a gatekeeper at a level crossing over a highway is not increased by the fact that there is an accommodation crossing near it.[27]

778 Railway undertakers must take reasonable care to avoid injuring members of the public at a level crossing. If they do something which would lead a reasonable man to believe that it is safe to cross the line and the plaintiff thereupon attempts to cross and is run into by a train, there is evidence of negligence against the railways. Examples of this have occurred where the railway's gatekeeper, on being asked by a carman at night if the line was clear, replied: " Yes, come on," and the carman came on and was run into by a train [28]; where the level crossing gates across the carriageway were left open and a pedestrian, in attempting to cross the line, was run over [29]; where a man, calling one night to inquire after his wife at the gatekeeper's lodge and being told that she was not there, proceeded to cross the line without receiving any warning from the gatekeeper that a train was approaching, and was killed [30]; where a wicket gate, usually kept locked when a train was about to pass, was left unlocked and a pedestrian went through and was run over by a train.[31]

779 Apart from the provision of gates, the railway undertakers must take reasonable precautions for the protection of persons using the crossing. The omission to whistle or otherwise give warning of the approach of the train may be evidence of negligence according to the circumstances,[32] but there is no obligation to whistle in every case.[33] Where a horse and

[24] *Williams* v. *G.W. Ry.* (1874) L.R. 9 Ex. 157. See further on this point Chap. 18, dealing with breach of statutory duty. For cases of injury to cattle through neglect of fencing, see also Chap. 10.
[25] *Wyatt* v. *G.W. Ry.* (1865) 34 L.J.Q.B. 204.
[26] *Cliff* v. *Midland Ry.* (1870) L.R. 5 Q.B. 258; *Stubley* v. *L. & N.W. Ry.* (1865) L.R. 1 Ex. 13; *Newman* v. *L. & S.W. Ry.* (1890) 7 T.L.R. 138.
[27] *Liddiatt* v. *G.W. Ry.* [1946] K.B. 545 (level crossing 160 yards from accommodation crossing, south gate of which is visible to gatekeeper—gatekeeper opened level crossing when south gate open, and plaintiff's heifer was killed by a train—railway company not liable).
[28] *Lunt* v. *L. & N.W. Ry.* (1866) L.R. 1 Q.B. 277.
[29] *N.E. Ry.* v. *Wanless* (1874) L.R. 7 H.L. 12.
[30] *Smith* v. *S.E. Ry.* [1896] 1 Q.B. 178.
[31] *Mercer* v. *S.E. & C. Ry.* [1922] 2 K.B. 549.
[32] *Dublin, Wicklow and Wexford Ry.* v. *Slattery* (1878) 3 App.Cas. 1155; *James* v. *G.W. Ry.* (1867) L.R. 2 C.P. 634n.; *Gray* v. *N.E. Ry.* (1883) 48 L.T. 904.
[33] *Ellis* v. *G.W. Ry.* (1874) L.R. 9 C.P. 551; *Newman* v. *L. & S.W. Ry.* (1890) 7 T.L.R. 138.

cart was being driven over a level crossing, at a place from which it was impossible to see the line until the crossing was reached, owing to the line being in a cutting and curved before it reached the crossing, it was held that a whistle board placed so near to the crossing that it would only take twelve-and-a-half seconds for the train to be on the crossing after blowing the whistle at the board was evidence of negligence against the railways.[34]

The driver or rider of a wheeled vehicle may be found to be negligent if he does not comply with the provisions of the Highway Code,[35] which are:

" THE ROAD USER AND RAILWAY LEVEL CROSSINGS

780 **General**

(141) Never drive " nose to tail " over any level crossing. Never drive on to one unless you can see that the road is clear on the other side. Never stop on or immediately beyond any level crossing.

Level crossings with gates or full barriers

(142) Many level crossings have gates, or barriers with skirts, that are operated by an attendant and go right across the road. Some also have flashing red warning lights. Do not cross the railway once the lights have started to flash.

(143) Some level crossings with gates, but no attendant, have small red and green warning lights. Open *both* gates before you cross with a vehicle or animals, and close them after you. Do not cross when the red light is showing, as a train is coming. There is a special railway telephone and if you are driving a very wide, or a long, or a slow-moving vehicle, or are herding animals, you must first phone the signalman to ask him to let you cross. When you have crossed, phone the signalman again to let him know you are over.

(144) Some level crossings have gates but no attendant or warning lights. At such crossings, stop, look both ways, listen and make sure there is no train coming. Open *both* gates before you cross with a vehicle or animals, and close them after you. If there is a special railway telephone, phone the signalman to make sure it is safe for you to cross.

Open level crossings

(145) At level crossings with no gates, or attendant, or warning lights, stop, look both ways, listen, and make sure there is no train coming before you cross. Always " Give Way " to trains.

(146) Some level crossings with no gates or attendant have flashing red stop lights. When the red lights flash you must stop and wait. Do not cross the railway—a train will reach the crossing soon after the lights begin to flash. The lights will go out when it is safe to cross.

[34] *Jenner* v. *S.E. Ry.* (1911) 105 L.T. 131.

[35] Road Traffic Act 1960, s. 74 (5). The most recent of which Code was issued with the authority of Parliament. (Resolutions passed December 1968.)

Automatic half-barrier level crossings

(147) These crossings have automatic barriers across the left side of the road. The trains work the barriers, which fall just before the train reaches the crossing. Flashing red stop lights and bells warn you when the barriers are about to come down. *Do not move on to the railway once these warning signals have started*—the train cannot stop and will be at the crossing in about half a minute. Wait at the " Stop " line. If you are on foot, wait at the barrier, or the broken white line on the road or footpath, or by the wicket gate. *Never zig-zag round the barriers*—you may be killed, and endanger other lives. If the barriers stay down and the red lights continue to flash after a train has gone by, another train is coming, so you should still wait.

(148) There are special railway telephones at these crossings. If the barriers stay down at any time for more than three minutes without a train arriving, phone the signalman for advice. If you are driving a very wide, or a long, or a slow-moving vehicle (one which cannot cross at more than 5 m.p.h.) or are herding animals, you must first phone the signalman to ask him to let you cross. When you have crossed, phone the signalman again to let him know you are over.

(149) If your vehicle stalls, or breaks down, or if you have an accident on the crossing.

First: get your passengers out of the vehicle and clear of the crossing; then phone the signalman immediately.

Second: if possible, push the vehicle clear of the crossing.

If the red lights and bells start, stand well clear of the crossing.

(150) If you are crossing when the red lights and bells start, *keep going*."

781 A person who crosses the line without first looking to see if a train is approaching may be prevented from recovering on the ground of negligence, particularly if the line is straight and he has an uninterrupted view along the line.[36] When the railway crosses a footpath, a person who attempts to use the footpath by crawling under a train which is standing on the line, and is injured through the train moving off, cannot recover against the railways even though no warning is given that the train is about to start.[37]

782 **Accommodation crossings.**[38] When a train is approaching an accommodation crossing, reasonable care must be used, but there is no duty to drive so that the train can be stopped within the limit of the driver's vision.[39] The degree of care to be exercised is not so high as that required where it is a public level crossing which is being approached. Further, where the driver of a tractor had sustained fatal injuries when he collided

[36] *Ellis* v. *G.W. Ry.*, *supra*; *Davey* v. *L. & S.W. Ry.* (1883) 12 Q.B.D. 70; *Skelton* v. *L. & N.W. Ry.* (1867) L.R. 2 C.P. 631; *Stubley* v. *L. & N.W. Ry.* (1865) L.R. 1 Ex. 13.

[37] *French* v. *Hills Plymouth Co.* (1908) 24 T.L.R. 644.

[38] For the duty owed where the person using a private level crossing is in fact a trespasser, see *Commissioner for Railways* v. *Quinlan* [1964] A.C. 1054.

[39] *Knight* v. *G.W. Ry.* [1943] K.B. 105 (the whistle was sounded where the whistle board was placed).

with a train at an accommodation level crossing on a foggy morning, it was held that the railway authorities were not bound to take any special precautions in foggy conditions.[40] The railway undertakers " need not at common law go so far as to turn an accommodation crossing into a public level crossing, with all the statutory obligations incident thereto; but they must do all that could reasonably be required of them, in the way of warnings, whistles and so forth, to reduce the damage to people using the crossing." [41] Also, when they know that the public are using a private road crossing, they are under a duty to take reasonable care to make the crossing safe. A notice, " Beware of the trains," is not enough.[42]

There is a duty not to expose users of the crossing to any perils beyond those ordinarily inherent in the user of an accommodation crossing. Normally, if there is nothing in the layout of the crossing to call for special precautions, the railway undertakers will not be liable in the absence of negligence on the part of the crew of the train. The duty of the engine driver is not the same as that of the driver of a motor-car. In particular, he is not bound to look out for traffic approaching from the side, such as motor-vehicles approaching a crossing.[43]

When the railway undertakers agreed with contractors to construct and maintain a temporary level crossing over a railway line to enable timber to be carried across the line their duty was to take reasonable precautions for the safety of persons using the crossing in connection with the haulage of timber, and failure to take those precautions would render them liable for the death of a lorry driver killed by a railway engine when he was driving a load of timber.[44]

783 **Persons present on the track.** Although the engine driver's duty was different from that of the driver on a road[43] nevertheless he must take reasonable care to keep a look out along the track ahead in order to avoid persons who may be on or near the rails and thereby in danger.[45] If there be a duty to warn in the circumstances then it is one's duty to make the warning effective if there be reasonable means of so doing. Thus an engine driver was found to be negligent in giving only a short blast on his whistle instead of a long one when driving along a dangerous part of the track on a dark and stormy morning. However, the wagon examiner that he struck was held to be two-thirds to blame for not looking

[40] *Hazell* v. *British Transport Commission* [1958] 1 W.L.R. 169. This followed the decision in *Kemshead* v. *British Transport Commission* [1958] 1 W.L.R. 173n., where a car, having reached the crossing, the gates of which had been left open, proceeded immediately over it in foggy conditions and was struck by a train.

[41] *Lloyds Bank Ltd.* v. *Railway Executive* [1952] 1 All E.R. 1248, *per* Denning L.J. (Railway Executive held liable for breach of statutory duty in failing to employ a gatekeeper, and for common law negligence in failing to have a whistle board—deceased negligent and damages reduced to one-fourth).

[42] *Smith* v. *Smith and The Railway Executive* [1948] W.N. 276.

[43] *Lloyds Bank* v. *British Transport Commission* [1956] 1 W.L.R. 1279; see also *Trznadel* v. *British Transport Commission* [1957] 1 W.L.R. 1002, 1006, *per* Morris L.J.

[44] *Anderson* v. *John M. MacDonald Ltd.* (1954) 104 L.J. 762.

[45] *Conway* v. *B.T.C.* (1962) 106 S.J. 78.

behind him in order to keep a proper look out for engines.[46] Where an employee of the railway undertakers was injured by a passing train whilst he was walking to work along the track the engine driver was held not to have been negligent in the circumstances in failing to see him.[47] A driver is not under any duty to keep any special look out for animals, which may have strayed on to the track.[48]

784 **Engine blowing off steam.** Where an engine blew off steam at a railway station and frightened a horse on a road leading from the station, the railway undertakers were held not liable, because they were not bound to screen the railway from the road or to refrain from blowing off steam at a station.[49] But where an engine blew off steam at a level crossing where there was considerable traffic and frightened a horse waiting to cross over the lines, the railway undertakers were liable.[50]

785 **Shunting.** When shunting operations are taking place, railway undertakers are under a duty to give warning to persons on the line likely to be injured if no warning is given. Failure to give such warning or to look out for persons whose presence on the line ought to be anticipated is evidence of negligence.[51] They are " under a duty to conduct their shunting operations with due care for the safety of all persons lawfully going over the level-crossing on business bent." [52] Railway undertakers which own and work lines in a dockyard are under no obligation before shunting to shut the dock gates opening onto a public street.[53] Conducting noisy shunting operations when a number of cattle are being driven on a siding near to the place where the shunting is going on, so as to frighten the cattle, is evidence of negligence.[54]

Where a chargeman examiner was examining a damaged wagon which was stationary in the sidings and was suddenly shunted into so violently that he was startled and fell injuring himself, it was held that as the plaintiff's injury was foreseeable the defendants were liable for their shunter's negligence in allowing abnormal shunting, which had produced such an unnecessarily loud and violent crash.[55]

(b) *Road Carriage*

786 **Duty generally.** The law set out in the section above relating to railways

46 *Geddes* v. *B.R.B.* (1968) 112 S.J. 194.
47 *Trznadel* v. *B.T.C., supra.* But where workmen are working on the maintenance of the permanent way itself, see the provisions of the Railway Employment (Prevention of Accidents) Act 1900 and the appropriate Rules 1902 (No. 616) and *Judson* v. *B.T.C.* [1954] 1 W.L.R. 585; *Reilly* v. *B.T.C.* [1957] 1 W.L.R. 76; *Hicks* v. *B.T.C.* [1958] 1 W.L.R. 493; *Cade* v. *B.T.C.* [1959] A.C. 256.
48 *Beddie* v. *B.T.C.* (1957) 74 Sh.Ct.Rep. 130.
49 *Simkin* v. *L. & N.W. Ry.* (1888) 21 Q.B.D. 453.
50 *M.S.J. & A. Ry.* v. *Fullarton* (1863) 14 C.B.(N.S.) 54.
51 *Jones* v. *G.W. Ry.* (1930) 47 T.L.R. 39; *Paul* v. *G.E. Ry.* (1920) 36 T.L.R. 344; *Grant* v. *G.W. Ry.* (1898) 14 T.L.R. 174.
52 *Ross* v. *Railway Executive*, 1948 S.C.(H.L.) 58, *per* Lord Uthwatt (deceased killed while crossing railway line between wagons during shunting—he " walked into a danger which was obvious to an ordinary man "—Railway Executive not liable).
53 *Clark* v. *N.B. Ry.* (1912) S.C. 1.
54 *Sneesby* v. *L. & Y. Ry.* (1875) 1 Q.B.D. 42.
55 *Slatter* v. *British Railways Board* (1966) 110 S.J. 688, 710.

applies, with the necessary modifications, to road carriage. The carriers' liability as to the condition of the vehicle which the intending passenger enters as a lawful visitor is under the Occupiers' Liability Act 1957 and, as already explained,[56] the duty owed is the common duty of care.

787 **Collisions.** Liability for a collision on the highway depends on the negligence of those in charge of the public vehicles. A passenger in a public conveyance who is injured in a highway collision can recover against the owners of the vehicle in which he is travelling if there be any negligence on the part of those in charge of it which contributed towards the collision happening even though there may also have been negligence on the part of some other person.

It has been held that if the driver is driving with reasonable care his employers are not liable if a passenger is struck by the projecting arm of a lamp-post, a tree or similar object. Accordingly, an omnibus company were held not liable when a passenger on top of an omnibus was struck by a fire alarm finger post, flush with the kerb, fixed on an electric light standard, when it was not found that the driver with reasonable care ought to have seen it[57]; when a similar accident occurred in which the passenger was struck by the projection on a street lamp[58]; and where a passenger was hit by the overhanging branch of a tree and there was no evidence that the driver was driving too near to the trees or that he had any reason to suspect that they were overhanging.[59] But if the driver knew that the trees were a potential source of danger and that they might overhang the highway, he should give them a wide berth.[60] In these cases of a collision between a passenger on the vehicle and a stationary object on the highway the mere fact of the collision is evidence of negligence against the proprietors of the vehicle, throwing upon them the burden of proving that it occurred without negligence on the part of any person for whose acts they are responsible.[61] If the driver of a horse-drawn vehicle inadvertently strikes a passenger with his whip it is evidence of negligence.[62]

88 **Defective apparatus.** If a passenger in a tramcar[63] is injured through a trolley arm becoming detached from the wire and striking him on the head, it is evidence of negligence against the tramway company. But where the company proved that their car was in good order, properly worked, and

[56] *Ante*, § 740 and, generally, Chap. 8.
[57] *Simon* v. *London General Omnibus Co.* (1907) 23 T.L.R. 463.
[58] *Hase* v. *London General Omnibus Co.* (1907) 23 T.L.R. 616.
[59] *Trinder* v. *G.W. Ry.* (1919) 35 T.L.R. 291.
[60] *Hale* v. *Hants & Dorset Motor Services* [1947] 2 All E.R. 628 (the trees were planted by the Poole Corporation, who were held liable for allowing them to overhang the highway, the liability being apportioned two-thirds to the Corporation and one-third to the motor company).
[61] *Isaac Walton & Co.* v. *Vanguard Motorbus Co.* (1908) 25 T.L.R. 13; *Barnes U.D.C.* v. *London General Omnibus Co.* (1908) 100 L.T. 115; *Ellor* v. *Selfridge & Co. Ltd.* (1930) 46 T.L.R. 236; *Radley* v. *L.P.T.B.* [1942] 1 All E.R. 433 (plaintiff succeeded where omnibus collided with overhanging branch).
[62] *Ward* v. *London General Omnibus Co.* (1873) 42 L.J.C.P. 265.
[63] For the law relating to tramways see the 4th edition: *Charlesworth on Negligence*, § 304.

every possible precaution had been taken to secure the safety of passengers, it was held that the prima facie case of negligence had been rebutted.[64] If the wheel of an omnibus is wrenched off by tramlines, it is prima facie evidence of negligence against the omnibus company.[65]

789 **Injury caused by one passenger to another.** It is the duty of those in charge of public conveyances to take reasonable care to prevent them from being overcrowded,[66] and also to take reasonable care to prevent persons who are likely to be dangerous to other passengers, by reason of disease, drunkenness, or declared intention to use violence, to enter the vehicle. Where a man in an obviously drunken condition was allowed to enter a tramcar and he pushed a woman down from the top of the vehicle so that she was injured and a baby in her arms was killed, it was held that the owners were liable.[67]

790 **Stopping and starting.** Public conveyances must be started and stopped with reasonable care. Accordingly it is evidence of negligence if they start off in motion with a jerk and a passenger is injured.[68] Again, it has been held to be an act of negligence to start when the passenger still has one foot on the step and before he has completed the act of boarding the vehicle.[69] When an omnibus has stopped in answer to a signal, the conductor should not start it again until he has seen that there are no more passengers wanting to alight.[70] If the vehicle starts too soon because of a passenger ringing the bell which is the signal to start, there is no evidence of negligence unless it is proved that, in the circumstances, the loss of control of the bell was negligence on the part of the conductor.[71] Such negligence was found when the conductor was absent from the platform for an appreciable interval.[72]

When the plaintiff's husband asked the conductor to stop at the next stop and the conductor rang the bell and told the husband to wait until the bus stopped, but the bus stopped some twenty yards from the next stop for traffic reasons, so that the husband got off followed by the plaintiff who was injured owing to the bus starting again as she was alighting, the bus company was held liable on the ground that the conductor should not have allowed the plaintiff and her husband to alight without first warning the driver that they were doing so.[73]

791 If a vehicle stops and then jerks on again while a passenger is alighting,

64 *Newberry* v. *Bristol Tramways Co.* (1912) 107 L.T. 801.
65 *Lilly* v. *Tilling Ltd.* (1912) 57 S.J. 59.
66 *Pickering* v. *Belfast Corpn.* [1911] 2 Ir.R. 224. See also *ante*, § 754, dealing with overcrowding on railways.
67 *Murgatroyd* v. *Blackburn Tramways* (1887) 3 T.L.R. 451.
68 *Geeves* v. *London General Omnibus Co.* (1901) 17 T.L.R. 249.
69 *Brien* v. *Bennett* (1839) 8 C. & P. 724; *Steele* v. *Belfast Corpn.* [1920] 2 Ir.R. 125; *Wilkie* v. *L.P.T.B.* [1947] 1 All E.R. 258.
70 *Mottram* v. *S. Lancashire Transport Co.* [1942] 2 All E.R. 452, 453.
71 *Wagner* v. *West Ham Corpn.* (1920) 37 T.L.R. 86; *Mottram* v. *S. Lancashire Transport Co., supra.*
72 *Davies* v. *Liverpool Corpn.* [1949] 2 All E.R. 175.
73 *Prescott* v. *Lancashire United Transport Co.* [1953] 1 W.L.R. 232.

it is evidence of negligence.[74] It is not negligence on the part of a passenger to stand on the footboard waiting for a vehicle to stop, when a signal to stop has been given. Where a signal to stop was given and the passenger went onto the footboard in readiness to alight, but the driver disregarded the signal so that the passenger was thrown off the footboard, it was held that the passenger's claim succeeded, because the driver was negligent in disregarding the signal and the conductor was negligent in not remaining on the platform for the answer to the signal.[75] Again, a passenger who, having requested the conductor to stop the tram at a specified stopping place, goes onto the platform as the tram slows down and is thrown off by its sudden acceleration can recover.[76] If the signal to stop is given by the passenger and not by the conductor, it is not negligence on the conductor's part to be on the top when the passenger comes on to the platform in readiness to alight.[77] If no signal to stop has been given, it is negligence on the part of the passenger to stand on the step in anticipation of the tram stopping.[78]

792 **Boarding and alighting from vehicle in motion.** If a passenger attempts to board a vehicle in motion he does so at his own risk, and the only duty of those in charge of the vehicle is not to act in reckless disregard of his safety. Where a drunken man attempted to get onto a tramcar in motion and the conductor pushed him off so that he fell and was injured, it was held that he could not recover damages, because he was wrongfully attempting to force himself onto the tram when he was drunk and had put the conductor in a difficulty in which he had not acted with such want of care as to cause the accident.[79] On the other hand, when a vehicle slowed down at a stopping place but, as it was full, did not stop and a man jumped onto the step although he was prevented from entering by the conductor, it was held that as he got off, thereby injuring himself, at a time when it had increased its speed, owing to the refusal of the conductor to stop the vehicle for him to alight, there was evidence of negligence on the part of the conductor.[80]

A passenger who alights from a vehicle which is still in motion may be guilty of negligence.[81] If, however, the door by which he is to alight is opened by the driver or conductor and he is forced out by the pressure of passengers behind, then his action in damages will succeed.[82] Where a passenger on a double decker bus was injured when he was thrown out through the open folded door of the vehicle from the platform, on which

[74] *Holland* v. *North Metropolitan Tramways* (1886) 3 T.L.R. 245.
[75] *Hall* v. *London Tramways* (1896) 12 T.L.R. 611; see also *Watt* v. *Glasgow Corpn.*, 1919 S.C. 300.
[76] *Anderson* v. *Belfast Corpn.* [1943] N.I. 34.
[77] *Martin* v. *Dublin United Tramways* [1908] 2 Ir.R. 13; *Mottram* v. *S. Lancashire Transport Co.* [1942] 2 All E.R. 452.
[78] *Caldwell* v. *Glasgow Corpn.*, 1936 S.C. 490; *Jude* v. *Edinburgh Corpn.*, 1943 S.C. 399.
[79] *Delany* v. *Dublin United Tramways* (1892) 30 L.R.Ir. 725.
[80] *Cullen* v. *Dublin United Tramways* [1920] 2 Ir.R. 63.
[81] *M'Sherry* v. *Glasgow Corpn.*, 1917 S.C. 156. See now the effect on the common law of the Law Reform (Contributory Negligence) Act 1945, and *post*, Chap. 16.
[82] *Pickering* v. *Belfast Corpn.* [1911] 2 Ir.R. 224.

he was standing preparatory to alighting, it was held by the House of Lords that the defendants were not liable. As there were other sufficient handholds, their failure to provide a central pillar in the doorway or else to institute a system whereby the door was kept closed until the vehicle had become stationary was not negligent in the circumstances.[83]

The Highway Code provides: " (21) Do not get on or off a bus unless it is standing at a recognised bus stop. If you want to get on a bus at a request stop, give a clear signal for the bus to stop, and do not try to get on until it has done so. When you get off a bus and want to cross the road, wait until the bus has moved off, and you have a clear view of the road."

793 **Statutory duties.** Much of the common law duty of drivers, conductors and passengers aforesaid has been embodied as statutory duty under the Public Service Vehicles (Conduct of Drivers, Conductors and Passengers) Regulations 1936.[84] By regulation 4: " A driver or a conductor, when acting as such, . . . (c) shall take all reasonable precautions to ensure the safety of passengers in or on or entering or alighting from the vehicle." Accordingly where the conductor controls the door of a public service vehicle, he should not cause it to be opened before the vehicle stops.[85] Whilst this regulation imposes a duty of care with regard to passengers, who are entitled to enter the vehicle, none is imposed with regard to a passenger who attempts to board the vehicle when it is in motion[86] and any intending passenger who does so attempt to board an omnibus not at a bus stop but either stopped at traffic lights or whenever it was stationary elsewhere, he must do so at his own risk.[87] The receipt of a signal to proceed given by the conductor cannot absolve the driver of an omnibus from his duty to take reasonable care for an intending passenger's safety so that where a driver moved off while a passenger was still in the act of climbing aboard civil liability was established sounding in damages for the injury sustained.[88]

794 **Damage caused by driving.** The driver owes a duty to passengers to drive with reasonable care. This duty is owed both to seated and to standing passengers, whether the latter are holding on or not.[89] A sudden swerve which causes injury to a passenger is evidence of negligence,[90] but the mere fact that a passenger is flung through the open door is not.[91] A sudden application of the brakes causing damage to a passenger is evidence of negligence, but where it was done to avoid running over a dog, the driver was held not liable, as he had acted with reasonable care in an emergency.[92] Where, however, the driver knew that the passenger

83 *Wyngrove* v. *Scottish Omnibuses*, 1966 S.C.(H.L.) 47.
84 S.R.O. 1936 No. 619.
85 *Nicholson* v. *Goddard* (1954) 118 J.P. 394.
86 *Reid* v. *MacNichol* 1958 S.L.T. 42.
87 *Police* v. *Okoukwo* [1954] Crim.L.R. 869.
88 *McLaughlin* v. *Glasgow Corporation* (1963) 79 Sh.Ct.Rep. 172.
89 *Western Scottish M.T. Co.* v. *Allam* [1943] 2 All E.R. 742.
90 *O'Hara* v. *Scottish M.T. Co.*, 1941 S.C. 363; *Doonan* v. *S.M.T. Co.*, 1950 S.C. 136.
91 *Johnstone* v. *Western S.M.T. Co.* (1955) 105 L.J. 762.
92 *Parkinson* v. *Liverpool Corpn.* [1950] 1 All E.R. 367.

was not yet seated and it was found that he had not exercised the necessary care and skill, the driver was held liable.[93] Driving an omnibus at such a speed as to cause a passenger in poor health to become ill, is not negligence, because the driver is entitled to assume normal health in his passengers.[94]

795 **Compulsory insurance against third party risks.** A motor omnibus or other motor-vehicle must not be used on the road unless there is in force a policy of insurance covering the user of the vehicle against third-party risks.[95] Such risks cover liability in respect of the death of or bodily injury to any person caused by or arising out of the use of the vehicle on a road, but are not bound to include liability to a servant of the user for injury arising out of or in the course of his employment or, unless passengers are carried for reward, liability for injury caused to persons carried on or getting on to or off the vehicle.[96] Judgment against any person insured against these third-party risks must be satisfied by the insurers.[97] There are numerous statutory provisions relating to this insurance to which reference for fuller information on this subject should be made.[98] If the insured under a policy of insurance becomes bankrupt or makes an arrangement with his creditors or, being a company, goes into liquidation, his rights under the policy vest in the third party and can be enforced against the insurers.[99] For claims against the Motor Insurers Bureau see *ante*, § 176.

796 **Contracts restricting liability.** A contract restricting liability in respect of the death or bodily injury to a passenger in a public service vehicle is void.[1] See generally Chapter 16 " Contracting out of liability for negligence," § 1086 *et seq.*, *post.*

797 **Hackney carriage passengers.** A person who accepts another as a passenger in a hackney carriage or other road vehicle is bound to exercise reasonable care for the safety of the passenger and of whatever he brings with him into the vehicle.

Under the London Hackney Carriages Acts the registered proprietor of a hackney carriage is liable for the negligence of the driver, whether or not the relation of master and servant exists between them.[2] So, if the passenger is injured or his luggage is lost owing to the negligence of the driver, the proprietor is liable.[3] Liability is imposed not only

[93] *Sutherland* v. *Glasgow Corpn.*, 1951 S.C. 1.
[94] *Walker* v. *Pitlochry Motor Co.*, 1930 S.C. 565.
[95] Road Traffic Act 1960, s. 201.
[96] *Ibid.* s. 203. See, however, the effect of the Motor Vehicles (Passenger Insurance) Act 1971, which comes into force December 1, 1972.
[97] *Ibid.* s. 207.
[98] Road Traffic Act 1960, ss. 201–214.
[99] Third Parties (Rights against Insurers) Act 1930, s. 1. This transfer is (subject to the provisions of s. 207 of the Road Traffic Act 1960) subject to the rights of the insurer against the assured.
[1] Road Traffic Act 1960, s. 151. In cases such as old age pensioners who have " free passes " see *Gore* v. *Van Der Lann* [1967] 2 Q.B. 31. See article " Strange case of Mrs. Gore " (Odgers) 86 L.Q.R. 69.
[2] *Keen* v. *Henry* [1894] 1 Q.B. 292; *King* v. *London Improved Cab Co.* (1889) 23 Q.B.D. 281; *Venables* v. *Smith* (1877) 2 Q.B.D. 279.
[3] *Powles* v. *Hider* (1856) 6 E. & B. 207.

on the licensed proprietor but also on the actual proprietor, so that where a hackney carriage was owned by the defendant and her son, but the son alone was registered as proprietor, it was held that the defendant was liable.[4] Under the Town Police Clauses Act 1847, ss. 37–48,[5] the registered proprietor of a hackney carriage is liable for the negligence of the driver while plying for hire.[6]

798 **Gratuitous rides.** A person who gratuitously gives another a ride in his vehicle is liable to that other person for any damage caused by the driver's negligence. His liability is the same if, instead of driving himself, he allows another person to do so.[7] He is under a duty to warn his passenger of a danger known to him but unknown to his passenger, such as a low bridge dangerous to persons inside the vehicle.[8]

(c) *Ships*

799 **Duty of shipowners.** The duty of shipowners towards passengers is largely governed by the provisions of the Merchant Shipping Acts 1894 to 1970, the terms of which it is not proposed to discuss, and, as regards the condition of the vessel, by the Occupiers' Liability Act 1957 as already explained.[9] The passengers' rights against the shipowners are also usually regulated by contract. Apart from such statutory provisions and contractual obligations, the duty of a shipowner is similar to that of a railway authority.

A shipowner owes a duty to the passenger to take reasonable care to provide safe access to the ship. Where, therefore, passengers were taken to a hulk from which they were to board a steamship, and the plaintiff, after descending a ladder in the hulk in order to reach the steamship, fell down an open hatchway, which was unguarded and imperfectly lighted, it was held that he could recover, although the shipowner had only the right to use the hulk, on the ground that the plaintiff was invited to use it.[10] On the other hand, where a passenger, in embarking on a ship, slipped from the gangway which was three inches above the deck and fractured her ankle, and claimed that the gangway was not properly lighted and that there was no one to help her off the gangway, it was held that the shipowners, who had embarked thirty thousand passengers during the year with no more precautions at night and in all states of the tide, were not liable.[11]

[4] *Gates* v. *Bill & Son* [1902] 2 K.B. 38.
[5] Repealed as to public service vehicles, Road Traffic Act 1930, Sched. V, in turn repealed by the Statute Law Revision Act 1950. The law as to hackney carriages applies to motor-vehicles: Road Traffic Act 1960, s. 256.
[6] *Bygraves* v. *Dicker* [1923] 2 K.B. 585.
[7] *Pratt* v. *Patrick* [1924] 1 K.B. 488; *Samson* v. *Aitchison* [1912] A.C. 844; *Smith* v. *Harris* [1939] 3 All E.R. 960; *Miller* v. *Liverpool Co-operative Soc. Ltd.* [1940] 4 All E.R. 367 (affirmed [1941] 1 All E.R. 379n.). For liability for acts of agents, see Chap. 14.
[8] *Lewys* v. *Burnett & Dunbar* [1945] 2 All E.R. 555.
[9] *Ante*, § 740 and, generally, Chap. 8.
[10] *John* v. *Bacon* (1870) L.R. 5 C.P. 437.
[11] *Cameron* v. *L.M.S. Ry.* (1936) 54 Ll.L.R. 95.

800 On board the ship itself reasonable care must be taken for the safety of passengers. Where there was no ladder provided to enable a lady in an upper berth to descend, and the stewardess placed a chair for the purpose on which the lady slipped and injured herself, it was held that the shipowners were liable because it was their duty "to provide means by which passengers might get out of their berths without danger of falling."[12] Again, where the porthole glass in a cabin was not properly secured, but was revolving at a high speed, so that when the passenger attempted to draw the curtains aside the glass caught his hand and injured it, the shipowners were held to be negligent.[13] Similarly, reasonable care must be taken to provide accommodation for passengers' luggage, so that where luggage was stowed in a vacant lavatory which became flooded owing to the overflow of water from the adjoining lavatory, it was held that the shipowners were liable.[14]

If a passenger slips on the floor of the passage outside his cabin, owing to its being made slippery by washing, and he sees the washing taking place, there is no negligence on the part of the shipowners,[15] but "wholly different considerations would arise if the steward had gone away leaving the floor wet and slippery without taking steps to warn perambulating passengers of its condition."[16]

(d) *Aircraft*

801 **Liability of aircraft owner.** At common law the liability of the owner of an aircraft does not differ from that of the owner of a highway vehicle. An aircraft when at rest is quite harmless, and although when in motion or flight it is a potential source of danger, it resembles in this respect a motor-vehicle and a railway train. An aircraft in motion is not an inherently dangerous thing or a thing dangerous in itself,[17] and therefore the principle of *Rylands* v. *Fletcher*[18] does not apply to it. The result is that, apart from the statutory provisions explained below, liability for aircraft is based on negligence.

An aircraft company were held liable when a man, seeing his wife and daughter off, was led to a position by one of the servants of the company and killed by one of the revolving propellors. The occupiers of the airfield were held not liable.[19]

The owners' liability as to the condition of the aircraft, which the intending passenger enters as a lawful visitor, is under the Occupiers' Liability Act 1957 and, as already explained,[20] the duty owed is the common duty of care.

12 *Andrews* v. *Little & Co.* (1887) 3 T.L.R. 544.
13 *Jones* v. *Oceanic Steam Navigation Co.* [1924] 2 K.B. 730 (the company were however absolved from liability by the conditions of the contract).
14 *Upperton* v. *Union-Castle Mail Steamship Co.* (1902) 19 T.L.R. 687.
15 *Beaumont-Thomas* v. *Blue Star Line* [1939] 3 All E.R. 127.
16 *Beaumont-Thomas* v. *Blue Star Line* [1939] 3 All E.R. 127, *per* Goddard L.J. at p. 135.
17 See *Fosbroke-Hobbes* v. *Airwork Ltd.* [1937] 1 All E.R. 108, 112, *per* Goddard J.
18 (1866) L.R. 1 Ex. 265; 3 H.L. 330; 37 L.J.Ex. 161.
19 *Waring* v. *East Anglian Flying Services Ltd.* [1951] W.N. 553.
20 And see *Chisholm* v. *British European Airways* [1963] 1 Lloyd's Rep. 626.

802 **Duty to passengers during flight.** In *Chisholm* v. *British European Airways*,[21] the captain of an aircraft received notice of an approaching storm and, accordingly, the passengers were told to remain seated and to fasten their seat belts. As the plaintiff passenger left her seat to go to the toilet the aircraft encountered severe turbulence and plunged violently causing the plaintiff to stumble, fall and injure herself. The defendants were held not to be liable by Fenton Atkinson J., on the ground that they had taken reasonable care for the plaintiff's safety as a result of having given her adequate warning to remain seated.

803 **Civil Aviation Act 1949.** The Civil Aviation Act 1949,[22] s. 40, provides: "(1) No action shall lie in respect of trespass or in respect of nuisance, by reason only of the flight of an aircraft over any property at a height above the ground, which, having regard to wind, weather, and all the circumstances of the case is reasonable, or the ordinary incidents of such flight, so long as the provisions of Part II and this Part of this Act and any Order in Council or order made under Part II or this Part of this Act are duly complied with; (2) where material loss or damage[23] is caused to any person or property on land or water by, or by a person in, or an article or person falling from, an aircraft while in flight, taking off,[24] or landing, then unless the loss or damage was caused or contributed to by the negligence of the person by whom it was suffered, damages in respect of the loss or damage shall be recoverable without proof of negligence or intention or other cause of action, as if the loss or damage had been caused by the wilful act, neglect, or default of the owner of the aircraft:

Provided that where material loss or damage is caused as aforesaid in circumstances in which—

(*a*) damages are recoverable in respect of the said loss or damage by virtue only of the foregoing provisions of this subsection; and

(*b*) a legal liability is created in some person other than the owner to pay damages in respect of the said loss or damage;

the owner shall be entitled to be indemnified by that other person against any claim in respect of the said loss or damage."

The burden of proving that the loss or damage was caused by or contributed to by the negligence of the injured party is on the owner of the aircraft.[25]

804 **Imposition of absolute liability.** The effect of section 40 is to impose an absolute liability on the " owner " of the aircraft as explained in the Act, subject only to the qualified defence of contributory negligence. The Act clearly contemplates that the owner is liable, although the damage or loss has been caused by the wrongful act, neglect or default of a third

21 *Ante*, § 740 and, generally, Chap. 8.
22 For the control of licensing see the Civil Aviation (Licensing) Act 1960. Further see Air Navigation (Amendment) Order 1960 (S.I. 1960, No. 2410).
23 The expression " loss or damage " includes, in relation to persons, loss of life and personal injury: Civil Aviation Act 1949, s. 63 (3).
24 As to the meaning of " taking off," see *Blankley* v. *Godley* [1952] 1 All E.R. 436n.
25 *Cubitt* v. *Gower* (1933) 47 Ll.L.R. 65.

party. Even if the damage or loss is caused by an " act of God," [26] the reference to liability " without proof of negligence or intention or other cause of action " seems to indicate that the owner would still be liable.

The owner's liability, however, is confined to material loss or damage to any person or property on land or water, and does not include loss or damage to person or property in the air. Liability for damage in the air will accordingly depend on proof of negligence.[27]

A person who is liable to pay damages for loss or damage " caused on any one occasion to persons or property on land or water by, or by a person in, or an article or person falling from, an aircraft while in flight, taking off or landing," may take proceedings to limit his liability to the amount set out in the Fifth Schedule to the Civil Aviation Act 1949.[28] No such proceedings can be taken if the loss or damage has been caused by his wilful misconduct or the wilful misconduct of his servants or agents, unless, in the latter case, the loss or damage occurred without his actual fault or privity.[29] Also, a person who is not the owner of the aircraft concerned and was in, or in possession or control of, the aircraft without the authority or permission of the owner, cannot take proceedings to limit his liability.[30]

5 **Compulsory insurance against third-party risks.** It is an offence to fly or cause or permit any other person to fly an aircraft unless there is in force in relation to the flying of the aircraft by the person in question a policy of insurance against the liability set out above.[31] Judgment recovered against the person insured must be satisfied by the insurer, subject to the conditions in the Act.[32]

6 **Liability of hirer of aircraft and others.** The absolute liability set out above is imposed on the owner of the aircraft. But, where any aircraft, " has been bona fide demised, let or hired out for any period exceeding fourteen days to any other person by the owner thereof, and no pilot, commander, navigator or operative member of the crew of the aircraft is in the employment of the owner," the owner of the aircraft is freed from liability, and the hirer is subject to it as if he were the owner.[33]

Liability for damage or loss caused by a person other than the owner, such as a pilot, a hirer who has hired the aircraft for a period not exceeding fourteen days, or a passenger who drops an article from the aircraft, is not covered by the provisions of the Civil Aviation Act 1949, and consequently depends on negligence. Such a person, if he is in the aircraft

[26] For the meaning of this expression, see Chap. 9, *ante*, § 429 *et seq.*

[27] Regulations can be made for the prevention of collisions at sea between seaplanes and between seaplanes and vessels on the surface of the water: Civil Aviation Act 1949, s. 52.

[28] Civil Aviation Act 1949, s. 42.

[29] *Ibid.* s. 42 (1). This does not affect any limit imposed by contract or by the Carriage by Air Act 1961.

[30] Civil Aviation Act 1949, s. 42 (3).

[31] *Ibid.* s. 43, which is the equivalent to the provisions of the Road Traffic Act 1960, s. 201, in the case of motor-vehicles used on the road.

[32] *Ibid.* Sched. VI, para. 2.

[33] Civil Aviation Act 1949, s. 49 (2).

with the permission of the owner, can take proceedings to limit his liability as explained above.[30]

807 **International carriage by air.** In contracts of international carriage by air, as defined in Schedule I, Article 1 of the Carriage by Air Act 1961,[34] the liability of the carrier for each passenger is limited to 250,000 francs (about £6,000) unless a larger sum has been agreed upon.[35] The carrier is not liable for the death of or bodily injury to a passenger if he proves that he and his servants and agents have taken all necessary measures to avoid the damage, or that it was impossible for them to take such measures.[36] However, a carrier cannot avail himself of the limited liability provisions of Article 22 if it is proved that the damage resulted from an act or omission of the carrier, his servants or agents done with intent to cause damage or recklessly and with the knowledge that damage would probably result, provided that the servant or agent was acting within the scope of his employment.[37] Breach of a contract of international carriage causing death gives a right of action to the dependants of the passenger suing under the Fatal Accidents Acts,[38] but their damages are limited to 250,000 francs.[39] It has been held that under Articles 17 and 20 the burden of disproving negligence lies on the defendants [40] and in an action under Article 17, the damages, though limited to 250,000 francs, are not limited to their pecuniary loss.[41]

808 **Res ipsa loquitur.** When negligence is in question, the doctrine *res ipsa loquitur* applies as well to aircraft as to other vehicles. Where, therefore, an aircraft took off and crashed just outside the aerodrome " well before it had attained the height at which the journey would be performed," the doctrine was applied and the owners were held liable for the death of a passenger in the aircraft at the time of the crash.[42]

(e) *Hovercraft*

809 **General introduction.** Hovercraft are but one of the large class of vehicles, best known collectively as " Ground effect machines " (G.E.M.s) which are characterised by having a significant proportion of their weight supported by forces arising from air pressures or suction developed around

[34] Which substantially reproduced Schedule 1 to the Carriage by Air Act 1932. Whilst the Act of 1961 as a whole came into force on receiving the Royal Assent (June 22, 1961) it could not become effective until s. 1, which gives the force of law to the Convention and repeals the Carriage by Air Act 1932, came into force on June 1, 1967, by virtue of the Carriage by Air (Convention) Order 1967 (S.I. 1967 No. 479).

[35] Carriage by Air Act 1961, Sched. I, Art. 22.

[36] Carriage by Air Act 1961, Sched. I, Art. 20; Civil Aviation Act 1949, s. 54.

[37] Carriage by Air Act 1961, Sched. I, Art. 25.

[38] *Ibid.* s. 3, Sched. I, Art. 17.

[39] *Grein* v. *Imperial Airways Ltd* [1937] 1 K.B. 50 (decided according to the Carriage by Air Act 1932, which limited the carrier's liability to 125,000 francs).

[40] *Chisholm* v. *B.E.A.*, *supra.*

[41] *Preston* v. *Hunting Air Transport Ltd.* [1956] 1 Q.B. 454 (infant children, suing in respect of their mother's death, awarded £400 for damage other than financial loss), which was distinguished by Megaw J. in *Pevec* v. *Brown* (1964) 108 S.J. 219 when he held that no damages can be awarded to an orphaned infant child for the fact that he will receive less care from a nurse than from his mother, financial loss only being recoverable.

[42] *Fosbroke-Hobbes* v. *Airwork Ltd.* [1937] 1 All E.R. 108.

the craft. As their name suggests they are restricted to operation in close proximity to the varied surfaces of the Earth which they profile as they travel about suspended on a cushion of air. Most of the G.E.M.s operating today are of the peripheral jet type known in the U.K. as " Air cushion vehicles " (A.C.V.s) and it was this class, more commonly called the Hovercraft [43] which was first successfully demonstrated as a working scale model in the nineteen fifties by the brilliant radio engineer, boat builder and designer Sir Christopher Cockerell C.B.E., from whose outstanding efforts most, if not all, of the present British activity in this sphere stem. Next came the original Hovercraft with its thirty foot hull and centrally mounted vertical air intake which was effectively demonstrated by the aircraft firm of Saunders-Roe Ltd. in June 1959 but it was not until the early nineteen sixties that suitable craft were developed and built which were capable of commercial operation.

Now the Cockerell patents are controlled by Hovercraft Development Ltd., a subsidiary of the National Research Development Corporation, which is an independent public body established by Act of Parliament.[44] The Government further continue to play an important part in A.C.V. research and development through the research establishments of the Ministry of Technology, notably the National Physical Laboratory as well as the Royal Aircraft Establishment and the Interservices Hovercraft Trials Unit based at Lee-on-Solent.

10 **Statute law.** The first comparable efforts by Parliament to match the ingenuity of Cockerell and his successors in the creation of a suitable code, which would apply, were however not so brilliant; indeed, they were quite unimaginative and inept for their purpose. Under the heading of " Hover vehicles " section 19 of the Road Traffic Act 1962 [45] illustrated quite plainly the absence of any profound thoughts or progressive ideas by providing that for the purposes of the principal Act of 1960 a hover vehicle: (a) shall be a motor vehicle, whether or not it is adapted or intended for use on roads; but (b) shall be treated (subject to the Minister's powers to make regulations [46]) as not being a vehicle of any of the classes or descriptions defined in section 253 (2) to (8) of the said principal Act.[47] So the matter lay until the passing of the Hovercraft Act 1968 [48] the object of which was to recognise the hovercraft as a vehicle of an entirely new kind altogether, which is neither a ship nor an aircraft. Accordingly by section 1 wide powers are given to make Orders in Council for regulating

[43] S. 4 (1) of the Hovercraft Act 1968, s. 59 defines a hovercraft as: " a vehicle which is designed to be supported when in motion wholly or partly by air expelled from the vehicle to form a cushion of which the boundaries include the ground, water or other surface beneath the vehicle ".

[44] The Development of Inventions Act 1967.

[45] Which section came into force on September 28, 1962, by virtue of S.I. 1962 No. 2088. These provisions are repeated in s. 101 of the Road Traffic Regulation Act 1967.

[46] None has been made.

[47] Which is repeated in s. 99 of the Road Traffic Regulation Act 1967.

[48] Which came into force on August 26, 1968, with the exception of s. 4 (3), which by virtue of s. 7 (2) " shall come into operation on such date as the Board of Trade may appoint by order made by statutory instrument." To date no such order has been made.

hovercraft, particularly as regards their registration and safety; liability for damage caused by or involving their use[48a]; investigation of accidents; the regulation of noise and vibration; the application of enactments relating to other forms of transport and of general maritime law; and the application of certain enactments limiting liability for damage. Certain enactments relating to Admiralty Jurisdiction are applied to hovercraft by section 2, which further enables provision to be made by Order in Council for modifying or excluding the application of those enactments in prescribed cases.

811 **Duty generally.** Until indications are given by Parliament to the contrary, there is no reason to suppose that the operators of hovercraft are in any different position from the operators of any other methods of transport and carriage already considered so far as concerns the duty of care that is owed. It follows that they are under a duty to use reasonable care and skill in the provision and maintenance of their craft and the provision and maintenance of their premises *e.g.* their hoverports [49] as well as their being under an obligation to devise a safe means of operation so as to prevent accidents, be these collisions with other hovercraft or otherwise. They are also liable for the negligence of their pilots and others who are concerned with the management and movement of their craft in operation.

3—HIGHWAY USERS AND COLLISIONS

812 **Duty of driver of vehicle.** The duty of a person who drives or rides a vehicle on the highway is to use reasonable care to avoid causing damage to persons, vehicles or property of any kind on or adjoining the highway. Reasonable care in this connection means the care which an ordinarily skilful driver or rider would have exercised under all the circumstances. The steps to be taken to perform this duty of taking reasonable care have been laid down in a more detailed form in several sets of circumstances which are of commonplace occurrence, but, as in other spheres of negligence, the law continues to develop by improving constantly that standard of ordinary reasonable care required in modern traffic conditions if the desirable object of avoiding accidental injury is to be achieved. As an illustration of this trend towards a very much higher standard of care being observed by highway users an important safety measure was introduced by the Road Safety Act 1967, Part 1 of which created the offence of driving or being in charge of a motor-vehicle on a road or other public place with blood-alcohol concentration above a prescribed limit.[50]

[48a] See Hovercraft (Civil Liability) Order 1971, which became operative on June 9, 1971. It applies to the carriage of passengers and baggage by hovercraft the principles of liability applying to their carriage by air, with modifications, but applies to the carriage of cargo by hovercraft and to third party liability in respect of hovercraft the principles, with modifications, that apply in maritime law.

[49] Defined by s. 4 (1) as meaning: " any area, whether on land or elsewhere, which is designed, equipped, set apart or commonly used for affording facilities for the arrival and departure of hovercraft."

[49a] As regards a learner driver, see § 858a, *post*.

[50] s. 7.

813 **The Highway Code.** Originally the Road Traffic Act 1930, s. 45, provided that the Minister of Transport should prepare a code, called the " Highway Code," comprising such directions as appeared to him to be proper for the guidance of persons using roads. This section is replaced by section 74 of the Road Traffic Act 1960, which provides that the Highway Code shall continue to have effect but it may be revised from time to time by the Minister as he thinks fit. The current revised edition of the Highway Code was issued in 1968. The effect of this code is set out in section 74 (5) of the 1960 Act as follows:

" A failure on the part of a person to observe a provision of the Highway Code shall not of itself render that person liable to criminal proceedings of any kind, but any such failure may in any proceedings (whether civil or criminal, and including proceedings for an offence under this Act) be relied upon by any party to the proceedings as tending to establish or to negative any liability which is in question in those proceedings."

14 The effect of this subsection appears to be that failure by any person to observe any provision of the Highway Code is prima facie evidence of negligence on the part of that person. This, however, is not quite clear as there are certain of the provisions, particularly those relating to pedestrians, non-observance of which would not appear to be negligence. For example, paragraph 1, to the effect that on a footpath the pedestrian is not to walk next to the kerb with his back to the traffic, deals with conduct on the part of a pedestrian which is not negligence at common law, and it cannot be supposed that the Act intended to make so important a change as to alter the common law in this respect. Greer L.J. has said [51]: " The code is not binding as a statutory regulation; it is only something which may be regarded as information and advice to drivers. It does not follow that, if they fail to carry out that which is provided for by the code, they are necessarily negligent. It only provides that they may be found to be negligent if they do not carry out the provisions of the code. Nor is it sufficient excuse for them to say, in answer to a claim for negligence: 'We did everything that is provided for in the code.'" On the other hand compliance with the provisions of the Highway Code does not necessarily absolve a person from being guilty of negligence.[52]

5 **Statutory regulations under Road Traffic Act 1960.** In addition to the Highway Code there are various regulations made under the Road Traffic Act 1960, s. 64, regulating the use and construction of motor-vehicles on roads. Failure to comply with these regulations is a matter to be taken into account in deciding whether there is negligence.

The driver or rider of a vehicle on the road may have observed the

[51] *Croston* v. *Vaughan* [1937] 4 All E.R. 249, 252.

[52] *White* v. *Broadbent and B.R.S.* [1958] Crim.L.R. 129. See also (traffic lights incidents) *Godsmark* v. *Knight Bros.* (*Brighton*), *The Times*, May 12, 1960; *Tingle Jacobs & Co.* v. *Kennedy* [1964] 1 W.L.R. 638n.

Highway Code and all statutory regulations and still be guilty of negligence. Speaking of the regulations requiring motor-cars to be fitted with a stop-light, Scott L.J. said[53]: " I cannot think that the mechanical directions contained in S.R. & O. 1935, No. 897, were intended to relieve drivers from what I may call common-sense action in emergencies," adding: " I think that the code and the regulations contained in S.R. & O. 1935, No. 897, still leave upon every driver a common law duty of taking appropriate action outside the code and the regulations in circumstances where it becomes essential in the interest of safety."

816 **Rule of the road.** The rule of the road is that when two vehicles are approaching each other from opposite directions, each must go " on the left or near side of the road for the purpose of allowing " the other to pass.[54] Failure to observe this rule is prima facie evidence of negligence.[55] No doubt, if there is no other traffic on the road, the driver of a vehicle may drive on the crown of the road or even on his offside, but, if so, he must keep a better lookout and use more care than if he were driving on his proper side[56]; if, while he is driving otherwise than on his near side, other traffic approaches and is put in a position of having to act quickly in an emergency, as a result of which a collision occurs, he will be liable because of his negligence in driving on the wrong side of the road.[57] For the effect of white lines see *post*, § 819.

This rule applies to the riders and drivers of animals as well as of vehicles.

The Highway Code expresses the rule as follows: " Keep to the left except when you intend to overtake, or turn right, or when you have to pass stationary vehicles or pedestrians in the road."[58] Similarly, with regard to horses which are ridden the code provides: " If you are riding a horse, keep to the left."[59] As to led horses see *post*, § 846.

817 The fact that a collision occurs on a driver's wrong side of the road is not conclusive evidence of negligence against him, because the circumstances may be such as to make it reasonable for him to depart from the ordinary rule of the road,[60] but it throws upon him the burden of proving the circumstances which made it reasonable for him to depart from the ordinary rule.

It has been said that " the rulc as to the proper side of the road

[53] *Croston* v. *Vaughan* [1937] 4 All E.R. 249, 261. *Cf. Wintle* v. *Bristol Tramways and Carriage Co.* (1917) 86 L.J.K.B. 240, 936.
[54] Highways Act 1835, s. 78, which imposes a penalty for breach of the section. The Act adopts the old common law rule of the road.
[55] *Chaplin* v. *Hawes* (1828) 3 C. & P. 554.
[56] *Pluckwell* v. *Wilson* (1832) 5 C. &. P. 375; *Aston* v. *Heaven* (1797) 2 Esp. 533.
[57] *Chaplin* v. *Hawes, supra.*
[58] Highway Code, para. 29.
[59] Para. 138.
[60] *Wayde* v. *Lady Carr* (1823) 2 Dowl. & Ry. 255; *Wallace* v. *Bergius*, 1915 S.C. 205 (vehicles A and B approach each other from opposite directions on the same side of the road, A on its proper side and B on its wrong side, and when collision is imminent, A swerves to its wrong side, B at the same time swerving to its proper side causing a collision—B is liable to A).

does not apply with respect to foot-passengers; and as regards the foot-passengers the carriages may go on whichever side of the road they please." [61] The rule, so stated, however, is misleading. The rule of the road is, no doubt, primarily a rule regulating the course of vehicles passing each other, but it leads to the result that all persons, including pedestrians, may reasonably expect that vehicles will be driving on or near their near side of the road in anticipation of meeting approaching traffic, and those persons will regulate their actions accordingly. A pedestrian must keep a careful lookout, both before and during the crossing of a road,[62] but if a vehicle on its wrong side of the road collides with a pedestrian, the driver must explain how his position on the road is consistent with the exercise of reasonable care on his part.[63] When traffic is held up, no attempt should be made to gain a forward position by encroaching on the offside of the road, or as the Highway Code expresses it " in a traffic hold-up, do not try to ' jump the queue,' [64] by cutting into another lane, or by overtaking the vehicles waiting in front of you."

818 **Motorways.** The motorways are " special roads " provided or to be provided in pursuance of a scheme under the Special Roads Act 1949, s. 1,[65] and the Highways Act 1959, s. 11. Motorways are the first efforts to bring speed with safety for modern traffic requirements and to relieve the congested conditions of the country's main road systems. Accordingly they are so designed to exclude all sharp bends, crossroads, roundabouts and traffic-lights. Any driver who desires to join or leave a motorway can only do so from the left-hand side, whilst all crossing traffic and vehicles which require to turn right are carried across by overhead bridges or underpasses beneath the roadway itself. The result of all these provisions is that it is possible to maintain higher average speeds compared with other main roads. A special section, " Motorway Driving " is included in the Highway Code since safety on motorways is of first importance and it is essential that all who use them should observe strictly these additional rules. The Road Traffic Act 1960, s. 37, provides for regulations to be made to limit the classes of vehicles which may use these roads [66] and there are special rules which apply to the traffic on them contained in the Motorways Traffic Regulations 1959.[67] Some types of vehicle, specifically excluded from the motorways, are: pedal-cycles; motor-cycles not exceeding 50 c.c. capacity; invalid carriages; certain slow-moving vehicles carrying oversized loads (except by special

61 *Cotterill* v. *Starkey* (1839) 8 C. & P. 691, *per* Patteson J.; see also *Lloyd* v. *Ogleby* (1859) 5 C.B.(N.S.) 667.
62 See Highway Code, paras. 6–12 which seem to embody the common law rules.
63 See *M'Kechnie* v. *Couper* (1887) 14 R. 345; *Clerk* v. *Petrie* (1879) 6 R. 1076; *Smith* v. *Browne* (1891) 28 L.R.Ir. 1; *M'Knight* v. *General Motor Carrying Co.*, 1936 S.C. 17.
64 Highway Code, para. 58.
65 Ss. 1–8 have been repealed by the Highways Act 1959, s. 312 (2), (3), Sched. XXV, and replaced by the provisions of that Act).
66 Sched. II to the Special Roads Act 1949, as amended by the Special Roads (Classes of Traffic) Order 1959, S.I. 1959, No. 1280.
67 S.I. 1959, No. 1147.

permission) and agricultural vehicles. Pedestrians, learner drivers and animals are not permitted on motorways either. There is a speed limit of 70 m.p.h. imposed upon the motorways' users except for the vehicles drawing certain types of trailer in which case the speed must not exceed 40 m.p.h. (Motor Vehicles (Speed Limits on Special Roads) Regulations 1959 [68]), and vehicles must be driven in the one direction only.

819 **White line.** A white line [69] has specifically been made a "traffic sign" by section 51 (1) of the Road Traffic Act 1960.[70] A double white line along the middle of the road is of particular significance, because if the nearer line is a continuous one, the vehicle must keep to its own side of it and is prohibited from crossing or straddling it. On the other hand, if the nearer line is a broken one, a vehicle may cross in certain circumstances although the mere presence of a broken line does not mean that it is safe for a vehicle to overtake. Failure to comply with the indication given by a "traffic sign" is an offence under the Act.[71]

820 **Overtaking.** Overtaking must be done on the right-hand or offside of the vehicle overtaken except when the driver in front has signalled that he is going to turn right, but this rule does not necessarily apply at roundabouts, or on one-way roads.[72] Nevertheless, when on a motorway, since the right-hand lanes are free from slow-moving as well as right-turning vehicles, overtaking on the left must never take place.[73] The driver or rider of the overtaking vehicle, before attempting to overtake, should see that it is safe to do so, and should be specially careful at dusk or in fog or mist when it is more difficult to judge speed and distance.[74] A driver should not overtake at or when coming to a corner or bend, a road junction, a pedestrian crossing, the brow of a hill, a level crossing, a hump-backed bridge, or where the road narrows, when to do so would force another vehicle to swerve or to reduce speed or if double unbroken white lines or double white lines with an unbroken line nearest the driver have to be crossed or there is a NO OVERTAKING sign.[75] Well before a driver overtakes, changes direction, slows down or stops, the rear mirror must be used then a signal given to give a clear indication of intention.[76] In all cases it is the duty of the person overtaking to allow an adequate margin of safety between his vehicle and the vehicle overtaken, and to overtake only when he can do so without causing danger to other traffic.[77] A driver who overtook a stationary bus at some traffic lights

[68] S.I. 1959, No. 1279.
[69] See Highway Code, paras. 50–54.
[70] Overruling *Evans* v. *Cross* [1938] 1 K.B. 694.
[71] s. 14.
[72] *Ibid.* para. 66, embodying the common law rule.
[73] *Ibid.* para. 116.
[74] Highway Code, para. 63. A driver was entitled to assume that he could overtake without danger if what he was overtaking gave not the slightest sign that it was going to do something other than what an ordinary motorist might expect: *Clark* v. *Wakelin* (1965) 109 S.J. 295.
[75] *Ibid.* para. 69; *Joseph Eva Ltd.* v. *Reeves* [1938] 2 K.B. 393.
[76] Highway Code, para. 31.
[77] *Leaver* v. *Pontypridd U.D.C.* (1911) 76 J.P. 31; *Umphray* v. *Ganson Bros.*, 1917 S.C. 371.

as they were changing to green and struck the plaintiff who was in the process of crossing the road in front of the bus was held liable on the basis that it was negligent to overtake the bus where he did and that in the circumstances he should have waited until it was half way across the cross-road before attempting to pass it.[78] Having completed the overtaking, the driver should not cut-in, that is, he should not pull in sharply in front of the moving vehicle which he has just overtaken.[79] Animals should be passed slowly, given plenty of room, and, if necessary, or if signalled to do so, the driver should stop.[80]

A driver should use reasonable care while he is being overtaken, and must use reasonable care not to swerve outwards so as to get in the way of the vehicle overtaking him.[81] He should not accelerate while he is being overtaken[82] but if he does, the driver of the overtaking vehicle should fall behind and not attempt to race him. He should allow others to overtake if they want to do so.[83]

If a public conveyance be stationary or about to stop, the driver of the overtaking vehicle ought to anticipate that passengers are likely to be alighting, and should be specially careful to keep a good lookout for them.[84]

821 **Speed.** It is the duty of the driver or rider of a vehicle to travel at a speed which is reasonable under the circumstances. In determining what is reasonable, the nature, condition, and use of the road in question, and the amount of traffic which is actually at the time, or which might reasonably be expected to be on it are important matters to be taken into consideration.[85] The Highway Code provides: "(33) Never break the speed limits for the road or for your vehicle. . . . (34) Never drive so fast that you cannot stop well within the distance you can see to be clear. Go much more slowly if the road is wet or icy, or if there is fog. . . . (40) Drive slowly near schools. . . . (42) When coming to a zebra crossing, be ready to slow down or stop to let people cross. . . ." If the driver of a vehicle sees a pedestrian in time to avoid a collision but does not slacken speed because he thinks there will be no collision if the pedestrian moves normally, and the pedestrian, owing to age or infirmity, does not do so and a collision occurs, the driver will be liable.[86] The maximum permitted speed of certain motor-vehicles is regulated by statute,[87] and if that speed

78 *Shepherd* v. *West (H.) & Son Ltd.* (1962) 106 S.J. 391 (on the question of damages only this case was considered by the House of Lords at [1964] A.C. 326).
79 Highway Code, para. 65.
80 *Ibid.* para. 49. See *Downing* v. *Birmingham & Midland Trams* (1888) 5 T.L.R. 40.
81 See *Milliken* v. *Glasgow Corpn.*, 1918 S.C. 857.
82 Highway Code, para. 67.
83 Highway Code, para. 29.
84 *Christie* v. *Glasgow Corpn.*, 1927 S.C. 273. See Highway Code, para. 38, for further instances of pedestrians who may suddenly emerge.
85 Road Traffic Act 1960, s. 2, which creates three separate offences and imposes penalties upon conviction; they are: (1) driving recklessly; (2) driving at a speed dangerous to the public; (3) driving in a manner dangerous to the public. S. 3 likewise creates two separate offences and provides penalties; they are: (1) driving without due care and attention; (2) driving without reasonable consideration for other persons using the road.
86 *Daly* v. *Liverpool Corpn.* [1939] 2 All E.R. 142.
87 Road Traffic Act 1960, s. 24.

is exceeded it means that a case of negligence is established against the driver.[88] Again, it is an offence to drive a vehicle at a speed exceeding thirty miles an hour on a road in a built-up area, that is, a road where there are street lamps not more than two hundred yards apart or a road to which the speed limit has been applied by order of the Minister of Transport [89]; it is also evidence of negligence to exceed the speed limit in a built-up area, because other traffic and persons in the area may be assumed to regulate their conduct in the expectation that the law will be obeyed.[88]

Where a plaintiff was injured by the negligent driving of a policeman who was riding a motor-cycle in pursuance of his police duties at 60 m.p.h. along a road where the permitted speed was restricted to 40 m.p.h., McNair J. held that a policeman, like any other driver of a motor-vehicle, owes a duty to drive with due care and attention and without exposing members of the public to unnecessary danger and that section 3 of the Road Traffic Act 1934, did not affect his civil liability (now section 25 of the Road Traffic Act 1960).[90] Further where a police constable in the execution of his duty must necessarily exceed the speed limit he must exercise a degree of care and skill proportionate to his speed and remember that the ordinary road user in a built-up area will not expect a motor-vehicle to be driven along at such a speed. It is desirable in such circumstances that particular care should be given to audible or other warning or approach.[91]

822 **Vehicle following another.** The driver of a vehicle following another should allow a sufficient space between the vehicles in which to deal with the ordinary exigencies of traffic. As the Highway Code puts it, " Leave enough space between you and the vehicle in front so that you can pull up safely if it slows down or stops suddenly. The safe rule is never to get closer than the overall stopping distance (set out in the table of shortest stopping distances). But on the open road, in good conditions, a gap of one yard for each m.p.h. of your speed may be enough. On wet or icy roads the gap should be much more. Drop back if an overtaking vehicle fills the gap in front of you." [92] If the driver follows this rule and the leading vehicle stops so suddenly so that he is unable to avoid it, he may not be liable for the damage caused to that vehicle.[93] Whether the leading vehicle will be liable depends on whether the sudden stop was due

88 *Kingman* v. *Seager* [1938] 1 K.B. 397; *Bracegirdle* v. *Oxley* [1947] 1 All E.R. 126. See also the provisions of the Civil Evidence Act 1968, s. 11, which places the burden on the defendant of disproving negligence where he has been convicted of an offence, which is relevant to the issue.

89 Road Traffic Act 1960, s. 19, certain roads, although provided with street lamps, have been freed from the speed limit by Order. In such cases signs to that effect are fixed to the lamp-posts. See also ss. 20 and 21. See Highway Code, para. 33.

90 *Gaynor* v. *Allen* [1959] 2 Q.B. 403.

91 *Dyer* v. *Bannell* (1965) 109 S.J. 216.

92 para. 35.

93 *Brown and Lynn* v. *Western S.M.T. Co.*, 1945 S.C. 31.

to the driver's negligence or to some other cause,[94] *e.g.* where the defendant applied her brakes violently in order to avoid hitting a pheasant, which ran across the road in front of her car, so that the motorist following her was unable to avoid a collision, the defendant was held to be liable.[95] On the other hand where the leading vehicle came to a gradual halt due to a blockage in the fuel system and was run into from behind, it was held that such a breakdown was a foreseeable emergency and the following vehicle's driver was negligent in failing to anticipate that it might have to slow down or stop.[96] However, a driver who intends to slow down, albeit suddenly, whilst driving along a motorway, is under no duty to give any warning of his intention, it being the duty of those following behind to keep clear.[97]

823 **Lookout.** It is the duty of the driver or rider of a vehicle to keep a good lookout. He must look out for other traffic which is or may be expected to be on the road, whether in front of him, behind him or alongside of him, especially at crossroads, junctions and bends,[98] and for traffic-light signals and traffic signs including lines marked on the highway. Disregard of traffic signals and failure to keep a proper lookout is evidence of negligence. When there are pedestrians about, the driver or rider must be ready in case they step from a street refuge or a footpath, or from behind a vehicle or other obstruction, and also be prepared for children, knowing that they may be expected to run suddenly on to the road.[99] When passing a standing vehicle or other obstruction which prevents a clear view of oncoming traffic or pedestrians, care should be taken and a good lookout kept.

A collision with a stationary vehicle on the highway in the daylight is prima facie evidence of negligence. When a tractor came out of a field into a country lane, which was a highway, and collided with a stationary car facing the direction from which the tractor was coming, it was held the tractor driver was liable.[1] The driver was in a legal dilemma. "Either there was room to pass or there was not. If there was room to pass, then the fact that he damaged the plaintiff's vehicle in passing was prima facie evidence of negligence. If there was no room to pass, then he was negligent in attempting to do so when there was no room."[2]

824 **Reversing.** A motorist, before reversing or turning round on the highway, should satisfy himself that it is safe to do so. The Highway Code provides: " (85) Before you reverse make sure that there are no pedestrians—particularly children—or obstructions in the road behind

94 See *Smith* v. *Harris* [1939] 3 All E.R. 960; *Sharp* v. *Avery* [1938] 4 All E.R. 85 (leader of two motor-cycles held liable for leading into a position of danger).
95 *Gussman* v. *Gratton-Storey* (1968) 112 S.J. 884.
96 *Rowlands* v. *Street*, *The Times*, November 22, 1962.
97 *Jungnickel* v. *Laing* (1966) 111 S.J. 19.
98 *Springett* v. *Ball* (1865) 4 F. & F. 472.
99 See Highway Code, paras. 38–41.
1 *Randall* v. *Tarrant* [1955] 1 All E.R. 600.
2 *Randall* v. *Tarrant* [1955] 1 All E.R. 600, *per* Jenkins L.J. at p. 605.

you. Be especially careful about the ' blind area ' behind you—that is, the part of the road which you cannot see from the driving seat. (86) If you cannot see clearly behind, get someone to guide you when you reverse. (87) Never reverse from a side road into a main road."[3]

825 **Collisions in centre of road.** When there is a collision in the highway between two motor-vehicles and there is no evidence pointing to one driver being more to blame than the other, the proper inference is that they are both to blame.[4] So, when there was a collision in the centre of crossroads of equal status and after the accident the defendant said to a policeman, " I was going along the road and we met in the middle," it was held there was a prima facie case that both drivers were to blame. The plaintiff was an innocent passenger and as the defendant called no evidence it was held that the plaintiff recovered in full against the defendant.[5] However, where there was a head-on collision and each party said that he was on his correct side of the road and that it was the other who had swerved but the trial judge was unable to say that one account was more probably correct rather than the other, then the claim and the counterclaim should both be dismissed.[6] When a collision occurred either through the gross negligence of a motorist or through the gross negligence of a motor-cyclist and the judge was unable to say which and dismissed both the claim and the counterclaim, it was held that he should either have made up his mind which was to blame or have held both equally to blame.[7]

826 **Pedestrian crossings.** Crossings should be approached with care. " It is the duty of persons," said Pollock C.B.,[8] " who are driving over a crossing for foot-passengers which is at the entrance of a street, to drive slowly, cautiously, and carefully; but it is also the duty of a foot-passenger to use due care and caution in going upon a crossing at the entrance of a street, so as not to get among the carriages, and thus receive injury."

The Highway Code provides: " (42) When coming to a zebra crossing be ready to slow down or stop to let people cross. You must give way once they have stepped on to the crossing. Signal to other drivers that you mean to slow down or stop " and " (45) At pedestrian crossings controlled by lights, or by a police officer or traffic warden, give way to pedestrians who are still crossing when the signal is given for vehicles to move."

827 Under the Pedestrian Crossings Regulations 1954,[9] special pedestrian

[3] See *M'Knight* v. *General Motor Carrying Co.*, 1936 S.C. 17.

[4] *Baker* v. *Market Harborough Industrial Co-operative Socy.* [1953] 1 W.L.R. 1472 (two motor-vehicles, going in opposite directions, collided in the dark, in the centre of road, both drivers being killed. There was no evidence pointing to one driver being more blameworthy than the other—held, both to blame). That rule would seem to apply even if it be perfectly feasible that neither party was negligent. *Davison* v. *Leggett* (1969) 113 S.J. 409.

[5] *France* v. *Parkinson* [1954] 1 W.L.R. 581.

[6] *Nesterczuk* v. *Mortimore* (1965) 39 A.L.J.R. 288.

[7] *Bray* v. *Palmer* [1953] 1 W.L.R. 1455.

[8] *Williams* v. *Richards* (1852) 3 Car. & Kir. 81.

[9] S.I. 1954, No. 370, amended by Pedestrian Crossings (England) (Amendment) Regs. 1966 (No. 492). See also Road Traffic Regulation Act 1967, ss. 21–23 and ss. 24, 25; School

crossings, usually called " zebra crossings," marked with two or more lighted beacons, black and white stripes and studs to indicate the limits of the crossing, can be made. The effect of such crossings, when made, is that the driver of every vehicle approaching a crossing must, unless he can see that there is no foot-passenger thereon, proceed at such a speed as to be able if necessary to stop before reaching the crossing, and the driver of every vehicle at or approaching a crossing where traffic is not for the time being controlled by a police constable, traffic warden or by light signals must allow free and uninterrupted passage to any foot-passenger who is on the carriage way at the crossing, and every such foot-passenger has precedence over all vehicular traffic at the crossing The effect of these regulations is that if the driver of a vehicle can see, by exercising reasonable care, that there is a pedestrian on the crossing, it is no defence for him to prove that the pedestrian did not look to see that his vehicle was approaching before starting to use the crossing.[10] Specifically, regulation 4 provides: " Every foot passenger on the carriage-way within the limits of an uncontrolled crossing shall have precedence within those limits over any vehicle and the driver of the vehicle shall accord such precedence to the foot passenger, if the foot passenger is on the carriageway within those limits before the vehicle or any part thereof has come onto the carriageway within those limits." Whether or not this regulation created an absolute duty fell to be considered by the Divisional Court in *Burns* v. *Bidder*.[11] The conclusion was reached that on a true construction of regulation 4 the duty imposed was not absolute in all circumstances and that there was no breach in conditions where the driver of a motor-vehicle failed to accord precedence to a pedestrian solely because his control of the vehicle was taken from him by the occurrence of an event outside his possible or reasonable control and in respect of which he was in no way at fault. Thus, for example, a latent defect in the vehicle's braking system may be a good defence. Further if a pedestrian suddenly steps from the footpath onto a crossing just as a vehicle is about to go onto the crossing, so as to give the driver no opportunity of avoiding a collision, provided he is driving with reasonable care having regard to the presence of the crossing, there may be no negligence or breach of statutory duty on his part, and the driver could

Crossing Patrol Order 1954 (No. 681); Pedestrian Crossing Regs. 1958 (No. 305); (Amendment) Regs. 1959 (No. 2296); Pedestrian Crossing (Push Button Control) Regs. 1962 (No. 425). Traffic Signs (School Crossing Patrols) (England and Wales) Regs. 1964 (No. 1859). See *Hoy* v. *Smith* [1964] 1 W.L.R. 1377.

10 *Bailey* v. *Geddes* [1938] 1 K.B. 156. This case appeared to decide that when a pedestrian is hit on a crossing by a motor-vehicle, it was not open to the court to find that there was any contributory negligence on the part of the pedestrian. In the cases cited in note 12 the C.A. held that it did not do so.

11 [1967] 2 Q.B. 227. *Cf.* the decision of Megaw J. in *Kozimor* v. *Adey* (1962) 106 S.J. 431 who said that there was an absolute duty so that a driver was in breach of the regulation, if in fact he collided with or interfered with the free passage of any pedestrian, and the only possible exception was if a suicidal pedestrian deliberately walked in front of a vehicle. He could only be certain of avoiding a breach by approaching the crossing at such a slow speed that he could stop in time to avoid any conceivable use of it by any conceivable pedestrian, however unexpected and however foolish. Nevertheless it is submitted that the view of the Divisional Court is to be preferred.

be found not liable,[12] although more usually the responsibility for causing the accident will be shared between the pedestrian and driver in similar circumstances.[13]

828 For the pedestrian the Highway Code provides: "(13) You have no priority at a zebra crossing until you have stepped on it, but, when you do, traffic must give way to you. Always allow vehicles plenty of time to slow down or stop before you start to cross, especially if the road is wet or icy. (14) Although drivers must give way to you once you are on the crossing, look right and left as you cross—even if one driver has given way, another might not have seen you, or might try to overtake."

Where the driver of an omnibus approaching a crossing was unable to see whether there was a pedestrian on the crossing or not because a taxicab obscured his view and a pedestrian came on the crossing from behind the taxicab at a time when the omnibus was so near that a collision could not be avoided, it was held that the driver was in breach of the regulations and liable, but that the pedestrian was also negligent in crossing without first seeing that the traffic lights were in her favour and consequently both parties were equally to blame.[14]

829 **Traffic lights.** It is an offence under section 14 of the Road Traffic Act 1960,[15] for any driver or cyclist to disobey a traffic light signal and it is an offence under section 15 of the Act for any pedestrian likewise to disobey a police constable's directions, when he is engaged in regulating the vehicular traffic in the road. If a pedestrian starts to cross a road on a pedestrian crossing while the lights are in his favour, he should be allowed free and uninterrupted passage over the crossing, even though the lights change in the meantime. But if there is a refuge in the road and when the pedestrian reaches the refuge the lights change, it will be negligence on the part of the pedestrian to step into the road without using due care.[16] The Highway Code provides: "(47) When turning at a road junction give way to pedestrians who are crossing." Where the plaintiff pedestrian had begun to cross the road at a junction controlled by traffic lights, which were in his favour, and the defendant's motor-car emerged from a side road, then turned to its right and struck the plaintiff, who had almost reached the centre of the road refuge, it was held that the defendant was wholly liable, the plaintiff being under no duty to safeguard himself against such atrocious driving.[17]

12 *Chisholm* v. *London Passenger Transport Board* [1939] 1 K.B. 426; *Sparks* v. *Edward Ash Ltd.* [1943] K.B. 223. See also *Knight* v. *Sampson* [1938] 3 All E.R. 309.

13 *e.g. Maynard* v. *Rogers* (1970) 114 S.J. 320 (pedestrian $\frac{2}{3}$: motorist $\frac{1}{3}$).

14 *L.P.T.B.* v. *Upson* [1949] A.C. 155. See also *Gibbons* v. *Kahl* [1956] 1 Q.B. 59; *Levine* v. *Morris* [1970] 1 W.L.R. 71.

15 (Amended by the Road Traffic Regulation Act 1967, Sched. 6); Traffic Signs Regs., 1964. reg. 34 (1) (*a*) (S.I. 1964, No. 1857); see *Ryan* v. *Smith* [1967] 2 Q.B. 893 (where the motor car was already partially over the stop line when the lights were at green before it had to stop but it proceeded farther after the signals changed to red).

16 *Wilkinson* v. *Chetham-Strode* [1940] 2 K.B. 310. See also the provisions of the Highway Code, paras. 6, 7 and 10. *Cf.* where pedal cyclist enters crossing on green light but the lights change: *Radburn* v. *Kemp, The Times*, July 6, 1971.

17 *Frank* v. *Cox* (1967) 111 S.J. 670.

Crossing a road in disobedience to a traffic light is negligence. A driver crossing when the lights are in his favour is under no duty to look out for traffic crossing in disobedience to the lights, but if he sees such traffic he must use reasonable care to avoid a collision.[18]

830 **Road junctions.** When coming from a side road into a main road, the driver or rider of a vehicle should select such a moment as will allow him to enter the main road with safety. The Highway Code[19] provides: " (70) Always approach a junction with great care and be ready to stop. Before crossing or turning, look right then left, then right again. Do not go on until you are sure it is safe, and that you will not block the road. Do not rely on signals to go on given by anybody except a police officer or traffic warden. (71) At a junction with double broken white lines across the road (it may also have a Give Way sign) you must slow down and be ready to stop to let traffic on the major road go by first. (72) You must stop at a junction with a Stop sign and double unbroken white lines across the road. Wait for a safe gap in the traffic before you go on." Further it is an offence to disobey a " Slow " or a " Halt " sign.[20] The effect of these rules is that although the vehicle on the minor road must give way to the vehicle on the major road[21] it is also the duty of the vehicle on the major road when approaching a minor road to do so with caution,[22] but if the possibility of danger is reasonably apparent, then for the driver of the vehicle on the major road to take no precautions in such circumstances is negligence.[23] In *McIntyre* v. *Coles* Sellers L.J. said: " It is a well recognised and conventional practice, rather than a rule, that where vehicles are approaching in that way with a risk of collision or where there is doubt as to the priority, the vehicle which has the other on its right-hand side is the give-way vehicle. It may not be established as obligatory but it is a very salutary guiding rule.[24] The Highway Code

18 *Eva* v. *Reeves* [1938] 2 K.B. 393; *Ward* v. *L.C.C.* [1938] 2 All E.R. 341 (fire-engine not entitled to disregard traffic lights); *Knight* v. *Cooper Supply Services* (1965) 109 S.J. 358 (the driver entering crossroads with the lights in his favour was not guilty of contributory negligence if he collided with another vehicle entering the crossing against the lights); *Davis* v. *Hassan* (1967) 117 New L.J. 72; *Butters* v. *Fenner & Co.* (1967) 117 New L.J. 213; *Ramoo* v. *Gan Soo Swee* [1971] 1 W.L.R. 1014.

19 See also *Macandrew* v. *Tillard*, 1909 S.C. 78; *Campbell* v. *Train*, 1910 S.C. 475.

20 Road Traffic Act 1960, s. 14. *Tollhurst* v. *Webster* (1936) 53 T.L.R. 174; *Anderson* v. *St. Andrews Ambulance Assn.*, 1943 S.C. 248, where the effect of the " Slow, Major Road Ahead " sign is discussed. The sign " Slow " means proceed at such a speed that you can stop if, when you get to the crossing, you find somebody in the process of crossing or about to cross: *Buffel* v. *Cardox* (*Great Britain*) *Ltd.* [1950] 2 All E.R. 878n.

21 In *Harding* v. *Hinchcliffe*, *The Times*, April 8, 1964, the defendant, waiting in his motor-car to drive out of the minor road and seeing a bus driver signal on the major road indicating an intention to turn left, moved forward and collided with a motor-cyclist who was in the act of overtaking the bus, their respective presences being unknown to the other. It was held that the defendant was negligent in not waiting until he could see that the major road was clear and in that he should have anticipated that there might have been a vehicle behind the bus.

22 See also *Robertson* v. *Wilson*, 1912 S.C. 1276; *M'Nair* v. *Glasgow Corpn.*, 1923 S.C. 398; *Hutchinson* v. *Leslie*, 1927 S.C. 95.

23 *Lang* v. *London Transport Executive* [1959] 1 W.L.R. 1168. See also *Williams* v. *Fullerton*, *The Times*, March 14, 1961, where the Court of Appeal held that a driver on a major road approaching a junction was under a duty to look out for and guard against excessive speed by drivers on minor roads. *Watkins* v. *Moffatt* (1967) 111 S.J. 719.

24 [1966] 1 W.L.R. 831, 834.

also provides: " (78) Well before you turn right use your mirror to make sure you know the position and movement of traffic behind you. When it is safe, give a right turn signal and, as soon as you can do so safely take up a position just left of the middle of the road or in the space marked for right-turning traffic. If you can, leave room for other vehicles to pass on the left. Wait until there is a safe gap between you and any oncoming vehicle; then make the turn but do not cut the corner. Remember—Mirror—Signal—Manoeuvre. (80) Well before you turn left, use your mirror and give a left turn signal. Do not swing out to the right before or after the turn. Make sure a cyclist or a motor cyclist is not coming up from behind on your left."

831 **Roundabouts.** The Highway Code provides: " (81) Give way to traffic coming from your immediate right, unless road markings indicate otherwise, but keep moving if the way is clear. (82) Unless the approach road and the roundabout itself are clear, or local conditions, or road markings indicate otherwise, you should:

when turning left

Approach in the left-hand lane; keep to that lane in the roundabout and leave by that lane. Use the left turn indicator on approach and through the roundabout.

when going forward

Approach in the left-hand lane; keep to that lane in the roundabout. Use the left turn indicator at the exit before the one to be taken. If conditions dictate (for example, if the left-hand lane is blocked) approach in the right-hand lane; keep to that lane in the roundabout. Use the left turn indicator at the exit before the one to be taken.

when turning right

Approach in the right-hand lane; use the right turn indicator before entering the roundabout and maintain this signal while keeping to the right-hand lane in the roundabout; change to the left turn indicator at the exit before the one to be taken.

(83) When going forward or turning right, leave the roundabout in the left-hand lane of the exit road unless conditions dictate use of right-hand lane. (84) When in a roundabout, look out for vehicles crossing in front of you to leave by the next exit."

832 **Signals.** The driver or rider of a vehicle should give the proper signal before he moves out or overtakes, before he stops, slows down or changes his direction and all signals should be given clearly and in good time to give an indication of intention to other users of the highway. He must watch out for the signals of other drivers and act promptly. Further, he must make certain that the direction indicator if it be used gives the signal intended, and that it is cancelled immediately after use.[25] Failure

[25] Highway Code, paras. 26, 27 and 28.

to do so is evidence of negligence.[26] He should obey the signals given by police constables or traffic wardens regulating traffic[27]; but reliance on signals to proceed given by unauthorised persons[28] will be no defence if, without such signals, it would have been negligence to proceed.[29]

A motor-vehicle may be fitted with a stop-light for the purpose of intimating the intention of the driver of the vehicle to stop or slow down. The application of the stop-light does not absolve the driver of the vehicle from the necessity of giving a hand signal of his intention to stop or slow down when the circumstances render it necessary to do so, and a driver has been held to be negligent who failed to give a hand signal, although the stop-light was properly operated.[30] But the provision of stop-lights and direction indicators, whilst not compulsory, is subject to regulations.[31]

833 **Lights.** In the hours of darkness (*i.e.* the time between half an hour after sunset and half an hour before sunrise[32]) it is necessary for the driver or rider of a vehicle to carry lights so as to indicate his position on the road and the direction in which he is going or intending to go. To indicate its position, every vehicle (except, *post*) is required by statute to carry two front lamps, each showing a white light visible from a reasonable distance, and two rear lamps showing a red light visible for a reasonable distance.[33] Every vehicle on any road must also carry attached to it two unobscured and efficient red reflectors each facing to the rear[34] unless it is one of a class which has been exempted by a regulation made by the Minister of Transport[35]; a horse-drawn agricultural vehicle is required to carry one front light which must be attached to the offside of the vehicle; a bicycle, without a sidecar, a tricycle and an invalid carriage are required to carry one front lamp showing a white light; whilst only a single lamp showing a red light to the rear and only a single red reflector are necessary in the case of a bicycle or tricycle not propelled by mechanical power or of a bicycle so propelled but not having a

[26] The duty of the driver of a vehicle with a left-hand drive is discussed in *Daborn* v. *Bath Tramways Motor Co.* [1946] 2 All E.R. 333.

[27] Road Traffic Act 1960, s. 14.

[28] If such person, standing beside his parked motor-vehicle, elects to give a signal to another motorist, although he is under no obligation to give any signs at all, as a result of which the latter overtakes the stationary vehicle he owes a duty to him to give him an accurate signal, which will not result for example in him driving forward into head-on collision with another vehicle approaching from the opposite direction: *Grange Motors (Cwmbran)* v. *Spencer* [1969] 1 W.L.R. 53.

[29] Highway Code: "(70) Do not rely on signals to go on given by anybody except a police officer or traffic warden."

[30] *Croston* v. *Vaughan* [1938] 1 K.B. 540. *Cf. Jung Nickel* v. *Laing* (1966) 111 S.J. 19.

[31] Motor Vehicles (Construction and Use) Regulations 1969 (S.I. 1969, No. 321) regs. 31 and 32.

[32] Road Transport Lighting Act 1957, s. 17. Both this Act and the Road Transport Lighting (Amendment) Act 1958 have been amended and explained by the Road Transport Lighting Act 1967. Further see Road Vehicles Lighting Regulations 1959 (S.I. 1959, No. 1869), the Road Vehicles Lighting Regulations 1964 (S.I. 1964, No. 205); Road Vehicles Lighting (Amendment) Regulations 1965 (S.I. 1965, No. 870).

[33] Road Transport Lighting Act 1957, s. 1 (1).

[34] *Ibid.* s. 1 (2).

[35] *Ibid.* s. 10 (3).

sidecar.[36] Amber-coloured reflectors on the pedals of bicycles and tricycles are permitted.[37]

834 When a vehicle carries a load projecting laterally, a lamp showing a white light must be carried so that no part of the load projects outwards more than twelve inches from the lamp,[38] and if the load projects to the rear, a lamp showing a red light must be carried, so that no part of the load projects to the rear more than three and a half feet from that lamp.[39] When a vehicle is drawing one or more vehicles, the vehicle or vehicles being drawn need not carry lamps showing lights to the front and only the rearmost vehicle need show the requisite red reflectors[34] and red lights[33] to the rear.[40]

To indicate direction, it is an offence to show a red light to the front and to show any light, other than a red light, to the rear, except that, when reversing, a white light may be shown on the rear of the vehicle.[41] It is permitted, however, that a vehicle can carry a lamp showing a light to the rear for the purposes of internal illumination, number-plate illumination, trafficator signals, taximeter, and, in the case of public passenger vehicles illuminated destination boards.[42]

Breach of the statutory duty to carry the lights prescribed by the Road Transport Lighting Acts does not of itself give a person who suffers damage in consequence thereof any right to damages.[43] This is because the duty is a public duty only, punishable by the penalties prescribed by the Acts, and not a duty enforceable by any individual aggrieved. Driving in the dark without proper lights, however, is evidence of negligence.[44] This is because " a driver must make allowance for the appearance on the road of lorries and other vehicles, and he must exercise common prudence by showing such an amount of light as would warn an approaching vehicle of the driver and his trolley; and it may well be that, where it is the prevailing custom to carry two lights, as was the case on this road, . . . an approaching vehicle might rely on such custom and be prevented from taking the necessary precautions by reason of the absence of such extra light." [45] Accordingly, failure to carry the usual lights, which misleads the driver of another vehicle and causes a collision, is negligence,[46] and likewise if lights are used in a manner which deceives such driver. Thus where the defendants' lorry was parked on the offside of the road at night with its headlamps on and it was run into by the plaintiff, each party

36 *Ibid.* s. 6.
37 Road Transport Lighting (Amendment) Act 1958, s. 1 (1).
38 Road Transport Lighting Act 1957, s. 8 (1).
39 *Ibid.* s. 8 (2).
40 *Ibid.* s. 9.
41 *Ibid.* s. 2 (1).
42 *Ibid.* s. 2 (2).
43 *Clarke* v. *Brims* [1947] K.B. 497; *West* v. *Lawson Ltd.*, 1949 S.C. 430.
44 *Baker* v. *Longhurst & Sons Ltd.* [1933] 2 K.B. 461, 464, *per* Scrutton L.J.
45 *Wintle* v. *Bristol Tramways and Carriage Co. Ltd.* (1917) 86 L.J.K.B. 240, 242, 936, *per* Ridley J.
46 *Pressley* v. *Burnett*, 1914 S.C. 874; *Wintle* v. *Bristol Tramways and Carriage Co Ltd.* *supra.*

was held equally to blame in negligence for the accident.[47] Upon arrival at the scene of a fire the brigade parked their fire engine close to the kerb and used only the blue flashing warning lights on top of the fire engine and not the red warning light, although such was available. It was held by the Court of Appeal that as the fire brigade's first duty was owed to those in peril from fire there was no negligence in failing to use the red warning light but that in any event the blue flashing lights were sufficient warning to approaching traffic.[48]

835 In a claim alleging the negligence of the person responsible for a motor-vehicle which, whilst standing unlit on a road at night, was involved in an accident, it was for that person to show that he had taken all reasonable steps to avoid creating or prolonging that vehicle's presence.[49] When a lorry was properly provided with a rear light which later went out without the driver's knowledge, and, without negligence on his part, a collision with an overtaking vehicle in the dark occurred it was held not to impose liability on the lorry owner.[50] Also where the lighting system of a car failed completely through no fault of the driver and it was run into whilst stationary near a street light during the process of its being towed by a lorry, the presumption of negligence which arises from the presence of an unlit car on the road at night was rebutted.[51]

It is negligence to drive a vehicle with inadequate lights so that the driver cannot see an obstruction or traffic on the road in front of him in time to stop or avoid it.[52]

836 **Headlamps.** The Highway Code provides: "(89) If you are dazzled by approaching headlamps slow down or stop; (90) When it is dark, drive so that you can stop well within the distance you can see in your headlamps to be clear ahead; (91) Use dipped headlamps at night in built-up areas unless the street lighting is so good that they are not needed. (92) You must use headlamps on all roads where there is no street lighting." As far as the general law is concerned, while it is not negligence to drive with bright headlights, there may well be circumstances under which the failure to dip headlights is negligence, as, for example, if the headlights are so bright as to dazzle an approaching motorist in front of whom is a pedestrian within such a distance that the approaching motorist collides with him, though he is exercising reasonable care.[53] The Highway Code also provides: "(93) Dip your headlamps when meeting other vehicles or road users, and before they dazzle the driver of a vehicle travelling

[47] *Chisman* v. *Electromation (Export)* (1969) 113 S.J. 246.
[48] *Amos* v. *Glamorgan C.C.* (1967) 66 L.G.R. 166.
[49] *Moore* v. *Maxwells of Emsworth* [1968] 1 W.L.R. 1077 the Court of Appeal held that the presumption of negligence arising from the presence of an unlit vehicle on a road after dark was rebutted by the evidence.
[50] *Maitland* v. *Raisbeck* [1944] K.B. 689 (the driver of the overtaking vehicle, a bus, was not negligent, so that the injured passengers in the bus had no remedy).
[51] *Parish* v. *Judd* [1960] 1 W.L.R. 867.
[52] *Pronek* v. *Winnipeg, Selkirk and Lake Winnipeg Ry.* [1933] A.C. 61.
[53] *Saville* v. *Bache* (1969) 113 S.J. 228 (a driver is under a duty to dip his headlights unless there is some good reason for keeping them on at full beam).

in the same direction in front of you; (94) Use your headlamps in daytime mist or fog if the light is bad—to see and be seen.[54] (95) The flashing of headlamps has the same meaning as sounding your horn—to let another road user know you are there." [55]

However a vehicle which stops to allow another vehicle to move across its intended path by flashing its headlights was held to mean only " come along so far as I am concerned " and was not intended to exonerate the crossing vehicle's driver from satisfying himself that it was safe to continue crossing, *e.g.* from some other vehicle overtaking the vehicle which had stopped.[56]

837 **Sounding horns.** Sounding a horn or a bell may be useful to warn other traffic of the approach of a vehicle, but it does not absolve the driver or rider of his duty to take care or give him the right of way.[57] The omission to sound a horn or a bell is " a collateral fact only, and not an independent act of negligence " [58]; by itself it is not evidence of negligence, but it may be taken into account, with other circumstances, in determining whether the driver or rider was negligent.

Normally there is no need to hoot the horn when overtaking another vehicle which is going straight ahead but there is a need if there is a movement of the overtaken vehicle such as to put the overtaking driver on inquiry as to what it is going to do.[59]

838 **Defective vehicle.** The driver or rider of a vehicle is bound to use reasonable care to keep it under proper control, and this involves a duty to use reasonable care to keep it in proper condition so that proper control can be exercised. There is no absolute duty to keep the vehicle in proper condition. Accordingly, where, owing to a defect in the axle of a motor-lorry, a wheel came off while the lorry was being driven in the highway and damaged a van, and it was proved that the lorry had, two days before, been returned from the makers where it had been overhauled and repaired, the owners of the lorry were held not liable.[60]

The owner of a vehicle must take such steps as a prudent owner would take to keep his vehicle in proper repair. If he fails to take such care so that the vehicle is defective, for example, if the steering of a motor-car becomes so worn that the driver cannot control the car,[61] it is evidence

[54] The defendant's contention that it was not necessary to use dipped headlights during fog failed in the circumstances in the case: *Burgess* v. *Hearn, The Guardian,* March 25, 1965.

[55] Highway Code, para. (95).

[56] *Clarke* v. *Winchurch* [1969] 1 W.L.R. 69.

[57] The Motor Vehicles (Construction and Use) Regulations 1969 (S.I 1969, No. 321), require the horn to be in working order. The horn must not be sounded at night (11.30 p.m.–7 a.m.) in a built-up area. See Highway Code, para. (96).

[58] *Per* McCardie J. in *Wintle* v. *Bristol Tramways and Carriage Co. Ltd.* (1917) 86 L.J.K.B. 240.

[59] *Holdack* v. *Bullock Bros.* (*Electrical*) *& Co.* (1965) 109 S.J. 238.

[60] *Phillips* v. *Britannia Hygienic Laundry Co.* [1923] 1 K.B. 539, affirmed [1923] 2 K.B. 832. *Stennett* v. *Hancock* [1939] 2 All E.R. 578 is a similar case. But see now the Motor Vehicles (Tests) Regulations 1960 (S.I. 1960, No. 1083).

[61] *Hutchins* v. *Maunder* (1920) 37 T.L.R. 72, where the defendant was held liable, although he was not negligent in failing to discover the defect. In this respect, this case goes too far. See *Phillips* v. *Britannia Hygienic Laundry Co., supra.* In *The European* (1885) 10 P.D. 99,

of negligence on his part. The vehicle must also be of such size and design that it can be safely used on the road. " If a man places on the streets a vehicle so wholly unmanageable as necessarily to be a continuing danger to other vehicles, either at all times or under special conditions of weather, I have no doubt he does it at his peril, and that he is responsible for injuries arising therefrom, even though there has been no negligence in the management of his vehicle." [62] But where a furniture van, while being driven along the road, was blown over by the wind onto the plaintiff's stationary car, it was held that the van owner was not liable, as the van was of a type in common use and the owner neither knew nor had reason to think that it was likely to be blown over.[63] Not only must proper care be taken to see that the vehicle is in a roadworthy condition before it is used on the road, but proper care must also be taken to see that it is properly loaded. When a vehicle was sent out with a load which was negligently secured and was driven under a low bridge so that the load was thrown off and injured a person in the highway, the owner was held liable.[64]

839 If the owner or his servant is driving the vehicle, the fact that the vehicle overturns on the highway,[65] that a wheel comes off,[66] that a tyre bursts,[67] or that any part of the vehicle breaks and causes a collision,[68] is evidence on which, in the absence of a satisfactory explanation, negligence on the part of the owner can be found. Where a fatal accident occurred because of a sudden brake failure, due to the collapse of that part of the brake fluid pipe which had corroded unobserved at a hidden and inaccessible point, and despite the owners' reliance upon careful weekly visual inspections, the House of Lords held that the owners had failed to discharge the onus of proving that in all the circumstances, which they knew or ought to have known, they had taken all steps that were necessary to avoid danger.[69]

840 **Skidding.** The fact that a vehicle, such as a motor-car, is liable to skid on the road in certain circumstances does not make it a nuisance to use that vehicle on the road.[70] It does, however, make it incumbent on the driver to use additional care proportioned to the greater risk, both with regard to his driving and also to the condition of his tyres.

If a vehicle, driven in the roadway, collides with a fixed object or a pedestrian on the footpath, the mere fact of the accident is evidence

it was held that to sail a ship with a patent steam steering gear, which got out of order and caused a collision, a few days after a previous breakdown of the gear, was negligence, although the gear had been overhauled in the meantime.

62 *Wing* v. *London General Omnibus Co.* [1909] 2 K.B. 652, 665, *per* Fletcher Moulton L.J.

63 *Shaw* v. *B.G. Services* (1939) 6 L.J.N.C.C.R. 226.

64 *Farrugia* v. *G.W. Ry.* [1947] 2 All E.R. 565.

65 *Halliwell* v. *Venables* (1930) 99 L.J.K.B. 353.

66 *Phillips* v. *Britannia Hygienic Laundry Co.* [1923] 1 K.B. 539. It is not, by itself, evidence of negligence on the part of the repairers: *Britannia Hygienic Laundry Co.* v. *Thornycroft* (1926) 95 L.J.K.B. 237.

67 *Barkway* v. *South Wales Transport Co.* [1950] 1 All E.R. 392, 394, 395.

68 *Templeman* v. *Haydon* (1852) 12 C.B. 507; *Welsh* v. *Lawrence* (1818) 2 Chit. 262; *Cotterill* v *Starkey* (1839) 8 C. & P. 691.

69 *Henderson* v. *Henry E. Jenkins & Sons* [1970] A.C. 282.

70 *Wing* v. *L.G.O. Co.* [1909] 2 K.B. 652; *Parker* v. *L.G.O. Co.* (1909) 101 L.T. 623.

of negligence against the driver, even if it is proved that his vehicle skidded onto the footpath.[71] In the past the mere fact of a skid was thought to be a neutral circumstance helping neither party. It was no defence to the driver to prove that his vehicle skidded, and equally it was no evidence of negligent driving on his part.[72] The fact of a skid may suggest that the driver was driving too fast or applied his brakes too suddenly having regard to the road conditions prevailing at the time, so as to be evidence of negligence on his part; but the skid may be consistent with the exercise by the driver of all due caution, and may be due either to the negligence of a third party or to inevitable accident.[73] Nevertheless the modern approach has been firmly asserted by McKenna J. who expressed the view correctly that an unexplained and violent skid may itself be evidence of negligent driving.[74]

841 **Opening doors.** It is negligence to open the door of a vehicle so as to strike a pedestrian or cyclist on the highway without first taking reasonable care to see that it is safe to open the door. The Highway Code provides: "(98) Before opening any door of a vehicle make sure there is no one on the road, pavement or footpath close enough to be hit by the door. Be particularly careful about cyclists. Get out on the side nearer the kerb whenever you can, and make sure your passengers (especially children) do so, too."

842 **Leaving vehicles on highway.** If a vehicle is left on the highway, there is a duty on the person in charge of it to leave it in such a place that it will not be a danger to other users of the highway.[75] The Highway Code expresses the duty as follows:

"(97) Do not park or let your vehicle stand:

1 Where you see these signs:
no parking;
clearway;
yellow lines beside the kerb (see page 43);
double white lines in the middle of the road.

2 Where it would make it difficult for others to see clearly; that is, at or near a:
junction;

71 *Isaac Walton & Co.* v. *Vanguard Motorbus Co.* (1908) 25 T.L.R. 13; *Barnes U.D.C.* v. *L.G.O. Co.* (1908) 100 L.T. 115; *Ellor* v. *Selfridge & Co. Ltd.* (1930) 46 T.L.R. 236; *Liffen* v. *Watson* (1939) 161 L.T. 351 (the report in [1940] 1 K.B. 556 deals solely with damages); *Laurie* v. *Raglan Building Co.* [1942] 1 K.B. 152. The pavement should give security for those persons using it from vehicles using the road and if a pedestrian be injured by a vehicle overlapping the pavement, *e.g.* by a projecting door handle, then the driver may be liable in negligence: *Watson* v. *Whitney & Co.* [1966] 1 W.L.R. 57: *Ottley* v. *L.T.B.*, *The Times*, January 21, 1966 (a pedestrian's foot was run over at a bus stop).

72 *Laurie* v. *Raglan Building Co.*, *supra.*

73 *Hunter* v. *Wright* [1938] 2 All E.R. 621.

74 *Richley* v. *Faull* [1965] 1 W.L.R. 1454; see article: "A skid as evidence of Negligence" (Simmons) 130 J.P.J. 283.

75 It is an offence under the Road Traffic Act 1960, s. 16, to leave a vehicle on any road in such a position or in such circumstances as to be likely to cause danger to other persons using the road.

bend[76];
brow of a hill;
hump-back bridge;
level crossing.

3 Where it would be a danger to other road users; that is:
at or near a bus stop;
on a pedestrian crossing, or on either side of it;
at or near a school entrance;
on a footpath, pavement or cycle path;
on the right-hand side of the road at night (except in a one-way street)[77];
where it would hide a traffic sign.

4 Where it would hold up traffic or inconvenience others; that is:
on a narrow road;
on flyovers, in tunnels or in underpasses (unless there are signs to say you must park there);
on fast main roads (except in a lay-by);
on motorways (except on the hard shoulder in an emergency);
on a single track road, or in a passing place on such a road;
outside a private entrance for vehicles.

5 Where emergency vehicles stop, or go in and out:
hospital entrances;
doctors' entrances;
fire stations;
fire hydrants.

6 Where you would make the road narrow:
opposite an island;
alongside another parked vehicle;
opposite another parked vehicle if this would narrow the road to less than the width of two vehicles;
near road works.

Make sure you always park your vehicle safely. Walk a few more yards rather than cause an accident."

843 It has been held that it is negligence to leave a motor-car unattended on a fairly steep slope, when the hand brake was out of order and the only thing to keep the car in position was a block of wood underneath the wheel[78]; to leave a motor-car unattended on a very steep gradient, so that it remained at rest for half an hour and then, for some unexplained reason, started down the hill[79]; and to leave a motor-lorry at the top of a steep and narrow street unattended, with the engine running, and without

76 When a driver overshot the turning which he was intending to take, then stopped his car on a bend on the main road where he was run into by a motor cyclist, the motorist was held 80 per cent. to blame for the collision: *Waller* v. *Levoi* (1968) 112 S.J. 865.

77 This is now an offence under Regulation 96 of the Motor Vehicles (Construction and Use) Regulations 1969 (S.I. 1969, No. 321).

78 *Martin* v. *Stanborough* (1924) 41 T.L.R. 1.

79 *Parker* v. *Miller* (1926) 42 T.L.R. 408.

taking proper precautions to secure it.[80] Where a lorry broke down at night and was parked on a clearway with the rear lights on but was run into from behind by the plaintiff, it was held that, the lorry being immobile, the driver was not negligent in failing to take it into a side road or on to the verge. Further, in the absence of any evidence of such a practice amongst lorry owners, it was held not to be negligent in failing to provide a torch or flashing light, which would give an earlier warning than the obligatory rear lights of the vehicle itself.[81]

If a motor-vehicle is left standing unattended in a level part of the highway, there is no liability on the owner if trespassers, in attempting to move the vehicle, start it and back it into a shop window.[82] Similarly, if an unhorsed van is left unattended, the owner is not liable if children climb onto the van and are injured.[83]

844 **Horse cases.** It is negligence to leave a horse-drawn vehicle unattended on the highway, and if the horse bolts the owner will be prima facie liable.[84] He will also be prima facie liable if children, playing with the horse, are injured.[85] Where a horse and cart were left standing unattended in the street and a passer-by struck the horse, causing it to back against a shop window, the owner of the horse was held liable, Tindal C.J. saying: " If a man chooses to leave a cart standing in the street he must take the risk of any mischief that may be done." [86] This dictum requires the limitation that the damage must not be too remote. If a horse is tethered in the street, reasonable care must be taken to tether it securely and in such a place that it does not cause damage. Even if it is tethered in a stable or yard adjoining the street, reasonable care must be taken to prevent it from going on the highway.[87]

It is not negligence to remove goods from a cart without putting a person to hold the horse's head.[88]

845 It is negligence to harness to a van a horse which is too big for it and where, under those circumstances, the horse was rubbed against the cross-bar of the shafts of the van and, startled by a slight collision, collided with a stationary omnibus, the owner was held liable.[89] Where a man was driving a gig with a young and spirited horse, without a curb rein, and while he was between a coach and a wagon his horse became frightened, and he pulled the wrong rein and a collision occurred,

[80] *Hambrook* v. *Stokes Bros.* [1925] 1 K.B. 141.
[81] *Butland* v. *Coxhead* (1968) 112 S.J. 465.
[82] *Ruoff* v. *Long & Co.* [1916] 1 K.B. 148.
[83] *Donovan* v. *Union Cartage Co.* [1933] 2 K.B. 71.
[84] *Gayler & Pope Ltd.* v. *B. Davies & Son Ltd.* [1924] 2 K.B. 75, where the cases are reviewed: *Cutler* v. *United Dairies (London) Ltd.* [1933] 2 K.B. 297; *Haynes* v. *Harwood & Son* [1935] 1 K.B. 146. See also *Aldham* v. *United Dairies (London) Ltd.* [1940] 1 K.B. 507.
[85] *Lynch* v. *Nurdin* (1841) 1 Q.B. 29.
[86] *Illidge* v. *Goodwin* (1831) 5 C. & P. 190. Tindal C.J.'s dictum was quoted with approval by the C.A. in *Engelhardt* v. *Farrant* [1897] 1 Q.B. 240.
[87] *Deen* v. *Davies* [1935] 2 K.B. 282.
[88] *Hayman* v. *Hewitt* (1798) Peake's Add.Cas. 170.
[89] *Burkin* v. *Bilezikdji* (1889) 5 T.L.R. 673.

he was held liable.[90] It has been held to be negligence to spur a horse while it is passing so near to another horse that it is able to kick out and strike it or the man leading it,[91] and to harness to a coach a horse without a kicking strap when there are marks of kicks on the panel of the coach.[92] If a horse is being ridden along a narrow road, the driver of a vehicle must exercise great caution in passing it, his duty being to slow down and to give it a wide berth. Should this latter precaution be impracticable because of another vehicle approaching him then the driver should wait before attempting to pass the horse.[93]

846 **Led animals.** The rule of the road as to led horses or other animals is different from the rule applicable to ridden or driven horses or vehicles. The Highway Code expresses it as follows: " (138) If you are riding a horse keep to the left. If you are leading a horse while riding another you should also keep to the left and keep the led animal on your left. (139) If you are on foot, and leading an animal on a road that has no footpath, walk on the right-hand side of the road. Keep between the animal and the traffic, and keep it close to the edge of the road." This is presumably intended to embody the common law rule, which is that the horse should be led along the right-hand or offside of the road with the man who is leading it on the left-hand or near side of the horse.

It is the duty of a person leading or driving an animal or a number of animals along the highway to take reasonable care that they do not cause damage to other users of the highway or to property adjoining the highway.[94] If cattle are driven along the highway it is the duty of the owner to keep them under proper control and to employ an adequate number of persons to enable them to be kept under control.[95] Accordingly, where a drover failed to keep a heifer under proper control, so that she tossed a woman who was walking along the pavement, the owner was held liable.[96] Again, where there was a collision in the highway after dark between a motor-car and one of a number of cows driven by a drover, judgment was given against the owner of the cow on a finding by the jury that the drover was negligent, the negligence alleged being that the cow was not kept under proper control and the drover did not show a light or shout or otherwise give warning.[97] Driving sheep or cattle in the highway after

90 *Wakeman* v. *Robinson* (1823) 1 Bing. 213.
91 *North* v. *Smith* (1861) 10 C.B.(N.S.) 572.
92 *Simson* v. *L.G.O. Co.* (1873) 8 C.P. 390.
93 *Burns* v. *Ellicott* (1969) 113 S.J. 490.
94 *Deen* v. *Davies* [1935] 2 K.B. 282.
95 See Highway Code, para. (140) which recommends that if the driver is accompanied by another person the latter should be sent along the road to warn drivers at places such as bends and brows of hills, where the drivers may not be able to see them. However the failure to provide an extra drover on the crest of the next rise of an undulating country road along which livestock were being driven, in order to warn approaching traffic who would be obscured from vision in the dips of the roadway was held not to be a negligent omission: *Graham* v. *Crawford* [1964] N.Z.L.R. 668.
96 *Pinn* v. *Rew* (1916) 32 T.L.R. 451.
97 *Turnbull* v. *Wieland* (1916) 33 T.L.R. 143. *Cf. Ludlam* v. *W. E. Peel & Son* (1939) 83 S.J. 832, where the owner succeeded.

dark without a light is not, of itself, evidence of negligence.[98] The Highway Code, however, provides: " (140) If you are herding animals along or across the road. . . . Carry lights after sunset."

847 In *Turner* v. *Coates* [99] a young unbroken colt was being taken along the highway after dark. It was not led, but was allowed to go loose between a mare which was being led by a boy in front and a trap which was being driven by its owner, a farmer, behind. A cyclist came along the road in the opposite direction and the colt, startled by the light, ran across the road and collided with the cyclist. It was held that the farmer was liable for his negligence in sending the colt on the highway without exercising proper control, and for failing to give warning to the cyclist of the presence of the colt.

As regards the motorist who meets animals on the highway it is recommended that he goes slowly when driving past giving them plenty of room and being prepared to stop if necessary. Care should be taken not to frighten animals by sounding the horn or revving up the engine. A watch must be kept for animals being led on the motorist's side of the road especially at a left-hand bend where extra care should be taken.[1]

848 **Dog on highway.** A collision with a dog in the highway imposes no liability on the owner of the dog, unless there is evidence of a mischievous propensity on the dog's part or the owner has been negligent in allowing the dog to be loose.[2] Thus in *Gomberg* v. *Smith* [3] a shop keeper, came out of his shop adjoining a highway in a built-up area, after dark with his St. Bernard dog, which was not on a lead, whereupon it ran across the road, hotly pursued by its owner. The dog then rushed back across the highway, collided with and damaged a van driven by the plaintiff which was travelling slowly and on its correct side of the road. The dog owner was held liable in negligence for the damage suffered since the law which applied to escape of animals on to a highway [4] was inapplicable where an owner had deliberately brought the dog on to the highway and he, in failing to control his dog had not fulfilled his duty to take reasonable care that he owed towards other highway users. But a person who causes or permits a dog to be on a designated road, *i.e.* a road specified by an order made by the local authority in whose area the

[98] *Catchpole* v. *Minster* (1913) 109 L.T. 953; *Turner* v. *Coates* [1917] 1 K.B. 670; 86 L.J.K.B. 321.

[99] [1917] 1 K.B. 670.

[1] Highway Code, para. (49).

[2] *Gibb* v. *Comerford* [1942] Ir.R. 295; *Milligan* v. *Henderson*, 1915 S.C. 1030; *Hines* v. *Tousley* (1926) 70 S.J. 732. Only in exceptional circumstances is there negligence in allowing a dog to be loose on the highway, as in *Pitcher* v. *Martin* [1937] 2 All E.R. 918 (dog on lead breaks away from person leading and entangles pedestrians in the lead—owner liable). See also *Jones* v. *Owen* (1871) 24 L.T.(N.S.) 587 (coupled greyhounds injure pedestrian—owner liable). In the absence of special circumstances which may include such things as topographical features (*per* Ormerod L.J.) and the fact that if a dog were known to shoot out of a gate on to the highway more like a missile (*per* Donovan L.J.) the owner of a dog is under no duty to prevent it straying on to a highway so that there is no difference here from any other domestic animals: *Ellis* v. *Johnstone* [1963] 2 Q.B. 8.

[3] [1963] 1 Q.B. 25.

[4] As from October 1, 1971, see the provisions of the Animals Act 1971, s. 8; § 852, *post*.

road is situated, without its being held on a lead commits an offence.[5] In the event of a driver of a vehicle having to take sudden avoiding action to save running over a dog, which ran across his path, it was held that he was not liable for the injuries sustained by his passenger, since he had acted with reasonable care in the agony of the moment.[6] The Highway Code provides: " (136) Do not let your dog out on its own. When you take it for a walk on the road, keep it on a lead. (137) If you have an animal in your car, keep it under control. Make sure it cannot disturb you while you are driving. Do not let a dog out of a car on to the road unless it is on a lead."

849 **Straying livestock.**[7] If cattle, while being driven along the highway, stray from the highway into a shop or other property adjoining the highway, it is evidence of negligence that they were not being kept under proper control, either because of an inadequate number of persons being employed to drive them or from carelessness on the part of those employed.[8] On the other hand, if there is no negligence on the part of the drover, there is no liability for the trespass of the animal in entering property adjoining the highway. So, where an ox was being driven through the streets of a country town and, without any negligence on the part of those in charge of it, entered a shop which adjoined the street and did damage, the owner was held not to be liable.[9]

50 Although a person committed an offence under the Highway Act 1864,[10] s. 25, if his cattle were found straying on the highway, it had been held that there was no liability at common law if cattle were negligently allowed to stray onto the highway and there collided with a vehicle. Accordingly, the owner of the animal was held not liable in the following cases—where a young horse, placed in a field with defective fences, escaped and ran across the road, colliding with the riders of a tandem bicycle[11]; where some cows escaped from a field through an open gate and collided with a cyclist[12]; where some sheep, placed in a field with defective hedges, escaped and collided with a motor-car[13]; where some fowls were allowed to stray on the highway and, being frightened by a dog, flew across the road and collided with a cyclist[14]; where a sow, allowed to stray on the highway, jumped up from the side of a hedge as a horse and van were about to pass a motor-car, causing the horse to shy and collide with the motor-car[15]; where two horses passed through a gate on a farm

[5] Road Traffic Act 1960, s. 220.
[6] *Parkinson* v. *Liverpool Corporation* [1950] 1 All E.R. 367.
[7] For the state of the law after October 1, 1971, see the effect of the Animals Act 1971, § 852, *post*.
[8] See *Gayler and Pope Ltd.* v. *Davies & Son* [1924] 2 K.B. 75, 87. See Highway Code, para. (140).
[9] *Tillett* v. *Ward* (1882) 10 Q.B.D. 17. See now s. 5 (5) of the Animals Act 1971.
[10] Now repealed by the Highways Act 1959, s. 311, Sched. XXIII.
[11] *Jones* v. *Lee* (1911) 106 L.T. 123.
[12] *Ellis* v. *Banyard* (1911) 106 L.T. 51.
[13] *Heath's Garage Ltd.* v. *Hodges* [1916] 2 K.B. 370.
[14] *Hadwell* v. *Righton* [1907] 2 K.B. 345.
[15] *Higgins* v. *Searle* (1909) 100 L.T. 280.

onto the highway and collided in the dark with a motor-car [16]; when a cyclist at night in the " blackout " collided with a horse which had got onto the highway through a gap in the fence [17]; when calves, driven from a field into the farmyard, escaped from the farmyard into the highway and, being frightened by the starting of the engine of a lorry, collided with a cyclist [18]; where a horse in a field jumped the hedge separating the field from the highway and landed on a motor-cyclist riding along the highway [19]; where an escaped cow knocked down the plaintiff on the highway as he was walking over a zebra crossing.[20]

851 The decisions, all prior to October 1, 1971, quoted in the preceding paragraph are based on the propositions (1) a landowner is under no duty (a) to maintain a fence to prevent his animals from straying on the highway [21]; (b) to prevent his animals from straying upon the highway; (2) an owner of an animal is not liable in the absence of *scienter*, for damage done by a tame animal which is contrary to its ordinary nature. But, " if an animal's owner knows that it has shown a tendency to run into cyclists or other passengers on the highway, it cannot avail him to say that it was not vice, but a frolicsome disposition, or perhaps, mere blundering, which caused the harm." [22] Nevertheless where two fillies, found to be playful but not vicious, were kept by the owners in a field across which ran a public footpath without hedge or fencing, and they galloped across to the plaintiff, who was walking along it, pranced around her, bumped into and knocked her down thereby causing her injuries, her claim failed because the animals had not been proved to have had a " vicious propensity " to the knowledge of the owners and negligence had not been proved.[23]

The difference in the legal position between animals straying and animals brought onto the highway is that " there is no duty to prevent

[16] *Hughes* v. *Williams* [1943] K.B. 574.

[17] *Searle* v. *Wallbank* [1947] A.C. 341. See articles: " *Searle* v. *Wallbank*, the Legislative Struggle " (North) 30 Conv. 44; " Negligence and the rule in *Searle* v. *Wallbank* " (Glover) 53 Law Guardian 11.

[18] *Wright* v. *Callwood* [1950] 2 K.B. 515.

[19] *Brock* v. *Richards* [1951] 1 K.B. 529.

[20] *Thorp* v. *King Bros.* (*Dorking*) *Ltd.*, *The Times*, February 23, 1957.

[21] *Searle* v. *Wallbank*, *supra*. This was only arrived at after several differences of opinion. Bankes J. in *Jones* v. *Lee*, *supra*, at p. 126, Buckley L.J. in *Ellis* v. *Bunyard*, *supra*, at p. 53, and Cozens-Hardy M.R. (p. 376) and Neville J. (p. 381) in *Heath's Garage Ltd.* v. *Hodges*, *supra*, expressed the opinion that there was no such obligation, while Vaughan Williams L.J. in *Jones* v. *Lee* at p. 54, expressed the opposite opinion, to which Kennedy L.J. in *Jones* v. *Lee*, and Pickford L.J. in *Heath's Garage Ltd.* v. *Hodges* at p. 379, also appeared to incline. In *Brackenborough* v. *Spalding U.D.C.* [1942] A.C. 310, 321, it was said the point was open. In *Hughes* v. *Williams*, *supra*, the C.A. held that it was bound by authority to hold that there was no duty to fence. The rule in *Searle* v. *Wallbank* was held to have no application to the situation in which the animal is under direct human control but strayed on to the highway as a foreseeable reaction to a fright it received: *Bativala* v. *West* [1970] 1 Q.B. 716.

[22] *Searle* v. *Wallbank*, *supra*, *per* Lord du Parcq at p. 359.

[23] *Fitzgerald* v. *E. D. & A. D. Cooke Bourne* (*Farms*) *Ltd.* [1964] 1 Q.B. 249. To impose on the owners a duty to guard against a possibility that the fillies would accidentally injure someone lawfully on the highway would be to impose too high a duty, namely a duty higher than the standard of care of an ordinary careful owner.

animals straying on the highway, but if brought on the highway, reasonable care must be exercised to control them." [24]

All the earlier authorities concerned the straying of " cattle " and until *Ellis* v. *Johnstone* [25] there had been no reported case which decided specifically whether or not a dog is also a domestic animal. In *Gomberg* v. *Smith*,[26] both Pearce L.J. and Davies L.J. inclined to the view that the owner's immunity with regard to the escape of cattle and the like did not extend to dogs but such expressions were *obiter dicta.* However Lord Maughan in *Searle* v. *Wallbank* [27] had regarded dogs which he classed together with " cats, pigs and fowls " as being in the same category as horses and cattle as far as the application of the rule is concerned, namely that an occupier of land adjoining a highway is under no obligation to fence to prevent such animals from straying on to the highway. However such debate is no longer of importance in view of the provisions of the Animals Act 1971 set out in the next paragraph, which are not in any way restricted to " cattle " or " livestock " as a class of animals.

52 **Animals Act 1971.**[28] This Act received the Royal Assent on May 12, 1971, and came into operation on October 1, 1971. By virtue of section 13 (3), gives effect with certain modifications to the recommendations contained in the Law Commission's report on Civil Liability for Animals.[29]

The above stated common law rules, which excluded or restricted a person's duty to take care to avoid damage being caused by animals straying on the highway, are abrogated by section 8 (1) which provides: " So much of the rules of the common law relating to liability for negligence as excludes or restricts the duty which a person might owe to others to take such care as is reasonable to see that damage is not caused by animals straying on to a highway is hereby abolished." Section 8 (2) allows a defence by enacting that " (2) Where damage is caused by animals straying from unfenced land to a highway a person who placed them on the land shall not be regarded as having committed a breach of the duty to take care by reason only of placing them there if—

(*a*) the land is common land, or is land situated in an area where fencing is not customary, or is a town or village green; and

(*b*) he had a right to place the animals on that land."

53 **Cyclists.** The rules set out above relating to road users generally equally apply to cyclists. The Highway Code provides extra rules for them as follows:

" (131) Do not start off, turn right or left, or pull up without first glancing behind to see it is safe. Give a clear signal of what you mean to do.

24 *Ibid. per* Lord Porter, p. 356, quoting Romer L.J. in *Deen* v. *Davies* [1935] 2 K.B. 282. See, as an example, *Gomberg* v. *Smith* [1963] 1 Q.B. 25. Further see article: 233 L.T. 255.
25 [1963] 2 Q.B. 8.
26 *Supra.*
27 *Supra* at p. 352.
28 See Chap. 10 " Animals " for a fuller consideration of the Act.
29 Law Commission Paper No. 13.

(132) Do not ride more than two abreast. Ride in single file on busy or narrow roads.

(133) On busy roads, if you want to turn right, it is often safer to pull well into the left side of the road and wait for a safe gap in the traffic in both directions before you start to cross.

(134) While riding:

(a) always hold the handlebar and keep your feet on the pedals;
(b) do not hold on to another vehicle or another cyclist;
(c) do not carry a passenger unless your cycle has been built or altered to carry one;
(d) do not ride close behind another vehicle;
(e) do not carry anything which may affect your balance;
(f) do not lead an animal.

(135) If there is an adequate cycle path beside the road, ride on it."

854 **Pedestrians.** It has been laid down that a foot-passenger, though he may be infirm from disease, has a right to walk in the carriageway and is entitled to the exercise of reasonable care on the part of persons driving vehicles along it.[30] Lord Dunedin has said that " there was all the difference between the case of a man run into on a railway and that of a man run into on the road. In the latter case the man had an absolute right to be there and it was the duty of drivers of vehicles not to run him down." [31] The Highway Code provides: (1) Where there is a pavement or suitable footpath, use it. Do not walk next to the kerb with your back to the traffic. Look both ways before you step into the road. (2) Where there is no suitable footpath, walk on the right-hand side of the road—it is safer to face oncoming traffic. Keep as close as possible to the side of the road, and do not walk more than two abreast. Take care at right-hand bends, and keep one behind the other if possible. (3) If you have children with you, walk between them and the traffic. Do not let them run into the road. (4) You can be more easily seen in the dark or in poor light if you wear or carry something white, or light-coloured, or reflective. This is important on country roads without footpaths. (5) A group of people marching on the road should keep to the left. There should be look-outs in front and at the back. At night the look-out in front should carry a white light, and the one at the back should carry a red light.

855 Although a pedestrian is entitled to walk along the carriageway, he is only entitled to the exercise of reasonable care on the part of drivers of vehicles. If, therefore, there is a pavement or suitable footpath, the driver of a vehicle, driving at a reasonable speed and keeping a proper lookout, may reasonably expect that a pedestrian, not crossing the road, will be walking on the footpath, and if a collision occurs, especially at dusk or in the dark, the pedestrian's claim may fail on the ground that

30 *Boss* v. *Litton* (1832) 5 C. & P. 407.
31 *Craig* v. *Glasgow Corpn.* (1919) 35 T.L.R. 214, 216.

there is no negligence on the part of the driver.[32] In blackout conditions during wartime a pedestrian walking in the highway must take more care than if such conditions did not prevail, and bear in mind that if he keeps a proper lookout a vehicle will be more visible to him than he is to the vehicle.[33]

A pedestrian owes a duty to other highway users to move with due care. " When a man steps from the kerb into the roadway, he owes a duty to traffic which is approaching him with risk of collision to exercise due care." [34] Accordingly where a pedestrian stepped out into the path of a motor scooter so that the rider fell off his machine and was killed, the pedestrian was held liable in negligence.[35] However a pedestrian, who suffered from attacks of petit mal was held not to be guilty of negligence when she had stepped off a pavement in a state of automatism and caused an accident, there being no evidence that she had received any medical advice discouraging her from going out alone for a walk.[36] Now a pedestrian is under a duty to comply with traffic directions given by a police constable in uniform.[37]

856 As regards the pedestrian's duty in crossing the road the Highway Code provides: " (6) *Kerb Drill.* Before you cross, stop at the kerb, look right, look left, look right again. When the road is clear, walk across at right angles but keep looking out for traffic. Cross the road as quickly as you can, but do not run. (7) Where pedestrian crossings, central islands traffic lights, subways or footbridges are provided, use them.[38] If you cross the road elsewhere, make sure you can see clearly both ways. (8) Try not to cross the road between, or in front of, parked vehicles, because drivers on the road may not be able to see you. If you have to cross near parked vehicles, stop at their outside edge and do your kerb drill. (9) Before crossing a one-way street, do your kerb drill and make sure you know which way the traffic is moving. (10) Where there is an island in the road, cross first to the island and wait there until the second half of the road is clear. Then finish crossing. (11) At night, cross the

[32] See *Tidy* v. *Battman* [1934] 1 K.B. 319; *Scott* v. *M'Intosh*, 1935 S.C. 199, and *cf. Page* v. *Richards & Draper* (1920), unreported, set out in *Tart* v. *G. W. Chitty & Co.* [1933] 2 K.B. 453.

[33] *Franklin* v. *Bristol Tramways & Carriage Co. Ltd.* [1941] 1 K.B. 255. This case lays down no rule of law; *Sparks* v. *Edward Ash Ltd.* [1943] K.B. 223, 237, 240. " The observations in that judgment seem to me to voice a truism, namely, that when it is pitch dark, everyone on a highway, whether he is driving or walking or riding, must be more alert and exercise more care than he needs to do when there is brilliant sunshine," *per* MacKinnon L.J. See also *Cowan* v. *Robertson*, 1941 S.C. 502; *M'Geown* v. *Greenock Motor Services*, 1943 S.C. 33.

[34] *Nance* v. *British Columbia Electric Ry.* [1951] A.C. 601, 611, *per* Lord Simon; see article " Liability of Pedestrian," 110 S.J. 934.

[35] *Barry* v. *McDonald* (1966) 110 S.J. 56; the driver of a motor-car does not have to drive in the constant expectation that a pedestrian may at any moment project himself into the path of his car from behind a vehicle in a line of traffic on his right, which is moving in the opposite direction: *Nolan* v. *Marsh Motors and Holzberger* [1965] Q.L.R. 490.

[36] *Green* v. *Hills* (1969) 113 S.J. 385.

[37] Road Traffic Act 1960, s. 15.

[38] Nevertheless in *Snow* v. *Giddins* (1969) 113 S.J. 229, a plaintiff crossing a busy road on foot was held not to be guilty of negligence in failing to use a pedestrian crossing, some 15 yards down the road, but was found 25 per cent. to blame for the accident, which befell him, in crossing over at a point where there was no central island refuge.

road near a lighted street lamp if there is no convenient pedestrian crossing or traffic signal. (12) Do not cross the road where there are guard rails, except through the gaps. Do not walk outside the guard rails."

857 **Defences.** There have been set out above a number of acts or omissions which have been described as evidence of negligence. This means that on proof of any of them the tribunal to decide facts, whether judge or jury, may, but not must, come to the conclusion that there is negligence on the part of the person responsible for the act or omission. That negligence, if found, is not necessarily conclusive of the issue of responsibility for the damage, because it may be shown that there was contributory negligence on the part of the plaintiff so that the damages have to be apportioned,[39] or that the negligence of a third party was the real cause of the damage. Evidence of negligence may also be rebutted by proving inevitable accident.[40]

858 **Suing more than one defendant.** A collision may be due to the negligence of more than one person, in which case an action can be brought against them all jointly, severally, and in the alternative. Judgment may then be given against one or more, but no more than the amount of damages awarded can be recovered. If judgment is obtained against one party whose negligence was responsible for the collision, he may obtain contribution from any other party whose negligence also was responsible.[41] If more than one defendant is joined and judgment is obtained against one only, the costs payable by the plaintiff to the successful defendants may be ordered to be included in the costs payable by the unsuccessful defendant to the plaintiff, provided that it was reasonable for the plaintiff to join the successful defendants.[42] If the defendants before or at the trial attempt to throw the responsibility for the collision upon each other, it will usually be held that the plaintiff was reasonable in joining them all.

If more than one defendant is sued and the facts proved are such that a reasonable inference is that one, if not both, of the defendants was negligent, one defendant should not be dismissed from the case on the ground that he has no case to answer, but the whole of the evidence against both defendants should be heard before a decision is given.[43]

858a **Duty of learner driver.** In *Nettleship* v. *Weston*[44] the Court of Appeal held that a learner driver owed the same duty of care to a person teaching her to drive as is owed by every driver on the road.[45] That standard is not lowered by reason of the instructor's knowing that the learner is not experienced.

[39] Chap. 16, § 1019.
[40] Chap. 16, § 1079.
[41] Law Reform (Married Women and Tortfeasors) Act 1935, s. 6; Chap. 13, *post*, § 890 *et seq.*
[42] *Bullock* v. *L.G.O. Ltd.* [1907] 1 K.B. 264.
[43] *Hummerstone* v. *Leary* [1921] 2 K.B. 664.
[44] *The Times*, July 1, 1971. See article: " One Law for All " (Weaver) 121 New L.J. 634.
[45] See § 812, *ante*. For the duty of the supervisor of the learner driver, see *e.g. Rubie* v. *Faulkner* [1940] 1 K.B. 571, 575, *per* Hilbery J.

Chapter 13

PARTIES

859 **Generally.** Subject to the various exceptions and qualifications considered below, all persons are entitled to sue and are liable to be sued in negligence and/or breach of statutory duty just the same as in actions in tort generally.

1.—The Crown

860 **At common law.** The position at common law was that the Crown could not be sued in tort either by an action against it or by an action against its servants in a representative capacity.[1] The individual wrongdoer could be sued for any wrong he had personally committed or to which he was directly privy as by having given orders for its performance,[2] but not otherwise, because the relationship of master and servant does not lie between superior and subordinate officials, as they are all fellow servants of the Crown. Accordingly, the Postmaster-General was held not to be liable for the negligence of a sectional engineer in the Post Office service when the plaintiff was injured by falling on the footway, the pavement not having been properly relaid after it had been taken up to allow a telegraph cable to be repaired.[3]

861 **Crown Proceedings Act 1947.** By virtue of the Crown Proceedings Act 1947 the Crown's immunity in tort was brought to an end whereby it may now be sued as of right, *inter alia*, in actions for negligence. It is provided by section 2 (1):

" Subject to the provisions of this Act, the Crown shall be subject to all those liabilities in tort to which, if it were a private person of full age and capacity, it would be subject:—

(*a*) in respect of torts committed by its servants or agents [4];

(*b*) in respect of any breach of those duties which a person owes to his servants or agents at common law by reason of being their employer; and

(*c*) in respect of any breach of the duties attaching at common law to the ownership, occupation, possession or control of property [5];

Provided that no proceedings shall lie against the Crown by virtue of paragraph (*a*) of this subsection in respect of any act or omission of a servant or agent of the Crown unless the act or omission would apart

[1] *Raleigh* v. *Goschen* [1898] 1 Ch. 73; *Hutton* v. *Secy. of State for War* (1926) 43 T.L.R. 106; *Roper* v. *Public Works Comrs.* [1915] 1 K.B. 45; *Tobin* v. *The Queen* (1864) 16 C.B.(N.S.) 310.

[2] *Mackenzie-Kennedy* v. *Air Council* [1927] 2 K.B. 517, 533.

[3] *Bainbridge* v. *Postmaster-General* [1906] 1 K.B. 178.

[4] Agent includes an independent contractor, s. 38 (2).

[5] See now the common law as replaced by the Occupiers' Liability Act 1957. *Ante*, Chap. 8.

from the provisions of this Act have given rise to a cause of action in tort against that servant or agent or his estate."

862 **The Sovereign.** The Act specifically provides by section 40 (1) that nothing in it shall apply to proceedings by or against or authorise proceedings in tort to be brought against the Sovereign in a private capacity at all.

863 **Torts committed by servants or agents.** It is clear from section 2 (1) of the Act that the Crown is made vicariously liable for those torts committed by its servants in the course of their employment. It is liable also for those torts committed by its independent contractors where the circumstances only are such that the private employer similarly would be liable.[6] The proviso is notable in that it ensures that the Crown can avail itself of such defences as act of state,[7] and the exercise of statutory or prerogative powers.

The Crown's liability for the torts of its officers including any servant or Minister of the Crown is limited to those cases where the officer is appointed by it directly or indirectly and at the material time is paid wholly out of the Consolidated Fund, moneys provided by Parliament or a fund equivalent thereto in respect of his duties as its officer.[8] This provision has the effect of excluding liability for the police and other public officers who are either appointed or paid by local or other public authorities.[9] However in the case of the police, although a constable is neither the servant of the Crown, the police authority nor of the chief constable, the Police Act 1964, s. 48, provides that the Chief Officer of Police of any area shall be liable in respect of torts committed by constables under his control in the performance of their functions in the like manner as a master is liable in respect of torts committed by his servants in the course of their employment. The Chief of Police is made a joint tortfeasor[10] with the peccant police constable but any damages and costs awarded against him are met out of the police fund.

864 It is settled law since *Mersey Docks Trustees* v. *Gibbs*[11] that the mere fact that a body has been created by statute for public purposes does not mean that it is a servant or agent of the Crown. Accordingly, in *Tamlin* v. *Hannaford*,[12] the Court of Appeal held that the nationalised railways' authority was not a servant or agent of the Crown, the proper

6 *Ibid.* s. 40 (2) (*d*).

7 There is no principle in our law which permits the Crown in time of peace to act for the public good as it thinks best: *Entick* v. *Carrington* (1765) 19 St.Tr. 1029. The Crown must be prepared to justify before the courts the legality of any act which interferes with the person or property of the subject. This does not apply when the plaintiff is a non-resident alien and the wrong is suffered elsewhere than in British territory. See *Buron* v. *Denman* (1848) 2 Ex. 167; *R.* v. *Bottrill* [1947] K.B. 41, at p. 57.

8 Crown Proceedings Act 1947, s. 2 (6).

9 *Stanbury* v. *Exeter Corp.* [1905] 2 K.B. 838 (agricultural inspector); *Fisher* v. *Oldham Corp.* [1930] 2 K.B. 364 and *Lewis* v. *Cattle* [1938] 2 K.B. 454 (police officers).

10 See generally Joint tortfeasors, § 891, *post*.

11 (1866) L.R. 1 H.L. 93. See also *Bank Voor Handel en Scheepvaart* v. *Administrator of Hungarian Property* [1954] A.C. 584.

12 [1950] 1 K.B. 18.

inference being, at any rate in the case of a commercial corporation, that it acted on its own behalf, although it was subject to control by a government department.

The Act of 1947 provides by section 2 (3), " Where any functions are conferred or imposed upon an officer of the Crown as such either by any rule of the common law or by statute, and that officer commits a tort while performing or purporting to perform those functions, the liabilities of the Crown in respect of the tort shall be such as they would have been if those functions had been conferred or imposed solely by virtue of instructions lawfully given by the Crown." Section 2 (4) gives the Crown the benefit of any statutory provisions which negative or limit the amount of the liability of a government department or Crown officer.

865 **Breach of statutory duty.** The Crown is also liable for breach of statutory duty. By section 2 (2), " Where the Crown is bound by a statutory duty which is binding also upon persons other than the Crown and its officers, then, subject to the provisions of this Act, the Crown shall, in respect of a failure to comply with that duty, be subject to all those liabilities in tort (if any) to which it would be so subject if it were a private person of full age and capacity." Seemingly this proviso was included in order to prevent the creation of a new branch of the law of tort by converting constitutional and administrative law into a collection of duties owed to individuals.[13] No difficulty arises where the particular statute expressly provides that it binds the Crown such as the Factories Act 1961.[14] It is to be noted that the Act itself, by section 4 (2) and (3) provides that the provisions relating to contribution and indemnity contained in section 6 of the Law Reform (Married Women and Tortfeasors) Act 1935 and those relating to contributory negligence contained in the Law Reform (Contributory Negligence) Act 1945 shall bind the Crown. Further, by section 6, it is enacted that the similar provisions contained in the Maritime Conventions Act 1911 shall bind the Crown, too. However difficulties may well arise where the statute is silent as to its application to the Crown since the Act preserves the common law principle of construction that the Crown is not bound by a statute in the absence of express words or necessary implication. Nevertheless the provisions of the Fatal Accidents Acts 1846 to 1908 and the Law Reform (Miscellaneous Provisions) Act 1934 section 1 are generally regarded as binding on the Crown.

866 **Judicial acts.** Section 2 (5) excludes proceedings against the Crown " in respect of anything done or omitted to be done by any person while discharging or purporting to discharge any responsibilities of a judicial nature vested in him, or any responsibilities which he has in connection with the execution of judicial process." It follows that no liability attaches

[13] Glanville Williams, *Crown Proceedings*, p. 48.

[14] s. 173. Other relevant Acts are the Law Reform (Personal Injuries) Act 1948 (s. 4); the Law Reform (Limitation of Actions) Act 1954 (s. 5), although the Limitation Act 1963 is silent on the matter it is submitted that it must also bind the Crown; the Occupiers' Liability Act 1957.

itself to the Crown for torts that may be committed by judges, magistrates and those others executing judgment, who exceed the limits of their immunity. In Hood Phillips, *Constitutional Law*, it is suggested that this exception probably does not extend to government officers exercising " quasi-judicial " functions.[15]

867 **The Post Office.** By the Post Office Act 1969 [16] the postal service is now administered by a commercial completely independent public authority known as the Post Office. Accordingly, section 9 of the Crown Proceedings Act 1947 is repealed although the exemptions from and conditions of the liability of the Post Office are now very similar indeed to those formerly governing the Crown's liability as set out above.

The general rule that no proceedings in tort shall lie against the Post Office in respect of loss or damage suffered by any person is embodied in section 29 (1) as regards: " (*a*) anything done or omitted to be done in relation to anything in the post or omission to carry out arrangements for the collection of anything to be conveyed by post; (*b*) failure to provide, or delay in providing, a telecommunication service, apparatus associated therewith or a service ancillary thereto; (*c*) failure, interruption, suspension or restriction of a telecommunication service or a service ancillary thereto or delay of, or fault in, communication by means of a telecommunication service; or (*d*) error in, or omission from, a directory for use in connection with a telecommunication service." Section 29 (2) expressly preserves the immunity of officers and servants of the Post Office, including such agents as a sub-postmaster or telephone exchange attendant, from " any civil liability for any loss or damage in the case of which liability of the Post Office therefor is excluded by the foregoing subsection." The immunity further extends to any person engaged in the carriage of mail and to any officer, servant, agent or sub-contractor of such person.[17] Section 30 subjects the Post Office to a liability in respect of registered inland packets in similar terms to those that formerly applied to the liability of the Crown. Proceedings under this section must be commenced within twelve months of the date of posting [18] and, unless the court gives leave to the contrary, which it may do in certain circumstances, relief under the section is only available to the sender or the addressee of the packet " whether or not he is the person damnified by the injury complained of." [19]

868 **Her Majesty's Forces.** By section 10 (1) of the Crown Proceedings Act 1947 it is provided that no act or omission of a member of the armed forces on duty shall subject either him or the Crown to liability in tort for causing the death of another person or for causing personal injury to another person who is a member of the armed forces, provided that the latter is either on duty or is on any land, premises, ship or vehicle being

[15] 4th ed., p. 362.
[16] Which came into force on October 1, 1969.
[17] *Ibid.* s. 29 (3), overruling thereby *Moukataff* v. *B.O.A.C.* (1967) 1 Lloyd's Rep. 396.
[18] s. 30 (1).
[19] s. 30 (5).

used for the purposes of the armed forces of the Crown, and the Minister of Pensions [20] certifies that the death or injury will be treated as attributable to service for pension purposes.[21] By virtue of the proviso to the subsection, exemption from liability extends to the actual tortfeasor unless the court is satisfied that the act or omission complained of was not connected with the performance and execution of his duties as a member of those forces. Section 10 (2) provides a similar exemption from liability in tort where the death or personal injury has been sustained by a member of the armed forces in consequence of the nature or condition of any land, premises, ship, aircraft, or vehicle being used for the armed forces' purposes or in consequence of the nature or condition of any equipment or supplies used for those purposes.

Sections 5 to 8 [22] deal with the ships, docks, harbours and canals owned or occupied by the Crown. The position of the Crown seems to be similar to that of a private owner or occupier so that, by way of example the provisions relating to limitation of liability contained in the Merchant Shipping Acts 1894 to 1970 apply equally in those cases which involve its vessels.[23]

869 **Government departments.** In the *Home Office* v. *Dorset Yacht Co. Ltd.*[24] seven Borstal boys who were working on an island under the control and supervision of three officers, left the island by night, boarded, cast adrift and damaged the plaintiffs' yacht which had been moored offshore. The respondents brought an action for damages against the appellant government department alleging negligence which they particularised as being that, knowing of the boys' criminal records and their records of previous bids to escape from Borstal institutions, and knowing that craft such as the plaintiffs' were moored offshore, the officers had failed to exercise any effective control or supervision over the boys. The appellants denied that they owed the respondents any duty of care with respect to the detention of the boys or to the manner in which they were treated, employed, disciplined, controlled or supervised. At the trial of the preliminary issue whether or not on the facts pleaded the appellants owed a duty of care either as alleged or at all, Thesiger J. answered that question in the affirmative and the Court of Appeal dismissed an appeal by the Home Office. On further appeal the House of Lords in dismissing the appeal [25] held that the Borstal officers had owed the plaintiffs a duty to take such care as was reasonable in all the circumstances, including the due exercise

[20] See now Ministry of Social Security Act 1966, s. 2 (3) and S.I. 1968, No. 1699 where the Secretary of State for Social Services has taken over the functions.

[21] See *Adams* v. *War Office* [1955] 1 W.L.R. 1116 (soldier killed during a gunnery exercise).

[22] s. 5 has been amended by the Merchant Shipping (Liability of Shipowners and Others) Act 1958, s. 8 (5).

[23] s. 5. See *The Truculent* [1952] P. 1 where the Admiralty, on behalf of the Crown sought to limit liability in respect of claims for damage including loss of life which arose out of a collision in January, 1950 between H.M. Submarine *Truculent* and the Swedish steamship *Divina*, during the hours of darkness.

[24] [1970] A.C. 1004. See articles: "Escaping Borstal boys and the immunity of office" (Hamson) 27 C.L.J. 273; "Borstals and the public" (Henderson) 1969 S.L.T. 81.

[25] *Supra*, affirming the C.A. [1969] 2 Q.B. 412 but with Viscount Dilhorne dissenting.

of discretion with regard to Borstal training policy, with a view to preventing the boys under their control from causing damage to the plaintiffs' property if that were a happening of which there was a manifest risk if they neglected that duty. It was also held that public policy did not require that there should be immunity from an action such as the plaintiffs' and that accordingly the question of law had rightly been answered in the affirmative.

Another example of where a government department was held to owe a duty of care and, indeed, was found to be liable in negligence, occurred in *Levine* v. *Morris and Ministry of Transport*,[26] when it was decided that the Ministry owed a duty of care to motorists in the siting of their road signs. Where motorists may inadvertently leave the road and collide with such signs, the duty is to select the site which is equally good as regards visibility but which involves the lesser hazard to the motorist. However, in practice, this need for special siting will arise only where the configuration of the road makes it foreseeable that there is an above average risk of a vehicle leaving the road's surface.

2.—Foreign Sovereigns, Ambassadors, Public Officials, and Visiting Forces

870 **Foreign sovereigns.** No action lies against a foreign sovereign, unless he submits to the jurisdiction, for any tort committed by him. This immunity attaches not only to foreign sovereigns and states but extends to departments of foreign states irrespective of any independent legal status.[27] Lord Atkin stated: " The courts of a country will not implead a foreign sovereign, that is, they will not by their process make him against his will a party to legal proceedings whether the proceedings involve process against his person or seek to recover from him specific property or damages." [28] Accordingly the only remedy for injuries and damage caused by a foreign sovereign is to invoke such diplomatic action on the part of the British Government. If the status of a foreign sovereign is in doubt the question may be resolved by the court seeking information from the Secretary of State on behalf of the Crown, whose certificate is conclusive.[29] However the sovereign's immunity ceases upon the termination of his sovereign status.[30]

871 **Ambassadors and public officials.** The law regarding diplomatic immunity is contained now in the Diplomatic Privileges Act 1964 [31] which gives the force of law to the Vienna Convention on Diplomatic Relations of 1961, which are set out in a Schedule to the Act. The main provisions of the Act and Convention bearing upon actions in tort concern (*a*) the

[26] [1970] 1 W.L.R. 71.
[27] *Krajina* v. *Tass Agency* [1949] 2 All E.R. 274 (telegraphic news agency); *Baccus S.R.L.* v. *Servicio Nacional Del Trigo* [1957] 1 Q.B. 438 (department of the Spanish Ministry of Agriculture having its own independent corporate existence).
[28] *Compania Naviera Vascongado* v. *S.S.* " *Cristina* " [1938] A.C. 485, at p. 490.
[29] *Cf.* s. 4 of the Diplomatic Privileges Act 1964.
[30] *Munden* v. *Brunswick* (*Duke of*) (1847) 10 Q.B. 656 (abdication).
[31] *Empson* v. *Smith* [1966] 1 Q.B. 426; Samuels (1964) 27 M.L.R. 689.

immunity of diplomatic agents *i.e.* the head of a mission and members of its staff having diplomatic rank; (*b*) the duration of such immunity and (*c*) the waiver of such immunity.

2 **Visiting forces.** By virtue of the Visiting Forces Act 1952 [32] the Secretary of State for Defence has been authorised to make arrangements [33] for the settlement of claims against members of visiting forces from the Commonwealth and states which are parties to the North Atlantic Treaty.[34] The scheme takes effect whereby claims in respect of acts or omissions of members of visiting forces will be satisfied by the payment by the Minister, out of moneys provided by Parliament, of such amounts as may be adjudged by any United Kingdom court, or agreed between the claimant and the Minister.[35] Nevertheless such a scheme does not appear to create any right of action against the Minister. Otherwise the same exemptions, privileges and immunities which apply to the Crown in respect of the home forces apply similarly to visiting forces.[36]

3.—CORPORATIONS AND UNINCORPORATED ASSOCIATIONS

3 **Corporations, directors and members.** A corporation can sue and be sued in negligence, in the same way as an individual [37]; but the directors of a limited company cannot be held liable for the torts of the servants by reason of their position as directors, unless they were responsible for ordering the acts to be done or the omissions to be made. They may, however, be liable if there are facts from which an inference can be drawn that the relationship of principal and agent has been established between the directors and the company, although the mere fact that their being the sole directors and shareholders is insufficient.[38] The members of a corporation are not as such liable for torts committed by the corporation, which as a body corporate is a personality distinct from its members. Nevertheless it cannot be doubted that a servant or agent by whom a corporation commits a tort is personally liable to the same extent as any other servant or agent who commits a tort in the service or on behalf of a principal or employer.

4 **Unincorporated associations and trade unions.** In *Taff Vale Ry.* v. *Amalgamated Society of Railway Servants* [39] it was held by the House of Lords that a registered trade union, though not a corporate body, was a legal entity having sufficient of the characteristics of a juristic person to enable it to be sued in tort for the wrongful acts or omissions of its officials. However by virtue of section 4 of the Trade Disputes Act 1906

[32] s. 9.
[33] The existing arrangements are summarised in Street, *The Law of Torts* 2nd ed. p. 473.
[34] The Crown by Order in Council may designate a country as being one to which the provisions of the Act or any of them apply: Visiting Forces Act 1952, s. 1 (2).
[35] *Ibid.* s. 9 (1).
[36] *Ibid.* s. 8. See Visiting Forces and International Headquarters (Application of Law) Order 1965 (S.I. 1965, No. 1536).
[37] *National Telephone Co. Ltd.* v. *The Constables of St. Peter Port* [1900] A.C. 317, even if the corporation seemingly is engaged in an *ultra vires* undertaking (at p. 321).
[38] *Rainham Chemical Works* v. *Belvedere Fish Guano Co.* [1921] 2 A.C. 465; *Performing Right Soc.* v. *Ciryl Syndicate* [1924] 1 K.B. 1.
[39] [1901] A.C. 426.

it is provided that, " an action against a trade union, whether of workmen or master, or against any members or officials thereof on behalf of themselves and all other members of the trade union, in respect of any tortious act [40] alleged to have been committed by or on behalf of the trade union, shall not be entertained by any court." Whilst the protection given is not confined to torts which are committed in contemplation of furtherance of a trade dispute, the Act does not protect officials of a trade union from their personal liability for wrongful acts.[41] The principle in the *Taff Vale* case has been held to cover a registered Friendly Society [42] and a Trustee Savings Bank [43] but not an ordinary members' club which is neither incorporated nor proprietary. An unincorporated association normally can only be sued by means of a representative action under R.S.C. Ord. 15, r. 12, provided that the members whose names appear on the writ are persons who may fairly be taken to represent the body of club members, and that they and all the other club members have a common interest in resisting the claim.[44] There are cases in which it may be possible to prove that the actual wrongdoer was the servant or agent of a particular member or members such as the committee.[45] Usually the members of the committee of a members' club owe no duty of care towards the club's members since there is no real distinction between them but it may be that an officer of the club, such as the steward, is personally liable for negligence to a member. If he be appointed by the committee then he is appointed in fact by all the members operating through the committee, and thus may be deemed to be the agent of each member to carry out with all reasonable care those things he is required to do. In this respect he does owe a duty to each member to take reasonable care and to carry out his duties without negligence.[46]

Since a trade union is a legal entity it has the correlative right to sue in its registered name.[47]

875 **Partners.** By the Partnership Act 1890 partners are made jointly and severally liable for the torts of any one of them whilst acting in the ordinary course of the business of the firm or when acting with the authority of his co-partners.[48] R.S.C. Ord. 81, rr. 1 & 2 permit partners to sue and be sued in the name of their firm. Where a plaintiff sues one partner and accepts a sum in full discharge of all claims and disputes between them he cannot then sue the other partner in respect of the same matter.[49]

40 Breaches of contract are not protected: *Bonsor* v. *Musicians' Union* [1956] A.C. 104.
41 *Rookes* v. *Barnard* [1964] A.C. 1129.
42 *Longdon-Griffiths* v. *Smith* [1951] 1 K.B. 295.
43 *Knight and Searle* v. *Dove* [1964] 2 Q.B. 631.
44 *Campbell* v. *Thompson* [1953] 1 Q.B. 445. See Lloyd, " Actions Instituted by or against Unincorporated Bodies " (1949) 12 M.L.R. 409; (1953) 16 M.L.R. 359.
45 *Brown* v. *Lewis* (1896) 12 T.L.R. 455 (members of committee of Blackburn Rovers Football Club personally liable for defective stand).
46 *Prole* v. *Allen* [1950] 1 All E.R. 476.
47 *National Union of General & Municipal Workers* v. *Gillian* [1946] K.B. 81; *Willis* v. *Brooks* [1947] 1 All E.R. 191; *B.M.T.A.* v. *Salvadori* [1949] Ch. 556.
48 ss. 10 and 12. See also *Hamlyn* v. *Houston* [1903] 1 K.B. 81; *Mercantile Credit Co. Ltd.* v. *Garrod* [1962] 3 All E.R. 1103; *Meekins* v. *Henson* [1964] 1 Q.B. 472.
49 *Howe* v. *Oliver, Haynes, Third Party* (1908) 24 T.L.R. 781.

4.—HUSBAND AND WIFE [50]

876 **Actions between spouses.** At common law a husband could not sue his wife in tort at all whilst the wife's action in tort against her husband was limited to that " for the protection and security of her property." [51] A radical change in the law was brought about by the Law Reform (Husband and Wife) Act 1962, which came into force on August 1, 1962, whereby, in consequence of the recommendations of the Law Reform Committee,[52] each of the parties to a marriage has the like right of action against the other as if they were not married.[53] There is however one qualification namely that where an action in tort is brought by one of the parties to the marriage against the other during the subsistence of the marriage, the court may stay the proceedings if it appears either that no substantial benefit will accrue to either party from the continuance of the action or the question before the court could be more conveniently disposed of under section 17 of the Married Women's Property Act 1882.[54]

877 **Law Reform (Married Women and Tortfeasors) Act 1935.** At common law a married woman could not sue or be sued unless her husband were joined in the action with her be it as the plaintiff or the defendant. As a result the husband, as a necessary if unwilling party to the proceedings for torts committed by his wife, was liable to pay damages for such wrongdoings by her. Since the passing of the Law Reform (Married Women and Tortfeasors) Act 1935 both these rules have been abolished. By virtue of section 1, a married woman may be sued for her torts and sue herself in all respects as if she were a *feme sole* whilst by section 3 it is provided that a husband shall not, by reason only of his being her husband, be liable in respect of any tort committed by his wife be it before or during the marriage.[55]

5.—MINORS [56]

878 **Capacity to sue.** A minor's capacity to sue is no different from that of an adult although there is a procedural requirement that he must sue by his next friend, who usually is either of his parents.[57] In the event of a parent being sued by the minor, *e.g.* for personal injuries sustained whilst travelling in a vehicle which was caused by the negligent driving of the parent, he would then sue through the other parent or by another relative who would be willing to undertake the responsibility on the child's behalf.

[50] See generally Chap. 14 concerning those instances where one spouse may be deemed to be the servant or agent of the other. See also § 924, *post*.
[51] Married Women's Property Act 1882, s. 12.
[52] Ninth Report (1961) Cmnd. 1268.
[53] *McLeod* v. *McLeod* (1963) 113 L.J. 420.
[54] *Supra.*
[55] Which reverses the decision of the H.L. in *Edwards* v. *Porter* [1925] A.C. 1; *Barber* v. *Pigden* [1937] 1 K.B. 664.
[56] The Family Law Reform Act 1969, Part 1 of which reduces the age of majority from 21 years to 18 years, came into force on January 1, 1970, in this regard and thereafter such persons under that full age will become known as " minors " instead of " infants " as hitherto. See article: " Age of majority 18 " (Samuels) 113 S.J. 763.
[57] R.S.C. Order 80 r. 2.

879 **Pre-natal injuries.** In the United States and Canada, actions have been permitted to be brought by infants, who have suffered pre-natal injuries, and provided that the necessary elements of a particular tort such as negligence or trespass to the person can be proved on its behalf, these actions can succeed.[58] Although there is still no direct authority on this subject in English law there is no valid reason why such an action should not be brought successfully. Certainly the inference is that such an action would be entertained and in *S.* v. *Distillers Co.* (*Biochemicals*)[59] where Hinchcliffe J. was required to assess damages in two representative actions arising out of that all too large a number of children, who were born pitifully deformed after their mothers had taken the drug thalidomide as a tranquilliser during their pregnancies, no attempt was made by the defendants to avoid liability altogether by asserting that the children had no causes of action, although negligence was firmly denied for the purposes of a compromise settlement.

880 **Capacity to be sued.** The defence of infancy or minority as such is unknown to the law of tort and save that a minor must appear by his guardian *ad litem*[57] he may be sued in tort and be found liable as if he were of full age.[60] Nevertheless the age of the minor may be highly relevant since in negligence in order to make him liable it must be proved that he failed to show that amount of care reasonably to be expected from a child of that age.[61] It is insufficient for a plaintiff to prove that an adult, had he acted the same way in the like circumstances, would have been guilty of negligence.

Often the consideration arises in practice[62] whether it is worth while suing a minor in tort since he may have no assets to satisfy any judgment that the injured plaintiff may obtain. In the main it is usually worth while since in our present affluent society a judgment debtor without funds may acquire them later on during his adult life. He may be sued on the judgment or execution may be issued on it up to six years from its date, or even at some later date having first obtained the leave of the court.[63] Where a judgment has been obtained against a minor which is ordered, usually, to be paid by instalments it is an abuse of process for him to file his petition in bankruptcy.[64]

For parents' responsibility for their children's torts, see *post*, § 945.

6.—PRISONERS AND BANKRUPTS

881 **Prisoners.** Criminals, when undergoing custodial sentences, have precisely the same rights of action for torts as any one else leading a

[58] *Prosser on Torts*, 3rd ed., pp. 354–357; *Montreal Tramways* v. *Leveille* [1933] 4 D.L.R. 337.
[59] (1969) 113 S.J. 672.
[60] *Gorely* v. *Codd* [1967] 1 W.L.R. 19.
[61] This seems to be implicit from the reasoning in the decisions concerned with contributory negligence of children. See *Lynch* v. *Nurdin* (1841) 1 Q.B. 29; *Harrold* v. *Watney* [1898] 2 Q.B. 320; *Liddle* v. *Yorkshire C.C.* [1934] 2 K.B. 101, 125, *per* Greer L.J.; *Yachuk* v. *Oliver Blais Ltd.* [1949] A.C. 386.
[62] *e.g.* by a pillion passenger on a motor cycle or scooter, whose only remedy lies against the negligent youthful rider, who can have no insurance backing for such liability.
[63] R.S.C. Ord. 46, rr. 2, 4.
[64] *Re a Debtor* [1967] Ch. 590.

blameless life, which seems to be the effect of the Criminal Justice Act 1948,[65] although the Home Secretary is free to decide on the merits of each case whether a prisoner should be allowed to initiate legal proceedings or to seek legal advice to that end.[66] In genuine cases the necessary permission to proceed is always given in practice, even where proceedings may be against the Crown itself.[67] A prisoner, equally, may be made a defendant for the purpose of being sued in tort. See *ante*, § 869 for actions against the Home Office in respect of damage caused by escaped prisoners.

882 **Bankrupts.** Bankrupts may be sued in tort whether committed before or during bankruptcy since they are in no special position in this respect. The bankrupt remains liable to be sued, the Bankruptcy Act 1914[68] providing that demands in the nature of unliquidated damages arising otherwise than by reason of a contract, promise or breach of trust are not provable against the trustee in bankruptcy. Where a plaintiff has a right of action in tort against the estate of a deceased tortfeasor but the estate is insolvent, under the Law Reform (Miscellaneous Provisions) Act 1934[69] he may prove in the administration of the estate for unliquidated damages.

883 **Capacity to sue.** A distinction has to be drawn between a tort committed against the bankrupt's person and his property. A right of action in respect of a tort resulting in personal injuries remains with the bankrupt and does not pass to the trustee[70] whilst a right of action resulting in damage to the bankrupt's estate passes to the trustee. If the tort has resulted in damage both to the bankrupt's person and his estate, the right of action in so far as it results in personal injuries remains in him whilst that damage to the estate will pass to the trustee.[71] In a case of this sort the trustee and the bankrupt can either bring separate actions or may join as plaintiffs in the same action in which event the damages will have to be assessed under the two heads of damage separately.[72]

7.—PERSONS OF UNSOUND MIND

884 **Persons of unsound mind.** There would appear to be no distinction between the liability of a person of unsound mind in an action for negligence and that of a young minor in the like action.[73] Therefore it is a question of fact for the court to determine in each case whether he was sufficiently self-possessed to be capable of taking reasonable care in the circumstances. Nevertheless some considerable caution is needed in

[65] s. 70 of which amended the Forfeiture Act 1870.
[66] *The English Prison and Borstal Systems* (Fox, 1952) p. 220; see also Prison Rules S.I. 1964, No. 388, rule 34 (8).
[67] *Ellis* v. *Home Office* [1953] 2 Q.B. 135; *Goody* v. *Odham Press Ltd.* [1967] 1 Q.B. 333.
[68] s. 30 (1).
[69] s. 1 (6).
[70] *Beckham* v. *Drake* (1849) 2 H.L.C. 579; *Ex p. Vine* (1878) 8 Ch.D. 364 (the bankrupt may spend damages he has recovered in the maintenance of himself and his family).
[71] *Rose* v. *Buckett* [1901] 2 K.B. 449; *Wenlock* v. *Moloney* [1965] 1 W.L.R. 1238.
[72] *Wilson* v. *United Counties Bank* [1920] A.C. 102.
[73] See under " Minors," *ante*, §§ 878–880.

making this approach to any given problem since in cases of negligence normally the applicable standard of care is the objective one.[74] By way of illustration a motorist who drove his car negligently could not escape liability by pleading by way of his defence that his unsoundness of mind was the cause of his failure to exercise the care and skill of a reasonably competent driver.

Where a person is a patient within the meaning of the Mental Health Act 1959 he must bring his action by his next friend [75] otherwise there are no special rules that apply in the case of a person of unsound mind. However no action in respect of acts done in pursuance of the provisions of that Act may be brought without the leave of the High Court.[76]

8.—ASSIGNEES

885 **Assignees.** A right of action for damages in respect of a tort is not capable of assignment, on the grounds of public policy.[77] As Lord Abinger said: " It is a rule—not of our law alone, but of that of all countries, that the mere right of purchase shall not give a man a right to legal remedies. The contrary doctrine is nowhere tolerated, and is against good policy." [78] On the other hand an assignment of the damages to be recovered in an action in tort is capable of being properly made since it is an assignment not of a bare cause of action but of property, namely, the fruits of an action as and when recovered.[79] Provided that the assignee has given written notice of the assignment to the third party, in compliance with section 136 of the Law of Property Act 1925, the assignee can sue in his own name and, further, he can enforce his right of action against the third party.[80]

9.—PERSONAL REPRESENTATIVES

886 **Executors and administrators.** What falls to be considered here is the question whether a cause of action survives the death of the injured person, which is quite distinct from the other question namely whether the act of causing the death of a person gives any, if so what, right of action for damages to his dependants. This latter is dealt with in detail in Chapter 19.

887 **Actio personalis moritur cum persona.** At common law a personal action died with the parties to the cause of action,[81] thus an action for negligence had to be begun during the joint lifetime of the person injured

[74] *White* v. *White* [1950] P. 39, *per* Denning L.J. at p. 59.
[75] R.S.C. Ord. 80 r. 2.
[76] Mental Health Act 1959, s. 141 (2). See application in *Buxton* v. *Jayne* [1960] 1 W.L.R. 783; *Moore* v. *Commissioner of Metropolitan Police* [1968] 1 Q.B. 26.
[77] *Defries* v. *Milne* [1913] 1 Ch. 98. *Cf. Dawson* v. *Great Northern and City Ry.* [1905] 1 K.B. 260.
[78] *Prosser* v. *Edmonds* (1835) 1 Y. & C. 481, 497. See also, *per* Farwell L.J. in *Defries* v. *Milne, supra.*, at p. 110; *Glegg* v. *Bromley* [1912] 3 K.B. 474.
[79] *Glegg* v. *Bromley, supra.*
[80] *Compania Colombiana de Seguros* v. *Pacific Steam Navigation Co.* [1965] 1 Q.B. 101.
[81] Law Revision Committee's Interim Report 1934 (Cmd. 4540).

and the tortfeasor. Even after such an action had been so commenced if either of the parties died before a verdict had been obtained, the action abated and could not be continued or recommenced by or against the deceased's personal representatives.

888 **Law Reform (Miscellaneous Provisions) Act 1934.** Before the passing of this Act it was commented upon frequently that it was cheaper to kill a man than to maim him.[82] The growth of motor traffic and the increasing number of accidents on the road highlighted this defect in the law, since a person injured in a collision due to the negligence of another driver might still find himself left without remedy, despite the existence of compulsory insurance[83] if the negligent defendant had been killed or had died subsequently. Accordingly, the Act made sweeping changes by providing, in this regard, that in future on the death[84] of any person all causes of action subsisting against or vested in him shall survive against, or, as the case may be, for the benefit of, his estate. On the other hand the Act does not abolish the common law rule that it is no tort to cause the death of another, but once death has occurred an existing cause of action can then descend to the personal representatives to pursue. In *Rose* v. *Ford*[85] the House of Lords held that a right of action for damages for loss of expectation of life survived to the personal representative, since a living person can claim damages for such loss, thus with the right vested in him in his lifetime, the same passes on to his personal representative after death. Even where the death is instantaneous the action will still descend to the personal representative since the cause of action is the negligence which has caused the death and not the fact of death itself.[86]

10.—JOINT AND SEVERAL TORTFEASORS[87]

889 **Joint and several torts.** Three situations can arise where two or more wrongdoers have committed torts which have caused damage to a plaintiff and these are: (1) where the wrongdoers are joint tortfeasors, (2) where they are several independent tortfeasors causing the same damage to him, and (3) where they are several independent tortfeasors but cause different damage to him. In this latter instance each wrongdoer is liable only for that part of the damage caused by him, whilst if one of a number of joint tortfeasors or one of several tortfeasors causing the same damage is sued alone then, subject to any right he may have to contribution from the other tortfeasors, he is liable for the whole of the damage, even though he may have been responsible merely for just a small part of it.[88]

[82] For comment of this maxim see *H. West & Son Ltd.* v. *Shephard* [1964] A.C. 326, *per* Lord Reid at p. 342.
[83] See Road Traffic Act 1930.
[84] Which includes subsequent suicide: *Pigney* v. *Pointers Transport Services* [1957] 1 W.L.R. 1121.
[85] [1937] A.C. 826.
[86] *Morgan* v. *Scoulding* [1938] 1 K.B. 786.
[87] The leading work on this subject is Glanville Williams' *Joint Tort and Contributory Negligence*.
[88] *Clark* v. *Newsham* (1847) 1 Ex. 131, 140; *Longdon-Griffiths* v. *Smith* [1951] 1 K.B. 295.

Prior to the passing of the Law Reform (Married Women and Tortfeasors) Act 1935 the distinction between situations (1) and (2) above was important since if there were a joint tort committed there could be only one action and one judgment obtained by the plaintiff for the whole of the amount of the damage suffered.[89] Accordingly judgment being obtained against one joint wrongdoer acted as a bar to any further action against any of the others, despite the fact that the judgment may have remained unsatisfied.[90] However this rule never applied in the case of there being several independent tortfeasors where each wrongdoer was responsible for a distinctly separate tort, since successive actions could then be brought against them, even where the plaintiff's damage was incapable of being apportioned between them.[91]

890 **Law Reform (Married Women and Tortfeasors) Act 1935.** This rule was abolished by section 6 of the Act which provides that:

"(1) Where damage is suffered by any person as a result of a tort (whether a crime or not)—(a) judgment recovered against any tortfeasor liable in respect of that damage shall not be a bar to an action against any other person who would, if sued, have been liable as a joint tortfeasor in respect of the same damage; (b) if more than one action is brought in respect of that damage by or on behalf of the person by whom it was suffered, or for the benefit of the estate, or of the wife, husband, parent or child, of that person, against tortfeasors liable in respect of the damage (whether as joint tortfeasors or otherwise) the sums recoverable under the judgments given in those actions by way of damages shall not in the aggregate exceed the amount of the damages awarded by the judgment first given; and in any of those actions, other than that in which judgment is first given, the plaintiff shall not be entitled to costs unless the court is of opinion that there was reasonable ground for bringing the action";

The effect of these provisions is that successive actions, subject to the aforesaid safeguards, may be brought against joint as well as several tortfeasors, who are liable in respect of the same damage to the plaintiff. By R.S.C. Order 15, rule 4 (1) all the tortfeasors may be made defendants in the same action regardless of whether they are joint or several causing the same damage to the plaintiff,[92] although under rule 4 (3) it is not imperative for him to sue all joint tortfeasors in the same action.[93] If judgment be obtained against one only, the costs which the plaintiff has to pay to the successful defendant can be added to the costs which he

[89] *London Association for Protection of Trade* v. *Greenlands* [1916] 2 A.C. 15.

[90] *Brinsmead* v. *Harrison* (1872) L.R. 7 C.P. 547 (the tort became submerged in the judgment); *Parr* v. *Snell* [1923] 1 K.B. 1; *Ash* v. *Hutchinson & Co.* [1936] Ch. 489.

[91] *The Koursk* [1924] P. 140. In the absence of evidence upon which to apportion the damages, they are usually apportioned equally between the tortfeasors; *Bunkview Mill* v. *Nelson Corpn.* [1942] 2 All E.R. 477, 483, which was reversed on other grounds [1943] 1 K.B. 337.

[92] See *Payne* v. *British Time Recorder Co. Ltd.* [1921] 2 K.B. 1, *per* Scrutton L.J. at p. 15, and Supreme Court Practice 1970, 15/4/4. The court has a discretion to order separate trials in certain circumstances.

[93] The defendant cannot compel the plaintiff to join other persons liable with him in tort. He can however apply to join such other person as a third party.

can recover from the unsuccessful defendant, if the court decides that he acted reasonably in joining the successful defendant as a party.[94] If judgment be obtained against more than one defendant, the plaintiff can recover the amount of his judgment from either or both of the defendants, provided he does not obtain more than the full amount of his judgment altogether, and he is not obliged to apportion the amount recovered among the various defendants. Among themselves, however, the defendants may recover contribution.

891 **Joint tortfeasors.** Wrongdoers are deemed to be joint tortfeasors within the meaning of the rule where the cause of action against each of them is the same, namely that the same evidence would support an action against them, individually.[95] As Sargant L.J. expressed it: "There must be a concurrence in the act or acts causing damage not merely a coincidence of separate acts which by their conjoined effect cause damage." [96] Accordingly they will be jointly liable for a tort which they both commit or for which they are responsible because the law imputes the commission of the same wrongful act to two or more persons at the same time. This occurs in cases of (a) agency, (b) vicarious liability [97] and (c) where a tort is committed in the course of a joint act whilst pursuing a common purpose agreed between them.[98]

An almost classic example of this latter situation is to be found in the facts of *Brooke* v. *Bool* where the defendant landlord went to investigate the smell of gas in the plaintiff's lock-up shop, taking his lodger with him to assist him in tracing the leaking pipe. The elderly defendant examined the lower part of the gas pipe with a naked light whilst the younger man climbed on top of the shop's counter with his naked light and was commencing to examine the upper part of the gas pipe when a severe explosion occurred. The defendant was held liable for the negligent acts of his lodger to the plaintiff shopkeeper for the loss and damage she had suffered.[99]

On the other hand wrongdoers will not be held jointly liable for a tort where each is responsible for a different *injuria* although the two *injuriae* happen to produce the same *damnum*[1]; they can only be jointly liable where the *injuriae* as well as the *damnum* are the same.[2] Many cases can

94 *Bullock* v. *London General Omnibus Co.* [1907] 1 K.B. 264; *Besterman* v. *British Motor Cab Co.* [1914] 3 K.B. 181.

95 *Brunsden* v. *Humphrey* (1884) 14 Q.B.D. 141, *per* Bowen L.J. at p. 147, quoting from older authorities.

96 *The Koursk* [1924] P. 140, at p. 159.

97 See *post*, Chap. 14.

98 See *Brooke* v. *Bool* [1928] 2 K.B. 578, at pp. 585, 586, *per* Salter J.

99 *Supra.*

1 *The Koursk*, *supra*, at p. 156 where Scrutton L.J. adopted as correct, the passage in *Clerk and Lindsell* (see now the 13th ed., § 179): " but mere similarity of design on the part of independent actors, causing independent damage is not enough; there must be concerted action to a common end." Still less will persons be joint tortfeasors when there is not even similarity of design, but independent wrongful acts accidentally resulting in one damage.

2 *e.g. King* v. *Sadler* (1969) 114 S.J. 192 (the plaintiff was injured by carbon monoxide gas which escaped from the boiler room below the hotel room where he was staying. He

be found in which the same damage is caused by independent and separate wrongful acts of several persons, for example where a plaintiff, a passenger travelling in a motor-car, sustains single damage as a result of the combined negligence of two or more motor-car drivers, who are not engaged in any common design, such as racing each other along the road.[3]

892 **Several tortfeasors causing different damage.** In contrast, where two or more tortfeasors cause different damage to the same plaintiff the causes of action against each wrongdoer are quite distinct and are required to be kept separate from one another. Thus the plaintiff is able to recover from each tortfeasor only that part of his damage which is attributable to the negligence of the particular defendant concerned.[4]

893 **Release.** The release of one joint tortfeasor releases all the others. Accordingly where a claim against several defendants, which is based upon the same facts, has been framed in alternative ways, if the plaintiff decides to accept a sum paid into court by one of the defendants in satisfaction of one of the causes of action, the whole of the claim against all the defendants comes to an end where the damages recoverable upon all the claims are the same and the sum so accepted is sufficient to cover these damages.[5] This full release would seem to be effective even though this may not have been the intention of the parties. A. L. Smith L.J. expressed the view on this point: " It is, we think, clear law, that a release granted to one joint tortfeasor, or to one joint debtor, operates as a discharge of the other joint tortfeasor or the other joint debtor, the reason being that the cause of action, which is one and indivisible, having been released, all persons otherwise liable thereto are consequently released." [6] This rule applies equally where the release has been made under deed or by way of accord and satisfaction.[7]

894 On the other hand a covenant or other agreement not to sue one of the joint tortfeasors does not operate as a release to the others, the reason being that the joint action is still alive.[8] Thus such a contract merely prevents it from being enforced against the particular tortfeasor with whom the plaintiff entered into the agreement not to sue. In *Gardiner* v. *Moore*[9] Thesiger J. held, *inter alia*, that while the release of one joint tortfeasor, whether by deed or by way of accord and satisfaction, released

claimed damages for negligence against the hotel owner and the gas board which was responsible for servicing the boiler. Sir Jocelyn Simon P. held that the board were in breach of their contract with the owner and in breach of their duty of care to the plaintiff; that the hotel owner was also in breach of duty to the plaintiff and that, on the facts liability should be apportioned equally between the two defendants).

[3] *The Koursk*, *supra*; *Drinkwater* v. *Kimber* [1952] 2 Q.B. 281, *per* Morris L.J. at p. 292.

[4] *Performance Cars Ltd.* v. *Abraham* [1962] 1 Q.B. 33; *Baker* v. *Willoughby* [1970] A.C. 467.

[5] *Beadon* v. *Capital Syndicate* (1912) 28 T.L.R. 427; *Clark* v. *Urquhart* [1930] A.C. 28 and see R.S.C., Ord. 22, r. 3 (3).

[6] *Duck* v. *Mayeu* [1892] 2 Q.B. 511, at p. 513.

[7] *Thurman* v. *Wild* (1840) 11 A. & E. 453.

[8] *Duck* v. *Mayeu*, *supra*, at p. 513, *per* A. L. Smith L.J. The distinction is well established, even if it be a technical one: *Cutler* v. *McPhail* [1962] 2 Q.B. 292.

[9] [1969] 1 Q.B. 55.

all others the same principle did not apply to a case with several tortfeasors. The form of release will be construed as being a mere agreement not to sue, if it contains an express or implied reservation of the right to proceed against the others, since otherwise the reservation would be wholly ineffective.

895 **Contribution between tortfeasors.** At common law, in the absence of an express or implied agreement for indemnity or contribution, permitted where it was not contrary to public policy, if an action were brought for a joint tort or for several torts causing the same damage one tortfeasor who had paid the whole of the damage could not recover any part of that sum that he had paid from the others. As Lord Goddard commented: " How some rules of law arose is not always known. For instance, except for the fact that in 1799 Lord Kenyon C.J. laid it down categorically in *Merryweather* v. *Nixan* [10] that there was no contribution between joint tortfeasors, no one has ever discovered whence the rule came, but it remained the law till abrogated by the Law Reform (Married Women and Tortfeasors) Act 1935." [11] By section 6 (1) (*c*) of this Act it is provided that where damage is suffered by any person as a result of a tort (whether a crime or not): " any tortfeasor liable in respect of that damage may recover contribution from any other tortfeasor who is, or would if sued have been, liable in respect of the same damage, whether as a joint tortfeasor or otherwise, so, however, that no person shall be entitled to recover contribution under this section from any person entitled to be indemnified by him in respect of the liability in respect of which the contribution is sought." It follows that if a plaintiff chooses to sue one tortfeasor only as a defendant the latter is entitled to claim against any other tortfeasor not so made a party to the action by bringing third-party proceedings against him. In such event the third party then becomes a party to the action with the same rights in respect of his defence against any claim made against him just as if he had been sued in the first instance by the defendant. However, it is only on the defendant being made liable that the defendant then has any cause of action against the third party. This was explained by Cassels J. " The position is quite clear. The proceedings by the defendant against the third party are independent of and separate from the proceedings by the plaintiff against the defendant, except that, when the defendant is made liable to the plaintiff, he then has his right open against the third party to establish, if he can, that he possesses a right to indemnity and contribution from that third party." [12]

10 (1799) 8 T.R. 186. See also *Romford Ice & Cold Storage Co. Ltd.* v. *Lister* [1956] 2 Q.B. 180 and [1957] A.C. 555 (on appeal). (Where one servant negligently injured another servant of the same employer, the H.L. held the employer entitled to a full indemnity from the servant on the ground that " the negligence was the negligence of the defendant and in those circumstances he is not entitled to anything by way of mitigation.") See also " Servant's obligation to indemnify master; an Australian note." Fridman, 106 L.J. 342.

11 *Carmarthenshire C.C.* v. *Lewis* [1955] A.C. 549, at p. 560.

12 *Hordern-Richmond Ltd.* v. *Duncan* [1947] K.B. 545, at p. 552. See R.S.C., Ord. 16, for the procedure involved.

896 **Who may claim contribution.** It is to be noted that the right to contribution only exists in favour of " any tortfeasor liable in respect of that damage." This was but one of the problems requiring clarification in the interpretation of this section of the Act which was faced by the House of Lords in *Wimpey* v. *B.O.A.C.*[13] The natural meaning of the word " liable " in this context is that the tortfeasor claimant to contribution must have committed a tort in respect of which he had been held liable to the plaintiff in the action by a court. However, when the matter was before the Court of Appeal both Singleton L.J. and Morris L.J. considered that word was not so limited to that meaning but it included the tortfeasor who had properly admitted liability to the person who had suffered damage without the necessity of having been held liable by a court.[14] In this event, Singleton L.J. added: " In such a case he would have to prove: (a) that he was a tortfeasor; and (b) that he was liable at the time he paid. And it would be open to the one against whom contribution was claimed to raise any defence which was open to the one who claimed contribution." [15] Since the law encourages the reaching of reasonable settlements this must be so, otherwise a tortfeasor would be compelled to defend an action to the end merely in order to establish his right to contribution, which cannot be the correct intention of the Act.

897 **From whom contribution may be claimed.** Contribution can only be recovered " from any other tortfeasor, who is, or would if sued have been, liable in respect of the same damage." Accordingly it cannot be recovered by the defendant from a person sued but against whom the plaintiff has failed in his action because, for example, at the time when the plaintiff commenced his proceedings, he was statute barred under the Limitation Acts.[16] Likewise contribution cannot be recovered if the person from whom it is claimed would not have been liable in an action brought against him.[17] Nevertheless, unlike the state of affairs in *Wimpey* v. *B.O.A.C.* where both the tortfeasors, namely the appellant and the respondent,

[13] [1955] A.C. 169.

[14] [1953] 2 Q.B. 501, at p. 510, and at p. 523. In the H.L., only Lord Reid mentioned this point, *supra*, at p. 186.

[15] *Ibid.* at p. 510.

[16] *Wimpey* v. *B.O.A.C.*, *supra*; *cf. Morgan* v. *Ashmore, Benson, Pease & Co.* [1953] 1 W.L.R. 418.

[17] As an example see *Knapp* v. *Railway Executive* [1949] 2 All E.R. 508 (a car driver accidentally hit a level crossing's gate, which was not securely fixed as it should have been under an Act of 1844, whereby it swung back across the track and was struck by an approaching train, injuring the train driver. The train driver sued his employers as well as the car driver but the latter settled the claim for £400. The C.A. held that since the relevant section of the 1844 Act was intended for the benefit of the highway users only it could not be relied upon by the train driver employed by the railway authority. Therefore since the train driver had no right of action under the section, the car driver likewise had no right so was not entitled to contribution from the railway authority). Further examples used to be found in those cases concerning the negligence of a husband or wife causing damage to the other when, prior to the passing of the Law Reform (Husband and Wife) Act 1962, one spouse could not sue the other in tort (see *ante*, § 876) so that a third party tortfeasor could not claim contribution from him or her as the case may be: *Chant* v. *Read* [1939] 2 K.B. 346; *Drinkwater* v. *Kimber* [1952] 2 Q.B. 281. A similar situation seems to arise under s. 10 (1) of the Crown Proceedings Act 1947 (see *ante*, § 861) where a serviceman on duty is injured by the combined negligence of a civilian and another serviceman.

had been sued by the injured plaintiff who, although he had succeeded against the appellant, had failed against the respondents (his employers), uncertainties have arisen as regards cases where the co-tortfeasor has not been sued to judgment by the plaintiff at all. Thus conflicting views have been expressed concerning the effect of the words "would, if sued, have been liable" in reaching the corollary namely "when?," if it be established that the co-tortfeasor would have been liable to the plaintiff at one particular time but not at some other moment. Such a problem faced McNair J. in *Harvey* v. *R. G. O'Dell Ltd.* (*Galway, Third Party*),[18] where he concluded that in view of the differences in opinion expressed by the Law Lords in *Wimpey's* case it is only binding authority for a case where a plaintiff had actually failed to establish liability against the tortfeasor, who was then sought to be made further liable by the defendant to contribute. McNair J. held that the words "if sued" do not have any temporal connotation but simply mean "if sued at any time." Accordingly he allowed the claim to contribution to succeed, its having been claimed by the defendant against the estate of a deceased tortfeasor, where neither the plaintiff's writ against the defendants, his employers, nor the defendants' notice claiming contribution was issued within six months of the grant of letters of administration to the deceased's administratrix.[19] In the result any tortfeasor who is required to contribute is not entitled to rely upon any limitation which, if an action were brought against him by the plaintiff instead, would have been available to him as a defence to that claim.

898 **Assessment of the amount of contribution.** Section 6 (2) of the Law Reform (Married Women and Tortfeasors) Act 1935 provides that "In any proceedings for contribution under this section the amount of the contribution recoverable from any person shall be such as may be found by the court to be just and equitable having regard to the extent of that person's responsibility for the damage; and the court shall have power to exempt any person from liability to make contribution, or to direct that the contribution to be recovered from any person shall amount to a complete indemnity." It follows that the court may order contribution amounting to a complete indemnity or, if one uses the alternative approach, it may exempt a person from liability altogether to make contribution.[20] Where an employer is liable because an independent contractor employed by him has failed to take reasonable care, the tendency is to give the employer contribution amounting to a full

[18] [1958] 2 Q.B. 78; see also *Hart* v. *Hall & Pickles Ltd.* [1969] 1 Q.B. 405 (where the plaintiff's claim against the second defendants was dismissed for want of prosecution, the first defendants were still entitled to maintain their claim for contribution).

[19] This is the limitation period prescribed by the Law Reform (Miscellaneous Provisions) Act 1934, s. 1 (3) (*b*). See Chap. 16, § 1150, *post* and *Airey* v. *Airey* [1958] 2 Q.B. 300. Further see *Morgan* v. *Ashmore, Benson, Pease & Co. Ltd.*, *supra*, criticising *Merlihan* v. *Pope (A.C.) Ltd.* (*Pagnello, Third Party*) [1946] K.B. 166, which was also doubted in *Hordern-Richmond Ltd.* v. *Duncan* [1947] K.B. 545.

[20] *e.g. Ryan* v. *Fildes* [1938] 3 All E.R. 517; *Lister* v. *Romford Ice and Cold Storage Co. Ltd.* [1957] A.C. 555.

indemnity.[21] The same is the case when the master is vicariously liable to a third party, not one of his servants,[22] but not when there is also some negligence on the part of the master himself.[23] This subsection has brooked criticism, in particular from Scott L.J. who remarked: " The subsection is, it is true, illogical, because it assumes the joint liability of two tortfeasors, which indeed is the postulate of the proceedings for contribution; but goes on to give the Court power to exempt one of such persons from liability to make any contribution at all, or, conversely, to make the other person pay the whole. In Admiralty the Maritime Conventions Act, 1911, is worked in this country, as I know is the case also in the jurisdiction of other countries which have the proportional rule, by apportioning the blame for injury done in the main action, and the curious ambiguity created by s. 6 of the 1935 Act cannot arise; but in spite of the illogical details of the language of subsection 2, I think that that section should be read as giving the judge, on the evidence that he has heard, complete jurisdiction to assess the blame of each tortfeasor just as if he had held them liable as defendants to the plaintiff only for that portion of the blame." [24]

899 Where a court finds that several defendants are liable as joint tortfeasors in damages to the plaintiff and a defendant so found liable applies for contribution, it is the duty of the court under section 6 (2) to make an assessment of the contribution which each defendant found liable should make according to his demonstrated share of blameworthiness. Moreover in making such an assessment the court must assess the damage as between those tortfeasors who have been found liable for it, regardless of any possible liability for negligence contributing to it of some other person who is not a party to the action and has not been found liable.[25]

There has also been some controversy whether the Act contemplates that damages should properly be assessed on the basis of causation or on the basis of the respective degrees of blameworthiness of the tortfeasors. Certainly the latter approach accords with the practice under the Maritime Conventions Act 1911[26] although Lord Pearce has expressed the view

[21] *Whitby* v. *Burt, Boulton & Hayward Ltd.* [1947] K.B. 918. It was conceded in *Honeywill & Stein Ltd.* v. *Larkin Bros. Ltd.* [1934] 1 K.B. 191 that the negligent contractors were liable to their employers either in contract or for negligence but see *Daniel* v. *Rickett Cockerell & Co.* [1938] 2 K.B. 322 and *Wilkinson* v. *Rea Ltd.* [1941] 1 K.B. 688, where such full contribution was not given.

[22] *Semtex* v. *Gladstone* [1954] 1 W.L.R. 945.

[23] *Jones* v. *Manchester Corpn.* [1952] 2 Q.B. 852. In *Daniel* v. *Rickett Cockerell & Co.* [1938] 2 K.B. 322 it was held that as the employer of the independent contractor was not entirely free from blame for the damage suffered the liability fell to be apportioned under the Act.

[24] *Croston* v. *Vaughan* [1938] 1 K.B. 540, at p. 565 (a woman driver pulled up violently and faster than a car usually did as well as failing to give a hand signal of her intention, which caused a chain of collisions from behind).

[25] *Maxfield* v. *Llewellyn* [1961] 1 W.L.R. 1119.

[26] See Williams, *Joint Torts*, pp. 157–158; Chapman, " Apportionment of Liability between Tortfeasors " (1948) 64 L.Q.R. 26 (" Causation itself is difficult enough, degrees of causation would really be a nightmare!"). It was adopted in *Weaver* v. *Commercial Process Co.* (1947) 63 T.L.R 466. For cases adopting the former alternative approach see *Smith* v. *Bray* (1939) 56 T.L.R. 200; *Collins* v. *Hertfordshire C.C.* [1947] K.B. 598.

that no true apportionment can be reached unless both those factors are borne in mind.[27] It is only in very exceptional cases that an appellate court should interfere with the trial judge's apportionment, when the trial judge's findings of fact have been accepted and there has been no error of law.[28]

900 Any issues of contribution between co-defendants, including apportionment, however, can be disposed of at the conclusion of the proceedings in which judgment is given against them, even if separate proceedings for contribution have not been instituted.[29]

Contribution between defendants who are already parties to an action is enforced by serving third-party notices under Order 16. It may, however, be enforced by making an application in court to the trial judge immediately after judgment, without serving any such notice.[30] This course, however, should not be adopted when issues as to discovery arise, such as the administration of interrogatories.[31] In the case of a person who is not already a party to the action the procedure set out in Order 16 applies. A written offer of contribution made by one joint tortfeasor to another before trial, has no effect on the order for costs when no costs have been incurred by the parties failing to agree the apportionment.[32]

901 **Limitation period for contribution proceedings.** Since the right of contribution is a right *sui generis* and not a cause of action in tort at all, the limitation period prescribed in such circumstances was once held to be six years.[33] However time does not begin to run until the cause of action for contribution under the Act accrues, which is normally when judgment has been given in the plaintiff's favour. Since such a state of affairs was so wholly out of line with the general policy of the limitations of actions it was felt necessary to remedy the situation. As a result by section 4 (1) of the Limitation Act 1963 it is provided that where a tortfeasor becomes entitled after July 31, 1963 to a right to recover contribution in respect of any damages from another tortfeasor, no action to recover contribution shall be brought after the end of two years from the date on which that right accrued to the first tortfeasor. Section 4 (2) goes on to provide that the date on which the right to recover contribution accrued " shall be ascertained as follows, that is to say —

27 *The Miraflores* v. *The Abades* [1967] 1 A.C. 826 and see also the view of Lawton J. in *Randolph* v. *Tuck* [1962] 1 Q.B. 175, 185; *Brown* v. *Thompson* [1968] 1 W.L.R. 1003. For a case under the Law Reform (Contributory Negligence) Act 1945, s. 1 (1), see views of Lord Reid in *Stapley* v. *Gypsum Mines Ltd.* [1953] A.C. 663, at p. 682.

28 *The MacGregor* [1943] A.C. 197, followed in *Ingram* v. *United Automobile Services Ltd.* [1943] K.B. 612; *Vickers* v. *E. Gomme Ltd.* [1957] 1 W.L.R. 656. A table, showing some decided apportionments set out, is to be found in Williams, *Joint Torts*, p. 159.

29 *Croston* v. *Vaughan, supra*; *Bell* v. *Holmes* [1956] 1 W.L.R. 1359. See *Calvert* v. *Pick* [1954] 1 W.L.R. 456 where Gerrard J. refused to apportion contribution between defendants after the plaintiffs had settled their actions but had agreed to retain one of their names on the record to keep the action alive so that the court might determine the issue of the proportion of damages.

30 *Burnham* v. *Boyer and Brown* [1936] 2 All E.R. 1165; *Croston* v. *Vaughan, supra*; followed in *Bell* v. *Holmes, supra*.

31 *Clayson* v. *Rolls-Royce Ltd.* [1951] 1 K.B. 746.

32 *Basted* v. *Cozens Sutcliffe Ltd.* [1954] 1 W.L.R. 1069.

33 *Harvey* v. *O'Dell Ltd.* [1958] 2 Q.B. 78.

(*a*) if the tortfeasor is held liable in respect of that damage by a judgment given in any civil proceedings or an award made on any arbitration, the relevant date shall be the date on which the judgment is given, or the date of the award, as the case may be;

(*b*) if, in any case not falling within the preceding paragraph, the tortfeasor admits liability in favour of one or more persons in respect of that damage, the relevant date shall be the earliest date on which the amount to be paid by him in discharge of that liability is agreed by or on behalf of the tortfeasor and that person, or each of those persons, as the case may be; and for the purposes of this subsection no account shall be taken of any judgment or award given or made on appeal in so far as it varies the amount of damages awarded against the tortfeasor."

In cases of fraud, disability and mistake a certain saving is given by section 4 (3).

902 **Contractual indemnity and the Act.** In practice contracts are frequently entered into between two parties which enable one of them to recover from the other an indemnity or some amount of contribution in the event of his becoming liable to a third party to pay damages for negligence or breach of statutory duty. This arises not only in cases where there is a separate policy of insurance cover but where there is an indemnity clause contained in some specific contract, such as when there has been the hire of some valuable item of plant or piece of equipment.[34] The principle involved in such cases is in no way dependent upon the provisions of the Law Reform (Married Women and Tortfeasors) Act 1935 since its roots are much older and deeper in history.[35] However problems have arisen as to their enforceability where the indemnity sought in respect of the tortious act happens to be a criminal offence as well.

903 Although the general principle at common law is expressed as: *ex turpi causa non oritur actio*, clearly the opening words of section 6 (1) of the Act, *viz.* " Where damage is suffered by any person as a result of a tort (whether a crime or not) . . .," constitute an exception to the rule. The importance of this becomes apparent when it is realised that so many actions for damages for personal injuries are brought where the allegations raised against the defendants concern breaches of their statutory duty *e.g.* under the Factories Act 1961 and/or the mass of regulations made thereunder, which also amount to criminal offences and are punishable as such, irrespective of the issues of civil liability.[36] Section 6 (4) (*c*) goes on to provide that the Act shall not render enforceable any agreement for indemnity which would not have been enforceable if the Act had never been passed. At common law, on the broad rule of public policy,

[34] Typically, as in *Wright* v. *Tyne Improvement Commissioners* [1968] 1 W.L.R. 336 (a crane).

[35] *Mowbray* v. *Merryweather* [1898] 2 Q.B. 640.

[36] For example the Construction (Lifting Operations) Regulations 1961 (S.I. 1961, No. 1581) in *Arthur White (Contractors) Ltd.* v. *Tarmac Civil Engineering Ltd.* [1967] 1 W.L.R. 1508, where nothing, incidentally, turned upon the fact that the first defendants, being liable for breach of statutory duty, were also guilty of a criminal offence.

no person can claim reparation or indemnity under a policy of insurance for the consequences of a criminal offence where his own wicked and deliberate intent is an essential ingredient in it.[37] Nevertheless in developing spheres of law, for example, such as that relating to road traffic, where motor insurance against third party risks became compulsory under the Road Traffic Act 1930,[38] the necessity of protection of innocent victims from the dire consequences of accidents involving motor vehicles has resulted in the courts readily holding that contracts of insurance are valid and enforceable. This is so even where the motorist has been guilty of driving in a manner which has amounted to a grave criminal offence [39]; thus insured drivers have been held entitled to indemnity under their insurance policies notwithstanding that their gross negligence also amounted to the crime of manslaughter.[40] It would seem therefore that the test to be applied in each case is not so much whether the act giving rise to liability was both criminal and tortious but rather to determine whether or not it was a deliberate wrongful act. In conclusion, a contractual indemnity against liability in respect of an unintentional tort is valid, even if the tort happens further to amount to a criminal offence. See Chapter 16, § 1098 *et seq.*, *post*, which deals more fully with indemnity.

904 **Master and servant.** It is an implied term in a servant's contract of employment that he shall exercise reasonable care in the performance of his duty to his master. Accordingly where a servant, a lorry driver, was negligent in the course of his employment as a result of which the employers were held to be vicariously liable and had to pay damages in respect of the servant's negligence, it was held that they were entitled to recover the amount of these damages from their servant in an action against him for breach of contract.[41] An employer, nevertheless, cannot rely upon the servant's or his contractor's breach of contract to recover the whole amount of the damages awarded against him, which he has had to pay if he himself or by another servant has also been guilty of negligence. In such circumstances his only remedy is to sue for contribution from the

[37] *Beresford* v. *Royal Insurance Co. Ltd.* [1938] A.C. 586.
[38] See now s. 201 of the Road Traffic Act 1960.
[39] *Hardy* v. *Motor Insurers' Bureau* [1964] 2 Q.B. 745.
[40] *Tinline* v. *White Cross Insurance Association Ltd.* [1921] 3 K.B. 327; *James* v. *British General Insurance Co. Ltd.* [1927] 2 K.B. 311.
[41] *Lister* v. *Romford Ice & Cold Storage Co.* [1957] A.C. 555 (it was held that there was no implied term in the contract of service that the driver was entitled to be indemnified by the employer either if the employer was in fact insured or was required by the Road Traffic Act to be insured, or if, as a reasonable and prudent person, he ought to have been insured). *Semtex* v. *Gladstone* [1954] 1 W.L.R. 945. See *Harvey* v. *R. G. O'Dell* (*Galway, Third Party*) [1958] 2 Q.B. 78 where it was held that *Lister's* case, *supra*, had no application where the servant was not actually carrying out the duties for which he was employed; *Gregory* v. *Ford* [1951] 1 All E.R. 121 (implied term in contract of service that employer would comply with the compulsory obligation to insure against third party risks). However Paull J. reserved his opinion whether this case remained good law since *Lister's* case, *supra*, and in *Vandyke* v. *Fender* [1969] 2 Q.B. 581 at p. 594 he applied " The principle—both at common law and under the Law Reform (Married Women and Tortfeasors) Act 1935—that an innocent principal is prima facie entitled to recover from his agent any moneys he has had to pay out by reason of the negligence of the agent." However the decision of Paull J. on third party liability was reversed by the C.A. [1970] 2 Q.B. 292 but leave to appeal to the H.L. was granted.

servant as a tortfeasor under the Act.[42] It will be seen from the above and these previous paragraphs that a master is jointly and severally liable for a tort which has been committed by his servant whilst acting in the course of his employment. It is now necessary to consider the scope of this vicarious liability [43] where in certain circumstances a person will be liable for the tort of another even though he has neither authorised nor ratified the tort.

[42] *Jones* v. *Manchester Corpn.* [1952] 2 Q.B. 852; *Daniel* v. *Rickett, Cockerell & Co.* [1938] 2 K.B. 322 (where Hilbery J. held that the employer of an independent contractor was not entirely free from blame, so that the damage fell to be apportioned under the Act of 1935). See article: " The Right to Indemnity between Master and Servant " (Jolowicz) (1956) C.L.J. 101; (1957) C.L.J. 21.

[43] The legal concept of vicarious liability requires three parties: the injured party, a person whose act or default caused the injury and a person vicariously liable for the latter's act or default: *Boyle* v. *Kodak* [1969] 1 W.L.R. 661, *per* Lord Diplock. See articles " Mixed and Vicarious Liability " (Barak), 29 M.L.R. 160: " Vicarious Liability Confined " (Fridman), 117 New L.J. 373.

CHAPTER 14

VICARIOUS LIABILITY

05 **Growth of the doctrine of vicarious liability.** The doctrine of vicarious liability has its roots in the early common law but it was not until the time of Sir John Holt, 1642–1710, that the development of these rules to meet the requirements of a more modern age began, which task of adaptation was effectively advanced by the great judges during the era of Queen Victoria's reign. Certainly by the turn of this century it was clearly established that the liability of a master was based not on the fiction that he had impliedly commanded his servant to do what he had done tortiously but on the more safe and simple ground that it had been done in the scope of or during the course of his employment or authority. Although this relationship of master and servant is by far the most important of the various cases in which vicarious liability is recognised by the law it is not confined merely to it. It follows that those for whose negligence a person may be liable must be considered under the headings of: (1) servants (2) agents (3) his children and (4) independent contractors.

1.—SERVANTS

06 **Distinction between servants and independent contractors.** A servant is one who is bound to obey any lawful orders given by the master as to the manner in which his work shall be done. The master retains the power of controlling him in his work, and may direct not only what he shall do, but how he shall do it.[1] Whether the employment is by the day or by the job, and whether the amount of wages or salary paid is great or small, is of little assistance in determining the existence of a contract of service.[2] " The test to be generally applied lies in the nature and degree of detailed control over the person alleged to be a servant." [3] " In ascertaining who is liable for the act of a wrongdoer, you must look to the wrongdoer himself or to the first person in the ascending line who is the employer and has control over the work. You cannot go further back, and make the employer of that person liable." [4]

An independent contractor, as opposed to a servant, is one who carries on an independent employment in the course of which he

[1] *Sadler* v. *Henlock* (1855) 4 E. & B. 570, 578, *per* Crompton J.; *Simmons* v. *Heath Laundry Co.* [1910] 1 K.B. 543; *Yewens* v. *Noakes* (1860) 6 Q.B.D. 530.

[2] *Sadler* v. *Henlock*, *supra*; *Performing Right Society Ltd.* v. *Mitchell and Booker* (*Palais de Danse*) *Ltd.* [1924] 1 K.B. 762.

[3] *Per* McCardie J. in the case last cited. It has been suggested ((1957) 6 I.C.L.Q. 162) that: " a better test to establish liability for a particular person's tort was whether he could be regarded as a member of the defendant's organisation." See also (1957) 20 M.L.R. 98.

[4] Willes J. in *Murray* v. *Currie* (1870) L.R. 6 C.P. 24, 27.

contracts to do certain work.[5] He may, by the terms of his contract, be subject to the directions of his employer, but apart from the contract he is his own master as to the manner and time in which the work shall be done.[6] If, in order to carry out the work, he has to engage and pay workmen or other servants on his own behalf and not as agent for another, there is a strong presumption that he is an independent contractor even though his employer has reserved the right to dismiss any workmen employed on his work.[7]

907 It is sometimes said that a servant is employed under a contract of service while an independent contractor is employed under a contract for services,[8] but this gives no assistance in determining whether a person is a servant or not because in all contracts of service it is the services of the servant which the master contracts to procure.

In more modern times, perhaps, the fullest discussion on this topic is to be found in the judgment of MacKenna J. in *Ready Mixed Concrete (South East) Ltd.* v. *Ministry of Pensions and National Insurance*[9] where after a full review of the authorities, including those outsides England, he held that a contract of service exists if (i) the servant agrees that, in consideration of a wage or other remuneration, he will provide his own work and skill in the performance of some service for his master; (ii) he agrees, expressly or impliedly that in the performance of that service he will be subject to the other's control in a sufficient degree to make that other master; and (iii) the other provisions of the contract are consistent with its being a contract of service.[10] Nevertheless whatever formula is sought to explain the apparent difficulties in drawing distinctions probably all avenues lead to the acceptance of the view of Somervell L.J. that " one perhaps cannot get much beyond this: ' was his contract a contract of service within the meaning which an ordinary person would give to the words? '. "[11]

908 A labourer, or other person carrying on an unskilled occupation, if employed to do work himself will usually be a servant, and accordingly

5 *Allen* v. *Hayward* (1845) 7 Q.B. 960, where the contractor was described as a " person carrying on an independent business, such as the commissioners were fully justified in employing to perform works which they could not execute for themselves, and who was known to all the world as performing them "; *Laugher* v. *Pointer* (1826) 5 B. & C. 547; *Quarman* v. *Burnett* (1840) 6 M. & W. 499.

6 *Steel* v. *S.E. Ry.* (1855) 16 C.B. 550; *Hardaker* v. *Idle D.C.* [1896] 1 Q.B. 335.

7 *Reedie* v. *L. & N.W. Ry.* (1849) 4 Ex. 244. Compare *Performing Right Society Ltd.* v. *Mitchell and Booker (Palais de Danse) Ltd. supra*, where the contract was made with the members of the band individually and they were held to be servants.

8 See, *e.g. Stevenson Jordan & Harrison Ltd.* v. *MacDonald & Evans* [1952] 1 T.L.R. 101, 111, *per* Denning L.J.; *Collins* v. *Hertfordshire C.C.* [1947] K.B. 598, 615, *per* Hilbery J.

9 [1968] 2 Q.B. 497; See Atiyah, *Vicarious Liability in the Law of Torts* (1967) pp. 37, 38.

10 *Ibid.* p. 515, whence the learned judge considered it unnecessary to enlarge upon (i) and (ii) but went on to explain (iii) at some length by giving five examples of what he meant by provisions *inconsistent* with the nature of a contract of service.

11 *Cassidy* v. *Ministry of Health* [1951] 2 K.B. 343, 352, 353 quoting the question, *inter alia*, as posed by Buckley L.J. in *Simmons* v. *Heath Laundry Co.* [1910] 1 K.B. 543, 553. See also, *per* Roskill J. in *Argent* v. *Minister of Social Security* [1968] 1 W.L.R. 1749 at p. 1760; *Market Investigations Ltd.* v. *Minister of Social Security* [1969] 2 Q.B. 173.

a labourer employed to clean out a drain on his employer's land,[12] and the owner of a horse and cart employed by the day to cart stones,[13] are servants. On the other hand, if he is not obliged to do the work in person but may engage others to do it, as where he lets on hire to a local authority a horse and driver to drive a watering cart,[14] he will usually be an independent contractor because he is carrying on a separate business of his own.

09 As a general rule, a person carrying on a skilled occupation as a separate business is not a servant; so, a plumber employed to mend a cistern,[15] a gas-fitter employed to mend a gas pipe,[16] a licensed drover employed to drive cattle in a district where the employment of a licensed drover is compulsory,[17] a stevedore employed to load or unload a ship,[18] an auctioneer conducting a sale on the premises of the person who employs him,[19] a music teacher who gives lessons to people either at her own house or at the houses of her pupils,[20] and a commercial traveller paid by commission,[21] have been held not to be servants. When the defendants, who had contracted with the owners of a theatre to produce a variety programme, made an agreement with variety artists to appear in the programme, it was held that the variety artists were not the defendants' servants.[22] Persons carrying on skilled occupations who are not carrying on a separate business will be servants, as a schoolmaster employed by a local education authority,[23] a musician employed at a dance hall.[24] A doctor employed by a hospital, whether he is full time or part time, is a servant.[25]

10 **Servant of one employer lent to another employer.** A servant may be the general servant of one person, and yet his services may be temporarily put at the disposal of another, who may be described as the particular employer. In such a case, although the general employer may pay the servant, select him for the work in question and have the power of dismissing him, the particular employer may in some circumstances be liable for the servant's negligence while engaged in his particular employment. "That the servant of A may, on a particular occasion, and for a particular purpose, become the servant of B, notwithstanding that he

[12] *Sadler* v. *Henlock* (1855) 4 E. & B. 570.
[13] *O'Donnell* v. *Clare C.C.* (1913) 47 I.L.T. 41.
[14] *Jones* v. *Liverpool Corporation* (1885) 14 Q.B.D. 890.
[15] *Blake* v. *Woolf* [1898] 2 Q.B. 426.
[16] *Rapson* v. *Cubitt* (1842) 9 M. & W. 710.
[17] *Milligan* v. *Wedge* (1840) 12 A. & E. 737. Otherwise in a district where it is not compulsory: *Turnbull* v. *Wieland* (1916) 33 T.L.R. 143.
[18] *Murray* v. *Currie* (1870) L.R. 6 C.P. 24.
[19] *Walker* v. *Crabb* (1916) 33 T.L.R. 119.
[20] *Simmons* v. *Heath Laundry Co.* [1910] 1 K.B. 543.
[21] *Egginton* v. *Reader* (1936) 52 T.L.R. 212.
[22] *Fraser-Wallas* v. *Waters* [1939] 4 All E.R. 609.
[23] *Smith* v. *Martin and Hull Corporation* [1911] 2 K.B. 775.
[24] *Performing Right Society Ltd.* v. *Mitchell and Booker* (*Palais de Danse*) *Ltd.* [1924] 1 K.B. 762.
[25] *Bolam* v. *Friern Hospital Management Committee* [1957] 1 W.L.R. 582. For the law relating to such persons, see *ante*, Chap. 7.

continues in A's service and is paid by him, is a rule recognised by a series of decisions." [26] " When one person lends his servant to another for a particular employment, the servant, for anything done in that particular employment, must be dealt with as the servant of the man to whom he is lent, although he remains the general servant of the person who lent him." [27] Whether or not the servant has become *pro hac vice* the servant of the particular employer is a question of fact in each case.[28] Lord Dunedin said categorically that the facts of one case can never rule another case and are only useful so far as similarity of facts are a help and a guide to decision,[29] although " it has been sought to find some general idea, or perhaps mere catchword, which may serve as a clue to solve the problem." [30] It is often a question of some difficulty to know whether at a given time the servant was in the service of the general employer or of the particular employer, so as to make the particular employer liable for the servant's negligence, and it is not easy to reconcile the later decisions with the earlier. The modern tendency is to hold that, in general, the servant remains the servant of the general employer. This is illustrated in *J. Young & Co.* (*Kelvinhaugh*) v. *O'Donnell*,[31] where the House of Lords held that the employers of a crane driver who had been negligent, whilst on hire, had failed to shift the prima facie responsibility from themselves as the general employer to the hirer as the temporary employer.

911 At one time the view prevailed that the main, if not the sole, test was the extent of the right of controlling the servant. This was stated by Bowen L.J. in *Donovan* v. *Laing Syndicate* [32]: " We have only to consider in whose employment the man was at the time when the acts complained of were done, in this sense, that by the employer is meant the person who has a right at the moment to control the doing of the act." So, too, Lord Dunedin said: " Payment is not everything; it is a circumstance pointing to who is the employer, but the real test is control." [33] Later, Lord Wright suggested [34] that control was not the test, but that the question was whether the servant was transferred or only the use and benefit of his work. More recently, the House of Lords

[26] Lord Watson in *Union Steamship Co. Ltd.* v. *Claridge* [1894] A.C. 185, 188.

[27] *Per* Cockburn C.J. in *Rourke* v. *White Moss Colliery* (1877) 2 C.P.D. 205, 209.

[28] *M'Cartan* v. *Belfast Harbour Commissioners* [1911] 2 I.R. 143 (H.L.).

[29] *Ibid.* p. 149. For examples see: *Donovan* v. *Laing Construction* [1893] 1 Q.B. 629; *Bain* v. *Central Vermont Ry.* [1921] 2 A.C. 412; *Bull* v. *West African Shipping Agency etc. Co.* [1927] A.C. 686; *Clelland* v. *Lloyds Ltd.* [1938] 1 K.B. 272; *Mersey Docks & Harbour Board* v. *Coggins & Griffith* (*Liverpool*) *Ltd.* [1947] A.C. 1; *Herdman* v. *Walker* (*Tooting*), *City Plant Hirers* (*Third Party*) [1956] 1 W.L.R. 209; *Brogan* v. *William Allan Smith & Co. Ltd.*, 1965 S.L.T. 175; *McGregor* v. *Duthie & Sons & Co. Ltd.*, 1966 S.L.T. 133.

[30] *Per* Lord Wright in *Century Insurance Co. Ltd.* v. *Northern Ireland Road Transport Board* [1942] A.C. 509, 515.

[31] 1958 S.L.T. 46.

[32] [1893] 1 Q.B. 629. Bowen L.J.'s judgment has been constantly quoted and approved, *e.g.* by the H.L. in *M'Cartan* v. *Belfast Harbour Comrs.* [1911] 2 Ir.R. 143, and *Century Insurance Co.* v. *N.I. Road Transport Board* [1942] A.C. 509. See, however, the criticism of it in *Mersey Docks and Harbour Board* v. *Coggins & Griffith* (*Liverpool*) *Ltd.* [1947] A.C. 1.

[33] *Bain* v. *Central Vermont Ry.* [1921] 2 A.C. 412.

[34] In *Century Insurance Co. N.I. Road Transport Board, supra*, at p. 516, following Bowen L.J. in *Moore* v. *Palmer* (1886) 2 T.L.R. 781, 782.

in *Mersey Docks and Harbour Board* v. *Coggins & Griffith* (*Liverpool*) *Ltd.*[35] re-established the test of control in the sense that the right of control means the right to control the way in which the act involving negligence was done. Whilst this case establishes no universal and conclusive test to be applied, Lord Porter stated: " Many factors have a bearing on the result. Who is paymaster, who can dismiss, how long the alternative service lasts, what machinery is employed, have all to be kept in mind." [36]

912 The following propositions may be derived from the cases:

1. The presumption is that the servant remains the servant of the general employer, the burden of proof being on those who assert the contrary. This burden is a heavy one and can only be discharged in quite exceptional circumstances.[37]

2. The employer at the material time is that employer who can tell the servant not only what he has to do, but also the way in which he is to do it. If the servant when doing the negligent act is merely exercising the discretion vested in him by the general employer and not obeying detailed directions given by the particular employer, he remains the servant of the general employer.[38]

3. The contract between the employers may provide that the servant shall be the servant of the particular employer. This contract is not conclusive. It cannot be used " to contradict the fact, if it is the fact, that the complete dominion and control over the servant has not passed from one to the other." [39]

4. If the servant is not employed to work or drive any machine, vehicle or animal belonging to the general employer, it is easier to find that he has become the servant of the particular employer.

This is seen by comparing the cases in which a driver with a vehicle

[35] [1947] A.C. 1, *per* Viscount Simon at p. 12, Lord Porter at p. 17, Lord Uthwatt at p. 23.

[36] *Ibid.* at p. 17 (this passage was applied in *The Polartank* [1948] Lloyds Rep. 108 and *The Panther and The Ericbank* [1957] P. 143).

[37] *Mersey Docks and Harbour Board* v. *Coggins & Griffith* (*Liverpool*) *Ltd.*, *supra*; *Century Insurance Co.* v. *N.I. Road Transport Board* [1942] A.C. 509. The burden was discharged in *Gibb* v. *United Steel Ltd.* [1957] 1 W.L.R. 668, where a dock labourer, who was the general servant of a harbour board and was injured while working on premises of which they were the owners and occupiers, was held to be *pro hac vice* the servant of master stevedores for whom he was working at the time of the accident. The burden was not discharged in *J. Young & Co.* (*Kelvinhaugh*) v. *O'Donnell*, 1958 S.L.T. 46; where a crane and its driver, who acted negligently, was on hire.

[38] *Mersey Docks and Harbour Board* v. *Coggins & Griffith* (*Liverpool*) *Ltd. supra.* See also *Denham* v. *Midland Employers' Mutual Assurance Ltd.* [1955] 2 All E.R. 561 (unskilled labourer, lent by general employer to particular employer, injured by negligence of particular employer's servants is not " under a contract of service " with the particular employer within the meaning of an insurance policy).

[39] *Mersey Docks and Harbour Board* v. *Coggins & Griffith* (*Liverpool*) *Ltd.*, *supra*, *per* Lord Simonds at p. 20. As to the effect of the servant's consent to the transfer, see *ibid.*, *per* Lord Uthwatt at p. 22, *Century Insurance Co.* v. *N.I. Road Transport Board*, *supra*, at p. 516, *per* Lord Wright. In both these cases there was a contract purporting to decide in whose employment the servant was, but little importance was attached to the contracts by the H.L. See also *Denham* v. *Midland Employers' Mutual Assurance Ltd.*, *supra*, *per* Denning L.J. at p. 564. In *Bain* v. *Central Vermont Ry.* [1921] 2 A.C. 412, the contract was treated as decisive. See also *Poulson* v. *Jarvis & Sons Ltd.* (1919) 36 T.L.R. 160; *Malley* v. *L.M.S. Ry.*, 1944 S.C. 129, 136.

or animal has been hired with those in which the driver alone has been hired.

When the owner of a carriage hired a pair of horses and a driver from a livery-stable, it was held that the driver was the servant of the livery-stable keeper and not of the owner of the carriage.[40] The same result was arrived at in a case where the owner of the carriage always had the same driver, and provided a livery for his use, with the result that while the driver was changing his livery he left the horses unattended and an accident occurred.[41] But where the owner of the carriage had his own horses and hired a driver alone, it was held that the driver was the servant of the owner of the carriage.[42] Similarly, when the owner of a motor-car hired a chauffeur from a garage, the chauffeur was held to be the servant of the car owner and not of the garage.[43] Again, when the purchaser of a motor-car agreed with the vendor that the vendor should supply a driver to drive the car to a particular destination, and an accident was caused through the driver's negligence, it was held that the driver was the purchaser's servant because the purchaser, being in the car at the time, had control of the driver.[44] But, when a motor-car was left with the manufacturers for repair and was then driven by a servant in the general employment of the manufacturers to take the owner to a railway station the servant was held not to be in the particular employment of the owner, on the ground that the owner had no right to control the manufacturers' servant.[45]

An electrician lent by his general employer to a particular employer to work in a factory was held to be the servant of the particular employer,[46] but where a ship was being unloaded at a jetty, the operation being under the general control of the jetty owners, and carried out partly by their servants working a grab and partly by trimmers employed by contractors, it was held that the trimmers had not passed into the service of the jetty owners.[47]

5. When the servant is employed to work or drive any machine, vehicle or animal belonging to the general employer, he exercises the discretion in its management delegated to him by the general employer and, subject to what is stated above, remains the servant of the general employer.

913 There are a number of cases dealing with the hire of a vehicle and driver. In almost all these cases the hirer gives instructions to the driver where he is to go and generally controls his actions in much the same way as if he was in his own employment. The driver, however, remains the

[40] *Laugher* v. *Pointer* (1826) 5 B. & C. 547, *per* Littledale J. and Abbott C.J., whose opinion was subsequently adopted in *Quarman* v. *Burnett* (1840) 6 M. & W. 499.
[41] *Quarman* v. *Burnett, supra.*
[42] *Jones* v. *Scullard* [1898] 2 Q.B. 565.
[43] *Bowie* v. *Shenkin*, 1934 S.C. 459.
[44] *Perkins* v. *Stead* (1907) 23 T.L.R. 433.
[45] *Chowdhary* v. *Gillot* [1947] 2 All E.R. 541.
[46] *Garrard* v. *A. E. Southey & Co.* [1952] 2 Q.B. 174.
[47] *Johnson* v. *A. H. Beaumont Ltd.* [1953] 2 Q.B. 184.

servant of the general employer unless there are quite exceptional circumstances pointing to the contrary.

914 Where a local authority hired a horse and driver to drive a watering cart, their property, it was held that the driver was not their servant, although their instructor told him what streets to water.[48] Where a company, in order to deliver goods to their customers, contracted with the defendant for the supply to them each working morning during the year of vans, horses and drivers, the drivers to be employed and paid by the defendant, who was to receive an inclusive sum for each van, horse and driver supplied, it was held that the drivers were the servants of the defendant and not of the company, although the company directed their work during the day.[49] Where the defendants let on hire an engine and driver, and the hirers directed where the engine was to go and what loads it should haul, it was held that the driver was the defendants' servant, because they appointed, paid and could dismiss him, the hirers merely having the right of telling him where he was to go.[50] Again, where the Ministry of Munitions were engaged in discharging steel billets from a ship into railway trucks, and contracted with the defendants for the supply of a man and two horses to haul the trucks from the shed, where they were loaded, to railway lines outside, it was held that the man was the servant of the defendants and not of the Ministry, although he received his instructions from the Ministry's representative.[51] When a lorry and driver were hired to a firm of furniture-removers, who could instruct the driver where to go and when, but had no power to dismiss him, it was held that the driver was the servant of the general employers.[52] When a transport undertaking let on hire a lorry and driver to a petroleum company under a contract providing that the driver should accept the orders of the company regarding the delivery of petrol and all matters incidental thereto, and the petrol caught fire while it was being delivered from the lorry to a tank, owing to the driver's negligence, the transport undertaking was held liable.[53] When a van and driver were hired to a firm to deliver goods to their customers, the driver being instructed as to the parcels to be delivered but being free to deliver them in the order he thought fit, the driver was held to be the servant of the general employers.[54]

48 *Jones* v. *Liverpool Corpn.* (1885) 14 Q.B.D. 890; *Mileham* v. *Borough of Marylebone and Latter* (1903) 67 J.P. 110, is a similar case.
49 *Waldock* v. *Winfield* [1901] 2 K.B. 596.
50 *Dewar* v. *Tasker & Sons Ltd.* (1907) 23 T.L.R. 259; C.A. reversing Div.Ct.
51 *Poulson* v. *Jarvis & Sons Ltd.* (1919) 89 L.J.K.B. 305.
52 *Willard* v. *Whiteley* [1938] 3 All E.R. 779. Similar cases are *Dowd* v. *W. H. Boase & Co. Ltd.* [1945] K.B. 301; *Nicholas* v. *F. J. Sparkes & Son* [1945] K.B. 309n.; *Marney* v. *Campbell, Symonds & Co. Ltd.* [1946] W.N. 72; *O'Reilly* v. *I.C.I. Ltd.* [1955] 1 W.L.R. 1155.
53 *Century Insurance Co.* v. *N.I. Road Transport Board* [1942] A.C. 509 (there was a contract relating to the service dealing with the question whose servant the driver was, but the H.L. attached no decisive importance to it).
54 *Bontex Knitting Works Ltd.* v. *St. John's Garage* [1943] 2 All E.R. 690, affd. [1944] 1 All E.R. 381.

The only case of this kind in which a different result has been arrived at is *Leggott & Son* v. *Normanton*.[55] There the defendants were in the habit of hiring from the plaintiffs, who were haulage contractors, motor-wagons with drivers, and the drivers received their instructions from the defendants and remained throughout the day under their orders; it was held that the drivers were the servants of the defendants. In view of the decisions quoted above, it must be taken that *Leggott & Son* v. *Normanton* was wrongly decided.[56]

915 There is a group of cases dealing with the hiring of cranes and similar pieces of machinery and men to work them.

Where colliery owners, who had started to sink a shaft at their colliery, agreed with a contractor that he should continue the work and that they should place at his disposal an engine with an engineer to work it, the engineer being in their general employment and paid by them, it was held that the engineer, who by his negligence injured some of the other workmen, was the servant of the contractor because he was under the orders and control of the contractor when the injuries were caused.[57] Again, where the owners hired out a crane, together with a man to work it, to a firm of wharfingers for use in loading ships at the wharf, it was held that, although the crane-man was selected and paid by the crane-owners, he was to be regarded as the servant for the time being of the wharfingers, because he was subject to their control.[58] On the other hand, in numerous later cases,[59] on facts which seem to be indistinguishable, the crane-man concerned has been held to remain the servant of the general employers.

When a ship was being unloaded by a stevedore who, in addition to his own workmen, employed and paid some of the ship's crew to assist him, it was held that the crew while so employed were the stevedore's servants.[60] But when the contract between the shipowner and the stevedore provided that the shipowner should provide one winch-driver and one hatchman for each hatch being discharged, and there was nothing in the contract or in the evidence to suggest that the winch-driver should be under the control of the stevedore, it was held that he was the servant of the shipowner.[61]

916 The circumstances may show that there was no intention to transfer the servant from the general employer to the particular employer, as

[55] (1928) 98 L.J.K.B. 145.
[56] In *Willard* v. *Whiteley* [1938] 3 All E.R. 779, the C.A. tentatively expressed this view.
[57] *Rourke* v. *White Moss Colliery* (1877) 2 C.P.D. 205.
[58] *Donovan* v. *Laing Syndicate* [1893] 1 Q.B. 629.
[59] *Mersey Docks and Harbour Board* v. *Coggins & Griffith (Liverpool) Ltd.* [1947] A.C. 1; *M'Cartan* v. *Belfast Harbour Comrs.* [1911] 2 Ir.R. 143; *Cairns* v. *Clyde Navigation Trustees* (1898) 25 R. 1021; *Ainslie* v. *Leith Docks Comrs.*, 1919 S.C. 676; *Moore* v. *Palmer* (1886) 2 T.L.R. 781. In *Holt* v. *W. H. Rhodes & Son Ltd.* [1949] 1 All E.R. 478, where a crane and driver were hired to stevedores, the C.A. ordered a new trial to decide whether the control of the operation had passed to the stevedores. See also the House of Lords decision in *J. Young & Co. (Kelvinhaugh)* v. *O'Donnell*, 1958 S.L.T. 46.
[60] *Murray* v. *Currie* (1870) L.R. 6 C.P. 24.
[61] *Union Steamship Co.* v. *Claridge* [1894] A.C. 185.

where an apprentice was sent by his employers to work with some contractors, who were installing plant on his employers' premises, as part of his training and not in response to any request for men by the contractors.[62]

917 **Particular employer's interference with the work.** Even though the servant remains the servant of the general employer, the particular employer may make himself liable for the servant's negligence. This occurs when he takes the control entirely away from the general employer and instructs the servant to do a specific act which he would not have done without those instructions. As Parke B. puts it: "It is undoubtedly true that there may be special circumstances which may render the hirer of job-horses and servants responsible for the neglect of a servant, though not liable by virtue of the general relation of master and servant. He may become so by his own conduct, as by taking the actual management of the horses, or ordering the servant to drive in a particular manner, which occasions the damage complained of, or to absent himself at one particular moment, and the like." [63] "If however the hirers intervene to give directions as to how to drive which they have no authority to give, and the driver *pro hac vice* complies with them, with the result that a third party is negligently damaged, the hirers may be liable as joint tortfeasors." [64]

It has been held that when a man rode upon the box of a carriage, hired from the general employer and driven by his servants, he made himself responsible for the negligence of the postilions because "with a full view of all that was taking place and not interfering" he assented to their act,[65] but this seems to go much too far.[66] The liability of the particular employer can only be based upon assumption of control and not upon passive acquiescence.

918 **Liability of general employer to particular employer for negligence of servant.** If a servant in the general employment of one person is temporarily in the employment of another, it follows that the particular employer cannot claim from the general employers for damage caused by the negligence of the servant while in his employment. A wooden motor ship required repairs at Shanghai, and the engineer obtained the services of some of the dock company's workmen to do the necessary work. The engineer required the use of candles and, by the negligence of a workman, the ship caught fire. It was held that, as the workman

62 *Clelland* v. *Edward Lloyd Ltd.* [1938] 1 K.B. 272.
63 *Quarman* v. *Burnett* (1840) 6 M. & W. 499, 507. See also, *per* Lush J. in *Poulson* v. *Jarvis & Sons Ltd.* (1919) 36 T.L.R. 160.
64 *Per* Lord Simon in *Mersey Docks and Harbour Board* v. *Coggins & Griffith* (*Liverpool*) *Ltd.* [1947] A.C. 1, 12.
65 *McLaughlin* v. *Pryor* (1842) 4 Man. & G. 48. *Burgess* v. *Gray* (1845) 1 C.B. 578 (owner of premises employs contractor to make drain communicating with sewer—heap of rubbish left, over which passer-by in highway falls—employer liable) was decided on the ground of personal interference by the employer, but seems rather a case of a contractor employed to interfere with the highway.
66 *Pike* v. *London General Omnibus Co.* (1891) 8 T.L.R. 164.

committed his act of negligence at the time when he was employed by the shipowners, there was no liability upon his general employers, the dock company.[67]

919 **Liability of particular employer to general employer for negligence of servant.** Conversely, if the servant, while in the service of the particular employer, negligently causes damage to the general employer, the particular employer is liable. So, where a lighter, manned by two lightermen, was let on hire to a ship for the purpose of loading it and, owing to the negligence of the lightermen in being absent during the night, the lighter got adrift and was damaged, it was held that the shipowners were liable for the damage to the lighter.[68] Similarly, where a motor-lorry with a driver was let on hire by the general employers, a firm of haulage contractors, to the particular employers, and, owing to the negligence of the driver, the lorry was driven under a tunnel so that the load became jammed and the lorry was damaged, it was held that the particular employers were liable for the damage to the lorry.[69]

920 **Persons who are not servants.** Nurses supplied by a nursing association on the terms that they were to obey the directions of the patient's medical man and were to be regarded as employed by the person engaging the nurse are not the servants of the nursing association so as to make the association liable for the negligence of the nurse during an operation.[70] The resident medical staff and the nurses at a hospital are not the servants of the surgeon operating at the hospital.[71]

Persons appointed by a local authority to perform statutory or common law duties are not the servants of the local authority while performing those duties. So an inspector appointed under the Diseases of Animals Acts,[72] and a police constable appointed by the watch committee,[73] have each been held not to be servants of the local authority. Further it has been held that the relationship of master and servant did not exist between the State and a sergeant in one of the Defence forces.[74] On the other hand, special constables employed by a railway company under powers contained in a private Act of Parliament are the servants of the company.[75] An engineer appointed by a board of guardians, whether he was a servant of the board or not, did not fix the board with liability for his negligence towards the recipients of poor law relief from the guardians.[76] A scoutmaster and a cub mistress in charge of

[67] *Société Maritime Française* v. *Shanghai Dock and Engineering Co.* (1921) 37 T.L.R. 379.
[68] *A. H. Bull & Co.* v. *West African Shipping Co.* [1927] A.C. 686.
[69] *Leggott & Son* v. *Normanton* (1928) 98 L.J.K.B. 145. The correctness of this decision on the question who the employer was is questioned above, § 914.
[70] *Hall* v. *Lees* [1904] 2 K.B. 602. For the position of doctors and nurses at a hospital, see Chap. 7.
[71] *Morris* v. *Winsbury-White* [1937] 4 All E.R. 494.
[72] *Stanbury* v. *Exeter Corpn.* [1905] 2 K.B. 838.
[73] *Fisher* v. *Oldham Corpn.* [1930] 2 K.B. 364. See also *Att.-Gen. for New South Wales* v. *Perpetual Trustee Co. Ltd.* [1955] A.C. 457. And see the Police Act 1964 and *ante*, § 863.
[74] *Att.-Gen. and Minister for Defence* v. *Ryans' Car Hire* (1964) 101 I.L.T.R. 57.
[75] *Lambert* v. *G.E. Ry.* [1909] 2 K.B. 776.
[76] *Tozeland* v. *West Ham Union* [1907] 1 K.B. 920.

schoolboys at an outing to Whipsnade Zoo were not servants of the Boy Scouts Association.[77]

21 **Persons who are servants.** There is an inference that a person is employed as a servant and not as an independent contractor where, despite his special skills needed to fulfil his duties, he comes under the direct supervision or personal control of his employer and does not purport to exercise some independent employment.[78] An example of this is to be found in a case of school-teachers who are employed, paid and liable to be dismissed by a local education authority and there thus exists the relationship of master and servant between them. Accordingly the local authority, as the employer, is vicariously liable for acts and omissions of the schoolmaster in the course of his employment.[79] So, where a schoolmistress punished a boy by boxing his ear thereby causing deafness, the employers were held liable.[80] For the employer in the case of county schools and in voluntary schools reference should be made to section 24 of the Education Act 1944.[81] In the case of endowed schools—which are usually known as public schools—the governors of the school are the employers; in private schools the proprietor of the school is the employer. The relationship of master and servant does not exist between the headmaster and under-masters in schools controlled by the local education authority; they are all servants of the education authority or the managers and consequently the headmaster is not liable for the negligence of a pupil-teacher or other subordinate master.[82] The Public Schools Act 1868, s. 13, provides that in the case of schools to which the Act applies,[83] all masters are appointed by and hold office at the pleasure of the headmaster, but that does not make the under-masters the servants of the headmaster. In private schools, unless the headmaster is the owner of the school, there will be no relationship of master and servant between him and the under-masters.

Although a headmaster is not liable for the acts of an under-master as his servant, he is liable if he delegates to an under-master, as his agent, some duty cast upon him which he ought to have performed himself but the under-master has performed negligently, under the maxim: "*delegatus non potest delegare*."

Under the same category may come doctors and the like professional employees. However, a local education authority are not liable for the negligence of a doctor or a surgeon in the carrying out of an operation on a pupil, provided they engage a competent person to perform the operation,[84] unless the doctor or surgeon is in their employment.

77 *Murphy* v. *Zoological Society of London, The Times,* November 14, 1962.
78 *Smith* v. *Martin and Hull Corpn.* [1911] 2 K.B. 775; *Fryer* v. *Salford Corpn.* [1937] 1 All E.R. 617.
79 *Smith* v. *Martin and Hull Corpn., supra.*
80 *Ryan* v. *Fildes* [1938] 3 All E.R. 517.
81 Amended by the Education Act 1959 in other respects.
82 *Crisp* v. *Thomas* (1890) 63 L.T. 756.
83 Eton, Winchester, Westminster, Charterhouse, Harrow, Rugby and Shrewsbury.
84 *Davis* v. *L.C.C.* (1914) 30 T.L.R. 275.

922 At one time it was considered that hospital authorities were not vicariously liable for the negligence of members of their medical staff since the element of control over their methods of working was lacking where the staff were employed to exercise their professional skills according to their own discretion, without being bound to obey the authorities' directions.[85] However, the modern view is to the contrary so that radiographers,[86] house surgeons,[87] whole-time assistant medical officers [88] and, probably, anaesthetists on the staff [89] have been held to be servants for whose negligence the hospital authority would ordinarily be vicariously liable.

The exact position as regards visiting consultants and surgeons is probably of no practical importance now because of the coming into force of the National Health Service Act 1946, since by section 3 it is the duty of the Minister to provide *inter alia* " medical, nursing or other services required at or for the purposes of hospitals " and " the services of specialists." Accordingly as the hospital authority itself is under a primary duty to its patients it cannot discharge that duty simply by delegating its performance to somebody else whether independent contractor or servant.[90] Nor is the hospital authority's statutory duty discharged by the appointment of competent doctors, nurses and specialists.[91]

Course of the Employment

923 **Meaning of the term.** A master is liable for the negligence of the servant if committed in the course of his employment, but is not liable for negligence committed outside the scope of his employment. Lynskey J. stated: " It is well settled law that a master is liable even for acts which he has not authorised provided that they are so connected with the acts which he has authorised that they may rightly be regarded as modes, although improper modes, of doing them. On the other hand, if the unauthorised and wrongful act of the servant is not so connected with the authorised act as to be a mode of doing it but is an independent act the master is not responsible for, in such a case the servant is not acting in the course of his employment but has gone outside it." [92] An act is done in the course of the employment not only when the servant is actually doing the work, which he is employed to do, but also when the act is an incident in performing something he is employed to do and when he is about business which concerns the master and the servant.[93]

85 *Hillyer* v. *St. Bartholomew's Hospital* [1909] 2 K.B. 820, *per* Farwell L.J. at p. 825.
86 *Gold* v. *Essex C.C.* [1942] 2 K.B. 293.
87 *Collins* v. *Hertfordshire C.C.* [1947] K.B. 598.
88 *Cassidy* v. *Ministry of Health* [1951] 2 K.B. 343.
89 *Roe* v. *Minister of Health* [1954] 2 Q.B. 66.
90 *Gold* v. *Essex C.C., supra, per* Lord Greene M.R. at p. 301 and, *per* Goddard L.J. at p. 309; *Cassidy* v. *Ministry of Health, supra,* at pp. 362–365, *per* Denning L.J.; *Roe* v. *Minister of Health, supra,* at p. 82, *per* Denning L.J.
91 *Razzel* v. *Snowball* [1954] 1 W.L.R. 1382.
92 *Marsh* v. *Moores* [1949] 2 K.B. 208, at p. 215.
93 *Staton* v. *N.C.B.* [1957] 1 W.L.R. 893, where a servant, cycling on his master's land to draw his pay at the pay office after he had finished his work, was held to be in the course of his employment because " it was most clearly an act essentially incident to his employment." He negligently collided with a third party and the master was held liable for his

A servant does not cease to act in the course of his employment unless he has plainly gone beyond the bounds.[94] In one sense it may be said that it is never within the scope of a servant's employment to commit an act of negligence. " In all these cases it may be said, as it was said here, that the master has not authorised the act. It is true, he has not authorised the particular act, but he has put the agent in his place to do that class of acts, and he must be answerable for the manner in which the agent has conducted himself in doing the business which it was the act of his master to place him in." [95] If the servant is doing negligently something which he was employed to do carefully, the negligent act is in the course of his employment and the master is liable.[96] However, in determining whether or not a servant's wrongful act is done in the course of his employment it is necessary that a broad view of all the surrounding circumstances should be taken as a whole and not restricted to the particular act which causes the damage.[97] There is no simple test which can be applied to cover every set of circumstances, so that it remains essentially a question of fact for decision in each case.[98]

924 **Basis of liability.** The exact basis of this liability need not be discussed here.[99] It has been suggested that " the master's liability for the negligence of his servant is not a vicarious liability but a liability of the master himself owing to his failure to have seen that his work was properly and carefully done," [1] and that when a master is held liable for the negligence of his servant in driving a lorry " he is himself under a duty to see that care is exercised in the driving of the lorry on his business." [2] This, however, is not the way in which the master's liability for his servant's negligence has been put in the past, and whatever a master's duty may be to his servant, which in many cases is a personal one, it has never been held that he owes a personal duty to third parties, except in cases of dangerous things and dangerous chattels. Whatever the basis,

negligence. Had the servant been on the highway and not on his master's land, Finnemore J. expressed the opinion that he would not have been in the course of his employment. See *O'Reilly* v. *National Rail and Tramway Appliances Ltd.* [1966] 1 All E.R. 499 and *Kay* v. *I.T.W. Ltd.* [1968] 1 Q.B. 140. See also article " In the Course of Employment " (Fridman) (1967) 117 New L.J. 850.

94 *County Plant Hire* v. *Jackson and Lane Bros.* (*Builders*) (*Third Party*) (1970) 8 K.I.R. 989, C.A.

95 *Per* Willes J. in *Barwick* v. *English Joint Stock Bank* (1867) L.R. 2 Ex. 259, 266.

96 In 6 I.C.L.Q. 162 two tests are discussed: (1) " In Continental law at least one wide positive rule has been established: if there is a relation in time, space and as to the nature of the act between employment and act there will be liability "; (2) " this test asks the question whether the employment created or increased the opportunity for committing the tort; if the answer is positive, the tort will be regarded as being within the course of employment."

97 *e.g. Century Insurance Co.* v. *Northern Ireland Road Transport Board* [1942] A.C. 509.

98 *Per* Finnemore J. in *Staton* v. *N.C.B.* [1957] 1 W.L.R. 893, 895.

99 It is discussed in *Pollock on Torts*, 15th ed., p. 60 *et seq.*; *Salmond on Torts*, 8th ed. pp. 654–657. *Winfield on Tort*, 15th ed., p. 620. See also " Vicarious Liability, and the Master's Indemnity," 20 M.L.R. 220, 437, by Glanville Williams and, by the same author, " Vicarious Liability: Tort of the Master and the Servant," 72 L.Q.R. 522.

1 *Broom* v. *Morgan* [1953] 1 Q.B. 597, 609, *per* Denning L.J.

2 *Ibid.* p. 608. See the clear and convincing comment on this by C. J. Hamson in (1954) C.L.J. 45. Denning L.J.'s view was rejected by the H.L. in *Staveley Iron & Chemical Co. Ltd.* v. *Jones* [1956] 1 All E.R. 403.

however, it is clear that the master " is liable vicariously for the negligent act of the servant done in the course of his employment." [3] If the servant is not liable, the master cannot be vicariously liable for his act or omission, whatever his own personal liability may be. The only exception to this was under the old common law where the servant was the spouse of the person injured by his or her negligence. However by virtue of the provisions of the Law Reform (Husband and Wife) Act 1962 [4] whereby this immunity from being sued was removed, this exception no longer applies.

925 **Vehicle entrusted to servant to be driven or used.** When a vehicle belonging to the master is entrusted to the servant to be driven or used in any other way, the master is liable if the servant be negligent while using the vehicle either wholly or partly on the master's business or in the latter's interest but not if he be negligent while using it for any other purposes, even though the servant has the master's permission to use it for those purposes.[5] Diplock J. said: " I think that the true test can be expressed in these words: was the [servant] doing something that he was employed to do? If so, however improper the manner in which he was doing it, whether negligent . . . or even fraudulent . . . or contrary to express orders . . . the master is liable. If, however, the servant is not doing what he is employed to do, the master does not become liable merely because the act of the servant is done with the master's knowledge, acquiescence or permission." [6] It is presumed that the vehicle is being used for the master's purposes if the servant has authority to use it at all.[7] Deviation from the master's orders does not necessarily prevent the user from being for the master's purposes; it is a question of degree. With reference to a servant driving a horse and cart, Parke B. said: " If the servants, being on their master's business, took a detour to call upon a friend, the master will be responsible. . . . The master is only liable where the servant is acting in the course of his employment. If he was going out of his way, against his master's implied commands, when driving on his master's business, he will make his master liable; but if he was going on a frolic of his own,[8] without being at all on his master's business, the master will not be liable." [9]

926 Where the master, a wine merchant, sent his carman and a clerk with a horse and cart to deliver some wine and bring back some empty

[3] *Broom* v. *Morgan*, *supra*, *per* Hodson L.J. at p. 612.
[4] For the previous position at common law, see *Charlesworth on Negligence*, 4th ed., § 157.
[5] See *Launchberry* v. *Morgans* [1971] 2 W.L.R. 602. The law puts a special responsibility on the owner of a motor-vehicle who permits it to go onto the road in the charge of another person, be it his wife, his servant, his friend or anyone else.
[6] *Hilton* v. *Thomas Burton* (*Rhodes*) *Ltd.* [1961] 1 W.L.R. 705, at p. 707.
[7] *Laycock* v. *Grayson* (1939) 55 T.L.R. 698.
[8] As Lord Denning M.R. said in *Morris* v. *C. W. Martin & Sons Ltd.* [1966] 1 Q.B. 716, at p. 724: " or on a ' joyride ' (to come into the 20th century)." For the limits of the application of the words: " a frolic of his own," see *Allen* v. *Aeroplane & Motor Aluminium Castings Ltd.* [1965] 3 All E.R. 377.
[9] *Joel* v. *Morison* (1834) 6 Car. & P. 501; *A. & W. Hemphill* v. *Williams* (1966) 110 S.J. 549.

bottles, and the servants, on their return, when about a quarter of a mile from the office, drove in another direction on business of the clerk's and negligently ran over the plaintiff, it was held that the master was not liable.[10] But " I am very far from saying, if the servant when going on his master's business took a somewhat longer road, that owing to this deviation he would cease to be in the employment of the master, so as to divest the latter of all liability; in such cases, it is a question of degree as to how far the deviation could be considered a separate journey." [11] When the carman, after his day's work was done, returned the horse and cart to the shop and obtained the stable key but, instead of putting the horse in the stable, drove on a journey of his own and injured the plaintiff on his return, it was held that the master was not liable.[12] Likewise his liability was avoided where the servants of a demolition contractor were permitted to use a van for any reasonable purpose of their own, such as going to get refreshment whilst out on a job, and the van overturned during the return journey from a café several miles away from their work site.[13] A servant who, in the course of making a journey for his master's purposes, goes off on a journey of his own so as to be outside the course of his employment may return to the course of his employment when he has finished his own journey and has resumed the journey for his master's purposes.[14]

If the servant is making a journey on the master's business, the fact that he is also doing business of his own on the same journey will not take him out of his employment.[15] But if he makes a journey on his own business, the fact that he does some small service for his master on his return, (*e.g.* by collecting two empty beer casks for which he received a penny each from his master) does not render the journey one which was made in the course of his employment.[16]

927 **Servant leaving vehicle unattended.** A carter, in charge of his master's horse and cart for the day, is acting in the course of his employment if he leaves his horse and cart unattended during the dinner hour, so that the horse runs away and an accident occurs.[17] Similarly, if he leaves his horse and cart with a boy who goes with him to deliver parcels and the boy, contrary to his master's orders, drives the cart and has an accident,

10 *Storey* v. *Ashton* (1869) L.R. 4 Q.B. 476.

11 *Per* Cockburn C.J. at pp. 479–480.

12 *Mitchell* v. *Crassweller* (1853) 13 C.B. 237.

13 *Hilton* v. *Thomas Burton (Rhodes) Ltd.* [1961] 1 W.L.R. 705. For a similar case see *Harvey* v. *R. G. O'Dell Ltd.* [1958] 2 Q.B. 78, where, on the facts, the employer was held liable.

14 *Creer* v. *Brightside Foundry and Engineering Co.* (1942) 35 B.W.C.C. 9.

15 *Patten* v. *Rea* (1857) 2 C.B.(N.S.) 606.

16 *Rayner* v. *Mitchell* (1877) 2 C.P.D. 357. See also *Hancock* v. *Operating and Vending Machine Co. Ltd.* (1938) 31 B.W.C.C. 209 (collector of money from automatic machines who has a van which it is his duty to return to employers' garage at night, after finishing his day's collecting, spends three hours in public-houses, when he changes copper into silver and notes in accordance with his instructions, and has accident when driving back—not in the course of his employment).

17 *Whatman* v. *Pearson* (1868) L.R. 3 C.P. 422. See also *Gayler & Pope* v. *B. Davies & Son* [1924] 2 K.B. 75.

he is in the course of his employment to look after the horse and cart during the day, and his master will be liable for the damage.[18]

928 **Servant permitted to use master's vehicle for his own purposes.** The fact that a servant is permitted to use his master's vehicle does not make the master liable for the servant's negligence in using that vehicle, unless it is being used for the master's business.[19] So, where the master lent his van-driver his private motor-car for the purpose of taking friends to the theatre and an accident occurred through the van-driver's negligence, the master was held not liable, because the motor-car was not being used for the master's purposes.[20] Again, where a boy was allowed to use a bicycle, belonging to his employers, to go home during his dinner hour and he negligently ran into the plaintiff, it was held that the employers were not liable.[21]

If the servant has not permission to use the vehicle, the case is an even stronger one. A servant who, without his employer's knowledge or consent, takes his motor-car or carriage for purposes of his own and by negligent driving causes damage to a third party, does not render his employer liable.[22] But if a superior servant gives orders to an inferior servant of the same employer to drive a vehicle for the superior servant's private business and not for the employer's business, and the inferior servant is negligent, the employer is liable, because the inferior servant still remains his servant and is in the course of his employment in obeying the orders of the superior servant.[23] Likewise where an employee is given the use of a car by his employer on condition that if he drove to work in it he should drive other employees to work too, free of charge, he so drives the car during the course of his employment and the employers are vicariously liable for his negligent driving.[24]

929 **Servant permitted to use own vehicle whilst on master's business.** The fact that a servant uses his own vehicle instead of his master's transport does not allow the master to escape liability for the servant's negligence in using that vehicle, if the servant was engaged on the master's business at the time. Where the master authorised the servant to use his own motor-cycle combination to carry a fellow servant as a passenger, whilst on the master's business, the master was held liable for the injuries sustained by that fellow servant due to the servant's negligent driving.[25]

[18] *Engelhardt* v. *Farrant & Co.* [1897] 1 Q.B. 240.
[19] *Hilton* v. *Thomas Burton* (*Rhodes*) *Ltd.* [1961] 1 W.L.R. 705.
[20] *Britt* v. *Galmoye* (1928) 44 T.L.R. 294.
[21] *Higbid* v. *Hammett* (1932) 49 T.L.R. 104.
[22] *Sanderson* v. *Collins* [1904] 1 K.B. 628. In this action the plaintiff and defendant were bailor and bailee, but this does not affect the law stated in the text. The bailee may be liable to the bailor for damage to the article bailed even though the bailee's servant was using it for his own purposes at the time it was damaged. *Aitchison* v. *Page Motors* (1935) 154 L.T. 128.
[23] *Irwin* v. *Waterloo Taxi-Cab Co. Ltd.* [1912] 3 K.B. 588.
[24] *Vandyke* v. *Fender* [1969] 2 Q.B. 581.
[25] *Harvey* v. *R. G. O'Dell Ltd.* [1958] 2 Q.B. 78. This case was distinguished in *Nottingham* v. *Aldridge and another* [1971] 3 W.L.R. 1. In this case the Post Office was held not liable for the negligence of one of its employees driving a fellow employee to their place of

930 **Delegation of authority by servant in charge of vehicle.** Apart from express authority, a driver or other servant in charge of his employer's vehicle has no authority to delegate his control of the vehicle to another. As Parke B. said: " If you think the servants lent the cart to a person who was driving without the defendant's [the master's] knowledge, he will not be responsible." [26] Where the driver of the defendant's omnibus was ordered by the police to cease driving, on the ground that he was drunk, and a bystander was thereupon authorised by the driver and the conductor to drive home, it was held that the employer was not liable. Neither the driver nor the conductor had any actual authority to employ a substitute, and they could not be agents of necessity because they might first have communicated with the defendant.[27] Again, when the driver of a motor-car, while he ascertained the cause of a noise in the car, delegated the driving to a man, not a servant of the defendant, by whose negligence an accident occurred, it was held that the defendant was not liable because there was no necessity to keep the car going while the driver examined the engine.[28]

931 **Driving by conductor and others.** If the driver of a vehicle, without delegating his duties to another, allows another person to drive, it is negligence for which his employer is responsible. When the driver of an omnibus, at the end of the journey, allowed the conductor to turn the omnibus in readiness for the next journey and sat next to him while he was driving, it was held that there was evidence of negligence on the part of the driver when the conductor negligently killed a person on the footpath.[29] The employer was not liable for the negligence of the conductor, who had no authority to drive, but he was liable for the negligence of the driver in allowing an unskilled man to drive. But the employer is not liable if the conductor, at the end of the journey and while the driver is away for his dinner, drives the omnibus and negligently causes damage, because there is no negligence on the part of the driver.[30] If the driver negligently leaves his vehicle unattended in the highway, the employer will be liable for all damage which is the consequence of that negligence and is not too remote. It has been held that if the driver is drunk, a collision caused by another drunken man driving in his place is too remote.[31] If a horse and cart are left unattended on the highway,

work in a car not owned by the Post Office, even though the employee who was driving received a mileage allowance and an additional allowance for his passenger.

26 *Joel* v. *Morison* (1834) 6 Car. & P. 501.

27 *Gwilliam* v. *Twist* [1895] 2 Q.B. 84.

28 *Harris* v. *Fiat Motors Ltd.* (1906) 22 T.L.R. 556. Reversed on other grounds, 23 T.L.R. 504.

29 *Ricketts* v. *Thomas Tilling Ltd.* [1915] 1 K.B. 644; *Marsh* v. *Moores* [1949] 2 K.B. 208.

30 *Beard* v. *London General Omnibus Co.* [1900] 2 Q.B. 530; distinguished in *Kay* v. *I.T.W. Ltd.* [1968] 1 Q.B. 140, since the servant's attempted removal of the visiting lorry which was causing the obstruction of the employer's warehouse access was done so that he could complete his task of bringing his employer's vehicle into the warehouse; thus it was held to be an act done in the course of his employment for which the employers were vicariously liable.

31 *Mann* v. *Ward* (1892) 8 T.L.R. 699. This case was criticised in *Engelhardt* v. *Farrant* [1897] 1 Q.B. 240, but as a decision on the question of remoteness of damage it seems quite sound.

damage caused by a third party driving it is not too remote,[32] but if a motor-vehicle, and not a horse and cart, is so left, it is too remote.[33]

932 **Master not liable to persons invited into vehicle by servant.** A servant in charge of a vehicle is not acting in the course of his employment if he invites his friends or other persons to come into the vehicle. If, owing to his negligence, such a person is injured while in the vehicle, the master is not liable. To the contrary, if the driver's foreman, within the scope of his ostensible authority, consents to the driver inviting a person onto his vehicle, the invitation will not be outside the course of the driver's employment.[34]

Where the plaintiff, at the request of the driver of the defendant's milk float, got into the float to help an injured boy, also a servant of the defendant, and was herself injured owing to the driver's negligence, it was held that the defendant was not liable, as the existence of an emergency gave the driver no authority to invite the plaintiff into the float.[35] Again, where a carrier contracted to carry the plaintiff's luggage in a cart and the plaintiff, with the permission of the carrier's servant but without any authority from the carrier, got into the cart which subsequently broke down, the carrier was held not liable.[36] When the employer expressly instructed his driver not to allow other persons to travel on his van and had notices to the same effect displayed in the van, he was held not liable to a person carried as a passenger in the van who was injured by the driver's negligence, on the ground that it was outside the scope of the driver's employment to carry the passenger, so that the employer owed no duty to him.[37] When the driver of a tractor, which was unsafe for passengers and was not intended to carry them, allowed a child to ride upon the tractor, the employer was held not liable for injuries sustained by the child when he fell while the driver was driving too fast round a bend.[38]

933 **Servant's disobedience of orders.** The fact that a servant disobeys the orders of his master does not necessarily mean that he is acting outside

[32] *Engelhardt* v. *Farrant, supra,* itself criticised by Lord Sumner in *Weld-Blundell* v. *Stephens* [1920] A.C. 956, 989.
[33] *Ruoff* v. *Long & Co.* [1916] 1 K.B. 148.
[34] *Young* v. *Edward Box & Co. Ltd.* [1951] 1 T.L.R. 789 (driver of defendants' lorry with consent of his foreman, such consent being within the ostensible scope of the foreman's authority, though not authorised by defendants, gave a lift to one of the defendants' workmen who was injured through the driver's negligence—defendants held liable).
[35] *Houghton* v. *Pilkington* [1912] 3 K.B. 308.
[36] *Lygo* v. *Newbold* (1854) 9 Ex. 302.
[37] *Twine* v. *Bean's Express Co.* [1946] 1 All E R. 202; affd. 175 L.T. 131. *Conway* v. *George Wimpey & Co. Ltd.* [1951] 2 K.B. 266 is a similar case to the same effect, in which Asquith L.J. said, " taking men other than the defendants' employees on the vehicle was not merely a wrongful mode of performing an act of the class which the driver in the present case was employed to perform, but was the performance of an act of a class which he was not employed to perform at all." *Twine* v. *Bean's Express Co.* is criticised in 17 M.L.R. 102, but *cf.* 62 L.Q.R. 113, 316 and 72 L.Q.R. 542. It was followed and approved by the C.A. in *Conway* v. *George Wimpey & Co. Ltd.* See also 67 L.Q.R. 152; 15 M.L.R. 84.
[38] *Nixon* v. *Cairns* [1944] N.I. 21, following *Houghton* v. *Pilkington, supra.*

the course of his employment.[39] The distinction is between an order which limits the *scope* of the employment, the disobedience to which means that the servant is not in the course of his employment, and an order which limits the *method* in which the duties of the servant shall be performed, the disobedience to which does not mean that the servant is outside his employment. For example, an order that a van driver shall not allow any person to travel in his van, notice of which is displayed on the van, is an order limiting the scope of the servant's employment with the result that a breach of the order involves the master in no liability.[40] On the other hand, an order to employees not to use uninsured motor-cars merely limits the way in which the work is to be performed, so that the liability of the employer is not excluded if damage is caused when the order is disobeyed.[41] As explained above [42] it is essential to avoid the approach of isolating the wrongful act of the servant from its surrounding facts in order to determine whether or not it was done in the course of his employment. Indeed, the necessity of taking the broad view of all the circumstances is well illustrated by the following contrasting cases. In *Ilkiw* v. *Samuels* [43] a lorry driver employed by a transport company drove their lorry to a sugar warehouse for loading and, whilst there, he permitted a sugar stacker employed at the warehouse to move the lorry for him so that the load could be sheeted, without first checking the man's competence to drive the vehicle. The latter in fact was quite incompetent and he was unable to stop the vehicle so that the plaintiff was crushed and injured. It was held that the defendants were liable in that their driver had been negligent in allowing the other workman to drive the lorry which act had taken place in the course of his employment, because he was employed not only to drive but also to take charge and control of it in all circumstances during the times when he was on duty, and he remained in charge of it even when he was not sitting at the controls.[44] This was so even though he was forbidden to allow anyone to drive his lorry, especially the servant of some other employer. In this case, however, no attempt was made to make liable the employers of the workman, whose negligent mismanagement of the visiting lorry was the actual primary cause of the accident. On the other hand, the employers of a servant whose negligent driving did cause an accident in similar circumstances were successfully sued in *Kay* v. *I.T.W. Ltd.*[45] In this case the driver of a fork lift

[39] The New Zealand Court of Appeal in *Att.-Gen.* v. *Hartley* [1964] N.Z.L.R. 785 held that it is not enough to decide whether what was done was a prohibited act since prohibition may either limit the scope of the employment or merely regulate the conduct of the employee within its sphere.

[40] *Twine* v. *Bean's Express Co.* [1946] 1 All E.R. 202; affd. 175 L.T. 131; *Conway* v. *George Wimpey & Co. Ltd., supra.*

[41] *Canadian Pacific Ry.* v. *Lockhart* [1942] A.C. 591.

[42] *Ante*, § 923.

[43] [1963] 1 W.L.R. 991. (See criticism of this case in " Liabilities Arising from Employment " (Fridman) (1966) 116 New L.J. 775. See also *Ricketts* v. *Thos. Tilling Ltd.* [1915] 1 K.B. 644.

[44] *Ibid.* p. 998, *per* Willmer L.J. and, *per* Danckwerts L.J. at p. 1002, but *cf.* the reasoning of Diplock L.J. at pp. 1003–1006.

[45] [1968] 1 Q.B. 140; *East* v. *Beavis Transport Ltd.* [1969] 1 Lloyd's Rep. 302.

truck found that his sole means of access to his employers' warehouse was blocked by a visiting lorry and, without attempting to make any inquiry where the lorry driver was or what he should do, he entered into the cab of the vehicle, started the motor and so negligently reversed the lorry that he pinned the plaintiff storekeeper up against the doors causing him severe personal injuries. His object in so acting was to clear an entrance to the warehouse for the fork lift truck where he was required to place it when not in use, but if this driving were to be considered in abstract without having regard to the surrounding facts it would not have been within the course of his employment. Such a narrow approach to the problem would be wrong but the dividing line, at times, will be difficult to discern. As Sachs L.J. pointed out: " The trouble in a case such as the present is, of course, that there are instances in which the dividing line can be very thin between acts which constitute a wrong and indeed a very stupid mode of doing an authorised act and acts which involve doing something which the employee has no business at all to be doing. Whether the line ought to be drawn by examining the question in terms of degree or in terms of kind has been discussed. I do not propose to say more on that point save this, that in either case the line should be drawn fairly high in favour of the innocent sufferer injured by the act of somebody who was employed by the defendant employer and who was seeking to further that employer's interests."[46]

934 An order to the servant to make a journey in the master's lorry which is performed by using a private car is not an order limiting the scope of the employment.[47] In *Limpus* v. *London General Omnibus Co.*[48] an omnibus driver drove his omnibus across the road in front of a rival omnibus, thereby causing it to overturn. His employers had issued written instructions that their drivers were not to race or obstruct other omnibuses, but they were nevertheless held liable, Willes J. saying: " It may be said that it was no part of the duty of the defendants' servant to obstruct the plaintiff's omnibus, and moreover the servant had distinct instructions not to obstruct any omnibus whatever. In my opinion those instructions are immaterial. If disobeyed, the law casts upon the master a liability for the act of his servant in the course of his employment; and the law is not so futile as to allow a master, by giving secret instructions to his servant, to discharge himself from liability. Therefore, I consider it immaterial that the defendants directed their servant not to do the act. Suppose a master told his servant not to break the law, would that exempt the master from responsibility for an unlawful act done by his servant in the course of his employment? "

935 Garage proprietors who employed a man as a general garage hand,

46 *Ibid.* at p. 156.
47 *McKean* v. *Raynor Bros.* [1942] 2 All E.R. 650.
48 (1862) 1 H. & C. 526, at p. 539. Even fraud in the method of carrying out his employment is an act done in the course of the employment, whether it was committed for the master's benefit or not: *Lloyd* v. *Grace, Smith & Co.* [1912] A.C. 716. See also *Ward* v. *L.G.O. Co.* (1873) 42 L.J.C.P. 265, and *United Africa Co. Ltd.* v. *Saka Owoade* [1955] A.C. 130.

part of his duties being to assist in moving cars out of the way of other cars in the garage but who was forbidden to drive and had no driving licence, were held liable for the man's act in driving the van into the highway so as to back it into the garage clear of the access to the petrol pumps, on the ground that he was doing an act within the scope of his employment, though he was doing it in an unauthorised way.[49] But where a contractor told his carters to tip rubbish at a particular place and nowhere else, and, in breach of their orders, they tipped it on the plaintiff's land, it was held that the act was outside the sphere of their employment and the contractor was not liable.[50]

Where a servant placed a loaded gun on a harvester in disobedience to his master's instructions and the gun fired accidentally and injured the driver, it was held[51] that the master was liable. The " scope " of employment must be construed liberally and accordingly the master was vicariously liable for his servant's act in adding a further danger to the risk of the work.

Where a solicitor's clerk, contrary to his orders, used the lavatory in his employer's private room and negligently left the tap running, it was held that the employer was not liable because " the prohibition is material as showing the local limit of the clerk's duties."[52] But where a clerk used a lavatory which he was allowed to use, his employer was held liable for his negligence in omitting to turn off the tap.[53]

936 **Servant smoking during work.** If a servant smokes during his work and damage is thereby caused, a question arises whether the smoking is in the course of his employment so as to make his employer liable. In *Williams* v. *Jones*[54] a carpenter employed to make a signboard, while engaged on his work, lighted his pipe with a shaving, which he dropped among the other shavings, and thereby set fire to a shed which had been lent to his employer by the plaintiff. It was held, by a majority, that the employer was not liable, on the ground that the act of smoking was not in any way connected with the making of the signboard. This decision must be regarded today as of doubtful authority. If a servant is working among shavings or other inflammable materials, he is under a duty to use reasonable care not to cause a fire. This was expressly held in *Jefferson* v. *Derbyshire Farmers Ltd.*,[55] where a youth employed in a garage, while drawing benzol from a drum, lit a cigarette and threw the match onto the floor, thereby lighting some petrol on the floor which

49 *L.C.C.* v. *Cattermoles* (*Garages*) *Ltd.* [1953] 1 W.L.R. 997.
50 *Rank Ltd.* v. *Craig* [1919] 1 Ch. 1.
51 *Spencer* v. *Curtis Bros.* (1962) 106 S.J. 390.
52 *Stevens* v. *Woodward* (1881) 6 Q.B.D. 318.
53 *Ruddiman* v. *Smith* (1889) 60 L.T. 708.
54 (1865) 3 H. & C. 602. Erle C.J., Keating and Smith JJ.; Blackburn and Mellor JJ. dissenting.
55 [1921] 2 K.B. 281. *Williams* v. *Jones* was distinguished on the ground that the negligent act of the carpenter in that case was unconnected with his work. As the smoking was an act of negligence only because he was working in a place where shavings and other inflammable material were about, it is difficult to separate the negligence from the employment.

set fire to the benzol and burnt down the garage. The employers were held liable on the ground that the youth was bound to use reasonable care in doing his work and "to smoke and throw a lighted match on the floor while doing this work was not to do the work with reasonable care."[56] This decision supports the dissenting judgment in *Williams* v. *Jones* of Blackburn J. who said: "It is said that Davies, the servant, was not employed by his master to smoke or to light his pipe, and that is no doubt true; but the act of lighting a pipe was in itself a harmless act; it only became negligent and a breach of duty towards the plaintiff because it was done when using his shed and working there amongst inflammable materials. . . . It seems to me, therefore, that it was negligence in the course of his employment."[57] The view of the minority in *Williams* v. *Jones* was preferred in *Century Insurance Co.* v. *Northern Ireland Road Transport Board*,[58] where the employers were held liable for the act of the driver of a lorry containing petrol who lit a cigarette while petrol was being transferred from the lorry to a tank, threw the match away and caused a fire and an explosion. Therein Lord Wright pointed out: "I think what plausibility the contrary argument might seem to possess results from treating the act of lighting the cigarette in abstraction from the circumstances as a separate act."[59] But where an explosion of firedamp in the National Coal Board's mine occurred as a result of a miner lighting a cigarette, an act prohibited by section 35 of the Coal Mines Act 1911, the Court of Session, Inner House, held that the miner who caused the explosion was not acting in the course of his employment when he lit the cigarette, since he had no business to be in the waste to which he had retired to smoke.[60]

The result is that the master will be liable if the servant's smoking is merely a negligent way of performing his employment. A prohibition against smoking, express or implied, affects the method in which the servant is to perform his duties and does not limit the scope of the employment.

937 **Servant's dishonesty or other acts causing damage.** At one time it was considered that a master could not be held vicariously liable for a theft perpetrated by his servant on the ground that such an act necessarily must have been outside the course of his employment.[61] That was so until recently when the Court of Appeal in *Morris* v. *C. W. Martin & Sons Ltd.*,[62] in what must be accepted as a far-reaching decision of importance, took vicarious liability for the acts of a servant unnecessarily far beyond the original conception of the law. In this case the plaintiff sent her

56 *Per* Bankes L.J. at p. 286.
57 (1865) 3 H. & C. 602, at p. 610.
58 [1942] A.C. 509.
59 *Ibid.* at p. 519.
60 *Kirby* v. *N.C.B.*, 1958 S.L.T. 47. See now the Mines and Quarries Act 1954, ss. 66 and 67.
61 *Cheshire* v. *Bailey* [1905] 1 K.B. 237; *Mintz* v. *Silverton* (1920) 36 T.L.R. 399. *Cf. Abraham* v. *Bullock* (1902) 86 L.T. 796.
62 [1966] 1 Q.B. 716. See articles: "The Thieving Lorry Driver" (1965) 109 S.J. 1021 and "Liabilities Arising from Employment" (Fridman) (1966) 116 New L.J. 719; 775; 857. See also *Mendelssohn* v. *Normand Ltd.* [1970] 1 Q.B. 177, C.A.

mink stole to a furrier for cleaning and it was arranged with her permission that the fur would be delivered to the defendants, who specialised in such cleaning work. Unfortunately an employee of the defendants was given the task of cleaning the fur, which he promptly stole when it had been handed over to him for custody, there having been no reason to suspect his honesty although he had only recently entered the defendants' employment. Upon the owner's suing, the defendants were held liable mainly on the ground that as their own duty as bailees for reward was to protect the goods from theft and depredation if they entrusted that duty to a servant or agent, they were responsible for the servant's breach of it, notwithstanding that the breach was a criminal act. Some emphasis was given to the fact that the fur was stolen by the very servant whom the defendants as bailees for reward had employed to take care of it and clean it. The suggestion emerged that had the theft of the fur been committed by some other servant the result would have been different because it would not have been possible to hold that it had been stolen by that employee through whom the defendants had chosen to discharge their duty of care.[63] If this be the correct approach then in cases of theft by an employee the preliminary question to be asked is whether or not the stolen goods had been put in the custody of the servant by the master. If they had been, it follows that the theft must have been committed in the course of his employment for which the employers will be vicariously liable unless there be some contractual provision excluding liability. On the other hand if the goods were not put in the thief's custody, the master will not be vicariously liable for the loss although he could well be liable on some other ground such as a breach of his own duty as bailee. Where goods have been bailed to the master which are damaged by the servant's negligence, whilst acting in the course of his employment, there can be no question but that the master is liable to their owner. The same would apply even where the servant may be using the goods for his own purposes.[64] For servants who cause injury as a result of indulging in horse-play, practical jokes and general skylarking about, see Chapter 6 § 210, *ante*.[65]

38 **Examples of acts in the course of employment.** Whether the negligent act of the servant is done in the course of his employment depends on the nature of the employment in each case. In the following cases the

[63] *Ibid.*, *per* Diplock L.J. at p. 737 and *per* Salmon L.J. at p. 740.

[64] *Aitchison* v. *Page Motors Ltd.* (1935) 154 L.T. 128; See observations by Lord Denning M.R. upon this case also the moot case discussed in *Morris* v. *C.W. Martin & Sons Ltd.* [1966] 1 Q.B. 716, 724–725. Further see the interesting problem raised in *Clerk & Lindsell*, 13th ed. § 227 concerning these decisions.

[65] *Smith* v. *Crossley* (1951) 95 S.J. 655 (compressed air pipe forced up an apprentice's rectum); *Hudson* v. *Ridge Manufacturing Co.* [1957] 2 Q.B. 348 (wrist broken when seized from behind and thrown to the ground); *Coddington* v. *International Harvester Co. of Great Britain Ltd.* (1969) 6 K.I.R. 146 (lighted inflammable spirit in a tin kicked about, which spilled and burned the plaintiff); *Chapman* v. *Oakleigh Animal Products* (1970) 114 S.J. 432 (schoolboy, working during his holidays, was instructed by three older employees to put his fingers up the spout of a meat grinding machine, whereupon the starter button was pressed and the machine operated injuring his hand).

act was held to be *in* the course of the employment: When a lighterman, under whose management the defendant's barge was sent to a wharf to be loaded, in order to get his barge alongside, moved the plaintiff's barge into such a position that it was damaged when the tide went down [66]; when iron was carted to a wharf where it was to be loaded into a ship by stevedores and the foreman of the stevedores, being dissatisfied with the unloading of the iron by the carters, himself got into the cart and negligently threw out some iron, injuring the plaintiff [67]; when the carter of a coal merchant, in order to deliver coals at a customer's premises, removed an iron plate in the footway which covered the entrance into the coal cellar, and the plaintiff fell into the opening and was injured [68]; when a school-teacher at a public elementary school told a pupil to poke the fire and draw out the damper in a room used by the teachers for their own convenience, and the pupil's pinafore was set on fire [69]; when the defendant's servants, authorised by their employment to burn weeds, burnt them on land adjoining but not belonging to the defendant, so that the fire spread on to the adjoining land and did damage [70]; when a carter, off duty, seeing a boy with his hand on a bag of sugar which was being carried on one of his employer's wagons gave the boy a cuff and so caused him to be run over by the wagon [71]; where three employees were determined to play a practical joke on a schoolboy, working during his holidays, and instructed him to put his hand up the spout of a mincer, which they then started up.[73]

939 **Examples of acts not in the course of employment.** In the following cases the act was held to be *not* in the course of the employment: When a gas inspector, who was not a repairer, attempted to remedy a defect in a gas meter by a pocket knife, and left the knife open when he went to get proper tools, so that the plaintiff's son, aged between three and four years, was able to get at the knife and was injured [74]; when a housemaid, employed to light the fires but not to clean the chimney, finding the fire difficult to light, lit some straw to clean the chimney and set the house on fire [75]; when a lorry driver stopped at a wayside café and crossed one section of a dual carriageway on foot to get refreshment (an act done while he was employed and with his employer's permission), a collision between him and a motor-cyclist, for which he was in fact to

[66] *Page* v. *Defries* (1866) 7 B. & S. 137.
[67] *Burns* v. *Poulsom* (1873) L.R. 8 C.P. 563.
[68] *Whiteley* v. *Pepper* (1876) 2 Q.B.D. 276.
[69] *Smith* v. *Martin and Hull Corpn.* [1911] 2 K.B. 775.
[70] *Goh Choon Seng* v. *Lee Kim Soo* [1925] A.C. 550.
[71] *Poland* v. *Parr* [1927] 1 K.B. 236.
[73] *Chapman* v. *Oakleigh Animal Products* (1970) 114 S.J. 432 where it was held that as the plaintiff was bound to obey his seniors' instructions in the circumstances the employers owed him a duty of care and the argument that the fellow employees were not acting in the course of their employment could not avail them. *Cf.* n. 61, *ante*.
[74] *Forsyth* v. *Manchester Corpn.* (1912) 29 T.L.R. 15.
[75] *M'Kenzie* v. *M'Leod* (1834) 10 Bing. 385.

blame, was held not to be in the course of his employment so as to make his employer liable to the motor-cyclist on the ground that the lorry driver was not discharging any duty to his employer at the time when the accident occurred[76]; where a miner illegally lit a cigarette underground in a place where he had no business to be at all and caused an explosion of firedamp.[77]

A fellow employee who was given to playing practical jokes was held to have acted outside the scope of his employment and accordingly the employers were not vicariously liable. He had deliberately but not maliciously pushed a tin of burning spirit towards a man who had kicked it away hastily so that the tin had overturned and had burnt the plaintiff, but since the practical joker had never previously been guilty of any dangerous behaviour towards his colleagues the employers were not negligent in continuing to employ him up to the time of the accident, although they knew of his propensity for " fooling about."[78]

2.—Agents

941 **Who is an agent?** An agent is one authorised to act on behalf of another, but it is not necessary that there should be a contract with him, as in the case of a servant. Examples are the friends, spouse or the children of the principal. On the other hand neither scoutmaster nor cub mistress in charge of schoolboys at an outing to Whipsnade Zoo were agents of the Boy Scouts Association.[79] A principal is liable for the negligence of his agent while acting in the course of his authority.[80] The law stated above relating to servants applies equally to agents, except that the scope of the agent's authority is, in practice, construed more strictly than the scope of a servant's employment.

A person may be the agent of another so as to make that other liable for his negligence, although he is a mere volunteer.[81] Indeed, in most of the cases in which the principal has been held liable for the negligence of his agent, the agent has been a volunteer. In *Brooke* v. *Bool*[82] the

[76] *Crook* v. *Derbyshire Stone Ltd.* [1956] 1 W.L.R. 432. See comment on this case in [1956] C.L.J. 156. This case was not followed in *Stewart's (Edinburgh) Holdings* v. *Lord Advocate*, 1966 S.L.T. 86, where it was held in similar circumstances that the army driver was not exclusively on his own business; accordingly, his employers were liable, applying *Harvey* v. *O'Dell* [1958] 2 Q.B. 78.

[77] *Kirby* v. *National Coal Board*, 1958 S.L.T. 47. See *ante*, § 936.

[78] *Coddington* v. *International Harvester Co. of Great Britain* (1969) 113 S.J. 265. However, *cf.* the situation in *Chapman* v. *Oakleigh Animal Products, supra,* where the employers were held to be vicariously liable. See Chap. 6 § 210, *ante*, and nn. 65 and 73.

[79] *Murphy* v. *Zoological Society of London, The Times*, November 14, 1962.

[80] See the interesting article, " Liability for the negligence of another—servant or agent," by B. J. Brooke-Smith, 70 L.Q.R. 253. See also *Scarsbrook* v. *Mason* [1961] 3 All E.R. 767, where the driver was the agent of all the passengers.

[81] A volunteer may be a " servant," at all events so as to make him a fellow servant within the now repealed doctrine of common employment. *Degg* v. *Midland Ry.* (1857) 1 H. & N. 773; *Potter* v. *Faulkner* (1861) 1 B. & S. 800; *Bass* v. *Hendon U.D.C.* (1912) 28 T.L.R. 317; *Heasmer* v. *Pickfords Ltd.* (1920) 36 T.L.R. 818, *sed quaere*. See the criticism of these cases in *Radcliffe* v. *Ribble Motor Services* [1939] A.C. 215, 247.

[82] [1928] 2 K.B. 578.

defendant was the owner of a lock-up shop, and lived next door to it. A lodger told the defendant that there was a smell of gas in the shop, and thereupon the defendant and the lodger went into the shop to investigate the escape. The lodger carried a naked light, which caused an explosion, and the defendant was held liable to the tenant of the shop, because the lodger was acting as his agent in trying to discover the escape of the gas.

941 **Friend driving motor-car in owner's presence.** The owner of a motor-car who allows his friend to drive it in his presence makes the friend his agent and is liable for his negligence in driving. In *Wheatley* v. *Patrick* [83] the defendant borrowed a horse and gig and went for a drive with a friend. During the excursion he allowed the friend to drive and by the friend's negligence the plaintiff was injured. The defendant was held liable on the ground that he was responsible for his friend's negligence. Again, where the defendant was attempting to sell his motor-car and took the son of the prospective purchaser with him, it was held that the defendant was liable for the negligence of the son while driving the car in his presence, because the possession and control of the car was in the defendant.[84] The same result was arrived at where the defendant, the owner of the motor-car, sat beside one of his friends who drove and, by his negligence, injured the plaintiff, also a passenger in the car.[85] Where the son of the owner of a motor-car negligently drove it, and the owner himself was not in the car but his driver, without whom he did not permit his son to drive the car, was sitting beside the son, it was held that the owner was liable for his son's negligence.[86]

When a servant, in control of a car for the purposes of his employment, allows a third party to drive it and an accident occurs through the third party's negligence the master is liable, on the ground that the servant is in control of the car on behalf of the master.[87] Lord Tucker said [88]: " It is now well settled that the person in control of a carriage or motor-vehicle—though not actually driving—is liable for the negligence of the driver over whom he has the right to exercise control."

942 **Owner not in car.** If the agent has authority to drive a motor-car on behalf of or for the purposes of the owner (whether wholly or partly on the owner's business or in the owner's interest) and in the course of that authority negligently causes damage, the owner of the car will be liable, as principal, even though he was not present in the car at the time.[89] On the other hand, if the owner permits another to use the

[83] (1837) 2 M. & W. 650.
[84] *Samson* v. *Aitchison* [1912] A.C. 844.
[85] *Pratt* v. *Patrick* [1924] 1 K.B. 488.
[86] *Reichardt* v. *Shard* (1914) 31 T.L.R. 24. This case and those in notes 83–85, *supra*, were followed in *Trust Co. Ltd.* v. *De Silva* [1956] 1 W.L.R. 376.
[87] *Trust Co. Ltd.* v. *De Silva, supra.*
[88] *Ibid.* p. 380.
[89] *Thompson* v. *Reynolds* [1926] N.I. 131 (brother of owner rides motor-cycle from repairer's shop to owner's garage—agent); *Hewitt* v. *Bonvin* [1940] 1 K.B. 188, at p. 191, *per* du Parcq L.J. See *Launchberry* v. *Morgans* [1971] 2 W.L.R. 602. The law puts a special

car for his own purposes and not for the purposes of the owner, that other will not be an agent. Where however a parent gave the use of his vehicle to someone else for the purpose of driving his child, the test of whether that person was acting on the parent's behalf and for the parents' purposes depended on whether the proposal for the use of the car originated from the parent, in which case the driver was acting as his agent, or from the sixteen-year-old child, in which case the driver was not acting as the parent's agent.[90] Where the owner of the car, being unable to drive, had her son to drive it for her and after she had been driven home from a party by her son, the son drove the car to the garage at his own house, where the car was kept, and had an accident on the way, the mother was held liable on the ground that the son was her agent.[91] If a parent owns and pays for the running expenses of a motor-car and allows his children, living at home with him, to drive the car, the children will usually be his agents; but if one child has not been allowed to drive and has not been provided with a driving licence, that child will not be the parent's agent.[92] In *Parker* v. *Miller*[93] the defendant, the owner of a motor-car, went for a drive with a friend. The defendant got out of the car and allowed the friend to drive on to his house. On arriving at his house, which was on a gradient, the friend negligently left the car so that it ran down the gradient and caused damage. The defendant was held liable on the ground that the friend was his agent and that, although he was no longer in the car, he still had the right of control. Again, when a motor-car was driven by a friend of the owner with the intention of reaching Monte Carlo where the owner was to join him so that they could use the car for a holiday together, the friend was held to be the owner's agent even before the owner had joined him.[94] " The owner is also liable if . . . the driver is, with the owner's consent, driving the car . . . partly for his own purposes and partly for the owner's purposes." [95]

A commercial traveller who sells goods on commission for his principal, and who drives his own motor-car, in respect of which he receives from his principal a weekly sum towards the running expenses, is not an agent so as to make his principal liable for his negligence in driving the car.[96]

3 **Loan of a car.** If the owner of a motor-car lends his car to a friend to be used for the friend's purposes,[97] or allows his son[98] or his servant[99]

responsibility on the owner of a motor-vehicle who permits it to go onto the road in the charge of another person, be it his wife, his servant, his friend or anyone else. See article: "Vicarious liability and the 'family car'" (Kidd) 121 New L.J. 529.

[90] *Carberry* v. *Davies* [1968] 1 W.L.R. 1103. In the case *Klein* v. *Caluori* [1971] 1 W.L.R. 619, the owner of a car was held not liable when it was borrowed by a friend who, when ordered to return it, ran into a stationary car, as the friend was not his agent even though acting on his orders to return the car.

[91] *Smith* v. *Moss* [1940] 1 K.B. 424.

[92] *Gibson* v. *O'Keeney* [1928] N.I. 66.

[93] (1926) 42 T.L.R. 408.

[94] *Ormrod* v. *Crosville Motor Services Ltd.* [1953] 1 W.L.R. 1120.

[95] *Per* Denning L.J., *ibid.* p. 1122.

[96] *Egginton* v. *Reader* (1936) 52 T.L.R. 212.

[97] *Daniels* v. *Vaux* [1938] 2 K.B. 203.

[98] *Hewitt* v. *Bonvin* [1940] 1 K.B. 188.

[99] *Britt* v. *Galmoye* (1928) 44 T.L.R. 294.

to use his car for their own purposes, he does not make them his servants or agents so as to be liable for their negligence. This is because the bailor of a chattel is not liable for negligence of the bailee in his use of the chattel. But where a car owner had lent his car for a few days to a prospective purchaser, the owner was held vicariously liable for the latter's negligent driving since it was to the advantage of the owner, who had wanted to sell the vehicle, to allow the other to test-drive it, hence the other was driving it partly if not wholly on the owner's business or for the owner's purposes.[1]

944 **Ownership of car evidence of agency.** The fact that the defendant is the owner of the motor-car in question is evidence that it was being driven by him or his servant or agent at the material time.[2] Such evidence, of course, is not conclusive, but may be rebutted by proving who was actually driving at the time.

3.—CHILDREN

945 **Liability of parent.** A parent as such is not liable for the negligence of his child,[3] unless the child is his servant or agent.[4] A parent, however, is liable for his own negligence and he is under a duty to exercise such control over his children as a prudent parent would exercise. The age of the child, however, is a material factor to be taken into account.[5] Accordingly when a father presented his son, aged fifteen, with an airgun and the boy broke a window and, a few months later, shot the plaintiff in the eye, it was held that the father was liable.[6] Similarly where a father allowed his son aged twelve to possess a .410 shotgun, but did not instruct him on the proper handling of the gun when he was in the presence of others, the father was held liable when a child was shot, although he had forbidden his son to use the gun with other children present.[7] Also a father of a boy aged fifteen was held liable for failing to take reasonable care to ensure that his son did not use an airgun in such a way as to injure other persons.[8] On the other hand, a father who allowed his son aged thirteen to have an air rifle on condition he did not use it outside the house, and had a large cellar in which the rifle could be used, was held not liable when, in disobedience to his orders, his son fired the rifle in an alleyway

1 *Wong it Yong* v. *Lim Gaw Teong* [1969] 1 M.L.J. 79.
2 *Barnard* v. *Sully* (1931) 47 T.L.R. 557.
3 *North* v. *Wood* [1914] 1 K.B. 629; *Donaldson* v. *McNiven* [1952] 2 All E.R. 691; *Gorely* v. *Codd* [1967] 1 W.L.R. 19.
4 *Sullivan* v. *Creed* [1904] 2 Ir.R. 317.
5 The Family Law Reform Act 1969, Part 1 of which reduced the age of majority from 21 years to 18 years, came into force on January 1, 1970, in this regard and thereafter such persons under that full age have become known as " minors " instead of " infants." See article: " Age of majority 18 " (Samuels) 113 S.J. 763.
6 *Bebee* v. *Sales* (1916) 32 T.L.R. 413. See also Chap. 9, Airguns.
7 *Newton* v. *Edgerley* [1959] 1 W.L.R. 1031. See also note on this case in 76 L.Q.R. 15.
8 *Court* v. *Wyatt, The Times,* June 25, 1960, Donovan J. stating in his judgment that a parent's duty included giving instructions that the gun should never be pointed, loaded or unloaded, at other persons and certainly never should be fired at anybody. A child should not be trusted with a gun at all if it be known to the parent that the child was not to be relied upon to obey instructions or heed warnings. See article based on this case in 28 Sol. 166.

and injured a boy aged five. The precautions taken were suitable and would have been adequate, but for the son's disobedience.[9]

The duty of a parent to control his children would appear to be at least as stringent as that of a schoolmaster, which is said to be that of a "careful father." [10] If, therefore, the children of X are playing with other children in the house or on the land occupied by X, X's liability towards the other children for injuries inflicted on them by his own children will presumably be the same as that of a schoolmaster for injuries inflicted by one of his pupils on another.[11]

The father of a child of four years of age was held to be jointly guilty of negligence with the motorist when the child was injured, since the father had failed to look after the child properly by allowing him to walk on the left hand side of the highway, so that he had his back to oncoming traffic.[12]

4.—INDEPENDENT CONTRACTORS

946 **No liability for negligence of independent contractor.** An employer is not vicariously liable for the negligence of an independent contractor or his servants in the execution of his contract. "Unquestionably, no one can be made liable for an act or breach of duty, unless it be traceable to himself or his servant or servants in the course of his or their employment. Consequently, if an independent contractor is employed to do a lawful act, and in the course of the work he or his servants commit some casual act of wrong or negligence, the employer is not answerable." [13] For example, if a man has his lorry repaired by competent motor repairers,[14] or his lift repaired by competent engineers [15] or his premises rewired by experienced electrical contractors [16] or has a large hawthorn tree cut down and removed from his front garden by an apparently competent tree felling contractor,[17] in each case he is not liable for damage caused by their negligent work. Likewise a building owner who engages an architect, whom he reasonably believes to be competent is not in general responsible for the architect's negligence, since he has no control over the manner in which the architect does his work.[18]

9 *Donaldson* v. *McNiven* [1952] 2 All E.R. 691; *Gorely* v. *Codd* [1967] 1 W.L.R. 19.

10 *Per* Lord Esher M.R. in *Williams* v. *Eady* (1893) 10 T.L.R. 41. See Chap. 7 § 297, *ante*.

11 See *Williams* v. *Eady*, *supra* (phosphorus left where boys could get at it); *Jackson* v. *L.C.C.* (1912) 28 T.L.R. 359 (heap of rubbish in playground); *Chilvers* v. *L.C.C.* (1916) 32 T.L.R. 363 (children playing with toy soldiers); *Jones* v. *L.C.C.* (1932) 48 T.L.R. 368; *Langham* v. *Governors of Wellingborough School* (1932) 101 L.J.K.B. 513 (children injured in playing games), and Chap. 7.

12 *McCallion* v. *Dodd* [1966] N.Z.L.R. 710.

13 *Pickard* v. *Smith* (1861) 10 C.B.(N.S.) 470, *per* Williams J. See also *Allen* v. *Hayward* (1845) 7 Q.B. 960; *Steel* v. *S.E. Ry.* (1855) 16 C.B. 550; *Wilson* v. *Hodgson's Kingston Brewery* (1915) 85 L.J.K.B. 270.

14 *Phillips* v. *Britannia Hygienic Laundry* [1923] 1 K.B. 539; affd. [1923] 2 K.B. 832; *Stennett* v. *Hancock* [1939] 2 All E.R. 578.

15 *Haseldine* v. *Daw & Son Ltd.* [1941] 1 K.B. 343.

16 *Green* v. *Fibreglass Ltd.* [1958] 2 Q.B. 245. *Cook* v. *Broderip* (1968) 112 S.J. 193 (nor was there a breach of the flat owner-occupier's duty under section 2 of the Occupiers' Liability Act 1957).

17 *Salsbury* v. *Woodland* [1970] 1 Q.B. 324.

18 *Clayton* v. *Woodman & Son (Builders) Ltd.* [1962] 2 Q.B. 533 (the C.A. held the architects not liable, either). See 78 L.Q.R. 107.

947 **Exceptions.** The employer, however, is liable for his own act or neglect and, accordingly, if he contracts with an independent contractor to do some act which he is not entitled to do, or to perform some duty which is thrown upon him, either by statute or common law, he will be liable for the way in which the contractor has performed the act or the duty, even though it be done negligently. Salmon J. expressed this view thus: " There are, of course, cases where, by virtue of a contract or by the operation of law, an obligation may be imposed on a man to do an act or to ensure that it is done and done carefully. In such cases the defendant cannot shelter behind any independent contractor, whom he may have employed. If he breaches the obligation he is liable, not in negligence, but in contract . . . or by reason of some breach of duty other than a duty to take care. . . ." [19] In such cases the contractor may be regarded as the agent of the employer to perform the primary duty of the employer himself [20] whose liability in such circumstances cannot be vicarious, properly so called.[21] It follows that the employer is liable because he has himself broken his own duty and not because he is liable for his contractor's negligence. This principle is conveniently summarised by Denning L.J. in these words: " I take it to be clear law, as well as good sense, that, where a person is himself under a duty to use care, he cannot get rid of his responsibility by delegating the performance of it to someone else, no matter whether the delegation be to a servant under a contract of service or to an independent contractor under a contract for services. Lord Blackburn laid that down on many occasions, see *Tarry* v. *Ashton* [22]; *Dalton* v. *Angus* [23]; and *Hughes* v. *Percival* [24]; and so have other great judges. . . ." [25] Even so in these cases the employer is not liable for the casual or collateral negligence of the contractor or his servants.[26]

948 **Unlawful act.** If the employer has contracted with the contractor to do an act which the employer is not entitled to do, such as a public nuisance, a private nuisance, or a trespass, the employer is liable for the resulting damage. Where a gas company, with no statutory powers for breaking up the highway, made a contract with a firm of contractors to dig trenches in the streets in order to lay gas pipes, and the contractors negligently left on the footway a heap of stones, over which the plaintiff fell and was injured, it was held that the gas company were liable. The ground of the decision was that the act was illegal and that the contractors were only doing what the gas company had instructed

[19] *Green* v. *Fibreglass Ltd.* [1958] 2 Q.B. 245, 250.
[20] See Chapman, 50 L.Q.R. 71, for a discussion of the principle underlying this liability and *cf.* Glanville Williams, " Liability of Independent Contractors " [1956] C.L.J. 180 for a different view.
[21] *Daniel* v. *Rickett, Cockerell & Co. Ltd.* [1938] 2 K.B. 322, 325.
[22] (1876) 1 Q.B.D. 314, 319.
[23] (1881) 6 App.Cas. 740, 829.
[24] (1883) 8 App.Cas. 443, 446.
[25] *Cassidy* v. *Ministry of Health* [1951] 2 K.B. 343, at p. 363.
[26] *Post*, § 959.

them to do.[27] " Though it may be that if the workmen employed had been careful in the way in which they heaped up the earth and stones the plaintiff would have avoided them, still I think the nuisance which the defendants employed the contractors to commit was the primary cause of the accident." [28] Similarly, if a contractor is employed to erect a building which infringes the adjoining owner's ancient lights or is a trespass upon the land of another, the employer is liable.[29]

949 **Contractor employed to perform a duty thrown by law on employer.** If an employer who has a duty to perform, either by statute or at common law, makes a contract with an independent contractor for the performance of that duty instead of doing it himself he is liable for the negligence of the independent contractor in the performance of the duty. But there can be cases where the contractors thereby owe a duty of care to the employee and will be held jointly liable with the employers.[30] In such an event the employers may become entitled to recover those damages awarded against themselves from the contractors as the measure of damages for breach of contract.[31] The cases in which a duty is thrown upon the employer are, (i) in relation to dangerous things, (ii) dangers on the highway, (iii) duties imposed by statute and, (iv) where an act involves special risk of damage.

950 (i) *Dangerous things.* When the employer is under the absolute duty which attaches to the ownership of dangerous things.[32] A person who builds a reservoir is liable for damage caused by the escape of water, even though he employed a contractor to construct it.[33] The employer who employs a contractor to do an act involving the creation of or the interference with a dangerous thing—as if the contractor is employed to burn brushwood on the employer's land and does so negligently so that the fire spreads to the adjoining land and does damage,[34] or photographers are employed to take a photograph which can only be taken by flashlight [35]—is liable for the negligence of the contractor in not preventing the dangerous thing from causing damage. Ship repairers who use an oxyacetylene burner on the strength of a certificate, issued by a consulting engineer employed by them, that the vessel is " gas free," are liable for the damage caused by an explosion owing to the negligence of the consulting engineer in failing to make a proper inspection before issuing his certificate.[36] " Where the introduction of implements or substances dangerous in themselves, such as flame-bearing

[27] *Ellis* v. *Sheffield Gas Consumers Co.* (1853) 2 E. & B. 767.
[28] *Per* Wightman J. *Cf. Clarke* v. *J. Sugrue & Sons Ltd., The Times,* May 29, 1959.
[29] *Upton* v. *Townend* (1855) 17 C.B. 30.
[30] *Driver* v. *William Willett (Contractors)* [1969] 1 All E.R. 665.
[31] *Sims* v. *Foster Wheeler Ltd.* [1966] 1 W.L.R. 769.
[32] See Chap. 9.
[33] *Rylands* v. *Fletcher* (1868) 3 H.L. 330; 37 L.J.Ex. 161. If the water is collected in a domestic cistern and escapes owing to the negligence of a plumber, an independent contractor, employed to mend the cistern, the employer is not liable: *Blake* v. *Woolf* [1898] 2 Q.B. 426.
[34] *Black* v. *Christchurch Finance Co.* [1894] A.C. 48.
[35] *Honeywill & Stein Ltd.* v. *Larkin Bros. Ltd.* [1934] 1 K.B. 191.
[36] *The Pass of Ballater* [1942] P. 112.

instruments or explosives, are necessarily incidental to the work to be performed a contractor is equally bound by an unescapable duty.... He has not merely a duty to take care but a duty to provide that care is taken. It is, therefore, a matter of no importance in these classes of case whether he delegates the duty to a servant or to a sub-contractor. The burden of the duty cannot be thrown off, and if care has not been taken, wherever the fault may lie, and however he may have protected himself by special covenant with the individual or contractor equally in fault, he is liable in law to a party who has suffered by the default."[37] A local authority, who employ a contractor to make a sewer near to the mains of a gas company, are liable for the negligence of the contractor in interfering with the foundations of the gas main so as to cause an escape of gas.[38]

951 (ii) *Dangers on the highway.* When the employer employs the contractor to perform, upon or adjoining the highway, work which is likely to involve danger to persons using the highway. Where a local authority employed a contractor to make up a highway, and the contractor negligently left a heap of soil, unlighted and unprotected, upon the highway so that the plaintiff, in the dark, fell over the heap and was injured, the local authority were held liable.[39] A. L. Smith L.J. approved the statement of the trial judge Bruce J. who had said: " When a person employs a contractor to do work in a place where the public are in the habit of passing, which work will, unless precautions are taken, cause danger to the public, an obligation is thrown upon the person who orders the work to be done to see that the necessary precautions are taken, and, if the necessary precautions are not taken, he cannot escape liability by seeking to throw the blame on the contractor."[40] This duty at common law is recognised by the provisions of section 1 (3) of the Highways (Miscellaneous Provisions) Act 1961, in dealing with the statutory defence available to the highway authority in an action against them for damage resulting from their failure to maintain a highway. Therein it is provided that it shall not be relevant to prove that the highway authority had arranged for a competent person to carry out or supervise the maintenance of the part of the highway to which the action relates unless it is also proved that the authority had given him proper instructions with regard to the maintenance of the highway and that he had carried out the instructions.

[37] *Ibid. per* Langton J. at p. 117.
[38] *Hardaker* v. *Idle District Council* [1896] 1 Q.B. 335.
[39] *Penny* v. *Wimbledon U.D.C.* [1899] 2 Q.B. 72. Similar cases are *Burgess* v. *Gray* (1845) 1 C.B. 578 (contractor employed to dig drain communicating with sewer in highway, leaves heap of rubbish over which plaintiff falls—employer liable); *Gray* v. *Pullen* (1864) 5 B. & S. 970 (trench improperly filled in by contractor); *Clements* v. *Tyrone C.C.* [1905] 2 Ir.R. 542 (contractor repairing road leaves heap of stones); *The Snark* [1900] P. 105 (wreck in navigable river left unlighted by contractor); *Bright* v. *Att.-Gen.* (1971) S.J. 226 (white lines negligently removed from road's surface). But *cf.* the position where public works contractors were laying a drain and a length of rope was left on the highway by an independent contractor, over which rope the plaintiff tripped and fell. Lord Parker C.J. held that the defendants were not liable for this act of the independent contractor since the defendants did not know that the rope was on the highway nor did they choose to leave it there: *Clarke* v. *J. Sugrue & Sons Ltd.*, *The Times*, May 29, 1959.
[40] [1898] 2 Q.B. 212, at p. 217.

52 Further illustrations of the above principle are afforded by the following cases: where a telephone company, engaged in laying telephone wires along a street, contracted with a plumber to do certain work and were held liable for the act of the plumber's servant in negligently dipping a lamp into a cauldron of melted solder, thereby causing an explosion which injured a passer-by [41]; where the occupier of a house from which a lamp was suspended over the street was held liable for the negligence of an independent contractor in failing to repair the attachment, as a result of which the lamp fell and injured a person passing along the street [42]; and where a contractor was employed to drive a heifer and calf along the highway, the employer was held liable when the heifer tossed a dog and injured a passer-by, on the ground that a heifer, with a calf, might become dangerous on meeting a dog.[43]

If a contractor is employed to deliver goods at premises of which the employer is not the occupier, there is no liability on the employer if the contractor, in course of delivery, creates some danger in the highway and injures a passer-by. So, when a brewery company employed a contractor to deliver beer to a public-house, of which they were not the occupiers, and the contractor negligently left open the cellar flaps, over which a boy tripped as he was walking along the street, the brewery company were held not liable.[44] On the other hand, if the employer is the occupier of the premises he will be liable if the work he has employed the contractor to do involves the opening of a cellar flap or similar thing or the creation of a heap of soil, coals or the like, in the highway.[45]

53 The principle stated above is not confined to dangers created on the highway; it extends to dangers created in any place where persons are lawfully passing. Accordingly, when the occupier of a refreshment room at a railway station employed a contractor to deliver coals down a coal hole in the platform, and the contractor negligently left the flap open, as a result of which a railway passenger was injured, it was held that the occupier was liable.[46]

However, work carried out near to a highway, which may cause injury to persons on the highway, such as felling a hawthorn tree in a front garden, does not constitute an exception to the general rule that an

41 *Holliday* v. *National Telephone Co.* [1899] 2 Q.B. 392. *Cf. Hardaker* v. *Idle District Council* [1896] 1 Q.B. 335.

42 *Tarry* v. *Ashton* (1876) 1 Q.B.D. 314.

43 *Pinn* v. *Rew* (1916) 32 T.L.R. 451.

44 *Wilson* v. *Hodgson's Kingston Brewery Co.* (1915) 85 L.J.K.B. 270.

45 *Pickard* v. *Smith* (1861) 10 C.B.(N.S.) 470; *Daniel* v. *Rickett Cockerell & Co. Ltd.* [1938] 2 K.B. 322 (in this case the employer recovered substantial contribution from the independent contractor).

46 *Pickard* v. *Smith, supra. Cf. Cunard* v. *Antifyre Ltd.* [1933] 1 K.B. 551, 562, *per* Talbot J. *Welfare* v. *London & Brighton Ry.* (1869) L.R. 4 Q.B. 693 (passenger in railway station injured by fall of zinc from roof which was being repaired by a contractor, railway company not liable) must be taken to have been wrongly decided. In *Pickard* v. *Smith* the railway company would have been liable because they were occupiers, see Chap. 8. In spite of Williams J.'s opinion to the contrary (p. 477) the contractor would have been liable; see *Whiteley* v. *Pepper* (1877) 2 Q.B.D. 276.

employer of an independent contractor is not responsible for the contractors' act or omissions.[47]

954 (iii) *Statutory duty*. When the employer employs the contractor to perform an absolute duty, which is thrown by statute upon the employer, the performance of it cannot be delegated to enable liability to be evaded.[48] It makes no difference whether the duty is owed to the public at large or just to a section of it; the same principle applies.[49] Where a railway company were authorised by statute to construct a bridge, provided that it would open so as to allow vessels to pass along the river, and employed contractors who constructed a bridge which would not open, the railway company were held liable.[50] Again, where a local authority had undertaken the cleansing of cesspools under the Public Health Act 1875, and employed contractors to do the work, they were held liable for the act of the contractors in wrongfully depositing the sewage upon the plaintiff's land, Buckley L.J. saying: " They [the local authority] owed a duty to use all reasonable skill and care so to dispose of and deposit this sewage as not to injure or cause damage to any person. They were at liberty to employ a contractor to do the work, but if the contractor failed to do that which it was the duty of these defendants to do or get done, then these defendants are liable." [51]

Similarly, where an employer is under a duty to fence dangerous [52] machinery under the Factories Act 1961 and to provide safe means of access [53] he cannot escape liability by delegating the performance of his duty to an independent contractor. Further, a carrier of goods by sea has not fulfilled his statutory duty to use due diligence even where he has employed a competent ship repairer and thereafter has had this work inspected in the usual way by a Lloyd's surveyor.[54]

But in *Driver* v. *William Willett* (*Contractors*) [55] it was held that a person who contracts with employers to act as their consultant safety and inspecting engineer in connection with their business also owes a duty of care to the latter's employees. Thus where there had been breaches of the various Building Regulations and the employers had been held liable to an injured workman of theirs, the independent contractor was also held to be liable since he had contractually undertaken the duties of a safety officer under the regulations. Accordingly, the employers were entitled to recover that proportion of damages awarded against themselves from the independent contractor as damages for breach of contract.[56]

47 *Salsbury* v. *Woodland* [1970] 1 Q.B. 324.
48 *The Pass of Ballater* [1942] P. 112, 117.
49 *Mulready* v. *J. H. & W. Bell Ltd.* [1953] 2 Q.B. 117.
50 *Hole* v. *Sittingbourne & Sheerness Ry.* (1861) 6 H. & N. 488.
51 *Robinson* v. *Beaconsfield R.D.C.* [1911] 2 Ch. 188, at pp. 197, 198.
52 *Groves* v. *Wimborne* (*Lord*) [1898] 2 Q.B. 402.
53 *Hosking* v. *De Havilland Aircraft Co. Ltd.* [1949] 1 All E.R. 540. But for the position under the Building Regulations, unless the employers had not divested themselves of the control of the work, see *Donaghey* v. *Boulton & Paul Ltd.* [1968] A.C. 1.
54 *Riverstone Meat Co. Pty. Ltd.* v. *Lancashire Shipping Co. Ltd.* [1961] A.C. 807.
55 [1969] 1 All E.R. 665.
56 Applying *Sims* v. *Foster Wheeler Ltd.* [1966] 1 W.L.R. 769.

955 (iv) *Act involves special risk of damage.* This arises when the employer employs a contractor to do work which in its very nature involves in the eyes of the law a special danger to another.[57] In such a case the employer is liable for the negligence of his independent contractor, and if the act is one which involves special danger of nuisance, is liable for nuisance.[58] If, therefore, the owner of a house, from which the owner of the adjoining house has a right of support, employs a contractor to pull down his house, he is liable for any damage caused to the adjoining house by the failure of the contractor to provide proper support.[59] Where the owner of a building, the ground floor of which had been let to the plaintiff, employed a contractor to demolish the building above the ground floor, he was held liable to the plaintiff for damage caused through dust and broken bricks entering his premises in the execution of the work.[60] Again, where the tenant of the first floor of a building employed an independent contractor to make structural alterations to that floor and caused a nuisance to the tenant of the second floor from the dust and noise set up by the alterations, the employer was held liable.[61] The principle of the decision was expressed by Slesser L.J. to be: " If the act done is one which in its very nature involves a special danger of nuisance being complained of, then it is one which falls within the exception for which the employer of the contractor will be responsible if there is a failure to take the necessary precautions that the nuisance shall not arise."

In these cases there is a duty upon the employer not to do the damage in question, and this duty is broken either by infringing some right of property, such as an easement of support, or by committing a nuisance.

Where the plaintiffs had agreed to allow the local authority to demolish a lean-to adjacent to their warehouse and, due to the delay in making good the security of the premises, thieves successfully broke in and stole stocks of tobacco, it was held that since all the parties knew of the warehouse's contents the local authority was liable for the loss inasmuch as the loss had occurred through the neglect of the contractors as its agents, but the latter were held to be joint tortfeasors.[62]

956 **Bailment.**[63] In the absence of an express term to the contrary a bailee will be liable for loss or damage to the goods, which had been caused by his independent contractor. Thus where the plaintiff's goods were damaged by sea water due to the unseaworthiness of the defendant's ship and it had been proved that this state of affairs was caused solely

57 There is liability under the rule in *Rylands* v. *Fletcher* (1868) L.R. 3 H.L. 330 for the acts of an independent contractor.

58 See *Balfour* v. *Barty-King* [1957] 1 Q.B. 496. See also the note of this case by T. Ellis Lewis in [1957] C.L.J. 132. *Honeywill & Stein Ltd.* v. *Larkin Bros.* [1934] 1 K.B. 191.

59 *Bower* v. *Peate* (1876) 1 Q.B.D. 321; *Dalton* v. *Angus* (1881) 6 App.Cas. 740; *Hughes* v. *Percival* (1883) 8 App.Cas. 443. In the latter case Lord Blackburn said that the proposition of Cockburn C.J. in *Bower* v. *Peate* at p. 326, was too broadly stated.

60 *Odell* v. *Cleveland House Ltd.* (1910) 26 T.L.R. 410.

61 *Matania* v. *National Provincial Bank* [1936] 2 All E.R. 633.

62 *Stanners* v. *High Wycombe Corporation* (1968) 67 L.G.R. 115. See further, *ante*, § 891.

63 Generally see *Morris* v. *C. W. Martin & Sons Ltd.* [1966] 1 Q.B. 716 and the examples given by Lord Denning M.R. at pp. 725–727.

by the negligence of a servant of an independent contractor, namely, a firm of ship-repairers, the House of Lords nevertheless held the defendants liable in spite of their duty under the bill of lading contract being limited to exercising due diligence in making the ship seaworthy.[64] Again, a bailee for reward, namely, a warehouseman, would still have been held liable for the negligence of a servant of independent contractors, who were security guards, if the Court of Appeal had been satisfied that it was his negligence in the discharge of his duties which had been the cause of the theft of the plaintiff's valuable lorry load of whisky.[65] There is no implied right to sub-contract where the bailment is of valuable goods for carriage.[66]

957 **Lessor and lessee.** The lessor of land let on a building lease does not stand to his lessee in the relation of employer to independent contractor. So, if the lessee, in pursuance of the covenants contained in his lease, proceeds to erect buildings on the land demised, the lessor is not liable for damage caused by the negligence of the lessee or his contractor during the work.[67]

958 **Occupiers' Liability.** The position at common law, where an occupier was not held liable to a licensee who was hurt by a danger which had been created by an independent contractor and of which the occupier had no knowledge,[68] has been altered by the Occupiers' Liability Act 1957. By section 2 (4) it is provided that: " In determining whether the occupier of premises had discharged the common duty of care to a visitor, regard is to be had to all the circumstances, so that (for example) . . . (*b*) where damage is caused to a visitor by a danger due to the faulty execution of any work of construction, maintenance or repair by an independent contractor employed by the occupier, the occupier is not to be treated without more as answerable for the danger, if in all the circumstances he had acted reasonably in entrusting the work to an independent contractor and had taken such steps (if any) as he reasonably ought in order to satisfy himself that the contractor was competent and that the work had been properly done." See generally Chapter 8.

959 **Casual or collateral negligence.**[69] Even when an employer is liable for the negligence of an independent contractor in doing what he has contracted to do, he is not liable for the casual or collateral negligence of the contractor. The latter's collateral negligence does not involve the employer in a breach of his non-delegable duty, hence the employer

[64] *Riverstone Meat Co. Pty. Ltd.* v. *Lancashire Shipping Co. Ltd.* [1961] A.C. 807. But *cf. Leesh River Tea Co. Ltd.* v. *British India Steam Navigation Co. Ltd.* [1967] 2 Q.B. 250.

[65] *B.R.S. Ltd.* v. (*Arthur V.*) *Crutchley & Co. Ltd.* [1968] 1 All E.R. 811, *per* Lord Pearson at p. 820 and, *per* Sachs L.J. at p. 824.

[66] *Garnham, Harris & Elton Ltd.* v. *Alfred W. Ellis* (*Transport*) *Ltd.* [1967] 1 W.L.R. 940.

[67] *Hurlstone* v. *London Electric Ry.* (1914) 30 T.L.R. 398.

[68] *Morgan* v. *Girls Friendly Society* [1936] 1 All E.R. 404.

[69] The distinction between these and other negligence was adversely criticised by Sachs L.J. in *Salsbury* v. *Woodland* [1970] 1 Q.B. 324, C.A. at p. 348, who found that he derived no assistance from it at all.

is exempt from liability because the act done is outside the scope of the duty imposed on him and not so much because it could not have been foreseen or precautions taken against its occurrence. Lord Blackburn in *Dalton* v. *Angus*[70] said: " Ever since *Quarman* v. *Burnett*[71] it has been considered settled law that one employing another is not liable for his collateral negligence unless the relation of master and servant existed between them. So that a person employing a contractor to do work is not liable for the negligence of that contractor or his servants. On the other hand, a person causing something to be done, the doing of which casts on him a duty, cannot escape from the responsibility attaching on him of seeing that duty performed by delegating it to a contractor." Commenting on this Lindley L.J. said: " Lord Blackburn in this passage contrasts a contractor's negligence, which he calls ' collateral,' with failure on the part of a contractor to perform the duty of his employer. For the first the employer is not liable; for the second he is, whether the failure is attributable to negligence or not."[72]

60 The following explanations of what amounts to casual or collateral negligence have been given: " Where the act complained of is purely collateral, and arises incidentally in the course of the performance of the work, the employer is not liable, because he never authorised that act "[73]; " If the contractor performs their duty for them, it is performed by them through him, and they are not responsible for anything more. They are not responsible for his negligence in other respects, as they would be if he were their servant. Such negligence is sometimes called casual or collateral negligence "[74]; " When a person, through a contractor, does work which from its nature is likely to cause danger to others, there is a duty on his part to take all reasonable precautions against such danger, and he does not escape from liability for the discharge of that duty by employing the contractor if the latter does not take these precautions. I desire to point out that accidents arising from what is called casual or collateral negligence cannot be guarded against beforehand, and do not come within this rule "[75]; " Before a superior employer could be held liable for the negligent act of a servant of a sub-contractor it must be shown that the work which the sub-contractor was employed to do was work the nature of which, and not merely the performance of which, cast on the superior employer the duty of taking precautions."[76]

61 From this it appears that the distinction is between negligence in fulfilling a duty which is thrown upon the employer, when the employer is liable, and negligence which is merely incidental to and does not arise

70 (1881) 6 App.Cas. 740, 829.
71 (1840) 6 M. & W. 499.
72 *Hardaker* v. *Idle D.C.* [1896] 1 Q.B. 335, 342.
73 Pollock C.B. in *Hole* v. *Sittingbourne & Sheerness Ry.* (1861) 6 H. & N. 488.
74 Lindley L.J. in *Hardaker* v. *Idle D.C., supra,* at p. 340.
75 Romer L.J. in *Penny* v. *Wimbledon U.D.C.* [1899] 2 Q.B. 72, 78.
76 Fletcher Moulton L.J. in *Padbury* v. *Holliday & Greenwood Ltd.* (1912) 28 T.L.R. 494.

directly out of the duty to be fulfilled, when the employer is not liable.[77] Examples of the former are the cases cited above in connection with dangers in the highway,[78] such as leaving a heap of stones unlighted and unguarded. On the other hand, if a workman employed in road works negligently leaves " a pickaxe, or such-like, in the road," the negligence is collateral and the employer of the contractor is not liable,[79] and likewise if he leaves a length of rope on the highway.[80] So, where a sub-contractor was employed to put metallic casements into the windows of a building, and one of his servants left a tool on the window sill, and the window was blown to by the wind, so that the tool fell and struck a man passing along the highway, the contractor was held not liable on the ground that the injury was caused by an act of collateral negligence on the part of the sub-contractor's servant.[81]

962 In *Reedie* v. *L. & N.W. Ry.*[82] the railway company employed a contractor to make a bridge. They were held not liable for the negligence of a workman of their contractor in letting a stone fall from the bridge onto the plaintiff. Although not based on collateral negligence, the decision was subsequently considered by Lindley L.J.[83] to be an example of collateral negligence. It may be doubted whether this is correct, because the duty of a person who is building a bridge over a highway is to see that reasonable care is taken not to drop things on the highway, and the negligence of the workman is negligence directly arising from what the contractor was employed to do.[84] In *Holliday* v. *National Telephone Co.*,[85] due to the negligence of a plumber who was employed as an independent contractor carrying out work on a public street, an explosion occurred as a result of him dipping his benzoline lamp into a caldron of molten solder so that the plaintiff, a passer-by, was splashed by the molten metal. The Divisional Court[86] gave judgment in the defendants' favour on the ground that the negligence of the plumber was collateral but the Court of Appeal reversed this decision on the ground that the negligence arose out of the very act which he was employed to perform on the defendants' behalf.[87] On the other hand, if the contractor was negligent in bringing steel girders or other materials to the site, or in leaving a horse and cart which had been used in connection with the work

[77] Collateral negligence raised as a specific defence succeeded in *Thompson* v. *Anglo-Saxon Petroleum Co. Ltd.* [1955] 2 Lloyd's Rep. 363.
[78] *Ante*, § 951.
[79] *Per* A. L. Smith L.J. in *Penny* v. *Wimbledon U.D.C.* [1899] 2 Q.B. 72.
[80] *Clarke* v. *J. Sugrue & Sons Ltd.*, *The Times*, May 29, 1959.
[81] *Padbury* v. *Holliday & Greenwood Ltd.*, *supra*; *Pearson* v. *Cox* (1877) 2 C.P.D. 369 (plasterer's servant left tool on window so that it fell into the street, employer of plasterer held not liable) is a similar case.
[82] (1849) 4 Ex. 244.
[83] *Hardaker* v. *Idle D.C.* [1896] 1 Q.B. 335.
[84] See *Kearney* v. *L.B. & S.C. Ry.* (1871) L.R. 6 Q.B. 759.
[85] [1899] 2 Q.B. 392.
[86] [1899] 1 Q.B. 221.
[87] *Supra*, *per* A. L. Smith L.J. at p. 400; *Darling* v. *Att.-Gen.* [1950] 2 All E.R. 793. See further, *per* Denning L.J. in *Cassidy* v. *Ministry of Health* [1951] 2 K.B. 343, 365.

unattended on the highway, the employer would not be liable, because his duty is confined to the erection of the bridge.

When the Ministry of Fuel and Power, under statutory powers, entered a field to bore for coal, the act of their independent contractor in leaving a heap of timber in the field, which injured a horse grazing there, was held not to be collateral negligence, on the ground that the Ministry owed to the occupier of the field a duty to take reasonable care from which they could not absolve themselves by employing an independent contractor.[88]

[88] *Darling* v. *Att.-Gen.* [1950] 2 All E.R. 793.

CHAPTER 15

PROOF OF NEGLIGENCE

1.—PROOF GENERALLY

963 **Burden of proof.** In an action for negligence, as in every other action, the burden of proof falls upon the plaintiff alleging it.[1] Hence it is for the plaintiff to give evidence of the facts on which he bases his claim to the redress which he seeks from the court. His evidence may consist of facts proved or admitted, and after it is concluded two questions arise, (1) whether on that evidence negligence may be reasonably inferred, and (2) whether, assuming it may be reasonably inferred, it is in fact inferred.[2] These two questions do not necessarily arise for decision at the same time. The first question usually arises at the conclusion of the plaintiff's case, although it may also arise at the conclusion of the whole of the evidence, and is a question of law. The second question arises at the conclusion of the whole of the evidence, and is a question of fact.[3] During the course of a trial, however, the *provisional* burden of proof, which is raised by the state of the evidence, may shift to the other side to rebut any presumption so raised, but the *legal* burden, from which the provisional burden must be distinguished, rests upon the person alleging negligence throughout.[4] Negligence is proved on a preponderance of probabilities.[5] This onus does not require the elimination by the plaintiff of every conceivable possibility of how the accident may have happened without the fault of the defendant but what is adduced in evidence on behalf of the plaintiff must go further than pure guesswork and reach the field of legal inference. As Lord Macmillan said, " the dividing line between conjecture and inference is often a very difficult one to draw. A conjecture may be plausible, but it is of no legal value, for its essence is that it is a mere guess. An inference in the legal sense, on the other hand, is a deduction from the evidence, and if it is a reasonable deduction it may have the validity of legal proof."[6] For the burden of proof of contributory negligence, see Chap. 16, *post*, at § 1017.

[1] See *Donoghue* v. *Stevenson* [1932] A.C. 562, *per* Lord Macmillan, at p. 622.
[2] *Metropolitan Ry.* v. *Jackson* (1877) 3 App.Cas. 193, 197, *per* Lord Cairns.
[3] *Ryder* v. *Wombwell* (1868) L.R. 4 Ex. 32, *per* Willes J., quoted by Lord Blackburn in *Metropolitan Ry.* v. *Jackson, supra*, at p. 207. " It has always been considered a question of law to be determined by the judge, subject, of course, to review, whether there is evidence which, if it is believed, and the counter evidence, if any, not believed, would establish the facts in controversy. It is for the jury to say whether and how far the evidence is to be believed."
[4] *Brown* v. *Rolls-Royce Ltd.* [1960] 1 W.L.R. 210, *per* Lord Denning, at pp. 215, 216.
[5] *Dawson* v. *Murex Ltd.* [1942] 1 All E.R. 483; *Horabin* v. *B.O.A.C.* [1952] 2 All E.R. 1016, 1021; *Bonnington Castings Ltd.* v. *Wardlaw* [1956] 1 A.C. 613; *Clarke* v. *E. R. Wright & Son* [1957] 1 W.L.R. 1191; *Brown* v. *Rolls-Royce Ltd., supra, per* Lord Denning.
[6] *Jones* v. *G.W. Ry.* (1930) 144 L.T. 194 at p. 202.

964 **Submission of no case.** On a submission by the defence that there is no case to answer, the practice is for the judge, before giving a ruling, to require the defendant to elect whether he will call evidence or not.[7] The whole of the evidence should be before the court when the judge is asked to rule no case, and consequently if the defendant elects to call evidence the ruling should only be given after his evidence has been called.[8] The reason for the practice is that if a ruling in favour of the defendant is reversed on appeal, the expense and delay of a new trial is saved, because the defendant cannot say that his evidence has not been put before the court.[9] If the judge does not put the defendant to his election, and no election in fact takes place, the defendant can call his evidence as if no submission had ever been made.[10] The duty of the appellate court, whether on appeal from a judge with a jury or a judge alone, is to assess the position realistically and to consider the whole of the evidence, including that of the defendant, for it would be a denial of justice to a plaintiff if the court made its assessment artificially on part of the evidence as it stood at the conclusion of his case when the judge made his ruling. Where, therefore, a defendant had of his own volition chosen to give evidence when he could have stood on his submission, and then had appealed against the judge's ruling, even if the submission of no case may have been wrongly rejected the Court of Appeal were not restricted to a consideration of the evidence called on behalf of the plaintiff only.[11] However when the appellate court orders a retrial, the defendant is no longer bound by his previous submission of no case to answer.[12]

965 **Facts more consistent with defendant's negligence than other causes.** There is evidence of negligence if the facts proved and the inferences to be drawn from them are more consistent with negligence on the part of the defendant than with other causes.[13] Negligence may be reasonably inferred

[7] It is discretionary: *Marbé* v. *G. Edwardes (Daly's Theatre) Ltd.* [1928] 1 K.B. 269; *Alexander* v. *Rayson* [1936] 1 K.B. 169, 178; *Young* v. *Rank* [1950] 2 K.B. 510.

[8] *Parry* v. *Aluminium Corpn. Ltd.* [1940] W.N. 44; *Laurie* v. *Raglan Building Co. Ltd.* [1942] 1 K.B. 152; *Alexander* v. *Rayson* [1936] 1 K.B. 169, 178. In *W. H. Müller & Co.* v. *Ebbw Vale Steel Co.* (1936) 52 T.L.R. 655, Branson J. held that the C.A. in *Alexander* v. *Rayson*, *supra*, did not intend to lay down any general rule, and ruled that there was no case to answer without requiring an undertaking from the defendants to refrain from calling evidence, but in view of the later decisions this must be taken to be erroneous.

[9] See *Practice Direction (Submission of no Case)* [1962] 1 W.L.R. 227, *per* Parker L.C.J.

[10] *Yuill* v. *Yuill* [1945] P. 15.

[11] *Payne* v. *Harrison* [1961] 2 Q.B. 403.

[12] *Storey* v. *Storey* [1961] P. 63. Ormerod L.J. said (at p. 69): " It was further submitted on behalf of the wife that even if there should be a new trial the husband should none the-less be bound by his election and should not be allowed to give evidence. This proposition is quite untenable. If there is to be a rehearing, the wife may well put her case differently, or call further evidence, and the husband cannot be denied the opportunity of giving in evidence his version of the events in question "; *Horton* v. *Horton* [1960] 1 W.L.R. 987.

[13] *Ellor* v. *Selfridge & Co. Ltd.* (1930) 46 T.L.R. 236; *McGowan* v. *Stott* (1923) reported 99 L.J.K.B. 357, *per* Atkin L.J. See also *per* Willes J. in *Daniel* v. *Metropolitan Ry.* (1868) L.R. 3 C.P. 216, reversed L.R. 5 H.L. 45: " It is necessary for the plaintiff to establish by evidence circumstances from which it may fairly be inferred that there is reasonable probability that the accident resulted from the want of some precaution which the defendants might and ought to have resorted to."

from facts which make it more probable that it was negligence on the part of the defendant which caused the damage in question than any other cause. For example, if a steamship under way runs down a ship at her moorings in broad daylight, there is evidence of negligence against the steamship [14]; if a motor-vehicle mounts the footpath and collides with a pedestrian or a permanent structure, such as a lamp-post, on the pavement, there is evidence of negligence against the driver [15]; if a motor-car while being driven along a highway overturns for no apparent cause,[16] or strikes a pedestrian in the back while he is walking along the highway at night,[17] there is evidence of negligence against the driver; if a passenger in a railway train is injured by the sudden and violent stopping [18] or starting [19] of the train, there is evidence of negligence against the railway company; if a tramcar is driven along a narrow road and crushes a man with a truck who has pulled his truck into the side of the road so as to allow the tramcar to pass, there is evidence of negligence against the tram company [20]; if an omnibus is so driven that it is upset as a result of a wheel being wrenched off by tramlines in the highway, there is evidence of negligence on the part of the driver of the omnibus.[21] It is, of course, always open to the defendant to call evidence contradicting or nullifying the inference which may be drawn from the plaintiff's evidence.

On the other hand, where a plaintiff averred that he had slipped down a muddy or crumbling earthwork bank at his place of work and, as a result, claimed damages from his employers for negligence but his employers called a witness who proved that the plaintiff had in fact slipped and fallen down a nearby gully, it was held, upon accepting the evidence of this latter witness, that this was so radical a departure from the pleadings as to disentitle the plaintiff from succeeding.[22]

966 If the plaintiff's evidence is equally consistent with negligence on the part of the defendant as with other causes, there is no evidence of negligence, and judgment cannot be given against the defendant. " The party seeking to recover compensation for damage must make out that the party against whom he complains was in the wrong. The burden of proof is clearly upon him, and he must show that the loss is to be attributed to the negligence of the opposite party. If at the end he leaves the case in even

14 *The City of Peking* (1888) 14 App.Cas. 40; *The Annot Lyle* (1886) 11 P.D. 114; *The Merchant Prince* [1892] P. 179.

15 *Isaac Walton & Co.* v. *Vanguard Motorbus Co.* (1908) 25 T.L.R. 13; *Barnes U.D.C.* v. *London General Omnibus Co.* (1908) 100 L.T. 115; *Ellor* v. *Selfridge & Co. Ltd.* (1930) 46 T.L.R. 236.

16 *Halliwell* v. *Venables* (1930) 99 L.J.K.B. 353.

17 *Page* v. *Richards and Draper* (unreported) referred to in *Tart* v. *Chitty* [1933] 2 K.B. 453, 457.

18 *Angus* v. *London, Tilbury and Southend Ry.* (1906) 22 T.L.R. 222.

19 *Metropolitan Ry.* v. *Delaney* (1921) 90 L.J.K.B. 721.

20 *Leaver* v. *Pontypridd U.D.C.* (1911) 76 J.P. 31 (H.L.).

21 *Lilly* v. *Tilling* (1912) 57 S.J. 59.

22 *Waghorn* v. *G. Wimpey & Co.* [1969] 1 W.L.R. 1764. This case was distinguishable from the facts in *John G. Stein & Co. Ltd.* v. *O'Hanlon* [1965] A.C. 890 where the House of Lords held that the departure was not sufficient to entitle the defendants to succeed without more in their defence of the plaintiff's claim for damages for personal injuries.

scales, and does not satisfy the court that it was occasioned by the negligence or default of the other party, he cannot succeed."[23] Accordingly, it was held that where the driver of an omnibus, having seen a woman cross in front of his bus, turned round to speak to the conductor, but the woman turned back to avoid another vehicle and was run over by the omnibus, there was no evidence of negligence because the evidence was equally consistent with the existence or non-existence of negligence on the part of the driver.[24] The plaintiff, however, is not bound to give evidence negativing contributory negligence on his part; once the plaintiff has given evidence showing a prima facie case of negligence on the part of the defendant, the burden of proof of contributory negligence is on the defendant.[25] This, of course, is not the case if the plaintiff's evidence itself shows contributory negligence on his own part.

67 **Causal connection between defendant's negligence and damage essential.** The plaintiff's evidence also must show that on the balance of probabilities the most likely cause of the damage was the defendant's negligence and not the negligence of any other person.[26] For instance, if a motor-van has been repaired and, two days afterwards, a wheel comes off while it is being driven by a servant of the owners, there is no evidence of negligence against the repairers because, although the facts suggest negligence on the part of somebody they do not point to negligence on the part of the repairers rather than of the driver or owner.[27] Again, where a chauffeur was injured through the fall of a pane of glass above the garage at which he was employed, and the circumstances were such as to show negligence on the part of somebody, but not necessarily personal negligence on the part of his employer, it was held that he could not recover.[28] If a lineman, working on an electrical installation, is electrocuted without any breach of the statutory regulations the mere fact of his death is no evidence of negligence on the part of anyone.[29] Where an upright in a scaffold was not vertical, contrary to regulation 10 (1) of the Building (Safety, Health and Welfare) Regulations 1948 and a scaffolder tried to remedy the defect in a way found by the court to be "fantastically wrong" and was injured, it was held he could not recover because his injury was caused solely by his own

[23] Lord Wensleydale in *Morgan* v. *Sim* (1857) 11 Moo.P.C. 307, 312. See also *Cotton* v. *Wood* (1860) 8 C.B.(N.S.) 568, *per* Erle C.J.; *Hammack* v. *White* (1862) 11 C.B.(N.S.) 588; *Wakelin* v. *L. & S.W. Ry.* (1886) 12 App.Cas. 41; *Brown* v. *Rolls-Royce Ltd.* [1960] 1 W.L.R. 210.

[24] *Cotton* v. *Wood, supra.*

[25] *Wakelin* v. *L. & S.W. Ry., supra, per* Lord Watson at p. 47; *Craig* v. *Glasgow Corpn.* (1919) 35 T.L.R. 214, *per* Lord Finlay; *Holland* v. *North Metropolitan Tramways* (1886) 3 T.L.R. 245; *Dublin, Wicklow and Wexford Ry.* v. *Slattery* (1878) 3 App.Cas. 1155, 1180, *per* Lord Penzance; *Caswell* v. *Powell Duffryn Associated Collieries Ltd.* [1940] A.C. 152, 172, *per* Lord Wright.

[26] *Donoghue* v. *Stevenson* [1932] A.C. 562, *per* Lord Macmillan at p. 622; *Gardiner* v. *Motherwell Machinery & Scrap Co.* [1961] 1 W.L.R. 1424 (a case of causation of industrial dermatitis). See generally Chap. 3.

[27] *Britannia Hygienic Laundry Co.* v. *Thornycroft* (1925) 95 L.J.K.B. 237. See also *Smith* v. *Midland Ry.* (1887) 57 L.T. 813; *Russell* v. *L. & S.W. Ry.* (1908) 24 T.L.R. 548; *Daniel* v. *Metropolitan Ry.* (1871) L.R. 5 H.L. 45.

[28] *Cole* v. *de Trafford* (*No.* 2) [1918] 2 K.B. 523.

[29] *Youngman* v. *Pirelli General Cable Works* [1940] 1 K.B. 1.

negligence and not by the defendant's breach of statutory duty.[30] Where a plaintiff was injured in the course of his employment due to the employers' negligence which had left him with a weak left leg, but some three weeks later, as he was about to descend a flight of stairs, he felt a twinge suddenly in the injured leg, which made him jump down several steps, whereby his right leg was injured, the Session Court held that there had been an intervening act which had broken the chain of causation. Further, as the second accident had not been caused by the original negligence of his employers, the resulting injury to the right leg was not the natural and probable or the natural and direct result of their negligence.[31] The plaintiff must also show that the damage was the result of the defendant's negligence, because negligence without proof of damage is not actionable.[32]

968 **Principal cause of the accident.** In *Bonnington Castings Ltd.* v. *Wardlaw* [33] where the pursuer was subjected in his work to the inhalation over a period of years of minute particles of silica, which accumulated gradually in his lungs causing pneumoconiosis, it was found that he had been exposed to two different sources of the invisible silica dust. Some of the dust came from one source, against which no complaint could be made, but some of the dust came from another source, which arose from breach of statutory duty and it was held to be sufficient to establish liability. Lord Reid said [34]: " The disease is caused by the whole of the noxious material inhaled and, if that material comes from two sources, it cannot be wholly attributed to material from one source or the other . . . and the real question is whether the dust from the swing grinders materially contributed to the disease. . . . A contribution which comes within the exception *de minimis non curat lex* is not material, but I think that any contribution which does not fall within that exception must be material." It follows that in an action for damages for breach of statutory duty or negligence it is not necessary to prove that the breach alleged was the whole or main cause of the accident, because it is sufficient to show that it materially contributed to the damage.[35]

969 **Cause of accident unknown.** It is not necessary for a plaintiff to give direct evidence of negligence. He may prove his case partly by direct and partly by indirect or circumstantial evidence. In some cases the facts of an accident are unknown, and the plaintiff to succeed must then prove facts

[30] *Norris* v. *W. Moss & Sons Ltd.* [1954] 1 W.L.R. 346.

[31] *McKew* v. *Holland & Hannen & Cubitts* (*Scotland*), 1969 S.L.T. 101, affirmed by the H.L. [1969] 3 All E.R. 1621. By way of contrast *cf. Wieland* v. *Cyril Lord Carpets* [1969] 3 All E.R. 1006.

[32] *Metropolitan Ry.* v. *Jackson* (1877) 3 App.Cas. 193. See further, Chap. 3.

[33] [1956] A.C. 613.

[34] At p. 621. For presumption of causation, see *Gardiner* v. *Motherwell Machinery Co.* [1961] 1 W.L.R. 1424. (When a man, who has not previously suffered from a disease, contracts such disease, after being subjected to conditions likely to cause it, and when he shows that it starts in a way typical of disease caused by such conditions, there is a prima facie presumption that his disease was caused by those conditions.)

[35] See also *Clarkson* v. *Modern Foundries Ltd* [1958] 1 All E.R. 33, where part of the exposure to the noxious dust occurred over a number of years outside the time limit for bringing the action for damages.

from which an inference of negligence on the part of the defendant may be reasonably inferred. "It is a mistake to think that because an event is unseen its cause cannot be reasonably inferred."[36] The facts, however, must be such as to put the matter beyond a mere surmise or conjecture; they must lead to an inference which is a reasonable deduction from the facts actually observed and proved. "If the evidence establishes only that the accident was possibly due to the negligence to which the plaintiffs seek to assign it, their case is not proved. To justify the verdict which they have obtained the evidence must be such that the attribution of the accident to that cause may reasonably be inferred. If a case such as this is left in the position that nothing has been proved to render more probable any one of two or more theories of the accident, then the plaintiff has failed to discharge the burden of proof incumbent upon him. He has left the case in equilibrium, and the court is not entitled to incline the balance one way or the other."[37]

970 By way of illustration of the practical application of these principles, it has been held that there was evidence of negligence on the part of the defendants where a bargeman was found drowned in a dock to which he had been navigating two loaded barges. One of the barges was found moored to the quay of the dock, but the other was not. There were no chains or ladders at the dock walls to help persons who fell into the water to get out. Some other people had been drowned in the dock, and complaint had been made to the dock company of the dock's dangerous condition.[38] Where an explosion occurred at a cartridge factory, the cause being unknown, the jury found that the owners of the factory were negligent in neglecting to supply suitable machinery and not taking proper precautions to prevent an explosion. It was held to be a reasonable inference that the explosion occurred rather from some irregularity in the working of the machinery than from any other cause, so that the jury's verdict was upheld.[39] A man was driving two cows along a road which was imperfectly lighted. The night was not dark, but it was cloudy. A tram was being driven along the road at a considerable speed. The driver saw nothing until he was quite close to the cows; he then applied his brake but the tram grazed a cow; shortly afterwards he felt a bump and, on getting down, found the man unconscious on the tramcar's near side. The man remembered nothing of the accident. It was held that, although no one saw the accident, the reasonable inference was that the man was injured by being knocked down by the tram owing to the driver's negligence in not keeping a proper lookout.[40] A workman left one part of his employer's works to go to another part. Shortly after he left, he was found dead between the buffers of two railway wagons. The wagons were on a siding. At the place where the accident happened there was a clear view up and

[36] Lord Buckmaster in *Jones* v. *G.W.Ry.* (1930) 47 T.L.R. 39, 41.
[37] Lord Macmillan in *Jones* v. *G.W.Ry.*, *supra*, at p. 45.
[38] *Moore* v. *Ransome's Dock Committee* (1898) 14 T.L.R. 539.
[39] *McArthur* v. *Dominion Cartridge Co.* [1905] A.C. 72.
[40] *Craig* v. *Glasgow Corpn.* (1919) 35 T.L.R. 214.

down the rails for more than 100 yards. The railway company were shunting these wagons and employed a man to give warning before shunting operations began. No warning was given because no one was seen. There were always wagons on the siding, but shunting operations were intermittent. It was usual for workmen to cross the siding. It was held that the facts warranted the inference that the death was caused by the railway company's negligence.[41] Two motor-cyclists collided on the highway. One was killed and neither the other nor anyone else could give evidence as to what happened. After the accident, both cycles were found interlocked on the deceased's proper side of the road, the deceased being ten feet away, also on his proper side of the road. The road surface on the other man's side of the road was very rough, but on the deceased's side was much better. It was held that there was evidence of negligence against the other man.[42]

971 On the other hand it has been held that there was no evidence of negligence on the part of the defendants when they owned two docks, East and West, where a boilermaker, working at the East dock, left to go to the latrine but was never seen alive again. His body was subsequently found in the West dock. When he left there was a dense fog; his route was along ground surrounded on three sides by water and then over a bridge. Chains were placed about twelve feet from the water's edge, but there was a gap in the chains opposite the place where the body was found. The deceased knew the docks well.[43] A railway company's line crossed the highway by a level crossing at which there were the usual gates and a watchman who was on duty from 8 a.m. to 8 p.m. From the gates the approach of a train could be seen for nearly half a mile, and on the crossing itself for a mile. A man was found dead on the line near the crossing, and had obviously been killed by a train. The engine which killed him carried the usual lights, but did not whistle when approaching the crossing. There was no evidence when the deceased got onto the line. It was held that there were no materials from which an inference could reasonably be drawn that the death was due to the negligence of the railway company.[44] A prisoner was arrested about 6 p.m. and was confined in a wooden lockup in a small rural municipality in British Columbia. About 7 p.m. another prisoner was put in the same lockup. Both prisoners were searched and deprived of matches on being arrested. About 9 p.m. a fire broke out in the lockup and the first prisoner was burnt to death. The municipality employed one policeman, who at the time of the fire was performing other duties, and did not arrive on the scene until half an hour after the fire had started. The fire appeared to have originated in the lockup, but there was no evidence as to its cause. Matches could have been handed to the prisoners through a window by persons passing outside. It was held that the probable inference was that the fire was started by one or other of the prisoners, and

[41] *Jones* v. *G.W.Ry.* (1930) 47 T.L.R. 39.
[42] *Alexander* v. *Anderson* [1933] N.I. 158.
[43] *Mersey Docks and Harbour Board* v. *Procter* [1923] A.C. 253.
[44] *Wakelin* v. *L. & S.W. Ry.* (1886) 12 App.Cas. 41.

there was no evidence of negligence against the municipality.[45] Two motor-cars travelling in opposite directions collided. There was no witness of the accident except the defendant's driver, the plaintiff's having since died. After the accident the cars were found not touching, each on its own side of the white line and practically level with each other. The plaintiff's car was pointing diagonally to its offside, the defendant's car was pointing diagonally to its nearside. The front part of the plaintiff's car was damaged on both sides. The defendant's car had damage on its off-side and in the front of the off-side. The suggestion was that the defendant's car had been on its wrong side and had swerved across the front of the plaintiff's car to get to its proper side. It was held that the damage was consistent with either car being at fault and there was no evidence that the defendant's car was ever on its wrong side of the white line.[46]

972 **Cause of accident where several defendants.** Difficulties arise from time to time in the application of the rule that the onus rests on the plaintiff to prove that the negligence of the defendant caused the accident where the acts of two or more defendants are involved in the responsibility for it. This can be illustrated in those cases where two sportsmen together carelessly discharged their shot guns so that the plaintiff was injured by a single pellet, which equally could have come from either gun but not from both, although it was impossible to say from which one.[47] In such circumstances it has been held that where the careless act of each defendant has prevented the plaintiff from discovering which caused him the damage then on common-sense grounds and as a matter of policy both defendants were liable.[48] In certain cases undoubtedly the trial judge is entitled to dismiss the plaintiff's claim if there be no evidence from which he can infer negligence on the part of one or other or both of the defendants but if the inference be that one or other or both have been negligent then the plaintiff has made out a prima facie case against either, or both defendants. Nevertheless the trial judge was not entitled to dismiss the claim on the ground that he was unable to decide which party was in the right since it was an essential part of his duty to come to a definite conclusion on the evidence.[49] Accordingly where two motor-vehicles, going in opposite directions, collided during the hours of darkness in the centre of the road as a result of which both the drivers were killed, it was held that the proper inference was that both were equally to blame, there being no evidence pointing to one driver being any more blameworthy than the other.[50]

45 *McKenzie* v. *Chilliwack Corpn.* [1912] A.C. 888.

46 *Hollington* v. *F. Hewthorn & Co. Ltd.* [1943] 2 All E.R. 35.

47 *e.g. Oliver* v. *Mills*, 144 Missouri 852 (1926); *cf. R.* v. *Salmon* (1880) 6 Q.B.D. 79; *Mohan* v. *R.* [1967] 2 A.C. 187.

48 *Cook* v. *Lewis* [1952] 1 D.L.R. 1 (two hunters one or other of whom fired the shot which wounded the plaintiff). See Hogan " *Cook* v. *Lewis* Re-examined " (1961) 24 M.L.R. 331.

49 *Bray* v. *Palmer* [1953] 2 All E.R. 1449 (each vehicle swerved but collision still occurred in the centre of the road—new trial ordered).

50 *Baker* v. *Market Harborough Industrial Co-operative Society Ltd.* [1953] 1 W.L.R. 1472. *Per* Denning L.J. that even assuming one of the vehicles was over the centre line, and thus to blame, the absence of any avoiding action by the other vehicle made that vehicle also to blame.

Similarly in another fatal accident where there was a collision at crossroads, both roads being of equal status, or on the brow of a hill, in the absence of special circumstances, the inference to be drawn was that both the deceased drivers had been equally negligent so that the innocent passenger has a prima facie case against both drivers or either of them.[51] This rule seems to apply even if it be perfectly feasible that neither was negligent.[52]

973 **Ownership of car evidence that owner was driving.** In an action for negligence arising out of a motor car collision, the fact of ownership of the motor car is prima facie evidence that the motor car, at the material time, was being driven by the owner or by his servant or agent.[53] This inference is rebuttable.[54] In such an action it is not competent to ask the driver a question to obtain an answer showing that he has been negligent on some other occasion, or a question merely showing that he has been involved in some other collision for which it is not alleged that he was to blame. Questions can, however, be asked to test his credibility as a witness or his skill and competence as a driver, and such questions cannot be excluded merely because they show that the driver has been involved in previous accidents.[55]

974 **Civil Evidence Act 1968.**[56] The law which deals with hearsay evidence in civil actions has been substantially altered by the provisions of the Civil Evidence Act 1968, Part 1 of which gives effect, with some modifications to the recommendations in the Thirteenth Report of the Law Reform Committee on this subject matter.[57] It provides for hearsay evidence to be admissible only by virtue of a statutory provision or by agreement[58] and the principle is that out-of-court " first hand " hearsay evidence whether oral or documentary will generally be admissible subject to certain rules of court,[59] whilst " second hand " or multiple hearsay evidence generally will only be admissible in certain limited situations. It follows that a statement can be used to prove a fact asserted therein if it had been observed by the maker but not normally to prove a fact which had been related to him by someone else.

Section 2 (1) provides that: " In any civil proceedings a statement

51 *France* v. *Parkinson* [1954] 1 W.L.R. 581.
52 *Davison* v. *Leggett* (1969) 113 S.J. 409.
53 *Barnard* v. *Sully* (1931) 47 T.L.R. 557.
54 *Rambarran* v. *Gurrucharran* [1970] 1 W.L.R. 556.
55 *James* v. *Audigier* (1932) 48 T.L.R. 600; affd. 49 T.L.R. 36.
56 1968, c. 64. Certain provisions of which came into force on October 25, 1968, others on December 2, 1968, and those remaining provisions which relate to the admissibility of hearsay evidence in the High Court came into operation on October 1, 1969, and the consequential additions to R.S.C., Ord. 38. The Civil Evidence Act 1968 (Commencement No. 2) Order 1969 (S.I. 1969 No. 1104) also brought s. 20 (2) of the Act into force which repeals ss. 1 and 2 of the Evidence Act 1938 as well as s. 6 (2) (*b*) and part of s. 6 (1). See articles " Civil Evidence Act 1968 " (Newark and Samuels), 31 M.L.R. 668; " Hearsay and the Civil Evidence Act 1968 " (Newark and Samuels), 119 New L.J. 812; " Evidence of Conviction in Civil Proceedings " (Miller) 121 New L.J. 573, 598 and 622. The Act has been brought into force in the county court from February 16, 1970.
57 Cmnd. 2964.
58 s. 1.
59 s. 2.

made, whether orally or in a document or otherwise, by any person whether called as a witness in those proceedings or not, shall, subject to this section and to rules of court, be admissible as evidence of any fact stated therein of which direct oral evidence by him would be admissible."[60] Both " statement " and " document " are defined in section 10 which provides that a " statement " includes any representation of fact, whether made in words or otherwise, whilst a " document " is widely cast to include, in addition to a document in writing, such things as maps, plans, graphs, drawings, photographs, recording tapes, films and micro-films.

975 Statements made would be admissible in the following cases, which it is submitted would be decided differently now; by a driver of a motor-car, involved in a collision, to a police officer [61]; by the mother, since deceased, of a witness [62]; by the master, first and second officers of the defendant ship-owners [63]; by a tyre tester and fitter employed by the defendant owners of an omnibus [64]; and by a domestic servant employed by the parents of a girl, aged four years, to look after the child together with their other children.[65] A statement by an independent witness, who has since died, to the police is admissible, and so is his evidence in a deposition in the police court, although it has not been signed.[66] Particulars of an accident supplied by a workman on a form provided by his approved society to support a claim for workmen's compensation were held admissible after his death in a subsequent action for negligence.[67] An order may be made in chambers, before trial, that statements made by a witness who has since gone abroad shall be admitted as evidence.[68]

The provisions of this part of the Act also cover (a) a previous statement made by a witness, as evidence of any fact stated therein, of which direct oral evidence by that witness would have been admissible [69]; (b) certain records [70]; (c) certain statements produced by a computer [71]; (d) certain hearsay evidence which was formerly admissible at common law.[72] As regards the admissibility of evidence going towards the credibility of the maker of statements admitted under section 2 or 4 of the Act, this is dealt with by the provisions of section 7.

[60] See *Ford* v. *Lewis* [1971] 1 W.L.R. 623 for consideration of where and when the trial judge should or should not exercise his discretion to admit in evidence a statement produced in circumstances which did not satisfy the requirements of s. 2 (1) of the Act, no notice having been given to the opposition's legal advisers as required by R.S.C., Ord. 38, rr. 21, 22 & 23.

[61] *Robinson* v. *Stern* [1939] 2 K.B. 260; *Bowskill* v. *Dawson* [1954] 1 Q.B. 288; *Friend* v. *Wallman* [1946] 2 All E.R. 237.

[62] *Holton* v. *Holton* [1946] 2 All E.R. 534.

[63] *Bain* v. *Moss Hutchinson Line Ltd.* [1949] 1 K.B. 51.

[64] *Barkway* v. *South Wales Transport Co. Ltd.* [1950] 1 All E.R. 392.

[65] *Evon* v. *Noble* [1949] 1 K.B. 222.

[66] *Bullock* v. *Borrett* [1939] 1 All E.R. 505.

[67] *Jarman* v. *Lambert & Cooke Contractors Ltd.* [1951] 2 K.B. 937.

[68] *Friend* v. *Wallman*, *supra.*

[69] s. 3.

[70] s. 4.

[71] s. 5.

[72] s. 9.

976 Part II of the Act, by sections 11 to 13,[73] gives effect, with modifications, to the recommendations contained in the Law Reform Committee's Fifteenth Report.[74] It reverses the rule in *Hollington* v. *F. Hewthorn & Co.*[75] by making a conviction by a court in the United Kingdom or a court-martial (whether in the United Kingdom or elsewhere) admissible as evidence in subsequent civil proceedings for the purpose of proving, where relevant, that the person so convicted committed the offence in question.[76] Such convicted person shall be taken conclusively to have committed the offence for the purposes of the civil action unless the contrary be proved by him.[77] This operates to shift the legal burden of proof requiring the party affected to prove, on a balance of probability, that he was innocent. The civil court is not entitled to find that that person is in fact innocent solely because the judge would have reached a different conclusion on the evidence. When a conviction has been confirmed on appeal and the evidence before the judge in the civil case is substantially the same, then the conviction for all practical purposes is conclusive.[78]

Where a judge had overlooked the provisions of section 11 and thus had failed to direct his mind to the fact that the burden of proof had been transferred to the convicted defendant to disprove negligence, the plaintiff, on appeal, was entitled to judgment in the circumstances.[79]

977 **Servant not agent to make admissions of negligence.** An admission of negligence by a servant is not evidence against his employer, unless the servant has express authority to make the admission.[80] The admission may, however, be part of the *res gestae* and, if that is so, it is evidence. On this point, Bailhache J. said: " In this case the *res gestae* was a single act—namely, the collision with the motor car. In such a case words, even spoken words, do not become part of the *res gestae*, unless they are made at the time and are the natural consequence of the collision, words which spring out of the collision, so to speak, inevitably and almost without the

73 Brought into force on December 2, 1968, by the Civil Evidence Act 1968 (Commencement No. 1) Order 1968 (S.I. 1968 No. 1734).

74 Cmnd. 3391.

75 [1943] 1 K.B. 587 (evidence could not be given that one of the drivers concerned in the collision was convicted of an offence under the Road Traffic Acts in respect of that accident). See article: " The Civil Evidence Act " (Phelan) (1970) 120 New L.J. 230.

76 s. 11 (1).

77 s. 11 (2). See *Wright* v. *Wright*, *The Times*, February 15, 1971.

78 *Stupple* v. *Royal Insurance Co.* [1970] 1 W.L.R. 124, affirmed by the C.A. [1971] 1 Q.B. 50 where Lord Denning M.R. added that the Act did not merely shift the *evidential* burden but it shifted the *legal* burden of proof. The weight to be given to a previous conviction was essentially for the judge at the civil trial. Just as he had to evaluate the oral evidence of a witness, so he should evaluate the probative force of a conviction. At the end of the day the judge must ask himself whether the conviction had been overthrown. If not, the conviction stood and proved the case. The decision was approved and followed in *Taylor* v. *Taylor* [1970] 1 W.L.R. 1148 and *Wright* v. *Wright* (1971) 115 S.J. 173.

79 *Wauchope* v. *Mordecai* [1970] 1 W.L.R. 317.

80 *Johnson* v. *Lindsay* (1889) 5 T.L.R. 454 (workman asked, " Why did you not hook the bucket securely? "; the answer, " We were in a hurry," is not admissible); *Burr* v. *Ware U.D.C.* [1939] 2 All E.R. 688 (in a collision case, interrogatories cannot be administered to the defendants asking them to admit statements made by their driver at an inquest). An admission by a servant that he would have acted differently, had the allegations of the other party been correct, is not binding on the master: *Glasgow Corpn.* v. *Muir* [1943] A.C. 448, 455; *Connachan* v. *S.M.T. Co.*, 1946 S.C. 428, 436.

will of the speaker, and are, at any rate, spontaneous. The words must, of course, be strictly germane to the collision." [81]

2.—RES IPSA LOQUITUR

978 **Res ipsa loquitur.** A special application of the principle that there is evidence of negligence if the facts proved are more consistent with negligence on the part of the defendant than with other causes is found in the cases in which the maxim *res ipsa loquitur* applies.[82] These cases are where the plaintiff proves the happening of the accident and nothing more. It may be that he cannot prove more, but whether he can or not he does not prove any specific act or omission on the part of the defendant.[83] The mere happening of the accident speaks for itself, since it may be more consistent with negligence on the part of the defendant than with other causes and, if that is so, the court may find negligence on the part of the defendant unless he gives a reasonable explanation to show how the accident may have occurred without negligence on his part. The maxim is not a rule of law. It is " no more than a rule of evidence affecting onus. It is based on common sense, and its purpose is to enable justice to be done when the facts bearing on causation and on the care exercised by the defendant are at the outset unknown to the plaintiff and are or ought to be within the knowledge of the defendant." [84]

979 **Meaning of res ipsa loquitur.** Kennedy L.J. explains the meaning of *res ipsa loquitur* as follows [85]: " The meaning, as I understand, of that phrase . . . is this, that there is, in the circumstances of the particular case, some evidence which, viewed not as a matter of conjecture, but of reasonable argument, makes it more probable that there was some negligence, upon the facts as shown and undisputed, than that the occurrence took place without negligence. The *res* speaks because the facts stand unexplained, and therefore the natural and reasonable, not conjectural, inference from the facts shows that what has happened is reasonably to be attributed to some act of negligence on the part of somebody; that is, some want of reasonable care under the circumstances. *Res ipsa loquitur* does not mean, as I understand it, that merely because at the end of a journey a horse is found hurt, or somebody is hurt in the streets, the mere fact that he is hurt implies negligence. That is absurd. It means that the circumstances are, so to speak, eloquent of the negligence of somebody who brought

[81] *Tustin* v. *Arnold & Sons* (1915) 84 L.J.K.B. 2214. See *Davies* v. *Fortior Ltd.* [1952] 1 All E.R. 1359 (workman fell from a platform into a bath of acid, as a result of which he died. Within a short time, variously estimated to be between a few seconds to two minutes, after being helped from the bath, he kept repeating " I should not have done it." This was held admissible as part of the *res gestae*).

[82] See " A Ramble with *res ipsa loquitur*," (Ellis Lewis) (1951) 11 C.L.J. 74, and " *Res ipsa loquitur*: The Australian Exprience," (O'Connell) (1954) C.L.J. 118; (1959) 109 L.J. 36 and 120 New L.J. (Fridman) 181; " *Res ipsa loquitur*: a closer look," (Morgan) 114 S.J. 346.

[83] A plaintiff who tenders evidence directed to proving the defendant guilty of any particular act of negligence is not thereby precluded from relying upon the doctrine: *Anchor Products* v. *Hedges* (1966) 115 C.L.R. 493 (Australian High Court). The maxim does not have to be pleaded: *Bennett* v. *Chemical Construction* (*G.B.*) (1970) 115 S.J. 550.

[84] *Barkway* v. *South Wales Transport Co. Ltd.* [1950] 1 All E.R. 392, 399, *per* Lord Normand.

[85] *Russell* v. *L. & S.W. Ry.* (1908) 24 T.L.R. 548, 551.

about the state of things which is complained of." Later, he adds: "*Res ipsa loquitur* in this sense; the circumstances are more consistent, reasonably interpreted without further explanation, with your negligence than with any other cause of the accident happening."

980 The maxim comes into operation: (1) on proof of the happening of an unexplained occurrence; (2) when the occurrence is one which would not have happened in the ordinary course of things without negligence on the part of somebody other than the plaintiff; and (3) the circumstances point to the negligence in question being that of the defendant rather than that of any other person. The third requirement is usually fulfilled by showing that the instrument causing the damage was in the management and control of the defendant at the time of the occurrence, but this is not essential.[86]

When an object or an operation is under the control of two persons, not in law responsible for the acts of each other, opinions differ whether the maxim applies. In *Roe* v. *Minister of Health*,[87] McNair J. expressed the opinion that in such a case the maxim does not apply because the *res* does not speak of negligence against either person individually. Denning L.J. differed,[88] on the ground that in such a case the plaintiff can call on each of the persons for an explanation.

981 **Cause must be unknown.** The doctrine of *res ipsa loquitur* does not apply when the cause of the accident is known. "The *res* can only speak so as to throw the inference of fault upon the defender in some cases where the act of the defender is unexplained."[89] Again, "if the facts are sufficiently known, the question ceases to be one where the facts speak for themselves, and the solution is to be found by determining whether on the facts as established, negligence is to be inferred or not."[90] For example, if a pedestrian is struck on the head by a cricket ball, driven out of the field by a batsman in the course of a cricket match, the maxim has no application because all the facts of the occurrence are known, and the court must decide whether those facts constitute negligence on the part of the defendant or not.[91]

982 **Things falling from buildings.** In the leading case of *Scott* v. *London and St. Katherine Docks Co.*[92] where the plaintiff, an officer in the customs, was lawfully passing in front of a warehouse in a dock when six bags of sugar lowered by the dock company's servants fell upon him, it was held

[86] See *McGowan* v. *Stott* (1923), reported in note to *Halliwell* v. *Venables*, 99 L.J.K.B. 353, 357, where the C.A. said that the dictum of Fletcher Moulton L.J. in *Wing* v. *L.G.O.* [1909] 2 K.B. 652 that *res ipsa loquitur* only applied when "the direct cause of the accident and so much of the surrounding circumstances as was essential to its occurrence, were within the sole control and management of the defendants, or their servants," went too far. See *e.g. Lloyde* v. *West Midlands Gas Board* [1971] 1 W.L.R. 749 (liable for gas explosion where apparatus was not under the Board's exclusive control).

[87] [1954] 2 Q.B. 66, 70.

[88] [1954] 2 Q.B. 66, 82. See also *Cook* v. *Lewis* [1952] 1 D.L.R. 1.

[89] *Milne* v. *Townsend* (1890) 19 R. 830, *per* Lord Adam, quoted by Scrutton L.J. in *Langham* v. *Governors of Wellingborough School* (1932) 101 L.J.K.B. 513.

[90] *Barkway* v. *South Wales Transport Co. Ltd.* [1950] 1 All E.R. 392, 395, *per* Lord Porter. See also to the same effect, *Bolton* v. *Stone* [1951] A.C. 850, 859.

[91] *Bolton* v. *Stone, supra.*

[92] (1865) 3 H. & C. 596.

that the accident was prima facie evidence of negligence against the dock company. The principle was stated by Sir William Erle C.J. delivering the judgment of the Court of Exchequer Chamber in these terms: " There must be reasonable evidence of negligence. But where the thing is shown to be under the management of the defendant or his servants, and the accident is such as in the ordinary course of things does not happen if those who have the management use proper care, it affords reasonable evidence, in the absence of explanation by the defendants, that the accident arose from want of care." [93] Similarly, where a person was walking in the highway past the shop of the defendant, who was a dealer in flour, when a barrel of flour fell upon him, it was held that the accident was prima facie evidence of the defendant's negligence, Pollock C.B. saying: " So in the building or repairing a house, or putting pots on the chimneys, if a person passing along the road is injured by something falling upon him, I think the accident alone would be prima facie evidence of negligence." [94] The fall of the ceiling of a theatre on a member of the audience is prima facie evidence of negligence on the part of the occupiers of the theatre.[95] If a packing-case belonging to the defendant is propped against the wall of the defendant's house and falls on a passer-by in the street,[96] or a brick falls out of a railway bridge and strikes a person on the highway,[97] in both these cases there is prima facie evidence of negligence, in one case against the owner of the packing-case, and in the other case against the railway company.

983 **Extraneous things found in manufactured goods.** If an article, manufactured by the defendant, is found to contain something which would not be present if due care in manufacture had been taken, as for example where a stone was found in a Bath-bun made by the defendant,[98] there is evidence of negligence. This is so, even though the article is handled by others before it reaches the person injured, if it is more probable that the defect was due to faulty manufacture than to other causes, as in the case of woollen underwear which was found to contain a chemical irritant which could hardly have got there except by negligence in manufacture.[99] On the other hand, where a glass windscreen on a motor-car broke without any apparent cause twelve months after the buyer had had the car, it was held that the breaking alone was no evidence of negligence against the maker of the windscreen.[1]

[93] *Ibid.* at p. 601.
[94] *Byrne* v. *Boadle* (1863) 2 H. & C. 722, 728. See also *Walsh* v. *Holst & Co. Ltd.* [1958] 1 W.L.R. 800; *Hardy* v. *Thames & General Lighterage* [1967] 1 Lloyd's Rep. 228. See also note at 74 L.Q.R. 472.
[95] *Pope* v. *St. Helen's Theatre Ltd.* [1947] K.B. 30.
[96] *Briggs* v. *Oliver* (1866) 4 H. & C. 403.
[97] *Kearney* v. *L.B. & S.C. Ry.* (1871) L.R. 6 Q.B. 759. *Cf. Palmer* v. *Bateman* [1908] 2 Ir.R. 393, where the prima facie case was successfully rebutted by the defendant. *Welfare* v. *London and Brighton Ry.* (1869) L.R. 4 Q.B. 693 (plaintiff went to a railway station to inquire about trains when a roll of zinc fell through a hole in the roof and injured him—held no evidence of negligence) must be taken to be wrongly decided as the accident certainly called for an explanation from the railway company.
[98] *Chapronière* v. *Mason* (1905) 21 T.L.R. 633.
[99] *Grant* v. *Australian Knitting Mills* [1936] A.C. 85.
[1] *Evans* v. *Triplex Safety Glass Co.* [1938] 1 All E.R. 283.

984 **Railway cases.** The mere happening of an accident was held to be evidence of negligence against the railway authority concerned in the following cases: where a railway-carriage broke down or ran off the rails,[2] where a collision occurred between two trains on the defendant company's line,[3] where a train ran into a station's buffers,[4] where the door of the carriage suddenly opened when a passenger looked out of the window [5] (but not where the door in a corridor-compartment containing numerous passengers suddenly opened),[6] where the train stopped suddenly and with a jerk and flung the passengers across the carriage,[7] and where a railway embankment supporting the line gave way and the train was wrecked.[8] On the other hand, the mere fact that a passenger's hand is jammed in a carriage door without warning being given before closing the door was held to be no evidence of negligence.[9]

985 **Highway cases.** It has been suggested that *res ipsa loquitur* does not apply to cases of collision on the highway, because "every vehicle has to adapt its own behaviour to the behaviour of other persons using the road, and over their actions those in charge of the vehicle have no control. Hence the fact that an accident has happened either to or through a particular vehicle is by itself no evidence that the fault, if any, which led to it was committed by those in charge of that vehicle," [10] but such a broad proposition cannot be supported, as there are many highway collisions in which the accident itself suggests a reasonable probability of negligence in one of the parties rather than the other. "Where both parties are moving and have a right to move, prima facie the mere fact that those moving bodies run into each other is not evidence of negligence. . . . When you get to the case of a man standing still in the highway in broad daylight and run into, I think myself that would be prima facie evidence of negligence of the driver of the vehicle that ran into him."[11] Even in the case of moving vehicles which collide, the mere happening of the accident may be evidence of negligence against one of them, as where one vehicle runs into another from behind in

[2] *Dawson* v. *Manchester, Sheffield and Lincolnshire Ry.* (1862) 5 L.T. 682; *Flannery* v. *Waterford, etc., Ry.* (1877) Ir.R. 11 C.L. 30.

[3] *Skinner* v. *L.B. & S.C. Ry.* (1850) 5 Ex. 787; *Carpue* v. *L. & B. Ry.* (1844) 5 Q.B. 747, 751; *Ayles* v. *S.E. Ry.* (1868) L.R. 3 Ex. 146 (train belonging to company A collided with train belonging to company B, which had running powers over company A's line—held evidence of negligence against company A).

[4] *Burke* v. *Manchester, Sheffield and Lincolnshire Ry.* (1870) 22 L.T. 442.

[5] *Gee* v. *Metropolitan Ry.* (1873) L.R. 8 Q.B. 161: *Hamer* v. *Cambrian Ry.* (1886) 2 T.L.R. 508; *Dudman* v. *North London Ry.* (1886) 2 T.L.R. 365; *Adams* v. *L. & Y. Ry.* (1869) L.R. 4 C.P. 739; *Toal* v. *N.B. Ry.* [1908] A.C. 352 (passenger on platform struck by open carriage-door); *Inglis* v. *L.M.S. Ry.*, 1941 S.C. 551.

[6] *Easson* v. *L.N.E.R.* [1944] K.B. 421.

[7] *Angus* v. *London, Tilbury and Southend Ry.* (1906) 22 T.L.R. 222.

[8] *G.W. Ry. of Canada* v. *Braid* (1863) 1 Moo.P.C. (N.S.) 101; criticised in *Czech* v. *General Steam Navigation Co.* (1867) L.R. 3 C.P. 14, but followed in *City of Montreal* v. *Watt and Scott* [1922] 2 A.C. 555.

[9] *Drury* v. *N.E. Ry.* [1901] 2 K.B. 322; *Benson* v. *Furness Ry.* (1903) 88 LT. 268; *Metropolitan Ry.* v. *Jackson* (1877) 3 App.Cas. 193.

[10] *Wing* v. *London General Omnibus Co.* [1909] 2 K.B. 652, *per* Fletcher Moulton L.J., at p. 664; adversely commented on in *McGowan* v. *Stott* (1923), reported in note to *Halliwell* v. *Venables*, 99 L.J.K.B. 353, 357.

[11] *McGowan* v. *Stott, supra, per* Scrutton L.J.

daylight, when there can be no doubt that the accident itself calls for an explanation from the overtaking vehicle.[12] A violent swerve,[13] a violent skid [14] and the sudden stopping [15] of an omnibus causing injury to a passenger have all been held to be prima facie evidence of negligence, but the accidental ejection of a passenger through an open door while the omnibus was in motion has not been so held.[16]

986 If a motor-vehicle under the control of the defendant or his servant overturned for no apparent cause while being driven along the highway, that fact alone was evidence of negligence against the defendant,[17] and so was the fact that it left the road and fell down an embankment.[18] The result was the same if such a vehicle got onto the footpath and there knocked down a lamp-post [19] or other erection,[20] or a pedestrian,[21] or if it projected over the footpath and knocked down a pedestrian.[22] There is no difference in this respect between a motor-vehicle driven by the defendant and a horse ridden or driven by the defendant. Some of the older cases appear to give countenance to the view that if a horse came on the footpath and collided with a pedestrian there was no evidence of negligence against the person in charge, but on examination it will be found that they do not go as far as this.

987 **Horse cases.** In *Hammack* v. *White* [23] a horse ridden by the defendant swerved from the roadway onto the footpath and killed a pedestrian. The plaintiff's evidence, however, proved that the defendant was doing his best to hold the horse in and doing all he reasonably could to avoid the accident. The court, accordingly, held that there was no evidence of negligence, but Willes J. said: " Here was a man riding on the foot-pavement and therefore prima facie in the wrong," although the evidence as a whole rebutted that prima facie presumption. *Manzoni* v. *Douglas* [24] was a similar case, where a horse drawing a brougham swerved on to the footway and injured the plaintiff. Here, again, the evidence for the plaintiff was held to rebut any inference of negligence which might otherwise have arisen, but in the course of his judgment Lindley J. said: " To hold that the mere fact of a

12 *Tart* v. *Chitty & Co.* [1933] 2 K.B. 453; *Baker* v. *Longhurst & Sons Ltd.* [1933] 2 K.B. 461 (in these cases, the question was whether the plaintiff in driving into a vehicle from behind was guilty of contributory negligence, and it was held that the fact of the collision alone was evidence of such negligence; it is not, of course, conclusive: *Tidy* v. *Battman* [1934] 1 K.B. 319; *Morris* v. *Luton Corpn.* [1946] 1 K.B. 114).

13 *O'Hara* v. *Scottish Motor Traction Co.*, 1941 S.C. 363; *Doonan* v. *S.M.T. Co. Ltd.*, 1950 S.C. 136; *Ludgate* v. *Lovett* [1969] 1 W.L.R. 1016.

14 *Richley* v. *Faull* [1965] 1 W.L.R. 1454.

15 *Parkinson* v. *Liverpool Corpn.* [1950] 1 All E.R. 367.

16 *Johnstone* v. *Western S.M.T. Co.* (1955) 105 L.J. 762.

17 *Halliwell* v. *Venables* (1930) 99 L.J.K.B. 353; *Liffen* v. *Watson* (1939) 161 L.T. 351.

18 *Barkway* v. *South Wales Transport Co. Ltd.* [1950] 1 All E.R. 392; *Elliott* v. *Young's Bus Services Ltd.*, 1945 S.C. 445.

19 *Isaac Walton & Co.* v. *Vanguard Motorbus Co.* (1908) 25 T.L.R. 13.

20 *Barnes U.D.C.* v. *L.G.O. Co.* (1908) 100 L.T. 115.

21 *Ellor* v. *Selfridge & Co.* (1930) 46 T.L.R. 236; *Hunter* v. *Wright* [1938] 2 All E.R. 621 (defendant rebutted the presumption of negligence).

22 *Laurie* v. *Raglan Building Co. Ltd.* [1942] 1 K.B. 152.

23 (1862) 11 C.B.(N.S.) 588.

24 (1880) 6 Q.B.D. 145, 153.

horse bolting is *per se* evidence of negligence would be mere reckless guesswork." This seems to ignore the problem, which is on proof by the plaintiff that the defendant's horse driven by the defendant got on to the footpath and injured the plaintiff, is the plaintiff entitled to succeed in the absence of an explanation by the defendant? Until the defendant gives his explanation it may not even be known that the horse has bolted, and even if it has bolted that fact would seem to call for some explanation from the driver to show how it happened consistently with his driving with reasonable care and skill. In *Gayler and Pope Ltd.* v. *B. Davies & Son Ltd.* [25] McCardie J., after reviewing the authorities, expressed the opinion that the unexplained collision on the footpath between a horse and a pedestrian is prima facie evidence of negligence on the part of the person in charge of the horse, and that the dictum of Lindley J., quoted above, went too far. It is submitted that the view of McCardie J. is right.

It is clear that on proof given by a plaintiff that the defendant's horse, harnessed to a cart, was running away unattended upon the highway, as a result of which the plaintiff was injured, a prima facie case of negligence is established, for such facts are " more consistent with the absence of ordinary care in superintending the horse than with such care having been used." [26] In the case of a loose horse, its presence on the highway unattended in a town has been held evidence of negligence, [27] but not in the country. [28]

988 **Unattended vehicles.** Although it may have been negligence to leave an unhorsed van unattended on a level road, the mere fact that an accident was caused to a child playing on the van was not of itself evidence of negligence causing injury to the child. [29] Similarly, it may have been negligence to leave a steam-lorry unattended in the street, but a collision by that lorry with a shop front when the lorry was being driven by trespassers was not, by itself, evidence of negligence causing injury to the shop. [30] On the other hand, the mere fact that a motor-car, left unattended, ran off down a hill, was itself evidence of negligence against the person in control of the car. [31]

989 **Other cases.** The maxim has been held to apply where the trolley arm of a tram was plucked from a standard and struck a passenger on the

[25] [1924] 2 K.B. 75. *Cf. Snee* v. *Durkie* (1903) 6 F. 42, where it was held that where a runaway horse and carriage runs down a person in daylight in a public street the presumption is that the owner of the horse and carriage is in fault: *Simson* v. *L.G.O. Co.* (1873) L.R. 8 C.P. 390, where the mere fact that a horse kicked through the front panel of an omnibus and injured a passenger was held evidence of negligence.

[26] *Watson* v. *Weekes* (unreported), *per* Smith J., referred to in *Tolhausen* v. *Davies* (1888) 57 L.J.Q.B. 392; affd. 58 L.J.Q.B. 98; *Gayler and Pope Ltd.* v. *B. Davies & Son Ltd.*, *supra*; *Haynes* v. *Harwood* [1935] 1 K.B. 146.

[27] *Deen* v. *Davies* [1935] 2 K.B. 282.

[28] *Searle* v. *Wallbank* [1947] A.C. 341; *Jones* v. *Lee* (1911) 106 L.T. 123; *Ellis* v. *Banyard* (1911) 106 L.T. 51 (cows).

[29] *Donovan* v. *Union Cartage Co.* [1933] 2 K.B. 71.

[30] *Ruoff* v. *Long & Co.* [1916] 1 K.B. 148.

[31] *Parker* v. *Miller* (1926) 42 T.L.R. 408; *Martin* v. *Stanborough* (1924) 41 T.L.R. 1.

head [32]; where a crane toppled over [33]; where a trawler sent to be examined on the defendant's slipway and put on to a cradle by the defendant's servants, suddenly fell over on her side and was damaged [34]; where a machine was delivered to a railway company for carriage and was afterwards found to be damaged [35]; where a coupling in a railway train had parted [36]; where an aeroplane crashed to the ground just as it had become airborne after it had taken off but before it had attained the height at which the flight would be performed [37]; where a barrel of petrol supplied by the sellers burst as it was rolling down a skid while it was being unloaded at the buyer's yard [38]; where a surgeon after an operation left a swab in the body of his patient [39]; where a patient went into hospital to be cured of two stiff fingers and came out with four stiff fingers [40]; when an explosion of plant managed by the defendants occurred [41]; when a rope broke at a haulage way [42] and at a hoist,[43] where moorings, let by the defendants for mooring the plaintiff's yacht, parted so that the yacht broke adrift [44]; and where the defendant's barge left its moorings, drifted uncontrolled down the river and collided with a ladies' rowing eight [45]; but NOT where livestock was sent by railway and found damaged on arrival [46]; where a schoolboy during the morning " break " while going along a corridor in the school building was hit in the eye by a golf ball, driven by another schoolboy in the playground, which had entered the corridor by the doorway [47]; where a tube was found in the bladder of a patient some weeks after an operation was performed upon him by a surgeon, and doctors and nurses at a hospital, in addition to the surgeon himself, had been from time to time engaged in removing and replacing the tube [48]; where the patient's jaw was broken and part of the root left in the jaw by a dentist in extracting a tooth [49]; or where a lineman, working at an electrical installation, came in contact with an electrically charged wire and was killed.[50]

32 *Newberry* v. *Bristol Tramways Co.* (1912) 107 L.T. 801.
33 *Swan* v. *Salisbury Construction Co.* [1966] 1 W.L.R. 204.
34 *Reynolds* v. *Boston Deep Sea Fishing and Ice Co.* (1921) 38 T.L.R. 22; affd. 38 T.L.R. 429.
35 *United Machine Tool Co.* v. *G.W. Ry.* (1914) 30 T.L.R. 312.
36 *Ballard* v. *N.B. Ry.*, 1923 S.C. 43.
37 *Fosbroke-Hobbes* v. *Airwork Ltd.* [1937] 1 All E.R. 108; *Zerka, Romley and Alex* v. *Lau-Goma Airways* (1960) 23 D.L.R. (2d) 145 (where the Ontario Court of Appeal held that the doctrine applied in the case of a passenger aeroplane whose engine failed shortly after it became airborne).
38 *Marshall* v. *Russian Oil Products*, 1938 S.C. 773.
39 *Mahon* v. *Osborne* [1939] 2 K.B. 14.
40 *Cassidy* v. *Ministry of Health* [1951] 2 K.B. 343.
41 *Moore* v. *R. Fox & Sons* [1956] 1 Q.B. 596.
42 *Turner* v. *National Coal Board* (1949) 65 T.L.R. 580 (the prima facie case was rebutted and the defendants succeeded).
43 *Birchall* v. *Bibby & Sons Ltd.* [1953] 1 All E.R. 163 (on proof that the rope had been deliberately cut, it was held that the defendants had rebutted the prima facie case against them and were not bound to prove that it had not been cut by one of their servants).
44 *The Quercus* [1943] P. 96.
45 *Newby* v. *General Lighterage Co. Ltd.*, *The Times*, March 3, 1955.
46 *Russell* v. *L. & S.W. Ry.* (1908) 24 T.L.R. 548.
47 *Langham* v. *Governors of Wellingborough School* (1932) 101 L.J.K.B. 513.
48 *Morris* v. *Winsbury-White* [1937] 4 All E.R. 494.
49 *Fish* v. *Kapur* [1948] 2 All E.R. 176.
50 *Youngman* v. *Pirelli General Cable Works* [1940] 1 K.B. 1.

990 **Rebuttal of presumption of negligence.** When a prima facie case of negligence against the defendant has been established under the doctrine of *res ipsa loquitur*, the defendant can rebut that case by proving that he was not negligent, even though he cannot prove how the accident happened.[51] Lord Dunedin has said, " If the defenders can show a way in which the accident may have occurred without negligence, the cogeny of the fact of the accident by itself disappears, and the pursuer is left as he began, namely, that he has to show negligence. I need scarcely add that the suggestion of how the accident may have occurred must be a reasonable suggestion." [52] Where a barge, towed by a tug, collided with the abutment of a bridge, it was held that the accident itself raised a prima facie case of negligence against the tug, but on the tug showing that the collision might equally well have been caused by the negligence of the men on the barge in not making the breast rope fast, judgment was given in favour of the tug. Langton J. saying: " If they [the defendants] give a reasonable explanation, which is equally consistent with the accident happening without their negligence as with their negligence, they have again shifted the burden of proof back to the plaintiffs to show—as they always have to show from the beginning—that it was the negligence of the defendants that caused the accident." [53] In *Colvilles Ltd.* v. *Devine* [54] the defenders had installed a new system for the manufacture of steel by the injection of oxygen into converters which involved bringing the gas from a source a mile away by means of a pipe which belonged to a third party. At the defenders' main intake there was a filter to remove foreign bodies from the oxygen and from that point a hose belonging to the defenders took the gas to a lance by means of which it was injected into the molten metal in the converters. The pursuer was working on a platform some 75 yards away from the converter where a violent explosion occurred which gave him a fright and caused him to jump down to the ground, as a result of which he was injured. Lord Guest expressed the opinion that the defenders " are absolved if they can give a reasonable explanation [55] of the accident and show this explanation was consistent with no lack of care on their part. . . . But this explanation only carries the [defenders] halfway to success. The

[51] *Woods* v. *Duncan* [1946] A.C. 401; *Walsh* v. *Holst & Co. Ltd.* [1958] 1 W.L.R. 800 and article founded on this decision in 22 M.L.R. 82; *Ludgate* v. *Lovett* [1969] 1 W.L.R. 1016 and article founded on this decision: " *Res ipsa loquitur*: a closer look." (Morgan) 114 S.J. 346.

[52] *Ballard* v. *N.B. Ry.*, 1923 S.C. 43, 45, quoted with approval in *Langham* v. *Wellingborough School* (1932) 101 L.J.K.B. 513, and in many other cases. These dicta were not followed in *Moore* v. *Fox & Sons* [1956] 1 Q.B. 596 where it was held that it was not enough for the defendants merely to show that the accident could have happened without negligence on their part. See the comment on this case by T. Ellis Lewis in [1956] C.L.J. 150, and in 73 L.Q.R. 408. The author, so far from not liking the case as is stated in 73 L.Q.R. 408, welcomes it as stating what he had always thought the law was. The defendants must show that they had taken all reasonable precautions to ensure that the accident did not happen. See *Esso Petroleum Co. Ltd.* v. *Southport Corporation* [1956] A.C. 218, 243, *per* Lord Radcliffe.

[53] *The Kite* [1933] P. 154 at p. 170. See also *The Mulbera* [1937] P. 82.

[54] [1969] 1 W.L.R. 475.

[55] *i.e.* " A plausible explanation," as spoken to by Lord Simonds in *Woods* v. *Duncan* [1946] A.C. 401, 441.

explanation to be available as a defence must be consistent with no negligence on their part." [56] Lord Donovan explained the onus in this way: "It was for the [defenders] to show that the accident was just as consistent with their having exercised due diligence as with their having been negligent. In that way the scales which have been tipped in the pursuer's favour by the doctrine of *res ipsa loquitur* would be once more in balance, and the pursuer would have to begin again and prove negligence in the usual way." [57]

990a In considering the effect of a reasonable explanation, it must be remembered that on a case of *res ipsa loquitur* being put forward there are two points to be considered, the first whether the *res* proved amounts to prima facie evidence of negligence, which is a question of law, and the second whether the negligence should be held to be proved, which is a question of fact. If the prima facie case of negligence is established against A it is still open to A to show that the facts equally establish a case against B, so that the inference of negligence on A's part should not be drawn against A. In such a case, A would be entitled to succeed, unless A and B are sued in the same action jointly, severally and in the alternative, when A would not be entitled to judgment until B's case also was heard. [58] In a separate action against A, his explanation, if supported by the facts, would rebut the presumption raised by the doctrine of *res ipsa loquitur*. An explanation, however, unsupported by the facts, is not enough. For example, the unexplained overturning of an omnibus into a ditch is *res ipsa loquitur*. If the explanation put forward is that the accident was due to a burst tyre, this explanation by itself will not do, it must be supported by evidence not only proving the fact of the burst tyre but also that the burst was not due to any negligence on the part of the defendants. [59] Again, if the explanation advanced is that there was a latent defect in some part of the material concerned, the burden is on the defendant to prove it. [60] A latent defect is a defect which cannot be detected by reasonable care and skill, and the burden of proving it is on the person relying on it. [61] "If the cause is ascertained and is proved to be latent, negligence is excluded, but where the cause is not ascertained the difficulty of excluding negligence is proportionately increased, and the defendant may fail because he cannot give any account of the occurrence sufficient to exclude negligence." [62] Where it was sought to rely on a latent defect as the sole cause of an accident the onus was on the defendant to establish that and to show that the accident had occurred despite proper maintenance having been carried out

56 *Ibid.* at pp. 477, 478.
57 *Ibid.* at p. 479.
58 *Hummerstone* v. *Leary* [1921] 2 K.B. 664.
59 *Barkway* v. *S. Wales Transport Co. Ltd.* [1950] 1 All E.R. 392.
60 *Marshall* v. *Russian Oil Products*, 1938 S.C. 773.
61 *Readhead* v. *Midland Ry.* (1869) L.R. 4 Q.B. 379; *Marshall* v. *Russian Oil Products*, 1938 S.C. 773; *Ritchie* v. *Western Scottish Motor Traction Co.*, 1935 S.L.T. 13.
62 *Marshall* v. *Russian Oil Products*, *supra*, *per* Lord Justice-Clerk Aitchison at p. 791.

by them.[63] In *Henderson* v. *Henry E. Jenkins & Sons* [64] a sudden escape of brake fluid from a hole in a pipe in the hydraulic braking system resulting from corrosion of that pipe, which could not have been seen on a visual inspection with the pipe *in situ*, caused a brake failure when the respondent's heavily ladened lorry was descending a steep hill so that it ran out of control and killed the deceased. The House of Lords held that the lorry owners could not rely on the defence of a latent defect not discoverable by the exercise of reasonable care unless they proved that they had taken all reasonable care in the circumstances. In order to do that they had to show that there were no special circumstances in the past use of the vehicle to indicate that it might have been subjected to a corrosive agent resulting in the corrosion of the pipe, which they had failed to prove. Again, if the negligence alleged is the sudden swerve of a vehicle, the prima facie case of negligence established by proof of the swerve is not rebutted by the mere suggestion that the swerve may have been necessary to avoid a pedestrian in the highway, but full proof is required.[65]

991 When *res ipsa loquitur* applies it is not strictly necessary for the defendant to disprove negligence; it is enough for him to neutralise the effect of the presumption raised by the *res*, but in practice the difference between neutralising the effect of the prima facie case and disproving negligence is so small as to be immaterial. The court has to judge, after all the evidence has been put before it, whether the facts establish that, on balance, the plaintiff has proved his case.[66]

3.—THE TRIAL OF A CAUSE OF ACTION [67]

992 **Duty of judge.** When a case is tried by a judge and jury, it is the duty of the judge to decidew hether there is any evidence from which negligence on the part of the defendant may be reasonably inferred, and if he decides that there is any such evidence, then it is the duty of the jury to decide whether or not the defendant was negligent. The judge must not withdraw the case from the jury merely because, in his opinion, the jury ought not to infer negligence.[68] On the other hand, he must not leave it to the jury to say whether or not there is negligence unless there is evidence on which a finding of negligence can legally be based, because it would " place in the hands of the jurors a power which might be exercised in the most arbitrary manner, if they were at liberty to hold that negligence might be inferred from any state of facts whatever." [69]

[63] *Pearce* v. *Round Oak Steel Works* [1969] 1 W.L.R. 595 where the Court of Appeal held, applying *Davie* v. *New Merton Board Mills* [1959] A.C. 604, that it was not enough to show that the accident was caused by a latent defect; the defendants had to show that it would have occurred despite all reasonable care on their part.

[64] [1970] A.C. 282. This decision illustrates the modern attitude of the courts. *viz.* of leaning against this defence succeeding where it is without merit, and a plaintiff, who is wholly blameless, has suffered damage.

[65] *O'Hara* v. *Central S.M.T. Co.*, 1941 S.C. 363; *Ludgate* v. *Lovett* [1969] 1 W.L.R. 1016.

[66] *Swan* v. *Salisbury Construction Co.* [1966] 1 W.L.R. 204.

[67] For jurisdiction generally of the court, see Chap. 17.

[68] *Bridges* v. *North London Ry.* (1874) L.R. 7 H.L. 213; *Metropolitan Ry.* v. *Jackson* (1877) 3 App.Cas. 193.

[69] Lord Cairns L.C. in *Metropolitan Ry.* v. *Jackson, supra.*

993 It has sometimes been said [70] that if there is only a scintilla of evidence, the judge should withdraw the case from the jury. If by scintilla is meant that there is no evidence on which twelve reasonable men could find negligence on the part of the defendant, then the proposition is correct, but if scintilla means that there is only very slight evidence of negligence, then it goes too far, because the judge must leave the case to the jury if there is any evidence of negligence at all, and must not substitute his own judgment of the weight of the evidence for that of the jury.[71]

994 The negligence in question which is alleged at the trial must, of course be negligence causing the accident.[72] If there is no causal connection between the negligence and the damage, there is no evidence of negligence to go to the jury. So, where owing to the negligence of the railway company a railway carriage was overcrowded and a passenger's hand was caught in the door as it was being shut by a porter, it was held that the injury to the passenger was not the result of the company's negligence, and the case ought to have been withdrawn from the jury.[73]

If any evidence of negligence is given on the part of the plaintiff the case must be left to the jury, even if the defendant calls other, and what the judge may think more cogent, evidence contradicting that of the plaintiff. In *Dublin, Wicklow and Wexford Ry.* v. *Slattery* [74] the negligence alleged was the failure to whistle when a railway engine approached a crossing, in consequence of which the plaintiff's husband was killed. The plaintiff's evidence consisted of three witnesses who swore that they did not hear any whistle, while on behalf of the defendants were called the engine driver and nine other witnesses, all of whom swore that the whistle was sounded. The jury found for the plaintiff, and the House of Lords held that as there was contradictory evidence on facts the case was properly left to the jury.

The question in each case is, " what is the reasonable inference from

[70] *Toomey* v. *L.B. & S.C. Ry.* (1857) 3 C.B.(N.S.) 146, 150, *per* Williams J.; *Ryder* v. *Wombwell* (1868) L.R. 4 Ex. 32; *Banbury* v. *Bank of Montreal* [1918] A.C. 626, 670.

[71] In *Metropolitan Ry.* v. *Jackson, supra*, Lord Blackburn quotes Willes J. in *Ryder* v. *Wombwell, supra*: " It was formerly considered necessary in all cases to leave the question to the jury, if there was any evidence, even a scintilla, in support of the case; but it is now settled that the question for the judge (subject, of course, to review) is, as stated by Mr. Justice Maule in *Jewell* v. *Parr* (13 C.B. 909 at p. 916), ' not whether there is literally no evidence but whether there is none that ought reasonably to satisfy the jury that the fact sought to be proved is established.' " This passage was also quoted by Lord Macmillan (dissenting) in *Jones* v. *G.W. Ry.* (1930) 47 T.L.R. 39, and stated to be " clearly the right view." It is submitted that this is not so, because the question is not whether there is any evidence which *ought* reasonably to satisfy the jury, but whether there is any evidence which *could* reasonably satisfy the jury: *Bridges* v. *North London Ry., supra*; *Metropolitan Ry.* v. *Jackson, supra*; *Metropolitan Ry.* v. *Wright* (1886) 11 App.Cas. 152. The accident must furnish " data from which an inference *can* reasonably be drawn that, as a matter of fact," the accident was occasioned by the defendant's negligence, *per* Lord Hailsham in *Jones* v. *G.W. Ry., supra*.

[72] See generally, Causation in Chap. 3.

[73] *Metropolitan Ry.* v. *Jackson, supra*.

[74] (1878) 3 App.Cas. 1155. In this case, the question of the verdict being against the weight of evidence, which would have been ground for a new trial, was not open on the appeal: Lord Cairns, p. 1165. See also *Smith* v. *S.E. Ry.* [1896] 1 Q.B. 178.

the known facts?" The jury, after taking into consideration all the evidence, decide whether in their opinion the defendant was guilty of negligence or not.[75]

In the vast majority of actions nowadays where the plaintiff alleges a breach of duty owed him, be it at common law or under some statute, the trial takes place before a judge alone, who hears the evidence then decides both the issues of law and fact.

In cases of personal injuries jury trials should only be ordered in exceptional circumstances [76] and not necessarily just because the injuries are so serious that the damages will be very substantial indeed.[77]

995 **Costs.** Normally costs follow the event, subject to any payment into court by the defendant, upon the application of the successful party. Nevertheless where an action in negligence, *inter alia*, is commenced in the High Court which could have been commenced in the county court, if the plaintiff recovers a sum less than £500 he is only entitled to costs taxed on the appropriate county court scale. Moreover, if the plaintiff only recovers a sum less than £100, then he shall not be entitled to any costs of the action at all, unless, of course, he had properly brought his action in the county court in the first instance.[78]

4.—APPEALS

996 **Setting aside verdict of jury.** If there was evidence to go to the jury and no misdirection by the judge, the verdict of the jury can only be set aside if it was one which could not reasonably have been found on the evidence before them. The principle is stated by Lord Halsbury [79] to be: "If a court—not a Court of Appeal in which the facts are open for original judgment, but a court which is not a court to review facts at all—can grant a new trial whenever it thinks that reasonable men ought to have found another verdict, it seems to me that they must form and act upon their own view of what the evidence in their judgment proves. That, I think, is not the law. If reasonable men *might* find (not 'ought to' as was said in *Solomon* v. *Bitton* [80]) the verdict which has been found, I think no court has jurisdiction to disturb a decision of fact which the law has confided to juries, not to judges." [81]

If, at the conclusion of the plaintiff's case, the defendant had taken the point that there was no evidence to go to the jury and his submission was overruled, he is not prevented on appeal from taking the point that there was no case to go to the jury, by the fact that he calls evidence on his own

[75] *Jones* v. *G.W. Ry.* (1930) 47 T.L.R. 39.
[76] *Ward* v. *James* [1966] 1 Q.B. 273.
[77] *Watts* v. *Manning* [1964] 1 W.L.R. 623.
[78] County Courts Act 1959, s. 47, as amended by s. 4 of the Administration of Justice Act 1969.
[79] *Metropolitan Ry.* v. *Wright* (1886) 11 App.Cas. 152, 156.
[80] (1881) 8 Q.B.D. 176.
[81] See also to the same effect *Com. for Railways* v. *Brown* (1887) 13 App.Cas. 133; *Phillips* v. *Martin* (1890) 15 App.Cas. 193; *Avis* v. *G.E. Ry.* (1892) 8 T.L.R. 693; *Dallas* v. *G.W. Ry.* (1893) 9 T.L.R. 344.

behalf; in such a case, however, the appellate court, in considering whether there was evidence to go to the jury, is entitled to take into account the whole evidence, called on both sides, and not only the evidence called for the plaintiff.[82]

997 **Settlement during hearing.** With the Court of Appeal's approval, an appeal may be settled by the parties on terms which vary the judgment against which the appeal has been made, even during the course of the hearing of the appeal.[83]

From the High Court

998 A decision on a question of fact given by a judge sitting in the High Court is not subject to the same rule as the verdict of a jury. On appeal, the Court of Appeal rehears the case on the evidence before the judge, and it has full power to substitute its own judgment on a question of fact as well as on a question of law for that of the trial judge.[84] When the facts are not in dispute, although the inference to be drawn from those facts is disputed, the Court of Appeal is in the same position to come to a conclusion as the trial judge.[85] When the facts are in dispute, and the decision of the trial judge is based on his estimate of the credibility of witnesses who have given evidence before him, the Court of Appeal " must, in order to reverse, not merely entertain doubts whether the decision below is right, but be convinced that it is wrong." [86] " The procedure on an appeal from a judge sitting without a jury is not governed by the rules applicable to a motion for a new trial after a verdict of a jury. In such a case it is the duty of the Court of Appeal to make up its own mind, not disregarding the judgment appealed from and giving special weight to that judgment in cases where the credibility of witnesses comes into question, but with full liberty to draw its own inference from the facts proved or admitted, and to decide accordingly." [87] Later in *Thomas* v. *Thomas* [88] Lord Thankerton laid down the principles governing appellate courts in these terms: " I. Where a question of fact has been tried by a judge without a jury, and there is no question of misdirection of himself by the judge, an appellate court which is disposed to come to a different conclusion on the printed evidence, should not do so unless it is satisfied that any advantage enjoyed by the trial judge by reason of having seen and heard the witnesses, could not be sufficient to explain or justify the trial judge's conclusion; II. The appellate court may take the view that, without having seen or heard the witnesses, it is not in a position to come to any satisfactory conclusion on the

[82] *Jenner* v. *South Eastern Ry.* (1911) 27 T.L.R. 445.
[83] *Vacwell Engineering Co.* v. *B.D.H. Chemicals* [1970] 3 W.L.R. 67.
[84] Ord. 58, r. 1. *Coglan* v. *Cumberland* [1898] 1 Ch. 704.
[85] *Montgomery & Co.* v. *Wallace-James* [1904] A.C. 73.
[86] *The Julia* (1860) 14 Moo.P.C. 210, 235, *per* Lord Kingsdown. See also to the same effect, *Clarke* v. *Edinburgh and District Tramways*, 1919 S.C.(H.L.) 35; *SS. Hontestroom* v. *SS. Sagaporack* [1927] A.C. 37; *Powell* v. *Streatham Manor Nursing Home* [1935] A.C. 243; *Flower* v. *Ebbw Vale Steel Co.* [1936] A.C. 206.
[87] Viscount Cave L.C. in *Mersey Docks & Harbour Board* v. *Proctor* [1923] A.C. 253.
[88] [1947] A.C. 484.

printed evidence; III. The appellate court, either because the reasons given by the trial judge are not satisfactory, or because it unmistakably so appears from the evidence, may be satisfied that he has not taken proper advantage of his having seen and heard the witnesses, and the matter will then become at large for the appellate court. It is obvious that the value and importance of having seen and heard the witnesses will vary according to the class of case, and, it may be, the individual case in question."[89] In *Benmax* v. *Austin Motor Co. Ltd.*[90] Lord Reid quoted with approval these three principles and considered that the whole passage of Lord Thankerton's judgment referred to cases where the credibility or reliability of one or more witnesses had been in dispute and where a decision on these matters had led the trial judge to come to his decision on the case as a whole. He added: " But in cases where there is no question of the credibility or reliability of any witness, and in cases where the point in dispute is the proper inference to be drawn from proved facts, an appeal court is generally in as good a position to evaluate the evidence as the trial judge, and ought not to shrink from that task, though it ought, of course, to give weight to his opinion." [91]

999 When a trial judge has apportioned blame between a defendant, guilty of negligence, and a plaintiff, guilty of a degree of contributory negligence, the Court of Appeal will not interfere with that apportionment unless there has been an error of principle or a misapprehension of material fact, because it requires a very strong case to justify an appellate court substituting its own discretion for that of the trial judge where the same view was taken of the law and the facts.[92] But the Court of Appeal, if satisfied that the apportionment is clearly wrong, should intervene to alter it.[93]

Likewise, if an appeal is brought against the amount of damages awarded by a judge sitting alone, the appellate tribunal will not interfere unless damages were assessed on a wrong principle, or weight has been given to evidence which ought to have been disregarded,[94] or unless the judge has " misapprehended the facts or has for these or other reasons made a wholly erroneous estimate of the damage suffered." [95]

1000 Leave to adduce further evidence on appeal will only be granted: (1) if it be shown that the evidence could not have been obtained with reasonable diligence for use at the trial; (2) if the further evidence be such that, if given, it would properly have an important influence on the result of the case, although it need not be decisive; and (3) if the evidence be such as is

[89] *Ibid.*, at pp. 487, 488.
[90] [1955] A.C. 370.
[91] *Ibid.*, at p. 375.
[92] *Brown* v. *Thompson* [1968] 1 W.L.R. 1003.
[93] *Kerry* v. *Carter* [1969] 1 W.L.R. 1372, approving the observations of Lord Sterndale M.R. in *The Karamea* [1921] P. 76, 78 and explaining *Brown* v. *Thompson, supra.* See also *Chisman* v. *Electromation (Export)* (1969) 6 K.I.R. 456; *Jennings* v. *Norman Collison (Contractors)* [1970] 1 All E.R. 1121.
[94] *Owen* v. *Sykes* [1936] 1 K.B. 192. See Chap. 3.
[95] *Davies* v. *Powell Duffryn Associated Collieries* [1942] A.C. 601, 617, *per* Lord Wright. See also *Naylor* v. *Yorkshire Electricity Board* [1968] A.C. 529.

presumably to be believed.[96] Where the further evidence sought to be adduced was evidence which (a) could not with reasonable diligence have been obtained for use at the trial, because it had not been communicated to the plaintiff or his legal advisers for use and (b) was not " available " for use at the trial because it was not and could not have been known to those who caused the witnesses (whose additional evidence was now " available ") to be called at the trial, the plaintiff's appeal was allowed and a new trial was ordered.[97] However, in a case where, if the fresh evidence were true, the plaintiff had perpetrated a gross fraud the court should not allow such a practice to succeed; thus a new trial would not be ordered.[98] Despite the general principle that damages were assessed at the trial once and for all, although the plaintiff might finally suffer greater loss than was anticipated, an appellate court has power, in exceptional cases, to hear evidence of something which had altered the effect of an order of the court below since it was made, if the particular exigencies of justice clearly outweighed the general undesirability of so doing.[99]

1001 **Appeal direct to House of Lords.** Part II [1] of the Administration of Justice Act 1969 [2] makes provision for appeals to be made direct to the House of Lords from the High Court in civil proceedings, subject to certain conditions. Section 12 provides for an appeal to go direct to the House of Lords if all the parties consent, where the proposed appeal raises a question of law of general public importance, involving either the construction of a statute or statutory instrument or an issue on which the court of trial is bound by a previous decision of the Court of Appeal or of the House of Lords. Under the section the trial judge or a Divisional Court must certify that the appeal is one in which the " leap-frog " procedure would be appropriate and section 13 requires application for leave to appeal then to be made to the House of Lords.

From the County Court

1002 The County Courts Act 1959,[3] s. 108, gives a right of appeal from the

96 *Ladd* v. *Marshall* [1954] 1 W.L.R. 1489; in a road accident case a material point was whether there was a stationary vehicle at a particular part of the road. The solicitor to one of the parties made certain inquiries of witnesses but did not inquire until after the trial concerning the evidence of a potential witness who lived immediately opposite the locus. The C.A. refused an application for leave to adduce the evidence of such person on the appeal: *Delaney* v. *Douglas* (No. 1) [1969] 3 All E.R. 1454. *Power* v. *Standard Triumph Motor Co. Ltd., The Times,* December 10, 1970. See article 121 New L.J. 645.

97 *House* v. *Haughton Brothers* (*Worcester*) *Ltd.* [1967] 1 W.L.R. 148.

98 *Power* v. *Standard Triumph Motor Co. Ltd., supra.*

99 *Murphy* v. *Stone-Wallwork* (*Charlton*) *Ltd.* [1969] 1 W.L.R. 1023, applying *Curwen* v. *James* [1963] 1 W.L.R. 748. The H.L. in *Mulholland* v. *Mitchell* [1971] 2 W.L.R. 93 held that the C.A. had an unfettered discretion to admit fresh evidence although that discretion would only be exercised in exceptional cases, one possible ground being that (as here) the basis on which the award of damages was made had been suddenly and materially falsified by a dramatic change in circumstances. See article: " Fresh evidence on assessment of damages, " 115 S.J. 164.

1 Which came into force on January 1, 1970, by virtue of the Administration of Justice Act 1969 (Commencement No. 1) Order 1969 (S.I. 1969, No. 1607).

2 1969, c. 58.

3 As amended by the Administration of Justice Act 1969, the material Part I of which came into force on May 26, 1970, by virtue of the Administration of Justice Act 1969 (Commencement No. 2) Order 1970 (S.I. 1970 No. 672) whereby the jurisdiction of the county courts

decision of a county court judge only on a point of law or upon the admission or rejection of evidence, with the result that " there is no power to review a decision of fact arrived at in the county court by any other tribunal than the county court itself." [4] An appeal lies only when there was no evidence on which the judge could reasonably arrive at his decision.[5] Where, however, the damage claimed in an action of tort exceeds £200 an appeal may be brought on a question of fact.[6]

An award of damages is a question of fact, so that no appeal lies even if the damages awarded are inadequate or excessive,[7] unless the judge took into account something which he ought not to take into account or of which there is no evidence or unless the amount claimed exceeds £200.

In contrast to an appellant in the Court of Appeal who cannot raise a point which he did not raise in the county court the respondent can take any point in support of a judgment, which he had obtained, whether previously argued or not, unless the point had been abandoned by him in the court below.[8]

in contract and tort, *inter alia*, is increased from £500 to £750. For future convenience by virtue of s. 10 the monetary limits of the county court's jurisdiction may be raised by Order in Council, subject to an affirmative resolution of both Houses of Parliament.

[4] Lord Halsbury in *Smith* v. *Baker* [1891] A.C. 325, 333. The Court of Appeal will not entertain a point of law not put forward in the county court unless it goes to the county court's jurisdiction or to illegality except in wholly exceptional circumstances: *Oscroft* v. *Benabo* [1967] 1 W.L.R. 1087.

[5] *Cousins* v. *Lombard Bank* (1876) 1 Ex.D. 404; *Baker* v. *Longhurst & Sons* [1933] 2 K.B. 461.

[6] County Courts Act 1959, s. 109. The Court of Appeal expressed the view that as a general matter a plaintiff should state whether or not his claim exceeds £200: *Leslie* v. *Liverpool Corporation* [1959] 3 All E.R. 898. A defendant's entitlement to appeal on a question of fact depends upon whether he has counterclaimed more than £200: *Ward* v. *M.W. Garages (Ramsgate)* (1966) 110 S.J. 688.

[7] *Shave* v. *J. W. Lees (Brewers) Ltd.* [1954] 3 All E.R. 249 (£750 awarded when C.A. thought the utmost should have been £150); *Henderson* v. *Clifford Watmough & Co.* (1939) 161 L.T. 233.

[8] *Thomas* v. *Marconi's Wireless Telegraph* [1965] 1 W.L.R. 850, approving *Waller & Sons Ltd.* v. *Thomas* [1921] 1 K.B. 541.

CHAPTER 16

DEFENCES AND DISCHARGES FROM LIABILITY

003 **Generally.** The failure to prove each of the essential ingredients of actionable negligence [1] will always afford a complete defence to the plaintiff's claim. Accordingly, if the plaintiff fails to prove that a duty of care was owed to him or that there was a breach of the duty of care which was owed or that his damage was caused by such breach, then his claim for damages must be dismissed.

Besides these, it is necessary to consider (1) contributory negligence, although it is no longer a defence as such but merely affects the measure of damages; (2) agreement to run the risk of injury, namely, *volenti non fit injuria*; (3) inevitable accident; (4) contracting out of liability for negligence, and (5) limitation of action.

1.—CONTRIBUTORY NEGLIGENCE

004 *Meaning of contributory negligence.* The expression " contributory negligence " is too firmly established to be disregarded, but unless properly understood it is apt to be misleading. It applies solely to the conduct of a plaintiff. It means that there has been an act or omission on the part of the plaintiff which has materially contributed to the damage, the act or omission being of such a nature that it may properly be described as negligence, although negligence is not given its usual meaning.

Contributory negligence is an expression meaning " negligence materially contributing to the injury," [2] the word " contributory " being regarded " as expressing something which is a direct cause of the accident." [3] However, the word " negligence " is not used in its usual meaning. Negligence ordinarily means breach of a legal duty to take care, but as used in the expression " contributory negligence " it does not mean breach of duty. It means the failure by a person to use reasonable care for the safety of himself or his property, so that he becomes " the author of his own wrong." [3] For example, if a railway train draws up at a platform which is not long enough for the train, a passenger in a carriage which is short of the platform owes no duty to the railway company not to alight, but if he gets out without looking where he is going it is contributory negligence on his part.[4] A workman on a ship owes no duty to the shipowner not to fall down an open hatchway negligently left unfenced by the shipowner, but if his fall is due to his own carelessness he is guilty of contributory negligence.[5] A member of the public owes no duty to a railway company to

1 Chap. 1, § 20, *ante*.
2 Lord Porter in *Caswell* v. *Powell Duffryn Associated Collieries Ltd.* [1940] A.C. 152, 186.
3 Parke B. in *Bridge* v. *Grand Junction Ry.* (1838) 3 M. & W. 244. See also the judgment of Lord Maugham in *R.* v. *Southern Canada Power Co.* [1937] 3 All E.R. 923, 930.
4 *Sharpe* v. *Southern Ry.* [1925] 2 K.B. 311.
5 *Dew* v. *United British Steamship Co.* (1929) 98 L.J.K.B. 88.

look out for approaching trains when he crosses the railway by means of a public level-crossing, but if he omits to do so and is injured his conduct amounts to contributory negligence.[6]

1005 The difference in the meaning of " negligence " as applied to a plaintiff and a defendant is pointed out by Atkin L.J.[7] where he said: " The doctrine of contributory negligence cannot, I think, be based upon a breach of duty to the negligent defendant. It is difficult to suppose that a person owes a duty to anyone to preserve his own property. He may not recover if he could reasonably have avoided the consequences of the defendant's negligence." [8] To the same effect said Lord Parmoor [9]: " I do not think that the question of contributory negligence depends upon any breach of duty as between the plaintiff and a negligent defendant; it depends entirely on the question whether the plaintiff could reasonably have avoided the consequences of the defendant's negligence." So, also, du Parcq L.J. said: " The doctrine of contributory negligence ' cannot be based upon a breach of duty to the negligent defendant.' " [10] More recently, Lord Simon said [11]: " When contributory negligence is set up as a defence, its existence does not depend on any duty owed by the injured party to the party sued, and all that is necessary to establish such a defence is to prove . . . that the injured party did not in his own interest take reasonable care of himself and contributed, by this want of care, to his own injury. For when contributory negligence is set up as a shield against the obligation to satisfy the whole of the plaintiff's claim, the principle involved is that, where a man is part author of his own injury, he cannot call on the other party to compensate him in full."

1006 Some cases which appear to indicate the view contrary to that stated in the preceding paragraphs may be noticed, premising that they do not affect the law as stated above. In *Becker* v. *Medd* [12] the defendant was the plaintiff's agent in England. Owing to the failure of the defendant to supervise a clerk, a servant of the plaintiff, considerable sums of money were lost to the plaintiff through the defalcations of the clerk. The jury found the defendant " very negligent " and also found that the plaintiff was guilty of negligence which partly contributed to the loss. The Court of Appeal held that there was no contributory negligence on the plaintiff's part, because he owed no duty to the defendant, Lord Esher saying: " The person who had undertaken the duty could not say that he had been negligent in the performance of that duty, but that the other person was guilty of contributory negligence in not finding him out." Although it was

6 *Davey* v. *L. & S.W. Ry.* (1883) 12 Q.B.D. 70.
7 *Ellerman Lines Ltd.* v. *Grayson Ltd.* [1919] 2 K.B. 514, 535, 536, in a judgment affirmed in the H.L. [1920] A.C. 466.
8 This passage was quoted with approval by Bucknill L.J. in *Davies* v. *Swan Motor Co.* [1949] 2 K.B. 291, 309.
9 [1920] A.C. 466, 477.
10 *Lewis* v. *Denye* [1939] 1 K.B. 540, 554; see also *Ross* v. *McQueen* [1947] N.I. 81, *per* MacDermott J.
11 *Nance* v. *British Columbia Electric Ry.* [1951] A.C. 601, 611.
12 (1897) 13 T.L.R. 313.

based on the ground that the plaintiff owed no duty to the defendant, the decision is readily explainable on the ground that the plaintiff was entitled to rely on the proper discharge by the defendant of his duty, and was not lacking in due care for his own interests if he failed to discover that the defendant did not discharge it.

1007 In *Compania Mexicana de Petroleo* v. *Essex Transport Co.*[13] stevedores were engaged in loading kerosene and gasoline into a ship. They did it by means of a tray which, owing to their negligence, dislodged an iron beam, causing it to fall to the bottom of the hold. In falling, it struck something which caused a spark, resulting in an explosion. The contributory negligence relied upon was that the shipowners had failed to bolt the beams in position before the loading began. It was held that this was not contributory negligence, and Scrutton L.J. said: " I do not see any duty of the ship towards the stevedores to provide that the ship should be fit to withstand the negligence of the stevedores." Here, again, it is clear that all that is meant is that the shipowners were entitled to rely on the stevedores to carry out their duty properly and were not bound to take precautions for the safety of the ship on the assumption that the stevedores were careless and incompetent people. This is the same conclusion as that arrived at in *Grayson Ltd.* v. *Ellerman Lines Ltd.*,[14] where ship repairers were doing work on a ship which contained an inflammable cargo. The repair work involved the use of red-hot rivets and, owing to the negligence of one of the repairers' servants, a rivet fell into the hold and caused a fire. The repairers contended that the omission of the shipowners to close the hatches was contributory negligence which prevented them from succeeding. This failed on the ground that it was for the repairers themselves to see that all necessary precautions were taken, Atkin L.J. giving the following illustrations of the principle: " If a workman is sent to my house containing inflammable material to work with fire, am I to remove the source of danger, or is he to take precautions which will avoid danger? If a man come to my premises containing an oil tank is he to abstain from smoking in its vicinity or am I to remove the oil tank? And if he chooses to smoke there am I precluded from recovering because I did not remove the oil tank but allowed him to continue at his peril? "[15]

1008 In *Vaile Bros.* v. *Hobson Ltd.*[16] the plaintiffs sued for breach of contract to repair a carburettor in a lorry. In the county court it was held that, although there had been a breach of contract, the plaintiffs were guilty of contributory negligence in not connecting the engine switch of the lorry, which would have prevented or minimised the damage. On appeal, it was held, following *Becker* v. *Medd*,[17] that the plaintiffs owed no duty to the defendants, so that no question of contributory negligence arose. As this

[13] (1929) 141 L.T. 106.
[14] [1920] A.C. 466.
[15] [1919] 2 K.B. 514, 535.
[16] (1933) 149 L.T. 283.
[17] (1897) 13 T.L.R. 313.

was an action for breach of contract, and as contributory negligence is only a defence to actions based on negligence, no question of contributory negligence could arise and, as in the other cases quoted above, the plaintiffs were entitled to rely on the due performance of their contract by the defendants.

1009 Although contributory negligence does not necessarily mean that the plaintiff is in breach of some duty this " is not to say that in all cases the plaintiff who is guilty of contributory negligence owes to the defendant no duty to act carefully." [18] In nearly all collision cases each party owes to the other a duty to take reasonable care and in many master and servant cases a servant owes a statutory duty to take some specified precaution. In current forensic usage such conduct is commonly described as " contributory negligence," although it might be more accurate to omit the word " contributory " and express it as " negligence " and " breach of statutory duty " respectively. In practice it is unnecessary to draw the distinction owing to the definition of " fault " in the Law Reform (Contributory Negligence) Act 1945, which includes negligence, breach of statutory duty and contributory negligence. In the remainder of this section, "contributory negligence " will be used in the sense of " fault " as defined in the 1945 Act, unless the contrary is indicated.

1010 **Taking a reasonable risk not contributory negligence.** The fact that the plaintiff has to take a risk does not amount to contributory negligence on his part if the risk is one created by the negligence or breach of statutory duty of the defendant, and it is one which a reasonably prudent man in the plaintiff's position would take. Accordingly, where a trench was made at the only entrance to a mews and was unfenced, leaving a narrow passage by which the plaintiff, a cabman, could get out his horse, and the horse while being led out slipped into the trench and was killed, a direction " whether the plaintiff acted as a man of ordinary prudence would have done, or rashly in defiance of warning " was upheld.[19] On the other hand, a slight inconvenience, such as sitting in a railway carriage with the door open for three minutes, has been held not to justify a passenger in running the risk of falling out of the train by attempting to shut the door of the carriage while the train was in motion.[20] When a slide was placed for lowering casks from vans in the street to a warehouse in such a way as to block up the footway, so that pedestrians had either to climb over the slide, go into the roadway near the heads of the van horses, or wait until the slide was removed, and the plaintiff, in attempting to get over the slide, fell and was injured, it was held that the plaintiff was entitled to recover, on the

18 *Nance* v. *British Columbia Electric Ry.* [1951] A.C. 601, 611.

19 *Clayards* v. *Dethick* (1842) 12 Q.B. 439. The jury found for the plaintiff. Lord Bramwell criticised this case in *Lax* v. *Darlington Corpn.* (1879) 5 Ex.D. 28, 35, and *MacMahon* v. *Field* (1881) 7 Q.B.D. 591, 594, but the direction to the jury seems to be beyond criticism. It was approved and followed by Cockburn C.J. in *Thompson* v. *N.E. Ry.* (1862) 2 B. & S. 119 and in *Billings & Sons Ltd* v. *Riden* [1958] A.C. 240. See also *Baker* v. *T. E. Hopkins & Sons Ltd.* [1959] 1 W.L.R. 966.

20 *Adams* v. *L. & Y. Ry.* (1869) L.R. 4 C.P. 739.

jury's finding that he had acted reasonably and prudently.[21] Stacking hay near a railway, the sparks from which set the hay on fire, does not amount to contributory negligence if " there is nothing to show that there was a risk which a reasonable man ought not to have taken in placing the stacks so near the railway." [22] Where a policeman used his patrol car as a road block against a motorist escaping arrest, who drove at high speed into the police vehicle, it was held that there was no contributory negligence on the policeman's part, although public duty does not, of itself, relieve him of the obligation to take reasonable care for his own safety.[23]

1011 A tenant of a house with a defective ceiling, which the landlord had agreed to repair, is not prevented from recovering when the ceiling falls and injures her, if her conduct in using the room with knowledge of the danger is reasonable under the circumstances.[24] Similarly, when the occupier of a requisitioned house reported a crack in the ceiling to the local authority but continued to use the kitchen until the ceiling fell and injured her, she was not prevented from recovering on the ground that " she was not free to avoid the danger. She had to stay there and live in her kitchen." [25] Also, a tenant who opens a window with one broken sash cord and is injured through the breaking of the other cord can sue the landlord for breach of statutory duty to keep the house fit for human habitation as long as her conduct in attempting to open the window was reasonable and not blameworthy.[26] The " rescue " cases discussed in an earlier section also illustrate this principle.[27]

1012 **Dilemma created by another's negligence.** If one party by his negligence places another in a position of danger in which it is necessary for that other to act quickly in order to extricate himself, it is not contributory negligence if that other fails to act in a way which is shown on reflection to have been the best way out of the difficulty. As Lord Hailsham put it [28]: " Mere failure to avoid the collision by taking some extraordinary precaution does not in itself constitute negligence: the plaintiff has no right to complain if in the agony of the collision the defendant fails to take some step which might have prevented a collision unless that step is one which a reasonably careful man would fairly be expected to take in the circumstances." In *Jones* v. *Boyce* [29] owing to the negligence of the defendant a coach in descending a slope became unmanageable, and the plaintiff, fearing the

21 *Lee* v. *Nixey* (1890) 63 L.T. 285.
22 *Groom* v. *G.W. Ry.* (1892) 8 T.L.R. 253, Mathew J.
23 *Hambley* v. *Shepley* (1967) 63 D.L.R. (2d) 94.
24 *Porter* v. *Jones* [1942] 2 All E.R. 570.
25 *Greene* v. *Chelsea B.C.* [1954] 2 Q.B. 127, 140, *per* Denning L.J.
26 *Summers* v. *Salford Corpn.* [1943] A.C. 283.
27 See § 67 *et seq.* For contributory negligence in rescue cases, see § 1051, *post.*
28 *Swadling* v. *Cooper* [1931] A.C. 1, 9.
29 (1816) 1 Starkie 493 (the coach did not overturn and had he remained on board he would not have been hurt). See also *Scott* v. *Shepherd* (1773) 2 Wm.Bl. 892 (lighted squib thrown by defendant into a crowd of people); *Brandon* v. *Osborne Garrett & Co.* [1924] 1 K.B. 548; *Maclenan* v. *Segar* [1917] 2 K.B. 325; *Sayers* v. *Harlow U.D.C.* [1958] 1 W.L.R. 623 (some degree of contributory negligence found in the way the plaintiff chose to escape from a locked lavatory); and an article founded on this decision: 21 M.L.R. 677.

coach would overturn, jumped off and was injured. Lord Ellenborough's direction was: " To enable the plaintiff to sustain the action, it is not necessary that he should have been thrown off the coach; it is sufficient if he was placed by the misconduct of the defendant in such a situation as obliged him to adopt the alternative of a dangerous leap, or to remain at certain peril."

Again, in *Chaplin* v. *Hawes* [30] a turnpike road had two gates, one for each line of traffic, and the plaintiff, riding a horse, made for his proper gate at the same time as the defendant's cart made for the same gate, which was its wrong gate, whereupon the plaintiff, thinking the defendant would give way, continued on his way, although he could have stopped, and a collision occurred. The plaintiff was held entitled to recover, Best C.J. saying: " On the sudden, a man may not be sufficiently self-possessed to know in which way to decide; and in such a case I think the wrongdoer is the party who is to be answerable for the mischief, though it might have been prevented by the other party's acting differently."

1013 The rule stated in the preceding paragraph has frequently been applied in maritime cases,[31] and is put by Lord Birkenhead in this way: " A.'s negligence makes collision so threatening that though by the appropriate measure B. could avoid it, B. has not really time to think and by mistake takes the wrong measure. B. is not held to be guilty of any negligence and A. wholly fails." [32] So, if two motorists, A. and B., are approaching each other from opposite directions, A. on his proper side of the road and B. on his wrong side, and they get so close together that a collision is inevitable, then if A. drives on to his wrong side and at the same time B. goes to his proper side of the road, so that a collision occurs on A.'s wrong side, A. can recover from B., because A.'s action was due to the position of difficulty into which he was put by B.'s negligence.[33]

This principle is often referred to as the doctrine of alternative danger and Lord Sumner said it " refers to personal danger. It has not been extended to danger to property." [34] This is based on the words of Montague Smith J.: " If the negligence of a railway company puts a passenger in a situation of alternative danger, that is to say, if he will be in danger by remaining still, and in danger if he attempts to escape, then, if he attempts to escape, any injury that he may sustain in so doing is a consequence of the company's negligence." [35] The suggested restriction, however, seems

[30] (1828) 3 Car. & P. 554.

[31] *The Bywell Castle* (1879) 4 P.D. 219; *Stoomvaart Maatschappy Nederland* v. *P. & O. Steam Nav. Co.* (1880) 5 App.Cas. 876; *The Tasmania* (1890) 15 App.Cas. 223, 226, *per* Lord Herschell; *U.S. Shipping Board* v. *Laird Line* [1924] A.C. 286; *The Highland Loch* [1912] A.C. 312; [1911] P. 261.

[32] *Admiralty Comrs.* v. *SS. Volute* [1922] 1 A.C. 129, 136.

[33] *Wallace* v. *Bergius*, 1915 S.C. 205.

[34] *Singleton Abbey* v. *SS. Paludina* [1927] A.C. 16, 28; *contra* Lord Phillimore, who dissented. *Collins* v. *Middle Level Comrs.* (1869) L.R. 4 C.P. 279 (doubted by Lord Sumner), relied on to show that the principle applies to danger to property, is not applicable in this connection because (1) there was no sudden emergency, (2) the act complained of had not to be done as the result of a quick decision.

[35] *Adams* v. *L. & Y. Ry.* (1869) L.R. 4 C.P. 739, 742.

somewhat arbitrary, and there does not appear to be any ground for so limiting the principle. The principle is, indeed, only an extension of the more general principle that a plaintiff who takes a risk is not prevented from recovering if the risk is one which a reasonably prudent man in his position would take.[36]

14 **Plaintiff " trapped " by defendant's conduct.** There are cases when a plaintiff is entitled to rely on the conduct of the defendant. If, in one of those cases, he does rely on it and so fail to take the care he otherwise would have done, it is not contributory negligence on his part. For example, in *Gee* v. *Metropolitan Ry.*[37] the plaintiff leant against the door of a railway carriage when the train was in motion and the door flew open and he fell out. It was held that he could recover, although he had not examined the door, because he was entitled to assume that the door was properly shut. The defendant may make a representation, express or implied, that a place is safe and then the plaintiff may rely upon it and so fail to take less than his usual care, as in the " invitation to alight " cases at railway stations.[38] Leaving the gates open at a level crossing " amounts to a statement and a notice to the public that the line is at that time safe for crossing," so that a person on the highway is entitled to assume it is safe to cross without taking further precautions.[39] Where, at a level crossing, the wicket-gate was kept locked when trains were expected, the fact that it is unlocked throws a person, who knows the practice, off his guard so that he is not guilty of contributory negligence if he crosses the line after passing through the gate.[40] When a local authority, during a wartime blackout, had an illuminated sign in the highway indicating the access to an air-raid shelter but failed to illuminate it so that the plaintiff, who knew that the sign was kept lit, was misled and in the dark fell into the entrance, it was held that there was no contributory negligence but " he was trapped through the light being out." [41]

5 There is no general rule that a person is entitled to rely on the proper discharge by others of their duty to take care. The driver of a motor-car, however, crossing when the traffic lights are in his favour, is not negligent in failing to anticipate that another driver will attempt to cross against the lights.[42] Again, it has been held that a stevedore, working on a ship on which repairers were also working and in the course of that work had uncovered the hatches, on returning from his lunch, finding that the repairers had gone and the lights removed, was entitled to assume that the

[36] *Ante*, § 1010.
[37] (1873) L.R. 8 Q.B. 161, quoted with approval in *Grant* v. *Sun Shipping Co* [1948] A.C. 549, 563, by Lord du Parcq. A somewhat similar case in *Brookes* v. *L.P.T.B.* [1947] 1 All E.R. 506. For cases on shutting doors, see *ante*, § 757.
[38] *Ante*, § 759 *et seq. Bridges* v. *North London Ry.* (1874) L.R. 7 H.L. 213; *L.T. & S. Ry.* v. *Glasscock* (1909) 19 T.L.R. 305.
[39] *North Eastern Ry.* v. *Wanless* (1874) L.R. 7 H.L. 12.
[40] *Mercer* v. *S.E. & C. Ry.* [1922] 2 K.B. 549.
[41] *Knight* v. *Sheffield Corpn.* [1942] 2 All E.R. 411.
[42] *Joseph Eva Ltd.* v. *Reeves* [1938] 2 K.B. 393; *Ward* v. *L.C.C.* [1938] 2 All E.R. 341; *Davis* v. *Hassan* (1967) 117 New L.J. 72.

repairers had fulfilled their statutory duty of replacing the hatch covers and was not guilty of contributory negligence in acting on that assumption without first trying to see that they had done so.[43] This, however, must be regarded as an example of the exceptional position of workmen in relation to contributory negligence (discussed, *post*, § 1045) and is not a general rule. For example, when the plaintiff stepped from an automatic lift, remained for a few seconds, then, without looking backwards, re-opened the door and fell down the lift shaft, thinking that he could only open the door when the lift was there, it was held, reversing Atkinson J. that there was contributory negligence on his part.[44]

1016 **Standard of care in contributory negligence.** The standard of care in contributory negligence is the same as that in negligence.[45] Were that not so, the absurd position would be reached that the party who managed to be the first to start the action, and so get himself into the position of plaintiff, would have an advantage over the other who, perforce, had to be defendant. " Although contributory negligence does not depend on a duty of care, it does depend on foreseeability. Just as actionable negligence requires the foreseeability of harm to others, so contributory negligence requires the foreseeability of harm to oneself. A person is guilty of contributory negligence if he ought reasonably to have foreseen that, if he did not act as a reasonably prudent man, he might hurt himself; and in his reckonings he must take into account the possibility of others being careless." [46] There is an exception to this in the case of accidents to workmen (discussed, *post*, § 1045).

It has been suggested that, " it is both in accordance with common sense and with good morals to hold that a man need not pay as much attention to his own safety as he does to the safety of others," and an illustration is given, " thus the inadvertence of a pedestrian who may step from the pavement into the road is not comparable to that of a driver who is proceeding at such a speed that he cannot stop within a reasonable distance. It is one thing to take a slight inadvertent risk with one's own life, even though one is not entitled to endanger it deliberately; it is an entirely different thing to risk the life of another by taking insufficient care." [47] There are some cases in which a man may pay little or no attention to his own safety such as the " rescue " cases,[48] but such cases are exceptional and, as a rule, do not include those in which the man is claiming damages from another for causing him personal injury. He cannot expect another to compensate him for such part of his damage as is attributable to his failing to take as much care for himself as he expects others to take of him. The pedestrian who steps by inadvertence from the pavement to the road

[43] *Grant* v. *Sun Shipping Co. Ltd.* [1948] A.C. 549.
[44] *Kerry* v. *Keighley Electrical Engineering Co.* [1940] 3 All E.R. 399. See Williams, *Joint Torts and Contributory Negligence*, p. 384, for a discussion of this.
[45] *A. C. Billings & Sons Ltd.* v. *Riden* [1958] A.C. 240.
[46] *Jones* v. *Livox Quarries Ltd.* [1952] 2 Q.B. 608, 615, *per* Denning L.J.
[47] 71 L.Q.R. 165.
[48] See § 67, *ante*, and § 1051, *post*.

owes a duty to exercise due care [49] and his failure to do so may cause serious injury to person [50] and property. A person's duty to take reasonable care of himself is enhanced by his knowledge of the risks involved.[51]

17 **Burden of proof of contributory negligence.** The burden of proving contributory negligence is on the defendant; it is not for the plaintiff to disprove it. " If the defendant's negligence or breach of duty is established as causing the death, the onus is on the defendants to establish that the plaintiff's contributory negligence was a substantial or material co-operating cause." [52] Further, it was explained by du Parcq L.J., " In order to establish the defence of contributory negligence, the defendant must prove first, that the plaintiff failed to take ' ordinary care of himself,' or, in other words, such care as a reasonable man would take for his own safety, and, secondly, that his failure to take care was a contributory cause of the accident." [53] The amount of care which a plaintiff may reasonably be expected to take necessarily varies with the circumstances and with the conditions actually prevailing at the material time.

18 **Effect of contributory negligence.** At common law the effect of contributory negligence on the part of the plaintiff was that the defendant succeeded in the action. Thus, in *Butterfield* v. *Forrester* [54] the defendant placed a pole across the highway. The plaintiff, riding as fast as his horse would go, collided with the pole and was injured. Judgment for the defendant was upheld, Lord Ellenborough C.J. saying: " A party is not to cast himself upon an obstruction which has been made by the fault of another, and avail himself of it, if he do not himself use common and ordinary caution to be in the right. . . . One person being in fault will not dispense with another's using ordinary care for himself. Two things must concur to support this action, an obstruction in the road by the fault of the defendant, and no want of ordinary care to avoid it on the part of the plaintiff."

19 The common law was that there had to be a judgment either for the plaintiff or for the defendant and there was no provision for apportioning the loss between them. When one of the parties alone was negligent, judgment had to be given against the other, but when both were negligent, the defendant could only be made liable if his negligence was the cause—what has been variously described as the " real cause," " effective cause," and " direct cause," " substantial cause," " decisive cause," " proximate

[49] *Nance* v. *British Columbia Electric Ry.* [1951] A.C. 601, 611, *per* Lord Simon, expressly disapproving a statement to the contrary by Denning L.J. in *Davies* v. *Swan Motor Co. (Swansea) Ltd.* [1949] 2 K.B. 291.

[50] As in *Carmarthenshire C.C.* v. *Lewis* [1955] A.C. 549, where a boy of four strayed on to the road and the driver of a lorry was killed in trying to avoid him.

[51] *Hicks* v. *British Transport Commission* [1958] 1 W.L.R. 493.

[52] Lord Wright in *Caswell* v. *Powell Duffryn Associated Collieries Ltd.* [1940] A.C. 152, 172. See also *Wakelin* v. *L. & S.W. Ry.* (1886) 12 App.Cas. 41, 47, *per* Lord Watson, and, *ante*, § 966, and Lord Green M.R. in *Stimson* v. *Standard Telephone & Cables Ltd.* [1940] 1 K.B. 342, where, says Williams (*Joint Torts and Contributory Negligence*, p. 387), the distinction between causation and contributory negligence " and the general effect of the distinction upon the burden of proof was beautifully explained."

[53] *Lewis* v. *Denye* [1939] 1 K.B. 540, 554.

[54] (1809) 11 East 60.

cause," " immediate cause "—of the accident. As Lord Sumner said,[55] " the inquiry is an investigation into responsibility." Liability was a question of fact and the question was, Whose negligence was the real or substantial cause of the accident? [56]

The law now recognises that responsibility for an accident may be shared between the parties and makes provision in such a case for the damages to be apportioned between them. This is done by the Law Reform (Contributory Negligence) Act 1945,[57] section 1 of which provides:

" 1.—(1) Where any person suffers damage [58] as the result partly of his own fault [59] and partly of the fault of any other person or persons, a claim in respect of that damage shall not be defeated by reason of the fault of the person suffering the damage, but the damages recoverable in respect thereof shall be reduced to such extent as the court [60] thinks just and equitable having regard to [61] the claimant's share in the responsibility for the damage: . . ."

1020 Section 1 " does not create a right of action; it removes an obstacle." [62] Where, therefore, a married woman was injured in a collision between a van driven by her husband and a motor-car driven by K., the collision being due to the negligence of both drivers, it was held that K. could not recover any part of the damages he had had to pay to the wife from the husband because it was not " damage " within the meaning of subsection (1).[63]

[55] *British Columbia Electric Ry.* v. *Loach* [1916] 1 A.C. 719, 728.

[56] *Swadling* v. *Cooper* [1931] A.C. 1, where the direction of Humphries J. " Whose negligence was it that substantially caused the injury " was approved.

[57] In *Ginty* v. *Belmont Building Supplies Ltd.* [1959] 1 All E.R. 414, Pearson J. said at p. 424: " The Law Reform (Contributory Negligence) Act applies only in a case where the accident is caused partly by the fault of the plaintiff and partly by the fault of somebody else . . . the common law principle is still valid to this extent, that, if the accident is wholly caused by the plaintiff's own fault he is disentitled to recover." See also *Rushton* v. *Turner Brothers Asbestos Co. Ltd.* [1960] 1 W.L.R. 96.

[58] " Includes loss of life and personal injury ": s. 4.

[59] " Means negligence, breach of statutory duty or other act or omission which gives rise to a liability in tort or would, apart from this Act give rise to the defence of contributory negligence ": s. 4. " Fault " in the wording of s. 4 does not mean some fault which fell short of negligence: *Jones* v. *Price*, *Guardian*, March 1, 1963. In *Quinn* v. *Burch Brothers (Builders) Ltd.* [1966] 2 Q.B. 370 it was held that for the provisions of the Law Reform (Contributory Negligence) Act 1945 to apply to a contract there had to be a breach of some term, which imported a duty not to be negligent; the mere fact that there had been an avoidable breach of contract by the defendants did not by itself constitute negligence or " fault " within the meaning of s. 1 (1), so it was held that the plaintiff was not entitled to succeed in his claim for damages.

[60] " Means, in relation to any claim, the court or arbitrator by or before whom the claim falls to be determined ": s. 4.

[61] " The words ' have regard to ' call for the exercise of a broad judgment and any arithmetical conclusion is qualified by what is deemed to be fair and reasonable ": Lord Simon in *Palser* v. *Grinling* [1948] A.C. 291, 315. See also *Newport B.C.* v. *Monmouthshire C.C.* [1947] A.C. 520, 534.

[62] *Drinkwater* v. *Kimber* [1952] 2 Q.B. 281, *per* Singleton L.J. at p. 288 (the claim of the defendant was really a claim to contribution but as such a claim could not succeed under s. 6 of the Law Reform (Married Women and Tortfeasors) Act 1935 due to the inability of a wife being able to sue her husband, the defendant sought to achieve the same end by claiming damages against the husband and bringing into play s. 1 of the Act of 1945). But see now the provisions of the Law Reform (Husband and Wife) Act 1962 which has overruled *Drinkwater* v. *Kimber, supra.*

[63] *Drinkwater* v. *Kimber* [1952] 2 Q.B. 281.

The language of this subsection is similar to that of section 6 (2) of the Law Reform (Married Women and Tortfeasors) Act 1935[64] and bears some resemblance to that of section 1 (1) of the Maritime Conventions Act 1911.[65]

The effect of the Act is that, in the cases to which it applies, the jury (or the judge as the case may be) must decide, (1) was the damage the result (a) of the plaintiff's fault, or (b) of the defendant's fault, or (c) partly of the plaintiff's fault and partly of the defendant's fault, (2) the total damages which would have been recoverable had the plaintiff not been at fault, and (3) when both parties are found to be at fault, the extent to which the plaintiff's damages are to be reduced.

The working of the Act will be seen from the following illustrations:

21 A, in the daylight, walking along the highway falls into an unfenced excavation which he could have avoided had he been looking where he was going. The court finds that his responsibility for the damage was three-quarters and assesses the damages at £400. A will recover one-quarter of his damages, namely, £100.

B and C, riding motor-cycles, come into collision at a crossroads and both are found equally to blame. B loses his leg and his damages are assessed at £2,500. C escapes lightly and his damages are only £100. There is a claim and a counterclaim. B will recover £1,250 from C, and C £50 from B.

The result is that there are now two questions which must be decided, first, whether one or more, and which, of the parties were at fault as a result of which the damage was caused, and secondly, if so, in what proportions should they bear the damage.

22 **Fault.** The reference in subsection (1) to damage as the result partly of . . . fault, means: " caused partly by the fault of " the person concerned. The common law doctrine of contributory negligence was based on causation, and causation has been held to be the basis of apportioning fault under the Maritime Conventions Act 1911.[66] " If contributory negligence is not regarded from the point of view of causation it is difficult to see how damage comes to be divided under the Admiralty rule which is adopted in ordinary cases of injury in other systems of jurisprudence, and which

64 " In any proceedings for contribution under this section the amount of the contribution recoverable from any person shall be such as may be found by the court to be just and equitable having regard to the extent of that person's responsibility for the damage; . . ." The responsibility (if any) of any other person, not before the court, should not be taken into account. In *Maxfield* v. *Llewellyn* [1961] 3 All E.R. 95, 96, Ormerod L.J. said: " The court must have regard to a person's responsibility for the damage, having regard to the parties who are before the court and whose share of the damage can be taken into account who have had the opportunity of putting arguments for and against their share of blame and generally of being heard in the action. . . . It is the duty of the court on finding more than one defendant liable to make an assessment of the contribution, which each defendant should make according to his share of blameworthiness."

65 " Where, by the fault of two or more vessels, damage or loss is caused to one or more of those vessels, to their cargoes or freight, or to any property on board, the liability to make good the damage or loss shall be in proportion to the degree in which each vessel was in fault: . . ."

66 *Anglo-Newfoundland Development Co.* v. *Pacific Steam Navigation Co.* [1924] A.C. 406; *The Vectis* [1929] P. 204.

persons of authority think should be adopted in ours." [67] " The existence of fault on the part of one of the ships is no reason for apportionment unless it in part caused the damage." [68] Construing the words " in fault " in section 1 (1) of the Maritime Conventions Act 1911, Pickford L.J. said, " That must be ' in fault ' so far as causing or contributing to the collision." [69] Also, with reference to the 1945 Act, Denning L.J. has said,[70] " causation is the decisive factor in determining whether there should be a reduced amount payable to the plaintiff." Causation is fully discussed in Chapter 3.

1023 In considering what is the *cause* of an accident " Causation is to be understood as the man in the street, and not as either the scientist or the metaphysician would understand it." [71] " One may find that as a matter of history several people have been at fault and that if any one of them had acted properly the accident would not have happened, but that does not mean that the accident must be regarded as having been caused by the faults of all of them. One must discriminate between those faults which must be discarded as being too remote and those which must not. Sometimes it is proper to discard all but one and to regard that as the sole cause, but in other cases it is proper to regard two or more as having jointly caused the accident. I doubt whether any test can be applied generally." [72] What the causes of an accident were is a question of fact and, as the passage just cited shows, no test has yet been formulated to enable this question to be decided. In *Stapley* v. *Gypsum Mines Ltd.*[73] two men were ordered to take down an unsafe roof in a mine. After attempting it for a time they gave it up and Stapley returned to work under the unsafe roof, when it fell and killed him. In the House of Lords two members thought that the sole cause of the accident was the act of Stapley in returning to work under a roof which he knew to be unsafe, but three members held that it was only partly the cause, the other part being the act of his fellow workman in leaving the roof.

1024 **The last opportunity rule.** It was thought at one time that there existed a rule known as the rule of the last opportunity which could be applied to determine whose fault caused the accident.[74] The rule was, " When an accident happens through the combined negligence of two persons he

[67] Lord Atkin in *Caswell* v. *Powell Duffryn Associated Collieries Ltd.* [1940] A.C. 152, 165, 166.
[68] Lord Finlay in *The Karamea* [1922] 1 A.C. 68, 71, 72, quoted with approval by Lord Wright in *SS. Heranger* v. *SS. Diamond* [1939] A.C. 94, 104.
[69] *The Peter Benoit* (1915) 84 L.J.P. 87, 91.
[70] *Davies* v. *Swan Motor Co. (Swansea) Ltd.* [1949] 2 K.B. 291, 326.
[71] Lord Wright in *Yorkshire Dale SS. Co.* v. *Minister of War Transport* [1942] A.C. 691, 706. See also *Sigurdson* v. *British Columbia Electric Ry.* [1953] A.C. 291, 299; " Causation and Responsibility in English Law " by Lord Wright [1955] C.L.J. 163.
[72] *Stapley* v. *Gypsum Mines Ltd.* [1953] A.C. 663, 681, *per* Lord Reid.
[73] *Supra*; followed, *Williams* v. *Sykes & Harrison Ltd.* [1955] 1 W.L.R. 1180; *Hodkinson* v. *Wallwork & Co.* [1955] 1 W.L.R. 1195. The case of *Stapley* v. *Gypsum Mines Ltd., supra*, gives authoritative guidance on the question of causation, but beyond that it decides nothing: *per* Lord Reid, *Imperial Chemical Industries Ltd.* v. *Shatwell* [1965] A.C. 656, 670.
[74] See, for an account of this, Williams, *Joint Torts and Contributory Negligence*, pp. 223–280. " Salmond invents the last opportunity rule " *Salmond on Torts*, 15th ed., p. 687.

alone is liable to the other who had the last opportunity for avoiding the accident by reasonable care," [75] which was the principle in *Davies* v. *Mann.*[76]

In *Davies* v. *Mann* [76] the plaintiff hobbled an ass and turned it loose on the highway, when it was run into by the defendant's wagon driven " at a smartish pace " and killed. Lord Abinger stated the law to be: " As the defendant might, by proper care, have avoided injuring the animal, and did not, he is liable for the consequences of his negligence, though the animal may have been improperly there," Parke B. adding: " Were this not so, a man might justify the driving over goods left on a public highway, or even over a man lying asleep there, or the purposely running against a carriage going on the wrong side of the road." Again, in *Radley* v. *L. & N.W. Ry.*[77] the defendants, the railway company, were in the habit of taking full trucks from the siding of the plaintiffs and returning empty trucks there. Over the siding was a bridge, and the plaintiffs left for return to the siding a truck containing another truck, the combined height of which exceeded the height of the bridge. The defendants pushed this truck towards the bridge and, on feeling resistance, continued to push and so brought down the bridge. The trial judge directed the jury that unless the accident was caused solely by the defendants' negligence and without any contributory negligence on the part of the plaintiffs, they must find for the defendants. The jury found contributory negligence on the part of the plaintiffs and judgment was accordingly entered for the defendants, but on appeal a new trial was ordered on the ground of misdirection, Lord Penzance saying: " Though the plaintiff may have been guilty of negligence, and although that negligence may, in fact, have contributed to the accident, yet if the defendant could in the result, by the exercise of ordinary care and diligence, have avoided the mischief which happened, the plaintiff's negligence will not excuse him."

25 In *British Columbia Electric Ry.* v. *Loach* [78] a horse-drawn wagon was driven onto a level crossing, but the driver, who was not keeping a proper lookout, failed to notice an approaching train and the train, owing to defective brakes, could not stop, so that a collision occurred, and the railway authority was held liable. Here, the wagon would appear to have had the last opportunity of avoiding the accident, but, to fit into the rule of the last opportunity, the case was explained by saying that a person who by his negligence has deprived himself of the last opportunity of avoiding the accident is to be deemed in law to have had the last opportunity. It is unnecessary to go further into this rule, the weakness of which was that it meant finding out who had the last opportunity for avoiding the accident rather than whose negligence caused it, since it was not followed in

[75] *Service* v. *Sundell* (1929) 99 L.J.K.B. 55, *per* Scrutton L.J., quoting *Salmond on Torts,* 6th ed., p. 95.
[76] (1842) 10 M. & W. 546.
[77] (1876) 1 App.Cas. 754.
[78] [1916] 1 A.C. 719.

Swadling v. *Cooper* [79] and was rejected in *The Volute.*[80] There, Lord Birkenhead said: " The question of contributory negligence must be dealt with somewhat broadly and upon common-sense principles as a jury would probably deal with it. And while no doubt, where a clear line can be drawn, the subsequent negligence is the only one to look to, there are cases in which the two acts come so closely together, and the second act of negligence is so much mixed up with the state of things brought about by the first act, that the party secondly negligent, while not held free from blame under the Bywell Castle rule, might, on the other hand, invoke the prior negligence as being part of the cause of the collision so as to make it a case of contribution." [81] An illustration of the application of this is the Admiralty case of *The Eurymedon,*[82] where the *Corstar* sued the *Eurymedon* for damages for collision. The *Corstar* was lying at anchor athwart the fairway, and a collision occurred between her and the *Eurymedon* from the failure of the *Eurymedon* to keep a proper lookout. It was held that both vessels were equally to blame.

1026 Finally, in the *Boy Andrew* [83] Lord Simon said: " The suggested test of ' last opportunity ' seems to me inaptly phrased and likely in some cases to lead to error, as the Law Revision Committee said in their report (Cmd. 6032 of 1939, p. 16): ' In truth there is no such rule—the question, as in all questions of liability for a tortious act, is, not who had the last opportunity of avoiding the mischief, but whose act caused the wrong? ' " In that case the S.R. was attempting to overtake the B.A. and was passing too close, when the B.A. changed her course in front of the S.R. and a collision occurred. The B.A. was held two-thirds to blame and the S.R. one-third.

1027 As a principle of law the rule of the last opportunity—if it ever existed—is now dead, but it may sometimes be a useful test to apply in deciding, as a matter of fact, whether an accident was caused by the fault of one or both of the parties. The chronological order of events is important and may well be decisive, as in *Davies* v. *Mann* [84] and *British Columbia Electric Ry.* v. *Loach,*[78] and the 1945 Act does not, as a matter of law, compel the tribunal of fact to find that when both parties are negligent there must of necessity be an apportionment of the damages. It is still necessary to find out whose act caused the wrong, whether it is a combination of the acts of both parties or the sole act of one of them. " I am persuaded that it is still part of the law of this country that two causes may both be necessary preconditions of a particular result—damage to X—yet the one may, if the

[79] [1931] A.C. 1.
[80] [1922] 1 A.C. 129. See also *Anglo-Newfoundland Development Co.* v. *Pacific Navigation Co.* [1924] A.C. 406.
[81] [1922] 1 A.C. at p. 144.
[82] [1938] P. 41.
[83] [1948] A.C. 140, 149. See also, to the same effect, *Grant* v. *Sun Shipping Co.* [1948] A.C. 549, 563, *per* Lord du Parcq, *Davies* v. *Swan Motor Co. Ltd.* [1949] 2 K.B. 291, and *Harvey* v. *Road Haulage Executive* [1952] 1 K.B. 120, where Denning L.J. (at p. 126) said that the the last opportunity rule " cannot survive the effect of the Law Reform (Contributory Negligence) Act 1945." See also " Contributory Negligence," by Lord Wright, 13 M.L.R. 1.
[84] (1842) 10 M. & W. 546.

facts justify that conclusion, be treated as the real, substantial, direct or effective cause, and the other dismissed as at best a *causa sine qua non* and ignored for the purpose of legal liability. This is a doctrine affirmed by your Lordship's House and not, in my view, displaced by the Law Reform (Contributory Negligence) Act 1945." [85] An illustration of this is *Sigurdson* v. *British Columbia Electric Ry.*[86] where S., wanting to drive from one side of the street to the other, after beginning to turn, stopped on a street car track in the centre of the road. The driver of the street car had an unobstructed view, but did not see S. until he was seventy-five feet away, so that there was a collision. The jury found the street car driver was negligent in not keeping a proper lookout, but that S. was not negligent. The decision, after being reversed on appeal, was upheld by the Judicial Committee. They disapproved the proposition that " where one party A actually knows of the dangerous situation created by the negligence of another B and fails by the exercise of reasonable care thereafter to avoid the danger A is, generally speaking, solely liable, but that if A by reason of his own negligence did not actually know of the danger, or by his own negligence or deliberate act has disabled himself from becoming aware of the danger, he can only be held liable for a proportion of the resulting damage." On the question of fact the Judicial Committee might have come to a different conclusion, but they held that the jury were not prevented in law from arriving at that conclusion if they thought fit. Again, if the effective cause of the accident is the plaintiff's own negligence he is not entitled to recover any damages.[87] So, where a scaffold was erected which was in breach of the Building Regulations in that one of the uprights was not vertical but the plaintiff, a scaffolder, tried to remedy the defect in a manner described as " fantastically wrong " which caused the scaffold to collapse, whereby he was injured, it was held there was no causal connection between the breach of statutory duty and the plaintiff's injury, and the plaintiff failed to recover.[88] Further, where a workman put his hand deliberately into the moving parts of a crushing machine in order to clean the grooves out, although the employers were in breach of their statutory duty under section 14 (1) of the Factories Act 1937 [89] by their failure to fence, they were held not to be liable in damages, because the cause of the accident in the sense of the operative act and effective cause was the workman's own negligence.[90]

28 **Fault causing the damage.** In considering " fault " what must be ascertained is the fault causing the damage; this may not necessarily be the same as the fault causing the accident which in turn caused the damage. In *Davies* v. *Swan Motor Co.*,[91] a collision took place between an omnibus

[85] Lord Asquith in *Stapley* v. *Gypsum Mines* [1953] A.C. 663, 687.
[86] [1953] A.C. 291. See the interesting note on this case by C. J. Hamson in [1954] C.L.J. 42.
[87] *C.P. Ry.* v. *Fréchette* [1915] A.C. 871.
[88] *Norris* v. *W. Moss & Sons Ltd.* [1954] 1 W.L.R. 346.
[89] Reproduced in Factories Act 1961.
[90] *Rushton* v. *Turner Brothers Asbestos Co. Ltd.* [1960] 1 W.L.R. 96.
[91] [1949] 2 K.B. 291.

and a dust-cart, owing to the negligence of the drivers of both vehicles, in which the plaintiff's husband was killed. He had been standing on the steps of the dust-cart, where he was forbidden to be, and was crushed in the collision, which was in no way caused or contributed to by his presence there. It was nevertheless held that his death was contributed to by his negligence in riding in a forbidden position and the damages payable to his widow were reduced by one-fifth. Similarly, when the plaintiff, employed by the defendants, was, contrary to orders, riding on the back of a traxcavator, which was run into from behind by a dumper negligently driven by another employee of the defendants, the plaintiff was found guilty of contributory negligence, on the ground that he had unreasonably and improperly exposed himself to this particular risk, even though his conduct was not a cause operating to produce this particular accident.[92] A further illustration is *Cork* v. *Kirby Maclean Ltd.*,[93] where an epileptic, who had been warned by his doctor not to work at heights, without telling his employers of this, worked on a platform some twenty feet above the ground when he had a fit, fell to the ground and was killed. The employers were in breach of their statutory duty in not providing toe boards and hand rails, and it was held that the epileptic's conduct and the employers' breach of duty were equally causes of the accident, so that the responsibility for the accident should be equally shared between them.

A moped rider who failed to wear a crash helmet was held to have contributed to his damage to the extent of 15 per cent.[93a]; but a plaintiff who failed to wear an available seat belt in a motor car was not held guilty of contributory negligence when he sustained injury in a motor accident.[94]

1029 **Apportionment of damages.** The 1945 Act provides that when both parties are at fault the plaintiff's damages are to be reduced " having regard to the claimant's share in the responsibility for the damage." The use of the word " responsibility " is intended to exclude the more remote causes of the damage and to concentrate on the responsible causes. To quote Lord Wright in a case decided before the 1945 Act [95]: " The decision . . . must turn not simply on causation but on responsibility; the plaintiff's negligence may be what is often called *causa sine qua non*, yet as regards responsibility it becomes merely evidential or matter of narrative if the defendant acting reasonably could and ought to have avoided the collision." For example, if a man lying drunk in the highway is run over in daylight by a motorist there are two causes of the accident, one on each side, but the parties would not be held to be equally responsible for the accident.[96]

" Share in the responsibility for the damage " therefore means share of

[92] *Jones* v. *Livox Quarries Ltd.* [1952] 2 Q.B. 608.
[93] [1952] 2 All E.R. 402. Also *Laszczyk* v. *N.C.B.* [1954] 1 W.L.R. 1426.
[93a] *O'Connell* v. *Jackson*, 121 New L.J. 618.
[94] *MacDonnell* v. *Kaiser* (1968) 68 D.L.R. (2d) 104; *Grier* v. *Kujama* [1970] 1 Lloyd's Rep. 364.
[95] *M'Lean* v. *Bell* (1932) 48 T.L.R. 467, 469.
[96] See *Davies* v. *Mann* (1842) 10 M. & W. 546, *per* Parke B.; *Paul* v. *G.E. Ry.* (1920) 36 T.L.R. 344.

the blame causing the damage, and the damages are to be apportioned on the basis of blameworthiness. This is expressed by Denning L.J.: " Whilst causation is the decisive factor in determining whether there should be a reduced amount payable to the plaintiff, nevertheless, the amount of the reduction does not depend solely on the degree of causation. The amount of the reduction . . . involves a consideration, not only of the causative potency of a particular factor, but also of its blameworthiness." [97]

30 In *Smith* v. *Bray*,[98] Hilbery J. expressed the view that apportionment should be based on causation, while in *Weaver* v. *Commercial Process Co. Ltd.*[99] Hallett J. put it on the basis of culpability. The present weight of authority is against the basis of causation and is in favour of the basis of blameworthiness.[1] In *Stapley* v. *Gypsum Mines Ltd.*[2] Lord Reid said: " A court must deal broadly with the problem of apportionment and in considering what is just and equitable must have regard to the blameworthiness of each party, but ' the claimant's share in the responsibility for the damage ' cannot, I think, be assessed without considering the relative importance of his acts in causing the damage apart from his blameworthiness." This seems to agree with the passage quoted above from Denning L.J. that in apportioning damage the " causative potency " of a party's acts must be considered as well as his blameworthiness and, indeed, blameworthiness can only be determined after the causative potency of the acts of both parties has been carefully considered.[3]

31 Under the Maritime Conventions Act 1911 when the court apportions the damages and the findings of fact are accepted by the appellate court, the apportionment, in the absence of error of law, will be altered only in very exceptional cases.[4] A similar conclusion has been arrived at when the apportionment is under the Law Reform (Married Women and Tortfeasors) Act 1935.[5] The position is the same under the Law Reform (Contributory Negligence) Act 1945—" as a rule an appellate body does not interfere with the discretion exercised by the judge who tried the case." [6]

[97] *Davies* v. *Swan Motor Co. Ltd.* [1949] 2 K.B. 291, 326.

[98] (1939) 56 T.L.R. 200. He applied the causation test in *Collins* v. *Hertfordshire C.C.* [1947] K.B. 598.

[99] (1947) 63 T.L.R. 466. See the note on this by S. Chapman in 64 L.Q.R. 26.

[1] Williams, *Joint Torts and Contributory Negligence*, p. 290.

[2] [1953] A.C. 663, 682. See the comment on this passage by C. J. Hamson in [1954] C.L.J. 40.

[3] When making an apportionment under the Law Reform (Contributory Negligence) Act 1945, Devlin J. considered two tests and gave effect to both in assessing the bus driver's contribution to be one-third towards the accident suffered by the plaintiff. These were: (1) the " causative potency " test, *i.e.* equal division of responsibility, and (2) the " blameworthiness " test, *i.e.* 20 per cent.: *Cavanagh* v. *London Transport Executive, The Times*, October 23, 1956.

[4] *The MacGregor* [1943] A.C. 197, reversing the C.A. and not following *The Testbank* [1942] P. 75. The same principle was held to apply to the findings of negligence and contributory negligence: *Brown* v. *Thompson* [1968] 1 W.L.R. 1003.

[5] *Ingram* v. *United Automobile Services Ltd.* [1943] K.B. 612; *Maxfield* v. *Llewellyn* [1961] 3 All E.R. 95.

[6] *National Coal Board* v. *England* [1954] A.C. 403, 420, *per* Lord Porter. In this case, however, the H.L. altered the apportionment of the trial judge of one-half to the workmen to one-quarter. Also in *Stapley* v. *Gypsum Mines Ltd.* [1953] A.C. 663, the trial judge's apportionment was altered.

1032 **Costs.** Costs are not usually awarded to the parties in accordance with the degree of responsibility attributed to each.[7] When a plaintiff succeeds, but his damages are reduced, he may nevertheless recover his full costs against a defendant who has not admitted that he has been himself partly at fault.[8]

1033 **Contributory negligence of children.**[9] When a child is negligent, in the sense that he could by the exercise of reasonable care have prevented or avoided the damage in question, he cannot recover full compensation; but in considering what is " reasonable care " the age of the child must be considered. Infancy as such is not a " status conferring right," [10] so that the test of what is contributory negligence is the same in the case of a child as of an adult, modified only to the extent that the degree of care to be expected must be proportioned to the age of the child.

Nevertheless the conduct of an infant plaintiff cannot amount to contributory negligence if it is no more than can be expected of a child of his age. Thus in *Jones* v. *Lawrence* [11] where a seven-year-old boy, without looking to his right or left, ran out from behind a parked van across a road, in order to reach a fun-fair, and collided with a motor-cyclist, he was held not to be guilty of contributory negligence. Evidence was accepted by Cumming-Bruce J. that children of that age are prone to forget what they had been taught about road safety, if something else be uppermost in their minds.

There is no age below which, as a matter of law, it can be said that a child is incapable of contributory negligence. Expressions are to be found referring to children " too young to be capable of contributory negligence," [12] or " of such a tender age as to be regarded in law as incapable of contributory negligence," [13] but these must be taken to be referring to children found on the facts of a particular case to be so young that contributory negligence cannot be attributed to them.

1034 In *Lynch* v. *Nurdin*,[14] the defendant negligently left his horse and cart unattended in the street. The plaintiff, aged seven, got upon the cart in play, another child led the horse on, and the plaintiff was thrown down and injured. The defendant was held liable. It was contended that the plaintiff

[7] *The Salabangka* [1943] P. 13.

[8] *McCarthy* v. *Raylton Productions Ltd.* [1951] W.N. 376 (plaintiff one-third successful awarded full costs); *Smith* v. *L.M.S. Ry.*, 1948 S.C. 125 (plaintiff three-fourths successful awarded full costs); *Howitt* v. *Alexander & Sons*, 1948 S.C. 154 (plaintiff one-third successful awarded full costs); *Smith* v. *W. H. Smith & Sons* [1952] 1 All E.R. 528 (both to blame, no costs); see also *Jay & Sons* v. *Veevers Ltd.* [1946] 1 All E.R. 648.

[9] See articles: " Children and Negligence " (Scott) 116 New L.J. 1394 and (Fridman) 117 New L.J. 35; " Children and Contributory Negligence," 100 I.T.L. 425. The principles under which a young child may be guilty of contributory negligence were considered in *Speirs* v. *Gorman* [1966] N.Z.L.R. 897, Supreme Court.

[10] *Glasgow Corpn.* v. *Taylor* [1922] 1 A.C. 44, 67, *per* Lord Sumner.

[11] [1969] 3 All E.R. 267.

[12] *Per* Hamilton L.J. in *Latham* v. *Johnson* [1913] 1 K.B. 398, 416; 82 L.J.K.B. 258.

[13] *Per* Greer L.J. in *Liddle* v. *Yorkshire* (*North Riding*) *C.C.* [1934] 2 K.B. 101, 125. In *Phipps* v. *Rochester Corpn.* [1955] 1 Q.B. 450 Devlin J. considered the meaning of " tender years."

[14] (1841) 1 Q.B. 29.

was guilty of contributory negligence, in that he could have prevented the accident by the exercise of ordinary care, but Lord Denman C.J. said: " Ordinary care must mean that degree of care which may reasonably be expected from a person in the plaintiff's situation; and this would evidently be very small indeed in so young a child." This has always been regarded as an authoritative statement of the law relating to the contributory negligence of children.[15]

The principle so laid down seems to have been followed in *Yachuk* v. *Oliver Blais Co. Ltd.*[16] There, a boy of nine, with his brother aged seven, obtained petrol from the defendants by untruly stating the purpose for which he wanted it. He set fire to the petrol and was injured. The trial judge found contributory negligence on his part, but this finding on appeal was set aside on the principle that [17] if one gives to a child an explosive substance and the child, with a limited knowledge in respect of the likely effect of the explosion, is tempted to meddle with it to its injury, it cannot be said in answer to a claim on behalf of the child that he did meddle to his own injury, or that he was tempted to do that which a child of his years might be reasonably expected to do."

1035 The defence of contributory negligence failed or was not raised in the following cases: Where a child of three and a half was run over in the street [18]; where a child aged thirteen and a half years emerged from behind a stationary lorry, the driver of which had stopped, signalled to other traffic and had invited her to cross over the road, which she commenced to do without looking out but was struck by an overtaking vehicle [19]; where a child of four, in crossing over a railway bridge, did not walk straight forward but slid along by placing his back against the fencing of the bridge, and fell backwards through an opening in the fencing [20]; where a girl aged ten leant against a protecting bar round the opening of an area, when it gave way and she fell into the area [21]; where a child of four climbed onto a fence adjoining the highway, and the fence collapsed [22]; where a girl of nearly fourteen was sent by her schoolmistress to poke a fire in an adjoining room, when her pinafore caught fire [23]; where a boy of twelve, employed at a railway bookstall, was run over when crossing the railway lines instead of going over the bridge [24]; where a child of seven was poisoned by eating poisonous berries of attractive appearance in a public park [25]; where

[15] *Harrold* v. *Watney* [1898] 2 Q.B. 320, 322, *per* A. L. Smith L.J.; *Glasgow Corpn.* v. *Taylor*, *supra*; *Cooke* v. *Mid. G.W. Ry. of Ireland* [1909] A.C. 229; *Liddle* v. *Yorkshire* (*North Riding*) *C.C.*, *supra*, *per* Slesser L.J. at p. 129; see also *Yachuk* v. *Oliver Blais Co. Ltd.* [1949] A.C. 386.

[16] [1949] A.C. 386.

[17] Expressed by McRuer J.A. [1945] Ont.Rep. 33.

[18] *Gardner* v. *Grace* (1858) 1 F. & F. 359. " The doctrine of contributory negligence does not apply to an infant of tender age ": *per* Channell B.

[19] *Gough* v. *Thorne* [1966] 1 W.L.R. 1387.

[20] *Lay* v. *Midland Ry.* (1875) 34 L.T. 30.

[21] *Jewson* v. *Gatti* (1886) 2 T.L.R. 441.

[22] *Harrold* v. *Watney* [1898] 2 Q.B. 320.

[23] *Smith* v. *Martin and Hull Corpn.* [1911] 2 K.B. 775.

[24] *Robinson* v. *W. H. Smith & Son* (1901) 17 T.L.R. 423.

[25] *Glasgow Corpn.* v. *Taylor* [1922] 1 A.C. 44.

a boy of seven fell off a high wall adjoining the highway [26]; where a girl of seventeen, employed to work a machine for filling soda water bottles, was injured by the bursting of a bottle having failed to wear a mask provided to prevent such an injury [27]; where a boy of ten kicked a bundle of straw into a threshing machine and caught his foot in the moving machinery.[28] On the other hand, a youth of nineteen who was injured while working a circular saw provided at instructional classes of a local authority was held not entitled to recover, as the nature of the saw was perfectly obvious to him,[29] and a child of seven who pulled at a cellar flap negligently left open by the defendant, so that it fell upon him and injured him, was held not entitled to recover, on the ground that his tender years made no difference to the fact that he had contributed by his own negligence to his damage.[30]

1036 In a number of cases children have failed to recover on the ground that there was no negligence on the part of the defendants, so that the question of contributory negligence did not arise. Such cases are: Where a child of three and a half strayed upon a railway line and was injured by a passing train [31]; where a boy of four placed his fingers in a machine, exposed by the defendant for sale in a public place, and his fingers were crushed by the turning of the handle by his brother aged seven [32]; where a boy of nine and a half trapped his fingers in the shafts of a roller secured by a strong rope which was cut by another boy [33]; where a boy of seven, in playing with an unhorsed van left in a public street, fell off and was injured [34]; where a child aged one year and nine months, allowed to play on a piece of land used for tipping rubbish, strayed onto a railway line and was injured.[35]

1037 The Scottish courts have been readier to find contributory negligence in children than the English courts. They have held contributory negligence where a child of four years and eight months, who was not looking where he was going, was run over by a tram,[36] and where a child of five ran against an obstruction in the street.[37] It may be doubted whether the English courts would be prepared to find that children of such an age could

26 *Liddle* v. *Yorkshire (North Riding) C.C.*, *supra*, *per* Greer and Slesser L.JJ. on the assumption that there was negligence (which was not found) on the part of the defendants.
27 *Crocker* v. *Banks* (1888) 4 T.L.R. 324. See also *Grizzle* v. *Frost* (1863) 3 F. & F. 622.
28 *Holdman* v. *Hamlyn* [1943] K.B. 664.
29 *Smerkinich* v. *Newport Corpn.* (1912) 76 J.P. 454.
30 *Hughes* v. *Macfie* (1863) 2 H. & C. 744. The reason given cannot now be considered satisfactory.
31 *Singleton* v. *E.C. Ry.* (1859) 7 C.B.(N.S.) 287.
32 *Mangan* v. *Atterton* (1866) L.R. 1 Ex. 239. This case was doubted, *Clark* v. *Chambers* (1878) 3 Q.B.D. 327, and now would probably be decided otherwise.
33 *Bailey* v. *Neal* (1888) 5 T.L.R. 20.
34 *Donovan* v. *Union Cartage Co.* [1933] 2 K.B. 71.
35 *Schofield* v. *Bolton Corpn.* (1910) 26 T.L.R. 230.
36 *Cass* v. *Edinburgh Tramways*, 1909 S.C. 1068.
37 *Plantza* v. *Glasgow Corpn.*, 1910 S.C. 786. Other cases where contributory negligence was found are: *Grant* v. *Caledonian Ry.* (1870) 9 Macph. 258 (six years); *Fraser* v. *Edinburgh Tramways* (1882) 10 R. 264 (six years).

be guilty of contributory negligence.[38] The only defence open in such cases would be that the defendant was not negligent or that his negligence was not the cause of the accident.

038 The doctrine of identification as laid down in *Waite* v. *North Eastern Ry. Co.*[39] whereby an infant plaintiff was so identified with the adult in charge of him that at common law he was disentitled to recover damages if that adult's negligence contributed towards the happening of the accident, could no longer be considered as good law and in the view of Swift J. was not now part of the law of England.[40] Thus if a child is injured partly through the negligence of the defendant and partly through the negligence of the person in charge of the child, the defendant is liable for the whole damage.[41] Accordingly, where a child, in his grandfather's charge, was crossing the road, and the grandfather startled by the approach of the defendants' omnibus, released the child's hand so that the child was run over, the defendants were held liable, although it was found that there was some degree of negligence also on the part of the grandfather.[42] Again, if a child is injured partly by the negligence of the defendant and partly through the negligence of another child, he can recover the whole of the damage from the defendant, as where a child was injured by his playmate pulling down a cellar flap negligently left open by the defendant.[43]

039 In cases turning on the existence of an invitation or licence it may be that an injured child cannot recover owing to his not being included as a visitor.[44] This occurred in *Burchell* v. *Hickisson*[45] where a child, aged four, went with his sister to the defendant's house. The house was approached by a flight of steps, and the child was left at the bottom while his sister went up the steps. The child, however, attempted to go up the steps, but fell into the area owing to defective rails. The child was held unable to recover, as the invitation did not extend to him unaccompanied by an adult. An infant who is a trespasser cannot generally recover damages.[46]

[38] See *per* Hamilton L.J. in *Latham* v. *Johnson* [1913] 1 K.B. 398, 413. In *Andrews* v. *Freeborough* [1967] 1 Q.B. 1, 8, Willmer L.J. said of a child of eight years that even if she had stepped off the kerb into the path of the defendant's motor-car, " I should have needed a good deal of persuasion before imputing contributory negligence to the child having regard to her tender age."

[39] (1858) E.B. & E. 719, 728.

[40] *Oliver* v. *Birmingham and Midland Omnibus Co.* [1933] 1 K.B. 35, 38, with which Macnaghten J. agreed at p. 41. See also *Mills* v. *Armstrong, The Bernina* (1888) 13 App. Cas. 1.

[41] However see now the provisions of the Law Reform (Married Women and Tortfeasors) Act 1935 and Contribution between tortfeasors, generally, Chap. 12.

[42] *Oliver* v. *Birmingham and Midland Motor Omnibus Co., supra,* not following *Waite* v. *N.E. Ry., supra.*

[43] *Abbott* v. *Macfie* (1863) 2 H. & C. 744.

[44] The duty to children who are visitors (whether invitees or licensees under the old common law) since January 1, 1958, is the common duty of care by the Occupiers' Liability Act 1957. S. 2 (3) (*a*) provides that among the circumstances of the case, which have to be considered " an occupier must be prepared for children to be less careful than adults." Meanwhile this Act does not alter the law affecting trespassers, whether they be children or not.

[45] (1880) 50 L.J.Q.B. 101. See the full discussion of this principle by Devlin J. in *Phipps* v. *Rochester Corpn.* [1955] 1 Q.B. 450. For the law prior to January 1, 1958, relating to invitees and licensees, see 3rd ed., Chap. 9, pp. 190–221.

[46] *Hardy* v. *Central London Ry.* [1920] 3 K.B. 459; *Robert Addie & Sons* v. *Dumbreck* [1929] A.C. 358; for further discussion of this, see Chap. 7.

1040 **Contributory negligence of infirm persons.** The duty to take care is based on the normal so that only when it is known that the abnormal is present is there a duty based on abnormality. For example, when a man is known to have only one eye there may be a duty to him which would not be owed to a two-eyed man.[47] " A measure of care appropriate to the inability or disability of those who are immature or feeble in mind or body is due from others, who know of or ought to anticipate the presence of such persons within the scope and hazard of their own operations." [48] A different question arises, however, when contributory negligence is considered. An abnormal man owes the same duty of care to others as a normal man, so that the driver of a motor-vehicle who runs over a pedestrian cannot set up as a defence that he suffers from defective eyesight or other physical defect which prevented him from avoiding the accident. If two motor-vehicles come into collision, both drivers are judged by the same standards and it does not avail one to show that by reason of his having only one eye, one arm or one leg he was unable to drive as skilfully as a driver with no physical defects. When, therefore, the contributory negligence consists of a breach of duty, mental or physical infirmity has no effect on liability. A deaf driver of a motor-vehicle, whose infirmity has caused or contributed to a motor accident, cannot be better off as plaintiff than he would have been as defendant. Whichever he is, his conduct must be judged by an objective standard based on the normal.

1041 When the contributory negligence does not consist of a breach of duty but is due to the failure of the plaintiff to take reasonable care for his own safety, ought his physical defects to be taken into consideration? Lord Wright said: " a blind or deaf man who crosses the traffic on a busy street cannot complain if he is run over by a careful driver who does not know of and could not be expected to observe and guard against the man's infirmity." [49] In this illustration, the blind or deaf man fails in his action, not because of his contributory negligence, but because there is no breach of a duty to take care on the part of the driver. Again, when the Post Office, under statutory powers, opened a manhole in the pavement and placed the usual light wooden guard round it, it was held that they were not liable to a blind person who collided with the guard and fell into the manhole.[50] Here, again, there was no breach of statutory duty on the part of the Post Office, so that the question of contributory negligence did not arise. Nevertheless in *Haley* v. *London Electricity Board* [51] the House of Lords held that it was the duty of those engaged in operations on the

[47] *Paris* v. *Stepney Borough Council* [1951] A.C. 367.
[48] *Glasgow Corpn.* v. *Taylor* [1922] 1 A.C. 44, 67, *per* Lord Sumner. This dictum was applied in *Haley* v. *London Electricity Board* [1965] A.C. 778.
[49] *Bourhill* v. *Young* [1943] A.C. 92, 109.
[50] *Pritchard* v. *Post Office* [1950] W.N. 310, distinguished and criticised in *Haley* v. *London Electricity Board, supra*, and n. 51.
[51] [1965] A.C. 778. See articles based on this case: " Duty Owed to Blind Pedestrians," 108 S.J. 82. " Duty Owed to Blind Pedestrians " (Harris) 108 S.J. 998; " The Duty of Care Re-examined " (Powell-Smith) 114 L.J. 801; " Duty to the Blind and Otherwise Disabled," 236 L.T. 3.

pavement of a highway to take reasonable care not to act in a way likely to endanger other persons who might reasonably be expected to walk along the pavement. Such duty was owed to blind persons if the operators foresaw or ought to have foreseen that blind persons might walk along the pavement and was in no way different from the duty owed to persons with sight, although the carrying out of the duty might involve extra precautions in the case of blind pedestrians. However in discharging that duty of care towards blind persons the operators were entitled to assume that such persons would take reasonable precautions for their own protection for example by using a stick in order to ascertain if there were anything in his way and by stopping if his stick touched some unfamiliar object over which otherwise he might fall.

A driver of a vehicle in the highway who drives near to a pedestrian in the expectation that the pedestrian will get out of the way in time, but the pedestrian does not because he is deaf and cannot hear the approach of the vehicle,[52] or is elderly and cannot move quickly enough,[53] has been held liable when he cannot stop in time to avoid a collision. In these cases there has been a breach of duty on the part of the driver and the conduct of the pedestrians has been held not to be contributory negligence.

1042 In every operation in which it is necessary to give a warning to persons "within the scope and hazard" of the operation, the failure of those persons to heed it, because being deaf they cannot hear it, being blind they cannot see it, or from some other infirmity they cannot take advantage of it, appears not to amount to contributory negligence on their part.[54] When a woman, almost blind, in walking along the footpath put her foot into an unguarded opening, with a pipe three feet high projecting from it, caused by the removal of a hydrant cover, it was held that her claim succeeded.[55] "On a question of contributory negligence you are entitled to take into account the defective eyesight or other infirmity of a person who meets with an accident."[56]

1043 Drunkenness has to be disregarded in considering contributory negligence. It is no excuse for failing to take reasonable care to prove that the person in question was unable to take proper care owing to the influence of drink or drugs. A drunken man cannot demand from his neighbour a higher standard of care than a sober man or plead drunkenness as an excuse for not taking the same care of himself when drunk as he would have taken when sober.[57] If a passenger in a motor-car is himself drunk so that he does not realise that the driver of the car is also drunk and allows himself to be driven, he is guilty of contributory negligence in the event of a collision.[58]

52 *Gaffney* v. *Dublin United Tramways* [1916] 2 Ir.R. 472; *Smith* v. *Browne* (1891) 28 L.R.Ir. 1.
53 *Daly* v. *Liverpool Corpn.* [1939] 2 All E.R. 142.
54 See *Paul* v. *G.E. Ry.* (1920) 36 T.L.R. 344 (deaf man killed during shunting operations).
55 *M'Kibbin* v. *Glasgow Corpn.*, 1920 S.C. 590.
56 Lord Salvesen at p. 597.
57 See *M'Cormick* v. *Caledonian Ry.* (1903) 5 F. 362 (drunken man killed on railway).
58 See the Australian case of *Insurance Commissioner* v. *Joyce* (1948) 77 C.L.R. 39 noted in 65 L.Q.R. 20.

1044 It is not easy to understand on what principle the view can be taken that the standard of care in contributory negligence on the part of old, young or infirm persons, depending as it does on foreseeability, can differ from that of normal persons. It may well be, however, that as the standard of care is based on the foreseeability of damage to normal people, although it is known that the halt, the maim and the blind, the deaf, the old and the pregnant woman exist, some measure of compensation is given to them for their exclusion from consideration when the general principle of liability is formulated by extending somewhat in their favour the rules of contributory negligence.

1045 **Contributory negligence of workmen.**[59] As has been pointed out,[60] the standard of care in contributory negligence is the same as that in negligence. An exception, however, occurs in the case of workmen who suffer accidents in the course of their employment from breach of statutory duty.[60a] It is instructive to see how this came about, prior to the passing of the Law Reform (Contributory Negligence) Act 1945.

In *Caswell* v. *Worth* [61] an action was brought for personal injuries sustained by the plaintiff, a workman, owing to the neglect of his employer to fence dangerous machinery, as required by statute. The employer pleaded that the plaintiff " wilfully, wrongfully and improperly, against the will and contrary to the express command of defendants " set the machinery in motion and was injured. On demurrer, it was held that this was a good plea. Lord Campbell said: " The statute was clearly not intended to protect persons employed in factories from the consequences of their own misconduct," and referred to *Butterfield* v. *Forrester* [62] as laying down that " the want of ordinary care in avoiding an injury disentitles the party injured from suing." Coleridge J. said: " The action must be subject to the rules of common law; and one of these is, that a want of ordinary care, or wilful misconduct on the part of the plaintiff, is an answer to the action." In *Senior* v. *Ward* [63] an action brought under the Fatal Accidents Acts by the dependants of a miner against an owner of a coal mine for breach of statutory duty, in not testing the cage before allowing the workmen to descend, failed on the ground of the contributory negligence of the deceased. The contributory negligence relied on was that the deceased, knowing that there had been a fire the day before and that the rope might have been damaged, and being warned by the banksman that he had better examine the rope before descending, disregarded the warning. In *Clarke* v. *Holmes* [64] it was held that knowledge of the danger on the part of the servant was not of itself contributory negligence, because " knowledge is only an ingredient in negligence." In that case, machinery had been fenced when the workman entered his employment but subsequently became

59 See articles both entitled: " Employees' contributory negligence " (Whincup) (1968) 118 New L.J. 972 and (Hawke) (1971) 121 New L.J. 1199.

60 *Ante*, § 1016.

60a See Chapter 18, § 1216, *post*.

61 (1856) 5 E. & B. 849.

62 (1809) 11 East 60.

63 (1859) 1 E. & E. 385.

64 (1862) 7 H. & N. 937.

unfenced. The jury found that there was no contributory negligence on the plaintiff's part, and the defendant was accordingly held liable, although "if a jury should find that a party complaining had materially contributed to the injury by his own rashness, the action could not be maintained, inasmuch as it is well established that a plaintiff who has materially contributed to his own injury, by his own negligence, cannot recover, although he may show negligence in the opposite party."[65]

046 In *Britton* v. *Great Western Cotton Co.*[66] a workman was killed through being caught in an unfenced flywheel. The jury negatived contributory negligence, and the employers were held liable. Channell B. agreed with Bramwell B. "with the distinction between a statutory and a common law liability, not by any means questioning the proposition, however, that in either case, contributory negligence on the part of the person injured would afford a defence," and Piggott B. said: "Although there may be a statutory duty imposed on the employer, the workman must still be careful of his own safety." In *Groves* v. *Wimborne*[67] the plaintiff's arm was caught in an unfenced cog-wheel, and there was no contributory negligence on his part, but Vaughan Williams L.J. said: "No one would contend, if there were contributory negligence, that such negligence on the part of the plaintiff would not be an answer to a claim by him for damages in respect of an injury occasioned through the neglect of his master to perform the absolute statutory duty. It would be an answer for the reason that in fact the damage to the plaintiff would not be caused by the failure of the master to perform the absolute statutory duty, but because it would not have happened but for that and something else, namely, the contributory negligence of the plaintiff." In *Dew* v. *United British Steamship Co.*[68] the plaintiff, a coal trimmer working on a ship, fell down an open and unfenced hatchway and the jury found that he was negligent in not taking sufficient precautions, knowing of the open hatchway. All the members of the Court of Appeal[69] held that contributory negligence prevented him from succeeding.

047 In *Higgins* v. *Harrison*[70] the plaintiff was employed on a machine and told to pick up the capsules, which came out at the back of the machine and sometimes dropped on the floor. She interpreted that as an order to get hold of any capsules she could find anywhere, and put her hand in the machine, while it was working, and was injured. It was held that she could not recover because of her contributory negligence. In *Flower* v. *Ebbw Vale Steel, Iron and Coal Co.*[71] the plaintiff was injured owing to dangerous machinery not being fenced. The trial judge (Lawrence J.) said that the question was: "Whether the plaintiff by the exercise of that degree of care

[65] *Per* Cockburn C.J.
[66] (1872) L.R. 7 Ex. 130.
[67] [1898] 2 Q.B. 402, 419.
[68] (1929) 98 L.J.K.B. 88.
[69] Scrutton L.J. at p. 91, Greer L.J. at p. 96, Sankey L.J. at p. 97.
[70] (1932) 25 B.W.C.C. 113.
[71] [1936] A.C. 206.

which an ordinary prudent workman would have shown in the circumstances could have avoided the result of the defendants' breach of duty. . . . In considering whether an ordinary prudent workman would have taken more care than the injured man, the tribunal of fact has to take into account all the circumstances of work in a factory and . . . it is not for every risky thing which a workman in a factory may do in his familiarity with the machinery that a plaintiff ought to be held guilty of contributory negligence." [72] He found that the cause of the accident was the plaintiff's disobedience to orders and gave judgment for the defendants. The Court of Appeal affirmed his judgment, but the House of Lords reversed it, on the ground that disobedience to orders was not proved. Lord Wright expressed the view that contributory negligence in connection with breach of statutory duty meant something more than ordinary negligence and meant misconduct, such as disobedience to orders.[73] In *Craze* v. *Meyer-Dunmore Bottlers' Equipment Co.*[74] the Court of Appeal, after considering the decision of the House of Lords in *Flower* v. *Ebbw Vale Steel, Iron and Coal Co.*, reiterated the view that contributory negligence in its ordinary sense was a defence to an action for breach of statutory duty, and rejected an argument that it was necessary to prove disobedience to orders or misconduct on the part of the workman. In *Caswell* v. *Powell Duffryn Associated Collieries Ltd.*,[75] the House of Lords recognised that contributory negligence was a defence to an action for breach of statutory duty, Lord Atkin saying: " I cannot therefore accept the view that the action for injuries caused by breach of statutory duty differs from an action for injuries caused by any other wrong," pointing out that contributory negligence is based on " the concept of causation " and that " the omission by the plaintiff to use ordinary care may be the sole cause of the injury." Lord Wright added that " some carelessness or inattention to his own safety " was not contributory negligence and that " the jury have to draw the line where mere thoughtlessness or inadvertence or forgetfulness ceases and where negligence begins." In *Lewis* v. *Denye* [76] a circular saw was not securely fenced and the workman was injured. His injury, however, was caused by his failure

[72] [1934] 2 K.B. 132, 139, 140. This test was approved by the H.L. in *Caswell* v. *Powell Duffryn Collieries Ltd.* [1940] A.C. 152, and in *Lewis* v. *Denye* [1940] A.C. 921, and several later cases, *e.g.* see *John Summers & Sons Ltd.* v. *Frost* [1955] A.C.. 740 The casual inadvertence of a workman is not necessarily negligence on his part: *Kansara* v. *Osram (G.E.C.)* [1967] 3 All E.R. 230; *Ryan* v. *Manbre Sugars* (1970) 114 S.J. 492 (failed to avoid stepping on a step which he knew to be slippery).

[73] This seems to be based (pp. 214, 215) on the view in *Caswell* v. *Worth* (1856) 5 E. & B. 849 of Lord Campbell who, however, did not lay down that it was necessary to prove that the workman knowingly and wilfully incurred the risk, but decided, on demurrer, that the facts alleged in the plea showed a knowing and wilful incurring of the risk by the plaintiff which, *a fortiori*, was a defence. See also *Imperial Chemical Industries Ltd.* v. *Shatwell* [1965] A.C. 656.

[74] [1936] W.N. 217.

[75] [1940] A.C. 152, 166 disapproving the decision of the High Court of Australia in *Bourke* v. *Butterfield, Lewis Ltd.* (1926) 38 C.L.R. 354. An illustration of this concept of causation is *Ginty* v. *Belmont Building Supplies Ltd.* [1959] 1 All E.R. 414, where the plaintiff and the employer were in breach of their statutory duty, yet he was not entitled to recover damages against his employer because the fault was the plaintiff's, and there was no fault on the part of the employer which went beyond or was independent of the plaintiff's own omission. However, see *Stocker* v. *Norprint* (1971) 10 K.I.R. 10.

[76] [1940] A.C. 921.

to use a " push stick " and therefore he did not recover, Lord Simon saying: " Negligence in the workman causing or contributing to the accident is a defence in an action alleging that the occupier did not fence securely." [77]

1048 In considering what amounts to contributory negligence on the part of a workman, in addition to the words of Lawrence J. quoted above,[78] the following words of Goddard L.J. are relevant: " I always directed myself to be exceedingly chary of finding contributory negligence where the contributory negligence alleged was the very thing which the statutory duty of the employer was designed to prevent." [79]

1049 The result was that before the passing of the Law Reform (Contributory Negligence) Act 1945 the test for ascertaining whether the workman was guilty of contributory negligence in cases of breach of statutory duty was that laid down by Lawrence J. as explained in *Caswell's* case. Its effect was that carelessness, thoughtlessness, forgetfulness or error of judgment on his part which would have constituted negligence by him as the servant of his employer and rendered his employer liable for his conduct was not regarded as contributory negligence on his part when he suffered an accident. No doubt this was due to the fact that until 1945 contributory negligence was a complete defence to an action for breach of statutory duty, and this was felt to bear rather hardly on the injured workman. Since 1945, however, when damages can be apportioned according to the degree of fault, a different attitude might have been adopted and the workman's position equated to that of all other persons. This, however, was not done. Instead, Sachs L.J. has reiterated that in determining whether a workman's carelessness amounted to contributory negligence where his employers were in breach of statutory duty it had been held that the acts of workmen must not be judged too severely, because, if there were too strict a standard imposed on workmen the effect would be to defeat the object of the regulations. That principle applied also where the workman's carelessness had overstepped the boundary between inadvertence and negligence and the court had to assess culpability. The courts, he argued, must be careful not to emasculate the protection given by the regulations by a sidewind through apportionment; thus the workman must not be judged too harshly for a momentary error where there was a continuing breach of the law by his employers.[80] It has been assumed that Lawrence J.'s words applied equally to common law negligence, but Lord Tucker has said, " I doubt very much whether they were ever intended or could properly be applied to a simple case of common law negligence such as the present where there was no evidence of workpeople performing repetitive work under strain or for long hours at dangerous machines." In *Staveley Iron & Chemical Co.*

77 *Ibid.* p. 930.
78 *Ante,* § 1047.
79 *Hutchinson* v. *L.N.E. Ry.* [1942] 1 K.B. 481, 488. See also to the same effect Lord Greene M.R. in *Hopwood* v. *Rolls-Royce Ltd.* (1947) 176 L.T. 514, 520.
80 *Mullard* v. *Ben Line Steamers Ltd.* [1970] 1 W.L.R. 1414. See also Chap. 18, § 1216, *post.*

Ltd. v. *Jones*,[81] where these words were used, a crane driver lowered a chain so that the load could be lifted. When this was done, the crane driver should have taken the strain, so as to ensure that the load was central, but she did not do so, and the load swung towards the plaintiff and injured him. He succeeded in his action on the ground that the crane driver was negligent and there was no contributory negligence on his part. Where a skilled rigger had adopted a method of lifting that was obviously less safe than the method he would have used had the employers provided the necessary and proper tackle, he was not held guilty of contributory negligence, since due to his employers' negligence he had been prevented from adopting a preferable method.[82] Where a workman carried out his work at a lathe in a manner in which he had been trained by his employers but was injured because this method was in fact dangerous it was held that as the defendants were negligent it did not lie in their mouth to criticise the plaintiff by saying that he ought to have acquired sufficient skill during his five years of employment to realise that in the particular circumstances there was a risk.[83] If a workman fails to choose the safer of two possible means of access he is not necessarily guilty of contributory negligence.[84]

1050 In addition to the cases cited in the preceding paragraphs, illustrations of the principle that a workman will not be considered to have been guilty of contributory negligence although other persons in similar circumstances would have been are: *Grant* v. *Sun Shipping Co.*,[85] *Thurogood* v. *Van den Berghs & Jurgens Ltd.*,[86] *Charles* v. *S. Smith & Sons (England) Ltd.*,[87] *Richard Thomas & Baldwins Ltd.* v. *Cummings*,[88] *John Summers & Sons Ltd.* v. *Frost*.[89] On the other hand contributory negligence to the amount stated has been found to exist in: *Cakebread* v. *Hopping Bros. Ltd.*[90] (woodworking operator, 50 per cent.), *Davies* v. *Swan Motor Co.*[91] (dustman on dustcart, 20 per cent.), *Hilton* v. *F. H. Marshall & Co., Ltd.*[92] (circular saw operator, 25 per cent.), *Clifford* v. *Challen & Son Ltd.*[93] (failure to use protective cream, 5 per cent.), *Cork* v. *Kirby Maclean Ltd.*[94] (painter fails to disclose he suffers from epileptic fits and has been told not to work on heights, 50 per cent.), *Jones* v. *Livox Quarries Ltd.*[95] (quarryman travelling on traxcavator contrary to orders, 20 per cent.), *Smith* v.

81 [1956] A.C. 627, 647. See also the comment on this case in [1956] C.L.J. 158.
82 *Machray* v. *Stewarts & Lloyds Ltd.* [1965] 1 W.L.R. 602.
83 *Herton* v. *Blaw Knox* (1968) 6 K.I.R. 35 applying *General Cleaning Contractors* v. *Christmas* [1953] A.C. 180.
84 *Fowler* v. *B.R.B.* [1969] 1 Lloyd's Rep. 231.
85 [1948] A.C. 549.
86 [1951] 2 K.B. 537.
87 [1954] 1 W.L.R. 451.
88 [1955] A.C. 321.
89 [1955] A.C. 740.
90 [1947] K.B. 641.
91 [1949] 2 K.B. 291.
92 [1951] W.N. 81. *cf. Kerry* v. *Carter* [1969] 1 W.L.R. 1372 where plaintiff aged 18½ was held by the C.A. to have been 2/3 to blame.
93 [1951] 1 K.B. 495.
94 [1952] 2 All E.R. 402.
95 [1952] 2 Q.B. 608.

Chesterfield & District Co-operative Socy.[96] (pastry rolling machine operator, 60 per cent.), *Stapley* v. *Gypsum Mines Ltd.*[97] (quarryman, 80 per cent.), *Harrison* v. *Metropolitan-Vickers Ltd.*[98] (coremaker in foundry, 50 per cent.), *National Coal Board* v. *England*[99] (miner, 50 per cent.), *Jones* v. *Richards*[1] (threshing machine operator, 33⅓ per cent.), *Haynes* v. *Qualcast (Wolverhampton) Ltd.*[2] (failure to wear protective clothing, 75 per cent.), *Hicks* v. *British Transport Commission*[3] (shunter riding on locomotive steps, 50 per cent.), *Heffer* v. *Rover Car Co.*[4] (fooling about with petrol during the luncheon break at his employer's premises, 50 per cent.), *Mullard* v. *Ben Line Steamers Ltd.*[5] (working in a hold in darkness knowing there was an open hatch, 33⅓ per cent.).

1051 **Contributory negligence in rescue cases.** In rescue cases[6] the rescuer cannot be exonerated from a proportion of blame however bravely he may have acted if as a matter of fact he acted unreasonably in all the circumstances. Further, as Morris L.J. said in *Baker* v. *T. E. Hopkins & Son Ltd.*[7] " If a rescuer acts with a wanton disregard of his own safety it might be that in some circumstances it might be held that any injury to him was not the result of the negligence that caused the situation of danger." Nevertheless the courts may be very reluctant to find such a stalwart person guilty of contributory negligence who has suffered loss or damage himself whilst attempting to save the life of another from a position of peril of a kind which had invited rescue and had been created by the defendants' negligence. In assessing the situation a court would always take into consideration and make due allowance for the lack of time available to him for deliberation of the consequences of his so acting and bear in mind that he would have been all too conscious of the fact that his chances of success of his attempt would have diminished moment by moment if he had tarried.

1052 **Appellate court's interference with findings of contributory negligence.** Only in the event of a substantial misjudgment of the factual basis of the apportionment by the trial judge would the Court of Appeal reassess the apportionment.[8] See generally Chapter 15, § 996, *ante*.

2.—AGREEMENT TO RUN THE RISK: " VOLENTI NON FIT INJURIA "[9]

1053 **Meaning of volenti non fit injuria.** A person who makes an agreement with another, either expressly or by implication, to run the risk of injury

96 [1953] 1 W.L.R. 370.
97 [1953] A.C. 663.
98 [1954] 1 W.L.R. 324.
99 [1954] A.C. 403.
1 [1955] 1 W.L.R. 444.
2 [1958] 1 W.L.R. 225, reversed on other grounds by the House of Lords [1959] A.C. 743.
3 [1958] 1 W.L.R. 493.
4 *The Times*, November 26, 1964.
5 *Supra.*
6 See further § 67 *et seq., ante.*
7 [1959] 1 W.L.R. 966, 977.
8 *Jennings* v. *Norman Collison (Contractors)* [1970] 1 All E.R. 1121.
9 See on this subject generally, Williams, *Joint Torts and Contributory Negligence*, Chap. 12: D. M. Gordon, 61 L.Q.R. 140. See also article by Benson: 115 S.J. 181.

caused by that other cannot recover for damage caused to him by any of the risks he agreed to run. This is what is expressed, somewhat clumsily if not conveniently, by the maxim " *volenti non fit injuria*."

1054 **To be distinguished from contributory negligence.** The distinction between consent and contributory negligence prior to 1945 was, perhaps, of no practical importance since at common law they were both complete defences to the plaintiff's claim. It is now necessary to be able to distinguish them since consent is still a total defence whilst contributory negligence operates mainly to reduce damages in proportion to the degree of fault by virtue of the provisions of the Law Reform (Contributory Negligence) Act 1945 as explained *ante*, § 1019 *et seq.* The most important example of this distinction is that contributory negligence always has been a defence to a breach of statutory duty but until recently consent was never a defence at all in such a case.[10] As a result of the House of Lords decision in *I.C.I. Ltd.* v. *Shatwell*, [11] however, a limited exception has now emerged to the rule that a person cannot consent to dispense with a statutory duty imposed on the defendant namely unless it can amount to a waiver of his right of action and provided always that this does not contravene public policy. Lord Reid dealt with the subject matter in this way: " More recently it appears to have been thought in some quarters that, at least as between master and servant, *volenti non fit injuria* is a dead or dying defence. That I think is because in most cases where the defence would now be available it has become usual to base the decision on contributory negligence. Where the plaintiff's own disobedient act is the sole cause of his injury it does not matter in the result whether one says 100 per cent. contributory negligence or *volenti non fit injuria.* But it does matter in a case like the present. If we adopt the inaccurate habit of using the word " negligence " to denote a deliberate act done with full knowledge of the risk it is not surprising that we sometimes get into difficulties. I think that most people would say, without stopping to think of the reason, that there is a world of difference between two fellow-servants collaborating carelessly so that the acts of both contribute to cause injury to one of them, and two fellow-servants combining to disobey an order deliberately though they know the risk involved. It seems reasonable that the injured man should recover some compensation in the former case but not in the latter. If the law treats both as merely cases of negligence it cannot draw a distinction. But in my view the law does and should draw a distinction. In the first case only the partial defence of contributory negligence is available. In the second *volenti non fit injuria* is a complete defence if the employer is not himself at fault and is only liable vicariously for the acts of the fellow-servant. If the plaintiff invited or freely aided and abetted his fellow-servant's disobedience, then he was *volens* in the fullest sense. He cannot complain of the resulting injury either against the fellow-servant or against

10 *Baddeley* v. *Earl of Granville* (1887) 19 Q.B.D. 423.

11 [1965] A.C. 656, followed in *O'Reilly* v. *National Rail and Tramway Appliances Ltd.* [1966] 1 All E.R. 499. Further see Master and Servant Cases, §§ 1059, 1060, *post.*

the master on the ground of his vicarious responsibility for his fellow-servant's conduct."[12]

055 By way of further distinction between the two concepts, a plaintiff may be truly *volens* even where he may have been taking very great care for his own safety, whilst for him to be found guilty of contributory negligence he must have been careless for his own safety. Again, a plaintiff may be held to have been guilty of contributory negligence where he ought to have known of the danger which confronted him even if in point of fact he did not know of it. To the contrary, as is shown in the next paragraphs he cannot be held to have been *volens* unless it can be proved that he had full knowledge both of the nature and extent of the risk involved.

056 **Express and implied agreement.** Cases of an express agreement are to be found when passengers in a railway train or ship agree either not to claim at all if they are injured by the negligence of the servants of the railway authority or shipping company, or to limit their claim to a certain sum.[13] Liability in such a case depends on the terms of the contract. In cases of implied agreement the chief difficulty is not the terms of the agreement, but whether any such agreement is to be inferred at all. The most important question is whether a person, who knows of a risk and then deliberately incurs it, can be said to have made an implied agreement to take the risk of harm upon himself and so be prevented from recovering. So, where an infant defendant exhibited a notice on the facia panel in his motor-car stating that passengers rode in it at their own risk and that he would not be liable for personal injuries, loss or damage, however caused (he being uninsured against such risks) it was held by John Stephenson J. that the infant plaintiff, knowing of this notice and appreciating its terms, impliedly agreed to exempt the defendant from liability having persuaded the latter to take him on a journey by offering to contribute towards the cost of the petrol.[14] In regard to premises after January 1, 1958, the Occupiers' Liability Act 1957, s. 2 (5), provides: "The common duty of care does not impose on an occupier any obligation to a visitor in respect of risks willingly accepted as his by the visitor (the question whether a risk was so accepted to be decided on the same principles as in other cases in which one person owes a duty of care to another)."

57 **Effect of knowledge of danger.** In answering the above question, the first point is that the courts will not find the existence of an implied agreement unless the person who is alleged to have made it had full knowledge of the nature and extent of the risk to be run.[15] The other point is, that

[12] *Ibid.*, at pp. 672, 673.

[13] See *Richardson, Spence & Co.* v. *Rowntree* [1894] A.C. 217; *Thompson* v. *L.M.S. Ry.* [1930] 1 K.B. 41, and see § 1086 *et seq.*

[14] *Buckpitt* v. *Oates* [1968] 1 All E.R. 1145. However *cf. Geier* v. *Kujawa* [1970] 1 Lloyd's Rep. 364, and *Bennett* v. *Tugwell* [1971] 2 W.L.R. 847—plaintiff failed to recover where notice displayed on dashboard, even though owner of car comprehensively insured. See generally the effect of exemption clauses, *post*, § 1108. Article "Liability for Passengers" (Ingman) 120 New L.J. 881.

[15] *Osborne* v. *L. & N.W. Ry.* (1888) 21 Q.B.D. 220.

although the plaintiff had full knowledge of the nature and extent of the risk and, with that knowledge, in fact incurred it, he will not be prevented from recovering unless the circumstances are such as to show that in incurring the risk he did it on the terms that the loss should fall on him and not on some other person. This is because, as has often been pointed out,[16] the maxim is " *volenti non fit injuria* " and not " *scienti non fit injuria.*" Knowledge of the risk is therefore only one of the elements which has to be taken into account, with the other circumstances, in deciding whether the inference that the plaintiff agreed to take the risk upon himself can be drawn. As Lord MacDermott put it,[17] " Evidence of knowledge may sometimes be evidence of assumption of risk, but in the nature of things this need not always be so. Each case must be judged on its own facts." This was first laid down by the House of Lords in *Smith* v. *Baker*.[18]

1058 In *Smith* v. *Baker* a workman was employed by the defendants to drill holes in the rock in a cutting. Near him was a crane, which was used for lifting stones and then swinging them over the workman's head. He knew of the danger but continued at work, and was eventually injured by a stone which fell from the crane. The jury found that he was not guilty of contributory negligence and did not voluntarily undertake a risky employment, and accordingly he was held entitled to succeed, Lord Halsbury saying: " In order to defeat the plaintiff's right by application of the maxim relied on, who would otherwise be entitled to recover, the jury ought to be able to affirm that he consented to the particular thing being done which would involve the risk, and consented to take the risk upon himself." [19] Lord Watson put it as follows: " The question which has most frequently to be considered is not whether he [the plaintiff] voluntarily and rashly exposed himself to injury, but whether he agreed that, if injury should befall him, the risk was to be his and not his master's." [20]

1059 **Master and servant cases.** In master and servant cases based on common law negligence the defence of *volenti non fit injuria* must be applied with caution.[21] This is because " a real assent to the assumption of the risk without compensation must be shown by the circumstances. . . . If, however, a man acts under the compulsion of a duty, such consent should rarely, if ever, be inferred, because a man cannot be said to be ' willing ' unless he is in a position to choose freely." [22] It failed in the following cases: Where a driver was kicked by a horse which he knew to be savage and about which he had complained to his foreman [23]; where a workman, employed by one employer was injured by a bolt negligently dropped by a

[16] *Yarmouth* v. *France* (1887) 19 Q.B.D. 647, *per* Lord Esher M.R.; *Thomas* v. *Quartermaine* (1887) 18 Q.B.D. 685, *per* Bowen L.J.
[17] *Kelly* v. *Farrans Ltd.* [1954] N.I. 41, 47.
[18] [1891] A.C. 325, overruling *Thomas* v. *Quartermaine, supra*, which can only be supported, if at all, on the ground that there was no negligence on the part of the defendants.
[19] *Ibid.* at p. 338.
[20] *Ibid.* at p. 355.
[21] *Bowater* v. *Rowley Regis Corpn.* [1944] K.B. 476.
[22] *Merrington* v. *Ironbridge Metal Works Ltd.* [1952] 2 All E.R. 1101, 1103, *per* Hallett J.
[23] *Yarmouth* v. *France* (1887) 19 Q.B.D. 647.

workman, employed by another employer, who was working above him in the same building [24]; where a workman, in descending from an elevated tramway, from which no ladder or other safe means of descending was provided, slipped and was killed [25]; where a dock labourer engaged in loading a ship was unable to climb up the iron hold ladders, which were blocked, and climbed up a rope ladder, which swung, as a result of which he fell off and was injured [26]; where a schoolmaster was injured by the bursting of a heating apparatus which he knew to be defective and about which he had complained to the school managers [27]; where a commercial traveller was injured in starting a motor-car supplied by his employers, when he knew the starting gear was defective and had complained about it [28]; where a carter was injured owing to the running away of his horse, which he knew had run away on previous occasions, and he had protested against driving the horse.[29] It succeeded where a workman, employed in repairing a house which he knew was damaged by blast, was injured by the collapse of a floor [30]; where scaffolding was moved contrary to the foreman's explicit orders whilst the plaintiff deliberately had remained on top of the platform for the ride along [31]; where a plaintiff purposely struck an unexploded shell with a sledgehammer, although he had recognised what it was, because he had been dared to do it by his fellow employee by way of an amusement.[32]

1060 On the other hand the maxim has no application to an action founded on a breach of statutory duty [33] with the limited exception explained by the House of Lords where the consent may be deemed to be a waiver of a right of action.[34] In such circumstances the employers of the party who has so consented may take the benefit and rely upon that waiver as their total defence to the claim made against them provided they were not themselves at fault. This is very clearly illustrated by the facts in *I.C.I. Ltd.* v. *Shatwell* [35] where two brothers, who were both experienced shot-firers, combined to disobey a statutory order deliberately though they well knew the risk involved of carrying out a continuity test on the electrical circuit connected to the detonators in the defendant's quarry without first taking cover in a proper shelter. As a result there was an explosion in which they were both severely injured and in due course one of them sued his employers on account of the other brother's breach of statutory duty. The

[24] *Thrussell* v. *Handyside* (1888) 20 Q.B.D. 359.
[25] *Williams* v. *Birmingham Battery and Metal Co.* [1899] 2 Q.B. 338.
[26] *Monaghan* v. *Rhodes & Son* [1920] 1 K.B. 487.
[27] *Abbott* v. *Isham* (1920) 90 L.J.K.B. 309.
[28] *Baker* v. *James* [1921] 2 K.B. 674.
[29] *Bowater* v. *Rowley Regis Corpn.* [1944] K.B. 476.
[30] *Taylor* v. *Sims* [1942] 2 All E.R. 375 (another and, it is submitted, a better ground for the decision was that the employer owed no duty to see that the house was safe to work in).
[31] *Bolt* v. *Wm. Moss & Sons* (1966) 110 S.J. 385.
[32] *O'Reilly* v. *National Rail & Tramway Appliances Ltd.* [1966] 1 All E.R. 499.
[33] *Baddeley* v. *Earl of Granville* (1887) 19 Q.B.D. 423. See further § 1215, *post*.
[34] *I.C.I.* v. *Shatwell* [1965] A.C. 656. See § 1054, *ante*.
[35] *Supra*. See articles founded on *I.C.I. Ltd.* v. *Shatwell*: "Breach of Statutory Duty by Workman: Acceptance of the Risk," (Munkman) 114 L.J. 715; "*Volenti Non Fit Injuria*—Detestable Maxim?," (Goodman) 235 L.T. 607; "*Volenti Non Fit Injuria*," 1965 S.L.T. 137; "Causation, Contributory Negligence and *Volenti Non Fit Injuria*," (Atiyah) 43 Can.Bar R. 609.

employers could only be held liable upon the basis of vicarious liability since they were not blameworthy even technically in any respect, the duty being on the two shot-firers personally.[36] They were held not liable for the reason that, although A could not consent to absolve B from his statutory duty, A by his acts had deprived himself of his right to sue B whereupon the employers were entitled to the benefit of that resulting non-actionability through such waiver. Lord Pearce observed: " On the facts it was an implied term (to the benefit of which the employers are vicariously entitled) that George would not sue James for any injury that he might suffer, if an accident occurred. Had an officious bystander raised the possibility, can one doubt that George would have ridiculed it? "[37]

The general result may be summed up in the words of McCardie J.[38]: " The matter is now beyond argument, for in *Smith* v. *Baker* the House of Lords held that knowledge of a danger or defect is evidence, but only evidence, of an agreement by a servant to take the risk upon himself. It does not of itself debar him from remedy. The question is ever one of fact—namely, whether the plaintiff has voluntarily undertaken and contracted to accept the risk for himself."

1061 **General application of the maxim.** The cases hitherto quoted have arisen out of the relation between master and servant but the maxim is general in its operation and has no special application to such cases.[39] In *Osborne* v. *L. & N.W. Ry.*[40] the plaintiff was injured by falling on steps leading to the platform of a railway station. The steps were covered with snow which had been trodden down and frozen over, and the plaintiff admitted that he knew they were dangerous in that condition. The jury found no contributory negligence on the part of the plaintiff, and it was held that the plaintiff was entitled to succeed, the maxim *volenti non fit injuria* having no application. Wills J. said: " If the defendants desire to succeed on the ground that the maxim ' *volenti non fit injuria* ' is applicable, they must obtain a finding of fact ' that the plaintiff freely and voluntarily, with full knowledge of the nature and extent of the risk he ran, impliedly agreed to incur it.' "[41] This statement of the law was expressly approved by the Privy Council in *Letang* v. *Ottawa Electric Ry.*,[42] where the facts were very similar, and may be taken accurately to state what must be proved for this defence to succeed. In *Slater* v. *Clay Cross Co. Ltd.*[43] where the plaintiff was injured due to the negligence of the defendants' engine driver as she was walking along a narrow tunnel on a railway track despite

[36] *Ibid.*, *per* Lord Reid at pp. 674, 675; *per* Lord Hodson at pp. 682, 683; *per* Lord Pearce at pp. 683, 687 and *per* Lord Donovan at p. 692.

[37] *Ibid.*, at p. 688. Further see Lord Donovan at p. 693.

[38] In *Baker* v. *James* [1921] 2 K.B. 674, 683.

[39] *Smith* v. *Baker* [1891] A.C. 325, *per* Lord Halsbury at p. 337, and *per* Lord Herschell at p. 360.

[40] (1888) 21 Q.B.D. 220.

[41] *Ibid.*, at pp. 223, 224, following the words of Lord Esher M.R. in *Yarmouth* v. *France* (1887) 19 Q.B.D. 647, 657.

[42] [1926] A.C. 725, 731.

[43] [1956] 2 Q.B. 264. See *Smith* v. *Austin Lifts Ltd.* [1959] 1 W.L.R. 100, 119.

her knowledge of the danger involved. Denning L.J. said: " Although it may be said that she voluntarily took the risk of danger from the running of the railway in the ordinary and accustomed way, nevertheless she did not take the risk of negligence by the driver. Her knowledge of the danger is a factor in contributory negligence, but is not a bar to the action." [44]

1062 In *Cutler* v. *United Dairies Ltd.*[45] the defendants negligently used a restive horse to draw a van. The horse bolted and went into a field adjoining the plaintiff's garden, when it was caught by the driver, who tried to pacify it. As it continued restive, the driver shouted for help and the plaintiff thereupon attempted to hold the horse, when it suddenly reared and threw him to the ground, causing him injury. Horridge J. put the question to the jury: " Did the plaintiff, freely and voluntarily, with full knowledge of the nature of the risk he ran, impliedly agree to incur it? " To which the jury answered " no," and judgment was thereupon entered for the plaintiff. The Court of Appeal reversed the decision on the ground that there was no evidence on which the jury could answer the question in the negative, and also that the plaintiff's act was a fresh intervening cause, breaking the chain of causation between the negligence and the damage. The second ground alone [46] was sufficient to decide the case in favour of the defendants, and it may well be doubted whether, in the face of the finding of the jury, it could be said that as a matter of law a tribunal was bound to find that the facts showed an implied agreement to take the risk of injury upon himself. It was not doubted that the question put to the jury was the correct one.

1063 **Spectators and participants in sporting activities.** As Diplock L.J. observed: " It is a remarkable thing that in a nation where during the present century so many have spent so much of their leisure in watching other people take part in sports and pastimes there is an almost complete dearth of judicial authority as to the duty of care owed by the actual participants to the spectators." [47] In *Wooldridge* v. *Sumner* [48] an experienced horseman, while taking part in a competition for heavyweight hunters at a horse show, galloped his horse so fast around a corner of the arena that its centrifugal force caused it to follow a wide arc sweeping out to the edge of the course. The horse temporarily got out of control and plunged down a line of potted shrubs bordering the arena to a point where the plaintiff, a photographer, was standing, who having no experience of horses, took fright, stepped back and stumbled into the path of the

44 *Ibid.*, at p. 271.
45 [1933] 2 K.B. 297. *Cf. Haynes* v. *Harwood* [1935] 1 K.B. 146, *post*, § 1071.
46 Scrutton L.J. seemed to regard " *volenti non fit injuria* " as the principal defence, while Slesser L.J. thought " *novus actus interveniens* " the more important.
47 *Wooldridge* v. *Sumner* [1963] 2 Q.B. 43, 65.
48 *Supra.* Although this case is capable of much criticism both on the law and the facts (see Prof. Goodhart 78 L.Q.R. 490) its authority must cause reconsideration of the earlier decisions concerning sports. See articles based on this decision: " Volunteers and Rescuers," 234 L.T. 159; " Injuries to Spectators in the Course of Sporting Activities," 25 M.L.R. 738; " The Sportsmen's Charter," 78 L.Q.R. 490. Distinguished in *Quire* v. *Coates* [1964] S.A.S.R. 294 and *Rootes* v. *Shelton* (1947) 41 A.L.T.R. 172.

animal. Diplock L.J. added " The practical result of this analysis of the application of the common law of negligence to participant and spectator would, I think be expressed by the common man in some such terms as these: ' A person attending a game or competition takes the risk of any damage caused to him by any act of a participant done in the course of and for the purposes of the game or competition notwithstanding that such act may involve an error of judgment or a lapse of skill, unless the participant's conduct is such as to evince a reckless disregard of the spectator's safety.' [48a] The spectator takes the risk because such an act involves no breach of the duty of care owed by the participant to him. He does not take the risk by virtue of the doctrine expressed or obscured by the maxim *volenti non fit injuria*. . . . In my view, the maxim in the absence of expressed contract has no application to negligence simpliciter where the duty of care is based solely upon proximity or ' neighbourship ' in the Atkinian sense. The maxim in English law presupposes a tortious act by the defendant. The consent that is relevant is not consent to the risk of injury but consent to the lack of reasonable care that may produce that risk, and requires on the part of the plaintiff at the time at which he gives his consent full knowledge of the nature and extent of the risk that he ran." [49]

1064 On the other hand as between participants themselves in *Rootes* v. *Shelton* [50] it was held that where a participant in a game or pastime is injured by the act or omission of another participant, the existence and extent of a duty of care are to be determined in the light of all the circumstances, including the risks, which may reasonably be inferred to have been accepted by the fact of participation. The rules of the game are a relevant but not a conclusive factor. A water skier brought an action against the driver of the towing speed boat, where he, one of a group of skiers which included the driver, was performing a complicated manoeuvre and was injured by a collision with a stationary obstruction of which the driver had given him no warning. It was held that the onus was on the driver to establish voluntary acceptance of a risk not inherent in the pastime. Nevertheless consent may sometimes be implied between persons engaged in sport.[51] As Lord Denning M.R. said: " I agree that in an ordinary fight with fists there is no cause of action to either of them for any injury suffered. The reason is that each of the participants in a fight voluntarily takes upon himself the risk of incidental injuries to himself. *Volenti non fit injuria.* But he does not take on himself the risk of a savage blow out of all proportion to the occasion. The man who strikes a blow of such severity is liable in damage unless he can prove accident or self-defence." [52] In *Cleghorn* v. *Oldham* [53] the plaintiff was carrying the defendant's golf clubs during a game between the defendant and the plaintiff's brother, when the plaintiff was struck by a golf club owing to the negligence of the defendant,

[48a] A competitor in a race " is expected to go as fast as he can, so long as he is not foolhardy," per Lord Denning M.R. in *Wilks* v. *Cheltenham Homeguard Motor Cycle and Light Car Club* [1971] W.L.R. 668, at p. 670.

[49] *Ibid.*, at pp. 68, 69. [50] (1947) 41 A.L.J.R. 172. [51] *R.* v. *Coney* (1882) 8 Q.B.D. 534.

[52] *Lane* v. *Holloway* [1968] 1 Q.B. 379, 386, 387. [53] (1927) 43 T.L.R. 465.

who was demonstrating a stroke to the brother. Swift J. gave judgment for the plaintiff on the ground that " no authority had been cited for the proposition that a person ever took the risk of anybody being negligent unless there was an express agreement on proper facts to that effect." [54] However, where a golfer had hooked his tee-shot and his ball had struck the plaintiff, who was another player on the golf course playing about 200 yards ahead, his action failed on other grounds namely that the consequences were not foreseeable, alternatively the risk was so slight of such a happening that it could be ignored in all the circumstances.[55]

1065 By way of distinction the occupiers of the premises or the promoters of the sport on such premises do owe a duty of care to their lawful visitors who include both the spectators, invited to watch, and the participants themselves. The duty is the " common duty of care " as explained in Chapter 8.[56] Accordingly it is a question of fact in each case whether or not the spectator or participant has agreed to take upon himself the relevant risk.[57] For example, a rugby footballer was held willingly to have accepted the risks of playing the game on the defendants' ground which, although it complied with the bye-laws of the Rugby Football League, had a concrete wall running at a distance of 7 feet 3 inches away from and along the touchline.[58] On the other hand, where the plaintiff was injured through slipping on the polished floor of a hall in which physical training classes were conducted, it was held that he did not agree to take upon himself the risk of slipping upon a floor which was not reasonably fit for the purpose of physical training.[59]

Where a plaintiff, a ballet dancer of good physique, had enrolled in one of the defendant local authority's judo classes and in his first lesson had his arm broken during the course of a contest, it was held that since the instructor had allowed the pupils to " run before they could walk " and had permitted a practice to turn into a competition, the defendants were liable since the risk of injury was a foreseeable consequence to which the plaintiff had not consented. This decision was reversed by the Court of Appeal not on the principle involved but only on the facts.[60]

1066 **Other cases of acceptance of ordinary risks.** A fireman, attending a fire in the course of his duty, although he undertakes to bear the ordinary risks of a fire does not undertake to accept without compensation the risk of an explosion caused by the negligence of the occupier of the building on

[54] The reference to " express " agreement must be a slip, as the agreement may be implied. A visitor to a golf course takes the course as he finds it and accepts the risk of the game. If he is injured, but there is no negligence in the design or construction of the course or in the conduct of another player, he has no remedy: *Potter* v. *Carlisle and Cliftonville Golf Club Ltd.* [1939] N.Ir. 114.

[55] *Brewer* v. *Delo* (1967) 117 New L.J. 575.

[56] See especially § 372 *et seq., ante.*

[57] See § 364, " *Volenti non fit injuria.*"

[58] *Simms* v. *Leigh Rugby Football Club* [1969] 2 All E.R. 923.

[59] *Gillmore* v. *L.C.C.* [1938] 4 All E.R. 331.

[60] *Conrad* v. *Inner London Education Authority* (1966) 116 New L.J. 1630; on appeal (1967) 111 S.J. 684.

fire.[61] Likewise a policeman who uses his vehicle as a road block against an escaping motorist does not voluntarily assume the risk of injury resulting therefrom when that motorist drives at high speed into the police car.[62] Where the plaintiff delivered a valuable fur coat to the defendants' shop, where it was put on display in the shop window but left there all day and night, and was stolen in a " smash and grab " raid it was held that the defendants had been negligent in taking an unjustifiable risk and they could not rely upon the principle of *volenti*.[63] Lord MacDermott sums up the position in these words [64]: " The question raised by a plea of *volenti non fit injuria* is not whether the injured party consented to run the risk of being hurt, but whether he consented to run that risk at his own expense so that he and not the party alleged to be negligent should bear the loss in the event of injury. In other words, the consent that is relevant is not consent to the risk of injury but consent to the lack of reasonable care that may produce that risk."

From these cases it will be seen that voluntary exposure to risk on the part of the plaintiff is not, of itself, a defence to an action for negligence against the defendant, but its only relevance is that it may be evidence of an agreement by the plaintiff to bear any loss due to that risk.

1067 **Nature of the agreement.** Whether the agreement must be a legal contract has not been considered except in master and servant cases. It has been held that when an employer is under a duty to his workmen imposed by statute, the maxim *volenti non fit injuria* does not apply, because the maxim only applies when there is an agreement between the parties and it is not open to an employer to contract out of statutory duty which he owes to his workmen.[65] An infant has been held not to be bound by the maxim when he exempted his employer by deed from liability for negligence and the deed was held to be void because it was not for the infant's benefit.[66] These instances seem to indicate that the agreement must be a contract enforceable at law.[67]

1068 **Volenti non fit injuria and inevitable accident.** The nature of the defence of *volenti non fit injuria* having been explained, it is necessary to consider it in connection with three different sets of circumstances, premising that in all these circumstances there is negligence on the defendant's part.[68] If

[61] *Merrington* v. *Ironbridge Metal Works Ltd.* [1952] 2 All E.R. 1101.
[62] *Hambley* v. *Shepley* (1967) 63 D.L.R. (2d) 94.
[63] *Saunders (Mayfair) Furs* v. *Davies* (1965) 109 S.J. 922.
[64] *Kelly* v. *Farrans Ltd.* [1954] N.I. 41.
[65] *Baddeley* v. *Granville* (1887) 19 Q.B.D. 423; *Davies* v. *Thomas Owen & Co.* [1919] 2 K.B. 39; *Wheeler* v. *New Merton Board Mills* [1933] 2 K.B. 669.
[66] *Olsen* v. *Corry* [1936] 3 All E.R. 241.
[67] Williams, *Joint Torts and Contributory Negligence*, p. 312, inclines to the opposite view.
[68] In *Smith* v. *Baker* [1891] A.C. 325, Lord Bramwell, who dissented, said (p. 344): " In the course of the argument I said that the maxim ' *volenti non fit injuria* ' did not apply to a case of negligence; that a person was never *volens* that he should be injured by negligence—at least, unless he specially agreed to it; I think so still." In so far as this means that the maxim is no defence in an action of negligence unless there is an agreement, express or implied, to take the risk of injury by negligence it is accurate; otherwise it seems to go too far.

there is no negligence on the defendant's part, then, as far as the subject-matter of this book is concerned, there is no need to rely on this defence. A person who is injured by inevitable accident, *e.g.* by a horse which bolts and runs onto the footpath, knocking him down, is prevented from recovering not because he has agreed to take the risk of such accidents upon himself, but because there is no negligence on the part of the defendant.[69] Similarly, an onlooker at a cricket or football match or at any other sport who is injured by the ball or the players, in the course of the game, getting among the spectators cannot recover without proving negligence,[70] and, when there is negligence, he is not debarred from recovering on the ground of *volenti non fit injuria.*[71] The three cases are: (1) where the plaintiff does not see a danger created by the negligence of the defendant, although he ought to have seen it; (2) where the plaintiff does see the danger and decides to run the risk of it; and (3) where the plaintiff sees the danger and agrees to exempt the defendant from liability.

1069 **[1] Plaintiff does not see danger.** The plaintiff does not see a danger created by the negligence of the defendant, although he ought to have seen it if he had taken reasonable care. This is contributory negligence on the part of the plaintiff and whether or not it will prevent the plaintiff from recovering in full depends on the ordinary law of contributory negligence.[72] In such a case the maxim has no application because the plaintiff, owing to his own negligence, does not know there is a risk to be run.

1070 **[2] Plaintiff sees danger and decides to run the risk.** The plaintiff does see a danger created by the negligence of the defendant, and decides to run the risk of it. If, after deciding to run it, he does not exercise reasonable care he is guilty of contributory negligence and may be unable to recover in full on that ground. If, on the other hand, there is no contributory negligence on his part after making his decision, the question arises, Does his decision to run the risk of itself prevent him from recovering damages? The answer is that it does not prevent him from recovering, provided that his conduct under all the circumstance was that of a reasonable man.[73] If a reasonable man would not have run the risk, then the person running it is guilty of

[69] If "*volenti non fit injuria*" were a defence in such a case "no person ever ought to have been awarded damages for being run over in London streets; for no one (at all events some years ago, before the admirable police regulations of later years) could have crossed London streets without knowing that there was a risk of being run over," *per* Lord Halsbury in *Smith* v. *Baker*, *supra*, at p. 337. For inevitable accident, see Chap. 26.

[70] *Hall* v. *Brooklands Auto-Racing Club* [1933] 1 K.B. 205 (motor-car at motor racing course leaves the track and injures spectator); *Potter* v. *Carlisle and Cliftonville Golf Club Ltd.* [1939] N.I. 114; *Murray* v. *Harringay Arena Ltd.* [1951] 2 K.B. 529 (child spectator at ice hockey match injured by the puck leaving the arena, without negligence, fails).

[71] *Cleghorn* v. *Oldham* (1927) 43 T.L.R. 465; *Welsh* v. *Canterbury and Paragon Ltd.* (1894) 10 T.L.R. 478; *McKee* v. *Malcolmson* [1925] N.I. 120.

[72] *Ante*, § 1004 *et seq.*

[73] *Clayards* v. *Dethick* (1848) 12 Q.B. 439, which was followed in *Behrens* v. *Bertram Mills Circus Ltd.* [1957] 2 Q.B. 1. See also *Adams* v. *L. & Y. Ry.* (1869) L.R. 4 C.P. 739; *Lee* v. *Nixey* (1890) 63 L.T. 285; *Robson* v. *N.E. Ry.* (1875) L.R. 10 Q.B. 271; *Rose* v. *N.E. Ry.* (1876) 2 Ex.D. 248; *Porter* v. *Jones* [1942] 2 All E.R. 570; *Summers* v. *Salford Corpn.* [1943] A.C. 283; *Sayers* v. *Harlow U.D.C.* [1958] 1 W.L.R. 623. *Ante*, § 1010. See also *per* Lord Halsbury in note 69, *ante*, § 1068.

contributory negligence. To say that a person, who, by negligence, creates any risk or danger, however slight, thereby imposes upon those who decide to take the risk the burden of acting at their peril, is clearly wrong. At what point the risk becomes great enough to throw the burden of it upon the person running it is a question of degree and, therefore, of fact, depending on whether or not it was reasonable to run it. In any event this is a question of contributory negligence and is wrongly dealt with as a case of *volenti non fit injuria*. In *Torrance* v. *Ilford U.D.C.*[74] the plaintiff's horse was drawing a heavy load along a road in the defendant's district. The road was under repair, and covered with five inches of granite stones which had not been rolled in. The plaintiff's driver drove the horse over the stones, as a result of which it strained itself and died. The jury found that the defendants were negligent, and that the driver could not by taking reasonable care have avoided the consequences of the defendant's negligence. Judgment was thereupon given for the plaintiff, but this was reversed on appeal, on the ground that the driver had elected to run the risk. It is submitted that the question should have been whether the driver's conduct was reasonable under the circumstances, and that, on the jury's finding, judgment should have been entered for the plaintiff or a new trial ordered. The defence of *volenti non fit injuria* failed in *Behrens* v. *Bertram Mills Circus Ltd.*[75] Devlin J. saying: " If a man is on the highway and he sees elephants approaching in procession, the law does not require him to elect between turning down a side street or accepting the risk of their misbehaviour if he goes on; but if he sees them stampeding and remains where he is because he considers that he has as much right to the highway as they have, he might fail to recover."

1071 **Rescue cases.** Further illustrations of the principle stated in the preceding paragraph are to be found in those cases in which a plaintiff, in no danger himself deliberately runs the risk of danger, negligently created by the defendant, in order to rescue some third party. The plaintiff in such cases can recover if his conduct was, under the circumstances, that of a reasonable man, and was the natural and probable consequence of the defendant's negligence.[76]

In *Brandon* v. *Osborne, Garrett & Co.*[77] a husband and wife were in a shop, when a skylight broke owing to the defendant's negligence and a portion of the glass fell and struck the husband. The wife was not in danger but, reasonably believing her husband to be in danger, she clutched her husband's arm and tried to pull him away, as a result of which she was injured. Swift J. in giving judgment for the wife, said: " It seems to me that where a person sustains injury through a combination of acts, some done by the defendants and some by himself, it is for the jury to say, having regard to the whole of the circumstances, whether (1) the injury is the

[74] (1909) 25 T.L.R. 355.
[75] [1957] 2 Q.B. 1, 20.
[76] Further see Contributory negligence in rescue cases § 1051, *ante*.
[77] [1924] 1 K.B. 548.

natural and probable consequence of the defendants' act, and (2) whether the plaintiff has been guilty of contributory negligence."[78] He explains what he means by contributory negligence in this connection by saying: "If she [the wife] did something which a reasonable person in the circumstances ought not to have done she would not be entitled to damages, but if what she did was done instinctively and was in the circumstances a natural and proper thing to do, I think she is entitled to recover."[79] As has been pointed out,[80] it is not necessary for the act to be done instinctively, but it is necessary that it should be "a natural and proper," or in other words a reasonable, thing to do, and in considering whether or not an act is reasonable the fact that is it instinctive is an element to be taken into account.

1072 The decision in *Brandon* v. *Osborne, Garrett & Co.*[77] was approved by the Court of Appeal in *Haynes* v. *Harwood*,[81] where the plaintiff was a policeman who rushed out of a police station and stopped the defendants' horses which were bolting down a street, in which there were a large number of people, including children. The defendants' horses had bolted due to their being negligently left unattended in the street, and the plaintiff was injured in stopping them. It was held that the plaintiff could recover, as his injuries were the natural and probable consequences of the defendants' negligence, and the maxim "*volenti non fit injuria*" did not apply. In this case there was much discussion of a suggested legal or moral duty to save life which was put in peril by the negligence of the defendant. It is quite clear that there is no legal duty on a person to take active steps to prevent another from being injured by the negligence of a third person.[82] The so-called moral duty, which depends on the relationship of the rescuer to the rescued and the imminence and gravity of the danger, is merely an element which has to be taken into account in deciding whether the act of the rescuer was the reasonable and probable consequence of the defendants' negligence. If the person endangered is unable, by reason of age, infirmity or ignorance of the impending danger, to save himself, it is a natural and probable consequence of the negligence creating the danger that some other person will try to rescue the person in danger. As Maugham L.J. said: "In deciding whether such a rescuer is justified in putting himself into a position of such great peril, the law has to measure the interests which he sought to protect and the other interests involved. We have all heard of the reasonable man whom the law postulates in certain circumstances; the reasonable man here must be endowed with qualities of energy and courage, and he is not to be deprived of a remedy because he has in a marked degree a desire to save human life when in

[78] *Ibid.*, at p. 555.
[79] *Ibid.*, at p. 552.
[80] *Haynes* v. *Harwood* [1935] 1 K.B. 146, *per* Greer L.J. at p. 158, and *per* Maugham L.J. at p. 164.
[81] [1935] 1 K.B. 146.
[82] *Per* Swift J. in *Brandon* v. *Osborne, Garrett & Co., supra*, at p. 554; *per* Maugham L.J. in *Haynes* v. *Harwood, supra*, at p. 161.

peril. So regarded, the present plaintiff was not acting unreasonably in the risks he took." [83] The same result would follow even if the rescuer were not a policeman.[84] A ship, which comes to the scene of a collision between two ships in order to rescue life, and is itself damaged through one of the other ships colliding with it, is not prevented from recovering on the ground that it had voluntarily assumed the risk.[85]

1073 Whether a right of action arises at the suit of the "rescuer" when the negligent act is committed by the person whom he attempts to rescue was considered by Barry J. in *Baker* v. *T. E. Hopkins & Sons Ltd.*[86] where he observed: "Were I called upon to decide it I should with some hesitation and doubt have taken this view: Although no one owes a duty to anyone else to preserve his own safety yet if by his own carelessness a man puts himself into a position of peril of a kind that invites rescue he would in law be liable for any injury caused to someone whom he ought to have foreseen would attempt to come to his aid." On appeal Morris L.J.[87] said that if a man "... actuated by an impulsive desire to save life acts bravely and promptly and subjugates any timorous over-concern for his own well-being or comfort, I cannot think that it would be either rational or seemly to say that he freely and voluntarily agreed to incur the risks of the situation which had been created by [another man's] negligence." The facts were that where a doctor, attempting to rescue the lives of two men working down a well, who had been overcome by carbon monoxide poisoning, himself became affected and died, his administrators were not prevented from recovering damages. In *Videan* v. *British Transport Commission* [88] Lord Denning M.R. stated: "the right of the rescuer is an independent right and is not derived from that of the victim. The victim may have been guilty of contributory negligence—or his right may be excluded by contractual stipulation—but still the rescuer can sue. So also the victim may, as here, be a trespasser and excluded on that ground, but still the rescuer can sue. Foreseeability is necessary, but not foreseeability of the particular emergency that arose." [89]

1074 An attempt to save property may be the natural and probable consequence of the defendant's negligence and, if it be, the person making the attempt will not be prevented from recovering unless, in the circumstances, he assumed an unreasonable risk. A servant, employed to watch premises and guard them from fire, who, on finding that a fire had broken out, went out and gave warning and then returned and was burnt, succeeded on the ground that he was performing his duty and was not a volunteer.[90] When a guard of a goods train was fatally injured in trying to save his train from

[83] *Haynes* v. *Harwood, supra*, at p. 162.
[84] *Morgan* v. *Aylen* [1942] 1 All E.R. 489.
[85] *The Gusty and The Daniel M.* [1940] P. 159.
[86] [1958] 1 W.L.R. 993 at p. 1004.
[87] [1959] 1 W.L.R. 966 at p. 976.
[88] [1963] 2 Q.B. 650; see article: "*Au Secour*," 97 I.L.T. 355.
[89] *Ibid.*, at p. 669.
[90] *D'Urso* v. *Sanson* [1939] 4 All E.R. 26.

a collision with some wagons which had run away owing to the defendants' negligence, his representatives were held entitled to recover on the finding that his attempt to save his employers' property was justifiable and a natural and probable consequence of the defendants' negligence.[91] Again, where a servant of some wagon repairers, on seeing that a railway company's wagon was on fire, went to try to extinguish the fire and was injured, he was held entitled to recover.[92]

1075 **[3] Plaintiff sees the danger and exempts defendant from liability.** The plaintiff sees the danger created by the negligence of the defendant, and agrees, expressly or by implication, to exempt the defendant from liability for any damage caused to him through that danger. This is the only case in which *volenti non fit injuria* applies, and its effect is to prevent the plaintiff from recovering. It is sometimes said that the maxim applies if the plaintiff consents to run the risk. This is accurate, as long as it is understood that consent means an agreement.[93] It has also been said that the maxim rather implies an election on the part of the plaintiff, than a contract. For the reasons given above, a plaintiff is entitled to elect to run a risk rather than have his liberty of action curtailed, provided that his conduct is reasonable.

1076 Apart from the case of a contract, the plaintiff only becomes a "volunteer" so as to be prevented from recovering, when he has done something to break the chain of causation between the defendant's negligence and the damage, so that he is "a new intervening cause."[94] The principles determining what is a new intervening cause are the same whether the cause in question is the act of the plaintiff or of a third party, and there is no necessity for invoking the maxim in such a case. In *Ilott* v. *Wilkes*[95] the plaintiff was a trespasser who was shot by a spring-gun, after entering the defendants' wood with the knowledge that spring-guns were set there. It was held that he could not recover, because the maxim applied and he had voluntarily exposed himself to the risk. In this case the plaintiff was a "volunteer," in the sense that the trespass was both wrongful and deliberate, but it would seem that the maxim has no application. A trespasser cannot recover for injuries he sustains through the condition of the land or buildings on which he trespasses, not because he voluntarily exposes himself to the risk, but because the owner owes no duty to a person whom he has neither invited nor permitted to come on his property. In addition, a landowner must not set a trap or do any act with the intention of injuring a trespasser[96]; if he does so, the fact that he warns the trespasser in advance will not alter his legal liability.

91 *Steel* v. *Glasgow Iron and Steel Co.*, 1944 S.C. 237.
92 *Hyett* v. *G.W. Ry.* [1948] 1 K.B. 345.
93 *Ante*, § 1056.
94 *Cutler* v. *United Dairies* [1933] 2 K.B. 297 is an example of this.
95 (1820) 3 B. & Ald. 304; in *Dann* v. *Hamilton* [1939] 1 K.B. 509 Asquith J. expressed the opinion that the case was rightly decided on this point.
96 *Bird* v. *Holbrook* (1828) 4 Bing. 628; *Hillen* v. *I.C.I.* (*Alkali*) *Ltd.* [1936] A.C. 65, 70, *per* Lord Atkin.

1077 In the cases considered in the preceding paragraphs, the defendant by his negligence, created the danger before the plaintiff acted and the question then was whether by his action in the face of that danger the plaintiff had assumed an unreasonable risk. There may, however, be cases when the plaintiff acts first and the defendant's negligence follows after, when the question will be whether the plaintiff, in view of the defendant's possible subsequent negligence, is prevented from recovering. This occurred in *Dann* v. *Hamilton*,[97] where the plaintiff, knowing that the defendant was drunk, nevertheless went as a passenger in a motor-car driven by the defendant and was injured in a collision caused by the defendant's drunkenness. The plaintiff succeeded and the maxim was held not to apply in such a case. It was suggested that in a case of extreme drunkenness on the part of a defendant, a plaintiff in similar circumstances might be defeated by the maxim.[98]

It would appear that the maxim has no application in a case of this kind, but that the right of the plaintiff to succeed in full depends on whether his conduct amounts to contributory negligence or not.[99]

1078 Where a plaintiff walked along a narrow tunnel on a railway track over land owned and occupied by the defendants, when she was struck and injured by a train driven by the defendants' servant, it was held that the driver was negligent in failing to observe instructions to whistle and to slow down when entering the tunnel. Accordingly the plaintiff recovered, but subject to a deduction of 40 per cent. of the damages.[1] On the defence of *volenti non fit injuria*, *Dann* v. *Hamilton* [97] was followed, Denning L.J. saying [2]: " Applying that decision to this case, it seems to me that when this lady walked into the tunnel, although it may be said that she voluntarily took the risk of danger from the running of the railway in the ordinary and accustomed way, nevertheless she did not take the risk of negligence in the driver. Her knowledge of the danger is a factor in contributory

[97] [1939] 1 K.B. 509. Reference was made to *Woodley* v. *Metropolitan District Ry.* (1877) 2 Ex.D. 384, 394, where Mellish L.J. said: " A man is employed . . . to scrape a particular street, and for the space of a fortnight he has the opportunity of observing that a particular hansom cabman drives his cab with extremely little regard for the safety of the men who scrape the streets. At the end of a fortnight the man who scrapes the streets is negligently run over by the cabman. An action is brought . . . and the cabman says in his defence: ' You know my style of driving, you had seen me drive for a fortnight; I was only driving in my usual style.' ' Yes, but your usual style of driving is a very negligent style, and my having seen you drive for a fortnight has nothing to do with it.' It will not be disputed that the scraper of the streets . . . is entitled to maintain his action."

[98] *Ibid.*, at p. 518.

[99] Asquith J., when Lord Asquith, pointed out in 69 L.Q.R. 317 that not only was contributory negligence not pleaded but that he encouraged counsel for the defence to ask for leave to amend by adding this plea, but that he did not do so. In *Dawrant* v. *Nutt* [1961] 1 W.L.R. 253 it was held that any person using a highway owed a duty to other users to take reasonable care of himself, and the plaintiff in travelling as a passenger in a motor-cycle combination knowing that it was not showing any lights in front was in breach of this duty and was, accordingly, guilty of some degree of contributory negligence, *viz.*, one quarter. Likewise in *Prior* v. *Kyle* (1965) 52 D.L.R. (2d) 272 where a 17 year-old female passenger continued to accompany the defendant in his motor-car, although she knew that he had agreed to race another, but was injured in a head-on collision during the speeding, it was held that she was guilty of contributory negligence to the extent of one quarter.

[1] *Slater* v. *Clay Cross Co. Ltd.* [1956] 2 Q.B. 264.

[2] *Ibid.* at p. 271.

negligence, but is not a bar to the action." A patient who submits to a surgical operation agrees to accept the risk of the operation but not the additional risk of the surgeon's negligence. However, surgical operations can be justified according to the circumstances both on the basis that consent nullifies wrongfulness and on necessity.[3] A man who, from drunkenness or any other cause, lies down in the middle of a busy street does not agree to accept the risk of being run over but, if he be, his failure to recover damages in full will be on the ground of contributory negligence. If the maxim does not apply when a passenger allows himself to be driven by a man who is, to his knowledge, half drunk, it is difficult to see how it can apply if the driver is completely drunk. In the latter case, the passenger's conduct would be extremely rash, but at the most could only be contributory negligence.[4]

For the important distinctions between *volenti non fit injuria* and contributory negligence, see *ante*, §§ 1054, 1055.

3.—INEVITABLE ACCIDENT

1079 **Meaning of inevitable accident.** In an action based on negligence it is, of course, open to a defendant to prove that there was no negligence on his part, and he will then succeed in the action. If, however, the facts proved by the plaintiff raise a prima facie case of negligence against the defendant, the burden of proof is then thrown upon the defendant to establish facts negativing his liability, and one way in which he can do this is by proving inevitable accident.

Inevitable accident is where a person, in doing an act which he lawfully may do, causes damage without either negligence or intention on his part. In maritime cases it has been described as follows: " An inevitable accident in point of law is this: *viz.*, that which the party charged with the offence could not possibly prevent by the exercise of ordinary care, caution, and maritime skill." [5] As to other cases, Lopes L.J. after quoting: " Inevitable accident is that which the party charged with the damage could not possibly

[3] *Bravery* v. *Bravery* [1954] 1 W.L.R. 1169 (consent to sterilisation). Where anaesthesia was administered against a patient's express wish see *Beausoleil* v. *La Communauté des Soeurs de la Charité de la Providence* (1964) 53 D.L.R. (2d) 65.

[4] In the Australian case of *Insurance Commissioner* v. *Joyce* (1948) 77 C.L.R. 39, noted in 65 L.Q.R. 20, *Dann* v. *Hamilton* was dissented from and not followed, but the court in *Joyce's* case appear to have drawn no distinction between voluntarily running a known risk and voluntarily agreeing to relieve the other party from liability if the risk resulted in injury. In the Canadian case of *Miller* v. *Decker* [1957] 9 D.L.R. (2d) 1, the Supreme Court of Canada by a majority decision held that the right time to test the question whether the appellant accepted the risk was when the plan was originally formulated, in this case to " go beering " together, and not when the appellant and the respondent left a dance hall already in a drunken state having thus put their plan into effect. The appellant in these circumstances was *volens* and therefore could not recover. On the other hand in *Stein* v. *Lehnert* (1962) 31 D.L.R. (2d) 673, the plaintiff accepted the defendant's invitation for an evening out, going to a night club, where the defendant became drunk. On the way home, the defendant crashed his car and injured the plaintiff. The Manitoba Court of Appeal held that although there was contributory negligence on the part of the plaintiff she did not come within the *volens* rule. The test of *volens* was whether the plaintiff agreed to absolve the defendant from his duty to take care and not whether she willingly ran the risk of danger from his driving whilst intoxicated.

[5] *The Marpesia* (1872) L.R. 4 P.C. 212, 220, citing Dr. Lushington in *The Virgil* (1843) 2 W.Rob. 201.

prevent by the exercise of ordinary care, caution, and maritime skill," has said: " I know no distinction as regards inevitable accident between cases which occur on land and those which occur at sea." [6] It is doubtful whether much advantage is gained by the continued use of the expression " inevitable accident." To quote the words of Lord Greene [7]: " I do not feel myself assisted by considering the meaning of the phrase ' inevitable accident.' I prefer to put the problem in a more simple way, namely, has it been established that the driver of the car was guilty of negligence? "

1080 The principle on which inevitable accident is a defence was expressed by Blackburn J. in these terms: " Traffic on the highway, whether by land or sea, cannot be conducted without exposing those whose persons or property are near it to some inevitable risk; and that being so, those who go on the highway or have their property adjacent to it, may well be held to do so subject to their taking upon themselves the risk of injury from that inevitable danger; and persons who by the licence of the owner pass near to warehouses where goods are being raised or lowered, certainly do so subject to the inevitable risk of accident. In neither case, therefore, can they recover without proof of want of care or skill, occasioning the accident; and it is believed that all the cases in which inevitable accident has been held an excuse for what prima facie was a trespass, can be explained on the same principle, *viz.*, that the circumstances were such as to show that the plaintiff had taken that risk upon himself." [8] This explanation, however, cannot be considered to be satisfactory. The danger from traffic on the highways arises largely from the negligence of the drivers of vehicles and of other persons on the highway and only to a very small extent from inevitable accident. In any event, it cannot be said, in any ordinary sense, that a person on the highway agrees to take upon himself the risk of inevitable accident but not the risk of negligence. [9] He may have to run the risk of damage caused by inevitable accident, but this is not the result of agreement but of necessity. The true view is that loss must lie where it falls, unless it can be shown that it was caused by a breach on the part of some other person of a duty to take care, or of some duty making it wrongful for him to have inflicted the loss upon the person who has suffered it.

1081 Apart from Admiralty cases, the reported cases in which the defence of inevitable accident has succeeded are few, owing to the question being almost entirely one of fact, but the defence itself is quite well established. In *Fawkes* v. *Poulson & Son* [10] the plaintiff was a boilermaker working in the hold of a ship and the defendants were stevedores, who were letting down bales into the hold by means of a crane. In doing so, a bale slipped

[6] *The Schwan* [1892] P. 419, 434.
[7] In *Browne* v. *De Luxe Car Services* [1941] K.B. 549, 552.
[8] *Fletcher* v. *Rylands* (1866) L.R. 1 Ex. 265, 286. Compare with this his similar statement of the law, as Lord Blackburn in *River Wear Comrs.* v. *Adamson* (1877) 2 App.Cas. 743, 767.
[9] See *per* Lord Halsbury in *Smith* v. *Baker* [1891] A.C. 325, 337.
[10] (1892) 8 T.L.R. 725. The test in *The Marpesia, supra,* was applied. It is difficult to understand how the C.A. felt themselves able to set aside the verdict of the jury on the facts as reported.

out of the chain by which it was secured and injured the plaintiff. The jury found for the plaintiff but, on appeal, the verdict was set aside, on the ground that it was inevitable accident, because " the evidence showed that it was practically impossible always to prevent the bales from slipping out of the chain." There is no inevitable accident unless the defendant can prove that something happened over which he had no control and the effect of which could not have been avoided by the exercise of care and skill.[11] Where a tramway company had statutory powers to run steam trams with running powers over the lines of another company and, owing to the defective state of the points of the other company's lines, one of their trams ran off the lines and injured the plaintiff, who was on the highway, it was held that the plea of inevitable accident failed because the defendant company ought to have inspected the lines before sending their tram along it.[12] On the other hand, when a passenger in a tram was struck on the head by a trolley arm which was plucked from the standard and fell upon him, and it was proved that the system of electric traction employed was the best known, the apparatus was in perfect order, and there was no negligence on the part of the tram company's servants, the defence of inevitable accident was made out, and it was held that the passenger could not recover.[13] It is inevitable accident to prove that a highway collision has been caused by a latent defect in one of the colliding vehicles.[14]

982 In addition to being a defence in actions of negligence, inevitable accident is a defence in trespass to the person, and in trespass to land or goods on or adjoining the highway. In *Stanley* v. *Powell* [15] the plaintiff, who was a member of a shooting party, fired at a pheasant and one of the pellets glanced off the bough of a tree and wounded the plaintiff, who was carrying cartridges and game for the party. The jury found that the defendant was not negligent in firing as he did and accordingly, on the ground that in trespass to the person either negligence or intention must be established, judgment was given for the defendant. Similarly, damage caused by horses bolting without any negligence on the part of the driver and trespassing upon the adjoining land,[16] and cattle driven without negligence and also trespassing upon adjoining land [17] has been held to be due to inevitable accident and not to be actionable.

983 **Burden of proof.** The burden of proof of inevitable accident is upon the

[11] *The Albano* [1892] P. 419, *per* Lord Esher M.R.

[12] *Sadler* v. *S. Staffordshire and Birmingham Tramways* (1889) 23 Q.B.D. 17. " The jury acquitted the tramway company of negligence, but they were held liable because they could not prove inevitable accident ": *Southport Corpn.* v. *Esso Petroleum Co. Ltd.* [1954] 2 Q.B. 182, 199, *per* Denning L.J.

[13] *Newberry* v. *Bristol Tramways Co.* (1912) 107 L.T. 801.

[14] *Winnipeg Electric Co.* v. *Geel* [1932] A.C. 690, 694.

[15] [1891] 1 Q.B. 86. The forcible comment on this case by Landon in *Pollock on Torts*, 15th ed., p. 128, deserves more attention than it received from the C.A. in *National Coal Board* v. *Evans* [1951] 2 K.B. 861, where *Stanley* v. *Powell* was approved.

[16] *Holmes* v. *Mather* (1875) L.R. 10 Ex. 261; *Manzoni* v. *Douglas* (1880) 6 Q.B.D. 145; *Hammack* v. *White* (1862) 11 C.B.(N.S.) 588; *Gayler & Pope Ltd.* v. *Davies & Son* [1924] 2 K.B. 75. For a discussion of these cases see *ante*, § 987.

[17] *Tillett* v. *Ward* (1882) 10 Q.B.D. 17.

defendant or the other person setting it up.[18] " The burden rests on the defendants to show inevitable accident. To sustain that the defendants must do one or other of two things. They must either show what was the cause of the accident, and show that the result of that cause was inevitable; or they must show all the possible causes, one or other of which produced the effect, and must further show with regard to every one of these possible causes that the result could not have been avoided. Unless they do one or other of these two things, it does not appear to me that they have shown inevitable accident." [19] Although *Stanley* v. *Powell* [20] has decided that inevitable accident was a good defence to an action of trespass, in *Fowler* v. *Lanning* [21] Diplock J. stated that he regarded the decision as neutral on the question of onus of proof and went on to extend *Stanley* v. *Powell* by holding that a plaintiff must always prove intention or negligence on the part of a defendant in such an action for the injuries sustained. " The onus of proving negligence, where the trespass is not intentional, lies on the plaintiff, whether the action be framed in trespass or in negligence. This has been unquestioned law in highway cases ever since *Holmes* v. *Mather* [22] and there is no reason in principle . . . why it should be any different in other cases. It is, indeed, but an illustration of the rule that he who affirms must prove, which lies at the root of our law of evidence." [23] The defence of inevitable accident need not be specially pleaded in actions based on negligence, but if it is brought forward on new facts likely to take the opposite party by surprise, an adjournment may be granted.[24]

1084 **Sudden death.** The sudden death of the driver of a motor-vehicle from heart failure, as the result of which an accident is caused, is inevitable accident.[25] Even sudden death or sudden illness, however, may give rise to liability if there is negligence in not having someone at hand to take over in such an emergency. This happened in *The Saint Angus* [26] when the owners of a motor-ship which collided with a steamship, owing to the fainting of the master at the wheel, were held liable because there was no person on deck to take over from him. Nevertheless in *Waugh* v. *Allan* [27] it was held that a reasonable man in the driver's position would have thought that his earlier symptoms related merely to a gastric attack and not to coronary thrombosis and he would not have expected his driving ability to be impaired so as to cause danger to other road users. In this

18 *The Merchant Prince* [1892] P. 179, where in broad daylight the *Merchant Prince* ran into a ship at anchor in the Mersey. See the discussion on this case in *Esso Petroleum Co. Ltd.* v. *Southport Corpn.* [1956] 2 W.L.R. 81.
19 [1892] P. 179, 189, *per* Fry L.J.
20 [1891] 1 Q.B. 86.
21 [1959] 1 Q.B. 426.
22 (1875) L.R. 10 Ex. 261.
23 At p. 439. Similar decisions have been given in the Canadian case of *Walmsley* v. *Humenick* [1954] 2 D.L.R. 232, and the New Zealand case of *Beals* v. *Hayward* [1960] N.Z.L.R. 131.
24 *Rumbold* v. *L.C.C.* (1909) 25 T.L.R. 541.
25 *Ryan* v. *Youngs* [1938] 1 All E.R. 522. But in *Boomer* v. *Penn* (1965) 52 D.L.R. (2d) 673 the defendant, a diabetic, failed to prove that his driving was not a conscious act of will, hence the defence of inevitable accident failed.
26 [1938] P. 225.
27 1963 S.C. 175. The decision was affirmed by the House of Lords, 1964 S.C.(H.L.) 162.

case a lorry driver was held not to be liable when he lost control of his vehicle as a result of a heart attack, mounted the pavement and struck a pedestrian, thereby injuring him.

085 **Inevitable accident and act of God.** Inevitable accident is not the same as "act of God." "Act of God" is the opposite of the act of man and is something "due to natural causes directly and exclusively without human intervention," [28] while inevitable accident is not restricted in any such way.

4.—CONTRACTING OUT OF LIABILITY FOR NEGLIGENCE

086 **Contracting out.** A person, by contract, may relieve himself from liability for his own negligence and the negligence of those for whom he is vicariously liable. Such a contract may be made before or after damage is caused. In certain cases, however, contracting out of liability for negligence is prohibited either by statute or at common law.

(a)—*Prohibition of Contracting Out by Statute*

087 **Carriage of Goods by Sea Act 1924.** The Carriage of Goods by Sea Act 1924, Schedule, Article III (8), contains the following in relation to the carriage of goods by sea:

"Any clause, covenant or agreement in a contract of carriage relieving the carrier or the ship from liability for loss or damage to or in connection with goods arising from negligence, fault or failure in the duties and obligations provided in this Article or lessening such liability otherwise than as provided in these Rules, shall be null and void and of no effect.

"A benefit of insurance or similar clause shall be deemed to be a clause relieving the carrier from liability."

088 **Road Traffic Act 1960.** The Road Traffic Act 1960,[29] s. 151, contains the following provision as to the carriage of passengers in a public service vehicle:

"A contract for the conveyance of a passenger in a public service vehicle shall, so far as it purports to negative or to restrict the liability of a person in respect of a claim which may be made against him in respect of the death of, or bodily injury to, the passenger while being carried in, entering or alighting from the vehicle, or purports to impose any conditions with respect to the enforcement of any such liability, be void."

089 **Transport Act 1962.** The Transport Act 1962 which provides for the re-organisation of the nationalised transport undertakings previously carried on under the Transport Act 1947 and replaces the British Transport Commission by four public authorities, namely: (1) British Railways; (2) London Transport; (3) British Transport Docks; and (4) British

[28] Mellish L.J. in *Nugent* v. *Smith* (1876) 1 C.P.D. 423, 444. For "act of God" see § 429.

[29] This provision does not apply to a person who travels "on a free pass": *Wilkie* v. *L.P.T.B.* [1947] 1 All E.R. 258. Nevertheless a free pass cannot protect the negligent driver because he is not one of the parties to the contract: *Genys* v. *Matthews* [1966] 1 W.L.R. 758. See also *Gore* v. *Van der Lann* [1967] 2 Q.B. 31 (likewise a bus conductor). Article "Strange case of Mrs. Gore" (Odgers), 86 L.Q.R. 69. Also Motor Vehicles (Passenger Insurance) Act 1971, which comes into force December 1, 1972, and applies to non-service vehicles.

Waterways, by section 43 (7) contains the following provision: "The Boards shall not carry passengers by rail on terms or conditions which—(*a*) purport, whether directly or indirectly, to exclude or limit their liability in respect of the death of, or bodily injury to, any passenger other than a passenger travelling on a free pass,[29] or (*b*) purport, whether directly or indirectly, to prescribe the time within which or the manner in which any such liability may be enforced, and any such terms or conditions shall be void and of no effect."

1090 **Carriage by Air Act 1961.** The Carriage by Air Act 1961,[30] in relation to international carriage by air, by Articles 17–30 in the First Schedule provides for the liability of the carrier, and by Article 23 (1):

"Any provision tending to relieve the carrier of liability or to fix a lower limit than that which is laid down in this Convention shall be null and void, but the nullity of any such provision does not involve the nullity of the whole contract, which shall remain subject to the provisions of this Convention."

1091 **Companies Act 1948.** The Companies Act 1948, s. 205, avoids provisions in articles or contracts relieving officers and auditors from liability as follows:

"Subject as hereinafter provided, any provision, whether contained in the articles of a company or in any contract with a company or otherwise, for exempting any officer of the company or any person (whether an officer of the company or not) employed by the company as auditor from, or indemnifying him against, any liability which by virtue of any rule of law would otherwise attach to him in respect of any negligence, default, breach of duty or breach of trust of which he may be guilty in relation to the company shall be void:

Provided that— . . .

(*b*) notwithstanding anything in this section, a company may, in pursuance of any such provisions as aforesaid, indemnify any such officer or auditor against any liability incurred by him in defending any proceedings, whether civil or criminal, in which judgment is given in his favour or in which he is acquitted or in connection with any application under section 448 of this Act in which relief is granted to him by the court."

1092 **Building Societies Act 1962.** The Building Societies Act 1962, s. 92, is in similar terms and avoids any provision in the rules or in any contract whereby any director, member of the committee of management, manager, secretary or officer of the society, or any auditor, is exempted from or indemnified against liability for negligence.

1093 **Solicitors Act 1957.** A solicitor can make an agreement in writing with his client as to his remuneration for contentious business [31] but by section

[30] Carriage by Air (Supplementary Provision) Act 1962; Orders 1967 (Nos. 479, 480, 803–810); Carriage by Air (Non-International Carriage) (United Kingdom) Order 1952 (S.I. 1952 No. 158).

[31] As to the difference between contentious and non-contentious business, see *Re A Solicitor* [1956] 1 Q.B. 155.

60 (4) of the Solicitors Act 1957 " A provision in the agreement that the solicitor shall not be liable for negligence, or that he shall be relieved from any responsibility to which he would otherwise be subject as a solicitor, shall be void."

1094 **Law Reform (Personal Injuries) Act 1948.** The Law Reform (Personal Injuries) Act 1948 provides:

" 1.—(3) Any provision contained in a contract of service or apprenticeship, or in an agreement collateral thereto (including a contract or agreement entered into before the commencement of this Act [32]), shall be void in so far as it would have the effect of excluding or limiting any liability of the employer in respect of personal injuries caused to the person employed or apprenticed by the negligence of persons in common employment with him."

(b)—*Prohibition at Common Law*

1095 **Public policy.** A duty which is imposed by common law or statute for the protection of a particular person or class of persons can, in general, be waived, the maxim being " *cuilibet licet renuntiare juri pro se introducto.*" In the case of a statute, it is a question of the construction of the particular statute whether or not contracting out is permissible.[33] In the case of a common law duty, contracting out is permissible unless it is against public policy. " Everyone many waive the advantage of a law made solely for the benefit or protection of him as an individual in his private capacity, but this cannot be done if the waiver would infringe a public right or public policy." [34] Perhaps the Occupiers' Liability Act 1957 [35] provides the best illustration not only because its main purpose was to provide new rules to replace the rules of the common law but because by section 2 (1) specifically it enacted that: " An occupier of premises owes the same duty, the common duty of care, to all his visitors, *except* in so far as he is free to and does extend, restrict, modify or exclude his duty to any visitor or visitors by agreement or otherwise." [36]

A contract by a workman not to claim compensation from his employers under the Employers' Liability Act 1880 [37] was not against public policy.[38] However contracting out of the Workmen's Compensation Act 1925 was forbidden,[39] except to a strictly limited extent.

096 **Master cannot contract out of statutory duty for workman's benefit.** Contracting out of a statutory duty imposed on an employer for the protection of his workmen is contrary to public policy and void. When a miner was killed owing to the breach by his employer of a duty imposed by the Coal Mines Regulation Act 1872 it was held that it was no defence

[32] July 5, 1948.
[33] *Salford Guardians* v. *Dewhurst* [1926] A.C. 619.
[34] *Bowmaker Ltd.* v. *Tabor* [1941] 2 K.B. 1, 6, *per* Goddard L.J.
[35] See generally Chap. 8.
[36] As to this section see § 347, *ante*.
[37] Now repealed by the Law Reform (Personal Injuries) Act 1948.
[38] *Griffiths* v. *Earl of Dudley* (1882) 9 Q.B.D. 357.
[39] S. 1 (3) (repealed by the National Insurance (Industrial Injuries) Act 1946).

to prove that the miner knew of the breach and voluntarily incurred the risk of it.[40] Wills J. in delivering the leading judgment, said: " If the supposed agreement . . . comes to this, that the master employs the servant on the terms that the latter shall waive the breach by the master of an obligation imposed on him by statute, and shall connive at his disregard of the statutory obligation imposed on him for the benefit of others, as well as of himself, such an agreement would be in violation of public policy and ought not to be listened to." [41] So, too, in a later case Slesser L.J. said: " Common employment may at least be argued as a kind of *volenti non fit injuria*, but any other kind of obligation which the workman takes upon himself cannot be used as a defence if in fact there is a breach of the statutory duty." [42]

1097 **Not contrary to public policy to contract out of liability for negligence.** There does not appear to be any instance in which it has been held that contracting out of liability for common law negligence is contrary to public policy.[43] Railway companies, in the past, habitually inserted in excursion and other cheap tickets a condition exempting them from liability for negligence. This practice has now been discontinued, but while it existed there was no doubt about the validity of the contracts thereby made.[44] On the other hand the Merchant Shipping Acts 1894–1958 entitle the shipowners to limit their liability for any loss of life or any personal injury caused to persons carried on board their ships.[45]

1098 **Indemnity against negligence amounting to a crime.** It is usual to insure against liability for damage caused by negligence and breach of statutory duty, and the question arises whether these contracts are enforceable if the negligence or breach of duty is a crime. Bailhache J. said: " It is against public policy to indemnify a man against the consequences of a crime which he knowingly commits, and in the word ' crime ' I include the breach of any statutory duty which renders a man liable to fine or imprisonment." [46] So, too, Kennedy J. said: " If an act is manifestly unlawful, or the doer of it knows it to be unlawful, as constituting either a civil wrong or a criminal offence, he cannot maintain an action for contribution or for indemnity against the liability which results to him therefrom. An express promise of indemnity to him for the commission of such an act is

40 *Baddeley* v. *Granville* (1887) 19 Q.B.D. 423.
41 *Ibid.* at pp. 426, 427.
42 *Wheeler* v. *New Merton Board Mills* [1933] 2 K.B. 669, 695. See also *Davies* v. *Thomas Owen & Son* [1919] 2 K.B. 39. See Chap. 14 (doctrine of common employment has been abolished when the cause of action accrues after July 5, 1948).
43 See *Ludditt* v. *Ginger Coote Airways* [1947] A.C. 233. On the contrary, see the Occupiers' Liability Act 1957, s. 2 (1), where provision is made for such an eventuality. See § 345, *ante*.
44 See *Thompson* v. *L.M.S. Ry.* [1930] 1 K.B. 41; *Penton* v. *S. Ry.* [1931] 2 K.B. 103; *Nunan* v. *S. Ry.* [1924] 1 K.B. 223. But see now the provisions of s. 43 (7) of the Transport Act 1962.
45 Merchant Shipping Act 1894, s. 503, amended by Merchant Shipping Act 1948, s. 4 (3); Merchant Shipping (Liability of Shipowners and Others) Act 1958, ss. 1 (1), 2, 4–6, 8. For limitation of liability in respect of goods see Carriage of Goods by Sea Act 1924; *Leesh River Tea Co. Ltd.* v. *British India Steam Navigation Co. Ltd.* [1967] 2 Q.B. 250. For harbour authorities exemption see *The Ballyalton* [1961] 1 W.L.R. 929.
46 *Tinline* v. *White Cross Ins.* [1921] 3 K.B. 327, 331.

void." [47] Again, Greer L.J. said: " A person may insure himself against errors of law, but not against the commission of a crime." [48] On the other hand, the Law Reform (Married Women and Tortfeasors) Act 1935, s. 6 (1), provides: " Where damage is suffered by any person as a result of a tort (whether a crime or not) . . .[48] any tortfeasor liable in respect of that damage may recover contribution from any other tortfeasor who is, or would if sued have been, liable in respect of the same damage," and such contribution can amount, if the court so directs, to a complete indemnity.

1099 A contract to indemnify a motorist against third-party claims " for accidental personal injury " has been held not to be void as against public policy, in an action by the motorist for a declaration that he was entitled to be indemnified against a claim made on behalf of a person killed by him under circumstances amounting to manslaughter.[49] The manslaughter was the result of driving at an excessive speed, but the same result was arrived at when the manslaughter was the result of driving when drunk.[50] In both of these cases the crime was an act of negligence and " not the wilful or advertent doing of the act," [51] and on that ground it was held that there was not " that degree of criminality which in the doing of a known unlawful act makes it against public policy that the perpetrator should be indemnified in respect of it." [51]

When a solicitor took out a policy of insurance indemnifying him from loss arising from claims made against him " by reason of any neglect, omission or error " while acting in his official capacity, it was held that it was against public policy to allow a claim under the policy against a loss sustained through his having, without realising the fact, entered into a champertous agreement.[52]

The result seems to be that it is not against public policy to contract to indemnify a person against his negligence or breach of statutory duty, even though it amounts to a crime. If the person intentionally did the act which was a crime, it would probably not come within the terms of the indemnity,[53] but if it did, whether it would be against public policy to enforce the indemnity would depend upon the nature of the crime in question.[53a]

(c)—*Contracting Out before Damage is Caused*

1100 **General principle.** A contract exempting one of the contracting parties from liability for negligence is made in accordance with the ordinary principles of contract, but the application of those principles to certain contracts of frequent occurrence in negligence cases may be considered here.

47 *Burrows* v. *Rhodes* [1899] 1 Q.B. 816, 828.
48 *Haseldine* v. *Hosken* [1933] 1 K.B. 822, 837.
49 *Tinline* v. *White Cross Ins.* [1921] 3 K.B. 327.
50 *James* v. *British General Ins. Co.* [1927] 2 K.B. 311.
51 *Ibid. per* Roche J. at p. 323.
52 *Haseldine* v. *Hosken* [1933] 1 K.B. 822. See also *Beresford* v. *Royal Ins. Co.* [1938] A.C. 586 (contrary to public policy to recover on a life policy when assured commits suicide while sane); *Askey* v. *Golden Wine Co. Ltd.* [1948] 2 All E.R. 35 (no indemnity allowed) where it was pointed out that in the motor manslaughter cases " the act to be indemnified was one intended by the law that people should insure against."
53 As in *Haseldine* v. *Hosken*, *supra*.
53a *Gray* v. *Barr* [1971] 2 W.L.R. 1334 (husband shot dead wife's suspected lover).

1101 **Ticket cases.** In contracts of carriage, the ticket given by the carrier to the passenger on payment of the fare often contains a condition, or a reference to another document containing a condition, limiting the carrier's liability for negligence. In such cases, if the passenger knows of the condition and does not express his dissent from it he will be taken to agree to it and will be bound by it. If he does not know of the condition, he will be bound by it if the carrier has done all that was reasonably sufficient to give him notice of it, but not otherwise.[54]

Reasonable notice of a condition is given if the condition is printed on the face of the ticket,[55] although even then there may be special circumstances from the smallness of the type in which the condition is printed, the absence of any device drawing attention to it, and other printed matter tending to obliterate it, to justify a finding that reasonable notice has not been given.[56] If the ticket consists of a book of coupons it is reasonable notice to print the condition inside the book.[57] When the conditions are printed on the back of the ticket, a printed direction on the front, " see back," is sufficient notice of the conditions,[58] but not if the direction is obliterated by the stamping of the date on the ticket or otherwise.[59] In the absence of any direction to the back of the ticket, the notice may be held to be insufficient.[60] The conditions themselves need not be printed on the ticket, as long as there is a reference to some document, such as a timetable, where they are to be found.[61] The fact that there might be some small expense and possible delay in procuring a copy of the document containing the conditions is immaterial. It is also immaterial that the passenger cannot read the conditions owing to blindness or illiteracy,[62] or that he cannot understand them " on account of his exceptional ignorance or stupidity or carelessness." [63]

1102 Considerations similar to those set out in the preceding paragraphs apply to bailments. If an article is deposited in a left-luggage office or cloakroom or similar place and a ticket is given by the bailee containing conditions limiting his liability for negligence, the conditions are only binding if the bailee has done all that is reasonably sufficient to bring them to the bailor's notice.[64]

[54] *Parker* v. *S.E. Ry.* (1877) 2 C.P.D. 416; *Hood* v. *Anchor Line* [1918] A.C. 837; *Thompson* v. *L.M.S. Ry.* [1930] 1 K.B. 41. "Incorporation of Exemption Clauses" (Powell-Smith) 121 New L.J. 216.

[55] *Cooke* v. *Wilson (T.) Sons & Co.* (1915) 85 L.J.K.B. 888 (in which a jury's finding that insufficient notice was given was set aside); *Hood* v. *Anchor Line, supra.*

[56] *Richardson Spence & Co.* v. *Rowntree* [1894] A.C. 217; *Williamson* v. *North of Scotland, etc. Steam Navigation Co.*, 1916 S.C. 554; *Hooper* v. *Furness Ry.* (1907) 23 T.L.R. 451 (where the ticket was issued after the voyage commenced).

[57] *Burke* v. *S.E. Ry.* (1875) 5 C.P.D. 1; *Zunz* v. *S.E. Ry.* (1869) L.R. 4 Q.B. 539.

[58] *Penton* v. *Southern Ry.* [1931] 2 K.B. 103; *Thompson* v. *L.M.S. Ry., supra*; *Stirling* v. *L. & S.W. Ry.* (1895) 12 T.L.R. 69.

[59] *Sugar* v. *L.M.S. Ry.* [1941] 1 All E.R. 172.

[60] *Henderson* v. *Stevenson* (1875) L.R. 2 H.L.Sc. 470.

[61] *Thompson* v. *L.M.S. Ry.* [1930] 1 K.B. 41; *Gray* v. *L.N.E. Ry.* 1930 S.C. 989.

[62] *Thompson* v. *L.M.S. Ry., supra.*

[63] *Per* Mellish L.J. in *Parker* v. *S.E. Ry.* (1877) 2 C.P.D. 416, 423.

[64] *Van Toll* v. *S.E. Ry.* (1862) 12 C.B. (N.S.) 75 (railway cloakroom); *Harris* v. *G.W. Ry.* (1876) 1 Q.B.D. 515 (railway cloakroom); *Pratt* v. *S.E. Ry.* [1897] 1 Q.B. 718 (railway cloakroom); *Parker* v. *S.E. Ry., supra* (railway cloakroom); *Watkins* v. *Rymill* (1883) 10 Q.B.D. 178 (horse repository); *Gibaud* v. *G.E. Ry.* [1921] 2 K.B. 426 (railway cloakroom).

Where the plaintiff took a ticket of admission to a football ground and the ticket contained a condition that the defendants should not be liable for any injury to him caused by the overcrowding of the stand or the conduct of the spectators, it was held that the condition was only binding if the defendants had taken reasonable care to give notice of it to the plaintiff.[65]

1103 The principles set out in § 1101 above apply to tickets issued by carriers and bailees because it is well known that conditions are usually imposed in such contracts. In other cases the person attempting to contract out of his liability for negligence must go somewhat further. He must be able to prove that the other party to the contract either knew or ought to have known that the ticket or other document contained the terms of the contract. The nature of the contract may be such that it is not usual to attach conditions limiting liability for negligence, or the document may be such as to suggest that there are no conditions attached. An illustration of this principle is afforded by *Chapelton* v. *Barry U.D.C.*,[66] where the plaintiff took a chair on the beach for which he paid 2d., getting in return a ticket on which was printed: " The council will not be liable for any accident or damage arising from the hire of the chair." The chair collapsed injuring the plaintiff, who was held entitled to recover, notwithstanding the clause, on the ground that the ticket was only a receipt and that nobody in the circumstances of the case " would think for one moment that some conditions were being imposed upon him which would limit his ordinary rights or that the document he received when paying his 2d. was a contractual document." [67] Again in *Henson* v. *L.N.E.R.*,[68] the plaintiff, employed by a third party to repair wagons on the railway company's property, was injured by the negligence of the railway company. He had a " walking pass," authorising him to go on to the railway company's premises, on the back of which was a condition: " The L.N.E.R. shall not be responsible to the holder . . . in the event of any accident or injury, however caused, happening to him whilst upon the railway and the premises named herein." The plaintiff did not know of the condition, and it was held that he was not bound by it, because there was nothing to lead him to suppose that the pass was a contractual document, and reasonable notice of the condition had not been given to him.

104 A receipt for goods containing a statement of the condition of the goods received is evidence as to the state of the goods, but is not a contract. Where the sellers of a reconditioned motor-car, on delivering it to the buyer, got the buyer to sign a receipt that the car was in good condition " as seen, tried and approved," and a wheel came off the first morning the

65 *Skrine* v. *Gould* (1912) 29 T.L.R. 19 (the jury found that reasonable notice was not given, and the plaintiff succeeded).

66 [1940] 1 K.B. 532. *Thornton* v. *Shoe Lane Parking Ltd.* [1971] 2 W.L.R. 585 (ticket extracted from a machine at entrance to the defendants' automatically controlled car park; held, no adequate steps taken to bring conditions to the plaintiff's notice).

67 *Ibid. per* Goddard L.J. at p. 539.

68 [1946] 1 All E.R. 653.

car was used, causing the driver to be injured, it was held that the terms of the receipt were ineffectual to relieve the sellers from liability for the negligent performance of their duty to the buyer.[69]

(d)—*Effect of a Notice*

1105 **Effect of notice.** Sometimes a notice is affixed in the office or other premises[70] of one of the parties bearing words intended to exempt that party from liability for negligence. The effect of such a notice is that if it is brought to the notice of the other party before or at the time of the making of the contract it is incorporated in the contract and the parties are bound by its contents. Prior to the passing of the Carriers Act 1830 common carriers frequently exhibited a notice in their offices restricting their liability for loss of or damage to the goods carried, and it was held that such a notice had contractual force and did restrict their liability if it came to the knowledge of the customer when the contract was made.[71] If, however, the notice did not come to the customer's knowledge it was ineffectual.[72] Thus where a plaintiff left his car at the defendant's garage for repairs but had failed to see an exemption notice exhibited and the car was damaged by catching fire it was held that the plaintiff had not visited the premises often enough to be taken to know of the notice, which did not therefore affect the contract of bailment.[73]

A notice which only comes to the attention of the party on whom it is said to be binding after the contract is made, will form no part of the contract. When a guest engaged a room at an hotel and found in the bedroom a notice, " Articles of value, if not kept under lock, should be deposited with the manager," it was held that the notice formed no part of the contract, Bowen L.J. saying: " There was no action by [the plaintiff] upon the offer contained in the notice. There was, therefore, no contract." [74]

1106 Public service vehicles often have a notice to the effect that passengers alighting when the vehicle is in motion do so at their own risk. Such a notice is merely a warning, disregard of which may be contributory negligence, but does not form one of the terms of the contract. A notice on an omnibus so placed that it could only be ready by persons on the

[69] *Herschtal* v. *Stewart & Ardern Ltd.* [1940] 1 K.B. 155.

[70] Where an infant defendant exhibited a notice in his motor-car stating that passengers rode in it at their own risk and that he would not be liable for personal injuries, loss or damage, however caused (he being uninsured against such risks) it was held by John Stephenson J. that the infant plaintiff, knowing of this notice and appreciating its terms, impliedly agreed to exempt the defendant from liability having persuaded the latter to take him on a journey by offering to contribute towards the cost of the petrol: *Buckpitt* v. *Oates* [1968] 1 All E.R. 1145, but *cf. Geier* v. *Kujawa* [1970] 1 Lloyd's Rep. 364 and *Bennett* v. *Tugwell* [1971] 2 W.L.R. 847 (overridden by the Motor Vehicles (Passenger Insurance) Act 1971, which comes into force December 1, 1972). Further, see article: " Liability for Passengers " (Ingman) 120 New L.J. 881.

[71] *Kerr* v. *Willan* (1817) 6 M. & S. 150; *Nicholson* v. *Willan* (1804) 5 East 507; *Mayhew* v. *Eames* (1825) 3 B. & C. 601; *per* Blackburn J. in *Peek* v. *North Staffordshire Ry.* (1863) 10 H.L.C. 473, 496; *per* Wright J. in *Shaw* v. *G.W. Ry.* [1894] 1 Q.B. 373, 381; *per* McCardie J. in *Wade* v. *L. & N.W. Ry.* [1921] 1 K.B. 582, 591.

[72] *Rowley* v. *Horne* (1825) 2 Bing. 2.

[73] *Smith* v. *Taylor* [1966] 2 Lloyd's Rep. 231.

[74] *Huntly* v. *Bedford Hotel Co.* (1891) 7 T.L.R. 641; see also *Olley* v. *Marlborough Court Ltd.* [1949] 1 K.B. 532 (notice in bedroom not seen until after plaintiff is accepted as a guest, not part of the contract).

step, " Wait until the bus stops before alighting," was held not to " amount to a transfer of the risk of falling from the omnibus from the persons on the step to the owners of the omnibus." [75] A notice " Lions, dangerous " on the door of a lions' cage is a warning to persons who might open the cage that there are lions inside but not a warning that lions might put their paws through the bars and injure people.[76] In any case, such a warning is only material on the question of contributory negligence.

When a barge came to the defendants' wharf to load a cargo from the defendants' mill, on the wall of which was a notice headed " Notice to barge owners," containing conditions limiting the defendants' liability, it was held that the notice was no protection to the defendants. The notice board was faded and difficult to read and had not been observed by the plaintiffs' lightermen.[77] In any case, it would seem that the contract had been made before the plaintiffs had any opportunity of seeing the notice, so that it could not form part of the contract. Again, a warning notice on a jetty that the occupiers would not be liable for damage, even caused by their negligence, and that vessels could only lie at or off the jetty at their own risk, does not protect the occupiers unless they prove that some responsible representative of the owners of a vessel at the jetty had read the notice. A lighterman in charge of a barge is not such a representative.[78]

1107 A person using a short cut over the defendants' land in such circumstances as to be a licensee was held bound by the terms of a notice (giving warning that users did so at their own risk and would have no claim against the defendants for any damage caused to them) when she admitted that she had read part of the notice and could have read the rest, but was held not bound by another notice giving warning of engines and trucks on railway lines crossing the short cut, which she could have read but did not. The effect of the first notice was that she was not entitled to recover against the occupier when she was injured by shunting operations on the line carried out negligently by the occupier.[79]

(e)—*Construction of Exemption Contracts* [80]

1108 **General principles.** In construing a contract excepting liability for negligence regard must be had to the whole of the document, and not

[75] *Jude* v. *Edinburgh Corpn.*, 1943 S.C. 399, 402, *per* the Lord Ordinary (Stevenson).
[76] *Pearson* v. *Coleman Bros.* [1948] 2 K.B. 359, 369.
[77] *The Humorist* [1944] P. 28.
[78] *Cawood Wharton & Co. Ltd.* v. *Samuel Williams & Sons Ltd.* [1951] P. 270.
[79] *Ashdown* v. *Samuel Williams & Sons Ltd.* [1957] 1 Q.B. 409. (See now Occupiers' Liability Act 1957, s. 2 (4).) It was not necessary to prove that the licensee had read all the terms of the notice, when she knew that the notice contained conditions which affected her and reasonable steps had been taken to bring the conditions to her notice.
[80] See articles: " Law Commission's first report on exemption clauses," (Diamond) 35 M.L.R. 77; " Exemption clauses in the sale of goods: the Law Commission's proposals," (Schofield) [1970] J.B.L. 7; " Controlling exception clauses in contracts: the Law Commission's first attempt," (Coote) 34 Conv. 254.

merely to a portion of it.[81] If the contract expressly provides that there shall be no liability for negligence, the only question is whether the exception applies to the particular loss or damage.[82] When, however, there is no express mention of negligence the liability of the party relying on the exception should first be ascertained. If this liability is at most a liability for negligence, the contract will be construed as excepting liability for negligence as long as the language used is at all apt for the purpose. But if he is under some higher duty, such as that of an insurer, the contract will be construed as excepting liability for the higher duty and not for negligence, unless the terms are such as to show an intention to except liability both for the higher duty and for negligence. Scrutton L.J. in *Rutter* v. *Palmer* [83] said: " In construing an exemption clause certain general rules may be applied: First, the defendant is not exempted from liability for the negligence of his servants unless adequate words are used; secondly, the liability of the defendant apart from the exempting words must be ascertained; then the particular clause in question must be considered; and if the only liability of the party pleading the exemption is a liability for negligence, the clause will more readily operate to exempt him." The same principle is expressed by Somervell L.J.[84]: " General words in an exception clause do not ordinarily except the party seeking to rely on the exception from liability for his own negligence or that of his servants. There is an exception to what I may call that prima facie approach if on looking more closely into the subject-matter, it is found that substantially the only scope for the operation of the exception clause is the negligence of the servant of the person who is seeking the benefit of it. In that case although the words are general, it has been construed as excluding a liability for negligence."

1109 Common carriers are liable at common law for the loss of or damage to the goods carried without any negligence on their part, and there are numerous cases [85] in which it has been held that a clause in the contract

[81] *Calico Printers' Association* v. *Barclays Bank* (1931) 145 L.T. 51; *G.W. Ry.* v. *Royal Norwegian Govt.* (1945) 114 L.J.K.B. 337.

[82] As in *Rosin and Turpentine Import Co.* v. *B. Jacob & Son* (1910) 102 L.T. 81 and *G.W. Ry.* v. *Royal Norwegian Govt., supra* (" Tug-owner shall not, while towing . . . be liable for any personal injury or loss of life arising from any cause, including negligence " exempts tug-owner from liability for death of member of tug's crew owing to negligence). " If the clause contains language which expressly exempts the person in whose favour it is made . . . from the consequence of the negligence of his servants, effect must be given to this provision " (*Canada Steamship Lines* v. *The King* [1952] A.C. 192, 208, *per* Lord Morton).

[83] [1922] 2 K.B. 87, 92. Similar statements of the law are to be found in *Reynolds* v. *Boston Deep Sea Co.* (1922) 38 T.L.R. 429; *Calico Printers' Association* v. *Barclays Bank, supra; Beaumont-Thomas* v. *Blue Star Line* [1939] 3 All E.R. 127; *White* v. *John Warwick & Co.Ltd.* [1953] 1 W.L.R. 1285. See also *Ashdown* v. *Samuel Williams & Sons Ltd.* [1957] 1 Q.B. 409.

[84] *James Archdale & Co. Ltd.* v. *Comservices Ltd.* [1954] 1 W.L.R. 459, 461. (Contractors were employed on the terms that they should be liable for all damage arising out of or in the execution of the works, provided it was due to their negligence and subject, as to loss or damage by fire, to cl. 15 of the contract, which provided that loss or damage by fire should be borne by the employers. A fire, due to the negligence of the contractors, caused damage. It was held that the intention of the contract was that this damage should be borne by the employers.)

[85] See *D'Arc* v. *L. & N.W. Ry.* (1874) L.R. 9 C.P. 325; *Martin* v. *Great India Peninsular Ry.* (1867) L.R. 3 Ex. 9; *The Pearlmoor* [1904] P. 286.

of carriage, excepting liability for loss or damage, but not referring to negligence, does not exempt them from liability for negligence. In *Price* v. *Union Lighterage Co.*[86] a clause providing that a barge owner was to be under no liability " for any loss or damage to goods which can be covered by insurance " was held not to exempt the barge owner from liability for negligence, but only from liability without negligence. This is because when a clause in such a contract as this is capable of two constructions, one of which will make it applicable when there is no negligence on the part of the carrier or his servants and the other will make it applicable when there is such negligence, it requires special words to make the clause cover non-liability in case of negligence.[87]

110 **Words referring to causes.** Words which refer to the cause of loss or damage have been more readily held to exempt from liability for negligence even in the case of persons who are liable without negligence, than words which merely refer to losses, such as fire or theft. " Though, if you merely enumerate losses without dealing with causes, such a clause may not protect you from your own negligence, if you enumerate causes and suggest you are free from all losses however caused, that will protect you from your own negligence. The words that have been held to give protection are, ' Under any circumstances whatsoever,' ' In any circumstances,' ' Under any circumstances,' or ' any injury however caused.' "[88] When goods in a barge were damaged owing to the barge owner's negligence, and the contract exempted him from liability " for any damage to goods however caused which can be covered by insurance," it was held that the clause relieved him from liability, Phillimore L.J. saying " if the clause directs attention to the cause of loss and excludes all causes it gives sufficient protection."[89]

111 **Words referring to responsibility or liability.** When the only liability is for negligence, it has been held that the words " the company will not be in any way responsible for any article deposited " exempted a railway company from liability for loss of a bicycle deposited with them.[90] A clause in a contract for disposing of refuse by barge, " The Council shall not be held responsible for any damage or mischief caused by or through the refuse after it has been shot for disposal into the contractors' barge,"

86 [1904] 1 K.B. 412.
87 [1904] 1 K.B. 412, *per* Lord Alverstone at p. 414.
88 *Per* Scrutton L.J. in *Gibaud* v. *Great Eastern Ry.* [1921] 2 K.B. 426, 437.
89 *Joseph Travers & Sons Ltd.* v. *Cooper* [1915] 1 K.B. 73, 102. See also *Manchester, Sheffield & Lincolnshire Ry.* v. *Brown* (1883) 8 App.Cas. 703 (exemption from " all liability for loss or damage by delay or from whatever other cause arising " covers loss from negligence); *Taubman* v. *Pacific S.N. Co.* (1872) 1 Asp.M.L.C. 336 (no liability for loss of luggage " under any circumstances whatsoever " protects from loss caused by wilful default of crew); *Wilkie* v. *L.P.T.B.* [1946] 1 All E.R. 650; [1947] 1 All E.R. 258 (exemption from damage " however caused " exempts from liability for negligence); *Farr Ltd.* v. *Admiralty* [1953] 1 W.L.R. 965 (contract for the construction of a jetty provided " The contractor shall be responsible for . . . any loss or damage [to the works] . . . arising from any cause whatsoever " makes the contractor liable for damage caused by the negligence of an Admiralty vessel colliding with the piles of the jetty).
90 *Gibaud* v. *G.E. Ry.* [1921] 2 K.B. 426.

exempted the Council from damage caused by dangerous refuse, even though the condition of the refuse made it a breach of the implied condition that the goods contracted to be carried were safe.[91] Similarly, a clause " the contractors are not responsible for loss or damage by fire " exempted furniture removers from liability for furniture damaged by fire caused by their negligence,[92] and a clause " the company will not under any circumstances be responsible for any article " also had this effect.[93] The omission of the words " in any way " or " under any circumstances " may make all the difference, and a rule of a club " the proprietors shall not be responsible for any article of value " was held not to exempt from liability when the article was stolen as a result of the club's negligence in the selection of a night porter.[94] Somewhat similar words, however, were held to cover loss by negligence when articles brought by a member of a proprietary club into the club were missing.[95] On the other hand, a notice " the proprietors will not hold themselves responsible for articles lost or stolen unless handed to the manager for safe custody " did not relieve an hotel proprietor (not a common innkeeper) from loss through theft when there was negligence on his part. The notice was said to be only a warning.[96]

1112 The words " no liability whatever shall attach " to the defendants were held to exempt them from liability for negligence.[97] Similarly, a contract of carriage by air with a clause " passengers . . . are accepted for carriage only upon condition that the company . . . shall be under no liability in respect of or arising out of the carriage, and that passengers shall renounce for themselves, their representatives and dependants, all claims for compensation for injury (fatal or otherwise) . . . however caused, sustained on board the aircraft " prevents any action being brought by the personal representatives of a passenger killed when the aircraft crashed into a hill owing to the faulty navigation of the pilot.[98] When a cycle was hired under a contract providing " nothing in this agreement shall render the owners liable for any personal injuries to the riders of the machine hired," it was held the owners were exempted from liability in contract only and not from liability in tort.[99]

1113 **Customer's or owner's risk.** A garage keeper has been held to be protected from liability by the words " customers' cars are driven by our staff at customers' sole risk " when a customer's car was damaged by one of his

[91] *Burley* v. *Stepney Corpn.* [1947] 1 All E.R. 507.
[92] *Turner* v. *Civil Service Supply Assn.* [1926] 1 K.B. 50.
[93] *Fagan* v. *Green & Edwards Ltd.* [1926] 1 K.B. 102.
[94] *Williams* v. *The Curzon Syndicate Ltd.* (1919) 35 T.L.R. 475.
[95] *Orchard* v. *Connaught Club* (1930) 46 T.L.R. 214.
[96] *Olley* v. *Marlborough Court Ltd.* [1949] 1 K.B. 532.
[97] *Reynolds* v. *Boston Deep Sea Co.* (1922) 38 T.L.R. 429.
[98] *McKay* v. *Scottish Airways*, 1948 S.C. 254. See Carriage by Air Act 1961, *ante* § 1090.
[99] *White* v. *John Warwick & Co. Ltd.* [1953] 1 W.L.R. 1285. (The seat tilted forward and injured the rider, and a new trial was ordered to find whether this was due to the owners' negligence or not.)

drivers' negligence.[1] It was pointed out, however, that " there are two obvious limitations to be imposed upon the meaning of those words. First, ' staff ' must mean ' driving staff '; secondly, ' driven ' must mean driven for the purpose of the bailment, namely, the purpose of selling the car. The clause does not mean that the garage keeper is to be free from liability if a member of his clerical staff takes out the car for pleasure." [2] Similarly, a clause " all barges or vessels while in Chelsea Dock are at the sole risk of the owners " exempted the dock owners from liability for damage to the barge through their negligence.[3] Again, the words " all cars being left in all respects entirely at their owners' risk " protected the owners of a car park from loss of the car by their negligence.[4] A contract to accept a fur coat either for storage or resale on the terms " goods left at customers' risk " is apt to exclude liability for loss by negligence, but does not relieve the bailee from liability when no explanation of the loss is given. The bailee to succeed must prove either that the loss occurred in some way without his negligence or, alternatively, that it did occur by his negligence.[5] A contract " the owner of a vessel using the graving dock must do so at his own risk, it being hereby expressly provided that the company are not to be responsible for any accident or damage to a vessel . . . whilst in the graving dock " protected the dock owners from liability when the vessel was damaged owing to their negligence in supplying blocks unsuitable for supporting the vessel.[6] A passenger in a steamship under a contract providing that passengers took upon themselves " all risk whatsoever of the passage " bars any claim for damage caused by the negligence of the shipowners in washing the floor outside his cabin.[7] A contract for the carriage of a passenger on a railway " at his own risk " protected the railway company from liability for negligence.[8]

Where a laundry accepted goods on the terms " the maximum amount allowed for lost or damaged articles is twenty times the charge made for laundering," and some articles were lost in the wash owing to the laundry's negligence, it was held that the terms restricted their liability to the amount mentioned.[9]

1 *Rutter* v. *Palmer* [1922] 2 K.B. 87. But see *Smith* v. *Taylor* [1966] 2 Lloyd's Rep. 231 (where the defendant garage owner had not brought the notice to the car owner's attention, it was held that as the onus was on the defendant as bailee to prove that he had not been negligent which he had failed to do, the defendant was liable).

2 [1922] 2 K.B. 87, *per* Scrutton L.J. at p. 93.

3 *Forbes Abbott & Lennard Ltd.* v. *G.W. Ry.* (1927) 44 T.L.R. 97.

4 *Ashby* v. *Tolhurst* [1937] 2 K.B. 242.

5 *Woolmer* v. *Delmer Price Ltd.* [1955] 1 Q.B. 291. See also *J. Spurling Ltd.* v. *Bradshaw* [1956] 1 W.L.R. 461.

6 *Pyman Steamship Co.* v. *Hull & Barnsley Ry.* [1915] 2 K.B. 729. See also *The Stella* [1900] P. 161; *The Forfarshire* [1908] P. 339, where words " all transporting to be at owners' risk " were held not to protect from damage caused through negligence during transportation, would seem to be out of line with the later authorities quoted above.

7 *Beaumont-Thomas* v. *Blue Star Line Ltd.* [1939] 3 All E.R. 127.

8 *McCawley* v. *Furness Ry.* (1872) L.R. 8 Q.B. 57.

9 *Alderslade* v. *Hendon Laundry Ltd.* [1945] K.B. 189; applied in *Collins* v. *Richmond Rodeo Riding and Amundson* (1966) 56 D.L.R. (2d) 428. (A riding stable employee selected a horse for an inexperienced rider, which bolted because it was not suitable. In an action for damages it was held unnecessary for the plaintiff to prove that the horse was dangerous to the owner's knowledge since it was a case of negligence in supplying an unsuitable horse.

1114 **Excepting words accompanied by other words.** If the contract shows an intention to accept liability for negligence, the exception is not affected by other words not intended to have contractual force. Where lightermen received goods for carriage from the defendants on the terms " every reasonable precaution is taken for the safety of goods whilst in craft; they will not be liable for loss or damage, including negligence, which can be covered by insurance," it was held that the terms protected them from liability for negligence, Lord Loreburn saying that they meant " You must not suppose we are careless people, but we will not accept liability; you must insure if you wish to be protected, both from our own and our servants' negligence." [10] Similarly, when a bank was employed to collect the proceeds of the sale of goods on the terms " collections are undertaken at depositor's risk only," and also under a clause " if goods are not taken up please do your best . . . to insure them against fire," and the goods were not taken up and were uninsured owing to the bank's negligence, it was held that the bank were protected, because the earlier words exempted them from liability for negligence, and the later words imposed no obligation on them to insure.[11] On the other hand, if the various parts of the document are contradictory so that the meaning is ambiguous, the party relying on the exception will fail.[12] " These exempting clauses are nowadays all held to be subject to the overriding proviso that they only avail to exempt a party when he is carrying out his contract, not when he is deviating from it or is guilty of a breach which goes to the root of it . . . I would not like to say, however, that negligence can never go to the root of the contract." [13]

1115 **Exemption only applies to acts done in execution of the contract.** Exemption clauses only have effect while something is being done in the due execution of the contract. The act or omission giving rise to the loss or damage must be one of the kind contemplated by the contract, even if the contract has been negligently performed. " The principle is well known, and perhaps *Lilley* v. *Doubleday* [14] is the best illustration, that if you undertake to do a thing in a certain way, or to keep a thing in a certain place, with certain conditions protecting it, and have broken the contract by not doing the thing contracted for in the way contracted for, or not keeping the article in the place in which you have contracted to keep it, you cannot rely on the conditions which were only intended to protect you if you carried out the contract in the way in which you had contracted to do it." [15] So, in a contract of towage a clause whereby the tug-owner was not

Although the displayed notices stating: " Ride at own risk " were sufficient to exclude liability for breach of the implied contractual warranty, which had been broken, they were not sufficient to exclude liability in negligence found to exist because a party who wishes so to limit his liability for negligence must do that in the clearest of terms.)

10 *Rosin and Turpentine Import Co.* v. *B. Jacob & Sons* (1910) 102 L.T. 81.

11 *Calico Printers' Association* v. *Barclays Bank* (1931) 145 L.T. 51.

12 As in *Nelson Line* v. *Nelson & Sons* [1908] A.C. 16.

13 Denning L.J. in *J. Spurling Ltd.* v. *Bradshaw* [1956] 1 W.L.R. 461, 465.

14 (1881) 7 Q.B.D. 510.

15 *Per* Scrutton L.J. in *Gibaud* v. *G.E. Ry.* [1921] 2 K.B. 426, 435, quoted with approval by Atkin L.J. in *The Cap Palos* [1921] P. 458, 471 and the H.L. in *L. & N.W. Ry.* v. *Neilson* [1922] 2 A.C. 263.

responsible for " any damage or loss that may arise to any vessel or craft being towed . . . by any . . . negligence or default of the steam tug-owner " was held to have no application to a case when a tug-owner had temporarily given up the attempt to continue the towage and had left the duty to others.[16] " The exception extends to cover a default during the actual performance of the duties of the contract, and not to an unjustified handing over of those obligations to some one else for performance." [17] Where theatrical luggage and properties were consigned by rail under an owner's risk contract and, by the negligence of the railway company, the articles were sent to various destinations, instead of to the destination in the contract, it was held that the departure from the agreed transit prevented the railway company from relying on the terms of the contract.[18] Again, a clause in a contract by private carriers exempting them from liability for loss or damage was held to be no protection when there was a departure from the terms of the contract.[19] The contract was for a delivery which could be done in two and a half hours and was to be done immediately, and the departure consisted in the act of the driver in leaving the van unattended for an hour in the middle of the day, during which it was stolen. When clothes were sent to a cleaner under a contract which provided " whilst every care is exercised in cleaning . . . all orders are accepted at owner's risk . . . the proprietors' liability for loss is limited to an amount not exceeding ten times the cost of cleaning," it was held that it was a deviation from the contract to sub-contract the work, so that the cleaner was not exempted from liability when the clothes were lost at the sub-contractors.[20] Even if there is no departure from the contract, the condition as a matter of construction may only have a limited application. When an employee of the London Passenger Transport Board was given a pass to travel on the Board's vehicles with a condition that the Board were not to be liable for injury to him however caused, it was held that the condition must be limited to cases when the pass was being used for the contemplated purpose, namely to travel on the Board's vehicles, and could have no application to such cases as the employee being run over in the street or being injured while driving his own vehicle.[21]

116 **Effect of fundamental breach.** Where there has been a fundamental breach of contract by the defendants they cannot rely upon their limitation of liability clause contained in the contract. Thus where the defendants under a contract had designed and installed equipment in the plaintiffs' £150,000 factory for storing and dispensing a heavy wax but on the day that the equipment was switched on for testing it burst into flames destroying the whole factory, due to the defendants' negligence and breach of

[16] *The Cap Palos* [1921] P. 458.
[17] *Ibid. per* Lord Sterndale M.R. at p. 468.
[18] *L. & N.W. Ry.* v. *Neilson* [1922] 2 A.C. 263.
[19] *Bontex Knitting Works Ltd.* v. *St. John's Garage* [1943] 2 All E.R. 690, affd. [1944] 1 All E.R. 381.
[20] *Davies* v. *Collins* [1945] 1 All E.R. 247.
[21] *Wilkie* v. *L.P.T.B.* [1947] 1 All E.R. 258. See also *Rutter* v. *Palmer* [1922] 2 K.B. 87.

contract, it was held that they could not rely upon the exemption clause purporting to limit their liability to the total value of the contract, *viz.* £2,330.[22]

(f)—*Indemnity Cases*

1117 **Construction of clauses.** In construing indemnity clauses there are two points which commonly arise, first whether the clause covers the particular loss or damage and secondly whether the clause is restricted to third party claims or also covers claims by the party to whom the indemnity is given.[23]

A railway company granted to the plaintiffs a licence to use a portable gangway overhanging their railway lines on the terms that the plaintiffs would " indemnify the railway company against all claims and demands or liability whatsoever whether in respect of damage to person or property arising out of or in connection with the existence or user of the said gangway." Owing to the negligence of the railway company some trucks shunted down the line damaged one of the plaintiffs' lorries on the gangway. The plaintiffs sued the railway company for the damage and succeeded.[24] Three points were taken, (1) whether the clause covered claims by the plaintiffs against the railway company; (2) if so, whether it covered a claim founded on the railway company's negligence and (3) whether the damage arose out of or in connection with the user of the gangway. On the first point, MacKinnon J.[25] and the Court of Appeal [26] held that the word " indemnify " was inapt to exclude a claim by the plaintiffs, and at least was ambiguous and must be construed *contra proferentes.* On the second point, MacKinnon J. and Lord Warrington held that the words were wide enough to cover negligence on the part of the railway company, but Lord Sumner, with whom Lord Atkin agreed, took the contrary view. As the material words were " all liability whatsoever " it would seem, on the authorities quoted above,[27] that the view of MacKinnon J. and Lord Warrington is to be preferred. On the third point, MacKinnon J. and Sargant L.J. held that the damage arose out of the user of the gangway, but the House of Lords held that it did not, Lord Sumner saying [28]: " the liability was, as a matter of causation, wholly due to the acts and defaults of the railway company and did not arise at all out of or in connection with the presence or the user of the gangway." This construction seems to ignore the fact that damage may well arise out of the user of the gangway owing to the railway company's negligence, and that the presence or

[22] *Harbutt's " Plasticine " Ltd.* v. *Wayne Tank and Pump Co. Ltd.* [1970] 1 Q.B. 447. Article " Fundamental breach reappraised," (Clarke and Todd) 114 S.J. 610, 630. For other examples of the courts' policy of striking at exemption clauses wherever possible see *A. P. Salmon Contractors Ltd.* v. *Monksfield* [1970] 1 Lloyd's Rep. 387; *Farnworth Finance Facilities Ltd.* v. *Attryde* [1970] 1 W.L.R. 1053.

[23] For example a clause in a contract for gas supply whereby the consumer indemnifies the Gas Board against all claims for loss or injury due to any action or omission arising out of the supply of gas does not thereby indemnify the Board against its own negligence: *Lowery* v. *Vickers Armstrong* (*Engineers*) (1969) 8 K.I.R. 603, C.A.

[24] *G.W. Ry.* v. *J. Durnford & Sons Ltd.* (1928) 44 T.L.R. at p. 415.

[25] 43 T.L.R. 527.

[26] 43 T.L.R. 679.

[27] *Ante*, § 1111.

[28] 44 T.L.R. at p. 417.

absence of negligence on the part of the railway company is irrelevant to a consideration of the question whether the damage arose out of the existence of the gangway.

118 A clause in a towage contract whereby the shipowners agreed " to indemnify and hold harmless the Port Authority against all claim for . . . loss or damage arising in the course of and in connection with the towage . . . and whether caused or contributed to by any negligence . . . of the Port Authority " was held not to be an indemnity against party and party claims but only against third party claims.[29] It was further held that a collision with the wall of the cutting between two docks, caused by the negligence of the Port Authority's lock foreman in signalling two ships to enter the cutting at opposite ends at the same time, was not damage in connection with the towage.

119 An indemnity clause can cover party and party claims in addition to third party claims if it is expressed in sufficiently wide terms. A contract for the reconstruction of a railway bridge provided, " the contractor shall be responsible for and provide against all risks and contingencies whatever that may arise in respect to the works and shall be liable to make good and pay for . . . any . . . loss or injury of or to any person . . . and any loss of life caused in connection with the works and shall indemnify the company . . . in respect of any such accident." It was held that this bound the contractor to indemnify the railway company against claims made by the contractor's workmen against the railway company for injuries caused by their negligence. It was further held that an accident to the contractor's workmen caused by a carriage door swinging open as a train crossed the bridge was an accident in connection with the works.[30] Lord Atkin said: " It is a mistake to try to imply in the language of the clause a causal relation limited to causes which arise directly out of the works." Similarly, in a ship repairing contract which provided that the repairers " shall be responsible for and shall save harmless and indemnify the company from and against all actions, claims, losses and expenses whatsoever in respect of loss of life or personal injury or loss of or damage to property howsoever caused arising out of or in any way attributable to the execution of the works," it was held that the repairers were liable to indemnify the shipowners from damage caused by the capsizing of the ship, owing to the repairers' negligence.[31]

20 A railway company let premises to a tenant, the agreement containing a clause: " The tenant agrees to bear the risk of and be responsible for all damage injury or loss whatsoever howsoever and wheresoever caused

[29] *The Carlton* [1931] P. 186.

[30] *Furness Shipbuilding Co.* v. *L.N.E. Ry.* (1934) 50 T.L.R. 257. *G.W. Ry.* v. *J. Durnford & Sons Ltd., supra*, was distinguished on the ground that " the contract in question was not a contract such as this is, in which all the risks were imposed upon the one party, the licensee; on the contrary, there was a large range of liability which was left to be determined by ordinary common law " (Lord Atkin).

[31] *G.W. Ry.* v. *Port Talbot Dry Dock Co.* [1944] 2 All E.R. 328.

arising directly or indirectly out of or in connection with the use of the said premises or sustained by him or his workmen servants or agents while working or being on the company's line of railway or sidings and whether such damage injury or loss be caused by the act neglect or default of the company or the company's servants or agents or otherwise," with an agreement to indemnify the railway company. The tenant had a workman who, while repairing wagons on the railway company's property, was injured by the railway company's negligence. It was held that although the workman was not on the premises under any licence conferred by the tenancy agreement and his presence was not in any way connected with the tenancy, the words of the clause were unambiguous and the tenant was liable to indemnify the railway company.[32] On the other hand, an indemnity in a tenancy agreement against all damage to property however caused " which but for the tenancy hereby created . . . would not have arisen " is confined to liabilities arising solely out of the relationship of landlord and tenant. It does not prevent the tenant from recovering for damage caused to goods in the demised premises set on fire by sparks from the landlord's locomotives.[33] A licence to occupy railway premises which provided . . . " The licensees will be responsible for and will release and indemnify the [licensors] and their servants and agents from and against all liability for personal injury (whether fatal or otherwise) . . . (except when proved to have been caused solely by the neglect or default of the [licensors] their servants or agents) and which, but for the permission hereby granted, would not have arisen " entitles the licensors to an indemnity when the fatal injury was caused partly by the negligence of the deceased and partly by the negligence of the licensors.[34]

1121 A clause in a contract for the hire of a crane providing, " the driver . . . supplied by owners shall be responsible for driving or operating the plant but shall use it and be under the direction and supervision of the hirer who shall be responsible for his action as though the driver were in the hirer's direct employ " renders the hirer liable to indemnify the owner against damages awarded against the owner for the negligence of the driver while driving the crane when on hire.[35] An indemnity clause, " Where work is carried on . . . the company's premises or any other site or place specified by the company the contractor shall be liable for and shall indemnify the company against every claim against the company under any statute or at common law for . . . (b) death, and (c) personal injury arising out of or in connexion with the carrying out of the contractor's work and from any

[32] *Henson* v. *L.N.E. Ry.* [1946] 1 All E.R. 653.

[33] *John Lee & Son* v. *Railway Executive* [1949] 2 All E.R. 581.

[34] *Warrellow* v. *Chandler & Braddick* [1956] 1 W.L.R. 1272 (which followed *John Lee & Son* v. *Railway Executive, supra*). The deceased was on the railway premises at the time of his death and it was held that unless the deceased man was there under the licence he would have been a trespasser and would have had no cause of action, as the duty of the licensors arose out of the relationship of licensee and licensor and therefore the licensors were entitled to an indemnity. See however Chap. 8 on liability to trespassers.

[35] *Herdman* v. *Walker (Tooting) Ltd.* [1956] 1 W.L.R. 209 following Lord Porter in *Mersey Docks & Harbour Board* v. *Coggins & Griffith* [1947] A.C. 1, 15.

cause other than the negligence of the company or its employee " is an indemnity against claims for breach of statutory duty by whomsoever committed, so long as there is no negligence on the part of the company.[36] In *Arthur White (Contractors) Ltd.* v. *Tarmac Civil Engineering Co.*[37] it was held that the owners of a mechanical excavator crane were entitled to a full indemnity from the hirers where an accident was caused by their driver's negligence in two different respects, *viz.*: the negligent operation of the machine (the hirer's responsibility under the contract) and the negligent maintenance of the machine (the owners' responsibility under the contract). The House of Lords considered that on the true construction of the clause of the contract it was the clear intention of the parties that as between themselves, the driver was " for all purposes " in connection with his employment in the working of the plant to be regarded as the servant or agent of the hirers, thus the latter were liable for his negligence in all respects. Where an indemnity was given by the hirers to the owners of a crane " to bear the risk of and be responsible for all damage, injury or loss whatsoever, howsoever and whensoever caused arising directly or indirectly out of or in connection with the hiring or use of the crane," the Court of Appeal held that, even although there was no blameworthy cause as far as the use of the crane was concerned, nevertheless the indemnity could be invoked because if the crane had been out of use and idle there would have been no accident at all. As it was, since an accident had happened, in the occurrence of which the moving crane had played some part, the resulting loss to the owners arose directly or at least indirectly out of or in connection with the use of a crane.[38]

1122 An indemnity given against personal injury claims by a contractor's workmen against the contractor on the terms " you shall take reasonable precautions to prevent accidents and to comply with all statutory requirements, also have all your gear regularly and properly tested and not use improper or inadequate gear " means that the contractor himself shall take reasonable precautions, but does not include his servants, so that if his servants fail to take reasonable precautions the contractor is nevertheless entitled to an indemnity. Further an indemnity cannot be claimed against the owner of a machine by a hirer, whose workman had been injured by its collapse, in the absence of an express or implied warranty to service and maintain it.[39] Again, the use of gear meant its use in the contractor's business not the incidental use of it by one of his servants.[40] In the third party proceedings in *Smith* v. *Vange Scaffolding & Engineering Co. Ltd.*[41]

[36] Although breach of statutory duty may in some cases fall within the term " negligence," in this clause a distinction was drawn between statutory liability and negligence: *Murfin* v. *United Steel Companies Ltd.* [1957] 1 W.L.R. 104.

[37] [1967] 1 W.L.R. 1508.

[38] *Wright* v. *Tyne Improvement Commissioners* [1968] 1 W.L.R. 336.

[39] *Hadley* v. *Droitwich Construction Co. Ltd.* [1968] 1 W.L.R. 37.

[40] *T. F. Maltby Ltd.* v. *Pelton Steamship Co. Ltd.* [1951] 2 All E.R. 954n.

[41] [1970] 1 W.L.R. 733. (The plaintiff was employed as a scaffolder by the first defendants who were independent scaffolding contractors working on a building site where the second defendants were the main contractors. The plaintiff was walking back from his place of

the second defendants claimed an indemnity from the first defendants under a contract between them for " Any liability . . . arising in common law or statute . . . in respect of personal injuries . . . arising out of the execution of the work . . . by reason of any act, default, or omission " on the part of the first defendants. McKenna J. held that the first defendants were liable to indemnify the second defendants under this clause of the contract, which made them liable in respect of personal injuries arising by reason of their default or omission, the plaintiff's injuries being sufficiently connected with the first defendants' omission to make them liable.

1123 **Servant cannot rely on exemption contract made by employer.** A servant cannot rely on an exemption contract made by his employer as he is not a party to the contract. Where the plaintiff, who was injured while on a cruise owing to the negligence of the master and the boatswain of the ship, could not sue the shipowners, because their contract exempted them from liability for negligence, but sued the master and the boatswain, it was held that the defendants could not claim the benefit of the exemption contract.[42] On the same principle, when the London Passenger Transport Board issued the plaintiff with a free pass containing a condition that neither the Board nor their servants should be liable to him for injury however caused, and he was injured by the negligent driving of one of the Board's omnibuses, it was held that the condition did not protect the omnibus driver in an action against him by the plaintiff.[43]

(g)—*Contracting Out after Damage is Caused*

1124 **Effect of receipt.** After damage is caused, a person not under disability is under no restriction as to the contract he makes in respect of it with the party under liability to him. There is no requirement similar to that in the Workmen's Compensation Act 1925,[44] s. 23, requiring the approval of the court. The person injured by the negligence of another may be paid a sum of money in satisfaction of his claim and give a receipt expressed to be in full discharge of his claim. The question then arises whether the acceptance of the money and the giving of the receipt prevent him from bringing an action for damages against the person in whose favour the receipt has been given.

1125 A receipt is evidence of the payment of a sum of money. It does not amount to a contract, even though it may set out that the money acknowledged to be received is in full discharge of the claims therein referred to. In *Lee* v. *L. & Y. Ry.*[45] the plaintiff, who had been injured in a railway accident owing to the railway company's negligence, signed a receipt headed " Mr. Lee's claim " in these terms: " Received from the Lancashire

work to a changing hut at dusk to knock off work, when he tripped and fell over a welding cable, left suspended a few inches above the gound by an employee of the second defendants, whereby he sustained personal injuries.)

42 *Adler* v. *Dickson* [1955] 1 Q.B. 158.
43 *Cosgrove* v. *Horsfall* (1945) 62 T.L.R. 140.
44 Now repealed by the National Insurance (Industrial Injuries) Act 1946.
45 (1871) L.R. 6 Ch.App. 527.

and Yorkshire Railway Company the sum of £400 in discharge of my claim in full upon that company for all loss sustained and incurred by the late accident at Miles Platting, September 25, 1865, including all expenses attending the same." Mellish L.J. said [46]: " I had some little doubt in the course of the argument whether it might not be said that this document amounted to an agreement . . . but on looking at the document I am convinced it is simply a receipt. It simply states a fact—it does not state an agreement or purport to bind either of the parties to any terms whatever; it simply acknowledges that a sum of money was received, and then states in respect of what it was received, *viz.*, in satisfaction of the damages the plaintiff had sustained in the collision." It was accordingly held that the receipt did not prevent the plaintiff from suing for damages and proving, if he could, that the receipt was not given in full discharge of his claim.

126 As the receipt is not a contract, evidence can be given of any agreement made between the parties for the settlement of the injured party's claim. The receipt itself is evidence of the agreement, but " when once it was found that in our law a document which had not the effect of an estoppel was not an agreement, the matter was at large, and all the facts as they stood at the time the document was signed might be proved in evidence and the conclusion as to its true effect must be drawn from them."[47] If the evidence proves that the injured person agreed to take the sum paid in full satisfaction of any claim he may have against the payer in respect of his injuries, he will be unable to maintain an action, even though his bargain is an improvident one. " No doubt a man might well be ready to take a certain sum in satisfaction of such injuries as he was sensible of, which would not be any equivalent for serious and permanent injuries. Still, if in fact a man has done so, he is bound by his bargain." [48]

127 The test to be applied was stated by Mellish L.J. to be " Did the man, bona fide and fairly, knowing what he was about, receive the sum in satisfaction of his claims ? " He added that the answer " was found by considering the whole of the circumstances under which the money was received." [49] If the real agreement was that the sum was received in satisfaction of the damage known to exist at the time, but not of possible future damage, an action for such future damage will lie.[50] It is for the party relying on the agreement to prove that the person accepting the money did so on the understanding that no further payment would be made by the payer in

[46] *Ibid.* p. 534.
[47] *Per* Collins L.J. in *Ellen* v. *G.N. Ry.* (1901) 17 T.L.R. 453.
[48] *Per* Erle C.J. in *Rideal* v. *G.W. Ry.* (1859) 1 F. & F. 706. In *N.B. Ry.* v. *Wood* (1891) 18 R.(H.L.) 27, the injured party was held to his bargain under the following circumstances: he was injured in a railway accident and nine days afterwards accepted £27 in full discharge of all claims, signing a receipt to that effect, without taking any medical or legal opinion as to his condition. Eighteen months afterwards, nervous symptoms developed, in respect of which the court of first instance awarded him £500 damages. The H.L. held that the evidence did not establish that he did not understand what he was doing, or that he had reserved his rights in case he did not get better, and dismissed the action.
[49] *Lee* v. *L. & Y. Ry.* (1871) L.R. 6 Ch.App. 527, 536.
[50] *Lee* v. *L. & Y. Ry.*, *supra*; *Ellen* v. *G.N. Ry.* (1901) 17 T.L.R. 453.

respect of the same accident. The injured party must understand and know at the time that he is accepting it in full and final satisfaction and discharge.[51]

1128 A receipt which is obtained by fraud is not binding on the party giving it.[52] So, where a passenger, injured in a railway collision, accepted three guineas in full satisfaction of his claim and executed a release under seal, on the fraudulent representation of the railway company's servant that his injuries were of a trivial and temporary character, it was held that the release was no bar to the action.[53]

A receipt does not act as an estoppel. " After all, a receipt does not in itself create an estoppel of any sort or kind. You are at liberty to take all the circumstances surrounding it into consideration, and ask yourself the question what was the real intention of the parties when the receipt was given and taken." [54] On the other hand a receipt under seal would act as an estoppel.

When a receipt is given and accepted " without prejudice," the presumption is that the signer of the receipt reserves all his rights against the person in whose favour it is given. In all cases evidence can be given to show in what sense those words were used by the parties.[55]

1129 When the injured person is an infant, a contract discharging the wrongdoer from all liability to the infant is binding only if it is for the infant's benefit. In *Mattei* v. *Vautro* [56] an infant brought an action against the defendant for wages and damages for false imprisonment. He afterwards accepted 30s. in full discharge and gave a receipt which the jury held to have been given voluntarily and in settlement of all his claims. His next friend continued the action, and it was held that effect ought not to be given to the agreement on the ground that it was not for the infant's benefit. The question whether or not an agreement to compromise is for the infant's benefit has to be decided on the facts known at the time when the agreement was made.[57] A binding compromise of an infant's claim can only be made with the approval of the court.[58]

(h)—*Effect of Contract on Liability to Third Parties*

1130 **Contracting out and liability to third parties.** When a person has made a contract exempting him from liability for negligence, it remains to consider what effect that contract has on his liability towards third parties. For example, a vehicle may be hired to a person on the terms that the owner is

51 *Lee* v. *L. & Y. Ry.* (1871) L.R. 6 Ch.App. 527 at p. 538.
52 *Stewart* v. *G.W. Ry.* (1865) 2 D.J. & S. 319.
53 *Hirschfeld* v. *L.B. & S.C. Ry.* (1876) 2 Q.B.D. 1.
54 *Oliver* v. *Nautilus Steam Shipping Co. Ltd.* [1903] 2 K.B. 639, 648, *per* Vaughan Williams L.J. To the same effect is *Huckle* v. *L.C.C.* (1910) 26 T.L.R. 580, affd. 27 T.L.R. 112.
55 *Oliver* v. *Nautilus Steam Shipping Co. Ltd., supra*; *Unsworth* v. *Elder Dempster Lines Ltd.* [1940] 1 K.B. 658.
56 (1898) 78 L.T. 682. See also *Stephens* v. *Dudbridge Ironworks Co.* [1904] 2 K.B. 225.
57 *Stimpson* v. *Standard Telephones and Cables Ltd.* [1940] 1 K.B. 342; *Murray* v. *Schwachman Ltd.* [1938] 1 K.B. 130.
58 R.S.C., Ord. 80, r. 10.

not to be responsible for damage caused by any defect, and, owing to a defect, someone in the vehicle on the invitation of the hirer may be injured; or a manufacturer may sell a chattel on the same terms, and the ultimate user, with whom the manufacturer has no contract, may be injured.

1131 If the contract is made with a person who is the agent of the injured man, it is binding on the principal who can only recover for his injuries in accordance with the contract conditions. In *G. T. Ry. of Canada* v. *Robinson* [59] the respondent travelled on the railway in charge of a horse at half fare under a " special livestock contract " containing a condition exempting the railway company from liability for negligence. The ticket was paid for, obtained and signed by the horse-owner in the presence of the respondent, who put it in his pocket without reading it or knowing the conditions. The respondent was injured owing to the railway company's negligence, but it was held that he was prevented from recovering damages by the conditions of the contract, Lord Haldane saying [60]: " If the contract is one which deprives the passenger of the benefit of a duty of care which he is prima facie entitled to expect that the company has accepted, the latter must discharge the burden of proving that the passenger assented to the special terms imposed. This he may be shown to have done either in person or through the agency of another. Such agency will be held to have been established when he is shown to have authorised antecedently or by way of ratification the making of the contract under circumstances in which he must be taken to have left everything to his agent. In such a case it is sufficient to prove that he has been content to accept the risk of allowing terms to be made without taking the trouble to learn what was being agreed to."

1132 In *Fosbroke-Hobbes* v. *Airwork Ltd.*[61] an aeroplane was hired and crashed owing to the pilot's negligence, injuring the passengers. A question arose as to whether a condition in the contract made with the hirer, exempting the owner from liability for negligence, prevented the other passengers from recovering, and Goddard J. said [62]: " If a person engages a means of conveyance for himself and his guests and the party who contracts to supply the conveyance stipulates that he is to be exempt from liability, or imposes any class of condition, the guest cannot be in any better position than his host, whether the owner of the vehicle knows guests are to be carried or not . . . The obligations of the owner cannot be increased by the fact that the person with whom he has made his contract chooses to bring along persons who are in no contractual relation with the owner." As in the case last quoted, the host must be taken to be the agent of the guest, and the guest's remedy, if any, must be against the host.

59 [1915] A.C. 740.
60 *Ibid.* p. 747.
61 [1937] 1 All E.R. 108.
62 *Ibid.* p. 112. The condition was held not to be binding on any of the parties.

1133 It is provided by the Occupiers' Liability Act 1957 [63] that when an occupier of premises (including any fixed or movable structure and any vessel, vehicle or aircraft) is bound by contract to permit persons who are strangers to the contract to enter or use the premises, the duty of care which he owes to them as his visitors cannot be restricted or excluded by that contract but (subject to any provision of the contract to the contrary) includes the duty to perform his obligations under the contract, whether undertaken for their protection or not, in so far as those obligations go beyond the obligations otherwise involved in that duty. The duty, however, does not, (unless expressly so provided) have the effect of making an occupier who has taken all reasonable care answerable to strangers to the contract for dangers due to the faulty execution of any work of construction, maintenance or repair or other like operation by persons other than himself, his servants and persons acting under his direction and control. A stranger to the contract means a person not for the time being entitled to the benefit of the contract as a party to it, or as the successor by assignment or otherwise of a party to it, and accordingly includes a party to the contract who has ceased to be so entitled. This applies to all contracts, whenever entered into, but in so far as the common duty of care [64] owed by an occupier is enlarged it only applies to contracts made after January 1, 1958.

The effect of this is that in cases such as *G.T. Ry. of Canada* v. *Robinson* [65] the respondent, if governed by English law, would not be prevented by the terms of his employers' contract with the railway company from recovering. Similarly, in *Fosbroke-Hobbes* v. *Airwork Ltd.*[66] the hirer's guest would not be prevented by the conditions of the ticket from recovering. A servant of the contracting party is a " stranger to the contract " within the meaning of section 3 (3).

1134 Apart from any question of agency, a contract by the wrongdoer with one party, relieving him from liability for negligence, will not affect his liability to persons who are not parties to the contract. In *Haseldine* v. *Daw & Son* [67] a firm of lift repairers contracted with the owner of a building to keep the lift in repair on the terms that they should not be liable for accidents. Owing to their negligence, a visitor to the building was injured in the lift, but it was held that their contract was no defence. Goddard L.J. said [68]: " It is, however, argued that it is not right that a repairer who, as in the present case, has stipulated with the person who employs him that he shall not be liable for accidents, should none the less be made liable to a third person. The answer to this argument is that the duty to the third party does not arise out of the contract, but independently of it. It is, for instance, a common thing nowadays for a garage proprietor to stipulate that customers' cars are driven by him only at the sole risk of

63 S. 3.
64 *Ibid.* s. 2.
65 [1915] A.C. 740.
66 [1937] 1 All E.R. 108.
67 [1941] 2 K.B. 343. See also *Rochman* v. *J. & E. Hall Ltd.* [1947] 1 All E.R. 895.
68 [1941] 2 K.B. p. 379.

the customer. But if, while driving a customer's car, he runs into and injures a pedestrian, the contract he has made would afford no answer to the latter's claim."

1135 Further, a wrongdoer who is a sub-contractor cannot avail himself of any contractual limitation of liability made between the main contracting parties.[69] Likewise where there is a limitation of liability contained in a contract made between A and B relating to A's goods and there is another contract made between B and C relating to the carriage of such goods which also contains a similar provision limiting liability, C cannot avail himself of either provision in an action against him by A in negligence, since there is no contract between them at all.[70]

5.—LIMITATION OF ACTION

1136 **Generally.**[71] The expiry of the period of limitation under the Limitation Act 1623 did not extinguish in any case the right of the plaintiff but it did bar his remedy, and whilst certain alterations have been made by statute subsequently,[72] the Limitation Act 1939 still preserves that principle by merely imposing a time limit within which the plaintiff's action must be brought. The act is procedural so that, subject to what is provided in the Act itself, its operation may be regulated by Rules of Court. By way of example, the rules may provide for the circumstances in which a writ and subsequent pleadings may be amended after the relevant period of limitation has expired.[73] Lord Denning M.R. observed, " in my opinion, whenever a writ has been issued within the permitted time,[74] but is found to be defective, the defendant has no right to have it remain defective. The court can permit the defect to be cured by amendment: and whether it should do so depends on the practice of the court. It is a matter of practice and procedure. As such it can be altered by the Rule Committee under section 99 (1) (*a*)[75] of the Supreme Court of Judicature (Consolidation)

[69] *Midland Silicones Ltd.* v. *Scruttons Ltd.* [1962] A.C. 446; *Genys* v. *Matthews* [1966] 1 W.L.R. 758.

[70] *Lee Cooper Ltd.* v. *C. H. Jeakins & Son* [1967] 2 Q.B. 1; *Garnham, Harris & Elton Ltd.* v. *A. W. Ellis (Transport) Ltd.* [1967] 1 W.L.R. 940; *Moukataff* v. *B.O.A.C.* [1967] 1 Lloyd's Rep. 396. See, however, the provisions of the Carriage by Air Act 1961, Sched. 1, Art. 25A.

[71] See articles: " Limitation of Actions," (Glover) 116 New L.J. 1222, 1242; " Problems of limitation ": " 1. Personal injuries—suing out of time," (Goodman) 119 New L.J. 500; " 2. Fraud and Mistake," 119 New L.J. 546; " 3. Disabilities—Custody of parent," 119 New L.J. 618; " 4. Acknowledgments," 119 New L.J. 738; " 5. Amendment of pleadings," 119 New L.J. 814; " 6. Exclusion by contract or estoppel," 119 New L.J. 872.

[72] So far as concerns real property, by the Real Property Limitation Act 1833, see now the Limitation Act 1939, s. 16; and by s. 3 of the 1939 Act whereby the title to personalty may become extinguished once the limitation period has expired.

[73] *Rodriguez* v. *R. J. Parker* [1967] 1 Q.B. 116; *Mitchell* v. *Harris Engineering Co. Ltd.* [1967] 2 Q.B. 703.

[74] It should be emphasised that a writ served on a first defendant within twelve months is not valid for service on a second defendant after the expiration of that period: *Jones* v. *Jones* [1970] 2 Q.B. 576.

[75] Which provides that Rules of Court may be made for " regulating and prescribing the procedure . . . and the practice to be followed in . . . the High Court."

Act 1925."[76] Now under the new Rules of the Supreme Court[77] there is a wide discretion[78] to permit amendments even if, in the result, a defendant may be deprived of a defence under the Act, when compared with the restrictions of the former practice which leaned generally towards allowing a defendant to insist upon retaining a benefit that had accrued under the Limitation Act.[79]

1137 Nevertheless in *Braniff* v. *Holland & Hannen and Cubitts* (*Southern*) *Ltd.*[80] the Court of Appeal refused leave to a plaintiff to amend his writ so as to add a second defendant, after the expiry of the period of limitation applicable to his cause of action, holding that the fact that under R.S.C., Order 20, r. 5, amendments were to be permitted in certain specific cases although the statutory period had run did not mean that there had in general been a relaxation of the rule that the courts would not, except in special circumstances, allow an amendment to be made which would take away a defence that had arisen under the Limitation Act. The court also held that, since there were no special circumstances, the case fell into the same class as that in which a plaintiff sought to renew an expired writ after the expiry of the limitation period and the judge had been entitled in his discretion properly to dismiss the plaintiff's appeal against the master's decision.

1138 A defendant must plead specifically that the action is out of time, if he desires to rely upon the defence of limitation to bar the action.[81] The Act does not confer any right on him[82] other than to plead the defence, should he be so minded to do. It has been pointed out by Nield J. that "the Act does not provide that after such period the plaintiff's remedy shall be extinguished or even wholly cease to be enforceable, and indeed the remedy is not extinguished, nor does it wholly cease to be enforceable; for if a defendant elects not to plead the Statute of Limitations, the remedy may be pursued after the period of limitation. Further than that, the benefit which a defendant derives from the Statute of Limitations is not, I think, properly described as a substantive benefit but really is merely as a right to plead a defence if he chooses to do so that the plaintiff is barred from prosecuting his claim."[83]

1139 Vaughan Williams L.J. has emphasised that "a Statute of Limitations

[76] *Mitchell* v. *Harris Engineering Co. Ltd.* [1967] 2 Q.B. 703, at p. 718 E.
[77] R.S.C., Ord. 20, r. 5.
[78] *Ibid.* r. 5 (3) and (5) to some extent limit the discretion, which in any event would be exercised with considerable care in order to avoid an injustice.
[79] *Marshall* v. *L.P.T.B.* [1936] 3 All E.R. 83; *Batting* v. *L.P.T.B.* [1941] 1 All E.R. 228; *Hilton* v. *Sutton Steam Laundry* [1946] K.B. 65; *Davies* v. *Elsby Brothers* [1961] 1 W.L.R. 170.
[80] [1969] 1 W.L.R. 1533. Widgery L.J. at p. 1541 expressed his disagreement with the dictum of Lord Denning M.R. in *Chatsworth Investments Ltd.* v. *Cussins* (*Contractors*) *Ltd.* [1969] 1 W.L.R. 1, 5, to the effect that the court ought to permit an amendment whenever it is just to do so, even although such amendment may deprive a defendant of his defence of limitation. Further, see the effect of *Lucy* v. *Henleys Telegraph Works Co. Ltd.* [1970] 1 Q.B. 393 for cases falling under the provisions of the Limitation Act 1963.
[81] R.S.C., Ord. 18, r. 8 (1).
[82] *Mitchell* v. *Harris Engineering Co. Ltd.*, *supra*, at p. 718 B.
[83] *Rodriguez* v. *R. J. Parker* [1967] 1 Q.B. 116, at p. 136. See also *Seabridge* v. *H. Cox & Sons* (*Plant Hire*) *Ltd.* [1968] 2 Q.B. 46.

cannot begin to run unless there are two things present—a party capable of suing and a party liable to be sued." [84] If therefore the wrongdoer is entitled to diplomatic immunity [85] at the time of the tort, time will not begin to run against the plaintiff until the former's immunity ceases,[86] since at the time when the cause of action arose there was no defendant capable of being sued. Where all the ingredients of the cause of action exist but the precise identity of the wrongdoer is unknown to the plaintiff, this fact make no difference and it does not prevent time running. Thus where a car was stolen by some unknown thieves the plaintiff's cause of action in conversion became statute-barred six years later although he never had had the opportunity of suing any known defendant.[87] In the case of actions in tort against the estates of deceased persons, where there are no personal representatives, see § 1150, *post*.

1140 **Periods of limitation.** The Limitation Act 1939,[88] s. 2 (1), as amended by the Law Reform (Limitation of Actions, etc.) Act 1954, s. 2 (1), provides: " The following actions shall not be brought after the expiration of six years from the date on which the cause of action accrued, that is to say:—

" (*a*) actions founded on simple contract or on tort. . . . Provided that, in the case of actions for damages for negligence, nuisance or breach of duty (whether the duty exists by virtue of a contract or of provision made by or under a statute or independently of any contract or any such provision) where the damages claimed by the plaintiff for the negligence, nuisance or breach of duty consist of or include damages in respect of personal injuries [89] to any person, this subsection shall have effect as if for the reference to six years there were substituted a reference to three years."

The proviso applies to all causes of action which arose on or after June 4, 1954.

The effect of this seems to be that when the damage caused by negligence consists of personal injuries to any person and also damage to property there will be two periods of limitation, three years in respect of the personal injuries and six years in respect of the damage to property, unless one action is brought for both heads of damage, in which case it appears that the period of limitation for both heads will be three years. This seems to follow from *Brunsden* v. *Humphrey*,[90] where it was held that in the case of a highway collision an action for damages for the personal

[84] *Thomson* v. *Lord Clanmorris* [1900] 1 Ch. 718, 728, 729.
[85] See Chap. 13, § 871.
[86] *Musurus Bey* v. *Gadban* [1894] 1 Q.B. 533.
[87] *R.B. Policies at Lloyd's* v. *Butler* [1950] 1 K.B. 76. See article " First Catch your Defendant—Limitation and the Unknown Tortfeasor," (Goodman) (1966) 29 M.L.R. 366. Also see *Clark* v. *Forbes Stuart* (*Thames Street*) *Ltd.* (*Intended Action*) [1964] 1 W.L.R. 836.
[88] The rules for the limitation of actions for damages for personal injury claims have been further modified by the Limitation Act 1963, see § 1151, *post*.
[89] " Includes any disease and any impairment of a person's physical or mental condition." Law Reform (Limitation of Actions, etc.) Act 1954, s. 2 (3).
[90] (1884) 14 Q.B.D. 141. See also *Barnes* v. *Pooley* (1935) 51 T.L.R. 391.

injuries did not bar a subsequent action for damages to the vehicle sustained in the same collision, on the ground that the two heads of damage gave rise to different causes of action.

1141 In *Letang* v. *Cooper* [91] an attempt to bring an action outside the three-year limitation period based on trespass to the person failed where the plaintiff's legs were accidentally run over by a car as she lay on the grass sun-bathing. It was held that her only cause of action arose in negligence, which action had been statute-barred after the lapse of time, but even if the cause of action were trespass to the person, then the words " breach of duty " in the proviso added to section 2 (1) of the Act of 1939 covered such a cause of action and the action should have been brought within the three-year limitation period. The same was held to apply in the case of an intentional trespass to the person. Thus where, on August 26, 1960, the infant plaintiff was playing with a water pistol by the side of a road and some water struck the defendant on the hair as he was working in a hole so that he wrongfully threw a handful of cement at her, injuring her eye, her writ issued on August 25, 1966, was held to be statute barred.[92] However, as has already been indicated, the Statute of Limitations does not confer any right on the defendant, its only imposing a time limit on the plaintiff. Accordingly where a writ, though defective, had been issued within the limitation period and " an amendment to correct the name of a party " within the meaning of R.S.C. Ord. 20, r. 5 (3), in a case where there had been a genuine mistake which did not mislead the defendants was sought, it was held by the Court of Appeal that the master and judge had correctly exercised their discretion to grant the amendment outside the limitation period.[93] Although the proceedings must be commenced within the required period provided by the statute, it is not necessary to serve the writ within that period. However it must be served during the period of its validity [94] and where a new defendant is added within the limitation period to a writ which has been served already on the original defendants the plaintiff still has twelve months during which it must be served on the new defendant.[95]

1142 **When time begins to run.** In an action of negligence, the cause of action accrues at the time when the damage is actually caused, even though its

91 [1964] 2 Q.B. 53.
92 *Long* v. *Hepworth* [1968] 1 W.L.R. 1299.
93 *Mitchell* v. *Harris Engineering Co.* [1967] 2 Q.B. 703, 718 B.
94 R.S.C., Ord. 6, r. 8 (1). This 12 months' period may be extended by order of the court (sub-r. (2)) but this jurisdiction to extend will only be exercised sparingly: *Battersby* v. *Anglo-American Oil Co. Ltd.* [1945] K.B. 23; *Heaven* v. *Road and Rail Wagons Ltd.* [1965] 2 Q.B. 355.
95 *Rodriguez* v. *Parker* [1967] 1 Q.B. 116; *Chatsworth Investments Ltd.* v. *Cussins (Contractors) Ltd.* [1969] 1 W.L.R. 1. On the other hand *cf. Braniff* v. *Holland & Hannen and Cubitts (Southern) Ltd.* [1969] 1 W.L.R. 1533, where the C.A. refused leave for the writ to be amended to include a second defendant after the expiry of the period of limitation. Further see *Lucy* v. *Henleys Telegraph Works Co. Ltd.* [1970] 1 Q.B. 393. R.S.C., Ord. 20, r. 5, which was first introduced in 1964, has given the court a wide discretion to allow amendments even if the result may deprive a defendant of a defence under the Act. This discretion however will doubtlessly be exercised with care. See § 1136, *ante.*

consequences may not be apparent until later. As a general rule the dates of the damage and the negligence will be the same but circumstances can occur otherwise.[96] Accordingly, by way of illustration of the latter, where a person is injured by a chattel which has been negligently manufactured he may sue the manufacturer within the three-year period which begins to run from the date of the injury, even though more than three years may well have expired since the chattel in question was produced and had left the maker's factory premises.[97] On the other hand where the negligence constitutes a breach of contract, despite the fact that such negligence may also be tortious, time begins to run from that negligent act and not from the time when the damage actually results.[98] Thus in *Howell* v. *Young*,[99] a solicitor was sued for negligence in representing that certain mortgages were sufficient security for a loan. More than six years after the alleged negligence damage was suffered and an action was begun, to which the solicitor pleaded that it was statute-barred. The plea was upheld, Holroyd J. saying: " I think it makes no difference in this respect whether the plaintiff elects to bring an action of assumpsit founded upon a breach of promise, or a special action on the case founded upon a breach of duty. The breach of promise or of duty took place as soon as the defendant took the insufficient security. Whether the plaintiff, therefore, elect to sue in one form of action or another, the cause of action, which in either form is substantially the same, accrued at the same moment of time. The breach of duty, therefore, constituting a cause of action, it follows that the Statute of Limitations is a bar to this action, unless the special damage alleged in the declaration constitute a new cause of action." It was held that it did not do so. This case was followed in *Archer* v. *Catton & Co. Ltd.*,[1] where a workman between 1923 and 1940 had worked in a confined space in which a quantity of brick-dust was given off. In 1943, for the first time, he found himself suffering from chest trouble

[96] The statement of the law by the author in his editions was: " In an action of negligence, the cause of action accrues at the time of the negligence, because it is then that the damage is caused, even though its consequences may not be apparent until later," which was applied in *Archer* v. *Catton & Co. Ltd.* [1954] 1 W.L.R. 775. It is submitted that although this statement by the author is correct, it could be misleading. See the comments upon this passage by both Sellers L.J. and Pearson L.J. in *Cartledge* v. *E. Jopling & Sons Ltd.* [1962] 1 Q.B. 189, 197, 206.

[97] An extreme example could be found where vintage port had become contaminated negligently by arsenic during production and prior to bottling by the producer so that no damage was suffered until the wine was consumed, perhaps, some 25 years or more later.

[98] *Bagot* v. *Stevens Scanlan & Co. Ltd.* [1966] 1 Q.B. 197 (architect employed in March 1955 to supervise the laying of a drainage system on the plaintiffs' land, which work was completed by February 1957, when the architect's supervisory duty ceased. On April 2, 1963, a writ was issued alleging in the statement of claim that the architect had failed to exercise reasonable care in effecting the duty under the contract, with the result that several of the pipes comprised in the drainage system broke in 1961, causing water to escape and cause damage. On the preliminary issue whether time under the Limitation Act 1939 ran from the date of the last act of negligence alleged or the date when damage first occurred it was held by Diplock L.J. (the trial judge) that as the duty arose out of contract alone, the action was statute-barred since the cause of action arose, if at all, from the earlier date).

[99] (1826) 5 B. & C. 259. See also *Smith* v. *Fox* (1848) 6 Hare 386; *Bean* v. *Wade* (1885) 2 T.L.R. 157; *Hughes* v. *Twisden* (1886) 55 L.J.Ch. 481; *Wood* v. *Jones* (1889) 61 L.T. 551; *Merlihan* v. *Pope* [1946] K.B. 166.

[1] [1954] 1 W.L.R. 775. *Cf. Clarkson* v. *Modern Foundries Ltd.* [1957] 1 W.L.R. 1210.

caused by the dust. In 1949 he started proceedings, but it was held that his claim was statute-barred as the cause of the action was complete by 1940.

1143 The possibility in personal injury cases that a cause of action could accrue unbeknown to a plaintiff, who was totally unaware that he had suffered any damage at all so that when he did discover its existence it was then too late, because his cause of action had in the meantime become statute-barred, was highlighted in *Cartledge* v. *E. Jopling & Sons Ltd.*[2] The plaintiffs, who were steel dressers in the defendants' factory, contracted pneumoconiosis after they had inhaled noxious silica dust to which they had been exposed over a period of many years as a result of the negligence and breach of statutory duty of the defendants. However, as there had been no breach of the defendants' duty during the relevant period of years of limitation immediately preceding the commencement of proceedings, the plaintiffs had already suffered their actionable personal injuries to their lungs so that their actions had become statute-barred before they had even been made aware that they had contracted the disease. The law in personal injury cases has now been altered by the Limitation Act 1963 [3] in the light of this apparent injustice.

1144 As regards the computation of time of limitation, the day on which the cause of action arose, generally, is excluded but the day when the action is begun is included.[4] Care must be exercised, nevertheless, where the last day of the limitation period falls on a day when the court offices are closed. The writ in such circumstances must be issued on the day previous to the holiday, since it will be too late then if it be issued on the subsequent day.[5] A further point is that once the period of limitation has begun to run in respect of a cause of action in tort it is not broken by any disability,[6] which subsequently accrues, and it makes no difference that at any one time over the material period there was nobody in existence capable of pursuing the action.[7] It follows that where a person, who has a vested cause of action, has died before he has commenced proceedings and no personal representatives have been appointed until time has expired, the action will be statute barred.[8]

1145 **Effect of fraudulent concealment.** Where the right of action is concealed by the fraud of the defendant or his agent or of any person through whom

[2] [1963] A.C. 758. See also *Brazier* v. *Ministry of Defence* [1965] 1 Lloyd's Rep. 26, where it was held that when a syringe needle had broken in the plaintiff's buttock during the giving of a penicillin injection in 1956, this invasion of the buttock by a foreign body with potentially serious consequences in the future was sufficient of itself to complete an accrual of an action. By 1960 the action of negligence had been statute-barred even although the broken needle-point had only recently shifted its position and had penetrated the groin which had required operative removal and treatment.

[3] See further, § 1151, *post*.

[4] *Marren* v. *Dawson Bentley & Co.* [1961] 2 Q.B. 135. *Cf. Goldsmith's Co.* v. *West Metropolitan Ry.* [1904] 1 K.B. 1 *per* Mathew L.J. at p. 5, which was applied in *Stewart* v. *Chapman* [1951] 2 K.B. 792 but distinguished in *Hare* v. *Gocher* [1962] 2 Q.B. 641.

[5] *Morris* v. *Richards* (1881) 45 L.T. 210; *McGowan* v. *Middleton* (1883) 11 Q.B.D. 464.

[6] See § 1146 *et seq.*, *post*, for greater detail of "disability."

[7] *Smith* v. *Hill* (1746) 1 Wils. 134; *Homfray* v. *Scroope* (1849) 13 Q.B. 509.

[8] *Penny* v. *Brice* (1865) 18 C.B. (N.S.) 393; *Boatwright* v. *Boatwright* [1873) L.R. 17 Eq. 71.

he claims or his agent, the period of limitation does not begin to run until the plaintiff has discovered the fraud or could with reasonable diligence have discovered it.[9] No degree of moral turpitude was necessary to establish fraud,[10] since it covered conduct, which having regard to the relationship of the parties, was unconscionable such as where solicitors employed on her behalf concealed from the plaintiff an offer by an electricity company to pay a sum of money for the death of her husband who had been electrocuted in the kitchen of their house.[11] In these circumstances the period of limitation did not begin to run in respect of the solicitors' negligence so that her cause of action was not statute barred.

146 **Extension of limitation period in case of disability.** The Limitation Act 1939, s. 22, provides: " If on the date when any right of action accrued for which a period of limitation is prescribed by this Act, the person to whom it accrued was under a disability, the action may be brought at any time before the expiration of six years . . . from the date when the person ceased to be under a disability or died, whichever event first occurred, notwithstanding that the period of limitation has expired. Provided that—

(*a*) this section shall not affect any case where the right of action first accrued to some person (not under a disability) through whom the person under a disability claims;

(*b*) when a right of action which has accrued to a person under a disability accrues on the death of that person while still under a disability, to another person under a disability, no further extension of time shall be allowed by reason of the disability of the second person."

" (2) [added by the Law Reform (Limitation of Actions, etc.) Act 1954, s. 2 (2)]. In the case of actions for damages for negligence, nuisance or breach of duty (whether the duty exists by virtue of a contract or of provision made by or under a statute or independently of any contract or any such provision) where the damages claimed by the plaintiff for the negligence, nuisance or breach of contract consist of or include damages in respect of personal injuries to any person,—

(*a*) the preceding provisions of this section shall have effect as if for the words ' six years ' there were substituted the words ' three years '; and

(*b*) this section shall not apply unless the plaintiff proves that the person under disability was not, at the time when the right of action accrued to him, in the custody of a parent." [12]

As a general rule persons under a disability therefor have the same time, after they cease to be under the disability, within which to bring an

[9] Limitation Act 1939, s. 26. *G. L. Baker Ltd.* v. *Medway Building & Supplies Ltd.* [1958] 1 W.L.R. 1216; *Eddis* v. *Chichester Constable* [1969] 2 Ch. 345.

[10] *Beaman* v. *A.R.T.S. Ltd.* [1949] 1 K.B. 550, 567.

[11] *Kitchen* v. *Royal Air Force Association* [1958] 1 W.L.R. 563; *Clark* v. *Woor* [1965] 1 W.L.R. 650 (inferior bricks) ; *Applegate* v. *Moss* [1971] 1 Q.B. 406 (defective unsafe foundations).

[12] " Parent " has the same meaning as in the Fatal Accidents Act 1846 as extended by the Law Reform (Miscellaneous Provisions) Act 1934, by virtue of s. 31 (1) of the Limitation Act 1939. Accordingly it includes besides the infant's mother and father, a stepmother, a stepfather, grandmother, grandfather, as well as illegitimate and adoptive relationships.

action whether for damages for personal injuries or for other damages as persons not under a disability. A person is under a disability " while he is an infant,[13] or of unsound mind, or a convict subject to the operation of the Forfeiture Act 1870 [14] in whose case no administrator or curator has been appointed under that Act." [15]

1147 The disability under section 22 does not prevent an infant or person of unsound mind from bringing an action if he is otherwise able to do so. The section only extends the limit of time within which the action can be brought.[16] An infant can bring an action by his next friend as soon as the cause of action accrues,[17] and will usually be well advised to do so when he has a cause of action in negligence, instead of waiting until he is of age when he may have difficulty in procuring evidence owing to the lapse of time. A person of unsound mind sues by his committee or next friend.[18] When a person, certified as a lunatic in 1912 and detained in an asylum until 1921, escaped and brought an action in 1922 claiming damages for negligence on the part of the doctor who certified him, and the jury found that he was not of unsound mind in 1912 and that the doctor was negligent, it was held that the action was barred because the plaintiff was not " *non compos mentis* " at the date of the negligent certification.[19] Now, however, a person is conclusively presumed to be of unsound mind (a) while he is liable to be detained or subject to guardianship under the Mental Health Act 1959, and (b) while he is receiving treatment as an in-patient in any hospital or mental nursing home within the meaning of the Act without being liable to be detained thereunder,[20] being treatment which follows without any interval a period during which he was liable to be detained or subject to guardianship.

In *Kirby* v. *Leather* [21] the plaintiff, aged twenty-four years, failed to wear a crash helmet whilst riding his motor scooter so that he sustained particularly severe head injuries after he had collided with a van. He was rendered fully unconscious for several weeks but eventually recovered consciousness to some degree. Nevertheless the medical evidence was that he suffered continuously from mental illness due to a brain trauma, which rendered him paranoic and aggressive, with defective comprehension and memory,

[13] As from January 1, 1970, a person shall attain full age on attaining the age of eighteen instead of on attaining the age of twenty-one: s. 1 (1) Family Law Reform Act 1969, c. 46 and the Family Law Reform (Commencement No. 1) Order 1969, S.I. 1969 No. 1140.

[14] The Forfeiture Act 1870, ss. 6 to 30, is repealed by the Criminal Justice Act 1948, so that a convict is no longer a person under a disability within the meaning of the Limitation Act 1939, s. 22.

[15] Limitation Act 1939, s. 31 (2).

[16] *Forbes* v. *Smith* (1855) 11 Ex. 161.

[17] R.S.C., Ord. 80, r. 2.

[18] R.S.C., Ord. 80, r. 3.

[19] *Harnett* v. *Fisher* [1927] A.C. 573.

[20] Limitation Act 1939 s. 31 (3), as amended by s. 149 (1) and Sched. VII to the Mental Health Act 1959 (*supra*), was passed to meet such a case as *Harnett* v. *Fisher*, *supra*.

[21] [1965] 2 Q.B. 367. See also *Penrose* v. *Mansfield* (1971) 115 S.J. 309. (Because a passenger, whose brain was severely damaged in a car crash, failed to prove that he was incapable of managing his affairs in relation to the accident a month after it had happened, he could not succeed in his claim for damages against the driver after the action was begun a month outside the three years' limitation period.)

and that he was, owing to his mental state, virtually unemployable and the prognosis was that he would so remain. In these circumstances the Court of Appeal held that a person was of unsound mind for the purposes of section 31 (2) of the Limitation Act 1939 if by reason of mental illness he was incapable of managing his affairs in relation to the accident, which was the subject-matter of his claim, as a reasonable man would do.[22]

1148 The exception to the general rule aforesaid is in actions of damages for personal injuries when time still runs from the moment when the cause of action accrues irrespective of the disability unless the plaintiff proves that he was not at that material time " in the custody of a parent." [23] In cases of persons of unsound mind it is difficult to attach any sensible meaning to the phrase, and, as Danckwerts L.J. observed, " I can only conclude that the draftsman must have had in mind the case of a harmless imbecile or mongol who could be expected to be actually in the custody of his parents." [24] Thus a young adult of twenty-four years of age was held not to be in his mother's custody at the time of the accident, which had caused his mental illness, although afterwards he continued to live with her in her home and to be looked after by her for all his needs.[25] In cases of infancy no particular problem arises normally where the minor is living at home, is dependent upon and is effectively looked after by his parent or parents [26] but problems have been raised where the minor has been living away from home or living a substantially independent life. In *Hewer* v. *Bryant* [27] a boy of fifteen and the son of a veterinary surgeon, after leaving school, and going to a farm training centre for residential training, went to a farm for his

[22] *Ibid., per* Lord Denning M.R. at p. 383, who added: " It is similar to the test where a guardian *ad litem* or a next friend is appointed under the new R.S.C. Ord. 80, r. 1. That states that a person under a disability means 'a person who by reason of mental disorder is incapable of managing and administering his property and affairs.' " Winn L.J., however, at p. 386 added the caution " that care must be taken not to confuse the decision which has been announced in these judgments with any such proposition . . . as this, that there can be a suspension of the running of the statutory limitation period during such time as an injured person is unconscious or ill or in a state of delirium without more being shown."

[23] See note 12 to § 1146, *ante*, for persons included in the meaning of " parent."

[24] *Kirby* v. *Leather* [1965] 2 Q.B. 367, 386.

[25] *Kirby* v. *Leather, supra.*

[26] In *Todd* v. *Davison* [1971] 2 W.L.R. 898 (H.L.) affirming [1971] 1 W.L.R 267. In a reserved judgment Dunn J. rejected the argument that the expression used in the subjective test laid down by the Court of Appeal in *Hewer* v. *Bryant, post,* namely one of " effective care and control " went beyond the fact of mere physical control and that in each case the Court ought to determine as a fact the *quality* of that care and control, *i.e.* whether the child had parents so circumstanced who could be relied on to take all proper steps and action on his behalf, he being *inops concilii.* Briefly the facts were that in 1962 the plaintiff then aged six years sustained very serious brain damage in a motor accident but his parents, who were both of very limited intelligence, of defective character and in poor circumstances, singularly failed in their duties to do anything about pursuing an action for damages on the child's behalf, beyond taking cursory advice, until pressed into doing something about it by the good offices of the Dr. Barnardo's organisation. In due course a writ was issued on June 19, 1968, and the court heard the preliminary issue whether or not the claim was statute barred. Following the leapfrogging procedure provided by the Administration of Justice Act 1969, on appeal direct to the House of Lords it was held, dismissing the appeal, that the words denoted a state of fact and it sufficed if the circumstances were such that a parent was in a position to exercise powers of control should he desire so to do, as would be the case where the child was in his care.

[27] [1970] 1 Q.B. 357.

practical training where he lived on the farm and received a working wage but was not in receipt of any allowance from his father. In August 1962 he suffered severe personal injuries when a truck in which he was a passenger left the road whilst being driven by the defendant who was a fellow trainee of the plaintiff. After the accident the plaintiff's father had considered whether or not to issue a writ as the plaintiff's next friend but had decided against it. However upon the boy's attaining his majority in December 1967 a writ claiming damages for personal injuries caused by the alleged negligent driving of the defendant was issued in January 1968. The question whether the plaintiff's claim was statute barred, since the writ had been issued over three years after the accident, was tried as a preliminary issue. Relying upon section 22 of the Limitation Act 1939, as amended by section 2 (2) of the Law Reform (Limitation of Actions, etc.) Act 1954, the plaintiff contended that at the time when his right of action accrued, some five years and more previously, he was under the disability of infancy and was not in the custody of a parent. The Court of Appeal, in reversing the decision of Paull J.,[28] held that as there was no rule of law that a father had custody of his children until they had become twenty-one years of age, it was a question of fact whether or not an infant is in the effective care and control of a parent. The same view had been taken by Melford Stevenson J. in *Brook* v. *Hoar* [29] in holding that as section 22 (2) (*b*), as amended, contemplated the possibility of an infant not being in the custody of a parent and, since there was no reason to assume that an infant must be in the custody of a parent until either he attained his majority or both his parents died, it was a question of fact in each case whether an infant was in the custody of a parent. Since the plaintiff had been enjoying complete economic independence from both his parents and freedom to live as and where he chose, it was held that he was not at the time when the action accrued in the custody of a parent. Likewise in *Duncan* v. *Lambeth London Borough Council* [30] Donaldson J. held the plaintiff not to be in the custody of a parent when the circumstances were such that the father could not reasonably be expected to have taken such action to prosecute her claim as could be expected of him if the claim were his own, because the plaintiff was in the care of the defendants in one of their homes.

1149 **Effect of death.**[31] When the negligence of one person causes the death of another, an action by or on behalf of the dependants under the Fatal Accidents Acts must be brought within three years of the death.[32] An action by the personal representative of the deceased for damage to his

[28] [1969] 1 Q.B. 415.
[29] [1967] 1 W.L.R. 1336 (18-year-old boy, who had his own key of the front door to his parent's home, where he lived, enjoyed economic and social independence. He was described by his father as a " young lodger " who gave his mother money for his keep).
[30] [1968] 1 Q.B. 747 (three-year-old girl, who was received into the care of the L.C.C. under s. 1 of the Children Act 1948 and was placed in a home in Croydon where she was visited regularly by her father who was well aware that she had been injured as a result of a bowl of hot soup being carried by a servant of the home and being spilled over her.
[31] See Chap. 19, § 1281, *post*, Limitation of Action.
[32] Law Reform (Limitation of Actions, etc.) Act 1954 s. 3.

estate under the Law Reform (Miscellaneous Provisions) Act 1934 is governed by the Limitation Act 1939, s. 2, as amended by the Law Reform (Limitation of Actions, etc.) Act 1954, s. 2 (1). If, therefore, the action consists of or includes damages in respect of loss of expectation of life, it must be brought within three years of the negligence, nuisance or breach of duty, but if it only consists of damages in respect of the deceased's real or personal property, it can be brought within six years. If the action is begun before the grant of administration, a subsequent grant does not relate back so as to validate the proceedings.[33]

But to enable a plaintiff to bring such an action the deceased must have been able to bring an action at the date of his death [34] so that if at that date his right of action is already barred, *e.g.* under the Limitation Act 1939 the right of action under the Fatal Accidents Acts is also barred.[35] If, however, the deceased died before his right of action was barred, it would appear that an action under the Fatal Accidents Acts may be brought, provided that three years have not elapsed since the death of the deceased, even though his right of action would have become barred meanwhile, if he had survived.[36] In addition where, at the date of his death, the deceased could have fulfilled the requirements of the Limitation Act 1963 [37] as suitably modified to fit the circumstances this latter Act applies so that with the leave of the court an action under the Fatal Accidents Acts can be brought within one year of the deceased's death.[38] For the position of fatal cases under the Carriage by Air Act 1961, see § 1162, *post*, and under the Maritime Conventions Act 1911, see § 1163, *post*.

1150 On the death of a person who is liable to be sued for negligence, the cause of action survives against his estate.[39] Prior to the coming into force of the Proceedings Against Estates Act 1970 [40] unless proceedings were actually pending at the date of his death, they had to be taken not later than six months after representation had been taken out, otherwise they would have been barred by virtue of the Law Reform (Miscellaneous Provisions) Act 1934, s. 1 (3), as amended by the Law Reform (Limitation of Actions, etc.) Act 1954, s. 4, which clearly constituted a period of limitation.[41] Where an action is one for which a period of limitation is already

33 *Ingall* v. *Moran* [1944] K.B. 160. See also *Hilton* v. *Sutton Steam Laundry* [1946] K.B. 65; *Burns* v. *Campbell* [1952] 1 K.B. 15.
34 Fatal Accidents Act 1846, s. 1.
35 *Williams* v. *Mersey Docks and Harbour Board* [1905] 1 K.B. 804.
36 *Venn* v. *Tedesco* [1926] 2 K.B. 227 following *British Columbia Electric Ry.* v. *Gentile* [1914] A.C. 1034.
37 Fully considered § 1151, *post*.
38 See Limitation Act 1963, s. 3.
39 Law Reform (Miscellaneous Provisions) Act 1934, s. 1 (1).
40 1970, c. 17, came into force on January 1, 1971, by virtue of the Proceedings Against Estates Act 1970 Commencement Order 1970, No. 1860.
41 For example: *Cambria Garages* v. *Lodge* (1966) 110 S.J. 724. (Where a plaintiff issued a writ claiming damages for negligence more than six months after the grant of letters of administration, the defendant administratrix contended that the claim was time-barred under s. 1 (3) of the Law Reform (Miscellaneous Provisions) Act 1934. The plaintiff then relied on the fact that the address of the deceased and the administratrix was wrongly stated in the grant as to the county of residence but it was held that since it could not be

prescribed, the period of limitation that is prescribed by the Limitation Act 1939 is excluded by the provisions of section 32. This is well illustrated in *Airey* v. *Airey* [42] where letters of administration were only taken out six years after the defendant's death in an accident, in which the plaintiff also was injured; it was held that her action was not statute-barred because she had still commenced proceedings within six months of the taking out of letters of administration, even though proceedings against the deceased himself would have been effectively barred had he been alive when the proceedings were commenced. In the court below Diplock J. took the opportunity of pointing out that, " it would seem, therefore, that today, although so long as a tortfeasor lives no action can be brought against him for damages for personal injuries after three years have passed since the cause of action arose, the moment he dies, however long after the cause of action arose, an action can be brought for the tort against his personal representative, since the only limitation period for such an action is six months after the appointment of his personal representative. A cause of action does not cease to exist because a limitation period has expired, and the original cause of action would therefore be one subsisting against the tortfeasor at the time of his death, and would survive against his estate by virtue of section 1 (1) of the Act of 1934." [43] The Court of Appeal carefully avoided becoming involved in having to make any pronouncement upon this corollary.[44] In its Report " Proceedings against Estates " [45] the Law Commission recommended the abolition of this rule that proceedings must be commenced within six months of the date when the personal representatives took out representation to the deceased's estate in respect of tortious actions against estates of deceased persons, so that the ordinary periods of limitation applicable in cases of tort should apply regardless of the fact of the tortfeasor's death. Effect was given to this recommendation by the Proceedings Against Estates Act 1970.[46] By section 2 it is enacted that rules of court may make provision: (a) for enabling proceedings to be commenced against the estate of a deceased person (whether by the appointment of a person to represent the estate or otherwise) where no grant of probate or administration has been made; (b) for enabling proceedings purporting to be commenced against a person who has died to be treated as having been commenced against his estate; and (c) for enabling any proceedings commenced or treated as commenced against the estate of a

alleged that the misdescription would justify a revocation of the grant, the grant was good and thus the defence under s. 1 (3) was unanswerable.)

[42] [1958] 2 Q.B. 300: The plaintiff sustained injuries on February 24, 1951, whilst a passenger in the car driven by her son who was killed in the accident. Letters of administration to the son's estate were not taken out until March 18, 1957, and on September 9, 1957, the plaintiff issued a writ against the administrator of the son's estate, namely, the father. (A further complication arose in this case concerning the father's own claim for damages, since he too was injured in the same accident.)

[43] [1958] 1 W.L.R. 734.

[44] *Ibid.* at p. 743 and [1958] 2 Q.B. 300, 315.

[45] (1969) Law Com. No. 19.

[46] *Supra*, n. 42, s. 1 of which repealed s. 1 (3) of the Law Reform (Miscellaneous Provisions) Act 1934 and ss. 4 and 7 (2) of the Law Reform (Limitation of Actions, etc.) Act 1954 (which relaxed those restrictions imposed by the Act of 1934).

deceased person to be maintained (whether by substitution of parties, amendment or otherwise) against a person appointed to represent the estate or, if a grant of probate or administration is made, against the personal representatives.[47]

151 **Limitation Act 1963.**[48] Following the decision of the Court of Appeal in *Cartledge* v. *E. Jopling & Sons Ltd.*,[49] which was subsequently affirmed by the House of Lords,[50] a committee was set up by the Lord Chancellor to consider the particular problems raised. The committee under the chairmanship of Edmund Davies L.J. in due course of time reported [51] as a result of which the Act was passed.[52] Although it has been described as a "very complicated and obscure" [53] Act, its main provisions [54] are that, where damages are claimed which consist of or include damages in respect of personal injuries, including any disease or impairment of a person's physical or mental condition or in respect of a person's death, a person may apply for the leave of the court to bring an action after the expiration of the prescribed three-year limitation period if he had remained ignorant of certain facts relating to his cause of action throughout the whole or for the most part of that period. Once leave has been obtained, then provided the conditions laid down in section 1 (3) have been proved by the plaintiff to have been fulfilled at the trial, the Act operates to prevent the expiry of the three-year limitation period from affording a defence to the action.[55] By section 6 there is given retrospective effect to causes of action which accrued before the passing of the Act.

152 **Application for leave of court.** The leave of the court may be sought by an application made at any stage of the proceedings,[56] although usually this will be made before such proceedings commence.[57] Section 2 (1) specifically provides that any application for leave shall be made *ex parte*, except in so far as rules of court may otherwise provide in relation to applications

[47] For the procedure prior to the Proceedings Against Estates Act 1970 for having the court appoint a personal representative where there was no person who could be sued as a defendant in connection with a deceased tortfeasor's estate, see *In the Estate of Simpson* (*deceased*); *In the Estate of Gunning* (*deceased*) [1936] P. 40; *Re the Goods of Knight* [1939] 3 All E.R. 928.

[48] The Law Commission has published Law Com. No. 35 "Limitation Act 1963. Advice to the Lord Chancellor under s. 3 (1) (*e*) of the Law Commissions Act 1965," Cmnd. 4532.

[49] [1962] 1 Q.B. 189.

[50] [1963] A.C. 758; § 1143, *ante*.

[51] (1962) Cmnd. 1829.

[52] 1963, c. 47, which came into operation on July 31, 1963.

[53] *Re Pickles* v. *N.C.B.* (*Intended Action*) [1968] 1 W.L.R. 997 *per* Lord Denning M.R. at p. 1000; also *Goodchild* v. *Greatness Timber Co. Ltd.* [1968] 2 Q.B. 372 *per* Salmon L.J. at p. 381. See articles "Limitation Act 1963," (Dworkin) (1964) 27 M.L.R. 199; "Limitation Act 1963," (Jolowicz) (1964) Camb.L.J. 47; "Limitation of Actions," (Glover) 116 New L.J. 1222 and 1242; "Problems of Limitation: Part 1, Personal Injuries—Suing Out of Time," (Goodman) 119 New L.J. 500.

[54] Further, the Act limits the time within which proceedings for contribution may be brought under the Law Reform (Married Women and Tortfeasors) Act 1935. See article on the Limitation Act 1963: (1964) 108 S.J. 22.

[55] s. 1 (1).

[56] *Ibid.*

[57] *In re Clark* v. *Forbes Stuart* (*Thames Street*) *Ltd.* (*Intended Action*) [1964] 1 W.L.R. 836 *per* Pearson L.J. at p. 841; *Cozens* v. *North Devon Hospital Management Committee* [1966] 2 Q.B. 330 *per* Salmon L.J. at p. 348.

which are made after the commencement of a relevant action.[58] Where such an application is made before the commencement of any relevant action, the court shall grant leave but only if, on evidence adduced by or on behalf of the plaintiff in a supporting affidavit to the summons whence it appears in the absence of evidence to the contrary, (a) that the plaintiff would be able to establish his cause of action apart from the defence of limitation and (b) that the requirements of section 1 (3) would be satisfied.[59] Section 2 (4) then goes on to provide that no appeal shall lie from any decision of the Court of Appeal on an appeal against a decision on an application under this section. However, unlike the normal situation relating to *ex parte* orders, no application from an intended defendant who desires to set aside an order granting leave can be entertained.[60] On the other hand a judge in chambers should not grant leave as a matter of course but " should carefully scrutinise the case to see if it is a proper one for leave." [61] Notwithstanding the fact that leave has been granted it is open to the defendant, when proceedings have been commenced, to take any objection that the requirements of the Act have not been fulfilled,[62] which in a suitable case may be dealt with as a preliminary issue.[63] Section 1 (3) as amended by the Law Reform (Miscellaneous Provisions) Act 1971,[63a] section 1 (1) provides: " The requirements of this subsection are fulfilled in relation to a cause of action if it is proved that the material facts relating to that cause of action were or included facts of a decisive character which were at all times outside the knowledge (actual or constructive) of the plaintiff until a date which was not earlier than three years before the date on which the action was brought."

1153 " Material facts " are defined in section 7 (3) as being any one or more of the following categories of fact *viz.*:— " (*a*) the fact that personal injuries resulted from the negligence, nuisance or breach of duty constituting that cause of action; (*b*) the nature or extent of the personal injuries resulting from that negligence, nuisance or breach of duty; (*c*) the fact that the personal injuries so resulting were attributable to that negligence, nuisance

[58] The *ex parte* summons is made to a judge in chambers in person: R.S.C., Ord. 110, r. 1 (1); *Harkness* v. *Bell's Asbestos Ltd.* [1967] 2 Q.B. 729.

[59] s. 2 (2). S. 2 (3) further provides that where the application is made after proceedings have been begun, the evidence must additionally satisfy the judge that, until after the commencement of the action, it was outside the plaintiff's knowledge, actual or constructive, that the matters constituting his cause of action had occurred after the expiry of three years from its accrual.

[60] *Cozens* v. *North Devon Hospital Management Committee* [1966] 2 Q.B. 330.

[61] *Goodchild* v. *Greatness Timber Co. Ltd.* [1968] 2 Q.B. 372 *per* Lord Denning M.R. at p. 380. To the like effect, see *per* Salmon and Edmund Davies L.JJ., *ibid.* at pp. 381, 382.

[62] *In re Clark* v. *Forbes Stuart* (*Thames Street*) *Ltd.* (*Intended Action*) [1964] 1 W.L.R. 836, *per* Lord Denning M.R. at p. 839: " This court, therefore, cannot decide finally whether the requirements of the Limitation Act 1963 are fulfilled. It can only be provisional. It must be open to the defendants, if and when they are served with a writ, to take the point, both on fact and law, that the requirements of the Act are not fulfilled." *Ibid., per* Pearson and Salmon L.JJ. at p. 842; *Cozens* v. *North Devon Hospital Management Committee, supra.*

[63] *Goodchild* v. *Greatness Timber Co. Ltd., supra, per* Lord Denning M.R. at p. 380.

[63a] This Act came into operation August 1, 1971. As to the transitional provisions see s. 3 and Schedule 2.

or breach of duty, or the extent to which any of those personal injuries were so attributable." Moreover such material facts relating to a cause of action shall be taken, at any particular time, to have been facts of " a decisive character " according to section 7 (4) if " they were facts which a reasonable person, knowing those facts and having obtained appropriate advice [64] with respect to them, would have regarded at that time as determining, in relation to that cause of action, that (apart from any defence under section 2 (1) of the Limitation Act 1939 or so much of section 3 of the Fatal Accidents Act 1846 as requires actions under that Act to be commenced within three years after the death of the deceased) an action would have a reasonable prospect of succeeding and of resulting in the award of damages sufficient to justify the bringing of the action." Also the plaintiff must prove that a material fact of a decisive character was outside his " knowledge (actual or constructive) " until a date not earlier than three years before the action was begun. In this regard three conditions must be satisfied by the plaintiff before the requirement can be fulfilled. They are: " (a) he did not then know that fact; (b) in so far as that fact was capable of being ascertained by him, he had taken all such action (if any) as it was reasonable for him to have taken before that time for the purpose of ascertaining it; and (c) in so far as there existed, and were known to him, circumstances from which, with appropriate advice [64] that fact might have been ascertained or inferred, he had taken all such action (if any) as it was reasonable for him to have taken before that time for the purpose of obtaining appropriate advice with respect to those circumstances." [65]

1154 The working of the Act may be illustrated by the following decisions:—

In *Goodchild* v. *Greatness Timber Co. Ltd.*[66] it was held that a plaintiff ought to be allowed to bring an action after three years had expired only if he could not reasonably have thought that he had a worthwhile action previously. In this case the plaintiff alleged that his injury had worsened in a manner which, according to the medical evidence, could not have been foreseen and that it was a fact " of a decisive character " within section 7 (4) of the Act. Upon the trial of this preliminary issue, however, it was held that as the plaintiff knew within the three-year period that his personal injuries were not trivial and he had had a reasonable opportunity of bringing a worthwhile action, the fact pleaded was not " of a decisive character."

In *Clark* v. *Forbes Stuart* (*Thames Street*) *Ltd.* (*Intended Action*) [67] it was held by the Court of Appeal on an *ex parte* application that in an action for negligence against the occupier of certain premises, his identity

[64] " Appropriate advice " is defined in s. 7 (8) as meaning " the advice of competent persons qualified, in their respective spheres, to advise on the medical, legal and other aspects of that fact or those circumstances as the case may be." Incorrect advice from a trade union may be a ground for extending the limitation period: *Drinkwater* v. *Joseph Lucas* (*Electrical*) [1970] 3 All E.R. 769. *Quaere* whether it can be a ground for extending the limitation period that the plaintiff had failed to pursue his claim because he mistakenly believed that it was statute-barred. *Ryan* v. *Carr and Marples Ridgeway & Partners* (1971) 115 S.J. 206.

[65] s. 7 (5).

[66] [1968] 2 Q.B. 372.

[67] [1964] 1 W.L.R. 836.

was a " material fact of a decisive character " within the meaning of sections 1 (3) and 7 (3) (*c*) of the Limitation Act 1963. Since the plaintiff had made out a prima facie case that he was ignorant of such material fact his time for suing was extended under that Act beyond the usual three years in personal injury claims.

In *Newton* v. *Cammell Laird & Co.* (*Shipbuilders & Engineers*) [68] where a deceased workman had learned in 1965 that he was suffering from asbestosis caused by his work with the defendants from 1943–1955 but had died without taking legal advice, the Court of Appeal held that constructive knowledge that he had a cause of action was not to be implied to the deceased under section 7 (5) (*b*) and (*c*). Thus, by applying the subjective test required by the Act, it was not reasonable to expect a dying man who was daily growing weaker to seek legal advice and since his widow had obtained leave to bring an action within twelve months from his death and had brought her action, it was not statute barred.

In *Re Pickles* v. *National Coal Board* (*Intended Action*) [69] the proposed plaintiff had been employed by the proposed defendants as a miner at one of their collieries between the years 1947 to 1960 when he decided to change his employment in order to become a machine operator. By February 1966 he had felt ill and a few months later, after consulting his doctor, he discovered the true extent of his illness. In due course he applied for leave under the Limitation Act 1963 which was refused. The Court of Appeal in allowing the appeal and granting leave to the appellant workman, held that by his putting the history of an injury before his Trade Union [70] he can be said to have taken all reasonable action (1) to ascertain the attributability of negligence or breach of statutory duty and (2) to obtain advice as to it, within the meaning of section 7 (5) (*b*) and (*c*) of the Act. Although his doctor had informed him that he had silicosis in July 1966, which fact he had reported to his Union, the latter delayed in giving him advice until July 1967 hence it was from that date and not July 1966 that the twelve-month period [70a] prescribed by section 1 (3) began to run so that he had until July 1968 in which to issue his writ.

1155 On the other hand, where widows had begun actions against the former employers of their husbands, who had died from cancer of the bladder, caused by the carcinogenic substance used at their work, and the employers had joined I.C.I. Ltd. as third parties, the widows were barred by section 3 (4) of the 1963 Act from joining the latter as co-defendants, since the actions against them had not been commenced within the obligatory twelve-month period from the men's deaths. [71]

[68] [1969] 1 W.L.R. 415.

[69] [1968] 1 W.L.R. 997. See also *Smith* v. *Central Asbestos Co. Ltd.* [1971] 3 W.L.R. 206.

[70] Incorrect advice from a trade union may be a ground for extending the limitation period *Drinkwater* v. *Joseph Lucas* (*Electrical*) [1970] 3 All E.R. 769.

[70a] Now it is " 3 years." See s. 1 (1) of the Law Reform (Miscellaneous Provisions) Act 1971 and § 1152, *ante*.

[71] *Lucy* v. *W. T. Henleys Telegraph Works Co.* [1970] 1 Q.B. 393; See *Braniff* v. *Holland & Hannen & Cubitts Ltd.* [1969] 1 W.L.R. 1533 for a similar situation as regards amendment of the writ, after the limitation period had expired, to bring in a second defendant, although the first defendant had been refused leave to commence third party proceedings.

1156 **No suspension once time has started to run.** When the period of limitation in respect of a cause of action in tort has started to run it is not broken either by any subsequent disability, which may have intervened, or by the fact that at some stage in the time there was no one who could sue.[72] Where a person has a vested cause of action but dies before he can begin his proceedings and no personal representative has been appointed until after the time limit has expired, the action is barred.[73] Further, a right of action for negligence once statute-barred cannot be revived by acknowledgment.[74]

1157 **No extension of time for defendant.** The former disability of the defendant during his absence beyond the seas [75] has been repealed [76] and there is now no disability which prevents time from running against a defendant.

1158 **Public authorities.** Actions against public authorities were required by the Public Authorities Protection Act 1893, s. 1, as amended by the Limitation Act 1939, s. 21, to be commenced " before the expiration of one year from the date on which the cause of action accrued." These provisions were repealed by the Law Reform (Limitation of Actions, etc.) Act 1954, s. 1, as from June 4, 1954, so that public authorities are no longer in any different position from any other person.

1159 **The Crown.** The period of limitation against the Crown in respect of actions founded on tort is the same as that in actions of tort against private persons.[77]

1160 **Waiver of protection.** The benefit of the Limitation Acts can be waived by the person who would otherwise be protected by it.[78]

1161 **Contributory negligence.** The Law Reform (Contributory Negligence) Act 1945, s. 1 (5), provides: " Where, in any case to which subsection (1) of this section applies, one of the persons at fault avoids liability to any other such person or his personal representative by pleading the Limitation Act 1939 or any other enactment limiting the time within which proceedings may be taken, he shall not be entitled to recover any damages or contributions from that other person or representative by virtue of the said subsection."

This subsection contemplates the case of one person at fault avoiding liability to another person at fault, but while it refers to the personal representative of the second-named person it does not refer to the personal

[72] *Smith* v. *Hill* (1746) 1 Wils. 134; *Doe* d. *Duroure* v. *Jones* (1791) 4 T.R. 300; *Homfray* v. *Scroope* (1849) 13 Q.B. 509.
[73] *Rhodes* v. *Smethurst* (1838) 4 M. & W. 42 and (1840) 6 M. & W. 351; *Penny* v. *Brice* (1865) 18 C.B.(N.S.) 393; *Boatwright* v. *Boatwright* (1873) L.R. 17 Eq. 71.
[74] *Hurst* v. *Parker* (1817) 1 B. & Ald. 92; *Short* v. *McCarthy* (1820) 3 B. & Ald. 626. See also Limitation Act 1939, s. 23.
[75] Administration of Justice Act 1705, s. 18, and Mercantile Law Amendment Act 1856, s. 12.
[76] *i.e.* by the Limitation Act 1939, s. 34, Sched.
[77] Limitation Act 1939, s. 30; Crown Proceedings Act 1947, s. 30; Law Reform (Limitation of Actions, etc.) Act 1954, s. 5.
[78] *Lubovsky* v. *Snelling* [1943] 2 All E.R. 577.

representative of the first-named. If, therefore, the personal representative of one of the parties at fault avoids liability to the other party at fault by pleading the Limitation Act 1939, as amended, it is a possible construction of the subsection that the personal representative in such a case could still recover damages under the Law Reform (Contributory Negligence) Act 1945. Presumably, however, the ordinary rule will apply by which a personal representative has no higher rights than the deceased whom he represents, with the result that the personal representative avoiding liability would be unable to recover.[79]

1161a **Contribution between tortfeasors.** The Law Reform (Married Women and Tortfeasors) Act 1935, s. 6, provided for claims to contributions between tortfeasors but made no provisions for the limitation of such claims. Since a claim for contributions under the Act is not a claim in tort,[80] before the Limitation Act 1963 was passed such claim had to be brought within six years of their accrual. Now the Act of 1963 [81] has reduced that period to two years from the date when the right to recover contribution accrued, which date shall be ascertained as: " (*a*) if the tortfeasor is held liable in respect of that damage by a judgment given in any civil proceedings, or an award made on any arbitration, the relevant date shall be the date on which the judgment is given, or the date of the award, as the case may be; (*b*) if, in any case not falling within the preceding paragraph, the tortfeasor admits liability in favour of one or more persons in respect of that damage, the relevant date shall be the earliest date on which the amount to be paid by him in discharge of that liability is agreed by or on behalf of the tortfeasor and that person, or each of those persons, as the case may be." [82] In regard to the above the same section goes on to provide that no account is to be taken of any judgment or award given on appeal in so far as the amount of damages awarded against the tortfeasor may be varied. On the other hand, where a tortfeasor settles a claim made against him without any admission of liability the position concerning when time begins to run in respect of contribution proceedings necessarily remains in considerable doubt.

1162 **Carriage by Air Act 1961.**[83] Since the Act enacts that the provisions of the Convention known as " the Warsaw Convention as amended at The Hague, 1955 " should have the force of law, section 5 (1) provides that " No action against a carrier's servant or agent which arises out of damage to which the Convention relates shall, if he was acting within the scope of his employment, be brought after more than two years, reckoned from the

[79] See, on the subsection generally, Williams, *Joint Torts and Contributory Negligence*, pp. 337–339.

[80] *Post Office* v. *Official Solicitor* [1951] 1 All E.R. 522; *Littlewood* v. *George Wimpey & Co. Ltd.* [1953] 2 Q.B. 501; *sub nom. George Wimpey & Co. Ltd.* v. *B.O.A.C.* [1955] A.C. 169; *Harvey* v. *R. G. O'Dell Ltd.* [1958] 2 Q.B. 78.

[81] 1963, c. 47, which came into force on July 31, 1963.

[82] s. 4 (2). *Cf.* the like provisions in the Carriage by Air Act 1961, s. 5 (2).

[83] Whilst the Act of 1961 as a whole came into force on receiving the Royal Assent on June 22, 1961, it could not become effective until s. 1 came into force on June 1, 1967, by virtue of the Carriage by Air (Convention) Order 1967 (S.I. 1967 No. 479).

date of arrival at the destination or from the date on which the aircraft ought to have arrived, or from the date on which the carriage stopped," which embodies Article 29 of the Convention and certainly applies in all cases of non-fatal accidents. Conversely, in cases of fatalities the position under the Act is the same as under the Fatal Accidents Acts since by section 3 " References in section 1 of the Fatal Accidents Act 1846 as it applies in England and Wales, and in Northern Ireland, to a wrongful act, neglect or default shall include references to any occurrence which gives rise to a liability under Article 17 . . ." Hence actions in respect of deaths caused by any such occurrence, being in effect ordinary actions under the Fatal Accidents Acts, will be subject to those ordinary rules for limitation in such cases, namely three years. Where there is such an apparent divergence between the provisions of the Act and those of the Convention the former must prevail over the latter so that Article 29 cannot have any bearing upon actions brought on behalf of dependants of deceased persons who have been killed in some common flying disaster or another.

1163 **Maritime Conventions Act 1911.** The Act by section 8 provides, *inter alia*, that no action shall be maintainable to enforce any claim against the owners of a vessel in respect of any damages for loss of life or personal injuries suffered by any person on board another vessel caused by negligence of the former vessel, unless proceedings are commenced within two years from the date when the damage or loss or injury was caused. However, this period may be extended by the court to such extent and on any such conditions as in its absolute discretion it thinks fit,[84] and it must be extended where the court is " satisfied that there has not during such period been any reasonable opportunity of arresting the defendant vessel within the jurisdiction of the court, or within the territorial waters of the country to which the plaintiff's ship belongs or in which the plaintiff resides or has his principal place of business." [85] In *The Alnwick* [86] the Court of Appeal held that the alteration of the general law by the Law Reform (Limitation of Actions, etc.) Act 1954 did not affect the provisions of the 1911 Act. Accordingly where the Act applies, it is exclusive of other periods of limitation so that the period which is appropriate to the case of a death on board one vessel caused by the negligence of another ship is two years and not three years as provided in normal fatal accident cases. Nevertheless in the circumstances of any culpable delay on the part of defendants the two-year limitation will be extended in the court's discretion by virtue of the aforesaid proviso to section 8.[87] In *Navarro* v. *Larrinaga Steamship Co. Ltd.*[88] where the administratrix of the estate of a deceased mariner, who lost his life in a sea collision between the *Niceto de Larrinaga* in which he was serving and the *Sitala*, sued the owners of the former vessel for damages for

[84] See *The Kashmir* [1923] P. 85; *The Arraiz* (1924) 132 L.T. 715; *The Vadne* [1959] 2 Lloyd's Rep. 480 for the principles on which the court will exercise its discretion.
[85] See proviso to s. 8, Maritime Conventions Act 1911.
[86] [1965] P. 357.
[87] *The Alnwick, supra.*
[88] [1966] P. 80.

loss of life, it was held that since section 8 of the Act only applied to actions against other vessels and not to actions against the vessel in which the damage, loss or injury had occurred, the normal three-year limitation period for actions under the Fatal Accidents Acts, as amended, applied.

1164 **Nuclear Installations Act 1965.**[89] Section 15 (1) enacts that: " notwithstanding anything in any other enactment," a claim under the Act shall not be entertained, " if made at any time after the expiration of thirty years from the relevant date," which date is that of the occurrence that gave rise to the claim and not of the infliction of damage. The limitation period begins to run from the date of the last occurrence, where it was either a continuing one or was one of a succession in the circumstances specified. Further, where a claim arises in respect of injury or damage caused by an occurrence involving nuclear matter stolen from, or lost, jettisoned or abandoned by the person whose breach of statutory duty under the Act gave rise to the claim it is provided by section 15 (2) that the limitation period in such circumstances is the period of twenty years. This period is to be calculated " beginning with the day when the nuclear matter in question was so stolen, lost, jettisoned or abandoned."

[89] See generally Chap. 9, § 564 *et seq.*, *ante*.

CHAPTER 17

NEGLIGENCE COMMITTED ABROAD

1165 **Generally.** Negligence committed abroad, just as any other tort, except one which is concerned with injury to interests in land, has always been actionable in England, provided that the defendant is within the jurisdiction,[1] namely the area of the territorial jurisdiction of the High Court.[2] On the other hand if the defendant is outside the jurisdiction the Rules of the Supreme Court do not permit the service of a writ or notice of it out of the jurisdiction although there are certain limited exceptions, concerning which the court has a discretion to give leave.[3] By way of example, where a tort has been committed outside the jurisdiction by several persons jointly, only one of whom is domiciled or ordinarily resident within the court's jurisdiction, leave may be given where the persons outside the jurisdiction are necessary or proper parties thereto.[4] As indicated above the jurisdiction to grant leave to serve out of the jurisdiction is entirely discretionary in all cases,[5] and the question which is the *forum conveniens* for the trial is a matter to be considered by the court when exercising such discretion.[6] A defendant served with a writ of summons is competent to apply to the court to set aside the writ on the ground that the cause of action did not arise within the jurisdiction of the court, before the plaintiff obtains leave to proceed.[7] In *Jackson* v. *Spittall* [8] it was held that " cause of action " did not mean the *whole* cause of action but the act on the part of the defendant which gave the plaintiff his cause of complaint. This must be of considerable importance in those negligence cases where the breach of duty takes place in one country but the essential damage, which completes the cause of action, is actually suffered in another. Indeed, an allied point

[1] *Re Busfield* (1886) 32 Ch.D. 123 *per* Cotton L.J. at p. 131: " Generally courts exercise jurisdiction only over persons who are within the territorial limits of their jurisdiction." The court has no jurisdiction in a cause if a person who is a necessary party has not been served with the process and it has no jurisdiction over a person who has not been served therewith unless there has been a submission to the jurisdiction.

[2] Its limits embrace the whole of England and Wales and Berwick upon Tweed (*cf. R.* v. *Cowle* (1759) 2 Burr. 834) but it does not extend to Scotland, the Isle of Man or the Channel Islands or any places beyond the seas: *Davison* v. *Farmer* (1851) 6 Exch.Rep. 242. It includes territorial waters up to the three-mile limit: *The Mecca* [1895] P. 95, *per* Halsbury L.C. at p. 105; *Carr* v. *Fracis Times & Co.* [1902] A.C. 176.

[3] R.S.C., Ord. 11, r. 1 sets out the cases where service abroad is allowed. Where leave has been granted to serve a writ out of the jurisdiction it is not competent for the plaintiff to join it with another claim in respect of which leave to serve the writ out of the jurisdiction could not have been granted: *Waterhouse* v. *Reid* [1938] 1 K.B. 743. But where an action is maintainable at the option of the plaintiff either in tort or contract he may take advantage of the rule: *Matthew* v. *Kuwait Bechtel Corpn.* [1959] 2 Q.B. 57.

[4] Ord. 11 r. 1 (j); *Witted* v. *Galbraith* [18931] 1 Q.B. 577.

[5] *Johnson* v. *Taylor Bros. & Co.* [1920] A.C. 144, 153; *Rosler* v. *Hilbery* [1925] Ch. 250, 259.

[6] *Logan* v. *Bank of Scotland* [1906] 1 K.B. 141. That proceedings are already pending elsewhere is a most material consideration in exercising discretion: *The Hagen* [1908] P. 189, 202.

[7] See now R.S.C., Ord. 12, r. 8.

[8] (1870) L.R. 5 C.P. 542.

arose for consideration by the Judicial Committee of the Privy Council in *Distillers Co. (Bio-Chemicals) Ltd.* v. *Thompson* [9] where it was held that the respondent child, a girl born without arms and without normal eyesight in New South Wales, who claimed that her disabilities were due to her mother having taken a preparation manufactured by the appellants, an English company, had a cause of action which arose within the jurisdiction of the New South Wales court. The preparation which contained the drug thalidomide was sold by another company in Australia, where the appellants did not carry on business. Lord Pearson considered seriatim the three theories: (1) that the " cause of action " must be the whole cause of action, so that every ingredient of it must have occurred within the jurisdiction; (2) that it was necessary and sufficient that the last ingredient which completed the cause of action occurred within the jurisdiction; and (3) that the act which gave the plaintiff her cause of complaint must have occurred within the jurisdiction. The first theory was ruled out by the principle in *Jackson* v. *Spittall.* [8] The second seemed to be wrong as a theory, since the last event might happen in a particular case to be the determining factor on its own merits but not because it was the last event. In negligence the happening of damage to the plaintiff was a necessary ingredient in the cause of action, and it was the last event completing the cause of action. But the place where it happened might be quite fortuitous and should not by itself be the sole determinant of jurisdiction. The right approach was, when the tort was complete, to look back over the series of events constituting it and to ask where in substance did the cause of action arise. The third theory was the rule laid down in *Jackson* v. *Spittall.* [8] In the majority of cases the place where the defendant was negligent was the same as where the negligence proceeded to cause the damage. Lord Pearson adverted to the fact that in the present case there was the alleged negligence by the English defendants in New South Wales causing injury to the plaintiff in New South Wales. The alleged negligence was in the defendants' failure to give a warning that the goods would be dangerous if taken by an expectant mother in the first three months of pregnancy. The warning could have been given by their putting a warning notice on each package as it was made up in England or it could have been given by communication to persons in New South Wales, including those responsible for its distribution and application such as the medical practitioners, the wholesale and retail chemists, as well as to the patients and purchasers. In the circumstances the plaintiff was entitled to complain of the lack of such communication in New South Wales as negligence by the defendants in New South Wales causing severe injury to her there; thus the cause of action arose within the jurisdiction of the court.

1166 **When foreign torts are actionable.** For foreign torts to be actionable in England two conditions must be fulfilled which were formulated by Willes J. as: " First, the wrong must be of such a character that it would have

9 [1971] 2 W.L.R. 441. See article " The Place of the Tort " (Scott) (1971) 121 New L.J. 693.

been actionable if committed in England. . . . Secondly, the act must not have been justifiable by the law of the place where it was done." [10] These two rules must be considered further in detail.

167 **[1] Act must be actionable by English law.** Willes J. pointed out that the authority for the rule was derived from the Judicial Committee of the Privy Council in *The Halley* [11] which pronounced against a suit in Admiralty founded upon a liability by the law of Belgium for collision caused by the act of a pilot whom the shipowner was compelled by the local law to employ and for whom, therefore, as not being his agent, he was not responsible by English law.[12] It follows that the law which will be applied in order to determine the existence and extent of the defendant's liability is the law of England, namely the *lex fori* and not the law of the place where the tort was committed, namely the *lex loci delicti.* Thus where a wrong is committed abroad, the injured party, seeking his redress by bringing his action in England, can recover damages assessed according to the law of England, the place of trial, not merely as to quantum, which was a matter of procedure, but also as to the heads of damage, which were matters of substantive law.[13]

168 **[2] Act must not have been justifiable where done.** This rule has occasioned much difficulty for the courts owing to the use of the words " not justifiable " when relating them to the nature of the justification abroad which would thereby prevent the action being maintained in England. The meaning of " justifiable " as interpreted by the court becomes apparent in considering the following two cases. In *Phillips* v. *Eyre* [14] the plaintiff brought an action for assault and false imprisonment against the Governor of Jamaica, who pleaded successfully that since the plaintiff's grievances complained of, *viz.*, his arrest made in connection with the suppression of a rebellion, an Act of Indemnity had been passed by the legislature of Jamaica and assented to by the Crown, which declared the arrest to have been lawful. At the trial hearing in the Court of Queen's Bench, Cockburn C.J. said: " It appears to us clear that where by the law of another country an act complained of is lawful, such act, though it would have been wrongful by our law if committed here, cannot be made the ground of an action in an English Court." [15] This is so, whether the act complained of that has been committed abroad is either lawful by the law of that foreign country at the

[10] *Phillips* v. *Eyre* (1870) L.R. 6 Q.B. 1 at pp. 28, 29; approved by Lord Macnaghten in *Carr* v. *Fracis Times & Co., supra* at p. 182. However in *Chaplin* v. *Boys* [1971] A.C. 356 Lord Hodson said that it was necessary to permit some flexibility in applying the language of Willes J. " which is to be applied as ' a general rule ' and not invariably " (p. 378). *Aliter* Lord Donovan who expressed the view that he was content with the rule as enunciated by Willes J. " and would leave it alone " (p. 383). For facts see § 1170, *post.*

[11] (1868) L.R. 2 P.C. 193. But see now the Pilotage Act 1913, s. 15, where the owner and master are made liable for the negligent navigation of a pilot who is made compulsory in waters to which the Act extends. *The Arum* [1921] P. 12; *G.W. Ry.* v. *S.S. Mostyn* (*Owners*) [1928] A.C. 57.

[12] *Ibid.* at p. 29.

[13] *Chaplin* v. *Boys, supra.*

[14] *Supra.*

[15] (1869) 4 Q.B. 225, 239.

time of its commission or was subsequently rendered lawful by legislation *ex post facto*. Then in *Machado* v. *Fontes* [16] which concerned an alleged libel upon the plaintiff contained in a pamphlet in the Portuguese language published in Brazil, it was held by the Court of Appeal that an action would lie in this country in respect of an act committed outside the jurisdiction if the act is wrongful both in this country and in the country where it is committed. Further it was held that it mattered not that libel was not a cause of action for damages in Brazil but was solely a criminal offence consequently the plaintiff was entitled to sue for damages in England although he would not have been entitled to an award of damages at all in Brazil.

1169 However, rigid adherence to these two rules enunciated by Willes J. has resulted in injustice being perpetrated. Perhaps the worst example in modern times is to be found in *M'Elroy* v. *M'Allister* [17] where the pursuer's husband, who was resident in Glasgow, died in a road accident in England, his death being caused by the negligence of the defender who also resided in Scotland. The factors resulting in misfortune to the widow were clearly analysed in the following passage: " If the accident had happened in Scotland the pursuer could have recovered substantial damages in respect of solatium and patrimonial loss. If the action had been brought in England, she could have recovered substantial damages as a dependant under the Fatal Accidents Acts 1846–1908 and as executrix for the deceased for loss of expectation of life under the Law Reform (Miscellaneous Provisions) Act 1934. It was held, however, by a full court of seven judges (Lord Keith dissenting) that she could only recover £40 in respect of funeral expenses, that being the only point at which Scottish and English law coincided. The claim for solatium failed because English law does not recognise such a claim for wrongful death. The claim under the Fatal Accidents Acts failed because the action was begun more than twelve months after the accident, contrary to section 3 of the Act of 1846. The claim under the Law Reform (Miscellaneous Provisions) Act 1934 failed because by Scots law all rights of action vested in an injured person (as opposed to his family) for personal injuries due to negligence die with the injured person, unless he had instituted proceedings before his death." [18]

1170 In *Chaplin* v. *Boys* [19] the respondent sustained serious injuries in a road accident in Malta which had been caused by the negligence of the appellant. Both parties were members of H.M. Armed Forces stationed in that country at the time of the accident although they normally resided in England. In due course the respondent brought an action in England, the

[16] [1897] 2 Q.B. 231; overruled by the H.L. in *Chaplin* v. *Boys, supra* (*per* Lord Hodson and Lord Wilberforce; but Lord Donovan and Lord Pearson were prepared to accept the wide meaning attaching to " not justifiable " under that decision).

[17] 1949 S.C. 110, which Lord Guest considered in *Chaplin* v. *Boys, supra*, to have been rightly decided.

[18] Morris, *Cases on Private International Law*, 3rd ed., p. 287.

[19] *Supra*. See articles on this decision: " *Chaplin* v. *Boys* or the maze of Malta," (Nygh) 44 A.L.J. 160.

only issue being whether the damages were to be assessed according to the law of Malta, where he could have sued the appellant but had he done so since Maltese law only allowed for pecuniary loss he could have recovered merely his special damage, agreed at £53, or by the law of England, under which he could also recover substantial general damages for pain, suffering, loss of amenities and future financial loss. Milmo J. at the trial awarded the respondent general damages in accordance with English law which the Court of Appeal affirmed by a majority.[20] On further appeal the House of Lords have unanimously dismissed the appeal holding that the respondent bringing his action in England could recover damages assessed by the law of this country not merely as to quantum but also as to the heads of damage.

171 Firstly, on the question what was the applicable law of tort Lord Hodson considered that, although in general in an action for personal injury the *lex loci delicti* determined the rights and liabilities of the parties where in respect to the particular issue some other country had a more significant relationship with the occurrence and the parties, the local law of that state would be applied. It accordingly followed in his lordship's view that, in agreeing with Lord Denning M.R.[21] he would " treat the law of England as applicable since even though the occurrence took place in Malta this was overshadowed by the identity and circumstances of the parties, British subjects temporarily serving in Malta." [22] Then as regards these rules in *Phillips* v. *Eyre* [23] the House of Lords generally reaffirmed them, Lord Wilberforce stating, " I would, therefore, restate the basic rule of English law with regard to foreign torts as requiring actionability as a tort according to English law, subject to the condition that civil liability in respect of the relevant claim exists as between the actual parties under the law of the foreign country where the act was done." [24] It follows from the above that the present effect of the rule is that the unjustifiable act must be actionable at least as a civil wrong in the country of commission. Later in his judgment Lord Wilberforce added: " Given the general rule . . . as one which will normally apply to foreign torts, I think that the necessary flexibility can be obtained from that principle which represents at least a common denominator of the United States decisions, namely, through segregation of the relevant issue and consideration whether, in relation to that issue, the relevant foreign rule ought, as a matter of policy or, as Westlake said, of science, to be applied. For this purpose it is necessary to identify the policy of the rule, to inquire to what situations, with what contacts, it was intended to apply; whether not to apply it, in the circumstances of the instant case, would serve any interest which the rule was devised to meet. This technique appears well adapted

[20] [1968] 2 Q.B. 1.
[21] *Supra*, at p. 36.
[22] [1971] A.C. 356 at p. 380.
[23] (1870) L.R. 6 Q.B. 1.
[24] *Ibid.* at p. 389, thereby disapproved *Machado* v. *Fontes*, *supra*.

to meet cases where the *lex delicti* either limits or excludes damages for personal injury: it appears even necessary and inevitable." [25]

1172 On the other hand the exception to the general rule in *Phillips* v. *Eyre* [23] which most concerned the House of Lords was the potential problem raised of searching around for the forum offering the best advantages to the litigant. Lord Donovan, with a particular reference to *Machado* v. *Fontes* expressed his concern in saying: "we do not need to alter the rule laid down by Willes J. It is enough to say that the case in question, while within the rule, was an abuse of it; and that considerations of public policy would justify a court here in rejecting any such future case of blatant 'forum shopping.' I may say I am assuming that the parties were Brazilian though the report does not say so." [26]

Following the diversity of judicial opinion expressed in *Chaplin* v. *Boys* both in the House of Lords as well as the Court of Appeal, the Lord Chancellor has appointed a committee under the chairmanship of Lord Diplock to consider the whole question of the law to be applied in relation to foreign torts. It is clearly desirable to achieve as wide a measure of agreement with the relevant rules of other jurisdictions concerned with the same problems, by formulating proposals for reform and restatement of English law which can be given effect by legislation. [27]

1173 **Limitation of action.** If the foreign law touches only the remedy or the procedure for enforcing that obligation then that is no valid reason for barring an action commenced in England. [28] Conversely if the foreign law extinguishes the right altogether then it will act as an effective bar in this country as well. [29]

1174 **Fatal Accidents Acts.** The Fatal Accidents Acts 1846 to 1959 [30] apply for the benefit of the representatives of a deceased alien as well as for those of a British subject, at all events against a British tortfeasor where the deceased could have maintained an action in England on a cause of action which arose abroad. Accordingly such representatives of a deceased foreigner have a right of action against the owners of a British ship the negligence of whose servants caused his death on the high seas. [31]

[25] *Ibid.* at p. 391.
[26] *Ibid.* at p. 383.
[27] See article: "Towards a Modern Applicable Law in Tort," (Graveson) (1969) 85 L.Q.R. 505; also note in (1969) 27 Camb. L.J. 201.
[28] *Huber* v. *Steiner* (1835) 2 Bing.N.C. 202; *Harris* v. *Quine* (1869) L.R. 4 Q.B. 653.
[29] *Per* Willes J. *Phillips* v. *Eyre* (1870) L.R. 6 Q.B. 1, 29. *Cf. Walpole* v. *Canadian Northern Ry.* [1923] A.C. 113; and the Limitation Act 1939, s. 3 (2) where the title of a person to a chattel is extinguished.
[30] See further Chap. 19 generally and § 1275, *post*.
[31] *Davidsson* v. *Hill* [1901] 2 K.B. 606.

CHAPTER 18

STATUTORY DUTY AND BREACH

175 **General Principle.** A statutory duty not infrequently gives rise to a liability to a civil action. This liability is *sui generis* and quite independent of any other form of tortious liability. It has been on occasions referred to as " statutory negligence " which may be a direct result of the fact that most commonly in certain classes of civil actions allegations of common law negligence are made which run parallel with and/or often substantially overlap the corresponding allegations of breaches of statutory duty that were owed to the plaintiff. However the existence of a statutory duty does not necessarily relieve an employer of his common law duty of care owed to his workmen although " in very many cases, it would be difficult, if not impossible, to maintain that an employer who had complied with regulations had been negligent at common law." [1] Nevertheless the mere existence of a statutory duty may indicate that a particular risk ought to have been foreseen and thus can be relied upon in order to establish negligence. On the other hand in *Chipchase* v. *British Titan Products Co. Ltd.*[2] it was unsuccessfully argued that where, on the facts, the case lies just outside the protection of the statutory duty the court ought to take the provisions of the relevant regulations into account on the question of negligence.

The classes of breach of statutory duty must now be considered.

1.—CLASSES OF BREACH OF STATUTORY DUTY

176 **Classes of breach.** Categories of liability arising out of a breach of statutory duty were classified by Willes J.[3] as follows: " There are three classes of cases in which a liability may be established founded upon a statute. One is, where there was a liability existing at common law, and that liability is affirmed by a statute which gives a special and peculiar form of remedy different from the remedy which existed at common law; there, unless the statute contains words which expressly or by necessary implication exclude the common law remedy, the party suing has his election to pursue either that or the statutory remedy. The second class of cases is, where the statute gives the right to sue merely, but provides no particular form of remedy: there, the party can only proceed by action at common law. But there is a third class, *viz.*, where a liability not existing at common law is created by a statute which at the same time gives a special and particular remedy for enforcing it."

77 **Liability at common law affirmed by statute giving a special remedy.** In cases where there is liability at common law it has been held that where a

[1] *Franklin* v. *Gramophone Co. Ltd.* [1948] 1 K.B. 542, *per* Somervell L.J. at p. 558; *N.C.B.* v. *England* [1954] A.C. 403.
[2] [1956] 1 Q.B. 545.
[3] *Wolverhampton New Waterworks Co.* v. *Hawkesford* (1859) 6 C.B.(N.S.) 336, 356.

statute creates or regrants rights of property, such as the right to a market, any infringement of those rights can be restrained by injunction, unless the statute expressly provides to the contrary.[4] Again, although the Salmon and Freshwater Fisheries Act 1923 [5] imposes penalties upon persons who put into waters containing fish any poisonous matter or trade effluent, the owner of a fishery who suffers damage in consequence of any such matter or effluent being put into the waters where his fishery exists can enforce his ordinary common law right and bring an action for damages.[6] If the conservators of a river are empowered by Act of Parliament to levy duties upon goods in barges navigating the river with a right to detain barges if the duty is not paid, they are not prevented from bringing a common law action of debt for the duties instead of resorting to their statutory remedy.[7]

1178 The Gasworks Clauses Act 1847, s. 20,[8] gave a summary remedy to gas companies whose lamp-posts or other works were damaged by providing that compensation not exceeding £5 could be recovered before any two justices. This remedy, however did not preclude gas companies from suing for such damage at common law instead of taking summary proceedings under the Act.[9] But if they elected to proceed under the Act and were awarded compensation, they could not afterwards sue at common law for the balance of their damage. The words of the Act were that the compensation shall be " by way of satisfaction " and this was construed as meaning " in full satisfaction."[10]

1179 The Corn Production Act 1917, s. 4, provided that an employer who failed to pay a workman in agriculture the minimum wage provided by the Act should be liable to a penalty. It was held that this did not prevent the workman from suing for arrears of wages based on the statutory minimum, because the penalty " is additional to any other right which the workman would, by ordinary law possess to recover his statutory wages." [11]

1180 As a general rule, if the statute provides a special remedy by which compensation can be awarded to the injured party, that remedy, although it does not exclude the common law remedy, cannot be resorted to if compensation is actually awarded. The London Hackney Carriage Act 1843, s. 28, provides that every driver of a hackney carriage or stage-coach who by carelessness or wilful misbehaviour damages person or property shall be liable to a fine, and that the justices on the hearing of the case may adjudge to the injured party " as and for compensation " a sum not exceeding £10. It has been held that an award of compensation under the Act, though inadequate, is a bar to an action at common law.[12] On the other

4 *Stevens* v. *Chown* [1901] 1 Ch. 894.
5 Now the Salmon and Freshwater Fisheries Acts 1923–1965.
6 *Nicholls* v. *Ely Beet Sugar Factory* [1936] Ch. 343.
7 *G.W. Ry.* v. *Sharman* (1892) 61 L.J.Q.B. 600.
8 Repealed by the Gas Act 1948.
9 *Crystal Palace Gas Co.* v. *Idris & Co.* (1900) 82 L.T. 200.
10 *Birmingham Corpn.* v. *Allsopp* (1918) 88 L.J.K.B. 549.
11 *Waghorn* v. *Collison* (1922) 91 L.J.K.B. 735.
12 *Wright* v. *London General Omnibus Co.* (1877) 2 Q.B.D. 271. See also *Birmingham Corpn.* v. *Allsopp*, *supra*, and Interpretation Act 1889, s. 33.

hand, where the Merchant Shipping Act 1854 provided that a seaman who failed to join his ship could be punished by imprisonment and also by forfeiture of part of his wages, it was held that such a provision was inconsistent with the owner's common law right to sue the seaman for damages for breach of contract and that such an action was not maintainable, although no proceedings had been taken under the Merchant Shipping Act.[13]

1181 **Statute creates a duty, but gives no remedy.** In the class of cases where a statute imposes a duty, but provides no remedy by which the duty can be enforced, the general rule is that an action for damages can be brought, provided that the person suing is one of a class intended to be benefited by the duty.[13a] " For, if it were not so, the statute would be but a pious aspiration." [14] In *Couch* v. *Steel* [15] Lord Campbell said: " The Statute of Westminster the Second [13 Edw. 1, c. 50], gives a remedy by action on the case to all who are aggrieved by the neglect of any duty created by statute: see 2 Inst. p. 486, and in Com. Dig. tit. Action upon Statute, F, it is laid down that ' in every case where a statute enacts or prohibits a thing for the benefit of a person, he shall have remedy upon the same statute for the thing enacted for his advantage, or for the recompense of a wrong done to him contrary to the said law.' " Similarly, in *Doe* d. *Bishop of Rochester* v. *Bridges*,[16] it is said: " If an obligation is created [by statute], but no mode of enforcing its performance is ordained, the common law may, in general, find a mode suited to the particular nature of the case." " Where there is a duty imposed by statute and someone is injured by reason of a breach of that duty, in the absence of any penalty, or remedy provided in the statute itself, normally an action will lie." [17] The result is that if no remedy is provided by the statute an action for damages may be brought by the injured party (coming within a class for whose benefit the duty was imposed), provided that he has suffered special damage, that is, damage beyond that suffered by the public at large.[18] An injunction can also be obtained at the suit of the Attorney-General, in a suitable case.

1182 If the duty imposed by statute can be enforced by a statutory remedy which is imperfect, as opposed to inadequate, an action for breach of duty may be brought. " If the statute creates such a duty which remains to be performed after the remedy provided by the statute has expired, the court must infer that the continuing duty was not intended to become one of imperfect obligation, but must hold that an action at law will arise on the cesser of the statutory remedy." [19]

[13] *Great Northern Fishing Co.* v. *Edgehill* (1883) 11 Q.B.D. 225. This decision is inconsistent with the later case of *Crystal Palace Gas Co.* v. *Idris & Co.*, *supra*, and seems wrong in principle.

[13a] Article: " Breach of Statutory Duty as Cause of Action " (Samuels) 121 New L.J. 610.

[14] *Cutler* v. *Wandsworth Stadium Ltd.* [1949] A.C. 398, *per* Lord Simonds at p. 407.

[15] (1854) 3 E. & B. 402. See also to the same effect Kennedy L.J. in *Dawson* v. *Bingley U.D.C.* [1911] 2 K.B. 149, 159.

[16] (1831) 1 B. & A. 847.

[17] *Square* v. *Model Farm Dairies* (*Bournemouth*) *Ltd.* [1939] 2 K.B. 365, 375, *per* Slesser L.J.

[18] *Nicholls* v. *Ely Beet Sugar Factory* [1936] Ch. 343; explaining *Fraser* v. *Fear* (1912) 107 L.T. 423.

[19] *Pulsford* v. *Devenish* [1903] 2 Ch. 625, *per* Farwell J. (liquidator of company liable to creditor for non-performance of statutory duty).

By the Education Act 1902, s. 7,[20] it is provided that " the school board shall maintain and keep efficient every school provided by " them. Where a pupil at a public elementary school fell in the playground through his foot being caught in a hole in the asphalt pavement, it was held that he could sue the education authority for breach of their statutory duty to maintain and keep efficient the school.[21] " As members of the public, if they are injured by neglect of a statutory duty with regard to a place where they are expected to play, they are entitled to make those upon whom the statute has imposed the duty responsible for injuries sustained by them through breach of such duty." [22]

1183 Railway companies, dock companies, canal companies and local authorities carrying out similar undertakings are usually under a statutory duty to make and maintain their works. The result is that " where a duty to do a work is imposed by statute on a corporate body, there will generally follow a liability to pay damages caused by negligence in doing that work. But it turns on the statute in each case." [23] The liability is the same whether the subject-matter of complaint is in the performance or the omission of a statutory duty; accordingly, a railway company which neglected to repair a canal [24] and a dock company which failed to repair a road over a swing bridge [25] were each held liable to an injured party. Further, a farmer was able to recover damages for the flooding of his land from the local authority who were responsible under a statutory duty to maintain the drains on the highway, which they had neglected to do.[26]

1184 The Railways Clauses Consolidation Act 1845 imposes various duties upon railway companies with regard to fencing their railways from the highway and the adjoining land. Under section 46, where a railway passes underneath a highway, the railway company must maintain a bridge and approaches over the railway. If the surface is not perfectly maintained, so that damage is caused to passing traffic, the railway company are liable.[27] Under section 47, where a railway crosses a public road on the level, the company are bound to erect and maintain gates so as to fence in the railway and prevent cattle or horses passing along the road from entering upon the railway. Accordingly, if a horse strays from a field, gets into the road and is killed on the railway owing to defective fences, the railway company are liable.[28] Under section 61, where a railway crosses any highway other than

[20] Re-enacted, Education Act 1921, s. 17. See now the Education Acts 1944 to 1959. An action will lie for breach of s. 10 of the 1944 Act: *Reffell* v. *Surrey C.C.* [1964] 1 W.L.R. 358.

[21] *Ching* v. *Surrey C.C.* [1910] 1 K.B. 736; *Abbott* v. *Isham* (1920) 90 L.J.K.B. 309.

[22] *Per* Fletcher Moulton L.J. in *Ching* v. *Surrey C.C.*, *supra*, at p. 743.

[23] *Per* Scrutton L.J. in *Boynton* v. *Ancholme Drainage and Navigation Comrs.* [1921] 2 K.B. 213, 232. See also *Mersey Docks Trustees* v. *Gibbs* (1866) L.R. 1 H.L. 93; *Geddis* v. *Bann Reservoir* (1878) 3 App.Cas. 430.

[24] *Blundy, Clark & Co.* v. *L.N.E. Ry.* [1931] 2 K.B. 334.

[25] *Guilfoyle* v. *Port of London Authority* [1932] 1 K.B. 336.

[26] *Att.-Gen.* v. *St. Ives R.D.C.* [1960] 1 Q.B. 312.

[27] *Swain* v. *Southern Ry.* [1939] 2 K.B. 560.

[28] *Charman* v. *S.E. Ry.* (1888) 21 Q.B.D. 524; *Fawcett* v. *York and N. Midland Ry.* (1851) 16 Q.B. 610.

a public carriage-way on the level, the company are to make sufficient approaches and fences where the highway crosses the railway line. This duty, like the duty under section 47, is one which is owed to the public at large, so that on a horse straying onto the highway and from there onto the railway, where it is injured, the railway company are liable to the owner.[29]

1185 On the other hand, under section 68 the railway company are only bound to erect and maintain fences " for the accommodation of the owners and occupiers of lands adjoining the railway." The effect of this limitation is that breach of this duty is actionable only at the suit of such owners or occupiers or their licensees,[30] and not at the suit of the general public.[31] Accordingly, if cattle, which are straying upon a highway adjoining the railway, get onto the railway owing to defective fences, the railway company are not liable under this section [32]; also, if cattle stray from a field not adjoining the railway into a field which does adjoin, and from there get onto the railway owing to defective fences, the railway company are not liable.[33] On the same principle, if cattle stray onto the railway line from an adjoining field, owing to defective fences, the railway company are not liable for breach of statutory duty to a passenger in a train who is injured through a collision between the train and the cattle.[34] Similarly, a section in an Act providing for the erection and maintenance of gates at a level crossing so that highway users " shall not be exposed to any danger or damage by the passing of any carriages or engines along the " railway is " designed to protect the public against the railway and not the railway against the public." Where, therefore, the level crossing gate was not securely closed but was opened by the negligence of a motorist who caused it to swing across the railway and injure the driver of a train, who subsequently recovered damages from the motorist, it was held that the engine driver had no right of action against the railway, so that the motorist could not recover contribution from the railway.[35]

1186 Where a local authority, in the discharge of their duty under the Public Health Act 1875 incorrectly marked the position of a fire-plug, so that when a fire broke out in the plaintiff's premises there was delay in obtaining water for the fire brigade with the result that the plaintiff suffered more damage than he would otherwise have done, the local authority were held liable.[36] Similarly, where a local authority negligently performed their

[29] *Parkinson* v. *Garstang and Knott End Ry.* [1910] 1 K.B. 615.
[30] *Dawson* v. *Midland Ry.* (1872) L.R. 8 Ex. 8.
[31] The defendants were held to owe no duty of care under s. 68 of the Railways Clauses Consolidation Act 1845 to the plaintiff, whose house was too far away from their accommodation bridge, notwithstanding her lawful user of the approach roads and the bridge, over which there was a public right of way: *Greenhalgh* v. *British Railways Board* [1969] 2 Q.B. 286.
[32] *Manchester, Sheffield and Lincolnshire Ry.* v. *Wallis* (1854) 14 C.B. 213; *Luscombe* v. *G W. Ry.* [1899] 2 Q.B. 313.
[33] *Ricketts* v. *E. & W. India Docks Ry.* (1852) 12 C.B. 160.
[34] *Buxton* v. *N.E. Ry.* (1868) L.R. 3 Q.B. 549.
[35] *Knapp* v. *Railway Executive* [1949] 2 All E.R. 508; decided on s. 274 of the Brighton and Chichester Railway Act 1844.
[36] *Dawson* v. *Bingley U.D.C.* [1911] 2 K.B. 149.

statutory duties with regard to lighting a street, so that the plaintiff's motor-car collided with an inadequately lighted street refuge, the local authority were held liable.[37] They were also held liable where they provided lighting which was inadequate at the entrance to an arch over the highway, as a result of which a van driver, driving under the arch, was killed.[38]

2.—WHEN AN ACTION MAY BE BROUGHT

1187 **Statute creates right and gives special remedy.** Where the statute creates a liability not existing at common law and provides a particular remedy for enforcing it, the question arises whether the particular remedy provided is the only remedy, or whether there is, in addition, a right of action for damages based on the breach of the statutory duty. As statutory duties deal with a great variety of matters of varying degrees of importance and are directed to a number of different objects, it is impossible to give a simple affirmative or negative answer to this question. Everything depends on the object and intention of the statute.[39] Liability " must, to a great extent, depend on the purview of the legislature in the particular statute, and the language which they have there employed." [40]

1188 The prima facie rule in this class of cases is that the special remedy provided by the statute is the only remedy: " Where an Act creates an obligation and enforces the performance in a specified manner, we take it to be a general rule that performance cannot be enforced in any other manner." [41] This rule, however, always yields to the proper construction of the statute and too much importance must not be attached to it. " When an Act imposes a duty of commission or omission, the question whether a person aggrieved by a breach of the duty has a right of action depends on the intention of the Act. Was it intended to make the duty one which was owed to the party aggrieved as well as to the State, or was it a public duty only? That depends on the construction of the Act and the circumstances in which it was made and to which it relates. One question to be considered is, Does the Act contain a reference to a remedy for breach of it? Prima facie if it does that is the only remedy. But that is not conclusive. The intention as disclosed by its scope and wording must still be regarded, and it may still be that, though the statute creates the duty and provides a penalty, the duty is nevertheless owed to individuals." [42]

[37] *Baldock* v. *Westminster City Council* (1918) 88 L.J.K.B. 502; *Carpenter* v. *Finsbury Borough Council* [1920] 2 K.B. 195; *Polkinghorn* v. *Lambeth B.C.* [1938] 1 All E.R. 339.

[38] *Carpenter* v. *Finsbury Borough Council, supra.*

[39] *Black* v. *Fife Coal Co. Ltd.* [1912] A.C. 149, *per* Lord Kinnear at p. 165: " We are to consider the scope and purpose of the statute and in particular for whose benefit it is intended." See also article: " The Effect of Penal Legislation in the Law of Tort," (1960) 23 M.L.R. 233.

[40] *Per* Lord Cairns C. in *Atkinson* v. *Newcastle Waterworks Co.* (1877) 2 Ex.D. 441, 448.

[41] *Doe* d. *Bishop of Rochester* v. *Bridges* (1831) 1 B. & A. 847, 859, *per* Lord Tenterden C.J.; *Pasmore* v. *Oswaldtwistle U.D.C.* [1898] A.C. 387; *Cutler* v. *Wandsworth Stadium Ltd.* [1949] A.C. 398; *Monk* v. *Warbey* [1935] 1 K.B. 75; *Stevens* v. *Jeacocke* (1847) 11 Q.B. 731; *Institute of Patent Agents* v. *Lockwood* [1894] A.C. 347; *Barraclough* v. *Brown* [1897] A.C. 615.

[42] *Per* Atkin L.J. in *Phillips* v. *Britannia Hygienic Laundry* [1923] 2 K.B. 832, 841.

189 **Considerations determining whether action lies.**[43] It has been said, " No universal rule can be formulated which will answer the question whether in any given case an individual can sue in respect of a breach of statutory duty." [44] In addition to the general rules set out in the preceding section, however, the most important matters to be taken into consideration appear to be: (a) Is the action brought in respect of the kind of harm which the statute was intended to prevent? (b) Is the person bringing the action one of the class which the statute desired to protect? (c) Is the special remedy provided by the statute adequate for the protection of the person injured? If the first two are answered in the affirmative and the third in the negative then, in most cases, the individual can sue.

(a) *Is the Action Brought in Respect of the Kind of Harm which the Statute was Intended to Prevent?*

190 **Harm statute intended to prevent.** The Road Traffic Act 1960, s. 201,[45] provides that a person who permits a motor-car to be used by another who is not insured against third party risks is liable to penalties. Accordingly, where the owner of a motor-car lent his car to a friend who was not insured, and in consequence of the friend's negligence a third party was injured, it was held that the owner was liable to the third party in damages for the amount he would have recovered from the insurers if the friend had been insured, on the ground that the section " was passed for the purpose of giving a remedy to third persons who might suffer injury by the negligence of the impecunious driver of a car." [46] An auctioneer who sells an uninsured and unlicensed car and allows it to be driven away by the purchaser does not cause or permit the purchaser to drive within the meaning of section 201 and so is not liable to a person injured by the purchaser's negligent driving.[47] Only the owner of a motor-vehicle can be liable under section 201, because he is the only person who can forbid another to use it.[48]

191 Where a water company was obliged by statute to supply water to the inhabitants of Newcastle and to keep their pipes to which fire-plugs were fixed charged with water at a certain pressure, under the penalty of a fine, it was held that they were not liable to a person whose premises were

43 This paragraph was approved and adopted by Veale J. in *Reffell* v. *Surrey C.C.* [1964] 1 W.L.R. 358, 362.

44 *Solomons* v. *Gertzenstein Ltd.* [1954] 2 Q.B. 243, 266, *per* Romer L.J. *Cf. ibid.* p. 253: " Attempts to lay down a principle have, as it seems to me, been unsuccessful," *per* Somervell L.J.

45 s. 201 (1) and (2), replaced s. 35 (1) and (2) of the Road Traffic Act 1930, respectively.

46 *Monk* v. *Warbey* [1935] 1 K.B. 75; *Houston* v. *Buchanan*, 1940 S.C.(H.L.) 17 (vehicle insured for commercial purposes, but not for private purposes—owner's brother given unrestricted permission to drive—owner liable when driven for private purposes, although he did not know it was being so used); *Daniels* v. *Vaux* [1938] 2 K.B. 203 (mother allowed son to drive car, and on insurance policy lapsing, told him to pay the premiums himself—not liable for damage caused when uninsured). Likewise a cause of action civilly will lie for a breach of certain regulations relating to traffic, *e.g.* the Traffic Signs Regulations, and General Directions 1964 (S.I. 1964 No. 1857) reg. 23 (2) (*a*): *Kelly* v. *W.R.N. Contracting Ltd.* [1968] 1 All E.R. 369.

47 *Watkins* v. *O'Shaughnessy* [1939] 1 All E.R. 385.

48 *Goodbarne* v. *Buck* [1940] 1 K.B. 771.

destroyed by fire in consequence of their failure to keep a sufficient pressure of water in the pipes to enable the fire to be extinguished. Lord Cairns said that if they were liable in the action " they would virtually become gratuitous insurers of the safety from fire, so far as water is capable of producing that safety, of all the houses within the district over which their powers were to extend," and held that the statute could not have intended any such result.[49] Similarly, where an action was brought against a gas company for breach of their duty under the Gasworks Clauses Act 1871 [50] to supply gas sufficient in amount and in purity to satisfy the requirements of the Act (the breach of which was enforced by a penalty), it was held that the only remedy of a consumer was to proceed for the penalty.[51] But where the Waterworks Clauses Act 1847 provided that if a water company broke up the pavement of a street they should reinstate it and make it good under payment of penalties,[52] it was held that a person walking along the street who was injured owing to the failure of the water company to make good the pavement could recover damages.[53] Darling J. dealing with this point said: " I do not think that because there is the power to sue the defendants for penalties they are not liable to be sued for negligence in the doing of the work, provided it be proved that the negligence resulted in injury to a plaintiff." [54] In *Close* v. *Steel Company of Wales Ltd.*[55] the House of Lords has held that the duty to fence " every dangerous part of any machinery " in section 14 (1) of the Factories Act [56] does not give rise to liability if a part of the machine or some fragment of the material being worked upon flies out and hurts the operator, since the provisions of the section are designed solely for the protection of the operator himself from coming into contact with the dangerous moving parts of the machinery itself. Nor does the duty to fence extend to dangers due to the machinery breaking down or behaving erratically in some unexpected manner nor from materials which are in motion in the machine [57] nor to prevent the operator's tools from coming into contact with such machinery.[58]

1192 Where by an order made under the Contagious Diseases (Animals) Act 1869 a ship should have had pens provided to enable it to carry sheep, and

[49] *Atkinson* v. *Newcastle Waterworks Co.* (1877) 2 Ex.D. 441, 446; *Johnston* v. *Consumers' Gas Co. of Toronto* [1898] A.C. 447 is a somewhat similar case. But *cf. Dawson & Co.* v. *Bingley U.D.C.* [1911] 2 K.B. 149.

[50] Which was repealed by the Gas Act 1948.

[51] *Clegg, Parkinson & Co.* v. *Earby Gas Co.* [1896] 1 Q.B. 592; *Stevens* v. *Aldershot, etc., District Lighting Co.* (1933) 102 L.J.K.B. 12 is a somewhat similar case to the same effect.

[52] See now the Public Utilities Street Works Act 1950.

[53] *Hartley* v. *Rochdale Corpn.* [1908] 2 K.B. 594; a similar case is *Withington* v. *Bolton Borough Council* [1937] 3 All E.R. 108.

[54] *Ibid.* at p. 598.

[55] [1962] A.C. 367. See further *Nicholls* v. *F. Austin (Leyton) Ltd.* [1946] A.C. 493; *Kilgollan* v. *Wm. Cooke & Co. Ltd.* [1956] 1 W.L.R. 527; *Rutherford* v. *R. E. Glanville & Sons Ltd.* [1958] 1 W.L.R. 415. Distinguished in *Littler* v. *G. L. Moore (Contractors) Ltd.* [1967] 1 W.L.R. 1241; *Millard* v. *Serck Tubes Ltd.* [1969] 1 W.L.R. 211. See articles (1969) 85 L.Q.R. 458 (Goodhart) and (1969) 32 M.L.R. 438 (Hendy). See also *Cross* v. *Midland Steel Co. Ltd.* [1965] A.C. 343; *Johnson* v. *F. E. Callow (Engineers) Ltd.* [1970] 2 Q.B. 1.

[56] A decision under the 1937 Act replaced now by the 1961 Act.

[57] *Eaves* v. *Morris Motors Ltd.* [1961] 2 Q.B 385. Article (1962) 25 M.L.R. 98–108 (Howells).

[58] *Sparrow* v. *Fairey Aviation Co. Ltd.* [1964] A.C. 1019.

in consequence of the non-provision of the pens some of the sheep were washed overboard, it was held that no action would lie for the neglect of this provision, on the ground that the object of the statute and order was to prevent the spread of contagious disease among animals and not to protect them against the perils of the seas.[59] The Motor Cars (Use and Construction) Order 1904 limits the weight and size of motor-cars used on the highway, prescribes the nature of the brakes and lamps to be fitted and also provides that " the motor-car and all the fittings thereof shall be in such a condition as not to cause, or to be likely to cause, danger to any person on the motor-car or on any highway." A penalty is imposed for breach of the regulations.[60] The defendant's motor-car, in breach of the regulation quoted above, had a defective axle which broke, as a result of which a wheel came off and damaged the plaintiff's vehicle. It was held that the plaintiff had no cause of action, because the regulations imposed obligations of various kinds, some relating to the maintenance of the highway and others dealing with the safety of the public, all of which were punishable by the same fine and, having regard to the existing remedies available against persons using vehicles on the highway, it could not have been intended by the statute to give additional remedies to private individuals.[61] The sale of a motor-vehicle with defective brakes in breach of the Road Traffic Act 1960, s. 68 [62] and the Motor Vehicles (Construction and Use) Regulations 1955 [63] does not give the buyer a right of action against the seller, because the aim of this legislation is not to protect the buyer.[64] Mere failure to carry a red rear-light on a car, contrary to the Road Transport Lighting Act 1957 [65] gives no right of action civilly to a person who collides with the car.[66] The Road Traffic Act 1960, s. 102 (3), provides that if a provisional licence holder fails to comply with the conditions prescribed (*inter alia*) by the Motor Vehicles (Driving Licences) Regulations 1963,[67] he shall be liable on summary conviction to a penalty. Where a learner driver without a qualified driver being present swerved across the road, overturned the car and injured his passenger, it was held that the breach of statutory requirements with respect to learner drivers did not of itself give a cause of action.[68]

193 Where a local authority were under a statutory duty to keep the streets in their area " properly swept and cleansed " and to remove " all street refuse," which was defined as including snow, under penalty of a fine, it was held that they were under no liability to a person who fell in the street

59 *Gorris* v. *Scott* (1874) L.R. 9 Ex. 125. See *Grant* v. *N.C.B.* [1956] 2 W.L.R. 752.
60 See now the Motor Vehicles (Construction and Use) Regulations 1969 (S.I. 1969, No. 321).
61 *Phillips* v. *Britannia Hygienic Laundry* [1923] 2 K.B. 832.
62 This section replaced the Road Traffic Act 1934, s. 8.
63 S.I. 1955, No. 482.
64 *Badham* v. *Lambs Ltd.* [1946] K.B. 45; *Vinall* v. *Howard* [1954] 1 Q.B. 375. See now subsection (5), which is statutory affirmation of these two decisions.
65 As amended by the Act of 1958, which repealed the Road Transport Lighting Act 1927.
66 *Clarke & Wife* v. *Brims* [1947] K.B. 497; *West* v. *Lawson Ltd.*, 1949 S.C. 430.
67 S.I. 1963 No. 1026.
68 *Verney* v. *Wilkins* (1962) 106 S.J. 879.

in consequence of their failure to remove the snow, because the statute disclosed no intention to provide a private right of action in such a case.[69]

1194 A by-law prohibiting, under penalty of a fine, dogs being brought into a park unless they are under proper control is intended to protect the park, the plants growing in it and the comfort and convenience of those using the park, and gives no right of action to a member of the public when there is a breach. When an uncontrolled Alsatian dog jumped a fence and injured the plaintiff, an action for breach of statutory duty failed.[70]

(b) *Is the Person Bringing the Action One of the Class which the Statute Desired to Protect?*

1195 **Person statute desired to protect.** The statute may have been designed to protect a particular class of persons, but this is not essential in order to give a right of action.[71] " The question is not to be solved by considering whether or not the person aggrieved can bring himself within some special class of the community or whether he is some designated individual. The duty may be of such paramount importance that it is owed to all the public. It would be strange if a less important duty, which is owed to a section of the public, may be enforced by an action, while a more important duty owed to the public at large cannot. The right of action does not depend on whether a statutory commandment or prohibition is pronounced for the benefit of the public or for the benefit of a class." [72] At the same time, if on the true construction of the statute it appears that the statute was passed for the benefit of a particular section of the community, of which the plaintiff is one, strong ground is afforded for coming to the conclusion that the action will lie.

1196 The Merchant Seamen Act 1844, s. 18,[73] required every ship to keep on board " a sufficient supply of medicines suitable to accidents and diseases arising on sea voyages," under the penalty of a fine. The defendant, in breach of the statute, neglected to keep a proper supply of medicines on board, as a result of which the plaintiff's health suffered. The plaintiff was held entitled to recover on the ground that, " The enactment provides a benefit for the seamen; and, according to the plaintiff's allegations in the second count, the defendant has violated this enactment; and thereby the plaintiff, being a seaman on board, was deprived of that benefit, and his health was injured." [74] Again, where the use of adjoining mines in the

[69] *Saunders* v. *Holborn District Board of Works* [1895] 1 Q.B. 64. Mathew J. based his judgment solely on the ground of the intention of the statute, but Charles J. also relied on the ground that the local authority were not liable for nonfeasance. On this latter point, see the provisions of the Highways (Miscellaneous Provisions) Act 1961.

[70] *Newman v. Francis* [1953] 1 W.L.R. 402.

[71] *Monk* v. *Warbey* [1935] 1 K.B. 75; *Ching* v. *Surrey C.C.* [1910] 1 K.B. 736.

[72] *Per* Atkin L.J. in *Phillips* v. *Britannia Hygienic Laundry* [1923] 2 K.B. 832, 841.

[73] Repealed and re-enacted in the Merchant Shipping Act 1894, s. 200.

[74] *Couch* v. *Steel* (1854) 3 E. & B. 402. Much of the reasoning in this case was dissented from in *Atkinson* v. *Newcastle Waterworks Co.* (1877) 2 Ex.D. 441, and *Cowley* v. *Newmarket Local Board* [1892] A.C. 345, but it " may properly be cited as an authority ": *R.* v. *Hall* [1891] 1 Q.B. 747, 769. It was quoted with approval in *Simmonds* v. *Newport, etc., Co.* [1921] 1 K.B. 616. See also *Solomons* v. *Gertzenstein Ltd.* [1954] 2 Q.B. 243, pp. 254, 265.

Forest of Dean was regulated by statute and the rules made thereunder, compliance with the rules being enforced by injunction and, the plaintiffs and the defendant being occupiers of adjoining mines, the defendant ceased to work his engines in his mine, contrary to the rules, as a result of which the plaintiffs' mine was flooded, it was held that the plaintiffs had a right of action for damages, because the statutory right which was infringed had been given to the plaintiffs for their personal benefit.[75]

197 The Waterworks Clauses Act 1847, s. 35, requires statutory undertakers to provide and keep in their pipes a supply of pure and wholesome water sufficient for the domestic use of the inhabitants of the district within their limits of supply. This duty is owed only to the ratepayers and not to people living with them, so that when water infected by typhoid bacillus caused the daughter of a ratepayer to contract typhoid fever it was held that the daughter had no right of action for breach of statutory duty.[76]

198 Under the Factories Acts the occupiers of a factory are required under a penalty of a fine to fence dangerous machinery. Breach of this statutory requirement renders them liable to an action at the suit of a workman[77] in the factory injured in consequence of the breach.[78] "Where a statute provides for the performance by certain persons of a particular duty, and someone belonging to a class of persons for whose benefit and protection the statute imposes the duty is injured by failure to perform it, prima facie, and if there be nothing to the contrary, an action by the person so injured will lie against the person who has so failed to perform the duty."[79] Similarly, the failure of the occupier of a coal mine to comply with the provisions of the Coal Mines Acts, as a result of which a workman is injured, renders the occupier liable to an action by the injured workman.[80] "Now the object of the present statute [the Coal Mines Regulation Act 1887] is plain. It was intended to compel mine owners to make due provision for the safety of the men working in their mines, and the persons for whose benefit all these rules are to be enforced are the persons exposed to danger. But when a duty of this kind is imposed for the benefit of particular persons, there arises at common law a correlative right in those persons who may be injured by its contravention. Therefore I think it is quite impossible to hold that the penalty clause detracts in any way from the

[75] *Ross* v. *Rugge-Price* (1876) 1 Ex.D. 269.

[76] *Read* v. *Croydon Corpn.* [1938] 4 All E.R. 631 (an action lay for common law negligence).

[77] The class of "workman" not intended to be protected includes: a workman working for his own private purposes after normal working hours; *Napieralski* v. *Curtis* (*Contractors*) *Ltd.* [1959] 2 All E.R. 426. But a workman who in working hours leaves his allotted tasks for a private purpose is so entitled to protection: *Uddin* v. *Associated Portland Cement Manufacturers Ltd.* [1965] 2 Q.B. 582. Nevertheless if a person engages in some act which he knows to be dangerous and to be in breach of the regulations designed for his protection he is liable to be treated as falling outside the ambit of the statutory duty: *Hillen* v. *I.C.I.* (*Alkali*) *Ltd.* [1934] 1 K.B. 455. (Docks Regulations 1925, reg 34 (*b*).)

[78] *Groves* v. *Wimborne* [1898] 2 Q.B. 402.

[79] *Ibid.*, *per* Vaughan Williams L.J. at p. 415.

[80] *Britannic Merthyr Coal Co.* v. *David* [1910] A.C. 74; *Black* v. *Fife Coal Co.* [1912] A.C. 149; *Watkins* v. *Naval Colliery Co.* [1912] A.C. 693. See now the Mines and Quarries Act 1954 to the same effect.

prima facie right of the persons for whose benefit the statutory enactment has been passed to enforce the civil liability." [81]

1199 However a fireman who was electrocuted whilst engaged in fighting a fire in a factory was held to have no cause of action for the breach of the regulations involved, since these were limited to the protection of " persons employed " [82]; likewise, a building contractor is not liable under the various Building Regulations [83] to a self employed craftsman working for him, who was not by contract obliged to work on an operation to which the statutory regulations applied, [84] nor to a clerk of works employed by a local authority. [85] On the other hand under the same regulations a head contractor has been [86] held liable to the employee of a sub-contractor and a sub-contractor has been held liable to the employee of a head contractor. [87] The failure of builders to comply with the provisions in the Building Regulations, requiring any part of the premises in which any person is habitually employed to be covered so as to prevent workmen from being struck by falling material, was held to entitle a workman who was struck by a falling brick, in the absence of such a cover, to obtain damages from the builders. [88] Further, it should be observed that the expression " any person " contained in section 29 of the Factories Act 1961 comprehends all those people who enter factory premises in order to work for the purposes of the occupiers, so that a window cleaner, who was employed as an independent contractor by them was held to be entitled to the protection of its provisions. [89] But the seller of a machine which was not securely fenced contrary to section 17 (2) of the Factories Act 1937 [90] owed no duty to a workman who subsequently used the machine in the buyer's factory. [91] For actions by workmen for breach of statutory duty, see *post*, § 1222 *et seq.*

1200 The duty imposed under the London Building Acts to keep and maintain means of escape in case of fire is imposed principally for the benefit of a particular class, namely, persons in the building, and those persons have a right of action, although penalties are also imposed for breach of the duty. [92]

1201 Where a statute prohibited persons from sending to market diseased animals, knowing that they were diseased, under penalty of a fine, and the defendant, in breach of the statute, sent to market pigs which were

81 *Per* Lord Kinnear in *Black* v. *Fife Coal Co.*, *supra*, at pp. 165, 166.
82 *Hartley* v. *Mayoh & Co.* [1954] 1 Q.B. 383. But *cf. Canadian Pacific Steamboats Ltd.* v. *Bryers* [1958] A.C. 485.
83 See generally these regulations set out fully in *Redgrave's Factories Acts*, 21st ed., pp. 552–645.
84 *Herbert* v. *Harold Shaw Ltd.* [1959] 2 Q.B. 138.
85 *Wingrove* v. *Prestige & Co.* [1954] 1 W.L.R. 524.
86 *Mulready* v. *J. H. & W. Bell Ltd.* [1953] 2 Q.B. 117, distinguished in *Kearney* v. *Eric Waller Ltd.* [1967] 1 Q.B. 29.
87 *Simmons* v. *Bovis Ltd.* [1956] 1 W.L.R. 381; *Clay* v. *A. J. Crump & Sons Ltd.* [1964] 1 Q.B. 533.
88 *Kearns* v. *Gee, Walker & Slater Ltd.* [1937] 1 K.B. 187. *Cf. Bailey* v. *Ayr Engineering and Constructional Co. Ltd.* [1959] 1 Q.B. 183.
89 *Wigley* v. *British Vinegars Ltd.* [1964] A.C. 307.
90 Now re-enacted by s. 17 (2), Factories Act 1961.
91 *Biddle* v. *Truvox Manufacturing Co.* [1952] 1 K.B. 101 following *Badham* v. *Lambs Ltd.* [1946] K.B. 45, *ante*, § 1192.
92 *Solomons* v. *Gertzenstein Ltd.* [1954] 2 Q.B. 243.

suffering from typhoid fever, as a result of which the plaintiff, who bought the pigs, suffered damage from his own pigs becoming infected with the disease, it was held that no action lay.[93] "The Act was passed for the benefit of the general public; it has nothing to do with the bargains of particular persons."[94] Again, where sheep were straying on the highway and their owner was subsequently fined for allowing them to stray contrary to the Highway Act 1864,[95] s. 25, it was held that this breach of statutory duty gave no right of action to a motorist whose car was overturned owing to the presence of the sheep on the road.[96] Also the Road Traffic Act 1930,[97] s. 35, imposed no duty on an employer to his servant to see that the motor-vehicle driven by the servant in the course of his employment was insured against third party risks.[98] Similarly, the statutes of forcible entry[99] make it unlawful on pain of imprisonment to enter upon land "with strong hand" or "with multitude of people." This, however, gives no right of action to a person who is forcibly ejected, any remedies he may have being limited to the common law actions of trespass and assault.[1] A statute regulating fishing in St. Ives Bay was held to give no right of action for damages to a fisherman whose catch had been anticipated, contrary to the statute, by another fisherman, on the ground that the statute merely imposed a penalty for the act done and imposed no duty owed to the plaintiff.[2] A breach of the Betting and Lotteries Act 1934, s. 11 (2),[3] which was intended to regulate the conduct of betting on race-tracks, did not give a bookmaker injured thereby any right of action.[4]

1202 A statute may impose a duty on the seller of goods as to the quality of the goods he sells and may impose a penalty for breach of that duty. This duty is owed to the purchaser only, and not to others who may suffer damage by its breach. The purchaser, however, will not be entitled to sue for breach of statutory duty when he already has a remedy for breach of contract[5] or when the object of the penal legislation was not to protect the purchaser.[6]

93 *Ward* v. *Hobbs* (1878) 4 App.Cas. 13. But *semble* an action would lie for negligence.
94 *Ibid., per* Lord O'Hagan at p. 28.
95 See now Highways Act 1959.
96 *Heath's Garage Co.* v. *Hodges* [1916] 2 K.B. 370.
97 Amended by the Road Traffic Act 1956, s. 29 (1), which provided a defence to such employee for the offence thus committed if the vehicle was not so insured. See now Road Traffic Act 1960, s. 201.
98 *Gregory* v. *Ford* [1951] 1 All E.R. 121. Followed in *Semtex Ltd.* v. *Gladstone* [1954] 2 All E.R. 206; *Lister* v. *Romford Ice Co. Ltd.* [1957] A.C. 555. However, in each of these cases at common law an implied term was found in the contract of service that the employer will insure as required by s. 35 (1) of the Act of 1930.
99 5 Ric. 2, st. 1, c. 8.
1 *Hemmings* v. *Stoke Poges Golf Club* [1920] 1 K.B. 720; *Harvey* v. *Brydges* (1845) 14 M. & W. 437, *per* Parke B.; *Beddall* v. *Maitland* (1881) 17 Ch.D. 174, 188, *per* Fry J.
2 *Stevens* v. *Jeacocke* (1847) 11 Q.B. 731. See the explanation of this case in *Couch* v. *Steel* (1854) 3 E. & B. 402. *Quaere*, whether the case would now be decided in the same way.
3 This provision is unaffected by the Betting and Gaming Act 1960.
4 *Cutler* v. *Wandsworth Stadium Ltd.* [1949] A.C. 398.
5 *Square* v. *Model Farm Dairies (Bournemouth) Ltd.* [1939] 2 K.B. 365 (milk containing typhoid germs—no action for breach of statutory duty by purchaser or his family).
6 *Badham* v. *Lambs Ltd.* [1946] K.B. 45 (penalties only remedy); *London Armoury* v. *Ever-Ready (Great Britain) Ltd.* [1941] 1 K.B. 742 (seller's breach of Merchandise Marks Act 1926, s. 1, gave no right of action to importers of foreign goods).

A person who contravenes the provisions of the Merchandise Marks Acts 1887 to 1953 was held not liable in a civil action brought by a rival trader.[7]

(c) *Is the Special Remedy Provided by the Statute Adequate for the Protection of the Person Injured?*

1203 **Special remedy.** In *Couch* v. *Steel* [8] Lord Campbell said: " As far as the public wrong is concerned, there is no remedy but that prescribed by the Act of Parliament. There is, however, beyond the public wrong, a special and particular damage sustained by the plaintiff by reason of the breach of duty by the defendant, for which he has no remedy unless an action on the case at his suit be maintainable: and the question is, whether the penalty annexed to the offence concludes the plaintiff who has sustained a special and particular damage, as well as the public, though no part of the penalty is payable to him. If the performance of a new duty created by Act of Parliament is enforced by a penalty, recoverable by the party grieved by the non-performance, there is no other remedy than that given by the Act, either for the public or the private wrong; but, by the penalty given in the Act now in question, compensation for private special damage seems not to have been contemplated. The penalty is recoverable in case of a breach of the public duty, though no damage may actually have been sustained by anybody; and no authority has been cited to us, nor are we aware of any, in which it has been held that, in such a case as the present, the common law right to maintain an action in respect of a special damage resulting from the breach of a public duty (whether such duty exists at common law or is created by statute) is taken away by reason of a penalty, recoverable by a common informer, being annexed as a punishment for the non-performance of the public duty." This opinion was criticised in *Atkinson* v. *Newcastle Waterworks Co.*[9] as laying down a proposition which was much too wide. It was, however, quoted with approval by the Court of Appeal in *Simmonds* v. *Newport, etc., Co.*,[10] and, though too broadly stated, may be taken as accurately laying down that an important, though not a conclusive, element in determining whether an action lies for breach of a statutory obligation, is whether or not the penalty imposed for non-performance of that obligation is payable to the injured party. In *Groves* v. *Wimborne*,[11] Vaughan Williams L.J. dealt with the point as follows: " If it be found that the remedy so provided by the statute is to enure for the benefit of the person injured by the breach of the statutory duty, that is an additional matter which ought to be taken into consideration in dealing with the question whether the legislature intended the

[7] *Bollinger* v. *Costa Brava Wine Co. Ltd.* [1960] Ch. 262, 287. See now the Trade Descriptions Act 1968, s. 41 (2), Sched. 2.
[8] (1854) 3 E. & B. 402, 412. For the facts of this case, see *ante*, § 1196.
[9] (1877) 2 Ex.D. 441, *per* Lord Cairns L.C. at pp. 447, 448.
[10] [1921] 1 K.B. 616, *per* Bankes L.J. at pp. 624, 625.
[11] [1898] 2 Q.B. 402, 416.

statutory remedy to be the only remedy. But again, the fact that the legislature has provided that that remedy shall enure, or under some circumstances shall enure, for the benefit of the person injured, is not conclusive of the question, and, although it may be a cogent and weighty consideration, other matters also have to be considered."

1204 By the Merchant Shipping Act 1854 the master of a ship was required to give a seaman a certificate of discharge, and on his refusal to do so, he was liable to a fine of £10, the whole or part of which might be applied in compensating the seaman. The refusal of the master to give a certificate gave a seaman no right of action for damages, because "£10 might be an abundant compensation for any wrong done to a seaman by withholding the certificate." [12]

1205 In *Beckford* v. *Hood* [13] an action for damages was brought for an infringement of the statute 8 Anne, c. 21, which gave the author of a book the sole right of printing and publishing it, the remedy for infringement being an action for penalties by an informer. It was held that the author could sue for damages, Lord Kenyon stating the law as follows: "The statute having vested that right in the author, the common law gives the remedy by action on the case for the violation of it. Of this there could have been no doubt made, if the statute had stopped there. But it has been argued that, as the statute in the same clause that creates the right has prescribed a particular remedy, that and no other can be resorted to. And if such appeared to have been the intention of the legislature I should have subscribed to it however inadequate it might be thought. But their meaning in creating the penalties in the latter part of the clause in question certainly was to give an accumulative remedy: nothing could be more incomplete as a remedy than those penalties alone; for without dwelling upon the incompetency of the sum, the right of action is not given to the party grieved but to any common informer. I cannot think that the legislature would act so inconsistently as to confer a right, and leave the party whose property was invaded without redress."

1206 By the Coal Mines Act 1911, [14] s. 96 (2), all persons employed in a mine were entitled to have delivered to them a statement showing how the amount of their wages was arrived at, and a penalty was imposed for contravention of the Act. It was held that this duty could be enforced not only by proceedings for the penalty, but also by an action at the suit of a person employed, for a declaration and for damages. [15]

(d) *Other Considerations*

1207 **Damage the result of breach of duty.** In *Bonnington Castings Ltd.* v.

[12] *Vallence* v. *Falle* (1884) 13 Q.B.D. 109, 112.
[13] (1798) 7 T.R. 620.
[14] See now the Mines and Quarries Act 1954 although this particular section has not been reproduced.
[15] *Simmonds* v. *Newport Abercarn Black Vein Steam Coal Co. Ltd.* [1921] 1 K.B. 616. As to an action for damages, see *per* Atkin L.J. at p. 631.

Wardlaw [16] the House of Lords laid down that unless the statute or regulation provides to the contrary, the burden rests on the plaintiff to prove on a balance of probabilities that the breach of duty caused or materially contributed to his damage. Lord Reid stated: " It would seem obvious in principle that a pursuer or plaintiff must prove not only negligence or breach of duty but also that such fault caused or materially contributed to his injury and there is ample authority for that proposition both in Scotland and in England. I can find neither reason nor authority for the rule being different where there is a breach of statutory duty. The fact that Parliament imposes a duty for the protection of employees has been held to entitle an employee to sue if he is injured as a result of a breach of that duty, it would be going a great deal farther to hold that it can be inferred from the enactment of a duty that Parliament intended that any employee suffering injury can sue his employer merely because there was a breach of duty and it is shown to be possible that his injury may have been caused by it." [17] To the like effect Viscount Simonds in *McWilliams* v. *Sir William Arrol & Co.*[18] stated: " I do not doubt that it is part of the law of Scotland as it is part of the law of England that a causal connection must be established between a breach by an employer of his duty at common law or under a statute and the damage suffered by his employee: see, for example, *Bonnington Castings* v. *Wardlaw*. If a contrary principle is thought to be established in *Roberts* v. *Dorman Long & Co. Ltd.*[19] I cannot reconcile that case with *Wardlaw*." Thus where an experienced steel erector fell to his death, his widow's action failed owing to the inability to establish a causal connection between his employers' failure to provide the deceased with a safety belt and the happening of the accident. On the evidence it was highly probable that the deceased would not have worn the safety belt even if it had been provided and it was held that there was no obligation on the employers to encourage and exhort him so to do.[20] The breach by a motorist of a statutory duty to have a red light in the rear of his motor-car would be no ground for an action for damages by a person who collided with the front of the car.[21]

From the above it would follow that where the effective cause of the accident is the deliberate act of folly by the employee, then the employer may avoid liability altogether.[22] For causation generally, see Chapter 3.

1208 **Other remedy available.** Although the statute may provide a special

[16] [1956] A.C. 613; *Quinn* v. *Cameron & Roberton Ltd.* [1958] A.C. 9, 23. See also *Nicholson* v. *Atlas Steel Co. Ltd.* [1957] 1 W.L.R. 613; *Clarke* v. *E. R. Wright & Son* [1957] 1 W.L.R. 1191; *Clarkson* v. *Modern Foundries Ltd.* [1957] 1 W.L.R. 1210; *Corn* v. *Weir's (Glass) Ltd.* [1960] 1 W.L.R. 577.

[17] *Ibid.* p. 260.

[18] [1962] 1 W.L.R. 295, 301.

[19] [1953] 1 W.L.R. 942.

[20] *McWilliams* v. *Sir William Arrol & Co., supra.*

[21] See *Phillips* v. *Britannia Hygienic Laundry* [1923] 2 K.B. 832, *per* Bankes L.J. at pp. 839, 840.

[22] *Rushton* v. *Turner Brothers Asbestos Co. Ltd.* [1960] 1 W.L.R. 96; *Horne* v. *Lec Refrigeration Ltd.* [1965] 2 All E.R. 898. Such employee may however succeed in proving negligence, *e.g. Nolan* v. *Dental Manufacturing Co. Ltd.* [1958] 1 W.L.R. 936.

remedy for breach of statutory duty, it may also provide that this remedy is not to be the only remedy. For example, in *Pickering* v. *James* [23] it was held that an action would lie by a person who had lost an election through the failure of a returning officer to perform his duty under the Ballot Act 1872 [24] whereby votes cast for the plaintiff were disallowed for want of the official mark on the ballot paper. A penalty for breach of duty was provided by the Act, but it was expressly enacted to be in addition to any other liability.

3.—THE EXTENT OF STATUTORY DUTY

1209 **Statutory duty usually absolute.** The extent of a statutory duty is a question of the construction of the particular statute, and on proof that the duty has not been performed, action will lie, when it lies at all, without proving lack of care or diligence on the part of the person on whom the duty is imposed. The mere non-performance of the act which the statute requires a person to perform is itself negligence on the part of that person. Lord Atkin dealt with the matter as follows: " The employer is alleged to have committed a breach of a duty owed by him to his servant to take a particular precaution (namely, support of the roof) for his servant's safety whereby the servant was injured. In my opinion, that state of facts constitutes negligence of the employer; and I am unable to conceive of any accurate definition of negligence which would exclude it. All that is necessary to show is a duty to take care to avoid injuring; and if the particular care to be taken is prescribed by statute, and the duty to the injured person to take the care is likewise imposed by statute, and the breach is proved, all the essentials of negligence are present." [25]

1210 The duty of a railway company to make and maintain fences under section 68 of the Railways Clauses Consolidation Act 1845 is absolute, so that the company are liable for failure to perform that duty whether they are otherwise negligent or not.[26] This duty, however, is not to maintain such a fence as no cattle will get through, it is only to maintain a fence to prevent cattle from straying. So, where some calves were separated from their dams and penned on one side of a railway track and their dams were penned on the other side, and the dams broke through the fence, which was as strong as an ordinary farm fence, got on the line and were killed, derailing the train, it was held that the railway were not liable for killing the dams and were entitled to recover the cost of repairs to the train and the track.[27]

1211 Various statutes impose a duty upon undertakers to make and maintain works such as canals, reservoirs, drains, railways and the like, and a difference of opinion is found in the authorities as to whether this duty is an

23 (1873) L.R. 8 C.P. 489.
24 See now the Representation of the People Act 1969.
25 *Lochgelly Iron and Coal Co.* v. *M'Mullan* [1934] A.C. 1, 9.
26 *Buxton* v. *N.E. Ry.* (1868) L.R. 3 Q.B. 549, *per* Lush J.; *Dixon* v. *G.W. Ry.* [1897] 1 Q.B. 300, *per* Lopes L.J.
27 *Cooper* v. *Railway Executive* [1953] 1 W.L.R. 223.

absolute one or not. It is clear that if the duty imposed upon the undertaker by the statute is properly carried out there is no breach of statutory duty, and in consequence no action for damages can be brought. "I take it, without citing cases, that it is now thoroughly well established that no action will lie for doing that which the legislature has authorised, if it be done without negligence, although it does occasion damage to anyone; but an action does lie for doing that which the legislature has authorised, if it be done negligently." [28] Accordingly, if the statute authorises the construction of works and damage is inevitably caused, that is, is caused in spite of all reasonable care and skill being used, the statutory undertaker is not liable [29]; but if the damage is not inevitable and could have been prevented had all reasonable care and skill been taken, the undertaker is liable.[30] It would seem from this, that, if by statute an undertaker is bound to repair and maintain works, he is bound to maintain them so as to cause no more damage to others than was inevitable at the time when they were originally constructed, at the least; and that if, after a lapse of time, more damage is caused owing to the works not being properly maintained, as, for example, by the collapse of the wall of a canal, it is no defence for him to prove that by the exercise of reasonable care and skill he could not have detected the imminence of the danger. If the duty is to maintain and repair, failure to fulfil that duty is negligence,[31] and there seems to be no justification for reading into the statute a duty merely to use reasonable care and skill to maintain and repair the works.

1212 Nevertheless, there is a considerable body of authority for the view that the duty referred to is not an absolute one, but is only a duty to use reasonable care and skill. In *Blundy, Clark & Co.* v. *L.N.E. Ry.*,[32] a railway company were under a statutory duty to keep and maintain the River Ure navigation and all works belonging thereto well and sufficiently repaired. A lock, part of the works, collapsed causing damage to the plaintiffs. The cause of the collapse was the insufficiency of the original foundations, with the result that the soil beneath the foundations was washed away, so that the walls subsided. As no outward indication of this state of affairs was visible, it was held that there was no failure of reasonable care and skill on the railway company's part.[33] It was admitted by the plaintiffs that under the statute the railway company's duty was not absolute, and, accordingly, the point being discussed was not actually decided, but all the members of the court agreed that the admission was rightly made, basing their opinion on various cases relating to local authorities.

[28] Lord Blackburn in *Geddis* v. *Proprietors of Bann Reservoir* (1878) 3 App.Cas. 430, 455, 456.
[29] *Vaughan* v. *Taff Vale Ry.* (1860) 5 H. & N. 679 (sparks from locomotive engine).
[30] *Manchester Corpn.* v. *Farnworth* [1930] A.C. 171 (fumes from generating station cause damage to farm).
[31] See *per* Lord Wright in *Lochgelly Iron and Coal Co.* v. *M'Mullan* [1934] A.C. 1, 25, on statutory duty generally. See also *Sephton* v. *Lancashire River Board* [1962] 1 All E.R. 183.
[32] [1931] 2 K.B. 334.
[33] The railway company were held to have been negligent in delaying to repair the lock.

1213 In *Hammond* v. *Vestry of St. Pancras*,[34] a local authority were under a duty to keep the sewers vested in them so as not to be a nuisance. The duty under the statute was explained by Brett J.: " The words of section 72 [35] are susceptible of either meaning, that an absolute duty is cast upon the defendants, or that they are only bound to exercise due and reasonable care. What, then, is the proper rule of interpretation? The defendants are a public body having a duty imposed upon them by parliament to do a thing which even with the exercise of the utmost care and diligence may not always be capable of being done. . . . It would seem to me to be contrary to natural justice to say that parliament intended to impose upon a public body a liability for a thing which no reasonable care and skill could obviate. The duty may notwithstanding be absolute: but, if so, it ought to be imposed in the clearest possible terms. The intention of the legislature is to be gathered from the language used and the subject-matter. Where the language used is consistent with either view, it ought not to be so construed as to inflict a liability, unless the party sought to be charged has been wanting in the exercise of due and reasonable care in the performance of the duty imposed." [36] It may be noted that the duty was to keep the sewers so as not to be a nuisance, and that liability for nuisance does not depend on the omission to exercise due care and skill.[37] The decision, however, has been followed in various cases decided under sections 15, 16 and 17 of the Public Health Act 1875 [38] where the duty is to keep sewers in repair,[39] and also in a case decided under section 35 of the Waterworks Clauses Act 1847.[40]

1214 Support for the opposite view is to be found in the opinion of Atkin L.J. in *Boynton* v. *Ancholme Drainage Commrs.*,[41] where he held that a statute providing that Commissioners should make, maintain and repair certain drains " imposes upon the Commissioners an absolute obligation to maintain, repair, and keep in repair such drainage works as in the judgment of themselves and their engineer are proper and necessary for the drainage of the Ancholme Level." The duty of a railway company to make and maintain fences for the accommodation of the owners and occupiers of lands adjoining the railway, has also been held to be an absolute duty.[42] But see, *ante*, § 1209, and *post*, § 1219.

[34] (1874) L.R. 9 C.P. 316.

[35] Metropolis Local Management Act 1855, s. 72, was repealed by the Public Health (London) Act 1936.

[36] In *Makin* v. *L.N.E. Ry.* [1943] K.B. 467, 471, Lord Greene M.R. said: " I certainly cannot read those words in their context as imposing any impediment on the court if, on the true construction of the particular section before it, it finds that the obligation imposed is absolute."

[37] *Rapier* v. *London Tramways* [1893] 2 Ch. 588.

[38] These sections are repealed and re-enacted by Public Health Act 1936.

[39] *Bateman* v. *Poplar Board of Works* (1887) 37 Ch.D. 272; *Stretton's Derby Brewery Co.* v. *Mayor of Derby* [1894] 1 Ch. 431; *Lambert* v. *Lowestoft Corpn.* [1901] 1 K.B. 590.

[40] *Read* v. *Croydon Corpn.* [1938] 4 All E.R. 631.

[41] [1921] 2 K.B. 213, 234, 235; see also *Makin* v. *L.N.E. Ry.* [1943] K.B. 467 (duty imposed on a canal company to make compensation for damage caused by accident, held to be absolute).

[42] *Buxton* v. *N.E. Ry.* (1868) L.R. 3 Q.B. 549, *per* Lush J.; *Dixon* v. *G.W. Ry.* [1897] 1 Q.B. 300, *per* Lopes L.J. See *Cooper* v. *Railway Executive* [1953] 1 W.L.R. 223.

4.—DEFENCES TO ACTION FOR BREACH OF STATUTORY DUTY [43]

1215 **Volenti non fit injuria.** In actions by workmen against their employers for breach of statutory duty, the principle *volenti non fit injuria* is no defence,[44] because it only applies when there is an agreement between the parties, and it is not open to an employer to contract out of a statutory duty which he owes to his workmen. Nevertheless the House of Lords has held in *Imperial Chemical Industries Ltd.* v. *Shatwell* [45] that whilst the defence of " *volenti* " is not available to the employers where they were in breach of their own statutory duty, there is nothing to prevent them relying on such a defence where they themselves were not in breach of any relevant statutory duty and were not vicariously in such breach, through the neglect of another person in authority, whose orders the plaintiff was obliged to obey or who owed the plaintiff a different duty of care.

In any event the plaintiff must still prove causation and if he has in fact voluntarily assumed the risk he may find much difficulty in proving his case, despite the defendant being in breach of his own statutory duty.[46]

In all other cases, whether it is a defence depends on whether it is possible to contract out of the statutory duty or not. It is not possible to contract out of the statutory duties set out §§ 1087–1094, so that in those cases the principle *volenti non fit injuria* will be no defence. In all other cases it will be a defence.

1216 **Contributory negligence.** Contributory negligence on the part of the plaintiff is a defence to an action for breach of statutory duty, subject to the provisions of the Law Reform (Contributory Negligence) Act 1945. This applies in master and servant cases [47] as well as in other cases,[48] but Lord Wright in *Caswell* v. *Powell Duffryn Collieries Ltd.*[49] laid down the authoritative guidance in the case of workmen that the courts should give " due regard to the actual conditions under which men work in a factory or mine, to the long hours and the fatigue, to the slackening of attention which naturally comes from constant repetition of the same operation, to the noise and confusion in which the man works, to his pre-occupation in what he is actually doing at the cost perhaps of some inattention to his own safety." It follows that a measure of the plaintiff's own carelessness may be overlooked by the court but, as was pointed out by Pearce L.J. in *Jenner* v. *Allen West & Co. Ltd.*,[50] " In each case it is a

[43] See Chap. 16 for " Defences " in more detail.

[44] *Baddeley* v. *Granville* (1887) 19 Q.B.D. 423; *Davies* v. *Thomas Owen & Co.* [1919] 2 K.B. 39; *Wheeler* v. *New Merton Board Mills* [1933] 2 K.B. 669.

[45] [1965] A.C. 656.

[46] *Bonnington Castings Ltd.* v. *Wardlaw* [1956] A.C. 613; *Nolan* v. *Dental Manufacturing Co. Ltd.* [1958] 1 W.L.R. 936; *Rushton* v. *Turner Brothers Asbestos Co. Ltd.* [1960] 1 W.L.R. 96.

[47] *Lewis* v. *Denye* [1940] A.C. 921; *Dunn* v. *Birds Eye Foods Ltd.* [1959] 2 Q.B. 265.

[48] *Ellis* v. *L. & S.W. Ry.* (1857) 2 H. & N. 424; *Parkinson* v. *Garstang & Knott End Ry.* [1910] 1 K.B. 615. In *Bailey* v. *Geddes* [1938] 1 K.B. 156, it was held that it was difficult, if not impossible, for contributory negligence to exist at a pedestrian crossing, but this was disapproved in *Sparks* v. *Edward Ash Ltd.* [1943] K.B. 223.

[49] [1940] A.C. 152, 178, 179. To the same effect, see *per* Lord Atkin at p. 166.

[50] [1959] 1 W.L.R. 554, 561. "Employees' Contributory Negligence," (Whincup) 118 New L.J. 972. See *Mullard* v. *Ben Line Steamers* [1970] 1 W.L.R. 1414, § 1049.

question of fact whether or not a breach of . . . (statutory duty) . . . by an employer through the fault of an employee gives rise to any claim by that employee. An employer can defeat such claim if he can say: ' I am in breach of the regulations because of, and only because of, your default. I, myself, have not failed in any respect (apart from my vicarious default through your wrongful act) and my breach is co-terminous with yours.' " On the other hand once it has been established that both the plaintiff and the defendant had been in breach of their statutory duty, then " however venial the fault of each of them they must share between them the responsibility for the whole of the damage," according to Lord Diplock.[51]

1217 **Act of God.** Whether or not an act of God [52] is a defence to an action for breach of statutory duty is a question of construction of the statute in question.[53] In *River Wear Commissioners* v. *Adamson* [54] Lord Cairns said: " If a duty is cast upon an individual by Common Law, the act of God will excuse him from the performance of that duty. No man is compelled to do that which is impossible. . . . If, however, a man contracts that he will be liable for the damage occasioned by a particular state of circumstances, or if an Act of Parliament declares that a man shall be liable for the damage occasioned by a particular state of circumstances, I know of no reason why a man should not be liable for the damage occasioned by that state of circumstances, whether the state of circumstances is brought about by the act of man or by the act of God. There is nothing impossible in that which, on such an hypothesis, he has contracted to do, or which he is by the statute ordered to do, namely, to be liable for the damages." Lord Blackburn, also in the same case, after citing *Paradine* v. *Jane* [55] said [56]: " The really important part of the decision is that where a contract is made which does not either expressly or impliedly except the act of God, the Courts could not introduce that exception by intendment of law; and that makes strongly against the supposition that, in construing a statute where the Legislature might have expressed, but did not express, such an exception, the Court should introduce it. And there is no case cited, and as far as I can find no case exists, in which such a doctrine is laid down." In a later case [57] Lord Dunedin dissented from the view " that the exception of an act of God to a duty or liability cast on a person by the common law is equally true of a duty or liability cast on him by an Act of Parliament," but Lord Blanesburgh, on the analogy of *Rylands* v. *Fletcher*,[58] said that

[51] *Boyle* v. *Kodak Ltd.* [1969] 1 W.L.R. 661, 674.

[52] For the meaning of the expression " act of God," see § 429, *ante*.

[53] *Makin* v. *L.N.E. Ry.* [1943] K.B. 467 (act of God no defence on the construction of a statute imposing an obligation on a canal company to pay compensation for damage caused by " accident "); *Rothes* v. *Kirkcaldy Waterworks Commrs.* (1882) 7 App.Cas. 694, *Witham Outfall Board* v. *Boston Corp.* (1926) 136 L.T. 756, 760.

[54] (1877) 2 App.Cas. 743, 750.

[55] (1647) Alleyn 26.

[56] At p. 771. See also *per* Lord Gordon, at p. 777.

[57] *G.W. Ry.* v. *Owners of SS. Mostyn* [1928] A.C. 57, 74; Lord Dunedin dissented, but this does not affect his opinion on the point set out.

[58] (1868) L.R. 3 H.L. 330.

liability was always subject " to the reservation that the damage is not attributable to an act of God." [59]

1218 In the case of an absolute statutory duty, it would seem that the legislature has intended to throw the loss resulting from failure to perform that duty upon the person on whom the duty is imposed rather than upon the person on whom the loss falls. If there is a causal connection between the loss sustained and the statutory duty, and both the sufferer and the person under duty are free from moral blame, the existence of the duty would appear to throw the loss upon the person burdened with the duty rather than on the original sufferer.

1219 **Independent act of a third party.** Whether or not the independent act of a third party [60] is a defence is also not free from doubt. If an absolute statutory duty is the same as an absolute common law duty, it is clear that it is a defence.

In *Groves* v. *Wimborne*,[61] Vaughan Williams L.J. said: " An obvious answer to an action against the master in such a case would be that the cause of the damage to the plaintiff was not the failure by the master to perform his statutory duty, but the particular action of someone else." If, however, the " particular action of someone else " is one which the master ought to have foreseen and guarded against, the master, notwithstanding, will be liable.[62] Again, in *Cooper* v. *Railway Executive* [63] Devlin J. said that the Railways Clauses Consolidation Act 1845, s. 68, imposed " an absolute obligation in this sense, that the Railway Executive is absolutely bound to maintain a fence, and it is no answer to say that some accident or act of a trespasser has made the fence defective."

1220 On principle, it would seem that this defence rests on the same basis as the defence of act of God, and if one is available, both are available. Therefore, it is submitted that if A is bound by statute to maintain a fence, either against dangerous machinery or as between a field and his railway, and the fence is broken, either by the deliberate act of X or the act of God, as a consequence of which damage is caused to B, to whom the statutory duty is owed, A is liable to B because it is the existence of A's works which has rendered necessary the existence of the statutory duty.

1221 **Delegation of duty.** Lastly it remains to be considered whether delegation of duty can be a defence in the light of the general principle that, if a duty has been cast on a person to perform, he cannot escape the responsibility for seeing to its performance by employing an independent contractor.[64] Obviously if there be a breach of statutory duty it will not be a

[59] *Ibid.* at p. 104. See also *per* McCardie J. in *R.* v. *Marshland, Smeeth and Fen District Commrs.* [1920] 1 K.B. 155, 167; where, however, it is not clear that the duty was held to be absolute.

[60] For the meaning of this expression, see § 439, *ante*.

[61] [1898] 2 Q.B. 402, 418.

[62] *Northwestern Utilities Ltd.* v. *London Guarantee and Accident Co.* [1936] A.C. 108.

[63] [1953] 1 W.L.R. 223, 228.

[64] *Dalton* v. *Angus* (1881) 6 App.Cas. 740, 829, *per* Lord Blackburn.

defence that a contractor was employed to fulfil it, unless delegation itself can be regarded as a fulfilment of the obligation, which, in turn, depends upon the true construction of the statute concerned.[65]

Where the delegation by the employers is to the plaintiff himself, the modern view is that such delegation of performance is not in itself a defence but is a material circumstance to be taken into consideration in deciding the question of whether the plaintiff has discharged the burden of proof of causation.[66] In *Ginty* v. *Belmont Building Supplies Ltd.*[67] Pearson J. said, on this point, " In my view the important and fundamental question . . . is not whether there was a delegation, but simply the usual question: ' Whose fault was it? ' "[68]

5.—EXAMPLES OF STATUTORY DUTY

1222 Since the statutory duty is set out in a multitude of statutes and statutory regulations it is not possible within the compass of this book to deal with it in much detail. It is proposed therefore to give no more than a mere introduction and general outline of the more important or recurring features of the duty, particularly those Acts that have fallen to be considered by the courts or those which involve a very large section of the working community.

(a) *The Factories Act* 1961

1223 **Application of Factories Act.** The Factories Act 1961[69] contains a number of provisions designed to secure the safety of workers in factories. It only applies (s. 172) to factories as defined by this Act (s. 175) and does not apply to quarries or mines. In deciding whether premises are a factory within the Act the premises as a whole must be considered, and though premises part of which are incidentally used for manual labour will not be a factory, they will be if the manual labour is used to make an article for gain as the essence of the operation.[70] Such things as a hospital kitchen,[71] a technical institute,[72] a restaurant within the curtilage of a factory for the use of the executive and administrative staff,[73] a chemist's shop where a

[65] *Gray* v. *Pullen* (1864) 5 B. & S. 970; *Hole* v. *Sittingbourne Ry.* (1861) 30 L.J.Ex. 81. See *Mulready* v. *J. H. & W. Bell Ltd.* [1953] 2 Q.B. 117, although the C.A.'s reasoning was disapproved of by the H.L. in *Donaghey* v. *Boulton & Paul Ltd.* [1968] A.C. 1.

[66] *Bonnington Castings Ltd.* v. *Wardlaw* [1956] A.C. 613; *Ross* v. *Associated Portland Cement Manufacturers Ltd.* [1964] 1 W.L.R. 768, 777.

[67] [1959] 1 All E.R. 414.

[68] *Ibid.* at pp. 423, 424. This view was approved by the C.A. in *McMath* v. *Rimmer Bros. (Liverpool) Ltd.* [1962] 1 W.L.R. 1. Further, in *Ross* v. *Associated Portland Cement Manufacturers Ltd., supra*, Lord Reid, at p. 777, said: " If the question is put in that way one must remember that fault is not necessarily equivalent in this context to blameworthiness. The question really is whose conduct caused the accident, because it is now well established that a breach of statutory duty does not give rise to civil liability unless there is proved a causal connection between the breach and the plaintiff's injury." See also *Boyle* v. *Kodak Ltd.* [1969] 1 W.L.R. 661.

[69] Which came into force on April 1, 1962, and repealed the Factories Acts 1937–1959. See article: " Some Sociological Aspects of Strict Liability and the Enforcement of Factory Legislation " (Carson), 33 M.L.R. 396.

[70] *Paul Popper Ltd.* v. *Grimsey* [1963] 1 Q.B. 44.

[71] *Wood* v. *L.C.C.* [1941] 2 K.B. 232.

[72] *Weston* v. *L.C.C.* [1941] 1 K.B. 608.

[73] *Thomas* v. *British Thomson-Houston Ltd.* [1953] 1 W.L.R. 67.

porter is employed in manual labour,[74] an omnibus depot,[75] a prison,[76] a pump house of a waterworks,[77] an apron of a hangar at an airfield,[78] have been held not to be a factory. But a canteen in the factory,[79] or an office,[80] a barge, moored to a backyard of a lighterage company's premises, a dock transit shed used for temporary storage of goods awaiting collection by consignors,[81] a workshop behind a radio shop where a radio engineer repaired wireless sets in conjunction with the shop business,[82] and the premises of a photographic agency where glazed prints were made from purchased negatives with a view to supplying them for reproduction in newspapers and magazines [83] were held to be a factory.[84]

1224 **Who is liable.** By section 155 liability for breach of duty is imposed by the Act not on the employer of the workmen but on the occupier [85] of the factory, unless it is provided that the owner shall be liable. There is no statutory definition of occupier, but more often than not in fact he will be the employer of the persons working in the factory and will be the person who is in legal possession of the premises be it as the owner or merely the

74 *Joyce* v. *Boots Cash Chemists* [1950] 2 All E.R. 719, affd. [1951] 1 All E.R. 682.

75 *Jones* v. *Crosville Motor Services Ltd.* [1956] 1 W.L.R. 1425.

76 *Pullin* v. *Prison Commissioners* [1957] 1 W.L.R. 1186; *Keatings* v. *Secretary of State for Scotland*, 77 Sh.Ct.Rep. 113.

77 *Longhurst* v. *Guildford, Godalming & District Water Board* [1961] 1 Q.B. 408 (even if such pump house be attached to a filter plant and if such plant be a factory—which was doubted by the Court of Appeal). Affirmed by the House of Lords [1963] A.C. 265. But a pump house within the curtilage of a factory used for pumping water for the purpose of a process carried on at a factory is part of a factory. *Newton* v. *John Stanning & Son* [1962] 1 W.L.R. 30.

78 *Walsh* v. *Allweather Mechanical Grouting Co. Ltd.* [1959] 2 Q.B. 300, although it was within the close, curtilage or precincts of the hangar it was also " a place . . . solely used for some purpose other than the processes carried on in the factory " within section 151 (6) of the 1937 Act.

79 *Luttman* v. *I.C.I. Ltd.* [1955] 1 W.L.R. 980.

80 *Cardiff Revenue Officer* v. *Cardiff Assessment Committee and Western Mail Ltd.* [1931] 1 K.B. 47. *Cf. Powley* v. *Bristol Siddeley Engines Ltd.* [1966] 1 W.L.R. 729 where the " administration block " adjoining and within the perimeter of a factory was not excluded by s. 175 (6) of the Act from being a part of the factory, because the activities carried out there, such as designing, drawing and technical development, were processes incidental to the work of the factory. However, where an office is excluded, the Offices, Shops and Railway Premises Act 1963 will apply to it. See § 1267, *post.*

81 *Fisher* v. *Port of London Authority* [1962] 1 W.L.R. 234.

82 *J. & F. Stone Lighting & Radio* v. *Haygarth* [1966] 1 Q.B. 91. The fact that in doing work with his hands a man uses his technical knowledge and skill does not prevent it from being " manual work " within s. 175 (1) of the Act so long as his work is not primarily or predominantly work of a different kind (*e.g.* intellectual activities) to which work with the hands is merely accessory.

83 *Paul Popper Ltd.* v. *Grimsey* [1963] 1 Q.B. 44.

84 *Moor* v. *Greenhithe Lighterage Co.*, *The Times*, January 28, 1961. The areas of a quayside at the docks being used for the storage and assembly of steel components by sub-contractors engaged in the construction of a floating oil dock, were a factory within the meaning of the definition section since a close need not have any boundary wall or fence and the assembly of the steel parts into larger components was the making of an article: *Barry* v. *Cleveland Bridge Engineering Co. Ltd.* [1963] 1 All E.R. 192.

85 *Rippon* v. *Port of London Authority* [1940] 1 K.B. 858; *Smith* v. *Cammell Laird & Co.* [1940] A.C. 242. Under s. 161, the occupier of the factory can exempt himself from punishment on conviction of the actual offender. Whether this also exempts him from liability to pay damages, see *Riddell* v. *Reid* [1943] A.C. 1. When the factory, or part of it, has been destroyed and exclusive possession is handed over to a contractor for rebuilding, the owner is not the occupier of that part of the factory which has been handed over. *Cox* v. *S. Cutler & Co. Ltd.* [1948] 2 All E.R. 665 (contractor reconstructing a ruined gas-holder); *Street* v. *British Electricity Authority* [1952] 2 Q.B. 399.

tenant. In *Ramsay* v. *Mackie* [86] Lord MacLaren said: " While the language is wide in order to prevent evasion yet ' occupier ' plainly means the person who runs the factory . . ., who regulates and controls the work, which is done there and who is responsible for the fulfilment of the provisions of the Factory Act within it." The emphasis, however, must be upon the control of the premises and not merely upon the work as this dictum may suggest. By section 163 the owner or hirer of a machine used in a factory is deemed the occupier of the factory so far as concerns a person employed in connection with that machine. In such a case the actual occupier is not liable for a breach of the requirements of the Act committed by the notional occupier. [87]

225 **Delegation.** The duty imposed by the statute on the occupier of the factory or on some other person may be fulfilled by delegating its performance to an official, a foreman or some other competent person. [88] In such a case, failure of performance on the part of the person to whom the duty has been properly delegated does not discharge the occupier or the other person from liability to third parties, [88] but it does relieve him from liability to the person to whom the duty has been delegated. [89] In *Jenner* v. *Allen West & Co. Ltd.* [90] Pearce L.J. said: " In each case it is a question of fact whether or not a breach of . . . (statutory duty) . . . by an employer through the fault of an employee gives rise to any claim by that employee. An employer can defeat such a claim if he can say: ' I am in breach of the regulations because of, and only because of, your default. I myself have not failed in any respect (apart from my vicarious default through your wrongful act) and my breach is co-terminous with yours.' " In *Smith* v. *Baveystock & Co. Ltd.* [89] the plaintiff was an experienced circular saw operator who was working a circular saw fitted with a guard in accordance with the regulations. The adjustment of the guard on his own saw was delegated to him. He was injured while operating the saw and it was held that, if the injury was due to the improper adjustment of the saw, he could not recover because performance of the statutory duty had been properly delegated to him. Again, where contractors delegated to their foreman, an experienced steel erector, the duty of selecting a ladder and the foreman selected a ladder which was not " of adequate strength," contrary to the Building Regulations, as a result of which he was injured, they were held not liable on the ground that " the only person who was to blame in this matter was the plaintiff." [91] In *Ross* v. *Associated Portland Cement*

[86] (1904) 7 F. (Ct. of Sess.) 106; see *Meigh* v. *Wickenden* [1942] 2 K.B. 160 (receiver for debenture holders was held liable since he alone could have sanctioned expenditure in the factory on such things as safety requirements because he was " complete master of the affairs of the company ").

[87] *Whalley* v. *Briggs Motor Bodies Ltd.* [1954] 2 All E.R. 193.

[88] *Vincent* v. *Southern Ry.* [1927] A.C. 430, 437, *per* Lord Cave.

[89] *Smith* v. *Baveystock & Co. Ltd.* [1945] 1 All E.R. 531; *Barcock* v. *Brighton Corpn.* [1949] 1 K.B. 339.

[90] [1959] 1 W.L.R. 554 at p. 561. See *McMath* v. *Rimmer Bros.* (*Liverpool*) [1962] 1 W.L.R. 1.

[91] *Johnson* v. *Croggan & Co. Ltd.* [1954] 1 W.L.R. 195; *Hammill* v. *Camborne Water Co.* (1964) 108 S.J. 335 (where a labourer failed to have his ladder footed).

Manufacturers,[92] by way of contract a chargehand steel erector was repairing a wire safety net, suspended below an aerial ropeway, using a ladder resting against the netting, when he was catapulted backwards due to a partial collapse of the supporting wires. It was held that the employers could not wholly escape liability since the plaintiff's decision to use the ladder was a decision reached by him on the basis that no more suitable equipment was available. However, this case was distinguished in *Richardson* v. *Stephenson Clarke*[93] where the plaintiff, who was a foreman of considerable experience at his employers' quay, instructed a mobile crane driver to move a large conveyor. It was within the foreman's knowledge that adequate lifting equipment was available, but an obviously inadequate sling with shackles was used instead, which broke during transit, so that the plaintiff was crushed by the falling conveyor. Nield J., in holding that the employers had not been negligent, considered that they were entitled to leave the selection of equipment to an experienced and competent workman.

1226 The onus of establishing delegation is on the employer and is a heavy one.[94] It is not enough to give instructions as to how to do the work in accordance with the statutory duty, it is necessary to make it clear expressly or by implication, that the statutory duty is being delegated.[95] In *Byers* v. *Head Wrightson*[96] Elwes J. held that the principle that a plaintiff could not recover damages for a breach of statutory duty established vicariously against his employer, by reason of the plaintiff's own act or omission in breach of the statutory duty, had no application to the case where the task of appraising what was necessary to be done, in order to do a certain job of work, was beyond the plaintiff's competence. It has been held that delegating the duty of working a crane to a workman is not the same as delegating to him the duty of seeing that it is not overloaded.[97]

Whether delegation, when proved, is a complete defence to the person on whom the statutory duty is placed or whether it is only an element to be taken into account when assessing damages to be awarded to the delegate who has failed to comply with the duty is in dispute. In *Cakebread* v.

[92] [1964] 1 W.L.R. 768.

[93] [1969] 1 W.L.R. 1695.

[94] *Beal* v. *E. Gomme Ltd.* (1949) 65 T.L.R. 543; *Hilton* v. *F. H. Marshall & Co. Ltd.* [1951] W.N. 81. In *Ginty* v. *Belmont Building Supplies Ltd.* [1959] 1 All E.R. 414 at pp. 423 and 424, Pearson J. said: " There have been a number of cases . . . in which it has been considered whether or not the employer delegated to the employee the performance of the statutory duty . . . in my view, the important and fundamental question in a case like this is . . . simply the usual question: Whose fault was it? . . . If the answer to that question is that in substance and reality the accident was solely due to the fault of the plaintiff, so that he was the sole author of his own wrong, he is disentitled to recover." See also *Rushton* v. *Turner Brothers Asbestos Co. Ltd.* [1960] 1 W.L.R. 96; *Boden* v. *Moore*, 105 S.J. 510; *Stocker* v. *Norprint* (1971) 10 K.I.R. 10.

[95] *Manwaring* v. *Billington* [1952] 2 All E.R. 747. There is a vital distinction between the need to instruct a craftsman on how to avoid obvious dangers and the need to instruct him about the application of the regulations in situations where no danger is apparent. There is a duty to forestall, if the employers can, breaches of regulations: *Boyle* v. *Kodak Ltd.* [1969] 1 W.L.R. 661.

[96] [1961] 1 W.L.R. 961.

[97] *Gallagher* v. *Dorman Long & Co.* [1947] 2 All E.R. 38.

Hopping Bros.,[98] Tucker L.J. adhered to the latter view and said that he could imagine that some courts might put as much as 90 per cent. of the blame on the workman; but in *Stapley* v. *Gypsum Mines Ltd.*[99] Singleton L.J., after considering this view, said: "If they [the employers] have properly placed on the employee the task of performing it and the failure is his, I do not see why their proportion of the responsibility should be more than nominal." A similar view was later expressed by Pilcher J.[1] who held that in such circumstances the delegate's claim failed.

227 **Burden of proof.** The burden of proof in actions by workmen against their employers for breach of statutory duty is the same as that imposed on all other plaintiffs, but as the question has sometimes given rise to difficulty, a short discussion is necessary.

228 The basic principle is stated by Lord Macmillan [2]: "The mere fact that at the time of an accident to a miner his employers can be shown to have been in breach of a statutory duty is clearly not enough in itself to impose liability on the employers. It must be shown that the accident was causally associated with the breach of statutory duty." It often happens, however, that the circumstances of the accident are unknown or only imperfectly known so that it is a matter of inference whether the breach of statutory duty has caused the accident. In such a case, it was suggested that there was a rule to be applied, namely, "If there is a definite breach of a safety provision imposed on the occupier of a factory, and a workman is injured in a way which could result from the breach, the onus of proof shifts on to the employer to show that the breach was not the cause. We think that that principle lies at the very basis of statutory rules of absolute duty." [3] In that case, a circular saw was not fenced in accordance with the regulations and the operator of the saw had injuries which were obviously caused by the saw. How the accident happened was unknown, but, in the absence of any other evidence, it seems an obvious inference that the injuries were caused by the breach of duty, as the court held, without the necessity of invoking the rule stated above.

229 It has now been decided that no such rule exists.[4] "No distinction can be drawn between actions for common law negligence and actions for

[98] [1947] K.B. 641.

[99] [1952] 2 Q.B. 575, 586. The decision in the C.A. was reversed in the H.L. [1953] A.C. 663, but no comment, adverse or otherwise, was made on this passage.

[1] *Johnson* v. *Croggan & Co. Ltd.* [1954] 1 W.L.R. 195.

[2] *Caswell* v. *Powell Duffryn Associated Collieries Ltd.* [1940] A.C. 152, 168.

[3] Scott L.J. in *Vyner* v. *Waldenberg Bros. Ltd.* [1946] K.B. 50, 55. A somewhat similar view had been expressed by Goddard L.J. in *Lee* v. *Nursery Furnishings Ltd.* [1945] 1 All E.R. 387. See also *Stimson* v. *Standard Telephones & Cables Ltd.* [1940] 1 K.B. 342. Scott L.J.'s rule was applied in *Hughes* v. *McGoff & Vickers Ltd.* [1955] 1 W.L.R. 416, where a length of pipe fell from a platform on a scaffold which was not provided with toe-boards, contrary to the regulations. But see now *Bonnington Castings Ltd.* v. *Wardlaw* (*post*) which Lord Keith considered overruled these earlier decisions but commented (at p. 625), "I think most, if not all, of the cases which professed to lay down or to recognise some such rule could have been decided as they were on simple rules of evidence."

[4] *Bonnington Castings Ltd.* v. *Wardlaw* [1956] A.C. 613, which overruled *Vyner* v. *Waldenberg Bros. Ltd.* (*supra*) in so far as it held that the onus is on an employer to show that the breach of a safety regulation was not the cause of an accident.

breach of statutory duty in this respect. In both the plaintiff or pursuer must prove (a) breach of duty and (b) that such breach caused the injury complained of." [5] " The employee must in all cases prove his case by the ordinary standard of proof in civil actions: he must make it appear at least that on a balance of probabilities the breach of duty caused or materially contributed to his injury." [6] So, where in a factory, in breach of their statutory duty, [7] the occupiers did not take all practicable measures to protect workmen from inhaling dust and a workman became tuberculous and claimed that his disease was made active by the breach, it was held there was no presumption in his favour and he had not discharged the burden of proof. [8] The fact that the breach might have been a cause was not enough to change the burden of proof. It was for the plaintiff to prove that it was the cause. Again, when a workman, cutting off bolts from an engine, was not supplied with goggles contrary to the regulations and received an eye injury which he claimed was caused by a flying bolt but which the judge refused to find was so caused, it was held that there was no presumption to induce the judge to find that it was. [9] In *Cork* v. *Kirby Maclean Ltd.*[10] Singleton L.J. said that Scott L.J.'s words " cannot be accepted as a true statement of the onus in every case arising under the Factories Act " and the court overruled the trial judge who had held that breach of statutory duty to have a handrail and toeboards to a platform twenty feet above ground threw the burden of proving that an epileptic who fell in a fit would have fallen even had those safeguards been provided. But in *Allen* v. *Aeroplane and Motor Aluminium Castings Ltd.*,[11] where the facts showed that there had been a breach of statutory duty, because of which the accident had happened or without which it would not have done so, and that the employee was injured thereby, liability was established notwithstanding that he had not given an acceptable version of how the accident had occurred. Once employers are fixed with the knowledge that an irregular practice is taking place, such as using a squeezy bottle to squirt coolant liquid into the interior of a workpiece on a centre lathe, they must be taken to foresee the risk of injury.[12]

[5] *Per* Lord Tucker, at p. 624. See generally § 20, *ante*.

[6] *Per* Lord Reid, at p. 620.

[7] s. 47 (1) of the 1937 Act: see now s. 63 (1) of the Factories Act 1961 which came into force on April 1, 1962.

[8] *Mist* v. *Toleman & Sons* [1946] 1 All E.R. 139.

[9] *Watts* v. *Enfield Rolling Mills Ltd.* [1952] 1 All E.R. 1013. In *Nolan* v. *Dental Manufacturing Co. Ltd.* [1958] 1 W.L.R. 936, the plaintiff had not established that the injury to his eye was caused by the defendants' breach of statutory duty because he had not proved that he would have worn the goggles if they had been provided; but the defendants were in breach of their common law duty not only to provide goggles, but also to give orders that they were to be worn, and to supervise the workmen to a reasonable extent to ensure that the orders were obeyed. See *McWilliams* v. *Sir William Arrol Co.* [1962] 1 W.L.R. 295, where a workman failed to prove that he would have worn a safety belt even if one had been provided.

[10] [1952] 2 All E.R. 402.

[11] [1965] 1 W.L.R. 1244; Diplock L.J. observed at p. 1248 " Nor do I think that the expression ' a frolic of his own,' which is relevant for the purpose of making a master vicariously liable for the torts of his servant, has any relevance to the question of whether a master is liable to his servant either for breach of statutory duty or at common law."

[12] *Johnson* v. *F. E. Callow* (*Engineers*) *Ltd.* [1970] 2 Q.B. 1 (affirmed by H.L. [1971] A.C. 335).

230 **To whom the duty is owed.** Subject to any provision to the contrary in any particular section, the duty under the Factories Act is owed not only to persons employed by the occupier of the factory, but also to all persons working in the factory, whether employed by the occupier or not.[13] All persons lawfully working or being in the factory are entitled to the protection of the Act.[14] Thus in *Uddin* v. *Associated Portland Cement Manufacturers Ltd.*[15] it was held that a person employed was entitled to the protection of the statutory provisions even though he was not actually working or acting within the scope of his employment at the relevant time. Thus where the plaintiff had left his allotted tasks for a private purpose, namely, a frolic of his own to catch a pigeon sitting behind an unfenced shaft high up off the ground and whilst in the process of leaning over he got caught in the moving shaft, his employers were found to be liable. However, in *Herbert* v. *Harold Shaw Ltd.*[16] the Court of Appeal held that an independent contractor who was not by contract obliged to work on an operation to which statutory regulations applied, is not a " workman " or a " person employed." Further, in *Napieralski* v. *Curtis* (*Contractors*) *Ltd.*,[17] where a workman was injured whilst operating a circular saw which was not securely fenced within the meaning of section 14 (1) of the Factories Act 1937 (now the Factories Act 1961), and reg. 10 (c) of the Woodworking Machinery Regulations 1922 [18] for his own private purposes and after normal working hours, it was held that the defendants owed no duty to him because at the time of the accident he was not " employed " but was voluntarily engaged in manual labour and he was not " working " on the premises within the meaning of the phrase " person employed or working on the premises " in section 14 (1) as he was not then working under any contract of service. Conversely in *Smith* v. *Supreme Wood Pulp Co. Ltd.*,[19] although the plaintiff driver did not use an unfenced circular saw in the course of his employment, had no authority to use it and used it entirely for his own purposes, it was held that he was not, in relation to it, a

[13] *John Summers & Sons Ltd.* v. *Frost* [1955] A.C. 740, *per* Lord Simonds; *Smith* v. *Cammell Laird & Co. Ltd.* [1940] A.C. 242; *Manchester Ship Canal Co.* v. *D.P.P.* [1930] 1 K.B. 547, 556; *Hawkins* v. *Thames Stevedore Co.* [1936] 2 All E.R. 472; *Lavender* v. *Diamints Ltd.* [1949] 1 K.B. 585 (owed to an independent contractor working in factory), which was approved by the House of Lords in *Wigley* v. *British Vinegars Ltd.* [1964] A.C. 307. See *per* Viscount Kilmuir at p. 324: " What is meant by the words ' any person ' which appear in both subsections? They cannot be of entirely general application: I agree that a policeman who enters a factory in pursuit of a felon, or a fireman who enters to put out a fire is not within the section, although he is a ' person ' and he is ' working.' I think one must exclude, for example, the film actor who enters the factory where a scene in which he is playing is to be shot although he again is a ' person ' and the factory is a place in which he is to work. In my view, the true distinction is between those who are to work for the purposes of the factory and those who are not. Clearly, maintenance of the factory is work for the purpose of the factory, while the arrest of a felon or the putting out of a fire is not, though it may benefit the factory indirectly."

[14] *Ward* v. *Coltness Iron Co.*, 1944 S.C. 318.

[15] [1965] 2 Q.B. 582. This decision was followed by the C.A. in *Allen* v. *Aeroplane & Motor Aluminium Castings Ltd.* [1965] 1 W.L.R. 1244.

[16] [1959] 2 Q.B. 138.

[17] [1959] 2 All E.R. 426.

[18] S.R. & O. 1922 No. 1196.

[19] [1968] 3 All E.R. 753.

trespasser and was thus within the class of persons entitled to the benefit of the statutory duty of protection.

1231 **Ventilation** (s. 4). This section is confined to defects of ventilation [20] and is aimed at requiring the circulation of fresh air efficiently. Devlin J. said that it is " dealing with the circulation of fresh air which gets rid of impurities which come into the air, whereas section [47] [21] is dealing with the methods of stopping impurities from ever getting into circulation at all." [22]

When there is a breach of section 4 by failing to produce adequate ventilation, the occupiers of the factory are liable if their failure exposes the workman to a greater degree of risk than otherwise would have been the case and contributed to his pneumoconiosis to an extent that was material and not negligible. " A contribution is material unless the maxim ' de minimis ' can be applied to it." [23]

1232 **Lighting** (s. 5). This section imposes a duty to maintain sufficient and suitable lights in every part of a factory in which persons are working or passing.[24] In *Lane* v. *Gloucester Engineering Co.*[25] it was held that there was no breach of the Act or regulations where the general standard of illumination was over 0·5 foot-candles at floor level but less in the shadow of the piece of machinery where the tie-bar was lying, over which the plaintiff had tripped, whilst he had been crossing the floor to switch on more light in order to read his newspaper before work had begun. In *Thornton* v. *Fisher & Ludlow Ltd.*[26] it was held that the "effective provision" of "sufficient and suitable lighting" within the meaning of the section requires such lighting to be switched on whenever the natural lighting is insufficient.

1233 **Fencing dangerous machinery.** Every flywheel directly connected to any prime mover [27] and every moving part of any prime mover (except electric generators, motors and rotary converters and every flywheel directly connected thereto when they are in such a position or of such construction as to be as safe to every person employed or working on the premises as if they were securely fenced) must be securely fenced whether the flywheel or prime mover is situated in an engine-house or not (s. 12). Every part of the

[20] *Ebbs* v. *James Whitsun & Co. Ltd.* [1952] 2 Q.B. 877; *Coote* v. *Eastern Gas Board* [1953] 1 Q.B. 594.
[21] Factories Act 1937 re-enacted by s. 63 of the 1961 Act.
[22] *Graham* v. *Co-operative Wholesale Society Ltd.* [1957] 1 W.L.R. 511 at p. 522.
[23] *Nicholson* v. *Atlas Steel Co. Ltd.* [1957] 1 W.L.R. 613, *per* Lord Simonds at p. 616 applying the test laid down in the House in *Bonnington Castings Ltd.* v. *Wardlaw* [1956] A.C. 613.
[24] See further Factories (Standards of Lighting) Regulations 1941 (S.R. & O. No. 94).
[25] [1967] 1 W.L.R. 767.
[26] [1968] 1 W.L.R. 655. See also *Rawding* v. *London Brick Co.* (1970) 9 K.I.R. 194.
[27] Means " every engine, motor, or other appliance which provides mechanical energy derived from steam, water, wind, electricity, the combustion of fuel, or other source ": s. 176.

transmission machinery [28] must be securely fenced unless it is in such a position or of such construction as to be as safe to every person working on the premises as it would be if securely fenced (s. 13). Otherwise as to machinery [29] which is not defined in the Act (other than that it " includes any driving-belt ") section 14 provides:

" (1) Every dangerous part of any machinery other than prime movers and transmission machinery, shall be securely fenced unless it is in such a position or of such construction as to be as safe to every person employed or working on the premises as it would be if securely fenced." [30]

Section 16 provides: " All fencing or other safeguards provided in pursuance of the foregoing provisions of this Part of this Act shall be of substantial construction, and constantly maintained [31]; and kept in position while the parts required to be fenced or safeguarded are in motion or use, [32] except when any such parts are necessarily exposed for examination

[28] Means " every shaft, wheel, drum, pulley, system of fast and loose pulleys, coupling, clutch, driving belt, or other device by which the motion of a prime mover is transmitted to or received by any machine or appliance ": s. 176.

[29] The term " machinery " was considered by the Court of Appeal in *Quintas* v. *National Smelting Co. Ltd.* [1961] 1 W.L.R. 401 where it was held that a rope way, consisting of an overhead travelling cable with large buckets attached at regular intervals and used for the purpose of transporting material from one part of a factory to another, was " plant " and not " machinery " within the meaning of s. 14 (1). See also 77 L.Q.R. 149. The term, however, was held to include a mobile crane, even though cranes are specifically dealt with in s. 27 of the Act: *Liptrot* v. *British Railways Board* [1969] 1 A.C. 136, so that every dangerous part of it must be securely fenced. The decision in *Cherry* v. *International Alloys* [1961] 1 Q.B. 136 (a petrol driven truck) has therefore been overruled. A grinding machine with an 8 foot long flexible shaft connecting the 7 inch cutting wheel to a small portable electric motor which could be plugged into any convenient electricity supply was " machinery " requiring to be fenced: *Lovelidge* v. *Anselm Odling & Sons Ltd.* [1967] 2 Q.B. 351. The drill of an electric drill in *Millard* v. *Serck Tubes* [1969] 1 W.L.R. 211 was held to be a dangerous part of machinery which was required to be fenced.

[30] For the meaning of this, see s. 15, and the regulations made by the Secretary of State. An unfenced shaft 13 feet above the ground is not in such a position as to be equally safe to every person working in the factory as if it were securely fenced: *Atkinson* v. *L.N.E. Ry.* [1926] 1 K.B. 313. Also, *Hodkinson* v. *Wallwork* [1955] 1 W.L.R. 1195. In *Foster* v. *Flexible Metal Co.* (1967) 4 K.I.R. 49 Paull J. held that where a guard for dangerous machinery is available but is not in position, the machinery cannot be said to be fenced within the meaning of s. 14.

[31] Means " maintained in an efficient state, in efficient working order, and in good repair ": s. 176.

[32] " In use " means " running as it was meant to run and doing the work it was meant to do "; " in motion " means " running as it was meant to run but not doing the work it was meant to do," *per* Lord Porter in *Richard Thomas & Baldwins Ltd.* v. *Cummings* [1955] A.C. 321. In that case, the power was cut off and the machine was being rotated by hand to enable adjustments to be made. In doing this, the plaintiff's finger was trapped between the belt and a pulley. It was held there was no breach of s. 16. In *Knight* v. *Leamington Spa Courier* [1961] 2 Q.B. 253 where a plaintiff was injured by a printing press which he was cleaning, having first set it in a slow motion specifically intended for carrying out that work, it was held by the Court of Appeal that in borderline cases the movement which made dangerous those parts of a machine " in motion or in use " within s. 16 was a question of degree and that there was no breach of duty in this case since it would be unreal for the employers to take precautions to have the guard, which usually covered the dangerous parts, lowered into position whilst the machine was being cleaned. Also it was held there was no breach of statutory duty when a workman was moving rollers around by means of an inching button during the course of cleaning the machine and he caught his hand in a nip: *Finnie* v. *John Laird & Son*, 1967 S.L.T. 243. But see *Conboy* v. *King & Hutchings* (1963) 61 L.G.R. 516 (machine being rotated by an inching device is " in motion or in use " within the section). See also *Kelly* v. *Dale Ltd.* [1965] 1 Q.B. 185 and a similar case *Stanbrook* v. *Waterlow & Sons* [1964] 1 W.L.R. 825. In *Mitchell* v. *W. S. Westin* [1965] 1 W.L.R. 297 the Court of Appeal followed *Knight* v. *Leamington Spa Courier* (*ante*) where the dangerous parts of a machine were being moved slowly and intermittently for the

and for any lubrication or adjustment [33] shown by the examination to be immediately necessary, and all such conditions as may be specified in regulations made by the Minister are complied with."

1234 What is a dangerous part of machinery is a question of degree and of fact.[34] Wills J. suggested the following test: "Machinery or parts of machinery is or are dangerous if in the ordinary course of human affairs danger may be reasonably anticipated from the use of them without protection. No doubt it would be impossible to say that because an accident had happened once therefore the machinery was dangerous. On the other hand, it is equally out of the question to say that machinery cannot be dangerous unless it is so in the course of careful working. In considering whether machinery is dangerous, the contingency of carelessness on the part of the workman in charge of it, and the frequency with which that contingency is likely to arise, are matters that must be taken into consideration." [35] In a later case this test was adopted and extended by du Parcq J. who said: "A part of machinery is dangerous if it is a possible cause of injury to anybody acting in a way in which a human being may be reasonably expected to act in circumstances which may be reasonably expected to occur." [36] Lord Cooper has put it: "The necessary and sufficient consideration for the emergence of the duty to fence imposed by section [14] of the Factories Act is that some part of the machinery should be 'dangerous.' The question is not whether the occupiers of the factory knew that it was dangerous; nor whether a factory inspector had so reported; nor whether previous accidents had occurred; nor whether the victims of these accidents had, or had not, been contributorily negligent. The test is objective and impersonal. Is the part such in its character, and so circumstanced in its position, exposure, method of operation and the like, that in the ordinary course of human affairs danger may reasonably be anticipated from its use unfenced, not only to the prudent, alert and skilled operative

purpose of repairs or adjustments. To be "in use" the machinery must be in use for its ordinary commercial purpose and not accidentally put in motion during some repair work being carried out on it: *Horne* v. *Lec Refrigeration* [1965] 2 All E.R. 898. On the other hand, see the different considerations where machinery is liable to be cleaned by women and young persons (s. 20): *Denyer* v. *Charles Skipper & East* [1970] 1 W.L.R. 1087.

33 This does not include the process of tool setting: *Nash* v. *High Duty Alloys Ltd.* [1947] K.B. 377.

34 In *Hindle* v. *Birtwistle* [1897] 1 Q.B. 192, 196, Wright J. in the concluding judgment said: "The mere fact that the shuttle will sometimes fly out, and that when it flies out it is dangerous, is not enough. It is a question of degree and of fact in all cases whether the tendency to fly out is a tendency to fly out often enough to satisfy a reasonable interpretation of the word 'dangerous.'" Also see *Carr* v. *Mercantile Produce Co.* [1949] 2 K.B. 601, where the machine was held not to be dangerous. In *Close* v. *Steel Company of Wales* [1961] 3 W.L.R. 319, the House of Lords held that the bit of an electric drill which suddenly shattered, flung out its broken particles and struck the operator's eye was not a dangerous part of machinery within s. 14. See notes on this case, 76 L.Q.R. 478, and 105 S.J. 997.

35 *Hindle* v. *Birtwistle* [1897] 1 Q.B. 192, 195. See the comment on this by Slesser L.J. in *Higgins* v. *Harrison* (1932) 25 B.W.C.C. 113, 125. Also, *Stimson* v. *Standard Telephones and Cables* [1940] 1 K.B. 342, 360.

36 *Walker* v. *Bletchley Flettons Ltd.* [1937] 1 All E.R. 170, 175. Later explained in *Stimson* v. *Standard Telephones and Cables Ltd., supra.* Lord Reid in *John Summers & Sons Ltd.* v. *Frost* [1955] A.C. 740 suggested the substitution for "possible" of "reasonably foreseeable cause of injury." See also *Carey* v. *Ocean Coal Co.* [1938] 1 K.B. 365; *Williams* v. *Sykes & Harrison Ltd.* [1955] 1 W.L.R. 1180.

intent upon his task, but also to the careless or inattentive worker whose inadvertent or indolent conduct may expose him to risk of injury or death from the unguarded part?" [37] A machine is dangerous if danger should reasonably be anticipated from its use without protection.[38] Whether a machine could be held to be dangerous in connection with the material or article on it was considered by Pearce L.J. in *Eaves* v. *Morris Motors* [39] where he said: " Although *Bullock* v. *G. John Powers* (*Agencies*) *Ltd.*[40] does not allow us to equate dangers from the nature of the material (namely, the sharp edge of the bolts) to dangers from the machinery, it does not compel us when deciding whether machinery is dangerous to disregard the nature of the machine when it is doing its normal appointed task, or from holding it to be dangerous if that task clearly involves danger from its juxtaposition with its normal materials. If a moving arm of the machine does not project and is therefore safe when the machine is empty, but projects dangerously when the machine is supplied with its proper material, it can obviously be labelled as dangerous machinery. And if it creates a dangerous nip when supplied with its normal material and when working normally (or in a foreseeable manner) I see no reason in principle why the court cannot consider the machinery dangerous, even if that nip is only created by the juxtaposition of material and machinery. For in that case it is not the nature of the material and it is not the material itself which causes the danger. The danger is caused by the design of the machine itself working normally with harmless material." In *Midland and Low Moor Iron and Steel Co.* v. *Cross* [41] it was held that the question whether a part of machinery was a dangerous part within the meaning of section 14 (1) must be determined on consideration of the machine when in normal operation doing the work which it was designed to do ordinarily. Accordingly the leading-in rollers of a power-driven hand-fed bar-straightening machine, where there was created a dangerous nip between them and the moving metal bar, ought to have been fenced.

235 Machinery is dangerous if it is a reasonably foreseeable source of danger to a person acting even carelessly, if the carelessness is of a kind which may be reasonably expected to occur from time to time. If the carelessness is quite outside ordinary expectation, the fact that the machine has caused injury to the person who has committed such carelessness is not conclusive proof that it is a dangerous machine. Where, therefore, a girl, told to pick up capsules from the floor, put her hand in a machine which was working, and it was proved that there had been four similar unfenced machines in

[37] *Mitchell* v. *N. British Rubber Co.*, 1945 S.C.(J.) 69, 73, quoted with approval in *John Summers & Sons Ltd.* v. *Frost* [1955] A.C. 740.

[38] *Per* Caldecote C.J. in *Kinder* v. *Camberwell Corpn.* [1944] 2 All E.R. 315, 317 (hand-operated pressing machine injures workman, owing to handle unexpectedly springing up—machines of that type never fenced and have been used without accident for twenty years—evidence that handle might fly up if wiring improperly done, wire broke, or too much paper put into machine—breach of s. 14).

[39] [1961] 2 Q.B. 385 at pp. 395, 396, approved by the H.L. in *Midland and Low Moor Iron and Steel Co. Ltd.* v. *Cross* [1965] A.C. 343.

[40] [1956] 1 W.L.R. 171.

[41] *Supra.*

use in the factory for sixteen years, without any accidents and without any requirement from the factory inspector that they should be fenced, it was held that the machines were not dangerous machines.[42]

1236 A distinction must be drawn between materials or articles, which were dangerous when in motion in a machine, and machinery itself, which was dangerous when in motion. The obligation under section 14 (1) to fence securely did not require that materials or articles should be fenced,[43] but there is a power under the concluding words of the section to make regulations requiring them to be fenced.[44] Further, this obligation did not extend to preventing tools held in the operator's hand from coming into contact with such machinery.[45] A duty to fence under section 14 (1) did not arise merely by reason of the dangerous proximity of a moving part of a machine to a stationary extraneous object.[46]

1237 The duty imposed by sections 12, 13 and 14 is an absolute one.[47] The machinery must be securely fenced, but there has been a difference of judicial opinion as to the standard to be applied. In *Burns* v. *Joseph Terry & Sons Ltd.*,[48] the Court of Appeal, by a majority, decided that the standard was to fence the machinery so as to give security from such dangers as might reasonably be anticipated. Denning L.J., dissenting, said that

[42] *Higgins* v. *Harrison* (1932) 25 B.W.C.C. 113; see also *Carr* v. *Mercantile Produce Co.* [1929] 2 K.B. 601.

[43] *Eaves* v. *Morris Motors* [1961] 2 Q.B. 385 (finger cut when removing two bolts, which had been milled, from the vice on a traversing table which unexpectedly began to move back towards the milling wheels, so that the plaintiff had to snatch his hands away), following *Nicholls* v. *Austin (Leyton) Ltd.* [1946] A.C. 493, and *Bullock* v. *G. John Power (Agencies) Ltd.* [1956] 1 W.L.R. 171. In *Lewis* v. *High Duty Alloys* [1957] 1 W.L.R. 632, Ashworth J. said: " No statutory obligation is imposed on factory owners where the danger arises indirectly through the conjunction of part of the machine with some part of the materials," but this decision was not followed by the H.L. in *Midland and Low Moor Iron and Steel Co. Ltd.* v. *Cross* [1965] A.C. 343, it being held that where a machine was being worked as it was designed to work and a part of the machine (not merely the material being worked) became dangerous from the operation of the machine, that part was required to be fenced securely. In dismissing the appeal, the earlier decision of Lynskey J. in *Hoare* v. *M. & W. Grazebrooke Ltd.* [1957] 1 W.L.R. 638 was affirmed and adopted by the House of Lords. In *Johnson* v. *F. E. Callow (Engineers) Ltd.* [1971] A.C. 335 (affirming the C.A. [1970] 2 Q.B. 1) the H.L. held that in considering whether a part is dangerous within s. 14 (1) regard must be had to the operation of the machine and any unsafe practice which is prevalent amongst the operators. A part of a machine may be dangerous because of its juxtaposition to another part of it or to a moving workpiece or the material being worked. See " Fencing of Machinery: Damage due to presence of materials," by John Munkman (1957) 107 L.J. 324.

[44] s. 14 (5). Willmer L.J. commenting at p. 665 in *Eaves* v. *Morris Motors* (*supra*) said, " The subsection would be unnecessary and indeed nonsensical if it were permissible to regard the (materials or articles) as themselves forming part of the machine."

[45] *Sparrow* v. *Fairey Aviation Co. Ltd.* [1964] A.C. 1019 (a lathe operator applied a tool to " blend off " the burring of a drilled hole in the sealing for a petrol filler cap, when the tool accidently caught against the jaws of the chuck and injured his finger). A decision to the contrary was given in *Johnson* v. *J. Stone & Co. (Charlton) Ltd.* [1961] 1 W.L.R. 849 (a band sawyer, who presented a metal casting to a vertical saw from the wrong side, which he knew, and dislodged a revolving pulley, injured his hand), but this was prior to the House of Lords decision in *Close* v. *Steel Company of Wales Ltd.* [1962] A.C. 367.

[46] *Pearce* v. *Stanley-Bridges* [1965] 1 W.L.R. 931; *Hindle* v. *Joseph Porritt & Sons* [1970] 1 All E.R. 1142.

[47] *John Summers & Sons Ltd.* v. *Frost* [1955] A.C. 740; *Miller* v. *William Boothman & Sons Ltd.* [1944] K.B. 337; *Groves* v. *Wimborne* [1898] 2 Q.B. 402; *Dunn* v. *Birds Eye Foods Ltd.* [1959] 2 Q.B. 265.

[48] [1951] 1 K.B. 454.

foreseeability was not the test, but that the duty was to erect and maintain an effective barrier to prevent any employee from making contact with the machine. In *John Summers & Sons Ltd.* v. *Frost* [49] the majority of the House of Lords approved of the decision in *Burns*' case, Lord Reid saying: " the object of fencing is to remove the danger which would exist in its absence, and I would hold that a dangerous part is securely fenced if, and only if, the presence of the fence makes it no longer dangerous within the meaning of that word as it is used in this section [s. 14]." [50] Foreseeability of danger is therefore the test not only of the dangerous character of the machinery but also of the adequacy of the fencing. Nevertheless where the failure to fence properly the dangerous parts of a drilling machine had caused an accident, the fact that the accident had happened in a way which could not reasonably have been foreseen was wholly irrelevant and did not affect the question of the defendant's certainty of liability.[51]

In accordance with this, when transmission machinery was fenced but the fencing did not extend all the way up to the top of the overhead driving shaft and while the machine was being worked the belt broke, lashed out over the fence and struck the operator, there was held to be no breach of section 13.[52]

238 The duty to fence is an obligation to screen or shield the machine so as to prevent the body of the operator from coming in contact with it, and does not include the duty of protecting the operator from being struck by any flying part of the machine itself or of the material on which the machine is working.[53] Where, therefore, a girl, working at a circular saw which was properly fenced, was injured by a piece of wood thrown off by the saw, it was held that there was no breach of the section.[54] Lord Simonds saying: " The fence is intended to keep the worker out, not to keep the machine or its product in." [55] Likewise where a workman was struck and injured in the eye whilst operating an electric drill, the bit of which suddenly shattered, flinging out its broken particles, there was held to be no breach of statutory duty.[56] However Lord Goddard added that " if in a factory there is a

49 [1955] A.C. 740.
50 *Ibid.* p. 765.
51 *Millard* v. *Serck Tubes Ltd.* [1969] 1 W.L.R. 211. See generally Chap. 3,
52 *Carroll* v. *Andrew Barclay & Sons Ltd.* [1948] A.C. 477.
53 *Close* v. *Steel Company of Wales Ltd.* [1962] A.C. 367 where the House of Lords held by a majority that the earlier decisions and dicta of the Court of Appeal could not be supported in so far as they departed from the clear view expressed by the House in *Nicholls*' case. These cases were: (1) *Dickson* v. *Flack* [1953] 2 Q.B. 464 (where a vertical spindle moulding machine was used which was liable to throw out parts when in use). (2) *Newnham* v. *Tagart, Morgan & Coles Ltd., The Times*, July 20, 1956 (where a bandsaw broke and a piece flew out); and (3) *Rutherford* v. *R.E. Glanville & Sons* (*Bovey Tracey*) *Ltd.* [1958] 1 W.L.R. 415 (where the guard, lifted by the force of a carborundum wheel, which broke whilst revolving at a high speed, struck the workman).
54 *Nicholls* v. *F. Austin* (*Leyton*) *Ltd.* [1946] A.C. 493. Material used in the machine need not be fenced: *Bullock* v. *John Power* (*Agencies*) *Ltd.* [1956] 1 W.L.R. 171. See also *Kilgollan* v. *William Cooke & Co. Ltd.* [1956] 1 W.L.R. 527, where it was held that the defendants were not in breach of s. 14 by not fencing a machine from which, as they knew, pieces of wire were from time to time ejected. The defendants were held liable at common law.
55 *Nicholls* v. *F. Austin* (*Leyton*) *Ltd.* [1946] A.C. 493 at p. 505.
56 *Close* v. *Steel Company of Wales Ltd.* [1962] A.C. 367.

machine which it is known from experience has a tendency to throw out parts of the machine itself or of the material on which it is working, so as to be a danger to the operator, the absence of a shield to protect him may well afford him a cause of action at common law." [57] The duty to fence may be modified or extended with respect to any class of factory by special regulations made by the Minister under section 76, and a number of such regulations have been made. For example, under regulation 10 of the Woodworking Machinery Regulations 1922, the guard on a circular saw must extend to a point as low as practicable at the cutting edge of the saw. A saw so guarded must of necessity leave part of the cutting edge exposed when the saw is in use for cutting but it has been held that if the guard complies with the regulations there is no breach of statutory duty.[58] If, however, the regulations provide that the most efficient guard is to be provided, it is not enough to provide a guard to protect the operator, but a guard must be provided to protect other persons working in the factory as well.[59]

1239 A machine is not securely fenced if the workman can get his hand through the guard without any real difficulty.[60] Where, therefore, a girl working on a pastry rolling machine deliberately put her hand underneath the guard to push some dough against the moving rollers, it was held that the machine was not securely fenced.[61] The words " securely fenced " mean fenced at the time of the accident. A machine fitted with a fence which was raised at the time of the accident is not fenced.[62] A guard which can be lifted or removed is not a secure fence if it is lifted or removed at the time of the accident.[63] On the other hand, a guard which has been forced off or removed in some exceptional way inconsistent with the reasonable though careless use of the machine would not be a breach of the statute. The duty to fence is not discharged by providing guards necessary for securely fencing the machinery and putting the responsibility for using them upon the workmen.[64] When the guard is one which requires adjustment, and the workman is injured because of inaccurate adjustment, the occupier is liable although the workman was at fault in not making the adjustment.[65] But if the duty of making the adjustment is expressly and

[57] *Ibid.* p. 390.

[58] *Miller* v. *William Boothman & Sons Ltd.* [1944] K.B. 337. In *John Summers & Sons Ltd.* v. *Frost* [1955] A.C. 740 the H.L. held that this case was rightly decided. When the saw is not used for sawing but is left running while the operator removes off-cuts from the bench, and the operator is injured by the unfenced edge, there is no breach of s. 14. *Stringer* v. *Automatic Woodturning Co. Ltd.* [1956] 1 W.L.R. 138.

[59] *Harrison* v. *Metropolitan Plywood Co.* [1946] K.B. 255. This case, decided on the construction of the regulations, must be contrasted with *Nicholls* v. *F. Austin (Leyton) Ltd., supra*, decided on s. 14.

[60] *Wood* v. *L.C.C.* [1940] 4 All E.R. 149, *per* Tucker J. The decision was reversed on other grounds [1941] 2 K.B. 232.

[61] *Smith* v. *Chesterfield Co-operative Socy.* [1953] 1 W.L.R. 370 (the girl was held 60 per cent. to blame).

[62] *Smith* v. *Morris Motors Ltd.* [1950] 1 K.B. 194.

[63] *Charles* v. *S. Smith & Sons (England) Ltd.* [1954] 1 W.L.R. 451.

[64] *Thomas* v. *Thomas Bolton & Sons Ltd.* (1928) 139 L.T. 397.

[65] *Lay* v. *D. & L. Studios Ltd.* [1944] 1 All E.R. 322; *Vyner* v. *Waldenberg Bros. Ltd.* [1946] K.B. 50. *Leach* v. *Standard Telephones and Cables* [1966] 1 W.L.R. 1392 (where a plaintiff

properly delegated to an experienced workman, who is injured because of his failure to make the necessary adjustment, the occupier is not liable.[66] Further, a " fence must not merely guard against accident but must be such as takes into account human weaknesses which include, as well as forgetfulness and inadvertence, an inclination sometimes to run minor risks and to take short cuts. Some degree of recklessness (as well as carelessness) has to be foreseen. The fence need not be constructed so as to keep out a determined man, but I think it must be such as will deter a man who, in pursuit of a short cut, is willing to run a minor risk." [67] If a dangerous machine is securely fenced when working forwards, but remains dangerous when being worked backwards, the duty is not discharged.[68] If it is commercially impracticable or mechanically impossible to fence the machine securely, it is still a breach of duty to leave it unfenced, and a workman who is injured in such circumstances can recover damages, because " if a machine cannot be securely fenced while remaining commercially practicable or mechanically useful the statute in effect prohibits its use." [69]

240 The machinery referred to in sections 12, 13 and 14 means machinery used [70] in the factory for the work carried on there and not machinery made or repaired in the factory for others in the ordinary course of the work of the factory. Where, therefore, a workman was cleaning a piece of machinery made in a factory, in which the work of making machinery was carried on, and was injured, it was held that there was no statutory duty to fence such machinery and the workman failed to recover.[71]

241 **Construction and sale of new machinery.** (s. 17): the seller of new machinery which does not comply with the requirements of section 17 (1)

set a guard much too high on a mechanical saw, his breach was not wholly co-extensive with his employers' breach, since even if the guard had been set as low as possible it would still not have been fully effective and this failure to fence securely was not a duty which the employers could vicariously discharge only through the plaintiff himself).

66 *Smith* v. *Baveystock & Co.* [1945] 1 All E.R. 531. As to delegation, see *ante*, § 1225. If a proper guard is not provided, the fact that its adjustment is left to an experienced workman will be no defence: *Cakebread* v. *Hopping Bros. Ltd.* [1947] K.B. 641.

67 *Quintas* v. *National Smelting Co. Ltd.* [1960] 1 W.L.R. 217, 222, *per* Devlin J. Reversed on other grounds [1961] 1 W.L.R. 401.

68 *Pursell* v. *Clement Talbot Ltd.* (1914) 111 L.T. 827.

69 *Davies* v. *Thomas Owen & Co. Ltd.* [1919] 2 K.B. 39, *per* Salter J. This was doubted by Lord Simon C. in *Lewis* v. *Denye* [1940] A.C. 921, 932, but expressly approved by the C.A. in *Miller* v. *William Boothman & Sons Ltd.* [1944] K.B. 337, 341, and followed in *Fowler* v. *Yorkshire Electric Power Co. Ltd.* [1939] 1 All E.R. 407; *Dennistoun* v. *Greenhill Ltd.* [1944] 2 All E.R. 434; *Mackay* v. *Ailsa Shipbuilding Co.*, 1945 S.C. 414; and *Pugh* v. *Manchester Dry Docks Co.* [1954] 1 W.L.R. 389. Finally, it was approved by the H.L. in *John Summers & Sons Ltd.* v. *Frost* [1955] A.C. 740, where it was held that a grindstone must be securely fenced even though, as appeared to be the case, it would make the machine unusable. The machine, to be used at all, had to have an exposed edge to cut or grind the stone, and the H.L. suggested that the only way in which the machine could be legally used was for regulations to be made under s. 60 as had been done in the case of circular saws.

70 Notwithstanding that the sack hoist concerned had not been taken into commercial use, since it was an independent entity of machinery, which had been completely installed in the factory, the statutory fencing requirements apply and thus the absence of fencing constituted a breach of statutory duty. *Irwin* v. *White, Tompkins & Courage Ltd.* [1964] 1 W.L.R. 387. This decision of the House of Lords was applied by the Court of Appeal in *Stanbrook* v. *Waterlow & Sons* [1964] 1 W.L.R. 825.

71 *Parvin* v. *Morton Machine Co.* [1952] A.C. 515. See also *Thurogood* v. *Van den Berghs & Jurgens Ltd.* [1951] 2 K.B. 537.

commits an offence and is liable to be fined, but does not owe any duty to men employed in a factory occupied by the purchaser. He is not liable in damages to anyone who is injured through his breach of statutory duty.[72]

1242 **Hoists and lifts.** (s. 22): the obligation imposed by this section is an absolute one. When a lift fell and injured the lift operator, the cause of the fall being a latent defect in the shafting, the occupiers of the factory were held liable.[73] Similarly, when the lift fell owing to the failure of the brakes to hold it, and inspection could discover no defect in the brakes or any reason for their failure, the occupier was also held liable.[74] Where the plaintiff inserted his hand through the outer gate of a lift in order to close the inner gate properly and as he did so the lift moved injuring his hand, likewise the occupier was held liable.[75]

1243 **Good construction.** Part II of the Act is constantly referring to the " construction " of various parts of the factory and the material used in it. The guard required in section 16 must be " of substantial construction," every lift must be (s. 22) " of good mechanical construction," lifting tackle must be (s. 26) " of good construction " and so must (s. 27) lifting machines, steam receivers (s. 35 (4)) and steam boilers (s. 32 (5)); floors and passages must be (s. 28) " of sound construction," and so must air receivers (s. 36 (3)) and gas holders (s. 39).

" Construction " means the original construction of whatever is in question as opposed to its subsequent maintenance. For example, a ladder in which the rungs were fixed by screws was held to be soundly constructed although the screws subsequently failed owing to corrosion.[76] " Sound construction " means well made for what the article is and does not mean good or sound construction for some practicable purpose.[77] It does not include design.[78] It might well be thought to include the material of which it was made because a thing can hardly be said to be of good construction if it is made of faulty material, but in many places in the Act the words " of sound material " are conjoined with the words " of good construction," as in sections 22, 26, 27, 32 (5) and 35 (4). This suggests

72 *Biddle* v. *Truvox Engineering Co. Ltd.* [1952] 1 K.B. 101.

73 *Whitehead* v. *James Stott Ltd.* [1949] 1 K.B. 358.

74 *Galashiels Gas Co.* v. *Millar* [1949] A.C. 275.

75 *Blakeley* v. *C. & H. Clothing Co.* [1958] 1 W.L.R. 378, their obligation being to provide the lift with gates of a character which, when shut, would prevent people from coming into contact with the lift when it was moving.

76 *Cole* v. *Blackstone & Co.* [1943] K.B. 615.

77 *Beadsley* v. *United Steel Cos.* [1951] 1 K.B. 408; *cf. Mayne* v. *Johnstone & Cumbers Ltd.* [1947] 2 All E.R. 159, where it was held that the " sound construction " of a floor under s. 25 of the 1937 Act meant " sound " for the purpose for which it was to be used. See also *Gledhill* v. *Liverpool Abattoir Ltd.* [1957] 1 W.L.R. 1028, 1033: " Good construction " does not import suitability for some particular purpose either.

78 *Gibby* v. *East Grinstead Gas Co.* [1944] 1 All E.R. 358, *per* Scott L.J. But it was held by the Court of Appeal that though the words " of sound construction " did not necessarily and in all cases exclude any reference to design, they were prima facie to be construed in their ordinary sense of " well built " or " well made ": *Hawkins* v. *Westinghouse Brake & Signal Co. Ltd.* (1959) 109 L.J. 89. The plaintiff tripped over a step an inch or two in height formed by the edge of a manhole cover next to a grating used for surface water drainage in the kerbside of a factory roadway, and the Court of Appeal made similar observations, as stated above.

that the Act is drawing a distinction between the actual materials used in the construction of the thing in question, which are only required to be sound when the section expressly so provides, and the actual work required to be done to make those materials into the finished product, which must be good or sound, but it is doubtful whether any such distinction can safely be drawn. There seems to be no difference between " good, " " sound " and " substantial " construction, but " good mechanical construction " seems to limit the construction which must be good to that part of the product which can properly be described as mechanical.

244 **Sound material.** Hoists and lifts (s. 22), chains, ropes and lifting tackle (s. 26), lifting gear (s. 27), steam boilers (s. 32 (5)), and steam receivers (s. 35 (4)) must be of sound material. This does not mean only that the material appears to be sound on reasonable inspection.[79] There is an absolute duty to use material which is sound, even though it is unsound from a latent defect not discoverable on reasonable examination. The time at which the material must be sound is at the time of construction. Its subsequent deterioration is not a breach of the duty to use sound material.

245 **Adequate strength.** The plant and appliances referred to in the last paragraph are also required to be " of adequate strength." This means adequate for the work for which the occupier of the factory requires it to be used. Failure of the appliance, such as the parting of a cable used with an overhead crane, is prima facie but not conclusive evidence of breach of the statutory duty. It is not conclusive evidence, because it is open to the occupier to prove that the appliance failed, not because it was not of adequate strength, but from some other cause.[80]

246 **Free from patent defect.** Chains, ropes and lifting tackle (s. 26), lifting gear (s. 27), steam boilers (s. 32 (5)), and steam receivers (s. 35 (4)) must be free from patent defect. This is an absolute obligation. A makeshift sling, constituting lifting tackle, formed from chains of different lengths is not free from patent defect.[81]

247 **Properly maintained.** A number of sections, such as sections 22, 27, 28, 32 (5), 35 (4), 36 (3) and 39, require that plant and appliances be properly maintained.[82] " Maintained " is defined in section 176 as meaning " maintained in an efficient state, in efficient working order and in good repair." The obligation is an absolute one and not merely to take reasonable care. It is to maintain the subject-matter in a good state of repair and denotes the continuance of a state of working efficiency.[83] In the case of a thing such as a floor, the obligation is to keep it in good repair and the

[79] *Whitehead* v. *James Stott Ltd.* [1949] 1 K.B. 358.
[80] *Reilly* v. *Beardmore & Co.*, 1947 S.C. 275.
[81] *Dawson* v. *Murex Ltd.* [1941] 2 All E.R. 784.
[82] " Properly maintained " means that the parts, etc., of every lifting gear must not only be of good construction, sound material, adequate strength and free from patent defect, but as regards each one of these things must continue to be in all these conditions: *Gledhill* v. *Liverpool Abattoir Ltd.* [1957] 1 W.L.R. 1028, 1035. See now s. 27 of the 1961 Act.
[83] *Galashiels Gas Co. Ltd.* v. *Millar* [1949] A.C. 275.

requirement of keeping it in an efficient state adds little if anything to this. Under the 1937 Act if the floor was temporarily dangerous, for example, by having some slippery substance upon it or by its being cumbered by things resting upon it, it could not be said that it was not properly maintained.[84] As Lord Reid said [85]: " I do not think that maintaining a floor includes keeping dangerous things away from it." But under the 1961 Act there are the additional words to the section [86] " and shall so far as is reasonably practicable be kept free from any obstruction and from any substance likely to cause persons to slip." In *Dorman Long* (*Steel*) *Ltd.* v. *Bell* [87] where a workman fell whilst walking over some metal plates lying on the floor upon which a film of slag dust had settled making their surface slippery, it was held that the appellants' statutory duty required them to prevent the presence of, or remove, slippery substances on which anyone on the floor was likely to step and it was immaterial whether or not the slippery substance was itself actually in contact with the floor. A workman who was injured by the presence of a chattel placed upon the floor could not recover on the ground that the floor had not been properly maintained.[88]

1248 **As far as practicable; impracticable; reasonably practicable.** In many places in the Act and in the regulations made under it [89] there is a duty to take some safety measure " as far as practicable," or to take " all practicable steps " to provide against some danger. " Practicable " is not the same as " possible " but involves some qualification of what is possible. The definition in the *Oxford English Dictionary*, " capable of being carried out in action," " feasible," has been adopted in two cases,[90] and expresses the distinction between what it is possible to do, perhaps in very exceptional conditions and in very favourable circumstances on rare occasions, and what can be done in practice by anyone with proper equipment, care and skill who sets out to do it. It is possible, for example, for a man to run a stated distance in record time, because it has been done, but it is not practicable to run that distance in that time because no other person, even the record holder himself, has been able to do it before or since. The definition in *Webster's Dictionary* " possible to be accomplished with known means and known resources " has also been approved.[91] In considering what is practicable, questions of cost are to be eliminated,[92] but

84 *Latimer* v. *A.E.C. Ltd.* [1953] A.C. 643.

85 *Ibid.* p. 658. See also *Payne* v. *Weldless Steel Tube Co.* [1956] 1 Q.B. 196.

86 s. 28 (1).

87 [1964] 1 W.L.R. 333.

88 *Woods* v. *W. H. Rhodes & Son Ltd.* [1953] 2 All E.R. 658. A different decision in this case now would depend upon the evidence in consideration of the words " reasonably practicable."

89 See ss. 28 (1), 29 (1), 31 (1) and (2), 63. Building Regs. 1948, reg. 79.

90 *Lee* v. *Nursery Furnishings Ltd.* [1945] 1 All E.R. 387 by Goddard L.J.; *Adsett* v. *K. and L. Steelfounders & Engineers Ltd.* [1953] 1 W.L.R. 733, by Singleton L.J.

91 *Adsett's* case, *supra*, p. 779; *Knight* v. *Demolition & Construction Co. Ltd.* [1953] 1 W.L.R. 981, 986, affd. [1954] 1 W.L.R. 563.

92 *Adsett* v. *K. and L. Steelfounders & Engineers Ltd.* [1953] 1 W.L.R. 137, 142, *per* Parker J.

regard must be had to the state of knowledge at the material time, particularly of scientific knowledge.[93] Where a defendant is under a duty to take " all practical measures " to obviate some risk, this could well include a duty to supervise and, if necessary, enforce the use of protective equipment provided.[94]

249 On the other hand " impracticable " is used on occasions to give relief from a statutory obligation. In such event the word must be interpreted strictly and has been held to mean something more than just " not reasonably practicable." [95] The fact that compliance with the obligation may involve unreasonable time or expense or both is quite irrelevant.[96] Nevertheless there is a clear distinction between " impracticable " and " impossible " in that in the former some degree of reason is introduced and it involves some regards for practice.[97]

If the statute requires such safety measures to be taken as are " reasonably practicable " the standard of care is lower than if the word " practicable " only is used. The cost of any necessary safety measures can be weighed against the risk and the expected efficacy of the measures. Asquith L.J. put it,[98] " ' Reasonably practicable ' is a narrower term than ' physically possible ' and seems to me to imply that a computation must be made by the owner, in which the quantum of risk is placed on one scale and the sacrifice involved in the measures necessary for averting the risk (whether in money, time or trouble) is placed in the other; and that if it be shown that there is a gross disproportion between them—the risk being insignificant in relation to the sacrifice—the defendants discharge the onus on them. Moreover, this computation falls to be made by the owner at a point of time anterior to the accident." In considering what is reasonably practicable, the employer must take into account the period of time over which the danger is spread, and the time, trouble and expense of the safeguards which would be required; if the latter are disproportionate to the period of the risk it will not be reasonably practicable to take them.[99] Accordingly where the statutory duty is a duty of doing what is reasonably practicable, there may not be very much difference between this standard

93 *Ibid.* [1953] 1 W.L.R. 773, 780, *per* Singleton L.J. *Richards* v. *Highways Ironfounders Ltd.* [1957] 1 W.L.R. 781.

94 *Crookall* v. *Vickers-Armstrong* [1955] 1 W.L.R. 659.

95 *Brown* v. *N.C.B.* [1962] A.C. 574, 598.

96 *Moorcroft* v. *Thomas Powles & Sons Ltd.* [1962] 3 All E.R. 741; *Cork* v. *Kirby Maclean Ltd.* [1952] 1 All E.R. 1064.

97 *Jayne* v. *N.C.B.* [1968] 2 All E.R. 220, 223.

98 *Edwards* v. *N.C.B.* [1949] 1 K.B. 704, 712, quoted and amplified by Jenkins L.J. in *Marshall* v. *Gotham Ltd.* [1952] 2 All E.R. 1044 and approved by Lord Reid in *Marshall* v. *Gotham Ltd.* [1954] A.C. 360, 373. See also *Jenkins* v. *Allied Ironfounders Ltd.* [1970] 1 W.L.R. 304; *Wraith* v. *N.C.B.* [1954] 1 W.L.R. 264, 270; *Gregson* v. *Hick Hargreaves & Co.* [1955] 1 W.L.R. 1252; *Walsh* v. *N.C.B.* [1956] 1 Q.B. 511; " Whether or not some precaution is ' reasonably practicable ' will depend on a number of considerations. Cost is one and I think that any risk inherent in providing the precaution is another ": Parker L.J. in *Trott* v. *W. E. Smith (Erectors) Ltd.* [1957] 1 W.L.R. 1154 at p. 1163.

99 *Coltness Iron Co.* v. *Sharp* [1938] A.C. 90; approved by Lord Oaksey in *Marshall* v. *Gotham, supra.*

and the common law standard of taking reasonable care in all the circumstances. The Court of Appeal on the one hand has indicated that the standard is much the same in the two cases,[1] then in another decision has gone on to say that the statutory obligation places a stricter obligation on the defendant than does the common law.[2] Further it has been held that to make a place as safe as is reasonably practicable is almost, if not quite, the same as the common law duty owed by a master to his servant when working on his master's premises.[3] The burden of proving that a particular safety measure is not reasonably practicable is on the occupier.[4]

1250 **Lifting tackle and lifting machines.** (ss. 26, 27): these sections provide for the construction and use of lifting tackle and lifting machines.[5] If tackle, in accordance with the provision of the section, is provided, there is no breach of duty if the workman fails to use it but uses instead some tackle which is unsuitable for the purpose.[6] A makeshift sling, formed from a number of chains of different lengths, is not free from patent defect.[7] The word " use " is not confined to the use authorised by the factory owners, hence where their servant misused certain lifting tackle which he knew had not been provided for that purpose and injured the plaintiff the owners were still liable.[8]

If a lifting machine is loaded beyond the safe working load and an accident is caused, the fact that the operator was wrong in his estimate of the load will not, of itself, prevent him from recovering damages.[9] A defective cable which conducts electricity to a crane is not a breach of section 27 (1).[10]

1 *Jones* v. *N.C.B.* [1957] 2 Q.B. 55.

2 *Trott* v. *W. E. Smith (Erectors) Ltd., supra.*

3 *McCarthy* v. *Coldair Ltd.* [1951] W.N. 590, where the Court of Appeal adopted as being applicable equally to the Factories Act the words of Tucker L.J. in *Edwards* v. *N.C.B., supra,* at p. 710: " In every case it is the risk that has to be weighed against the measures necessary to eliminate the risk." See also *McWilliams* v. *Sir William Arrol & Co.* [1962] 1 W.L.R. 295.

4 *Nimmo* v. *Alexander Cowan & Sons Ltd.* [1968] A.C. 107, but with Lord Reid and Lord Wilberforce dissenting. See *Dorman Long (Steel) Ltd.* v. *Bell* [1964] 1 W.L.R. 333 where Lord Reid earlier had declined to consider the question of where the onus of proof lay. Further, see *Callaghan* v. *Fred Kidd & Son (Engineers) Ltd.* [1944] K.B. 560, 565; *Sheppey* v. *Shaw & Co. Ltd.* [1952] W.N. 249. The onus of proving that it is not reasonably practicable to provide a safety measure is on the person on whom the duty is imposed (*Walter Wilson & Son* v. *Summerfield* [1956] 1 W.L.R. 1429), subject always to the construction of the regulations (*Marshall* v. *Gotham Co. Ltd.* [1954] A.C. 360, 374, *per* Lord Tucker, not following the dicta of Scott L.J. in *Callaghan* v. *Fred Kidd & Son (Engineers) Ltd.* [1944] K.B. 560, 565). See article: " Who Proves the Practicability " 116 New L.J. 1419.

5 By s. 27 (1), the obligation imposed on the occupiers is that " all parts and working gear . . . of every lifting machine shall be of good construction, sound material, adequate strength and free from patent defect. . . ." The Court of Session, Outer House, held that it was irrelevant whether the defect was patent or latent since the requirements of good construction, sound material and adequate strength were not qualified by the latter requirement that there should be no patent defect: *McNeil* v. *Dickson and Mann*, 1957 S.L.T. 364. The pursuer's husband was killed when a crane jib collapsed as a result of a gear wheel breaking due to a latent defect, metal fatigue. (*Cf.* this decision with the view expressed in Munkman's *Employer's Liability*, 7th ed., pp. 260–263.)

6 *Beadsley* v. *United Steel Companies Ltd.* [1951] 1 K.B. 408.

7 *Dawson* v. *Murex Ltd.* [1941] 2 All E.R. 784.

8 *Barry* v. *Cleveland Bridge & Engineering Co.* [1963] 1 All E.R. 192.

9 *Gallagher* v. *Dorman Long & Co. Ltd.* [1947] 2 All E.R. 38.

10 *Gatehouse* v. *John Summers & Sons Ltd.* [1953] 1 W.L.R. 742. But in *Evans* v. *Sanderson Bros. and Newbould* (1968) 112 S.J. 293 it was held that as the electrical points which

The duty imposed by section 27 (7) is absolute.[11] It is broken if the crane hits some object near the workman, such as a drill, which is dislodged and causes him injury.[12]

251 **Floors, passages and stairs.** By section 28 (1) it is provided that: " All floors, steps, stairs, passages and gangways [13] shall be of sound construction and properly maintained [14] and shall, so far as is reasonably practicable, be kept free from any obstruction and from any substance likely to cause persons to slip." Accordingly, the duty under the first part of the subsection is absolute; but an employer will avoid liability if the workman has been the author of his own misfortune and the employer has not done anything which is co-extensive with the latter's act.[15] Further, the employer will not be liable where there is no proof of any causal connection between his acts and the presence of the obstructions on the floor.[16]

252 On the other hand as the duty imposed by the second part of the subsection is qualified by the words " so far as is reasonably practicable," the effect of this qualification is that in deciding whether there has been a breach of statutory duty the risk of injury must be balanced against the

were controlled by buttons on a pendulum control of an electric crane were defective there was a breach of s. 27, since they were part of the lifting machinery, which should have been of good construction and properly maintained.

11 *Lotinga* v. *N.E. Marine Engineering Co.* [1941] 2 K.B. 399. *Hunter* v. *Glenfield & Kennedy*, 1947 S.C. 536. See also *Ward* v. *Coltness Iron Co.*, 1944 S.C. 318. An " overhead travelling crane " within the meaning of s. 27 (7) is a crane which travels overhead, and does not include a crane which runs on rails at ground level although part of the structure, the crab, travels on the girder overhead: *Carrington* v. *John Summers & Sons Ltd.* [1957] 1 W.L.R. 504 (the defendants were held liable for common law negligence).

12 *Holmes* v. *Hadfields Ltd.* [1944] K.B. 275.

13 For cases in which these five words " floors "; " steps "; " stairs "; " passages "; and " gangways " have been considered, see: *Hosking* v. *De Havilland* [1949] 1 All E.R. 540 (plank across a duct was held to be a gangway) likewise *Hudson* v. *Acme Flooring and Paving Co. Ltd.* (*1904*) (1963) 107 S.J. 234, C.A.; *Morris* v. *Port of London Authority* (1950) 84 Lloyd's Rep. 564 (floor of a gantry came within the ambit of the section) but see *Tate* v. *Swan Hunter & Wigham Richardson Ltd.* [1958] 1 W.L.R. 39 (planks on gantry were not a floor); *Harrison* v. *Metro-Vickers Electrical Co. Ltd.* [1954] 1 W.L.R. 324 (sand surface of a factory was a floor) whilst *Newberry* v. *Joseph Westwood & Co.* [1960] 2 Lloyd's Rep. 37 (workman walking on mother earth, pushing a heavily laden truck on rails into a shed on a wharf was not walking along a floor, passage or gangway) and likewise *Sullivan* v. *Hall Russell & Co. Ltd.* 1964 S.L.T. 192 (earthen surface of an open-air wood-yard was held not to be a floor); In *Pengelley* v. *Bell Punch Co. Ltd.* [1964] 1 W.L.R. 433, which was reversed on other grounds by the C.A. (1964) 108 S.J. 461, it was held that the storage place for large reels was a part of the floor. In *Thornton* v. *Fisher & Ludlow Ltd.* [1968] 1 W.L.R. 655 it was held that a 30 foot wide roadway running through a factory was not a passage or gangway within the meaning of s. 28 although it was undoubtedly a means of access within the meaning of s. 29. (Diplock L.J. dissented.)

14 The construction of all floors, etc., must be sound and they must be maintained in that condition so as to be safe for the persons using them. In each case safety is a question of degree and fact; *Payne* v. *Weldless Steel Tube Co.* [1956] 1 Q.B. 196. In deciding whether or not a floor is of sound construction and is properly maintained, regard must be had to the purposes for which the premises are intended to be used: *Mayne* v. *Johnstone & Cumbers* [1947] 2 All E.R. 159; *Fisher* v. *Port of London Authority* [1962] 1 W.L.R. 234 (broken stair in a stairway of a transit shed).

15 *Hudson* v. *Acme Flooring and Paving Co. Ltd.* (*1904*) (1963) 107 S.J. 234, C.A. (experienced workman chose a defective plank to use for a gangway); following *Ginty* v. *Belmont Building Supplies Ltd.* [1959] 1 All E.R. 414; *McMath* v. *Rimmer Bros.* (*Liverpool*) *Ltd.* [1962] 1 W.L.R. 1.

16 *Fairfield Shipbuilding & Engineering Co. Ltd.* v. *Hall* [1964] 1 Lloyd's Rep. 73.

steps necessary to eliminate that risk.[17] Where an occupier has allowed grease to drop on to the factory floor, in this case from an overhead crane, in order to avoid liability for an accident due to slipping he must establish that it was not possible to avoid the likelihood of slipping by any measure which (a) was practicable, *i.e.* which was capable of being taken, and (b) would not involve such expense or other effort and exertion in time and labour as was unreasonable.[18] Thus it was held that as precautions to keep the floor of a corporation bus depot free from patches of oil were reasonably practicable, the failure to take such precautions amounted to a breach of the section.[19] As regards the words " kept free " the House of Lords have held that the subsection requires the defendants to keep a floor free both by preventing things getting on to it and by removing things which have got on to it.[20] The words " any obstruction " mean something which, though not forming part of the floor, is on the floor but is not normally there since its presence there is not for any particular purpose.[21] Hence a vertical angle-iron projection, being part of a machine fixed to the concrete floor in a foundry, was held not to be an obstruction[22]; likewise a mould, placed on the gangway floor in a factory, its being a convenient and proper place for it,[23] some heavy reels of paper lying on a floor,[24] and where a trolley, used to bring materials for lathes, was left at the edge of a gangway it was held not to be an " obstruction " within the section, although it was actually a necessary and reasonable obstruction of the gangway.[25] Conversely, plates, which were in fact pit covers but had been removed for the purpose of certain maintenance work in the pits, were held to constitute an obstruction where they had been laid temporarily on the factory floor at a slight angle.[26] A " gate " lying covered or partially covered by some sand which constituted the surface of the floor in the moulding shop of the respondent's foundry shop was also held to be an obstruction.[27] The words

[17] See *ante*, § 1248. See also *Vinnyey* v. *Star Paper Mills Ltd.* [1965] 1 All E.R. 175 where a workman fell during the mopping up operations following the spillage of a viscous fluid on a factory floor due to some carelessness of the workman in making a proper pipe connection. It was held that the plaintiff could not recover because it was not reasonably foreseeable that a workman brought to the scene of the mess and charged with so simple a duty of cleaning it up would slip in the course of performing that task. There was no breach of statutory duty where there was a slippery substance lying for about ten minutes on the floor of the sausage department in a factory after a table had been washed down and the plaintiff had slipped upon it and fell just as a cleaner was about to start mopping and cleaning the floor. The words of the section did not mean that the floor must be kept absolutely free at all times but all reasonable measures must be taken to keep it free: *Braham* v. *J. Lyons & Co.* [1962] 1 W.L.R. 1048.

[18] *Williams* v. *Painter Bros.* (1968) 5 K.I.R. 487.

[19] *Fern* v. *Dundee Corporation*, 1964 S.L.T. 294.

[20] *Fairfield Shipbuilding & Engineering Co. Ltd.* v. *Hall, supra.*

[21] Lord Denning in *Pengelley* v. *Bell Punch Co. Ltd.* [1964] 1 W.L.R. 1055, 1058 defined an obstruction as " something on the floor that has no business to be there, and which is a source of risk to persons ordinarily using the floor." See also *Mooney* v. *B.M.C. (Scotland) Ltd.*, 1970 S.L.T. 24n.

[22] *Drummond* v. *Harland Engineering Co. Ltd.*, 1963 S.C. 162.

[23] *Churchill* v. *Louis Marx & Co.* (1964) 108 S.J. 334, C.A.

[24] *Pengelley* v. *Bell Punch Co. Ltd., supra.*

[25] *Marshall* v. *Ericsson Telephones Ltd.* [1964] 1 W.L.R. 1367.

[26] *Dorman Long (Steel) Ltd.* v. *Bell* [1964] 1 W.L.R. 333.

[27] *Jenkins* v. *Allied Ironfounders Ltd.* [1970] 1 W.L.R. 304, but it was held that it was not reasonably practicable to ensure that the floor was constantly kept free from such " gates."

" any substance likely to cause persons to slip " were held to include rain water lying on a passage floor which did indeed cause a person to slip and fall.[28] In *Hall* v. *Fairfield Shipbuilding & Engineering Co.*[29] where a workman had slipped on a small piece of metal rod lying on the floor, the employers argued that the duty of keeping the floor clear was limited not only by the words " so far as is reasonably practicable," but also by the words " likely to cause persons to slip." The result was therefore to give this part of the section a limitation to those parts of the floor which were likely to be trodden on, but this was rejected by the court which held that the words qualified only the word " substance " and so did not limit the amount of floor at all which had to be kept free. Where dust produced a slippery surface the fact that it was not in contact with the floor was held to be immaterial since the dust was covering the metal plates lying upon the floor.[30]

1253 In *Powley* v. *Bristol Siddeley Engines Ltd.*[31] Megaw J. held that the statutory duty under section 28 was a higher duty than that at common law.

Under section 28 (2) a handrail must be provided for a staircase which owing to the condition of the surface of the steps or other special circumstances is specially liable to cause accidents. The term " staircase " was not apt to describe three steel steps about three feet high giving access and egress to a platform, such steps being removable.[32] The words " specially liable " mean " more than usually liable," and " special circumstances " imply circumstances continually arising. A history of fifteen years without an accident is strong evidence that there is no breach of the subsection.[33]

By section 28 (4) openings in floors must be securely fenced unless fencing is impracticable. Similar provisions are contained in the Building Regulations 1948, reg. 30, and the Shipbuilding and Ship-repairing Regulations 1960, reg. 26. An inspection pit,[34] a space at the edge of a floor [35] and a hole cut in the sand bed of a foundry [36] are openings in the floor, but the space between the edge of a gallery and the wall of a bay in which a bridge was going to be placed,[37] and a dry dock [38] are not.

254 **Safe means of access and safe place of employment.** Whereas section 28 (1) deals with passages and stairs, including ladders, which in themselves

[28] *Taylor* v. *Gestetner* (1967) 2 K.I.R. 133.
[29] 1963 S.L.T. 37 but was reversed on another point by the H.L. [1964] 1 Lloyd's Rep. 73.
[30] *Dorman Long (Steel) Ltd.* v. *Bell*, *supra.*
[31] [1966] 1 W.L.R. 729 (employers failed within an hour of work starting to have some steps into an open courtyard leading to the administrative block of a factory cleared of ice).
[32] *Kimpton* v. *Steel Co. of Wales* [1960] 1 W.L.R. 527, reversing Edmund Davies J.'s decision (1959) 109 L.J. 362. A ramp over steps was not a staircase: *Roast* v. *Nortic Electrical* (1961) 111 L.J. 598.
[33] *Harris* v. *Rugby Portland Cement Co.* [1955] 1 W.L.R. 648.
[34] *Griffin* v. *London Transport Executive* [1950] 1 All E.R. 716; *Barrington* v. *Kent Rivers Catchment Board* [1947] 2 All E.R. 782.
[35] *Tate* v. *Swan Hunter & Wigham Richardson Ltd.* [1958] 1 W.L.R. 39.
[36] *Harrison* v. *Metropolitan-Vickers Electrical Co.* [1954] 1 W.L.R. 324.
[37] *Street* v. *British Electricity Authority* [1952] 2 Q.B. 399.
[38] *Bath* v. *British Transport Commissioners* [1954] 1 W.L.R. 1013.

are means of access, and with floors, which may well be used as a means of access, section 29 (1) is concerned with those unspecified things such as stagings and scaffolds, which have been erected for the purpose of getting to or at a place of work. It provides: " There shall, so far as reasonably practicable, be provided and maintained safe means of access to every place at which any person has at any time to work, and every such place shall, so far as is reasonably practicable, be made and kept safe for any person working there." As Denning L.J. has pointed out section 28 (1) " in regard to its specific means of access, imposes a higher obligation than section [29 (1)]. It enacts that they *shall be* properly maintained; whereas section [29 (1)] only requires that the means provided under it shall be maintained *so far as is reasonably practicable*." [39]

These latter italicised words qualify the duty to provide safe means of access and show that the duty is not absolute and the liability depends on whether or not the degree of risk outweighs the steps which are necessary to eliminate that risk.[40] In *Nimmo* v. *Alexander Cowan & Sons Ltd.*[41] the House of Lords held by a majority that the onus of proving that it was not reasonably practicable to keep the pursuer's place of work safe lay firmly upon the employers to discharge. The duty to provide and maintain a safe means of access is owed to every person working in the factory whether directly or indirectly employed by the occupier.[42] Furthermore the occupier will be liable even though the means of access belongs to independent contractors if it be used by the occupiers' workmen as well as those of the contractors.[43] The duty is a continuing and positive one to maintain the safety of the access,[44] whatever its form [45] and whatever other workmen are allowed to use it, even if it be not a recognised gangway.[46] There may be two or more means of access to a place of work and if they are all likely to be used, provisions of the section must be applied, but where " there is one safe route and the workman chooses another which it cannot reasonably be anticipated that he would choose " Devlin J. did not think that there could be any obligation in respect of that second route.[47] Nevertheless

[39] *Levesley* v. *Firth & Brown Ltd.* [1953] 1 W.L.R. 1206, 1209.

[40] *McCarthy* v. *Coldair* (1951) 2 T.L.R. 1226.

[41] [1968] A.C. 107 (Lord Reid and Lord Wilberforce dissenting); *Garner* v. *John Thompson (Wolverhampton) Ltd.* (1968) 112 S.J. 1006.

[42] *Whitby* v. *Burt, Boulton & Hayward Ltd.* [1947] K.B. 918; *Lavender* v. *Diamints Ltd.* [1949] 1 K.B. 585; *Whincup* v. *J. Woodhead & Sons* [1951] 1 All E.R. 387; *Wigley* v. *British Vinegars* [1964] A.C. 307. But s. 29 (1) has no application to a fireman acting in the course of his employment, because of the nature of his work: *Flannigan* v. *British Dyewood Co. Ltd.*, 1969 S.L.T. 223. On the other hand in *Keenan* v. *Rolls Royce*, 1970 S.L.T.(S.C.) 90 it was held that the duty extended to the careless and inattentive worker, whose inadvertent or indolent conduct may have exposed him to risk of injury, in the same way as the duties imposed by ss. 12–14.

[43] *Hosking* v. *De Havilland Aircraft Co. Ltd.* [1949] 1 All E.R. 540.

[44] *Callaghan* v. *Fred Kidd & Son (Engineers) Ltd.* [1944] 1 K.B. 560; *Alison* v. *Henry Bruce & Sons Ltd.*, 1951 S.L.T. 399.

[45] *McCarthy* v. *Coldair Ltd.*, *supra*; *Farquhar* v. *Chance Bros. Ltd.* [1951] W.N. 442; *Higgins* v. *Lyons & Co. Ltd.* (1941) 85 S.J. 93, C.A.

[46] *Hopwood* v. *Rolls Royce Ltd.* (1947) 176 L.T. 514, C.A.

[47] *Donovan* v. *Camell Laird & Co.* [1949] 2 All E.R. 82, 89. But see *Davies* v. *John G. Stein & Co. Ltd.*, 1965 S.L.T. 169 where there was an alternative place from which to work.

the duty imposed on the occupier is no more than to provide a way which will be safe when used with reasonable care and caution.[48]

1255 It is a question of fact and degree whether the means of access is "provided" or not. Where a workman had to work on a platform sixteen feet from the ground, the normal access to which, previously used by him, was by a ladder, of which there was a supply in store within reasonable distance of the platform, but the workman did not bother to fetch a ladder and tried to climb up and was killed, it was held a safe means of access had been provided.[49] As regards the word "maintain," until the decision of the Court of Appeal in *Levesley* v. *Firth & Brown* [50] there was a tendency for it to be construed as imposing a continuing duty to maintain the safety of the means of access.[51] However Denning L.J. said that, on a true construction, the section,[52] read together with the definition of "maintained" (contained in a later section) [53] did not impose "an absolute obligation to maintain safety, but a relative obligation to maintain efficiently. Once a safe means of access is provided, such as a passage or gangway, the occupier is not responsible for every temporary obstruction (such as a patch of oil or slipperiness) which may, through some accident or mischance, occur in it. If he has an efficient system, then to keep it clean and free from obstruction is all that can be reasonably demanded of him.[54] It is, indeed, all that is reasonably practicable. So regarded section [26] adds very little to the common law obligation between employers and workmen, and it has been so said on several occasions in this court." [55]

1256 "Safe" is the converse of dangerous and, as in those sections which apply to the fencing of dangerous machinery,[56] the test to be applied in each case of what is safe is that of reasonable foreseeability. Accordingly a means of access is not safe if it is a reasonably foreseeable cause of injury to anyone acting in a way that a human being may be reasonably expected

48 *Brown* v. *Redpath Brown & Co. Ltd.*, 1963 S.L.T. 219.
49 *Farquhar* v. *Chance Bros. Ltd.*, *supra*.
50 *Supra* (where the floor of a factory had a passageway marked by white lines and the plaintiff, when passing, found the way partly blocked by a lorry and in avoiding the lorry tripped over a piece of steel packing which projected into the way, he failed to recover damages because the obstruction was temporary and not a breach of the section).
51 *e.g. Callaghan* v. *Fred Kidd & Son* (*Engineers*) *Ltd.* [1944] K.B. 560 (tripped over some bars left lying on the factory floor near a grindstone although the obstruction was only temporary), which was thought to be decided wrongly in view of *Latimer* v. *A.E.C. Ltd.* [1953] A.C. 643.
52 Factories Act 1937, s. 26 (1), which corresponds to s. 29 (1) of the current 1961 Act.
53 *Ibid.* s. 152 (1) which corresponds to s. 176 (1) of the current 1961 Act.
54 *Cf.* the wording of this sentence with that reported in [1953] 2 All E.R. 869 [B].
55 *Levesley* v. *Firth & Brown Ltd.*, *supra*, at p. 1210. *Latimer* v. *A.E.C.* [1953] A.C. 643 (a gangway became slippery with a mixture of water and escaped cooling oil and had not been treated with sawdust); *Thomas* v. *Bristol Aeroplane Co.* [1954] 1 W.L.R. 694 (where the entrance to a factory was made slippery owing to a sudden fall of snow, which froze as it fell shortly before the men were due to start work, there was no breach of statutory duty); *Fawcett* v. *Smith's Dock Co.* [1951] 2 Lloyd's Rep. 299 (number of pipes on floor of a factory, was not a breach of statutory duty); *Woods* v. *W. H. Rhodes & Son Ltd.* (large wooden platform placed against wall of a shed but was dislodged when a door was opened).
56 See *ante*, § 1233 *et seq.*

to act in circumstances which may reasonably be expected to occur.[57] In order that a means of access may be safe it must be safe for all contingencies that can reasonably be foreseen, likely as well as unlikely, possible as well as probable,[58] the fact that human beings may not exercise a high degree of care for their own safety is a relevant matter to be taken into account.[59] However, a safe means of access does not become unsafe because of some isolated and extraneous act of negligence of another person such as where clouds of dust caused by the activities of a third party obfuscated a gangway, which was otherwise perfectly safe.[60]

The words " means of " which are added to " access " are probably to be construed as getting away from the idea of some definite track with an aspect of permanency.[61] Thus in *Gardiner* v. *Admiralty Commissioners* [62] where a workman carrying a bucket of boiling pitch tripped whilst walking across the deck of a vessel, which was undergoing repairs in the defender's shipyard, he was held to come within the protection of the subsection, its provisions being wide enough to cover means of access within a factory which passed over the article being manufactured or repaired.

1257 There is a distinction between a safe means of access and a safe place of work, although it is often difficult to distinguish between the two. Two examples are to be found in the facts of *Hopwood* v. *Rolls Royce Ltd.*[63] and *Dorman Long Ltd.* v. *Hillier*.[64] In the latter case Devlin J. commented on the judgment of Lord Greene M.R. in the former case: " it is said that a place may be, as I gather, at one and the same time both a means of access and a place of work. I should like to guard myself against saying that that proposition must now be regarded as authoritatively established. . . . If it can be held that a place may be at one and the same time a place of work and a means of access, then it is necessary to see for which purpose it is being used, or may require to be used, at the material time." Accordingly Devlin J. held that a workman moving about whilst at work is not using a means of access to a place where he has to work but it must be noted that the last words added to the subsection require that the working place as well as the means of access must also be kept safe.

[57] *Cf. Trott* v. *W. E. Smith (Erectors) Ltd.* [1957] 1 W.L.R. 1154 *per* Parker L.J. at p. 1162.
[58] *McCarthy* v. *Coldair Ltd., supra* (A ladder placed on a smooth surface and neither held nor stayed so that it slips while a man is climbing it, is not a safe means of access). See also *Canning* v. *Remington Rand Co.* (Ct. of Session) (1954) 104 L.J. 538; *Hill* v. *J. O. Buchanan Ltd.* 1965 S.L.T.(Notes) 24; *Garner* v. *John Thompson (Wolverhampton)* (1968) 112 S.J. 1006.
[59] *Sheppey* v. *Matthew T. Shaw & Co. Ltd.* [1952] 1 T.L.R. 1272.
[60] *Amis* v. *Smith's Dock Co. Ltd.* [1963] 1 Lloyd's Rep. 181.
[61] *Gardiner* v. *The Admiralty*, 1963 S.C. 399, *per* Lord Sorn.
[62] [1964] 1 W.L.R. 590 (H.L.).
[63] (1947) 176 L.T. 514. (Two workmen had to carry an aeroplane engine's cylinder head weighing some 89 lbs. to an inspection bench. As they started to move backwards with the load the plaintiff struck his foot against two other cylinder blocks which had been deposited on the floor during inspection, which caused him to stumble and fall so that his hand was badly crushed.)
[64] [1951] 1 All E.R. 357. (The workmen had to strip corrugated iron sheets off a factory roof, access to which was by way of a ladder and then by treading on purlin bars. One of the workmen had thus reached part of the roof and had removed a sheet and was standing on a purlin in the act of passing it down when he took a step backwards on to another sheet, which was perished, fell through it and was killed.)

The access must be to a place of work. A passage to a works canteen is not such a place [65] nor is the way to a lavatory.[66]

1258 Section 29 (2) provides: " Where any person has to work at a place from which he will be liable to fall a distance more than 6 feet 6 inches, then, unless the place is one which affords secure foothold and, where necessary, secure handhold, means shall be provided, so far as is reasonably practicable, by fencing or otherwise, for ensuring his safety." In order to give a meaning to the words " has to work " it would have to be established that the employer had ordered the workman to work at the place where he was injured or that it was the only practicable place where he could have performed the operation on which he was engaged which would be the equivalent of a compulsion to work there.[67] Accordingly where a workman, proceeding to repair a ventilator, fell from a high horizontal roof whilst lifting his ladders up on to it, it was held that the roof was a " place " at which he " had to work " and that a breach had been proved.[68]

In *Wigley* v. *British Vinegars Ltd.*[69] the House of Lords held that the " place from which " a window cleaner, using a ladder, is " liable to fall " within the meaning of the section is the ladder itself so that the section is complied with if the ladder provides secure foothold and, where necessary, secure handhold; meanwhile, a foothold does not fail to be secure merely because it is possible for someone to fall off it if the ladder otherwise be soundly constructed, properly positioned and was unlikely to slip. On the other hand the subsection is not intended to apply to a place where there is a secure foothold normally but from which a man may be thrown off by an abnormal occurrence, *viz.*, an explosion in the factory.[70]

1259 **Precautions with respect to explosive or inflammable dust, gas, vapour or substance.** (s. 31): section 31 (4) imposes an absolute duty and therefore it is irrelevant that the defendants did not know, in the events which happened, that an inflammable substance remained in the plant, tank or vessel.[71]

1260 **Accommodation for clothing.** (s. 59): failure to comply with the requirements of this section renders the occupier liable in damages. The obligation is not absolute, but in considering whether the accommodation is suitable the risk of theft must be taken into account.[72]

1261 **Removal of dust or fumes.** (s. 63): the duty under this section to take all

[65] *Davies* v. *De Havilland Aircraft Co.* [1951] 1 K.B. 50.
[66] *Rose* v. *Colvilles Ltd.*, 1950 S.L.T.(Notes) 72; *Cockady* v. *Bristol Siddeley Engines* (1965) 115 L.J. 661.
[67] *Davies* v. *John G. Stein & Co. Ltd.*, 1965 S.L.T. 169; but *cf. Cumming* v. *B.R.B.*, 1968 S.L.T. (Notes) 5.
[68] *Tisbury* v. *Ship Carbon Co. of Great Britain Ltd.* (1965) 109 S.J. 352.
[69] [1964] A.C. 307 approving *Lavender* v. *Diamints Ltd.* [1949] 1 K.B. 585.
[70] *Tinto* v. *Stewarts & Lloyds Ltd.*, 1962 S.L.T. 314.
[71] *Williams* v. *L. B. Holliday & Co. Ltd.* (1957) 107 L.J. 379.
[72] *McCarthy* v. *Daily Mirror Newspapers Ltd.* [1949] 1 All E.R. 801.

practicable [73] measures to protect workmen from inhaling dust or fumes involves, in a proper case, the provision of masks and the taking of steps to induce the workmen to wear them.[74] The obligation is not absolute, so that where the occupier has taken all measures for the protection of the workmen as were known to be possible at the time when the workman was injured he is not in breach of the section.[75] But he is in breach, if large amounts of dust are given off, the visible being harmless but the invisible dust being dangerous.[76] The burden of proving that the cause of his disease was the breach of the statute is on the workman and there is no presumption in his favour which the occupier has to rebut.[77] To come within the section, there must be given off either (1) a dust which is likely to be injurious or offensive to the persons employed in the sense of likely to be injurious according to the estimation of a reasonably well-informed factory occupier or which the actual occupier knew or ought to have known to be likely to be injurious, or (2) dust present, of any kind, in substantial quantities.[78] The obligation imposed by this section to take practicable measures to prevent dust accumulating in any workroom refers to an accumulation of deposited dust and not to dust settling on the skin of a workman.[79] The section does not apply to a boiler room which is not a workroom.[80]

In cases to which the Grinding of Metals (Miscellaneous Industries) Regulations 1925 as amended by the Blasting (Castings and Other Articles) Special Regulations 1949, apply, the section has no operative effect.[81]

1262 **Protection of eyes.** (s. 65): suitable goggles or protective screens must be provided to protect the eyes of the persons employed in the processes specified in regulations, being processes involving a special risk of injury to the eyes from particles or fragments thrown off in the processes. The Protection of Eyes Regulations 1938 [82] have been made under this section.

" Suitable " does not mean " perfect." It means suitable to protect the eyes in the process in which the man is employed. The obligation to provide suitable goggles is absolute but there is no absolute obligation that the goggles so provided shall ensure protection. So, when suitable goggles were provided but misted over and the workman partially removed them to

[73] *Ante*, § 1248. This must be judged in the light of the state of relevant knowledge at the date of the alleged breach; *Richards* v. *Highways Ironfounders* (*West Bromwich*) *Ltd.* [1955] 1 W.L.R. 1049.
[74] *Crookall* v. *Vickers-Armstrong Ltd.* [1955] 1 W.L.R. 659.
[75] *Adsett* v. *K. & L. Steelfounders & Engineers Ltd.* [1953] 1 W.L.R. 773.
[76] *Gregson* v. *Hick Hargreaves & Co. Ltd.* [1955] 1 W.L.R. 1252.
[77] *Mist* v. *Toleman & Sons* [1946] 1 All E.R. 139.
[78] *Ebbs* v. *James Whitsun & Co. Ltd.* [1952] 2 Q.B. 877; *Richards* v. *Highways Ironfounders* (*West Bromwich*) *Ltd.* [1957] 1 W.L.R. 781. The words " substantial quantity of dust " mean a substantial quantity of dust of which the occupier is or ought to be aware.
[79] *Graham* v. *Co-operative Wholesale Society Ltd.* [1957] 1 W.L.R. 511.
[80] *Brophy* v. *Bradfield Ltd.* [1955] 1 W.L.R. 1148.
[81] *Franklin* v. *Gramophone Co. Ltd.* [1948] 1 K.B. 542. For a case under the regulations, see *Bonnington Castings Ltd.* v. *Wardlaw* [1956] 2 W.L.R. 707.
[82] S.R. & O. 1938, No. 654.

clean them and, while he was doing so, a piece of metal entered his eye, there was no breach of the section.[83] Goggles which do not fit the workman are not suitable.[84]

1263 Goggles are " provided " if they are given to each man individually. Otherwise, " it would be necessary either that they should be put in a place where they come easily and obviously to the hand of the workman . . . or, at the very least, that he should be given clear directions where he is to get them." [85] Goggles are not " provided " if there be only one pair in the stores near to the three or four small grinders which all may be in operation at the same time by machine setters using the carborundum wheels for sharpening tools.[86]

The process specified in the regulations means a process carried on by the occupier. When an independent contractor was employed to make fresh bed-plates for machinery, the occupier was held not liable to one of the contractor's workmen who was injured when using a pneumatic pick to break up concrete owing to his not being provided with goggles.[87]

The process of " welding or cutting of metals by means of an electrical, oxyacetylene or similar process " applies only to a high temperature electrical process and not to a cold process.[88] " Plant," as used in the regulations, is not restricted to the plant of the occupier but means any object of a general kind which is riveted or bolted and from which cold rivets may be cut out or cut off.[89] Removing " runners " or " gates " from castings is not fettling metal castings,[90] nor is chipping a groove in a dressed and machined casting.[91]

1264 **Lifting excessive weights.** (s. 72): a person shall not be employed to lift, carry or move any load so heavy as to be likely to cause injury to him. Where the plaintiff, who had only one leg, and who, to his employers' knowledge had suffered from a previous strain, had been instructed to ask for assistance which was readily available should he ever require it to lift lengths of heavy chain, but failed to do so, his action for damages failed. At common law the employers were entitled to permit him to judge

[83] *Daniels* v. *Ford Motor Co. Ltd.* [1955] 1 W.L.R. 76. See also *Marshall* v. *Babcock & Wilcox*, 1961 S.L.T. 259, where the Lord President (Clyde) said, at p. 261, that regulation 8 (1) (c) of the Iron and Steel Foundries Regulations 1953 (S.I. 1953, No. 1464) " did not impose an absolute duty. What it requires is suitable protection to meet the dangers inherent in pouring molten metal. The requirement of suitability is related to the dangers envisaged in the operation. The goggles supplied did meet these dangers and as a protection they were complete. If suitability means something which has no inconveniences or drawbacks of any kind, as the pursuer's argument involves, then his construction of the regulation would mean that the defenders had a duty imposed upon them to do the impossible."

[84] *Lloyd* v. *F. Evans & Sons Ltd.* [1951] W.N. 306.

[85] *Finch* v. *Telegraph Co. Ltd.* [1949] 1 All E.R. 452, 454, *per* Devlin J.

[86] *Nolan* v. *Dental Manufacturing Co. Ltd.* [1958] 1 W.L.R. 936.

[87] *Whalley* v. *Briggs Motor Bodies Ltd.* [1954] 2 All E.R. 193 (the contractor was liable under s. 139 as the notional occupier of the factory).

[88] *Rees* v. *Bernard Hastie & Co. Ltd.* [1953] 1 Q.B. 328; *Hunter* v. *Singer Manufacturing Co. Ltd.* (1954) 104 L.J. 58.

[89] *Watts* v. *Enfield Rolling Mills Ltd.* [1952] 1 All E.R. 1013.

[90] *Williams* v. *Falkirk Iron Co. Ltd.* [1951] 1 All E.R. 294n.

[91] *Prophet* v. *Platt Bros. & Co.* [1961] 2 All E.R. 644.

whether or not he needed any help with the chains since he was the best and only judge of his own particular strength and capacity to do the job safely.[92]

1265 **Duties of persons employed.** (s. 143): persons employed must use any safety appliance provided. " It would, I think, be unfortunate if little or no responsibility were to be placed on the workmen themselves. Once a proper guard is provided, then the men are just as responsible as the occupier for seeing that it is used." [93] Where an experienced asbestos sheeter failed to use boards provided for his use on the factory roof where he was required to work, and fell through as a result, he did something likely to endanger himself and was therefore in breach of both subsections.[94]

The duty imposed on the workman that he shall not " wilfully interfere with or misuse " a machine, means " a perverse intermeddling " and not a mere " touching " or " misplacing " of a safety appliance.[95]

1266 **Power to make special regulations for safety.** (s. 76): the Minister, if he " is satisfied that any manufacture, machinery, plant, equipment appliance, process or description of manual labour is of such a nature as to cause risk of bodily injury to the persons employed[96] or any class of those persons," can " make such special regulations as appear to him to be reasonably practicable and to meet the necessity of the case." He can also " modify or extend . . . any provisions . . . imposing requirements as to health or safety." This power has been held to enable him to modify section 14 (relating to fencing),[97] and section 63 (relating to dust),[98] and it applies generally to any safety requirements in Parts I, II, and IV of the Act. Similar powers were contained in the Factory and Workshop Act 1901 and regulations made under the powers conferred by that Act continue in force until they are varied or revoked by an order made under the 1937 Act (s. 159), and now under the 1961 Act (s. 183 and 6th Schedule).

Under these powers, numerous regulations have been made and breach of these regulations imposes the same liability as breach of statutory duty. However these regulations are beyond the scope of this book.

92 *Peat* v. *N. J. Muschamp & Co.* (1969) 7 K.I.R. 469, C.A. *Per* Widgery L.J. where, however, such loads are of differing sizes, shapes and weights, an employer might be expected to give an employee some guidance as to when he should or should not seek assistance.

93 *Norris* v. *Syndic Manufacturing Co. Ltd.* [1952] 2 Q.B. 135, *per* Denning L.J. Failure to make use of appliance would be a ground for reducing damages.

94 *Ginty* v. *Belmont Building Supplies Ltd.* [1959] 1 All E.R. 414 (s. 119 (1) and (2) under the 1937 Act).

95 *Charles* v. *S. Smith & Sons (England) Ltd.* [1954] 1 W.L.R. 451.

96 The words " persons employed " are not limited to persons who are employed by the factory occupier or owner but include men doing work in the factory by whomsoever they are employed: *Massey-Harris-Ferguson (Manufacturing) Ltd.* v. *Piper* [1956] 2 Q.B. 396. See to the same effect, *Bryers* v. *Canadian Pacific Steamships Ltd.* [1957] 1 Q.B. 134 (a member of the crew of a ship, working on the ship while it is being repaired in a dry dock, is within the category of persons protected by the Shipbuilding Regulations 1931). This decision of the Court of Appeal was affirmed in *Canadian Pacific Steamships Ltd.* v. *Bryers* [1958] A.C. 485. Note that the 1931 Regulations have now been revoked by the Shipbuilding and Ship-Repairing Regulations 1960. Further see § 1230, *ante*.

97 *Miller* v. *William Boothman & Sons Ltd.* [1944] K.B. 337, approved by H.L. in *John Summers & Sons Ltd.* v. *Frost* [1955] A.C. 740.

98 *Franklin* v. *Gramophone Co. Ltd.* [1948] 1 K.B. 542.

(b) *The Offices, Shops and Railway Premises Act 1963*

1267 **Application of the Act.** The Offices, Shops and Railway Premises Act 1963 [99] received the Royal Assent on July 31, 1963, and by August 1, 1964, the majority of the sections had come into force by virtue of statutory instrument.[1] The Act followed, after fourteen years of silence and the relative inaction of successive governments, the recommendations of the Gowers Committee which reported in March 1949.[2] Its object was to set standards of health, welfare and safety for employees [2a] in office, shop and railway premises estimated to cover the employment of about eight million people engaged in the non-industrial field. These standards frequently follow those laid down for factories by the Factories Act 1961 and it will be noted that the wording of the latter Act has been adhered to quite deliberately where it was deemed relevant to the scope of this Act. However these two Acts are intended mutually to be exclusive in that no part of this Act applies to any premises which, for the purposes of the Factories Act 1961, form part of a factory.[3] This Act is like the Factories Act also in that its provisions are enforceable by criminal process whilst certain of its provisions, which are designed to promote safety, give rise to civil liability for damages.[4] On the other hand as regards a breach of a health provision, although the matter is not settled beyond doubt, the preponderance of authority is strongly in favour of permitting an action for damages in an appropriate case.[5] The expressions: " office premises "; " shop premises " and " railway premises " are all elaborately defined in section 1. Section 18 provides that no young person, namely a person who has not attained the age of eighteen, " shall clean any machinery used as, or forming, part of the equipment of the premises if doing so exposes him to risk of injury from a moving part of that or any adjacent machinery." Where a sixteen-year-old youth cleaned the blade of a bacon slicer by a dangerous and unauthorised method in the defendants' shop as a result of which he cut off the tip of a finger it was held that he had been " exposed to risk of injury from a moving part of machinery " within the meaning of the section.[6] Whether the operation is one which consists of " cleaning " is a pure question of fact. Thus in *Taylor* v. *Dawson* (*Mark*) *& Son Ltd.*[7] a child who was removing fluff from some rollers of a moving machine was

[99] Which superseded the Offices Act 1960, introduced by Mr. Richard Marsh, M.P. as a Private Member's Bill.

[1] The Offices Shops and Railway Premises Act 1963 (Commencement No. 1) Order 1964 (S.I. 1964 No. 191). See article on the Act, 114 L.J. 20.

[2] Cmnd. 7664. However the recommendations concerning the railway industry are given only limited effect whilst those which concerned theatres received no legislation in this Act.

[2a] Not for shop-customers: *Reid* v. *Galbraith's Stores* (1970) S.L.T.(Notes) 83.

[3] s. 85 (1).

[4] *Groves* v. *Wimborne* (*Lord*) [1898] 2 Q.B. 402; *Britannic Merthyr Coal Co. Ltd.* v. *David* [1910] A.C. 74; *Black* v. *Fife Coal Co. Ltd.* [1912] A.C. 149.

[5] This is so under the Factories Act 1961 hence by parity of reasoning for a breach of a cognate provision of the Act an action in damages will lie. See *McCarthy* v. *Daily Mirror Newspapers Ltd.* [1949] 1 All E.R. 801; *Nicholson* v. *Atlas Steel Foundry and Engineering Co. Ltd.* [1957] 1 W.L.R. 613; *Clarkson* v. *Modern Foundries Ltd.* [1957] 1 W.L.R. 1210.

[6] *Dewhurst* (*J. H.*) *Ltd.* v. *Coventry Corpn.* [1970] 1 Q.B. 20.

[7] [1911] 1 K.B. 145.

held to be cleaning the machine, since the fluff would have clogged it up, despite the fact the fluff was intended to be collected and sold because it had a commercial value. In order for a part of a machine to be " a moving part " within the meaning of the section it does not have to be in motion or in use at the relevant time.[8] Section 19 goes on to deal with the training and supervision of persons working at dangerous machines, which is similar in terms to those contained in the Factories Act 1961 [9] which, although it applies only to " young persons," imposes no duty on such a person whereby he would become disentitled to claim against his employers.[10]

1268 Section 23 provides that: " No person shall, in the course of his work in premises to which this Act applies, be required to lift, carry or move a load so heavy as to be likely to cause injury to him." In *Kinsella* v. *Harris Lebus Ltd.*[11] it was held that the provision was designed to give protection against excessive weight lifting only and that 145 lbs. was not likely to cause injury to an experienced man setting about the task in a sensible and normal manner. However, as the employers' system of work had left the individual employee to decide whether or not he needed assistance they had not in the circumstances discharged their duty of care which they owed to the plaintiff.

Section 67 provides that it shall be a defence for a person charged with a contravention of the Act to prove that he " used all due diligence " to secure compliance with that provision. Whilst this may enable an occupier to escape his criminal liability it cannot be a defence to his civil liability unless, of course, the employee alone was responsible for causing the breach of statutory duty and as a result thereby sustained his injury.[12]

(c) *The Agriculture (Safety, Health and Welfare Provisions) Act 1956*

1269 **Application of the Act.** This Act, which came in force on July 5, 1956, is the first Act to provide comprehensively for securing the safety and protection of farm workers and children arising out of the use, in connection with agriculture, of vehicles, machinery and implements. It is based on certain recommendations of the Gowers Committee, which reported in March 1949,[13] following a wide inquiry on health, welfare and safety generally in non-industrial employment of which this Act and the Offices, Shops and Railway Premises Act 1963 were the more important, if belated, products. Section 24 (1) defines " agriculture " as including dairy farming, the production of any consumable produce which is grown for sale or for consumption or other use for the purposes of a trade or business or of any

8 *Kelly* v. *John Dale Ltd.* [1965] 1 Q.B. 185 (under the comparable sections of the Factories Act 1961).
9 *Viz.*, s. 21.
10 *M'Cafferty* v. *Brown*, 1950 S.C. 300.
11 (1963) 108 S.J. 14, C.A. (which concerned the corresponding section of the Factories Act 1961, *viz.*, s. 72).
12 See *Gallagher* v. *Dorman Long & Co. Ltd.* [1947] 2 All E.R. 38, C.A.
13 Cmnd. 7664.

other undertaking (whether carried on for profit or not), and the use of land as grazing meadow or pasture land or orchard or osier land or woodland or for market gardens or nursery grounds. Meanwhile section 1 of the Act authorises the making of regulations for the protection of " workers employed in agriculture against risks of bodily injury or injury to health arising out of the use of any machinery, plant, equipment or appliance, the carrying on of any operation, the use of any process or the management of animals, for securing to such workers safe places to work in and safe means of access thereto and for protecting them against risks of bodily injury arising out of their falling through apertures in floors or walls, or from their work places, or while ascending or descending staircases or ladders." It follows that, before the Act could become fully effective regulations had to be made to cover the various headings (*a*) to (*h*) contained in subsection (3), and many of these have been made now.

1270 The Act also allowed for the making of orders [14] to repeal the Chaff-Cutting Machines (Accidents) Act 1897 and the Threshing Machines Act 1878. This earlier Act of 1878 provided for the fencing of steam threshing machines, and liability is imposed not only on the owner of the machine but also on the person for whose service or benefit it is worked. Where the operator of the machine left the feeding box but failed to close the protective door as it was his duty to do, and, on his return, took an incautious step so that his leg went through the feeding mouth and was injured, both the owner of the machine and the farmer were held liable. The farmer was given a complete indemnity against the owner, and the operator was held one-third to blame.[15] Now the Act of 1897 has been repealed by the Chaff-Cutting Machines (Accidents) Act 1897 (Repeal) (Appointed Day) Order 1961,[16] which appoints July 14, 1961, as the day on which it is repealed; similarly the Act of 1878 has been repealed by the Threshing Machines Act 1878 (Repeal) (Appointed Day) Order 1961,[17] which appoints August 1, 1961, as the day on which it is repealed. From those specified dates the Acts are replaced by the Agriculture (Stationary Machines) Regulations 1959 [18] and the Agriculture (Threshers and Balers) Regulations 1960,[19] respectively.

14 *Ibid.* s. 1 (7).
15 *Jones* v. *Richards* [1955] 1 W.L.R. 444.
16 S.I. 1961, No. 1108.
17 S.I. 1961, No. 1109.
18 S.I. 1959, No. 1216.
19 S.I. 1960, No. 1199.

CHAPTER 19

THE FATAL ACCIDENTS ACTS

1.—NATURE OF THE ACTION

1271 **Nature of the action.**[1] The Fatal Accidents Acts 1846 to 1959 give a right of action to certain specified dependants of a deceased person for the pecuniary loss they have suffered from the death of that person.

Lord Campbell's Act, *viz.*, the Fatal Accidents Act 1846, s. 1,[2] provides: "... whensoever the death of a person shall be caused by wrongful act, neglect, or default, and the act, neglect, or default is such as would (if death had not ensued) have entitled the party injured to maintain an action and recover damages in respect thereof, then and in every such case the person [3] who would have been liable if death had not ensued shall be liable to an action for damages, notwithstanding the death of the person injured, [and although the death shall have been caused under such circumstances as amount in law to felony]."

The Act gives a new cause of action, which is not the same as the deceased would have had if he had been injured and not killed.[4] "The statute ... gives to the personal representative a cause of action beyond that which the deceased would have if he had survived, and based on a different principle." [5] The principle on which it is based is that of giving to the dependants, for the financial loss they have sustained through the death statutory compensation payable by the wrongdoer. Death is essentially the cause of action.[6] The damages recoverable do not form part of the estate of the deceased,[7] so as to pass by his will or on an intestacy, and are not measured by the loss his estate has sustained by his death.

1272 To maintain an action under the statute there must be proved (1) that the deceased person was injured by the wrongful act, neglect or default of the defendant; (2) that he died in consequence of such injury; (3) that at the time he died he had a right to recover damages; and (4) that the beneficiaries have suffered pecuniary loss from his death.[8] All these things must

1 See article: " Fatal Accidents—Damages " (Hoskins) (1967) 117 New L.J. 4.

2 The words in square brackets are repealed by the Criminal Law Act 1967, s. 10 (2) and Sched. 3.

3 Includes bodies politic and corporate: s. 5.

4 *Seward* v. " *Vera Cruz* " (1884) 10 App.Cas. 59 *per* Lord Blackburn, at pp. 70, 71: " an action which ... is new in its species, new in its quality, new in its principle, in every way new."

5 *Per* Erle C.J. in *Pym* v. *Great Northern Ry.* (1863) 4 B. & S. 396.

6 *Seward* v. " *Vera Cruz* " *supra, per* Lord Selborne at p. 67.

7 See *Marginson* v. *Blackburn B.C.* [1939] 2 K.B. 426.

8 Somewhat surprisingly Crichton J. held that the widow and children of a deceased criminal were not entitled to maintain claims under the Fatal Accidents Acts for loss of support from his " earnings," since such claims arose *ex turpi causa*: *Burns* v. *Edman* [1970] 2 Q.B. 541. It is submitted that this cannot be the correct approach to such a problem. See further the pertinent comments, in the article: " Damages—The Sins of the Fathers," 119 New L.J. 1083, with which the editor agrees.

be proved, and failure in any one of them is fatal to the cause of action.[9] A breach of contract causing death is an act, neglect or default within the meaning of the statute.[10]

1273 **The death.** The action lies " notwithstanding the death of the person injured, [and although the death shall have been caused under such circumstances as amount in law to felony]." [11] This will include the case of suicide committed by the injured person as a result of insanity due to the defendant's negligence,[12] and of a suicide even when he was not at the time insane according to the test of the M'Naughten Rules where such death was directly traceable to the injuries sustained in the accident for which the defendants were responsible.[13]

1274 **Right of deceased to sue had death not ensued.** As it must be shown that the deceased, had he not died, would have been able to maintain the action, it follows that the defence can set up anything which would have negatived the right of the deceased himself to bring the action,[14] so that at one time both contributory negligence [15] and common employment [16] were defences. Now, the contributory negligence of the deceased will not defeat the claim of the dependants but may cause their damages to be reduced. By the Law Reform (Contributory Negligence) Act 1945, s. 1 (4), " Where any person dies as a result partly of his own fault and partly of the fault of any other person or persons, and accordingly if an action were brought for the benefit of the estate under the Law Reform (Miscellaneous Provisions) Act 1934 the damages recoverable would be reduced under subsection (1) of this section, any damages recoverable in an action brought for the benefit of the dependants of that person under the Fatal Accidents Acts, 1846 to [1908], shall be reduced to a proportionate extent." If the deceased had, during his lifetime, by contract relieved the defendant from liability for his wrongful act, neglect or default, an action cannot be successfully brought under the statute. Accordingly, when a passenger on a steamship took a ticket containing a condition: " The company will not be responsible for

[9] *Nunan* v. *Southern Ry.* [1923] 2 K.B. 703, *per* Swift J.; affd. [1924] 1 K.B. 223.
[10] *Grein* v. *Imperial Airways Ltd.* [1937] 1 K.B. 50.
[11] Fatal Accidents Act, s. 1. The words in square brackets are repealed by the Criminal Law Act 1967, s. 10 (2) and Sched. 3.
[12] See *Withers* v. *L.B. & S.C. Ry.* [1916] 2 K.B. 772 and *Dixon* v. *Sutton Heath & Lee Green Colliery* (1930) 23 B.W.C.C. 135, decisions under the Workmen's Compensation Acts. For a discussion of the meaning of insanity in this connection see A. G. Davis in 59 L.Q.R. 202.
[13] *Pigney* v. *Pointers Transport Services Ltd.* [1957] 2 All E.R. 807. (a man, injured through his employers' negligence, suffered from anxiety neurosis and depression and committed suicide 18 months later). In *Farmer* v. *Rash* [1969] 1 W.L.R. 160, where it was in issue whether or not the suicide's death was directly traceable to the injuries received in the accident, Willis J. concluded that, as the likelihood of the executor succeeding under the Fatal Accidents Acts claim was so remote, he would decline to apportion any of the damages under those Acts but awarded the whole under the Law Reform (Miscellaneous Provisions) Act 1934. (The deceased was normally of a naturally cheerful disposition but became increasingly depressed after the accident so that a year later he killed himself by slashing his wrists and taking an overdose of pills.)
[14] See *per* Scrutton L.J. in *Nunan* v. *Southern Ry.* [1924] 1 K.B. 223, 228.
[15] *Senior* v. *Ward* (1859) 1 E. & E. 385; *Nunan* v. *Southern Ry.*, *supra.*
[16] *Coldrick* v. *Partridge, Jones & Co.* [1910] A.C. 77.

. . . any loss or damage arising from the perils of the sea . . . or from any act, neglect or default whatsoever of the pilot, master or mariners," and was drowned owing to the negligent navigation of the company's servants, the dependants were held to have no cause of action.[17] Again, where the deceased had a free pass issued on the condition that the defendants were " relieved from all responsibility for any injury, delay, loss, or damage, however caused, that may be sustained by the person or persons using this pass," and was drowned owing to the negligence of the defendant's servants, it was held that the condition prevented his dependants from recovering damages.[18] On the other hand, a contract by the deceased for a passage by air on the terms: " Passengers . . . are accepted for carriage only upon condition that, except in so far as liability is expressly provided for in these conditions of carriage, no liability whatsoever is accepted by the carriers . . . and upon condition that (except in so far as liability is expressly provided for in these conditions) the passenger renounces for himself and his representatives all claims for compensation for damage in connection with the carriage " and " carriers are not liable if they prove that they and their agents have taken all necessary measures to avoid the damage, or that it was impossible for them to take such measures," does not entirely exclude all liability to the passenger, and accordingly his dependants can recover damages if the carrier fails to prove that he has taken all necessary measures to avoid damage or that it was impossible to take such measures.[19] A contract made by the deceased limiting the amount of damages payable on his death is not binding on the dependants.[20]

1275 The dependants cannot sue if the deceased in his lifetime compromised his claim for damages in respect of the act which later resulted in his death,[21] or if the provisions of some statute have taken away any claim he would have had in his lifetime and substituted other rights,[22] or if the deceased's cause of action has been barred by the Statutes of Limitation in his lifetime.[23]

The dependants of a deceased alien can sue when the circumstances are such that they could have sued had he not been an alien.[24]

2.—BY WHOM ACTION CAN BE BROUGHT

1276 **By whom action can be brought.** The Fatal Accidents Act 1846,[25] s. 2,

[17] *Haigh* v. *Royal Mail Steam Packet Co.* [1883] W.N. 151. *Griffiths* v. *Dudley* (1882) 9 Q.B.D. 357, is another case of contracting out.

[18] *The Stella* [1900] P. 161.

[19] *Grein* v. *Imperial Airways Ltd* (1935) 52 T.L.R. 28, reversed on other grounds [1937] 1 K.B. 50.

[20] *Nunan* v. *Southern Ry.* [1923] 2 K.B. 703, and *post*, § 1295.

[21] *Read* v. *Great Eastern Ry.* (1868) L.R. 3 Q.B. 555. *Cf. Nunan* v. *Southern Ry.*, *supra.*

[22] *Walpole* v. *Canadian Northern Ry.* [1923] A.C. 113 (right barred by the Workmen's Compensation Act of British Columbia); *McColl* v. *Canadian Pacific Ry.* [1923] A.C. 126 (right barred by Railway Act of Canada).

[23] *Williams* v. *Mersey Docks and Harbour Board* [1905] 1 K.B. 804; *British Columbia Electric Ry.* v. *Gentile* [1914] A.C. 1034. Further, see s. 4—time within which action must be brought, *post*, § 1281.

[24] *Davidsson* v. *Hill* [1901] 2 K.B. 606.

[25] For a situation where the deceased person's administratrix herself subsequently dies see *Voller* v. *Dairy Produce Packers Ltd.* [1962] 1 W.L.R. 960.

provides: " Every such action . . . shall be brought by and in the name of the executor or administrator of the person deceased. . . ."

The Fatal Accidents Act 1864, s. 1, provides: " If and so often as it shall happen . . . in any of the cases intended and provided for by the said Act [1846 Act], that there shall be no executor or administrator of the person deceased, or that there being such executor or administrator no such action as in the said Act mentioned shall within six calendar months after the death of such deceased person . . . have been brought by and in the name of his or her executor or administrator, then and in every such case such action may be brought by and in the name or names of all or any of the persons (if more than one) for whose benefit such action would have been, if it had been brought by and in the name of such executor or administrator; and every action so to be brought shall be for the benefit of the same person or persons, and shall be subject to the same regulations and procedure, as nearly as may be, as if it were brought by and in the name of such executor or administrator."

1277 If there be no executor or administrator, one of the dependants may bring an action within six months, without first waiting to see if a personal representative will be appointed.[26] If an administrator is subsequently appointed and brings an action, the court will not stay an action already brought by a dependant in good faith before the date of the appointment.[27] An action brought by the plaintiff as administrator before letters of administration are taken out is a nullity, and a subsequent grant does not relate back so as to validate the action.[28] A dependant suing as administrator before obtaining a grant will not be allowed to amend his pleadings to enable him to sue as a dependant if the effect of the amendment would be to deprive the defendant of the opportunity of pleading that the action is out of time.[29] If the plaintiff, before taking out administration, sues as " widow and administratrix " without specifying the identity of those whom she represents, the claim under the Fatal Accidents Acts will be good,[30] but if she is described in the writ as the administratrix and in the statement of claim as the widow and administratrix of the deceased, the action must be dismissed if administration has not been taken out before the issue of the writ.[31]

1278 The Fatal Accidents Act 1846, s. 3, provides, ". . . not more than one action shall lie for and in respect of the same subject matter of complaint." This does not prevent the personal representative, who has recovered damages for the benefit of the dependants under the Fatal Accidents Acts, from bringing a subsequent action for damage to the estate of the deceased. The action may be either in contract at common law, as where a railway

26 *Holleran* v. *Bagnell* (1879) 4 L.R.Ir. 740.
27 *M'Cabe* v. *G.N. Ry. of Ireland* [1899] 2 Ir.R. 123.
28 *Ingall* v. *Moran* [1944] K.B. 160.
29 *Hilton* v. *Sutton Steam Laundry* [1946] K.B. 65; *Burns* v. *Campbell* [1952] 1 K.B. 15.
30 *Stebbings* v. *Holst & Co. Ltd.* [1953] 1 All E.R. 925.
31 *Finnegan* v. *Cementation Co. Ltd.* [1953] 1 Q.B. 688.

season ticket-holder was killed by the negligence of the railway company, and it was held that an action for damages caused through his being unable to attend to his business during illness and for the expenses of medical attendance and nursing was not barred by the recovery of damages under the Fatal Accidents Acts,[32] or in tort under the Law Reform (Miscellaneous Provisions) Act 1934 for the loss of expectation of life.[33]

An action under the Fatal Accidents Acts can be made the subject of an application for summary judgment under Order 14.[34]

3.—FOR WHOSE BENEFIT THE ACTION IS BROUGHT

1279 **Persons to benefit.** The Fatal Accidents Act 1846, s. 2, further provides: " Every such action shall be for the benefit of the wife, husband, parent, and child of the person whose death shall have been so caused. . . ." The word " parent " includes father, mother, grandfather, grandmother, stepfather and stepmother, and " child " includes son, daughter, grandson, grand-daughter, stepson and step-daughter.[35] A posthumous child is included,[36] and so is an illegitimate child and an adopted child.[37] It will be noted that originally brothers and sisters *inter alia* of the deceased were not included, but this omission has been remedied now by the Fatal Accidents Act 1959 where the class of persons for whose benefit or by whom an action may be brought has been extended to include " any person who is, or is the issue of, a brother, sister, uncle or aunt of the deceased person."

The plaintiff must deliver full particulars of the person or persons on whose behalf the action is brought, and the nature of the claim made,[38] but he is not required in his statement of claim to negative the existence of other dependants.[39]

1280 Only one action can be brought on behalf of the dependants,[40] so that a dependant who is neither a plaintiff nor a person named in the particulars as a person on whose behalf the action is brought at the time when judgment is given has no claim against the wrongdoer. He cannot bring a

[32] *Leggott* v. *G.N. Ry.* (1876) 1 Q.B.D. 599; *Bradshaw* v. *L. & Y. Ry.* (1875) L.R. 10 C.P. 189; *Potter* v. *Metropolitan Ry.* (1875) 32 L.T. 36.
[33] *May* v. *McAlpine & Sons* [1938] 3 All E.R. 85.
[34] *Dummer* v. *Brown* [1953] 1 Q.B. 710.
[35] Fatal Accidents Act 1846, s. 5.
[36] *The George and Richard* (1871) L.R. 3 A. & E. 446.
[37] Fatal Accidents Act 1959, which repealed but re-enacted the Law Reform (Miscellaneous Provisions) Act 1934, s. 2 (1), which added these persons.
[38] Fatal Accidents Act 1846, s. 4. The particulars are properly set out in the statement of claim. *Stebbings* v. *Holst & Co. Ltd.* [1953] 1 All E.R. 925; *Cooper* v. *Williams* [1963] 2 Q.B. 567.
[39] *Barnes* v. *Ward* (1850) 9 C.B. 392.
[40] Fatal Accidents Act 1846, s. 3. This does not affect the position where a plaintiff desires to join several claims in one action, although leave must first be obtained under R.S.C., Ord. 15, r. 1 (1) (*c*), and, where such joinder will not cause inconvenience, it may be allowed (reversing *Tredegar* v. *Roberts* [1914] 1 K.B. 283, where the joinder was not allowed under the former rule). Thus where arising out of the same accident a widow has a claim in her personal capacity for personal injuries and also a claim as administratrix of the estate of her husband under the Fatal Accidents Acts and the Law Reform (Miscellaneous Provisions) Act she may now obtain leave to join these claims in one action, and leave in such cases will normally be granted as a matter of course.

second action. The dependants not named cannot appear by counsel at the trial and give evidence of dependency or apply to be joined as parties [41]; but they may apply to be named as dependants in the particulars.[42] Thus a widow was permitted to intervene in and to be added as one of the persons for whose benefit the action was brought in an action brought by the deceased's illegitimate child, who had taken out a summons to approve a settlement and to stay all further proceedings. It was held by the Court of Appeal that an irregularity which can be cured is never a nullity and that a stay of proceedings is not equivalent to a discontinuance or to a judgment for the plaintiff or the defendant, but might be removed on proper grounds being shown.[43] The plaintiff sues as trustee for the dependants as a class [44] and it is therefore his duty to set out in the particulars the names of all persons claiming to be dependants and to put before the court the evidence on which they base their claims. Failure to do this will render him liable in equity to account to the dependant for the sum the dependant would have received if he had been included in the particulars as a dependant.[45] Possibly, also, the person claiming to be a dependant can obtain an order against the plaintiff compelling the plaintiff to add him as a dependant.[46]

4.—TIME WITHIN WHICH ACTION MUST BE BROUGHT

281 **Limitation of Action.** The Fatal Accidents Act 1846, s. 3 (as amended by the Law Reform (Limitation of Actions, etc.) Act 1954, s. 3) provides: " every such action shall be commenced within three years after the death of such deceased person." [47] Time therefore runs from the death and not from the date of the wrongful act, neglect or default which is the subject of the complaint.[48] But to enable a plaintiff to bring such an action the deceased must have been able to bring an action at the date of his death,[49] so that if at that date his right of action is already barred, *e.g.* under the Limitation Act 1939 the right of action under the Fatal Accidents Acts is also barred.[50] If, however, the deceased died before his right of action was barred, it would appear that an action under the Fatal Accidents Acts may be brought, provided that three years have not elapsed since the death of the deceased, even though his right of action would have become barred meanwhile, had he survived.[51]

5.—THE MEASURE OF DAMAGES

282 **Measure of Damages.** The Fatal Accidents Act 1846, s. 2, provides:

41 *Steele* v. *G.N. Ry.* (1890) 26 L.R.Ir. 96; *Johnston* v. *G.N. Ry.* (1887) 20 L.R.Ir. 4 (where evidence on behalf of the dependant was allowed).

42 *Per* Lord Atkin in *Avery* v. *L.N.E. Ry.* [1938] A.C. 606, 613.

43 *Cooper* v. *Williams, supra.*

44 *Bradshaw* v. *L. & Y. Ry.* (1875) L.R. 10 C.P. 189, *per* Grove J.

45 *Condliff* v. *Condliff* (1874) 29 L.T. 831.

46 *Per* Lord Atkin in *Avery* v. *L.N.E. Ry.* [1938] A.C. 606, 613.

47 There may be a contract not to plead this section: *Lubovsky* v. *Snelling* [1944] K.B. 44.

48 *British Columbia Electric Ry.* v. *Gentile* [1914] A.C. 1034; *Venn* v. *Tedesco* [1926] 2 K.B. 227.

49 Fatal Accidents Act 1846, s. 1.

50 *Williams* v. *Mersey Docks and Harbour Board* [1905] 1 K.B. 804.

51 *Venn* v. *Tedesco* [1926] 2 K.B. 227; following *British Columbia Electric Ry.* v. *Gentile* [1914] A.C. 1034.

" in every such action the jury may give such damages as they may think proportioned to the injury resulting from such death to the parties respectively for whom and for whose benefit such action shall be brought."

The measure of damages is the pecuniary loss suffered by the dependants as a result of the death. " What the court has to try to ascertain in these cases is: How much have the widow and family lost by the father's death? " [52] No damages can be given for the mental sufferings they have undergone or by way of solatium for their wounded feelings or the pain and suffering of the deceased.[53] The pecuniary loss in question means the actual financial benefit of which the dependants have in fact been deprived, whether the benefit was a result of a legal obligation or of what may reasonably have been expected to take place in the future. It is the amount of the pecuniary benefit which it is reasonably probable the dependants would have received if the deceased had remained alive.[54] " Legal liability alone is not the test of injury in respect of which damages may be recovered under Lord Campbell's Act . . . the reasonable expectation of pecuniary advantage to the relation remaining alive may be taken into account. . . and damages may be given in respect of that expectation being disappointed." [55] Accordingly, where the deceased was a bachelor, aged twenty-seven, living away from his parents' home, and he used to make gifts worth about £20 a year to his parents, the parents were held entitled to damages on his death.[56] The pecuniary advantage need not have been received in the form of money or goods, but may have been derived from services rendered by the deceased. So, a workman was held entitled to recover damages for the death of his wife, because she used to do his housekeeping and on her death he had to employ and pay a housekeeper who was not able to manage as economically as his wife used to do.[57] If, however, the services rendered by the deceased were paid for by the dependant at the ordinary rate of wages, there will be no pecuniary loss from the death, as the dependant will be able to employ another person to do the same work at the same price. This occurred where a father employed his son as a bricklayer at the ordinary rate of wages and it was held that on the death of the son the father suffered no pecuniary loss.[58]

1283 The pecuniary benefit derived from the deceased must have arisen from

[52] *Heatley* v. *Steel Company of Wales Ltd.* [1953] 1 W.L.R. 405, *per* Lord Goddard C.J. at p. 408.

[53] *Blake* v. *Midland Ry.* (1852) 18 Q.B. 93; *Davies* v. *Powell Duffryn Associated Collieries Ltd.* [1942] A.C. 601, 607, *per* Lord Wright: " There is no question here of what may be called sentimental damage, bereavement or pain and suffering. It is a hard matter of pounds, shillings and pence, subject to the element of reasonable future probabilities."

[54] *Pym* v. *G.N. Ry.* (1863) 4 B. & S. 396, *per* Erle C.J. In *Preston* v. *Hunting Air Transport* [1956] 1 Q.B. 454, in addition to financial loss, £400 was awarded for " damage possibly of a more intangible character by reason of the loss of their mother."

[55] *Dalton* v. *S.E. Ry.* (1858) 4 C.B.(N.S.) 296, *per* Willes J.

[56] *Ibid.* The jury awarded £80 to the father and £40 to the mother.

[57] *Berry* v. *Humm & Co.* [1915] 1 K.B. 627. The jury awarded £50 of which Scrutton J. apportioned £35 for loss of services and £15 for extra cost of management by a housekeeper. *Cf. Feay* v. *Barnwell* [1938] 1 All E.R. 31 (£625 awarded). In *Burgess* v. *Florence Nightingale Hospital* [1955] 1 All E.R. 511, £2,000 was awarded for loss of the wife's services.

[58] *Sykes* v. *N.E. Ry.* (1875) 44 L.J.C.P. 191.

the relationship and not from any other cause. Where a man and his wife were professional dancing partners, earning jointly more than the sum they would each have earned separately, and the wife died from the defendant's negligence, it was held that the loss to the husband of the value of his wife as a dancing partner, assessed at £2,500, could not be taken into account.[59] On the other hand, where the plaintiff had been employed by her late husband's private company, which was a " one-man " business, at a yearly salary in the £600–£800 range but had lost this income since the company could no longer function without the deceased, the Court of Appeal valued her services to the company at £200, which fell to be deducted, and held that as the balance of her salary represented a pecuniary benefit derived from the marital status she was entitled to recover damages for such loss.[60]

When a husband and wife, each with separate incomes, are living together and sharing their expenses so that their joint expenses are less than twice the expenses of each living separately, each confers a financial benefit on the other so that on the death of the wife the husband is entitled to damages.[60]

When the deceased had covenanted to pay his mother an annuity of £200 during their joint lives, it was held that the jury were entitled to take into account the probable duration of the lives of the deceased and his mother and to award the present value of such an annuity, not on the basis that it was as valuable as a government annuity or one secured by a good insurance company, but having regard to the manner in which it was secured and the circumstances of the covenantor.[61]

284 A reasonable expectation of pecuniary benefit can be established by showing that the deceased has in the past contributed to the support of the dependants, and from that fact it can be inferred that the support would be continued in the future. If the deceased had not attained his full earning capacity, damages can be given on the assumption that his contributions would increase as his earning capacity increased. So, where a father was old and getting infirm and the son was young and earning good wages and assisted his father in some work for which the father was paid 3s. 6d. a week, it was held that the father was entitled to damages on the death of the son.[62] Again, where the deceased was a boy fourteen years old who had earned 4s. a week for a year or two but was unemployed at his death, it was held that his father, a working mason, was entitled to damages.[63] Also, where the deceased was an unmarried man twenty-nine years old

[59] *Burgess* v. *Florence Nightingale Hospital*, *supra*. See also *Grzelak* v. *Harefield and Northwood Hospital Management Committee* (1968) 112 S.J. 195.

[60] *Malyon* v. *Plummer* [1964] 1 Q.B. 330. In assessing her damages one of the considerations to be disregarded is the increase in value of her shares in the company as a result of an insurance by the company on her husband's life, because s. 2 (1) of the Fatal Accidents Act 1959 applies to that benefit.

[61] *Rowley* v. *L. & N.W. Ry.* (1873) L.R. 8 Ex. 221.

[62] *Franklin* v. *S.E. Ry.* (1858) 3 H. & N. 211. An award by the jury of £75 was held by the court to be excessive.

[63] *Duckworth* v. *Johnson* (1859) 4 H. & N. 653. The jury awarded £20.

whose father was nearly blind and injured in his head and legs, and the deceased had helped his father five or six years before when the father was out of work for six months, a ruling by the trial judge that there was no evidence of pecuniary loss to the father was overruled on appeal.[64]

1285 It is not necessary that the deceased should have been actually earning wages at the death if there is a reasonable expectation that wages will be earned in the future, with the result that financial benefit will accrue to the dependants. Accordingly, where the deceased was a girl of sixteen who was nearing the completion of her apprenticeship as a dressmaker and would then have been likely to make substantial earnings in the near future, it was held that her parents were entitled to damages.[65] " The fact of past contribution may be important in strengthening the probability of future pecuniary advantage, but it cannot be a condition precedent to the existence of such a probability." [66] On the other hand, a mere speculative possibility of pecuniary benefit in the future is not enough. Where the deceased was a boy of four and the father was in business earning about £1,000 a year, it was held that there was no reasonable expectation of pecuniary benefit.[67] " The boy was subject to all the risks of illness, disease, accident and death. His education and upkeep would have been a substantial burden to the plaintiff for many years if he had lived. He might or might not have turned out a useful young man. He would have earned nothing till about sixteen years of age. He might never have aided his father at all. He might have proved a mere expense. I cannot adequately speculate one way or the other." [68]

Damages for dependent children are to be assessed as a broad question of fact for a jury [69] and no damages can be awarded to an orphaned child for the fact that he will receive less care from a nurse than from his mother, since it is only the financial loss which is recoverable.[70] Where a wife and an infant daughter are both claimants under the Acts but the wife dies soon after the husband from unallied causes with the husband's fatal accident, the dependency of the daughter should be separately assessed.[71]

In the case of illegitimate children, it is sufficient proof of pecuniary loss to show that they were living with the deceased, their father, and their mother (who was not a dependant because she was unmarried) and derived benefit out of the housekeeping allowance made by their father to their mother.[72]

1286 **Loss of expectation of pecuniary advantage.** Damages are awarded for

64 *Hetherington* v. *N.E. Ry.* (1882) 9 Q.B.D. 160.
65 *Taff Vale Ry.* v. *Jenkins* [1913] A.C. 1; *Wathen* v. *Vernon* [1970] R.T.R. 471.
66 *Per* Lord Moulton in the case last cited.
67 *Barnett* v. *Cohen* [1921] 2 K.B. 461.
68 *Ibid. per* McCardie J. at p. 472.
69 *Kassam* v. *Kampala Aerated Water Co.* [1965] 1 W.L.R. 668.
70 *Pevec* v. *Brown* (1964) 108 S.J. 219.
71 *Moore* v. *Babcock & Wilcox* [1966] 3 All E.R. 882. (On the facts, that assessment would be on the footing that if her father had lived but her mother had died, she would have stayed at home and would not have gone out to work for some years ahead.)
72 *Phipps* v. *Cunard White Star Ltd.* [1951] 1 T.L.R. 359.

the loss of expectation of pecuniary advantage so that in all cases the amount of the pecuniary loss sustained is a question of fact. The mere existence of the relationship of husband and wife or parent and child is not enough to show pecuniary loss, and does not even raise a presumption of such loss.[73] The fact that a husband and wife are living apart is not conclusive evidence that there is no pecuniary loss,[74] but where a wife is living in adultery it is difficult, if not impossible, to prove any such loss.[75] A wife may be partially dependent on her husband and suffer financial loss on his death, even though she has a substantial private fortune.[76] Again, on her husband's death a widow may obtain employment and earn enough to support herself, but may still have been substantially dependent on him during his lifetime.

An action cannot be maintained by the dependants for nominal damages.[77]

287 In ascertaining the pecuniary loss in cases in which the deceased lived with the dependants, as in the case of a husband or a son, it is necessary to take into account the cost of maintaining the deceased.[78] There must also be taken into account the expectation of life of the deceased and of each of the persons claiming to be dependants.[79] If, before trial, one of the dependants has died, compensation can only be awarded for her actual loss and not for the loss she would have suffered had she continued to live throughout the period of her normal expectation of life.[80] In determining the extent of the pecuniary loss the dependant's future prospects after the death of the deceased must necessarily be taken into account however distasteful that may seem at times. Accordingly where a widow's expectation of life was held to be lower than average for her age due to her

[73] *New Monckton Collieries* v. *Keeling* [1911] A.C. 648; *Lee* v. *SS. Bessie* [1912] 1 K.B. 83. (These are cases under the Workmen's Compensation Act, but the principle is equally applicable to the Fatal Accidents Acts.) But where a mother lived with her son's family, doing all the housework and caring for the children whilst her son and daughter-in-law went out to work, in return for which services the mother received her board, lodging and pocket-money, it was held, upon her death, that as there had been a benefit to the son during her lifetime which arose out of their relationship, he was entitled to recover damages for his loss under the Fatal Accidents Act: *Saikaley* v. *Pelletier* (1966) 57 D.L.R. (2d) 394.

[74] *Harrison* v. *L. & N.W. Ry.* (1885) Cab. & El. 540.

[75] *Stimpson* v. *Wood* (1888) 57 L.J.Q.B. 484.

[76] *Shiels* v. *Crookshank* [1953] 1 W.L.R. 533 (a Scottish case and not a decision on the Fatal Accidents Acts).

[77] *Duckworth* v. *Johnson* (1859) 4 H. & N. 653.

[78] *Duckworth* v. *Johnson* (1859) 4 H. & N. 653; *Tamworth Colliery Co.* v. *Hall* [1911] A.C. 665, a case under the Workmen's Compensation Act 1906, where, on this point, the same principles are applicable. In *Pigney* v. *Pointers Transport Services Ltd.* [1957] 2 All E.R. 807, a man, injured through his employers' negligence, suffered from anxiety neurosis and depression and, 18 months after his accident, committed suicide while sane. As his death was directly traceable to his accident, his widow was awarded damages. She was 53 and he was 55, her dependency (after giving credit for the cost of food) being between £5 and £6 a week. She was awarded £1,800 and funeral expenses.

[79] *Price* v. *Glynea and Castle Coal Co.* (1915) 9 B.W.C.C. 188, 198 *per* Bray J.; *Barnett* v. *Cohen* [1921] 2 K.B. 461. In *Hall* v. *Wilson* [1939] 4 All E.R. 85 the possibility of the deceased being killed in war or in air-raids was taken into account, but in *Bishop* v. *Cunard White Star Ltd.* [1950] P. 240 no reduction was made on account of the hazards of life at sea during war.

[80] *Williamson* v. *John I. Thornycroft & Co. Ltd.* [1940] 2 K.B. 658.

chronic ill health her period of dependency for the future was proportionately reduced.[81] Prior to August 1, 1971, the possibility of the widow remarrying had to be taken into account and her prospects of remarriage assessed, since in the event of such happening her dependency, even if it did not disappear completely, would be considerably reduced.[82] Now by virtue of section 4 (1) of the Law Reform (Miscellaneous Provisions) Act 1971 [82a] in assessing damages payable to a widow in respect of her husband's death in any action under the Fatal Accidents Acts "there shall not be taken into account the remarriage of the widow or her prospects of remarriage." On the other hand a widower's prospects of remarriage still must be assessed,[83] although the considerations may be slightly different. A collateral problem has to be faced in the case of children where the surviving parent remarries. When infant children have been accepted by their stepfather as children of the family, upon their widowed mother's remarriage, their dependency necessarily has been affected since her new husband has incurred a statutory legal obligation to give them financial support, which must be taken into account in assessing the children's claims individually for dependency under the Fatal Accidents Acts. Their damages in these circumstances must be based so as to compensate them for the risks of loss in the future and ought not to be assessed on the loss of support of a father.[84] In *Curwen* v. *James* [85] where a widow had remarried before the time for appealing had expired, the Court of Appeal

[81] *Whittome* v. *Coates* [1965] 1 W.L.R. 1285. But a widow is not obliged to submit to a medical examination: *Baugh* v. *Delta Water Fittings, The Times,* May 13, 1971.

[82] *Davies* v. *Powell Duffryn Associated Collieries Ltd.* [1942] A.C. 601, 617, *per* Lord Wright; *Nance* v. *British Columbia Electric Ry.* [1951] A.C. 601, 615; *Miller* v. *B.R.S. Ltd.* [1967] 1 W.L.R. 443; *Buckley* v. *John Allen & Ford (Oxford) Ltd.* [1967] 2 Q.B. 637. (The dictum of Phillimore J., however, was disapproved by the C.A. in *Goodburn* v. *Cotton* [1968] 1 Q.B. 845.) See articles on Remarriage and Damages: 235 L.T. 172 and 18 N.I.L.Q. 422.

[82a] This Act, which received the Royal Assent on July 1, 1971, followed on from the unanimous opinion of the Committee on Personal Injuries Litigation, Cmnd. 3691, paras. 378–379.

[83] *Collins* v. *Noma Electric Co.* (1962) 106 S.J. 431 (widower with six children was awarded £2,391 for the dependency proved in respect of his deceased wife, his children's mother); *Jeffery* v. *Smith, The Times,* March 11, 1970 (widower, aged 51, with three children aged nine, six and three years respectively, claimed damages for the deceased's death quantified as the cost of employing a woman to look after the children and the home at a wage of £10/week, net, living in. Melford Stevenson J. considered the possibility of the widower remarrying and other imponderables then awarded £5,200 damages. Salmon L.J. thought that the "multiplier of 10" was perhaps on the high side but the C.A. declined to interfere with the award. Sir Frederick Sellers commented that the case illustrated the value to a young family of a wife aged 38 and mother. Without the award the plaintiff could not have afforded the expense and he would, indeed, have been in a dilemma if he had no remedy for his wife's death.

[84] *Reincke* v. *Gray* [1964] 1 W.L.R. 832, *per* Sellers L.J. at p. 835. For the statutory obligation see the relevant provisions in the Matrimonial Proceedings (Magistrates' Courts) Act 1960, s. 16, and the Matrimonial Causes Act 1965, ss. 34 and 46, as amended by the Divorce Reform Act 1969, Sched. 1, which came into operation on January 1, 1971. See also *Rawlinson* v. *Babcock & Wilcox Ltd.* [1967] 1 W.L.R. 481. For the situation prior to the imposition of a statutory obligation on a stepfather see *Mead* v. *Clarke Chapman & Co. Ltd.* [1956] 1 W.L.R. 76.

[85] [1963] 1 W.L.R. 748. (The C.A. stated that when the exigencies of justice clearly outweigh the general undesirability of admitting evidence of matters which alter the effect of an order of the court below as to damages, the appellate court has power in exceptional circumstances to hear it.) Approved by the H.L. in *Murphy* v. *Stone Wallwork (Charlton)* [1969] 1 W.L.R. 1023.

admitted such evidence at the hearing of the appeal and, as a result, reduced the assessment of damages to a figure which the trial judge would probably have awarded had he known that the remarriage was likely to have taken place as early as it did. Whilst it is clear that damages have to be assessed as at the date of the deceased's death nevertheless the court must take cognisance of subsequent events which throw light upon the realities of the situation [86] since the court must not speculate when it knows.[87] Accordingly where the plaintiff widow had died, some fourteen months after the deceased had been killed but before her action was ready for trial, the court was obliged to award to her estate only a comparatively small sum in the light of such a known fact.[88]

288 **Pecuniary gains resulting from the death.** The rule at common law in respect of the assessment of claims for damages under the Fatal Accidents Acts was that there had to be taken into account any pecuniary benefit accruing to the dependant, by reason of the death of the deceased, and such had to be set against the pecuniary loss suffered.[89]

289 However certain statutory exceptions to this rule at common law were first made in respect of contractual benefits by the Fatal Accidents (Damages) Act 1908 [90] and later made in respect of national insurance benefits by the Law Reform (Personal Injuries) Act 1948. These provisions have been replaced by the Fatal Accidents Act 1959 which came into force on January 29, 1959, and applies only to actions brought in respect of deaths occurring after that date. Section 2 provides: "In assessing damages in respect of a person's death in any action under the Fatal Accidents Act 1846 . . . there shall not be taken into account any insurance money, benefit, pension or gratuity which has been or will or may be paid as a result of the death." The Act of 1908 applied to all contracts of assurance or insurance, whether life, accident or any other form, and whether the contract was made by the deceased himself or by the dependants, but it did not apply to payments which were not contractual.[91] Death benefit paid under a pension scheme was not within this Act,[92] and so had to be

86 *Williamson* v. *John I. Thornycroft & Co. Ltd.* [1940] 2 K.B. 658; *Curwen* v. *James, supra*; *Dietz* v. *Lennig Chemicals Ltd.* [1969] 1 A.C. 170.

87 *Per* Harman L.J. in *Curwen* v. *James, supra*, at p. 753 and again in *Baker* v. *Willoughby* [1969] 2 W.L.R. 489, 497 (reversed on other grounds by the H.L. [1970] A.C. 467).

88 *Williamson* v. *John I. Thornycroft & Co. Ltd., supra.*

89 *Grand Trunk Ry.* v. *Jennings* (1888) 13 App.Cas. 800, 804; *Baker* v. *Dalgleish S.S. Co. Ltd.* [1922] 1 K.B. 361.

90 But where an employee died in a fire on his employer's premises, the employer having taken out a personal accident group policy, which insurance did not form any part of the terms of employment, the Court of Appeal held that the money was paid under a contract of insurance within the meaning of s. 1, although the employee had no right either at common law or in equity to the money paid by the insurance company to his employer: *Green* v. *Russell* [1959] 2 Q.B. 226. Accordingly the money did not fall to be deducted from the damages. See also *Baker* v. *T. E. Hopkins & Son Ltd.* [1958] 1 W.L.R. 993.

91 *Carling* v. *Lebbon* [1927] 2 K.B. 108.

92 *Smith* v. *British European Airways Corpn. Ltd.* [1951] 2 K.B. 893; *O'Neill* v. *S. J. Smith & Co. (Bideford) Ltd.* [1957] 1 W.L.R. 1204 where sums payable to the widow and children on the death of a miner under a mineworkers' pension scheme established under the Coal Industry Nationalisation (Superannuation) Regulations 1950 (S.I. 1950, No. 376), had to be taken into account in assessing the damages payable under the Fatal Accidents Acts and were not excluded by the Fatal Accidents (Damages) Act 1908, s. 1.

deducted, but a payment under a group life assurance scheme taken out by a company for the benefit of its employees was held to be within the Act and was not to be taken into account.[93] Any annual premiums paid by the deceased under the contract of insurance must be taken into account in estimating his net income for the purpose of calculating the pecuniary loss arising on his death.[94] Section 2 (2) of the Act of 1959 further expressly provides that " benefit " means: " benefit under the National Insurance Acts 1946 (as amended by any subsequent enactment, whether passed before or after the commencement of this Act) . . . and any payment by a friendly society or trade union for the relief or maintenance of a member's dependants; ' insurance money ' includes a return of premiums[95]; and ' pension ' includes a return of contributions and any payment of a lump sum in respect of a person's employment."

1290 It will be seen, therefore, that the Act of 1959 has considerably widened the categories of benefits which must not be taken into account to lessen damages and the wording is sufficient to exclude from the assessment of damages most of the pecuniary gains that a dependant most probably would receive, except, perhaps, by way of inheritance,[96] from the deceased himself, who had private capital. Where stocks and shares or comparable income producing investments are concerned and the dependant's interests are accelerated by the death, some deduction will have to be made, although care will be required in order to make sure that the sum deducted does not exceed the true financial gain to the dependants. Except in extreme cases where the whole of the family income is derived from the deceased's investments the value of such inheritance should not normally be deducted pound for pound.[97] However before any deduction is made the value of the inheritance firstly should be assessed net, namely after estate duty and, doubtlessly, capital gains tax have been taken into account.[98] Nevertheless, much must depend upon the nature of the inheritance and this is well illustrated in the decision of the Court of

[93] *Bowskill* v. *Dawson* [1955] 1 Q.B. 13.

[94] *Grand Trunk Ry.* v. *Jennings* (1888) 13 App.Cas. 800; *Baker* v. *Dalgleish Steam Shipping Co.* [1922] 1 K.B. 361, *per* Scrutton L.J.

[95] See also *Malyon* v. *Plummer* [1964] 1 Q.B. 330 (distinguishing *Burgess* v. *Florence Nightingale Hospital for Gentlewomen* [1955] 1 Q.B. 349). In assessing a widow's damages the consideration to be disregarded is the increase in value of her shares in a company as a result of an insurance by the company on her husband's life, because s. 2 (1) of the Fatal Accidents Act 1959 applies to that benefit. The excess of her salary from the company over the market value of her services was a benefit derived from her relationship to her husband as his wife and thus was a benefit lost by his death and to be taken into account in assessing her dependency on him.

[96] *Baker* v. *Dalgleish Steam Shipping Co.* [1922] 1 K.B. 361; *Peacock* v. *Amusement Equipment Co. Ltd.* [1954] 2 Q.B. 347.

[97] *Bishop* v. *Cunard White Star Co. Ltd.* [1950] P. 240, *per* Hodson J. at p. 248; *Rawlinson* v. *Babcock & Wilcox Ltd.* [1967] 1 W.L.R. 481, *per* Chapman J. at p. 486.

[98] *Baker* v. *T. E. Hopkins & Sons Ltd.* [1958] 1 W.L.R. 993 (affirmed [1959] 1 W.L.R. 966 although no appeal on this particular point); *Daniel* v. *Jones* [1961] 1 W.L.R. 1103, although the question of loss was one of fact for the jury, and although some arithmetical calculations were necessary, they did not provide a substitute for common sense. Accordingly the value of an estate should not in every case be set off, pound for pound, against the loss of income as a matter of precise arithmetical calculation.

Appeal in *Heatley* v. *Steel Company of Wales Ltd.*[99] where a widow had inherited the equity of redemption of the house wherein she and their four children had lived with her husband, the deceased. The question both posed and answered by Lord Goddard C.J. is, " what the court has to try to ascertain in these cases is: How much have the widow and family lost by the father's death? This is not a case where, by the death of the father, the widow will come into some large sum of money of which she never before had the handling. She will simply continue to live in this house and provide a home there for the children until it is sold, and if and when it is sold she will have to get another house. At any rate, her two younger children are likely to be living with her in this house or elsewhere for a long time, and her two elder children are still dependent on her. The court cannot see that there is really any sum to be deducted for the value of the house at all." Similarly no deduction fell to be made where the deceased's butcher's business and insurance policy moneys had passed to the widow. The debts of the business exceeded the money due by £549, but the deceased's father took over the business, paying nothing for it, but discharging all the debts so that had the widow kept the business she would have had to pay these debts out of the insurance policy moneys.[1] Likewise an infant dependant's damages should not be reduced by the fact of the benevolence of her uncle, who took her in and gave her money following the death of her mother who had died some fifteen months after the fatal accident that befell the child's father.[2]

291 Only the value of an accelerated receipt of the inheritance should be taken into account where a dependant had an expectation of inheriting sometime in the future.[3] Although there are cases where even this should not be done, *viz.*: where the deceased was a high earning frugal man who saved and, in his lifetime, provided very generously for his family, which was unusually well-knit and close together [4] or where, " having regard to the anticipated savings which might reasonably have been made by the deceased if he had lived " his dependants by his premature death inherited a much smaller sum than otherwise they would have done had he not been killed when he was.[5]

From the above it seems clear that the rule at common law has ceased to have very much practical effect. The exception concerning damages awarded for the benefit of the estate of the deceased under the Law Reform

99 [1953] 1 W.L.R. 405. See also *Bishop* v. *Cunard White Star Co. Ltd.* [1950] P. 240 where Hodson J. held that where the estate included a freehold house jointly occupied by the wife and husband, its value should not be taken into account. (The deceased was one of 334 officers and men of the Royal Navy who lost their lives when *H.M.S. Curacoa* collided with the *Queen Mary* and sank immediately.) However *cf.* the facts in *Voller* v. *Dairy Produce Packers Ltd.* [1962] 1 W.L.R. 960.

1 *Schneider* v. *Eisovitch* [1960] 2 Q.B. 430.

2 *Rawlinson* v. *Babcock & Wilcox Ltd.* [1967] 1 W.L.R. 481.

3 *Nance* v. *British Columbia Electric Ry.* [1951] A.C. 601, *per* Viscount Simon at p. 615; *Voller* v. *Dairy Produce Packers Ltd.* [1962] 1 W.L.R. 960; *Taylor* v. *O'Connor* [1971] A.C. 115.

4 *Daniels* v. *Jones* [1961] 1 W.L.R. 1103.

5 *Kassam* v. *Kampala Aerated Water Co. Ltd.* [1965] 1 W.L.R. 668, 673.

(Miscellaneous Provisions) Act 1934, must always be taken into account so far as they increase the share coming to any individual dependant under the will or on the intestacy of the deceased [6] and will fall to be deducted pound for pound.[7] A dependant who is not obtaining any benefit from the deceased's estate is not affected by any award of damages under that Act.

1292 **Method of calculating damages.** When the income of the deceased was derived from his own earnings, " it then becomes necessary to consider what, but for the accident which terminated his existence, would have been his reasonable prospects of life, work and remuneration; and also how far these, if realised, would have conduced to the benefit of the individual claiming compensation." [8] The manner of arriving at the damages is (a) to ascertain the net income of the deceased available for the support of himself and his dependants; (b) (i) to deduct therefrom such part of his income as the deceased was accustomed to spend upon himself, whether for maintenance or pleasure,[9] or (ii) what should amount to the same thing, to ascertain what part of his net income the deceased was accustomed to spend for the benefit of the dependants [10]; and then (c) to capitalise the difference between the sums (a) and (b) (i) or (b) (ii) (sometimes called the " lump sum " or the " basic figure ") by multiplying it by a figure representing the proper number of years' purchase.[11] This multiplier necessarily must remain a flexible figure for the judge to decide and is usually determined reasonably by having regard to the deceased's expectation of life, his age and health,[12] the probable duration of his earning capacity, the possibility of his earning capacity being increased or decreased in the future, the expectation of life of the dependants [13] and the probable duration of the continuance of the deceased's assistance to the dependants during their joint lives.[14] Much of the calculation necessarily

[6] *Davies* v. *Powell Duffryn Associated Collieries Ltd.* [1942] A.C. 601; *Ellis* v. *Raine* [1939] 2 K.B. 180.

[7] *Bishop* v. *Cunard White Star Ltd.* [1950] P. 240.

[8] *Grand Trunk Ry.* v. *Jennings* (1888) 13 App.Cas. 800, *per* Lord Watson at p. 804.

[9] *Davies* v. *Powell Duffryn Associated Collieries Ltd.* [1942] A.C. 601, 617, *per* Lord Wright.

[10] *Nance* v. *British Columbia Electric Ry.* [1951] A.C. 601, 614, *per* Lord Simon.

[11] In *Brennan* v. *Gale* [1949] N.I. 178 the C.A. in Northern Ireland expressed the opinion that the figure of sixteen years' purchase adopted by the C.A. in *Johnson* v. *Hill* (1945) 61 T.L.R. 398 approached the upper limit. In *Mallett* v. *McMonagle* [1970] A.C. 166, 177 Lord Diplock observed with approval that courts not infrequently have awarded 16 years' purchase of the dependency in cases where the deceased was aged 25 years, leaving a widow of a similar age, with three young children but it is seldom that this number of years' purchase ought to be exceeded. However, the " multiplier " is correctly determined if assessed by rule of thumb including such considerations as prospects of the widow's remarriage; it is doubtful whether actuarial or mathematical tables could be put in at all as admissible evidence directed to a precise calculation of the correct multiplier for the dependency: *Butler* v. *Amalgamated Removers & Transport* (1964) 108 S.J. 562.

[12] *e.g. Gilbertson* v. *Harland & Wolff Ltd.* [1966] 2 Lloyd's Rep. 190. The deceased was an active healthy man of 70, who would have gone on working until the age of 75, although, normally it must be assumed in the absence of contrary evidence a man would have retired at 65. See *Whittome* v. *Coates* [1965] 1 W.L.R. 1285, *per* Sellers L.J. at p. 1288.

[13] *Grzelak* v. *Harefield and Northwood Hospital Management Committee* (1968) 112 S.J. 195 where the dependants included the deceased's parents who were aged 77 and 80. Their multiplier was assessed as a three years' purchase.

[14] See *Grand Trunk Ry.* v. *Jennings, supra*; *Royal Trust Co.* v. *C.P. Ry.* (1922) 38 T.L.R. 899; *Davies* v. *Powell Duffryn Associated Collieries Ltd.* [1942] A.C. 601, 617; *Bishop* v. *Cunard*

must be in the realms of hypothesis " and in that region arithmetic is a good servant but a bad master " [15] since there are so often many imponderables.[16] In every case " it is the over-all picture that matters " and the court must try to assess as best as it can the loss suffered by each dependant having regard to all the circumstances but subject to the fact that " it is the wood that has to be looked at, and not the individual trees." [17] Thus in the case of a twenty-nine year old bachelor, living with his widowed mother to whom he paid £5 per week out of which she provided him with food, it was held that her damages under the Acts must not be assessed on the same basis as if she had been the deceased's widow. Since in all probability some day the deceased would have married and as he was under no legal liability to support his mother although in the future, from a sense of moral obligation he might have continued to give his mother something but probably less than he had contributed in the past, damages ought to be assessed on a correspondingly lower scale.[18]

93 **Other considerations.** In *Taylor* v. *O'Connor* [19] where the deceased was aged fifty-three years, was in good health, was devoted to his work as an architect and had been earning a very substantial income as a result of which the capital sum to be awarded to his dependants was bound to be high, the House of Lords had to consider the special factors of the incidence of tax and future inflation, which more usually do not arise. As regards the tax which would have to be paid by the dependants on the income derived from the award of a capital sum their Lordships held that that must be taken into account in its assessment. Lord Reid calculated the capital sum to be £53,000 [20] after observing that " this case is in a sense *British Transport Commission* v. *Gourley* [21] in reverse, for that case instructs us that we must see what the plaintiff really lost taking account of taxation. There damages had to be reduced if taxation was taken into account. Here they have to be increased," [22] by an amount necessary to counteract the shortfall caused by the fact that the interest income available to the dependants will be subject to tax as unearned income. However upon the

White Star Ltd. [1950] P. 240; *Nance* v. *British Columbia Electric Ry.* [1951] A.C. 601; *Heatley* v. *Steel Company of Wales Ltd.* [1953] 1 W.L.R. 405. The practical application of this method of calculation must obviously give results which vary according to the weight given to the different elements by the individual calculator. Nevertheless, the Court of Appeal has expressed the view that in assessing an award of damages the total sum to be awarded should be assessed at a round figure rather than at a figure based on actuarial calculation: *Whittome* v. *Coates* [1965] 1 W.L.R. 1285.

15 *Daniels* v. *Jones* [1961] 1 W.L.R. 1103, *per* Holroyd Pearce L.J. at p. 1110; *Kassam* v. *Kampala Aerated Water Co. Ltd.* [1965] 1 W.L.R. 668, *per* Lord Guest at p. 674. *Cf. Whittome* v. *Coates* [1965] 1 W.L.R. 1285, *per* Diplock L.J. at p. 1293.

16 *Rawlinson* v. *Babcock & Wilcox Ltd.* [1967] 1 W.L.R. 481, 489 where there were so many imponderables that Chapman J. weighed all factors as best he could but did not " profess to be a stockbroker or merchant banker or a computer, or even a psychiatrist."

17 *Daniels* v. *Jones, supra, per* Willmer L.J. at p. 1113.

18 *Dolbey* v. *Godwin* [1955] 1 W.L.R. 553.

19 [1971] A.C. 115.

20 This was so close to the award of £54,196 made by the trial judge Lyell J. as not to justify any interference with it.

21 [1956] A.C. 185.

22 *Ibid.* at pp. 476, 477.

consideration of the extent if any to which the prospect of future inflation should be taken into account in assessing the damages, varying views were expressed. Lord Reid thought that inflation was a relevant factor which ought not to be ignored [23] whilst Viscount Dilhorne and Lord Pearson considered that the only relevance of the prospect of future inflation was where it affected the interest rates to be assumed for the purpose of calculating the present value of the future payments which the dependants otherwise would have received had it not been for the deceased's death.[24] Upon the assumption that the capital sum awarded by the court would be invested partly in low yielding growth stocks and partly in stocks yielding more income and that tax would be paid at the then standard rate of 8s. 3d. in the pound, Lord Pearson thought that an average interest rate of 3 per cent. or 4 per cent. should be adopted for the purposes of the calculation. In the earlier decision of the House of Lords in *Mallett* v. *McMonagle* [25] on this same point Lord Diplock said: " In my view the only practicable course for courts to adopt in assessing damages awarded under the Fatal Accidents Acts is to leave out of account the risk of further inflation, on the one hand, and the high interest rates which reflect the fear of it and capital appreciation of property and equities which are the consequence of it, on the other hand. In estimating the amount of the annual dependency in the future, had the deceased not been killed, money should be treated as retaining its value at the date of the judgment, and in calculating the present value of annual payments which would have been received in future years, interest rates appropriate to times of stable currency such as 4 per cent. to 5 per cent. should be adopted."

Damages must be reduced if there has been contributory negligence on the part of the deceased, in accordance with section 1 (4) of the Law Reform (Contributory Negligence) Act 1945.

1294 **Funeral expenses.** By the Law Reform (Miscellaneous Provisions) Act 1934, s. 2 (3), it is provided: " In an action brought under the Fatal Accidents Acts 1846 to [1908], damages may be awarded in respect of the funeral expenses of the deceased person if such expenses have been incurred by the parties for whose benefit the action is brought." Funeral expenses do not include the cost of a tombstone but they do include the cost of embalming the body.[26] The expenses of mourning [27] and other

23 *Ibid.* at p. 477.

24 *Ibid.* at p. 485 and pp. 489–490.

25 [1970] A.C. 166 at p. 176.

26 *Hart* v. *Griffiths-Jones* [1948] 2 All E.R. 729. A tombstone has been held to be a funeral expense within the meaning of s. 36 of the Assurance Companies Act 1909; *Goldstein* v. *Salvation Army Ass. Socy.* [1917] 2 K.B. 291. Funeral expenses must be reasonable having regard to the position of the deceased; *Re Walter* [1929] 1 Ch. 647, 655. In *Stanton* v. *Ewart F. Youlden* [1960] 1 W.L.R. 543, a stone over a grave may properly be considered as part of the funeral expenses if it is a reasonable expenditure for the person in the position of the deceased and of the relatives who are responsible for the ordering of the stone; but in so far as it is merely a memorial set up as a sign of love and affection then it should not be included.

27 *Dalton* v. *S.E. Ry.* (1858) 4 C.B.(N.S.) 296.

ceremonial expenses incurred out of respect to the dead cannot be recovered.[28]

1295 **Effect of contract by deceased limiting damages.** A contract made by the deceased in his lifetime limiting the amount of damages recoverable by the dependants on his death is not binding on his dependants, because the dependants' claim is a new cause of action in which the measure of damages is different. Accordingly, where the deceased was a passenger on a railway train under a contract providing: " The liability of the company is limited to a sum not exceeding £100," and was killed by the negligence of the railway company, it was held that the dependants were not bound by the limit but could recover full damages.[29] Again, where a passenger in an aeroplane was carried under a contract subject to the Carriage by Air Act 1932, article 22 (1) of which provides: " The liability of the carrier for each passenger is limited to the sum of 125,000 francs," it was held that on his death by the carrier's negligence his dependants were not bound by the limit but could recover full damages.[30]

1296 **Apportionment of the damages.** The damages are to be apportioned among the dependants named in the particulars according to the degree of their pecuniary loss. By the Fatal Accidents Act 1846, s. 2, " the amount so recovered [in the action] after deducting the costs not recovered from the defendant, shall be divided amongst the before-mentioned parties in such shares as the jury by their verdict shall find and direct." If the action is tried by a judge alone, the judge makes the apportionment.[31]

However, as has been stated, each dependant's claim needs to be separately considered.[32] There is no question of there being any group compensation with the amount of damages of any one dependant member, whose claim is before the court, being regarded as a proportion of the limited whole sum.[33] Nevertheless the practice is for the damages to be assessed for the whole of the dependants in one lump sum and then divided among the appropriate dependants [34] in accordance with the pecuniary loss suffered by each individual dependant.[35] When a defendant decides to make a payment into court, he need not apportion it among the dependants; if then the plaintiff thinks it is insufficient but the jury find it is sufficient, the defendant is entitled to the verdict upon that issue.[36] It is no concern

[28] *Barnett* v. *Cohen* [1921] 2 K.B. 461.

[29] *Nunan* v. *Southern Ry.* [1924] 1 K.B. 223.

[30] *Grein* v. *Imperial Airways Ltd.* (1935) 52 T.L.R. 28, reversed on other grounds [1937] 1 K.B. 50.

[31] *Nunan* v. *Southern Ry.* [1923] 2 K.B. 703.

[32] *Dietz* v. *Lennig Chemicals Ltd.* [1969] 1 A.C. 170, *per* Lord Morris at p. 183, *e.g.* see *Williamson* v. *John I. Thornycroft & Co. Ltd.* [1940] 2 K.B. 658; *Voller* v. *Dairy Produce Packers Ltd.* [1962] 1 W.L.R. 960; *Rawlinson* v. *Babcock & Wilcox Ltd.* [1967] 1 W.L.R. 481.

[33] *Avery* v. *L. & N.E. Ry.* [1938] A.C. 606, *per* Lord Atkin at p. 612.

[34] See *Johnson* v. *Hill* [1945] 2 All E.R. 272; *Bishop* v. *Cunard White Star Ltd.* [1950] P. 240, 248, *per* Hodson J.; *Kassam* v. *Kampala Aerated Water Co. Ltd.* [1965] 1 W.L.R. 668, 672, *per* Lord Guest.

[35] *Pym* v. *G.N. Ry.* (1863) 4 B. & S. 396, 407; *G.T. Ry. of Canada* v. *Jennings* (1888) 13 App. Cas. 800, 803.

[36] Fatal Accidents Act 1864, s. 2.

of the defendant how the damages are apportioned among the dependants, and therefore no appeal will lie against the apportionment.[37]

1297 **Actions under the Law Reform (Miscellaneous Provisions) Act 1934.**[38] Section 1 (5) of the Law Reform (Miscellaneous Provisions) Act 1934 provides, " the rights conferred by this Act for the benefit of the estates of deceased persons shall be in addition to and not in derogation of any rights conferred on the dependants of deceased persons by the Fatal Accidents Acts, 1846. . . ." In practice it frequently occurs that actions for damages under the Fatal Accidents Acts and the Law Reform (Miscellaneous Provisions) Act 1934 are pleaded together in the same writ and statement of claim so are properly tried at the same time. Accordingly the problem arises what relationship the damages awarded under the one series of Acts should bear to the damages given under the other Act. If the persons entitled to the deceased's estate are not the same persons who are his dependants for the purposes of the Fatal Accidents Acts then in assessing the damages under these Acts no account needs to be taken of any damages awarded to the deceased's estate under the Act of 1934. On the other hand, where any dependant is also beneficially entitled to a share of the deceased's estate since section 1 (5) quoted above has not altered at all the general rule for the assessment of damages under the Fatal Accidents Acts, *viz.*: that any pecuniary benefit which accrues to the dependants as a result of the death must be set against their pecuniary losses suffered, this deduction must be made pound for pound to the extent of such entitlement. The pecuniary benefit which has to be taken into account when assessing the dependant's damages in these circumstances is the net value after estate duty and the administration expenses have been paid.[39] In *Rawlinson* v. *Babcock & Wilcox Ltd.*[40] the deceased met his death as a result of an accident for which the defendants admitted liability and it was agreed that the sum of £700 per annum represented the dependency of his widow and his fourteen year old daughter in the actions brought by the widow as his administratrix both on behalf of his estate and on behalf of herself and daughter as the only dependants. Unfortunately, she died before the trial so that the actions were continued by her administrators whereupon Chapman J. assessed the damages due to the widow under the Fatal Accidents Acts at £708. This became an irrelevant figure since it was a sum less than what she received as administratrix, namely £1,000 to which estate she alone was wholly entitled, so that no award was made under the Fatal Accidents Acts to her. However, when the damages payable under those Acts to the daughter came to be assessed, this £1,000, which presumably must have descended to her together with the remainder of her

[37] *Eifert* v. *Holt's Transport Co.* [1951] 2 All E.R. 655n.

[38] This Act lays down the general rule that on the death of any person all causes of action subsisting against or vested in him shall survive against or as the case may be, for the benefit of his estate (s. 1 (1)). See further, in detail Chap. 4 § 132, and § 143, *ante*.

[39] *Davies* v. *Powell Duffryn Associated Collieries Ltd.* [1942] A.C. 601; *Schneider* v. *Eisovitch* [1960] 2 Q.B. 430; *Voller* v. *Dairy Produce Packers Ltd.* [1962] 1 W.L.R. 960.

[40] [1967] 1 W.L.R. 481.

mother's estate, was not deducted, correctly it is submitted, since it had not been received by her as a pecuniary advantage in consequence of her *father's* death.

298 **Settlement of claims under the Fatal Accidents Acts.** In practice actions under the Acts are usually brought by the personal representatives of the deceased, since claims under the Law Reform (Miscellaneous Provisions) Act 1934 are conveniently included, but they cannot make a binding agreement with the defendant to accept a lump sum settlement to cover all the dependants unless (a) the court has sanctioned the agreement as being one for the benefit of each of the dependants, who are still minors at the time, and (b) each of the dependants, who is *sui juris* and desires to claim, has approved the agreement in so far as it affects him individually.[41] " Where, however, the administrator has with the approval of any dependant who is *sui juris* entered into an agreement with the defendant that the defendant should pay to that dependant (whom I shall call the settling dependant) a sum of money which is agreed to be sufficient as being proportionate to the injury suffered by the settling dependant, then the settling dependant is bound by the agreement as he would be if he personally entered into such agreement." [42]

299 In an appropriate case, it is only when the court's approval has been given that for the first time a binding agreement comes into existence. In *Dietz* v. *Lennig Chemicals Ltd.*[43] the deceased was killed in an accident on October 6, 1964, leaving a widow, the appellant, and a fifteen month old child whereupon she made a claim in negligence as administratrix on her own behalf and on behalf of the child against her late husband's employers, the respondents. The latter's solicitors offered to settle the proceedings for £10,000 and in August 1965 her solicitors wrote to the respondents' solicitors agreeing on her behalf to accept such offer " subject to the approval of the court." In pursuance of this agreement, a trust deed was drawn up and an application was made to the court by summons taken out on October 13, 1965, for the approval of the settlement and the terms of the trust deed at which date she was truly a widow but unbeknown to her solicitors before the hearing of this summons in fact she remarried. In due course, namely on November 12 at the hearing of the summons, the master made an order by initialling the summons, approving the settlement but before the consent order was drawn up the appellant's solicitors discovered that she had remarried whereupon they immediately informed the respondents' solicitors who then had the order set aside. The House of Lords held that the bargain entered into between the parties in August 1965 for the payment of a lump sum to cover the claims of the widow and the infant was not binding without the approval of the court and so was not a binding contract. Since the order of November 12 had not been drawn up, it had

41 *Jeffrey* v. *Kent C.C.* [1958] 1 W.L.R. 927.
42 *Ibid. per* Paull J. at p. 930.
43 [1969] 1 A.C. 170.

not been perfected and the respondents were entitled to have it set aside as their consent to its making had been induced by an innocent representation on behalf of the appellant that she was a widow at the date of the order.

All the dependants, who are *sui juris*, may make independent settlements before proceedings are commenced but once an action has been started and any infant is or infants are included in the dependants then it is no longer open to the widow to do so, since the damages awarded to her as well as those awarded to the infant dependants remain under the control of the court.[44] Where the only purpose of proceedings is to obtain the court's approval of an agreement which has already been reached between the parties, then the proceedings can properly be commenced by originating summons and no appearance need be entered by the defendants.[45]

1300 **Other Acts.** (1) By section 12 (1) of the Coal Mining (Subsidence) Act 1957 liability is imposed on the National Coal Board in respect of deaths caused by coal mining subsidence where, apart from the subsection, no action to recover damages for the death is otherwise maintainable. It is enacted, in effect, that the provisions of the Fatal Accidents Acts shall apply in such case but with the important distinction that the plaintiff is not required to prove that the death was caused by the Board's negligence.

The defences open to the Board are contained in subsection (2) which provides: " No liability shall attach to the Board under the foregoing subsection in respect of the death or disablement of any person as a result of an injury if:—

(*a*) at the time when that person incurred the injury he was a trespasser; or

(*b*) the injury was incurred underground in a mine of coal within the meaning of the Mines and Quarries Act 1954; or

(*c*) the injury was wholly attributable to the negligence of that person; and if the injury was partly attributable to the negligence of that person the liability of the Board under the foregoing subsection shall be reduced proportionately."

(2) The Carriage by Air Act 1961 gives the force of law to the Warsaw Convention as amended at The Hague, 1955, and replaces the Carriage by Air Act 1932. The carrier's liability under Article 17 for damage sustained in the event of the death of a passenger if the accident which caused the damage took place on board the aircraft or in the course of any of the operations of embarking or disembarking is not dependent upon proof of fault.[46] See further Chapter 12 § 807, *ante*, and Chapter 16 § 1162, *ante*.

[44] Administration of Justice Act 1965, s. 19.
[45] R.S.C. Ord. 80 r. 11.
[46] But see Art. 20: " The carrier is not liable if he proves that he and his servants or agents have taken all necessary measures to avoid the damage or that it was impossible for him or them to take such measures."

INDEX

[*All references are to paragraph numbers*]

THE COMMON LAW LIBRARY

Number 6

CHARLESWORTH
ON
NEGLIGENCE

FIRST SUPPLEMENT TO THE
FIFTH EDITION

Price £0.65p

SWEET & MAXWELL

THE COMMON LAW LIBRARY

Number 6

CHARLESWORTH
ON
NEGLIGENCE

FIRST SUPPLEMENT TO THE FIFTH EDITION

By

R. A. PERCY, M.A.

Barrister-at-Law of the Middle Temple
and North-Eastern Circuit;
A Recorder of the Crown Court

Up to date to March 1, 1974

LONDON

SWEET & MAXWELL

1974

Published in 1974 by
Sweet and Maxwell Limited of
11 New Fetter Lane, London
and printed in Great Britain
by The Eastern Press Limited
of London and Reading

Supplement only SBN 421 204 80X
Supplement (with Main Work) SBN 421 204 702

TABLE OF STATUTES

TABLE OF CASES CITED

CHARLESWORTH on NEGLIGENCE

FIRST SUPPLEMENT TO THE FIFTH EDITION

Chapter 1

MEANING OF NEGLIGENCE

CHARLESWORTH PARAGRAPH

9 **(2)—Negligence as careless conduct**

See article: " Contributory negligence and the duty of care " (Blackshaw) 116 S.J. 577.

16 **Actual damage necessary**

Where the plaintiffs were induced to take a lease of premises by the negligent misrepresentation of their estate agents that the net area was 948 square feet greater than it was in fact, they failed to prove any damage, since the evidence showed that the market value of the lease based on its actual area was in the range £52,000–£60,000 whilst they had only paid £54,000. *Carreras* v. *D. E. & J. Levy* (1970) 215 E.G. 707.

Chapter 2

THE DUTY TO TAKE CARE

1.—General Aspects of the Duty of Care

21 **The need for a duty of care to exist**

See article: " Duty of care in negligence: recently expressed policy elements " (Symmons) 34 M.L.R. 394; 528.

24 **Duty only exists when special relationship**

Note 15a. *Dutton* v. *Bognor Regis U.D.C.* [1972] 1 Q.B. 373 C.A.; reversing [1971] 2 All E.R. 1003 (a local authority whose surveyor approved a building's foundations although they did not comply with a by-law, may be liable to a subsequent owner for any deterioration of the building resulting from such negligence). See articles: " Local authority's liability for negligent approval of building construction," 35 Conv.(N.S.) 385; (Merritt) [1972] J.P.L. 69; " Duty of a council to take care," 136 L.G.Rev. 362; " Local authority's liability for negligence," 116 S.J. 264.

Auditors when acting as experts and not as arbitrators in valuing shares on a contract of sale as between shareholders owe no duty of care in respect of their valuation, since they are performing a quasi-judicial function and are immune on the ground of public policy. *Arenson* v. *Arenson* [1973] Ch. 346.

An authorised vehicle examiner owes a duty to carry out the M.O.T. test carefully and to deliver an accurate certificate. *Artingstoll* v. *Hewens Garages* [1973] R.T.R. 197.

A road user owes a duty of care to other road users, even to those who may be driving without care, but not those who are reckless. *Rouse* v. *Squires* [1973] Q.B. 889.

2.—Foreseeability of Damage

(a) *The Kind of Harm*

42 **Pecuniary and economic loss resulting from careless acts**

See articles: " Limitations on liability for economic loss caused by negligence: a pragmatic appraisal " (James) 12 J.S.P.T.L. 105; " Economic losses and negligence—the search for a just solution " (Harvey) 50 Can.Bar Rev. 580; " Damages for economic loss," 137 L.G.Rev. 6; " Negligence—loss of profits—economic loss " (Jolowicz) [1973] C.L.J. 20.

43 Note 10. Applied in *Spartan Steel and Alloys* v. *Martin & Co. (Contractors)* [1973] Q.B. 27.

44 **Pecuniary and economic loss resulting from careless statements**

See article: " Liability for negligent misstatements " (Samuels) 115 S.J. 646.

51 Note 42. See articles: " *Hedley Byrne* v. *Heller* in the Privy Council—the continuing story " (Phegan) 45 A.L.J. 20; " Pleadings, facts and the law relating to negligent advice " (Farmer) [1971] C.L.J. 189.

51–52 In *J. Nunes Diamonds* v. *Dominion Electric Protection Co.* (1972) 26 D.L.R. (3d) 699 the plaintiff diamond merchants sued the defendants for damages for the loss of a quantity of diamonds stolen from a safe, which had been protected by the defendants' burglar alarm installation. As the result of an earlier burglary from another firm's safe protected by an identical alarm system, the plaintiffs sought the advice of the defendants, who checked on their installation, found that it was efficient and, in their opinion, could not be circumvented, at the same time promising an investigation and report into the other system's failure. Prior to the plaintiffs' loss nothing further was communicated to the plaintiffs or their insurance broker. The Canadian Supreme Court held that these representations were not actionable in negligence because the defendants were not acting in any fiduciary or advisory capacity towards the plaintiffs.

(b) *The Carelessness Causing the Harm*

56 **Acts of omission**

Add to end of paragraph: On further appeal by H's dependants the Canadian Supreme Court held that, although the appeal failed, a host or owner and operator of a vessel is under a duty at common law to do the best he can in the circumstances to effect the rescue of a guest who has accidentally fallen overboard. *Sub nom. Horsley* v. *MacLaren*; *The Ogopogo* [1971] 2 Lloyd's Rep. 410.

See articles: " Rescuer as defendant—reversal of roles reversed " (Spencer) [1971] C.L.J. 193; " One rescuer's obligation to another: The Ogopogo lands in the Supreme Court of Canada " (Alexander) 22 U.T.L.J. 98.

(c) *The Kind of Person*

71 **An unborn child**

In *Watt* v. *Rama* [1972] V.R. 353 the Victoria Supreme Court held that the pre-natal injuries sustained by the plaintiff were not too remote since the injury to her pregnant mother, who was lawfully using the highway, was foreseeable. Where the injury does not arise contemporaneously with the negligence or where the plaintiff is not defined at that time, the duty of care is contingent only, but it crystallises when the plaintiff becomes defined.

A similar decision was made in *Duval* v. *Seguin* (1972) 26 D.L.R. (3d) 418, where the plaintiff child received serious brain injuries whilst she was still *en ventre sa mère,* and was held to be entitled to succeed in her claim for damages.

See articles: " Rights of an unborn child " (Brown) 21 I.C.L.Q. 789; " En ventre sa mère " (MacDonald) 70 L.S.Gaz. 1425; " Pregnant women and unborn children " (Williams) 117 S.J. 79; " Unborn child " (Rowe) 123 New L.J. 96; " Delicta in uterum " (Veitch) 24 N.I.L.Q. 40.

See also the Law Commission Published Working Paper No. 47: " Injuries to unborn children."

NOTE 12. The High Court has approved terms of settlement in 433 actions brought by children who suffered injuries as a result of the use of the drug thalidomide by their mothers during pregnancy. *Allen* v. *Distillers Co. (Biochemicals)* [1974] 2 W.L.R. 481, Geoffrey Lane J.

See article: " Thalidomide claims: law, fantasy and reform " (Franks) 117 S.J. 643.

CHAPTER 3

CAUSATION AND REMOTENESS OF DAMAGE

1.—CAUSATION

79 **What is the cause of an accident ?**

NOTE 21a. See § 56, *ante.*

2.—REMOTENESS OF DAMAGE

105 **Where The Wagon Mound principle has no application**

(a) Unforeseeable extent of damage

In *Robinson* v. *The Post Office* (1973) 117 S.J. 915, the plaintiff sustained a minor injury due to the defendants' negligence but, as a result of the plaintiff's receiving an anti-tetanus injection to which he was allergic, he suffered the rare complication of encephalitis, with grave consequences. Ashworth J. held that the doctor had acted negligently in administering the injection but that this had had no causative effect since even with proper precautions the encephalitis would not have been prevented. The C.A. in dismissing the respondents' appeal held that they could not rely on the negligence of the doctor as a *novus actus interveniens* and thus they were liable for all the plaintiff's disabilities. [Leave to appeal to the H.L. was given.]

See article: " Employers' Liability for effect of anti-tetanus injection " (Poole) 124 New L.J. 195.

107 In *Stephenson* v. *Waite Tileman* [1973] N.Z.L.R. 152 the plaintiff was injured on the hand by a frayed and rusty wire rope. Medical witnesses were agreed that an unknown virus had infected the wound, but one doctor held the view that it had caused irreversable brain damage whilst the other held the opinion that the plaintiff was suffering from traumatic neurosis to which he was susceptible. The C.A. held that in cases of especially susceptible plaintiffs the court must decide whether the initial injury is of a kind, type or character which ought reasonably to have been foreseen

and, if it were, the defendant is liable for the eventual consequences directly caused by it.

113 **Novus actus interveniens**

See article: " Novus actus interveniens: the present effect of Wagon Mound " (Millner) 22 N.I.L.Q. 168.

See *Robinson* v. *The Post Office* (1973) 117 S.J. 915, § 105, *ante*, and article thereon: " Employer's liability for effect of anti-tetanus injection " (Poole) 124 New L.J. 195.

120 **Reasonableness as a test as well as foreseeability**

NOTE 45. *West* v. *Hughes of Beaconsfield* [1971] R.T.R. 298 (held that it was foreseeable that a cyclist, who was knocked down by one vehicle, would be injured by another following).

124 **Acts done to minimise the plaintiffs' damage**

See article: " Plaintiff's duty to mitigate loss " (Glover) 121 New L.J. 713, 1092.

CHAPTER 4

DAMAGES

1.—INTRODUCTION

126 **General principles**

See articles: " Compensation for the injured " (Atiyah) 34 M.L.R. 432; " Reform of the law of damages for personal injuries " (Samuels) 123 New L.J. 1141. See also " Damages for personal injuries " (Samuels) 123 New L.J. 1009 for a review of the changes in the law over the preceding year or so.

The Law Commission has published its Report on Assessment of Damages in Personal Injury Actions. See article: " A significant study " (Woolf) 124 New L.J. 238.

129 **Minimising the damages**

However, it has been held that a plaintiff who, through ignorance, fails to claim benefits to which he is entitled, is not guilty of unreasonable failure to mitigate loss: *Eley* v. *Bedford* [1972] 1 Q.B. 155.

130 **Interference by appellate courts with awards of damages**

See *McCann* v. *Sheppard* [1973] 1 W.L.R. 540 and § 1000, *post*, where the C.A. had admitted fresh evidence which resulted in interference with an award of damages.

2.—HEADS OF DAMAGE AND ASSESSMENT

138 **Personal injuries**

In an action by a young spinster a sum will be awarded in respect of loss of marriage prospects and another sum will be awarded in respect of loss of future earnings. However, in assessing the latter, the court must have in mind that marriage usually involves a woman giving up her career for at least part of the time, thus reducing her future earnings by a substantial amount. After fixing the itemised awards the court should look at the grand total to see whether it accords with the pattern of other similar awards, making due allowance for the continually falling value of the pound sterling. *Harris* v. *Harris* [1973] 1 Lloyd's Rep. 445, C.A.

See articles: "Damages for lost amenities for a foot, a feeling or a function" (Ogus) 35 M.L.R. 1. The Law Commission has published its Report on Assessment of Damages in Personal Injury Actions. See article: "A significant study" (Woolf) 124 New L.J. 238.

148 **Assessment of damages**

NOTE 13. *Williams* v. *Scottish Gas Board,* 1972 S.L.T.(Notes) 66: "not less than £3,250 for the loss of an eye."

150 **Matters not to be taken into account in assessing damages**

Ex gratia payments from an employer to an injured person are not to be taken into account when assessing damages: *Cunningham* v. *Harrison* [1973] Q.B. 942.

153 **Financial loss**

Where the plaintiff through the fault of the defendant loses profits on a certain venture but later makes a profit on it, the profit actually made must be set off against the loss of profit claimed irrespective of whether the claim is based in contract or tort. Thus where the plaintiff, a driving school proprietor, was injured by the defendant's negligence and consequently could not finalise the purchase of a driving simulator for £7,000, but was able later to acquire a secondhand machine as bankrupt stock for £1,900 which he operated profitably, it was held that he must set off against his claim for loss of profit during the period without the machine, the extra profit he had made by buying the used simulator so cheaply and from its subsequent operation: *Bellingham* v. *Dhillon* [1973] Q.B. 304.

NOTE 34. *Donnelly* v. *Joyce* [1973] 3 W.L.R. 514 (mother gave up her part-time work in order to look after her 6-year-old son, injured by the defendant's negligent driving. Although she would have had no direct cause of action against the defendant her loss formed part of that incurred by the minor plaintiff and so was recoverable). In *Cunningham* v. *Harrison* [1973] Q.B. 942 the damages in respect of future nursing were reduced by the C.A. to take into account the likelihood of the plaintiff's receiving nursing under the National Health Service and the Chronically Sick and Disabled Persons Act 1970.

NOTE 39. But, on a claim for damages for personal injuries, a plaintiff must produce satisfactory accounts in order to substantiate a claim for loss of profits of a one-man business resulting from his injuries: *Ashcroft* v. *Curtin* [1971] 1 W.L.R. 1731.

154 **Loss of earnings**

See article: "Loss of earnings or earning capacity?" (Atiyah) 45 A.L.J. 228.

155 The C.A. in *Fairley* v. *John Thompson (Design and Contracting Division) Ltd.* [1973] 2 Lloyd's Rep. 40 held that the plaintiff was not entitled to an award for loss of future earnings unless this loss is sufficiently proved by evidence. In the absence of such proof, the plaintiff may still be entitled to compensation for loss of earning capacity as part of his general damages, but the distinction between the two types of award is important. See also *Field* v. *B.E.A.*, *The Times,* March 1, 1973, C.A.

156 **Damage to chattels**

In *Martindale* v. *Duncan* [1973] 1 W.L.R. 574 it was held that the plaintiff was entitled to recover the cost of hiring a replacement vehicle during the time he was awaiting the defendant's insurer's approval of the cost of repair to his own damaged car. In *Payton* v. *Brooks, The Times,* February 5, 1974, the C.A. held that where sufficient evidence had been given of a diminution in value of a damaged motor vehicle, such diminution could be recovered in addition to the cost of repairs.

157 See article: " Negligence—loss of profits—economic loss " (Jolowicz) [1973] C.L.J. 20.

See *Martindale* v. *Duncan* [1973] 1 W.L.R. 574, § 156, *supra.*

NOTE 61a. *Moore* v. *D.E.R.* [1971] 1 W.L.R. 1476. There can be circumstances where it may be reasonable for a plaintiff to replace a car, which has been " written off " due to the defendant's negligence, with a new car, as opposed to a secondhand car comparable to the damaged one.

NOTE 63. See article: " The status of ' The Edison.' " (Lawson) 124 New L.J. 240.

159 **Damage to land and buildings**

NOTE 67. But financial loss which is not the direct result of physical damage is too remote. *Spartan Steel and Alloys* v. *Martin* [1973] Q.B. 27. Thus where the defendants negligently cut an electricity cable causing interruption in the power supply to the plaintiffs' factory, the latter were entitled to the loss of the value of the metal in the course of processing and the loss of profit which would have been made on it, but they were not entitled to the loss of additional profits which would have been made on further lots of metal, which would have been processed in the hours until the power supply was restored.

163 **Damages for loss of consortium**

NOTE 89. In *Harris* v. *Nakhla* [1973] 4 C.L. 91 £400 was awarded for loss of consortium where the impairment of sexual relations only permitted the couple to practise intercourse to a limited extent, giving them little satisfaction, although there might have been some improvement once litigation was over.

165 **Reimbursement of a third party's losses**

See article: " Parent and child " (Wharam) 121 New L.J. 786.

Cunningham v. *Harrison* [1973] Q.B. 942; see § 167, *infra.* *Donnelly* v. *Joyce* [1973] 3 W.L.R. 514, see § 153, *ante*, and § 167, *infra.*

167 When a gravely injured husband is entitled to damages and his wife renders services to him instead of a nurse, he is entitled to recover compensation for the value of these services which he should hold on trust for her. Even though she may only be doing domestic duties in the home, all the extra attendance on her husband calls for compensation. *Cunningham* v. *Harrison* [1973] Q.B. 942. See also § 153, *ante.* In *Donnelly* v. *Joyce* [1973] 3 W.L.R. 514 the C.A. considered that it was erroneous doctrine that a plaintiff's right to recover damages in respect of money paid or the value of services rendered on his behalf by some other person can be brought into existence if, subsequent to the wrong-doing, a contract for re-imbursement is made between the plaintiff and the provider. Such a contract is *res inter alias acta* and irrelevant to the defendant's liability, which was established

in tort. Hence a minor plaintiff may recover against the defendant his mother's loss of wages incurred through her having to nurse him after his accident, although she had no direct cause of action for the money against the defendant. *Roach* v. *Yates* [1938] 1 K.B. 256 and *Liffen* v. *Watson* [1940] 1 K.B. 556 were applied but *Haggar* v. *de Placido* [1972] 1 W.L.R. 716 was disapproved.

170 **Interest**

The C.A. held that in commercial cases too, a party awarded damages is prima facie entitled to interest at a reasonable rate from the date when the sum should have been paid, unless there is some good reason shown for an exception to that rule. *Panchaud Frères S.A.* v. *Pagnan & Fratelli, The Times,* November 24, 1973.

171 A third party should pay interest from the date of issue of the third party notice only and not from the date of issue of the writ. *Slater* v. *Hughes* [1971] 1 W.L.R. 1438.

During 1972–73 the average rate of interest appears to have been 7 per cent. Since section 19 of the Finance Act 1971, which exempts for tax purposes interest on damages awarded for personal injuries or death, is intended to benefit the plaintiff, the court is not required to award a lower rate of interest. *Mason* v. *Harman* (1971) 115 S.J. 931.

176 **Motor Insurers' Bureau**

NOTE 43. *Motor Insurers' Bureau* v. *Meanen* (note) [1971] 2 All E.R. 1372; *Albert* v. *Motor Insurers' Bureau* [1972] A.C. 301.

CHAPTER 6

MASTER AND SERVANT AT COMMON LAW

1.—COMMON LAW DUTY OF MASTER

200 **General duty**

NOTE 9. The Employers' Liability (Compulsory Insurance) Act 1969 (Commencement) Order 1971 (No. 1116) brought the Act into operation on January 1, 1972. See also the Employers' Liability (Compulsory Insurance) General Regulations 1971 (No. 1117) which became operative on January 1, 1972, except for regulations 6 and 7, which took effect on January 1, 1973; and the Employers' Liability (Compulsory Insurance) Exemption Regulations 1971 (No. 1933) which became operative on January 1, 1972, specifying exemptions additional to those contained in section 3 of the Act itself.

See articles: "The Employers' Liability (Compulsory Insurance) Act 1969" (Simpson) 35 M.L.R. 63 and "Insurance and the fault principle: some recent developments" (Rowe) 123 New L.J. 736.

205 **(1) Safe place of work**

It may be sufficient to have a system whereby employees are themselves responsible for clearing away dangerous debris from the immediate vicinity of their work places. *Stanley* v. *Concentric (Pressed Products)* (1971) 11 K.I.R. 260, C.A.

211 **(3) Adequate plant and appliances**

Where a nurse sat on a chair which collapsed due to the fact that it had been weakened by woodworm, it was held that the employers were in breach of their duty to have a system of inspecting their furniture. *Baxter* v. *St. Helena Group Hospital Management Committee, The Times,* February 15, 1972.

213 **Provision of protective device or clothing**

In *Berry* v. *Stone Manganese and Marine Ltd.* (1971) 115 S.J. 966 Ashworth J. held that it was negligent to submit an employee to very loud noise without having tried to persuade him to wear protective ear muffs.

See article: " Liability for noise at work " (Samuels) 2 I.L.J. 78.

216 **(4) Safe system of work**

See article: " What is a safe system of work? " (Powell and Slater) 1 Industrial L.J. 135.

221 NOTE 35. *Berry* v. *Stone Manganese and Marine Ltd.* (1971) 115 S.J. 966. See § 213, *ante.*

222 NOTE 60. *Wright* v. *Dunlop Rubber Co.* (1971) 11 K.I.R. 311 affirmed
223 by C.A. (1973) 13 K.I.R. 255; and where employees were themselves responsible for clearing away dangerous debris from the immediate vicinity of their work places: *Stanley* v. *Concentric (Pressed Products)* (1971) 11 K.I.R. 260, C.A.

NOTE 70. *James* v. *Wellington City* [1972] N.Z.L.R. 70 (chimpanzee bit off finger of a zoo-keeper).

227 **No liability for ordinary risks of service**

See article: " Winter hazards and occupiers' liability " (Poole) 122 New L.J. 99.

3.—LIABILITY OF SERVANT TO MASTER

231 **Duty of servant to master**

Where the risk of a servant's negligence is covered by insurance, his employer should not seek to make that servant liable for it; at any rate the court should not compel him to allow an indemnifier to use his name to do so by subrogation. *Morris* v. *Ford Motor Co.* [1973] Q.B. 792.

See article: " Quo Vadis, Doctrine of Subrogation? " (Ahmed) 124 New L.J. 26.

CHAPTER 7

PERSONS PROFESSING SOME SPECIAL SKILL

1.—ACTIONS AGAINST SKILLED PERSONS GENERALLY

243 **Special relationships**

NOTE 39. See articles: " *Hedley Byrne* v. *Heller* in the Privy Council—the continuing story " (Phegan) 45 A.L.J. 20; " Fortunes of Hedley Byrne " (Hodgin) [1972] J.B.L. 27.

2.—ACCOUNTANTS AND AUDITORS

246 **Nature of the duty**

NOTE 50.; and 22 *Commercial Accountant* 180. " Professional liability of accountants and auditors." 167 Acct. 162; " Liability of accountants and auditors for negligent statements in company accounts." (Baxt) 36 M.L.R. 42.

247 **Duty depends on terms of employment**

Auditors when acting as experts and not as arbitrators in valuing shares on a contract of sale as between shareholders owe no duty of care in respect of their valuation, since they are performing a quasi-judicial function and are immune on the ground of public policy. *Arenson* v. *Arenson* [1973] Ch. 346. See article: "Striking out statement of claim: a comment on *Arenson* v. *Arenson*" (Glover) 123 New L.J. 703.

3.—Architects, Surveyors and Engineers

255 **Nature of the duty**

Note 76. In *Daisley* v. *B. S. Hall & Co.* (1972) 225 E.G. 1553 the surveyor was held to have been negligent in failing to report to his client, the plaintiff, the risk created by the combination of the poplar trees growing nearby and the clay sub-soil, where certain signs and cracks indicating shrinkage were already discernible in the house that the plaintiff was intending to purchase.

257 Note 82. In *Sutcliffe* v. *Thackrah* [1974] 2 W.L.R. 295 (reversing the C.A. [1973] 1 W.L.R. 888) an architect was held liable for negligently giving excessive interim certificates to the builder. Certifying such work is not to be equated to that function of an arbitrator so that *Chambers* v. *Goldthorpe* [1901] 1 K.B. 624 is overruled accordingly.

5.—Bankers

264 Note 12. *Commercial Banking Co. of Sydney* v. *R. H. Brown & Co.* [1972] 2 Lloyd's Rep. 360. (The High Court of Australia held that the bank's opinion was not honestly held by its manager concerning the business worthiness of its customer, a wool buyer.)

9.—Doctors, Surgeons, Physicians and Psychiatrists

272 **Nature of duty**

See article: "The negligent doctor" (Linden) 11 Osgoode Hall L.J. 31.

278 **Standard of care**

; failing to give warning to a patient, who had a tendency to phlebitis, of the dangerous side effects of an anti-coagulent drug he had prescribed. *Crichton* v. *Hasting* (1972) 29 D.L.R.(3d) 692.

14.—Quasi-Arbitrators

296 In *Arenson* v. *Arenson* [1973] Ch. 346 it was held that an expert, who performs a quasi-judicial function as between two parties, is immune on the ground of public policy from an action for negligence brought by either party.

See article: "Recovery for negligence" (Glover) 122 New L.J. 924.

15.—Schools and Schoolteachers

304 **Duty to exercise supervision**

A local authority was held to be vicariously liable for the negligence of a school crossing patrolman, who had failed to do all that he ought to have done in order to control and ensure the safety of school children crossing. *Toole* v. *Sherbourne Pouffes, Newport Corporation (Third Py.)* [1971] R.T.R. 479.

16.—Solicitors

310 **Nature of duty**

See articles: " Duty of care of the solicitor " (Samuels) 69 L.S.Gaz. 761; " Professional negligence, insurance and the Law Society " (Bates) 117 S.J. 494.

312 **Standard of care**

In *Duchess of Argyll* v. *Beuselinck* [1972] 2 Lloyd's Rep. 172 Megarry J. considered the question whether a higher standard of care should be expected of solicitors who held themselves out to be experts in a particular field, than of general practitioners. He appeared to favour the view that there should be, but came to no conclusion on the matter.

319 **Duty in non-contentious matters**

In addition a solicitor has been held negligent for mistakenly exchanging contracts before he had received the landlord's acceptance of the plaintiff as assignee, despite a clause in the lease which may well have made him unacceptable. *Transportation Agency* v. *Jenkins* (1972) 223 E.G. 1101.

322 **No duty to advise on business matters**

, or, when he has been retained to give general advice to the plaintiff, who was contemplating publishing her memoirs, so to advise her to enable her to avoid incurring a substantial tax liability by organising her affairs differently. *Duchess of Argyll* v. *Beuselinck* [1972] 2 Lloyd's Rep. 172.

324 **Measure of damages**

Note 87. *Simple Simon Catering* v. *Binstock Miller & Co.* (1973) 117 S.J. 529.

18.—Valuers and Estate Agents

327 Where an estate agent, who received his commission from the vendor of the property, was employed by the plaintiff gratuitously to find him a house on which there was a long term mortgage available, failed to check, so that the plaintiff bought a house on which the mortgage had less than one week to run, thereby suffering a loss, the estate agent was held to be liable in negligence. *Avery* v. *Salie* (1972) 25 D.L.R.(3d) 495.

Where a landlord suffered loss and damage due to non-payment of rent and the expense of evicting his tenant, who had entered into possession of the dwelling house without paying an advance rent or deposit by deceiving the inexperienced employee of the defendant firm of house agents, the latter was found liable in negligence. *Brutton* v. *Alfred, Savill, Curtis & Henson* (1970) 218 E.G. 1417.

Note 1. *Daisley* v. *B. S. Hall & Co.* (1972) 225 E.G. 1553. See § 255.

Chapter 8

DANGEROUS PREMISES

2.—The Person Liable for Dangerous Premises

341 **Liability of invitor or licensor not in occupation of premises**

Note 64. See now section 4 of the Defective Premises Act 1972, which supersedes the Occupiers' Liability Act 1957, s. 4, and makes provision for a landlord's liability for defects in the state of the premises that he has let where he has an obligation or the right to remedy such defects. He is now under a duty of care to see that other persons are reasonably safe from risk either as regards personal injury or damage to their property by such a defect.

3.—THE DUTY OWED

346 **What is the duty owed ?**

An occupier has been held not liable where a guest slipped on snow lying on the forecourt of the occupiers' hotel since, on the facts, nothing could have been done to render the forecourt less dangerous in the prevailing weather conditions. *Wood* v. *Morland & Co.* (1971) 115 S.J. 569.

See article: " Winter hazards and occupiers' liability " (Poole) 122 New L.J. 99.

347 **Extension, restriction, modification or exclusion of liability**

In *White* v. *Blackmore* [1972] 2 Q.B. 651 it was held that the organisers of a dangerous sport, namely a " jalopy " racing club meeting, may effectively exclude their liability to spectators for accidents arising from their breach of duty of care and their duty under the Occupiers' Liability Act 1957 by displaying notices warning the public of the danger and stating that it is a condition of admission that they are absolved from all liabilities for accidents " howsoever caused." The deceased, a member of the club, went to a meeting organised by the defendants as a competitor, but was unhappily killed whilst he was watching another race, when the wheel of a car caught in a safety rope and catapulted him about twenty feet away.

See article: " Occupiers' liability: effects of warning notice " (Glover) 123 New L.J. 938.

353 **Traps for children at common law**

NOTE 41. See further articles: "Child trespasser: an outmoded doctrine? " 115 S.J. 339 and " Trespassers still unprotected " (Samuels) 135 J.P.N. 736.

355 **Trespassing children**

But where the electricity authority maintained a highly dangerous electrical transmission system over the land of another, to which people generally resorted, and an eleven-year-old child climbed up a pole which was insufficiently cladded to prevent him doing so and suffered injury by electrical burning, it was held that the authority were liable: *Munnings* v. *Hydro-Electric Commission* (1971) 45 A.L.J.R. 378. See a similar decision in *Southern Portland Cement v. Cooper* [1974] 2 W.L.R. 152.

On the subject as a whole see now *British Railways Board* v. *Herrington* [1972] A.C. 877. The plaintiff, a six-year-old child who had been playing in a field which was frequently used by children and was open to the public, climbed through a gap in a fence adjoining the defendants' electrified railway lines and sustained severe personal injuries and burns when he came into contact with the " live " raised rail. The fence, through which the boy had climbed, was dilapidated and had been in such bad repair for a considerable length of time as a result of people using the gap as a short cut. A number of weeks before the accident, the defendants had reported the presence of children on the line but had taken no effective measures to prevent their trespassing from continuing. The defendants were held liable in negligence by the trial judge (Cairns J.) the C.A. (Salmon, Edmund Davies and Cross L.J.) and the H.L. (Lords Reid, Morris of Borth-y-Gest, Wilberforce, Pearson and Diplock). See further § 387–395, *post*.

See articles: "Child trespasser: verdict on Addie" 116 S.J. 706; "Child tresspassers—a new attempt to solve an insoluble problem" (Barrett) 136 L.G. Rev. 726; "Forgiving our trespassers" (Weaver) 124 New L.J. 92.

A local authority which had been warned of a danger on its land, such as a wall in imminent danger of collapse, by a member of the public telephoning, cannot evade liability merely because the message had failed to find its way to the appropriate department. *Melvin* v. *Franklins (Builders)* (1972) 71 L.G.R. 142, C.A.

The Law Commission has published its Working Paper No. 52: "Liability for damage or injury to trespassers and related questions of occupiers' liability."

360 **Warning and knowledge of dangers**

See *White* v. *Blackmore* [1972] 2 Q.B. 651 and § 347, *ante*.

See article: "Occupiers' liability: effect of warning notice" (Glover) 123 New L.J. 958.

370 **Contractual duty to persons entering the premises**

Nevertheless, when a person has been injured after entering premises by right of contract, he may sue the occupier in tort as well as in contract, where there was no express or implied term in the agreement restricting him to a claim in contract only. *Sole* v. *Hallt* [1973] Q.B. 574.

(a) *Spectacles and Entertainments*

375 **Duty as to the performance**

NOTE 28. *White* v. *Blackmore* [1972] 2 Q.B. 651. See § 347, *ante*. See article: "Occupiers' liability: effects of warning notice" (Glover) 123 New L.J. 938.

NOTE 31. See article: "Sportsman's charter revoked" (Kovats) 115 S.J. 824.

(b) *Landlord and Tenant*

377–379 **Obligation of landlord**

See now the effects of the Defective Premises Act 1972, which came into force on January 1, 1974, in particular section 4 which supersedes the Occupiers' Liability Act 1957, s. 4. See § 341, *ante*, § 401, *post*.

See also article: "Defective Premises Act 1972" (Samuels) 116 S.J. 910.

5.—TRESPASSERS

387–395 On the subject as a whole see now *British Railways Board* v. *Herrington* [1972] A.C. 877. The facts are summarised at § 355, *ante*. The House of Lords held that the test of liability is subjective in that the trespasser must take the occupier as he finds him and that the duty to a trespasser is a "humanitarian duty." Thus the occupier's duty will vary in all the circumstances, including his state of knowledge, ability and resources. Accordingly, the question whether an occupier is liable in negligence to a trespasser depends upon whether a conscientious, humane man with his knowledge, skill and resources could reasonably have been expected to have done or refrained from doing something before the accident which could have avoided it, or, in other words, he must act in a humane manner. The H.L. also expressed the view that *Addie* v. *Dumbreck* [1929] A.C. 358 would be decided differently today, the child succeeding in his action, and that the test of "intent or recklessness" laid down in *Addie* v. *Dumbreck* (*ante*) and

Commissioners for Railways v. *Quinlan* [1964] A.C. 1054 was too narrow, whilst the foreseeability test suggested by Lord Denning M.R. in *Videan* v. *British Transport Commission* [1963] 2 Q.B. 650 was too wide.

Herrington's decision was applied in *Pannett* v. *McGuinness & Co.* [1972] 2 Q.B. 599, where the C.A. held that in considering the question of an occupier's liability to a trespasser the court should take into account all the circumstances of the case and see then whether the occupier ought to have done more than he did. The plaintiff, a five-year-old boy, was severely burned in a bonfire of rubbish lit in the vicinity of a warehouse which was being demolished in a heavily populated area near a park where children were accustomed to play. The workmen in charge had frequently chased children, including the plaintiff, away, but despite this they had left the bonfire unattended and the boy had immediately gained access.

See articles: " Occupiers' and non-occupiers' duty towards trespassers " (Vennell) (1972) N.Z.L.R. 161; " Duty of care " (Seepersad) 122 New L.J. 1004. The Law Commission has published its Working Paper No. 52: " Liability for damage or injury to trespassers and related questions of occupiers' liability."

395 **Liability to a trespasser for negligence**

See articles: " Another trespassing child " (Weaver) 122 New L.J. 381; " Forgiving our Trespassers " (Weaver) 124 L.J. 92.

NOTE 25a: See articles: " Child trespasser: an outmoded doctrine? " 115 S.J. 339; " Child trespasser: verdict on Addie " 116 S.J. 706; " Child trespassers—a new attempt to solve an insoluble problem " (Barrett) 136 L.G.Rev. 726; " Recent developments in the law of occupiers and trespassers " (Keeler) 46 A.L.J. 444; " Occupiers' liability: the under-privileged neighbour " (Weaver) 122 New L.J. 221.

6.—LIABILITY FOR NEGLIGENT ACTS ON PREMISES

396 **Liability generally**

NOTE 35. *White* v. *Blackmore* [1972] 2 Q.B. 651. See § 347, *ante*.

399 **Nature of liability**

NOTE 49. *Otto's* case was overruled by the C.A. in *Dutton* v. *Bognor Regis U.D.C.* [1972] 1 Q.B. 373. See further § 401, *post*.

7.—LIABILITY OF VENDOR OR LESSOR

401 **Liability of vendor or lessor**

On the subject as a whole see now the effects of the Defective Premises Act 1972, which came into force on January 1, 1974; section 3 of which abolished the common law rule under which vendors (*Bottomley* v. *Bannister* [1934] 1 K.B. 458, and *Otto* v. *Bolton and Norris* [1936] 2 K.B. 46) and lessors (*Cavalier* v. *Pope* [1906] A.C. 428) of land had been held immune from liability for negligence, subject to a few exceptions, either in building or other works carried out on that land, which had taken place before the sale or letting, and in the absence of express contractual conditions.

The new law is set out in section 3 (1) and the limited situations where the section does not apply are set out in sub-section (2).

Even before the passing of this Act the C.A., in *Dutton* v. *Bognor Regis U.D.C.* [1972] 1 Q.B. 373, had regarded both *Bottomley* v. *Bannister* (*supra*) and *Otto* v. *Bolton and Norris* (*supra*) as being no longer good law and Lord Denning M.R. felt prepared to overrule them, whilst Sachs L.J. considered *Bottomley's* case had been superseded by *Donoghue* v. *Stevenson* [1932] A.C. 562 and that *Otto's* case was not binding on the court in any event.

See articles: "Defective Premises Act 1972" (Samuels) 37 Conv.(N.S.) 314 and 116 S.J. 910.

NOTE 52. *Sheldon* v. *West Bromwich Corporation* (1973) 25 P. & C.R. 360. Where a water tank in a council house had remained discoloured for some considerable time with the knowledge of the council and, later, the tank burst, the defendants were held to be in breach of their implied covenant under section 32 (1) of the Housing Act 1961 to keep in repair the installation for the supply of water.

402 See dicta of Lord Denning M.R. and Sachs L.J. in *Dutton* v. *Bognor Regis U.D.C.* [1972] 1 Q.B. 373 at pp. 394 and 401.

8.—LIABILITY OF NON-OCCUPIERS

403 **Liability of persons not in occupation**

See article: "Occupiers' and non-occupiers' duty towards trespassers" (Vennell) 1972 N.Z.L.J. 161.

CHAPTER 9

DANGEROUS THINGS: RYLANDS v. FLETCHER

2.—DEFENCES

(d) *Independent Act of Third Party*

440 **Meaning of "third party"**

Where the plaintiff's crops and cattle suffered damage as the result of oil pollution, caused by a leak from the defendants' trunk pipe line into a flooded watercourse as a result of the deliberate act of a trespasser maliciously drilling a hole in the pipe, the Trinidad and Tobago Court of Appeal held that the plaintiff's claim failed. *Mandraj and Mandraj* v. *Texaco Trinidad Inc.* (1969) 15 W.I.R. 251.

3.—WATER

469 **Canals**

Where barges on a canal frequently tied up against a wall abutting the plaintiff's factory, despite a notice displayed by the defendants forbidding this, and over the years the banging of these barges against this wall had caused water to seep through so that the wall's base collapsed and damaged the foundations of the factory, it was held that the defendants were liable. The basis of such liability was failing in their duty to take reasonable steps to prevent not only the heavy congestion at this point of the canal, but also the collisions which took place with the plaintiffs' wall. *Boxes* v. *British Waterways Board* [1971] 2 Lloyd's Rep. 183.

488 **Escape of water collected on roofs**

NOTE 37. Where much debris fell on to the flat roof of the plaintiff's premises in the course of building and it was allowed to remain there because of the defendant's faulty system of inspection and removal, causing the drains to become blocked so that flooding and damage occurred following a heavy rainstorm, the defendants were held liable in negligence, nuisance and under the rule in *Rylands* v. *Fletcher. Heintzman & Co.* v. *Hashman Construction* (1972) 32 D.L.R. 622.

4.—FIRE

493 **Fires Prevention (Metropolis) Act 1774**

It was held to be negligent where the defenders, in order to save on the costs of storage, had ignored the proper and well-known fire precaution of providing sufficient spacing between the bales of jute stacked in their warehouse, as a result of which overheating occurred and a fire started which spread to the pursuers' adjoining premises. *Scott* v. *MacKenzie Stewart,* 1972 S.L.T.(Notes) 69, applying *Morris* v. *West Hartlepool Steam Navigation Co.* [1956] A.C. 552.

526 **Liability of landlord or vendor of real property**

See now the effects of the Defective Premises Act 1972 and *Dutton* v. *Bognor Regis U.D.C.* [1972] 1 Q.B. 373, §§ 29 and 401 *et seq., ante.*

9.—NUCLEAR INSTALLATIONS

569 **Nuclear Installations Act 1965**

See also Nuclear Installations Act 1969.

CHAPTER 10

ANIMALS

572 **Principles of liability**

NOTE 9. See articles: " Animals Act 1971 " (Samuels) 115 S.J. 662 and 34 M.L.R. 550; (Passingham) 66 L.S.Gaz. 397.

1.—STRICT LIABILITY FOR DAMAGE DONE BY ANIMALS

579 **Liability for damage done by dangerous animals**

NOTE 60. Distinguished in *Morris* v. *Bailey* (1970) 13 D.L.R.(3d) 150 where the defendant allowed his collie dog to run at large, well knowing that it had a propensity to run up to people, barking furiously, although it stopped short of actually touching them.

Exceptions from liability

NOTE 1. See *James* v. *Wellington City* [1972] N.Z.L.R. 70 in which the New Zealand Supreme Court held that there is an exception to the general rule of strict liability for dangerous animals in that an employer must only take reasonable care not to subject his employees to unnecessary risks. Where a zookeeper in charge of the chimpanzees, came to the outside of the cage to pacify one of them and having done so had his finger bitten off as he turned to go, it was held that the defence applied, because he was employed to work amongst dangerous animals and must be presumed to have known and accepted that fact.

592 **Dogs**

See article: " Dogs and the law " (Samuels) 117 S.J. 238.

2.—LIABILITY FOR NEGLIGENCE

594 **Principles of liability**

NOTE 20. Distinguished in *Morris* v. *Bailey* (1970) 13 D.L.R.(3d) 150.

597 **Cases of negligence**

Where a three-year-old child was attacked by a number of Jack Russell Terrier puppies, the judge accepted expert evidence that dogs of that particular breed, when in groups, were highly dangerous and that no responsible dog breeder would allow such animals to be free to roam about, and found the owner liable in negligence, despite his having rebutted successfully a case of scienter. *Draper* v. *Hodder* [1972] 2 Q.B. 556.

3.—LIABILITY FOR TRESPASS

604 **Damages for livestock trespass**

NOTE 71. See article: " *Wormald* v. *Cole* lives? " (Horrocks) 123 New L.J. 255.

CHAPTER 11

DANGEROUS CHATTELS: DONOGHUE v. STEVENSON

2.—DUTY OF MANUFACTURER OF GOODS

Defences

644 **Inspection contemplated before use**

NOTE 3. *Otto* v. *Bolton* is no longer good law. See dicta of Lord Denning M.R. and Sachs L.J. in *Dutton* v. *Bognor Regis U.D.C.* [1972] 1 Q.B. 373.

CHAPTER 12

HIGHWAYS

1.—DANGERS ON OR ADJOINING THE HIGHWAY

675 **Duties in respect of a highway**

NOTE 1. As regards vehicles parked on the highway see § 842.

(a) *Dangers on the Highway*

676 **Obstructions on highway**

NOTE 2. Dictum of Romer L.J. in *Harper* v. *Haden & Sons* [1933] Ch. 298 applied by Bridge J. in *Dymond* v. *Pearce* [1971] R.T.R. 417, although his decision was varied on appeal [1972] 1 Q.B. 496. See also § 843, *post.*

See article: "Obstruction on the highway: liability for collision" (Samuels) 117 S.J. 422.

699 **Nature of the statutory duty**

See *Ford* v. *Liverpool Corporation* (1972) 117 S.J. 167 (the obstruction of a one-inch high ridge on the surface of the roadway, as opposed to its being on the pavement, must be expected, although personal injuries resulting therefrom were not to be expected).

See article: "Statutory liability for dangerous roads" (Hawke) 123 New L.J. 3.

700 A highway authority's duty under section 44 of the Highways Act 1959 is reasonably to maintain and repair the highway so that it is free of danger to all using it normally, taking into account the traffic reasonably expected to be on it and that drivers may make mistakes. *Rider* v. *Rider* [1973] Q.B.

505. However mere unevenness, undulations and minor potholes do not normally constitute a danger and the normal run of drivers does not include the drunk or the reckless person. *Rider* v. *Rider, supra,* was applied in *Rae* v. *Dunbarton C.C.*, 1973 S.L.T.(Notes) 23, Outer House (failure to alleviate the dangerous and wintry state of their road).

NOTE 31. Where a road is old and likely to break up, the highway authority must provide an extremely high standard of maintenance if the road be called upon to carry heavy traffic. *Bramwell* v. *Shaw* [1971] R.T.R. 167.

704 Examples of misfeasance

Rider v. *Rider* [1973] Q.B. 505, *supra.*

2.—DUTY OF CARRIERS

(a) *Railways*

763 Stopping and starting trains

The railway authority was held liable when the train, without audible warning, started to move off from the station so that the plaintiff, who had boarded it to help an elderly passenger on with his luggage, felt obliged to jump from the moving train as it was gathering speed, whereby he was injured. *Caterson* v. *Commissioner for Railways (N.S.W.)* (1973) 47 A.L.J.R. 249.

782 Accommodation crossings

NOTE 39. *Short* v. *British Railways Board*, 1974, 118 S.J. 101.

(d) *Aircraft*

807 International carriage by air

See article: "Compensation for death and injury in international air transport" (Martin) 67 Law Guardian 11.

(e) *Hovercraft*

810 Statute law

NOTE 48. Hovercraft Act 1968 (Commencement) Order 1972 (No. 979) brought section 4 (3) of the Act into operation on July 12, 1972.

3.—HIGHWAY USERS AND COLLISIONS

812 Duty of driver of vehicle

The duty of the instructor driver is to instruct the pupil in the correct and safe management of the vehicle and it is the duty of the pupil to use the best skill he has and to obey the instructor in so far as he has acquired the skill so to do. However in the absence of any stipulation to the contrary, the instructor must be held to accept those risks of driving with a learner driver which go with the skill the pupil has, to the instructor's knowledge, obtained. *Lovelace* v. *Fossum* (1971) 24 D.L.R.(3d) 561.

NOTE 49a. *Nettleship* v. *Western* [1971] 2 Q.B. 691.

NOTE 50. , namely 80 mg. per 100 ml.

813 The Highway Code

See article: "Breach of the Highway Code" (Glover) 123 New L.J. 244.

814 Whilst a breach of the Highway Code can be relied on in an attempt to show negligence or contributory negligence it is not to be elevated into a breach of statutory duty, which establishes automatically a cause of action or a defence. *Powell* v. *Phillips*, 116 S.J. 713. (The C.A. refused to find a plaintiff guilty of contributory negligence when she had failed to walk on a pavement at night in a poorly lit road but had walked in the roadway with her back to the oncoming traffic, wearing dark clothes and without carrying anything white in colour.)

817 **Rule of the road**

NOTE 62. *Hurt* v. *Murphy* [1971] R.T.R. 186. (The deceased was held one-fifth to blame for not continuing to look to her left as she crossed over the road.)

820 **Overtaking**

NOTES 71 and 76. *Goke* v. *Willett* (1973) 117 S.J. 468, C.A. (a hand signal in addition to a flashing trafficator signal may be necessary to distinguish between the intention of overtaking and either increasing or maintaining speed rather than the intention of reducing speed and then turning to change direction to the right).

NOTE 84. *Gambino* v. *Di Leo* (1971) 17 D.L.R.(3d) 167 (children emerged suddenly from behind an ice-cream truck).

822 **Vehicle following another**

NOTE 93. *Thompson* v. *Spedding* [1973] R.T.R. 312. (Both the plaintiff and the defendant drivers were held equally to blame.)

825 **Collisions in centre of road**

NOTE 4. *Baker* v. *Market Harborough Industrial Co-operative Socy.* was applied in *Howard* v. *Bemrose* [1973] R.T.R. 32, C.A.

829 **Traffic lights**

NOTE 17. Similarly where pedestrians were injured whilst crossing a road on a crossing marked by studs but with the traffic lights at green in favour of vehicular traffic, it was held that too much attention should not be paid to that fact, since the degree of blameworthiness to be attached to them may be very small, especially where the defendents' vehicle was approaching at a very fast speed. *Mulligan* v. *Holmes* [1971] R.T.R. 179 (20 per cent. contributory negligence).

NOTE 18. But a motorist who fails to realise that traffic lights are not functioning properly may be guilty of negligence. *Ramoo s/o Erulapan* v. *Gan Soo Swee* [1971] 1 W.L.R. 1014; *Sudds* v. *Hanscombe* [1971] R.T.R. 212, C.A.

830 **Road junctions**

NOTE 23. On the other hand a driver on the main road has no duty to take his foot off the accelerator pedal and poise it over the brake pedal just in case a car driven dangerously might come across his path out of a side road without stopping. *Humphrey* v. *Leigh* [1971] R.T.R. 363 (doubting the dictum of Ormerod L.J. in *Williams* v. *Fullerton*, 105 S.J. 280).

832 **Signals**

NOTE 30. *Goke* v. *Willett* (1973) 117 S.J. 468. See § 820, *ante*.

833 **Lights**

If a motorist stops his motor-car at night on a road in a position where it is only safe if exhibiting lights, O'Connor J. held that it was negligent to use the self-starter for prolonged periods, which had had the effect of dimming or extinguishing the compulsory lights altogether. *Young* v. *Chester* [1973] R.T.R. 319.

835 Where a car was left unlit because of lights failure on a clearway, which was well lit, the driver was held to be negligent in failing to display a warning sign but similarly the other driver, who had driven into the stationary vehicle, was found to be equally negligent in failing the keep a proper look out. *Lee* v. *Lever* [1974] R.T.R. 35, C.A. (*Parish* v. *Judd* [1960] 1 W.L.R. 867 considered).

836 **Headlamps**

A motorist who drives on dipped headlights for the convenience of oncoming traffic must travel at a speed which will enable him to deal with the ordinary problems of the highway. *Young* v. *Chester, supra.*

NOTE 56. *Leeson* v. *Bevis & Tolchard Ltd.* [1972] R.T.R. 373, C.A.

842 **Leaving vehicles on highway**

NOTE 75. *Watson* v. *Heslop,* 115 S.J. 308.

843 In *Watson* v. *Heslop, supra,* it was held that it was negligent to park at night on a busy main road if other traffic cannot pass easily. See also *Young* v. *Chester* [1973] R.T.R. 319.

Whilst the leaving of a large wide lorry on the road overnight, albeit under a street lamp and with a vehicle's own lights on, amounted to a nuisance by obstruction, nevertheless for a plaintiff to recover damages for personal injuries resulting from a collision with it, he must establish that the obstruction constituted a danger. *Dymond* v. *Pearce* [1972] 1 Q.B. 496. This case was applied in *Wills* v. *T. F. Martin (Roof Contractors)* 116 S.J. 145 to a skip, with lights, placed on the road. For cases involving skips which had not been or were inadequately lit so as to be visible instantly, see *Drury* v. *Camden London Borough Council* [1972] R.T.R. 391; *Saper* v. *Hungate Builders* [1972] R.T.R. 380.

See article: " Liability for obstructing the highway " (Poole) 115 S.J. 940.

846 **Led animals**

NOTE 95. However in *Andrews* v. *Watts* [1971] R.T.R. 484 the Divisional Court held that a cattle owner who herded his cattle on a road at night was guilty of negligence in failing to equip his drovers with some form of lamp or a reflector in accordance with paragraph 140 of the Highway Code.

851 **Straying livestock**

NOTE 23. Distinguished in *Morris* v. *Bailey* (1970) 13 D.L.R.(3d) 150.

854 **Pedestrians**

However in *Parkinson* v. *Parkinson* [1973] R.T.R. 193, C.A., it was held that it is not necessarily negligent for a pedestrian to walk on the nearside of a country road *viz.*: with his back to the oncoming traffic. Also see *Kerley* v. *Downes* [1973] R.T.R. 189; *Powell* v. *Phillips* [1972] 3 All E.R. 864. § 814, *ante.*

858a Duty of learner driver

Nettleship v. *Weston* [1971] 2 Q.B. 691. It is the duty of the pupil to use the best skill he has and to obey the instructor in so far as he has acquired the skill so to do. *Lovelace* v. *Fossum* (1971) 24 D.L.R.(3d) 561.

CHAPTER 13

PARTIES

1.—THE CROWN

866 Judicial acts

NOTE 15. But see *Arenson* v. *Arenson* [1973] Ch. 346. See also § 247, *ante.*

869 Government departments

Where a municipality is exercising legistlative or quasi-judicial powers, it may act beyond its powers in the ultimate view of a court, but it would be incredible to suggest in such circumstances that it owed a duty of care giving rise to liability in damages for its breach. Thus the Canada Supreme Court held that a builder who had spent money in reliance on a by-law which was later declared invalid at the instance of ratepayers' action, and thereby suffered loss and damage, had no cause of action. *Welbridge Holdings* v. *Metropolitan Corporation of Greater Winnipeg* (1971) 22 D.L.R.(3d) 470.

NOTE 24. *Home Office* v. *Dorset Yacht* was approved by the Ontario C.A. in *Schacht* v. *The Queen in Right of the Province of Ontario* (1972) 30 D.L.R.(3d) 641. (The Ontario police were required by statute to maintain a traffic patrol on highways and to their knowledge a well-lit barrier marking a detour had been knocked down, leaving a hazardous situation, but they took adequate steps to warn approaching motorists of the danger.)

CHAPTER 14

VICARIOUS LIABILITY

1.—SERVANTS

925 Vehicle entrusted to servant to be driven or used

In order to fix vicarious liability for the negligence of the driver of a motor-car or the owner of the vehicle, it must be shown that the driver was using it for the owner's purposes under delegation of a task or duty. *Morgans* v. *Launchberry* [1973] A.C. 127 (approving *Hewitt* v. *Bonvin* [1940] 1 K.B. 188).

See article: " Vicarious liability and the car owner: orthodoxy restored " (Kidd) 122 New L.J. 488.

929 Servant permitted to use own vehicle whilst on master's business

However the master is only vicariously liable for his servant's acts if the latter were carrying out a task or duty delegated to him by the master and not merely acting for the master's benefit or at his request, such as by attending a residential training centre. *Nottingham* v. *Aldridge; Prudential Assurance Co. (Third Party)* [1971] 2 Q.B. 739.

Where there is the special duty in a contract of employment to obey an emergency call at any hour, a servant has been held to be on duty whilst making his way to his place of work. *Blee* v. *L.N.E.R.* [1938] A.C. 126 (ganger called out to a derailment). *Stitt* v. *Woolley* (1971) 115 S.J. 708 (fireman attending promptly at the fire station in response to an emergency call).

NOTE 25. But see *Elleanor* v. *Cavendish Woodhouse Ltd.* (1972) 117 S.J. 14 (two salesmen returning home together after an evening's canvassing when an accident happened; it was held that the employer was vicariously liable).

931 **Driving by conductors and others**

NOTE 30. *Iqbal* v. *London Transport Executive, The Times,* June 7, 1973, C.A. (although a bus-conductor had been prohibited on many occasions from driving buses, he still attempted to drive a bus at a depot and injured a fellow employee, but the employers were held not liable for his negligence).

2.—AGENTS

942 **Owner not in car**

See now *Morgans* v. *Launchberry* [1973] A.C. 127. See § 925, *ante.*

NOTE 89. See article: "Family car" (Strachan) 115 S.J. 801; "Vicarious liability—motor vehicle—insurance" (Jolowicz) [1971] C.L.J. 195.

3.—CHILDREN

945 **Liability of parent**

Hahn v. *Conley* (1971) 45 A.L.J.R. 631. See § 1038, *post.*

See article: "Child v. Parent" (Rowe) 124 New L.J. 117.

CHAPTER 15

PROOF OF NEGLIGENCE

1.—PROOF GENERALLY

963 **Burden of proof**

NOTE 5. and it is actionable materially to increase the risk of another's injury, even if it cannot be proved that injury was definitely caused. In *McGhee* v. *National Coal Board* [1973] 1 W.L.R. 1, where the plaintiff was employed to do hot dusty work but had to cycle home caked with sweat and grime because the defendants had provided no showers or proper washing facilities, in breach of their duty, so that his exertions under such conditions appreciably increased the risk of contracting dermatitis, it was held that the defendants were liable even though the precise mechanism of the inception of the disease was not clearly understood.

972 **Cause of accident where several defendants**

NOTE 50. Applied in *Howard* v. *Bemrose* [1973] R.T.R. 32, C.A.

974 **Civil Evidence Act 1968**

See also the Civil Evidence Act 1972, which gives effect to the majority recommendations contained in the Seventeenth Report of the Law Reform Committee (Evidence of Opinion and Expert Evidence) Cmnd. 4489. Section

1 makes hearsay statement of opinions admissible in evidence in civil proceedings to substantially the same extent as hearsay statements of facts are so admissible under Part I of the Civil Evidence Act 1968. The Act came into force on January 1, 1973, except sections 1 and 4 (2)–(5) which come into force on June 1, 1974.

See articles: " Expert evidence in the Civil Evidence Bill " (Amies) 1972 R.V.R. 254; " Civil Evidence Act 1972 " (Newark and Samuels) 122 New L.J. 847.

NOTE 60. Distinguished in *Morris* v. *Stratford on Avon R.D.C.* [1973] 1 W.L.R. 1059.

2.—RES IPSA LOQUITUR

978 **Res ipsa loquitur**

NOTE 83. *Bennett* v. *Chemical Construction (G.B.)* [1971] 1 W.L.R. 1571. See article: " A glimpse of res ipsa loquitur " (Lall) 124 New L.J. 216.

980 **Meaning of res ipsa loquitur**

NOTE 86. However in *McLeod* v. *Glasgow Corporation,* 1971 S.L.T. 64, where the pursuer was injured when the lavatory pan in a public toilet, owned and occupied by the defenders, broke as he sat down upon it, it was held that as the allegedly defective apparatus had been in regular use by members of the public to the exclusion of the defenders and its employees the maxim did not apply.

3.—THE TRIAL OF A CAUSE OF ACTION

992 **Duty of judge**

It is the court's duty when deciding whether a civil action should be tried by a jury to act fairly to all parties to the action; the mere fact that a party mistakenly thinks that a judge alone would be biased against him is not a sufficient reason. *Williams* v. *Beesley* [1973] 1 W.L.R. 1295.

4.—APPEALS

From the High Court

1000 NOTE 99. The C.A. exercised its discretion to admit fresh evidence as to the intervening death of a successful plaintiff between an award of damages, for substantial loss of future earnings and amenities, and the hearing of an appeal against that award. *McCann* v. *Sheppard* [1973] 1 W.L.R. 540.

See article: " Judicial attitudes towards actuarial evidence " (Richards and Kidner) 124 New L.J. 105.

CHAPTER 16

DEFENCES AND DISCHARGES FROM LIABILITY

1.—CONTRIBUTORY NEGLIGENCE

1004 **Meaning of contributory negligence**

See article: " Widening scope of defence of contributory negligence (Spencer) 30 C.L.J. 27.

1015 **Plaintiff " trapped " by defendant's conduct**

NOTE 42. But a motorist who fails to realise that traffic lights are not functioning properly may be guilty of negligence. *Ramoo s/o Erulapan* v. *Gan Soo Swee* [1971] 1 W.L.R. 1014.

1028 **Fault causing the damage**

Where a passenger travelled in a motor-car and failed to wear the seat belt provided she was held to be guilty of contributory negligence to the extent of 5 per cent., although the driver had not encouraged her to wear it. *Pasternack* v. *Poulton* [1973] 1 W.L.R. 476. *Cf.* similar failures to wear seat belts where the findings of contributory negligence were: one-fifth in *Parnell* v. *Shields* [1973] R.T.R. 414; a quarter in *Toperoff* v. *Mor* [1973] R.T.R. 419 and one-third in *McGee* v. *F. Shaw & Co.* [1973] R.T.R. 409.

See articles: " Seat belts and contributory negligence " (Linden) 49 Can. Bar Rev. 475; " Road user and safety devices " 116 S.J. 440; " Why bother with that seat belt ? " (Kerse) 117 S.J. 45; " If only I'd worn my seat belt " (Lamming and Rowe) 123 New L.J. 288; " Some recent decisions on wearing seat belts " (Kerse) 117 S.J. 625.

However see *Lertora* v. *Finzi* [1973] R.T.R. 161 where it was held that in order to succeed in a finding of contributory negligence for failing to wear a safety belt it was also necessary to show that wearing it would have reduced the injuries.

NOTE 93a. Now reported [1972] 1 Q.B. 270.

1029 **Apportionment of damages**

The court having found contributory negligence on the part of the plaintiff may not disregard that negligence when awarding damages. *Boothman* v. *British Northrop* (1972) 13 K.I.R. 112, C.A.

1037 **Contributory negligence of children**

NOTE 36. A child of five years who ran across a main road and was struck by a motor-car was held to be equally to blame with the motorist. *McKinnell* v. *White,* 1971 S.L.T. 61.

1038 NOTE 42. *Cf. Hahn* v. *Conley* (1971) 45 A.L.J.R. 631 where the Australian High Court held that a grandfather owed no duty of care to his three-year-old granddaughter whom he had seen was unaccompanied and was attempting to cross a road when she was struck down by a passing motorist.

See articles: " Third-partying the parent " (Gibson-Watt) 122 New L.J. 280; " Child v. Parent " (Rowe) 124 New L.J. 117.

2.—AGREEMENT TO RUN THE RISK: " VOLENTI NON FIT INJURIA "

1056 **Express and implied agreement**

NOTE 14. *Birch* v. *Thomas* [1972] 1 W.L.R. 294. See article: " Does liability depend on insurance? " (Parsons) 122 New L.J. 348. But see now the Motor Vehicle (Passenger Insurance) Act 1971, which came into force December 1, 1972.

1057 **Effect of knowledge of danger**

NOTE 15. Followed by C.A. in *White* v. *Blackmore* [1972] 2 Q.B. 651.

1061 **General application of the maxim**

NOTE 40. Followed by C.A. in *White* v. *Blackmore* [1972] 2 Q.B. 651. See § 347, *ante*.

1063 **Spectators and participants in sporting activities**

NOTE 48a. See article: " Sportsman's charter revoked " (Kovats) 115 S.J. 824.

4.—Contracting Out of Liability for Negligence

(d) *Effect of a Notice*

1105 **Effect of notice**

NOTE 70. *Birch* v. *Thomas* [1972] 1 W.L.R. 294. See articles: " Volenti non fit injuria and passenger liability (Symmons) 123 New L.J. 373; " Effect of notice excluding liability " (Poole) [1973] J.P.L. 588; " Non-Contractual Exclusion Clauses—1 " (Dobson) 124 New L.J. 249.

It could not be said that the plaintiff had freely and voluntarily incurred the risk of negligence on the part of the defendants where he had been sent by his employers to use the defendants premises. *Burnett* v. *British Waterways Board* [1973] 1 W.L.R. 700.

(e) *Construction of Exemption Contracts*

1108 **General principles**

In *Gillespie Bros. & Co.* v. *Roy Bowles Transport* [1973] 1 Q.B. 400 the words " all claims or demands whatsoever " were held to constitute an agreement in express terms which would cover all claims without exception, including a claim arising from negligence. But see also *A.M.F. International* v. *Magnet Bowling* [1968] 1 W.L.R. 1028.

1113 **Customer's or owner's risk**

NOTE 8. *Birch* v. *Thomas* [1972] 1 W.L.R. 294.

1116 **Effect of fundamental breach**

NOTE 22. See article: " Fundamental breach—the aftermath of Harbutts' Plasticene " (Legh-Jones and Pickering) 87 L.Q.R. 515.

5.— Limitation of Action

1136 **Generally**

See article: " Limitation of actions: a construction problem " 116 S.J. 425, 591.

1144 **When time begins to run**

NOTE 5. However in *Pritam Kaur* v. *S. Russell & Sons* [1973] Q.B. 336 the C.A. held that where the last day for doing an act in the court office is a day on which the office is not open, the act is done in time if it be done on the next day when the office is open.

1145 **Effect of fraudulent concealment**

NOTE 11. *King* v. *Victor Parsons* [1973] 1 W.L.R. 29. See article: " Construction of house on unsound foundations: liability for damage: concealed fraud " (Sophian) 70 L.S.Gaz. 1399.

1151 **Limitation Act 1963**

See articles: " Limitation Act 1963—time to clear the air " (Watmore) 70 L.S.Gaz. 1707; " Personal Injuries—when time runs " (Watmore) 122 New L.J. 672; " Personal injury limitations—House of Lords interpretation " (Woolf) 122 New L.J. 824.

1152 **Application for leave of court**

NOTE 53: See article: " Limitation Act 1963: personal injuries—a reply " (Watmore) 122 New L.J. 936.

1153 See article: " Ignorance of cause of action " (Glover) 123 New L.J. 740.

1154 In *Smith* v. *Central Asbestos Co.* [1973] A.C. 518 it was held that the twelve-month period provided by the Limitation Act 1963 did not begin to run against an injured plaintiff until he knows not only that he has been injured by the fault of the proposed defendant but also that he has a worthwhile cause of action. The plaintiff had worked for his employers in their asbestos factory since 1952 and in 1964 he had discovered that he was suffering from asbestosis. Later he claimed disability benefit and received it but was then told by the Works Manager that having done so he could not claim damages from the employers. In 1967 the plaintiff sought legal advice and discovered that he had a right of action. Since the plaintiff had been ignorant of a material fact of a decisive character he was entitled to rely on the provisions of the Act.

Smith's case was followed in *Knipe* v. *British Railways Board* [1972] 1 Q.B. 361. The C.A. held that even if a plaintiff's cause of action in negligence had been exhausted by two periods of limitation he may yet take advantage of section 1 (3) of the Limitation Act 1963 by bringing an action within the prescribed period of discovering that he had a worthwhile cause of action.

In *Howell* v. *West Midlands Passenger Transport Executive* [1973] 1 Lloyd's Rep. 199, the C.A. held that leave should be granted where the plaintiff was ignorant of her legal rights and her inaction was induced by the wrong advice given her by claims assessors who had taken over the handling of the claim and had informed her that they could do no more for her.

See articles: " Personal injuries—when time runs " (Watmore) 122 New L.J. 672; " Limitation of actions: a construction problem " 116 S.J. 425, 591; " Asbestosis," 1972 S.L.T. 209.

CHAPTER 17

NEGLIGENCE COMMITTED ABROAD

1165 **Generally**

See article: " Place of the tort " (Scott) 121 New L.J. 693.

CHAPTER 18

STATUTORY DUTY AND BREACH

1.—CLASSES OF BREACH OF STATUTORY BREACH

1185 **Statute creates a duty, but gives no remedy**

Where the plaintiff's bullocks had escaped at an accommodation crossing, the gate of which had a defective lock, so that the beasts gained access to the tracks where they were injured and killed by a passenger train, the defendants were held not liable since there was no statutory duty to maintain and repair the gate. *Short* v. *British Railways Board,* 118 S.J. 101.

2.—WHEN AN ACTION MAY BE BROUGHT

(d) *Other Considerations*

1207 **Damage the result of breach of duty**

NOTE 16. See *McGhee* v. *National Coal Board* [1973] 1 W.L.R. 1, § 963, *ante.*

4.—Defences to Action for Breach of Statutory Duty

1216 **Contributory negligence**

Any apportionment of liability under section 14 of the Factories Act 1961 must take into account the degree to which breach of the section is deliberate, flagrant or continuous; where an employer's liability stems from such a breach the court must be careful not to emasculate the statute's provisions by apportionment: *McGuiness* v. *Key Markets* (1973) 13 K.I.R. 249, C.A.

5.—Examples of Statutory Duty

(a) *The Factories Act 1961*

1230 **To whom the duty is owed**

Note 15. , and approved by the H.L. in *Westwood* v. *Post Office* [1973] 3 W.L.R. 287.

Note 17. approved by C.A. in *Westwood* v. *Post Office* [1973] Q.B. 591 (although not further considered by the H.L. [1974] A.C. 1).

1231 **Ventilation** (s. 4)

An employer who fails to consider the relevant medical and other literature and, in particular, the 1965 Ministry of Labour's publication: " Dust and Fumes in Factory Atmospheres " and the ceiling limits contained therein, will not have taken " all practicable measures " to protect his employees against inhalation of injurious fumes within section 63 (1). Thus where a plaintiff contracted a bad lung condition after many years of work as an arc welder, during which time he was exposed to the prolonged inhalation of low concentrations of welding fumes containing oxides of nitrogen, it was held that his employers were liable. *Cartwright* v. *G. K. N. Sankey* (1973) 14 K.I.R. 339.

Note 23. *McGhee* v. *National Coal Board* [1973] 1 W.L.R. 1. See also §§ 963, 1207, *ante*.

1233 **Fencing dangerous machinery**

Note 32. *Joy* v. *News of the World* (1972) 13 K.I.R. 57 (a machine which is going very slowly is, nevertheless, " in motion ").

1239 *McGuiness* v. *Key Markets* (1973) 13 K.I.R. 249. See also § 1216, *ante*.

1258 **Safe means of access and safe place of employment**

See article: " Duty to guard a ' working place ' " (Poole) 116 S.J. 230.

1259 **Precautions with respect to explosive or inflammable dust, gas, vapour or substance** (s. 31)

Where the pursuer was injured in the course of his employment in the defender's scrap metal yard whilst using an oxy-acetylene cutter to open an old safe which suddenly exploded because, unknown to the defenders, it contained some nitro-glycerine, it was held that the section did not apply since the safe was stock in trade and not " plant " or a " vessel." *Haigh* v. *Charles W. Ireland Ltd.* [1974] 1 W.L.R. 43, H.L.

1261 **Removal of dust or fumes** (s. 63)

Cartwright v. *G. K. N. Sankey* (1973) 14 K.I.R. 339. In *Wallhead* v. *Ruston & Hornsby* (1973) 14 K.I.R. 285. The test for breach of statutory duty (the actual or constructive knowledge which would have been ascertained from literature or inquiries made by a reasonable prudent employer) was different from that at common law (information commonly known in the trade).

1262 **Protection of eyes** (s. 65)

NOTE 84. Goggles were held not to be suitable where there were gaps between the rims and the faces of those wearing them, as well as a large number of small holes near the rims. *Rodgers* v. *Geo. Blair & Co.* (1971) 116 S.J. 77.

1263 To fall within the provisions of section 65 the accident must be caused by an operation forming part of the "process specified": *Hay* v. *Dowty Mining Equipment* [1971] 3 All E.R. 1136.

The word "plant" denotes any part of the apparatus in a factory used in carrying on the industrial process undertaken on those premises but does not include any article on those premises for the purpose of its being subjected to that industrial process. *Haigh* v. *Charles W. Ireland Ltd.* [1974] 1 W.L.R. 43, H.L. See § 1259, *ante*.

(b) *The Offices, Shops and Railway Premises Act, 1963*

1267 **Application of the Act**

If a building as a whole constitutes office premises as defined by section 1 (2) (*b*), the protection of the Act extends to all parts of it and applies to employees, even when acting outside the course of their employment. *Westwood* v. *Post Office* [1973] 3 W.L.R. 287. (approving *Uddin* v. *Associated Portland Cement Manufacturers* [1965] 2 Q.B. 582). Accordingly the employers were held liable to their employee who was killed as the result of the defective construction of their lift motor room through which he had taken a short-cut, although he well knew that he had been forbidden to enter by a notice exhibited on the premises.

See article: "Workmen as trespassers," 70 L.S.Gaz. 1716.

At end of chapter add:

(d) *The Mineral Workings (Offshore Installations) Act 1971*

1270a **Application of the Act**

This Act, which received the Royal Assent on July 27, 1971, and came into force on May 1, 1972 (all except sections 4 and 5 which came into force on August 31, 1972), by virtue of Mineral Workings (Offshore Installations) Act 1971 (Commencement) Order 1972 makes provisions for the safety, health and welfare of persons on installations concerned with the underwater exploration and exploitation of mineral resources in the water surrounding the United Kingdom.

CHAPTER 19

THE FATAL ACCIDENTS ACTS

1.—NATURE OF THE ACTION

1272 **Nature of the action**

See article: "Wages of sin—Fatal Accidents Acts—dependency—proof—damages" (Fleming) [1973] C.L.Y. 17.

5.—The Measure of Damages

1282 **Measure of damages**

See article: " Widow's dependency (Glover) 122 New L.J. 75.

1285 A widow who had been in desertion of her husband and had thereby forfeited her right to any maintenance, must show some significant prospect, as opposed to a mere speculative possibility, of a reconciliation with him had he lived. *A. P. Davies (Suing as Widow and Administratrix of the Estate of Kenneth Stanley Davies)* v. *Taylor* [1972] 3 W.L.R. 801.

1286 **Loss of expectation of pecuniary advantage**

However in *Howitt* v. *Heads* [1973] 1 Q.B. 64 Cumming-Bruce J. (applying *Goodger* v. *Knapman* [1924] S.A.S.R. 347 and *Usher* v. *Williams* (1955) 60 W.A.L.R. 69) held that no deduction should be made for the possibility of the widow finding work in the future, *e.g.* when her children would be grown up, any more than it would have been for any private fortune she might have had.

Savings which have been set aside from a deceased husband's income should not be regarded as the widow's capital asset but as income, part of which would be spent for the husband's benefit. *Gavin* v. *Wilmot Breeden Ltd.* [1973] 1 W.L.R. 1117.

See article: " Savings as a factor in fatal accident damages " (Glover) 124 New L.J. 16.

Where, after a fatal accident to their parents, the orphaned children were being gratuitously cared for by a relative, it was held that such benevolence should be disregarded, despite the defendant's contentions that they had lost nothing in material terms by the loss of their mother, and judgment was given for the quantified loss of their mother's services as well. *Hay & Toone* v. *Hughes* (1973) 117 S.J. 915.

1287 See article: " The widow's claim " (Wharam) 121 New L.J. 1064—is not a widow under an obligation to mitigate her loss?

A widow's remarriage or prospects of remarriage are relevant considerations when assessing the damages payable to an infant child. *Thompson* v. *Price* [1973] Q.B. 838.

Note 82a. See *Wilson* v. *Dagnall* [1972] 1 Q.B. 509 where the C.A. held that no effect could be given to provisions of the Law Reform (Miscellaneous Provisions) Act 1971, the trial having taken place five days before it came into force, even though the appeal was heard after the commencement of the Act.

1293 **Other considerations**

Note 19. Applied in *Howitt* v. *Heads* [1973] 1 Q.B. 64 (no deduction should be made for a widow's possible future earnings any more than it would have been for any private fortune she might have had).

See article: " Judicial attitudes towards actuarial evidence " (Richards and Kidner) 124 New L.J. 105.